Studies in the Scriptures
1928-29

Volume 4
of
17 Volume Set

Studies in the Scriptures 1928-29

Volume 4
of
17 Volume Set

Arthur W. Pink

Sovereign Grace Publishers, Inc.
P.O. Box 4998
Lafayette, IN 47903
2001

A. W. Pink's Studies in the Scriptures,
Volume 4 of 17 Vols - 1928-29 - Paperback Edition
Copyright © 2001
By Jay P. Green, Sr.
All Rights Reserved

Volume 1 = ISBN 1-58960-233-1

Studies in the Scriptures -- 1928
Index

The Epixtle to the Hebrews		2
Gleanings in Exodus	Exodus 28:15-30	7
The Prophetic Parables of Matthew 13		11
Outside the Camp	Heb. 13:13	14
The Churches of God	1 Cor. 11:22	18
Children's Address		21
A Ray of Sunshine		23
God's Word About Giving		23
The Epistle to the Hebrews	Prophets 1:1-3	26
Gleanings in Exodus	Exodus 28:30	32
The Urim and Thummim	Neh. 7:63-65	36
The Prophetic Parables of Matthew 13		40
Spiritual Progress		43
The Epistle to the Hebrews	Prophets 1:1-3	50
Gleanings in Exodus	Exodus 28:40-43	56
The Prophetic Parables of Matthew 13		61
A Sacrifice of Praise	Heb. 13:15	65
Worldly Church Methods		68
The Epistle to the Hebrews		74
Gleanings in Exodus	Exodus 29:36-43	81
The Prophetic Parables of Matthew 13	Matthew 13:45, 46	86
The Means of Regeneration		91
The Epistle of the Hebrews		98
Gleanings in Exodus	Exodus 30:1-10	104
The Prophetic Parables of Matthew 13	Matthew 13:47-50	110
Life Out of Death	1 Peter 3:19-21	115
The Epistle to the Hebrews	Heb 1:10-13	122
Gleanings to Exodus	Exodus 30:11-15	129
The Prophetic Parables of Matthew 13		133
The Family of God	Isa. 54:13	136
The Gospel of God's Grace	Acts 20:24	140
Was Adam Saved?		143
The Epistle to the Hebrews		146
Gleanings in Exodus	Exodus 30:17-21	152
Taught of God	Isa. 54:13	158
Dead to Sin and Alive to God		161
Pray Always		167
The Epistle of the Hebrews		170
Gleanings of Exodus	Exodus 30:22-33	176
Great Peace	Isa. 54:13	181
Unclothed or Clothed	2 Corinthians 5:1	184

The Epistles to the Hebrews	Heb. 2:9-11	194
Gleanings in Exodus	Exodus 31:1-11	200
The Prophetic Scope of Matthew 24		205
The Christian's Greatest Need	Luke 10:42	209
"Get Thee Out."	Acts 7:3	215
The Epistles to the Hebrews	Heb. 2:11-13	218
Gleanings in Exodus	Exodus 31:13-18	224
The Path of the Just		229
The Way of the Wicked	Prov. 4:19	231
The Saving Look	Isa. 45-22	235
No Contradiction	John 1:18	238
Gracious Speech	Col. 4:6	239
The Epistle to the Hebrews	Heb. 2:14-16	242
Gleanings in Exodus	Exodus 32:1-10	248
Worship		252
Christ in Us	Col. 3:9-25; 4:1	255
Privilege and Responsibility	Deuteronomy 20:1-9	258
Touch Not Mine Anointed		260
Christ for All		262
The Epistle to the Hebrews		266
Gleanings in Exodus	Exodus 32:11-14	271
Worship		276
Worship		279
Sobriety		283
Christ as Master		284
Qualifications of a Preachers		285
Anxious Care		287

Studies in the Scriptures - 1929
Index

The Epistle to the Hebrews		2
Gleanings in Exodus	Exodus 32:15-29	7
Abraham's Call	Gen. 12	11
Romans 7		15
The Sympathy & Grace of Christ	Matt 14:1-21, Mark 6:30-44	17
One of Christ's Little Ones	Matt. 18:10	20
Jerusalem and Cyprus	Acts 13:13 and 15:38, 39	21
A Personal Word		23
The Epistle to the Hebrews	Heb. 3:7-12	26
Gleanings in Exodus	Exodus 32:38 to 33:2	32
Life of Abram	Gen. 12:1-3	35
Romans 7		39
Grapes of Eschol	Numbers 13	43

Laughter	Gen. 21:6, Luke 6:21	46
The Epistle to the Hebrews	Heb. 3:13-19	50
Gleanings in Exodus	Exodus 33:4-10	56
Abram's Compromises	Gen. 11:31, 32	60
A Threefold Salvation		64
A Personal Word		71
The Epistle to the Hebrews	Heb. 4:1-3	74
Gleanings in Exodus	Exodus 33:11-17	80
Abram's Obedience	Gen. 12:4-7	84
Provision for Perilous Times		88
A Model Christian		92
The Epistle to the Hebrews	Heb. 4:3-10	98
Gleanings in Exodus	Exodus 33:18-23	104
Abram's Worship	Gen. 12:7, 8	109
The Willful King	1 Sam. 8-31	113
The Epistle to the Hebrews	Heb. 4:11-16	122
Gleanings in Exodus	Exodus 34:1-7	128
Abram's Failure	Gen. 12:9, 10	133
The Servant-King		137
The Epistle to the Hebrews	Heb 5:1-4	146
Gleanings in Exodus	Exodus 34:8-17	152
Abram's Sin	Gen. 12:10-13	157
The Book of Nehemiah		161
A Personal Word		163
Self-Control		164
Important Notice		166
The Epistle to the Hebrews	Heb. 5:5-7	170
Gleanings in Exodus	Exodus 34:18-21	176
Sanctification by the Blood	Heb. 10:10, Heb. 13:12	185
Christ Our All in All		190
The Epistle to the Hebrews	Heb. 5:8-10	194
Gleanings in Exodus	Exodus 34:22-27	200
The Holy Spirit's Work		205
Matters of First Importance		211
The Epistle to the Hebrews	Heb. 5:11-14	218
Gleanings in Exodus	Exodus 34:28-35	225
The Holy Spirit's Work		230
Separation		234
The History of a Stanza		237
The Epistle to the Hebrews	Heb. 6:1-3	242
Gleanings in Exodus	Exodus 35-40	249
The Holy Spirit's Work		254
The Unity of Saints		259
Paticular Redemption	Matt. 20:28	263
The Epistle to the Hebrews	Heb. 6:4-6	266

Gleanings in Exodus 273
Justification 278
A Personal word 284
Holy Horror 285

Vol. VII.   JANUARY, 1928   NO. 1

STUDIES IN THE SCRIPTURES

"Search the Scriptures" John 5:

Copyright in all English-speaking Countries.

Editor: Arthur W. Pink, 15 Hurlstone Avenue, Summer Hill, N.S.W., Australia.
Hon. Agent in U.S.A.: Mr. C. S. Pressel, 559 Dupont Avenue, York, Penna.

FREE TO ALL WHO WILL READ IT

"For here have we no continuing city, but we seek one to come" (Heb. 13:14)

Another year has passed and gone. Numbers of our readers have experienced some radical changes, both in their circumstances and in their connections; changes which were sudden and unexpected. But they ought not to feel that some strange thing has happened to them. Nor should they be cast down because of them; even the changes which the unerring providence of Him who changes not (Mal. 3:6) orders for us, are among the "all things" which work together for the Christian's good.

"Change and decay in all around I see" says a well-known hymn. But these frequent changes make us fretful. Possibly that needs some qualification, for the natural man is a bundle of contradictions. One of the poets said, "Variety is the spice of life." In some moods we hanker after change. Monotony palls on one. Contentment is something few enjoy. On the other hand, the flesh loves to take its ease; and anything which disturbs our rest is resented. In a business position or in our place of residence we like to feel anchored, for a while at least. But God constantly reminds us that "*here* have we no continuing city."

The editor and his wife thought they had found a congenial church-home, and hoped to remain in it till the Lord came for them. But *He* willed otherwise. Our preaching was too scriptural for some of them. In Arminian "churches" our exposition of the sovereignty of God gave offense; in this Calvinistic "church" our enforcing ot the responsibility of man occasioned trouble. The deaconate and about fifty per cent. of the members deny that it is the duty of unregenerate sinners to repent and believe unto salvation. Though the Lord and His apostles (see Mark 1:15; 6:12; John 12:36) pressed these upon all, yet His servants to-day must not, because it is contrary to the denominational "Articles of Faith." We laboured hard to set before them the teachings of Holy Writ on the subject; but in vain. Moreover, their ideas of maintaining discipline were so different from what we believe the Word of God requires, that we felt there was only one course open to us: "Can two walk together, except they be agreed?" (Amos 3:3). We have, therefore, resigned; and (without any pressure from us) about forty per cent. of the membership have done likewise.

"Let us go forth therefore unto Him without the camp, bearing His reproach" (Heb. 13:13). This is the word God gave us; and we feel it is a timely one for many of His people to-day. We are now on the outside of all denominationalism. But blessed be the name of our Lord and Saviour, we are "with Him," and most blessedly is He manifesting Himself to His despised people. To bear *His* "reproach" is an unspeakable privilege and honour. We have endeavoured to organise on Scriptural lines, without any man-made "rules" or "articles of faith;" fully assured that the Scriptures are sufficient to "thoroughly furnish us unto *all* good works" (2 Tim. 3:16, 17). May the Lord make *His* way "plain" before all His dear people.

Returning now to our opening text, "For here have we no continuing city, but we seek one to come." The *connection* is clear. In the previous verse the apostle had said, "Let us go forth therefore unto Him without the camp, bearing His reproach." Now he advances a *reason* ("for") why Christians should willingly submit

(Continued on page 24.)

IMPORTANT NOTICES

Back numbers of each year of the magazine are yet obtainable at 5/- (1.25) per year. Bound at 7/6 (1.75) post paid. They will soon be out of print. Those in U.S.A. wanting them, please purchase from Mr. Pressel (see front cover page).

Advise promptly of change of address. This Magazine is published as a work of faith and labour of love. The Editor gladly gives his services. It is freely sent to all who will read it. No charge is made for it.

Christians who feel definitely led to do so, may have fellowship with us in this Ministry. Send only *Inter-National M.O.*

CONTENTS.

	Page
Hebrews	2
Gleanings in Exodus	7
Parables of Matt. 13	11
Outside the Camp	14
The Churches of God	18
Children's Address	21

THE EPISTLE TO THE HEBREWS.

1. Introduction.

Before taking up the study of this important Epistle let writer and reader humbly bow before its Divine Inspirer, and earnestly seek from Him that preparation of heart which is needed to bring us into fellowship with that One whose person, offices, and glories are here so sublimely displayed. Let us personally and definitely seek the help of that blessed Spirit who has been given to the saints of God for the purpose of guiding them into all truth, and taking of the things of Christ to show unto them. In Luke 24:45 we learn that Christ opened the understanding of the disciples "*that* they might understand the Scriptures." May He graciously do so with us, then the entrance of His words will "give light" (Psa. 119:130), and in *His* light *we* shall "see light."

In this opening article we shall confine ourselves to things of an introductory character, things which it is necessary to weigh ere we take up the details of the Epistle. We shall consider its addresses, its purpose, its theme, its divisions, its characteristics, its value, and its writer.

Before doing so, let us say that we expect to quote freely from other expositors, and where possible name them. In some cases we shall not be able to do so owing to the fact that extensive and long-distance travelling has obliged the writer to break up five libraries during the last twenty years. During those years he has read (and owned most of them) between thirty and forty commentaries on Hebrews, from which he has made notes in his Bible and taken helpful extracts for his own use when lecturing on this Epistle. As most of these commentaries have been disposed of, we can now do no more than make a general acknowledgment of help received from those written by Drs. J. Owen, J. Gill, Moses Stewart, Andrew Bonar, Griffith-Thomas, and Messrs. Pridham, Ridout, and Tucker. Let us now consider:—

1. *Its Addressees.*

In our English Bibles we find the words "The Epistle of Paul the Apostle to the Hebrews" as the address. Perhaps some of our readers are not aware that the titles found at the head of the different books of the Bible are *not* Divinely inspired, and therefore are not accounted canonical as are the contents. No doubt these titles were originated by the early scribes, when making copies of the original manuscripts—manuscripts, all traces of which have long since disappeared. In some instances these titles are unsatisfactory; in a few, grossly erroneous. As an example of the latter, we may refer to the final book of Scripture. Here the title is "The Revelation of St. John the Divine," whereas the opening sentence of the book itself designates it "The Revelation of Jesus Christ!"

While treating in general with the titles of the books of Scripture, we may note that in almost all of the Epistles there is a Divinely-named addressee in the opening verses. But we may add, the contents of each Epistle are *not* to be restricted to those immediately and locally addressed. It is important that the young Christian should grasp this firmly, so that he may be fortified against ultra-dispensational teaching. There are some, claiming to have great light, who would rob the saints to-day of the Epistle of James because it is addressed to "the Twelve Tribes which are scattered abroad." With equal propriety they might take from us the Epistles to the Philippians and Colossians because they were addressed only to the saints in those cities! The truth is that what Christ said to the apostles in Mark 13:17—"What I say unto *you*, I say unto *all*"—may well be applied to the whole of the Bible. *All* Scripture is needed by us (2 Tim. 3:16, 17), and all Scripture is God's word to us. Note carefully that while at the beginning of his Epistle to Titus Paul *only* addresses Titus himself (1:4), yet at the close of this letter he expressly says, "Grace be with you *all*" (3:15)!

Ignoring then the man-made title at the head of our Epistle, we are at once struck by the *absence* of any Divinely-given one in the opening verses. Nevertheless, its first sentence enables us to *identify* at once those to whom the Epistle was originally sent: see 1:1, 2. They to whom God spake through the prophets were the children of Israel, and it was also *unto them* He had spoken through His Son. In 3:1 we find a word which, however, *narrows* the circle to which this Epistle was first sent. It was not the Jewish nation at large which was addressed, but the "holy brethren, partakers of the heavenly calling" among them. Clear confirmation of this is supplied in the Epistles of Peter. His first was addressed, locally, to "the elect sojourners of the Dispersion (I:I) - Gk., "eklektois parepidenois diasporas"). His second Epistle (see 3:1) was addressed, locally and immediately, to the same company. Now in 2 Peter 3:15 the apostle makes specific reference to "our beloved brother Paul also according to the wisdom given unto him hath written *unto you.*" Thus all doubt is removed as to whom our Epistle was first sent.

The Epistle itself contains further details which serve to identify the addresses. That it was written to saints who were by no means young in the faith is clear from 5:12, that is was sent to those who had suffered severe persecutions (cf. Acts 8:1) is plain from what we read in 10:32. That it was addressed to a Christian community of considerable size is evident from 13:24. From this last reference we are inclined to conclude that this Epistle was first delivered to the church in Jerusalem (Acts II:22), or to the churches in Judea (Acts 9:31), copies of which would be made and forwarded to Jewish Christians in foreign lands. Thus, our Epistle was first addressed to those descendants of Abraham, who, by grace, had believed on their Saviour-Messiah.

2. *Its Purpose.*

This in a word, was to instruct Jewish believers that Judaism had been superceded by Christianity. It must be borne in mind that a very considerable proportion of the earliest converts to Christ were Jews by natural birth, who continued to labour under Jewish prejudices. In his early Epistles the apostle had touched several times on this point, and sought to wean them from an undue and now untimely attachment to the Mosaic institutions. But only in *this* Epistle does he deal fully and systematically with the subject.

It is difficult for us to appreciate the position, the time this Epistle was written, of those in Israel who had believed on the Lord Jesus. Unlike the Gentiles, who, for long centuries past, had lost all knowledge of the true God, and, in consequence, worshipped idols; the Jews *had* a Divine religion and a Divinely-appointed place of worship. To be called upon to *forsake* these, which had been venerated by their fathers for over a thousand years, was to make a big demand upon them. It was natural that even those among them who had savingly believed on Christ should want to retain the forms and ceremonies amid which they had been brought up; the more so, seeing that the Temple still stood and the Levitical priesthood still functioned. An endeavour had been made to link Christianity on to Judaism, and as Acts 21:20 tells us there were many thousands of the early Jewish Christians who were "zealous of the law"—as the next verses clearly show, the *ceremonial* law.

"Instead of perceiving that under the new economy of things, there was neither Jew nor Gentile, but, that, without reference to external distinctions, all believers in Christ Jesus were now to live together in the closest bonds of spiritual attachment in holy society, they dreamed of the Gentiles being admitted to the participation of the Jewish Church through means of the Messiah, and, that its external economy was to remain unaltered to the end of the world" (Dr. J. Brown).

In addition to their natural prejudices, the *temporal circumstances* of the believing Jews became increasingly discouraging, yea, presented a sore temptation for them to abandon the profession of Christianity. Following the persecution spoken of in Acts 8:1, that eminent scholar, Adolph Saphir—himself a converted Jew—tells us: "Then arose another persecution of the believers, especially directed against the apostle Paul. Festus died about the year 63, and under the high priest Ananias, who favoured the Sadducees, the Christian Hebrews were persecuted as transgressors of the law. Some of them were stoned to death; and though this extreme punishment could not be frequently inflicted by the Sanhedrim, they were able to subject their brethren to sufferings and reproaches which they felt keenly. It was a small thing that they confiscated their goods; but they banished them from the holy places. Hitherto they had enjoyed the privileges of devout Israelites: they could take part in the beautiful and God-appointed services of the sanctuary; but now they were treated as unclean and apostates. Unless they gave up faith in Jesus, and forsook the assembling of themselves together, they were not allowed to enter the Temple, they were banished from the altar, the sacrifice, the high priest, the house of Jehovah.

"We can scarcely realise the piercing sword which thus wounded their inmost heart. That by clinging to the Messiah they were to be severed from Messiah's people, was, indeed, a great and perplexing trial; that for the hope of Israel's glory they were banished from the place which God had chosen, and where the divine Presence was revealed, and the symbols and ordinances had been the joy and strength of their fathers; that they were to be no longer children of the covenant and of the house, but worse than Gentiles, excluded from the outer court, cut off from the commonwealth of Israel. This was indeed a sore and mysterious trial. Cleaving to the promises made unto their fathers, cherishing the hope in constant prayer that their nation would yet accept the Messiah, it was the severest test to which their faith could be put, when their loyalty to Jesus involved separation from all the sacred rights and privileges of Jerusalem."

Thus the *need* for an authoritative, lucid, and systematic setting forth of the real relation of Christianity to Judaism was a pressing one. Satan would not miss the opporunity of seeking to persuade these Hebrews that their faith in Jesus of Nazareth was a mistake, a delusion, a sin. Were *they* right, while the vast majority of their brethren, according to the flesh, among whom were almost all the respected members of the Sanhedrim and the priesthood, wrong? Had God *prospered* them since they had become followers of the crucified One? or, did not their temporal circumstances evidence that He was most displeased with them? Moreover, the believing remnant of Israel had looked for a speedy return of Christ to the earth, but thirty years had now passed and He had not come! Yes, their situation was critical, and there was an urgent need that their faith should be strengthened, their understanding enlightened, and a fuller explanation be given them of Christianity in the light of the O.T. It was to meet this need that God, in His tender mercy, moved His servant to write this Epistle to them.

3. *Its Theme.*

This is, the superabounding excellence of Christianity over Judaism. The sum and substance, the centre and circumference, the light and life of Christianity, is *Christ* Therefore, the method followed by the Holy Spirit in this Epistle, in developing its dominent theme, is to show the able superiority of Christ over all that had gone before. One by one the various objects in which the Jews boasted are taken up, and in the presence of the superlative glory of the Son of God they pale into utter insignificance. We are shown first, His superiority over the prophets 1:1-3. Second, His superiority over angels in 1:4 to 2:18 third His superiority over Moses in 3: 1-19. Fourth, His superiority over Joshua 4: 1-23. Fifth, His superiority over Aaron in 5:14 to 7:18. Sixth, His superiority over the whole ritual of Judaism, which is devolped by showing the surpassing excellency of the new covenant over the old, in 7:19 to 10:39. Seventh, His superiority over each and all of the O.T. saints 11:1 to 12:3. In the Lord Jesus. Christians have the substance and reality, of which Judaism contained but the shadows and figures.

If the Lord permits us to go through this Epistle—O that He may come for us before—many illustrations and examplifications of our definition of its theme will come before us. At the moment, we may note how frequently the comparative term "better" is used, thus showing the *superiority* of what we have in Christianity over what the saints of old had in Judaism. In Heb 1:4 Christ is "better than angels;" in 7: 19 mention is made of a "better hope;" in 7:22 of a "better testament" or "covenant; in 8:6 of "better promises;" in 9:23 of "better sacrifices;" in 10:34 of a "better substance;" in 11:16 of a "better country;" in 11:34 of a "better resurrection," and in 11:40 of the "better thing." So, too, we may observe the seven *great* things mentioned therein, namely: the "great salvation" (2:3), the "great High priest (4:14), tthe "great Tabernacle' (9:II) the "great fight of afflictions" (10:32) the "great recompense" (10:35), the "great cloud of witnesses" (12:1), the "great Shepherd of the sheep" (13:20).

Again; in contrast from what the believing Hebrews were called upon to *give up*, they were reminded of what they had *gained*. Note how frequently occurs the "we have"—a great High Priest (4:14, 8: 1), an anchor of the soul (6:19), a better and enduring substance (10:34), an altar (13:10). Once more, we may note how these

Hebrews were encouraged to forget the things which were behind and to press toward those which were before. All through this Epistle the *forward look* is prominent. In 1:6 and 2:5 mention is made of a "world (or 'habitable earth') to come;" in 6:5 of an "age to come;" in 8:10 of a "new covenant," yet to be made with the house of Israel; in 9:11 and 10:1 of "good things" to come; in 9:28 of a "salvation" to be revealed; in 10:38 of the coming Redeemer, in 11:14 and 13:14 of a "city" yet to be manifested.

Throughout this Epistle great prominence is given to the *Priesthood* of Christ. The centre of Judaism was its temple and the priesthood. Hence the Holy Spirit has here shown at length how that believers now have in Christ the substance of which these supplied but the shadows. The following passages should be carefully weighed:—2:17; 3:1; 4:14, 15; 5:6, 10; 6:20; 7:26; 8:1; 9:11; 10:21. "Though deprived of the temple, with its priesthood and altar and sacrifice, the apostle reminds the Hebrews, 'we have' the real and substantial temple, the great High Priest, the true altar, the one sacrifice, and with it all offerings, the true access into the very presence of the Most Holy" (A. Saphir).

4. Its Divisions.

These have been set forth so simply by Dr. J. Brown we cannot do better than quote from him: "The Epistle divides itself into two parts—the first, doctrinal; the second, practical—though the division is not so accurately (closely, A.W.P.) observed, that there are no duties enjoined or urged in the first part, and no doctrines stated in the second. The first is by far the larger division, reaching from the beginning of the Epistle down to the 18th verse of the 10th chapter. The second commences with the 19th verse of the 10th chapter, and extends to the end of the Epistle. The superiority of Christianity to Judaism is the great doctrine which the Epistle teaches; and constancy in the faith and profession of that religion, is the great duty which it enjoins."

5. Its Characteristics.

In several noticeable respects Hebrews differs from all the other Epistles of the New Testament. The name of the writer is omitted, there is no opening salutation, the ones to whom it was first specifically and locally sent are not mentioned. On the positive side we may note, that the typical teachings of the O.T. are expounded here at greater length than elsewhere; the priesthood of Christ is opened up, fully, only in this Epistle; the warnings against apostasy are more frequent and more solemn, and the calls to steadfastness and perseverance are more emphatic and numerous than in any other N.T. book. All of these things are accounted for by the fleshly nationality of those addressed, and the circumstances they were then in. Unless we keep these features steadily in mind, not a little in this Epistle will necessarily remain obscure and dark. Much of the language used, the figures employed, the references made, are only intelligible in the light of the O. T. Scriptures, on which Judaism was based. Except this be kept before us, such expressions as *"purged our sins"* (1:3), "there remaineth therefore a *sabbath-keeping* to the people of God (4:9), "leaving the principles of the doctrine of Christ, let us go on unto perfection" (6:1), "our bodies washed with pure water" (10:22), "we have an altar" (13:10), etc., will remain unintelligible.

The first time that *Christ* is referred to in this Epistle it is as seated at the right hand of the Majesty on high" (1:3), for it is with a *heavenly* Christ that Christianity has to do: note the other reference in this Epistle to the same fact—1:13, 8:1, 10:12, 12:2. In perfect accord with 1:3, which strikes the keynote of the Epistle, in addition to the heavenly Christ, reference is made to "the heavenly calling" (3:1), to "the heavenly gift" (6:4), to "heavenly things" (8:5), to "the heavenly Country" (11:16), to the "heavenly Jerusalem" (12:22), and to "the church of the First-born, whose names are written in Heaven" (12:23). This emphasis is easily understood when we remember that our Epistle is addressed to those whose inheritance, religious relationships, and hopes, had been all *earthly*.

In 13:22 there is a striking word which defines the *character* of this Epistle: "And I beseech you, brethren, suffer the word *of exhortation*, for I have written a letter unto you in few words." Upon this verse Saphir has well said, "The central idea of the Epistle is the glory of the New Covenant, contrasted with and excelling the glory of the old covenant; and while this idea is developed in a systematic manner, yet the aim of the writer throughout is eminently and directly practical. Everywhere his object is exhortation. He never loses sight of the dangers and wants of his brethren. The application to conscience and life is never forgotten. It is rather a sermon than an exposition. . . . In all his arguments, in every doctrine, in every illustration, the central aim of the Epistle is kept prominent—the exhortation to *steadfastness.*" This is, indeed, a peculiarity about Hebrews. In his other Epistles, the apostle rarely breaks in on an argument to utter an admonition or exhortation; instead, his well-nigh uniform method was to open with doctrinal exposition, and then base upon this a series of practical exhortations. But the unusual situation which the Hebrews were in, and the peculiar love that the writer bore to them (cf. Rom. 9:3) explains this exception.

What has just been said above accounts for what we find in Heb. 11. Nowhere else in the Bible do we find such a lengthy and complete description of *the life of faith.* But here a whole chapter, the longest in the Epistle, is devoted to it. The reason for this is not far to seek. Brought up in a system with an elaborate ritual, whose worship was primarily a matter of *outward* symbols and ceremonies; tempted as few ever have been to walk by sight, there was a special and most pressing need for a clear and detailed analysis and description of what it means to "walk by faith." Inasmuch as "example is better than precept," better because more easily grasped and because making a more powerful appeal to the heart, the Holy Spirit saw well to develop this important theme by an appeal to the history of saints recorded in the Scriptures of the Hebrews.

But it is most important that we recognise the fullness of the term *faith.* As Saphir well said, "Throughout Scripture faith means more than trust in Jesus for personal safety. This *is* the central point, but we must take care that we understand it in a true and deep manner. Faith, as the apostle explains in the Epistle to the Corinthians, is looking at the things which are not seen and temporal: it is preferring spiritual and eternal realities to the things of time, sense, and sin; it is leaning on God and realising His Word; it is the substance of things hoped for, the evidence of things not seem. Thus every doctrine and illustration of this Epistle goes straight to the heart and conscience, appeals to life, addresses itself to faith. It is one continued and sustained fervent and intense appeal to cleave to Jesus, the High Priest; to the substantial, true, and real worship. A most urgent and loving exhortation to be steadfast, patient, hopeful, in the presence of God, in the love and sympathy of the Lord Jesus, in the fellowship of the great cloud of witnesses."

Another prominent characteristic, concerning which there is no need for us now to enlarge upon, is the repeated *warnings* in this Epistle *against apostasy.* The most solemn and searching exhortations against the danger of falling away to be found anywhere in Holy Writ were given to these Hebrews. 2:1-3, most of the third and fourth chapters, 6:4-6, 10:26-29, 12:15-17 will at once occur to all who are familiar with the contents of this Epistle. The occasion for and the need of them has already been pointed out: the disappointing of the hopes the Hebrews had cherished, the persecutions they were then enduring, and the Divine judgment which was on the very eve of falling on Jerusalem (in A.D. 70) made them imperative.

6. *Its Value.*

Let us mention first its *evidential* value. The Epistle is particularly rich in proofs of the *verbal* inspiration of Scripture. This is seen in the way the apostle refers to the O.T., and the use he makes of it. Mark how in 1:5-9 when quoting from the Psalms, 2nd Samuel, Deuteronomy, he refers these utterances to God Himself—"He saith," vv. 6, 7, 8. So in 3:7 "the Holy Spirit saith." Observe how when quoting from the O.T. the apostle attentively weighs *every word,* and often builds a fundamental truth on a single expression. Let us cite a few from the many examples of this:

See how in 2:8 the apostle argues from the authority of the word "all." In 2:11, when quoting from Psalm 22, he deduces the conclusion from the expression "My brethren" that the Son of God took to Himself human nature. Observe that in 3:7-19 and 4:2-11, when quoting from Psalm 95, he builds on the words "To-day," "I have sworn," and "My rest;" also in 3:2-6 how his conclusions there are drawn from the words "servant," and "My house" in Numbers 11:7. His whole argument in chapter 8 is based on the word "new" found in Jer. 31:31. How blessedly he makes use of the words "My son" from Prov. 3:11 in 12:5-9! How emphatically he appeals in 12:26, 27 to the words "once more" in Hag. 2:11. Is it not abundantly clear that in the judgment of the apostle Paul the Scriptures were Divinely inspired even to the *most minute* expression?

The *evangelical* value of this Epistle has been recognised by Christians of all schools of thought. Here is set forth with sunlight clearness the preciousness, design, efficacy and effects of the great Sacrifice offered once and for all. Christ has Himself purged our sins (1:3); He is able to save "to the uttermost" (7:25); by His one offering He has "perfected forever the sanctified" (10:14); by His blood a new and living way has been opened for His people into the Holiest (10:19, 20): such are some of its wondrous declarations. Emphasising the inestimable worth of His redemptive-work, it is here that we read of an "eternal salvation" (5:9), "eternal redemption" (9:12), and of the "eternal inheritance" (9:15).

The *doctrinal* importance of this book is exceeded by none, not even by the Roman Epistle. Where its teachings are believed, understood, and embodied in the life, ritualism and legalism (the two chief enemies of Christianity) receive their death-blow. In no other book of Scripture are the sophistries and deceptions of Romanism so clearly and systematically exposed. So fully and pointedly are the errors of Popery refuted, it might well have been written *since* that Satanic system became established. Well did one of the Puritans say, "God foreseeing what poisonous heresies would be broached by the Papacy, prepared this antidote against them."

But perhaps its chief distinctive value lies in its exposition of the O.T. types. It is here we are taught that the Tabernacle and its furniture, the priesthood and their service, the various sacrifices and offerings, all pointed to the person, offices, and glories of the Lord Jesus. Of Israel's priests it is said, "who served unto the example and shadow of heavenly things" (8:5); the first tabernacle was "a figure for the time then present" (9:9); the ceremonial law had "a shadow of good things to come" (10:1). Melchizedec was a type of Christ (7:15), Isaac was a figure of Him (11:9), and so on. The details of these will be considered, D.V., in due course.

7. Its Writer.

This, we are fully assured, was the apostle Paul. Though he was distinctively and essentially the "apostle of the Gentiles" (Rom. 11:13), yet his ministry was by no means confined to them, as the book of Acts clearly shows. At the time of his apprehension the Lord said, "He is a chosen vessel unto Me, to bear My Name before the Gentiles, and kings, and the children of Israel" (Acts 9:15). It is significant that Israel is there mentioned *last*, in harmony with the fact that his Epistle to the Hebrews was written *after* most of his others to Gentile saints. That this Epistle *was* written by Paul is clear from 2 Peter 3:15. Peter was writing to saved Jews as the opening verses of his first Epistle intimates; the first verse of chapter 3 in his second Epistle informs us that this latter was addressed to the same people as his former one had been. Then, in vv. 15 he declares that his beloved brother Paul "also according to the wisdom given unto him hath written *unto you*." If the Epistle to the Hebrews be not *that* writing, where is it?

As this introduction is already longer than we had intended, we must reserve for our next article other evidences that Paul wrote this Epistle. In the meantime may the Spirit of truth stir up reader and writer to a closer study of its opening verses.

—*Arthur W. Pink.*

GLEANINGS IN EXODUS.

49. *The Breastplate* (*Ex.* 28:15-30).

In our last article we pointed out how that the garments of Aaron which were for "glory and for beauty" are seven in number. Six of these, the ephod, girdle, robe, broidered-coat, mitre, and goldencrown, were then briefly considered. Now, we are to meditate upon the remaining one, namely, the Breastplate. This was the chief and most costly of the high priest's vestments, the other garments being as it were a foundation and background for it, this central one pointing to the very *heart* of Christ Himself. Its importance is at once denoted by being mentioned first in Ex. 28:4. A description of it is furnished in 28:15-30. Let us ponder:

1. *Its Workmanship.*

This is described at length in vv. 15, 16, 21, 28, to which we would ask the reader to turn. From these verses it will be seen that the Breastplate itself was made of fine twined linen of cunning work (v. 15). From the remainder of v. 15 we gather that it was richly embroidered with the three colours there mentioned. It was foursquare in shape, and thus corresponded with both the brazen and incense altars. Its dimensions were "a handbreadth;" that is, from the tip of the little finger to the end of the outstretched thumb, a distance of about ten and a half inches, or half a cubit. It was "doubled" so as to give it strength and firmness, in order that it might sustain the weight of the precious stones.

"Two rings of gold were placed inwards, at the bottom of the breastplate: and two gold rings were attached to the ephod, just above the curious belt (girdle): so that the breastplate was bound to the ephod by a lace of blue, coupling these rings. Two wreathen chains of gold were fastened to the ouches, in which the onyx stones were set; and were also fastened, at their other two ends, to two rings at the top of the breastplate. Thus, the ephod, onyx stones, and breastplate were all linked together in one. It may here be observed that the translation 'at the ends' (28:14, 22) should, according to Gesenius, be rendered 'twisted work,' like the twisting of a rope, and the passage will then read thus: 'Two chains of pure gold twisted, wreathen work, shalt thou make them'" (G. Soltau).

2. Its Significance.

There are at least five things which serve as guides to help us ascertain the distinctive typical meaning of this part of the high priest's dress. First, its name: it is called the "breastplate of judgment" (v. 15). Second, the twelve gems set in it, on which were engraved the names of Israel's twelve tribes (vv. 17-21). Third, its inseparability from the ephod: "that the breastplate be not loosed from the ephod" (v. 28). Fourth, the place where the breastplate was worn: it was upon the high priest's "heart" (v. 20). Fifth, the mysterious "Urim and Thummin" which were placed in it (v. 30). As these will be considered separately, in detail, below, we shall now only generalise.

The purpose or design of the breastplate was to furnish a support to the precious stones which were set in it, as well as to provide a background from which their brilliant beauty might be displayed. Thus there is little or no difficulty in perceiving that which is central in this blessed type. On the jewels were inscribed the names of Israel's twelve tribes. Therefore, what we have foreshadowed here is Christ, as our great High Priest, bearing on His heart, sustaining, and presenting before God, His blood-bought people. There is a slight distinction to be drawn from what we have here and that which is set forth in Ex. 28:9-12. There, too, we have the names of Israel's tribes borne by their high priest before God. But there they are seen resting upon his "shoulders," whereas here (v. 29) they rest upon his heart. In the one it is the *strength* or power of Christ engaged on behalf of His helpless people; in the other, it is His *affections* exercised for them.

It will therefore be seen that it is, primarily, the perfect and lasting *security* of believers which is set forth in our present type. Both the power and the love of Christ are for them, guaranteeing their eternal preservation: "And Aaron shall bear the names of the children of Israel in the breastplate of judgment upon his heart when he goeth in unto the holy place, for a memorial before the Lord *continually*" (v. 29). Their position or standing before God was neither affected nor altered by their changing circumstances, infirmities or sins. Whenever Aaron went into the holy place, there on his heart were the names of all God's people. Emphasising this truth of *security*, note carefully how that their names were not simply written upon (so that their erasure was possible) the precious stones, but "engraved" (v. 21)!

Still emphasising the same thought, notice also how that each jewel was secured to the breastplate by a golden setting: "they shall be set in gold in their inclosings" (v. 20). Thus it was impossible for them to slip out of their places, or for any one of them to be lost! Mark, too, the provision made for firmly fixing in place the breastplate itself. This is brought before us in vv. 21-28. It was fastened by "chains at the ends of wreathen work of pure gold" (v. 22), and these were passed through "two rings of gold on the ends of the breastplate." Thus the people of God (as represented by their names) were *chained* to the high priest!

"The chains were wreathen and twisted like a rope, for both words are used; wreathen, interwoven. The same word is used in Judges 15:13, 14; 16:11, 12; Psa. 12:3; Hosea 1:4—cords of love. 'Twisted work' is Gesenius' translation of the Hebrew word, which our version gives, 'at the ends' (vv. 14, 22). Thus he would translate 'and two chains of pure gold, wreathen shalt thou make them, twisted work.' The object in adding the word 'twisted' to 'wreathen' appears to imply a combination of skill and strength, and that the breastplate might be indissolubly connected with the shoulder-stones. Every movement of the high priest's shoulder would affect the breastplate: and every beat of his heart which agitated the breastplate would be conveyed, by means of the wreathen chains, to the covering of the shoulders.

"There is a beautiful significance in this, reminding us how the mighty power of the arm of the Lord is intimately linked on with the tenderness of His heart of love. No action of His strength is disconnected from His counsels of mercy and grace towards His saints. He makes all things work together for good to them that love Him. His arm and His heart are combined in sustaining them in their high calling. He is able to keep them from falling, and to present them faultless before the presence of His glory with exceeding joy. They shall never perish, neither shall any pluck them out of the Shepherd's hand: and who shall separate them from His love?" (G. Soltau). How the double "span" or handbreadth in 28:16 confirms this!

3. Its Jewels.

These were twelve in number, one for each tribe, set in four rows of three each. They are enumerated in vv. 17-20. With respect to the identity of these precious stones but little is known. There have been many laboured attempts made by learned men to discover the real names of the gems; but, with the exception of four or five, most Biblical students acknowledge the subject to be involved in obscurity. But though we are unable to recognise these stones under their modern names, yet many blessed thoughts are suggested by them.

First, the fact the Jehovah selected gems to represent His people indicates how *precious* they are in His sight. How dear they were, is seen in the fact that He gave up His own beloved Son to die for them. Second, their *excellency* was prefigured. And how accurate the type! The believer's excellency or righteousness is not one of his own, but is imputed. So it is with precious stones. "Whatever beauty each has, the light alone brings it out; in the darkness it has none" (C. H. Bright). Thus it is with the saints: it is only as God sees them in Him who is the "true Light" that they are acceptable unto Him. Third, the perfect *knowledge* of the Lord regarding each disciple is intimated by the individualising of the tribes by name. "The Lord knoweth them that are His." "He calleth His own sheep by name." Such is the omniscience of our High Priest that all our wants are known to Him. Fourth, the *durability* of these stones symbolises the fact that the salvation purchased for sinners is an "eternal" one (Heb. 5:9).

Concerning each stone it has been well said, "Much, very much, of its beauty depends upon its *cutting*. Cut skilfully, so as to refract the rays of light from many sides, it sparkles with a beauty quite unknown to its natural condition. Thus, too, with believers; undoubtedly each one has some inherent characteristic difference, but only as the Divine hand in much patience and skill cuts and polishes the stone to catch and discover the colours of the Divine light which illuminates it doth it appear beautiful. Its beauty is not its own, but it has been endowed with capacity to appreciate and *reflect* the beauty of Him who is light and love; and it is to reflect the beauties of the perfect One that we have been chosen—'that in the ages to come He might *show* the exceeding riches of His grace in His kindness toward us through Christ Jesus' (Eph. 2:7). So when that day of manifestation of the glory of His grace comes, 'the nations shall walk in *her* light,'" Rev. 21:24 (C. H. Bright).

Twelve stones were set in it, all precious stones, but no two of them were alike. They were altogether different in form, hew, character, and also in beauty and value (according to man's estimation); but all of them were *gems* in the sight of God, one as much as another. They were each set in gold, and they rested equally upon the heart of Aaron, when he ministered before the Lord. Doubtless, these precious stones were gathered in lands far sundered. Some from the depths of the ocean it might be, and some from the dark mine. But whatever their variety, or the circumstances of their history, or the distance from which they were quarried, they were *united* upon the high priest's heart: diamond, jasper, and emerald were borne there equally and together for a memorial before the Lord.

What comfort, yea, what joy the realisation of this brings to the Christian. Let not the ruby (sardius) proudly think itself superior to the carbuncle; let not the jasper repine because it is not the diamond. Let us not compare ourselves with others. Each believer is accepted in the Beloved. Each believer is clothed with the righteousness of Christ. Each is complete in Him. Is it not enough thou art in the Breastplate, set in gold and borne upon His heart!

In conclusion, let us call attention to something which is exceedingly suggestive and significant concerning them as a whole. These jewels which adorned the Breastplate of the high priest of Israel also pointed backward to sinless Eden, and forward to the sinless New Jerusalem. The first precious stone mentioned in Scripture is the "onyx" (Gen. 2:12), and *this* was the gem which bore on each of Aaron's shoulders the "memorial" on which the names of God's people were graven (28:9-12), and to which the Breastplate was united (v. 25). While in Rev. 21:19-20 we learn that the foundations of the Heavenly City will be garnished with twelve precious stones. Thus the "onyx" stones on the high priest's shoulders look back to Gen. 2:10, which contained a hidden *promise* of the re-admission of God's people into the sinless state; while the Breastplate itself looked forward to Rev. 21, where the *fulfilment* of that promise is seen!

4. *Its Connections.*

The Breastplate was inseparably linked to the ephod. The latter was made for the former, and not the former for the latter. It was never to be separated from it: "that the Breastplate be not loosed from the ephod" (v. 28). The ephod was peculiarly and essentially the high priestly garment. "The names of God's people as borne upon the heart of the priest, shining out in all the sparkling lustre and beauty of the stones on which they are engraven. This symbolises the fact that believers are before God in all the acceptance of Christ. When God looks upon the great High Priest, He beholds His people upon His heart, as well as upon His shoulders, adorned with all the beauty of the One on whom His eye ever rests with perfect delight. Or, looking at it from another aspect, it might be said that Christ presented His people to God, in the exercise of His priesthood, as Himself. He thus establishes in His intercession His own claims upon God on their behalf. And with what joy does He so present them before God! For they are those for whom He has died, and whom He has cleansed with His own most precious blood, those whom He has made the objects of His own love, and whom finally He will bring to be forever with Him; and He pleads for them before God according to all the strength of these ties" (Ed. Dennett).

Thus the truth set forth by the Breastplate is inseparably united to the priestly ministry of Christ. "It is fastened to the ephod by chains of gold, by all that Christ is therefore as Divine. It is also an eternal connection as typified by the rings—the ring being without an end, and hence, an emblem of eternity. As Priest, Christ can never fail us. If He has once undertaken our cause, He will never lay it down. Surely this truth will strengthen our hearts in times of trial or weakness. We may be despondent, but if we look up we may rejoice in the thought that our place upon the heart and shoulders of Christ can never be lost" (Ed. Dennett).

"He preserves us, as that which He has on His heart, to God, He cannot be before Him without doing so, and whatever claim the desire and wish of Christ's heart has to draw out the favour of God, operates in drawing out that favour to us. The light and favour of the sanctuary—God as dwelling there—cannot shine out on him without shining on us, and that as an object presented by Him for it" (Mr. J. N. Darby).

5. *Its Name.*

It is called "the breastplate of judgment" (v. 15). This term occurs for the first time in Gen. 18:19, where God says to Abraham, concerning his sons, "They shall keep the way of the Lord, to do justice and judgment." Its next occurrence is in Ex. 21:1, where "judgments" signify the decrees or fiats of God—cf. Psalm 19:9. That which is here set forth is that the saints are represented by their High Priest according to God's mind concerning them. Expressing almost the same aspect of truth is that blessed word, "I know the thoughts that I think toward you, saith the Lord, thoughts of peace, and not of evil, to give you an expected end" (Jer. 29:11).

Closely connected with its name is what is said in v. 29: "And Aaron shall bear the names of the children of Israel in the breastplate of judgment upon his heart when he goeth in unto the holy place, *for a memorial* before the Lord continually." A remarkable word is this: A "memorial" is a reminder, for calling to remembrance. But does our Father in heaven need such? To inform His omniscience, no; but to delight His heart and satisfy His love, yes. And this, too, for the strengthening of our faith, that His people might know they have that in heaven for the staying of their hearts.

6. *Its Position.*

The Breastplate was placed over Aaron's heart. It is striking to observe that three times over we have these words "upon his heart" (vv. 29, 30, 30). As we have seen, the Breastplate was suspended from the shoulders by golden chains connected with the onyx stones, and from golden rings in the lower corners it was fastened to the girdle of the ephod by a lace of blue. Thus it was firmly secured over the heart of Israel's high priest. God's people were thus doubly represented: first, upon his shoulders, the place of strength; and then, upon his heart, the seat of affection. Lovely type was this of our Redeemer in His present heavenly ministry, exercising His power to uphold His poor people; and His deep, tender, unchangeable love embracing them, binding them close to His heart, and presenting them to the Father in the glory and preciousness of the splendour with which He is invested.

"This is precious, and oftentimes we need to refresh ourselves by 'considering' thus 'the Apostle and High Priest of our confession' (Heb. 3:1). There are times when we forget that we have One on high whom, in grace, cares for and watches over those who are treading the path of faith He once trod on earth. And there are times when, though we remember this, we limit either His love or His power. Precious, then, is it to be thus reminded that according to what He *can* do, His love makes us *willing* to do; and according to what His affection is, He hath strength to carry out what it dictates" (C. H. Bright).

It is beautiful to note in the Song of Sol. how the Bride says to her Beloved, "Set me as a seal upon Thine heart, as a seal upon Thine arm" (8:6): let my name be graven deep in Thine heart, where love is strong as death, which many waters cannot quench, which the floods of the Almighty have not drowned. And let my name be also graven in the seat of Thy power, that I may be upheld from sin and folly, that I may not be like the adulterer and adulteress who seek the friendship of the world. If such a prayer suited the desires of an earthy people, how much more may this petition express the devotion and the longings of Christ's heavenly people!

7. *Its Lace.*

"And they shall bind the breastplate by the rings thereof unto the rings of the ephod with a lace of blue, that it may be above the curious girdle of the ephod, and that the breastplate be not loosed from the ephod" (v. 28). What beautiful completeness this gives to our type! "Blue" is the *heavenly* colour, and "as long as His heavenly priesthood continues, so long is it inseparably connected with bearing us on the breastplate. Not that He will ever cease to love us, but when His church is *with* Him it will no longer need this care which the trials of the way call out. And surely to be *with* one who loves us is better than simply to be *remembered* by him, however faithful that remembrance may be. Christ is made a priest forever after the order of Melkeizedek. His priesthood has for the present an *intercessory* character, as typified in Aaron; but the time will come when—God's judgment upon the nations being executed—He will come forth as the Priest of the Most High God, not to intercede, but to *reward* (Gen. 14:18). At this time His *royal* priesthood will be in exercise, and ours too. 'King of righteousness' He will first be proved to be; then 'King of peace,' Heb. 7:2" (C. H. Bright).

May God be pleased to bless this little meditation to many of His people, and use it to make Christ more precious to them.
—*Arthur W. Pink.*

THE PROPHETIC PARABLES OF MATTHEW 13.

5. *The Mustard-seed.*

"Another parable put He forth unto them, saying, The kingdom of heaven is like to a grain of mustard-seed, which a man took, and sowed in His field: Which, indeed, is the least of all seeds: but when it is grown, it is the greatest among herbs, and becometh a tree, so that the birds of the air come and lodge in the branches thereof" (vv. 31:32).

It should be evident to all that our understanding of this parable hinges upon a correct interpretation of its three central figures: the mustard-seed, the great tree which sprang from it, and the "birds of the air" which came and lodged in its branches. *What* does each represent?

Now there are few passages of Scripture which have suffered more at the hands of commentators than the third and fourth parables of Matt. 13. They have been turned completely upside down; that is to say, they have been made to mean the very opposite of what the Lord Jesus taught. The main cause of this erroneous interpretation may be traced back to a wrong understanding of the expression "kingdom of heaven." Those who have failed in their definition of this term are, necessarily, all at sea, when they come to the details of these parables.

The popular and current explanation of these parables is that they were meant to announce the glorious success of the Gospel. Thus, that of the mustard-seed is regarded as portraying the rapid extension of Christianity and the expansion of the Church of Christ. Beginning insignificantly and obscurely, its proportions have increased immensely, until ultimately it shall cover the earth. Let us first show how untenable and impossible this interpretation is:

First, it must be steadily borne in mind that these seven parables form part of one connected and complete discourse whose teaching must necessarily be consistent and harmonious throughout. Therefore, it is obvious that this third one cannot conflict with the teaching of the first two. In the first parable, instead of drawing a picture of a field in which the good Seed took root and flourished in every part of it, our Lord pointed out that most of its soil was unfavourable, and that only a fractional proportion bore an increase. Moreover, instead of promising that the good-ground section of the field would yield greater and greater returns, He announced that there would be a decreasing harvest—"some an hundredfold, some sixty, some thirty." In the second parable, our Lord revealed the field as over-sown with "tares," and declared that these should continue until the harvest-time, which He defined as "the end of the age." This fixes beyond all doubt the evil consequences of the Enemy's work, and positively forbids the expectation of a world won to Christ during this present dispensation. Christ plainly warned us that the evil effects of the Devil's labours at the beginning of the age would never be repaired. The crop as a whole is spoiled! Thus this third parable *cannot* teach that the failure of things in the hands of men will be removed and reversed.

Second, the *figure* here selected by Christ should at once expose the fallacy of the popular interpretation. Surely our Lord would never have taken a mustard-seed, which afterwards became a "tree," ever rooting itself deeper and deeper in the earth, to portray that people whose calling, hope, citizenship, and destiny is *heavenly*. Again and again He affirmed that His people were "*not* of the world." Again, a great tree with its towering branches speaks of prominence and loftiness, but lowliness and suffering, not prominence and exaltation, are the present portion of the New Testament saints. The more any church of Christ climbs the ladder of worldly fame the more it sinks spiritually. That which is represented by this "tree" is *not* a people who are "strangers and pilgrims" down here, but a system whose roots lie deeply in the earth and which aims at greatness and expansion in the world.

Third, that which Christ here describes is a *monstrocity*. We are aware that this is denied by some, but our Lord's own words are final. He tells us that when this mustard-seed is grown it is the "greatest among *herbs*, and *becometh* a tree" (v. 32). "Herbs" are an entirely different specie from trees. That which distinguished them is that their stems never develop woody tissue, but live only long enough for the development of flowers and seeds. But this "herb" became a "tree;" that is to say, it developed into something entirely *foreign* to its very nature and constitution. How strange that sober men should have deemed this unnatural growth, this abnormal production, a fitting symbol of the *saints* of God in their corporate form!

Some tell us that the soil of Palestine is a most congenial one for the growth of mustard, and that it is quite common for it to develop into goodly-sized shrubs. But cannot the very ones who advance this as an objection to the pre-millennial interpretation of this parable see that it form an argument *against* what they contend for? Clearly the "field," all through Matt. 13, is *the world*. Is, then, "the world" a *favourable* place for the growth of that kingdom which Christ solemnly and expressly said was "*not* of this world" (John 18:36)? Is *this* world, where the flesh and the Devil unite in opposing all that concerns Christ and His interests, a *congenial* soil for Christianity? Either the world must cease to be what it is—"the enemy of God"—or the Seed must change its character, before the one will be favourable to the other. And this is just what our parable does teach: the "herb" becomes a "tree."

Fourth, the "birds" lodging in the branches of this tree makes altogether against the current interpretation. If Scripture be compared with Scripture it will be found that these "birds" symbolise Satan and his agents. Let not the reader be turned aside by the fact that the "dove," and in some passages the "eagle," represents that which is good. That which we must now attempt to define is the actual word "*birds*," or better, "*fowls*"—as the Greek word is rendered in v. 4. In Gen. 15:11 we are told that the "*fowls* came down upon the carcasses" (the bodies of the sacrifices) and that "Abram drove them away." Here, beyond doubt, they prefigure the efforts of Satan to render null and void the sacrifice of the Lord Jesus; but this, the Father (foreshadowed in Abraham) has prevented.

Again, in Deut. 28, where we have the curses which were to come upon Israel for their disobedience, we are told, "And thy carcase shall be meat unto all *fowls* of the air" (v. 26). The last time the term occurs in Scripture is in Rev. 18:2, where we are told that fallen Babylon becomes the "habitation of demons, and the hold of every foul spirit, and a cage of every unclean and hateful *bird*."

But we do not have to go outside of Matt. 13 itself to discover what Christ referred to under the figure of these "birds." The Greek word in v. 32 is precisely the same as that which is rendered "fowls" in v. 4, which are explained in v. 19 as "the wicked." How, then, can this great "tree" represent the true Church of Christ, while its branches afford shelter for the Devil and his emissaries?

Coming now to the positive side, if we let Scripture interpret Scripture, the great "tree" is easily identified. In Dan. 4:10-12 we read, "I saw, and behold *a tree* was in the midst of the earth, and the height thereof was great. The tree grew, and was strong, and the height thereof reached unto heaven, and the sight thereof to the ends of all the earth: The leaves thereof were fair, and the fruit thereof much, and in it was meat for all: the beasts of the field had shadow under it, and *the fowls* of the heavens dwelt in *the boughs* thereof, and all flesh was fed of it." Who cannot fail to see that we have in this vision of Nebuchadnezzar the *key* to our parable? In Daniel 4:20-22 we have the inspired interpretation of the vision: "The tree that thou sawest, which grew, and was strong. . . . it is thou, O king, that art grown and become strong, for thy greatness is grown, and reacheth unto heaven, and thy dominion to the ends of the earth." Thus, the "tree" was a figure of a mighty earthly kingdom or empire.

Again, in Ezek. 31 we have the same figure used: "Behold the "Assyrian was a *cedar* in Lebanon with fair branches, and with a shadowing shroud, and of an high stature; and his top was among the thick boughs. The waters made him great, the deep set him up on high with her rivers running round about his plants, and sent out her little rivers unto all the trees of the field. Therefore, his height was exalted above all the trees of the field, and his boughs were multiplied, and his branches became long because of the multitude of waters, when he shot forth. All the *fowls* of heaven made their nests in his boughs, and under his branches did all the beasts of the field bring forth their young, and under his shadow dwelt all great nations" (vv. 3-6). Thus a "tree," whose widespreading branches afforded lodgment for birds, was a familiar Old Testament figure for a mighty kingdom which gave shelter to the nations. So it is in our parable. The "tree" symbolises earthly greatness, worldly prominence, giving shelter to the nations.

The *history* of Christendom clearly confirms this. At the beginning, those who bore the name of Christ were but a despised handful. Judged by worldly standards, Christianity was unimportant and unworthy of serious consideration. Speaking generally, its adherents were not men of renown, culture, or worldly influence. There were few among the Lord's "little flock" of outstanding genius or social prominence; for the most part, they were unlettered, obscure, and poor. For, "God hath chosen the foolish things of the world to confound the wise; and God hath chosen the weak things of the world to confound the things which are mighty; and base things of the world, and things which are despised, hath God chosen, and things which are not, to bring to nought the things that are; that no flesh should glory in His presence" (1 Cor. 1:27-29).

Nevertheless, though at first the cause of Christ on earth was so uninfluential and insignificant, it was an object of intense hatred to Satan. Against Christianity he vented the full force of his fiendish malignity. Every weapon in his arsenal was employed in the effort to exterminate it. He stirred up men in authority and moved emperors to issue cruel edicts. Property was confiscated, Christians captured, imprisoned, fined, tortured, slain. Mercilessly and ceaselessly did the Devil seek to blot out the name of Christ from the earth. But the more it was persecuted, the more Christianity flourished. As one of the early "fathers" put it, "The blood of the martyrs was the seed of the Church."

Finding that force was of no avail, the Enemy changed his tactics. Failing to intimdiate as the roaring lion, he now sought to insinuate as the subtle serpent. Ceasing to attack from without, he now worked *from within*. In the first parable the assault was from without—the fowls of the air catchng away the Seed. In the second parable his activities were from within—he sowed his tares *among* the wheat. In the third parable we are shown the effects of this. Satan now moved worldly men to seek membership in the churches of God. These soon caused the Truth to be watered down, discipline to be relaxed, that which repelled the world to be kept in the background, and what would appeal to the carnal mind to be made prominent. Instead of affections being set upon things above, they were fixed on things below. Soon Christianity ceased to be hated by the unregenerate: the gulf between the world and the "Church" was bridged.

Persecution ceased, and the professed cause of the despised and rejected Saviour became popular. The distinctive truths of Christianity were abandoned, the Gospel was adulterated, the pilgrim character of professing saints ceased. More and more the wise and great of this world were attracted. By the fourth century the heads of the Roman Empire, instead of hating Christianity, perceived that it was a power for moral good in the governing of men, and so espoused it. In the days of Constantine the so-called Church and the State united, and became a vast political-religious system. Mind you, the courts of Caesar *had not changed* their character, nor become like the little "upper room" in Jerusalem, where the lowly Church of Christ, small as a grain of mustard, first assembled. It was professing Christianity which had changed. The lowly upper room had long been forsaken, and the honours of kings' courts coveted. And God granted their fleshly desire—just as long before He had given Saul to apostate Israel when they forsook the path of separation and wished to be like the surrounding nations.

Under these changed circumstances *professing* Christianity soon became *great* in the earth. Caves and caverns as places of worship gave place to costly church-houses and ornate cathedrals. The ritual was celebrated with a corresponding pomp. Its gorgeous vestments, its imposing ceremonies, its pompous priesthood, all lured the unregenerate; and multitudes applied for baptism. More and more the leaders sought after temporal power, and more and more were their longings gratified. In consequence, worldly-minded men were the ones who sought after and secured the highest offices. Hence we find the "birds," the agents of Satan, lodging in the *branches* of the "tree": they secured the positions of power and directed the activities of Christendom.

Thus we may discern in the first three parables of Matt. 13 a striking and sad forecast of the *development of evil*. In the first, the Devil caught away part of the good Seed. In the second, he is seen engaged in the work of imitation. Here, in the third, we are shown a corrupted Christianity affording him shelter.

N.B.—Several thoughts and expressions in this article have been borrowed from one by the late F. W. Grant.

—*Arthur W. Pink.*

OUTSIDE THE CAMP.

"Let us go forth therefore unto Him without the camp, bearing His reproach." (Heb. 13:13.)

The first thing calling for attention in our text is the word "therefore," which of necessity looks backward, pointing a conclusion from something that has been said previously. We need go no further back than verses 11 and 12 to find the premise from which the conclusion is drawn. There we read, "For the bodies of those beasts, whose blood is brought into the sanctuary by the high priest for sin, are burned without the camp. Wherefore Jesus also, that He might sanctify the people with His own blood, suffered without the gate. Let us go forth, therefore, unto Him without the camp." Now, in the 11th verse there is something that is exceedingly striking and solemn. The blood of those animals which were sacrificed was not always brought into the holy of holies and placed upon the mercy seat. It was the general custom to slay the animal in the outer court where the brasen-altar was, and to pour out its blood by the altar. If you turn to the first chapter of Leviticus several illustrations of that principle will be found there. "And he shall put his hand upon the head of the burnt offering; and it shall be accepted for him to make atonement for him. And he shall kill the bullock before the Lord: and the priests, Aaron's sons, shall bring the blood, and sprinkle the blood round about upon the altar that is by the door of the tabernacle of the congregation" (vv. 4, 5).

Continuing from Lev. 1: "And if his offering be of the flocks, of the sheep, or of the goats, for a burnt sacrifice; he shall bring it a male without blemish. And he shall kill it on the side of the altar northward before the Lord: and the priests, Aaron's sons, shall sprinkle his blood round about upon the altar" (vv. 10, 11). Now, if you read through the whole of the books of Exodus and Leviticus it will be found that this was the common custom: to sprinkle the blood of the animal which had been offered in sacrifice to God upon the altar in the outer court, not be take its blood inside the veil and place it upon the mercy-seat. But there was an exception. In Exodus 29:14 we read, "But the flesh of the bullock, and his skin, and his dung, shalt thou burn with fire without the camp:"—not upon the brasen-altar where the other sacrifices were consumed; this was to be burned with fire without the camp. It was a sin-offering. Now turn over to Leviticus 16:27, "And the bullock for the sin-offering, and the goat for the sin-offering, whose blood was brought in to make atonement in the holy place (not simply left outside at the altar in the outer court), shall one carry forth without the camp; and they shall burn in the fire their skins, and their flesh, and their dung."

During the Levitical economy God appointed many and various offerings and sacrifices for the Israelites to bring to Him. There was the burnt-offering, the meal-offering, the peace-offering, the trespass-offering, the passover-offering, the consecration-offering, and others; but the blood of none of them was carried within the veil and placed upon the mercy-seat. It was only that animal which was offered as a sin-offering to God, and whose body was burned *outside* the camp, whose blood was taken right into the holy place—typically opening up a way to God Himself.

Now if we turn back to Hebrews 13:11 you will understand that verse a little better: "For the bodies of those beasts whose blood is brought into the sanctuary by the high priest for sin, are burned without (outside) the camp." Why? That is something which is unutterably solemn. Outside the camp was the place beyond all ordered relationship with God. You recall from the book of Numbers that the centre of the camp was the tabernacle, and around that tabernacle were grouped the various tribes according to God's appointing. The camp was the place of ordered relationships to God, with God dwelling in the centre. Outside the camp was the place beyond all relationship to God, therefore it was the place that the leper was commanded to take, it was the place of the unclean. In other words, it was the place of distance from God, the place of divine judgment. And the antitype of that is seen at Calvary, where we hear the Sufferer on the central cross saying, "Why hast Thou forsaken Me?" It was the sin-offering being burned in the fires of God's wrath outside, away from God, the place of distance from God. It was the sin-offering being burned outside the camp. Hence we read in Hebrews 13:11:—"The bodies of those beasts whose blood is brought into the sanctuary by the high priest for sin are burned without the camp."

Do you see the meaning of the type, dear brethren and sisters? Listen closely: in connection with that offering whose blood opened a way to God Himself (was brought into the place where God was, and put on the mercy seat), the body of it was burned up outside the camp; no other body of an offering was. It was God there teaching us in the type that something more than death was necessary. All the other animals that were sacrificed at the brasen-altar died, but something more than death was necessary to bring you and me to God; something more than death by violence, for the animal at the brasen-altar was cut with a knife. What more than death was needed? "It is appointed unto men once to die, but after this the judgment"—the judgment of a sin-hating God. Ah, my brethren and sisters, Christ not only had to die, He not only had to lay down His life, but He had to come beneath the judgment of a sin-hating God, and that judgment is *banishment* from Him, separation from Him; that judgment is the place "outside the camp" where He was. Hence we read here in Hebrews 13:12:—"Wherefore Jesus also, that He might sanctify the people with His own blood, suffered without, suffered outside, outside the gate." The "gate" marked, of course, the limits of the City. He suffered outside the gate as One who was not regarded as being fit to be put to death in the City. In the eyes of the authorities He was such a vile wretch that their City would have been contaminated by executing Him within it; and so, as the last mark of shame and scorn, they led Him "outside" the City. Little did they know that they were fulfilling God's type! *That* was where the body of the animal whose blood was carried within must be burned—outside the camp. And so Jesus also, that He might sanctify (set apart) the people with His own blood, suffered without the gate. Only *such* blood could be carried into God; only such blood, the blood of a victim whose body was consumed outside the camp.

Now, I think there should be little difficulty in recognising the force of the "therefore" in our text. "Let us go forth therefore unto Him without the camp." In other words, if Jesus, the incarnate Son of God, in order to make an atonement for our sins, considered no sacrifice, no shame, no reproach too great for you and me, then let us therefore gladly submit to any little sacrifice that may be required from us if we are to be true to Him and His glory. "Let us . . . . therefore." Jesus took the place outside the camp;

shall we hesitate to? "Let us go forth therefore unto Him without the camp." In other words, we have, by matchless grace, been called unto fellowship with our Lord Jesus Christ—fellowship with Him now in sufferings, fellowship with Him soon in glory, for it is written, "If so be that we suffer with Him, that we may be also glorified together" (Rom. 8:17). "Let us go forth therefore unto Him without the camp, bearing His reproach." We are called upon to take up our cross and follow Him. Now, there are three things in the text that I want to briefly dwell upon.

First of all *a privilege* is set before us: "Let us go forth therefore unto Him." It is very important that we should carefully notice the order of the words in our text. It does not say, "Let us therefore go without the camp unto Him"; it says, "Let us go forth unto Him without the camp." What is the difference? I am very anxious that you should see this clearly for yourselves. Our text does not say, "Let us go forth therefore without the camp unto Him"; it says, "Let us go forth therefore unto Him without the camp." There are many in the past who have done that very thing: they have gone forth outside the camp, but it has only been to form another camp, more legalistic and more Pharisaical than Judaism itself. *Christ* must be the object, He must be the attraction. It is "unto *Him*" that we must go forth, otherwise it is no use leaving the camp.

"Let us go forth therefore unto Him"—unto Him who has ever been the Refuge of His people, unto Him who is sufficient for every situation, every emergency, every need that can arise; unto Him who is altogether lovely and who alone can satisfy the hearts of His people. "Let us go forth therefore unto Him," for *He* is "outside" the camp! We are shown that in Revelation 3:21, in that Laodicean epistle which so graphically describes conditions in Christendom to-day. There the Lord is represented on *the outside*. He says, "Behold, I stand at the door, and knock." He is on the outside, and that is why the call goes forth, "Let *us* go forth therefore *unto Him* without the camp." And, my brethren and sisters, to go forth unto "Him" cannot be loss; it must be gain!

In the second place, we not only have a privilege set before us (and to go forth unto Him *is* a privilege), but there is a duty enjoined upon us: "Let us *go forth* unto Him *without the camp*." To those to whom our text was first addressed, namely, the Hebrews, the converted Jews, going forth "without the camp" meant the forsaking of Judaism, with its temple, priesthood, and the whole of the ceremonial law. To them the word went forth, "You must leave it all; go forth unto Him without the camp." But why? Judaism had been appointed by God; Judaism was not a man-made, it was a God-appointed system. Why should His people be now called upon to leave it? Because Judaism had rejected Christ. There are more ways than one of rejecting Christ. God reminded us through one of the brethren in the opening prayer this morning that the Lord Jesus said, "He that receiveth you (My servant) receiveth Me, and he that receiveth Me, receiveth Him that sent Me. . . . He that despiseth you (My servant) despiseth Me; and he that despiseth Me despiseth Him that sent Me." *That* is what Judaism had done with Christ: "He came unto His own, and His own received Him not" (John 1:11). Judaism had rejected Christ, and Christ had rejected Judaism! He was now on the outside of it all.

At the beginning of His public ministry He said of the Temple, "Make not My Father's house an house of merchandise" (John 2:16). He *owned* the temple as God's house. But at the end, just before the cross, as He left the temple for the last time, He said, "*Your* house is left unto you desolate" (Matt. 23:38). He no longer owns it as God's house. He says, It is your house, and it is left unto you desolate. Judaism had rejected Christ. Christ rejected Judaism. And therefore, because Christ was now on the outside of Judaism, the Holy Spirit said to His people, "Let us go forth therefore unto Him without the camp." Why? Because the camp—Judaism: its temple, its priesthood, the whole system—was no longer owned of God. His glory had departed from it, His presence was no longer manifested there. It was a house left "desolate." Mind you, the house continued to stand for some years. The house itself was not destroyed until A.D. 70, but it was forsaken of God. So that this word in its first application to those to whom it came meant the turning of their backs upon Judaism, and in the case of those Hebrews it was a most searching, severe, flesh-harrowing test.

When God said to these believing Hebrews, "Go forth outside the camp," it meant separating themselves from their brethren according to the flesh who were still left in it. It meant forsaking a place of holy, happy memories, where God Himself had so often appeared in their midst to bless, but was now forsaken by Him. Yes, it was a searching, severe test, for the temple still stood, the outward form still went on. It was only those with discernment and the spiritual ear that could recognise the need for such a word as this, "Let us go forth therefore unto Him without the camp." But I want you to notice before I pass from this second point one striking, important, and radical difference in keeping with the change of dispensation. In Old Testament times "outside the camp" meant away from God; it meant being outside the circle of God's appointment, for that is what the camp was. "Outside the camp" under the Old Testament economy meant away from God and His house and His people. But there has been a change of dispensation, and everything is altered. It is the very opposite now. In this New Testament dispensation "outside the camp" is the place *where God is.*

But how are *we* to apply the exhortation of our text? Its first application was to the Hebrews in connection with Judaism; but Judaism has long since passed away! Has it? In one sense, yes. In another sense, no. Ceremonially, as a system, Judaism has passed away (in A.D. 70 when God used Titus to destroy Jerusalem); but in principle Judaism still remains. What characterised Judaism in the days of Christ and His apostles? What were the essential principles and marks of Judaism in His day? First of all, a system more or less orthodox, but devoid of life. That is what Judaism was. There was the temple; there was its priesthood, ordered more or less according to Scripture; but it was an orthodox system devoid of life. Secondly, Judaism was a system of clinging to "the traditions of the fathers," but refusing a further and fuller light. They were willing to receive the Old Testament —that is, their own interpretation of it— but the light of Christianity they did not want. That is what Judaism was, a clinging to the traditions of the fathers with no desire for further light, and turning their backs upon it when it was given them! Third, there was great strictness and punctuality in the observance of ordinances, but no unction or blessing. That is why in the Gospel of John, several times over, the feasts are called "the feasts *of the Jews*"—not "the Lord's passover," as in Exodus 12:27, but "the Jews' passover" (John 2:13)! The feast was still observed, and observed with great particularity; see John 18:28! O they were most punctilious in the observing of their rites and forms and ceremonies; *but* there was no life, no unction, no blessing in them. Just as those things characterised Judaism in the days of Christ and His Apostles, so these very things characterise Christendom to-day, denominationalism as such. That is true not of one, but of all of them. And while it is true that Romanism is that which gives us the extreme form of Judaism to-day, yet Rome has many daughters—dead-letter systems with their man-made creeds and *their* "articles of faith," which are as binding as the decrees of the Council of Trent. Yes, Rome has many daughters. The Counsels of Trent drawn up in 1545 are the final court of appeal with Rome. Those Counsels of Trent are like the laws of the Medes and Persians; they alter not. And Rome has many daughters, as the Denominational creeds and catechisms, rules and regulations sadly evidence.

"Let us go forth therefore unto Him without the camp." If any exercised soul is asking, How am I to know *what is* "the camp" and what is not the camp to-day? let me briefly suggest these answers: I will put them in the interrogative form. You may very soon discover which is the camp and which is not by answering these questions: Is *God* there? Is God's glory *manifested* there? Is God's presence *felt* there? If it is not, it is "the camp," and you are to leave it. "Go forth unto Him who is on the outside." Again, Is *His Word* supreme? Is the whole counsel of God, embraced in Old and New Testaments alike, the final court of appeal? If it is not, then it is "the camp," and you are called upon to leave it.

Now, the third thing in our text is *the sure consequence·* (are you prepared for it?), "bearing His reproach"—fellowship with a despised and rejected Christ. He bore reproach for us, scoffing rude; His holy face covered with the vile spittle of man; condemned to a convict's death; cast outside the city as unfit to die within its walls. Is it too much for Him to ask you and me to drink of the cup that He drank of and be baptised with the baptism that He was baptised with? "Let us go forth therefore unto Him without the camp, *bearing His reproach.*" You must expect it. You must be armed against it. You know the old saying, "Forewarned is forearmed." You remember those words concerning Moses in the same Epistle, chapter 11, verse 24:—"By faith Moses, when he was come to years, refused to be called the son of Pharaoh's daughter; choosing rather to suffer affliction with the people of God, than to enjoy the pleasures of sin for a season; esteeming the reproach of Christ greater riches than the treasures in Egypt."

Ah, my brethren and sisters, I want to dwell upon the verb for a moment. "Let us go forth therefore unto Him without the camp, bearing His reproach." I think that word includes three things: First of all, a willingness to suffer; secondly, a constancy in enduring it—not fleeing from, not seeking to escape, but "bearing" it; thirdly, it tells us of the spirit in which we should bear it: "suffering" His reproach —not retaliating, not opposing, but "bearing." When He was reviled, He reviled not again. We are to go forth meekly, passively "bearing," bearing His reproach. There is another thought, too: "bearing," not being crushed by it—carrying it. "If any will come after Me, let him deny himself, and take up his cross"—bearing it.

In closing, let me say, What a marvellous Book this is! There is a word in it suited to every circumstance that God's people can ever pass through in this world; a word directly fitted to every emergency that can arise, every need that can come. God has called many, if not all *of us*, to leave the camp, to go forth unto Him, to bear His reproach. But let our last thought be of *Himself*. "Let us go forth unto *Him*." O that we may go forth unto Him in our hearts—our affections set upon Him. O that we may go forth unto Him in our aim—nothing but His honour and glory before us. O that we may go forth unto Him in our ways—our methods, our work, our very "order" patterned after His will. O that it *all* may be "unto Him," then we shall have His blessings now and His public approval in the day to come.

N.B.—This was the first sermon preached by the Editor after he, with many of his dear Brethren and Sisters, had withdrawn from the Strict and Particular Baptists. May Divine grace now enable us to give Christ the pre-eminence in all things.— A.W.P.

THE CHURCHES OF GOD.

2. *Despising the Church.*

"Despise ye the church of God?" (1 Cor. 11:22).

The reference in the above text is to a local and visible church of Jesus Christ. In our last article we endeavoured to show from Scripture what such a church is, namely: a company of baptized believers, in organised relationship, publicly and corporately worshipping God according to the ways of His appointing. In this present one we shall seek to point out various ways in which the church of God is "despised" by different companies of people.

1. *It is despised by the world.*

There is no institution on earth that is so utterly despised by the world as is a true church of Christ which is scripturally ordered and conducted. "It is not only despised, but it is intensely hated. There is a clear distinction between despising and hating. You despise with the head; you hate with the heart. To despise is "to look down upon and lightly regard"; to hate is to have the spirit of murder. A church is despised and hated by the world just in proportion to its fidelity to the truth, and its loyalty to Christ. Neither the truth nor Christ was popular with the world, and His people need not expect to be, for, 'As He is so are we in this world.' Synagogues of Satan may be loved by the world, but the church that Jesus built, never. 'If ye were of the world, the world would love its own: but because ye are not of the world, but I have chosen you out of the world, therefore the world hateth you' (John 15:19)." (Pastor C. D. Cole.)

Let any church of Christ tighten the reins, let it hew closely to the lines God has marked out for it in Scripture: let its worship be modelled by Holy Writ, let its ordinances be administered, its discipline maintained, and all its work prosecuted according to the Word of God, and it will be, it *must* be, both despised and hated. To be more specific:

Let a church of God insist on a regenerated membership, demanding a credible profession of personal and real experience of God's great salvation, and it will soon be "despised." Let it *refuse* to receive those people that apply for membership who, though being of good moral character and social respectability, yet give no evidence of evangelical repentance and faith; and such a church will be regarded with contempt.

Let a church of God conform to the teaching of His Word upon the keeping of the Lord's supper. Let it refuse to act as though it were its *own*, to which they might properly "invite" whomsoever they pleased. Let it be recognised that the table is the *Lord's*, and therefore His church dare not receive to it any save those who possess the qualifications which *He* has stipulated, and refuse those who have not; and such a church will be "despised" as a company of narrow-minded bigots.

Let a church of God conduct its finances on Scriptural lines. Let it boldly affirm that *only* Christians may have fellowship with and part in supporting the cause of Christ. Let it affirm that those who despise and reject Him cannot give acceptably to God, and therefore that we cannot accept their money; and such a church will soon be looked upon as self-righteous Pharisees.

Let a church of God insist that all of its departments must be conducted according to God's Word, and it will be hated. Let a "Thus saith the Lord" be required for everything that is done in the Sabbath School, in the Sisters' work, in Missionary activities, and let it *refuse* the assistance and co-operation of worldlings, and such a church will be hated.

2. *It is despised by Christians on the outside.*

This is done by God's people, who deem His churches as of such little importance and value that they never join them. Some may say, I am not conscious of this; I do not see that my remaining a non-member *is* a "despising" of the church of God. Are you willing to be put to the proof? Then let us try and help you. Suppose you are attending some place of worship where you meet a number of the regular worshippers week by week and month by month, and they never speak to you. More, suppose you nod to them, and they give you the cold shoulder. *What conclusion would you draw?* This, that they had not much use for you; in a word, that they "despised" you. They might not say unkind things about you, they might not positively injure you; but by their *negative* conduct, by what they omitted, by their lack of respect, you would rightly conclude that they despised you. So, when I see real Christians continuing to slight the "church" itself—for the building in which it meets is merely the "churchhouse"—giving it the cold shoulder, holding aloof from it, then they *must* "despise" it. From the negative actions of such Christians I can only draw this conclusion. If they esteemed it, if they looked upon it as an honour and a privilege to be in membership, would they not promptly apply?

Now, to help such Christians see their duty, let us point out that the local church is the only institution on this earth that the Son of God has ordained and built. *He* organised no societies, no secret orders, no "lodges," no so-called "circles of fellowship"; but He did a "church." His will has been clearly made known that His people *should* be members of His "churches."

This comes out plainly in His teaching in the parable of the Net. Of the fishermen He said, "They drew to shore, and sat down, and gathered the good *into vessels*" (Matt. 13:48). In Matt. 18:15 to 17 He clearly intimated that a "brother" would be a member of a "church." In Acts 2:47 we are told that the Lord added "to the church." The Lord's will on this matter has further been clearly revealed in His Word concerning the "supper." "*Do* this in remembrance of Me" is His expressed command, and many of His people are not obeying. They cannot, while they remain outside of one of His own appointed churches, for Christ Himself has made this a *church ordinance,* as 1 Cor. 11:2 compared with 1 Cor. 1:2 plainly shows. Finally, those words found seven times over in Rev. 2 and 3, "He that hath an ear to hear, let him hear what the Spirit saith *unto the churches*," furnishes additional proof that God's people ought to belong to those institutions which His Spirit specifically addresses. If, then, your duty is clear and you are neglecting it, let us point out that in James 4:17 it is written, "Therefore to him that knoweth to do good, and doeth it not, to him it is *sin.*"

Of course, what has been said above does not apply to those children of God who are living in places where they are unable to obtain access to a true church of God, such as was defined and described in our preceding article. They should pray that it may please God to locate them where such a church *is* to be found.

3. *Despised by Christians on the inside.*

First, by unbecoming conduct. This is the local force of our text. The apostle points out to the Corinthians how that their disorderly walk was really a "despising" of the church of God. The reference was to the manner in which they had conducted themselves in the Assembly. What a warning is this for God's people to-day. How much all of us need to heed that word in Psa. 89:7: "God is greatly to be feared in the assembly of the saints, and to be *had in reverence* of all them that are about Him!" So, too, that word of the Saviour's, "Take heed how ye hear": with what demeanor, with what reverent awe; remembering that ye are listening to the holy and authoritative Word of God. Thus we may "despise the church of God" by looseness of conduct, carelessness of walk, irreverence, and lightness in its worship.

Second, by diverting honour from it to man-made societies. In Eph. 3:21 we read, "Unto Him be *glory in the church* by Christ Jesus throughout all ages." Therefore "the church" should have the credit, the honour, the glory for what is done and given by its members. Yet how often in a financial report we read, the church gave so much to foreign missions, the Sunday School so much, the Women's Aid so much, ad-nauseam. To divorce these departments from the church itself is to "despise" it. Christ has placed His glory in the church, and therefore His people should give it the glory which is its due. How striking is the language of 2 Cor. 8:23, "The messengers of the churches, *the glory of* Christ."

Third, by manifesting little or no interest in its prayer and "business" meetings. Remember that the word despise means to "think lightly of, to look down upon." Thus, if we rarely attend its weeknight meetings it must be because we lightly esteem their importance. If we are interested in the welfare of our church and are truly concerned for the honour of its Head, then shall we be anxious to see that its government and affairs are Scripturally conducted. If we do not, it must be because we "despise the church of God."

Fourth, by growing lax in its discipline. If we are jealous and zealous for the honour of God's house, we shall be anxious for its spirituality to be preserved. Those who take pride in their homes, see to it that they are kept clean and that everything is in its proper place. How much more so should this be the case in connection with *God's house,* that there, all things should be done "decently and in order." Remember the example set us by the Lord Jesus. Read the 2nd chapter of John's Gospel and see Him correcting the abuses of the Temple. If those in membership are willing to tolerate an ungodly and Christ-dishonouring walk on the part of some of their fellows, it must be because they "despise the church of God."

Fifth, by unnecessarily absenting ourselves from its worship of God. How many professing Christians to-day indulge in the habit of their godless neighbours by taking a two, four, or six weeks' "holiday," and either going to some pleasure resort, or away from where there are true "churches of God!" There is far more *worldliness* among God's people to-day than most of them are aware of. How many when they do go away for a "holiday" start out on the Saturday and return on the Monday! This looks as though they think more of their own ease than they do of the glory of God and the honour of His house. To such who may be guilty of these worldly practices we would ask them to answer this question before Him, "*Despise ye* the church of God?"

Sixth, by criticising its officers. How much complaining and fault-finding there often is among the members because their officers are "slow" or "old-fashioned" in their way of doing things! Have we forgotten how God manifested His displeasure against the children of Israel for "murmuring" against Moses and Aaron! Have we forgotten that it is written, "Thou shalt not speak evil of the ruler of thy people" (Acts 23:5)? What a needful word to-day is that in Heb. 13:17, "Obey them that have the rule over you, and submit yourselves; for they watch for your souls, as they that must give account, that they may do it with joy, and not with grief." Then pray for them, obey them, be respectful and loving to them, and then will they have "joy" and not "grief."

Seventh, by not allowing any other interests to take time, money, service, which should be given to "the church of God." Business interests, avoidable, cause some members to absent themselves from the mid-week services. Lodge meetings are allowed to keep others away: which shows plainly that they respect a man-made organisation and "despise the church of God." Going out shopping or visiting friends on the afternoon of the same day that the prayer-meeting is held, so that they are "too tired" to attend it that night, is another form of "despising the church of God."

If Romanists have made too much of "the church," clear it is that Protestants have made too little of it. We are creatures of extremes. The Papacy places salvation in the church, and makes her the custodian of God's truth. The church is nothing of the sort; it is to be in subjection to the truth: "Came the Word of God out from you? or came it unto you only?" (1 Cor. 14:36). Once again we would remind the reader that Scripture says, "Unto him be glory *in the church* by Christ Jesus throughout all ages." May there be increasing "glory" to Him in His churches, by all of their members cleaving more closely to the Scriptures and less and less "despising" the only institution on earth founded by our Saviour-God.

—*Arthur W. Pink.*

CHILDREN'S ADDRESS.

Below is the substance of a sermon preached by the Editor at a Sunday School Anniversary. We would suggest that those readers who have little ones should read this to them.

Whiter than Snow.

"Wash me, and I shall be whiter than snow" (Psa. 51:7). There are three points in this text which we shall briefly consider. First, the sinner's need of cleansing: the ones who need "washing" are those who are unclean. Second, this cleansing is done for sinners and not by them. Third, the effects of this cleansing.

1. *Our need of cleansing.* When David said "Wash me" he referred not to physical cleansing, but to spiritual. It was not his hands and face, but his heart, which needed "washing."

In God's sight we are all unclean. Sin defiles and pollutes: that is to say, sin makes us dirty, unfit for God's presence. If you were crossing the street on a very wet day and fell down, you know what would be the consequence. It would result in your clothes being soiled, and your hands and knees becoming muddy. You would be a filthy object.

Now, this is just how man became unclean. He had a fall. Adam and Eve, our first parents, fell from the position in which God placed them. They fell from a state of innocency. God made them clean in heart, and they became unclean. They disobeyed God, they sinned, and so became wicked and defiled. And all of Adam's children are wicked and defiled, too. "We are *all* as an unclean thing" (Isa. 64:6). "There is none that understandeth, there is none that seeketh after God, they are all gone out of the way, they are together become unprofitable; there is none that doeth good, no, not one" (Rom. 3:11, 12). Now, because of this, we all need washing; washing by God, so that we may be *made* clean.

Every one of us is born into this world with a sinful heart. God tells us that "the heart is deceitful above all things, and desperately wicked" (Jer. 17:9). Do you know why it is easier for each of us to do that which is wrong than that which is right? Do you know why it is harder to be good than naughty? It is because we are "naughty" *inside*, and God's word for "naughty" is *sin*.

"We are all as an unclean thing." If you are not sure whether your face is dirty or not, what is the best thing to do? Why, to gaze into a looking-glass. Now, the Bible is a spiritual looking-glass. In it God has given a true picture of what we are. And if we look into it we shall discover that we are unclean, and need washing.

Oh, children, our hearts are much blacker than we think. Often this is not seen till we grow up. Those wicked men that you sometimes hear about were once nice little children; but they were never washed by God!

2. *We cannot wash ourselves.* Not only does God's Word show us that we are dirty, sinful, but it also tells us that we cannot make ourselves clean. That is why, in our text, David asked *God* to wash him.

Did any of you ever try to wash a piece of coal and make it white? No, you would not be so silly. It would be an impossible task. Equally so is it for the sinner to cleanse himself. It is because of this that God sent His Son into the world, that Jesus Christ should die; for it was only by the shedding of His precious blood that anybody's sins *could* be washed away. Listen to what He says: "Without shedding of blood is no remission" (Heb. 9:22).

Now, in our text we hear a sinner praying to God, "Wash me." He knew that he could not wash himself. *God* must wash him or he never would be cleansed. I suppose most of you have seen a black man: well, all the soap and water in the world would not make his black face white. So there is nothing which we can do that will make ourselves clean.

It is because of this that we need to ask God to cleanse us. He is willing, if we really want Him to. If His Spirit has shown you how filthy and sinful you are, and made you feel your unfitness to go to Heaven, and put into your heart a desire for Him to cleanse you, then He is ready to do so. Is not that good news? Hear what He says in Isa. 1:18: "Though your sins be as scarlet, they shall be as white as snow; though they be red like crimson, they shall be as wool." This brings me to our next point:

3. *The results of God's cleansing.* "Wash me, and I shall be whiter than snow." Though some of you have never actually seen snow, yet you have a pretty good idea of what it looks like. It is one of the most beautiful things in Nature; it is one of the wonderful works of God. It is the whitest thing in all creation. It comes down from above, as though to tell us that Heaven is a place of perfect

purity; as indeed it is. Snow is of a wonderful colour: it is much whiter than anything man can make. A nice clean handkerchief looks yellow on the top of newly fallen snow. It is so white that when the sun shines upon it, it hurts the eyes to look at it. Yet in our text David says, "Wash me, and I shall be *whiter* than snow." But how is that possible? That is a question which some of the older folk would not find easy to answer. Let me now try and point out three respects in which a sinner who has been washed by God is made *whiter* than snow.

First, though snow is so spotlessly white, yet it does not cleanse what is beneath it. If there was a piece of waste ground on which garbage was thrown—dirty cans, old shoes, and other rubbish—and then the snow fell thick and covered them all over, yet they would still be there underneath. So it is with reformation. That is rather a long word for you little ones, isn't it? It means that effort or attempt which is made when the sinner seeks to *fit himself* for God. He tries to make himself nice and clean on the outside, but underneath he is still as sinful as ever. But when a sinner is cleansed by God and robed in the righteousness of Christ, he is "Clean every whit" (John 13:10). As we are told in 1 John 1:7, "The blood of Jesus Christ His Son cleanseth us from *all* sin." Thus, when God washes a sinner he is made "whiter than snow," because he is not only clean outwardly, but *all* defilement is removed from before his face.

Second, the whiteness of snow is only a created whiteness. Though snow is whiter than anything else in Nature, yet it does not partake of the actual purity of its Creator. God is the One who makes the snow, yet it is not as white as He is. But when God cleanses from sin, He clothes the sinner with a purity which is like His own nature. The righteousness which is given to a Christian is a *Divine* righteousness. As we are told in 2 Cor. 5:21, "For He hath made Him to be sin for us, who knew no sin; that we might be made the righteousness of God in Him." Thus the cleansed sinner is "whiter than snow" because he is made a "partaker of the Divine nature" (2 Peter 1:4), and is clothed with the righteousness of Christ (Phil. 3:9).

Third, though snow is beautifully white it does not remain so. How often has the preacher got up on a winter's morning and seen the ground all covered over with a carpet of spotless snow; and then the sun arose and began to melt it, the soot from the chimneys came down upon it, people walked over it, and it soon became slushy and dirty. By the end of the day that snow which was so gloriously white in the early morning was grimy and almost black by night-time. But how different is it with those who are washed by God! Though still sinful in themselves, yet *in Christ* they remain perfectly clean forever. "For by one offering He hath perfected forever them that are sanctified" (Heb. 10:14). "I know that, whatsoever God doeth, it shall be *forever*: nothing can be put to it, nor anything taken from it: and God doeth it, that men should fear before Him" (Eccl. 3:14). Thus the Christian is "whiter than snow," for his fitness for God's presence is an eternal one.

When the soldier pierced the side of Jesus we are told that "forthwith came there out blood and water" (John 19:34). The blood was to justify; the water was to sanctify. The blood was to satisfy the demands of God's justice; the water was to purify His believing people.

Oh, children, if, while I have been preaching, God has shown you that your heart is very unclean and filthy, and if you feel that you really want Him to make you whiter than snow, then ask God to cleanse *you*. Get alone in your room, get down on your knees, and say with David, "Wash me, and I shall be whiter than snow." May the Lord bless you.

—*Arthur W. Pink.*

Are you praying for God to use this Magazine?

Ask Him to bless it to many.

A RAY OF SUNSHINE.

A minister, whom the Master has been pleased to honour as a comforter of the saints, relates the following incident: In the earlier years of my Christian life I was accustomed to visit a poor district of a city in Scotland. One day I stepped into a hovel, dimly lighted and scantily furnished, but yet displaying a studied neatness and order. The only inmate, an aged woman, bowed down with infirmities, and almost blind, was seated near the fireplace. A few moments' conversation satisfied me that she was one of Christ's lowly ones, rich in faith, full of peace, and rejoicing in hope of the glory of God. After my own soul had been refreshed with her own gracious words, I asked, "And how do you spend the long day here?" "There is little difference to me," she replied, "between the hours of night and day, but they never seem long. There is One who abides with me, whose love makes it all light and joy to my soul. When I awake He is still with me, and the time seems too short to meditate on His perfections and to commune with Him. My neighbours are very kind, and when they come in to help me I have the privilege of telling them what He is to me, and of persuading them to taste and see that God is good. There is just one hour for which I watch. You see that window, she said, pointing to the four little panes that admitted the dim light into the apartment in which we sat. "For about an hour every day, when it is not cloudy, the sun shines in there. I then take my large-printed Bible and sit down in the sunlight, where I can see well enough to read, and a precious hour it is to me."

"I thought," said the minister when he related her little story, "I thought of the great sun, the centre of the solar system, sending his light and heat to so many distant worlds. I thought of all that he shone upon in this busy world—the fields of grain, and the golden fruits that were ripening in his heat—all the labours of man that were advancing in his light; and I felt sure that from his going forth from the ends of heaven, as a bridegroom coming forth from his chamber, as a strong man to run a race, in all his circuits to the end of it, he did no nobler service and none more so grateful to our Father in heaven, who causeth His sun to shine on the evil and on the good, than when, for a short hour, he sent a few beams into that little window, to light up the sacred page to the dim eyes of that poor old woman whom the world knew not."

—Scripture Testimony.

GOD'S WORD ABOUT GIVING.

"Remember the words of the Lord Jesus, how He said, It is more blessed to give than to receive" (Acts 20:35). "Give and it shall be given unto you" (Luke 6:38).

"Bring ye *all* the tithes into the storehouse . . . . and prove Me now herewith, saith the Lord of hosts, if I will not open you the windows of heaven, and pour you out a blessing, that there shall not be room enough to receive it" (Mal. 3:10).

"Lay *not* up for yourselves treasures upon earth . . . . but lay up for yourselves treasures in heaven" (Matt. 6:19 20). "But to do good and to communicate forget not: for with such sacrifices God is well pleased" (Heb. 13:16).

"But this I say, he which soweth sparingly shall also reap sparingly; and he which soweth bountifully shall reap also bountifully. Every man according as he prospereth in his heart so let him give; not grudgingly, or of necessity: for God loveth a cheerful giver. And God is able to make all grace abound toward you; that ye always having all sufficiency in all things, may abound to every good work" (2 Cor. 9:6-9).

"My God shall supply all your need according to His riches in glory by Christ Jesus" (Phil. 4:19). "Now concerning the collection for the saints, as I have given order to the churches of Galatia, so do ye. Upon the first day of the week let every one of you lay by him in store, as God hath prospered him" (1 Cor. 16:1, 2). "For the administration of this service not only supplieth the want of the saints, but is abundant also by many thanksgivings unto God" (2 Cor. 9:12). "Thanks be unto God for His unspeakable gift" (2 Cor. 9:15).

N.B.—Please see also:—2 Cor. 8:9; Gal. 6:6; Prov. 11:24, 25.

Compiled by three Chinese evangelists.

to the sufferings which faithfulness to and fellowship with Christ necessarily involve. The little sacrifices we may be called upon to make, ought not to unduly distress us. We are but "strangers and pilgrims" here: we have no permanent abode in this poor world. This is not our rest; our Home is above, and its joys will more than compensate us for what we suffer now. In the light of Holy Writ Christians ought not to be surprised at the vicissitudes of life. Let the reader turn to Numbers 33 and note particularly verses 1, 3, 5-11 and onwards. What is written large across that chapter? This: No resting-place in the Wilderness. And *we* are still in the wilderness, and frequently does God remind us of it. All that is earthly is transitory. Only that which is spiritual is permanent.

But *why* these frequent "changes," which so perturb the flesh? Because we are called unto "the fellowship of God's Son, Jesus Christ our Lord" (1 Cor. 1:9). This means something more than participating in His life and sharing His peace and joy. It means that we are called to share, in measure, His experiences—enduring the wrath of God, alone excepted. We are called upon to follow a rejected Christ: see John 10:4; Luke 22:28; etc.

What was *Christ's* experience in this world? Even as a little Child there was no rest for Him here; His parents had to take Him down into Egypt, to escape the wrath of Herod. Trace the record of His public ministry: He was ever on the move— "Who *went about* doing good" (Acts 10:38). We read in John 4:6, "Jesus therefore being *wearied* with His journey." We too must share this experience. If we are called unto fellowship with Him who had not where to lay His head, should we be surprised if, in our circumstances, we are frequently reminded that "here have we *no continuing city*"?

Why these frequent changes? Let the reader carefully ponder Deut. 32:11, 12, "As an eagle *stirreth up* her nest, fluttereth over her young, spreadeth abroad her wings, taketh them, beareth them on her wings: *so* the Lord alone did lead him." Thus does God still deal with His people. Why? To teach them to use their wings, that they may soar above the earth, and delight themselves in heavenly places. It is written, "Set your affection on things above, not on things on the earth" (Col. 3:2), and because we are so slow to obey, often God "stirs up" our earthly nests!

Notice how it is put in the text. It is not, "Here there *is* no continuing city," but "Here have *we* no continuing city"—as though believers are the only ones of whom this is true. In reality the worldling has here "no continuing city;" yet he *has* in his imagination and affections—he sets his heart on temporal things and *acts* as though he will enjoy them always. See Psalm 49:11; 2 Peter 3:4!

"But we seek one to come." We seek a "City," which is in striking contract from "the Camp," which also has no continuance. This "City" which Christians "seek" is the one mentioned in Heb. 10:34; 11:10; 12:28; Rev. 21:2. This City is also contrasted from the cities of the earth. The first "city" mentioned in Scripture is in Gen. 4:17; where is *it* now? Destroyed long ago by the flood! Where too are Nineveh, Thebes, Babylon? They were strong and stately in their time; but they are no more. Ours is "eternal in the heavens" (2 Cor. 5:1)!

Why do we "seek" *this* City? Because it is the Dwelling-place of God. Where He is, His children long to be. The Greek word here for "seek" is very emphatic, signifying an earnest seeking of the heart, as in Matt. 7:7. It implies a deep longing to obtain, and is rendered "desire" in Phil. 4:17. It is used of the Gentiles who "seek" the things of this world—seek with great determination and ardour. So it is with the true Christian: the more he is nauseated by this world, the more he longs for Heaven. How blessed is the promise, "Him that overcometh will I make a pillar in the temple of My God, and he shall *go no more out*" (Rev. 3:12)!

"We seek one to come." May this be increasingly true of each Christian reader during 1928. The time is short, beloved; "the night is far spent" (Rom. 13:12). Have we not already wasted far too much time in "seeking" the things of earth? "Set your affection on things above" (Col. 3:2). Press forward unto the things "which are before" (Phil. 3:13). Let this be our watchword for the New Year: "we *seek* one to come.'" Seek it by faith, with singleness of purpose; seek it in hope, by blessed anticipation, a hope that shall not make ashamed; seek it in love, with our hearts set upon it; seek it as strangers and pilgrims on earth, "for they that say (by their actions) such things declare plainly that they *seek* a Country" (Heb. 11:14). Thus shall we prove ourselves to be, indeed, the children of Abraham (Rom. 4:16), for "*he looked* for a city which hath foundations, whose builder and maker is God" (Heb. 11:10).

—*Arthur W. Pink.*

STUDIES IN THE SCRIPTURES

"Search the Scriptures" John 5: 39

Copyright in all English-speaking Countries.

Editor: Arthur W. Pink, 15 Hurlstone Avenue, Summer Hill, N.S.W., Australia.
Hon. Agent in U.S.A.: Mr. C. S. Pressel, 559 Dupont Avenue, York, Penna.

FREE TO ALL WHO WILL READ IT

THE LORDSHIP OF CHRIST.

"But sanctify in your hearts Christ as Lord" (1 Peter 3:15, R.V.).

In view of their context it is very striking to note that it was *Peter* whom the Spirit of God first moved to write these words. As he did so, his heart, no doubt, was filled with sorrow and deep contrition. In v. 14 he says "If ye suffer for righteousness' sake happy are ye: and be not afraid of their terror, neither be troubled." On a never-to-be forgotten occasion, *he* had been afraid of the "terror" of the wicked. In Pilate's palace the fear of man brought him a snare. But in our text he announces the Divine remedy for deliverance from the fear of man.

"But sanctify in your hearts Christ as Lord." In the light of its setting, this means, first of all, Let the awe and blessedness of the lordship of Christ possess your hearts. Dwell constantly on the fact that Christ *is* "Lord." Because He is "Lord" all power in heaven and earth is His, and therefore He is master of every situation, sufficient for every emergency, able to supply every need. When a Christian cowers and trembles in the presence of his enemies, it is because he doubts or has lost sight of the faithfulness and power of Christ. Let us seek grace to cherish in our hearts an abiding sense of Christ's lordship, and unswerving reliance upon His presence and power.

"But sanctify in your hearts Christ as Lord." Yet, let not the motive or purpose for obeying this precept be our own peace and comfort, but *His* honour and glory. To guard against the fear of man the saint is to cultivate the fear of the Lord, and that, that Christ Himself may be magnified. The Lord Jesus is glorified when His tried and persecuted people preserve a calm demeanour and immovable fortitude before all opposition. But remember this is possible only as our hearts are occupied with Him, and particularly with His lordship.

"But sanctify in your hearts Christ as Lord." Having pointed out the more direct force of these words as modified by their context, let us now dwell upon their wider application. How little professing Christians *do* dwell upon the lordship of Christ! What dishonouring and degrading conceptions many of them entertain of Him who is yet to be the Judge of all! How sadly inadequate are the real Christian's views of that One who has been given a name which is above every name! "That I may know (obtain a better knowledge of) Him" (Phil. 3:10) should be the daily longing of our hearts, and the earnest prayer of our lips. Not only do we need to *grow* in "grace," but also in "the knowledge of our Lord and Saviour Jesus Christ" (2 Peter 3:18).

How little we really know the Christ of God! "No one knoweth (perfectly) the Son, but the Father" (Matt. 11:27). Yet much, very much, has been revealed concerning Him in the Holy Scriptures. But how little we study those Scriptures with the definite object of seeking a better, deeper, fuller knowledge of the Lord Jesus!

(Continued on page 48.)

IMPORTANT NOTICES

Back numbers of each year of the magazine are yet obtainable at 5/- (1.25) per year. Bound at 7/6 (1.75) post paid. They will soon be out of print. Those in U.S.A. wanting them, please purchase from Mr. Pressel (see front cover page).

Advise promptly of change of address. This Magazine is published as a work of faith and labour of love. The Editor gladly gives his services. It is freely sent to all who will read it. No charge is made for it.

Christians who feel definitely led to do so, may have fellowship with us in this Ministry. Send only *Inter-National M.O.*

CONTENTS.

	Page
Hebrews	26
Gleanings in Exodus	32
The Urim and Thummim	36
Parables of Matt. 13	40
Spiritual Progress	43

THE EPISTLE TO THE HEBREWS.

2. The Superiority of Christ over the Prophets 1:1-3.

Before taking up the study of the opening verses of our Epistle, let us adduce further evidence that the apostle Paul was the writer of it. To begin with, note its Pauline *characteristics*. First, a *numerical* one. There is a striking parallel between his enumeration in Rom. 8:35-39 and in Heb. 12:18-24. In the former he draws up a list of the things which shall not separate the saint from the love of God which is in Christ Jesus. If the reader will *count* them, he will find they are seventeen in number, but divided into a seven and a ten. The first seven are given in v. 35, the second ten in vv. 38, 39. In Heb. 12:18-23 he draws a contrast between Mount Sinai and Mount Sion, and he mentions seventeen details, and again the seventeen is divided into a seven and a ten. In vv. 18, 19 he names seven things which the saints are *not* "come unto"; while in vv. 22 to 24 he mentions ten things they *have* "come unto," viz., to Mount Sion, the City of the living God, the heavenly Jerusalem, an innumerable company of angels, the general Assembly, the Church of the Firstborn, to God the Judge of all, to the spirits of just men made perfect, to Jesus the Mediator, to the Blood of sprinkling. Compare also Gal. 5:19-21, where the apostle, when describing the "works of the flesh," enumerates *seventeen*. So far as we are aware, no other epistle writer of the N.T. used this number seventeen in such a manner.

Again; the *terms* which he used. We single out one only. In Heb. 2:11 he speaks of the many *sons* which Christ is bringing to glory. Now Paul is the *only* N.T. writer that employs the term "sons." The others used a different Greek word meaning "children."

For *doctrinal* parallelisms compare Rom. 8:16 with Heb. 10:15, and 1 Cor. 3:1-3 with Heb. 5:12-14, and who can doubt that the Holy Spirit used the *same* penman in both cases?

Note a *devotional* correspondency. In Heb. 13:18 the writer of this Epistle says, "Pray for us." In his other Epistles we find Paul, more than once, making a similar request; but *no other* Epistle-writer is placed on record as soliciting prayer!

Finally, it is to be noted that *Timothy* was the companion of the writer of this Epistle, see 13:23. We know of no hint anywhere that Timothy was the fellow-worker of anyone else but the apostle Paul: that he companied with *him* is clear from 2 Cor. 1:1, Col. 1:1, 1 Thess. 3:1, 2.

In addition to the many Pauline characteristics stamped on this Epistle, we may further observe that it was written by one who had been in "bonds" (see 10:34); by one who was now sundered from Jewish believers (13:19)—would not this indicate that Paul wrote this Epistle while in his hired house in Rome (Acts 28:30)? Again; here is a striking fact, which will have more force with some readers than others: if the Epistle to the Hebrews was *not* written by the apostle Paul, then the N.T. contains only *thirteen* Epistles from his pen—a number which, in Scripture, is ever associated with evil! But if Hebrews was also written by him, this brings the total number of his Epistles to fourteen, i.e., 7 x 2—seven being the number of perfection and two of witness. Thus, *a perfect witness* was given by this beloved servant of the Lord to Jew and Gentile!

In the last place, there is one other evidence that the apostle Paul penned the Hebrews' Epistle which is still more conclusive. In 2 Thess. 3:17-18 we read, "The *salutation* of Paul with mine own hand, which is the token in *every* Epistle, so I write. the *grace* of our Lord Jesus Christ be with you all." Now, if the reader will turn to the closing verse of each of the first thirteen Epistles of this apostle, it will be found that this "token" is given in each one. Then, if he will refer to the close of the Epistles of James, Peter, John and Jude, he will discover a noticeable *absence* of it. Thus it was a *distinctive* "token" of the apostle Paul. It served to identify *his* writings. When, then, at the close of Hebrews we read *"grace be with you all"* the proof is conclusive and complete that none other than Paul's hand originally wrote this Epistle.

Ere passing from this point a word should be added concerning the distinctive *suitability* of Paul as the penman of this Epistle. In our little work "Why Four Gospels" (pages 20-22), we have called attention to the *wisdom* of God displayed in the selection of the four men He employed to write the Gospels. In each one we may clearly perceive a special personal fitness for the task before him. Thus it is here. All through the Epistle of Hebrews Christ is presented as the glorified One in Heaven. Now, it was *there* the apostle Paul first saw the Lord (Acts 26:19); who, then, was so well suited, so experimentally equipped, to present to the Hebrews the rejected Messiah at God's right hand! *He* had seen Him there; and with the exceptions of Stephen, and later, John of Patmos, he was the only one who had or has!

Should it be asked, *Why* is the apostle Paul's *name* omitted from the preface to this Epistle? a threefold answer may be suggested. First, it is addressed, primarily, to converted "Hebrews," and Paul was not characteristically or essentially an apostle *to them:* he was the apostle to the Gentiles. Second, the inscribing of his name at the beginning of this Epistle would, probably, have prejudiced many Jewish readers against it (cf. Acts 21:27, 28; 22:17-22). Third, the supreme purpose of the Epistle is to exalt Christ, and in this Epistle *He* is the "Apostle," see 3:1. Therefore the impropriety of Paul making mention of his own apostleship. But let us now turn to the contents of the Epistle:

VV. 1-3. These verses are not only a preface, but they contain a summary of the doctrinal section of the Epistle. The keynote is struck at once. Here we are shown, briefly but conclusively, the superiority of Christianity over Judaism. The apostle introduces his theme in a manner least calculated to provoke the antipathy of his Jewish readers. He begins by acknowledging that Judaism was of Divine authority: it was *God* who had spoken to their fathers. "He confirms and seals the doctrine which was held by the Hebrews, that unto them had been committed the oracles of God; and that in the writings of Moses and the prophets they possessed the Scripture which could not be broken, in which God had displayed unto them His will" (A. Saphir). It is worthy of note that the Gospels open with a summary of O.T. history from Abraham to David, from David to the Captivity, and from the Captivity to Jesus, the Immanuel predicted by Isaiah (see Matt. 1), and that the Epistles also begin by telling us that the Gospel expounded by the prophets had been "promised afore by God's prophets in the Holy Scriptures" (Rom. 1:1-3).

Having affirmed that God *had* spoken to the fathers by the prophets, the apostle at once points out that God has now spoken to us by His Son. "The great object of the Epistle is to describe the contrast between the old and new covenants. But this contrast is based upon their unity. It is impossible for us rightly to understand the contrast unless we know first the resemblance. The new covenant is contrasted with the old covenant, not in the way in which the light of the knowledge of God is contrasted with the darkness and ignorance of heathenism, for the old covenant is also of God, and is therefore possessed of Divine glory. Beautiful is the night in which the moon and the stars of prophecy and types are shining; but when the sun arises then we forget the hours of watchfulness and expectancy, and in the clear and joyous light of day there is revealed to us the reality and substance of the eternal and heavenly sanctuary" (A. Saphir). Let us now examine these opening verses word by word.

"God" (v. 1). The particular reference is to the Father, as the words "by (His) Son" in v. 2 intimate. Yet the other Persons of the Trinity are not excluded. In O.T. times the Godhead spoke by the Son, see Exodus 3:2, 1 Cor. 10:9; and by the Holy Spirit, see Acts 28:26, Heb. 3:7, etc. Being a Trinity in Unity, one Person is often said to work by Another. A striking example of this is found in Gen. 19:24, where Jehovah the Son is said to have rained down fire *from* Jehovah the Father.

"God . . . . spake" (v. 1). Deity is not speechless. The true and living God, unlike the idols of the heathen, is no dumb Being. The God of Scripture, unlike that absolute and impersonal "first Cause" of philosophers and evolutionists, is not silent. At the beginning of earth's history we find Him speaking: "God *said,* Let there be light: and there was light" (Gen. 1:4). "He spake and it was done, He commanded and it stood fast" (Psa. 33:9). To men He spake, and still speaks. For this we can never be sufficiently thankful.

"God who at sundry times . . . spake" (v. 1). Not once or twice, but many times, did God speak. The Greek for "at sundry times" literally means "by many parts," which necessarily implies, some at one time, some at another. From Abraham to Malachi was a period of fifteen hundred years, and during that time God spake frequently: to some a few words, to others many. The apostle was here paving the way for making manifest the superiority of Christianity. The Divine revelation vouchsafed under the Mosaic economy was but *fragmentary*. The Jew desired to set Moses against Christ (John 9:28). The apostle acknowledges that God *had* spoken to Israel. But *how?* Had He communicated to them the fulness of His mind? Nay. The O.T. revelation was but the refracted rays, not the light unbroken and complete. As illustrations of this we may refer to the *gradual* making known of the Divine character through His different titles, or to the prophesies concerning the coming Messiah. It was "here a little and there a little."

"God who . . . in divers manner spake" (v. 1). The majority of the commentators regard these words as referring to the *various ways* in which God revealed Himself to the prophets—sometimes directly, at others indirectly—through an angel (Gen. 19:1, etc.); sometimes audibly, at others in dreams and visions. But, with Dr. J. Brown, we believe that the particular point here is *how* God spake *to the fathers* by the prophets, and not how He has made known His mind to the prophets themselves. "The revelation was sometimes communicated by typical representations and emblematical actions, sometimes in a continued parable, at other times by separate figures, at other times—though comparatively rarely—in plain explicit language. The revelation has sometimes the form of a narrative, at other times that of a prediction, at other times that of an argumentative discourse; sometimes it is given in prose, at other times in poetry" (Dr. J.B.). Thus we may see here an illustration of the *sovereignty* of God: He did not act *uniformly* or confine Himself to any one method of speaking to the fathers. He spake by way of promise and prediction, by types and symbols, by commandments and precepts, by warnings and exhortations.

"God . . . spake in times past unto the fathers by the prophets" (v. 1). Thus the apostle sets his seal upon the Divine inspiration and authority of the O.T. Scriptures. The "fathers" here goes right back to the beginnings of God's dealings with the Hebrews—cf. Luke 1:55. To "the fathers" God spake "by," or more literally and precisely, "*in*" the prophets. This denotes that God possessed their hearts, controlled their minds, ordered their tongues, so that they spake not their own words, but *His* words—see 2 Peter 1:21. At times the prophets were themselves conscious of this, see 2 Sam. 23:2, etc. We may add that the word "prophet" signifies the mouthpiece of God: see Gen. 20:7, Ex. 7:1, John 4:19—she recognised *God* was speaking to her; Acts 3:21!

"God . . . hath in these last days spoken unto us by"—better "in" (His) Son" (v. 2). "Having thus described the Jewish revelation he goes on to give an account of the Christian, and begins it in an antithetical form. The God who spake to 'the fathers' now speaks to 'us.' The God who spake in 'times past,' now speaks in these 'last days.' The God who spake 'by the prophets,' now speaks 'by His Son.' There is nothing in the description of the Gospel revelation that answers to the two phrases 'at sundry itmes,' and 'in divers manners'; but the ideas which they necessarily suggest to the mind are, the *completeness* of the Gospel revelation compared with the imperfection of the Jewish, and the *simplicity* and clearness of the Gospel revelation compared with the multiformity and obscurity of the Jewish" (Dr. J. Brown).

"This manifesting of God's will by parts ('at sundry times,' etc.), is here (v. 1) noted by way of distinction and difference from God's revealing His will under the Gospel; which was all at one time, viz., the times of His Son's being on earth: for then the whole counsel of God was made known so far as was meet for the Church to know it while this world continueth. In this respect Christ said, 'All things that I have heard of My Father, I have made known to you' (John 15:15), and 'the Comforter shall teach you all things, and bring to your remembrance whatsoever I have said unto you.' The woman of Samaria understood thus much: 'When the Messiah is come, He will tell us *all* things' (John 4:25). Objection: the apostles had many things revealed to them later. Answer: those were no other things than what Christ had revealed before, while He lived" (Dr. Gouge).

The central point of contrast here is between the O.T. "prophets" and Christ "the Son." Though the Holy Spirit has not here developed the details of this contrast, we can ourselves, by going back to the O.T., supply them. Mr. Saphir has strikingly summarised them under seven heads. "First, they were many: one succeeded another: they lived in different periods. Second, they gave out God's revelation in 'divers manners'—similitudes, visions, symbols. Each prophet had his peculiar gift and character. Their stature and capacity varied. Third, they were sinful men—Isa. 6:5, Dan. 10:8. Fourth, they did not possess the Spirit constantly. The 'word' came to them, but they did not *possess* the Word! Fifth, they did not understand the heights and depths of their own message—1 Peter 1:10. Sixth, still less did they comprehend the whole of God's revelation in O.T. times. Seventh, like John the Baptist they had to testify 'I am not the Light I am only sent to bear witness of the Light.'" Now, the very opposite was the case in all these respects with the "Son." Though the revelation which God gave the prophets is equally inspired and authoritative, yet that through His Son possesses a greater dignity and value, for *He* has revealed all the secrets of the Father's heart, the fulness of His counsel, and the riches of His grace.

"In these last days" (v. 2). This expression is not to be taken absolutely, but is a contrast from "in time past." The ministry of Christ marked "the last days" *of the Mosaic dispensation*, Heb. 9:26 proves this, "but now, once (for all), in the *end* of the age (*not* the beginning of a *new* age) hath He appeared to put away sin by the sacrifice of Himself." To those who would raise a quibble over this, and object, You are inconsistent: first, you say these verses contrast Judaism and Christianity, the latter of which was an entirely new thing; now you tell us the ministry of Christ was the winding up of the old economy. Our answer is, The difficulty is more imaginary than real. God's truth cannot be compressed into the narrow compartments which men arbitrarily invent. Take the Lord's word to the Samaritan adultress: "the hour cometh and now is" (John 4:23, cf. 5:23). The truth is, there was an overlapping of dispensations, or, more correctly, the ministry of Christ marked a *transitional* period. This much on the *dispensational* meaning of the term. But no doubt it has a *doctrinal* force, too. That which the Holy Spirit was pressing upon the Hebrews was the *finality* of the Gospel revelation. Through the "prophets" God had given predictions and foreshadowings; in the Son, the fulfilment and substance. The "fulness of time" had come when God sent forth His Son (Gal. 4:4). He has nothing now in reserve. He has no further revelation to make. Christ is the *final* Spokesman of Deity. The written Word is now complete. In conclusion, note how Christ *divides history*: everything before pointed toward Him, everything since points back to Him; *He* is the Centre of all God's counsels.

"Spoken unto us" (v. 2). "The pronoun *us* refers directly to the Jews of that age, to which class belonged both the writer and his readers; but the statement is equally true in reference to all, in every succeeding age, to whom the word of this salvation comes. God, in the completed revelation of His will, respecting the salvation of men through Christ Jesus, is still speaking to all who have an opportunity of reading the N.T. or of hearing the Gospel" (Dr. J. Brown).

"In (His) Son" (v. 2). Christ is the "Son of God" in two respects. First, eternally so, as the second Person in the Trinity, very God of very God. Second, He is also the "Son" as incarnate. When He took upon Him sinless human nature He did not cease to be God, nor did He (as some blasphemously teach) "empty" Himself of His Divine attributes, which are inseparable from the Divine Being. "*God* was manifest in flesh" (1 Tim. 3:16). Before His birth, God sent an angel to Mary, saying, "He (the Word become flesh) shall be called the Son of God" (Luke 1:35). The One born in Bethlehem's manger was the *same* Divine Person as had subsisted from all eternity, though He had now taken unto Him another, an additional nature, the human. But so perfect is the *union* between the Divine and the human natures in Christ that, in some instances, the properties of the one are ascribed to the other: see John 3:13, Rom. 5:10. It is in the *second* of these respects that our blessed Saviour is viewed in our present passage—as the Mediator, and not in His essential Being. As the Mediator, the God-man, God "spake" in and through Him: see John 17:8, 14, etc.

Summarising what has been said, we may note how that this opening sentence of our Epistle points a threefold contrast between the communications which God has made through Judaism and through Christianity. First, in their respective *characters*: the one was fragmentary and incomplete; the other perfect and final.

Second, in the *instruments* which He employed: in the former, it was sinful men; in the latter, His holy Son. Third, in the *periods* selected: the one was "in time past," the other in "these last days," intimating that God has now fully expressed Himself, that He has nothing in reserve. But is there not here something deeper and more blessed? We believe there is. Let us endeavour to set it forth.

That which is central and vital in these opening verses is God *speaking*. A silent God is an unknown God: God "speaking" is God expressing, *revealing* Himself. All that we know or can now know of God is what He has revealed of Himself through His Word. But the opening verse of Hebrews presents a contrast between God's "speakings." To Israel He gave a revelation of Himself in "time past"; to them He also gave another in "these last days." *What*, then, was the *character* of these two distinct revelations?

As we all know, God's Word is divided into two main sections, the Old and the New Testaments. Now, it is instructive to note that the distinctive character in which God is revealed in them strikingly corresponds to those two words about Him recorded in the first Epistle of John: "God is light" (1:5); "God is love" (4:8). Mark attentively the order of these two statements which make known to us what God actually is in Himself.

"God is light." It was in this character that He was revealed in Old Testament times. What is the very first thing we hear Him saying in His Word? This: "Let there be light" (Gen. 1:3). In what character does He appear to our fallen first parents in Gen. 3? As "light," as the holy One, uncompromisingly judging sin. In what character was He revealed at the flood? As the "light," unsparingly dealing with that which was evil. How did He make Himself known to Israel at Sinai? As the One who is "light." And so we might go on through the whole Old Testament. We do not say that His love was entirely unknown, but most assuredly it was not fully revealed. That which was *characteristic* of the revelation of the Divine character in the Mosaic dispensation was God as *light*.

"God is love." It is in this character that He stands revealed in New Testament times. To make known His love God sent forth the Son of His love. It is only in Christ that love is fully unveiled. Not that the light was absent; that could not be, seeing that He was and is God Himself. The love which He exercised and manifested was ever an holy love. But just as "God is light" was the characteristic revelation in Old Testament times, so "God is love" is characteristic of the New Testament revelation. In the final analysis, *this* is the contrast pointed to in the opening verses of Hebrews. In the prophets God "spoke" (revealed Himself) as *light:* the requirements, claims, demands of His holiness being insisted upon. But in the Son it is the sweet accents of *love* that we hear. It is the *affections* of God which the Son has expressed, appealing to ours; hence, it is by the heart, and not the head, that God can be known.

"God . . . . hath in these last days spoken unto us by (His) Son." It will be noted that the word "His" is in italics, which means there is no corresponding word in the original. But the omission of this word makes the sentence obscure; nor are we helped very much when we learn that the preposition "by" should be "in." "God hath spoken in Son." Yet, really, this is not so obscure as at first it seems. Were a friend to tell you that he had visited a certain church, and that the preacher "spoke in Latin," you would have no difficulty in understanding what he meant: "spoke *in* Latin" would intimate that that particular language marked his utterance. Such is the thought here. "In Son" has reference to that which *characterised* God's revelation. The thought of the contrast is that God, who of old had spoken *prophetwise*, now speaks *sonwise*. The thought is similar to that expressed in 1 Tim. 3:16, "God was manifest in flesh," the words "in flesh" referring to that which characterised the Divine manifestation. God was not manifested in intangible and invisible ether, nor did He appear in angelic form; but "in flesh." So He has now spoken "in Son," Sonwisely.

The whole revelation and manifestation of God is now in Christ; He alone reveals the Father's heart. It is not only that Christ declared or delivered God's message, but that He *Himself* was and is God's message. All that God has to say to us is in His Son: all His thoughts, counsels, promises, gifts, are to be found in the Lord Jesus. Take the perfect life of Christ, His deportment, His ways; *that* is God "speaking"—revealing Himself— to us. Take His miracles, revealing His tender compassion, displaying His mighty power; they are God "speaking" to us. Take His death, commending to us the love of God, in that while we were yet sinners, He died for us; that is God "speaking" to us. Take His resurrection, triumphing over the grave, vanquishing him who had the power of death, coming forth as the "first fruits of them that slept"—the "earnest" of the "harvest" to follow; that is *God* "speaking" to us.

That which is so blessed in this opening sentence of the Hebrews' Epistle, and which it is so important that our hearts should lay hold of, is, that God has come out in an entirely new character—*Sonwise*. It is not so much that God speaks to us in *the* Son, but God addresses Himself to us in Sonlike character, that is, in the character of *love*. God might have spoken "Almightywise," as He did at Sinai; but that would have terrified and overwhelmed us. God might have spoken "Judgewise," as He will at the great white Throne; but that would have condemned us, and forever banished us from His presence. But, blessed be His name, He has spoken "Sonwise," in the *tenderest* relation which He could possibly assume.

What was the announcement from Heaven as soon as the Son was revealed? "Unto you is born"—what? Not a "Judge," or even a "Teacher," but "a Saviour, which is Christ the Lord" (Luke 2:11). There we have the *heart* of God revealed.

It is the *character* in which God "spoke" or revealed Himself which this opening sentence of our Epistle emphasises. He has appeared before us in the person of His beloved Son, to bring us a knowledge of the Divine affections, and this in order to engage our affections. In the very nature of the case there can be nothing higher. Through Christ God is now fully, perfectly, finally revealed.

We lose much if we fail to keep constantly in mind the fact that Christ is *God* —"God *manifest* in flesh." We profess to believe that *He is* Divine, the second person of the blessed Trinity. But it is to be feared that often we forget this when reading the record of His earthly life or when pondering the words which fell from His lips. How necessary it is when taking up a passage in the Gospels to realise that there it is God "speaking" to us "Sonwise," God's affections made known.

Take the familiar words of Luke 19:10, "The Son of man is come to seek and to save that which is lost." But who was this "Son of man?" It was *God* "manifest in flesh"; it was God revealing Himself in His "Son" character. Thus, this well-known verse shows us the *heart* of God, yearning over His fallen creatures. Take, again, that precious word of Matt. 11:28, "Come unto Me all ye that labour and are heavy laden, and I will give you rest." Those words were uttered by "Jesus of Nazareth," yet they illustrate what is said in Heb. 1:2: it was God "speaking" Sonwisely, i.e., bringing to poor sinners a knowledge of Divine affections. Let us re-read the four Gospels with this glorious truth before us.

Cannot we now discern the wondrous and blessed contrast pointed in the opening verses of Hebrews? How different are the two revelations which God has made of His character. In Old Testament times God "spoke," revealed Himself, according to what He is as *light;* and this, in keeping with the fact that it was "in the prophets" —those who made known His *mind*. In New Testament times God has "spoken," revealed Himself, according to what He is as *love;* and this, in keeping with the fact that it was "in Son" He is now made known. May we not only bow before Him in reverence and godly fear, but may our hearts be drawn out to Him in fervent love and adoration.

—*Arthur W. Pink.*

(Concluded from page 47.)

semblies of witches and other self-devoted victims of Satan, was to read the Word of God backward. Perhaps it was a fable designed to express the truth, that one of Satan's most plausible delusions to beguile unstable souls has always been to invert the order of God's lessons; to make the fruits of faith its warrant; to make that consecration of soul which is but the consequence of knowing that we are bought with a price, the path by which we are to travel back to peace with God, and so to begin with solemn vows and acts of self-dedication, as the method by which joy is to be experienced and assurance attained. Our fathers also supposed that to read a verse of Scripture in its natural order would in a moment break every spell, and put Satan and his assembled hosts to flight. And blessed would be the results if the children of God were but to open their eyes, to see that all the fulness of Christ is already theirs—that they are complete in Him, and that the assurance of the grace of God in Christ is the starting-point and not the terminus of the Christian race.

Waymarks in the Wilderness. 1865.

GLEANINGS IN EXODUS.

50. *The Urim and Thummim. Ex. 28:30.*

"The secret things belong unto the Lord our God: but those things which are revealed belong unto us and to our children forever" (Deut. 29:29). This seems to be a suitable passage with which to introduce our present inquiry. Things which Jehovah has not seen fit to make known unto us, it is presumption and impiety to attempt to pry into; hence the Christian needs constantly to pray, "Keep back Thy servant also from presumptuous sins" (Psa. 19:13). Let us not attempt to be wise above that which is written. Let us seek grace to be kept humble, from invading the prerogatives of the Most High, and from endeavouring to handle things which are "too wonderful" (Psa. 139:6) for us. "Now I know *in part*" (1 Cor. 13:12); let us be thankful for this "part," and leave it with God to grant us a fuller revelation in the Day to come.

On the other hand, let us not forget that the things which *are* revealed "belong" unto us. They are given for our instruction. They are given for us to study prayerfully and carefully. It is only by perseveringly comparing Scripture with Scripture that we learn what God *has* "revealed" in His Word. The Holy Spirit places no premium upon sloth. It is not the dilatory but the "diligent" soul who is "made fat" (Prov. 13:4). A rightly divided Word of Truth calls for a "workman" (2 Tim. 2:15), not a lazy man. It is because they spend, comparatively, so little time over the Scriptures, it is because they cannot truly say "I have esteemed the words of His mouth more than my necessary food" (Job 23:12), that the great majority of professing Christians have little or no conception of how much God has been pleased to reveal to us in His Word.

Now, in connection with the Urim and the Thummim there appear to be some things which God has seen fit to keep "secret," hence the profitless articles which many, who resorted to speculation, have written on the subject. Concerning the "Urim and the Thummim" no man, Jew or Gentile, knows, or can know, anything, save what God has "revealed" to us in His Word. But as the humble student attentively compares the different passages where they are mentioned, as he notes what is said therein, he discovers that God has been pleased to intimate to us not a little concerning their nature, use, and spiritual significance. Let us now note:—

1. *Their Names.*

Both words are in the plural number, though this (as is often the case in the Hebrew of the O.T.) is probably what is called the "plural of majesty"—used for the purpose of *emphasising* the importance or dignity of a thing. Thus, it is most likely that the "Urim" was but a single object, and the "Thummim" another; but of this we cannot be certain. There is no difficulty in ascertaining the English equivalent of these Hebrew terms. Urim signifies "lights" or "light," being the plural form of the word very frequently used for "light." In Isa. 31:9; 44:16; 47:14; 50:11; Ezek. 5:2 Urim is translated "fire" (its secondary meaning); while in Isa. 24:15 it is rendered "fires." Thummim means "perfections" or "perfection." In the Sept. these two words are translated by "delosis" and "aletheim," meaning "manifestation" and "truth."

It is surely striking that reference is made to these mysterious objects in the Old Testament just *seven* times. In Ex. 28:30, Lev. 8:8, Ezra 2:63, and Neh. 7:65 they are spoken of as the "Urim and Thummim," but in Deut. 33:8 the order is reversed "Thummim and Urim"; while in Num. 27:21 and 1 Sam. 28:6 "Urim" is mentioned alone. It is also to be noted that no command was given to Moses by Jehovah to "make" them; he was simply told to "put" (Heb. nathan "to give" them in the Breastplate). Let us next consider:

2. *Their Place.*

This is made known in Ex. 28:30, "And thou shalt put in the breastplate of judgment the Urim and the Thummim." From v. 16, "Foursquare it shall be doubled," we gather that the linen fabric of which the breastplate was composed was made in the form of a bag, in which (more literally "into which") the Urim and the Thummim were placed. Thus, they also were worn upon the high priest's heart. They would be under the twelve precious stones which bore the names of Israel's tribes, and linked, too, with the onyx stones on Aaron's shoulders.

3. *Their Use.*

This may be gathered from the different passages where they are mentioned. The first is in Num. 27:21, "And he shall stand before Eleazar the priest, who shall ask counsel for him after the judgment of Urim before the Lord: at his word they shall go out, and at his word they shall come in, both he, and all the children of Israel with him, even all the congregation."

From the above quotation it seems clear that, in certain circumstances, the mind of the Lord was conveyed through them. 1 Sam. 28:6 bears this out, for of Saul it is there said, "when he *enquired* of the Lord, the Lord answered him not, neither by dreams nor by Urim, nor by prophets." From these two passages we gather that by means of the Urim, or "light," in the breastplate of the high priest, counsel or prophetic guidance was obtained from God.

Further confirmation of this is found in Ezra 2. In vv. 61, 62 we are told, "And of the children of the priests: the children of Habaiah, the children of Koz, the children of Barzillai; which took a wife of the daughters of Barzillai the Gileadite, and was called after their name: These sought their register among those that were reckoned by genealogy, but they were not found: therefore were they, as polluted, put from the priesthood." Then it is added, "And the governor said unto them, that they should not eat of the most holy things till there stood up a priest with Urim and with Thummim," i.e., till one through whom the mind of the Lord was clearly revealed.

From these Scriptures the late Dr. Bullinger drew the following deductions: "The Urim and Thummim were probably two precious stones, which were drawn out as a lot to give Jehovah's judgment. 'The lot is cast into the lap (Heb. 'bosom'), but the whole judgment thereof is of the Lord' (Prov. 16:33)—bosom is here put for the clothing or covering over it: cf. Ex. 4:6, 7; Ruth 4:10. . . . Thus, these two placed in the 'bag,' and one drawn out, would give the judicial decision, which would be 'of the Lord.' Hence the breastplate itself was known as 'the breastplate of *judgment*' (v. 15), because, by that, Jehovah's judgment was obtained whenever it was needed. Hence, when the land was divided 'by lot' (Num. 26:55) Eleazar, the high priest, must be present (Num. 34:17 —cf. 27:21—Josh. 17:4). When he would decide it the lot 'came up' (Josh. 18:11), 'came forth' (Josh. 19:1), 'came out' (Josh. 19:17), i.e., 'out' or 'forth' from the bag of the ephod. In Ezra. 2:61-63 no judgment could be given unless the high priest were present with the breastplate, with its bag, with the lots of Urim and Thummim, which gave Jehovah's decision."

4. *Their Connections.*

First, as intimated above, they were deposited in the bag of the breastplate. Not only so, the very name of this important part of the high priest's vestments is taken therefrom, for it was termed "the breastplate of judgment," i.e., of decision, as giving God's mind. In striking accord with this, we may point out how that the word used in the Sept. version (the first translation ever made of the Old Testament into Greek) is "logeion," which means *oracle,* because by it the high priest obtained oracular responses from God.

Second, as pointed out in the preceding article, the breastplate was inseparably connected with, yea, formed an essential part of, the "ephod" itself—see Ex. 28:6, 7, 28 and our notes thereon. Now, the "ephod" was peculiarly the *prophetic* dress of the high priest. By means of it (that is, through the Urim and Thummim) he learned the counsel of God, and was thus able to declare what course the people should take, or what events were about to happen. Upon this, the late Mr. Soltau has most helpfully pointed out:

"Thus we find Saul, accompanied by Ahiah, the Lord's priest in Shiloh, wearing an ephod, commanding the ark to be brought, that he may ascertain the meaning of the tumult among the Philistines. But, instead of waiting to receive any response from God, he binds Israel with a curse and enters into the battle (1 Sam. 14:3, 19, 24). Abiathar, the only surviving priest of the line of Eli, fled to David with the ephod in his hand, having escaped the slaughter at Nob. David ascertained by this means the purpose of the men of Keilah to deliver him up to Saul (1 Sam. 23:6, 10). Again, in the affair at Ziglag, David consulted the Lord through Abiathar and the ephod, and obtained a favourable answer (1 Sam. 30:7, 8). On a subsequent occasion we read of David inquiring of the Lord, and obtaining answers (2 Sam. 2:1), and although in this instance the priest and ephod are not mentioned, yet judging from the previous instances it is probable that the same mode of inquiry was adopted."

5. *Their Significance.*

The twelve gems on which were graven the names of Israel's tribes were worn *upon* the heart of Aaron; the "Urim and the Thummim" were placed *within* the breastplate, beneath the precious stones. Thus they speak, first of all, of that which is found in the heart of the Lord Jesus. As said the apostle who leaned upon His bosom, "The Word became flesh and tabernacled among us, and we beheld His glory, the glory as of the only begotten of the Father, *full* of grace and truth" (John 1:14). "Light" and "Perfection" centre in Him who is our great High Priest.

In Christ Himself we see the antitype of the "Urim." "In Him was life, and the life was the *light* of men . . . .

that was the true Light, which lighteth every man that cometh into the world" (John 1:5, 9). Therefore did He say, "I am the light of the world: he that followeth Me shall not walk in darkness, but shall have the light of life" (John 8:12).

"God is light" (1 John 1:5), and Christ could say, "He that hath seen Me hath seen the Father" (John 14:9). Yes, He is the reality of which the Urim was the figure: the light of the knowledge of the glory of God shines "in the face of Jesus Christ" (2 Cor. 4:6).

In Christ we see the antitype of the "Thummim." Every "perfection" is found in Him, for He is *altogether* lovely" (Song of Sol. 5:16). Concerning His Deity, He is "over all, God blessed forever" (Rom. 9:5). Concerning His humanity, He is "that holy thing" (Luke 1:35). As the God-man, the Father said, "This is My Beloved Son." In His speech He was perfect: "grace is poured into Thy lips" (Psa. 45:2) testified the Spirit of prophecy. "Never man spake like this Man" (John 7:46), confessed His enemies. In His character He was flawless: "a lamb without spot and blemish" (1 Peter 1:19). In His conduct He was perfect: "I do *always* those things that please Him" (John 8:29). Yes, Christ is the reality of which the Thummim was the figure.

But is there not something else here, still more specific? We believe there is. "God is light" (1 John 1:5) and "God is love" (1 John 4:8), make known to us what God *is* in Himself. The *balance* between these, if we may so speak, was perfectly maintained and blessedly manifested by the incarnate Son. The love which He exercised was ever an holy love; the light which He displayed was never divorced from this love. In like manner, these two, the Urim and the Thummim—"light" and "perfection"—formed a unit, being *together* within the breastplate upon the high priest's heart. The antitype of this is found in John 1:14, already quoted. "Now, in this expression—'full of grace and truth'—we have, in brief, the two main thoughts of the breastplate. 'Truth' is the effect of the light, and God is light. Light is what manifests, brings out the truth, *is* the truth. Christ, the light of the world, is the truth come into it: everything gets its true character from Him. 'Grace,' while it is what it is in God, is *toward* man" F. W. Grant).

In addition to the names of these two objects (what they were in themselves) foreshadowing that which is in Christ, the purpose for which they were designed, the use to which they were put, also receives its typical fulfilment in Him. As we have seen, they were employed for communicating to the people a knowledge of God's mind and will concerning them. How blessedly this pointed to the Lord Jesus as "the wonderful Counseller" (Isa. 9:6)! In Him "are hid all the treasures of wisdom and knowledge" (Col. 2:3). And therefore could He say, "I am the Truth" (John 14:6). The mind and will of God are perfectly revealed to Him and by Him.

Christ's perfect knowledge of the Father's thoughts are clearly intimated in the following Scriptures: "For the Father loveth the Son and showeth Him *all* things that Himself doeth" (John 5:20)—there is no restraint, no reserve. "No one knoweth the Son save the Father; neither doth any know the Father, save the Son, and he to whosoever the Son willeth to reveal Him" (Matt. 11:27, R.V.). "The Father loveth the Son, and hath given *all* things into His hand" (John 3:35).

Christ's communication to His people of what the Father has given to Him is also without reserve. Speaking to His beloved disciples He says, "Henceforth I call you not servants; for the servant knoweth not what his lord doeth: but I have called you friends; for *all* things that I have heard of My Father I have made known unto you" (John 15:15). This is developed, in a doctrinal way, in the Epistle to the Hebrews: "God hath, in these last days, spoken unto us by *His Son*" (1:1, 2). Perfectly has Christ communicated to His people the mind of God; fully has He revealed the Father's heart. This, we take it, then, is the second great truth foreshadowed by the Urim and Thummim: the counsels of God are only to be learned through the Lord Jesus, our great High Priest; and those counsels (of grace) are inseparably connected with His own dear people—as symbolised by the Urim and Thummim and the twelve precious stones, bearing their names, being *together* in the breastplate.

Another blessed truth was also signified by the Urim and Thummim. When the people of God were doubtful as to what course they should follow, when they desired light upon their path, they could obtain it by coming to and seeking it from the high priest. "And he shall stand before Eleazar the priest, who shall *ask counsel for him*, after the judgment of Urim before the Lord" (Num. 27:21). "Thus we learn that the high priest not only bore the judgment of the congregation before the Lord, but also carried the judgment of the Lord to the congregation. Solemn, weighty, and most precious functions! All this we have, in divine perfectness, in our great High Priest, who has passed into the heavens; He bears the judgment of His people on His heart continually; and He, by the Holy Spirit, communicates to us the counsel of God, in reference to the most minute circumstances of our daily course. We do not want dreams or visions; if only we walk in the Spirit we shall enjoy all the certainty which the perfect 'Urim,' on the breast of our great High Priest, can afford" (C.H.M.).

Yet one other point remains to be considered in this striking type. In the quotation made above from Dr. Bullinger's works it will be seen that the Urim and Thummim played an important part in the allocation of Canaan to the different tribes in the days of Joshua. It was to them that God's mind was made known respecting Israel's portions in the promised land. The antitype of this is most blessed. Christ has purchased for Himself an inheritance (see Psa. 2:8, etc.). His inheritance, both the heavenly and earthly portions of it, He will share with His people, for they are "jointheirs" with Him (Rom. 8:17). In John 17 we find Him saying to the Father, "the glory which Thou gavest Me I have given them" (v. 22). The different positions which His people will occupy during the Millennium will be determined by the Lord Jesus. To one He will say, "have thou authority over ten cities" (Luke 19:17), to another, 'be thou over five cities" (Luke 19:19), and so on. Thus our Joshua (the Hebrew of "Jesus") will apportion the Inheritance according to the mind of God.

To sum up. In Christ, then, we have the reality of all that was foreshadowed by the Urim and Thummim. First, He is the "Light and Perfection" of God—the Brightness of His glory (Heb. 1:3). Second, in Christ the light and life, the righteousness and grace of God, meet together, and their balance is perfectly maintained. Third, Christ is the One in whom all the counsels of God find their Centre. Fourth, the counsels of God which centre in Christ are inseparably connected with His people. Fifth, to Christ and by Christ is made fully known the mind of God, for in Him are hid *all the treasures of wisdom and knowledge"* (Col. 2:3). Sixth, from Christ, by His Spirit, directions may be obtained for every step of our pilgrim journey. Seventh, by Christ the promised and purchased inheritance will be administered.

In conclusion, we may note a *dispensational* application which the Urim and Thummim had for the Jews. Ezra 2:63 informs us that there was no one with the Urim and Thummim to communicate the mind of God in the day of Israel's return from their Babylonian captivity. The company seen with Ezra typify the godly Jewish remnant in the Tribulation period. Though sustained by God, the Holy Spirit will not be on earth at that time, and they will be without many of the spiritual privileges which we now enjoy. But at the close of the time of Jacob's trouble, the Lord Jesus shall return to earth: "He shall build the temple of the Lord, and He shall bear the glory, and shall sit and rule upon His throne; and He shall be a priest upon His throne: and the *counsel* of peace shall be between them both" (Zeck. 6:13).

At the beginning of the Millennium, "It shall come to pass that the mountain of the Lord's house shall be established in the top of the mountains, and shall be exalted above the hills; and all nations shall flow unto it. And many people shall go and say, Come ye, and let us go up to the mountain of the Lord, to the house of the God of Jacob; and He will *teach* us of His ways, and we will walk in His paths; for out of Zion shall go forth the law, and the word of the Lord from Jerusalem. And He shall *judge* among the nations. . . . O house of Jacob, come ye, and let us walk in the *light* of the Lord" (Isa. 2:2-5). Then shall Israel enjoy that which, of old, was adumbrated by the Urim and Thummim in their high priest's breastplate.

—*Arthur W. Pink.*

N.B.—Having completed our own study of the subject, and after having looked in vain for any help from numerous commentaries ancient and modern, in the good providence of God we found an illuminating article in "Addresses on Hebrews," by P. R. Morford. This led us to follow up his suggestion of linking the "Urim and Thummim" with Hebrews 1 and 2; the results of which we give in a sermon preached thereon. The further and clearer distinction drawn between the spiritual significations of the Urim and Thummim explains the slight variations found in several Old Testament scriptures. In Num. 27:21 and 1 Sam. 28:6 only the "Urim" is mentioned, because that had to do, specifically, with God revealing Himself. In Deut. 33:8 the "Thummim" is mentioned first, in keeping with the thought of the verse as a whole.—A.W.P.

THE URIM AND THUMMIM.

Text, Neh. 7:63-65.

Our text has reference to an incident which occurred shortly after a remnant of the Jews had returned from captivity unto their own land. While in Babylon some of the Levites had married out of the priestly family, and were now unable to establish a pure genealogy, and as this alone gave right and title of access to God in priestly service, they were excluded from the priesthood. In consequence of this, they were debarred from eating of the holy things, yet this deprivation was not to continue for ever, but only "till there stood up a priest with Urim and Thummim."

The above passage in Nehemiah contains the last reference to "the Urim and the Thummim" in the Old Testament, and it is exceedingly striking to note that it pointed forward to the future. It was really a prophecy, a Messianic prophecy, a prophecy concerning Christ in His *priestly* character; a prophecy which intimated that the substance of that which was shadowed-forth by the Urim and Thummim would be found in Him. Now, as there is no hint in the remainder of the Old Testament of such a priest ever having appeared unto Israel, we are obliged to look in the New Testament for its fulfilment.

As we all know, the New Testament opens by bringing before us the true Priest, and presents Him appearing unto the very descendants of the Jewish remnant of Nehemiah's days. But, "He came unto His own, and His own received Him not" (John 1:11). He ministered unto them, but was hated by them. By wicked hands they took and crucified Him, and after His burial, demanded that His tomb be securely guarded. That was the last which the Nation saw of Him. Then God intervened: raised from the dead the despised and rejected One, and exalted Him to His own right hand.

Where sin had abounded, grace did much more abound. Instead of at once destroying the murderers of His Son, "the longsuffering of God *waited*," as it had before in the days of Noah (1 Pet. 3:20). Not only so, but an amnesty was proclaimed and the Gospel of peace was published. Unto the Jews Peter was sent to say, "Repent ye therefore, and be converted, that your sins may be blotted out so that the times of refreshing shall come from the presence of the Lord; and He shall send Jesus Christ, which before was preached unto you" (Acts 3:19, 20).

But of old God had said, "My Spirit shall not always strive with man" (Genesis 6:3). The period of "waiting" was almost ended. Thirty years had passed since the rejected Saviour had returned to His Father, and judgment was about to fall on the unrepentant Nation and destroy their wicked City. Many thousands of the Jews had believed the Gospel, but in order to avoid the reproach which going forth unto Christ outside the Camp involved, they still adhered to Judaism (Acts 21:20). Many of them were sorely tempted to abandon the Christian profession and give up their heavenly hope. It was then that God, in His mercy, moved the apostle Paul to write the Epistle to the Hebrews.

Though there is nothing in Scripture which is solely local or ephemeral, yet many of its details and references cannot be properly understood unless attention be paid to the condition and circumstances of those to whom each portion of the Scriptures was first sent. Notably is this the case with the Epistle to the Hebrews. That Epistle was first addressed to a people who had gone back spiritually (5:12), whose faith was wavering (3:6, 14), who had failed to take up their cross and follow a despised Christ (13:13); yet it was written not so much to rebuke as to win them. It was written to draw their hearts away from the venerable system to which they were attached, and to draw their affections to things above, where Christ sitteth on the right hand of God. With Christ was connected a new and living system which would supplant the lifeless order of Judaism, that was shortly to be destroyed by Titus.

The Hebrews' Epistle settles once for all questions which our text from Nehemiah should have raised in the minds of every godly Jew, namely, Has the promised Priest actually stood up? Has One having the "Urim and Thummim" really appeared? The ancient Aaronic order of priesthood was on the eve of passing away, had, then, a *new* order been inaugurated? Now, as all who have read the Hebrews' Epistle are aware, it is there (and there only in the New Testament) that the Priesthood of the Lord Jesus is so blessedly unfolded. As the first verse of the 8th chapter announces, "Now of the things which we have spoken this is the sum: We have such an High Priest, who is set on the right hand of the throne of the Majesty in the heavens." And as the details of this blessed Epistle are studied, it will be found that in Christ we have, without a doubt, the reality of which the Urim and Thummim were but figures.

Now, the two chief things to be borne in mind concerning the Urim and Thummim are these: the *purpose* they served, and the *place* they occupied. Each of these was before us this morning (see preceding article). The purpose they served was this: they were used to convey to God's people a knowledge of His mind (Num. 27:21). The place they occupied was the bag in the breastplate upon the high priest's heart (Exodus 28:30). Thus, they supplied intelligence of the Divine will, and they occupied the place of affection. Observe how the same two things meet us at the very beginning of the Hebrews' Epistle.

"God who .... spake in time past unto the fathers by the prophets, hath in these last days spoken unto us" (Heb. 1:1, 2). God "speaking" is God revealing Himself, God communicating a knowledge of His mind and heart. But *how* has God, in these last days, spoken "to us?" Through what channel has He made Himself known? or, better, in what character has He manifested Himself? The answer is, "In (His) Son." God has come out to us in the person of His Beloved, bringing to our hearts a knowledge of the Divine affections.

What is so wonderful to behold is, that in the first two chapters of Hebrews we find that which clearly answers to the Urim and Thummim on the high priest's heart; in other words, it is there we have the *antitype* of them. To enable you to see this the better for yourselves, let me repeat that these two Hebrew words are in the plural number—Lights and Perfections. The plural form conveys the thought of *intense* light, and the *sum* of perfection. If we bear these two things in mind we shall have no difficulty in recognising that the whole Epistle of Hebrews centres around the blessed truth that the promised Priest *has* appeared bearing these two marks: the "Urim and Thummim," or Lights and Perfections. Let us now consider:

1. *The Antiytpe of "the Urim."*

As soon as we open Hebrews 1, what meets our gaze? Surely this, "Intense Light." God is light (1 John 1:5), and it is here that Christ is presented to us as "the Brightness of His glory and the express Image of His person" (v. 3). Christ is the very effulgence, the outshining, the Revealer of God. What is His "glory?" It is His surpassing excellency, it is the sum of His perfections. Every attribute of God, every perfection of His being and character, is not only found in the Lord Jesus, but is displayed, manifested by Him. He is "the Word," uttering, expressing, showing what God *is*. He who is in the bosom of the Father "hath declared Him" (John 1:18), and so perfectly so, that He could say, "He that hath seen Me hath seen the Father" (John 14:9).

Urim means "light," intense light. By means of the Urim God's mind was made known to Israel. Thus, in the antitype, it is Christ as the "true Light" (John 1:5) revealing God. It is Christ bringing to light, making known what God is. And how wondrously, how blessedly, how perfectly He has done this? Turn for a moment to Luke 15:2, "And the Pharisees and scribes murmured, saying, This man receiveth sinners, and eateth with them." But *who* was that "Man?" None other than God Himself—"God *manifest* in flesh." Not till *then* had God been clearly, fully, perfectly, finally revealed.

Creation makes known some of God's attributes, but it does not reveal God Himself. The immensity of space hints at His infinity; the sustentation of the universe tells of His mighty power; the details of His handiwork reveal His consummate wisdom. But Nature does not reveal God Himself. There is an infinitely greater difference between learning of a man through his books and then becoming personally acquainted with their author, than there is between deducing the attributes of the Creator from His works and knowing Him in a personal way. Not till the Son became incarnate was the *heart* of God revealed—seeking, saving, receiving, eating with sinners.

"'This man receiveth sinners, and eateth with them.' It scandalised the religious people, who belonged to the order of things about to pass away (so little did they know God A.W.P.), but the Man who was there receiving sinners was in that very act setting forth what God is. The light of God shone in its intensity—bowels of mercy, tender compassion that yearned over the fall of His creature, and sought to win his heart in affection, that he might come into the joy of the blessed God. Christ in Luke 15 vindicated the heart of God and his actions: 'It was meet that we should make merry, and be glad,' v. 32." (Mr. P. R. Morford.)

It is blessed to see the Lord Jesus in Luke 15 vindicating God. Those words of the Father's concerning the prodigal are inexpressibly precious. "It was *meet*"— suited to My nature, in keeping with what I am, consonant to My purpose of grace. It was Christ making known that wondrous Love which passeth knowledge. Was not *that* "light," "intense light," almost blinding light? Yes, it is like trying to gaze into the face of the midday sun. We are overcome when we attempt to contemplate the love of God, revealed in Christ, to poor hell-deserving wretches. Truly, the light of the knowledge of the glory of God *shines* "in the face of Jesus Christ" (2 Cor. 4:6).

Now I ask, Does not the Lord Jesus manifest in Himself that which answers to, is the antitype of, the "Urim"? And every heart which *loves* Him must answer, Yes. But we can only enter into and appropriate it in Divine affection: it is only as our hearts go out to Him in love that we can really lay hold of His glorious place as Priest, and this will only be as we have the assurance of and rejoice in the knowledge that He has "By Himself purged our sins" (Heb. 1:3). Let me say that *this* must be settled in our hearts before we go any farther; we cannot appreciate what follows in this blessed Epistle till we *know* Christ as the One who has put away *our* sins. We cannot know Him as Priest, till we know Him as Saviour. Before He took His place on High, He went down into death to "purge our sins."

2. *The Antitype of "the Thummim."*

As we have already said, this Hebrew word means "perfection." The antitype of this is also to be found in Hebrews. It is striking to observe how prominent is *this* term in that Epistle. Observe it in the following passages: "To make the Captain of their salvation *perfect* through sufferings" (2:10); "And being made *perfect,* He became the Author of eternal salvation unto all them that obey Him" (5:9). "Therefore leaving the principles of the doctrine of Christ, let us go on unto *perfection.*" "For the law made nothing *perfect,* but the bringing in of a better hope *did"* (Heb. 7:19). "For by one offering He hath *perfected* for ever them that are sanctified" (10:14). "God having provided some better thing for us. that they without us should not be made *perfect"* (11:40). "But ye are come unto . . . the spirits of just men made *perfect"* (12:23).

Now the "perfection" spoken of in these passages is little understood to-day. Most Christians have a fairly intelligent grasp of the fact that God has made Himself known in Christ. But there is something else about Christ, equally wonderful and blessed, which many are very hazy about. Not only has God been presented to us in intense light in Christ, but we have been *presented to God* in that same blessed Person. God has come out to us in Christ; we have gone into God in Christ. He took our place on the cross; we now take His place before God in Heaven. It is the apprehension of Christ as the Representative of His people in Heaven, which will enable us to understand *what* "the Thummim" pointed forward to, namely, that "perfection" which is found in His glorious person.

Now just as in Hebrews 1: the Holy Spirit brings before us the antitype of the "Urim," so in Hebrews 2 He shows us the antitype of the "Thummim." In other words, in the first chapter we behold God, in Christ, coming out to us as the "light;" in the second chapter, we see the saints, in Christ, going in to God in "perfection." In Heb. 2:6 the question is asked. "What is man, that Thou art mindful of him?" The answer which is given is very remarkable, though it is little understood: "Thou madest him a little lower than the angels; Thou crownedst him with glory and honour, and didst set him over the works of Thy hands: Thou hast put all things in subjection under his feet" (vv. 7, 8).

Many have been puzzled by the above quotation from Psa. 8. *Of whom* was David speaking? To whom was the apostle, by his quotation, referring? The answer is: To a new order of man, of which the Lord Jesus is the Head; to *redeemed* man. Thus we are told, "But now we see not yet all things put under him. But we see Jesus, . . . crowned with glory and honour" (vv. 8, 9).

In Christ God has brought into view another order of "Man," one in whom not sin is found, nor even "innocence," but *perfection.* And what is God going to do with this Man? Yea, what has He already done with Him? Heb. 2:7-9 tells us: God has glorified Him, exalted Him above all. God has given this Man a place, *the* place in His very presence. This, Adam, even in his unfallen condition, did not have.

Now note what follows in Heb. 2:10: "For it became Him, for whom are all things, and by whom are all things, in bringing many sons unto glory to make the Captain of their salvation perfect through sufferings." Observe, first, that this verse begins with "for;" second, the words "in bringing," *not* "shall bring;" third, the name given to Christ. The place of perfection—"crowned with glory and honour" —is not occupied by Christ alone: He is there as our "Captain," Head, Leader. *He* is the true Joshua, leading God's people into the promised Inheritance.

What then is the result of this relationship? Heb. 2:11-13 tells us: "For both He that sanctifieth and they who are sanctified are *all of one;* for which cause He is not ashamed to call them *brethren,* Saying, I will declare Thy name unto My brethren, in the midst of the church will I sing praise unto Thee. And again, I will put My trust in Him. And again, Behold I *and* the children which God hath given Me."

Cannot we now *identify* the Lord Jesus as the One who has "stood up with Urim and Thummin"? Do not the first two chapters of the Epistle to the Hebrews bring Him before us as the One who has, first, presented the full light of God to our souls; and, second, presented us in "perfection" before God? O to realise that God has His eye not on us, but upon Christ; and that as God looks at Him He sees, for the first time, a Perfect Man— the "Second Man" (1 Cor. 15:47), the Head of the new creation; the "New Man" of Eph. 2:15, the "perfect Man" of Eph. 4:13!

3. *The Blessed Consequences of this.*

If the reader will turn back to and read carefully Neh. 7:63-65, he will see that there are three things which the Levites of those days were debarred from: first, proving their genealogy; second, their priestly place; third, enjoying their priestly portion. These three deprivations resulted from there being no Priest in their midst "with Urim and Thummim." Contrariwise, these *are* the very privileges which every true Christian should enjoy; alas, that so many do not. Let us look, briefly, at these three things.

1. *We may* now trace our "genealogy." Those in Nehemiah's day could not, because there was no priest with "Urim and Thummim." *They* could not approach God as priests until the great Priest appeared. To this day they are unable to. The Jews have their "rabbi's" (teachers), but they have no priests to present an offering unto God. Because they rejected the Saviour, Christ is not yet officiating as their "great High Priest." Having no Priest their "genealogy" is gone—no Jew on earth today can determine for certain which tribe he has descended from.

The same sad condition now extensively prevails, in a spiritual way, throughout Christendom. The *priesthood* of Christ, is largely an empty name, and there is little *priestly* exercise of Christians before God. Why is this? Because many of them are unable to trace *their* "genealogy." And much of modern Christianity encourages this deplorable state. Ask the average church-member if he is saved, and he is doubtful; at best he "hopes" so. He is taught that assurance is presumption. He is taught that a state of uncertainty is an evidence of spiritual humility.

How may we "trace our genealogy"? Only through Christ. *He* is the promised Priest who *has* "stood up" with "Urim and Thummim." Then, has He manifested *to you* the wondrous and intense light of God? Has He revealed to your needy heart the matchless and marvellous Love of God? Do you see in Him "perfection," *your* perfection? Do you see that *He* is the measure of your acceptance with God? that you are complete in Him (Col. 2:10), that you are "perfected" by Him (Heb. 10:14)? It is written, "For both He that sanctifieth and they who are sanctified *are all of one*" (Heb. 2:11). If you are resting on *that,* if you realise it by faith in your heart, then you *can* "trace your genealogy."

2. We should, in a practical way, occupy our place as priests before God. So far as their standing is concerned, by virtue of their union with Christ, *all* believers have been "made kings and priests unto God" (Rev. 1:6). But how many experimentally realise this? How many Christians exercise *priestly* functions before God? Why, the very expression sounds strange in most of their ears. *What* are "priestly" activities? 1 Peter 2:5 tells us: Christians are an holy priesthood "to *offer* up spiritual sacrifices, acceptable to God by Jesus Christ." Alas, the highest thought with most of them, even when they come together on the Sabbath, is to be ministered *unto,* to receive a blessing; they have little or nothing to *offer* God! And *what* should they "offer"? Hebrews 13:15 tells us, "By Him therefore let us offer the *sacrifice of praise* to God continually."

And why is it that so few of Gods children are really doing this? The principal reason is, because of the defective teaching, or rather, preaching, they sit under. While they are encouraged to tarry in 'the Slough of Despond,' while they are constantly occupied with their own miserable selves, there can be no "priestly" exercises, no enjoyment of "priestly" privileges, no "offering" of true praise unto God. These can not be till we can trace our genealogy. Praise and doubt will not dwell together.

The third consequence of being linked to the true Priest who *has* "stood up with Urim and Thummim" is that we are entitled to our "priestly" portion—we *may* "eat of the most holy things"—see text. As we are told in Heb. 13:10, *"We have an altar whereof they had no right to eat which serve the tabernacle."* Those who "serve the tabernacle" were the Jews of the apostle's day that still held fast to Judaism. The "we" at the beginning of the verse were those who believed in and were, by faith, following Christ. To-day the "we" finds its fulfilment in all true Christians.

"Eating" signifies laying hold of, appropriating, making our own; feeding upon, being refreshed by, gladdened and strengthened. But observe that they are "most *holy* things." The polluted cannot touch them; nor may Christians while walking arm in arm with the world. None have any right to them until they have found in Christ the true Priest with these two marks: One who has come out from God to reveal Him to our hearts; One who has gone back to God to present us in perfection before Him.

Thus the "Urim and Thummim" supply a valuable key to the Hebrew Epistle. It is there that we are shown their antitype; it is there that we get the blessed sequel to our text. In chapter 1 it is the "Urim," the *light* which is seen—Christ making God known. In chapter 2 it is the "Thummim" which is seen, Christ bringing men to God in his own *perfection*. The succeeding chapters are given to bring us consciously into the present possession of these revelations, that there may be wrought in us an answer, a response to God in our *affections* for His Son; a taking of our place "with Him" outside all that dishonours him.

—*Arthur W. Pink.*

THE PROPHETIC PARABLES OF MATTHEW 13.

6. *The Leaven.*

"Another parable spake He unto them: The kingdom of heaven is like unto leaven, which a woman took, and hid in three measures of meal, till the whole was leavened" (v. 33).

In the mercy of God we are not left to any human opinions or authority, nor is the meaning of the parables of Matt. 13 open to argument. Christ Himself explained for us the first two and the seventh, and it is obvious that the intervening four must be interpreted in strict accord with them. There is an unmistakable *unity* underlying the whole chapter. As there is a noticeable connection between the first two parables in relation to the *beginning* of the kingdom of heaven in its present form, so there is a close relation between the third and fourth which treat of its *extension* and *corruption*. The third gives us the *external* aspect or outward growth of the kingdom, the fourth reveals its *internal* aspect and secret corruption.

The popular interpretation of this parable regards the "leaven" as representing the Gospel and its power, the "woman" the Church. Here are the words of Dr. John Gill: "Leaven is everywhere else used in a bad sense . . . here it seems to be taken in a good sense, and the Gospel to be compared unto it." The "woman," he tells us, is "the church" or the ministers of the Gospel. Calvinists understand the "three measures of meal" to represent God's elect; Arminians understand them to prefigure all mankind. The latter expound the parable as follows: As the result of the Gospel, and by means of its assimilating power, the mass of humanity is ultimately to be penetrated, affected, and blest. So firmly is this belief embedded in the minds of church-goers that it is hard for them to tear loose from it.

It is apparent at once that our understanding and interpretation of this parable turns upon a correct definition of the "leaven." If this be a figure of the Gospel, and if the meal represents the human race, then it necessarily follows that, ultimately, *all* must be regenerated or at least reformed by the Evangel. But if the "leaven" be the symbol of corrupting evil, and the meal stands for the pure truth of God, and that this parable also supplies a picture of the Christian profession, then it necessarily follows that, ultimately, the truth of God is to be corrupted throughout Christendom. How are we to find out which of these is true? Only from the Holy Scriptures. Let us now examine the current interpretation of this parable in the light of the Word:

1. If the popular view be correct then, in this chapter, Christ flatly contradicts Himself. What He has said in the first three parables is dead against *world*-conversion or even *world*-reformation by means of Gospel preaching. In the first parable, instead of our Lord teaching that

the good Seed would bear fruit in *every* part of the field, He declared that most of its ground would prove uncongenial and unproductive. Nor was there any hint that later "sowers" would find conditions improved; rather did He intimate that things would get worse. In the second parable the picture which He drew of the coming Harvest expressly forbids such a thought, and positively excludes the idea of world-conversion in this Age. In the third parable He predicted that Christendom would develop into such a monstrosity that the Devil's agents would be afforded shelter in it and would rule over it. How then can this fourth parable teach the very opposite?

2. The post-millennial interpretation of this parable is flatly contradicted by what we are told in vv. 11, 35 of Matt. 13. There we learn that these parables are "mysteries of the kingdom of heaven," "things which have been kept secret from the foundation of the world." Dr. Gill echoes the teaching of the Reformers, and they have been re-echoed by later Calvinists, affirming that the "leaven" represents the Gospel. But that *cannot* be. Whatever may or may not be prefigured, the "Gospel" is the *last* thing which could possibly be in view. For this reason: the Gospel was *not* an unrevealed secret in O.T. times. Gal. 3:8 declares that the Gospel was "preached unto Abraham."

3. If the "leaven" represents the Gospel and the "meal" the human race, or, as Dr. Gill teaches, God's elect in their natural condition, then the figure which Christ here employed is a faulty one. And this in three different respects. First, in the way it works. *How* does "leaven" act? Why, it is simply placed in meal, and then it works of itself! That is all: just place it there, *leave it alone*, and it is bound to leaven the whole lump. But is *that* the way the Gospel works? Certainly not. Multitudes *have* received the Gospel, but it has had no effect upon them!

Second, in the actor here mentioned. It is a "woman" who places the leaven in the meal. But the Lord Jesus Christ has not committed His Gospel into the hands of *women*. There were none among the twelve, nor among the seventy whom He chose and sent forth. The preaching of the Gospel is a man's job. The part allotted to the sisters, and an important part it is, is to hold up the hands of their ministering brethren by prayer and supplication.

Third, in the effects it produces. When leaven is placed into meal it causes it to swell, it *puffs it up!* Is *that* what the Gospel does when it enters human hearts? No indeed. It produces the very opposite effect. It humbles, it abases.

4. The popular interpretation is contradicted by the plain facts of history and by present-day experience. Were the current explanations true, then we should be forced to acknowledge that this prediction of Christ's has failed in its accomplishment. The Gospel has now been preached for nineteen centuries, yet not a single nation or state, no, nor even city, town or village, has been completely evangelized—let alone won to Christ! If the popular view be the correct one, then the Gospel is a colossal and tragic failure.

5. To make the "leaven" a figure of the Gospel and its power, of that which is *good*, is to contradict every other passage in Scripture where this figure is used. Christ was speaking to a Jewish audience, and with their knowledge of the O.T. Scriptures none of them would ever dream that He had reference to something that was good. With the Jews "leaven" was ever a figure of evil.

The first time that "leaven," in its negative form, occurs in the Bible is in Gen. 19:3, where we are told that Lot "did bake *un*-leavened bread" for the angels, and that "they did eat." No doubt *leavened* bread was a common commodity in the wicked city of Sodom. Why then did not righteous Lot place some of *it* before the angels? Because he knew better. He must have known that they, like Peter, allowed "nothing common or unclean" to pass their lips. They would receive nothing with the least semblance of evil in it. Many congregations to-day are not nearly so careful about *their* food—their *soul-*food. They will readily swallow any rubbish that is handed them from the pulpit, and the sad thing is that they will do so *without any protest*. Why do they not go to the preacher and say, Why don't you give us the Bread of life?

In Ex. 12 it will be found that Jehovah commanded the Israelites to rigidly purge their houses of all "leaven" at the Passover season. Why was this if "leaven" be a type of that which is good? Ex. 34:25 tells us that God prohibited any "leaven" from accompanying offerings of blood. Lev. 2:11 informs us that "leaven" was also excluded from every offering of the Lord made by fire.

This parable in Matt. 13 is not the only occasion when the Lord Jesus employed this figure. *How* did He use it elsewhere?

In Matt. 16:11 we find Him saying to the disciples, "Beware of the leaven of the Pharisees and the Sadducees." There, it is plainly a figure for that which is *evil*. So in Luke 12:1 He said, "Beware ye of the leaven of the Pharisees which is hypocrisy." Would He then deliberately *confuse* His disciples by using it as the figure of *good* in Matt. 13?

The Holy Spirit has also used this same figure through the apostle Paul. In what manner? In 1 Cor. 5:6, 7 we read, "Know ye not that a little leaven leaveneth the whole lump? *Purge out* therefore the old leaven, that ye may be a new lump." Would they be told to "purge out" that which was *good?* The last passage in the N.T. in which "leaven" is mentioned is Gal. 5:7-9. Note there three things: first, it is called a "persuasion"—something which exerts a powerful and moving influence. Second, it *hinders* men "from obeying the truth." Third, it is expressly said to be *"not* from Him which calleth you." Thus, that which is a thing of fermentation—really, incipient purtifaction—is, throughout Scripture, uniformly a figure of corruption—evil. It is remarkable that the word "leaven" occurs just *thirteen* times in the N.T., a number always associated with evil and the work of Satan.

Objectors have appealed to two passages in the O.T. where "leaven" is employed in a *good* sense. But when examined it will be found that they are only seeming exceptions. The first is in Lev. 23:17. The two loaves presented unto the Lord at the Feast of Weeks were to be baken "with leaven." But there is no difficulty here. The Feast of Weeks foreshadowed what is recorded in Acts 2, where the "first fruits" of this dispensation are seen. The two "loaves" prefigured saved Jews *and* Gentiles. Inasmuch as the old nature *remains* in those who are born again, the "leaven" was needed in the loaves which represented these believers. Whenever the typical bread represented Christ it must be unleavened, wherever it typified His people it must be leavened.

The second passage is in Amos 4:5, "Offer a sacrifice of thanksgiving with leaven." This was the language of *irony*, which means it has a meaning the very opposite of what is said. You will sometimes hear a parent say to a wilful child, You do *that* and I will deal with you! Does he mean for the child to actually do it? No, the very reverse. So it is in Amos 4:5: the preceding verse proves it— "Come to Bethel, and transgress; at Gilgal multiply transgression; and bring your sacrifice every morning." Clearly it is the language of irony.

6. Let us now consider the "three measures of meal." Post-millennarians say that they represent the human race among whom the Gospel is working. If so, the "meal" is a figure of that which is *evil*. The human race is fallen, sinful, depraved; "the whole world lieth in the Wicked one" (1 John 5:19). Nor is the usual explanation supplied by Calvinistic commentators any better. They say the "meal" stands for God's elect in their natural state. But the analogy of faith is against them. Let our appeal be to the Scriptures.

"And Abram hastened into the tent unto Sarah, and said, make ready quickly three measures of fine meal, knead it, and make cakes upon the hearth" (Gen. 18:6). Did Abraham prepare for the Lord and His angels food out of that which symbolised evil? Note what is said in 1 Kings 17:14-16. God does not feed His servants on that which speaks of evil! Now *where* does "meal" for bread come from? Any child can answer: not from evil tares, but from good wheat. It is the product of the good Seed. Then that which is good, wholesome, nutritious, pure, can never be a figure of fallen and corrupt humanity.

In Gen. 18:6 the "three measures of meal" are a figure of *Christ's person*, just as the "tender calf" in v. 7 which was killed and dressed prefigured His work. The meal is a type of Him who is the Corn of wheat (John 12:24) and the Bread of life. And thus in the language of N.T. symbolry the "meal" stands for the *doctrine of Christ*.

7. The *action* of the "woman" in our parable exposes the error of the common interpretation. She "took," *not* "received"; and *hid* the leaven in the meal. Is this the way in which the servants of God preach His Gospel? Is the evangel something to be whispered in secret? Does God bid His servants act stealthily? No. The Lord has said to them, "What I tell you in darkness, that speak ye in light: and what ye hear in the ear, that preach ye upon the housetop" (Matt. 11:27).

Writing to the Corinthians, and describing the character of his own ministry, the apostle Paul said, "We faint not, but have renounced the hidden things of dishonesty, not walking in craftiness, nor handling the Word of God deceitfully, but by manifestation of the truth commending ourselves to every man's conscience in the sight of

God" (2 Cor. 4:2). But in our parable, the woman *is* acting dishonestly and deceitfully: she stealthily introduced a foreign and corrupting element into the meal. Her object was to effect its deterioration. If the reader will turn to Lev. 2:11 he will find that this "woman" was doing the very thing which the Word of God forbade her; and he will also observe that she *left out the oil*, which was the very thing the Scriptures enjoined!

Let us now turn, briefly, to the positive side, and give what we believe is the true interpretation. As already stated, the "three measures of meal" stand for Christ as the food of His people: Christ as presented in the written Word, therefore, the doctrine of Christ. The "woman" refers, primarily, to the Papacy, and generally, to all corruptors of God's truth. Romanism has many "daughters." It is most significant that the leading false cults in Christendom were originated by *women*. Modern Spiritualism was started in Boston, U.S.A., in 1848 by the Fox sisters. Seventh Day Adventism was founded by Mrs. White. Christian Science was organised by Mrs. Eddy. Theosophy was devised by Madame Blavatsky, and is now engineered by Mrs. Besant.

The "leaven" symbolises the corrupting of God's truth by the introduction of evil doctrine—compare Matt. 16:12. The unadulterated truth of God is too heavy for the natural man: the sovereignty of God, the helplessness of man, the awfulness of sin, the totality of human depravity, the eternal punishment of the wicked, are indigestible to the carnal mind. Therefore, Rome and her "daughters" have introduced the lightening "leaven," so as to make, what they hand out, more palatable to their dupes. And thus has history repeated itself. Of old God complained to Israel, "Ye offer *polluted* bread upon Mine altar" (Mal. 1:7). So to-day priestcraft and clericalism have corrupted the bread of God.

It is to be noted that the "three measures of meal" *were not removed*, nor was something else substituted in their place. Instead, a foreign element was mingled with it, an element which has slowly and gradually corrupted it. In 2 Thess. 2:4 the apostle Paul declared, "The mystery of iniquity doth *already work*." The leaven had started to act even then, and, as our Saviour declared, it would work till "the whole was leavened." How nearly this is the case to-day the majority of our readers are sadly aware. There are but few places to which an hungry child of God can now go and receive pure Bread. But thank God there *are* still a few such places. While the Holy Spirit remains on earth amongst the saints, God's truth *will be* proclaimed. While *He* is here, there is a *hindering* cause, preventing the "whole" from being "leavened." But at the Rapture the Hinderer will be "taken out of the way" (2 Thess. 2:7), and *then* the "whole" will be completely leavened. The "salt" will be removed, and nothing will be left to stay universal corruption.

—*Arthur W. Pink.*

SPIRITUAL PROGRESS.

We can imagine the son and rightful heir of a king through the crime of a usurper, brought up in poverty and in ignorance of his lineage and inheritance. We can imagine him struggling with the difficulties, animated by the little successes, and cast down by the little adversities of an humble lot, never aspiring beyond the obscurity to which he believed himself born. We can imagine him faithful and exemplary, and therefore esteemed in a sphere where he accounted himself the peer of subjects and servants. And then we can imagine the revolution which would be effected in his views of life, and in his whole character, if the truth regarding his parentage were revealed to him, and if he were assured of a speedy vindication of his rights. A certain dignity would be impressed upon his manners; he would become indifferent to the successes and discouragements which formerly influenced his happiness. And the qualities which had already won the esteem of men, though not in themselves changed, would bear a very different aspect in their new sphere; for it is one thing to occupy faithfully the place of a servant, and another thing to walk worthy of the destiny of a sovereign.

We can imagine a man living in certain relations to another, ignorant of important circumstances affecting their relationship, and of certain characteristics of the person to whom he is related, which if known would influence his whole conduct. A son, for example, might know nothing extraordinary in the claims of his father upon his love and respect. But should it come to his knowledge that, at a period antedating his intelligence, his father had been exposed to extraordinary suffering and danger on his account, and that he owed his life to his father's heroic and self-sacrificing affections; or if circumstances should develop a depth of affection and nobility of character which had lain concealed under his father's meek and unassuming manners, it is easy to imagine the emotion with which the son's heart would swell, and the ardor with which his gratitude would burn. Nor would the influence of such discoveries expire with the emotion of the hour when they were made. They would hallow the relationship for ever, and impart a new tone to the everyday discharge of filial duties.

Illustrations might be multiplied of the influence of our knowledge of the objects of our affections, upon our relations to them; and of the manner in which the discovery of circumstances in their history, and of traits in their character, may affect our happiness or our conduct. In doing so, we should probably speak to the experience of every reader. In too many cases we should revive the regrets with which our best friends are remembered because these discoveries were made too late, and we learned their worth and our obligations only when they had passed beyond the reach of our gratitude. The cases supposed are enough for our purpose; and we may only add that, in the first case, though he was a king's son, whether he knew it or not, he must be made acquainted with the fact before it could influence his conduct; in the case of a son saved by a father's heroism, his salvation was an accomplished fact, though he might never know of the danger from which he had been rescued, but he must be informed of it before it could awaken his gratitude; and so, though the father's love and worth were independent of the son's appreciation, he must know and appreciate them before they could win his reverence or admiration.

What we have supposed in these earthly relations has its counterpart in the spiritual relations of the Christian. When he first finds pardon and peace in believing, full to overflowing as the joy of it may be, he has yet almost everything to learn of the salvation in which he rejoices, and of the Saviour to whom he owes it. Take, for example, the thief on the cross; how little could he know of the doctrine of Christ, or of the privileges, life, and prospects of a believer! Enough for him that in the sinless Sufferer by his side, faith had discovered the Saviour of sinners; the Man who hung there in shame and agony faith had owned as Lord, and from these dying lips there had come, in the triumphant certainty of a divine promise, the assurance, "Thou shalt be with Me in paradise." Had he been spared to bear testimony to that Saviour in this world, he would, under the instruction of apostles and prophets, through the enlightenment of the Spirit of wisdom and revelation, have grown in grace, and in the knowledge of our Lord and Saviour. But as it was, his salvation was not incomplete because his knowledge of it was imperfect; his forgiveness was not according to his view of the blood which was there shed, but according to God's estimate of it his acceptance was not according to his knowledge of Christ, but according to what Christ is; and little as he understood of all that was included in his prayer and the Lord's reply, he shall be found at last perfect and glorious, made a king-priest unto God, to sit with Christ on His throne, and share His glory for ever. There is a vast difference between Saul, in the first bewilderment of salvation, asking, "Lord, what wilt Thou have me to do?" or when Ananias laid his hands upon him, and said, "Brother Saul, receive thy sight." And Paul, the veteran apostle, when, according to the wisdom given unto him, he wrote those epistles, in which are some things hard to be understood. But had the overpowering astonishment of that vision, or the overpowering joy of that deliverance dissolved the bonds of mortality, Saul of Tarsus would have been found beside the thief from the cross, made perfect in glory with Christ on the throne—the chief of sinners saved.

The abundance of the revelation vouchsafed to Paul, and the gifts bestowed upon him, contributed nothing to his salvation, which was perfect, whether he knew its extent or not. But the knowledge which contributed nothing to the salvation which grace brought, was of the highest importance in the service to which grace called him. So with every believer sent into the world. The love of God, the fulness of Christ, the perfection of salvation, are not dependent on our intelligence and appreciation of them; but our present enjoyment of them is. Their power to comfort, animate, and sanctify us must be in proportion to the clearness, certainty, extent, and accuracy of our knowledge of them. We can love God only as we know and believe the love God hath to us. We can be called to walk worthy of the vocation wherewith He hath called us, only as we, through His Spirit, "comprehend the length and breadth, and height and depth, and know the love of God, which passeth knowledge, that we may be filled with all the fulness of God." We can occupy the place of strangers and pilgrims only as we have been taught that we are a chosen generation, a royal priesthood, a holy nation, a peculiar people, that we should show forth the praises of Him who hath called us out of darkness into His marvellous light. The onward and upward path of the Christian is not a long and toilsome journey amidst fears and uncertainties, which may, peradventure, issue in salvation at last; but, to use once more the scriptural expression of the blessed truth, "the grace of God brings salvation," and then it is ours, in the fear of the Lord and in the power of the Spirit, to work out and manifest the salvation which grace has brought to us, and bestowed upon us. It is this outward manifestation of it that is probably meant to be expressed in the phrase, "our progressive sanctification," and it is as the Scriptures unfold to us that salvation and the grace which bestows it—what Christ is, and what we are in Christ—the character of God in His relations to us in Christ, and the glory in which these relations will be consummated, that they are made available as the instrument of the Spirit in promoting our practical holiness. As a matter of fact, it will be found that the spiritual progress of the believer is commensurate with his advancement in divine knowledge; not a merely formal knowledge either of doctrines or duties, but a knowledge of the truth conveyed to the quickened soul by the Spirit, which we have received "that we might know the things which are freely given us of God."

We cannot prescribe the order and method of the Spirit's procedure in this enlightenment and training of the soul; and there is always danger in citing individual instances of it, that we should be understood as exhibiting a model to which the experience of others must be conformed. But it is safe to say that the darkness which overshadows the lives of many of the children of God, and the direst conflicts of the most earnest souls, proceed from misconception of the character of God, erroneous views of our relations to Him, defective views of Christ and His work, and the interposition of humanly contrived terms between the soul and His grace. In like manner, the barrenness, worldly conformity, coldness, and inaction of the churches may be traced to low views of the grace of God, and ignorance of our standing, calling, and prospects in Christ. The explanation of every remarkable deliverance of struggling souls, of every signal accession of joy and strength, of every true revival in the Church, will be found in the enlightenment of that ignorance, the correction of these errors, in the disentanglement of the truth from the notions that have obscured it, and its application in living power to the heart. In the lives of some Christians there may be a steady progress in grace and knowledge which has no marked and memorable stages. But there are few of us who cannot recall sudden, and full, and thrilling manifestations of some aspects of the truth which have marked a new era in our spiritual history. We could mention more than one instance in which a transformation of life, which arrested attention and excited enquiry, has been explained, when the subjects of the change told how the truth of the coming and kingdom of the Lord had been received into a heart long closed against it by prejudice. "The joy of it," said one, "was like the joy of conversion. It has changed my views of all present relations, as well as of future prospects, and has made the Bible a book of new meanings as well as new interest." Another spoke in similar terms of a fresh influx of life, joy, and love, in the reading of the wonderful close of the Lord's intercession, "that the love wherewith Thou hast loved Me may be in them."

But very frequently these most marked epochs of the spiritual history of the children of God date from simpler, clearer, fuller views, and a firmer grasp of the fundamental truth of the sinner's justification and acceptance in Christ. In the annals of what may be called experimental Christianity, there is probably no more remarkable instance of joy in the Lord which anticipated heaven, of settled peace, calm rest in Christ, of unquestioning assurance of the divine faithfulness, and submission to the divine will, of deadness to the world, renunciation of self and devotion to the glory of God in a holy, loving, and Christ-like walk, than that of Mrs. Edwards, the wife of Jonathan Edwards, at whose request she wrote a statement of the gracious dealings of the Lord with her soul. The following is her account of the commencement and starting-point of the most noticeable era in her spiritual progress: "When Mr. Reynolds was at prayer this morning, in the family, I felt an earnest desire that in calling upon God he should say *"Father,"* or that he would address the Almighty under that appellation, on which the thought turned in my mind, Why can I say *"Father!"* Can I now at this time, with the confidence of a child, and without the least misgiving of heart, call God *"my Father!"* This brought to my mind two lines of Mr. Erskine's sonnet:

"I see Him lay His vengeance by,
And smile in Jesu's face."

"I was thus deeply sensible that my sins did loudly call for vengeance, but I then by faith saw God lay His vengeance by, and smile in Jesu's face. It appeared to be real and certain that He did so. I had not the least doubt that He then sweetly smiled upon me with the look of forgiveness and love, having laid aside all His displeasure against me, for Jesu's sake; which made me feel very weak and somewhat faint.

"In consequence of this, I felt a strong desire to be alone with God, to go to Him without having anyone to interrupt the silent and soft communion which I earnestly desired between God and my own soul; and accordingly withdrew to my chamber. It should have been mentioned before that I retired, while Mr. Reynolds was praying, these words, in Romans 8:34, came into my mind, 'Who is he that condemneth? It is Christ that died, yea, rather that is risen again, who is even at the right hand of God, who also maketh intercession for us,' as well as the following words, 'Who shall separate us from the love of Christ?' which occasioned great sweetness and delight in my soul. But when I was alone the words came into my mind with far greater power and sweetness; upon which I took the Bible, and read the words to the end of the chapter, when they were impressed upon my heart with vastly greater power and sweetness still. They appeared to me with undoubted certainty as the words of God, and as words which God did pronounce concerning me. I had no more doubt of it than I had of my being. I seemed, as it were, to hear God proclaiming thus to the world concerning me, *Who shall lay anything to thy charge?* and had it strongly impressed upon me how impossible it was for anything in heaven or earth, in this world or the future, ever to separate me from the love of God, which was in Christ Jesus."

Did space permit, it might be pleasant and profitable to extend this quotation, to the transport of joy of which this was the spring, and the life of devotion and holiness of which this was the starting-point, regarding which her distinguished husband says: "Now, if such things are enthusiasm and the offspring of a distempered brain, let my brain be possessed ever more of that happy distemper! If this be distraction, I pray God that the world of mankind may all be swayed with this benign, meek, beneficent, beautific, glorious distraction." But we must hasten to conclude these remarks with a chapter, hitherto unpublished, from a brother in Christ, who would shrink from having his name connected with it as courting notoriety, but who will rejoice and give thanks if it may be used of God to illustrate the connection between our spiritual progress and our advancement in the knowledge of the truth as it is in Jesus; and still more, if it should be instrumental in leading any child of God into the knowledge of what was the special object of the Holy Spirit in giving that epistle to the churches by the pen of the beloved apostle: "That ye also may have fellowship with us, and truly our fellowship is with the Father and with His Son Jesus Christ."

"I well remember the hour when my soul first realised these words in power: 'And truly our fellowship is with the Father and with His Son Jesus Christ.' Long before this I had known that the blood of Jesus Christ cleanseth from all sin; I had known somewhat of the power of death, burial, and resurrection with Christ. I had even known, through many failures confessed and forgiven, our perpetual priestly standing in confidence before God; and I had learned to be looking for that blessed hope, even the glorious appearing of the great God and our Saviour Jesus Christ. But here was an advancement in the knowledge of our Lord and Saviour—the knowledge of my companionship and community of interest with Him —and that my all was to be held in fellowship with the Father and the Son. And was I, by faith, to sit with Him evermore in heavenly places, a heavenly man not only with a destiny, but with a present fellowship far above angels, for a while walking in a world already doomed and about to be consumed? Was I to tread the every-day scenes of a life of toil and care, not only wearing my priestly garments, but carrying through them all the solemn consciousness of my fellowship with the Father and the Son, knowing the while that as Christ Himself is, so does the Father look upon me in this world?

"Like Daniel, I was left alone and saw this great vision, and there remained no strength in me; for my vigour was turned into corruption, and I retained no strength. But I heard the voice, 'O man, greatly beloved, fear not; peace be unto thee; be strong, yea, be strong.' And when He had spoken unto me, I was strengthened, and said, Let my Lord speak, for Thou hast strengthened me. God was giving me to know, in my poverty, the riches of the glory of His inheritance in the saints; in my weakness, the exceeding greatness of His power to usward who believe; and He was giving me to walk with a solemn yet joyous awe upon my spirit as one made a temple of the Holy Ghost. I found myself indeed a stranger and a pilgrim here, because I had found my citizenship, my companionship, my inheritance in heaven. My mission was now no longer in any wise to reform Egypt or its works, but with a chosen heavenly people to go out from it into the wilderness; to leave the dead in trespasses and sins to care for its own works of death, and to give myself to preach the Gospel of the glory of Christ —a ministry of life and reconciliation. My hopes could no longer be placed in dreams of human progress; national or party triumphs were nothing to me, except as they bore upon the coming kingdom. With the angelic choir, I could rejoice over one sinner that repenteth, and care little for the blood-stained victories that had so often thrilled my heart.

"While the Lots of the Church went down to dwell in Sodom, and even, like Lot, sat in the gate to judge the doomed people or reform them, I was brought to the top of the mountain to walk with Abraham in wondrous fellowship with the everlasting, glorious Jehovah, and to partake of His thoughts and counsels. I saw, indeed, that those of His people who had ventured into Sodom, and vexed their righteous souls by contact with its abominations, should, through sovereign grace, escape the fire as truly as those upon the mountain, but that it would be with the loss of their life-toil, their carefully gathered hay, wood, and stubble, and with shame and dishonour, saved by the strong hand of God, yet so as by fire, while their works were burned up. Such a walk was plainly impossible for one whose fellowship was with the Father and the Son; for 'if we say that we have fellowship with *Him*, and walk in darkness, we lie, and do not tell the truth.'

"As I walked among men, my spirit was chastened by holy fear—a dread of marring that for which I had been apprehended of Christ. I could now yield myself a willing servant to work out or manifest this salvation, knowing the while that it was God who had lifted me up to fellowship with Himself, and who was now working in me to will and to do of His good pleasure. Now that I was called to unbroken fellowship with Him, I saw that the bustle and toil of my works were to be replaced by a quiet and natural fruit-bearing, the vine producing all, while I, as a branch, might be honoured to bear the precious fruit. I saw I was to bear much fruit, not by struggling, but by abiding in Christ. This implied that other alliances should be severed. Separation from the world and its influences is necessary to the unhindered manifestation of God as a Father to us, as the Apostle says, 'Come out from among them and be ye separate, and touch not the unclean thing, and I will be a Father unto you, and ye shall be my sons and my daughters, saith the Lord Almighty.'

"I entered the scenes of my secular occupation with new feelings. Where once I desired to rule, I was taught to seek the lowly place which my Master chose. How differently, too, I was taught to meet wrong and insult! I could even love my opposers, when I remembered Him who had brought me into fellowship with Himself, who, when He was reviled, reviled not again. I could willingly suffer wrong when my spirit was subdued by the thought that I was placed on a more intimate footing with Christ than the angels that had never sinned, and that only a thin veil needed to be pierced, and I should stand in the unclouded presence of the great God and Saviour who had called me to be a partner, first of His suffering, and then of His glory, as one chosen to show the highest triumphs of grace before the universe.

"The lessons of independence and self-reliance, so carefully learned and so proudly cherished as the grand object of education, from the cradle upward, and only half discarded since my conversion, were now to be learned backward, and every day was to find me with less confidence in the flesh and a more single dependence on God. I now saw that we prevailed with God, and, therefore, with men, when compelled, by our very weakness, to cleave to Him in heart-broken reliance on His grace. Henceforth I was called to act in the power and spirit of a kingdom not of this age, living in the world in the joy of the anticipated glory of the world to come. . . ."

From such instances men have undertaken to construct theories of sanctification; they speak of second conversion, and incite restless, earnest souls to copy the outward actings of faith, and to imitate the accompanying emotions of these blessed discoveries of truth. Unhappily, nature is always disposed to reverse the order of the Gospel, and from the outward results to travel back to the inward grace. In the superstitions of our fathers, it was held that one of the most potent of the impious rites and incantations of the fabled as-

(Concluded page 31.)

How circumscribed is the scope of our studies! It is greatly to be feared that many form their conceptions of Christ from what is said of Him in the first four books of the New Testament. How rarely, comparatively speaking, does even their reading go beyond those books! How little they study the Epistles!

It needs to be pointed out that the Gospels treat of Christ's life during the days of His humiliation. They view Him in the form of a Servant, who came not to be ministered unto, but to minister. True it is that Matthew's Gospel sets forth the kingship of Him who was here as Jehovah's Servant; yet is it as the rejected King. True also, that John's Gospel portrays the Divine glories of the incarnate Son; yet as the One who was unknown in the world which He had made, and as received not by His own to whom He came (John 1:10, 11). It is not till we pass beyond the Gospels that we find the lordship of Jesus of Nazareth really made manifest.

On the day of Pentecost Peter said, "Let all the house of Israel know assuredly, that God hath made that same Jesus, whom ye have crucified, both Lord and Christ" (Acts 2:36). The humbled One is now the victorious One. He who was here in lowliness, has been exalted "far above all principality, and power, and might, and dominion, and every name that is named, not only in this world, but also in that which is to come" (Eph. 1:21). He who suffered His face to be covered with the vile spittal of men, has been given a name more excellent than the angels (Heb. 1:4). He whom man once crowned with thorns has been, by God, "crowned with glory and honour" (Heb. 2:9). He who hung, in apparent helplessness, upon the cross of shame, has taken His seat "on the right hand of the Majesty on high" (Heb. 1:3).

Now the New Testament Epistles, in contrast from the Gospels, are all written from the viewpoint of an *ascended* Christ. They treat of a glorified Saviour. And how much we lose by their neglect! Why is it that when Christ comes before our minds our thoughts at once turn back to the "days of His flesh"? Why is it that our hearts are so little occupied with the heavenly Christ? Why do we meditate so little upon His exaltation, His seat and session at God's right hand? Is it not because we read the Epistles so infrequently?

Many Christians, when they turn to the Epistles, find them so much more difficult than they do the four Gospels. Of course they do—because they are so unfamiliar with them! You know how it is when you enter a strange city: its lay-out, its streets, its suburbs, are unknown; and you find it hard to find your way about. Thus it is with the Epistles. You must live in them to become acquainted with their contents, then you will not feel that you are treading a difficult, because unknown, territory.

It is in the Epistles, and in *them alone,* we have set forth the distinctive character of Christianity. We have it not in the Gospels; the Acts is transitionary: most of the Revelation belongs to the future. The Epistles alone treat, essentially, of the present Dispensation. Yet in the international lessons for the Sunday School these are studiously ignored. Present-day preaching (?) rarely notices them. Christians, in their private reading of the Word, seldom turn to them. But, we repeat, in the Epistles only do we have Christianity expounded, for Christianity has to do with a risen, glorified, and enthroned Christ! Thus, if we are to heed the injunction of our opening text, we must spend much time in the Epistles.

Our closing word is an earnest appeal. Sunday-School-teachers and Christian parents, heed that word concerning children in Eph. 6:4: "Bringing them up in the nurture and admonition of *the Lord*"—not simply "Jesus"! Seek help from on high to be delivered from presenting to them an erroneous or inadequate view of the person of Christ. If you read to them from the Gospels, be careful to tell them that they treat of Christ's earthly life, during the days of His humiliation; but that now He is in Heaven, crowned with glory and honour.

Let the little ones' first conception of Christ be not only of Him as the Babe of Bethlehem and the Sufferer of Calvary, but also of Him as the One before whom the angels bow in worship. Tell them that Jesus of Nazareth was *"God* manifest in flesh," and that He is to be honoured even as the Father is honoured (John 5:23). Set before them an example of reverence when you speak to them of Him who is "the Brightness of God's glory and the express Image of His person (Heb. 1:3). Ever refer to Him as "the *Lord* Jesus Christ," and to help you, seek grace to daily "sanctify in your hearts Christ as Lord."

—*Arthur W. Pink.*

STUDIES IN THE SCRIPTURES

"Search the Scriptures" John 5: 39

Copyright in all English-speaking Countries.

Editor: Arthur W. Pink, 15 Hurlstone Avenue, Summer Hill, N.S.W., Australia.
Hon. Agent in U.S.A.: Mr. C. S. Pressel, 559 Dupont Avenue, York, Penna.

FREE TO ALL WHO WILL READ IT

A CALL TO SEPARATION.

2 Cor. 6: 14-18.

This passage gives utterance to a Divine exhortation for those belonging to Christ to hold aloof from all intimate associations with the ungodly. It expressly forbids them entering into alliances with the unconverted. It definitely prohibits the children of God walking arm-in-arm with worldlings. It is an admonition applying to *every* phase and department of our lives—religious, domestic, social, commercial. And never, perhaps, was there a time when it more needed pressing on Christians than now. The days in which we are living are marked by the spirit of compromise. On every side we behold unholy mixtures, ungodly alliances, unequal yokes. Many professing Christians appear to be trying how near to the world they may walk and wet go to Heaven.

"Be ye *not* unequally yoked together." This is a call to godly separation. In each dispensation this Divine demand has been made. To Abraham Jehovah's peremptory word was, "Get thee out of thy country, and from thy kindred, and from thy father's house." To Israel He said, "After the doings of the land of Egypt wherein ye dwelt, shall ye not do: and after the doings of the land of Canaan, whither I bring you, shall ye not do: neither shall ye walk in their ordinances" (Lev. 18:3). And again, "Ye shall not walk in the manners of the nation which I cast out before you" (Lev. 20:23). It was for their disregard of these very prohibitions that Israel brought down upon themselves such severe chastisements.

At the beginning of the New Testament we are shown the forerunner of Christ standing outside the organised Judaism of his day, calling on men to flee from the wrath to come. The Saviour announced that, "He calleth His own sheep by name, and leadeth them *out*" (John 10:3). On the day of Pentecost the word to believers was, "Save yourselves *from* this untoward generation" (Acts 2:40). Later, to the Christian Hebrews Paul wrote, "Let us *go forth* therefore unto Him without the camp" (13:13). In the Tribulation period, God's call to His people in Babylon will be, "Come out of her, My people, that ye be not partakers of her sins, and that ye receive not of her plagues" (Rev. 18:4).

"Be ye *not* unequally yoked together." This is God's word unto His people *to-day*. Nor does it stand alone. In Rom. 16:17 it is said, "Mark them which cause divisions and offences contrary to the doctrine which ye have learned, and *avoid* them." In 2 Tim. 2:20 we read, "In a great house there are not only vessels of gold and of silver, but also of wood and of earth; and some to honour, and some to dishonour. If a man therefore purge himself *from* these, he shall be a vessel unto honour, sanctified, and meet for the Master's use." 2 Tim. 3:5 speaks of those having a form of godliness, but denying the power thereof," then it is added, *"from such* turn away." What a word is that in 2 Thess. 3:14, "If any man obey not our

(Continued on page 72.)

IMPORTANT NOTICES

Back numbers of each year of the magazine are yet obtainable at 5/- (1.25) per year. Bound at 7/6 (1.75) post paid. They will soon be out of print. Those in U.S.A. wanting them, please purchase from Mr. Pressel (see front cover page).

Advise promptly of change of address. This Magazine is published as a work of faith and labour of love. The Editor gladly gives his services. It is freely sent to all who will read it. No charge is made for it.

Christians who feel definitely led to do so, may have fellowship with us in this Ministry. Send only *Inter-National M.O.*

CONTENTS.

	Page
Hebrews	50
Gleanings in Exodus	56
Parables of Matt. 13	61
A Sacrifice of Praise	65
Worldly Church Methods	68

THE EPISTLE TO THE HEBREWS.

3. The Superiority of Christ over the Prophets 1:1-3.

That which distinguishes the Hebrews' Epistle from all other books is that it has for its subject the superiority of Christianity over Judaism. Its theme is the superabounding excellency of the new covenant. The method followed by the Holy Spirit in developing His theme is to take Him who is the centre and circumference, the life and light of Christianity, even Christ, and hold before Him one object after another. As he does so, elevated, important, venerated, as some of those objects are, yet, in the presence of the "Son" their glories fade into utter insignificance.

Someone has suggested an analogy with what is recorded in Matthew 17. There we see Christ upon the holy Mount, transfigured before His disciples; and, as they continued gazing on His flashing excellency, they saw no man "save Jesus only." At first, there appeared standing with Him Moses and Elijah, and so real and tangible were they, Peter said, "If Thou wilt, let us make here three tabernacles; one for Thee, one for Moses, and one for Elijah." But as they looked "a bright cloud overshadowed them," and a Voice was heard saying, "This is My Beloved Son: hear *Him*" (Luke 9.35). How significant are the words that immediately followed: "And when the Voice was passed, Jesus was found *alone*." The glory associated with Moses and Elijah was so eclipsed by the infinitely greater glory connected with Christ, that they faded from view.

Now it is something very much like this that we see here, all through the Hebrews' Epistle. The Holy Spirit takes up one object after another, holds each one up, as it were, in the presence of the all-excellent "Son," and as He does so, their glory is eclipsed, and the Lord Jesus is "found *alone*." The prophets, the angels, Moses, Joshua, the Levitical priesthood, the Old Testament men of faith, each come into view; each is compared with Christ, and each, in turn, fades away before His greater glory. Thus, the very things which Judaism most highly esteemed are shown to be far inferior to what God has now made known in the Christian revelation.

In the opening verses the keynote of the Epistle is at once struck. As is usual in Scripture, the Spirit has placed the key for us over the very entrance. There we see an antithesis is drawn. There we behold a contrast between Judaism and Christianity. There we are shown the immeasurable superiority of the latter over the former. There we have brought before us the "Son" as the Speaker to whom we must listen, the Object on which to gaze, the Satisfier of the heart, the One through whom God is now perfectly and finally made known. God hath, in these last days, "spoken unto us in Son." As God is the *Source* from which all blessings flow, *He* is set before us in the very first word of the Epistle. As Christ is the *Channel* through which all blessing comes to us, *He* is mentioned next, and that, in His highest character, as "Son." The more these opening verses are prayerfully pondered, the more will their wondrous depths, exhaustless contents and unspeakable preciousness be made apparent.

In the preceding article we pointed out how that in the first two verses of Hebrews a contrast is drawn between Christ and the prophets. Israel regarded them with the highest veneration, and justly so, for they were the instruments Jehovah had condescended to employ in the giving forth of the revelation of His mind and will in Old Testament times. But Divine as were their communications, they were but introductory to something better and grander. The revelation which God made through them was neither complete nor final, as was hinted at in its fragmentary character: "in many parts and in many ways"

God, of old, spake to the fathers in the prophets. Over against this, as transcending and excelling the Old Testament revelation, God has, in these last days "spoken to us in Son," i.e., in Christianity has given a new, perfect, final revelation of Himself.

Thus, the superiority over Judaism of Christianity is here denoted in a twofold way: first, by necessary implication the latter, not being diverse and fragmentary, is one and complete; it is the grand consummation toward which the other was but introductory; it is the substance and reality, of which the former furnished but the shadows and types. Second, by the instruments employed: in the one God spoke "in the prophets," in the other "in (His) Son." Just as far as the personal glory of the Son excels that of the prophets, so is the revelation God made through Christ more sublime and exalted than that which He made under Judaism. In the one He was made known as *light*—the requirements, claims, demands of His holiness. In the other, He is manifested as *love*—the affections of His heart are displayed.

Now, to prevent the Hebrews from concluding that Christ was nothing more than another *instrument* through which God had "spoken," the Holy Spirit in the verses which we are now to take up, brings before us some of the highest and most blessed of our Saviour's personal excellencies. He there proceeds to exalt the Hebrews' conception of the Divine Prophet and Founder of the new economy. This He does by bringing into view seven of His wondrous glories. To the contemplation of these we now turn. Let us consider,

1. *His Heirship.*

"Whom He hath appointed Heir of all things" (v. 2). There are three things here claiming attention. First, the character in which Christ is viewed. Second, His appointment unto the inheritance. Third, the scope of the inheritance.

First, this declaration that God has appointed the Saviour "Heir of all things" is similar in scope to that word of Peter's on the day of Pentecost, "Therefore let all the house of Israel know assuredly, that God hath made that same Jesus, whom ye have crucified, both Lord and Christ" (Acts 2:36). In both passages the reference is to the honour which has been conferred upon the Mediator, and in each case the design of speaker or writer was to magnify the Christian revelation by showing the exalted dignity of its Author and Head.

That the title "Heir" is similar in force to "Lord" is clear from Gal. 4:1, "The heir, as long as he is a child, differeth nothing from a servant, though he be *lord* of all." Yet though there is a similarity between the terms "Heir" and "Lord," there is also a clear distinction between them; not only so, we may admire the Divine discrimination in the one used in Heb. 1:2. Strikingly does it follow immediately after the reference to Him as "Son," in fact furnishing proof thereof, for the son *is* the father's heir.

The word "heir" suggests two things: dignity and dominion, with the additional implication of legal title thereto. For its force see Gen. 21:10, 12; Gal. 4:1, etc. "An 'heir' is a successor to his father in all that his father hath. In connection with the Father and the Son, the supreme sovereignty of the One is nowise infringed upon by the supreme sovereignty of the Other—cf. John 5:19. The difference is only in the manner: the Father doeth all *by* the Son, and the Son doeth all *from* the Father" (Dr. Gouge). The title "Heir" here denotes Christ's proprietorship. He is the Possessor and Disposer of all things.

Second, unto an inheritance Christ was "appointed" by God. This at once shows us that the "Son" through whom God has revealed Himself, is here viewed not in His abstract Diety, but mediatorially, as incarnate. Only as such could He be "*appointed*" Heir; as God the Son, essentially, He could not be deputed to anything.

This "appointment" was in the eternal counsels of the Godhead. Two things are hereby affirmed: certainty and valid title. Because God has predestined that the Mediator should be "Heir of all things," His inheritance is most sure and absolutely guaranteed, for "the Lord of hosts hath purposed, and who shall disannul?" (Isa. 43:27); hath He not said, "My counsel *shall* stand, and I will do all My pleasure" (Isa. 46:10)! Again: because God has "appointed" the Mediator "Heir" we are assured of His indubitable *right* to this supreme dignity. That which is said of Christ's being made priest, in Heb. 5:5, may also be applied to this other dignity: Christ glorified not Himself to be an Heir, but He that saith to Him, "Thou art My Son, to-day have I begotten Thee," also "appointed" Him Heir.

Above we have said, This appointment was in the eternal counsels of the Godhead. With our present passage should be compared Acts 2:23, "Him, being delivered by the determinate counsel and foreknowledge of God, ye have taken, and by wicked hands have crucified and slain." Thus there were two chief things to which the Mediator was "appointed": sufferings (cf. also 1 Pet. 1:19, 20), and glory—cf. 1 Pet. 1:11. How this shows us that, from the beginning, *Christ* was the Centre of all the Divine counsels. Before a single creature was called into existence, God had appointed an "Heir" to all things, and that Heir was the Lord Jesus. It was the predestined *reward* of His voluntary humiliation; He who had not where to lay His head, is now the lawful Possessor of the universe.

This appointment of Christ to the inheritance was mentioned in O.T. prophecy: "Also I will make Him My **Firstborn**, higher than the kings of the earth" (Psa. 89:27). "Firstborn" in Scripture refers not so much to primogeniture, as to dignity and inheritance: see Gen. 49:3 for the first occurrence. It is remarkable to observe and most solemn to discover that, in the days of His flesh, Israel recognised Him as such: "*This* is the Heir come let us kill Him, and the inheritance shall be ours" (Mark 12:7), was their terrible language.

Third, a few words now on the extent of that Inheritance unto which the Mediator has been deputed: "Whom He hath appointed Heir of *all* things." The *manifestation* of this is yet future, but confirmation of it was made when the risen Saviour said to the disciples, "All power is *given* unto Me in heaven and in earth" (Matt. 28:18). At the beginning of the Millennium God shall say, "I will declare the decree (i.e., the "appointment"), Thou art My Son; this day have I begotten Thee. Ask of Me, and I shall give Thee the heathen for Thine inheritance, and the uttermost parts of the earth for Thy possession" (Psa. 2:7, 8). His proprietorship of mankind will be evidenced when He shall "sit upon the throne of His glory: and before Him shall be gathered all nations; and He shall separate them one from another, as a shepherd divideth his sheep from the goats" (Matt. 25:31, 32). His right to dispose of all will be witnessed at the great white throne. But it is when this world has passed away that His universal Heirship will be fully and eternally displayed: on the new earth shall be "the *throne* of God *and* of the Lamb" (Rev. 22:1)!

"How rich is our adorable Jesus! The blessed Lord, when He was upon the cross, had nothing. He had not where to lay His head; even His very garments were taken from Him. He was buried in a grave which belonged not to Him or to His family. On earth He was poor to the very last; none so absolutely poor as He. But as man, He is to inherit all things; as Jesus, God and man in one person. All angels, all human beings upon the earth, all powers in the universe, when asked, 'Who is Lord of all?' will answer, 'Jesus the Son of Mary'" (Saphir). Such is the reward which God has ordained for the once humiliated One.

But most wonderful of all is that word in Rom. 8:16, 17, "The Spirit Himself beareth witness with our spirits, that *we* are the children of God; and if children, then *heirs;* heirs of God, and joint-heirs with Christ." This the angels are not. It is because of their indissoluable union with Him that His people shall also enjoy the Inheritance which God has appointed unto the Son. Herein we discover the Divine discrimination and propriety in here speaking of Christ not as "Lord of all things," but "Heir." *We* can never be "joint-lords," but grace *has* made us "joint-heirs." Because of this the Redeemer said to the Father, "the glory which Thou gavest Me I have given *them*" (John 17: 22).

2. *His Creatorship.*

"By whom also He made the worlds" (v. 2). The Greek term for the last word is "aionas," the primary meaning of which is *ages*. But here, by a metonymy, it seems to be applied to matter, and signifies, the *universe*. "Aion properly denotes time, either past or future; and then comes to signify things formed and done in time —the world. . . . The aionas is plainly the synonym of the ta panta ("all things") in the preceding clause". (Dr. J. Brown). Two things incline us to this view. First, other scriptures ascribe creation to the Son: John 1:3; Col. 1:16. Second, this gives force to the previous clause: He was, in the beginning, appointed Heir of all things because He was to be their Creator. Col. 1:16 confirms this: "all things were created by Him and *for* Him."

"By whom also He made the worlds." Here is furnished clear proof of the Mediator's Diety: only *God* can create. This also is brought in for the purpose of emphasising the immeasurable value of the new revelation which God has made. Attention is focused on the One in whom and through whom God has spoken in the "last days." Three things are told us in v. 2 concerning Christ: first, we have His person—He is the "Son"; second, His dignity and dominion—He is the "Heir of all things"; third, His work—He has "made the worlds," heaven and earth. If, then, His dignity be so exalted, if His glory be so great, what must not be the word of such a "Son"! what the fulness of truth which God has made known to His people by Him!

3. His Effulgency.

"Who being the brightness of (His) glory" (v. 3). In this verse the Holy Spirit continues to set forth the excellencies of Christ, and in the same order as in the preceding one. First, the Divine dignity of His person, His relation to the Father—He is the Brightness of His glory. The Greek verb from which "brightness" is derived, signifies "to send forth brightness or light," and the noun here used, such brightness as cometh from light, as the sunbeams issuing from the sun. The term is thus used metaphorically. So ably has this been developed by Dr. Gouge we transcribe from his excellent commentary of 1650: "No resemblance taken from any other creature can more fully set out the mutual relation between the Father and the Son:

"1. The brightness issuing from the sun is the same nature that the sun is—cf. John 10:30. 2. It is of as long continuance as the sun: never was the sun without the brightness of it—cf. John 1:1. 3. The brightness cannot be separated from the sun: the sun may as well be made no sun, as have the brightness thereof severed from it—cf. Prov. 8:30. 4. This brightness though from the sun is not the sun itself —cf. John 8:42. 5. The sun and the brightness are distinct from each other; the one is not the other—cf. John 5:17. 6. All the glory of the sun is this brightness—cf. John 17:5; 2 Cor. 4:6. 7. The light which the sun giveth the world is by this brightness—cf. John 14:9. . . . Thus the Son is no whit inferior to the Father, but every way His equal. He was brightness, the brightness of His Father, yea, also the brightness of His Father's glory. Whatever excellency soever was in the Father, the same likewise was in the Son, and that in the most transplendent manner. Glory sets out excellency; brightness of glory, the excellency of excellency."

That which is in view in this third item of our passage so far transcends the grasp of the finite mind that it is impossible to give it adequate expression in words. Christ is the irradiation of God's glory. The Mediator's relation to the Godhead is like that of the rays to the sun itself. We may conceive of the sun in the firmament, yet shining not: were there no rays, we should not see the sun. So, apart from Christ, the *brightness* of God's "glory" could not be perceived by us. Without Christ, man is in the dark, utterly in the dark concerning God. It is in Christ that God is *revealed*.

4. His Being.

"The express image of His person," or, more literally, "the impress of His substance" (v. 3). The Greek for "express image" is a single word, and the verb from which it is derived signifies "to engrave," and in its noun form "that which is engraved," as the stamp on a coin, the print pressed on paper, the mark made by a seal. Nothing can be more like the original mold or seal than the image pressed out on the clay or wax, the one carrying the very form or features of the other. The O.T. saints did not perfectly "express" God, nor can angels, for they are but finite creatures; but Christ, being Himself God, could, and did. All that God is, in His nature and character, is expressed and manifested, absolutely and perfectly, by the incarnate Son.

"And the very impress of His substance." Here again we are faced with that which is difficult to comprehend, and harder still to express. Perhaps we may be helped to get the thought by comparing 1 Tim. 6:16 with Col. 1:15: "Dwelling in the light which no man can approach unto; whom no man hath seen, nor can see," "Who is the image of the invisible God." All true knowledge of God must come from His approach unto us, for we cannot by "searching" find Him out. The approach must come from *His* side, and it *has* come, "the only begotten Son, which is in the bosom of the Father, He hath declared Him" (John 1:18).

"The very impress of His substance." This is the nearest approach to defining God's essence or essential existence. The word "substance" means essential being or essential existence; but how little we know about this! God—self-existent: One who never had a beginning, yet full of all that we know of blessed attributes. And Christ, the incarnate Son, is the very "impress," as it were, of that substance. As we have said, the original term is taken from the impress of a seal. Though we had never seen the seal we might, from beholding the impress of it (that which is exactly like it), form a true and accurate idea of the seal itself. So Christ is the Impress of the substance of God, the One in whom all the Divine perfections are found. Though essentially Light, He is also the Outshining of the "Light"; though in Himself essentially God, He is also the visible Representation of God. Being "with God" and being God, He is also the Manifestation of God; so that by and through Him we learn what God is.

"The very impress of His substance." It is not enough to *read* Scripture, nor even to compare passage with passage; nor have we done all when we have prayed for light thereon; there must also be meditation, *prolonged meditation*. Of whom were these words spoken? Of the "Son," but as incarnate, i.e., as the Son of man; of Him who entered this world by mysterious and miraculous conception in the virgin's womb. Men doubt and deny this, and no wonder, when they have nothing but a corrupt reason to guide them. How can a sin-darkened understanding lay hold of, believe, and *love* the truth that the great God should hide Himself in a frail human nature! That Omnipotence should be concealed in a Servant's form! That the Eternal One should become an Infant of days! This is the "great mystery" of godliness, but to the family of God it is "without controversy."

But if the human mind, unaided, is incapable of grasping the fact of the great God *hiding* Himself in human form, how much less can it apprehend that that very hiding was a *manifestation*, that the concealing was a revealing of Himself—the Invisible becoming visible, the Infinite becoming cognisible to the finite. Yet such it was: "And the very impress of His substance." *Who was?* The incarnate Son, the Man Christ Jesus. Of *whose* "substance?" Of God's! But how could that be? God is *eternal*, and Christ *died!* True, yet He manifested His Godhood in the very way that He died. He died as none other ever did: *He* "laid down" His life. More, He manifested His Godhood by rising again: "destroy this temple" (His body) said He, "And I will raise it again"; and He *did*. His Godhead is now manifested in that "He is alive forever more."

But God is *immutable* and *self-sufficient*, and Christ *hungered and thirsted!* True; because He was made "in all things like unto His brethren," and because that from actual experience of these things, He might be able to "succor them that are tempted." Moreover, He manifested *His* self-sufficiency by miraculously feeding the five thousand, and by His absolute power over all Nature—ruling the winds and waves, blasting the fig tree, etc.

But God is *Lord of all*, and Christ was "Led as a lamb to the slaughter": He seemed so helpless when arrested and when hanging upon the Cross! But appearances are deceptive; sometimes it is a greater thing to withhold the putting forth of power than to exert it! Yet glimpses of *His* Lordship flashed forth even then. See Him in the Garden, and those sent to apprehend Him prostrate on the ground (John 18:6)! See Him again on the Cross, putting forth His power and "plucking a brand from the burning": it was the power of God, for nothing short of *that* can free one of Satan's captives! Yes, Christ *was*, ever was, the "very impress of His substance," "for in Him dwelleth all the fulness of the Godhead bodily" (Col. 2:9).

5. *His Administration.*

"Upholding all things by the word of His power" (v. 3). The Spirit of truth continues to describe the dignity and majesty of Him in whom God now "speaks" to us. Here is a declaration that is unequivocal in meaning and unlimited in its scope. Against the statement "by whom" God "made the worlds," it might be argued that, after all, the "Son" was only a minister, an agent whom God employed for that great work. In reply it would be sufficient to point out that there is no hint in Scripture of God ever having assigned to a mere creature, no matter how exalted his rank, a work which was in any wise comparable with the stupendous task of "making the worlds." But as if to anticipate such an objection, to show that the "Son" is high above the noblest and most honoured of God's ministers, it is here affirmed that "He upholdeth all things by the word of His power," that is, His *own* power; we may add that the Greek reads "His own" as in Matt. 16:26 —"his own soul"; and "His own house" (Heb. 3:6). The "upholding" of all things is a *Divine* work.

We have said that the term "Heir" connotes two things: dignity and dominion. In the opening clauses of v. 3 the dignity of the Mediator is set forth; here, it is His dominion which is brought before us. As it was said that He is appointed Heir of "all things," so are we now told that He upholds "all things"—all things that are visible or invisible, in heaven or earth, or under the earth; "all things" not only creatures, but all events.

The Greek word for "upholding" means to "carry or support," see Mark 2:3; it also signifies "to energise or impel," see 2 Pet. 1:21. It is the word used in the Sept. for "moved" in Gen. 1:2. That which is in view in this fifth glory of Christ is His Divine *providence*. "The term 'uphold' seems to refer both to preservation and government. 'By Him the worlds were made'—their materials were called into being, and arranged in comely order; and by Him, too, they are preserved from running into confusion, or reverting back into nothing. The whole universe hangs on His arm; His unsearchable wisdom and boundless power are manifested in governing and directing the complicated movements of animate and inanimate, rational, and irrational beings, to the attainment of His own great and holy purposes; and He does this by the word of His power, or by His powerful word. All this is done without effort or difficulty. He speaks, and it is done; He commands, and it stands fast" (Dr. J. Brown). What a proof that the "Son" is *God!*

He who appeared on earth in *servant* form, is the Sustainer of the universe. He is Lord over all. He has been given "power over all flesh" (John 17:2). The Roman legions who destroyed Jerusalem were *"His"* armies" (Matt. 22:7). The angels are *"His"* angels," see Matt. 13:41; 24:31. Every movement in heaven and earth is directed by Jesus Christ: "by Him all things consist" (Col. 1:17). He is not only at the head of the spiritual realm, but He "upholds *all things.*" All movements, developments, actions, are borne up and directed by the word of His power. Glimpses of this flashed forth even in the days of His flesh. The winds and the waves were subservient to His word. Sickness and disease fled before His command. Demons were subject to His authoritative bidding. Even the dead came forth in response to His mighty fiat. And all through the ages, to-day, the whole of creation is directed by the will and word of its Heir, Maker, and Upholder.

6. *His Expiation.*

"When He had by Himself purged our sins" (v. 3). Here is something still more wondrous. Striking is it to behold the point at which this statement is introduced. The cross was the great stumblingblock unto the Jews; but so far was the apostle from apologising for the death of the "Son," he here includes it as among His highest glories. And such indeed it was. The putting away of the sins of His people was an even greater and grander work than was the making of the worlds or the upholding of all things by His mighty power. His sacrifice for sins has brought greater glory to the Godhead and greater blessing to the redeemed than have His works of creation or providence.

"Why has this wonderful and glorious Being, in whom all things are summed up, and who is before all things the Father's delight and the Father's glory; why has this infinite light, this infinite power, this infinite majesty come down to our poor earth? For what purpose? To shine? To show forth the splendour of His majesty? To teach heavenly wisdom? To rule with just and holy right? No. He came to *purge our sins.* What height of glory! what depths of abasement! Infinite in His majesty, and infinite in His self-humiliation, and in the depths of His love. What a glorious Lord! And what an awful sacrifice of unspeakable love, to purge our sins by Himself"! (Saphir).

"By Himself purged our sins." This has reference to the atonement which He has made. The metaphor of "purging" is borrowed from the language of the Mosaic economy—cf. 9:22. The Greek word is sometimes put for the *means* of purging (John 2:6), sometimes for the *act* itself (Mark 1:44). Both are included here: the *merits* of Christ's sacrifice, and the *efficacy* thereof. The tense of the verb, the aorist, denotes a *finished* work, literally, "having purged." Another has suggested an additional and humbling thought which is pointed by this metaphor—the *filth* of our sins, which needed "purging" away. The contrastive and superlative value and efficacy of Christ's sacrifice is thus set before us. *His* blood is here distinguished from that of the legal and ceremonial purifications. None of them could purge away sins—10:4. All they did was to sanctify to "the purifying of the flesh" (9:13), *not* to the "purifying of the *soul"!*

"The manner and power of this purification form the subject of this whole Epistle. But in this short expression, 'by Himself He purged our sins,' all is summed up. By Himself; the Son of God, the eternal Word in humanity. Himself: the priest, who is sacrifice, yea, altar, and everything that is needed for full and real expiation and reconciliation. Here is fulfilled what was prefigured on the day of atonement, when an atonement was made for Israel, to cleanse them from all sins, that they may be clean from all their sins before the Lord (Lev. 16:30). Thus our great High Priest saith unto us, Ye are clean this day before God from all your sins. He is the fulfilment and the reality, because He is the Son of God. 'The blood of Jesus Christ His Son cleanseth us from all sin' (1 John 1:7). The church is purchased by the blood of Him who is God (Acts 20:28, with His own blood). Behold the perfection of the sacrifice in the infinite dignity of the incarnate Son. Sin is taken away. Oh, what a wonderful thing is this!" (Saphir).

7. *His Exaltation.*

"Sat down on the right hand of the Majesty on high" (v. 3). Unspeakably blessed is this. The One who descended into such unfathomable depths of shame.

who humbled Himself and became "obedient unto death even the death of the cross," has been highly exalted above all principality and power, and dominion, and every name which is named, not only in this world, but also in that which is to come. All-important is it, too, to mark carefully the connection between these two wondrous statements: *"when* He had by Himself purged our sins, *sat down* on the right hand on the Majesty on high." We cannot rightly think of the God-man as *where* He now is, without realising that the very circumstance of His being there, shows, in itself, that "our sins" are put away for ever. The present possession of glory by the Mediator is the conclusive evidence that my sins *are* put away. What blessed connection is there, then, between our peace of soul, and His glory!

"Sat down on the right hand of the Majesty on high." Three things are here denoted. First, high honour: "sitting," in Scripture, is often a posture of dignity, when superiors sit before inferiors: see Job 29:7, 8; Dan. 7:9, 10; Rev. 5:13. Second, it denotes settled continuance. In Gen. 49:24 Jacob said to Joseph that his "bow *sat* in strength," fittingly rendered "abode in strength." So in Lev. 8:35 "abode" is literally "sit." Though He will vacate that seat when He descends into the air (1 Thess. 4:16) to receive His blood-bought people unto Himself, yet it is clear from Rev. 22:1 that this position of highest honour and glory belongs to Christ for ever and ever. Third, it signifies rest, cessation from His sacrificial services and sufferings. It has often been pointed out that no provision was made for Israel's priests to sit down: there was no chair in the Tabernacle's furniture. And why? Because their work was never completed—see Heb. 10:1, 3. But Christ's work of expiation *is* completed; on the cross He declared, "It is *finished*" (John 19:30). In proof of this, He is now seated on High.

The term "the Majesty on high" refers to God Himself. "Majesty" signifies such greatness as makes one to be honoured of all and preferred above all. Hence it is a delegated title, proper to kings, cf. 2 Pet. 1:16. In our passage it denotes God's supreme sovereignty. It is brought in here to emphasise and magnify the exaltation of the Saviour—elevated to the highest possible dignity and position. The "right hand" speaks of power (Ex. 15:6), and honour (1 Kings 2:19). "On high" is, in the Greek, a compound word, used nowhere else in the N.T.; literally, it signifies, "the highest height," the most elevated exaltation that could be conceived of or is possible. Thus we are shown that the highest seat in the universe now belongs to Him who once had not where to lay His head.

It is to be observed that in vv. 2, 3 the Holy Spirit has, briefly, set forth the three great offices of the Mediator. First, His *prophetic*: He is the final Spokesman of God. Second, His *kingly*: His royal majesty—upholding all things, and that, by the word of His power, which affirms His absolute sovereignty. Third, His *priestly*: the two parts of which are expiation of His people's sins and intercession at God's right hand.

In conclusion, it should be pointed out how that everything in these opening verses of Hebrews is in striking contrast from what Israel enjoyed under the old economy. They had prophets; Christ is the final Spokesman of Deity. They were His people; He, God's "Son." Abraham was constituted "heir of the world" (Rom. 4:13); Christ is the "Heir" of the universe. Moses made the tabernacle; Christ, "the worlds." The law furnished "a shadow of good things to come"; Christ, is the Brightness of God's glory. In O.T. times Israel enjoyed theophanic manifestations of Christ; now, He is revealed as the Image of God's person. Moses bore the burden of Israel (Num. 11:11, 12); Christ, "upholds *all* things." The sacrifices of old took not sins away; Christ's sacrifice did. Israel's high priests never sat down; Christ has.

Arthur W. Pink.

GLEANINGS IN EXODUS.

51. *The Vestments of the Priests.*

Ex. 28:40-43.

"Thy testimonies are wonderful" (Psalm 119:129). The one who first penned these words had a much smaller Bible than we now have. Little more than the Pentateuch had been written in the Psalmist's time, yet his study of the first five books of Holy Writ moved David to wonderment as he pondered their contents. All that is said of the tabernacle and its priesthood, down to its minutest detail, is indeed "wonderful": wonderful in its depth, for there is much here which none has yet fathomed; wonderful in its freshness, for the Holy Spirit is ever revealing new beauties therein; wonderful in its preciousness, for the one in communion with its Author must say, "More to be desired are they than gold, yea, than much fine gold: sweeter also than honey or the honeycomb" (Psa. 19:10).

There is another and more comprehensive reason why God's testimonies are "wonderful," and that is, because they are concerned with Him whose name is called "Wonderful" (Isa. 9:6). Said the Lord Jesus, as He came into this world, "Lo I come—in the volume of the Book it is written *of Me*—to do Thy will O God" (Heb. 10:7). Hence, to the unbelieving Pharisees He said, "Search the Scriptures . . . . for they are they which testify of Me." The incarnate Word is the key to the written Word. It is the Person and Work of Christ which gives meaning and blessedness to what is found in the Old Testament types. "And beginning at Moses and all the prophets, He expounded unto them in all the Scriptures the things *concerning Himself*" (Luke 24:27).

But it is just because the Scriptures testify of Christ that He alone can expound them to us. Their Divine Inspirer must also be their Interpreter if we are to discern their spiritual import. As we read in Luke 24:45, "Then opened He their understanding, that they *might* understand the Scriptures." This is our deep need, too, to ask Him to anoint our eyes with eyesalve that we may see (Rev. 3:18). It is only as He *does* thus anoint our eyes, that we are enabled to discern in many an Old Testament character, ritual, symbol, wondrous and perfect foreshadowments of Himself. Oh that He may, increasingly, instruct both writer and reader.

"Thy testimonies are wonderful," wonderful also in their very *arrangement*. Again and again in the course of these articles upon Exodus we have called attention to this striking feature. In what is now to be before us, we have still another example. The *order* of the contents of Ex. 28 is most suggestive and significant. The whole chapter has to do with the priests and their vestments. First, in v. 1, before details are entered into, Aaron and his sons are seen together. This, as already pointed out, typified Christ and His people in their perfect union. Then, in vv. 2 to 39, we have described the robes and insignia of Aaron himself. Finally, in vv. 40-43, reference is made to the vestments of Aaron's sons. Who can fail to see here the handiwork of God? In all things Christ must have the pre-eminence: first the garments of the high priest are mentioned, then those of the priestly family!

"And for Aaron's sons thou shalt make coats, and thou shalt make for them girdles, and bonnets shalt thou make for them, for glory and for beauty" (v. 40). It is very striking and most blessed to mark that here we have repeated what was said in v. 2. There, we read how that Jehovah said to Moses, "And thou shalt make holy garments for Aaron thy brother, for glory and for beauty." So here in v. 40 the Lord gave instruction that Aaron's sons should also have robes made for them for "glory and for beauty." As pointed out in the previous articles, the various garments worn by Aaron, pointed to the inherent, essential and personal excellencies of our great High Priest. That which was prefigured in those worn by Aaron's sons was the graces with which Christ's people are endowed, by virtue of their association with Him.

All believers are priests. All Christians have been consecrated to and for Divine service; all have access to God, a place within the heavenly sanctuary. They have been made "kings and priests unto God" (Rev. 1:6). They are a "holy priesthood, to offer up spiritual sacrifices, which are acceptable to God by Christ Jesus" (1 Peter 2:5). They are also "a royal priesthood" (1 Peter 2:9), because united to Him who is King of kings. There is no Scriptural warrant at all for a separate priestly class among Christians; all have equal title to draw near to God (Heb. 10:22). Every Christian is a "priest," for he worships in a spiritual temple (Heb. 10:19), he stands at a spiritual altar (Heb. 13:10), he offers a spiritual sacrifice (Heb. 13:15). But to be priests to God necessitates holy garments. Those belonging to Aaron's "sons" were four in number, each of which we shall consider separately.

1. *Their Coats.*

"And for Aaron's sons thou shalt make coats" (v. 40). This receives amplification in Ex. 39:27, where we are told, "And they made coats of fine linen of woven work for Aaron and for his sons." As we have seen in earlier articles, the "fine linen" speaks of the spotless purity and holiness of Christ. "The robing of Aaron's sons is really the putting on of Christ; and this, in fact, brings them into association with Him; for the church possesses nothing apart from Christ. If believers, for example, are brought into the position of priests, and the enjoyment of priestly privileges, it is in virtue of their connection with Him. He is the Priest, and He it is that makes them priests (see Rev. 1:5, 6). Everything flows from Him. Thus, when Aaron is put into company with his sons, it is not so much that he becomes merged into the priestly family, but rather to teach that all the blessings and privileges of the priestly family are derived from Christ. But in order to do this they must first be invested with robes of glory and for beauty—robes which adorn them with the glory and beauty of Christ" (Ed. Dennett).

More specifically, these spotless linen coats of the priests set forth the *righteousness* with which the saints are clothed. Our own righteousnesses are as filthy rags (Isa. 64:6). But these have been removed, and in their place the "best robe" of Christ's righteousness has been placed upon us (Luke 15:22). This is strikingly and blessedly set forth in Zech. 3: "Now Joshua was clothed with filthy garments, and stood before the angel. And he answered and spake unto those that stood, before him, saying, Take away the filthy garments from him. And unto him He said, Behold, I have caused thine iniquity to pass from thee, and I will clothe thee with change of raiment" (vv. 3, 4). It is because of this that the believer sings, "I will greatly rejoice in the Lord, my soul shall be joyful in my God, for He hath clothed me with the garments of salvation, He hath covered me with the robe of righteousness, as a bridegroom decketh himself with ornaments, and as a bride adorneth herself with her jewels" (Isa. 61:10).

Of old it was said, "Let thy priests be clothed with righteousness; and let thy saints shout for joy. . . . I will also clothe her priests with salvation" (Psa. 132:9, 16). The answer to this is given in the New Testament, where we are told that God has made Christ to be "unto us wisdom, and righteousness, and sanctification, and redemption" (1 Cor. 1:30); and again, "For He hath made Him to be sin for us, who knew no sin; that we might be made the righteousness of God in Him" (2 Cor. 5:21).

"Aaron, as the high priest, appeared in the presence of the Lord in a representative character, personating, we may say, the whole nation of Israel, and upholding it in the glory and beauty required by God; bearing the names of the tribes on his shoulders and breastplate, graven on precious stones. His sons, the priests, stood in no such official dignity, but had access into the holy place and ministered at the altar on behalf of the people; not as representing them, but rather as leaders of their worship, and instructors of them in the holy things of God. They were types of one aspect of the church of God—the heavenly priesthood. In the Revelation, the four and twenty elders have a priestly standing; they form the heavenly council, being 'elders,' and therefore also judges. They are seated on 'thrones' because kings. They are clothed in white raiment as priests, and they have on their heads crowns of gold, that is, victors' crowns as chaplets (Rev. 4:4).

"The countless multitude are also seen clothed with white robes; a priestly company serving day and night in the temple (7:9). The Lamb's wife is seen arrayed in fine linen, clean and white (19:8). We have white raiment also alluded to in Rev. 3:4, 18 and 6:11. Thus the priestly dress of fine linen, and the garments of unsullied whiteness, represent the same thing—spotless righteousness. The standing of the believer in Christ before God not being his own righteousness, but the righteousness of God which is by faith" (H. W. Soltau).

Ere passing from this part of the priests' vestments, we need to be reminded that our desire and aim concerning our state should ever be an approximation unto our standing. The Christian's condition in this world ought to correspond to his position before God. Thus, while in Gal. 3:27 it is said, "For as many of you as have been baptized into Christ *have* put on Christ," in Rom. 13:14 we are exhorted *"put ye on the Lord Jesus Christ, and make not provision for the flesh, to fulfil the lusts thereof."* To do this we need to have the heart constantly engaged with Christ, remembering that He has left us "an example, that ye should follow His steps" (1 Peter 2:21). O to be more engaged with Him who is fairer than the children of men.

2. *Their Girdles.*

"And thou shalt make for them girdles" (v. 40). With this should be compared what we are told in 39:29, "And a girdle of fine twined linen, and blue, and purple, and scarlet, of needlework; as the Lord commanded Moses." Some have thought that because "girdle" is here found in the singular number that the reference must be to that alone which was worn by the high priest. But this is a mistake, *his* "girdle" is described in 28:8, and it will be seen by a careful comparison with 39:29 that it differed from those worn by the priests in this respect: his had "gold" in it, theirs did not.

It is only by comparing Scripture with Scripture that we can rightly interpret any figure or symbol. Two thoughts are suggested by the "girdle": it is an equipment for service, it is a means of strength.

First, we may note Luke 12:35, 36, "Let your loins be girded about, and your lights burning; and ye yourselves like unto men that wait for their Lord." This is an exhortation from Christ for His people to be ready for His return. Here two things are prefaced: they must be active in service and faithful in testimony. As another has said, "The hope of our Lord's return will not really abide in the heart unless we keep our loins girded, as engaged in the Master's work, and unless our light shines out before men. An inactive believer is sure to become a worldly-minded one. He will have companionship with men of the world, whose intoxicating pursuits of avarice, ambition, and pleasure deaden their hearts and consciences to all the truth of God. 'Occupy till I come' is another precept of the same kind as 'let your loins be girded.'"

Another New Testament exhortation where this figure of the "girdle" is used occurs in 1 Peter 1:13, "Wherefore gird up the loins of your mind, be sober, and hope to the end for the grace that is to be brought unto you at the revelation of Jesus Christ." Here believers are addressed as "strangers and pilgrims," passing through the wilderness on their way to the promised inheritance (vv. 1, 4). Two great motives are presented to them: the sufferings of Christ and the glory that shall follow (v. 11). Thus, in order to be constantly pressing onwards we must stay our minds upon Christ, ever contemplating Him in His two characters as the Victim and as the Victor. A man who fails to use the "girdle," allowing his garments to hang loose, is impeded in his movements and progress. Loose thoughts and wandering imaginations must be gathered in, and our hearts and understandings set upon the death, resurrection, and return of Christ, if we would pursue our journey with less distraction.

Eph. 6 informs us of the *nature* of our "girdle": "Wherefore take unto you the whole armour of God, that ye may be able to withstand in the evil day, and having done all, to stand. Stand, therefore, having your loins girt about *with truth*" (vv. 13, 14). Here the believer is contemplated in still another character. He is not only a priest to serve God, and a pilgrim journeying to another country, he is also a soldier, called on to "fight the good fight of faith" and to "wrestle" (v. 12). But no matter in what relationship he is viewed, the "girdle" is essential. It is striking to note that the "girdle" is mentioned *first* in Eph. 6:14-18, and that here the two separate thoughts suggested in connection therewith are combined. The whole strength of the warrior to stand and wrestle, depends upon the close fitting of his firm girdle. If his outer garments are loose and trailing (carelessness in his ways), or if his loins (the place of strength) be not supported and sustained by God's truth, Satan will soon overcome him, and instead of "standing"—experimentally maintaining his high calling in Christ—he will be cast down, to sink into the darkness of the world's delusions; ensnared either by its vanities and glittering honours, or its learned speculations of "vain philosophy" and "science falsely so called."

Our loins are to be "girt about with truth." The "girdle," then, speaks of the Word of God, particularly, all that centres in Christ and proceeds from Him. *This is the priest's equipment for service, the pilgrim's source of strength, the warrior's staying power.* Additional Scriptures which bring in the thought of *strength* in connection with the "girdle" are found in Rev. 1:13; 15:16. In the former, Christ is seen, "girt about the breasts with a golden girdle," the symbolic significance of this being, the binding of the ephod of blue—the robe of heavenly peace and love—about His heart, so that in the midst of searching words of reproof and warning, mercies might also proceed from "breasts of consolation." In the latter passage, golden girdles are seen about the breasts of the angels—to whom the vials of wrath are entrusted—indicating that their hearts needed strengthening for their terrible work of judgment. Thus, the "girdles" of the priests tell of that equipment and strength for service which is to be found in Christ.

3. *Their Bonnets.*

"And bonnets shalt thou make for them, for glory and for beauty" (v. 40). "And goodly bonnets of fine linen" (39:28). "The Hebrew word occurs only four times in the Old Testament, and is exclusively used for the head-dress of the priests. It is derived from a verb signifying 'elevation,' often used of a hill. They apparently differed from the mitre of the high priest, in the fact that they were *bound* round the heads of the priests, which is never said of the mitre. In Ex. 29:9 and Lev. 8:13 the margin of the A.V. correctly gives 'bind' for 'put.' They were probably rolls of fine linen, folded like a turban round the head. The word translated 'goodly' (Ex. 39:28) is worthy of notice. It is rendered 'tire' of the heads (Ezek. 24:17, 23); 'beauty' (Isa. 61:3); 'ornaments' (Isa. 61:10), and is derived from a verb signifying 'to beautify or glorify'" (Soltau).

There seems to be two thoughts suggested by these "bonnets," which, though at first glance seem widely dissimilar, are, nevertheless, closely related. From the etymology of the word, they speak of *elevation* or exaltation. On the other hand, from the general tenor of Scripture, the covering of the head betokens *subjection* (1 Cor. 11:4-10, etc). The orthodox Jew, to this day, always keeps his head covered in the synagogue; and even in private, when reading God's Word, he covers his head. How, then, are we to harmonize the two things, so different, suggested by this figure? Thus: the priesthood of believers speaks of the high position to which Divine grace has elevated them—they shall, in Heaven, lead the worship of angels. Yet, are they in subjection to Christ, for *He* will lead their praise (Psa. 22:22). Even now we are in subjection to the revealed will of God; and *this* is true dignity or elevation. We serve in the liberty of Christ, but as growing "up into Him in all things which is the Head, even Christ" (Eph. 4:15), avoiding the things mentioned in Col. 2:18, which tend unto the "not holding the Head" (Col. 2:19).

"These head-tires of white are said to be 'goodly' or 'ornamental.' There was nothing of display to attract the common gaze, but like the adorning recommended for Christian women (1 Peter 3:4, 5) they were types of the meek and quite spirit which in the sight of God is of great price. Like the holy women of old who trusted in God, and thus adorned themselves, in subjection to their own husbands" (Soltau). So these "bonnets" of the priests were for glory and beauty. True, complete subjection to God may be little admired by man, but they are lovely in the sight of Heaven.

4. *Their Breeches.*

"And thou shalt make them linen breeches to cover their nakedness; from the loins even unto the thighs shall they reach. And they shall be upon Aaron and upon his sons, when they come in unto the tabernacle of the congregation, or when they come near unto the altar to minister in the holy place; that they bear not iniquity, and die: it shall be a statute forever unto him and his seed after him" (vv. 42, 43). Before taking up the typical teaching of these verses attention should, perhaps, be called to one point in them which, by a comparison with Lev. 8:13, brings out the strict and high *moral* standard which God set before Israel. A careful reader of Lev. 8:13 will note an omission: Moses was ordered to "put" the coats, girdles, and bonnets upon Aaron's sons, but he was *not* told to "put" the "breeches" or trousers on them, even though they were his own nephews. Those, *they* would put on first, before they came to him to be formally invested with the other garments. They must not appear, even before one of their own sex, in the nude!

Unspeakably blessed is the *spiritual* purport of the present portion of our type, and most helpfully has it been presented by the one from whom we shall now quote. "The first result of the entrance of sin was to discover to man his nakedness (Gen. 3:7). The feeling of shame, a guilty feeling, crept over his soul; and his attention was immediately directed to some mode of quieting his confidence in this respect, that he might appear unabashed in the presence of his fellow. No thought of his fall as it regarded *God*, or of his inability to stand in His presence, occurred to him. And so it is to this day. The great object which men propose to themselves, is to quieten their own consciences, and to stand well with their neighbours. To this end they invent a religion. But as soon as we have to do with God, the conscience is convicted, and the guilt and shame which before were quieted, spring up within, and nothing can still the restless, uneasiness of the heart. We become aware that all things are naked and opened to the eyes of Him with whom we have to do. The soul in vain attempts concealment. The still, small voice of God sounds within, and drags the culprit out to stand before Him.

"It is here that a righteousness not our own becomes unspeakably precious to the soul. A covering that both blots out all sin, and forever clothes the sinner with spotless purity, which conceals from the searching eye of God all iniquity, and in so doing completely justifies the sinner before Him: Psalm 32:1, 2" (Soltau). Thus these "linen breeches" speak of that perfect provision which God has made for His people in Christ, that which has made an end of the flesh before Him: "Knowing this, that our old man is crucified with Him, that the body of sin might be destroyed, that henceforth we should not serve sin" (Rom. 6:6).

And what is the *practical* lesson to be drawn from the "breeches"? This: all that is of the flesh must be kept out of sight in our priestly activities. As another has said, "That which is of the flesh is bad anywhere, but it is most of all out of place in the holy service of God. What could be more dreadful than for such things as vanity, jealousy, emulation, or desire to make something of oneself, to come into what should be spiritual service? All that would be, indeed, 'the flesh of nakedness': it is not to be seen" (C. A. Coates). Striking are the words of v. 42: "To cover their nakedness from the loins even to the thighs." The whole strength of nature is to be concealed; that power of indwelling evil, which ever opposes God and seeks to mar our walk, must be covered.

Oh, that Divine grace may enable the writer and each Christian reader to put on, experimentally, the linen coat, girdle, bonnet, and breeches; to draw from Christ that strength which will enable us to "deny ungodliness and worldly lusts, and live soberly, righteously and goldly, in this present world" (Titus 2:12).

—*Arthur W. Pink.*

THE PROPHETIC PARABLES OF MATTHEW 13.

7. *The Treasure.*

"Again the kingdom of heaven is like unto treasure hid in a field; that which when a man hath found, he hideth, and for joy thereof goeth and selleth all that he hath, and buyeth that field" (Matt. 13: 44).

The common interpretation of this parable, both by Calvinists and Arminians, is as far removed from what I am fully assured is its true meaning as is the explanation they give of the earlier ones in Matt. 13. Dr. John Gill tells us that the treasure in this parable is "the Gospel," that the field in which the treasure is hidden is "the Scriptures," and that the man who sought and found the treasure is "an elect and awakened sinner." It is amazing how such an exegete of the Scriptures, and a man so deeply taught of God, could wander so far astray when he came to this parable. In the first place, the "field" is mentioned in two of the preceding parables—the field in which the good Seed was sown, and the field that was over-sown by tares; and in v. 38 of this very chapter Christ has told us the field is the *world.* Then why should it be supposed that the field means something entirely different in this fifth parable of the same chapter? Again, we have already had a "man" before us in the first two parables—a man who sowed good Seed in his field (v. 24). The Lord Jesus Himself has told us who that man is: "He that soweth the good seed is the Son of man" (v. 37). If, then, the man in the second parable represents the Son of man, why, in this fifth parable, without any word to the contrary, are we to understand him to point to someone entirely different?

Against the popular interpretation of the parable we advance these objections: First, if in this parable the Lord Jesus was setting forth the way of salvation, teaching that earnestness and diligence are needed on the part of an awakened sinner if he is to reach the treasure and make it his own (which treasure is hidden from the dilatory and careless), then how strange it is that it was not spoken in the hearing of *the multitude!* Instead, we are told that Christ had sent the multitude away, had entered the house and spoke this parable to His disciples only. Second, in this parable the treasure is hid in "the field," and, as we have seen, the field is the "world." In what possible sense is Christ or the Gospel hidden in the world? In the third place, when the man had found this treasure he hid it again: "the which when a man hath found, he hideth." If the treasure represents the Gospel and the field be the world, and if the man who is seeking the treasure be an awakened sinner, then our parable teaches that God requires the awakened sinner, after he has found peace and obtained salvation, to go out and hide it in the world! How absurd! Christ plainly told His disciples to let their light so shine that men might see their good works and glorify their Father which is in heaven. In the fourth place, in the parable we are told that after this man had found the treasure and then hid it again, that he went and "sold all that he had" and "bought it." *What* does an awakened sinner have to sell, and what it it that he *purchases?* Surely not the world! Such a loose interpretation may suit and satisfy lazy people who are too dilatory to carefully examine the parable for themselves, but it certainly will not do for those who, by the grace of God, have become prayerful and diligent students of the Word. We need hardly say that any interpretation that contains such absurdities must be promptly dismissed.

Now the first key to this parable is found in the fact that it was spoken by Christ after He had dismissed the multitudes and had taken His disciples into the house. This parable, unlike the four which precede it, was spoken to the disciples only. Those disciples must have been perplexed and dismayed at the gloomy picture which Christ had drawn of the form which His kingdom was going to assume in this world after His departure. He told them, or at least He had said in their hearing, that they would go forth and scatter the good Seed broadcast, but, with meagre results. The sowing which had been begun by Him was to be continued by them, and He had warned them that, though there should be a broadcast sowing throughout the field, only a fractional portion of the good Seed would take root and bear fruit. Second, He had said that the Devil would turn farmer and over-sow the field with tares. And they were forbidden to pluck them up: the tares and the wheat were to grow side by side until the harvest, and then the tares would be found in such quantities it would be necessary to bind them in "bundles!" Third, He had warned them that His professing cause on earth would develop so extensively and rapidly that it would be like a little mustard-seed growing up into a herb, ultimately becoming a tree, with widespreading branches; but that the Devil and his agents would find shelter in them; Fourth, He announced that into the meal, which was the emblem of His pure truth, a foreign and corrupting element would be introduced, stealthily and secretly, and the outcome should be that ultimately the whole of the meal would be leavened.

Yes, there was every reason for the poor disciples to be perplexed and dismayed. Then the Lord Jesus (it was just like Him), took them apart, and in the parables of the treasure and pearl He spoke words to reassure their hearts. He made known to them that, though the outward professing cause of Christianity upon earth would develop so tragically, yet there will be no failure on the part of God. He tells them there are two bodies, two elect peoples, who are inexpressibly precious in His sight, and that through them He will manifest the inexhaustible riches of His grace and glory—and that, in the two realms of His dominion—on the earth and in heaven. Two distinct elect companies, one the "treasure" hid in the field, symbolising the literal nation of Israel; the other, the one "pearl," symbolising the one body which has a heavenly calling, destiny, citizenship, and inheritance. The order of these next two parables is this: "To the Jew first, and also to the Greek." Therefore, the hidden treasure in the field, the symbol of Israel, is given before the pearl, which is the figure of the Church.

The second key which unlocks the parable before us, and the two which follow, is indicated in the way in which the Lord *divided* the whole series. There are seven parables in all, and He divided them into four and three: the four being spoken by the seaside in the hearing of the multitudes, the last three being spoken inside the house to the disciples only. Four is the number of the earth, the world. God has stamped "four" upon it. There are four points to the compass; four seasons to earth's year, and so on. Four then, is the number of the earth or the world; hence in the first four parables of Matthew 13 Christ has described the kingdom of heaven as it *appears in the world*, as it is manifested here on earth. Three is the number of the Holy Trinity, and therefore in the last three parables the kingdom is looked at from *God's* viewpoint. We have God's thoughts upon it, we are shown what God has in the kingdom—a hidden treasure, a pearl of great price.

With this somewhat lengthy introduction, let us take up the parable in detail. "Again, the kingdom of heaven is like unto treasure hid in a field." If Scripture be allowed to interpret Scripture there will be no difficulty whatever in discovering what this "hid treasure" actually and definitely signifies. Go back to Ex. 19:5. "Now therefore, if ye will obey My voice —it was the house of Jacob, the children of Israel that was addressed—and keep My covenant, then *ye* shall be a peculiar *treasure* unto me above all people: *for* all the *earth* is Mine"—corresponding with "the field" in which the "treasure" is found! Again, "For thou art a holy people unto the Lord thy God, and the Lord hath chosen thee to be a peculiar *treasure* unto Himself" (Deut. 14:2). The Hebrew in this verse is the same as in Exodus 19:5. Again, "When the Most High divided to the nations their inheritance (that means their earthly portion), when He separated the sons of Adam, He set the bounds of the people according to the number of the children of Israel. For the Lord's portion is His people; Jacob is the lot of His inheritance" (Deut. 32:8): that is, *here,* on earth, for the context is speaking solely about earthly things— the apportioning of the earth to the nations. Once more. "For the Lord hath chosen Jacob unto Himself, and Israel for His peculiar *treasure*" (Psa. 135:4). These passages have no reference at all to the saints of this present dispensation, or to the church which is the body of Christ, but speak of the earthly Israel according to the flesh. *They* are God's treasure on earth, His earthly elect people. Confirmation of *this* definition of the "treasure" in our parable, is found in the fact that never once in the twenty-one Epistles in the New Testament is the word "treasure" used of the Church! It is never applied to the saints of this present dispensation.

Now the first thing we are told in Matthew 13:44 about this treasure is that it was *hid* in a field, and the field was "the world" (see v. 38). This is precisely the condition in which God's *earthly* elect people were found at the beginning of His dealings with them. The parable starts with the treasure hid in the field, and the Old Testament begins with *Israel* hidden in the field! Who was the father of Israel according to the flesh? Abraham. Go back to the starting-point in Abraham's life. Where was he when God's hand was first laid upon him? Was he living in separation from the idolatrous people around him? No, he was hidden away among them—one of them! Take a later point in their early history. After Abraham came Isaac, and after Isaac Jacob, for Esau was not in the elect line. Look at Jacob, away from the promised land, an exile in Padan-aram, working for an unprincipled godless Gentile—for that is virtually what he was. Look at Jacob there among all the servants of Laban, *hidden*—nothing to indicate that he was one of the high favourites of God.

Proceed a little further. Abraham's and Jacob's descendants have become a numerous progeny, until they number some two million souls. Where are they to be found? Working in the brick-kilns of Egypt, a company of slaves. What was there to distinguish them? What was there to denote that they were God's peculiar treasure? Nothing, indeed: the treasure *was* "hidden." That is where the parable begins, and that is where their history as a nation began—buried, as it were, amid the rubbish of Egypt. That is why we read, "And it shall be, when thou art come in unto the land which the Lord thy God giveth thee for an inheritance, and possessest it, and dwellest therein; that thou shalt take of the first of all the fruit of the earth, which thou shalt bring of thy land that the Lord thy God giveth thee, and shall put it in a basket, and shalt go unto the place which the Lord thy God shall choose to place His name there . . . . And thou shalt speak and say before the Lord thy God, A Syrian *ready to perish* was my father" (Deut. 26:1, 5). Yes, the treasure was hidden in the field at the beginning. From Isa. 51:1, 2, we learn how, at a later point in the history of Israel, God reminded them of their lowly origin, of the humble start that they had as a people: "Hearken to Me, ye that follow after righteousness, ye that seek the Lord: look unto the rock whence ye are hewn, and to *the hole of the pit* whence ye are digged. Look unto Abraham your father, and unto Sarah that bear you." One other passage on this point: "For the Lord's portion is His people; Jacob is the lot of His inheritance. He found him in a desert land, and in the waste howling wilderness" (Deut. 32:10). There is their lowly origin mentioned again: the treasure was "hid," buried in the field.

Coming back to our text let us turn to the second detail in it: "Again, the kingdom of heaven is like unto treasure hid in a field; the which when a man *hath found*." That is the next point, the finding of the treasure. That is so very simple it needs no interpretation. The "man" here is Christ Himself—as the "man" is Christ in v. 24, see v. 37; and in the parable that follows, v. 45. The "finding" of the "treasure" by Christ refers to the days of His earthly ministry. We are told in John 1:11, "He came unto His own;" that does not mean His own spiritually, for we read that "His own received Him not." It was His own people according to the flesh. As He said to the Canaanitish woman in Matthew 15:24, "I am not sent but unto the lost sheep of the house of Israel." Christ, the Man, came to Israel, the Jews. His ministry was confined unto them. The "treasure" was "found"—it was no longer hidden when Christ came here. The Jewish nation was not as it was in the days of Moses in Egypt. The sons of Jacob were in their own land. They had their own temple; the priesthood was still intact. And it was to them, this Man, Christ, came.

"Again the kingdom of heaven is like unto treasure hid in a field; the which when a man hath found, he *hideth*." There is a distinct step in each clause. He "hideth" it. *That* is the most solemn word in the chapter, with the one exception of the furnace of fire. Remember what was before us in the 12th of Matthew, which furnishes the key to the 13th. In Matthew 12 Christ presented Himself to the Jews and the Jews rejected Him, and because of their rejection He rejected them. pronounced sentence of doom upon them —the evil spirit coming back and taking with him seven other spirits more wicked than himself, "Even so shall it be also unto this wicked generation." Then at the close of the chapter Christ intimated He would no longer acknowledge any bond or tie, any kinship except a spiritual one—"Whosoever shall do the will of My Father": it was Christ *severing* the link which, according to the flesh, bound Him to Israel. So here in the parable: first we have the treasure hid in the field: that was Israel's condition at the beginning of their national history in Old Testament times. Second, we have the Man coming to the treasure: that was the earthly ministry of Christ. Third, we have the treasure hid once more: that was Christ's *rejection* of Israel. The "hiding" of the treasure referred to the last dispersion and scattering of the Jews throughout the whole earth. And, so effectually *has* He "hidden" the treasure that ten out of the twelve tribes are still lost! Yes, they *are* hidden, so securely hidden that no man to this day knows where they are!

One passage of Scripture in proof of what we have said above on Christ's "hiding" Israel: "For they are a nation void of counsel, neither is there any understanding in them. O that *they* were wise, that *they* understood this, that they would consider their latter end" (Deut. 32:28, 29). How often is a sermon preached on this as though it applied to every man on earth, and his "latter end" is made to mean his death-bed! But the "latter end" here is of the nation of Israel, and it is the latter end of their history *on this earth*. Now read the next verse: "How shall one chase a thousand and two put ten thousand to flight, except their Rock had sold them, and the Lord had *shut them up?*" Yes, they "sold" *Him* for thirty pieces of silver. But "whatsoever a man soweth *that* shall he also reap," and *God* delivered them into the hands of the Gentiles! Their Rock "sold" them, and "the Lord shut them up." That is parallel with the treasure "hidden" again. They *are* "shut up." When a thing is shut up you cannot see it, it is hidden from sight.

Consider now the fourth point in our text: which is the most puzzling detail in the parable. Look at it closely: "Again, the kingdom of heaven is like unto treasure hid in a field; the which when a man hath found, he hideth, and for joy thereof goeth and selleth all that he hath, and buyeth that field." The purchase is made *after* the treasure had been "hidden," and, as we have seen, the hiding of the treasure had respect to Christ's judgment upon Israel and His dispersion of them throughout the earth. Turn now to John 11:51, 52: "And this he spake not of himself: but being high priest that year, he prophesied." What did he prophesy? "That Jesus should die for"—for whom?—"for that nation, and not for that nation only, but that He also should gather together in one the children of God that are scattered abroad." Now what could be plainer than that? We have *two* distinct objects there, two distinct companies — "that nation" and also the gathering together in one of "the children of God" that are scattered abroad. The gathering together in one of the children of God that are scattered abroad is what God is doing in this present dispensation, taking out of the Gentiles a people for His name, and gathering them together into one Body. That is what we have in the sixth parable—one pearl. But before that, we are told here in John 11:51, He also died for "that nation." This is what you have in the fifth parable, the earthly people, hid in the field, the world, the earth. This is God's *earthly* elect, "that nation." In the sixth parable, the pearl, you have His *heavenly* elect people, the one body.

But we are told in the parable that "for joy thereof He goeth and selleth all that He hath and *buyeth* that field." Turn to 2 Peter 2:1, "But there were false prophets also among the people, even as there shall be false teachers among you, who privily shall bring in damnable heresies, even denying the Lord that *bought* them." These false teachers are reprobates, yet this very verse says the Lord *bought* them. Many have created their own difficulty there in failing to distinguish between ransoming and redeeming. The Lord has "bought" the world, but He has *not* "redeemed" the world. There is a big difference between the two things. The first Adam was placed at the head of the world: God said "Have thou dominion over all"; and he lost it, he forfeited it; the Devil wrested it from his hands: and the last Adam, *as man*—"the second Man from heaven"—needed to purchase that which Adam had lost; therefore He bought *the field*. He has bought the whole world, but He has not redeemed it. Particular redemption is for God's elect only, but ransoming, purchasing, is much wider. He bought the field—"Denying the Lord that *bought* them"—you cannot get away from it. Now, then, He bought the field also because of the treasure that was hidden in it. The treasure in the field is Israel. The man in the parable is Christ. He went and sold all that He had. He who was rich became poor, and bought the field. Now that is mentioned *after* the re-hiding of the treasure in the field for this reason: the Jews do not enter into the value and the benefits of Christ's atonement until after this age is over. It is not until the

Millennium that Israel will enjoy the benefits of that purchase of His. He bought the field because of the treasure that was in it, and that is why the purchasing of the field is mentioned after the re-hiding of the treasure in it.

To summarise. First we have the treasure hid in the field: that takes us back to the beginning of Israel's history as a nation. Second, we have the Man finding that treasure; that is Christ coming to this earth and confining His message to the Jews in Palestine. Third, we have the Man hiding the treasure; that is Christ's judgment upon Israel because of their rejection of Him, referring to their dispersion abroad throughout the earth. Fourth, we have the Man purchasing the treasure and the whole field in which it was found, referring to the death of Christ. Now, have you noticed there is a fifth point omitted?—the logical completion of the parable would be the Man actually *possessing* the treasure that He purchased. He hid it, then He purchased it. Logically, the parable needs this to complete it—the Man owning and possessing the treasure. Why is that left out? Because *it lies outside the scope* of Matthew 13. This chapter, dealing with the "mysteries of the kingdom of heaven," has to do with the history *of Christendom.* It describes the cause of Christ on this earth during the period of His absence, and therefore there is nothing in this parable about the restoration of Israel and the Lord possessing His earthly treasure, because that comes *after* this dispensation is over, after the history of Christendom has been wound up, after the new age has been inaugerated, namely, the Millennium! How perfect is Scripture in its omissions! For passages treating of Christ's recovery and possession of the treasure see Amos 9:14, 15; Acts 15:17. In due time the Jews *shall be manifested* as God's peculiar "treasure" on "earth"—see Isaiah 62:1-4.
—*Arthur W. Pink.*

A SACRIFICE OF PRAISE.

"By Him therefore let us offer the sacrifice of praise to God continually, that is, the fruit of our lips giving thanks to His name" (Heb. 13:15).

The link of connection between this verse and the context is very blessed. In v. 13 the apostle had said, "Let us go forth therefore unto Him without the camp, bearing His reproach"—v. 14 coming in more or less parenthetically. Thus, though we are *outside* the camp, yet we have *Christ,* and "by Him" we may draw near to God, as priests, offering sacrifices which are well-pleasing to Him.

Our text points to one of the fundamental differences between what obtained under the old and the new covenants. Judaism consisted largely of carnal ordinances, an outward ritual, an appeal to the eye; everything was external. But Christianity is related to the inward and invisible, and is wholly spiritual. Christians have no active interest in the ceremonies of the Mosaic law. Have we then no temple, altar, sacrifice to bring before God? Yes! but all is spiritual. Christ is the substance of that which was shadowed-forth by the spectacular rites of Judaism. And to us the word is "By Him therefore let us offer the sacrifice of praise to God continually, that is, the fruit of our lips giving thanks to His name."

One can readily understand the Hebrews' need for such a word as this. They had been brought up under Judaism, the worship of which, not only consisted of an elaborate ritual, but was largely carried on by proxy. An Israelite had no direct approach unto God; he could draw near only through the Levitical priests. When he desired to express praise unto God he did so by bringing a burnt or meat-offering, for the Jews were required to bring not only sacrifices for sin, but also for thanksgiving. But now they were told that all of this belonged to the past.

A radical change had taken place. The temple had been forsaken of Jehovah, the priesthood was set aside; the offering of animals and birds was no longer acceptable to God. We can well imagine the state of their hearts and minds. What should they do? What was left for them? Could they no longer worship God? Were there no sacrifices they could bring? The Epistle to the Hebrews was written in the first instance, to meet these difficulties of Christian Jews. They *had* a priest (4:14); they *could* "draw near" (10:19-22); they *might* offer sacrifices to God (13:15, 16)—not animals and birds, but praise and thanksgiving, service, and ministry to others.

So with Christians to-day. But it needs to be emphasised that while there is nothing meritorious about such sacrifices, yet, the praise of our lips, if it proceeds from our hearts and is confirmed by our lives, and the bringing of our gifts, whether proceeding from plenty or poverty, *are* acceptable to God. Mark how the apostle speaks of a monetary contribution: "I am full, having received of Epaphroditus the things which were sent from you, an odour of a sweet smell, a sacrifice acceptable, *well-pleasing* to God." (Phil. 4:18). Mark how Peter speaks of the saints as "an holy priesthood, to offer up spiritual sacrifices, *acceptable* to God by Jesus Christ" (1 Peter 2:5). Let not a one-sided view of justification deprive us of this comforting and stimulating truth, that our worship, gifts, ministering to the poor of the flock are regarded by God with delight and are acceptable to Him. Let us now note.

1. *The Nature of this "Sacrifice."*

First, it is a *"sacrifice of praise."* Now, praise is more than thanksgiving. The latter is acknowledging God's gifts, the former is the heart occupied with the Giver Himself. There are times when even worldlings "thank" God for temporal mercies, but they never "praise" Him. Psa. 115:17 proves that: "The dead praise not the Lord." So in Psa. 22:22 Christ says, "In the midst of *the church* will I praise Thee."

Praise is the outflow of a heart which is occupied with God. Thus, only a redeemed people are capable of it. Israel never praised God while they were in Egypt. There they sighed and groaned (Ex. 2:23, 24). But when they were delivered from the house of bondage and their enemies had been destroyed, "*Then* sang Moses and the children of Israel this *song* unto the Lord" (Ex. 15:1). Mary was *praising* when she said, "My soul doth magnify the Lord, and my spirit hath rejoiced in God my Saviour" (Luke 1:46, 47). It is not a formal thing which we feel duty-bound to render, but a spontaneous outburst of the heart delighting itself in the Lord.

Second, it is *"the fruit of our lips,"* vocal, articulated "praise." It is not enough to feel adoring emotions in our hearts; they must be expressed with our mouths. That is why, in all ages, the saints of God have expressed their praise in holy songs or hymns. We none of us sing as much as we ought. Hear how worldlings pour forth their ungodly mirth; how often they shame us; *they* are not backward in singing. "Is any merry? let him sing psalms" (James 5:13). Let us say with David, "I will praise Thee, O Lord, with my whole heart; I will show forth all Thy marvellous works. I will be glad and rejoice in Thee; I will sing praise to Thy name, O Thou most High" (Psa. 9:1, 2).

Perhaps this expression "the *fruit* of our lips" strikes us as strange; but by comparing other Scriptures, the force of it may easily be perceived. By nature our lips are unclean: "Their throat is an open sepulchre; with their tongues they have used deceit; the poison of asps is under their lips: whose mouth is full of cursing and bitterness" (Rom. 3:13, 14). But by grace our lips have been cleansed, for the blood of Jesus Christ, God's son, "cleanseth us from *all* sin." A blessed illustration of this is found in Isa. 6. When that prophet saw the Lord on His throne and heard the seraphim crying, "Holy, holy, holy is the Lord of hosts," he was moved to say, "Woe is me! for I am undone; because I am a man of unclean lips, and I dwell in the midst of a people of unclean lips." But we are told, "Then flew one of the seraphim unto me, having a live coal in his hand, which he had taken with the tongs from off the altar: and he laid it upon my mouth, and said, Lo, this hath touched thy lips; and thine iniquity is taken away, and thy sin purged." What, then, should be the effects of this? Why, praise! Now "fruit" is a *living* thing, the product of the Holy Spirit. It is He who draws out our hearts in worship to God; therefore, is our praise designated "the fruit of our lips?"

Third, it is an *offering.* "Let us *offer* the sacrifice of praise." When a worshipping Israelite approached the Tabernacle or Temple, he did not come empty-handed; he brought an offering with him. So when Christians come together, they should have a higher aim in view than having their empty vessels filled and their hungry souls fed; with definite purpose of heart they should bring to God "a sacrifice of praise." Alas, that this is so often omitted!

But there are other thoughts suggested and other truths pointed by this word "offer." An Israelite was required to be most particular and punctillious about the "offering" which he brought. If it were a lamb, he was not allowed to bring the first one from the flock which his eye fell upon; it must be "without blemish and without spot." So our worship should be reverent, decent, whole-hearted.

Again, notice that our text does not say, "By Him therefore let us *bring* the sacrifice of praise to God," but let us "offer." An Israelite could not "offer" it, he only "brought" it; the *priest* offered. But Christians may not only bring, but "offer." Why? Because they have been made "kings and priests unto God" (Rev. 1: 6). Worship is a *priestly* act; the offering of praise to God is the exercise of our priestly functions and privileges. To refer once more to 1 Peter 2:5: we are there told that we are *"an holy priesthood, to* offer up spiritual sacrifices, acceptable to God by Jesus Christ." Let us now consider.

2. The Presenter of our "Sacrifice."

"By Him therefore let us offer the sacrifice of praise to God." The first two words of our text look back to vv. 12, 13, the reference being to the person of our blessed Lord. We pointed out at the beginning that only the *redeemed* can really offer praise to God; here is additional proof. Not only cannot the unconverted *serve* God acceptably, but, while they reject Christ, they cannot *worship* Him. As the Lord declared, "No man cometh unto the Father but by Me" (John 14:6). This was plainly taught under the O.T. types. The Israelite could not go in and worship Jehovah. Into the outer court alone could he enter; there he gave his offering to the priest, who was the one that then presented it before God.

A very solemn example and warning of approach unto God only by means of His appointed priest is to be found in 2 Chron. 26:16-21. There we are told of Uzziah that, "When he was strong, his heart was lifted up to his destruction: for he transgressed against the Lord his God, and went into the temple of the Lord to burn incense upon the altar of incense. And Azariah the priest went in after him, and with him four-score priests of the Lord, valiant men: And they withstood Uzziah the king, and said unto him: it appertaineth not unto thee, Uzziah, to burn incense unto the Lord, but the priests the sons of Aaron, that are consecrated to burn incense: Go out of the sanctuary; for thou has transgressed; neither shall it be for thine honour from the Lord God. Then Uzziah was wroth, and had a censer in his hand to burn incense: and while he was wroth to the priests the leprosy even rose up in his forehead before the priests in the house of the Lord, from beside the incense altar. And Azariah, the chief priest, and all the priests, looked upon him, and, behold, he was leprous in his forehead, and they thrust him out from thence; yea, himself hasted also to go out, because the Lord had smitten him. And Uzziah the king was a leper unto the day of his death, and dwelt in a several house, being a leper; for he was cut off from the house of the Lord." Yes, even royalty is required to submit to the appointments of the Lord God!

At the very threshold of worship, of offering anything to God, we begin with Christ. Without the Mediator it is impossible to approach Him. The great High Priest meets us at the door of the heavenly Sanctuary, as it were, and we place our sacrifices in His hands, that He may, in the sweet fragrance of *His* merits and perfections, present them to God. And how meet this is. All that God gives us is for Christ's sake; every spiritual blessing we enjoy was purchased for us at the Cross. How suitable is it, then, that in His name we offer our thanks and praise to God—"to offer up spiritual sacrifices, *by Jesus Christ"* (1 Peter 2:5).

"By Him therefore let us offer the sacrifice of praise to God." "By Him" signifies, then, in dependency upon Him, recognising that it is through Him alone we have access unto God. This is further strengthened and emphasised by the added "therefore" in our text. It looks back first to v. 12: because *He* has offered a sacrifice once for all, which has been accepted by God, we, too, may now offer a sacrifice of praise by Him. This "therefore" is also connected with v. 13: because we have gone forth "unto Him," then let us **by** Him offer a sacrifice of praise unto God. There is also a link between this "therefore" and v. 14: because we "seek" a City to come, let us *therefore* "offer a sacrifice of praise to God." Let us ponder now:

3. The Frequency of this "Sacrifice."

"By Him therefore let us offer the sacrifice of praise to God *continually."* This points another contrast from what obtained under Judaism, considered formally and corporately. The praise-sacrifices of the Law were only presented at particular times and particular places: see Lev. 23 where the "Feasts of the Lord" are described. But the Christian may, through Christ, offer a sacrifice of praise to God any time and anywhere.

This word "continually" is one which each of us needs to attentively treasure up in his heart. It is not enough to praise God only on the Sabbath; no such occasional rejoicing and worshipping as that should suffice. Does it mean *"every* morning and evening"? Assuredly, yet more: all through the day, "continually"—without ceasing. Does not the apostle say, "Rejoice in the Lord alway" (Phil. 4:4)! Let us say with the sweet singer of Israel, "I will bless the Lord at all times: His praise shall continually be in my mouth" (Psa. 34:1).

How this meets that oft-heard lament of Christians, "There seems so little that I can do for the Lord. I have no gift for preaching, I do not even feel qualified or called upon to be a Sunday School teacher. Then, too, my health is failing me, and I feel the weight of increasing years." As one wrote us recently, "I feel like a worn-out tool—of no more use; there are so many things I would love to do." Here, then, is a word for all such: "Let us offer the sacrifice of praise to God continually." When the apostles, in the Phillipian dungeon, could no longer preach, they could and did "praise"!

Many of David's most jubilant songs were written in times of persecution and distress. Those Christians who are most deficient in praise are not the suffering and afflicted ones, but those whose earthly path is smooth and easy, who fall into a languid and dull routine, whose hearts become forgetful of the Lord and His marvellous love. Then let the reader praise God continually: for His unspeakable gift, for His predestinating love, for His regenerating grace, for His unchanging faithfulness, for the blissful prospect which He has set before us in His Word, for His precious promises, for His tender forbearance with us, for the throne of grace to which we have access; for all that He is in Himself.

To help us, let it be pointed out, that praise is grounded upon an implicit confidence in God. There will not be the praise of our lips while our hearts are full of doubts: "My lips shall utter praise, when Thou hast taught me Thy statutes" (Psa. 119:171). Again, praise is the outcome of daily communion with God. There is little wonder that the praise of many Christians is so spasmodic when we consider how little fellowship they enjoy with the Lord. Live in communion with Him and you cannot help but praise Him: "Then were the disciples glad, when they saw the Lord" (John 20:20).

Once more: praise is the outflow of a real and spiritual joy in God and His salvation. There is a big difference between happiness and joy: the former is dependent upon our circumstances and surroundings, the latter is not so. Paul said, "As sorrowful, yet always rejoicing." The difference may be illustrated from the sea in a storm: its depths remain calm, even when its surface is agitated. Do not be satisfied with simply being a believer; covet joyousness. We lose our power when we lose our joy, for it is written, "The joy of the Lord is your strength" (Neh. 8:10).

Let us remember that praise is God's due. Shall our gracious and loving God be unpraised? Has He not given us abundant cause for us to "delight ourselves in Him"? Is it not written, "Give unto the Lord the glory due unto His name" (1 Chron. 16:29)! Again, praise is what God loves. Note the verse which comes right after our text: "For with such sacrifices is God *well pleased*." God delights in hearing the voice of melody. It is significant in this connection to note that when Israel's tribes were crossing the wilderness *Judah* (whose name means "praise") went first! Finally, it should be said that the cultivation of the spirit of praise will preserve us from many evils and enable us to bear more cheerfully the trials of life. The heart which is praising God is delivered from anxious care and self-centred gloom. Praise is Heaven anticipated.

"I would begin the music here
And so my soul should rise,
O for more heavenly notes,
To bear my passions to the skies."

—*Arthur W. Pink.*

WORLDLY CHURCH METHODS.

Few things more clearly illustrate the secularisation of the churches than their present methods of making appointments and carrying on their work. While Christ is, in theory, the recognised Head of the Church, He is too often deposed in and by church government. While great church gatherings are held and opened with prayer in His name, the arrangements are too often taken almost entirely out of His hands. When His guidance has been asked about ministerial and official lay appointments, wire-pulling, canvassing, and the courted influence of those in office and power, too often make it impossible for Him to answer such prayers. While there is a business side to the work of the Church, it is a Divine institution, and can only be successful in its mission when acting under the Divine guidance and power.

When someone said, "I have one brother who runs a business, and another who runs a church, and they both pay," he put into honest speech the mistaken spirit and methods of multitudes of churches in these days.

When our own circuit officers are needing and looking out for a new minister, how often do they enquire first about his spirituality of life and preaching, his knowledge of the Word of God, his appreciation of the preciousness of His Church to the

Saviour, and his passion for the saving of men? Eloquence is often more prized than spirituality, gifts than grace, scholarship than spiritual equipment, and the power to *draw*, more than the *power to save*. "There was a man sent from God, whose name was John." He stood on the threshold of a new dispensation, shook the hearts of Israel, and prepared the way for the coming King. And unless ministers are "sent from God" in these days they had better not be sent at all. When the Lord's judgment is sought and trusted, and church officers call the church together for prayer about the next minister, there will be fewer misfits and failures, and we shall cease to hear the familiar words about such men: "He is a very nice man, indeed, but he is not the man for here."

On the other hand, it is to be feared the kindred material considerations are often paramount in the minds of many ministers when seeking a fresh sphere of service. There is a strong suspicion abroad, that too often for family, residential, social and sometimes financial reasons the thing is really settled before the guidance of God has been asked for at all. And it is only too well known that people in positions of influence and power are constantly pestered to use them to help the suppliants into the sphere of work for which they are seeking. This is the world's way, of course, and its imitation in the churches is acting most disastrously upon "those that are without."

If the church be a *Christian church*, it is the purchase of the blood of Christ, and is precious in His sight. He knows and loves it as no one else can. He knows, too, just the kind of pastor it needs, and if asked and trusted by the church, He will send them the right man. If a minister is called of God to the work, He knows in what field he can labour most successfully. If the man's life-plan be taken from His Master, He will always, if asked, send him to the right church. This is simple, scriptural truth, and a matter of simple faith in God; and yet, both ministers and church officers stare at us as if we were mad, when we ask them if they thus left such appointments in the hands of God.

These same principles apply to the offices held by the laity in the churches, and the same mistakes are made in connection with their appointments. In order to hold the most menial office in the early church, a man had to be "of good report, full of the Spirit and of wisdom." That is, God's qualifications for such offices is *character*, while the churches often make it *cash*, or *social status*. Personally, I know of no grander men of God than the majority of our lay officials, and yet too often imperious, short-tempered, unspiritual men, and sometimes men who cross the lines of truthfulness, honesty, purity, and sobriety, hold office in churches where men of sterling Christian character and long service are passed by in their favour.

Such appointments are not the result of waiting upon God for guidance, and in view of spiritual influences and results, the effects of them are disastrous to the life and work of the church. Such unspiritual men know in their hearts their unfitness for such offices, and while they thank the minister who nominates them, they suspect him of material motives and a sacrifice of principle. That seriously limits the power of ministers to do them good from the pulpit.

And what shall we say of the worse than worldly, because often grossly, irreverent methods, now used to attract people to our places of worship? While "*preach the Word*" is the great command of God to all whom He sends as messengers, that Word is the last thing many of them consider likely to attract the people. Consequently, subjects and titles of addresses are often placarded that are utterly out of harmony with common reverence, and that make thoughtful outsiders turn away with scorn.

Lest the Word of God should be "dry," and " the crowd" would not come to hear it, it has to be set in a circle of attractions that appeal to "the flesh," and tickle the taste of the natural man. The "musical service" is perhaps the mildest form of this disease, and is designed to *draw* people of musical tastes and culture. "Madame So-and-so, the famous soprano," or "Mr. So-and-so, the celebrated tenor," will sing solos during the service, is a common form of announcement in these days, and the majority of church-goers seem to think that it is New Testament Christianity.

Sometimes a specially gifted choir is made the big attraction, and the Word and worship of God are made secondary in what is called "God's house." Clever and brilliant renderings are given as entertainments, while the audience, who should be worshipping God, sit and listen, and then pay for it in the collection. Anthems are sung which extol the Lord of hosts, the glory of His purposes, and the joy of His salvation, and often sung by people who in heart reject that Lord, and trample upon the very things of which they sing. Yet, in these days, this is called "worship." Of whom?

The worldliness of the churches is seen, too, in their growing obsequiousness to, and seeking for, the smile and patronage of the world's great ones. We know that "hated" was the world's attitude to our Lord when He was upon earth, and that He warned His people to expect the same treatment at the world's hands. We know that the same unbelieving world is refusing and rejecting Him still. We know that in aims, ambitions, ideals, pleasures, honours, and spirit, that the world is in bitter antagonism to the Spirit, purposes, and church of God. And yet its friendship, honours, and emoluments are sought and prized by the churches in the most deplorable ways.

The oneness of the church and the world in these things is now so far complete, that to take chairs on great church occasions, to lay foundation-stones, to open new churches, or to preside at the opening of bazaars the ambition in many churches is to secure royalties, or wealthy titled somebodys. We should have no quarrel with such methods if the Christian character of these big folks was commensurate with their wealth and social position, and if that was the main reason why the churches invited them. And it is probable, too, that there was never more titled and wealthy people in this land, who sincerely loved the Lord Jesus Christ, than there are now. For such Christians in such positions we thank God. But people of title, rank, and wealth, who make no profession of Christianity whatever, are, for the sake of these things, and the prestige they are supposed to give to the occasion, constantly invited to take a leading part in these ecclesiastical functions.

Of course, the world is true to its own, and such functions are reported in the Press without a word against these manifest incongruities. Can we wonder that the masses who think at all, but do not read the Word of God itself, are disgusted at what *they suppose to be Christianity?* Can we wonder that they look upon the whole church system as a humbug and a sham? Strangers at the fount of divine truth, and strangers to the real blessedness of a personal and loving fellowship with Christ, and seeing little else except the world masquerading and mumming under ecclesiastical names, the masses of the people are misled, and treat real Christianity as well as the worldly with indifferent and scorn.

We have no word to say, of course, either against titles or titled people as such. The taller the man the longer his shadow, and the higher our social status the wider our circle of influence. But what are such positions and titles to the exalted Son of God? In His sight the only "nobility" is *spirituality*, and the only "aristocracy" is *separateness from the world*. And what are the world's titles to the "sons of God?" What its smile compared to His? And what its honours, in view of abiding friendship and fellowship with Him? "One" is the church's "Master," even Christ, and His own are "all one in Him." If some of the world's great ones are His loved ones, welcome them to His church and in His service. But even then the honour is *theirs* of being a member of Christ's body "which is the church," and the highest dignity among men is that of being "co-workers together with God" in the interests of that church.

This is *the creed* of the churches. When it becomes *their practice*, they will see better days. When offices and honours are given rather to Christian character than to earthly possessions, and when they put loyalty to Christ before social status, and look at men in the light of Christ, they will win more of respect of decent outsiders, and less of their contempt, than they are doing now. And when the religious Press has less space and smaller type announcing the civic, municipal, and national honours bestowed upon the members of their respective communions, and rejoices more in the tokens of the smile of God upon their labours, more spiritually minded people will read them, and they will do much more than at present to stimulate and guide the churches to godly life and toil.

Extracts from Pastor Thomas Waugh, 1909.

"For what fellowship hath righteousness with unrighteousness? and what communion hath light with darkness? And what concord hath Christ with Belial? or what part hath he that believeth with an infidel? And what agreement hath the temple of God with idols?" How explicit and emphatic are the terms used here! No excuse whatever is there for failing to understand the terms of this exhortation, and the reason with which it is supported. "Fellowship, communion, concord, part, agreement" are so plain they require no interpreter. *All* unions, alliances, partnerships, entanglements with unbelievers are expressly forbidden to the Christian. It is impossible to find within the whole range of Holy Scripture plainer language on any subject than we have here. "Righteousness, unrighteousness, light, darkness; Christ, Belial"—what have they in common? What bond is there between them?

The contrasts presented are very pointed and searching. "Righteousness" is right doing; "unrighteousness" is wrong doing. The unerring and only standard of right doing is "the Word of Righteousness" (Heb. 5:13). By this alone is the Christian's life and walk to be regulated. But the worldling disregards and defies it. Then what "fellowship" can there be between one who is in subjection to God's Word with one who is not? "Light" and "darkness." God is light (1 John 1:5), and His saints are "the children of light" (Luke 16:8). But the children of the Wicked one are "darkness" (Eph. 5:8). What communion, then, can there be between members of families so dissimilar? "Christ" and "Belial"—what concord can there be between one to whom Christ is everything, and one who despises and rejects Him?

"For ye are the temple of the living God: as God hath said, I will dwell in them, and walk in them, and I will be their God, and they shall be My people." How blessed is this! First, we have the exhortation given, "Be ye not unequally yoked together"; second, the reason adduced, "for what fellowship hath righteousness with unrighteousness?"; third, the inducement proffered. This is a Divine promise, and it is striking to note it is a sevenfold one:—1) "I will dwell in them," 2) "and walk in them," 3) "And I will be their God," 4) "And they shall be My people," 5) "And I will receive you," 6) "And will be a Father unto you," 7) "And ye shall be My sons and daughters."

"I will dwell in them," is fellowship; "and walk in them," is companionship; "and I will be their God," is relationship. First, *in* them, then *with* them, now *for* them; and "if God be for us, who can be against us?" (Rom. 8:31). "And they shall be My people," is ownership, acknowledged as His. "And I will receive you," means being brought to the place of experimental and conscious nearness to God. "And will be a Father unto you" means "I will *manifest* Myself to you in this character, and impart to your hearts all the joys of such. "And ye shall be My sons and daughters" means, that such godly separation from the world will afford demonstration that we *are* His "sons and daughters."—Compare Matt. 5:44.

"Saith the Lord Almighty." This is the only time the Divine title "Almighty" is found in all the twenty-one Epistles of the New Testament! It seems to be brought in here for the purpose of emphasising the *sufficiency* of our Resource. As another has said, "Let any Christian act on the command of separation given in 2 Cor. 6:14-17, and he will find his path so beset with difficulties and so tending to arouse the hostility of all, that if his eyes are not kept fixed on the *Almighty* God who has thus called him out, he will surely have a breakdown." But let it be noted that these promises are *conditional*, conditional on obeying the preceding exhortations. Yet if the heart lays hold of this blessed inducement, then obedience to the command will be easy and pleasant.

—*Arthur W. Pink.*

N.B.—We are having this article set up, separately, in booklet form for distribution among Christians. Is not its message much needed to-day?

word by this epistle, note that man, and have *no* company with him!" How radical is the admonition of 1 Cor. 5:11, "Now I have written unto you not to keep company, if any man is called a brother be a fornicator, or covetous, or an idolator, or a railer, or a drunkard, or an extortionor: with such an one no not to eat."

"Be ye *not* unequally yoked together." We are fully persuaded that it is disregard of *this* commandment, for command it is, which is largely responsible for the low state which now obtains so generally among Christians, both individually and corporately. No wonder the spiritual pulse of many churches beats so feebly. No wonder their prayer-meetings are so thinly attended; Christians who are unequally yoked have no heart for prayer! Disobedience at this point is a certain preventative to real and whole-hearted devotion to Christ. No one can be an unshackled follower of the Lord Jesus who is, in any way, "yoked" to His enemies. He may be a truly saved person, but the testimony of his life, the witness of his walk, will not honour and glorify Christ.

"Be ye *not* unequally yoked together." This applies, first, to our *religious* or ecclesiastical connections. How many Christians are members of so-called "churches," where much is going on which they *know* is at direct variance with the Word of God —either the teaching from the pulpit, the worldly attractions used to draw the ungodly, and the worldly methods employed to finance it, or the constant receiving into its membership of those who give no evidence of having been born again. Believers in Christ who remain in such "churches" (?) are dishonouring their Lord. Should they answer: "Practically all the churches are the same, and were we to resign what could we do? We must go somewhere on Sundays." Such language would show they are putting their *own* interests before the glory of Christ. Better stay at home and read God's Word, than fellowship that which His Word condemns.

"Be ye *not* unequally yoked together." This applies to *membership in Secret Orders*. A "yoke" is that which *unites*. Those who belong to a "lodge" *are* united in solemn oath and covenant with their "brother" members. Many of their fellow-members give no evidence of being born again. They may believe in a "Supreme Being," but what love have they for God's Word? what is their relation to God's Son? "Can two walk together except they be agreed?" (Amos 3:3.) Can those who owe their all to Christ, both for time and eternity, have fellowship with those who "despise and reject" Him? Let any Christian reader who *is* thus unequally yoked get from under it without delay.

"Be ye *not* unequally yoked together." This applies to *marriage*. There are but two families in this world: the children of God, and the children of the Devil (1 John 3:10). If, then, a daughter of God marries a son of the Evil one, she becomes a daughter-in-law to Satan! If a son of God marries a daughter of Satan, he becomes a son-in-law to the Devil! By such an infamous step an affinity is formed between one belonging to the Most High and one belonging to His arch-enemy. "Strong language!" Yes, but not too strong. And O the bitter reaping from such a sowing. In every case it is the poor Christian who suffers. Read the inspired histories of Samson, Solomon, and Ahab, and see what followed *their* unholy alliances in wedlock. As well might an athlete, who attached to himself a heavy weight, expect to win a race, as a Christian to progress spiritually by marrying a worldling. O what watchfulness in prayer are needed in the regulation of our affections!

"Be ye *not* unequally yoked together." This applies to *business* partnerships. Disobedience at this point has wrecked many a Christian's testimony and pierced him through with many sorrows. Whatever may be gained of this world by seeking its avenues to wealth and social prestige, will but poorly compensate for the loss of fellowship with the Father and with His Son Jesus Christ. Read Prov. 1:10-14. The path which the disciple of Christ is called to tread is a narrow one, and if he leaves it for a wider road, it will mean severe chastenings, heart-breaking losses, and perhaps the forfeiting of the Saviour's "Well done" at the end of the journey.

We are to *hate* even the "garment"—figure of our habits and ways—spotted by the flesh (Jude 23), and are to keep ourselves "unspotted from the world" (James 1:27). What a searching and sweeping word is that in 2 Cor. 7:1, "Let us cleanse ourselves from *all* filthiness of the flesh and spirit, perfecting holiness in the fear of God." If any occupation or association is found to hinder our communion with God or our enjoyment of spiritual things, then it must be abandoned. Beware of "leprosy" in the *garment* (Lev. 13:47). Anything in my habits or ways which mars happy fellowship with the brethren or robs me of power in service, is to be unsparingly judged and made an end of—"burned," Lev. 13:52. Whatever I cannot do for God's glory must be avoided.

(Completed page 71).

STUDIES IN THE SCRIPTURES

"Search the Scriptures" John 5: 39

Copyright in all English-speaking Countries.

Editor: Arthur W. Pink, 15 Hurlstone Avenue, Summer Hill, N.S.W., Australia.
Hon. Agent in U.S.A.: Mr. C. S. Pressel, 559 Dupont Avenue, York, Penna.

FREE TO ALL WHO WILL READ IT

THE DUTY OF PRAYER.

"Men ought always to pray, and not to faint" (Luke 18:1).

In these words the Lord Jesus emphasised an aspect of prayer which is very rarely contemplated, and little understood. The Saviour here shows us that prayer belongs to the realm of *oughtness*. Prayer is something more than a blessed privilege, it is a pressing duty. It is not optional, but obligatory. It is not only a channel of grace, but a binding responsibility. And this, not simply when we feel in the mood, but "always"!

The O.T. shows plainly that one cause of God's punishing the wicked is their prayerlessness: "Pour out Thy wrath upon the heathen that have not known Thee, and upon the kingdoms that *have not called* upon Thy name" (Psa. 79:6). Daniel ascribes the evil which came upon the Jews as partly due to their neglect of prayer: "All this evil is come upon us, yet *made we not* our prayer before the Lord our God, that we might turn from our iniquities, and understand Thy truth. *Therefore* hath the Lord watched upon the evil, and brought it upon us: for the Lord our God is righteous in all His works" (Dan. 9:13, 14). Who then can doubt that God's chastenings to-day, both of individual Christians and of churches, is due to the same cause! He changes not, neither do the principles of His righteous government.

God requires that we should acknowledge our dependence upon Him and *seek* blessings at His hands. In His first discourse to the disciples, commonly called the Sermon on the Mount, we find Christ saying not a little on the subject of prayer: He ever maintained God's rights. *"Ask,"* He said, "and it shall be given unto you." "Pray ye therefore the Lord of the harvest" (Matt. 9:38). "Watch and pray lest ye enter into temptation" (Matt. 26:41) was His word to Peter. The same teaching is found in the Epistles: prayer is there enjoined both by example and by precept "Continue instant in prayer," is found in Rom. 12 side by side with "Be not conformed to this world," and "Owe no man anything." So "pray without ceasing" (I Thess. 5:17) is as much a command as "Quench not the Spirit"

Let us now endeavour to show the force of the "ought" in our text.

First, men ought always to pray, *because prayer is God's due*. This, because of the *relations* which He sustains to His children. God is our *Creator*. As such His claims upon us are absolute and universal. Prayer is the acknowledgement of our creaturehood. It is right that we should own our Maker's supremacy, bow before His high sovereignty take our proper place before Him. It is meet that we should acknowledge our dependency, own that we are insufficient of ourselves, and confess our deep need. Prayerlessness is the spirit of independency; it is refusal to admit our helplessness; it is the denial of our creaturehood.

God is our *King* (1 Tim. 1:17). It is proper for the subjects of an earthly king to pay him homage, to spread their petitions before him, and when they have offended, to sue for his clemancy. How much more should the subjects of the King of kings

(Concluded on page 96.)

IMPORTANT NOTICES

Back numbers of each year of the magazine are yet obtainable at 5/- (1.25) per year. Bound at 7/6 (1.75) post paid. They will soon be out of print. Those in U.S.A. wanting them, please purchase from Mr. Pressel (see front cover page).

Advise promptly of change of address. This Magazine is published as a work of faith and labour of love. The Editor gladly gives his services. It is freely sent to all who will read it. No charge is made for it.

Christians who feel definitely led to do so, may have fellowship with us in this Ministry. Send only *Inter-National M.O.*

CONTENTS.

	Page.
Hebrews	74
Gleanings in Exodus	81
Parables of Matt. 13	86
Means of Regeneration	91

THE EPISTLE TO THE HEBREWS.

4. *Christ Superior to Angels* (1:4-14).

One of the first prerequisites for a spiritual workman who is approved of God, is that he must prayerfully and constantly aim at a "rightly dividing" of the Word of Truth (2 Tim. 2:15). Pre-eminently is this the case when he takes up those passages treating of the person of the Lord Jesus Christ. Unless we "rightly divide" or definitely distinguish between what is said of Him in His essential Being" and what is predicated of Him in His official character, we are certain to err, and err grievously. By His "essential Being" is meant what He always was and must ever remain as God the Son. By His "official character" reference is made to what may be postulated of Him as Mediator, that is, as God incarnate, the Godman. It is the *same* blessed person in each case, but looked at in different relationships.

It is failure to thus rightly divide what is said in the Word of Truth concerning the Lord Jesus which has caused unregenerate men to entertain most dishonouring and degrading views of Him, and has led some regenerate men to err in their interpretation of many passages. As illustrations of the former we may cite some of the more devout unitarians, who, appealing to such statements as "My Father is greater than I" (John 14:28), "when all things shall be subdued unto Him, then shall the Son also Himself *be subject* unto Him that put all things under Him" (1 Cor. 15:28), etc., have argued that though the Son be superior to all creatures, yet is He inferior to the Father. But the passages cited do not relate to the "essential Being" of Christ, but speak of Him in His Mediatorial character. As an example of the latter we may mention how that such an able exegete as Dr. John Brown interprets the second half of Heb. 1:4 as referring to the essential Being of the Saviour.

Thus it will be seen that that to which we have drawn attention above is something more than an arbitary theological distinction; it vitally affects the forming of right views of Christ's person and a sound interpretation of many passages of Holy Writ. Now in His Word God has not drawn the artificial lines which man is fond of making. That is to say, the essential and the official glories of Christ are often found intermingling, rather than being separately classified. A case in point occurs in the first three verses of Heb. 1. First we are told that, at the close of the Mosaic dispensation, God spoke to the Hebrews by (in) His Son. Obviously this was upon earth, *after* the Word had become flesh. Thus the reference is to Christ in His *Mediatorial* character. Second, "whom He hath appointed Heir of all things" manifestly views Him in the same character, for in His essential Being no such "appointment" was needed—as God the Son "all things" *are* His. But when we come to the third clause, "by whom also He made the worlds" there is clearly a change of viewpoint. The worlds were made long before the Son became incarnate, therefore *this* postulate must be understood of Him in His eternal and essential Being.

The inquiring mind will naturally ask. *Why* this change of viewpoint? Why introduce this higher glory of the Son in the midst of a list of His Mediatorial honours?—for it is clear that the Holy Spirit *returns* to these in the clauses which follow in v. 3. The answer is not far to seek: it is to *exalt* the Mediator in our esteem: it is to show us that the One who appeared on earth in Servant form was possessed of a dignity and majesty which should bow our hearts in worship before Him. He who "by Himself purged our sins" is the same that "made the worlds." The crucified was the Creator! But this is not the only wonder set forth in this passage. In order to be crucified it was needful for the Creator to become man. The Son of God (though never ceasing to be such) became the Son of man, and this Man has been exalted to the right hand of the Majesty on high. So beautifully has the late Mr. Saphir written on this point we transcribe from him at length:—

"Is it more wonderful to see the Son of God in Bethlehem as a little babe, or to see the Son of man at the right hand of the Father? Is it more marvellous to see the Counsellor, the Wonderful, the Mighty God, the Prince of Peace, the Everlasting Father, a child born unto us, and a Son given unto us—or to see the Son of man, and in Him the dust of earth, seated at the right hand of God? The high priest entered once a year into the holy of holies, but who would have ventured to abide there, or take up his position next to the cherubim, where the glory of the Most High was revealed? But Jesus, the Son of man, ascended, and by His own power, and in His own right, as well as by the appointment of the Father, He is enthroned, crowned with glory and majesty. On the wings of omnipotent love He came down from heaven, but to return to heaven, omnipotence and love were not sufficient. It was comparatively easy (if I may use this expression of the most stupendous miracle) for the Son of God to humble Himself, and to come down to this earth; but to return to heaven, it was necessary for Him to be baptised with the baptism of suffering, and to die the death upon the accursed tree. Not as He came down did He ascend again; for it was necessary that He who in infinite grace had taken our position should bow and remove our burden and overcome our enemies. Therefore was His soul straightened to be baptised with His baptism; and therefore, from the first moment that He appeared in Jerusalem, He knew that the temple of His sacred body was to be broken, and He looked forward to the decease which He should accomplish on that mount. Not as He came did He ascend again; for He came as the Son of God; but He returned not merely as the Son of God, but as the Son of God *incarnate*, the Son of David, our brother and our Lord. Not as He came did He ascend again; for He came alone, the Good Shepherd, moved with boundless compassion, when He thought of the lost and perishing sheep in the wilderness; but He returned with the saved sheep upon His shoulders, rejoicing, and bringing it to a heavenly and eternal home. He went back again, not merely triumphing, but He who had gone forth weeping, bearing precious seed, who Himself had been sown, by His sacrifice unto death, returned, bringing His sheaves with Him. . . . It was when He had by Himself purged our sins that He sat down at the right hand of God; by the power of His blood He entered into the holy of holies; as the Lamb slain God exalted Him, and gave Him a name which is above every name."

Thus that which is prominent, yea, dominant, in this opening chapter in Hebrews is the *Mediatorial* glories of the Son. True, His essential glory is referred to in v. 2: "By whom also He made the worlds," but, as already stated, this is introduced for the purpose of exalting the Mediator in our esteem, to prevent us forming an unworthy and erroneous conception of His person. The One who "by Himself purged our sins" is the same person as made the worlds, it is He who is "the Brightness of God's glory, and the express Image of His substance." What ground, what cause have we for exclaiming, "Worthy is the Lamb that was slain to receive power and riches, and wisdom and strength, and honour and glory, and blessing" (Rev. 5:12)! To this the Godman is entitled. Because of this, God exalted Him to His own right hand. Having shown His infinite elevation above the prophets we have next revealed His immeasurable superiority over the angels.

"Being made so much better than the angels, as He hath by inheritance obtained a more excellent name than they" (v. 4). Before attempting to expound the details of this verse, it may be well for us first to enquire, *Why* does the Holy Spirit here introduce the "angels?" What was His particular purpose in showing Christ's superiority over them? To these questions a threefold answer, at least, may be returned:—

First, because the chief design of the Holy Spirit in this Epistle is to exalt the Lord Jesus, as the God-man, far above every name and dignity. In the next section (chapter 3) He shows the superiority of Christ over Moses. But to have commenced with Moses would not have gone back far enough, for Moses, the mediator, received the law by "the disposition of angels" (Acts 7:53). Inasmuch as angels are described in Holy Writ as "excelling in strength," and thus as far raised in the scale of being above man, it was necessary, in order to establish Christ's superiority over *all* created beings, to show that He was much better than they. To prove that God the Son was superior to angels were superfluous, but to show that the Son of man has been exalted high above them was essential if the Hebrews were to ascribe to Him the glory which is His due.

Second, the object before the Holy Spirit in this Epistle in presenting the supreme dignity and dominion of the Mediator was to demonstrate the immeasurable superiority of Christianity over Judaism. The method He has followed here is very striking and convincing. The old order or economy was given by "the disposition of *angels*" (Acts 7:53). Exactly what this means perhaps we cannot be quite sure, though there are several scriptures which throw light thereon, for in Deut. 33:2 we read: "The Lord came from Sinai, and rose up from Seir unto them; He shined forth from Mount Paran, and He came with ten thousands of saints"—"holy ones," i.e., "angels." Again, Psa. 68:17 tells us, "The chariots of God are twenty thousand, even thousands of angels: the Lord is among them, as in Sinai." Finally, Gal. 3:19 says, "Wherefore then serveth the law? It was added because of transgressions, till the Seed would come to whom the promise was made; and it was ordained *by angels* in the hand of a mediator." Thus, the glory of Jehovah at Sinai (the beginning of the Mosaic economy) was an angelic one, and the employment of angels in the giving of the law stamped a dignity and importance upon it. But the legal dispensation has been set aside by a new and higher glory revealed in "the Son," and Heb. 1 shows us the angels subservient to Him, and not only so, closes with the statement that they are now the *servants* of the present "heirs of salvation!"

Third, it was necessary to show the superiority of Christ (the Centre and Life of Christianity) over the angels, because the Jews regarded them as the most exalted of all God's creatures. And rightly so. It was as "the Angel of the covenant" (Mal. 3:1), the "Angel of the Lord" (Ex. 3.2), that Jehovah had appeared most frequently unto them. From earliest times angelic ministration had been a chief instrument of Divine power and medium of communication. It was "the Angel of the Lord" who delivered Hagar (Gen. 16:7), and who appeared to Abraham. Angels delivered Lot (Gen. 19:1). It was the Lord's "angel" who protected Israel on the passover-night (Num. 20:16). Thus the Jews esteemed angels more highly than man. To be told that the Messiah Himself, God the Son incarnate, had become *man* made Him, in their eyes, *inferior* to the angels. Therefore, was it necessary to show them from their own Scriptures that the Mediator, God manifest *in flesh*, possessed a dignity and glory as far excelling that of the angels as the heavens are higher than the earth.

"Being made so much better than the angels." This verse may be termed the text, and the remainder of the chapter, the sermon—the exposition and application of it. The first key to its meaning and scope lies in its first two words (which are but one in the Greek), "being made." Grammatically it seems almost a blemish to open a new paragraph with a participle; in truth, it demonstrates the perfections of the Spirit's handiwork. It illustrates a noticable difference which ever distinguishes the living works of God from the lifeless productions of man—contrast the several parts of a chair or table with the various members of the human body: in the one the several sections of it are so put together that its pieces are quite distinct, and the joints between them clearly perceptible; in the other, the ending of one member is lost in the beginning of the next. Our analogy may be commonplace, but it serves to illustrate one of the great differences between the writings of men and the Scriptures of God. The latter is a *living* organism, a body of truth, vitilised by the breath of God!

Though v. 4 begins a distinct section of the Epistle it is closely and inseparably united to the introductory verses which precede, and more especially to the final clauses of v. 3. Unless this be kept in mind we are certain to err in our interpretation of it. At the close of v. 3 Christ is presented as the One who has purged the sins of His people, in other words, as the Son of man, God incarnate, and it was *as such* He has been exalted to the right hand of the Majesty of high. There is now a Man in the glory. And it is this *Man*, the "second Man (1 Cor. 15:47) who has been made better than the angels," and who has obtained "a more excellent name than they." It is *this* which the opening participle makes clear, being designed to carry our thoughts back to what has been said at the close of v. 3.

"Being made so much better than the angels." To appreciate the force of this we must, briefly consider the *excellency* of the "angels." Angels are the highest of all God's creatures: heaven is their native home (Matt. 24:36). They "excell in strength" (Psa. 103:20). They are God's "ministers" (Psa. 104:4). Like a king's gentlemen-in-waiting, they are said to "minister *unto* the Ancient of days" (Dan. 7:10). They are "holy" (Matt. 25:21). Their countenances are like "lightening," and their raiment is as white as snow (Matt. 28:3). They surround God's throne (Rev. 5:11). They carry on every development of nature. "God does not move and rule the world merely by laws and principles, by unconscious and inanimate powers, but by living beings full of light and love. His angels are like flames of fire; they have charge over the winds, and the earth, and the trees, and the sea (the book of Revelation shows this—A.W.P.). Through the angels He carries on the government of the world" (Saphir).

But glorious as the angels are, elevated as is their station, great as is their work, they are, nevertheless, in subjection to the Lord Jesus *as Man;* for in His human nature God has enthroned Him high above all. "The apostle in the former verses proves Christ to be more excellent than the excellentest of men; even such as God extraordinarily inspired with his holy Spirit, and to whom he immediately revealed his will that they might make it known to others. Such were the priests, prophets, and heads of the people. But these, as all other men, notwithstanding their excellencies, were on earth mortal. Therefore he ascendeth higher, and culleth out the celestial and immortal spirits, which are called angels. Angels are of all mere creatures the most excellent. If Christ then be more excellent than the most excellent, He must needs be the most excellent of all. This excellency of Christ is so set out, as thereby the glory and royalty of His kingly office is magnified. For this is the first of Christ's offices which the apostle doth in particular exemplify: in which exemplification He giveth many proofs of Christ's divine nature, and showeth Him to be man as He is God also; and in the next chapter, so to be God as He is man also: 'like to his brethren' (2:17)" (Dr. Gouge).

"Being made so much better than the angels." Through Isaiah God had promised that the "Man of sorrows" who was to be "cut off out of the land of the living" for the transgression of His people, should be richly rewarded for His travail: "Therefore, will I divide Him a portion with the great and He shall divide the spoil with the strong" (53:12). In Psa. 68:18 He is represented as ascending "on high," and that, as a mighty conqueror leading captives in His train and receiving gifts for men. In Phil. 2 we learn that He who took upon Him the form of a servant and was made in the likeness of men, who became obedient unto death, even the death of the cross, "God also hath highly exalted Him and given Him a name which is above every name, that at (in) the name of Jesus (given to Him at His incarnation) *every* knee should bow, of things *in heaven* and in earth, and under the earth" (vv. 9-11). He has been "made so much better than the angels" first of all, by the *position* accorded Him—He is seated on the right hand of the Majesty on High: angels are *"round about* the Throne (Rev. 5:11), the Lamb is *on* the Throne!

"As He hath by inheritance obtained a more excellent name than they" (v. 4). "We who live in the West think a name of slight importance: but God always taught His people to attach great importance to names. The first petition in the Lord's prayer is, 'Hallowed be Thy name;' and all the blessings and privileges which God bestowed upon Israel are summed up in this, that God revealed unto them His name. The name is the *outward expression* and the pledge and seal of all that a person really and substantially is; and when it says that the Son of God has received a higher name than angels, it means that, not only in dignity, but in kind, He is high above them" (A. Saphir). "The descriptive designation given to Christ Jesus, when contrasted to that given to angels, marks Him as belonging to a higher order of beings. Their name is created spirits; His name is the only-begotten Son of God" (Dr. J. Brown).

"As He hath by inheritance obtained a more excellent name than they" (v. 4). When commenting on the first part of this verse we endeavoured to show that the reference is to the Father rewarding the Mediator for His sacrificial work, and attention was directed to the parallel supplied in Phil. 2:9-11. That passage begins by saying: "Wherefore God also hath highly exalted Him," and this finds its counterpart here in "being made so much better than the angels." Then follows the statement "and hath given Him a name which is above every name," the parallel being found in "a more excellent name than *they,*" i.e., the highest of all created beings. Finally, His *right* to this exalted name is to be owned by every knee bowing before it; so also the last clause of Heb 1:4 affirms Christ's right to His more excellent name. Is it not more than a coincidence that the corresponding passage to *Heb.* 1:4 is found in one of the apostle *Paul's* Epistles!

"He hath by inheritance obtained a more excellent name than they." This affirms the right of Christ to His more excellent name. The English rendering here seems slightly misleading. The Greek for "He hath by inheritance obtained" is a single word. It is a technical term relating to legal title, secure tenure. The right of inheritance which Sarah would not that the son of the bondwoman should have, is expressed by this word: "shall not the heir" (Gal. 4:30—"Shall not by inheritance obtain," or, "shall not inherit." Christ's right to His supreme dignity is twofold: first, because of the union between His humanity and essential Deity; second, as a reward for His mediatorial sufferings and unparalleled obedience to His Father.

"For unto which of the angels said He at any time, Thou art My Son?" (v. 5). Having affirmed the superiority of Christ over angels, the Holy Spirit now supplies proof of this, drawing His evidence from the O.T. Scriptures. The first passage appealed to is found in the second Psalm, and the manner in which it is introduced should be noted. It is put in the form of a question. This was to stir up the minds of those who read the Epistle. It is worthy of remark that this interrogative form of instruction is found quite frequently in the Pauline Epistles—e.g., 1 Cor. 9:4-10, Gal. 3:1-5—and much more so than any other N.T. writer. This method of teaching was often employed by the Lord Jesus, as a glance at the Gospels will show. Observe, too, how the question asked in our text assumes that the Hebrews were *familiar* with the entire contents of Scripture. The interrogative way of presenting this quotation was tantamount to saying: Judge for yourselves whether what I say be true—where in the Sacred Writings is there any record of God's addressing an angel as His "Son"? They could not thus judge unless they were well versed in the Word.

"Unto which of the angels said He at any time, Thou art My Son"? The answer is, To none of them. Nowhere in the O.T. Scriptures is there a single instance of God's addressing an angel as "My Son." It is true that in Job 38:7 the angels are termed "sons of God," but this simply has reference to their *creation*. Adam is termed a "son of God" (Luke 3:38) in the same sense. So, regenerated saints are "sons of God" by virtue of new creation. But no *individual* angel was ever addressed by the Father as "My Son." The Lord Jesus *was*, both at His baptism and His transfiguration. Herein we perceive not only His pre-eminence, but His uniqueness.

"Unto which of the angels said He at any time, Thou art My Son, this day have I begotten Thee" (v. 5)? This latter expression has occasioned not a little difficulty to some of the commentators, and, in the past, has been made the battleground of fierce theological fights. The issue raised was "the eternal *Sonship* of Christ." Those affirming understood "this day" (or "to-day")—the Greek is the same as in Luke 23:43—to be *timeless*, and "this day have I begotten Thee" to refer to the eternal generation of the Son by the Father. Much of the fighting was merely a strife "about *words*," which was to no profit. Though Scripture clearly teaches the Godhead and absolute Deity of the Son (Heb. 1:8, etc.) and affirms His eternality (John 1:1, etc.), it nowhere speaks of His eternal "sonship," and where Scripture is silent it behoves us to be silent too. Certainly *this* verse does not teach the eternal sonship of Christ, for if we allow the apostle to define his own terms, we read in Heb. 4:7, "He *limiteth* a *certain* day, saying in David, *To-day*," etc. This, it appears to us, illustrates the Spirit's foresight in thus preventing "to-day" in 1:5 being understood as a timeless, limitless "day"—eternity.

Further proof that the Spirit is not here treating of the essential Deity or eternal sonship of Christ is seen by a glance at the passage from which these words are taken. Heb. 1:5 contains far more than the mere quotation of a detached sentence from the O.T. The reference is to the second Psalm, and if the reader will turn to and read through it, he should at once see the striking propriety in the apostle's reference to it here. This is the *first* O.T. passage quoted in Hebrews, and like the first of anything in Scripture claims special attention because of its prime importance. Coming as it does right after what has been said in v. 4, namely, that He who, positionally, had been made lower than the angels, is now exalted above them, an appeal to the 2nd Psalm was most appropriate. That Psalm has two divisions and treats of the humiliation and exaltation of the Messiah! In v. 3 counsel is taken against Him; in vv. 10-12 kings and judges are bidden to pay homage to Him.

Now it is in this 2nd Psalm that the Father is heard saying to the Messiah, "Thou art My Son, this day have I begotten Thee" (v. 7). The whole context shows that it is the Father addressing the Son in time, not eternity; on earth, not in heaven; in His mediatorial character, not His essential Being. Nor is there any difficulty in the "to-day have I begotten Thee," the Holy Spirit having explained its force in Acts 13:33. There the apostle declared to the Jews that God had fulfilled *the* promise made unto the fathers, namely, that He had "raised up Jesus," i.e. had sent the Messiah unto them. Acts 13:33 has no reference to Christ's resurrection, but relates to His incarnation and manifestation to Israel—cf. Deut. 18:18, "I will *raise them up* a Prophet"; also Acts 3:26. It was not until Acts 13:34, 35 that the apostle brought in His resurrection "raised Him up *from the dead*." Thus in Acts 13 Psalm 2 is cited to prove the Father had sent the Saviour to Israel and His promise so to do had been fulfilled in the Divine incarnation. We may add that the word "again" in Acts 13:33 is not found in the Greek and is omitted in the R.V.! If further proof be needed that the *"This day* have I begotten Thee" refers to the *incarnation* of Christ, Luke 2:11 supplies it. "unto you is born *this day* in the city of David a Saviour, which is Christ the Lord"—could so much be said of any but the only-begotten Son of God? Thus "this day" is here, by an angel's voice expressly referred to the day of the Saviour's birth.

"This day have I begotten Thee." This, then, is another verse which teaches the *virgin-birth* of Christ! His humanity was "begotten" by God the Father. Though the Son of man, He was not begotten by a man. Because His very humanity was begotten by the Father it was said unto His mother, "That holy thing which shall be born of thee shall be called the Son of God" (Luke 1:35). It only remains to be added that Psalm 2:7 looks forward **to the Millennium** for its ultimate application: it is when Christ shall return to **earth and** set up His throne of glory **(Matt. 25:31)** that the eternal decree concerning Him shall then be "declared" or **publicly proclaimed**, and all will be compelled to own His sceptre.

"And again, I will be to Him a Father, and He shall be to Me a Son" (v. 5). The opening "and" connects this second quotation with the first; what follows clearly and conclusively fixes the scope of the first part of this verse. Here is indubitable proof that the Holy Spirit is speaking of Christ not according to His essential glory, but in His mediatorial character, as incarnate. Had the first part of v. 5 referred to the *eternal* relationship of the Son to the Father as practically all of the older (Calvinistic) commentators insist, it would surely be meaningless to add the quotation which follows—"I *will be*" does not take us back into the timeless past! Nor was there any occasion for the first Person of the Trinity to assure the Second that He would be "a Father unto Him." Clearly, it is the Father accepting and owning as His Son the One whom the world had cast out.

"And again, I will be to Him a Father and He shall be to Me a Son." This second quotation is from 2 Sam. 7:12-17, which forms part of one of the great Messianic predictions of the O.T. Like all prophecy it had a minor and major scope and receives a partial and ultimate fulfilment. Its first reference was to Solomon, who, in many respects, was a remarkable type of the Lord Jesus. But its chief application was to Christ Himself. That Solomon did not exhaust its fulfilment is clear enough from the language of v. 13 itself, for, as Dr. Brown has pointed out. "It refers to a son to be *raised up* after David had gone to be with his fathers. whereas Solomon was not only born but crowned before David's death; and the person to be raised up, whosoever he is. was to be settled 'in God's house and kingdom,' and his throne was to be 'established forever more',—words certainly not applicable, in their full extent, to Solomon." Doubtless none would have argued for an exclusive reference to Solomon had it not been for the words which follow in 2 Sam. 7:14. But competent Hebrew scholars tell us that "if he commit iniquity" may fairly be rendered "whosoever shall commit iniquity" and find their parallel in Psalm 89:30-33.

"I will be to Him a Father, and He shall be to Me a Son." This was God's promise concerning the Messiah, David's Son, a thousand years before He appeared on earth. "I will be to Him a Father." I will *own* Him as My Son, I will *treat* Him accordingly. This He did. In death He would not suffer Him to see corruption. He raised Him from the dead. He exalted Him to His own right hand. "And

He shall be to Me a Son": He shall act as such. And He did. He ever spake of Him as "Father," He obeyed Him even unto death, He committed His spirit into His hands.

"And again, when He bringeth in the Firstbegotten into the world, He saith, 'And let all the angels of God worship Him'" (v. 6). This is a quotation from Psalm 97:7, which in the Sept. reads, "Worship Him, all ye His angels." What a proof was this that the Son *had* been "made *so* much better than the angels": so far were these celestial creatures from approaching the glory of the incarnate Son, they are commanded to worship Him! But before we enlarge upon this, let us mark attentively the special character in which Christ is here viewed. Many are His titles, and none of them is without its distinctive significance. It is as "Firstbegotten" or "Firstborn" that the angels are bidden to render Him homage. As many are far from clear as to the precise value and meaning of this name, let us look at it the more closely. The Greek word, "protokokos," is found nine times in the N.T., eight of them referring to the Lord Jesus. It is manifestly a title of great dignity.

This N.T. title of Christ, like many another, has its roots in the O.T. Its force may be clearly perceived in Gen. 49:3, where Jacob says of Reuben, "Thou art my firstborn, my might, and the beginning of my strength, the *excellency of dignity,* and the excellency of power." Thus, the primary thought in it is not primogeniture, but dignity, honour, dominion. Note in Ex. 4:22 God calls Israel His "firstborn" because to them belonged the high honour of being His favoured people. In the great Messianic prediction of Psa. 89, after promising to put down His foes and plague them that hate Him (v. 23), and after the perfect Servant says "Thou art My Father, My God, and the Rock of My salvation" (v. 26), the Father declares, "I *will make Him* My Firstborn, higher than the kings of the earth" (v. 27). Clearly, then, this title has no reference whatever to the eternal origin of His Being, i.e. His "eternal Sonship," still less does it intimate His creation in time, as Russellites and others blasphemously affirm; but relates to the high position of honour and glory which has been conferred upon the Son of man because of His obedience and suffering.

The first occurrence of this term in the N.T. is in Matt. 1:25, "she brought forth her firstborn Son," and the second is parallel—Luke 2:7. That Mary had other sons is clear from Matt. 13:55. The Lord Jesus was not only the first in time, but the Chief, not only among but over them. In Romans 8:29 we read, that God has predestinated His elect to be conformed to the image of His Son in order that He might be the Firstborn among many brethren, i.e. their Chief and most excellent Ruler. In Col. 1:15 He is designated the "Firstborn of every creature," which most certainly *does not* mean that He was Himself the first to be created, as many to-day wickedly teach, for never does Scripture speak of Him as "the Firstborn of God," but affirms that He is the Head and Lord of every creature. In Col. 1:18 He is spoken of as "the Firstborn from the dead," which does not signify that He was the first to rise again, but the One to whom the bodies of His saints shall be conformed—see Phil. 3:21. In Heb. 11:28 this term is applied to the flower and might of Egypt. In Heb. 12:23 the Church in glory is termed "the Church of the Firstborn." This title then is synonymous with the "appointed Heir of all things." It is, however, to be distinguished from "Onlybegotten" in John 1:18, 3:16. This latter is a term of *endearment,* as a reference to Heb. 11:17 shows—Isaac was not Abraham's *only* "begotten," for Ishmael was begotten by him too; but Isaac was his *darling*: so Christ is God's "Darling" —see Psalm 22:20; 35:17.

"Under the law the 'firstborn' had authority over his brethren (cf. Rom. 8:29, A.W.P.), and to them belonged a double portion, as well as the honour of acting as priests; the firstborn in Israel being holy; that is to say, consecrated to the Lord. Reuben forfeiting his right of primogeniture by his sin, his privileges were divided, so that the dominion belonging to it was transferred to Judah and the double portion to Joseph, who had two tribes and two portions in Canaan by Ephraim and Manasseh (1 Chron. 5:1, 2); while the priesthood and the right of sacrifice was transferred to Levi. The word 'firstborn' also signifies what surpasses anything as of the same kind, as 'the firstborn of the poor' (Isa. 14:30); that is to say, the most miserable of all; and 'firstborn of death' (Job 18:13), signifying a very terrible death, surpassing in grief and violence. The term 'firstborn' is also applied to those who were most beloved, as Ephraim is called 'the firstborn of the Lord' (Jer. 31:9), that is, His 'dear son. In all these respects the application of 'firstborn' belongs to the Lord Jesus, both as to the superiority of His nature, of His office, and of His glory" (Robert Haldane).

"And again when He bringeth in the Firstbegotten into the world," etc. Commentators are divided as to the meaning and placing of the word "again," many contending it should be rendered, "When He shall bring in again into the habitable earth the Firstborn." There is not a little to be said in favour of this view. First, the Greek warrants it. In the second part of v. 5 the translators have observed the order of the original—"and Again, I will be unto Him," etc. But here in v. 6 they have departed from it—"And again, when He bringeth in" instead of "when He shall bring in again." Secondly, we know of nothing in Scripture which intimates that the angels worshipped the infant Saviour. Luke 2:13, 14 refers to them adoring God in heaven, and not His incarnate Son on earth. But Rev. 5:11-14 shows us all heaven worshipping the Lamb on the eve of His return to the earth, when He comes with power and glory. Scriptures which mention the angels in connection with Christ's second advent are Matt. 13:41; 16:27; 24:31; 25:31; 2 Thess. 1:7.

That v. 6 has reference to the second advent of Christ receives further confirmation in the expression "when He *bringeth* in the Firstbegotten into the world." This language clearly looks back to Jehovah putting Israel into possession of the land of Canaan, their promised inheritance. "Thou shalt *bring them in*, and plant them in the mountain of Thine inheritance" (Ex. 15:17). "To drive out the nations from before thee, greater and mightier than thou art, to *bring thee in*, to give thee their land for an inheritance" (Deut. 4:38). In like manner, when Christ returns to the earth, the Father will say to Him, "Ask of Me, and I shall give Thee the heathen for Thine *inheritance*, and the uttermost parts of the earth for Thy *possession*" (Psa. 2:8). Finally, the Psalm from which Heb. 1:6 quotes is clearly a *millennial* one, describing Christ's reign here on earth.

In addition to what has just been said on "when He *bringeth* in the firstborn" into the world we would call attention to what we doubt not, is a latent contrast here. It is set over against His *expulsion* from the world, at His first advent. Men, as it were, drove Him ignominiously from the world. But He will re-enter it in majesty, in the manifested power of God. He will be "brought into it" in solemn pomp, and the same world which before witnessed His reproach, shall then behold His Divine dominion. Then shall He come, "in the glory of His Father" (Matt. 16:27), and then shall the angels render gladsome homage to that One whose honour is the Father's chief delight. Then shall the word go forth from the Father's lips, "Let all the angels of God worship Him."

Our minds naturally turn back to the first advent and what is recorded in Luke 2. But there the angels praised the Sender, not the Sent: God in the highest was the object of their worship, though the moving cause of it was the lowly Babe. But when Christ comes back to earth it is the Firstborn Himself who shall be worshipped by them. It was to this He referred when He said, "When He shall come in His own glory, and in His Father's *and* of the holy angels." The "glory of the angels," i.e. the glory they will bring to Him, namely, their worship of Him. Then shall be seen "the angels of God ascending and descending upon the Son of man" (John 1:51). May we who have been sought out and saved by Him "worship" Him *now* in the time of His rejection.

—*Arthur W. Pink.*

GLEANINGS IN EXODUS.

52. *The Continual Burnt-offering.*

Ex. 29:36-43.

Having considered something of the typical teaching connected with the vestments of the priests as described in Ex. 28, we may observe that the next thing which the Holy Spirit brings before us is the consecration of Aaron and his sons, i.e. the ritual belonging to their induction into that sacred office. This is described at length in Ex. 29, a chapter which is rich in spiritual teaching. As, however, almost all of it is found again in Lev. 8, we shall defer a detailed study thereof—if the Lord wills—until we come to that book.

The two accounts given of the consecration of the priests is like unto the twofold description which we have of the tabernacle and its furniture: first, we are told what Moses was commanded *to* make; second, we learn what he actually *did* make. So with the priesthood: in Exodus we learn that this was a blessing which God *proposed* to bestow upon His redeemed, whereas in Leviticus (the tabernacle having been set up) we see the *execution* of His purpose—the activities of the priests there being seen. Moreover, as in the actual making of the tabernacle we read, "According to *all* that the Lord commanded Moses, so the children of Israel made all the work" (Ex. 39:42); in like manner we are told that, in connection with the appointing of the priesthood, "So Aaron and his sons did *all things* which the Lord commanded by the hand of Moses" (Lev. 8:36).

In order to link up our articles on Ex. 28 with the present one, which deals with the closing verses of chapter 29, and those which follow on chapter 30, we will give a brief outline of the ceremonies which were to be observed at the consecration of the priests. It is striking to note that there were exactly seven things done for them. First, they were *taken* "from among the children of Israel" (28:1). How plainly this points to the Father choosing His elect out of Adam's race— the initial step in connection with their salvation—is too obvious to need any enlarging upon. Second, they were *brought* unto the door of the tabernacle (29:4): the antitype of this is found in 1 Peter 3:18: "For Christ also hath once suffered for sins, the Just for the unjust, that He might bring us to God." Third, they were *washed* (29:4): this foreshadowed the believer's regeneration and sanctification by the Spirit (see John 3:5, Titus 3:5, Eph. 5:26). Fourth, they were *clothed* with their official vestments (29:4-9): this symbolised the putting on of Christ. Fifth, they were *anointed* (29:21): this pointed to the gift of the Spirit to the believer (2 Cor. 1:21; 1 John 2:27). Sixth, their *hands were filled* (29:24)—compare with this 1 John 1:1-3. Seventh, they were *sanctified* (29:44): this contemplates our setting apart unto God, see Rom. 6:13, 22.

It is indeed striking to see that in the above, Aaron and his sons took no active part at all; from first to last they were passive in the hands of another. They did not minister, but were ministered unto. Much was done for them and to them; but they themselves did nothing. Standing in God's stead, Moses did all for them. It was by his word that they were chosen and brought. It was by his hands they were washed. clothed and anointed. It was Moses also who brought the bullock for the sin-offering, as "the ram of consecration." So too the application of the blood to the several parts of their bodies was the work of Moses (v. 20). So with the wave-offering: Moses arranged its several parts (v. 22): he it was who "filled their hands"—he gave, they received (v. 24). Finally, it was Moses who received back from their hands and gave again to God what they had first been given (v. 25).

There were however four exceptions, striking and blessed ones; four things which God required Aaron and his sons to do. First, they were to "put their hands upon the head of the bullock" of the sin-offering (29:10), thus identifying themselves with the victim that was to be slain. Typically, this is the saints confessing, "But He was wounded for our transgressions, He was bruised for our iniquities: the chastisement of our peace was upon Him; and with His stripes we are healed" (Isa. 53:5). Second, they were to "put their hands on the head of the ram" (v. 15) which was a burnt-offering unto the Lord. This speaks of the believer's assurance of his acceptance in the Beloved. Third, they also placed their hands upon the head of the ram of consecration (v. 19). This foreshadowed the saints as set apart to and for God, in and by Christ— "For by one offering He hath perfected forever them that are set apart" (Heb. 10:14). Fourth, they were to *eat* the flesh of the ram and the shewbread (vv. 32:33). This set forth Christ as the Food of His people: their substance and life. It is as we contemplate and appropriate Christ without, that He is "formed" within us: see Gal. 2:20; 4:19.

A more direct link between the lengthy account furnished in Ex. 29 of the ceremonies connected with the consecration of the priests and the closing verses which form our present portion, is what is said in vv. 35-37: "And thus shalt thou do unto Aaron and to his sons, according to all things which I have commanded thee: seven days shalt thou consecrate them. And thou shalt offer every day a bullock for a sin-offering for atonement: and thou shalt cleanse the altar, when thou shalt make an atonement for it, and thou shalt anoint it, to sanctify it. Seven days thou shalt make an atonement for the altar, and sanctify it; and it shall be an altar most holy; whatsoever toucheth the altar shall be holy."

The fact that these particular ceremonies and the cleansing of the altar were to be repeated and kept up for seven days denotes that Christ's people are completely consecrated in Him (Col. 2:10), and that their altar is a perfect one. Both the consecration of the priests and the sanctification of the altar must alike be according to all the requirements of a holy God. "Approach now must be at a cleansed, anointed, and hallowed altar. It is the first time in Scripture that we read of a cleansed and anointed altar. Previously, the altar was according to the measure of the one who approached, but now approach must be cleansed from every feature of human imperfection—cleansed in all the efficacy of the sin-offering" (C. A. Coates). In other words, all acceptable worship now must be "in spirit and in truth."

This is the force of that word of Christ's, "But the hour cometh, and now is, when the true worshippers shall worship the Father in spirit and in truth: for the Father seeketh such to worship Him. God is spirit: and they that worship Him must worship Him in spirit and in truth" (John 4:23, 24). The Saviour was referring to that great change which would be brought in consequent upon His death. Though such worship shuts out all that is of the flesh, it makes room for all that is of the Spirit and of Christ.

And of what does this cleansed, anointed and sanctified "altar" speak? Clearly of Christ Himself: His blessed person. As we are told in Heb. 13:10, "We have an altar, whereof they have no right to eat which serve the tabernacle." Christ Himself is altar, sacrifice, and priest. *He* is "the Altar that sanctifieth the gift" (Matt. 23:19). Hence believers are now told, "*By Him* therefore let us offer the sacrifice of praise to God continually, that is the fruit of our lips, giving thanks to His name" (Heb. 13:15).

From the parallel Scripture in Lev. 8 we learn that the Lord's word to Aaron and his sons, in this same connection, was, "Therefore shall ye abide at the door of the tabernacle of the congregation day and night seven days, and keep the charge of the Lord, that ye die not." Upon this Mr. Saltau wrote: "They were to be habituated to abide before the Lord; and they were to realise the value of the sin-offering, as thus enabling them so to abide there. The seven days of their week of consecration may, in type, prefigure the whole of our earthly life: our whole week of service. We are to accustom ourselves to be in the presence of our God. Our life is to be spent there; only we have the privilege of abiding, not at the door, but in the very holiest of all. May we rejoice to use this wondrous liberty of access, and not only 'draw near,' but 'abide under the shadow of the Almighty.' And what will be our help and power for this? The sin-offering of atonement, constantly realised by the help of the Holy Spirit."

"Now this is that which thou shalt offer upon the altar; two lambs of the first year day by day continually. The one lamb thou shalt offer in the morning; and the other lamb thou shalt offer at even" (vv. 38, 39). In v. 42 we learn that this offering was called "a *continual* burnt-offering." That which was placed upon the altar was in perfect accord with its now anointed and hallowed character. The "burnt" offering is the highest type of sacrifice in Scripture. The first reference to it in the Word helps us ascertain its distinctive significance. In Gen. 22:2 we read that the Lord said unto Abraham, "Take now thy son, thine only Isaac, whom thou lovest, and get thee into the land of Moriah; and offer him there for a burnt-offering upon one of the mountains which I will tell thee of." That which is to be particularly noted there is the willingness and readiness of Isaac's conforming to his father's will. Thus, the central thought in this offering is *devotedness*. The Hebrew word for burnt-offering literally means, that which "goes up." It might well be designated "the ascending offering." The whole of it, consumed upon the altar, ascended to heaven as a sweet savor.

Lev. 1 furnishes full details concerning the burnt-offering. There we read, in v. 3, that the offerer should "offer it of his own voluntary will." This offering was really the basis of all the other sacrifices, as may be seen not only from the fact that it is given precedence in Lev. 1 to 5, but also because the altar itself took its name from this—"the altar of the burnt offering" (Ex. 40:10). It foreshadowed, therefore, the perfect devotedness of the Son to the Father, which was the basis or spring of the whole of His earthly life, ministry, and sacrificial death. He "glorified not Himself." When He spoke or acted it was ever the Father's honour He sought. He could say, "I came not to do Mine own will, but the will of Him that sent Me." He could say, "I have set the Lord always before Me" (Psalm 16:8). Eph. 5:2 speaks in the language of this particular type: "Christ also hath loved us, and hath given Himself for us, an offering and a sacrifice to God for a sweet-smelling savor."

"Now this is that which thou shalt offer upon the altar; two lambs of the first year, day by day continually. The one lamb thou shalt offer in the morning, and the other lamb thou shalt offer at even." Speaking after the manner of men, it was as though God would keep before Him a constant reminder of the devotedness of His blessed Son. Therefore a "lamb." rather than a bullock or ram (which prefigured Christ more in His strength and sufficiency) was appointed—suitably expressing His gentleness, and yieldedness to the will of God. And, too, that which was ever to be kept before His people also was, that which would set forth the *Godward* aspect of Christ's work. Though the Lord Jesus came here to atone for the sins of His people, it was only because it was the Father's will for Him so to do: cf. Heb. 10:7 with 10:10.

"Inasmuch as the offering before us was perpetual, God laid a foundation thereby on which Israel could stand and be accepted in all its fragrance and savour. It thus becomes no mean type of the position of the believer, revealing the ground of his acceptance in the Beloved; for just as the sweet savour of the continual burnt-offering ever ascended to God on behalf of Israel, so Christ in all His acceptability is ever before His eyes on behalf of His own. We can therefore say, 'As He is, so are we in this world' (1 John 4:17), for we are in the Divine presence in all the savour of His sacrifice, and in all the acceptance of His Person" (Ed. Dennett).

Nor should we lose sight of the *practical* teaching for our own souls in this morning and evening continual burnt-offering. Suitably has this been expressed by another: "God would encourage us to renew in our affections continually the terms on which He is with us. He would have every day to begin and end with a fresh sense of being with God and having God with us, in the sweet odor and acceptance of Christ. He never places His saints on any other ground before Him than that of Christ—the One who has perfectly glorified Him, and done all His will, and in whom He has infinite delight. He never departs from that; He never meets His saints on other or lower ground than that. And He would have the consciousness of it continually renewed on our side."

"And with the one lamb a tenth deal of flour mingled with the fourth part of an hin of beaten oil; and the fourth part of an hin of wine for a drink offering. And the other lamb thou shalt offer at even, and shalt do thereto according to the meat offering of the morning, and according to the drink offering thereof, for a sweet savour, an offering made by fire unto the Lord" (vv. 40:41). This was the accompaniment of the burnt-offering. The meal-offering is often spoken of as an appendix to it, thus, as "the burnt-offering and *its* meal-offering" (Lev. 23:13, 18; Num. 28: 28, 31; 29:3, 6, 9, etc.).

The "meat," or better "meal-offering" is described at length in Lev. 2. It foreshadowed the holy and perfect humanity through which the Son manifested His devotedness to the Father. Mingled with the meal was the fourth part of an hin of beaten oil. This shadowed forth the mystery of the supernatural birth of Christ, under the operation of the Holy Spirit: as said the angel to Mary, "The Holy Spirit shall come upon thee, and the power of the Highest shall overshadow thee: *therefore* also that holy thing which shall be born of thee shall be called the Son of God" (Luke 1:35). So, too, the whole of Christ's earthly life and ministry was permeated by the Holy Spirit. It was by the Spirit He was led into the wilderness to be tempted of the Devil (Matt. 4:1), and from the temptation He "returned in the power of the Spirit into Galilee" (Luke 4:14). It was by the Spirit He cast out demons (Matt. 12:28). It was through the Spirit that He offered Himself without spot to God (Heb. 9:14). And, even after His resurrection, it was "through the Spirit" He gave commandments unto the apostles (Acts 1:2).

Accompanying the burnt-offering there was also a drink-offering, which consisted of "the fourth part of an hin of wine." One of the significations of "wine," when it is employed emblematically, is *joy*—see Judges 9:13; Psalm 104:15. Thus, in our present type, the accompanying drink-offering speaks of the Father's joy in Christ—"This is My Beloved Son, in whom I am well pleased." But more: it was offered here by the Lord's people. Therefore it would also express *their* communion with the joy of God in the perfections and devotion of His Son. God would have us feast on that which delights Him. Beautifully is this brought out in the parable of the prodigal son. When the wanderer had returned in penitence, the Father said, "Bring hither the fatted calf, and kill; and let *us* eat, and *be merry*" (Luke 15:23)—figure of the Father and His child rejoicing together in Christ.

Striking are the words, in this connection, of v. 42: "This shall be a continual burnt-offering throughout your generations." Occupation with the devoted Son and His perfect humanity was to be continual, and every morning and evening the types of these were to be presented by Israel to God, accompanied by the fourth part of an hin of wine. Note again the words of v. 41: "And the other lamb thou shalt offer at even, and shalt do thereto according to the meat-offering of the morning, and according to the drink-offering thereof, for a sweet savour, an offering made by fire unto the Lord." Was not this continuous morning-offering the Lord saying to His people of old, "Rejoice in the Lord alway," and was not the repetition in the evening God's Old Testament *"again* I say, Rejoice" (Phil. 4:4)!

Gloominess in the Christian is not glorifying unto God. A long-faced believer is no commendation of Christ to those who know Him not. God does not desire His people to be miserable. Did He not move one of His apostles to say, "These things write we unto you, that your joy may be full" (1 John 1:4)? If the Christian *is* sad and miserable, the fault is entirely his own. The explanation thereof is furnished in the immediate context of the Scripture last quoted: "Our fellowship is with the Father, and with His Son, Jesus Christ" (1 John 1:3). As this fellowship is experimentally maintained, our joy *will be* "full." Lack of joy, then, is due to lack of fellowship with God.

And how is this to be remedied? Our present type tells us: begin and end each day with a fresh occupation of the heart with Christ, a concentrated meditation upon His excellencies—His devotedness to the Father, His dying love for us. But accompanying this there must be the "oil": it is only by the help and power of the Holy Spirit that we can truly "consider" Christ (Heb. 3:1 cf. John 16:14). And to the extent that we yield to and are filled with the Spirit, and to that extent only, shall we also be filled with joy—note how the "fourth part of an hin of wine" corresponds exactly to the "fourth part of an hin of oil" (v. 40)! To show that this is no mere coincidence, or unimportant detail, let the reader turn to Num. 15:6, 7 where he will find that though the quantities of the oil and wine are different, yet their proportions are the same! O that "the joy of the Lord" may be our strength (Neh. 8:10).

"This shall be a continual burnt-offering throughout your generations at the door of the tabernacle of the congregation before the Lord: where I will meet you, to speak there unto thee. And there I will meet with the children of Israel and they shall be sanctified by My glory" (vv. 42, 43). That which is so unspeakably blessed here is the Lord's repeated promise that He would *meet* with His people. The Hebrew word signifies "to meet as by appointment," and this, in the required manner and place.

"Moses was permitted in grace to meet Jehovah at the mercy-seat (Ex. 25:22); but the people could not pass beyond the door of the tabernacle of the congregation. It was here that the burnt-offering was presented on the brazen altar; and hence this was the meeting-place, on the ground of the sacrifice, between God and Israel. There could be no other possible place; just as now Christ forms the only meeting-place between God and the sinner. It is most important to see this truth—especially for those who are unsaved—that apart from Christ there can be no drawing nigh to God. 'I am the Way, the Truth, and the Life: no man cometh unto the Father, but by Me' (John 14:6). Mark well, moreover, that God cannot be approached except on the ground of the sacrifice of Christ. This is the truth foreshadowed in connection with the burnt-offering. If the cross, Christ crucified, be ignored, no relationships can be had with God, excepting those which may exist between a guilty sinner and a holy Judge. But the moment the sinner is led to take his stand upon 'the sweet savour' of the sacrifice of God, upon the efficacy of what Christ accomplished by His death, God can meet with him, in grace and love" (Ed. Dennett).

There is also a spiritual application of the blessed promise of vv. 42, 43 to the saints of God to-day, considered both singly and collectively. There is such a thing as God "meeting" with us in the *manifestation* of Himself to our hearts—alas, that so many experience this so infrequently. Where there is true soul-occupation with the person and work of Christ, in the power of the Spirit, there is also a making known of Himself (Luke 24:31). So, when the saints assemble for Divine worship, occupied not with their *own* needs, but with Christ's excellency—coming not to obtain a blessing, but to offer to God a sacrifice of praise; there is then such a gracious revelation of Himself that we are made to exclaim: "This is none other than the house of God, and this is the gate of heaven" (Gen. 28:17). O to know more of this blessed experience.

"And I will dwell among the children of Israel, and will be their God. And they shall know that I am the Lord their God, that brought them forth out of the land of Egypt, that I may dwell among them: I am the Lord their God" (vv. 45, 46). As in the previous verses God repeated His promise to "meet" with His worshipping people, so here He says, twice over, "I will dwell among them."

It was for this that Jehovah had delivered His people from Egypt: He could not "dwell" with them *there*. Nor could He dwell with Israel at all until they had been redeemed. This was something entirely new. God never "dwelt" with Adam, nor with Abraham. In the Song of Redemption (see Ex. 15:1, 13), Israel exclaimed, "Thou shalt bring them in, and plant them in the mountain of Thine inheritance, in the place, O Lord, Thou hast made for Thee to *dwell* in, the sanctuary" (15:17). To Moses God said, "Let them make Me a sanctuary; that I may dwell among them" (Ex. 25:8). Now, that promise was to be realised on the ground of the efficacy of the burnt-offering. Most blessed is it to mark God's purpose in thus dwelling in Israel's midst—"They shall know that I am the Lord their God." Equally precious is the promise which He has given us: "Lo, I am with you alway, unto the end of the age" (Matt. 28:20); and again, "I will never leave thee, nor forsake thee" (Heb. 13:5).

There is no doubt but that, prophetically, our present type looks forward to the second coming of Christ to this earth. Then will it be that "all Israel shall be saved: as it is written, There shall come out of Sion the Deliverer and shall turn away ungodliness from Jacob (Rom. 11:26). And again, "Thus speaketh the Lord of hosts, saying. Behold the man whose name is The Branch; and He shall grow up out of His place, and He shall build the temple of the Lord; even He shall build the temple of the Lord; and He shall bear the glory, and shall sit and rule upon His throne; and He shall be a priest upon His throne: and the counsel of peace shall be between them both" (Zech. 6:12, 13). Then will God say, "Sing and rejoice, O daughter of Zion; for, lo I come, and I will *dwell* in the midst of thee, saith the Lord" (Zech. 2:10). The ultimate fulfilment of our type will be seen on the new earth: "And I heard a great voice out of heaven saying, Behold, the tabernacle of God is with men, and He will *dwell* with them" (Rev. 21:3).

"But there is more than even dwelling with them: there is also relationship—'I will be their God.' It is not, be it remarked, what they shall be to Him, though they were His people by His grace; but what He will be to them. 'Their God'—words fraught with unspeakable blessings, for when God undertakes to become the God of His people, deigns to enter into relationship with them, He assures them that everything they need, whether for guidance, sustenance, defence, succour, yea, everything, is secure for them by what He is to them as their God. It was in view of the blessing of such a wondrous relationship that the Psalmist exclaims, 'Happy is that people whose God is the Lord'—Psalm 144:15" (Ed. Dennett). So, too, on the new earth it is said: "And they shall be His people, and God Himself shall be with them, and be their God" (Rev. 21:3). May the Lord use to His glory these musings upon this blessed type.

—*Arthur W. Pink.*

THE PROPHETIC PARABLES OF MATTHEW 13.

8. *The Pearl.*

"Again, the kingdom of heaven is like unto a merchant man, seeking goodly pearls: who, when he had found one pearl of great price, went and sold all that he had, and bought it" (Matt. 13:45, 46).

First of all, let us deal briefly with the popular and current interpretation of this parable. When we say "popular" we mean, particularly, that which has been given out principally (though not exclusively) by Arminians. The general conception of its meaning is this: Christianity is likened unto one who earnestly desired and diligently sought salvation. Ultimately his efforts were rewarded by his finding Christ, the Pearl of great price. Having found Him, as presented in the Gospel, the sinner sold all that he had: that is to say, he forsook all that the flesh held dear, he abandoned his worldly companions, he surrendered his will, he dedicated his life to God; and in that way, secured his salvation. The awful thing is that this interpretation is the one which, substantially, is given out almost everywhere throughout Christendom to-day. That is what is taught in the great majority of the denominational Sunday School periodicals. During the last twenty years I have examined scores of Sunday School teachers' aids in which an exposition of this parable has been found. The one which I have just given is an outline of that which has commonly been advanced.

Now, against that popular interpretation let us name three or four objections which are fatal to it. First, we are told this parable teaches that the sinner earnestly and diligently seeks salvation. But the truth is there has never been a single sinner on this earth who took the initiative in seeking salvation. The sinner *ought to* seek salvation, for he needs it badly enough. He ought to seek it, for God commands him so to do: "Let the wicked forsake his way, and the unrighteous man his thoughts: and let him return unto the Lord." "Seek ye the Lord while He may be found," is His command; but fallen man, the sinner in his natural state, never does and never will seek the Lord or His salvation.

How was it with the first sinner? When Adam sinned, and in the cool of the evening of that first awful day, the voice of the Lord was heard rolling down the avenues of Eden; what did he do? Did he hasten to the Lord and cast himself at His feet and cry for mercy? No, he did not seek the Lord at all; he fled. The first sinner did *not* "seek" God—the Lord sought him: "Adam, where art thou?" And it has ever been thus. How was it with Abraham? There is nothing whatever in Scripture to indicate that Abraham sought God; there is not a little to the contrary. He himself was a heathen, his parents idolaters worshipping other gods —as the last chapter of Joshua tells us— and the Lord suddenly appeared to him in that heathen city. Abraham had not been seeking God; it was God who sought him. And thus it has been all through the piece. When the Saviour came here He declared, "The Son of Man is come to seek and to save that which was lost" (Luke 19:10).

But perhaps there are some saying in themselves, "I cannot deny my own *experience;* I know quite well there *was* a time when I "sought the Lord." We do not deny it; what we would call attention to is, there was something *before* that. What *caused* you to "seek" the Lord? Ah, the truth is, you sought Him because *He* first sought you—just as truly as you love Him because He first loved you. It is not the sheep that seeks the Shepherd; it is the Shepherd who seeks the sheep; and having sought the sheep, He creates in the heart of that sheep a desire after Himself, then it begins to seek Him.

Thus, to make this parable teach that the natural man, an unconverted sinner, is seeking Christ, "the Pearl of great price," is to repudiate Scripture and to dishonour the grace of God. In Romans 3:11 are these words, and they are final: "There is none that seeketh after God." No, there is not one. There are multitudes that seek after pleasure, and seek after wealth, but there is none that seeketh after "God." *He* is the great Seeker. Oh that He may seek out some poor, needy souls now, and show them their need of Him, and create in their hearts a longing after Himself. O Spirit of God seek out Thine own.

In the second place, we are told in the popular interpretation of this parable, that, having sought and found Christ, the Pearl of great price, the sinner sells all that he has and buys it. But *that* cannot be, because the sinner has nothing to sell! Righteousness he has none, for Isa. 64:6 says that all our righteousnesses are as filthy rags. Goodness he has none, for Romans 3:12 tells us "There is none that doeth good, no, not one." Faith he has none, for *that* is God's "gift" (Eph. 2:8). The sinner has nothing to sell. The popular view of this parable turns God's truth upside down, for He declares that salvation is without money and without price (Isa. 55:1).

In the third place, to say that the sinner sells all that he has and *buys* the one pearl of great price—buys Christ—is positively awful! What a travesty! What a blasphemy! If there is one thing taught more clearly than anything else in Holy Writ, it is that salvation cannot be purchased by man: "Not by works of righteousness which we have done, but according to His mercy He saved us" (Titus 3:5). "The *gift* of God is eternal life" (Rom. 6:23). If it is a "gift" it is not to be sold or bartered.

Let us give now what we believe is the true interpretation of this parable. "Again, the kingdom of heaven is like unto a merchantman." The "man" referred to is Christ, as He is all through this chapter. The "man" that sowed the good Seed in the field in the first parable is Christ. The "man" referred to in v. 24 at the beginning of the second parable is Christ, and the "man" in this parable, the "merchantman," is the Lord Jesus. Now, notice five things concerning this "man."

First, he *desired* this goodly pearl: "the kingdom of heaven is like unto a merchantman seeking goodly pearls: who when he had found one pearl of great price went and sold all that he had, and bought it." The parable begins by intimating that the Merchantman had set his heart upon this pearl. The pearl represents His church in its entirety, and that people, that church, the Lord Jesus *desired*. This is something which altogether passes our comprehension. What was there in us poor, fallen, depraved, sinful creatures to awaken *His* desire?

"What was there in us
  That could merit esteem,
  Or give the Creator delight?
'Twas even thus, Father!
We ever must sing,
  For so it seemed good in Thy sight."
That is the only reason.

Now let us turn to two or three Scriptures which bear out this thought—Christ's desire for a people. "So shall the King greatly *desire* thy beauty" (Psa. 45:11). O wonder of wonders, that He, the King, should greatly desire poor, sinful worms of the earth! In the light of that, recall those blessed words of His in John 14—O how they lay bare the very heart of the Saviour—"Let not your heart be troubled: ye believe in God believe also in Me. In My Father's house are many mansions: if it were not so, I would have told you. I go to prepare a place *for you*." How that speaks forth His love for His own people! How precious they must be in His sight! "I go to prepare a place for you. And if I go and prepare a place for you, I will come again"—beautiful as that place may be, perfect as that place is, it does not satisfy the longing of His heart until that place is occupied *by those* for whom it is prepared. "I will go and prepare a place for you, and if I go . . . . . I will come again, and receive you unto Myself; that where I am, there ye may be also." How that tells out the intense desire of the heart of Christ which will not be satisfied until He has His own blood-bought people around Himself! Compare Eph. 5:25; Rev. 3:20! The parable then begins by intimating the desire of Christ for this "pearl."

The second thing is that He regarded this pearl as being of "great price." That is what has staggered so many of the commentators. Even Mr. Spurgeon used to think that such language could never be true of poor sinners of the earth, that it could only be appropriate of the Christ of God. It *is* staggering—that not only should Christ desire you and me, but that we should be of "great price" in His sight! It only illustrates what we are told in Isa. 55: "My thoughts are not your thoughts . . . . as the heavens are higher than the earth . . . . so are My thoughts than your thoughts." Yes, they are. Would any redeemed sinner have formed such a conception in his own mind if God's Word had never so told us—that we were of "great price" in His sight? No, I am sure none of us would; for God's people are not of "great price" in their own sight, let alone the sight of the Lord Himself. O think of it, that we were of "great price" in *His* sight! There is an intimation of this in that wonderful 8th chapter of Proverbs, where we are taken back into the eternal counsels of God, and are permitted to witness something of the relationship that existed between the Father and the Son before earth's foundations were laid: "Then I was by Him as One brought up with Him: And I was daily His delight." And then in the 31st verse we read the words of Christ, spoken prophetically or in anticipation: "My delights were with the children of men." "*My delights*": O my brethren and sisters in Christ, not only were we present in His thoughts, not only did we stand before His mind in the eternity of the past, but His *heart* was fixed on us; His affections went out to us. We were His "delights" even then. "My delights are with the sons of men." It may be asked, "Can you understand that?" And we say, No, dear friends, we cannot: our poor little minds are altogether inadequate for rising to such a level: we can only bow in wonderment and worship where we cannot understand.

In the third place, we are told that the Merchantman not only desired this pearl, and esteemed it of so great value, but He *sold all that He had*—words easily uttered, I am afraid sometimes glibly spoken. If our minds were incapable of rising to the level of the thought that has just been expressed, who amongst us is capable of gauging what it meant for the Lord of glory, the Creator of the universe, to sell all that He had? He who was rich for your sakes became poor—poorer than any of us have ever been; much poorer. So poor that He occupied a manger—that one day we might occupy a mansion. So poor that He had not where to lay His head—in order that you and I, who are amongst His favoured ones, might rest our heads forever on His sacred bosom. "He who was rich for your sakes became poor, that ye through His poverty might be rich."

In the fourth place, this Merchantman *sought* the pearl. "The kingdom of heaven is like unto a merchantman seeking." This points a contrast from what was before us in the preceding parable. In the fifth parable the treasure was "found": in the case of the pearl it was "sought." The distinction appropriately expresses the difference between God's earthly election, the Jews; and God's heavenly election, which are, for the most part, gathered out from the Gentiles (Acts 15:14). Turn to Eph. 2:17: "And came and preached peace to you which were afar off, *and* to them that were nigh." Were not *all* sinners "far off" from Him? Were there any sinners that were "nigh" to Him? In one sense, No. In another sense, Yes. *Spiritually* all of Adam's race were "far off" from Him, yet *dispensationally* the Jews were "nigh," and the Gentiles were "far off"; but they both needed the word of peace preached to them. He preached "peace to you which were far off (that is, the Gentiles) and to them that were nigh" (that is, the Jews).

Hence, in the first of these two parables the treasure was "found"; it did not need "seeking!" It was already in the land when the Christ of God became incarnate: the Jews were already there in outward covenant relationship with God—with the Word of God in their hands, the temple of God in their midst, and so on. But in the next parable, where the Gentiles are in view, *they* not only had to be "found," but they needed to be "sought!" *They* were "afar off" from God in every way. O the minute accuracy of Scripture!

Now notice in the next place, the Merchantman *bought* the "pearl." There is no need to enlarge on that, except perhaps to quote 1 Peter 1:18, 19, ". . . . not redeemed with corruptible things, as silver and gold, from your vain conversation received by tradition from your fathers; but with the precious blood of Christ, as of a lamb without blemish and without spot." It was at the Cross that He bought the pearl, and the price that He paid was His own precious blood.

Let us now consider the "pearl" itself, and admire the accuracy, beauty, and fulness of this figure that Christ selected for portraying His Church. First, notice its *unity*. "A Merchantman was seeking goodly pearls, and when he had found one pearl of great price." Let us observe, however, that this Merchantman had *several* pearls. He was seeking goodly pearls, and, of course, if *He* sought them He found each one. Yes, Christ has several pearls. There are quite a number of distinct companies among His redeemed. The Old Testament saints is one, and so on. But attention is here focussed on "one pearl" in particular: the unity of God's saints of this present dispensation is what is referred to, "In Christ there is neither Jew nor Greek, bond nor free, male nor female, for we are all *one*" (Gal. 3:28). Now, it is a significant fact that a pearl is the only gem whose unity cannot be broken without destroying it. I may take a diamond and cut it into two, then I have two diamonds. I may take a lump of gold and divide it into two, and I have two lumps of gold. But if I take a pearl and cut it into two, I have nothing; I have destroyed it! A pearl significantly stands for the unity of the saints of this present dispensation.

In the second place, a pearl is *the product of a living creature,* and it is the *only* gem that is. Not only so, but it is the result of *suffering*. Away down in the ocean's depths there lives a little animal encased in a shell: we call it an oyster. One day a foreign substance, a grain of sand, intrudes, and pierces its side. Now, God has endowed that animal with the faculty of self-preservation, like He has all others of His creatures, and it throws out, exudes, a slimy substance called nacre and covers the wound, repeating the process again and again. One layer after another of that nacre or mother-of-pearl is cast out by that little animal on the wound in its side, until ultimately there is built up what eventuates in a pearl. So that a pearl is the product of suffering. How wonderful the figure! How accurate the emblem! The Church, the saints of this dispensation, are the fruitage of the travail of Christ's soul. The pearl, we may say, is the answer to the injury that was inflicted upon the animal. In other words, it is the *offending* particle that ultimately becomes the object of beauty: that which injured the oyster becomes the precious gem. The very thing that injured the animal, the little grain of sand that intruded, is ultimately clothed with a beauty that is not its own and covered with the comeliness of the one that it injured. How manifestly is the Author of the Bible and the Saviour of our souls the Regulator of everything in nature. Yes, He saw to it, when He created the oyster, that it should furnish an appropriate type and figure of His Church.

In the third place, the pearl is an object that is formed *slowly and gradually*. It does not come into existence in a single day. There is a tedious process of waiting while the pearl is being slowly but surely formed. And so it has been with the Church. For nineteen centuries now that, of which the pearl is the figure and type, has been in process of formation by the power and grace of God. Just as the oyster covered the wound in its side and that which pierced it with one layer after another of the beautiful nacre, constantly repeating the process, so out of each generation of men on earth God has called a few and added them to that Church which He is now building for His Son.

In the fourth place, notice *the lowly origin* of that which is a type of the Church. That beautiful pearl originally had its home in the depths of the sea, amid its mire and filth, for that is where oysters congregate. They are the scavengers of the ocean. Down in the ocean's depths, amidst the mire, is that precious gem being formed. What a lowly origin! Yes, and that is to remind us, and to humble us with the remembrance of it, that we, who have by sovereign grace been made members of Christ, had by nature our origin in the filth and mire and ruin of the fall. Compare Eph. 2:11, 12.

In the fifth place, the pearl, as it is being formed down there in the ocean's depths, is *not seen by the eye of man*. It is a secret formation; none but God witnesses its building up. In like manner, that Church which Christ is now building, that body of His which is now in process of formation, is unknown and unseen by the world. I am not speaking of the visible churches, I am talking about that Church, which is now *being* built (see Eph. 2:21; 4:16, etc.), and which as it is being formed, like the oyster, is unseen by the eye of man. Your life is *hid* with Christ in God (Col. 3:3). Significant, too, is the fact that just as the pearl is found not in the mines of earth, but in the *sea*, so the Church of this dispensation is composed mainly of Gentiles—the "waters" figuring such, see Rev. 17:15.

In the sixth place, we learn from this figure that in the eyes of God that Church is *an object of value and beauty*. That little object, hidden from the eyes of men, is being fashioned into a precious gem, which shall yet reflect the light of heaven and become an object of beauty and admiration in the eyes of all who see it. Turn to 2 Thess. 1:10. "When He shall come to be glorified in His saints (not only in Himself), and to be admired in all them that believe." That is speaking in the language of the pearl. First, the Lord Jesus will "present to Himself a glorious church, not having spot or wrinkle, or any such thing; but it shall be holy and without blemish" (Eph. 5:27); second, when He returns to the earth itself, He will bring with him His complete and beautified Church and *it* will be an object of admiration to all who behold it. To a wondering universe Christ will yet display His glorified Church.

In the seventh place, see how in the figure Christ here selected, we have an intimation of *the honourable and exalted future* that the Church is yet to enjoy. That little object in the ocean's depths, unseen by the eye of men, which is being gradually built up, ultimately has a position and a place in the diadem of the king. That is the destiny of the pearl of great price: it becomes the jewel of royalty; for this it has been made. And so we are told, "When Christ, our life, shall appear, then shall *ye also* appear with Him in glory" (Col. 3:4). And again, "That in the ages to come (that is yet future) He might show the exceeding riches of His grace in His kindness toward us" (Eph. 2:7). Ah, my friends, many of God's people to-day may be poor and despised and hated by the prominent and great of this world, but just as surely as the pearl of great price of lowly origin ultimates in a position of dignity and honour and glory, so those who now are last shall be first.

In closing, let me sum up in two words of practical application. First, to the unconverted. O my unsaved friend, let this parable show you once and for all the utter impossibility and the needlessness of attempting to purchase your salvation, of seeking to win God's approval by some works and doings of your own. The pearl in this parable is not a Saviour whom the sinner has to "buy." "By grace are ye saved through faith; and that not of yourselves, it is the gift of God . . . . not of works lest any man should boast."

And what is the word to those of us who by the grace of God have been saved? This: the pearl has been purchased by Christ: we are the *purchased property* of another! Ye are not your own, but "bought with a price" (1 Cor. 6:20). To what extent is that Divine truth regulating our lives? How far is that fact dominating our daily walk? We are not our own; we belong to Christ! Do we realise that? Are we living day by day as though we realised it? Does our walk manifest it? Not our own—the property of another! Then should we not say, "For me to live is Christ?" Can any of us truthfully say it? "For me to live is *Christ?*" Is it true that I have only one aim, only one desire, only one ambition; all my efforts concentrated on the honouring, obeying, magnifying of Christ? O my friends, the poor preacher cannot honestly say it. By the grace of God he may say that *is* his *desire*. But O how far short he comes of attaining to it in his daily life. May God help all His people to realise in their souls that they are not their own: no longer free, no longer have the right to plan their own life, to say what they will do or what they will not do; no longer any whatever—the purchased property of Another. Our answer to that ought to be, "For me to live in Christ." O may Divine, enabling grace be granted to us so to live.

—*Arthur W. Pink.*

THE MEANS OF REGENERATION.

The doctrines of revelation form a connected whole, so that an error on any point affects a man's views on every other point. If the error stood isolated and independent, to regard it as trivial or innocuous would be an insult to the grace and wisdom of Him who has adapted His revelation to our necessities, so that it is all profitable, and there is neither redundancy nor defect in it. But when we consider the influence of one error as extending to every part of the great system of truth, with what prayerful caution should we watch over what we either receive or propagate as the truth of God!

On no subject would the diffusive influence of error be more easily shown than on the fundamental doctrine of regeneration. When we know what a man holds for truth on this subject, we can infer his whole creed. At present we only observe that when regeneration is represented as being a mere change of principles and conduct, or a change effected in our fallen nature—in "the flesh"—the representation strips of meaning every passage of Scripture relating to the believer's sonship, and every passage relating to the life which the believer receives in Christ. Our sonship it reduces to a nominal relationship, giving a certain legal status, according to the human notion of adoption; instead of exhibiting it as an actual relationship, resulting from "being born of God." Eternal life, which is the gift of God through Jesus Christ our Lord, it reduces to an awakening of the dormant energies, the development of the latent powers, and the rectification of the disordered affections of an already existing life.

Yet the language of Scripture is sufficiently explicit, both as to the condition of the natural man as absolutely destitute of life, and as to the communication to the believer of something which he did not previously possess, through Him who said to the Father: "Thou hast given Him power over all flesh, that He should give eternal life to as many as Thou hast given Him." The believer is said to have passed from death unto life, and it is expressly declared: "He that hath the Son *hath life,* and he that hath not the Son of God *hath not life."* This life can be enjoyed only in union with Christ, for "this life is in His Son," or still more emphatically: "Christ is our life."

This life is, in other words, the new nature which is styled "spirit," in contrast with the old nature, which is styled "flesh," and which is essentially enmity against God. "So, then, they that are *in the flesh* cannot please God. But ye (believers) are not in the flesh, but *in the spirit;* if so be that the Spirit of God dwell in you. Now, if any man have not the Spirit of Christ, he is none of His. And if *Christ be in you,* the body is dead because of sin, but the *spirit is life* because of righteousness." We cannot now speak of the relation between sin and death on the one hand, and between righteousness and life on the other. But let it be observed that He who is "our righteousness" is also "our life," and then it is evident that the unbeliever is as truly destitute of "the life" as he is destitute of righteousness, and he is destitute of both because he is "without Christ."

The production of this life in the believer is ascribed to the Holy Spirit, and spoken of as a creation as plainly as the first production of the world, when God "breathed into man's nostrils the breath of life, and man became a living soul." To create is not to effect a change in something which already exists; and to be born is not to undergo some modification of life, but to be brought into life. To be born anew is to be brought into that eternal life which is in the Son, and which, with reference both to its origin and its character, is called "spirit," in eternal contrariety to "the flesh." These preliminary observations seemed necessary to our examination of the doctrine of Scripture regarding the means of regeneration, because the prevailing misconceptions affect the greater number of those passages from which the doctrine is to be gathered.

In the narratives of the New Testament, where the ruin of man and our need of a Saviour are taught, the illustration is found in the case of someone whom the world would recognise as a representative of human excellence, such as the young ruler, of whom it is said at his coming, "when Jesus saw him He loved him," but in whom, as he went away sorrowful, it was seen that "with man it is impossible." Where the grace and sufficiency of the Saviour are taught, an example is taken from those whom the world would abandon as the chief of sinners, such as the infamous Zaccheus, whose very presence was regarded as contaminating; but in whom it was shown that "with God, all things are possible." Thus, it was to Nicodemus, a man of the Pharisees, and a ruler of the Jews, than whom, probably, no man had more whereof to boast in the flesh, that the Lord addressed the sweeping declaration, "except a man be born again he cannot see the kingdom of God." It is worthy of notice that the highest claims of legality and the loudest boast in the flesh, can never give peace and assurance to the soul. The young ruler and Nicodemus both prove this—they are evidently ill at ease, lest there might be some flaw in their claim—something omitted, or something done amiss. It has been expressed, "if salvation depended upon a movement of the eyelid, no one could ever be assured that it had been correctly done." Nicodemus felt the need of a teacher, but he was taught that he needed not a teacher, but a Saviour; not a rule of life, but life itself; not to be directed, but to be born again.

It is of little consequence to our present enquiry whether the question, "How can a man be born when he is old?" was the utterance of his ignorant perplexity or of his ignorant scorn. The Lord graciously and patiently taught him that He spoke of the production of a new life, differing in every respect from that which Nicodemus was vainly attempting to discipline for a kingdom, for the enjoyment of which he was as utterly incapacitated as the dead in their graves are for the enjoyment of this world. "Except a man be born of water and of the Spirit he cannot enter the kingdom of God." The import of "water" in this explanation may be more satisfactorily considered hereafter. For the present we remark that it cannot refer to baptism, since it is an explanation of being "born again," and since, if there were no other save the thief on the cross, we know positively of one who shall enter the kingdom of God without being baptised. Among men "there are exceptions to every general rule," because those who utter it are not omniscient and infallible. But if, when the Lord says, "except a man be born of water," He means, except a man be baptised; and we can yet show that there is so much as one exception to it, how could anyone be assured that there might not also be exceptions to the declaration that, "Whosoever believeth on Him shall not perish, but have everlasting life?"

The necessity of being thus born is shown by the fact that "that which is born of the flesh is flesh." Train it, torture it, discipline it, adorn it as you please, it is still "flesh," and can never be fitted for an inheritance which is incorruptible and undefiled, and which fadeth not away. The flesh is made manifest by its works which are these: Adultery, fornication, uncleanness, lasciviousness, idolatry, witchcraft, hatred, variance, emulations, wrath, strife, sedition, heresies, envyings, murders, drunkenness, revellings, and suchlike. And surely it is not necessary to argue further that that which is born of the flesh cannot enter the kingdom of God. Those only who are born of God can be heirs of God and joint-heirs with Christ; but they are, by that very fact, made meet for the inheritance, for "that which is born of the Spirit is spirit"; as unchangeably opposite to the flesh as light is to darkness, holiness to sin.

The life produced by the Spirit is indeed inexplicable to human reason. But the testimony of the Lord may convince a man of its reality, and that without it he cannot enter the kingdom of God. So Nicodemus understood, that, though a Hebrew of the Hebrews, as touching the law a Pharisee, touching the righteousness which is of the law, blameless; still, as he was born of the flesh and not of the Spirit, all his cherished hopes were vain. For we do not understand the question, "How can these things be?" as expressing his incredulity, but his felt need; as though he had asked, "What must I do to be saved?" And it is this question which the Lord answered, after He had reproved the guilty ignorance of a master in Israel, a blind leader of the blind.

The Lord's answer relates to the means by which the Spirit communicates life, which it greatly concerned Nicodemus to know, and not to the secret mode of the Spirit's operation, which created intelligence could never comprehend. The creature's knowledge of the Creator's works can never go beyond this, even in the natural world. Science can only collect the facts of existence; and any attempt to go beyond these is a presumptuous folly which science disclaims. As it has been expressed by a natural philosopher who treats of the limits of our knowledge of Nature: "We only know *that it is*, but *what*, or *how*, or *why* it is, transcends our powers." We can observe and record the facts concerning sowing the seed, its germination in the earth, the springing up of the plant, its progress to maturity, and its decay. But if we attempt to explore that vegetable life beyond these facts, or to discover *how* and *why* certain means or causes produce certain results, we at once find that we are beyond our province, and must return, baffled and humbled. Yet men who are baffled by the mystery of the existence of a blade of grass, will arrogantly demand to know the *what*, the *how*, and the *why* of this divine life, before they will listen to the doctrine of the Lord regarding the necessity of being born again, and regarding the means by which the Divine Agent accomplishes His creative work.

We have no theory or speculation wherewith to gratify such impertinent curiosity, but we have a plain answer to the honest enquirer after salvation: "As Moses lifted up the serpent in the wilderness, even so must the Son of Man be lifted up, that whosoever believeth in Him should not perish but have eternal life." Having eternal life is equivalent to being born again. In other words, as in nature, to be born is to be brought into life, so here to be born again is to be brought into eternal life; and, thus, the Lord teaches that whosoever believes in Him is born again. Let this be kept in mind on considering all the passages which connect faith in Him with the possession of everlasting life. In like manner let it be kept in mind in considering the passages which connect faith in Him with sonship, that to be a son of God is to be born of God: "As many as received Him, to them gave He power to become sons of God, even to them who believe on His name, which were born not of blood nor of the will of the flesh nor of the will of man, but of God."

Whatever, then, is the means of our belief in Him, must be the means of regeneration; and that is the Word of God—the Gospel—the testimony of God concerning His Son. "If we receive the witness of man, the witness of God is greater. For this is the witness of God which He hath testified of His Son. He that believeth on the Son of God hath the witness in himself; he that believeth not God hath made Him a liar, because he believeth not the record which God gave of His Son —and this is the record that God hath given to us eternal life, and this life is in His Son. He that hath the Son hath life, and He that hath not the Son of God hath not life." Our belief in Him is not acknowledging certain facts on historical evidence, nor certain general claims as supported by sound reasoning, but it is our reliance on Him as our Saviour, upon the testimony of God that "Whosoever believeth on Him shall not perish, but have everlasting life."

The lost are pointed to the Saviour, and the Word of God is: "Believe on the Lord Jesus Christ and thou shalt be saved." The guilty are pointed to the Lamb of God, who takes away the sin of the world, and the message of God is: "He that believeth on Him is justified from all things." *Here* are men dead in trespasses and sins, destitute of true life; *there* is Christ, the THE LIFE, a full and overflowing fountain of life, and the Word of God is: "He that believeth on the Son hath everlasting life." Faith connects the soul with the fountain of life, and the Word of God is the warrant and means of that faith—a mighty word, like that which said, "Let there be light," and light was—they that hear shall live. This word, therefore, is expressly spoken of in Scripture as the means of regeneration: "Of His own will begat He us with the Word of Truth." James 1:18. "Being born again, not of corruptible seed, but of incorruptible by the Word of God, which liveth and abideth for ever. . . . And this is the word which by the Gospel is preached unto you." 1 Peter 1:23.

The prevailing misconception of regeneration, that it is a change effected in the old man—in that which the Word of God styles "the flesh"—has led to another error regarding the means of regeneration. For, finding in the Scriptures such passages as those we have quoted from James and Peter, those who hold that regeneration is a change effected in the old man, have endeavoured to show that the truth revealed in the Gospel is adapted to produce such a change. In doing so, they state much that is Scripturally correct regarding the nature and tendency of the truth. They endeavour to show, for example, what must be the influence upon a man's character and conduct of the Gospel representation of his natural condition and prospects. He can no longer remain contented in such a condition, and the world can no longer hold out to him the promise of a satisfying portion. The revelation which the Gospel makes of the love of God must subdue his heart, and awaken a responsive love—according to the Scriptural maxim: "We love Him because He first loved us." The forgiveness which the Gospel proclaims must bind the soul by cords of gratitude to our Saviour-God; "having been forgiven much he will love much." The glory which the Gospel promises must far outweigh the attractions of a perishing world; so that relinquishing the pursuit of present vanities, he must press on to the enjoyment of immortal blessedness. And thus, they argue, the whole life and character must be so changed that the man may well be styled a new man.

Now, however correct and Scriptural these representations of the necessary influence of these truths whenever they are received, those by whom they are made overlook the important fact that the nature upon which the truths are supposed to operate is utterly incapable of discerning or receiving them, and is as incapable of being moved by the love of God or the attractions of heavenly things, as the dead in their graves are of being moved by the most eloquent address. "The natural man receiveth not the things of the Spirit of God, for they are foolishness unto him; neither can he know them, because they are spiritually discerned." It is true of believers, that they are influenced by these considerations; but then it is because "they have received not the spirit of the world but the Spirit which is of God, that they might know the things which are freely given them of God." It is true that believers love Him because He first loved us, but then it is because they are born of God. The love of Christ constraineth them that they live not unto themselves, but unto Him that died for them, and rose again; but then it is because they *live*. They set their affections upon things above; but then it is because they are risen with Christ.

We may here remark that we are very far from alleging, or even harbouring a suspicion that all those who make these representations, and who are labouring under these misconceptions, are themselves strangers to this life. On the contrary, they often speak of the influences of these blessed truths in such a way as to convey an irresistible conviction that they speak from experience, that they do know and believe the love God hath to us, and that they live more or less under the influence of heavenly things. And it is a truth in which we have all reason to rejoice that every believer is justified, born of God, sanctified, and saved, however imperfect his knowledge or conceptions may be of the salvation which he has found in Christ. How little, for example, must the thief on the cross have known or understood of those great truths which were revealed to Paul and by Paul; but he was as truly born of God, and was as truly an heir of God and a joint-heir with Christ, "Whosoever believeth that Jesus is the Christ, is born of God."

This admission will not be understood as rendering it a matter of little moment whether our views of this, or any other truth of God, are clear or obscure, Scriptural or philosophical, true or false. The dishonour to God, the torture inflicted upon anxious souls, the lifelong oppression and sorrow to the advocates of them, which have been occasioned by these misconceptions of the doctrine of regeneration, never can be known till the secrets of all hearts are revealed. Not a few of us could tell our own sad experience through years of darkness and doubts, from the very recollection of which we shrink. And it is from such an experience that we come to lift up an humble but earnest testimony to the truth, that while the Word of God is the incorruptible seed of that new birth, the means by which the Spirit of God accomplishes His new creation, regeneration is not in any sense a change effected in our ruined nature by the natural influence and tendency of the truth which presents new motives, new principles, new aims of life. It does all this, but it would present them, in vain, to a nature that is incapable of discerning them, utterly insensible to them, and irreconcilably opposed to them. To be born anew is to be brought into a new life; there is, indeed, a new creation, and it remains true after that has been accomplished, as before it, that which is born of the flesh is flesh, and that which is born of the Spirit is spirit; and down to the very instant of dissolution, it is true, in the experience of every believer, that the flesh lusteth against the spirit, and the spirit against the flesh.

The word, which is the means of regeneration, is the Gospel; the testimony of God which is the warrant and means of that faith which makes us one with Christ, who is our life, and in whom we have eternal life. To believe in Him is not more truly to be justified from all things than it is to be born of the Spirit, to have eternal life; to be a son of God. "For," says the apostle, "ye are all children of God by faith in Christ Jesus." And it is a blessed thought that our whole standing and relations, our righteousness and life, our title and claim, our peace, joy, strength, and hope, our all is in Him.

One important practical result of a distinct apprehension of the doctrine of Scripture on this subject will be the simplicity and directness of our testimony to perishing men. There is often a bewildering confusion in the manner in which the impenitent are addressed and the awakened are instructed on this subject; the effect of which was expressed by the venerable old man who was mentioned in the former essay on regeneration, who, apart from his conviction of the sufficiency of the sacrifice of Christ for sin, felt that before he had any warrant to look Christ-ward, he must undergo some change which he called being born again. Every one who has any acquaintance with the condition and mental exercise of awakened sinners, or of those who are in any manner concerned about salvation, knows how extensively perplexity and confusion on this matter prevail. "They are occupied," as it has been expressed, "with the process of regeneration instead of the Word which regenerates!" And too frequently those to whom they tell their perplexities are unprepared to tell them that as the Israelites were healed by looking at the serpent which Moses lifted up, the sinner now obtains life, is born again, by simply believing on the Son of Man crucified for our offences and raised again for our justification. He finds eternal life where and when he finds justification. They cannot be separated any more than sin and death can be separated. He that believes in Him is justified from all things, is born of God, has everlasting life. What remains for us is simply to proclaim the Gospel. The Word of God, assured that whenever a sinner receives that simple testimony concerning Jesus, the Christ, the Son of God, and so believes in Him, he is born of God.

The whole Scriptures unite in the testimony that the Spirit of God is the Agent, and the Word of God the means of regeneration. And the enquiry might readily be suggested whether, in saying, "Except a man be born of water and of the spirit he cannot enter the kingdom of God," the Lord did not refer to this agency and instrumentality. That the work is ascribed to the sole agency of the Spirit is evident from what follows, in which the Spirit alone is spoken of; and then in answering the question, "How can these things be?" There is no reference to the water, unless it be understood as a figurative expression of the only instrumentality employed by the Spirit in communicating new life. And we might properly inquire whether there is any thing in the Scriptures which countenances this figurative interpretation of the word water. It must be remembered that the introduction of new life does not destroy the personal identity of the sinner. He is born anew. It is not the introduction of a new person into the world. It is bringing life out of death, holiness out of sin. There is an old man to be put off, as well as a new man to be put on, and consequently there is the idea of purification as well as the idea of quickening, the washing of regeneration as well as the renewing of the Holy Spirit. The Word of God is frequently spoken of as the means of this purification. Thus Peter, in that passage where he speaks to believers of being born again by the Word of God, says, "Seeing ye have purified your souls in obeying the truth." "Ye are clean," said the Lord to His disciples, "through the word that I have spoken to you." Still more directly bearing on the point before us, Paul says, Ephesians 5: 25: "Christ also loved the church, and gave Himself for it, that He might sanctify and cleanse it with the washing of water by the Word." The difficulty which expositors have found in the passage grows out of the foregone conclusion that the washing of water means baptism; and understanding the apostle to state that the Lord cleanses His Church by baptism; they do not know how to dispose of the phrase, "by the word." It contradicts the whole tenor of Scripture to say that He cleanses the Church by baptism; it is entirely in harmony with the testimony of Scripture to say that He cleanses it by the Word, while "with the washing of water" is introduced as a lively figure of the process. Nicodemus certainly could not understand any illusion to an outward rite which was not then instituted, and could only have been bewildered by such reference in this explanation of a great Scripture truth. While, as a master of Israel, he might fairly be expected to understand a figure drawn from the treasury of Scripture in which God speaks of His own work: "Then will I sprinkle clean water upon you, and ye shall be clean; from all your filthiness, and from all your idols will I cleanse you." Ezekiel 36:25.

In these views of the Scriptural doctrine of regeneration, two things are established beyond cavil, on the Word of God: *First*—In a state of nature men are absolutely incapable of occupying a place in the kingdom of God. If what may be styled the legal disqualification of their guilt and condemnation as sinners were removed, and the gates of heaven were flung wide open to them, their nature—educate, train, and mould it as you may—is still essentially sinful, and they are without "the life" which exists there—the nature which is at home there. Heaven, if it could be entered, would, to such a being, prove the most terrible hell. *Second*—According to the provision which grace has made for the removal of guilt and the communication of life, the message of God to the sinner is: "Believe on the Lord Jesus Christ, and thou shalt be saved." The believer is at once justified from all things, and born of God. He who truly preaches the Gospel is sustained by the assurance that the glorious result is indeed the work of the Holy Spirit, and every sinner saved will recognise the working of His mighty power. But the office of the preacher is simply to point men to "the Son of Man lifted up, that whosoever believeth on Him, should not perish, but have everlasting life."

Waymarks in the Wilderness. 1865.

do so! Prayerlessness is a despising of the Ruler of the universe; it is refusing to pay Him homage, consult His will, seek His help. Prayerlessness is a slighting of the throne of the most High; it is a species of insubordination.

God is our *Benefactor*. Every good and every perfect gift is from above, and cometh down from the Father of lights. Every privilege we enjoy, every blessing that is ours, we owe to His goodness. Now a proper recognition of this is due from us. The least we can do is to own His beneficence, and thank Him for His favours. If you sent a valuable gift to a friend who received it, but made no acknowledgment, you would be grieved. Yet how often we treat God thus! Prayerlessness is base ingratitude.

God is our *Father*. It is proper that children should honour and respect their parents; when in need, it is right that they should make known their requests to them. Now, Christians are the children of God: therefore, it is fitting that they should seek His face, ask His counsel, desire His blessing. Not to do so is to ignore His Fatherhood and grieve His Spirit. Prayerlessness betrays a lack of filial respect and evidences the coldness of our hearts. Yes, "Men *ought* always to pray."

Second, we ought to pray, *because God is the Hearer and Answerer of prayer*. Even though He were to pay no attention to our petitions, it would still be our bounden duty to supplicate Him. But He deigns to listen. What condescension! What a mercy that His ear *is* open to our cries! And what a marvel that we are so unwilling to come to His throne of grace!

Both the O. and N.T. mention many answers to prayer. They are recorded for our inspiration. It was in answer to the prayer of Abraham that God delivered Lot from Sodom. It was in answer to the prayer of Jacob that God subdued Esau's enmity. It was in answer to Moses' prayer that God delivered Israel at the Red Sea, and gave them victory over the Amalekites in the Wilderness. In answer to prayer Samuel was given to Hannah; the Philistines were smitten (1 Sam. 7:8-11); Solomon obtained wisdom; Elijah shut up heaven that it rained not for three and a half years. It was in answer to prayer the Holy Spirit was poured out on the day of Pentecost. In view of such encouragements, verily, "Men *ought* always to pray."

Third, *because prayerlessness is sin!* While honest souls will acknowledge their deficiency, that they devote far less time to this holy exercise than they should, few realise the wickedness of a prayerless life. The general tendency to-day is to excuse it; to regard it as an infirmity; or, worse still, to attribute it to the unwillingness of the Holy Spirit to move them. The deep guilt of prayerlessness is little realised.

Consider what God has done for you, fellow-Christian. He so loved thee as to give His Son to die for thee; thou hast been redeemed at the cost of bloodshedding! He has begotten you by His Spirit, re-created you in His image, and given you a place in His family. He has rent the veil and made a way into the Holiest. He bids you draw near and hold converse with Him, especially to experience the joy and blessedness of fellowship with Him.

How have you requited Him? What use art thou making of this inestimable privilege? Do you proffer the excuse of lack of time? We *make* time for whatever really interests us! If a friend, whom you have not seen for a long time, comes from a distance and visits you, every thing is put on one side. Why? Because you are anxious to converse with him. But He who deigns to call us His "friends" is neglected!

Consider what this reveals. What a reproach it is to God! It indicates that our hearts enjoy not His presence. Oh, what a dishonour to the Father to say I cannot find time for fellowship with Him! How it demonstrates that our life is dominated by "the flesh!" What need has each of us to get down on our knees, confess to God this sin of prayerlessness, and earnestly seek His forgiveness. Entreat Him to subdue the workings of the flesh; ask Him to fill you with His Spirit, to give you a heart and will to heed our text, "Men ought always to pray."

Fourth, because *prayerlessness means a deficient spiritual life*. Prayerlessness makes Scripture-reading dull and unprofitable. The Bible is an unique Book, and it makes unique demands upon its readers. It utters God's voice, and it calls for a trained spiritual ear to recognise it. Prayer gives the needed preparation. Again; prayerlessness prevents growth in grace. The same principle holds good in the spiritual realm as in the natural: we cannot be healthy without exercise; and prayer is ordained of God to call into exercise all the faculties of the new man. Finally, prayerlessness is the certain precursor of blacksliding. It was at this point that poor Peter failed: instead of praying in the Garden, he went to sleep. The sad sequel is recorded for our learning and warning. For these reasons "Men *ought* always to pray."

—Arthur W. Pink.

VOL. VII.   MAY, 1928   NO. 5

STUDIES IN THE SCRIPTURES

"Search the Scriptures" John 5: 39

Copyright in all English-speaking Countries.

Editor: Arthur W. Pink, 15 Hurlstone Avenue, Summer Hill, N.S.W., Australia.
Hon. Agent in U.S.A.: Mr. C. S. Pressel, 559 Dupont Avenue, York, Penna.

FREE TO ALL WHO WILL READ IT

THE IMPORTANCE OF PRAYER.

"Ye have not, because ye ask not" (James 4:2).

While it is true that many Arminians have an erroneous conception of the design of prayer, supposing that it may even change God's purpose, and imagining that God's plans are regulated and His policy shaped by the supplications of His people, it is also true that not a few Calvinists have swung to the opposite extreme. They dwell so much on the invincibility of God's decrees, and the certainty of them being worked out, that some appear to regard it as a matter of little moment whether they pray or not. At any rate, there are certain Scriptures on the necessity, the importance, and the value of prayer, that seem to have little weight with them. We therefore present a number of impressive considerations for the thoughtful perusal of the Christian reader:—

First, the *importance* of prayer may be seen from the place which it had in the earthly life of the Lord Jesus. Nothing is clearer from the Gospel records than that Christ was a man of prayer, that He spent much of His time and strength in this holy exercise. In Mark 1:35 we read, "And in the morning, rising up a great while before day, He went out, and departed into a solitary place, and there prayed." How this should rebuke *our* prayerlessness! In Luke 6:12 we are told, "And it came to pass in those days, that He went out into a mountain to pray, and continued all night in prayer to God." How this shows us the need for spending *much time* on our knees! "Who in the days of His flesh, when He had offered up prayers and supplications with *strong crying and tears* unto Him that was able to save Him from death" (Heb. 5:7) What light this throws on the praying of the Saviour: no formal, mechanical petitions were His! And He has left us an example that we should "follow His steps"!

Second, the *importance* of prayer may be seen by the place which it now has in Christ's session at God's right hand. His praying did not cease when He left this earth: the work of intercession is that in which He is now principally engaged—see Rom. 8:34 and Heb. 7:25. Says Dr. Torrey, "I know of nothing that has so impressed me with a sense of the importance of praying at all seasons, being much and constantly in prayer, as the thought that that is the principal occupation at present of my risen Lord. I want to have fellowship with Him, and to that end I have asked the Father that whatever else He may make me, to make me at all events an intercessor, to make me a man who knows how to pray, and who spends much time in prayer." There are few things more calculated to impress Christians with the deep importance of praying than the consideration and realisation that *this* is the principal occupation of their risen Lord.

Third, the *importance* of prayer may be seen by the place which it held in the lives of the Apostles. None believed more strongly in the sovereignty of God and the fixity of His decrees than did Paul, yet so far was this from rendering him careless or lethargic about prayer that, with the exception of his Lord, he was

(Concluded on page 96.)

IMPORTANT NOTICES

Back numbers of each year of the magazine are yet obtainable at 5/- (1.25) per year. Bound at 7/6 (1.75) post paid. They will soon be out of print. Those in U.S.A. wanting them, please purchase from Mr. Pressel (see front cover page).

Advise promptly of change of address.

This Magazine is published as a work of faith and labour of love. The Editor gladly gives his services. It is freely sent to all who will read it. No charge is made for it.

Christians who feel definitely led to do so, may have fellowship with us in this Ministry. Send only *Inter-National M.O.*

CONTENTS.

	Page.
Hebrews	98
Gleanings in Exodus	104
Parables of Matt. 13	110
Life Out of Death	115

THE EPISTLE TO THE HEBREWS.

5. Christ Superior to Angels: 1:7-9.

The verses which are now to be before us continue the passage begun in our last article. As a distinctive section of the Epistle this second division commences at 1:4 and runs to the end of the second chapter. Its theme is the immeasurable superiority of Christ over the angels. But though the boundaries of this section are clearly defined, yet is it intimately related to the one that precedes. The first three verses of chapter one contain a summary of that which is afterwards developed at length in the Epistle, and, really, 1:4-14 is a setting forth of the proofs for the various affirmations made in vv. 2, 3. First, in v. 2, the One whom the Jewish nation had despised and rejected is said to be "Son," and in v. 5 we are shown that He against whom the kings of the earth did set themselves and the rulers take counsel together, is addressed by Jehovah Himself as "Thou art My Son." Second, in v. 2 the One who had been crucified by wicked hands is said to be "the Heir of all things," and in v. 6 proof of this is given: God affirmed that He is the "Firstborn"—the two titles being practically synonymous in their force.

Thus it will be seen that the method followed here by the Holy Spirit, was in moving the apostle to first make seven affirmations concerning the exalted dignity and dominion of Christ, and then to confirm them from the Scriptures. The proofs are all drawn from the Old Testament. From it He proceeds to show that the Messiah *was to be* a person superior to the angels. Psalm 2 should have led the Jews to *expect* "the Son" and Psalm 97:7 ought to have taught them that the promised Messiah was to receive the adoration of all the celestial hierarchies. In vv. 5, 6 the Spirit has established the superiority of Christ both in name and dignity; in the verses which follow He shows the inferiority of the angels in nature and rank.

"And of the angels He saith, Who maketh His angels spirits" (v. 7). This is a quotation from Psalm 104, the opening verses of which ascribe praise unto Jehovah as Creator and Governor of the universe. Its second and third verses apparently relate to the intermediary heavens, and the fourth verse to their inhabitants; verse five and onwards treats of the earth and its earliest history. The fact that the earth is mentioned right after the angels suggests that they are there viewed as connected with mundane affairs, as the servants God employs in regulating its concerns.

The Spirit's purpose in quoting this verse in Heb. 1 is evident: it was to point a contrast between the *natures* of the angels and the Son: they were "made"—created; He is uncreated. Not only were the angels created, but they were created by Christ Himself—"*Who* maketh" which looks back to the last clause of v. 2, "He (The Son) made the worlds:" it is the making of the worlds that Psalm 104 speaks of. Moreover, they are here termed not merely "the angels," but "*His* angels!" They are but "spirits," He is "God;" they are "His ministers." He is their Head (Col. 2:10).

"Who maketh His angels spirits." The Hebrew word for "spirits" in Psalm 104:4 and the Greek word rendered "spirits" in Heb. 1:7 has both a primary and secondary meaning, namely, spirits and "winds." It would seem from the words which follow "and His ministers a flame of fire"—that God is not only defining the nature of these celestial creatures, but is also describing their qualities and activities. Thus we are inclined to regard the words before us as having a double force. A threefold reason may be suggested why the angels are likened unto "winds." First, their power to render themselves invisible. The wind is one of the very few things in the natural world which is unseen by the eyes of man; so the angels are one of the very few classes of God's creatures that are capable of passing beyond the purview of man's senses. Second, because of their great power. Like as the wind when commissioned by God, so the angels are able to sweep everything before them (2 Kings 19:35). Third, because of the rapid speed at which they travel. If the reader will ponder carefully Dan. 10:21, 23, he will find that during the brief moments the prophet was engaged in prayer, an angel from the highest heaven reached him here on earth! Other analogies will be suggested by prayerful meditation.

"And His ministers a flame of fire" (v.7). Here, as always in Scripture, "fire" speaks of Divine judgment, and the sentence as a whole informs us that the angels are the executioners of God's wrath. A number of passages supply us with solemn illustrations of this fact. In Gen. 19:13 we read that the two angels said to Lot concerning Sodom, "*We* will destroy this place, because the cry of them is waxen great before the face of the Lord: and the Lord hath sent *us* to destroy it." Referring to God's judgments which fell upon Egypt we are told, "He cast upon them the fierceness of His anger, wrath and indignation, and trouble, *by* sending evil angels" (Psa. 78:48), by which we do not understand fallen angels, but "angels of evil," i.e. angels of judgment—compare the word "evil" in Isa. 45:7, where it is contrasted *not* with "good" but "peace." Again, in Matt. 13:41:42 we read, "The Son of man shall send forth His angels, and they shall gather out of His kingdom all things that offend, and them which do iniquity; and shall *cast* them into a furnace of fire; there shall be wailing and gnashing of teeth." Does not this passage throw light on Rev. 20:15?—"And whosoever was not found written in the book of life was *cast* into the lake of fire"—by whom, if not the angels, the executioners of God's wrath!

"And His ministers a flame of fire." Doubtless these words refer also to the brilliant brightness and terrifying appearance of the angels, when manifested in their native form to mortal eyes. A number of scriptures confirm this. Note how when Baalam saw the angel of the Lord that he "fell flat on his face" (Num. 22:31). Note how it is said of the angel who rolled back the stone of the Saviour's sepulchre that "his countenance was like lightning," and that "for fear of him the keepers did shake and become as dead men" (Matt. 21:3:4). This accounts for the "fear not" with which angels so frequently addressed different ones before whom they appeared on an errand of mercy: see Matt. 28:5; Luke 1:30; 2:10. Note how in proof the angels are "a flame of fire," we are told that when the angel of the Lord came to Peter, "*a light shined* in prison" (Acts 12:7)! Yea, so resplendent is an angel's brightness when manifested to men, that the apostle John fell at the feet of one to worship (Rev. 19:10)—evidently mistaking him for the Lord Himself, as He had appeared on the mount of transfiguration.

"But unto the Son He saith, Thy throne, O God is forever and ever" (v. 8). Here the Holy Spirit quotes from still another Psalm, the 45th, to prove the superiority of Israel's Messiah over the angels. How blessed and marked is the contrast presented! Here we listen to the Father addressing His incarnate Son, owning Him as "God." "Unto the Son He *saith*," that others might hear and know it. "Thy throne, O God." How sharp is the antithesis! How immeasurable the gulf which separates between creature and Creator! The angels are but "spirits," the Son is "God." They are but "ministers," His is the "throne." They are but "a flame of fire," the executioners of judgment, He the One who commands and commissions them.

"But unto the Son He saith, Thy throne, O God." This supplies us with one of the most emphatic and unequivocal proofs of the Deity of Christ to be found in the Scriptures. It is the Father Himself testifying to the Godhead of Him who was despised and rejected of men. And how fittingly is this quotation from Psalm 45 introduced at the point it is in Heb. 1. In v. 6 we are told that all the angels of God have received command to "worship" the Mediator, now we are shown the *propriety* of them so doing—He is "God!" They must render Divine honours to Him because of His very nature. Thus we may admire, once more, the perfect *order* of Scripture.

"But unto the Son, He saith, Thy throne O God is forever and ever." Difficulty has been experienced by some concerning the identity of the "throne" here mentioned. It is clear from what precedes and also from what follows in v. 9.—"Thy God," that the Son is here addressed in His mediatorial character. But is it not also clear from 1 Cor. 15:24-28 that there will be a time when His mediatorial kingdom will come to an end? Certainly not.

Whatever the passage in 1 Cor. 15 may or may not teach, it certainly does not contradict other portions of Gods Word. Again and again the Scriptures affirm the *endlessness* of Christs mediatorial kingdom: see Isa. 9:7; Dan. 7:13, 14; Luke 1:33; etc. Even on the new earth we read of "The *throne* of God *and* of the Lamb" (Rev. 22:1)!

If then it is not the mediatorial kingdom which Christ shall deliver up to the Father, *what* is it? We answer, His *millenial* one, His kingdom on *this* earth. In Luke 19:12 (the Gospel which, distinctively, sets forth His perfect humanity) Christ speaks of Himself as a "Nobleman" going into a far country to "receive for Himself a *kingdom* and to return," after which He added," when He was returned, having received the kingdom," etc. (v. 15). It is to this Matt. 25:31 refers, "When the Son of man shall come in His glory, and all the holy angels with Him, then shall He sit upon the throne of *His* glory." As in the days of His first advent, the second Person of the Trinity (incarnate) was more dishonoured than the Father or the Spirit, so, following His second advent He shall, for a season, be more honoured than They. Following the millennium, He shall, still in His character as "Son of man" (see John 5:27) "execute judgment," i.e., on His enemies. Then, having put down (by power, *not* having reconciled by grace) all opposing forces, He shall "*deliver up* the kingdom to. God" (1 Cor. 15:24)—observe that it is *not* "taken from" Him! i.e. the millennial kingdom.

That it is *not* the mediatorial kingdom which Christ shall deliver up to the Father is clear from 1 Cor. 15:28, where we are expressly told "then shall the Son also Himself be subject unto Him." As the Godman, the Mediator, He will be officially subservient to the Father. This should be evident. Throughout eternity the mediation of Christ will be needed to preserve fellowship between the Creator and the creature, the Infinite and the finite; hence five times over (the number of *grace*) in Holy Writ occur the words, "Thou art a Priest forever after the order of Melkizedek." But in His essential Being the Son will *not* be in subjection to His Father, as is clear from John 17:5.

Thus we trust it has been made clear that whereas the Messianic kingdom of the Son will be but temporal, His Mediatorial kingdom will be eternal. His kingdom on this earth will continue only for a thousand years, but His kingdom on the new earth will last forever. Blessed is it to observe that, even as Mediator, Christ is thus owned by the Father "Thy throne, *O God,* is forever and ever." How far above the angels that puts Him!

"A sceptre of righteousness is the sceptre of Thy kingdom" (v. 8). The apostle is still quoting from the 45th Psalm, and continuing to advance proofs of the proposition laid down in 1:4. There is no difficulty in perceiving how the sentence here cited contributes to his argument. The "sceptre" is the badge of royalty and the emblem of authority. An illustration of this is furnished in the book of Esther. When Ahasuerus would give an evidence of his authoritative favour unto Esther, he held out his sceptre to her (see Esther 5:2; 8:4). So here the "sceptre" is the emblem of royal power. "The Son is the King; the highest dignity belonging to the angels is that they hold the first rank among His subjects (Dr. J. Brown). The suffering Saviour is now the supreme Sovereign; the mighty angels are His servants.

"A sceptre *of righteousness* is the sceptre of Thy kingdom." This is very blessed. The sceptre of Christ's kingdom will be one not merely of power, arbitarily exercised, but a "righteous" one. "The Greek word joined by the apostle to the sceptre signifieth rectitude, straightness, evenness; it is opposed to wickedness, roughness, unevenness. So doeth the Hebrew word also signify; it is fitly applied to a sceptre, which useth to be straight and upright, not crooked, not inclining this way or that way; so as that which is set out by a sceptre, namely, government, is hereby implied to be right and upright, just and equal, not partially inclining to either side" (Dr. Gouge).

Of old the Triune God declared, "He that ruleth over men must be just, ruling in the fear of God" (2 Sam. 23:3). This has never yet been perfectly exemplified on earth, but ere long it will be. When the Lord Jesus shall return to Jerusalem and there establish His throne, He will order all the affairs of His kingdom with impartial equity, favouring neither the classes nor the masses. As the Anti-type of Melchizedek, He will be both "King of righteousness" and "King of peace" (Heb. 7:2). These are the two qualities which will characterise His reign. "Of the increase of His government and peace there shall be no end, upon the throne of David and upon His Kingdom, to order it and to establish it with judgment and with justice from henceforth even forever." Then will be fulfilled that ancient oracle. "Behold the days come, saith the Lord that

I will raise unto David a *righteous* Branch, and a king shall reign and prosper, and shall execute judgment and justice in the earth." (Jer. 23:5). The rewards He will bestow, the judgments He will execute, will be administered impartially. But let it not be forgotten that this is equally true of His government even now, though faith alone perceives it; in all dispensations it remains that "justice and judgment are the habitation of Thy Throne" (Psa. 89:14).

"Thou hast loved righteousness, and hated iniquity" (v. 9). The past tense of the verbs is to be carefully observed. It is still the Father addressing His Son, owning on high the moral perfections He had manifested here upon earth. The reference is to the Lord Jesus in the days of His humiliation. The words before us furnish a brief but blessed description both of His character and conduct. First, He loved righteousness. "Righteousness" signifies the doing of that which is right. The unerring standard is the revealed will of God. From that standard the incarnate Son never deviated. As a Boy of twelve He said, "Wist ye not that I must be about My Father's business?" (Luke 2:49—perform His pleasure, respond to His wishes. When replying to John's demur against baptizing Him, He replied, "Suffer it to be so now: for thus it becometh us to fulfil all righteousness" (Matt. 3:15). When tempted by the Devil to follow a course of selfwill, He answered, "It is written, Man shall not live by bread alone, but by every word that proceedeth out of the mouth of God" (Matt. 4:4). So it was all through: He "became *obedient* unto death, even the death of the cross" (Phil. 2:8).

"Thou has loved righteousness." This is much more than *doing* righteousness. These words reveal to us the spring of all Christ's actions, even devotedness and affection unto the Father. "I *delight* to do Thy will, O God" (Psa. 40:8), was the confession of the perfect One. "O how love I Thy law! it is My meditation all the day" (Psa. 119:97), revealed His attitude toward the precepts and commandments of Holy Writ. Herein we perceive His uniqueness. How often *our* obedience is a reluctant one! How often God's will crosses ours; and when our response is an obedient one, frequently it is joyless and unwilling. Different far was it with the Lord Jesus. He not only performed righteousness, but "loved" it. He could say, "Thy law is within My *heart*" (Psa. 40:8)—the seat of the affections. When a sinful creature is said to have God's law in his heart it is because He has *written* it there (see Heb. 8:10).

Because He loved righteousness, Christ "hated iniquity." The two things are inseparable: the one cannot exist without the other (Amos 5:5). Where there is true love for God, there is also abhorrence of sin. Illustrations of the Saviour's hatred of iniquity are found in His action at the close of the Temptation and in His cleansing of the Temple. Observe how, after meeting the vile solicitations of the Devil with the repeated "it is written," He, with holy abhorrence said, "Get thee hence, Satan" (Matt. 4:10). See Him, as the Vindicator of His Father's house, driving before Him its profane traffickers and crying, "Make not My Father's house an house of merchandise" (John 2:16). What must it have meant for One who thus loved righteousness and hated iniquity to tabernacle for thirty-three years in such a world as this! And what must it have meant for such an One to be "numbered with the transgressors" and "made sin" for His people!

"Thou hast loved righteousness and hated iniquity." This is true of Him still, for He changes not. "He that hath My commandments, he it is that loveth Me: and he that loveth Me shall be loved of My Father, and I will *love him*, and will manifest Myself to him" (John 14:21). So He still "hates": "So hast thou also them that hold the doctrine of the Nicolaitans which thing *I hate*" (Rev. 2:15). To what extent do these two things characterise you and me, dear reader? To the extent that we are really walking with Christ; no more, no less. The more we enjoy fellowship with Him, the more we are conformed to His image, the more shall *we* love the things He loves, and hate the things He hates.

"Therefore, God, Thy God, hath anointed Thee with the oil of gladness" (v. 9). The Spirit is still quoting from the 45th Psalm. The enemies of God's truth would discover here a "flat contradiction." In v. 8 the One spoken to is hailed as "God," on the throne. But here in v. 9 He is addressed as an inferior, "*Thy* God hath anointed Thee." How could the same person be both supreme and subordinate? If He Himself had a God, how could He at the same time be God? No wonder Divine things are "foolishness to the natural man!" Yet is the enigma easily explained, the seeming contradiction readily harmonised. The Mediator was, in His own person, both Creator and creature,

God and man. Once we see it is *as* Mediator, as the God-man, that Christ is here spoken to, all difficulty vanishes. It is this which supplies the key to the whole passage. Much in Heb. 1 cannot be understood unless it be seen that the Holy Spirit is there speaking not of the essential glories of Christ, but of His mediatorial dignities and honours.

"Therefore, God, Thy God, hath anointed Thee." Concerning this Dr. Gouge has well said, "Christ is God-man, God may be said to be His God three ways: 1. As Christ's human nature was created of God, and preserved by Him like other creatures. 2. As Christ was mediator, he is deputed and sent of God (John 3:34), and he subjected himself to God and set himself to do the will of God, and such works as God appointed him to do (John 4:34; 9:4). In these respects also God is his God. 3. As Christ, God-man, was given by God to be an head to a mystical body, which is the church (Eph. 1:22, 23); God, therefore, entered into covenant with him in the behalf of that body (Isa. 42:6; 49:8). Thus he is called the messenger (Mal. 3:1) and the mediator of the covenant (Heb. 8:6). Now, God is in an especial manner their God, with whom he doth enter into covenant; as he said unto Abraham, 'I will establish my covenant between me and thee,' etc., 'to be a God unto thee' (Gen. 17:7). As God made a covenant with Abraham and his seed, so also with Christ and His seed, which are all the elect of God. This is the 'seed' mentioned in Isa. 53:10. So by special relation between God and Christ, God is his God in covenant with him. God also is, in especial manner, the God of the elect through Christ."

"Therefore, God, Thy God, hath anointed Thee." While here on earth the Mediator owned that God *was* His God. He lived by His Word, He was subject to His will, He was entirely dependent on Him. "I will put My trust in Him" was His avowal (Heb. 2:13); yea, did He not declare, "I was cast upon Thee from the womb: Thou art My God from My mother's belly" (Psa. 22:10)! Many similar utterances of His are recorded in the Psalms. On the cross He owned His subjection, crying, "My God, why hast Thou forsaken Me?" Even after His resurrection we hear Him saying, "I ascend unto My Father and to your Father; and *My God*, and your God" (John 20:17). So now: though seated at the right hand of the Majesty on high, He is there making "intercession." So when He returns to this earth in glory, He will "ask" for the inheritance (Psa. 2:8). How this brings out the truth of His humanity, real Man, though true God. Mysterious, wondrous, blessed Person; upholding all things by the Word of His own power, yet in the place of intercession; Himself the "Mighty God" (Isa. 9:6), yet owning God as *His* God!

"Thy God hath anointed Thee with the oil of gladness." There is a plain reference here to the ancient method, instituted by God, whereby the kings of Israel were established in their office. Their coronation was denoted by the pouring of oil upon their heads: see 1 Sam. 10:1; 16:13; 1 Kings 1:39, etc. It was in allusion to this the kings were styled "anointed" (2 Sam. 19:21) and "the anointed of the Lord" (Lam. 4:20). "The apostle and Psalmist are both speaking of the Messiah as a prince, and their sentiment is 'God, even Thy God, hath raised Thee to a kingdom far more replete with enjoyment than that ever conferred on any other ruler. He has given Thee a kingdom which, for extent and duration, and multitude and magnitude of blessings as far exceeds any kingdom ever bestowed on man or angels as the heaven is above the earth'" (J. Brown).

Though we are assured that this anointing of Christ with the "oil of gladness" (following the mention of His "sceptre" and "kingdom" in v. 8) is a reference to His investiture on High with royal honours—the "blessing of the Lord" which the King of glory received at the time of His ascension (Psa. 24:5, and note carefully the whole Psalm)—yet we do not think this exhausts its scope. In addition, we believe there is also a reference to His being honoured as our great High Priest, for it is written, "He shall be a Priest upon His throne" (Zech. 6:13). Thus there is also a manifest allusion in our verse to what is recorded in Psa. 133. There we read, "Behold, how good and how pleasant it is for brethren to dwell together in unity! It is like the precious ointment upon the head, that ran down upon the beard, Aaron's beard: that went down to the skirts of his garments—cf. Ex. 30:25, 30. This is most precious, though its beauty is rarely perceived. How few see in these verses of Psa. 133 anything more than a word expressing the desirability and blessedness of saints on earth dwelling together in concord. But is *this* all the Psalm teaches? We trow not. What then is the analogy pointed between what is said in v. 1 and v. 2?

What is the meaning of "how good and how pleasant it is for brethren to dwell together in unity. *It is like* the precious ointment upon the head," etc?

What resemblance is there between brethren dwelling together in unity and the precious anointing-ointment which ran down from Aaron's head to the skirts of his garments? It seems strange that so many should have missed this point. As the high priest of Israel, Aaron foreshadowed our great High Priest. The anointing of his "head" prefigured the anointing of our exalted Head. The running down of the fragrant ungent even to the skirts of Aaron's garments, adumbrated the glorious fact that those who are members of the body of Christ partake of His sweet savor before God. The analogy drawn in Psa. 133 is obvious: the dwelling together of brethren in unity is "good and pleasant" not simply for the mere sake of preserving peace among them, but because it illustrates the spiritual and mystical union existing between Christ and His people. Our dwelling together in unity is "good and pleasant" not only, nor primarily, for our own well-being, but because it gives an outward manifestation, a concrete example of that invisible and Divine *oneness* which exists between the Head and the members of His body.

"Anointed Thee with the oil of gladness." As ever in the Old Testament, the "oil" was an emblem of the Spirit, and the anointing both of Aaron and of David were typifications of the enduement of Christ with the Holy Spirit. But the reference here is not (as some of the commentators suppose) to the coming of the Spirit upon Christ at the time of His baptism. This should be apparent from the structure of v. 9. The words "Thou hast loved righteousness and hated iniquity" look back to the earthly life of the Lord Jesus, as the past tense of the verbs intimate; the *"therefore*, God, even Thy God, hath anointed Thee," shows that this was the reward for His perfect work, the honouring of the humbled One. It is closely parallel with what we are told in Acts 2:36, "God hath made that same Jesus, whom ye have crucified, both Lord and Christ;" and Acts 5:31, "Him hath God exalted with His right hand to be a Prince and a Saviour."

"Anointed Thee with the oil of gladness" refers, we believe, to the Holy Spirit's being made officially subordinate to the Mediator. Just as the incarnate Son was subject to the Father, so is the Spirit now subject to Christ. Just as the Saviour when here glorified not Himself, but the Father, so the Spirit is here to glorify Christ (John 16:14). There are several scriptures which plainly teach the present official subordination of the Spirit to Christ: "But when the Comforter is come, whom *I will send* unto you from the Father" (John 15:26). That which took place on the day of Pentecost manifested the same fact: as His forerunner announced, "I indeed baptize with water, but *He* (Christ) shall baptize you with the Holy Spirit" (Mark 1:8). In Rev. 3:1 the Lord Jesus is referred to as "He that *hath* the seven Spirits of God," i.e. the Holy Spirit in the fulness of His perfections and the plentitude of His operations; "hath" to minister the Spirit unto His people. It is further proof that the suffering Saviour has been exalted to the place of supreme Sovereignty.

"Above Thy fellows." Opinion is divided among the commentators as to whether the reference be to angels or to Christians. Both the Hebrew word in Psa. 45:7 and the Greek word here signify "such as partake of one and the same condition." If it be borne in mind that the Holy Spirit is speaking here of Christ in His Mediatorial character, we are less likely to be stumbled by the thought of angels being termed His "fellows."

"They are styled His fellows in regard of that low degree whereunto the Son of God, Creator of all things, humbled Himself by assuming a creature nature; so that as He was a creature (Man), angels are His fellows" (Dr. Gouge). Nor must we overlook the fact that the chief design of the whole of this passage is to evidence the Mediator's superiority over the angels.

As already pointed out, the central thought of v. 9 is the investiture of Christ with *royal* honours, following right after the mention of His "sceptre" and "kingdom" in v. 8. Angels are also **rulers**; great powers are delegated to them; much of the administration of God's government is committed into their hands. But the Man Christ Jesus has been exalted high above them in this respect too. A close parallel is found in Col. 1:18, where it is said of the Lord Jesus, "that in all things He might have the pre-eminence." It is important to note that in the immediate context there, *angels* are mentioned in connection with "thrones, dominions principalities and powers" (v. 16)! But Christ has been given a "sceptre" and royal honours which exalt Him high above them all.

But what has been said above does not exhaust the scope of these closing words of Heb. 1:9. As is so often the case in Scripture (evidencing the exhaustless fulness of its words) there is at least a *double* reference in the term "fellows;" first to the angels, second to Christians—thus supplying a *link* with v. 14, where the "heirs of salvation" are more directly in view. That the term "fellows" applies also to believers is clear from Heb. 3:14 where "metochos" is specifically used of them: "For we are made *partakers* (fellows) of Christ," if we hold the beginning of our confidence steadfast unto the end."

Though the wondrous grace of God has so united His people to His beloved Son that "he that is joined unto the Lord is one spirit" (1 Cor. 6:17), yet we must carefully bear in mind that He is "the Firstborn (Chief) among many brethren" (Rom. 8:29). Though members of His body, He is nevertheless the Head. Though joint-heirs with Him, He is our Lord! So, too, though Christians have been "anointed" with the Spirit (1 John 2:20; 27), yet our blessed Redeemer has been "anointed with the oil of gladness *above* His fellows." The Spirit is now subject to His administration; not so to ours. Christ is the one who is "glorified," the Spirit is the Agent, we the vessels through which He works. Thus in *all* things Christ *has* "the pre-eminence."

It is indeed striking to see how much was included in that ancient oracle concerning the Messiah which the Spirit here quoted from Psa. 45. Let us attempt to summarise the content of that remarkable prophecy. First, it establishes His Deity, for the Father Himself owns Him as "God." Second, it shows us the exalted position He now occupies: He is on the throne, and there for ever. Third, it makes mention of His Kingship, the royal "sceptre" being weilded by Him. Fourth, it tells of the impartiality of His government and the excellency of His rule: His sceptre is a "righteous" one. Fifth, it takes us back to the days of His flesh and makes known the perfections of His character and conduct here on earth: He "loved righteousness and hated iniquity." Sixth, it reveals the place which He took when He made Himself of no reputation, as Man in subjection to God: "Thy God." Seventh, it announces the reward He received for such condescension and grace: "*Therefore*. . . . God hath anointed Thee." Eighth, it affirms He has the pre-eminence in all things, for He has been anointed with the oil of gladness "*above* His fellows." May the Spirit of God stir us up to search more prayerfully and diligently the volume of that Book in which it is written of Him.

—*Arthur W. Pink.*

GLEANINGS IN EXODUS.

53. *The Golden Altar, Ex.* 30:1-10.

There were two altars connected with the Tabernacle. Both were made of wood, but covered with a different metal: the one with brass, and so named after it "the brazen altar" (Ex. 38:30); the other with gold, and so called "the golden altar" (Ex. 39:38). The one was placed outside the building in the court, just before the entrance; the other was inside the holy place, and stood before the vail. These altars were closely connected, but served different uses. Their characteristic names point out their distinctive designs: the former being designated "the altar of burnt offering" (40:6), and was the place of sacrifice; the latter was termed "the altar of incense" (30:27), and was the place of worship. Both altars were needed to set forth our one and only Altar, of whom it is written, "we have an Altar, whereof they have no right to eat which serve the tabernacle" (Heb. 13:10).

Some have wondered why the incense altar was not mentioned in Ex. 25 and 26, where five of the other pieces of the Tabernacle's furniture are referred to, and where the holy place in which it stood is described. Three reasons may be suggested for this. First, the omission of the golden altar from those earlier chapters may have been because of what was typically set forth by the various holy vessels. Those enumerated in Ex. 25 and 26 speak of God in Christ coming out to His people, displaying the riches of His grace; whereas the two which are before us in Ex. 30 tell of the provisions God has made for us to go in to Him, expressing the fullness of His love. Beautifully has this been expounded by another:

"Why, then, does the Lord, when giving directions about the furniture of the 'holy place' omit the altar of incense, and pass out to the brazen altar which stood at the door of the Tabernacle? The reason I believe is simply this: He first described the mode in which He would manifest

Himself to man, and then He described the mode of man's approach to Him. He took His seat upon the throne as 'The Lord of all the earth' (Josh. 3:13). The beams of His glory were hidden behind the vail—type of Christ's flesh (Heb. 10:20); but there was the manifestation of Himself in connection with man, as in 'the pure table' and by the light and power of the Holy Ghost, as in the candlestick. Then we have the manifested character of Christ as a man down here on this earth, as seen in the curtains and coverings of the tabernacle. And, finally, we have the brazen altar as the grand exhibition of the meeting place between a holy God and a sinner. This conducts us as it were, to the extreme point, from which we return, in company with Aaron and his sons, back to the holy place, the ordinary priestly position, where stood the golden altar of incense. Thus the order is strikingly beautiful" (C.H.M.).

A second reason may be suggested as to why the description of the golden altar and the laver should have been postponed until the 30th chapter of Exodus was reached. This is plainly intimated in Ex. 28 and 29, where we have the appointment, investiture and consecration of the priesthood. Thus, the golden altar was not mentioned until there was a priest to burn incense thereon! It was at the laver the priests washed, and it was at the golden altar they ministered; there, too, it was where Aaron presented himself before Jehovah. Thus the contents of chapters 28 and 29 were needed to bring before us the priestly family before we learn of the two holy vessels with which they were more directly associated. So, too, experimentally, *we* apprehend that of which the preceding chapters speak, before we value that which chapter 30 sets forth.

A third reason lies in the application of the teaching of the holy vessels to believers. The primary application of each of them is to Christ Himself, but there is a secondary application to His people. As we shall yet seek to show, one of the fundamental things prefigured by the golden altar is *worship*, and as this is the highest exercise of our priestly privileges, suitably was this the last piece of furniture met with as the sons of Aaron approached unto Jehovah.

"Just as the golden altar was the last object to be reached in the journey from the gate to the vail which hid the mercy-seat from view, just so is *worship* the highest state to be reached on earth and the object for which all other things are preparations. The Father seeks worshippers (John 4:23), and this it was that led the Lord to go through Samaria to meet that sinner, to turn her heart from her sins, by filling it with the satisfying portion of grace, that she might meet the desires of Divine love and give that praise, that worship, that only a sinner (a cleansed sinner) can give. And this it was that led the Lord to take that larger journey from the heaven of light and peace down to the cross of suffering and shame. He sought sinners, He seeketh them still; seeketh them that, having tasted as no angel can possibly taste, the love of God, they might then from a heart overflowing with the consciousness of its indebtedness to the Saviour, and the appreciation of His own excellence, pour forth the fragrant incense of praise" (C. H. Bright).

1. Its Significance.

"And thou shalt make an altar to burn incense upon" (v. 1). It is striking to note that before anything is said about the materials of which the altar was made, its size and shape, or the position it was to occupy, we are first told of the purpose for which it was to be used. It is this which places in our hands a sure key to its spiritual interpretation. Attention is directed straight to the altar and the incense which was burned thereon. The altar speaks of Christ Himself, and the incense was a figure both of His intercession and the praises which He presents to God.

The fact that the golden altar comes before us in Exodus immediately after the investiture and consecration of Aaron and his sons, at once tells us that what is here portrayed is the ministrations of our great High Priest in the heavenly sanctuary. Though He is now seated at the right hand of the Majesty on high, yet He is not inactive. He is constantly engaged before God on behalf of His redeemed, presenting to the Father—in the sweet fragrance of His own perfections—both the petitions and worship of His people. The *position* occupied by the golden altar confirms this. It was not situated in the outer court —all connected with which adumbrated the manifestation of Christ here on earth; but in the holy place, which tells of Christ having gone in to appear before God on behalf of His people. Further confirmation that this is the central thought in our present type is supplied in the words at the close of v. 3: "And thou shalt make unto it a crown of gold round about." Thus, it is Christ in heaven, not on earth, "crowned with glory and honour" (Heb. 2:9).

Unutterably solemn is it to contemplate Christ at the brazen altar there made sin for us, suffering, enduring judgment, bowing His head beneath the awful storm of God's wrath. But unspeakably blessed is it to behold Him at the golden altar, risen from the grave, alive for evermore, maintaining the interests of His people before God's throne, presenting them in all His own excellency and preciousness. "If when we were enemies we were reconciled to God by the death of His Son, much more, being reconciled, we shall be saved by His life" (Rom. 5:10). This is the point which the Spirit of God reserves for the climax in His unanswerable reply to the challenge "Who shall lay anything to the charge of God's elect?" it is God that justifieth. Who is he that condemneth? it is Christ that died, yea rather, that is risen again, who is even at the right hand of God, who also maketh intercession for us" (Rom. 8:33, 34).

"Let my prayer be set forth before Thee as incense; and the lifting up of mine hands as the evening sacrifice" (Psa. 141:2). This gives us the emblematical meaning of "incense." So again in Rev. 5:8 we read, "having every one of them harps, and golden vails full of incense, which are the prayers of saints." The incense burned upon the golden altar, then, foreshadowed Christ in heaven, praying for His people. As we read in Heb. 7:25, "Wherefore He is able also to save them to the uttermost that come unto God by Him, seeing He ever liveth to make intercession for them." Christ's intercession is not for the purpose of completing the believer's justification, for that would show His sacrifice of the cross was insufficient; by that one offering He has perfected us forever (Heb. 10:14); rather does it crown it with glory and honour. The precious incense of our Lord's priestly intercession *maintains* us (through our wilderness journey) in the place of fullest acceptance as a sweet savor unto God.

A striking typical illustration of the wondrous efficacy of our great High Priest's intercession is furnished in Num. 16. There we see, first, how Korah and his company repudiated Aaron as their high priest, claiming equal nearness to God for all Israel, see v. 3. But a sinful people could have no standing before the Holy One save through the priest who offered the sacrifice. This, the rebellious people were made to feel (v. 35). The "gainsaying of Korah" (Jude 11), then, was the practical denial of Christ's person and sacrificial work. Then, in Num. 16, we also behold how the *grace* of God shone forth: Aaron the high priest was told to "take a censer, and put fire therein from off the altar, and put on incense, and go quickly unto the congregation, and make an atonement for them" (v. 46). Blessed was the sequel: "And he stood between the dead and the living; and the plague was stayed" (v. 48). What a foreshadowing of the mediatorial intercession of Christ, interposing on behalf of His erring people, and that, on the ground of His sacrificial death.

It is a mistake, made by most of the commentators, to limit the "incense" as pointing only to the Saviour's intercession; it includes also His offering of praise to God. Did He not say, "In the midst of the church will I sing *praise* unto Thee" (Heb. 2:12)? So also in Heb. 13:15 we are told, "*By Him*, therefore, let us offer the sacrifice of praise to God continually." He is the One who receives the praises of His people and presents them to God. So again in 1 Peter 2:5 we are told, "Ye also, as living stones, are built up a spiritual house, an holy priesthood, to offer us spiritual sacrifices, acceptable to God by Jesus Christ." Christ is the one who makes our worship acceptable to God. Therefore, the incense has to be burned upon the altar.

2. *Its Composition.*

"And thou shalt make an altar to burn incense upon it: of shittim wood shalt thou make it" (v. 1). This, as we have seen in earlier types, symbolised the perfect humanity of Christ. "This accacia wood, the emblem of the incorruptible and spotless humanity of the Son of God, entered into the composition of the altar of burnt-offering outside in the court, and was covered with brass, enabling it to endure the fire that consumed its victim. The same accacia wood entered into the composition of the table of shewbread; it also entered into the composition of the altar of incense, which was covered and crowned with gold, for no atonement for sin was ever offered or needed at that altar; all *that* was finished. It also entered into the composition of the ark of the covenant within the vail, identifying all these with the person and salvation-work of our Lord Jesus Christ, teaching us that His perfect humanity—made in all things like His brethren, sin excepted—in all the modifications of His covenant engagements and offices of our behalf, whether at His incarnation, His birth, His walk with God on earth, His death on the cross, or after His resurrection, when He was seen of His disciples for forty days, or after His ascension to the right hand of God, where He ever liveth to make intercession for us—was ever one and the same immortalised humanity in the person of our living and glorified Head, Substitute, and Representative" (Mr. Rainsford).

"And thou shalt overlay it with pure gold, the top thereof, and the sides thereof round about, and the horns thereof" (v. 3). This is very lovely, speaking, as it does, of that Divine glory into which the Man Christ Jesus has entered. As the sons of Aaron approached this altar figures of worshipping believers now drawing near to God—they would see nothing but the gold. So it is not a dead Christ on the cross who is the object of our worship, but a living Christ who has been "received up into glory" (1 Tim. 3:16). Therefore are we bidden "if ye then be risen with Christ, seek those things which are above, where Christ sitteth on the right hand of God: Set your affection on things above, not on things on the earth; for ye are dead, and your life is hid with Christ in God" (Col. 3:1-3). As another has said, "God saw only the gold—that which was suited to Him, suited to His own nature. The remembrance of this gives boldness when bowing in His presence. It is indeed a wondrous mercy that Christ is before the eye of God, and before the eye of the worshipper, Himself the meeting-place between God and His people, as well as the foundation of His people's acceptance" (Ed Dennet).

3. Its Dimensions.

"A cubit shall be the length thereof, and a cubit the breadth thereof; foursquare shall it be; and two cubits shall be the height thereof: the horns thereof shall be of the same" (v. 2). The dimensions of the golden altar differed considerably from those of the brazen altar, the latter being five cubits long, five cubits broad, and three cubits high (27:1). Herein we may see the wonderful accuracy of these types and their perfections down to the minutest detail. The brazen altar was much larger than the golden altar. The former foreshadowed the sacrificial death of Christ; the latter, His present ministry in heaven. But does He not now appear before God on behalf of *all* for whom He died? In one sense, yes; in another sense no. Representatively He does, actively He does not. John 11:51, 52 shows that He died for two distinct companies—"that nation (Israel) and the children of God scattered abroad—God's elect among the Gentiles. But at present Christ *is not* interceding for Israel, nor is He presenting their praises before God! It is only on behalf of the Church that He is now actively engaged: Israel will be taken up in the Day to come, and this will be at His return to the earth, as the brazen altar in the outer court denotes. Thus, there is a wonderful propriety in the golden altar, within the holy place, being smaller than the brazen altar.

May not the fact that it was but one cubit in *length* indicate to us that Christ needs not to repeat His plea on our behalf —once is sufficient, for the Father hears Him always (John 11:42). Though He ever liveth, it is not said, "He ever intercedeth." The tense of the verb (in the Greek) implies that Christ prayed but once for Peter in Luke 22:32. The *breadth* being one cubit would point to the "one body" as the *extent* of those for whom He now intercedes—"I pray not for the world" (John 17:9)! The *two* cubits of its height would perhaps denote that Christ presents to God both the praises of His saints which are now in heaven as those yet on earth. Its being "foursquare" tells us that the objects of His intercession are scattered abroad, reaching to the four corners of the earth. Though we may forget to remember His blood-brought ones in far distant places, He does not!

"Foursquare shall it be" (v. 2). In its application to Christ Himself this tells us that His intercession embraces *all* His people, "scattered abroad." In its application to us we find the New Testament equivalent in 1 Tim. 2:1, "I exhort, therefore, that, first of all, supplication, prayers, intercessions, giving of thanks, be made for all men." In Eph. 6:18 we are bidden to make supplication "for *all* saints." How little of this there is to-day! How self-centered we are, how narrow are our hearts! How little *our* "altar" answers to the foursquaredness of the incense altar! May the Lord enlarge our hearts.

4. Its Ornamentation.

"And thou shalt overlay it with pure gold, the top thereof, and the sides thereof round about, and the horns thereof" (v. 3). The "horn" is the symbol of power (Hab. 3:4), so that what we are shown here is Christ's intercessory power with God. A more literal rendering of the Hebrew would be, "Of itself shall be its horns:" all that Christ is in His wondrous person gives Him power with God; blessedly is this seen in John 17.

It will be noted that the number of its "horns" is not given. Many conclude that it had one at each corner, as had the brazen altar (38:2). As there is nothing in Scripture without spiritual significance, even its very omissions manifesting its Divine Authorship, we must enquire, Why has not the Holy Spirit told us there were *four* "horns" here? The answer is not far to seek. Four is the number of the earth, and the golden altar foreshadowed Christ's priestly ministry in Heaven; thus we may see that the *mention* of the "four horns" would have cast a blemish on the perfection of our type.

"And thou shalt make unto it a crown of gold round about" (v. 3). Three of the seven pieces of the tabernacle's furniture had a "crown" upon it. First, the ark of the covenant (25:11), in which were preserved the two tables of stone. This was the crown of the law, which Christ "magnified" and "made honourable" (Isa. 42:21). Second, the table of shewbread (25:24). This was the crown of fellowship: the Christian's highest honour and supremest privilege is to enjoy communion with Him who has been crowned with glory. Or, if we look at it from the dispensational viewpoint, the table with its twelve loaves would speak of Israel in a coming day, restored and in fellowship with Christ—this would be the crown of the kingdom. Here, in connection with the golden altar, it is the crown of the priesthood, and reminds us that Christ, our great High Priest, is seated upon "the Throne of Grace!"

5. *Its Rings and Staves.*

"And two golden rings shalt thou make to it under the crown of it, by the two corners thereof, upon the two sides of it shalt thou make it; and they shall be for places for the staves to bear it withal. And thou shalt make the staves of shittim wood, and overlay them with gold (vv. 4, 5). Thus provision was made for the altar to be carried with them as Israel journeyed from place to place—it was not stationary, so that they had to make pilgrimages to it. Typically, this tells us that God's pilgrims to-day, while they are here below, are enjoying the blessings of Christ's priestly intercession on high. *Two* "rings" are the number of *witness,* and speak of the Holy Spirit who is here to "testify" of Christ (John 15:26); their being of "gold" announces that He is a Divine person. The "staves" of wood, overlaid with gold, intimate that it is the God-man whom the Spirit is here to glorify.

In its practical application to us, the lesson taught by the rings and staves is both searching and blessed. It is only as we maintain our pilgrim character, in separation from that religious world which rejects Christ, that we can really appropriate and enjoy that which the golden-altar prefigured. There is a striking passage in Heb. 13 which speaks in the language of our present type: "Let us go forth therefore unto Him without the camp (man's organised Christianity), bearing His reproach. For here have we (in affections and aim) no continuing city, but (as pilgrims journeying) we seek one to come. By Him (the antitype of the altar) therefore let us offer the sacrifice of praise (the burning of incense) to God continually, that is, fruit of our lips giving thanks to His name" (vv. 13, 15).

6. *Its Use.*

"And Aaron shall burn thereon sweet incense" (v. 7). The altar was used for one thing only. We gather from Lev. 16: 12, 13 and Num. 16: 46 that the fire on which the incense was laid had been taken from off the brazen-altar, where the sin-offering was consumed. There was, therefore, a very intimate connection between the two altars: the activities of the latter being based upon those of the former; in other words, the incense was kindled upon that fire which had first fed upon the sacrifice; thus identifying the priest's service at both altars. This, in figure, tells us that our great High Priest pleads for no blessings which His blood has not purchased, and asks pardon from Divine justice for no sins for which He has not atoned. The measure of the blessings for which He pleads is God's estimate of the life which He gave. Note how in John 17, before He presents a single petition concerning His people, that Christ said, "I have glorified Thee on the earth; I have finished the work which Thou gavest Me to do" (v. 4). *That* was the foundation on which all His pleas were based and urged.

There are other scriptures where the two altars are linked together. As another has said, "Fittingly therefore does the Psalmist in speaking of the house for the lonely sparrow and a nest for the restless swallow, refer to these two altars. 'Yea, the sparrow hath found a house, and the swallow a nest for herself, where she may lay her young, even Thine *altars* O Lord of Hosts, my King and my God' (Psa. 84: 3). Both altars are thus connected together and form the solid and abiding rest for the poor and needy soul.

"Thus too, when Isaiah saw the glory

of the Lord in the temple, and the adoring seraphim with veiled faces celebrating the majesty of the thrice holy triune God, he was overwhelmed with the sense of his own and Israel's uncleanness, until one of those burning ones (suggesting, perhaps, the fire of God as seen in His executors of judgment) flew with a live coal which he had taken from off the altar, and touched his lips, saying, 'Lo, this hath touched thy lips; and thine iniquity is taken away, and thy sin purged' (Isa. 6: 7). The coal of Divine holiness had already consumed the sacrifice and was also consuming the sweet incense. Thus symbolically the prophet's lips were cleansed according to God's estimate of the value of the sacrifice and person of our Lord" (Mr. Ridout).

A most solemn contrast from this is presented in the opening verses of Lev. 10. There we are told, "And Nadab and Abihu, the sons of Aaron, took either of them his censer, and put fire therein, and put incense thereon, and offered strange fire before the Lord, which He commanded them not. And there went out fire from the Lord, and devoured them, and they died before the Lord" (vv. 1, 2), These sons of Aaron were consumed by Divine judgment because they "offered *strange* fire before the Lord," that is, the incense in their censers was not burned on fire taken from off the brazen altar, but was of their own kindling. They had departed from the plain word of Jehovah, who had already instructed them as to the mode of their worship. God was very jealous of His types (compare 2 Kings 5: 26, 27). By their actions Nadab and Abihu were signifying that worship may be offered to God on another foundation than acceptance through a crucified Christ; and for this He slew them.

The incense was to be kept sacredly for tabernacle service and he who manufactured any for his personal or family use had to pay the death-penalty for his presumption (30: 28). None but the priests of the seed of Aaron were allowed to handle it. When king Uzziah attempted to usurp the priest's office and daringly challenged the holy God by presuming to burn incense before Him, his impiety was severely punished—see 2 Chron. 26: 16-21. Even royalty must bow in abasement before Jehovah!

The composition and preparation of the sacred incense are specified in Ex. 30: 34, 35. Upon the nature, costliness, and distinctive typical import of the respective spices we cannot here comment. That which we would specially notice is the three things which are said about the incense as a whole. First, it was, "sweet" (v. 7). Exceedingly fragrant must have been its odour, telling of the acceptability and preciousness of Christ's intercessions and praises before God. Second, it was "pure" (v. 35): unlike ours, nothing whatever of the flesh enters into the priestly ministrations of the Redeemer. Third, it was "most holy" (v. 36): Christ's exercises within the heavenly sanctuary are in all the excellences of His peerless person. "Of each shall there be a like weight" (v. 34) should also be observed: no one grace or attribute predominates in the Lord Jesus, there is a perfect balance between all.

It is striking to see how the lighting of the lamps is here linked with the golden altar: "And Aaron shall burn thereon sweet incense every morning: *when* he dresseth the lamps, he shall burn incense upon it. And *when* Aaron lighteth the lamps at even, he shall burn incense upon it" (vv. 7, 8). The maintenance of the light was inseparably associated with the service of the altar. Typically, this tells us that the gift and ministry of the Holy Spirit (as the Spirit of Christ, Rom. 8: 9) is the consequence of the Saviour's intercession—cf. John 14: 16. In its practical application to believers we may see here a setting forth of the fact that, every fresh kindling or exercise of the Spirit in our hearts, results in new outbursts of praise unto God: our worship is ever in proportion to the manifestation of the Spirit's power.

"He shall burn incense upon it, a *perpetual* incense before the Lord throughout your generations" (v. 8). This is very blessed. The fire upon the altar was always burning and the fragrance from the sweet incense was continually rising. So Christ is ever before God, in all the merits of His person and value of His work, on His people's behalf. One third of our lives is spent in sleep; but He never slumbers: "He *ever* liveth to make intercession for us," and because of this He is "able to save unto the uttermost (to the end of their wilderness journey) them that come unto God by Him" (Heb. 7: 25). Thus the golden-altar is a pledge of our eternal security.

"Ye shall offer no strange incense thereon, nor burnt-sacrifice, nor meat-offering; neither shall ye pour drink-offering thereon" (v. 9). For the Levites to offer these upon *this* altar would be to confound it with the brazen-altar. The same sad mistake is made now when Christians gathered together for worship take their place at the cross, instead of within the rent vail. Instead of being occupied with our sins and Christ's sacrifice for them, we should be contemplating the Lord Jesus Himself as He appears in the presence of God for us; nothing short of this will enable us to occupy our true priestly position and exercise our joyous priestly functions.

"And Aaron shall make an atonement upon the horns of it once in a year with the blood of the sin-offering of atonement: once in the year shall he make atonement upon it" (v. 10). This is most blessed. The congregation of Israel could approach unto God only at the brazen-altar; but Aaron and his sons (figure of Christ and His heavenly people) came to the golden-altar, in the holy place. How this tells us that a position has been secured for us within the heavenly sanctuary in all the value of the sin-offering! This interpretation is confirmed by the fact that there is no mention of the golden-altar in Ezekiel's temple, which typifies Israel's millennial relations to God! But we also need to ponder this tenth verse from the practical viewpoint. Looked at thus its teaching is parallel with that word in Ex. 28: 38, "That Aaron may bear the iniquity of the holy things," cf. Lev. 5: 15. Our prayers are so faulty, our praises so feeble, our worship so far below the level of what it ought to be, that even our "holy things" needed to be cleansed by the blood of atonement. How humbling this is!

7. *Its Coverings.*

"And upon the golden altar they shall spread a cloth of blue, and cover it with a covering of badgers' skins, and shall put to the staves thereof" (Num. 4: 11). How this confirms what has been said above. The golden-altar being wrapped in a "blue" cloth speaks plainly of the present *heavenly* ministry of Christ. But this was not made known to the earthly people, as the *outer* covering of the badgers' skins indicates. May the Lord add His blessing to this meditation.

Arthur W. Pink.

THE PROPHETIC PARABLES OF MATTHEW 13.

The Dragnet.

Matthew 13: 47-50.

"Again the kingdom of heaven is like unto a net, that was cast into the sea, and gathered of every kind." We have previously pointed out that it is of first importance to carefully note the manner and method in which these seven parables are arranged, for their order supplies a key to their interpretation. The first one stands by itself, being distinguished from the other six which follow by the omission of the opening clause "the kingdom of heaven is like unto." The first parable is not a similitude of the kingdom of heaven; the last six are. The first parable treats of a preparatory work, done prior to the introduction of the kingdom of heaven in its present form; that introductory work being the broadcast sowing of the seed, first by the Lord Himself, afterwards by the apostles.

The six parables which follow are plainly divided into two threes. The first three were spoken by the Lord from the ship in the hearing of the multitude by the seaside, and therefore they give us the more public aspect of the kingdom of heaven in its present form—the kingdom of heaven in this world as it is *seen by men*. The last three parables were not spoken to the multitude nor were they uttered by the seashore, but were spoken by the Lord to the disciples only, and that within the house; intimating that they treat of the internal and hidden aspects of the kingdom of heaven, that which is *not* manifested before men in this world. So that the last three parables speak from the standpoint of *God's counsels.*

The first of the last three is the parable of the treasure hid in the field, a man for joy thereof buying the field—principally for the sake of the treasure that was hidden therein. The next parable, that of the pearl, also sought, desired, and purchased by the same man, the merchantman. Those two objects, the treasure and the pearl, intimate that there are *two* elect companies, dear unto God and precious unto His Son, purchased by Him: one an earthly people, the other a heavenly; through whom the wondrous riches of Divine grace and glory will yet be made manifest in the two great divisions of God's dominions—heaven and earth. The earthly people, spoken of under the figure of the treasure, being Israel, the literal Israel; the heavenly people, spoken of under the figure of the pearl, looking forward to the time when the body of Christ will be completed and He shall present to Himself a glorious Church. The order of these two parables, then, is, "to the Jew first and also to the Greek"—the treasure coming before the pearl.

But if these seven parables give us a prophetical outline of the course of Christendom, that is the history of the Christian profession throughout this dispensation, during the time of Christ's absence from the earth, one more parable is needed to complete the picture. The last parable is in one sense an amplification of the sixth. In the sixth parable there is only one man at work, one agent acting—the Merchant-man. He is the one who does all in connection with the pearl. But while it is true the Merchant-man, the Lord Jesus Christ, is *the* principal worker in connection with the gathering out of the saints during this dispensation, in His condescending grace He does not work alone. He has been pleased to call His own saints to have a part with Him in the prosecution of this work, in the accomplishing of God's counsels, in the gathering out of His elect people. Consequently, when we come to this seventh parable, for the first time, the number of the pronoun is changed. Notice this in v. 47: "Again the kingdom of heaven is like unto a net, that was cast into the sea, and gathered of every kind: which, when it was full, *they* drew to shore"—not "he" but "they." That is the first time we have "they" in the parables. Illustrations of what is thereby denoted are found in the Gospels in connection with Christ's miracles.

Take the first one that He performed—the turning of water into wine. This is a sermon in action. His mother came to Him and said, "They have no wine." Their own wine had given out. Now "wine" in Scripture is the symbol of joy—not exclusively, but that is one of its essential significations. "They have no wine." Christ alone can impart real joy to the heart; but in the working of the miracle He used servants. He said *to the servants*, "Fill the waterpots." He said to the servants, "Draw it forth." He said to the servants, Convey it to "the master of the feast." He deigned to use *them*, and in their obedience they became workers together with Him in the performing of that miracle.

Take again the feeding of the multitude. There was the famishing crowd: they had no food. Here was the Lord Jesus Christ. A few loaves and fishes were placed in His hands, and under His miraculous working-power those loaves and fishes were made to feed the hungry multitude. But what was the method that He followed? He did not hand the food *directly* to the crowd; He first gave to the disciples, and they distributed to the multitude. So that (we say it reverently) between the Lord Jesus Christ and the multitudes, and the wine and food, there is need of consecrated servants, to first receive from Him and then to hand out to others. Therefore we may see that if these seven parables furnish an outline of the history of this present dispensation, it is necessary to complete the picture by showing us that the Lord Jesus, in His condescending grace, uses others to the accomplishing of God's purpose and the executing of His counsels.

Now the details of this parable are so few in number and so simple that it seems they hardly call for explanation. First of all, there is the "net." Second, there is the "sea" into which the net is cast. Third, there are the "fishermen" themselves—they gather in. And fourth, there are the "fish" that are enclosed in the net.

It should be plain to all that the "net" itself is a symbol of the Gospel, the proclaiming and presenting Christ to the responsibility of men. Second, the "sea" into which the net is cast has the same meaning that it has in the first verse of the chapter: it stands for the nations as such, the Gentiles, and that is why the "sea" is here once more mentioned—because that which is specially characteristic of the present dispensation, in contradistinction from the dispensation that preceded it and the one which shall yet follow, is God's mercy turning *unto the Gentiles*: therefore we have the figure of the "sea" once more. The "fishermen," those who cast the net into the sea, are the Lord's gospellers, the evangelists, the preachers of the Word. That is clear by comparing Scripture with Scripture: in Matthew 4:19 and in Luke 5 the Lord Jesus said to His first disciples, "Follow Me and I will make you fishers of men," it is His own figure for His evangelists.

Now very briefly let us call attention to seven things connected with the parable. The first thing that has impressed us in studying it is this: the *inconspicuousness* of the fishermen. Observe that in the 47th verse they are not even mentioned: "The kingdom of heaven is like unto a net, that was cast into the sea, and gathered of every kind," while in the 48th verse Christ just refers to them as "they": "Which when it was full, *they* drew to shore." That is all that is said about them. How inconspicuous they are! In other words, those who have been so high'y honoured by God, and (it is an infinitely higher honour to be a servant of Christ than to be King of the British Empire) to have a part in the casting of this net into the sea, are here hidden from view, nothing is said about them, except they are just referred to once as "they." O how that rebukes and condemns the preacher-worship of the day! Turn for a moment to 1 Cor. 3: beginning at v. 4:—"For while one saith, I am of Paul; and another, I am of Apollos, are ye not carnal? Who then is Paul, and who is Apollos, but ministers by whom ye believed, even as the Lord gave to every man? I have planted, Apollos watered; but God gave the increase. So then neither is he that planteth *anything*, neither he that watereth." Do we realise that, my brethren? Do you realise that the one whom God has called to minister to you, is himself *nothing*—nothing at all, merely an empty vessel, that, unless the Lord comes, will soon crumble away to dust! But He, the One who deigns to bless, who places His treasure in earthen vessels, He is everything. O my brethren and sisters, it has impressed me deeply in studying this parable that the fishermen are hidden from sight. They are inconspicuous, they are mere nothings that God can dispense with as easily as He can use them. Do not imagine that the prosperity of any church depends upon the presence of some particular man in the pulpit. The Lord is not only able to continue and prosper His work, but to do so a hundredfold more *without* the most gifted preacher if He so pleases. The instrument is nothing. How that rebukes the preacher-worship of the day! May Almighty God deliver His people from it. May God in His grace (for He is a jealous God, who will not share His glory with another), preserve His people from giving any of the honour and glory to the mere instrument, the whole of which is due and belongs alone to Him. Just as surely as you begin to honour and glorify the instrument, the blessing of God will depart. Heed well this first point in our parable: the fishermen were hidden from sight. May they be hidden from sight in all the churches of God.

Secondly, *the object before* the fishermen in casting the net into the sea and drawing it forth again. This was simply to gather good fish. That was their one aim and design, the 48th verse shows that —"which when it was full, they drew to shore, and sat down, and gathered the good fish into vessels." It is true there were also some bad fish in the net, but these they cast away. It is the good fish they were out for. Now, while it is true the servant of God is under marching orders to "preach the gospel to *every* creature," nevertheless, that which he must ever keep steadily before him, those whom he must perseveringly seek out, and those he is called to minister unto, are *God's elect*. Though the servant of God is sent forth to preach the Gospel to all who come under the sound of his voice, yet he is not sent to draw a bow at a venture. God has not sent him forth so that the success of his labours is made dependent upon the caprice of man or the response of his will. No, the primary purpose of God in raising up His servants and sending them forth is, the good of His own elect. And that end is to be kept in view by those whom God calls upon to engage in His service, whether that work be in the mission-field or in the Sunday School class or in district visitation. God has called you to seek out those whom He has marked out from all eternity—the "good fish"

There are two Scriptures I want to refer to from the Epistles of Paul which bring *both* of these aspects before us. First, I Cor. 9:22, "I am made all things to *all* men, that I might by all means save some." In a general way that means this: Paul was carrying out his Divinely given commission and preaching the Gospel to every creature—the net was cast into the sea at large. Paul was made all things to all men. He welcomed an opportunity to preach the Gospel to the poor; but he did not miss an opportunity to preach God's Word to the prominent and eminent as well. He was primarily, "the apostle to the Gentiles" (Rom. 11:13), yet how often he preached to the Jews! He was made all things to all men. That is one side: that is the casting of the net "into-the-sea" aspect.

Now turn to 2 Tim. 2:10, which is a verse many Arminians do not seem to know is in the Bible at all; those who have been brought up under "Freewill" teaching need to look at it closely. These were the words of the apostle Paul in connection with his own ministry: "Therefore I endure all things *for the elect's sake*, that they may also obtain the salvation which is in Christ Jeusus." That was the object before the apostle's heart, that was the goal that he had in view. That was the aim of his ministry, that was what enabled him to endure such a great fight of afflictions. He endured all things "for the elect's sake." How that gives the aspect of the Gospel work portrayed in our parable! There is first the broadcasting of the net into the sea at large, and there is secondly the particular design in so doing. The purpose of it is to gather out the "good fish." So while you and I are called upon to preach the Gospel to every creature, let us not lose sight of the fact that God's purpose and our submission to it is the seeking out of the good fish, praying that God will use us to find His hidden ones. For, observe that, at first, God's elect are *hidden* from His servants, like the "good fish" in the sea; but as we labour in the Gospel they become *manifest*—they are *seen* in the "net!"

In the third place, we are told that the net gathered in of every kind. Coming back to Matt. 13:47, the last part of the verse: "that was cast into the sea, and gathered of *every* kind." Others besides "good fish" were enclosed. This reminds us once more that the main thing which is in view in our chapter is the Christian *profession*. Here we are shown *the effects* of Gospel preaching. Here we behold the results of the net being cast into the sea at large—the world-wide proclamation of the Gospel and the universal presentation of Christ unto men. The result is that there is a *mixed* profession. The net gathers in "of every kind." Just as at the beginning of the age there were the wheat and tares, so at the end of the age (to which this parable conducts us) there are bad fish as well as good.

Now in the fourth place, the fact that this net gathered in bad fishes as well as good ones was *no reflection* upon the skill of the fishermen. But on the other hand, they *were* responsible to distinguish between the good and the bad fish *after* they had entered the net, and they were responsible to separate the one from the other. That is an essential and important part of the work and duty of God's servants—to discriminate, to distinguish between the good and the bad fish. Mark it carefully: "which when it was full, (that is, the net) they drew to shore, and (what?) sat down" (v. 8). They sat down *before* they did anything with the fish. Before they attempted to do any sorting out and separating, they sat down: which indicates that this aspect of their work requires time, care, deliberation!

Now notice also in verse 48: "They gathered the good fish into vessels, but cast the bad away." That is all that the fishermen did with the bad; just cast them away. They had got into the net, but they were rejected. They would have nothing further to do with them. Nothing else is required of the fishermen, but just to cast them away. Such was Christ's word in Matthew 15:13, where the disciples came to Him and were speaking about the Pharisees, He said, "Every plant which My heavenly Father hath not planted, shall be rooted up. Let them alone." It is *not* our business to do the rooting up; just leave them alone, that is all; have no fellowship with them. Turn to Rom. 16:17, "Now I beseech you brethren, mark them which have caused divisions and offences contrary to the doctrine which ye have learned"—imprison them, torture them, burn them? No, God has never told His people, or His professing people, to do any such thing. Even if Rome were right in her doctrines, Scripture absolutely condemns her practices. How has *she* acted towards those who have differed from her doctrine? Here is what *Scripture* says, "Brethren mark them which cause divisions and offences contrary to the doctrine which ye have learned; and *avoid* them." That is all! Give them a wide berth; separate yourselves from them; have nothing to do with them, avoid them. *Do you* avoid them? If some man comes to the City with a great reputation, and the newspapers announce that he is teaching this, that, and the other, and huge crowds are being drawn, and a lot of people tell you he is such a nice man, yet you know he is teaching contrary to the doctrine that you have received; what do you do? Do you "avoid" him? I am afraid some of you don't. Many need this word. "Avoid them!" See also 2 John 10!

In the fifth place. These fishermen were to distinguish and discriminate between the good and the bad fish. Though they are not to be blamed for the entrance of the "bad" fish into the "net"—being under the waters they could not see what sort of fish entered; yet they have a responsibility concerning them once the net is drawn to land: then they are exposed to sight. It is not long before a professing Christian makes it *manifest* whether or not he has been really born again. It is concerning this God holds His servants responsible.

Perhaps some will ask, *How* are they able to do it? In what way are God's servants to distinguish the good fish from the bad? Has God left them to their own discretion in the matter? No, my friends. We need not lean unto our own understanding in anything. The Scriptures have been given that the man of God may be thoroughly furnished unto all good works, and in them God Himself has described the very marks by which we can distinguish good fish from bad!

Turn for a moment to Lev. 11:9, "These shall ye eat of all that are in the waters, whatsoever hath fins, and scales, in the waters, in the seas, and in the rivers, them shall ye eat. And all that have not fins and scales in the seas and in the rivers, of all that move in the waters, and of any living thing which is in the waters, they shall be an abomination unto you." Do you suppose that these verses contain nothing more than instructions to the Hebrews about their diet 3,000 years ago? Do you imagine that God has recorded in His eternal Word something with no other significance and importance than the mere regulating of the table of the Israelites in the past? I trust that by this time most of you have learned that there is a spiritual significance and value to *everything* in Scripture. There is not time now to expound this, but concerning the good fish there were two things, fins and scales—fins to propel them through the waters and aid their motion; scales to protect, to shield them from the pressure and action of the waters as they passed swiftly through them. Can you interpret it? God has given His people two things: armour to protect them, and also an inward power to propel them through the waters of this world. Those who give evidence of having on them the armour of light (Rom. 13:12; Eph. 6:13-17), corresponding to the "scales;" and those who make it manifest they are swimming against (instead of floating down) the tide of this world, furnish proof that they are "good fish."

In the sixth place, it should be carefully noted that the work of the fishermen did not cease when they drew the net to land. Something else yet remained for them to do. Look again at the parable: "Which when it was full, they drew to shore, and sat down, and *gathered* the good fish into"—a vessel? It does not say so; but "they gathered the good fish into *vessels*." Why? The work of the fishermen was not completed when they gathered the fish into the net, nor was it finished when they had separated the good from the bad: the good ones must be gathered into "vessels." Surely that does not need interpreting. The "good" fish represent believers; their being "gathered" speaks of association together—fellowship. Thus, the "vessels" are a figure of the local churches, where God's people are (or should be) united in the bonds of love, with common interests and aims.

May God impress this on many hearts. The revealed will of God is not completed when you have been drawn out of the waters of the world and separated from the bad fish. That is not sufficient. Some of you do not have as high a respect for those "vessels" as you ought to have. Some of you are satisfied to be good fish just swimming alone *by yourselves*. Why, my brethren and sisters manifestly the "vessels" here stand for *the local churches*, into which God has ordained and appointed (in His Word) that His people—after sovereign grace has drawn them out of the world and has manifested that He has made a difference between them and the bad fishes—need to be brought, into association and fellowship with other good fishes. And if you are outside one of those "vessels" you are outside the complete circle of God's will. Yes, it seems to me one of the most important lessons that this parable teaches is the gathering of the good fishes into vessels. Someone has suggested that the "vessels" referred to the "many mansions" in the Father's House. Why, the parables of this chapter go no farther than the Christian profession on *earth*, and certainly Gospel preachers will have nothing to do with the *placing* of God's saints on High!

I have only time now to mention the last point without elaborating—If this parable be studied closely it will be found that vv. 49 and 59 present two difficulties —those who have not studied it, will not have felt their force: "So shall it be at the end of the world (or of the age): the angels shall come forth, and sever the wicked from among the just." In the parable itself the work is done by the fishermen: but in the *interpretation* of the parable the work is done by "angels." Again, in the parable itself the good fish are separated from the bad, but when you come to the interpretation, the order is reversed: "they shall sever the wicked from among the just." So that in the interpretation the bad are separated from the good—the very opposite of the order in v. 48. For the present we leave these two points with you.

—*Arthur W. Pink.*

"Gleanings in Genesis," in two volumes, on which the Editor worked for six years, may be had from us for 12/6 post paid, or from Mr. Pressel for $2:50. Special attention is given in it to the types and prophecies of that book.

LIFE OUT OF DEATH.

An Exposition of 1 Peter 3:19-21.

It is easy to prove a charge against a man when his enemy sits as judge; and it is easy to establish any proposition which accords with the interests, prejudices, and habits of thought and feeling of those whom we address. Thus, a doctrine which falls in with the wishes of the carnal heart, or which flatters its self-righteousness, will be accepted on the most slender show of support from Scripture by those who demand an array of clear and unequivocal proofs in favour of every point of doctrine which exalts God and abases man. We have oftener than once had occasion to notice how much the opponents of what are called "the doctrines of grace" often rest on a defective translation, a doubtful reading, or a single phrase which is susceptible of a rendering favourable to their own notions. How much, for example, do the Arminian advocates of the doctrine of "perfection" rest upon a passage in our English Bible—"herein is our love made perfect"—though no ingenuity can defend it as a translation of the original text. How much have Arminian expositors and controversialists made of the phrase, "Who walk not after the flesh, but after the spirit," as modifying the triumphant language of faith, "there is therefore now no condemnation to them who are in Christ Jesus," in Romans 8:1! And yet it is universally conceded by all competent critics that the phrase is an interpolation without a shadow of authority.

In like manner, conclusions which are irreconcilable with the whole tenor of Scripture, first, respecting the condition of the departed, and, secondly, respecting the ordinance of baptism, have been maintained with confidence on no better grounds than a forced and unnatural interpretation of two clauses in the passage selected as the subject of this paper. The construction of the passage may be regarded as somewhat difficult. But it must be remembered that when an interpretation which coincides with the natural tendencies of the heart has once become familiar, it increases, if it does not create, the seeming obscurity of a passage. And so in this case the difficulty may be due rather to the reader's prepossessions, than to the construction of the passage itself.

Before entering upon an examination of the passage, let us glance at the scope of the context, if, haply, we may ascertain the object of the writer in introducing an allusion first to the deluge and then to baptism, between which there appears to be no natural connection. A prominent design of the Epistle was to comfort and sustain the churches of that day amid many persecutions and tribulations. The grounds of that encouragement are various, but are chiefly found in various aspects of Christ's sufferings. In the verse immediately preceding the passage before us, it is stated that He "once suffered for sins, the just for the unjust, that He might bring us to God." Here it is clearly implied that suffering is a necessary condition of our salvation. In no other way could He bring us to God but by suffering for sins. So imperative was the necessity, that even the Just One could not escape when He took up the cause of the unjust. He, indeed, was ever the Holy One and the Just, but He had assumed our nature —appeared "in the likeness of sinful flesh"—and as it has been expressed, "before He could save us after the power of an endless life. He needed Himself to be made perfect through suffering, and saved from death. The curse could pass away only through the exhaustion of its terrors on Him who bore it for our sakes. The whole life of the flesh must come to a bloody and perpetual end. He was *'put to death in the flesh!'* And then, that He might not after all lose the precious end for which He suffered, but as the 'quickening spirit' of the new creation might beget sons in His own heavenly likeness, and so bring us to God. He was Himself also, as an equally indispensable preliminary, *'quickened in spirit!'* Now behold the glorious issue of this triumph of Divine wisdom in bringing life out of death! He who descended so low for us 'is gone into heaven, and is on the right hand of God, angels, and authorities, and powers being made subject unto Him'—a pledge and exemplification of the glory which His suffering followers shall inherit!"

The quotation in the foregoing paragraph is from Dr. Lillie's lecture on the passage. An important variation from our English version will be noticed in the phrase "quickened in spirit," which is the proper translation of the language used by the Apostle, according to all critical editors of the Greek text. On account of its bearing on a subsequent point in our exposition, we add Dr. Lillie's observations on the phrase: "Before His manifestation in the flesh, and after His resurrection, our Lord Jesus Christ may be said to have lived in spirit. . . . This spiritual element was common to both conditions of His being. And in both the excellency of glory was the Divine; insomuch that, when

He who was put to death in flesh was quickened in spirit, it would be fully accordant with the analogy of Scripture to overlook the economical modification, and speak of Him as re-entering the glory which He had with the Father before the world was. Just as Immanuel could say of Himself 'Before Abraham was, I am. . . . I came from the Father, and am come into the world; again I leave the world and go to the Father;' so on the same ground of the unchangeable and all-pervading identity of His God-head—the same yesterday, to-day, and for ever—the inspired writers freely and everywhere represent Him, to whom they all bear witness, as remaining one and the same person through all historical transitions, and through every variety of experience and operation. In the bold, popular language of the New Testament, He who was in the beginning with God, by Whom God made the world, who spoke to Moses in Mount Sinai and led the tribes through the wilderness, was in the fulness of time born of a woman, died on Calvary, arose from the dead, and now liveth at the right hand of God."

The bearing of the Apostle's statement regarding the sufferings of Christ in this verse, on the object of the Epistle, evidently is, that it shows that in the accomplishment of God's purpose of grace toward us, salvation must be brought out of suffering, life out of death, and, we might add, joy out of sorrow, glory out of shame. The highest illustration of this principle is found in Christ's suffering for sins; but it runs through all God's dealings with us, individually and collectively, and is illustrated at every stage and in every aspect of our salvation. To illustrate this still further is, we believe, the design of the Apostle in his reference to the deluge and to baptism, to the consideration of which we now proceed.

The statement "by which" or, more strictly, "in which also He went and preached to the spirits in prison," has been regarded as the great difficulty in the passage. Where, when, to whom, and with what object did He preach? Our readers know the use which is made of the passage by the Roman Catholic Church, to support its doctrine of purgatory. The earlier fathers also held, and some Protestant commentators now hold, that the time of this preaching was the period which elapsed between His death and His resurrection; that then He descended into Hades—"the world of spirits"—and proclaimed salvation through His blood to the sinners who were carried away by the flood, or to all the unholy dead of former generations. Others, perceiving the inconsistency of such a supposition with the uniform testimony of Scripture regarding the doom and destiny of those who have died in their sins, have supposed that His mission to Hades had reference to the pious dead whom He went to deliver, as Roman Catholics say, from the fires of purgatory, or, as others say, from "the state of dim seclusion" in which they awaited the accomplishment of His sacrifice for sin.

Although the present subject does not require us to dwell on this last view, it may be interesting to notice that those who hold it point out a marked difference in the manner in which departed saints are spoken of before and after the resurrection of Christ. In the Old Testament they are said to go down to Sheol, or Hades, and it is alleged that a part of Hades was separated from the rest and allotted to the righteous—a division referred to in the parable of Dives and Lazarus, where Abraham and Lazarus are spoken of as separated by a vast and impassable chasm from the place of torment where Dives was. It was impossible, they say, that any of Adam's race should be admitted into the heavenlies until the great High Priest had entered with His own blood. The expectants of salvation were therefore reserved in Hades till the sacrifice was offered, and then He descended thither to announce their deliverence. Some have connected with this the opening of the grave, when He cried, "It is finished." But though the graves were then opened, the bodies of the saints did not come forth until He returned from His supposed mission to Hades and His resurrection from the dead. Then, it is alleged, He brought His ransomed people of all preceding ages from their place of waiting, and carried them up with Him in His ascent to the heavenlies; according to the description of His triumph, "When He ascended up on high, He led captivity captive." Thenceforth those who sleep in Jesus are never said to go down to Hades, but "to depart and be with Christ."

Whatever may be said in favour of such a view, it certainly receives no countenance from the passage before us. The time of His preaching could not be in the interval between His death and resurrection, for in that case He must be held to have been "quickened in spirit" when He died, and not when He rose again; while the phrase unquestionably refers to His resurrection. Those to whom He preached were not expectant saints, but disobedient sinners. And this brings us to a very plain answer to the question, *To whom* did He preach? To "the spirits in prison who formerly were disobedient when the longsuffering of God waited in the days of Noah while the ark was a preparing." But it also furnishes an answer to the question, *When* did He preach? For their disobedience evidently relates to the preaching and the time of the preaching to which they were disobedient must have been "while the ark was a preparing." The words, "spirits in prison," describe, not their condition when He preached to them, but their present condition in consequence of their disobedience.

"How," it may be asked, "could He be said to have gone and preached to them in the days of Noah?" We answer, He went not bodily, but "in spirit," for the words, "by which," in the commencement of verse 19, are properly "in which." That is to say, He went in spirit, and preached by the lips of Noah, just as, after He had ascended up on high, it is said He "came and preached peace to them which were afar off, and to them which were nigh" (Eph. 2:17), not in person, but by the apostles and evangelists endowed with His Spirit.

The disobedience and consequent doom of those to whom He preached in the days of Noah are introduced here to show these persecuted believers that the opposition of the world had been the same in all ages. There is a close analogy between the treatment both of the message and the messenger in the days of Noah, and in the days of a suffering church. And surely it was not without significance at such a time to intimate that those who had in a former age turned a deaf ear to the message of grace, were now spirits in prison, reserved to a more terrible judgment; while the *few*—the godly remnant—were saved by the very deluge which swept the ungodly away.

Here it is that our commentators miss the very point of the passage "in which (the ark) few, that is, eight souls, were saved by water." The impression is that the Apostle meant nothing more than that those eight souls were saved in the ark *from* the water, but he says that they were saved *"by* water." It has, indeed, been rendered "through water," that is, says Dr. Lillie, "they were carried clear through it;" but had that been intended, the Apostle would have said, "the water," that is, of the deluge. As it is, we have simply "water" as the means of their salvation. And this is made certain by the reading of the next verse adopted by Tischendorf and all the critical editors, *"which also in a figure now saves us."* The antecedent to "which" is "water," and the connection would be unmeaning unless, in the former case, the salvation had been by water.

We therefore ask, From what were they "saved by water?" The answer will be found in the condition of the earth at that time. "The earth also was corrupt before God, and the earth was filled with violence" Genesis 6:11. The remnant of righteousness was narrowed down to the limits of Noah's family, surrounded by corruption and violence, which threatened daily to engulf it. And it affords us another view of God's gracious regard for His elect in all His dealings with the world, when we see that the deluge, which we have been accustomed to regard only as His judgment on the ungodly, was at the same time specially designed for the salvation of His people. You will now perceive why it is introduced in this place. It is another exemplification of the principle of which we have spoken. It is life brought out of death, salvation brought out of destruction; and it is a foreshadowing of a more terrible judgment, with still more glorious results, Paul saw manifestly betokened amid the persecutions and tribulations which the Church of the Thessalonians endured; "seeing," said he, "it is a righteous thing with God to recompense tribulation to them that trouble you: and to you who are troubled rest with us when the Lord Jesus shall be revealed from heaven," etc., 2 Thess. 1:5-10.

The failure to see this point—the salvation of the few by the water which swept away their enemies—has occasioned the next great difficulty of the passage in its reference to baptism in verse 21: "The like figure whereunto baptism doth also now save." And it must be admitted that it is very difficult to extract any clear meaning from these words as they stand in our English Bibles. A question has been raised of a supposed resemblance between Christian baptism and the salvation of Noah and his family in the ark, of which angry disputants about what is called "the mode of baptism" have made a use which is equally puerile and unworthy on either side. Dr. Lillie, in at least better taste, says, "The comparison is not between baptism and the ark, nor yet generally between the Christian salvation through baptism and Noah's salvation through water, but between the baptismal use and import of water as it is here explained, and the action of the same element in relation to Noah and his company!" But then as he appears to us to have overlooked the truth on the latter point, he comes short of the true explanation in the former, when he adds: "It does seem absolutely to assert that *now*, as formerly, we too, as well as the inmates of the ark, lifted up on the swelling, but to them friendly waves, are saved through water, and that there is in the one case, as our version phrases it, a 'like figure' of the other."

We venture to say that if, in the case of Noah, there was no salvation intimated except his salvation from the destructive flood, nothing could be more unlike than the action of water from which, or "clear through which," he was carried in the ark, and the baptismal use and import of the same element; for no one surely can imagine that the Apostle designed to intimate that the baptised were rescued from any danger of perishing by water. According to the corrected text, Dr. Lillie renders the statement "which" (water) "in a like figure now saveth us also, even baptism." It is difficult to see how the word "like" comes into the translation, for the word antitupos has no such meaning as "the like figure" either in sacred or classical Greek. Nor is the word *"anti-type"* its proper English equivalent. It occurs only in one other passage in the New Testament, namely, in Hebrews 9:24, and *there* its meaning is not doubtful: "For Christ is not entered into the holy places made with hands, which are the *figures* (antitupa) of the true." And so we would render it here—"which also in a figure now saves us, even baptism."

Our answer to the question, Does baptism actually save us? Would therefore be, so far as this passage is concerned, no! it saves in a figure; that is, the baptismal use of water is emblematic of our salvation, which, in the passage itself, is said to be "by the resurrection of Jesus Christ." This answer is confirmed by the parenthesis in which the Apostle guards his statement from any ritualistic perversion: "Not the putting away of the filth of the flesh." It is not to be regarded as a ceremonial lustration, like the diverse washings under a legal economy; or, if you understand the "filth of the flesh" in the moral sense of that phrase, then the Apostle asserts that baptism is not in itself the means of our purification or regeneration; but it is "the answer of a good conscience toward God."

The word eperotema, which in our version is translated "answer," has puzzled commentators. It occurs nowhere else in the New Testament; elsewhere it means "question" or "inquiry," rather than "answer." Many have supposed that the Apostle alludes to some question which was put to the person about to be baptised. Others have supposed that he uses it in the sense in which it occurs in Greek authors as a legal term implying stipulation or engagement. Perhaps the word used in our translation is nearer the Apostle's meaning, for if it means an inquiry, it must be understood, not as the act of inquiry, but as the thing about which inquiry is made; and we have no word which expresses it better in such a connection than "answer." It is evident, at any rate, that the Apostle is thinking of the inward and spiritual reality of which baptism is an outward corresponding act or an emblem. That inward reality is "a good conscience." Now, no man can have a good conscience except as his heart is sprinkled from an evil conscience. It is only when sin is purged by the all-atoning blood that he has "no more conscience of sin." That blood alone can "purge the conscience from dead works to serve the living God." And baptism is an outward representation or expression of that inward reality.

Paul thus expounds the import of this ordinance in Romans 6: 3-5, "Know ye not that so many of us as were baptised into Jesus Christ were baptised into His death? Therefore, we are buried with Him by baptism into death; that like as Christ was raised from the dead by the glory of the Father, even so we also should walk in newness of life. For if we have been planted together in the likeness of His death, we shall be also in the likeness of His resurrection." And with this explanation of the figure baptism, it is easy to see why it is introduced in this connection. It is not because baptism is an emblem of the flood, or the flood a type of baptism. But, because both in the historical fact and emblematic ordinance, we have an exemplification of the principle which the Apostle would have these persecuted saints see exemplified also in the sufferings they were called to endure for the name of Jesus. Life brought out of death is the lesson in it all. This we see in the history of Him who is the author and finisher of our faith. He could bring us to God only by suffering for sins. Accordingly, He was put to death in the flesh. But then, behold the triumphant issue of suffering and death! He is quickened in spirit, and in the highest place of glory and honour He reigns supreme over all angels, authorities, and powers. But in the application of this to individual believers, they are regarded as identified with Him in His crucifixion and resurrection, and it is as one with Him, who, having been crucified for our offences, was raised again for our justification, that we stand before God justified from all things, having no more conscience of sin. This is what baptism signifies and represents—it is the outward response to God of a good conscience.

Nor is it alone as to our justification that it speaks, but also of a new life in Him who was quickened in spirit. "God, who is rich in mercy, for that great love wherewith He loved us, even when we were dead in sins, hath quickened us together with Christ." We have life, but it is life brought out of death. And according to the Apostle's unfolding of the import of baptism, it is just our practical identification with Christ in His death—"reckoning ourselves dead, indeed, unto sin"—and our consequent practical identification of ourselves with Christ in His resurrection—"reckoning ourselves alive unto God through Jesus Christ our Lord"—that constitutes our proper life here to the glory of the Father. Every step of our progress is but a putting off the old man and a putting on of the new man. And thus it is evermore a repetition of that principle which is exemplified in the commencement of it—life brought out of death—while hope goes out continually to the completion of it all in that glory which, as the result of His suffering for us, He has gotten from the Father and hath given to us. To this consummation, also, the figure baptism, as expounded by the Apostle, clearly points.

The bearing of all this upon the Apostle's design is surely not obscure. For while it all illustrates the general necessity of the case—that our salvation comes out of suffering, our life out of death—it most graciously assures the hearts of believers in all possible circumstances. "Thou art so knit to Him," says Leighton, "that His resurrection and glory secure thee thine, His life and thine are not two, but one as that of the head and members; and if He could not be overcome by death, thou canst not." Oh! that sweet word, "Because I live, ye shall live also." When we look at Him who has gone before us in the path to glory, and remember that He is the well-beloved Son, we need not think any sufferings into which the Church may fall strange or desperate. From the lowest depths to which He descended, follow Him to the glory in which He sits; and must we not conclude regarding His Church also, that the deeper her distress, she shall only rise the higher in the day of her final deliverence? "If we suffer with Him we shall also reign with Him."

From the character of the world through which our path lies, it is evident that persecution and hatred must await those who are one with Him. "If the world hate you," said our Lord, "ye know that it hated Me before it hated you." And this antagonism is very ancient. It dates from the days of "Cain, who was of that wicked one and slew his brother," and through all intervening time till the present it is seen that "he that was born after the flesh persecuted him that was born after the spirit;" precisely as when the Lord came in person to His own, His own received Him not, so when in spirit He went with the words of gracious warning to the men of Noah's day they were disobedient. But through all that opposition God is carrying forward His purpose to a sure accomplishment; He has His eye on His suffering people, and makes every thing tributory to their advantage. Their haughty enemies, nay, sometimes their own weak hearts, may conclude that He has forgotten a despised remnant. He may, He does, bear long with their persecutors. His long-suffering waits; but think you that He will not avenge His own elect that cry night and day unto Him? "I tell you," says the Lord, "that He will avenge them speedily." The flood came at last and swept away the world of the ungodly, and the issue of that judgment was the salvation of the "few," and it is to this issue—the salvation of His elect—that He is carrying forward all the affairs of this world. Little as it appears to carnal eyes, and though nothing enters less into the calculations of this world's sages, everything has reference to this grand result. "All things are yours," says the Apostle. Whether we regard its greatest interests and events in all their complications and variety, or regard its most trivial incidents in their simplicity and obscurity, "all things work together for good to them that love God, to them that are the called according to His purpose. "And what a summing up will it all have at last, when, from the wreck of all this world's grandeur, the smoke of the fire which destroys the adversaries, and the drifting chaff of its kingdoms broken in the threshing floor of God's righteous judgment, the Church shall shine forth in the glory of her Lord, and take her destined place as the queen consort of a regenerated universe.

Waymarks of the Wilderness, 1868.

probably the mightiest intercessor that the household of faith has had. We cannot fail, in reading his Epistles, to perceive that a very large part of his service consisted of earnest supplication on behalf of others. None was more fervent and persistent in prayer than he: "night and day praying exceedingly" (1 Thess. 3:10) he wrote. "Strive together with me in your prayers to God" he exhorted the Romain saints. And what an example he had set them: "without ceasing I make mention of you always in my prayers" (1:9), he had told them. He prayed for Israel that they might be saved (Rom. 10:1).

The prayer-life of the Apostle Paul is a wonderful study. What a long prayer-list he must have kept and constantly used! For the Ephesian saints he wrestled in prayer (1:16-19; 3:14-19). To the Philippians he wrote, "Always in every prayer of mine for you all making request with joy" (1;4), which shows that his supplications for them was not an irksome duty or burden, but a delight. To the Colossians he wrote, "We also, since the day we heard, do not cease to pray for you" (1:9), and again, "For I would that ye knew what great conflict I have for you, and for them at Laodicea, and for as many as have not seen my face in the flesh. . . . Although I be absent in the flesh, yet am I with you in the spirit" (Col. 2:1, 5). To the Thessalonian saints he declared, "Night and day praying exceedingly that we might see your face, and might perfect that which is lacking in your faith" (1 Thess. 3:10).

Nor was Paul the only one of the apostles who devoted himself so largely to this ministry of prayer. Of the others, it is recorded that they requested the early church to appoint deacons so that "we will give ourselves *continually* to prayer and to the ministry of the Word" (Acts 6:4). The order here is remarkable, prayer being mentioned *before* the preaching of the Word. What a place does this give to the work of intercession! If there is to be a return of apostolic power there must be the employment of apostolic methods!

Fourth, the *importance* of prayer may be seen from the fact that it is God's appointed channel for the bestowal of needed blessings. Christ taught His disciples to pray even for their daily bread. In the Epistles we are exhorted, "Let us therefore come boldly unto the throne of grace, that we may obtain mercy, and find grace to help in time of need" (Heb. 4:16). Who is there among God's children that does not feel his or her need of more grace? And whose fault is it that we have so little? Our opening text says, "Ye have not, because ye ask not." Why is our faith so weak, our love so feeble, our zeal so low? Why have we so little light from the Word? Why have we so little victory over sin and Satan? "Ye have not, because ye ask not." Here is the explanation of our weakness, our leanness, and our fruitlessness.

Fifth, the *importance* of prayer may be seen from the place that it is given in Ephesians 6. In v. 12 the Christian is told that his antagonists are not human, but Satanic he wrestles not against "flesh and blood," but against "the powers and rulers of darkness." Then, in v. 13, he is exhorted to take unto him the whole armour of God, which is described in the verses that follow. Finally, in v. 18, he is told to *pray* "always with all prayer and supplication in the Spirit, and watching thereunto with all perseverance and supplication for all saints' —weigh well the three "all's." Without this constant recourse to the Throne of Grace the other pieces of armour avail us not. In other words, we can gain the victory over Satan only by spending much time upon our knees. It is prayer which keeps the "armour" bright and fit for use. Before we can "put on" the armour of light, we must "awake out of sleep" (Rom. 13:11, 12), i.e., that slothful indifference to the importance and necessity of prayer.

The same principle holds good in connection with the assemblies of God's people as it does with individual Christians. Of the first church it is said, "They continued steadfastly in the apostles' doctrine and fellowship, and in breaking of bread, and *in prayers*" (Acts 2:42). There may be both oneness in doctrine and outward fellowship, but if prayer has little or no place in their corporate life, spirituality is bound to be at a low ebb. It has often been said, and rightly so, Power with men is the result of first having power with God. Whenever you find a church where saints are being blest and sinners saved, the prayer-meeting has a prominent place.

To all of this some may reply, But we cannot force ourselves to pray; we cannot really pray at all unless the Spirit prompts us! Quite true. But if we do not have the assistance of the Holy Spirit, the fault is entirely ours! Did not Christ say, "If ye then, being   how to give good gifts unto your children: how much more shall your heavenly Father give the Holy Spirit to them that *ask* him?" So here, "Ye have not because ye ask not!" The greatest obstacle is not our lack of ability, but of desire and will. Then let us pray more earnestly for the spirit of prayer.

—*Arthur W. Pink.*

VOL. VII.   JUNE, 1928   No. 6

STUDIES IN THE SCRIPTURES

"Search the Scriptures" John 5: 39

Copyright in all English-speaking Countries.

Editor: Arthur W. Pink, 15 Hurlstone Avenue, Summer Hill, N.S.W., Australia.
Hon. Agent in U.S.A.: Mr. C. S. Pressel, 559 Dupont Avenue, York, Penna.

FREE TO ALL WHO WILL READ IT

THE VALUE OF PRAYER.

"He that cometh to God must believe that He is, and that He is a rewarder of them that diligently seek Him" (Heb. 11:6).

The two chief reasons why God has appointed that His people should pray, are, that He should be glorified, and that they should be blest. These are the two great ends which God has ever had in view; these are the motives or considerations which regulate all His dealings. Prov. 16:4 announces, "The Lord hath made all things for Himself." Rom. 8:28 affirms, "All things work together for good to them that love God." Let us enlarge a little on these two things.

First, prayer is appointed that God should be glorified. How is this attained? Thus: prayer is the acknowledgment that God is on the throne, and that all things are in His hands. Prayer is the soul prostrating itself before its Maker, owning His exalted greatness. It is the heart's intelligent homage, adoring the perfections of the Divine character. It is a returning of thanks to the great Benefactor for His mercies. Thus, God is honoured by His creatures, through their bending the knee before Him and giving Him His rightful place.

Second, prayer is appointed for the blessing of God's people. Rightly engaged in, prayer is a wondrous means of grace to the soul. It calls into exercise the faculties of the new man and, by use, develops them. It brings blessing to every part of our complex being. There is nothing more quietening to the soul and restful to the nerves than a season of true waiting upon God. But its chief gain is the enriching of the spiritual life. Prayer calls down mercies which otherwise would not be given us.

Now in our text there are three things, right on the surface, concerning prayer. First, the *requirement* of prayer: we "must believe." Faith, confidence, trust, are essential; without these all praying is vain. To believe that God is means far more than to be satisfied that He exists, that there *is* a God. It means we "must believe that He is" ready to hear, willing to respond. Second, the *nature* of effectual prayer: "diligently seeking." God must be earnestly sought after. There must be a definite "drawing near" to Him in spirit; not formally and half-heartedly, but "diligently." Third, the *value* of prayer: "He is a Rewarder." Real prayer is not in vain; time thus spent is never wasted. The supplicant is a gainer in many ways. It is this last thought which we shall now seek to develop.

1. True prayer makes God more real to the soul. To many of us, I fear, God seems so unreal. We are fully assured of His existence, but our experimental acquaintance with Him is scanty indeed. He seems so far away. To what a small extent can any of us say "I *know* whom I have believed!" Now if God is to become a living reality to the soul, if the sense of remoteness is to be overcome, if we are to get better acquainted with Him experimentally, then we must constantly seek Him in prayer, we must dwell much in "the secret place," we must cultivate daily communion with Him.

(Concluded on Page 144)

IMPORTANT NOTICES

Back numbers of each year of the magazine are yet obtainable at 5/- (1.25) per year. Bound at 7/6 (1.75) post paid. They will soon be out of print. Those in U.S.A. wanting them, please purchase from Mr. Pressel (see front cover page).

Advise promptly of change of address.

This Magazine is published as a work of faith and labour of love. The Editor gladly gives his services. It is freely sent to all who will read it. No charge is made for it.

Christians who feel definitely led to do so, may have fellowship with us in this Ministry. Send only *Inter-National M.O.*

CONTENTS.

	Page.
Hebrews	122
Gleanings in Exodus	129
Parables of Matt. 13	133
The Family of God	138
Gospel of Grace	140

THE EPISTLE TO THE HEBREWS.

6. *Christ Superior to Angels*: Heb 1: 10-13.

The closing verses of Heb. 1 present a striking climax to the apostle's argument. They contain the most touching and also the most thrilling references to be found in this wondrous chapter. In it the Holy Spirit completes His proof for the superiority of the Mediator over the angels, proof which was all drawn from Israel's own Scriptures. Five times He had cited passages from the Old Testament which set forth the exalted dignities and glories of the Messiah. A sixth and a seventh is now quoted from the 102nd and the 110th Psalms, to show that He who had passed through such unparalleled humiliation and suffering, had been greeted and treated by God as One who was worthy of supremest honour and reward. The details of this will come before us in the course of our exposition.

It is very striking to observe how that the *character* of these seven quotations made by the Holy Spirit from the O.T. agree perfectly with the *numerical* position of each of them. One is the number of *supremacy*: see Zech. 14:9—there will be none other in that day to dispute the Lord's rule, for Satan will be in the Pit. So the first quotation in Heb. 1 brings out the supremacy of Christ over the angels as "Son" (v. 5). Two is the number of *witness*: see Rev. 11:3, etc. So the force of the second quotation in Heb. 1 is the unique relation of the Son to the Father borne witness to. Three is the number of *manifestation*, and in the third quotation we see the superiority of the Mediator manifested by the angels "worshipping" Him (v. 6). Four is the number of the *creature*, and in the fourth quotation the Holy Spirit significantly turns from Christ, who is more than creature, and dwells upon the inferiority of the angels (v. 7) who are "made." Five is the number of *grace*, and the fifth quotation brings before us the "throne" of the Saviour (v. 8), which *is* "the Throne of Grace" (Heb. 4:16). Six is the number of *man*, and the sixth quotation (vv. 10-2) contains God's response to the plaint of the Son of Man's being taken away "in the midst of His days." Seven is the number of completion and of *rest* after a finished work: see Gen. 2:3; and so the seventh quotation views Christ as now seated at God's right hand (v. 13), as the reward of His finished work. How perfect is every detail of Holy Writ!

The final verse of Heb. 1 furnishes the fullest demonstration of the superiority of Christianity over Judaism and the exaltation of Christ above the celestial hierarchies. So far are the angels below the Saviour, they are sent forth by Him to minister unto His people. The fact of this ministry, as well as the nature and value of it, are known to but few to-day. The subject is a most interesting as well as important one, and will well repay much fuller study than our limited space here permits us to indulge in. May the bare outline we attempt stimulate our readers to fill it in for themselves.

"And Thou, Lord, in the beginning, hast laid the foundation of the earth" (v. 10). The opening "and" shows that the apostle is continuing to advance proof of the proposition laid down in v. 4. This proof of Christ's excellency is taken from a work peculiar to God, creation. The argument is based upon a Divine testimony found in the Old Testament. The argument may be stated thus: The Creator is more excellent than creatures; Christ is the Creator, angels are creatures; therefore Christ is more excellent than angels. That Christ *is* Creator is here proved; that angels are creatures, has been shown in v. 7. This verse also completes the answer to a question which v. 4 may have raised in the minds of some, namely, what is the "more excellent name" which the Mediator has obtained? The reply is "Son" (v. 5), "God" (v. 8), "Lord" (v. 10).

"And Thou, Lord, in the beginning, hast laid the foundation of the earth." The Psalm from which this is quoted is a truly wondrous one; in some respects it is, perhaps, the most remarkable of the whole series. It lays bare before us the Saviour's very soul. Few, if any, of us would have thought of applying it to Christ, or even dared to, had not the Spirit of God done so here in Heb. 1. This Psalm brings before us the true and perfect humanity of Christ, and depicts Him as the despised and rejected One. It reveals Him as One who *felt,* and felt deeply, the experiences through which He passed. It might well be termed the Psalm of the Man of Sorrows. In it He is seen opening His heart and pouring out His grief before God. We lose much if we fail to attend carefully to the context of that portion which the Spirit here quotes. Let us go back to its opening verses:

"Hear My prayer, O Lord, and let My cry come unto Thee. Hide not Thy face from Me, in the day when I am in trouble; incline Thine ear unto Me: in the day when I call answer Me speedily. For My days are consumed like smoke, and My bones are burned as an hearth. My heart is smitten, and withered like grass; so that I forget to eat My bread. By reason of the voice of My groaning My bones cleave to my skin. I am like a pelican of the wilderness; I am like an owl of the desert. I watch, and am as a sparrow alone upon the housetop, Mine enemies reproach Me all the day, and they that are mad against Me are sworn against Me. For I have eaten ashes like bread, and mingled My drink with weeping. Because of Thine indignation and Thy wrath: for Thou hast lifted Me up, and cast Me down. My days are like a shadow that declineth; and I am withered like grass" (vv. 1-11).

The above quotation is a longer one than we are accustomed to make, but it seemed impossible to abbreviate without losing its pathos and its moving effects upon us. There we are permitted to behold something of the Saviour's "travail of soul." How it should bow our hearts before Him! These plaintive sentences were uttered by our blessed Redeemer either amid the dark shadows of Gethsemane, or under the more awful darkness of Calvary. But notwithstanding His awful anguish, mark the perfect confidence in God of this suffering One:

"But Thou, O Lord, shalt endure forever, and Thy remembrance unto all generations. Thou shalt arise and have mercy upon Zion: for the time to favour her, yea, the set time, is come. For Thy servants take pleasure in her stones, and favour the dust thereof. So the heathen shall fear the name of the Lord, and all the kings of the earth Thy glory. When the Lord shall build up Zion, He shall appear in His glory. He will regard the prayer of the destitute, and not despise their prayer. This shall be written for the generation to come: and the people which shall be created shall praise the Lord. For He hath looked down from the height of His sanctuary; from heaven did the Lord behold the earth; to hear the groaning of the prisoner to loose those that are appointed to death; to declare the name of the Lord in Zion and His praise in Jerusalem; when the people are gathered together, and the kingdoms to serve the Lord" (vv. 12-22). Blessed is it to behold here the Saviour looking away from the things seen to the things unseen: from the dark present to the bright future.

"He weakened My strength in the way; He shortened My days. I said O My God, take Me not away in the midst of My days" (vv. 23, 24). Here again we are permitted to hear the "strong crying" (Heb. 5:7) of Him who was "acquainted with grief" as none other ever was. Few things recorded in the Word are more affecting than this: that the Lord Jesus, the perfect Man, should, at the age of thirty-three, be deemed by men as unfit to live any longer. He had hardly entered upon man's estate when they crucified Him. Do you think *that* was nothing to Christ? Ah, brethren, He felt it deeply. Who can doubt it in the light of this awful plaint: "He weakened My strength in the way; He shortened My days. I said, O My God, take Me not away in the midst of My days." As Man He felt acutely this "cutting off" in His very prime.

Those words of the Saviour make manifest what He suffered in His soul. He was perfect Man, with all the sinless sensibilities of human nature. A very touching type of Christ's being cut off in the early prime of manhood is found in Lev. 2:14. Each grade of the meal-offering described in Lev. 2 pointed to the *humanity* of the Redeemer. Here in v. 14 Israel was bidden to take *"green* ears of corn dried by the fire" and offer it to the Lord as an offering. The "green ears of corn" (compare John 12:24 where Christ speaks of Himself under this figure) had not fully ripened, and so, were "dried by the fire"—symbol of being subjected to God's judgment. So it was with Christ. Man's sickle went over the field of corn and He was "cut off" in the midst of His days: when He was barely half of the "three score years and ten" (Psa. 90:10).

And what was Heaven's response to this anguished cry of the Saviour? The remainder of the Psalm records God's answer: "Thy years are throughout all generations. Of old hast Thou laid the foundation of the earth. And the heavens are the work of Thy hands. They shall perish, but Thou shalt endure, yea, all of them shall wax old like a garment; as a vesture shalt Thou change them, and they shall be changed: But Thou are the same, and Thy years shall have no end" (vv. 24-27).

"How marvellous is this! How incomprehensible this union of divine and human, of eternity and time, sadness and omnipotence! Do not wonder that such language of anguish, faintness and sorrow, of agonising faith, is attributed by the Holy Spirit to Jesus. Remember the life of Jesus was a life of faith, a real, true, and earnest conflict; and that, although He constantly took firm hold of the promises of God, yet His feelings of sorrow, His sense of utter dependence on God, His anxious looking forward to His last suffering, all this was a reality. He gained the victory by faith; He knew that He was, through suffering, returning to the Father He knew that as Son of Man and Redeemer of His people He would be glorified with the glory which He had with the Father before the foundations of the world were laid" (Saphir).

Let us examine closely the blessed reply of the Father to the plaintive petition of His suffering Son. "And, Thou, Lord." Before His incarnation, David, by the Spirit, called Him "Lord" (Matt. 22:43). At His birth, the angels who brought the first glad tidings of His advent to this earth, hailed Him as "Christ the Lord" (Luke 2:11). During His earthly ministry the disciples owned Him as "Lord" (John 13:13). So, too, is He often referred to in the Epistles (Rom. 1:8, etc.). But here, it is none other than the Father Himself who directly addresses as "Lord" that suffering Man, as He lay on His face in the Garden, sweating as it were great drops of blood. Thus may, and thus should, every believer also say of Him, "My Lord, and my God" (John 20:28), and *worship* Him as such.

"Thou, Lord, in the beginning." This phrase sets forth the *eternity* of the being of Him who became the Mediator. If Christ "in the beginning" laid the foundation of the earth, then *He* must be without beginning, and thus, eternal, compare (Prov. 8:22, 23).

"Hast laid the foundation of the earth." We have been deeply impressed with the fact that God has some good reason for referring in His Word to "the foundation" and "foundations" of the earth or the world more then twenty-five times. We believe it is to safeguard His people from the popular delusion of the day, namely, that the earth revolves on its axis, and that the heavenly bodies are stationary, only *appearing* to our sight to move, as the banks and trees seem to be doing to one seated in a rowing-boat or sailing-ship. This theory was first advanced (so far as the writer is aware) by Grecian heathen philosophers, echoed by Copernicus in the fifteenth century, and re-echoed by science "falsely so called" (see 1 Tim. 6:20) to-day. Alas, that so many of God's servants and people have accepted it. Such a conceit cannot be harmonised with "a *foundation*" so often predicated of the earth; which, necessarily, implies its *fixity!* Nor can such a theory be squared with the repeated statements of Holy Writ that the "sun moves" (Joshua 10:12), etc. The writer is well aware that this paragraph may evoke a pitying smile from some. But that will not move him. Let *God* be true and every man a liar. We are content to believe what *He* has said. Paul was willing to be a fool for Christ's sake (1 Cor. 4:10), and we are willing to be thought a fool for the Scripture's sake.

"And the heavens are the work of Thine hand" (v. 10). This seems to bring in an additional thought. In the preceding clause creation is ascribed to Christ; here the greatness of His power. The heavens being of so far vaster dimensions than the earth, suggests the omnipotency of their Maker.

"They shall perish, but Thou remainest" (v. 11). This verse makes mention of still another perfection of Christ, namely, His *immutability*. The earth and the heavens shall perish. The apostle John, in prophetic vision, saw "a new heaven and a new earth, for the first heaven and the first earth were passed away" (Rev. 21:1). But Christ "remaineth." He is "the same yesterday, and to-day, and forever."

"And they all shall wax old as doth a garment, and as a vesture shalt Thou fold them up, and they shall be changed" (vv. 11:12). This emphasises the mutability of the creature. Two resemblances are employed: first the earth may be said to "wax old as doth a garment" in that it is not to last forever, but is appointed to an end: see 2 Peter 3:10. The longer, therefore, it has continued, the nearer it approaches to that end; as a garment, the longer it is worn, the nearer it is to its end. May not the increasing number of earthquakes evidence that "old age" is fast coming upon it? Second, the heavens may be said to be "folded up as a vesture," inasmuch as Scripture declares "the heavens shall be rolled together as a scroll" (Isa. 34:4).

"*Thou* shall fold them up." This intimates Christ's absolute control over all creation. He that made all hath an absolute power to preserve, alter, and destroy all, as it pleaseth Him. He is the Potter, we are but the clay, to be moulded as He will. Our Lord Jesus Christ, being true God, is the Most High and supreme Sovereign over all, and He doeth all "that man may know that Thou, whose name is *Jehovah*, art the Most High over all the earth" (Psa. 83:18). "By the word of the Lord were the heavens made" (Psa. 33:6); by the same word shall they be folded up. The practical value of this for our hearts is plain; such a Lord may be safely trusted; such a Lord should be revered and worshipped. In what holy awe should He be held!

"But Thou art the same, and Thy years shall not fail" (v. 12). "The mutability of creatures being distinctly set out, the apostle returneth to the main point intended, which is Christ's immutability. It was before generally set down in the phrase, 'Thou remaineth.' Here it is illustrated in two other branches. Though all these three phrases in general intend one and the same thing, namely, immutability, yet, to show that there is no tautology, no vain repetition, of one and the same thing, they may be distinguished one from another:

"'Thou remaineth,' pointeth at Christ's eternity before all times; for it implieth his being before, in which he still abides. 'Thou art the same' delares Christ's constancy. There is no variableness with him; thus, therefore, he says of himself, 'I am the Lord, I change not' (Mal. 3:6). 'Thy years shall not fail' intendeth Christ's everlastingness; that he was before all times, and continueth in all ages, and will beyond all times so continue" (Dr. Gouge).

"But Thou art the same, and Thy years shall not fail." *This* was God's answer to the plaint of Christ's being, "cut off" in the midst of His days. As man, *His* "years" should have no end! As God the Son He *is* eternal in His being; but as Man, in resurrection, He received "life for evermore" (cf. Heb. 7:14-17). Do we really grasp this? For nineteen hundred years since the Cross, men have been born, have lived, and then died. Statesmen, emperors, kings have appeared on the scene and then passed away. But there is one glorious Man who spans the centuries, who in His own humanity bridges those nineteen hundred years. He has not died, nor even grown old; He is *"the same* yesterday, and to-day, and forever!"

"But Thou art the same, and Thy years shall not fail." What assurance was this for the believing of Israel who had been sorely perplexed at the "cutting off" of the Messiah, in the midst of His days! Humbled as He had been, yet was He the Creator. In servant form had He appeared among them, but He was and is the sovereign Disposer of all things. Died he had on the cross, but He was now "alive for evermore." Their own Scriptures bore witness to it: God Himself affirmed it!

And what is the practical application of this wondrous passage for us to-day! Surely this: first, such a Saviour, who is none other than Him who made heaven and earth, is a mighty Redeemer, "Able also to save them to the uttermost that come unto God by Him." Second, such an One, who is immutable and eternal, may be safely and confidently trusted; none can pluck out of *His* hand! Third, such an One, who is "Lord" over all, is to be held in holy awe and given the worship, submission, and service which are His due.

"But to which of the angels said He at any time, Sit on My right hand until I make Thine enemies Thy footstool?" (v. 13). This completes the proof of what the apostle had said in vv. 2, 3. The O.T. itself witnessed to the fact that the rejected Messiah is now seated at God's right hand, and this by the word of the Father Himself. The quotation is from the 110th Psalm, a Psalm quoted more frequently in the N.T. than any other.

Verses 13 and 14 belong together. In them another contrast is pointed between Christ and the angels. As an argument it may be stated thus: He that sitteth at God's right hand is far more excellent than ministers: Christ sitteth at God's right hand, and angels *are* "ministers;" therefore, Christ is far more excellent than they. The former part is proved in v. 13, the latter is shown in v. 14.

As D.V. the subject of v. 13 will come before us again and again in our studies in this Epistle, we will now offer only the briefest comment. The Speaker here is the Father; the One addressed is the Son, but in His mediatorial character, for it was as the Son of Man that God exalted Him. Further proof of this is supplied by "until *I* make Thine enemies Thy footstool." As mediatorial King and Priest, Christ is subservient to the Father; He is subject to Him who has "put all things under Him" (1 Cor. 15:27).

"*Until* I make." Christ is not to sit at God's right hand forever. 1 Thess. 4:16 says, "The Lord Himself shall descend from heaven with a shout," etc. He remains there throughout this present Day of Grace. Then, following a brief interval, His enemies shall be made His footstool. This will be at His return to the earth: see Rev. 19:11-21; Isa. 63:1-3, etc. Then Christ *Himself* will subdue His enemies: note the "He" in 1 Cor. 15:25; but it will be by the Father's decree, see Psa. 2:6-9.

"Are they not all ministering spirits, sent forth to minister for them who shall be heirs of salvation?" (v. 14). This verse presents a fact which should awaken in every Christian varied and deep emotions: Alas that, through lack of diligence in searching the Word, so many of the Lord's people are largely in ignorance of much that is said therein, and here referred to.

It should awaken within us a sense of *wonderment*. The angels are portrayed as *our* attendants! When we remember who and what they are—their exalted rank in the scale of being, their sinlessness, their wondrous capacities, knowledge and powers —it is surely an astonishing thing to learn that they should minister unto us. Think of it, the unfallen angels waiting upon the fallen descendants of Adam! The courtiers of Heaven ministering to worms of the earth! The mighty angels, who "excel in strength," taking notice of and serving those so far beneath them! Could you imagine the princes of the royal family seeking out dwellers in the slums and ministering to them, not once or occasionally, but constantly? But the analogy altogether fails. The angels of God are sent forth to minister unto redeemed sinners! Marvel at it.

It should awaken within us *fervent praise to God*. What an evidence of His grace, what a proof of His love, that He sends forth His angels to "minister" unto us! This is another of the wondrous provisions of His mercy, which none of us begin to appreciate as we should. It is another of the blessed consequences of our *union* with Christ. In Matt. 4:11 we read, "angels came and ministered unto Him." Therefore, because Divine grace has made us one with Him, they do so to us too. What a proof is this of our oneness with Him! Angels of God are sent forth to minister unto redeemed sinners! Bow in worship and praise.

It should deepen within us *a sense of security*. True, it may be abused, but rightly appropriated, how it is calculated to quieten our fears, counteract our sense of feebleness, calm our hearts in time of danger! Is it not written, "The angel of the Lord encampeth round about them that fear Him, and delivereth them;" then *why* be afraid? We doubt not that every Christian has been "delivered" many more times from the jaws of death by angelic interposition, than any of us imagine. The angels of God are sent forth to minister unto redeemed sinners. Then let the realization of this deepen within us a sense of the Lord's protecting care for entrusting us to His mighty angels.

"Are they not all ministering spirits, sent forth to minister for them who shall be the heirs of salvation?" (v. 14). Three things are to be considered: those to whom the angels minister, why they thus minister, and the form their ministry takes.

Those to whom the angels minister are here termed "heirs of salvation," an expression denoting at least four things. There is an Estate unto which God has predestinated His people, an inheritance —*willed* to them by God. This Estate is designated "salvation," see 1 Thess. 5:9, where our appointment unto it is mentioned. It is the consummation of our salvation which is in view, Heb. 9:28; 1 Pet. 1:3, 4. Well may this estate or inheritance be called "Salvation," for those who enter it are forever delivered from all danger, freed from all enemies, secured from all evils. This expression "heirs of salvation" also denotes our *legal rights* to the inheritance: our title is an indefeasible one. Further, it presupposes the coming in of *death*, Christ's death. Finally, it implies the *perpetuity* of it—'to him and his heirs forever.'

It is to these "heirs of salvation" that the angels minister. To enable us the better to grasp the *relation* of angels to Christians, let us employ an illustration. Take the present household of the Duke of York. In it are many servants, honoured, trusted, loved. There are titled "ladies" and "lords" of the realm, yet they are serving, "ministering,' to the infant Princess Elizabeth. At present, she is inferior to them in age, strength, wisdom and attainments; yet is she superior in rank and station. She is of the royal stock, a princess, possibly heir to the throne. In like manner, the heirs of salvation are now in the stage of their infancy; they are but babes in Christ; this is the period of their minority. The angels far excell us in strength, wisdom, attainments; yet are they our servants, they "minister" unto us. Why? Because we are high above them in birth, rank, station. We are chilren of God, we are joint-heirs with Christ, we have been redeemed with royal blood, yea, we have been made "kings and priests unto God" (Rev. 1:6). O how wonderful is our rank—members of the Royal family of Heaven, therefore are we "ministered" unto by the holy angels. What a calling is ours! What provision has Divine love made for us!

Let us now inquire, *Why* do they thus "minister" unto us? For what reason or reasons has God ordained that the angels should be our attendants? All His ways are ordered by perfect wisdom. Let us then reverently enquire as to His purpose in this arrangement.

First, is it not to exercise the graces of obedience and benevolence in the angels themselves? Such a task being assigned them constitutes a real test of their fidelity to their Maker. They are bidden to leave the glories of Heaven and come down to this poor sin-cursed earth; yes, oftentimes to seek out children of God in hovels and workhouses. What a test of their loyalty to God! Not only so, but what an opportunity is thus afforded for the exercise in them of the spirit of benevolence! As the angels are brought into contact with the frail and suffering children of God, how their sympathies must be drawn out! There are no such objects in Heaven, there is no distress or suffering there; and, methinks, that were the angels to be confined to that realm of unclouded bliss, they would be stoics—unable to sympathise with us poor afflicted creatures. Therefore, to cultivate both the spirit of obedience and of benevolence, God has commissioned them to "minister for them who shall be heirs of salvation."

Second, Has not God assigned to them this ministery in order to give them a closer acquaintance with His own wondrous grace and matchless love for poor sinners? The angels are not simply far-distant spectators of the out-working of God's wondrous purpose of mercy, but have been made, in part, the actual administrators of it! Thus, by virtue of this commission which they have received from Him, they learn in a practical way how much He cares for us.

Third, has not God assigned to them this ministry in order that there might be a closer bond between the different section of His family? That word in Eph. 3:15, refers, we believe, not only to the redeemed of Christ, but to all of Heaven's inhabitants—"of whom the whole family in heaven and earth is named." Yes, the angels are members of God's "family" too. Note how in Heb. 12:22, 23 the two great sections of it are placed side by side: "to an innumerable company of angels, to the general assembly and Church of the Fristborn." Thus, the angels are commissioned to minister for those who shall be heirs of salvation in order that there may be formed a closer bond of intercourse and sympathy between the two great sections of God's family.

Fourth, has not God assigned them this ministry in order to magnify the work of the Lord Jesus? The angels are not only subject to Christ as their Lord, are not only called on to worship Him as God, but they are also employed in watching over the safety and promoting the temporal interests of His redeemed. No doubt this fourth named reason is both the primary and ultimate one. How this magnifies the Saviour! Commissioning them to "minister for those who shall be heirs of salvation" is God's putting His imprimature upon the cross-work of Christ.

Let us now consider *how* the angels "minister" to us. First, in *protecting from temporal dangers*. A striking example of this is found in 2 Kings 6:15-17. Elisha and his servant were menaced by the king of Syria. His forces were sent out to capture them. An host compassed the city where they were. The servant was terrified; then the prophet prayed unto the Lord to open his eyes, "and the Lord opened the eyes of the young man; and he saw: and, behold, the mountain was full of horses and chariots of fire round about Elisha," which, in the light of Psa. 68:17 and Heb. 1:7, we know were the protecting angels of God. In the sequel we learn that the enemy was smitten with blindness, and thus the servants of God escaped. This was a concrete illustration of Psa. 34:7, "The angel of the Lord encampeth round about them that fear Him, and delivereth them."

Second, in *delivering from temporal dangers*. A case in point is that which is recorded of Lot: "And when the morning arose, then the angels hastened Lot, saying, Arise, take thy wife and thy two daughters which are here; lest thou be consumed in the iniquity of the city. And while he lingered, the men laid hold upon his hand, and upon the hand of his wife, and upon the hand of his two daughters; the Lord being merciful unto him, and they brought him forth, and set him without the city." How often angels have "hastened" us when in the place of danger, and "laid hold" of us while we lingered, perhaps the Day will reveal.

Another example is found in the case of Daniel. We refer to the time when he was cast into the lions' den. All Bible readers are aware that the prophet was miraculously preserved from these wild beasts, but what is not generally known is the particular instrumentality which God employed on that occasion. This is made known in Dan. 6:22: "My God hath sent His *angel*, and hath shut the lions' mouths, that they have not hurt me." What an illustration is this of Psa. 34:7, "The angel of the Lord encampeth round about them that fear Him, and delivereth them!"

Nor is angelic deliverance of God's people confined to Old Testament times. In Acts 5:17-19 we read, "Then the high priest rose up, and all they that were with him (which is the sect of the Sadducees) and were filled with indignation, and laid their hands on the apostles, and put them in the common prison. But the angel of the Lord by night opened the prison doors, and brought them forth." Again, in Acts 12:6-9 we read, "The same night Peter was sleeping between two soldiers, bound with two chains; and the keepers before the door kept the prison. And, behold, the angel of the Lord came upon him, and a light shined in the prison: and he smote Peter on the side, and raised him up, saying, Arise up quickly. And his chains fell off from his hands. And he went out, and followed him."

One other form which the ministry of angels takes in connection with their custody of God's children is brought before us in Luke 16:22: "And it came to pass, that the beggar died, and was carried by the angels into Abraham's bosom." To our natural feelings, a death-bed scene is often a most painful and distressing experience. There we behold a helpless creature, emaciated by disease, convulsed with pain, panting for breath; his countenance pallid, his lips quivering, his brow bedewed with a cold sweat. But were not the spiritual world hidden from us by a vail of God's appointing we should also see there the glorious inhabitants of Heaven surrounding the bed, waiting for God's summons, to convoy that soul from earth, through the territory of Satan, up to the Father's House. There they are, ready to perform their last office in ministering for those who shall be heirs of salvation. Then, Christian, why fear death?

It should be carefully noted that angels are mentioned in the plural number in Luke 16:22, so also are they in Psa. 91:11, 12: "For He shall give His *angels* charge over thee, to keep thee in all thy ways. They shall bear thee up in their hands, lest thou dash thy foot against a stone." There is nothing whatever in Scripture to support the Romish tradition of a single guardian angel for each person or Christian: the plural number in the above passages make directly against it.

"Are they not all ministering spirits, sent forth to minister for them who shall be heirs of salvation?" (v. 14). "This text wears an interrogative form; but it is just equivalent to a strong affirmation It is certain that no angel sits on the throne of God; it is certain that they are all *ministering* spirits. A minister is a servant—a person who occupies an inferior place, who acts a subordinate part, subject to the authority and regulated by the will of another. The angels are 'ministering spirits,' they are not *governing* spirits. Service, not dominion, is their province. In the first phrase there is an expression of their being God's ministers or servants; in the second, that He *sends forth*, commissions these servants of His to minister to those who shall be heirs of salvation. They are His servants, and He uses their instrumentality for promoting the happiness of His peculiar people. There is a double contrast. The Son is the co-ruler—they are servants; the Son sits—they are sent forth" (Dr. J. Brown).

Finally, it should be observed that "ministering spirits" is a title or designation. Not only do the angels render service to God's saints, but they have an *office* so to do. It is not simply that they "go forth" to minister for them, but they are "sent forth." They do not take this work upon themselves, but have received a definite charge or commission from their Maker. How this evidences, once more, the preciousness to Christ of those whom He purchased with His blood! O that our hearts may be bowed in wonderment and worship for this blessed provision of His love toward us while we are left in this wilderness scene. O that our fears may be removed, and our hearts strengthened by the realization that, amid the dangers and perils with which we are now surrounded, the angels of God are guarding and ministering both for and to us.

—Arthur W. Pink.

N.B.—Does not the reader desire fellow-Christians to share these good things? Why not speak of them to others? Why not loan out your copy, asking interested ones to write us for the magazine!—A.W.P.

GLEANINGS IN EXODUS.

54. *The Atonement Money*: Ex. 30:11-15.

The above versus present to us that which it is by no means easy to understand at first glance, and up to the point where God grants light upon them the more they are studied the more will the force of their difficulties be felt. That which is central in our present portion is Jehovah commanding His people to give "every man a ransom." This ransom was a *monetary* one, a half shekel of silver, and it was in order "to make an atonement for their souls." But this seems so utterly foreign to the general tone and tenor of Scripture that many have been sorely puzzled by it. How is our present passage to be harmonised with the words of Isa. 55:1, "without money and without price?" How may we interpret it so as not to clash with 1 Peter 1:18 "Forasmuch as ye know that ye were not redeemed with corruptible things as silver and gold?"

Nor is the presenting of money by the Israelites as a "ransom" and for "an atonement" the only difficulty here. The *position* occupied by our present passage seems a strange one. Israel were already a "redeemed" people. Had they not sung at the Red Sea, "Thou in Thy mercy hast led forth the people which Thou hast redeemed" (15:13)! Why, then, was a "ransom" price necessary now? Then, too, why introduce this strange ordinance between descriptions of the golden-altar and the laver; what possible connection was there between the three things? Surely our passage calls for prayer as well as study! May the God of all grace open now our eyes that we may be enabled to behold wondrous things out of His law.

In taking up our passage the first thing we must do is to ponder it in the light of its wider context; that is to say, consider carefully the particular book in which it is found. This is ever essential if we are rightly to ascertain the scope of any passage. Each book of Scripture has a prominent and dominant theme which, as such, is peculiar to itself, around which all its contents are made to centre, and of which all its details are but the amplification. As stated in our opening article upon Exodus, this book, viewed doctrinally, treats of *redemption*; that is its principal subject, its dominant theme.

This important and blessed truth of redemption is illustrated in Exodus by God's dealings with the children of Israel. First, we are shown their need of redemption—a people in captivity groaning in bitter bondage. Second, we behold the might and holiness of the Redeemer Himself—displayed in His plagues upon Egypt. Third, we see the character of redemption—purchased by blood, emancipated by power. Fourth, we learn the duty of the redeemed—obedience to the Lord. Finally, we have set before us the privileges of the redeemed—worshipping God in His holy habitation. Thus, we are enabled to see at the outset, that our present passage has to do with the people of God entering into the privileges of redemption. Bearing this in mind, let us now attend to the details of our passage.

"*When* thou takest the sum of the children of Israel after their number, *then* shall they give every man a ransom for his soul unto the Lord, when thou numberest them; that there be no plague among them, when thou numberest them" (v. 12). Observe the two words placed in italics. Whenever the Holy Spirit supplies a time-mark like this, it should be carefully pondered: often it supplies a valuable key to a passage—cf. Matt. 13:1; 25:1, etc.; such as the case here. The giving of this ransom-money was connected with the "numbering" of Israel: observe that a reference to this fact is made no less than five times in vv. 12-14. Here, then, is the next thing to be weighed as we seek to ascertain the spiritual meaning of this ordinance. What, then, are the thoughts connected with "numbering" in Scripture?

That this is no unimportant question is at once evidenced by the fact that the fourth book of the Old Testament is designated "Numbers:" its title being taken from the numberings of the children of Israel for war, for ministry, and for their inheritance in Canaan. Thus, a just apprehension of Jehovah's design in these numberings is essential to a spiritual understanding of the act. Now the most obvious thing suggested by "numbering" is *ownership*. Take one or two simple examples which illustrate this. It is natural for me to number the books in my own library; but I would never think of doing so with my neighbour's. A farmer numbers the sheep of his own flock, but not those belonging to another. *Property in*, and consequent *right over* are the thoughts connected with "numbering." So it is in the Scriptures: when God numbers or orders anything to be numbered, taking the sum of them denotes that they belong to Him, and that He has the sovereign right to do with them as He pleases. The action itself says of the things numbered, "These are Mine, and I assign them their place as I will." If the following passages be pondered it will be found that they confirm our definition.

"Lift up your eyes on high, and behold who hath created these things, that bringeth out their hosts by number, He calleth them all by names by the greatness of His might, for that He is strong in power; not one faileth" (Isa. 40:26). The reference here is to the heavenly bodies. God's ownership and sovereign disposings of them. So again in Psalm 147:4 we read, "He telleth the number of the stars; He calleth them all by their names."

Let us take now another kind of example: "Therefore will I *number* you to the sword, and ye shall all bow down to the slaughter" (Isa. 65:12). This passage does not, indeed, assert God's property *in* His enemies, but the expression "number you to the sword" asserts His power to dispose of them; and the other is clearly implied. The Lord "numbers" to the sword because He has "made all things for Himself: yea, even the wicked for the day of evil" (Prov. 16:4). A similar instance is found in the sentence pronounced on Belshazzar: "MENE, God hath numbered thy kingdom and finished it" (Dan. 5:26). This may suffice to show the meaning of the Divine sum-takings. They assert God's property rights and His power to do what He will with His own.

In the numberings of Israel it was God dealing with the people whom He had redeemed for Himself, appropriating what was His, and assigning to each and all their place before Him. This is what is made so prominent in the book of Numbers—Israel were *Jehovah's* soldiers and servants, and He distributed each as He pleased. As men of war belonging to the Lord, engaged in a warfare by which His name was to be glorified, it was for Him to muster the army for Himself: "The Lord is a Man of war: the Lord is His name" (Ex. 15:3). "The Lord strong and mighty, the Lord mighty in battle" (Psa. 24:8). All the hosts of heaven are His, and all the armies of the earth; therefore it is His prerogative to number them. How jealously the Lord guards this prerogative may be seen, with terrific force, in the history of David. He had been entrusted with the leading forth of the armies of the living God, and so long as he occupied his place before the hosts it was well; but at length David forgot God's glory, and sought his own:

"And Satan stood up against Israel and provoked David to number Israel. And David said to Joab and to the rulers of the people, Go, number Israel from Beersheba even to Dan; and bring the number of them to me, that I may know it. And Joab answered, The Lord make His people an hundred times so many more as they be; but my lord the king, are they not all my lord's servants? why then doth my lord require this thing? why will he be a cause of trespass to Israel? Nevertheless, the king's word prevailed against Joab. . . . and God was displeased with this thing; wherefore He smote Israel. And David said unto God, I have sinned greatly, because I have done this thing: but now, I beseech Thee, do away the iniquity of Thy servant; for I have done very foolishly" (1 Chron. 21:1-4, 7, 8).

It may be asked, What harm was there in thus numbering the people? Is not a census valuable? Yes, for men warring after the flesh and walking according to worldly principles; but even Joab, a man of iniquity, knew so well what the numbering of the army of the living God signified, that he protested against the act, as one flagrantly trenching upon the rights and glory of the Lord, that judgment was sure to follow; as it did. God will not give His glory to another. Alas, David forgot this, and brought evil upon Israel. There is only one King, the Captain of our salvation, who, being entrusted with the ordering of God's people, never forgets the Father's glory. And this is what is before us in our present type, as God said to Moses, "When *thou* takest the sum of the children of Israel:" it was only the typical mediator who could take the sum of God's people!

Above, we have pointed out how that the numberings of Israel recorded in the fourth book of Scripture set forth God's appropriation and ordering of a people whom He had redeemed for and unto Himself. It is this which supplies the key to our present portion. Appropriately is this *first* reference to the "numbering" of Israel found in that book which, doctrinally, treats of *redemption*; and significantly is it said at the beginning of the passage, "when thou takest the sum of the children of Israel after their number, they shall give every man a *ransom* for his soul" (v. 12). Thus, as usual, the key is hung right on the door for us! That which is central in this ordinance of the atonement-money is, that God *appropriates* His elect unto Himself only as a *ransomed* people. A clear proof of this has already been before us in Ex. 12 and 13, where we saw the "firstborn" secured by Him because ransomed to Him.

In Ex. 12 and 13 the "firstborn" were ransomed and secured by blood-shedding; here in Ex. 30 the children of Israel are owned as Jehovah's ("numbered") by "silver." The change of figure should occasion no difficulty. Twice in our passage is the money specifically termed "an *offering* unto the Lord." As was pointed out when commenting upon the silver sockets under the boards of the tabernacle's framework (26:19), the blood of the sacrifices more nearly exhibited the *mode* by which actual atonement was to be made for sin, but the "atonement-money" fitly proclaimed the *preciousness* of that by which sinners should be redeemed. Further confirmation of this is found in Num. 31:49-54, where we learn that the officers of Israel's hosts brought an offering of *gold* "to make an atonement." That our present passage does not stand alone may be seen by a reference to Num. 3:46-51; 18:15, 16, etc.

We learn best the meaning of our type by observing how the Holy Spirit sets it aside once the antitype has come in. Just as we see most clearly the typical meaning of the blood of bulls and goats when, in the presence of the "one sacrifice for sins" God declares it is not possible "that these should take away sins" (Heb. 10:4); so we get hold of the design of the atonement-silver and the atonement-gold (cf. Num. 31:49-54 where the term "gold" is found four times) when, beholding Him in whom is treasured up all redemption's wealth we are told, "Ye were not *redeemed* with corruptible things as silver and gold, from your vain conversation. . . . but with the precious blood of Christ, as of a lamb without blemish and without spot." Thus, the "*precious* blood" (an expression found nowhere else) in *this* connection, tells us that the "ransom" money prefigured the *costliness* of Christ's sacrifice, as the "blood" did the character of it.

Does not this satisfactorily dispose of the first difficulty in our passage to which we called attention at the beginning of this article? True, the Israelite was required to give a monetary ransom for his soul, but this no more signified that salvation might be secured by the sinner's own efforts than did the furnishing of a bullock or lamb imply that the offerer was thereby purchasing God's favour. Instead, it was the Lord teaching His people, in type and figure, of Him who alone could make an atonement for sin, namely Christ: the slaying of the offerer's sacrifice telling of the shedding of His blood, the bringing of the silver or gold speaking of the preciousness of that blood. That each was furnished by the Israelite himself only emphasised the truth that the sinner must, by faith, personally *appropriate* the Lord Jesus, and place Him between his sins and a holy God.

Let us notice next the amount required from each Israelite: "This they shall give, every one that passeth among them that are numbered, half a shekel, after the shekel of the sanctuary: (a shekel is twenty gerahs): an half shekel shall be the offering of the Lord" (v. 13). Thus we learn that the "ransom" stipulated consisted of half a shekel or ten gerahs. This detail in our type is not without its significance, rather does it throw light upon it as a whole.

Ten, as we have shown in previous articles, is the number of human responsibility, and here we see the "ransom" fully meeting this responsibility. Less than ten gerahs would not avail before God—note how the woman in Luke 15:8 was not satisfied with only nine pieces of silver! The sinner imagines that if he discharges his duties toward his fellow-man, that is all which can fairly be required of him; God and His claims are left entirely out of his calculations. But the Ten Commandments begin with man's relations with and responsibility to the Lord God. But where is the one who ever loved the Lord his God with all his heart, or even his neighbour as himself? Ah, there is only one, the Lord Jesus Christ. He it was who presented to God the required ransom: "Christ hath redeemed us from the curse of the law, being made a curse for us" (Gal. 3:13). He was also "made under the law, to redeem them that are under the law" (Gal. 4:4, 5). Though we could not pay the ten gerahs of our responsibility, Christ has paid in full for us: He kept the law perfectly, in thought and word and deed, and also suffered its penalty on our behalf; thus has He provided the perfect ransom.

"Half a shekel, after the shekel of the sanctuary" (v. 13). This is a most important detail. It was by the *standard* "shekel," which was kept there in the sanctuary, that all others were tested: each must be full up to the required weight. So it was with the antitype. The true Atonement has been weighed in the balances of the heavenly sanctuary and found of full value before the throne of God. The Father's acceptance of our Saviour's ransom was convincingly demonstrated when He raised Him from the dead, and afterwards exalted Him to His own right hand. Christ has fully discharged the whole of His people's debt, completely satisfied every demand of Divine holiness, and provided a sure and eternal standing-ground for us before God.

"Every one that passeth among them that are numbered, from twenty years old and above, shall give an offering unto the Lord.

The rich shall not give more, and the poor shall not give less than half a shekel, when they give an offering unto the Lord, to make an atonement for your souls" (vv. 14, 15). This is very striking.

"All were to pay alike. In the matter of atonement, all must stand on one common platform. There may be a vast difference in knowledge, in experience, in capacity, in attainment, in zeal, in devotedness, but the ground of atonement is alike to all. The great apostle of the Gentiles and the feeblest lamb in all the flock of Christ stand on the same level as regards atonement. This is a very simple and a very blessed truth. All may not be alike devoted and fruitful, but 'the precious blood of Christ,' and not devotedness or fruitfulness, is the solid and everlasting ground of the believer's rest. The more we enter into the truth and power of this the more fruitful shall we be" (C.H.M.).

"And thou shalt take the atonement money of the children of Israel, and shalt appoint it for the service of the tabernacle of the congregation" (v. 16). The "appointment" of this atonement-money is mentioned in Ex. 38:25-28: *it furnished the foundation* for the Tabernacle! The use to which this ransom money was put supplies additional confirmation of our interpretation of the type. The House of God rested upon the "silver sockets." Thus, the *foundation* of God's people being around Himself is *redemption*. That the silver from which these "sockets" was made was given by Israel at the time of their "numbering," was God, in figure, appropriating His elect unto Himself as a ransomed people.

If we be not ransomed, we are not His. If we are not before Him, in the value of the blood of Christ, we are not numbered to Him as the lot of His inheritance. "The necessity for that is strongly emphasised in that no man could be considered as His at all apart from the redemption money paid for each one. No exemption was made, and no excuse could be pleaded. The rich was not permitted to pay more, nor the poor less than the half shekel. A shekel is said to be equivalent to thirty pence or sixty-two cents. A half shekel each man had to pay alike. God is no respecter of persons and redemption views all men on the same level before God. The rich might think it but a trifle, but it could not be neglected; and none were so poor as to be unable to give it. The prominent thought is the *availability* of the ransom-price, so as to leave each one without excuse: If God is to have a ransomed people among whom He will dwell, it must be according to His, not their, thoughts.

"The price is to be half a shekel, or ten gerahs, according to the shekel of the sanctuary—the Divine estimation. Man might conceive that something else would be more suited for his redemption—his own works, his feelings, his worthiness, or his faithfulness. But God's holiness and righteousness would not permit poor man to be so deceived. The foundation must be according to God's estimation, the shekel must be according to the balances of the sanctuary" (Mr. Ridout).

"And thou shalt take the atonement money of the children of Israel, and shall appoint it for the service of the tabernacle of the congregation; that it may be a memorial unto the children of Israel before the Lord, to make an atonement for your souls" (v. 16). The mention here of the "memorial" is most blessed. A lasting testimony was before God that atonement had been made for the souls of His people. They might but feebly enter into the blessedness of redemption, but the "memorial" of it was ever before Jehovah. The antitype of this is brought before us at length in the Epistle to the Hebrews—Christ now at the right hand of God, there as the Representative of His people.

There is a practical application to be made of our type to Christians to-day. We are under deep and lasting obligations to *own* the redemption-rights of Christ. God ransomed Israel to Himself in Egypt, but after they had been brought on to redemption-ground, they were required to *acknowledge* the responsibility this entailed, by bringing their *ten* gerahs of silver. So often we dwell upon what Christ's ransom has freed us *from*; so little are we occupied with what His ransom has freed us *for*. By ransoming us Christ has acquired rights over us, and He is entitled to our recognition of this in a practical way. Our lives should ever evidence the fact that we are not our own. If they do not, we shall suffer from a "plague" (v. 12)—Divine righteousness will chasten us.

It only remains for us now to point out that the *order* of these types is Divinely perfect. In Ex. 28 and 29 we have seen the establishment of the priesthood, and in consequence, God dwelling in Israel's midst. Then we have had their worship, ascending to Him as a sweet savour (30:1-10). Now we are shown how the people themselves were *identified with* the holy service of the tabernacle *through redemption*. A lasting "memorial" of it remained before Jehovah: a permanent standing-ground was provided before Him in that which, in figure, spoke of the preciousness of the Lamb's atonement. O that we may be increasingly occupied with Him, and our responsibility to glorify Him in our spirits and bodies which are His by purchase right.

—Arthur W. Pink.

THE PROPHETIC PARABLES OF MATT. 13.

10. Review.

We have endeavoured to show in our exposition of Matt. 13 that the prophetic parables found therein contain an outline sketch of the history of Christendom, i.e., the circle of profession, that sphere where the authority of Christ is nominally owned. That which is in view, particularly in the first four parables, is the circle of human responsibility, and therefore it is a picture of *failure* which is presented to us. Look where you will, it is always the same; whenever God has committed anything to man as a responsible creature, he has failed in his trust.

God placed Adam in Eden on the ground of human responsibility—that is, on probation; and he fell. God gave to Noah the sword of magisterial authority, but he failed to govern himself. God committed to Israel the law, and they broke it: before Moses came down from the mount they had set up the calf and were worshipping it. God instituted priesthood in Israel, in the tribe of Levi, and Aaron and his sons were duly consecrated to their office; yet on the very next day two of Aaron's sons offered strange fire, and judgment fell upon them. God instituted kingship in Israel, and that also was a sorry failure, as the books of Kings and Chronicles bear witness. God endowed Nebuchadnezzar with great power and it turned his head: he became so bloated with his own self-importance that he made an image to himself and demanded that all should worship it.

And the Christian profession has been no exception. Paul announced that after his departure "grievous wolves should enter the flock," and they did. The evil introduced by Satan at the beginning of this dispensation has never been eradicated, nor will it be till harvest-time. Instead of things getting better, Scripture explicitly declares they will become "worse and worse"; until Christ will "spue out" the whole system that bears His name.

The seven parables of Matt. 13 divide into four and three, the usual division of a septenary series. The first four were spoken to the multitude on the seashore; the last three to the disciples within the house. Hence, the first four give us the *external* view of the history of Christendom; the last three treating of that which is internal or spiritual. The first four are arranged in two pairs, the first two giving us the *individual* aspect of things, the wheat and tares. The second pair set forth that which is collective and corporate, the mustard-tree and the leaven.

Again; the first parable shows us a "sowing"; the fifth and sixth reveal the resultant crop. In like manner, the second parable also shows us a "sowing," while the third and fourth describe the harvest which springs from it. Should it be asked, Why is the crop from the second sowing mentioned before that of the first? The answer is, this is in keeping with God's invariable method: "Howbeit, that was not first which is spiritual, but that which is natural; and *afterward* that which is spiritual" (1 Cor. 15:46). Cain was born before Abel, Ishmael before Isaac, Esau before Jacob. The nation of Egypt existed before Israel; Saul came to the throne before David, and so on.

Let us now briefly *review* the details of these parables. The first represents our Lord still here upon earth, in Servant-form, scattering broadcast the Seed of the kingdom. It intimates the ratio of the Gospel's success, and forewarns us that only a fractional portion thereof produces abiding results. It makes known, from the human side, the various hindrances which render most of the Seed unfertile. Thus, this parable plainly repudiates the popular delusion which supposes that this age will yet witness a universal reception of the Gospel; it positively forbids any expectation of a millennium brought about by human enterprise or the labours of Christ's servants. It declares that as the result of the opposition of the devil, the flesh and the world, most of the Seed is either caught away or choked, and general barrenness is the result. Nor is there any hint at the close of the parable that such opposition would cease or that the yield would increase; instead, the Lord affirmed that it would decrease from an hundred-fold down to thirty-fold. The *history* of the last nineteen centuries has fully corroborated the teaching of this parable and made manifest the fulfilment of Christ's prediction. Only a *fractional* proportion of people in any land, State, city, or village really receive the Gospel! Not only is this true in general throughout the world, but it applies with equal force to the religious sphere. Where is the church to-day which can carry on its work if the *faithful minority* were removed?

The second parable carries us forward to a point after Christ's ascension, and shows us dual forces at work in Christendom. These "dual forces" are named in vv. 24, 25. They are Christ (through His servants) sowing His "good Seed" and the Devil sowing his "tares." Through the unwatchfulness of the Lord's servants, while "men slept," the Enemy got in his work, and as the result the crop in the field, as a whole, is spoilt, and is to continue thus to the end of the age.

Some have experienced a difficulty in v. 27. In view of the fact that the "tares" so closely resemble the wheat that the one cannot be distinguished from the other till harvest-time, how was it that their presence was detected at such an early date? The difficulty is more imaginary than real. Note the difference between what is said in v. 25 and v. 27: in the former it was "men" that slept; in the latter, it was the "servants" who discovered the presence of the tares. These "servants" obviously refer to the *apostles,* who were endowed with the Holy Spirit to an extent than none others have been, and therefore possessed a discernment which none others have had since then.

But though the "tares" were detected, orders were given that they must not be removed; they were to "grow together" with the wheat until the harvest. It is a great pity that many with more zeal than knowledge have *ignored* this command of Christ's. This word of His at once exposes the uselessness, worthlessness, and unscripturalness of "reform" movements and efforts. Men have indulged the idle dream that they could improve the world by ridding it of noxious weeds; in other words, by the banishment of drunkenness and immorality, and the purifying of politics—as well might they attempt to purify the waters of the Dead Sea! Christ said, "*Let* both grow"; do not waste time in seeking to get rid of the "tares." "Preach the Gospel to every creature" is our marching-orders, and due attention to it will leave no time for seeking to root up weeds! Finally, it is blessed to note that the Enemy can neither injure the wheat nor prevent the garnering of it. The sowing of his tares was by God's permission.

The third parable carries us beyond the days of the apostles and anticipated the time when the outward character of professing Christianity underwent a radical change. That which had hitherto been despised, had become popular; that which was so insignificant in the world, assumed huge proportions. But instead of this being a great blessing, it was a fearful curse. So far from its being a triumph for the Gospel, it evidenced a victory of Satan. The little mustard-seed developed into a monstrosity, and produced that which gave shelter for the agents of the Devil. Instead of living as strangers and pilgrims here, professing Christians took part in politics and sought to reform the State. Instead of having as their hope the returning Christ, they sought to improve the world, and to such an extent did they imagine they had succeeded, it was announced that the millennium had commenced.

The parable of the leaven presents to us something still more tragic. Just as the mustard-tree depicted the *outward* corruption of the Christian profession, this fourth parable shows us the *inward* corruption of it. Into the "meal," which represents the pure doctrine of Christ, a foreign element was *stealthily* introduced. This was designed to make the food of God's people lighter and more palatable to the world; but it *corrupted* the same. The Lord announced that this evil process would continue until the whole was leavened. This cannot be completely realised while the Holy Spirit remains on earth; but how nearly this prophecy has become history shows us how very close at hand must be the time when He will take His departure.

But though these four parables give us a sad picture of the unfaithfulness of men, there has been no failure with God. That cannot be. In spite of all the breakdown in human responsibility, and notwithstanding Satan's opposition, God has been slowly but surely working out *His* "eternal purpose." "Known unto God are all His works from the beginning of the world," says Acts 15:18, and clear and abundant proof of this is furnished here in Matt. 13.

The fifth and the sixth parables bring before us the gracious and blessed work of Christ, securing for Himself *two* Objects which are inexpressibly precious to Him, namely, the "treasure" hid in the field and the "pearl" from the sea; which represent redeemed Israel and the Church of the present dispensation. This gives us the brighter side of things, and shows that, notwithstanding Satan's Divinely-permitted success, Christ *shall* yet "see of the travail of His soul and be satisfied" (Isa. 53:11).

In connection with the next parable there remain two points to be considered: first, Christ's interpretation of it, which is found in vv. 49:50. The careful reader will observe that this contains a principle similar to that found in connection with the interpretation of the second parable which is given in vv. 41-43. In the parable (itself) of the tares Christ went no farther than what actually takes place here on earth, see v. 30; the state in the next world of those represented by the tares *is not* revealed. But in the *interpretation* of this parable, which Christ gave to His disciples, their future destiny *was* made known, see vv. 39-43. Thus the interpretation *carries us farther* than do the details of the parable itself. This principle is also exemplified in a number of symbolic prophecies: Dan. 7 supplies a notable illustration—the explanations there given *going beyond* the symbols used.

It is thus in the seventh parable. In vv. 47, 48 the *final destiny* of neither the good nor the bad fish is given. Neither in the parable of the Tares nor of the Net does the *execution of judgment* form part of the parable itself. The reason of this is not far to seek. These parables all treat of the present dispensation, while the churches are on earth; God's judgment will descend *after* they have gone. Hence, in the parable itself the "tares" are left on the field (v. 30); and in the last parable the "bad fish" are left on the shore, that is, on earth (v. 48). This is clear from the fact that the "vessels" into which the "good fish are gathered" *are on earth*. The execution of judgment upon the "tares" and on the "bad fish" occurs at a *later* date, and this was indicated by Christ Himself, in His giving the interpretation separately and *after* the parable itself.

In further confirmation of what has just been said, it is to be noted that, *the fishermen* have nothing to do with the work of judgment. As Christ declared "at the end of the age (which will be more than seven years after the Rapture) the angels shall come forth," etc. (v. 49). Thus it is the "angels" who execute God's judgment—compare carefully Rev. 7:1, 8:1, 16:1, etc.

One other point connected with the last parable must be noted. In v. 49 we are told that "the angels shall come forth, and sever the wicked from among the just." This is the very opposite of what the fishermen do in v. 48: they, first, gather the good fish into vessels, and then cast the bad away. In both the parable of the Tares and of the Net the "angels' are occupied with the *wicked*. The "just" in v. 49 refer to the godly Jewish remnant who will be on earth, after the Church has been removed at the end of this age.

The very fact that Matt. 13 contains *seven* parables intimates that we have here a *complete* something, and that is, the history of the Christian profession on earth. In the prophetic outline presented by Christ, the salient points and principal epochs in this history are noticed. In the first, which is introductory, the earthly ministry of Christ is in view. The second, describes what took place in the days of the apostles. The third, brings us down to the fourth century, when the little mustard-seed became a great "tree," which pointed to the union between the State and professing Christianity in the days of Constantine. The fourth takes us to the end of the sixth century, and forecast the rise of the Papacy, the woman corrupting the meal.

After the fourth parable there is a manifest *break*, the Lord leaving the seaside and retiring within the house: thus He was *hidden* from the multitude! Marvellously and accurately does this correspond with the history of Christendom, for, following the establishment of Romanism, came the Dark Ages, when the multitudes were forsaken by Christ. After the break, come the next two parables spoken to the disciples only. These forecast the great Reformation in the days of Luther, Calvin, etc. Most significant is it that the central object in each is Christ seeking that which was *hidden* and bringing it to light. That which He first unearthed was the "treasure" hid in a field. How manifestly this found its parallel in the *recovery* of the precious Word of God which had for so long been kept back from the people! The parable of the "one pearl" anticipated the recovery of the blessed truth of the *oneness* in Christ of all God's people.

The seventh parable, as its position in the series indicates, treats of conditions at the *close* of this dispensation. In the light of this, how very significant are the words at the end of v. 47: "A net that was cast into the sea and gathered of every kind." No efforts are now being spared to attract fish of *"every* kind" into the various denominational "nets," and everything that would tend to frighten or keep away worldlings is carefully avoided. In modern "church" (?) services there is something to suit the tastes and meet the needs of all, *except* the true children of God! Social, economic, and diplomatic problems and issues are discussed to satisfy the political mind. Worldly amusements are introduced to attract the lovers of pleasure. Grand organs are put in and professional vocalists engaged to soothe and charm the aesthetic. Dramatic speakers, so-called "Evangelists," who are but religious showmen. are employed to please the sensation-monger. In short, everything that can please the flesh has been brought into the churches (?) to draw the crowds and thus catch fish of "every sort." Sad it is that so much time, money, and energy are wasted in such misguided and God-dishonouring efforts. Sinners do not need amusing and cheering, but showing their lost condition. The business of the ministers of the Gospel is not to tickle ears, but to preach that which, by the Spirit's application, will touch hearts and search consciences. Their duty is to make manifest the character of God, the awfulness of sin, the certainty of its punishment, and to bid their perishing hearers, "Flee from the wrath to come."

The next thing to happen will be the *removal* of God's saints from the earth, and their translation to heaven: see 1 Thess. 4:16, 17. Following this, after a brief interval, God will pour out His judgments upon the wicked, and then shall "the angels come forth, and sever the wicked from among the just, and shall cast them into a furnace of fire: there shall be wailing and gnashing of teeth" (vv. 49, 50). These verses will then receive a solemn and literal fulfilment. After this "then shall the righteous shine forth as the sun in the kingdom of their Father" (v. 43), i.e., the *upper* or heavenly department of Christ's millennial kingdom—John 1:51 implies the *two* spheres of the Messiah's Kingdom. May the Lord grant that each reader of these articles shall "find mercy of the Lord in that day" (2 Tim. 1:18).

—*Arthur W. Pink.*

THE FAMILY OF GOD.

"And all Thy children shall be taught of the Lord" (Isa. 54:13).

There is a wonderful variety in the works of God. "There is one glory of the sun, and another glory of the moon, and another glory of the stars: for one star differeth from another star in glory" (1 Cor. 15:41). So all flesh is not the same flesh; as 1 Cor. 15:39 declares, "There is one kind of flesh of men, another flesh of beasts, another of fishes, another of birds." So it is in every department of the natural world.

Take the food which the Creator has mercifully provided: what differences there are among vegetables, what varieties of fruit! Now, while one may be more partial unto a particular article of diet, yet the best results are obtained from a well-balanced menu. If one lives chiefly on meats, and ignores cereals, etc., he will be the loser. On the other hand, if he eats no meat and exists on vegetables and fruits, the body will lack that which meat alone can supply. It is the wise *proportioning* of the different foods which God has provided that furnishes the best results bodily.

So it is spiritually. In the Scriptures God has graciously supplied a variety of food for His children, and unless the pulpit observes this principle, then the congregation is likely to suffer either from spiritual indigestion or spiritual anaemia. A pulpit which confines itself to doctrinal preaching and neglects evangelism will necessarily result in a declining or decaying church. Life is perpetuated by propagation; families are built up by multiplication. If Zion does not travail, then no children are brought forth; and if there are no children, the local family will soon become extinct.

This *has* frequently happened. An hundred years ago there were many Calvinistic churches in England whose pulpit ministrations were restricted to the regenerate. There was no preaching of the Gospel to the unconverted. In consequence, many of those churches have ceased to exist, and others are dead but not yet buried. The same thing is true in America. In the Southern States those known as Primitive Baptists are rapidly dying out, the cause of their decaying being that they have no Gospel for the unregenerate. It is an unchanging law that, a church which ceases to evangelise must inevitably fossilize. As Christ said to the angel of the church at Ephesus: "Remember therefore from whence thou art fallen: and repent, and do the first works (preach the Gospel); or else I will come unto thee quickly, and will *remove* thy candlestick" (Rev. 2:5). This very thing has happened here in Australia. Two generations ago Strict and Particular Baptist churches were planted in three different States, and about a dozen of these churches were in Associational fellowship. In less than fifty years more than half of them have had their candlesticks "removed," and most of the remaining ones have ceased to send forth any light into the surrounding darkness!

On the other hand, a pulpit which entirely restricts itself to evangelism will soon turn the church into a nursery. Milk is suitable food for babes, but if they are to grow, something stronger and more substantial than milk is needed by them. If God's children are to be developed into "young men" and "fathers" and become of some use to the Lord and His people, they need building up in their faith; and one of the chief means to this end is *doctrinal* instruction. Thus only is the balance preserved.

Of course there is in Scripture something more than the proclamation of the Gospel and the exposition of doctrine. A large part of it is in the form of typical pictures, figurative foreshadowings, which richly repay prayerful study. A larger portion still is devoted to prophecy, making known things to come; this, too, should receive our attention. If we neglect prophecy, we are the poorer. "All Scripture is given by inspiration of God and is profitable"; all of it is needed by us. Then there are promises in Scripture to cheer drooping hearts; counsels to regulate the walk; exhortations to stir up the listless; rebukes and warnings for backsliders. The ministry of the pulpit should be as varied and many-sided as is the whole truth of God's Word.

These reflections may serve as an introduction to my present sermon, which will be a *doctrinal* one; strong doctrine, "high doctrine" some may term it. For the last few months most of my Sabbath-evening sermons have mainly been designed for the benefit of the unconverted. To-night I shall address myself principally to those who have, by grace, believed to the saving of their souls. After you have heard it, some may say that it conflicts with other sermons which have preceded it, that the preacher has contradicted himself. Such a charge will not occasion me any concern. My only aim is to conform to the Word of God. If I make assertions which are contrary to that Word, I trust that you will not only criticise, but condemn me. But I challenge any present to produce any statements from the previous sermons which I cannot back up from Scripture. If you doubt that, act like men—accept my challenge, come to me after the service, ask for the Scriptural proof for anything I have said which you think is unscriptural. If not, hold your peace, lest you be found talking of what you understand not, or be found fighting against God.

"And all thy children shall be taught of the Lord; and great shall be the peace of thy children" (Isa. 54:13). This language is most positive and emphatic: "All," not "some"; "shall be," not "ought to be"; "great shall be the peace of thy children," not merely "peace shall be their portion." Three questions naturally occur as we ponder this text: First, *who* constitute the members of this favoured family? Second, *what* is it that they are *all* "taught"? Third, *what is* this "great peace" which is their portion? I shall devote a separate sermon to each. To-night we shall spend the balance of the time in considering, *who* are the members of this favoured family?

Before coming to the direct answer, let me briefly refute a popular and widespread error on the subject, namely, the universal Fatherhood of God. This error has probably resulted from and grown out of the unfaithfulness of many preachers. Too often the pulpit has failed to separate between the precious and the vile. Many preachers have been guilty of taking numerous passages of Scripture which concern and are addressed only to the believing children of God, and have given them a general and indiscriminate application. Through fear of giving offence, they have failed to *label* their sermons. They have taken the "children's bread and cast it to the dogs." How often the ungodly are encouraged to repeat the Lord's prayer, which, as its opening words signify, is designed only for the family of God! Thus the impression has been given that all of Adam's descendants are the children of God—many of them wayward and unfaithful, yet still His children. Out of this has grown the popular figment of God's universal Fatherhood.

Scripture is directly, plainly, and uniformly opposed to such a delusion. It is true that at the beginning God created man in His own image and likeness. But man fell, and that image was broken and that likeness was marred. In Gen. 5:3 we read, "And Adam lived an hundred and thirty years and begat a son in his own likeness, after his image": since then, all his descendants are but fallen children of fallen parents.

"The field is the world; the good seed are the children of the kingdom; but the tares are the children of the wicked one" (Matt. 13:38). How plainly do these words of Christ expose and refute this modern error! The Jews believed that *they* were all children of God; their proud boast was "we have one Father, even God" (John 8:41). But mark our Lord's reply, "If God were your Father, ye would love Me: for I proceeded forth and came from God; neither came I of Myself, but He sent Me. Why do ye not understand

My speech? even because ye cannot hear My word. Ye are of your father the Devil."

Having brushed this rubbish out of the way, let us return to our text and ask, Who are the members of this favoured family, of whom it is said, "And all thy children shall be taught of the Lord; and great shall be the peace of thy children"? We answer:

1. *Those whom God eternally ordained to be such.* Are there a few present who are saying, "We do not want to hear about *that*"? But you must, if God is to be honoured; and I shall no more omit or whittle down this vital part of God's truth in order to please refined Arminians, than I shall leave out a free Gospel for "whosoever believeth" to gain the good will of hyper-Calvinists.

Turn to Eph. 1:5: "Having predestinated us unto the adoption of *children* by Jesus Christ to Himself, according to the good pleasure of His will." Here is the first answer to our question, Who are the favoured members of this family? In the eternal counsels of the holy Trinity, a certain definite number were singled out from among their fellow-sinners, and "predestinated to the adoption of children." Note well this is said to be "according to the good pleasure of *His* will." Here, we have revealed the cause of their predestination. It was not anything good or meritorious in the ones selected, either actual or foreseen; but proceeded solely from the sovereign pleasure of the Almighty. Hence, in Heb. 2:13, we hear Christ saying, "Behold I and the children which God hath *given* Me."

A striking illustration of this first point is found in the book of Exodus, in the demands which Jehovah made, through Moses, upon Pharoah. When commissioned to appear before Egypt's king, God told Moses to say unto him, "Let My people go, that they may hold a feast unto Me in the wilderness" (Ex. 5:1). Mark you, this was while the Hebrews was yet in bondage, *before* the blood of the lamb was shed and applied, before they were actually "redeemed" at the Red Sea. Yes, from the beginning, Jehovah owned them as "My people." They were His by the eternal election of His sovereign grace.

The same blessed truth was plainly signified in the words of the Lord Jesus in John 10: "I lay down My life for the sheep. And other sheep I have, which are not of this fold, them also I must bring, and they shall hear My voice; and there shall be one fold, one Shepherd" (vv. 15, 16). "This fold" referred to Judaism as it existed at the time when Christ was speaking. In it were some of His "sheep." But God's elect were not confined to the Jewish people. "Other sheep" also belong to Him, namely, the chosen of God scattered among the Gentiles. Them also He must seek, gather, and carry Home (Luke 15:4-6). But what is to be especially noted is, that when Christ spoke of the people of God among the Gentiles who were yet to be brought into the fold, He said of them, "Other sheep I *have*." Yes, they were *His* even then; His, by the eternal choice of the Father. So also in Acts 18:10 we find the Lord appearing to Paul, at the beginning of his evangelistic labours in Corinth, saying "I *have* much people in this city."

Who are the members of this favoured family? We answer:

2. *Those whom God has obtained by Redemption.* This is most strikingly brought out in John 11: 51-52: "This spake he not of himself: but being high priest that year, he prophesied that Jesus should die for that nation; and not for that nation only, but that also He should gather together in one the children of God that were scattered abroad." God, in His absolute sovereignty, sometimes makes use of strange and unlikely instruments. Here we find Him giving a blessed prophecy through the lips of one who hated His Son and condemned Him to death! "This spake he *not* of himself" at once refutes the heresy of the Freewillers, who insist that God never interferes with man's free agency, and never causes him to do anything against his natural inclinations. But here is one, among a number of examples, where He *did* so. Another illustration is furnished in Balaam.

This prophecy through Caiaphas made known the purpose of God in the death of His Son. First, it was a substitutionary death: "that Jesus should die *for*," in the stead of. Second, its scope was limited. Jesus did not die for "every body," but (a) "that Nation," and (b) "the *children of God* that were scattered abroad"—scattered throughout the world. Thus, they are spoken of as "children of God" *before* Christ died for them. His death was in order that they should be "gathered together in one," that is, that they should be brought on to resurrection-ground, united by a tie of blood, made one family.

The same precious truth is taught in Gal. 4: 4-6: "But when the fulness of time was come, God sent forth His Son, made of a woman, made under the law, to redeem them that were under the law, that we might receive the adoption of sons. And because ye are sons, God hath sent forth the Spirit of His Son into your hearts, crying, Abba, Father." The coming of Christ into the world and His being "made under the law," was in order to "redeem" a certain people who were under the law—under its condemning sentence, under its inexorable requirements, under it as a burden beyond their powers to sustain. And this redemption by Christ was that this people "might receive the adoption of sons." The law held them fast as condemned criminals; justice refusing to relinquish them. The ransom-price which justice demanded, must be paid. This price *was* paid, and, in consequence, all for whom it was paid are "the children of God" by redemption. The result of this is stated in v. 6: "Because ye are (not "in order that they should become") sons, God hath sent forth the Spirit of His Son into your hearts." They were "sons" before the Spirit came to indwell them!

Blessedly was this illustrated by God's dealings with the Hebrews in Egypt. He *delivered* them from their awful bondage. He brought His people out of Egypt with a high hand. He emancipated Pharoah's captives. He actually "redeemed" them. This is something more than the paying of a ransom-price. Redemption includes the act of deliverance of an enslaved people; the freeing from bondage of those who are Satan's usurped captives. Note how it is put in Zech. 9: 11: "As for Thee also, by the blood of Thy covenant I have sent forth *Thy* prisoners out of the pit wherein is no water." It is the Father speaking to the Son. The reference is to the rescuing of His elect out of the "horrible pit." And they are spoken of as Christ's "prisoners"!

Who are the members of this favoured family? We answer:

3. *Those whom God has created anew by Regeneration.* This is brought out in John 1: 12, 13: "But as many as received Him, to them gave He power to become *children of God* (R.V.), even to them that believe on His name: which were born not of blood, nor of the will of the flesh, nor of the will of man, but of God." This tells us *how* the elect become God's children experimentally.

With John 1: 12, 13 should be linked John 3: 5, 6: "Except a man be born of water and of the Spirit, he cannot enter into the kingdom of God. That which is born of the flesh is flesh, and that which is born of the Spirit is spirit." Note how this brings in the work of the third Person of the Godhead! First we have considered the Father's predestination; then, the Son's propitiation; now, the Spirit's regeneration. Here is a threefold cord which cannot be broken. First, we are "children": *elected* by the Father's choice. Second, we are "children": *legally* by the Son's redemption. Third, we are "children": *experimentally* by the Holy Spirit's quickening.

Who are the members of this favoured family? We answer:

4. *Those who are owned as such.* The Father owns the "children," by bestowing upon them His love: "Behold what manner of love the Father hath bestowed upon us, that we should be called children (R.V.) of God" (1 John 3: 1).

The Son owns the "children" by interceding for them: "Wherefore He is able also to save them to the uttermost that come unto God by Him, seeing He ever liveth to make intercession for them" (Heb. 7: 25).

The Spirit owns "the children," by indwelling them: "But ye are not in the flesh, but in the spirit, if so be that the Spirit of God dwell in you. . . . The Spirit Himself beareth witness with our spirit that we are the children of God" (Rom. 8: 9, 16).

Angels own the "children," by ministering unto them: "Are they not all ministering spirits, sent forth to minister for them who shall be heirs of salvation"? (Heb. 1: 14). "The angel of the Lord encampeth round about them that fear Him, and delivereth them" (Psa. 34: 7).

The Devil owns the "children," by accusing and attacking them. "For the accuser of our brethren is cast down, which accused them before our God day and night" (Rev. 12: 10). "Taking the shield of faith, wherewith, ye shall be able to quench all the fiery darts of the wicked" (Eph. 6: 16).

Who are the members of this favoured family? We answer:

5. *Those whose walk MANIFESTS their divine parentage.* "But I say unto you, Love your enemies, bless them that curse you, do good to them that hate you, and pray for them which despitefully use you, and persecute you; that ye may be (i.e. appear as such) the children of your Father which is in heaven" (Matt. 5: 44, 45).

"For as many as are led by the Spirit of God, they are the sons of God" (Rom. 8: 14). That is to say, as many as follow not the course of this world, lean not unto their own understandings, are not governed by the flesh; but are guided by the Spirit, through His revealed will in the Scriptures. Such make it evident that *they* are the children of God.

"We know that we have passed from death unto life because we love the brethren" (1 John 3:14)—love them with something purer than that which is attracted by a pleasing temperament, that which unites those of the same party views, that which is merely the sentiment of the flesh. As 1 John 5:2 puts it, "By this we know that we love the children of God, when we love God and keep His commandments." Thus the elect are created anew in God's likeness, and it is the manifestation of this which distinguishes the children of God from those who are of the world.

In closing, let me press on you this question: Are *you* really a member of this favoured family? Is the family likeness stamped upon you? Can others see the marks of election, redemption and regeneration upon you? Are your affections set upon things above, and not upon things on the earth? Are you walking by faith, and not by sight? Can you really say, "Whom have I in heaven but Thee, and there is none upon earth that I desire beside Thee"? Are you "Crucifying the flesh, with its affections and lusts"? Have you a "desire" to depart from this world, and "be with Christ, which is far better"? Are you walking in obedience to the Word: Christ says, "If a man love Me, he *will* keep My words" (John 14:23).

Are *you* really a member of this favoured family? There may be some trembling babe-in-Christ who hesitates before this question. Then let me try and help such an one by quoting Gal. 3:26, "Ye are all the children of God *by faith* in Christ Jesus." *This* is the Christian's "birth-mark." Reliance alone upon Christ and His shed blood is the first evidence of regeneration. If there is an exercised soul present who desires to *make* sure, then believe in Christ to-night: "As many as received Him, to them gave He power to become the sons of God, even to them that believe on His name" (John 1:12). Let those who, by grace, *have* believed on Him, daily and earnestly seek a closer conformity to the image of God's Son.

—*Arthur W. Pink.*

THE GOSPEL OF GOD'S GRACE.

"*To testify the Gospel of the grace of God*" (*Acts 20:24*).

These words formed part of the farewell address of the apostle Paul to the leaders of the church at Ephesus. After reminding them of his manner of life among them (vv. 18-21), he tells them of his forthcoming trip to Jerusalem, which was to eventuate in his being carried prisoner to Rome. He says, "And now, behold, I go bound in the spirit unto Jerusalem, not knowing the things that shall befall me there: save that the Holy Spirit witnesseth in every city, saying that bonds and afflictions abide me." And, then, in a truly characteristic word, he says, "But none of these things move me, neither count I my life dear unto myself, so that I might finish my course with joy, and the ministry which I have received of the Lord Jesus, to testify the Gospel of the grace of God." Wherever the providence of God might take him, whatever his circumstances might be, whether in bonds or enjoying his freedom, *this* should be his mission and message. And it is to this same ministry that the Lord of the harvest still calls and appoints His servants: to "testify the Gospel of the grace of God."

There is a continual need for recurring to the great fundamental of the faith, and as long as the age lasts the Gospel of God's grace must be preached. This need arises out of the natural state of the human heart, which is essentially legalistic. The cardinal error against which the Gospel has to contend, is the inveterate tendency of men to rely on and rest in their own performances. The great antagonist to the Truth is the *pride* of man, which causes him to imagine that he can be, in part at least, his own saviour. This error is the prolific mother of a multitude of heresies. It is by means of this falsehood that the pure stream of God's truth, passing through human channels, has been polluted.

Now the Gospel of God's grace is epitomised in Eph. 2:8, 9, "For by grace are ye saved, through faith; and that not of yourselves: it is the gift of God; not of works, lest any man should boast." All genuine reforms and revivals in the churches of God must have for their basis a plain declaration of this doctrine. The tendency of Christians is like that of the world, away from this truth, which is the very sum and substance of the Gospel. Those who have any acquaintance with "church history" know how sadly true this is. Within fifty years of the death of the last of the apostles, so far as we can now learn, the Gospel of God's grace almost ceased to be preached. Instead of evangelising, the preachers of the second and third centuries gave themselves to philosophising. Metaphysics took the place of the simplicity of the Gospel.

Then, in the fourth century, God mercifully raised up a man, Augustine, who faithfully and fearlessly proclaimed the Gospel of His grace. So mightily did God empower both his voice and pen that more than half of Christendom was shaken by him. Through his instrumentality there came an heaven-sent Revival. His influence for good stayed off the great Romish heresy for another century, and had the churches heeded his teaching, Popery had never been born. But, alas, they turned back to vain philosophy and science "falsely so-called."

Then came the Dark Ages, when for centuries the Gospel of God's grace ceased to be generally preached. Here and there feeble voices were raised, but most of them were soon silenced again by the Italian priests. It was not until the fifteenth century that the great Reformation came, and God raised up Martin Luther, who taught in no uncertain terms and tones that sinners are justified by faith, and not by works.

After Luther came a still more distinguished and honoured teacher, John Calvin. He was much more deeply taught in the truth of the Gospel, and pushed its central doctrine of grace to its logical conclusions. As Spurgeon put it, "Luther had, as it were, undammed the stream of truth, by breaking down the barriers, which had kept back its living waters, as in a great reservoir. But the stream was turbid and carried down with it much which ought to have been left behind. Then Calvin came, and cast salt into the waters, and purged them; so that there flowed on a purer stream to gladden and refresh souls and quench the thirst of poor lost sinners."

The great centre of all Calvin's preaching was the Grace of God, and it has been the custom ever since to designate as "Calvinists" those who emphasise what he emphasised. We do not accept that title without qualification, but we certainly are not ashamed of it. The truth which Calvin thundered forth with all his might, was identical with the truth which Paul had preached and set down in writing long centuries before. This was also the substance of Whitefield's preaching, which God honoured so extensively as to produce the Great Revival in his day. And I am assured there will be no breaking out on the right and on the left until there is more preaching of the Gospel of the Grace of God. Let us now consider that:

1. *The Gospel is a Revelation of the Grace of God.*

The "Gospel of the grace of God" is one of the Holy Spirit's appellations of that good news which the ambassadors of Christ are called upon to preach. Various names are given to it in the Scriptures. In Rom. 1: 1 it is called the "Gospel of God," for He is its Author. In Rom. 1: 16 it is termed the "Gospel of Christ," for He is its Theme. In Eph. 6: 15 it is designated the "Gospel of peace," for this is its Bestowment. In our text it is spoken of as the "Gospel of the Grace of God," for this is its Source.

Grace is a truth which is peculiar to the Divine revelation. It is a concept which the unaided powers of man's mind never rises to. Proof of this is seen in the fact that where the Bible has not gone "grace" is unknown. Very often missionaries have found, when translating the Scriptures into the native-tongues of the heathen, they were quite unable to discover a word which in anywise corresponded to the Bible word "grace." Grace is entirely absent from the great heathen religions, Brahmanism, Buddhism, Mohammedanism, Confucianism, Zoroastrianism. Even Nature does not teach "grace": break her laws and you *must* suffer the penalty.

What then is "grace"? First, it is evidently something very blessed and joyous, for our text speaks of the *"good news* of the grace of God." Secondly, it is manifestly the opposite of law: Law and Gospel are antithetical terms: "The law was given by Moses, but grace and truth came by Jesus Christ" (John 1: 17). It is significant that the word "Gospel" is never found in the O.T. Let us consider a few contrasts between them:

The Law manifested what was in man —sin; Grace manifests what is in God— love, mercy. The Law speaks of what man must do for God; Grace tells of what Christ has done for men. The Law demanded righteousness from men; Grace brings righteousness to men. The Law brought out God to men; Grace brings in men to God. The Law sentenced a living man to death; Grace brings a dead man to life. The Law never had a missionary; the Gospel of God's grace is to be preached to every creature. The Law makes known the will of God; Grace reveals the heart of God!

In the third place, Grace, then, is the very opposite of justice. Justice shows no favour and knows no mercy. Grace is the reverse of this. Justice requires that every one should receive his due; grace bestows on sinners that to which they are *not* entitled: pure charity. **Grace** is "something for nothing."

Now the Gospel is a *revelation* of this wondrous grace of God. It tells us that Christ has done for sinners that which they could not do for themselves—satisfied the demands of God's law. Christ has fully and perfectly met all the requirements of God's holiness, so that He can righteously receive every poor sinner that comes to Him. The Gospel tells us that Christ died not for good people, who never did anything very bad; but for lost and godless sinners, who never did anything good. The Gospel reveals to every sinner, for his acceptance, a Saviour all-sufficient: "able to save unto the uttermost them that come unto God by Him."

2. *The Gospel is a Proclamation of the Grace of God.*

The word "Gospel" is a technical one. It is employed in the N.T. in a double sense: in a narrower and in a wider one. In its narrower, it has reference to the heralding of the glorious fact that the grace of God has provided a Saviour for every poor sinner who feels his need of and by faith receives Him. In its wider, it comprehends the whole revelation which God has made of Himself in and through Christ; in this sense, it includes the whole of the N.T.

In proof of this double application of the term Gospel, will the reader please turn, first, to 1 Cor. 15: 1-3, and there he will find a *definition* of the Gospel in the narrower sense of the term: it is, that Christ died for our sins, was buried, and rose again. Then if he will turn to Rom. 1: 1 he will there find the term "Gospel" used in its wider sense, for there it includes the whole doctrinal exposition of that Epistle. When Christ bade His disciples, "Preach the Gospel to every creature," I do not think that He had reference to *all* that is found in the N.T., but simply to the fact that the grace of God has provided a Saviour for sinners. Therefore we say that the Gospel is a *proclamation* of the grace of God.

The Gospel affirms that "grace" is the sinner's *only* hope. Unless we are saved by grace, we cannot be saved at all. To reject a gratuitous salvation is to spurn the only one that is possible or available for lost sinners. Grace is God's provision for those who are so corrupt that they cannot change their own natures; so averse to God, they cannot turn to Him; so blind that they cannot see Him; so deaf that they cannot hear Him; in a word, so dead in sin, that He must open their graves and bring them on to resurrection-ground, if ever they are to be saved. Grace, then, implies that the sinner's case is desperate, but that God is merciful.

The Gospel of God's grace is for sinners in whom there is no help. It is exercised by God "*without* respect of persons," without regard to merit, without requirement of any return. The Gospel is not a word of good advice, but a message of good news. It does not speak of what man is to do, but tells of what Christ has done. It is not sent to good men, but to bad. Grace, then, is something that is worthy of God.

3. *The Gospel is a Manifestation of the Grace of God.*

The Gospel is the power of God unto salvation to everyone that believeth. It is the *chosen instrument* which God uses in the freeing and delivering of His people from error, ignorance, darkness, the power of Satan. It is by and through the Gospel, applied by the Holy Spirit, that His elect are emancipated from the guilt and power of sin. "For the preaching of the cross is to them which perish foolishness; but unto us which are saved it is the power of God. . . . But we preach Christ crucified, unto the Jews a stumblingblock, and unto the Greeks foolishness; but unto them which are called, both Jews and Greeks, Christ the power of God, and the wisdom of God" (1 Cor. 1: 18, 23).

Where evolution is substituted for the new birth, the cultivation of character for faith in the blood of Christ, development of will-power for humble dependence on God, the carnal mind may be attracted and poor human reason appealed to, but it is all *destitute of power* and brings no salvation to the perishing. There is no Gospel in a system of ethics, and no dynamic in the exactions of law.

But grace *works*. It is something more than a good-natured smile, or a sentiment of pity. It redeems, conquers, saves. The N.T. interprets grace as *power*. By it redemption comes, for it was by "the grace of God" that Christ tasted death "for every one" of the sons (Heb. 2: 9). Forgiveness of sins is proclaimed through His blood "according to the riches of His grace" (Eph. 1: 7). Grace not only makes salvation possible, but effectual. Grace is allpowerful. "My grace is *sufficient* for thee" (2 Cor. 12: 9)—sufficient to overcome unbelief, the infirmities of the flesh, the oppositions of men, the attacks of Satan.

This is the glory of the Gospel: it is the power of God unto salvation. In one of his books Dr. Jowett says, "A little while ago I was speaking to a New York doctor, a man of long and varied experience with diseases that afflict both the body and mind. I asked him how many cases he had known of the slaves of drink having been delivered by medical treatment into health and freedom. How many he had been able to 'doctor' into liberty and self-control. He immediately replied, 'Not one.' He further assured me that he believed his experience would be corroborated by the testimony of the faculty of medicine."

Doctors might afford a seeming and temporary escape, but the real bonds are not broken. At the end of the apparent but brief deliverance it was found that the chains remained. Medicine might address itself to effects, but the cause was as real and dominant as ever. The doctor has no cure for the drunkard. Medical skill cannot save him. But *grace* can! Without doctors, drugs, priests, penance, works, money or price, grace actually *saves*. Hallelujah! Yes, grace saves. It snaps the fetters of a life-time, and makes a poor sinner a partaker of the Divine nature and a happy and rejoicing saint. It saves not only from the bondage of fleshly habits, but from the curse of the Fall, from the captivity of Satan, from the wrath to come.

We close with a question and an appeal. What effect has this message on your heart? Does it melt it? Does it fill you with praise to God? Are you thankful to know that salvation *is* by "grace"? Can you see and do you appreciate the infinite difference there is between all of man's schemes for self-help and self-betterment and the "Gospel of the Grace of God"?

Has God's grace saved *you?* Or are you a stranger to it? Grace is your only hope. Unless God saves you by His grace, you will never be saved at all. There is no other alternative. "If by grace, then it is no more of works: otherwise grace is no more grace" (Rom. 11: 6). Then if you are yet in your sins, will you not cry from your heart, "Lord, be gracious *to me*"? May His Holy Spirit move you so to do "to the praise of the glory of His grace."

The above is the substance of a sermon preached by the Editor in Sydney.

—*Arthur W. Pink.*

WAS ADAM SAVED?

We know of nothing at all in Scripture that either directly affirms or indirectly hints at it. On the other hand, there appear to be a number of considerations which go to show he was not saved. First, he was the head of a fallen race, and it is written, "In Adam all die." Second, the Holy Spirit definitely contrasts Adam and all the represented from Christ and those He stood for: Rom. 5:12-19. Third, the line of the men of faith in Heb. 11 begins with Abel: the absence of Adam there is solemnly suggestive.

Appeal is made by some to Gen. 3:21. But this is far from being conclusive as a proof that Adam was saved. Did not Jehovah clothe our first parents with skins for the purpose of teaching them the worthlessness of their fig-leaf aprons? as well as to teach us the need for a covering Divinely provided? The closing verse of Gen. 3 not only sets aside the conclusion which many have drawn from Gen. 3.21, but, in the judgment of the writer, clearly evidences that Adam was not saved: "So he (the Lord God) *drove out* the man"! The only other references in Gen. to Adam after this are 4:1, 4:25, 26; 5:1-5!—A.W.P.

Possibly the above may sound, to some, like carnal presumption or Arminian error. Turn then to Job 22:21 and observe that there we are expressly told to "acquaint now thyself with Him." The best way to become "acquainted" with an earthly person is to be much in his company; so with God. Observe carefully the order in James 4:8: "Draw nigh to God, and He will draw nigh to you." Now as helps to this end, let us suggest several simple but important counsels.

First, make sure that you are *addressing God*: "He that cometh to God." When you get down on your knees to pray, before presenting any petitions to Him, seek to definitely realise in your soul that you are about to speak to the living God. "Prayer was made without ceasing of the church *unto God*" (Acts 12:5). The only prayer which has power is that which is consciously addressed to Him.

But is not *all* prayer "to God?" No; much so-called prayer, both private and public, is not unto Him. I fear that in much of our praying there is really little definite thought of God Himself. Our minds become so occupied with our needs that there is great danger of losing sight of the One before whom we spread them. It is only when we really come into *God's* presence, meet Him face to face, that He becomes real to the soul and that there is power in our prayers. Seek, then, to realise in your hearts, that you are actually presenting petitions to *God,* that *He* is listening to you.

"For through Him we both have access by one Spirit unto the Father" (Eph. 2:18). This is both humbling and blessed: it intimates our insufficiency, it tells of God's gracious provision. To obtain a real audience with God is only possible by the direct assistance of His Holy Spirit. Then look to Him for needed help; definitely seek His aid.

Be specific in your askings. We need not be surprised that many find so little joy in praying and have so little personal acquaintance with its potency. Their petitions are so vague and abstract, their supplications so indefinite and general that they would not recognise an answer if it were given. The prayers of the Bible were all to the point, and recorded for our learning.

Third, put your heart into your praying. "Strive together with me in prayers to God for me" (Rom. 15:30). The Greek verb is very significant; it signifies "to contend as an athlete," it means the putting forth of all our strength. "Labouring fervently for you in prayers" (Col. 4:12): what light this throws upon the manner in which the apostle Paul supplicated God! Much of our present-day praying is powerless because there is so little heart in it.

If these simple directions be heeded, prayer will cease to be a mere form and God will become more real to the soul. Herein, lies the first and foundational *value* of prayer: not simply the obtaining the things which we need, but realising that God is, and that He is a Rewarder of them that diligently seek Him. David had learned this, "In Thy *presence* is fulness of joy," that is, *now,* in our soul's experience.

2. It enriches the spiritual life of the Christian. Real prayer strengthens faith, for it is faith in exercise. Faith is a looking away from self and a being occupied with God; it is a laying hold of His promises and counting upon His fulfilment. Faith is extending empty hands to Heaven, to be filled with the riches of Divine grace. And for faith to grow, it must be exercised; and it is exercised chiefly in prayer. We pray so little because our faith is so weak; our faith is weak, because we pray so little.

Real prayer subdues the pride of our hearts. It is designed to humble us before God, to bow in meekness before Him. Prayer is appointed for the purpose of bringing our rebellious wills in subjection to God's perfect will. It teaches us to seek His mind, desire His glory, and be emptied of self-seeking.

Real prayer increases our joy. "Ask, and ye shall receive, that your joy may be full" (John 16:24). There are many "joys" spoken of in Scripture. There is the joy of salvation (Psa. 51:12), of assurance (Luke 10:20), of seeing sinners saved (Luke 15:6), of being wholly yielded up to God's will (John 15:11). There is also the joy of answered prayer. Great indeed is the gladness which fills the heart when a wondrous answer to prayer is given. To pray amid darkness and have God send light, to pray in the face of barriers and see God tear them down before you, to cry to Him in the midst of dire and urgent need and have God swiftly supply it, does indeed fill the heart with joy.

Real prayer prepares us to receive God's blessings. The Holy Spirit first creates a desire in the heart, leads us to ask, and then God gives. Thus we are the better enabled to see that He *is* the Giver. Thus, too, we appreciate His mercies the more when they are bestowed upon us. Yes, God *is* a "Rewarder of them that diligently seek Him." Then let us more frequently and more whole-heartedly "seek" Him.

—*Arthur W. Pink.*

VOL. VII.   JULY, 1928   NO. 7
STUDIES IN THE SCRIPTURES
"Search the Scriptures" John

Copyright in all English-speaking Countries.

Editor: Arthur W. Pink, 15 Hurlstone Avenue, Summer Hill, N.S.W., Australia.
Hon. Agent in U.S.A.: Mr. C. S. Pressel, 559 Dupont Avenue, York, Penna.

FREE TO ALL WHO WILL READ IT

SAVING EXPERIENCE.

"And knew the grace of God in truth" (Col. 1:6).

A saving experience is a personal acquaintance with God's salvation. There are many who talk about salvation, who are prepared to argue about it, but who have no personal experience *of* God's salvation. There are some whose views of salvation are orthodox, but whose lives show they are total strangers to God's salvation. It is one thing to have an intelligent understanding of it, it is quite another to have a heart knowledge of God's salvation. It is one thing to hear a preacher expounding the Gospel with scriptural precision and for the hearer to mentally assent to all that is said, but it is quite another to be actually saved. The religious world to-day is crowded with notionalists and formalists. There are tens of thousands of professing Christians with "a form of *godliness*"—which is much more than mere morality—yet are they without "the power thereof" (2 Tim. 3:5). Reader, are *you* one of them? Ask God to search your heart and show you.

Now any ministry which, under God, is helpful, must necessarily alternate between the presentation of the objective and subjective aspects of the Truth. There is a "balance" to be carefully observed here. A one-sided emphasis upon the objective—the Word without me—fosters pride and produces a hard and cold type of Christian. On the other hand, an undue stressing of the subjective side tends to mysticism or fanaticism. God "desireth truth in the *inward* parts" (Psa. 51:6). And unless writer or reader has it there, woe be to him—he is still "in the gall of bitterness and in the bond of iniquity." A Bible in the home is good; the Scriptures stored in the mind is still better; but the Word hid in the heart, is best of all.

Vital godliness is a thing of the heart. It is God beginning "a good work *in* you" (Phil. 1:6). It is having cause to confess with the apostle, "It pleased God, who separated me from my mother's womb, and called me by His grace, to reveal His Son *in me*" (Gal. 1:15, 16). It is a being able to say with Job, "I *have* heard of Thee by the hearing of the ear: but *now* mine eyes seeth Thee" (42:5); seeth Thee as a living reality; seeth Thee with the eyes of the heart; seeth Thee as the One with whom I have to do; as *my* God. Have you thus seen Him, dear reader? Has the testimony of Christ been "*confirmed* IN you" (1 Cor. 1:6)? If so, the language of our opening text applies to you.

Bishop H. C. Moule rendered the last clause of Col. 1:6 as follows: "Since the day when you heard and came spiritually to know the grace of God in its reality." and in his notes on the Greek verb he adds, "epegnote almost always, by usage and connection, in the New Testament means knowledge which goes deeper than the surface of facts; and so, continually, it is to be explained as the spiritual knowledge which sees the truth in the fact and finds the experience in the truth."

To "know the grace of God in truth" means to know it personally by experience. It is to know it in our hearts as a blessed reality. It is a knowledge of fact as opposed to theory. There are many who are charmed with the very concept of

(Concluded on Page 168)

IMPORTANT NOTICES

Back numbers of each year of the magazine are yet obtainable at 5/- (1.25) per year. Bound at 7/6 (1.75) post paid. They will soon be out of print. Those in U.S.A. wanting them, please purchase from Mr. Pressel (see front cover page).

Advise promptly of change of address. This Magazine is published as a work of faith and labour of love. The Editor gladly gives his services. It is freely sent to all who will read it. No charge is made for it.

Christians who feel definitely led to do so, may have fellowship with us in this Ministry. Send only *Inter-National M.O.*

CONTENTS.

	Page.
Hebrews	146
Gleanings in Exodus	152
Taught of God	158
Dead to Sin	161
Pray Always	167

THE EPISTLE TO THE HEBREWS.

7. Christ superior to Angels 2:1-4.

The title of this article is based upon the fact that the opening verses of Heb. 2 contain an exhortation based upon what has been said in chapter 1. Thus, our present portion continues the second section of the Epistle. Inasmuch as it opens with the word "Therefore" we are called upon to review that which has already been before us.

The first section of the Epistle, contained in its first three verses, may be looked at in two ways: both as forming an Introduction to the Epistle as a whole, and as a distinct division of it, in which is set forth the superiority of Christ over the prophets. In what follows, to the end of the chapter, we are shown the superiority of Christ over angels. This is affirmed in v. 4, and the proofs thereof are found in vv. 5 to 14. These proofs are all drawn from the O.T. Scriptures, and the completeness and perfection of the demonstration thus afforded is evidenced by their being *seven* in number. Thus, centuries before He appeared on earth, the Word of Truth bore witness to the surpassing excellency of Christ and His exaltation above all creatures.

As an analysis and summary of what these seven passages teach concerning the superiority of Christ over the angels, we may express it thus: 1. He has obtained a more excellent name than they vv. 4, 5. 2. He will be worshipped by them as the Firstborn v. 6. 3. He made them v. 7. 4. He is the Divine throne-sitter vv. 8, 9. 5. He is anointed above them v. 9. 6. He is the Creator of the universe, immutable and eternal vv. 10-12. 7. He has a higher place of honour vv. 13-14.

It is striking to note that these same seven quotations from the O.T. also furnish proof of the sevenfold glory of the Mediator affirmed in vv. 2, 3. There He is spoken of, first, as the "Son:" proof of this is supplied in v. 5, by a quotation from the 2nd Psalm. Second, He is denominated the "Heir:" proof of this is given in v. 6, where He is owned as the "Firstborn." Third, it is said in v. 2 that He "made the worlds:" proof of this is given in v. 10 by a quotation from the 104th Psalm. Fourth, He is called "the Brightness of God's glory:" in v. 9 an O.T. Scripture is quoted to show that He has been "anointed with the oil of gladness above His fellows." Fifth, He is the "express Image" of God's person: in v. 8 Scripture is quoted to show that the Father owned Him as "God." Sixth, in v. 3 it is said that He has "purged our sins": in v. 14 we have mention of "the heirs of salvation." Seventh, in v. 3 it is affirmed that He has "sat down on the right hand of the Majesty on high"; in v. 13 the 110th Psalm is quoted in proof of this. What an example is this of "proving all things" (1 Thess., 5:21), and that, by the Word of God itself!

Having set forth the excellency of Christ's Divine nature and royal function, the apostle now, in chapter 2, proceeds to show the reality and uniqueness of His humanity. In passing from the one to the other the Holy Spirit moves him to make a practical application to his hearers of what he had already brought before them, for the two things which ever concern and the two ends at which the true servant of God ever aims, are, the glory of the Lord and the spiritual good of those to whom he ministers. God's truth is not only addressed to our understanding, but to our conscience. It is designed not only to instruct, but to move us and mould our lives.

In one sense the first four verses of chapter 2 form a parenthesis, inasmuch as they interrupt the apostle's discussion of Christ's relation to angels, which is resumed in v. 5 and amplified in v. 9. But this digression, so far from being a literary blemish, is very beautiful. When is it that a well-trained mind ceases to think logically? or an instructed preacher to speak in orderly sequence? Is it not when his heart is moved? when his emotions are deeply stirred? So was it here with the apostle Paul. His great heart yearned for the salvation of his brethren according to the flesh; therefore, did his mind turn for a moment *from* the theme he was pursuing, to address himself to their consciences. He who said to the saints at Rome, "Brethren, my heart's desire and prayer to God for Israel is, that they might be saved" (10:1), could not calmly write to the Hebrews without breaking off and making an impassioned appeal to them. This, we shall, D.V., find he does again and again.

That which is central in our present parenthesis is an exhortation to give good heed to .the Gospel. This admonition is first propounded in v. 1, and then enforced in vv. 2-4. Two points are noted for the enforcing of this duty; one is the danger; the other, the vengeance, which is certain to follow on the neglect of the Gospel. The danger is intimated in the words, "Lest we should let them slip." The vengeance is hinted in the question, "How shall we escape"? This is emphasised by a solemn warning, namely, despisers of God were summarily dealt with under the law; therefore, those who shut their ears to the Gospel, which is so much more excellent, are, without doubt, treasuring up unto themselves wrath against the day of wrath (Rom. 2:4-5). We are now ready to attend to the details of our present portion.

"Therefore, we ought to give the more earnest heed to the things which we have heard, lest at any time we should let them slip" (v. 1). In this verse, and in those which immediately follow, the apostle specifies a duty to be performed in regard of that most excellent Teacher which God sent to reveal His Gospel unto them. This duty is to give more than ordinary heed unto that Gospel. Such is the force of the opening, "Therefore," which signifies, for this cause: because God has vouchsafed so excellent a Teacher, He must be the more carefully attended unto. The "therefore" looks back to all the varied glories which set forth Christ's excellency named in the previous chapter. Because He is God's "Son," therefore give heed. Because He is "the Heir of all things," therefore give heed. Because He "made the worlds," therefore give heed; and so on. These are so many grounds on which our present exhortation is based.

"*Therefore* is equivalent to, 'Since Jesus Christ is as much better than the angels, as He hath received by inheritance a more excellent name than they—since He is both essentially and officially inconceivably superior to these heavenly messengers, His message has paramount claims on our attention, belief, and obedience'" (Dr. J. Brown).

The eminency of an author's dignity and authority, and the excellency of his knowledge and wisdom, do much commend that which is spoken or written by him. If a king, prudent and learned, takes upon himself to instruct others, due attention and diligent heed should be given thereunto. "The Queen of the South came from the uttermost parts of the earth to hear the wisdom of Solomon" (Matt. 12:42), and counted those of his servants who stood continually before him and heard his wisdom, to be happy (1 Kings 10:8). But a greater than Solomon is here referred to by the apostle: therefore, we *ought* "to give the more earnest heed." It was usual with the prophets to preface their utterances with a "Thus saith the Lord," and thereby arrest the attention and awe the hearts of their hearers. Here the apostle refers to the person of the Lord Himself as the argument for hearing what He said.

"Therefore" *we* ought." "It is striking to see how the apostle takes the place of such as simply had the message, like other Jews, from those who personally heard Him; so completely was he writing, not as the apostle magnifying his office, but as one of Israel, who were addressed by those who companied with Messiah on earth. It was confirmed 'unto *us*,' says he, again putting himself along with his nation, instead of conveying his heavenly revelations as one taken out from the people and the Gentiles to which he was sent. He looks at what was their proper testimony, not at that to which he had been separated extraordinarily. He is dealing with them as much as possible on their own ground, though, of course, without compromise of his own" (Wm. Kelly).

"We *ought* to give the more earnest heed." Here the apostle addresses himself to the *responsibility* of his readers. Here is an exhortation to the performing of a specific duty. The Greek verb is very strong and emphatic; several times it is translated "must." Thus, in 1 Tim. 3:2, "A bishop must be blameless"; that is, it is his duty so to be. That to which the apostle here pointed was a necessity lying upon his readers. It is not an arbitrary matter, left to our own caprice, to do or not to do. "Give the more earnest heed," is something more than a piece of good advice; it is a Divine precept, and God has commanded us "to keep His precepts diligently" (Psa. 119:4). Thus, in view of His sovereignty, and His power and rights over us, we "*ought* to give the more earnest heed" to what He has bidden us do. Descending to a lower level, it is the part of wisdom so to do, and that for our own good; we "ought to earnestly heed the things which we hear" in order to our own happiness.

"To 'give heed' is to apply the mind to a particular subject, to attend to it, to consider it. It is here opposed to 'neglecting the great salvation.' No person can read the Scriptures without observing the stress that is laid on *consideration*, and the criminality and hazards which are represented as connected with inconsideration. Nor is this at all wonderful when we reflect that the Gospel is a moral remedy for a moral disease. It is by being believed it becomes efficacious. It cannot be believed unless it is understood; it cannot be understood unless it is attended to. Truth must be kept before the mind in order to its producing an appropriate effect; and how can it be kept before the mind, but by our giving heed to it" (Dr. J. Brown).

"The duty here intended is a serious, firm, and fixed settling of the mind upon that which we hear; a bowing and bending of the will to yield unto it; an applying of the heart to it, a placing of the affections upon it, and bringing the whole man into conformity thereunto. Thus it comprises knowledge of the Word, faith therein, obedience thereto, and all other due respects that may any way concern it" (Dr. Gouge).

"To the things which we have heard." To "hear" is not sufficient, there must be prayerful meditation, personal appropriation. No doubt the wider reference was to the Gospel, which these Hebrews had heard; though the more direct appeal was concerning that which the apostle had brought before them, in the previous chapter concerning the person and work of God's Son. To us, to-day, it would include all that God has said in His Word.

"Lest at any time we should let slip." There is a difficulty here in making quite sure of the Spirit's precise meaning. The expression "we should let slip" is one word in the Greek, and it occurs nowhere else in the N.T. The absence of the pronoun seems to be designed for the allowing of a *double* thought: lest we "let slip" the things we have heard, and, or, lest we ourselves slip away—apostatize.

"Lest at any time we let them slip." The danger is real. The effects of sin are stamped on our members; it is easy to recall the things of no value, but the things of God slip out of our mind. The fault is our own, through failing to give "the more earnest heed." Unless we "keep in memory" (1 Cor. 15:2), and unless we are duly informed by them, they slip away like water out of a leaky utensil.

"Lest haply we drift away." Understood thus, these words sound the first warning-note of this Epistle against apostasy, and this verse is parallel with 3:14; 4:1; 12:25. Perseverence in the faith, continuance in the Word, is a prime prerequisite of discipleship, see John 8:31; Col. 1:23, etc. Many who heard, and once seemed really interested in spiritual things, "concerning the faith *have* made shipwreck" (1 Tim. 1:19).

Thus, in the light of the whole context four reasons may be mentioned *why* we should give the more earnest heed to the things which God has spoken unto us: First, because of the glory and majesty of the One by whom He has communicated His mind and will, the Son. Second, because the message of Christianity is final. Third, because of the infinite preciousness of the Gospel. Fourth, because of the hopeless perdition and terrible tortures awaiting those who reject or let slip the testimony of God's wondrous grace.

"For if the word spoken by angels was stedfast, and every transgression and disobedience received a just recompense of reward" (v. 2). The apostle here advances another reason why the Hebrews ought to attend diligently to the Gospel. Having shown that such attention should be given because of the excellency of its Author and Publisher, and because of the benefits which would be lost through negligence, he now announces the certain vengeance of Heaven on its neglecters, a vengeance sorer than even that which was wont to be executed under the Law.

The opening "for" indicates that what follows gives a reason for persuading the Hebrews. The "if" has the force of "since," as in John 8:46; 14:3; Col. 3:1, etc. The "word spoken by angels" seems to refer to the Mosaic law, compare Acts 7:53; Gal. 3:19. "The only difficulty seems to arise out of the express declaration made by the sacred historian, that Jehovah spake all the words of the law. But the difficulty is more apparent than real. What lies at the foundation of the apostle's whole argument is *God* spake both the Law and the Gospel. Both the one and the other are of Divine origin. It is not the origin, but the *medium* of the two revelations which he contrasts. 'He made known His will by the ministry of angels in the giving of the law; He made known His will by the Son in the revelation of mercy.' It seems probable from these words that the audible voice in which the revelation from Mount Sinai was made, was produced by angelic ministry" (Dr. J. Brown).

Because the word spoken, ministerially, by angels was the Word of the Lord, it was "stedfast"—firm, inviolable, not to be gainsaid. Proof of this is furnished in the "and every transgression," etc. The distinction between "transgression" and "disobedience" is not easy to define. The one refers more to the outward act of violating God's law; the other, perhaps, to the state of heart which produced it. The words "receive a just recompense of reward" signify that every violation of God's law was punished according to its demerits. The term "reward" conveys the thought of "that which is due." Punishment for the breaking of God's law is not always administered in this life, but is none the less sure: see Rom. 2:3-9.

This verse sets out a most important principle in connection with the governmental dealings of God: that principle is that the Judge of all the earth will be absolutely just in His dealings with the wicked. Though the direct reference be to His administration of the Law's penalty in the past, yet, inasmuch as He changes not, it is strictly applicable to the great assize in the Day to come. There will be degrees of punishment, and those degrees, the sentence meted out to each rebel against God, will be on this basis, that every transgression and disobedience shall receive "a *just* recompense of reward." In brief, we may say that, punishment will be graded according to light and opportunity (Matt. 11:20-24; Luke 12:47, 48), according to the nature of the sins committed (John 19:11; Mark 12:38-40; Heb. 10:29), according to the number of the sins committed (Rom. 2:6, etc).

"How shall we escape, if we neglect so great salvation?" (v. 3). This verse evokes a number of questions to which, perhaps, no conclusive and final answers may be furnished. Who are referred to by the "we?" How shall we escape—*what*? Exactly what is in view in the "so great salvation?" In pondering these questions several considerations need to be steadily kept before us. First, the people to whom this Epistle was directly addressed and the circumstances in which they were then placed. Second, the central purpose of the Epistle and the character of its distinctive theme. Third, the bearing of the context on this verse and its several expressions. Fourth, light which other passages in this Epistle may shed upon it.

The relation between this verse and the preceding ones is evident. The apostle had just been pressing upon his brethren the need of their more earnestly giving heed unto the things which they had heard, which is more or less defined in the second half of v. 3: "which at the first began to be spoken by the Lord"—the reference being to His preaching of the Gospel. By a metonymy, the Gospel, that reveals and proclaims God's salvation, is here meant. In Eph. 1:13 it is styled "The gospel of your salvation," in Acts 3:26 the "word of this salvation," in Rom. 1:16 it is called "the power of God unto salvation to every one that believeth," and in Titus 2:11, "the grace of God which bringeth salvation." The Gospel dispensation is denominated "the Day of Salvation" (2 Cor. 6:2). Ministers of the Gospel are they "which show unto us the way of salvation" (Acts 16:17).

That under this word "salvation" the Gospel be meant, is also evident from the contrastive expression in v. 2—"the word spoken by angels." That word was spoken before the time of the Gospel's publication (note that the term "Gospel" is never once found in the O.T.), and obviously signified the Law. Fitly may the Gospel be styled "salvation:" first, because in opposition to the Law (which was a "ministration of condemnation" 2 Cor. 3:9), it is a ministration of salvation. Second, because the Author of the Gospel *is* "salvation" itself: see Luke 2:30, John 4:22, etc., where "salvation" is synonymous with "the Saviour." Third, because whatever is needful to a knowledge of salvation is contained in the Gospel. Fourth, because the Gospel is God's appointed means of salvation: see 1 Cor. 1:21. True, in O.T. times God's elect had and knew the Gospel—Gal. 3:16; Heb. 4:2—yet it was not publicly proclaimed and fully expounded. They had it under types and shadows, and in promises and prophecies.

The excellency of this salvation is denoted by the words "so great." The absence of any co-relative implies it to be so wondrous that its greatness cannot be expressed. Upon this Dr. J. Brown has well said: "The 'salvation' here, then, is the deliverance of men through the mediation of Jesus Christ. This salvation is spoken of by the Apostle as unspeakably great: not merely a great salvation, nor even *the* great salvation but 'so great salvation'—an expression peculiarly fitted to express his high estimate of its importance. And who that knows anything about that deliverance can wonder at the Apostle using such language?

"What are the *evils* from which it saves us? The displeasure of God, with all its fearful consequences in time and eternity; and 'who knows the power of His anger?' We must measure the extent of infinite power, we must fathom the depths of infinite wisdom, before we can resolve the fearful question. We can only say, 'According to Thy fear, so is Thy wrath.' The most frightful conception comes infinitely short of the more dreadful reality. A depravity of nature ever increasing, and miseries varied according to our varied capacities of suffering—limited in intensity only by our powers of endurance, which an almighty enemy can enlarge indefinitely, and protracted throughout the whole eternity of our being—these are the evils from which this salvation delivers.

"And what are the *blessings* to which it raises? A full, free, and everlasting remission of all our sins—the enjoyment of the paternal favour of the infinitely powerful, and wise, and benignant Jehovah—the transformation of our moral nature—a tranquil conscience—a good hope down here; and in due time, perfect purity and perfect happiness for ever in the eternal enjoyment of God.

"And *how* were these evils averted from us?—how were these blessings obtained for us? By the incarnation, obedience, suffering, and death of the Only-begotten of God, as a sin-offering in our room! And how are we individually interested in this salvation? Through the operations of the Holy Spirit, in which He manifests a power not inferior to that by which the Saviour was raised from the dead, or the world was created. Surely such a deliverance well merits the appellation, a 'so great salvation!'"

But this great salvation, which is made known in the Gospel, may be "neglected." While it is true that salvation is not only announced, but is also secured to and effectuated in God's elect by the Holy Spirit, yet it must not be forgotten that the Gospel addresses the *moral responsibility* of those to whom it comes. There is not only an effectual call, but a general one, which is made unto "the sons of men" (Prov. 8:4). The Gospel is for the sinner's *acceptance*, see 1 Tim. 1:15; 2 Cor. 11:4! The Gospel is more than a publication of good news, more than an invitation for burdened souls to come to Christ for relief and peace. In its first address to those who hear, it is a Divine mandate, an authoritative command, which is disregarded at the sinner's iminent peril. That it *does* issue a "command" is clear from Acts 17:30; Rom. 16:25, 26. That disobedience to *this* "command" will be punished, is clear from John 3:18, 1 Peter 4:17, 2 Thess. 1:8.

The Greek word here rendered "neglect" is translated "made light of" in Matt. 22:5. In this latter passage the reference is to the King making a marriage for His Son, and then sending forth His servants to call them which were bidden to the wedding. But they "made light of" the King's gracious overtures and "went their ways, one to his family, another to his merchandise." The parable sets forth the very sin against which the apostle was here warning the Hebrews, namely, failure to give earnest heed to the things which were spoken by the Lord, and neglecting His great salvation. To "neglect" the Gospel, is to remain inattentive and unbelieving. How, then, asks the apostle, shall such "escape?" "Escape" what? Why, the "damnation of Hell" (Matt. 23:33)! Such we take it is the first meaning and wider scope of the searching question asked in v. 3. Should it be objected. This cannot be, for in the "we" the apostle Paul manifestly included himself. The answer is, so also does he in the "we" of Heb. 10:26! That the "we" includes more than those who had really believed the Gospel will be clear from v. 4.

Coming now to the narrower application of these words and their more direct bearing upon the regenerated Hebrews whom the Holy Spirit was specifically addressing, we must consider them in the light of the chief design of this Epistle, and the circumstances in which the Hebrews were then placed; namely, under sore temptation to forsake their espousal of Christianity and to return to Judaism. Looked at thus, the "so great salvation" is only another name for Christianity itself, the "better thing" (Heb. 11:40) which had been brought in by Christ. Judaism was about to fall under the unsparing judgment of God. If, therefore, they turned from their allegiance to Christ and went back to that which was on the eve of being destroyed, how could they "escape" was the question which they must face?

Heb. 2:3 must be interpreted in harmony with its whole context. In the opening verse of chapter 2 the apostle is making a practical and searching application of all he had said in chapter 1, where he had shown the superiority of Christianity over Judaism, by proving the exaltation of Christ—the Center and Substance of Christianity—over prophets and angels. In 1:14 He had spoken of the "*heirs* of salvation" which, among other things, pointed to their salvation as being yet future. In one sense they had been saved (from the penalty of sin), in another sense they were still being saved (from the power of sin), in still another sense they were yet to be saved (from the presence of sin). But God ever deals with His people as *accountable* creatures. As moral beings, in contrast from stocks and stones, He addresses their responsibility. Hence, God's saints are called upon to give diligence to make their "calling and election sure" (2 Peter 1:10)—sure unto themselves, and unto their brethren. This, among other things, is done, by using the Divinely-appointed means of grace, and by perseverance and continuance in the faith: see John 8:31; Acts 11:23; 13:43; 14:22; 2 Tim. 3:14, etc.

The Christian life is likened unto a "race" set before us: 1 Cor. 9:24; Phil. 3:13, 14; 2 Tim. 4:7; Heb. 12:1. A "race" calls for self-discipline, personal exertion, perseverance. The Inheritance is set before us in promise, but it is written, "Ye have need of patience, that, after ye have done the will of God, ye might receive the promise" (Heb. 10:36). The "promise" is secured by faith and patience, by actually, "running" the race set before us. In the light of this, "neglect" would signify failure to "give diligence" to make our calling and election sure, failure to "press forward" and "run the race." If then we "neglect," how shall we "escape?" Escape *what*? Ah, note how abstractly the apostle worded it. He did not *specify* the "what." It all depends upon the state of the individual. If he be only a lifeless professor and continues neglecting the Gospel, Hell will be his certain portion. But if he be a regenerated believer, though a careless and worldly one, then lack of assurance and joy, profitlessness and fruitlessness, will be his portion; and then, how shall he "escape" the chastening rod of the holy Father? Thus, the question asked in our verse addresses itself to *all* who read the Epistle.

"Which at the first began to be spoken by the Lord, and was confirmed unto us by them that heard" (v. 3). This need not detain us long. Its central design is to emphasise the importance and need of heeding that which had been spoken by Christ: with it should be carefully compared Deut. 18:18, 19: Luke 9:35. Incidentally, the words "at the first *began*" intimates that Christ was the first Gospel-Preacher! The reference is to that which was preached first by Christ Himself, recorded in the Gospels; then, to that which was proclaimed by His apostles, reported in the book of Acts. The title here given to the Saviour, "Lord," emphasises both His dignity and authority, and intimates that the responsibility of the Hebrews was being addressed. Till Christ came and preached, "the people sat in darkness and in the shadow and region of death;" and when He began to preach, they "saw great light" (Matt. 4:16). With the "confirmed unto us" compare Luke 1:1, 2. The apostle was calling the Hebrews' attention to the *sureness* of the ground on which their faith rested.

"God also bearing witness, both with signs and wonders, and with divers miracles, and gifts of the Holy Spirit, according to His own will" (v. 4). The reference here is to the miracles wrought by God through the apostles in the early days of the Christian era. The book of Acts records many examples and illustrations of what is here said: see 5:9, 10; 13:11; 3:7; 9:40; 19:12, etc. The Gospel was first preached by the Lord Himself, then it was confirmed by the apostles, and then again by God Himself in such works as could not be performed but by a Divine power. "Bearing witness with" is a single word in the Greek, but a double compound. The simple verb signifies to witness to a thing as in John 1:7; the compound, to add testimony to testimony, or to add a testimony to some other confirmation; the double compound, to give a joint-testimony or to give-witness-together with one another. A similar compound is used in Rom. 8:16.

The means employed by God in thus confirming the witness of His servant are described by four terms: signs, wonders, miracles, gifts. The first three refer to the same things, though under different aspects. "Signs" denote the making more simple and evident that which otherwise could hardly be discerned; compare the use of the terms in Matt. 12:38; 16:1, and note the "see" and "show." "Wonders" points both to the striking nature of the "signs" and to the effects produced in those who beheld them: compare Acts 2:19; 7:36. "Miracles" refers to the supernatural power which produced the "signs" and "wonders." The Greek word is rendered "mighty deeds" in 2 Cor. 12:12. Thus, "miracles" are visible and wondrous works done by the all-mighty power of God, above or against the course of nature. Our text speaks of *"divers* miracles": many sorts of supernatural interpositions of God are recorded in the Acts.

An additional means employed by God in confirming the Gospel was "gifts of the Holy Spirit." The Greek word here rendered "gifts" means "divisions" or "distributions"; in the singular number it occurs in Heb. 4:12, where it is translated "dividing asunder." In its verbal form it is found in 1 Cor. 7:17, "God hath distributed to every man." Because these distributions of the Holy Spirit originated not in those by whom they were exercised and through whom they were displayed, they are not unfitly translated "gifts"; the reference being to the gifts extraordinary, manifested through and by the apostles. These "gifts" may also be seen in the book of Acts—the day of Pentecost, e.g., also in 1 Cor. 12:4 and what there follows. We may add that these "divers miracles and gifts of the Holy Spirit" were given by God *before* the N.T. was written. Now that the Scriptures are complete they are no longer needed, nor given.

"According to His own will." The forementioned divers miracles and distributions of gifts were ordered and disposed according to the sovereign pleasure of Deity. The act of distributing is attributed to God the Father in 1 Cor. 7:17, to the Son in Eph. 4:7, to the Spirit in 1 Cor. 12:11. The Greek signifies, "according to *His own* will." The will of God is the one rule by which all things are ordered that He Himself doeth, and whereby all things ought to be ordered that His creatures do. Scripture distinguishes between the secret and revealed will of God, see Deut. 29:29, where both are referred to. The secret will of God is called His "counsel" (Isa. 46:10), the "counsel of His will" (Eph. 1:11), His "purpose" (Rom. 8:28), His "good pleasure" (Eph. 1:9). The revealed will of God is made known in His Word, and is so called because, just as the ordinary means by which men make known their minds is by the word of their mouth, so the revelation of God's will is called "His Word." This revealed will of God is described in Rom. 12:2, and is primarily intended in the second clause of the Lord's prayer. Here in our text it is the secret will of God which is meant.

In these days of creature-pride and haughtiness, we need reminding that God is sovereign, conferring with none, consulting none; doing as *He* pleases. God's will is His only rule. As He creates, governs, and disposes all things, so He distributes the gifts of His Spirit "according to His own will." Should any murmur, His challenge is "Is it not lawful for Me to do what I will with Mine own?" Matt. 20:15). It is important to note that these gifts of the Spirit were distributed *not* "according to the faith" of those who received them—just as in the parable of the talents the supreme Sovereign distributed them unequally, according to His own good pleasure. May Divine grace bring both writer and reader into complete subjection to the secret will of God and obedience to His revealed will.

What has been before us in vv. 2, 3 tells us how firm and sure is the foundation on which our faith rests. In giving earnest heed to the Gospel, notwithstanding its unique and amazing contents, we are not following cunningly devised fables, but that which comes to us certified by unimpeachable witnesses. First, it began to be spoken by the Lord Himself. Though this was sufficient to make the Gospel "worthy of all acceptation," God mercifully, because of our weakness, caused it to be "confirmed" by those who had heard the Lord for themselves. The witness of these men was, in turn, authenticated by Divine displays of power through them such as was never seen before or since. Finally, additional attestation was furnished in supernatural outpourings of the Holy Spirit. Thus, God has graciously added witness to witness and testimony to testimony. How thankful we should be for these many infallible proofs! May this consideration of them result in the strengthening of our faith to the praise of the glory of God's grace.

—*Arthur W. Pink.*

GLEANINGS IN EXODUS.

55. *The Laver*: Ex. 30:17-21.

We are now to consider the seventh of the Tabernacle's holy vessels. Though given last in the Divine description of its various pieces of furniture, the Laver was really the second which met the priest in his way into the sacred building. It stood in the outer court, between the brazen-altar and the curtained wall which marked off the holy place. Though closely related to the brazen-altar, everything connected with the Laver was in striking contrast therefrom. The former was made of wood and brass; the latter of brass only. The one was square in shape; the other, most probably, was round. The dimensions of the altar are fully particularised; but no measurements are given in connection with the Laver. The former had rings and staves for carrying it; the latter had not. Instructions were given that the one should be covered when Israel journeyed from camp to camp; but nothing is said of this about the other. The altar was for fire; the Laver for water. The former received the sacrifices of all alike; the latter was for the priests alone. Thus everything about them was sharply distinguished.

That which is most prominent in connection with the Laver was its water for cleansing. "The figure of water is universally familiar, and represents one of the most important and necessary elements in the physical universe. We find it in the vast ocean, comprising by far the largest part of the earth's surface; and in our inland lakes and rivers, which form such exquisite networks both of beauty and convenience and of commercial value. We find it in the vapour of the skies; and the dews that gather about the vegetable creation, and preserve it from withering through the torrid summer. We find it forming the largest proportion of our own bodies. It is a figure of purity and refreshing; of quickening life and power; of vastness and abundance. Without it, life could not be for a single month maintained. And so we find it in the Bible as one of the most important symbols of spiritual things" (Dr. A. B. Simpson).

Even in Eden we find mention of a river "to water the garden" (Gen. 2:10), type of that river "the streams whereof shall make glad the city of God" (Psa. 46:4). This river went out from Eden to water the earth, being parted into four heads: figure of the temporal mercies of God flowing forth to all His creatures. Next, we read of the fearful waters of the Flood, being the instrument of God's unsparing judgment upon sin—compare the destruction of Pharaoh and his hosts by the same element: Ex. 14:1. Then we find it as preserving the life of Hagar and her son (Gen. 16:7, 21:19). Later, we find Jehovah furnishing water from the smitten rock for the refreshment of His people in the wilderness. Water has quite a prominent place in the ministries of Elijah and Elisha. It brought healing to Naaman (2 Kings 5), and saved Jehoshaphat's army from destruction (2 Kings 2).

So in the New Testament "water" is found in widely different connections. It is the element in which the believer is figuratively buried. It is found in connection with Christ's first miracle. From the pierced side of the Saviour there flowed "blood and water." Finally, in the last chapter of Holy Writ, we read of "a pure river of water of life, clear as crystal, proceeding out of the throne of God and of the Lamb" (v. 1). Thus, the contents of the Laver bring before us one of the most far-reaching and many-sided figures of Scripture.

The typical teaching of the Laver is rarely apprehended even among Christians, and their failure at this point has brought in much that is dishonouring to the Lord Jesus. Cleansing by blood and washing with water are sharply distinguished in the Old Testament types, but they are sadly confused in the thoughts of most churchgoers to-day. The sermons they hear, the hymns they sing, the prayers they utter, both express and add to the awful and Christ-dishonouring disorder of these last days. The thorough and prayerful study of the Tabernacle and all connected with it, would correct much which is now regarded as Scriptural, even in orthodox circles. But we will not anticipate. Let us now consider:

1. *Its Signification.*

This we may learn at once from the use to which it was put: "For Aaron and his sons shall wash their hands and their feet thereat" (v. 19). Thus we see at a glance it was designed for priestly purification. At the brazen-altar sins were dealt with and put away. At the golden-altar that which spoke of worship was presented to God. Midway between the two stood the Laver: at it the priests were required to wash their hands and feet, for communion with God necessitates not only acceptance but purification—a practical answering thereto.

There is therefore no difficulty at all in perceiving the spiritual meaning of the holy vessel which is now before us: happily the commentators are almost unanimous in their interpretation of this type. The Laver tells of the need of cleansing if communion with God is to be maintained: cleansing not from the guilt of sin, but from the defilements of the way. As already said, the question of sin was dealt with at the brazen-altar: *that* must be settled before there can be any approach unto God. Hence the brazen-altar was the *first* holy vessel to be met with in the outer court, being stationed just within the entrance. But having there slain the sacrifice and poured out its blood at the foot of the altar, the sons of Aaron were now able to advance; but ere they were ready to burn incense upon the golden-altar they must wash at the Laver. The need for this will be easily discerned.

Having officiated at the brazen-altar their hands would be unclean, smeared with blood. Moreover, as no shoes were provided for Aaron and his sons, the dust of the desert would soil their feet. These must be removed ere they could pass into the holy place; as it is said concerning the eternal Dwellingplace of God, "And there shall in no wise enter into it anything that defileth" (Rev. 21:27). The spiritual application of this to Christians to-day is obvious. The blood on the hands of Aaron and his sons evidenced that they had come into contact with *death*. So we, in our every-day lives, constantly have dealings with those who are dead in trespasses and sins, and their very influence defiles us. In like manner, our passage through this wilderness world, which lieth in the Wicked one (1 John 5:19), fouls our walk. There is therefore a daily need for these to be removed.

It is to be carefully noted that it was in their official character as priests, not merely as Israelites, that Aaron and his sons were required to wash their hands and feet at the Laver. Had they failed in this duty, they had still been Israelites, but they were disqualified for entering into the holy place and ministering before God. How clear and blessed is the typical teaching of this. The soiling of our hands and feet through association with the unregenerate, and in consequence sojourning in a world which knows not and loves not Christ, does not in any wise affect our perfect standing before God: "For by one offering He hath perfected *forever* them that are sanctified" (Heb. 10:14). But though the defilements of the way do not affect our standing, they *do* interfere with our communion with God. We cannot enter into our priestly privileges (1 Peter 2:5), nor discharge our priestly duties (Heb. 13:15), till we have been cleansed at the Laver. The Laver, like everything else in the Tabernacle, pointed to the Lord Jesus Christ, and tells of His sufficiency to meet our every need. It shows us that we must have recourse to Him for daily cleansing. This leads us to consider:

2. *Its Contents.*

"And thou shalt put water therein, for Aaron and his sons shall wash their hands and feet thereat: when they go into the tabernacle of the congregation, they shall wash with water" (vv. 18-20). Water and not blood was the element appointed and used for the purification of the priests. As that aspect of God's truth set forth in this detail of our type has largely been lost by the saints, we must examine it with doubly close attention.

In our present type the water within the Laver was plainly a figure of the written Word of God. This same figure is employed in the following passages: "Wherewithal shall a young man cleanse his way? by taking heed thereto according to Thy Word" (Psa. 119:9). "Except a man be born of water and of the Spirit, he cannot enter into the **kingdom of God**" (John 3:5). "Now ye are clean through the word which I have spoken unto you" (John 15:3). "Christ also loved the church, and gave Himself for it, that He might sanctify and cleanse it with the washing of water by the Word" (Eph. 5:25, 26). "According to His mercy He saved us, by the washing of regeneration, and renewing of the Holy Spirit" (Titus 3:5). "Let us draw near with a true heart in full assurance of faith, having our hearts sprinkled from an evil conscience, and our bodies washed with pure water" (Heb. 10:22). "Seeing ye have purified your souls in obeying the truth through the Spirit" (1 Peter 1:22).

Now, it is of first importance that we should discriminate between two distinct types. In Ex. 29:4 we are told, "And Aaron and his sons thou shalt bring unto the door of the tabernacle of the congregation, and thou shalt wash them with water." While in Ex. 30:19 we read, "Aaron and his sons shall wash their hands and feet thereat." The former was done *for* them; the latter was done *by* them. In the one they were completely washed all over; in the latter, it was only their hands and feet that were concerned. The former was never repeated; the latter was needed every time they would draw near the golden-altar. The one was a figure of regeneration, the other typified the Christian's need of daily cleansing. John 3:5; Titus 3:5; Heb. 10:22 give us the antitype of Ex. 29:4; Psalm 119:9, 1 Peter 1:22 speaks in the language of our present type.

The same distinction noted above is to be observed in the words of Christ to Peter: "He that is washed needeth not save to wash his feet, but is clean every whit" (John 13:10). The R.V. brings out the meaning of the Greek more accurately: "For he that is bathed needeth not save to wash his feet." The washing or bathing received at regeneration needs not to be repeated; the washing of the feet is all that is required to make us "clean every whit." The defilements of the way do not raise any need for me to be regenerated again: the new birth is once and for all. Nothing can affect it; nothing I do can cause me to become unborn; such a thing is impossible, both in the natural and spiritual realms.

But side by side with this blessed truth of a washing once for all, which needs not to be, and which, indeed, cannot be repeated, stands another truth of great practical importance. "He that is bathed needeth not save to *wash his feet*." This is what is so blessedly brought before us in John 13. The particular point there which we would now note is the Lord's words to Peter, when that disciple demurred at the thought of Christ washing his feet. To him the Saviour said, "If I wash thee not, thou hast no part with Me" (v. 8). Observe that Christ did not say *in* Me," but *"with* Me." "In Christ" refers to my spiritual state and standing before God; my acceptance. "With Christ" has to do with fellowship; communion with Him. For this there must be a removal of all that defiles, all that offends His holy eye. For this there must be a coming to Him and a placing of our feet in His hands—an humbling of ourselves before Him and an asking of Him to cleanse our walk. Thus the Laver points to Christ as the Cleanser of His people; its water to the Word which He uses for this.

3. *Its Position.*

"And thou shalt put it between the tabernacle of the congregation and the altar" (v. 18). As already stated, the Laver stood midway between the two altars. The priest's work at the brazen-altar was completed before he passed on to the Laver. This tells us that the question of our acceptance before God is not raised at the Laver. The interpretation and application of this detail is most important. That which the sons of Aaron needed for the removal of the dust of the desert was not blood, but water. So when the believer contracts defilement by treading the path of life through this world, it is *not* a fresh application of the blood of Christ which he needs, but the water of the Word.

Those Christians who speak and sing of re-applications of the blood of Christ unwittingly degrade His perfect sacrifice to the level of those offered under the Mosaic economy. Every time an Israelite transgressed God's righteous law, a fresh sin-offering was required. Why? Because the blood of bulls and goats could not take away sins (Heb. 10:4). But in contradistinction from those sacrifices, Christ has offered a perfect sacrifice for His people once for all (Heb. 9:26, 28). The blood He shed at Calvary has made full atonement; every claim of God's justice was there met, every demand of His holiness there fully satisfied. There is therefore now no need for any fresh sacrifice. The moment the convicted sinner has "faith in His blood" (Rom. 3:25), i.e., puts his trust in the redemptive-work of Christ as the alone ground of his acceptance before God, that moment is he cleansed "from *all* sin" (1 John 1:7). To him the Spirit saith, "There is therefore now no condemnation to them which are in Christ Jesus" (Rom. 8:1). In simple confidence he may now rest on the Divine declaration that "by one offering He hath perfected forever them that are sanctified" (Heb. 10:14).

True, an evil heart of unbelief still remains within him; true, "in many things we all offend" (James 3:2); but neither the presence of the old nature, nor its evil fruits, can invalidate our perfect standing before God, which rests upon our acceptance in Christ. We are "complete in Him" (Col. 2:10). He has already "made us meet to be partakers of the inheritance of the saints in light" (Col. 1:12). It is the realisation of this which establishes the heart. It is the recognition of this which keeps us in unclouded peace. It is the laying hold of this which fills us with thanksgiving and praise unto God. To ask Him for a re-application of the blood is to repudiate the fact that we stand "unblameable and unreproveable in His sight" (Col. 1:22). Nay, what is worse, it is to deny the efficacy and sufficiency of its once-and-for-all application to us.

What is needed by the exercised believer as he is conscious of the blemishes of his service (the "hands") and the failures of his walk (the "feet"), is to avail himself of that which the Laver and its water prefigured—the provision which God has made for us in His Word. What is needed by us is a practical appropriation of that Word to all the details of our daily lives. It is to seek grace and heed that Word, "He that sayeth he abideth in Him ought himself also so to walk, even as He walked" (1 John 2:6). It is only by obeying the truth, through the Spirit, that we purify our souls (1 Peter 1:22). Christ could say, "By the Word of Thy lips I have kept Me from the paths of the Destroyer" (Psa. 17:4); and such ought to be our experience, too. When we fail, then we must act upon 1 John 1:9.

It is important to note that the Laver stood in the outer court and not within the holy place, which was the chamber of worship. With this should be linked the fact that this vessel was only for the use of Aaron's sons. What is in view here is *priestly* activity, the removing of that which would otherwise disqualify them for service at the golden-altar. What an unspeakable insult unto Jehovah had they passed into the holy place with soiled hands and feet! For them it would have been fatal, as the twice repeated "that they die not" clearly denotes. In like manner, we cannot enter into the worship of God's house if we have not first washed at the

Laver; the confessing of our sins and the consequent practical cleansing should take place before—in the outer court. Failure at this point is to, morally, bring in "death." "But let a man examine himself, and *so* let him eat of that bread, and drink of that cup" (1 Cor. 11:28). This involves the taking account of our hands and feet, and washing at the Laver *before* coming to the Lord's table.

4. *Its Composition.*

"Thou shalt also make a Laver of brass" (v. 18). In the outer court everything was made of brass (really "copper"), or covered with brass: altar, laver, pillars, and pins. This was in sharp distinction from the vessels which stood in the inner chamber, which were all of or covered with gold. "It is Divine righteousness testing man in responsibility, and consequently testing man in the place where he is. Brass, on this account, is always found outside of the tabernacle; while gold, which is Divine righteousness as suited to the nature of God, is found within. But testing man, it of necessity condemns him, because he is a sinner; and hence it will be found to have associated with it a constant judicial aspect" (Ed. Dennett).

If the reader will refer back to Article 15 he will there find we have, at some length, entered into the meaning of this symbol. Without again bringing forward the proofs of our definition, we shall here make only the bare statement that "brass" speaks of *judgment*. The Laver, then, typifies Christ in His character of Judge. In John 5:22 we find Him saying, "The Father judgeth no man, but hath committed all judgment unto the Son"; and again, "and hath given Him authority to execute judgment also, because He is the Son of man" (5:27). Hence, in Rev. 1, where One like unto "the Son of man" is seen in the midst of the seven golden lampstands—judging—inspecting, passing sentence—we are told that His feet were "like unto fine *brass*" (v. 19).

Thus the Laver of brass presents the inflexible righteousness of Christ testing, judging His people, condemning that which mars their communion with God. But how blessed to remember that He also supplies that water which *removes* the very things which are condemned! "It is not the execution of judgment upon our Substitute, nor is it the infliction of judgment upon us; but it is the testing and trying of our ways by the Son of God according to the authority given Him to judge among His people, before He judges all the earth in a later day" (Mr. Ridout).

5. *Its Use.*

Strictly speaking, it was not the Laver itself that was used, but the water in it: "Aaron and his sons shall wash their hands and feet thereat," more literally, *"from it."* This, the sons of Aaron were to do for themselves. It speaks, then, of believers, in their priestly character, making practical application to all their ways of the Word of Christ (Col. 3:16). The water in the *brazen* Laver points to the believer *judging* himself, unsparingly, by that Word.

First of all, that Word should be used to *prevent* us falling into evil. God's Word has been given to us for "a lamp unto our feet and a light unto our path"; that is, to expose the snares of Satan and to reveal the path in which we should walk. O that more and more we may be able to say, "Thy Word have I hid in mine heart, that I might not sin against Thee."

Second, that Word is to be used in *cleansing* us from all defilement. We can only heed that exhortation in 2 Cor. 7:1—"Let us cleanse ourselves from all filthiness of the flesh and spirit"—by diligently attending to and daily obeying the precepts of Holy Writ. What a searching word is that in Rev. 22:14, "Blessed are they that wash (by the Word) their robes (emblematic of our external deportment), that they might have the right to the tree of life" (R.V.)!

Third, that Word is to be used for *refreshment*. Though we know of no other commentator who has called attention to this, yet we believe it is definitely taught in our present type. In Ex. 30:20 we are also told that Aaron's sons were required to wash with water "when they come near the altar to minister, to burn offering made by fire unto the Lord." This was upon the *brazen* altar. It seems to us that the thought here is not so much the removal of defilement, as it is that of coming to the altar in vigour or freshness, as the priests brought with them that which spoke of the highest aspect of Christ's work.

Water is used by us not only for cleansing, but to invigorate—nothing is more refreshing to tired feet than to bathe them. Is not this thought clearly seen in the *first* mention of the washing of feet in Scripture? "Let a little water, I pray you, be fetched, and wash your feet *and rest* yourselves under the tree" (Gen. 18:4). Note how the two angels refused to wash their feet in Lot's house (Gen. 19:2)—there was no refreshment for them in Sodom! The application to us of this detail in our type is plain: in order to minister before God as priests, we must first receive refreshment from His Word. It is by that alone we are "quickened"—revived and refreshed.

6. Its Manufacture.

It is striking to note the source from which the material for the Laver was obtained. This we are not told in our present passage, but have it made known in Ex. 38:8: "And he made the laver of brass, and the foot of it of brass, of the looking-glasses of the women assembling, which assembled at the door of the tabernacle of the congregation." These looking-glasses or mirrors were not like our modern ones, of glass and quicksilver, but were of highly polished brass or copper. Several lines of thought are pointed to by this important detail.

First, we may admire the lovely product which the grace of God, working in their hearts, brought forth. At the beginning, Jehovah bade Moses, "Speak unto the children of Israel, that they bring Me an offering of every man ("whosoever" 35:5) that giveth it willingly with his heart, ye shall take My offering" (25:8). Here we see the answer of the hearts of the daughters of Israel: they "willingly offered what might gratify vanity, to provide for that vessel of cleansing, that Jehovah's service and worship might not be hindered" (Mr. Ridout). In like manner, God's people to-day delight to give of their substance to the furtherance of His work. But how often the sacrificial giving of the sisters puts the brethren to shame!

Second, have we not here a beautiful foreshadowing of the Lord Jesus setting aside that which ministered to His glory, in order that He might provide cleansing for His people? He left the worship of angels in Heaven, and came here, to the "outer court," in servant form. He came not to be ministered unto, but to minister. It is exceedingly striking to observe that in the Gospels, the only record we have of any ministering to Him of their substance were devoted *women* (Luke 8:2, 3)! So, too, it was women, not the apostles (sad failure on their part!), who washed His feet with tears, and also anointed Him.

Third, the practical application to ourselves is very searching. The very material from which the Laver was made spoke of *surrender,* a willingness to part with what was calculated to make something of self; and this, in order that conditions of holy purity might be maintained in the priests. Thus we, too, must sacrifice what would minister to pride if we are to obtain that cleansing which fits for communion with God!

Fourth, the uselessness of worldly expedients may be seen here—the women had brought their mirrors from Egypt. "We are ever prone to be 'like a man beholding his natural face in a glass; for he beholdeth himself and goeth away, and straightway forgetteth what manner of man he was.' Nature's looking-glass can never furnish a clear and permanent view of our true condition. 'But whoso looketh into the perfect law of liberty, and continueth therein, he being not a forgetful hearer, but a doer of the work, this man shall be blessed in his deed' (James 1:23-25). The man who has constant recourse to the Word of God, and who allows that Word to tell upon his heart and conscience, will be maintained in the holy activities of the Divine life" (C.H.M.).

7. Its Omissions.

These were two in number, and very noticeable they are. First, no *dimensions* were prescribed for the Laver, nor are we told the quantity of water which it contained. A similar omission was observed in connection with the lampstand. The measurements of all the other vessels are given. The absence of any here in connection with the Laver and its water plainly denotes that an *unlimited* provision has been made by God for our cleansing. In Christ and His Word is sufficient to minister to our every need.

Second, no directions were given to Israel concerning the *covering* of the Laver while they journeyed from camp to camp. In Num. 4 we find instructions for the protection of the ark, the table, the lampstand, and both the altars; but nothing is said of the Laver. Does not the absence of any covering to this vessel strikingly accord with its typical character? Does it not tell us that the purifying Word is *ever* available, and that we need to use it daily in all our wilderness journeyings! Thus, we see again, that the omissions of Scripture (which the carnal mind would regard as defects) are profoundly significant.

We may also take note of the significant omission of further references to the Laver in the Old Testament. Only once is it referred to after the tabernacle was erected and furnished; and that is when it was anointed (Lev. 8:11). Not until we reach the book of Kings do we find that which took the place of the Laver in Solomon's temple, namely, the "molten sea" (1 Kings 7:23, etc.). Does not *this* omission silently testify to Israel's departure from the Word throughout their history! Probably the "Fountain" of Zech. 13:1 gives us the Millennial Laver.

That which in Heaven corresponds to the Laver is brought before us in Rev. 15:2, 3—cf. 1 Kings 7:23. Here the saints will no longer need to wash, but they are eternally reminded of the source of their purity. They are seen standing on a "sea" (Laver) of glass, "singing unto the Lamb." Altar and Laver will never be forgotten. The altar says, "without shedding of blood is no remission." The Laver announces "without holiness no man shall see the Lord." Both are witnessed to on High. As another has so beautifully said:

"Here we are permitted to look into the glory. There, in the heavenly sanctuary, is the throne of God and of the Lamb, as the ark was in the tabernacle. The hidden manna is there, answering to the table of shewbread. The seven Spirits of God are before the throne, answering to the candlestick; and the sea of glass, answering to that in Solomon's temple. Notice it is not now the laver filled with water—no need to remove defilement there; it is a sea of transparent glass, reminding us of the laver which has accomplished its work here. When all the redeemed of God are gathered there, the day of cleansing from defilement is over, no more need to wash one another's feet; no more need for the Lord's washing our feet, but there we stand with harps of God in our hands, nothing to hinder praise and worship. But the sea of glass, the witness and perpetual reminder of our cleansing, will flash forth there a continual remembrance of our Lord's gracious and humble service throughout our journey here" (Mr. Ridout).

—*Arthur W. Pink.*

TAUGHT OF GOD.

"And all Thy children shall be taught of the Lord" (Isa. 54:13).

In our first sermon upon this text we confined ourselves to one point, namely, *who* are the members of this favoured family? We answered: First, they are those whom God eternally ordained to be such, and therefore He predestinated them unto "the adoption of children by Jesus Christ to Himself" (Eph. 1:5). Second, they are those whom God hath legally obtained by redemption, being purchased by the Lord Jesus (Zech. 9:11; John 11:51, 52). Third, they are those whom God hath begotten through regeneration, creating them anew by His Holy Spirit (John 3:6; Gal. 4:6). Fourth, they are those who are owned as such: by the Father, the Son, the Holy Spirit, the angels, and the Devil. Fifth, they are those who manifest their Divine parentage by evidencing the marks of the Divine likeness.

In our present sermon we are going to consider *what* it is that the members of this favoured family are all taught. Before taking this up in detail, let me first say how profoundly thankful all real Christians should be *for* such Divine teaching; that amid the babel of tongues which now obtains in the religious world, there is one circle where Divine truth *is* known! In heathendom there are many religious systems, well established, hundreds of years old, numbering their devotees by the hundreds of millions. They differ widely in their teaching; yet each one claims to be the only true religion. In Christendom the confusion is equally bewildering: on every side new sects, isms, and systems are rising, each claiming superior enlightenment above all others. Because of this, some have been much puzzled over one of the petitions of the Lord's prayer in John 17, where the Saviour asked the Father that His people should be *one,* even as the Father and Son were one.

In view of this request of the Son's, the world is fond of chiding Christians with their differences and divisions. But I refuse to admit that these differences are as serious or as numerous as the ungodly allege. That there are radical differences among *professing* Christians I grant; but among the believing children of God, despite minor differences, there is a real, deep, fundamental and blessed unity among them. As I shall now proceed to point out, there is a firm agreement among the members of the family of God upon the great verities of the faith. This *must* be so, for they all have one infallible Teacher; and He never contradicts Himself. Consider now:

1. *They are all taught the Bible is a Divine Revelation.* I place this first because it is the foundation on which the Christian faith rests. The Spirit of God ever directs attention to the Word. That is one reason why He is called the Spirit of Truth—"when He, the Spirit of Truth, is come, He will guide you into all truth" (John 16:13). He is the "Spirit of Truth" not only because He is the Author of it, but also because He is the Expounder and

Applier of it. It is by the Word He convicts of sin, showing us our ruined, guilty, and lost condition. It is by the Word that He makes known to us the wondrous and merciful provision which God has made for poor sinners. It is through the Word that He makes known the way back to God. And as He does this, He creates in the heart a realisation that it is *God* who is speaking to us through that Word.

The man who calls into question the Divine Authorship of the Scriptures is yet dead in trespasses and sins. He may be highly educated, a person of great erudition, a scholar of many degrees; but if he regards the Bible as being merely the production of man, that is proof positive that he has never been born again, for it is written "he that hath received His testimony hath set to his seal that God is true" (John 3:33). Of the saints it is declared, "Ye have an unction from the Holy One, and *ye know* all things" (1 John 2:20). Therefore the "agnostic" (one who "knows not") no matter though he call himself a Christian, is devoid of such Divine "unction."

On the other hand, the Christian may be one who possesses little of the learning obtained in human schools, yet as he reads the Bible he perceives that it is a message from his Father; he realises in his heart that he is listening to a voice that is Divine. God's children are all taught that the Scriptures are "holy," that is, *separated* from all other writings: different not only in degree, but in kind. They are taught that the Bible is infallible, and therefore trustworthy. In resting upon its teachings, they know that they have a "thus saith the Lord" to go upon. They know the Scriptures are Divine because their language has a pungency and power which no other book possesses. They know that the Scriptures are Divine because there is a sweetness and preciousness in their contents which no other writings have for them. Because they know the Scriptures are Divine, the Bible is to them the Final Court of appeal; they bow to its authority.

2. *They are taught that by nature they are lost and hell-deserving sinners.* By their natural birth God's children are no better and no different from the children of the Devil. They were "shapen in iniquity and conceived in sin" (Psa. 51:5). They were born into this world "having the understanding darkened, being alienated from the life of God, through the ignorance that is in them, because of the blindness of their hearts" (Eph. 4:18). They were born with their backs to Heaven, and with their faces toward Hell. Because of this, they followed the evil desires of their wicked heart; they turned "every one to *his own* way" (Isa. 53:6) The fear of God was not before their eyes; for the honour of God they had no concern; His glory they sought not. Before regeneration, their lives were wholly sinful in thought, word, and deed. Their sins were more in number than the hairs of their heads.

But they were completely unconscious of this. They knew not the fearfulness of their condition. They were "by nature the children of wrath, even as others" (Eph. 2:3). They were "dead in trespasses and sins," and therefore quite insensible to the awfulness of their state. Then it was that God in His wondrous, sovereign grace, sent the Holy Spirit and opened their eyes so that they saw their ruined and guilty condition. The Spirit convicted them of sin, made them conscious of their vileness, revealed to them their unfitness to dwell with the thrice holy God. He brought them to a state of despair, so that they saw there was no help in themselves. He stript them of their own self-righteousness and made them mourn before God.

"And all Thy children shall be taught of the Lord." Yes, sooner or later each of His children is taught that he is condemned by God's righteous law, and that he is utterly powerless to make any atonement unto it. He is made to feel that he is a debtor to God, and that he has nothing whatever to pay with. He is revealed to himself as a spiritual leper, and taught that he can no more heal himself than can one who is such physically. He is *so* "taught" that he ceases to make any excuse for himself, and cries, "God be merciful to me a sinner."

This is one of the chief things which distinguishes the children of God from the children of the Devil. The ungodly can see no reason why they should be cast into the lake of fire. They may have made "mistakes," they may not be quite all that they should be, but they realise not that they are guilty of anything which merits everlasting woe. But how different with the regenerate! They marvel that they are not in Hell long ago. They know that if they were to receive their personal deserts, that endless weeping and wailing and gnashing of teeth are their well-earned portion.

3. *They are taught the depravity of their natures.* The Spirit of God not only convicts them of what they have done, but shows them what they are. They are taught the *source* from which their wickedness comes. They are taught that they are not sinners because they sin, but they sin because they are sinners. They are

made to realise that "in the flesh there dwelleth *no* good thing." They are made to **feel** that there is "no soundness (Isa. l: 6) in them. They are brought to see that "the heart is deceitful above all things, and desperately wicked" (Jer. 17:9). Because the tree is corrupt the fruit can only be evil. This is something of which the natural man is totally ignorant. He may, occasionally, condemn his ways, but never himself. That is why he is always vowing that he will do better in the future, resolving to "turn over a new leaf." But a child of God, who has been shown his sinful self, says with Isaiah, "Woe is me! for I am undone" (Isa. 6:5). He says with Job, "I abhor myself, and repent in sackcloth and ashes" (42:6).

No doubt there are varying degrees in this painful experience. God gives to some of His people a deeper realisation of their innate and total depravity than He gives to others. Yet the experience itself is shared by *all* the saints. They know that "out of the heart proceed evil thoughts, adulteries, fornications, murders, thefts, coveteousness, wickedness, deceit, lasciviousness, an evil eye, blasphemy, pride, foolishness; all these evil things come from *within*, and defile the man" (Mark 7:21-23). They know that, but for the restraining and subduing grace of God, they would actually commit these awful sins. They are all present in the heart in germ form, and will develop unless God prevents. As said an eminent saint of old, who witnessed a murderer going to the gallows, "There goes John Bradford, but for the grace of God." I believe that in most cases, though not in all, this solemn truth of our vitiated nature is realised by Christians more deeply *after* their convertion than before. Some Christians feel they are growing worse; really, it is God giving them a clearer sight of their sinful selves. Our daily prayer should be, "Show me myself," then "Show me Thyself."

4. *They are taught that Christ is their only hope.* Sooner or later, all of God's children are taught that their case is so desperate there is no hope in themselves. They are taught that the Ethiopian could change his skin or the leopard his spots, sooner than that the natural man could make himself into a spiritual one. They are taught that a disease more loathsome and incurable than leprosy cleaveth to them, and hence, that none but a Divine physician can heal them. They are taught to look away from self to Christ.
"Ask them whence their victory came,
They with *united breath*,
Ascribe their victory to the Lamb,
Their triumph to His death."

As the soul is made to feel the intolerable burden of its guilt, they are then given an ear to hear Christ saying, "Come unto Me all ye that labour and are heavy laden, and I will give you rest" (Matt. 11:28). They are made to cry with the repentant and dying thief, "Lord, remember me" (Luke 23:42). They exclaim like sinking Peter did, "Lord, save me" (Matt. 14:30).

5. *They are taught that their salvation is by grace alone.* The natural man is quite unable to follow a servant of God when he declares that our evil works have just as much to do with our salvation as have our good ones. The truth is that his heart is so full of pride and self-righteousness that he is incapable of appreciating the wondrous grace of God. His desire is to make God his debtor. His determination is to have some ground for boasting. Were salvation offered by God to men as a wage to be earned and a prize to be won, multitudes would compete for it. But because the Lord requires that man shall come to Him as a sinner, empty handed, as a pauper, to receive charity, few take this position before Him; and that few, only as they are "taught" by the Holy Spirit.

Each member of this Divinely-taught and favoured family is brought to see that God is everything, that man is nothing. They rejoice in the declaration that "By grace are ye saved through faith, and that not of yourselves; it is the gift of God, not of works lest any man should boast" (Eph. 2:8, 9). But here again there are degrees in which this is perceived by the understanding and realised in the soul; and in the experience of the Christian there are times when he feels more deeply than at others *what* a debtor he is to the grace of God. But every believing child of God has been taught that there was and is nothing whatever in him to merit esteem, nothing of or from him which deserves good at God's hand. The Holy Spirit has taught him that salvation is by grace alone, and the language of all the saints is, "Not by works of righteousness which we have done, but according to His mercy He saved us" (Titus 3:5). The Christian knows that his salvation is not partly of grace and partly of works, not begun by grace and perfected by works; but wholly of grace from first to last. Therefore our testimony is, "Not unto us, O Lord, not unto us, but unto Thy name give glory, for Thy mercy, and for Thy truth's sake" (Psa. 115:1).

6. *They are all taught the value of Prayer.* God has no dumb children. The Spirit of God, who indwells them, impresses upon their hearts the importance

of and their need for prayer. "Shall not God avenge His own elect, which cry day and night unto Him?" (Luke 18:7). The first thing recorded of Saul of Tarsus after his conversion was, "Behold, he prayeth" (Acts 9:11). Just as a living child enters this world with a cry, and continues to cry every time it is conscious of its needs: so the spiritual child finds his heart going out to God and unburdens himself to Him. What a word is that in Rev. 8:3: "Another angel came and stood at the altar, having a golden censer; and there was given unto him much incense, that he should offer it with the prayers of *all* saints upon the golden altar which was before the throne!"

But the Christian has to be "taught" the value of prayer; yea, he has to be taught *to* pray. As it is written, "We know not what we should pray for as we ought" (Rom. 8:26). Therefore do the saints still come to Christ saying, "Lord, *teach us* to pray" (Luke 11:1). It is true that many of us are very slow in responding to what we have been taught. Instead of asking for more light, most of us need to ask God to enable us to walk according to the light which He has already given us. Nevertheless, it remains true that the members of this favoured family are a praying people.

7. *They are all taught the necessity of a godly walk.* And this, not as a means to or contribution towards their salvation, but as an *evidence* that they have been saved. "As the body without the spirit is dead, so faith without works is dead also" (James 2:26). It is by bringing forth "much fruit" that their heavenly Father is glorified (John 15:8).

The members of this favoured family are not only shown the importance of a Christ-honouring walk, but they are also —in varying measure—empowered for such. "For we are His workmanship, created in Christ Jesus unto good works, which God hath before ordained that we *should* walk in them" (Eph. 2:10). It is written that, "The grace of God that bringeth salvation hath appeared to all men, *teaching us* that, denying ungodliness and worldly lusts, we should live soberly, righteously, and godly, in this present world" (Titus 2:11, 12). An *un*righteous professing Christian is an impostor. "Why call ye Me, Lord, Lord, and do not the things which I say?" is Christ's searching word to such.

Now, to be "taught" of God means far more than having the mind informed on these points. It means having a personal and experimental acquaintance with them. It is not sufficient for an hearer to say, "I approve of what the preacher is declaring; I cannot gainsay what he advances; I believe that he is sincere, and has the Scriptures on his side." No, though God's servant has preached to you with the precision, plainness, and power of the apostle Paul, yea, with the tongue of an angel; unless a miracle of grace has been wrought within you, unless your life has been revolutionised from centre to circumference, unless you now hate the things you once loved and love the things you hated, then his preaching is, *to you,* only "the savor of death unto death."

What avails it that you know God is sovereign, unless you know Him as *your* God? What avails it you know that Christ is an all-sufficient Saviour, and the only Saviour of sinners, unless *you* are trusting in Him? What avails it that you know God has a favoured people, unless you are sure that *you* are one of them? What avails it you know man is a fallen creature, unless you hate yourself and groan before God? What avails it that you subscribe to an orthodox creed, unless you have been born again? What avails it that you have a form of godliness, if you are a stranger to its power? Nothing! It is only like decking out a corpse in fine clothes. May the Spirit of God search your heart, open your eyes, grant you discernment to know which Path you are treading, which Family you belong to, which Place you will dwell in forever.

—*Arthur W. Pink.*

DEAD TO SIN AND ALIVE TO GOD.

The old conceit of "perfect holiness," "perfect love," or whatever be the terms in which its preposterous claims are clothed, makes its appearance among us with a somewhat modified terminology. This is due to the fact that it has found advocates whose previous theological education was not Arminian, addressing themselves to a class of inquirers who could not be approached except with the sound and semblance of evangelical truth. We do not propose to go into the history of this movement. But we may state it as an impression, that it arises naturally out of the habit of holding the doctrines of grace theoretically, while, practically, salvation is placed upon legal ground. In connection with this, we find mistaken notions of regeneration as a change in the old nature, rather than the birth of a new nature—a change which is only the commencement of a progressive sanctification which is to be consummated sooner or later within the limits of this life.

The greater number of us can only too well understand the torture of uncertainty as regards the great issues of life which drive men to seek some relief in the dream of another conversion and a higher life than that which they were leading. And it is a satisfaction to think that, amidst all the confusion and extravagance by which their guides have bewildered them, some of these tortured souls have been led to true rest in Christ Jesus; and, though they use the verbiage which is peculiar to the coteries in which they mingle, patient search for the reality which underlies their pretentious language and excited feelings may discover that "the blessing" in which they rejoice is an apprehension of what Christ is to the believer, and of the believer's standing and acceptance in Christ. When this is the case, they will gradually become ashamed of the extravagant claims which their language imports; they will be repelled by the egotism and excitement in which alone the delusion of "perfection" can exist; and they will seek a calm and lowly walk with God in more healthful association where the Lord, and not the creature of His hand, is exalted.

Doubtless the movement has been strengthened by accessions from another class whose case is far more sad, and whose advocacy of it is much more plausible and dangerous. There are those who have had "clear views," as they are called, of the plan of grace—of the ground of a sinner's justification in the sight of God, of the believer's standing in Christ, as well as of the work of the Holy Spirit in regeneration, and of the completeness of the new man in Christ. Not only could they make clear and scriptural statements of doctrine, they have known it in its power and preciousness. But they become too much occupied with the doctrine in the abstract, with the truth rather than with the True One. Perhaps they have become more or less inflated by the superior clearness of their views. The truth has then lost its living power in their souls, and they have fallen into a sluggish habit, and into the indulgence of unhallowed frames and habitual carnality, which they vainly attempt to excuse by a perversion of the truths which were once living and controlling. Ill at ease and self-condemned, they seek an explanation of their failure in some defect in the truth they have received. They cannot reject it as false, but they conclude that it was defective. And it is easy to understand how all this predisposes them to accept the notion that a man may believe in Christ for justification and so be justified; while yet it remains for him to believe in Christ for sanctification and so be sanctified; on the alleged "law of faith," by which they say, "God ordains to bestow freely on each soul, without any claim through works, that thing for which he will trust the Saviour." To superficial consideration, these words have a certain savor of grace; but in effect they undermine the very foundations of the gospel of the Grace of God, which brings, not a partial but a complete salvation, and which presents, not a divided Saviour but a whole Christ, "who of God is made unto us wisdom, and righteousness, and sanctification, and redemption."

We need not be surprised if those to whom sin is most hateful should be captivated by the thought of being done with it at once and for ever—the thought of being done with the conflict of the flesh warring against the Spirit, and done with "groaning being burdened." If, being imperfectly instructed, they are approached by those who claim superior spiritual intelligence as well as superior sanctity—who clothe their fancies in Scriptural phrases detached from their connection, silencing all questions by insinuating that all who differ from them are unilluminated, and that the mystery can only be understood when the state of sanctification is attained—and who, moreover, offer their own testimony of the enjoyment of this state as a matter of fact; if imperfectly instructed Christians are thus approached, it is not wonderful that they should eagerly embrace the delusion which would forestall the blessed hope that "we shall be like Him when we shall see Him as He is." They adopt the opinion that the wished-for state is attainable, though the greater number of them may never be able so far to impose upon themselves as to think that they have attained it. Those who are drawn into the vain pursuit of it are miserable; but far more to be pitied are those who become infatuated with the conceit of having attained it, and who seek every opportunity of professing their own sinlessness, not knowing that spiritual pride is the most aggravated form of sin, and that of those who say, "I am holier than thou," a holy God has said, "These are a smoke in My nostrils." One of the characteristics of true sanctity is unconsciousness of itself, with a still deepening humility in the clearer light of God's countenance.

We address ourselves now chiefly to those who are distracted by the supposition that this state of sinless perfection is attainable, and that it is their privelege to aspire to a place among the class who claim this pre-eminence over the commonplace Christians who have not attained this "higher and more abundant life." We address ourselves also to the earnest souls in our churches who are moved by their hatred of sin to lend a favourable ear to the advocates of this delusive holiness. While the assumption of peculiar sanctity by these teachers may place us at a disadvantage when we come to expose their delusion—for we are evidently precluded from putting forward a rival claim—we must not be regarded as advocating a low standard of Christian life, or as in any sense apologising for the sins of believers, which are the blackest and most inexcusable of all sins. But we insist upon the very truths of which the Apostle says, "These things write we unto you, that ye sin not." We aim to state the truth of God in opposition to the conceits of men, with the persuasion that this is the most effectual means of promoting holiness of life, purity as well as peace of heart, and so the glory of God in His people.

As we bring no rival claims to the boasted perfection of these teachers, so we cannot dispute with them the palm of superior illumination. We have no notions to present to our readers, with the charge that they shall kneel before God with their open Bible, with the resolution that they will never rise till they see these notions in the Word of God. Our office rather is to restore perverted passages and phrases of Scripture to the connections from which they have been detached, and not to force a meaning on the word, but to let the word itself be heard.

Though parallel and related passages must necessarily be noticed, we are more particularly called to inquire in what sense Christians are said to be *"dead to sin"*—words which occur in the sixth chapter of the Epistle to the Romans, a chapter which the advocates of "perfection" regard as their stronghold in teaching the doctrine and describing the experience. And we remark,

1. That it is affirmed of all believers as such. It does not describe the peculiar attainment of some Christians, or point us to a condition at which we are exhorted to aim; but presents a fact that is so true of all believers as to render it a monstrous thought that any of them should continue in sin that grace may abound. The same may be remarked of all the parallel and related passages in this chapter, and throughout the Scriptures—"dead with Christ," "buried, crucified, risen with Christ, quickened together with Christ." Indeed, it is remarkable that almost every passage which these teachers cite as describing the attainment of sinlessness, or entire consecration, is evidently applicable to all believers as such, and frequently makes it evident that no man can be a believer to whom it is not applicable. Thus, in the memorable passage, "Whosoever is born of God doth not commit sin; for his seed remaineth in him; and he cannot sin, because he is born of God." (1 John 3, 9.) However you understand the affirmation, "doth not commit sin," it is affirmed of all who are born of God; and, strong as the language is, "he cannot sin," it is predicated simply on the ground that he is born of God. We cannot dwell upon this passage in its connection, in order to show its force and bearing on the Christian life. But, if we are asked how is it to be reconciled with the statements of the Word of God regarding the sins of believers, or with the teaching of this very epistle, or with the humbling facts in the life of every Christian, we may only suggest an answer in Paul's explanation in his own case, not when he is excusing, but when he is bewailing his failure. "Now then it is no more I that do it, but sin that dwelleth in me." In another passage which the advocates of sinlessness often use, "They that are Christ's have crucified the flesh, with the affections and lusts," Gal. 5:24, we have not the distinction of a few to which we are exhorted to aspire, but a characteristic of all that are Christ's, a fact affirmed of them *as* His. To return to the phrase, "dead to sin," we remark,

2. That it is affirmed as a fact accomplished. It is not something that is to take place either slowly or by a sudden stroke in the advancing experience of the Christian; it is not a state after which he is called to aspire; it is the statement of a fact accomplished in the case of all believers. This is still more impressive in the Greek, where the verb is in what has been called the historic tense, and would be more accurately rendered in English, "who died to sin." The same thing is true of the parallel and related phrases, both in this chapter and throughout the epistles. Thus, in the passage, "If one died for all, then were all dead" (2 Cor. 5:14), it is the same tense, "then all died."

And again in the passage, "For ye are dead, and your life is hid with Christ in God" (Col. 3:3), it is the same tense, "For ye died." This is especially to be observed with reference to the much-abused texts which speak of the believer's crucifixion. It might be curious to trace the history of the metaphorical use of the word "crucify" in our language. Probably it might be traced to the mistaken use of these very passages of Scripture. However men came to speak of self-crucifixion, when, of all forms of death, crucifixion is the most impossible for a man to inflict upon himself, there is certainly no such thought in the New Testament. It is always a fact historically stated, never something to take place in the experience of the believer, or which the believer is exhorted to do. The expression, "Our old man is crucified with Him" (Romans 6:6), would be more accurately rendered "was crucified." So also Paul's confession, "I am crucified with Christ" (Gal. 2:20), should be, "I was crucified with Christ." And in the passage, "But God forbid that I should glory save in the cross of our Lord Jesus Christ, by whom the world is crucified unto me, and I unto the world" (Gal. 6:14), we have the same tense, "was crucified." In short, everywhere it is a transaction past, not in progress or in prospect. Without enumerating the passages, we may say generally that wherever we are said to be "raised," or "quickened," it is always a fact accomplished. In speaking of all these—death, crucifixion, burial, rising again—as being affirmed of all believers, and as facts accomplished, it is important to observe that it is always "with Christ," or "in Christ," that they died, were crucified, and were quickened; but we shall have occasion to notice this connection hereafter. Meanwhile, returning to the phrase, "dead to sin," we remark,

3. That, whatever be its meaning, it is affirmed of Christ as well as of believers. We have the same words in the first verse, "*we died to sin,*" and in the tenth verse, "For in that He died, *He died to sin* once." With this fact before us, let us look at the meaning which the teachers of perfection would put upon the phrase. They tell us that death to sin is "the death of the old life, with its passions, prejudices, preferences, animosities, uncleannesses, ambitions, envyings, idolatries, self-will, and self-seeking." This is what they claim may be accomplished in the believer, "not by the process of a gradual, never accomplished crucifixion of the flesh; not so much by a severing of this and that and the other member; not so much by cutting out the cancers—though this otherwise might be needful—but by dying in the centre of your existence to self."

We do not ask if any man can be sincere in claiming that he has so died; for there is no extravagance of which the deceitful heart may not persuade itself. But surely they must be startled at their own recklessness when they find it stated in the same words that Jesus "died to sin." The construction which they put upon the phrase will be seen to be impossible when attention is drawn to this fact. The whole context shows that it has the same meaning in both cases. On the fact that He died to sin, the whole argument depends. On the fact that they died with Him, their life and resurrection depend. And if this means their "dying in the centre of their being to self," the death of the old man, with its lusts and passions, "then the work of Christ is superseded, and they procure life by their own act. "The likeness of His death," in that case, means that His death was the pattern of that which they attempt to inflict upon themselves. Do they at all reflect when they speak of "our Lord's crucifixion being reproduced in the experience of His saints"?

But again, according to their view, it is sin that dies—the natural will dies in them. So they claim that they are "freed from sin," as the victims of oppression are freed by the death of the tyrant. From a similar confusion of thought, the most remarkable mistranslation has crept into our English version: "But now we are delivered from the law, *that being dead* wherein we were held"; as though the law of God were dead. Whereas the apostle says, "But now we are delivered from the law, *being dead* (or having died) *to that* wherein we were held." The expression "dead to the law" throws light on the expression "dead to sin." For it refers to death by the execution of the law's sentence. In Gal. 2:19 the apostle says, "For I, through the law, am dead to the law," and adds, "I was crucified with Christ." The sentence of the law was executed on Paul in the person of his substitute. But to return to the phrase, "dead in sin," we remark,

4. That it is in Christ and with Him that we died. The demand, "How shall we who died to sin live any longer therein?" may seem abrupt; and, as an answer to the question, "Shall we continue in sin,

that grace may abound?" it may be considered irrelevant; if there has been no previous reference to our having died.

This throws us back on the preceding context, where we are taught that all men were so in Adam that, when he sinned, they sinned, and the condemnation of that one offence fell on them all. Life, in its true sense, was lost, and they are found "dead in trespasses and sins," by nature "children of wrath." In his relation to his posterity, who were "in him" according to the constitution of nature, Adam was the type of Christ in His relation to all who are "in Him" according to the election of grace. The sin of the first Adam is met by the righteousness of the Second Adam, so that, "as by the disobedience of one many were made sinners, so by the obedience of One many shall be made righteous"; in order that, "as sin reigned unto death, even so might grace reign through righteousness unto eternal life, by Jesus Christ our Lord."

Those who were represented by either are said to have done what was done by their head—to have sinned in Adam, or to have obeyed in Christ. But the only righteousness that could avail for sinners must include the endurance of the irreversible sentence of the law; the only obedience available for them was obedience unto death, even the death of the cross. So that, as it is said of those who were in Adam, "'all sinned'" when he sinned; so it is said of those who were in Christ, "all died" when He died.

Now, the reader will see the importance of the previous remarks that it is affirmed of all believers, and not of an aristocracy among them, is affirmed of them all as a fact accomplished, that they "died to sin"; and that what is affirmed of them is affirmed of Him, "He died to sin once." It is not that sin died in them, for that would involve the blasphemy that sin died in Him. But we in Him died under the doom of sin, and then rose with Him to newness of life—a life which has its proper sphere in His relations to God; holy in its nature; having its interests in the things which are above, and its consummation in glory, when He who is our life shall appear.

All the parallel and related passasges fall in with this view. "Crucified" does not refer to the self-inflicted torture of ascetics and mystics who think it a penance and an agony to relinquish sin. "Crucified" refers to the shameful, painful, and cursed death of the cross, in which God executed, and the Mighty One endured, all that was due to the sins of those whom He represented. "Our old man was crucified with Him," when "God, sending His own Son in the likeness of sinful flesh and for sin, condemned sin in the flesh." And the object of this, "that the body of sin might be annulled, that henceforth we should not serve sin," is embraced in the apostle's shout of liberty, "There is, therefore, now no condemnation to them that are in Christ Jesus; for the law of the Spirit of life in Christ Jesus hath made me free from the law of sin and death."

We may be asked to show the bearing of this great transaction of the past upon our practical holiness. To carnal minds, complete immunity from the curse seems complete freedom to sin; and the assurance of abounding grace seems an encouragement in the career of wickedness. But the apostle addresses those who are born of the Spirit. If the Gospel revealed grace over-riding the claims of righteousness, obliterating or reversing the principles of God's righteous government, it might be charged with encouraging sin. But it reveals grace reigning through righteousness, makes a display of God's love above all that was witnessed in heaven, and of God's justice above all that shall be witnessed in hell. The Son of God bore our sins, not that in a sinful nature we might be free from wrath, but that in a holy nature we might be embraced with Himself in the love of God. And it is to this holy nature that the arguments and incentives of the Gospel are addressed.

They tell us that this is all "judicial," as though it were a mere legal form by which sinners escape. The infliction of the awful doom of sin on our Substitute was, indeed, a judicial act. But being "in Christ" is a vital relation; and so, since in Him we "died to sin," eternal life and the awards of perfect righteousness follow as necessarily as "death passed upon all men, for that all sinned" in Adam. There is a glorious issue to this dying to sin; "for he that has died is freed from sin," but not freed as the oppressed are freed by the tyrant's death. It is not the death of sin, but death *to* sin, that is spoken of, and the word rendered "freed" has no such meaning as they put on it. It is properly rendered in the margin "justified." And life as necessarily accompanies justification as death follows sin. The apostle's argument is, Can sin assert its authority over the new man, "Christ in you"? Can we make Christ the servant of sin? He calls on believers to act upon the reality of their life in Christ. "Reckon yourselves dead indeed to sin, but alive to God in Jesus Christ." They are to reckon it so because it is so. It is true of all believers that they died in sin, and therefore true that Christ lives in them. Though all who are Christ's live in the Spirit, it is still necessary to admonish them, "Let us also walk in the Spirit." Those who are "light in the Lord" still need to be admonished, "Walk as children of the light." So he charges those who can in truth reckon themselves dead to sin and alive to God, "Let not sin therefore reign in your mortal bodies, that ye should obey it in the lusts thereof." The tyrant is not dead, though dethroned, and would still reassert his authority. In the interests of holiness we are warned, "If we say that we have no sin, we deceive ourselves, and the truth is not in us." But sin is not to lord it over Christ's freemen. The flesh, by necessity of its nature, wars against the Spirit; but if "we walk in the Spirit, we shall not fulfil the lusts of the flesh."

Despondency and carnal security are equally unbecoming our state. We are not called to put on heavenly armour for a holiday parade. We are not veterans reposing on our laurels, fighting our battles over again amid the applause of fireside audiences. The war is not ended. And though, in the conflict, we are cheered by the certainty of victory through Him that loved us, the mighty power by which victory is achieved assures us that the conflict is momentous, and calls us to "watch and be sober."

The manner in which we "died to sin" tells us of the love of God; of the exceeding sinfulness of sin in us; calls us to live, not unto ourselves, but to Him that died for us, and rose again; summons us to glorify God in our bodies and our spirits, which are His. This death issues in a life the object of which is God Himself. The holiness to which we are called does not consist in negatives, but has both its essence and pattern in Christ Himself. The fact that we "died to sin" carries with it all the results of Christ's death, even a participation of life and likeness, which alone could constitute meetness for a joint heirship in glory and dominion. "Now we are the sons of God, but it doth not yet appear what we shall be." Now we have eternal life, but it is "hid with Christ in God." Now we have a sinless perfection, but it is not yet manifested in unhindered brightness. But if, meanwhile, even we who have received the first-fruits of the Spirit groan within ourselves, it only gives intensity to our longing for His appearing when "we shall be like Him, for we shall see Him as He is."

Those who are distracted by the vain promise of perfection, and who, having begun in the Spirit, have been seduced into the attempt to be made perfect in the flesh, may be assured that there is no possible disconnection of the blessed whole of salvation—no possible failure of its consummation. A whole Christ is presented to you; let Christ be everything to you. His blood brings purity as well as peace, and you cannot take the one without the other. The truth which might be considered as relating specially to our justification is the very truth which the Spirit uses to promote our practical holiness. Many who have wearied themselves in chasing the phantom of sentimental sinlessness have, in the language of one of them, "come to know that justification realised is the great vantage ground in striving after personal holiness, and that a happy consciousness of acceptance in the Beloved is the great incentive to true obedience." It is the same cross that speaks to us of pardon and peace through Him who put away sin by the sacrifice of Himself, that determines what the world is to us, and what we are to the world. It is looking to Him who is lifted up there, that we have life, and as dead with Him we are risen with Him to new relations and aims and hopes. "Since ye are risen with Christ, seek those things which are above, where Christ sitteth at the right hand of God. Set your affection on things that are above, where Christ sitteth at the right hand of God; for ye are dead, and your life is hid with Christ in God. When Christ, our life, shall appear, then shall ye also appear with Him in glory."

Waymarks in the Wilderness, 1871.

Are you still joining us in daily prayer for God to bring us into touch with more of His hungry and starved sheep; those who would rejoice in this ministry, if they knew of it?

PRAY ALWAYS.

The following occurred on Lake Erie nearly forty years ago:—

The principal personage in the narrative was a Christian sailor, John ———, employed as first mate under Captain ———, who had command of one of the two ships which some ambitious persons in Buffalo set afloat on Lake Erie during the fierce heat of speculation which raged like a forest-fire over the West for a few years prior to 1836.

Determined to lead the navigation of the season, the ship left Buffalo immediately after the harbour was cleared of ice, supposing, what was quite a usual occurrence, that the wind would carry the ice up the lake, break it up, and so disperse it that they would have no further trouble with it; but to their great surprise, as they neared the upper end of the lake, they found themselves moving between two immense fields of ice, that on the right extending apparently to the Canada shore, that on the left moving before the wind, slowly, but surely, down upon them.

The ship was not prepared for an Arctic encounter like this, and how to escape from their perilous position was, of course, an anxious question. But two courses presented themselves, and whether either of these was practicable remained to be seen. The first was to land on the ice, and so make their way to the Canada shore. Our hero, John ———, volunteered the attempt to reach the shore. It was, of course, fraught with fearful hazard; but he succeeded in making the exploration and in returning safely to the ship, but only to report that the ice was entirely detached from the shore, and that escape in that direction was impossible.

The second method was to reach the open water through the channel between the ice-fields in the ship's boats; but this idea was soon abandoned, for, at the rate the ice was moving before the wind, it was very certain the two fields would meet long before the boats could reach the open water, and, if caught, they would be crushed like egg-shells. What was to be done? Officers, sailors, passengers looked in silence and with pallid cheeks upon the approaching foe. In front, as far as could be seen, there was nothing but the narrow channel, and no wind to carry them through to the open water.

Under these circumstances, the Captain called the passengers, and as many of the crew as could be spared from the deck, into the cabin, made a plain statement of their danger, and of his entire want of power to afford them relief; and though not a professing Christian, said, "We are in the hands of God; if He does not interpose for us, there is no help, no hope. If any of you know how to pray, I wish you would do so." There sat that despairing company, with bowed heads, in dead silence—so still, you could hear your heart beat. In that terrible moment, John ———, the pious mate, raised his head, and just in a whisper said, "Let us pray." Officers, passengers, sailors, at once quietly went down on their knees, and naught was heard, except now and then a deep-drawn sigh or half-suppressed sob, while the converted sailor, in simple child-like language, told in the ears of Him who holds the winds in His fists, and the sea in the hollow of His hand, their exposure and danger, the interest they each had in their own lives and the lives and happiness of others—fathers, mothers, wives, children, and friends; humbly confessing their sins and just exposure to pain and penalty; and then with tearful penitence and loving trustfulness, supplicating mercy and deliverance through the crucified and exalted Redeemer.

After the prayer, the Captain and mate went on deck, and who can tell what were their thoughts or feelings when they saw that, during that solemn moment of penitent prayer, the wind had changed, and now, instead of blowing the crushing ice-field upon them, it was blowing the ship slowly, but surely, through that open channel? In the presence of that strange fact, the Captain and the mate uncovered their heads, and John ———, looking aloft at the nearly naked yards, said, "Shall I put some more canvas on her, Captain?" "No," said the Captain, "don't touch her; some One else is managing the ship." And so the unseen Hand did lead them through to the open water, and to their desired haven in safety.

We will not stop to do battle with the speculative theories of prayer which eminent scientists have latterly thrust into the face of Christendom. The incident, of the truth of which the reader can rest assured, shall be left to bear, uninterpreted, its own testimony to the truth that God hears and answers prayer. And therefore it is written, "Men ought always to *pray and not to faint.*"

—Food, 1887.

"grace." To those who are poor and wretched, salvation "without money and without price" appears very blessed and lovely. Yes, even the carnal mind is willing to assent to the *beauty* of "grace," while the heart is quite unacquainted with it. It is one thing to hear about grace, and to sing hymns upon it, it is quite another to "*know* the grace of God in truth."

To "know the grace of God in truth" is to have *tasted* that the Lord is gracious" (1 Peter 2:3). What a difference there is between admiring the luscious peach growing upon the tree, and *tasting* it! What a difference there is between a parched man seeing the running brook, and actually tasting of its limpid waters and quenching his thirst therefrom! So, what a vast difference there is between hearing the testimonies of others to the wondrous grace of God, and having for myself heeded that word "O, taste and see that the Lord is good" (Psa. 34:8)! To have "tasted that the Lord is gracious" is to *know* that He is, and to know this, not from the report of others, but from my own experience.

To know the grace of God in theory only, will not avail in the Day to come. When this world and all its works shall be burned up, when its very elements shall melt with fervent heat, only that will endure the searching test of God, which He Himself has wrought in us. Only that will enter Heaven which has come out of Heaven. Only that which the Divine hand has produced will satisfy the requirements of Divine holiness. "The flesh profiteth *nothing*" (John 6:63). "For in Christ Jesus neither circumcision availeth anything, nor uncircumcision, but a new creation" (Gal. 6:15). All the resolutions, efforts, religious activities of poor fallen man, are worthless and useless. Thus, to "know the grace of God in truth" is to experience it by the Spirit's power, applying it to the heart.

O, my reader, *what* is the ground of your confidence? Upon *what* are you resting your hopes? Is it something *you* have done? Is it something you imagine a preacher did for you? Is it some "decision" you have made, some "stand" you have taken? Or, is it something which *God* has done, not only *for*, but *in* you? Do you *know* that He has? Are you quite sure He has wrought a work in your heart which shall endure forever? You cannot afford to be uncertain; something more than a vague "hope so" is needed. The Saviour has faithfully and plainly warned us, "Many will say to Me in that day, Lord, Lord, have we not prophesied in Thy name? and in Thy name have cast out demons, and in Thy name done many wonderful works? And then will I profess unto *them*, I never knew you: depart from Me, ye that work iniquity" (Matt. 7:22, 23). O, my reader, search yourself in the presence of God. Better, ask *Him* to search you, for *your* heart is "deceitful above all things" (Jer. 17:9)!

The apostle said, "Since the day ye heard and *knew* the grace of God in truth." These Colossian saints "knew." Do *you*? Rest not satisfied with anything short of a definite, personal, positive assurance. Do you ask, How can I "know" it? Once more we must shut you up to God: only He can impart this knowledge. The preacher, the writer, cannot. We can neither argue nor persuade you into it. It is the Spirit of God who "beareth witness" with renewed spirits (Rom. 8:16). Does He bear witness with yours? If not, earnestly seek it. Cry unto God; cast yourself on His mercy; ask Him, for *Christ's* sake to grant you the experience of the Thessalonian Christians, to whom the apostle could say, "For our Gospel came not unto you in word only, but also *in power*, and in the Holy Spirit and in much assurance" (1 Thess. 1:5).

To "know the grace of God in truth" is also a progressive thing in the Christian's life. Above, we have emphasised the initial experience, the *saving* knowledge of it. But it is written, "He giveth more grace" (James 4:6). There is also a "growing in grace" (2 Peter 3:18), which is largely determined by the habitual cultivation of humility before God, for it is written "He giveth grace to the *lowly*" (Prov. 3:34). There is the heart becoming "established with grace" (Heb. 13:9), and that comes by reading, studying, meditating upon, appropriating unto ourselves the Word of God's grace (Acts 20:32). We are bidden to "be strong in the grace that is in Christ Jesus" (2 Tim. 2:1). Thus, in its wider meaning, to "know the grace of God in truth" is to prove by experience the blessedness of His promise "My grace is sufficient for thee" (2 Cor. 12:9).

In its ultimate sense, not till we are with Him in the Glory, when we shall no longer see through a glass darkly, but face to face; when we fully discover not only what we have been redeemed from, but redeemed for, shall we really "know the grace of God in truth." Then will be fulfilled that word in Eph. 2:7, "That in the ages to come He might show the exceeding riches of His grace in His kindness toward us through Christ Jesus."

—*Arthur W. Pink.*

STUDIES IN THE SCRIPTURES

"Search the Scriptures" John 5: 39

Copyright in all English-speaking Countries.

Editor: Arthur W. Pink, 15 Hurlstone Avenue, Summer Hill, N.S.W., Australia.
Hon. Agent in U.S.A.: Mr. C. S. Pressel, 559 Dupont Avenue, York, Penna.

FREE TO ALL WHO WILL READ IT

WHOLE-HEARTED TRUST.

"Trust in the Lord with all thine heart: Prov. 3:5.

One of the principal differences between the book of Psalms and the book of Proverbs is this: in the former we hear, for the most part, the saints addressing God, praising and petitioning Him; in the latter, it is God addressing His people, giving counsels for their walk. Though there is not a little in the book of Proverbs which is, in its ultimate scope (veiled), prophecy, yet its first application is of a practical nature, containing Divine precepts for the regulation of every branch of our earthly lives. In Prov. 3:5, 6 is found a word which is of great importance and value for our souls. Its weighty language impresses us at once, and the more it is prayerfully pondered, the more will the anointed eye discern the Divine wisdom which dictated it. It falls into four parts, to each of which we purpose devoting a separate article.

"Trust in the Lord with all thine heart." As the opening words of Prov. 3 plainly intimate, the contents of this chapter are addressed directly to the children of God. What, then, is the first implication of our present text? Surely a very humbling one —that we *need* such an admonition, that we have to be *told* to "Trust in the Lord." One had thought it were as natural for a Christian to trust in the Lord as it is to breathe. Alas, our experience has shown us otherwise. The sad and awful fact is that we are readier to trust in any one, yea, in any thing, rather than in the living God. That is why we need exhorting, "Trust in the Lord with all thine heart."

But exactly what is meant by "Trust in the Lord?" The Hebrew verb literally means to "lean upon." It conveys the idea of one who is conscious of feebleness and so turns and rests upon a stronger one for support. It presupposes confidence in and reliance upon the Lord. To "Trust in the Lord" means to count upon Him in every emergency, to look to Him for the supply of every need, to say with the Psalmist, "The Lord is my Shepherd, I shall not want." To "Trust in the Lord" means to confidently expect the fulfilment of His every promise, in His own good time and way. It means that we cast all our care upon Him, drawing from Him strength day by day and hour by hour, and thus proving the sufficiency of His grace. Thus, to "Trust in the Lord" means for the Christian *to continue* even as he commenced. When we first really turned to the Lord, conscious of our deep and desperate need, how did we act? We repudiated all confidence in self, abandoned all our own doings, and cast ourselves upon Him as our only hope and confidence. Now just as we acted when we first came to Him for salvation, so should we daily rely on Him for all needed wisdom, strength, and grace.

But what is meant by Trust in the Lord "with all thine heart?" I think three things are chiefly intended. First, it means giving unto God our *undivided* confidence, not looking to any other for help and relief. It was at this point Judah failed of old. Hear Jehovah's complaint against her, "And yet for all this her treacherous sister Judah hath not turned unto Me with her whole heart, but feignedly, saith the Lord" (Jer. 3:10). A parallel to our text is found in that word, "Wait thou *only* upon God" (Psa. 62:5). Second, it means *with child-like simplicity*. You know how a little

(Concluded on Page 192.)

IMPORTANT NOTICES

Back numbers of each year of the magazine are yet obtainable at 5/- (1.25) per year. Bound at 7/6 (1.75) post paid. They will soon be out of print. Those in U.S.A. wanting them, please purchase from Mr. Pressel (see front cover page).

Advise promptly of change of address. This Magazine is published as a work of faith and labour of love. The Editor gladly gives his services. It is freely sent to all who will read it. No charge is made for it.

Christians who feel definitely led to do so, may have fellowship with us in this Ministry. Send only *Inter-National M.O.*

CONTENTS.

	Page.
Hebrews	170
Gleanings in Exodus	176
Great Peace	181
Unclothed or Clothed	184
Godliness and a Sufficiency	190

THE EPISTLE OF THE HEBREWS.

8. Christ Superior to the Angels. 2:5-9.

The scope, the order of thought, and the logical bearings of our present passage are not so easily discerned as those we have already gone over. That it, the first part at least, picks up the thread dropped in 1:14 and continues to exhibit the superiority of Christ over angels, is clear from v. 5; but when we reach v. 9 we read of Jesus being "made a little *lower* than the angels." At first glance this seems to present a real difficulty, but, as is generally the case with such passages, in reality v. 9, taken as a whole, supplies the key to our present portion.

In 1:4-14 the Holy Spirit, through the apostle, has furnished a sevenfold proof of the superiority of Israel's Messiah over the angels. This proof, taken from their own Scriptures, was clear and incontrovertible. In 2:1-4 a parenthesis was made, opportunity being taken to give a solemn and searching application to the consciences and hearts of the Hebrews of what had just been brought before them: the authority of the Gospel was commensurate with its grace, and God would avenge the slightings of that which was first proclaimed by His Son, as surely as He had the refractions of that law which he had given by the mediation of angels. Now here in 2:5 and onwards an objection is anticipated and removed.

The objection may be framed thus: How could supremacy be predicated of One who became Man, and died? As we have shown in a previous article, the Jews actually regarded the angels with a higher veneration than the greatest of the "fathers"—Abraham, Moses, Joshua, and David. And rightly so; their own Scriptures declared that they "excel in strength." Thus a real difficulty was presented to them, in the fact that He whom the apostle affirmed had, by inheritance, obtained "a more excellent name" than angels, was known to them as "the Son of man," for man was a creature *inferior* to angels. Moreover, angels do not die, Christ had; how, then, could He be their superior?

The method followed by the Holy Spirit in meeting this objection and removing the difficulty is as follows: He shows (in v. 9) that so far from the humiliation and suffering endured by Christ tarnishing His glory, they were the meritorious cause of His exaltation. In support of this a remarkable quotation is made from the 8th Psalm to prove that God has placed *man*, and not angels, at the head of the future economy—the "world to come." The design of God in that economy is to raise "man" to the highest place of all among His creatures, and that design has been secured by Christ's becoming Man and dying, and thus obtaining for Himself and His people that state of transcendent dignity and honour which the Psalmist prophesied should be possessed by man in the Age to come.

Thus, those commentators are mistaken who suppose that in Heb. 2:5 the apostle begins to advance *further proof* of Christ's superiority over angels. Complete demonstration of this had been made in chapter 1, as the *seven* O.T. passages there cited go to show. True it is that what the apostle says in v. 5 makes manifest the exaltation of the Saviour above the celestial hierarchies, yet his purpose in so doing was to meet an objector. What we have in our present section is brought in to show that the evidence supplied in chapter 1 could not be shaken, and that the very objection which a Jew might make against it had been duly provided for and fully met in his own Scriptures. Thus may we admire the wisdom of Him who knoweth the end from the beginning, and maketh even the wrath of man to praise Him.

"For unto the angels hath He not put in subjection the world to come, whereof we speak" (v. 5). In taking up this verse three questions need to be duly pondered: What is here referred to in "the world to come?" What is meant by its being "put in subjection?" What bearing has this statement upon the apostle's argument? Let us endeavour to deal with them in this order.

Commentators are by no means agreed on the signification of this term "the world to come." Many of the older ones, who were post-millennavians, understood by it a reference to the present Gospel dispensation, in contrast from the Mosaic economy. Others suppose that it refers to the Church, of which Christ, and not angels, is the Head. Others look upon it as synonymous with the Eternal State, comparing it with the Lord's words in Matt. 12:32, "Whosoever speaketh against the Holy Spirit, it shall not be forgiven him, neither in this world, neither in the world to come." The objection against this last view is that the Greek word for "world" is quite different in Heb. 2:5 from that which is used in Matt. 12:32.

We believe the first key to the right understanding of this expression is to be found in the particular term used here by the Holy Spirit, translated "world." It is neither "kosmos," the common one for "world," as in John 3:16, etc.; nor "aion," meaning "age," in Matt. 13:39, Heb. 9:26, etc. Instead, it is "oikoumene," which, etymologically, signifies "habitable place"; but this helps us nothing. The word is found fifteen times in the N.T. In thirteen of them it appears to be used as a synonym for "earth." But in the remaining passage, namely, Heb. 1:6, light is cast upon our present verse. As we sought to show in our exposition of that verse, the words "when again He brings in the Firstborn into the world" (oikoumene) refer to the second advent of Christ to this earth, and point to His millennial kingdom. This, we are satisfied, is also the reference in 2:5.

The "world to come" was a subject of absorbing interest and a topic of frequent conversation among all godly Jews. Unlike us, the object of hope set before them was not Heaven, but a glorious kingdom on earth, ruled over in righteousness by their Messiah. This would be the time when Jerusalem should be no more "trodden down by the Gentiles," but become "a praise in all the earth"; when heathen idolatry should give place to "the knowledge of the glory of the Lord," filling the earth as the waters do the sea. In other words, it would be the time when the kingdom-predictions of their prophets should be fulfilled. Nor had there been anything in the teachings of Christ to show these expectations were unwarranted. Instead, He had said, "Ye which have followed Me, in the regeneration (Millennium) when the Son of Man shall sit in the throne of His glory, ye also shall sit upon twelve thrones, judging the twelve tribes of Israel. And every one that hath forsaken houses, or brethren . . . for My name's sake, shall receive an hundredfold," etc. (Matt. 19:28-30). Those who had believed in Him as the Saviour from sin, eagerly awaited the establishing of His kingdom on earth: see Acts 1:6.

There are comparatively few who realise that the work of Christ on this earth has been *interrupted*, interrupted by Israel's rejection of Him, and His consequent return to the Father. This very earth which was the scene of His sufferings, is also to be the witness of His glory. Many are the Scriptures which affirm this. Satan is now the "prince of this world," and under him are mighty hosts of evil beings, an organised army of fallen but powerful creatures: see Eph. 6:12, 13. That passage shows that the Devil's forces are permitted by God to exercise a tremendous influence in the present government of the world. But this state of things is not to continue till the end of time. Satan and his hosts are going to be deposed (see Isa. 24:21), and the government of this earth placed upon the shoulder of Another. A new order of things is to be established on this earth, here called the "world to come" because it is yet future. That order of things is to be not in the hands of angels, but of "man," and all things will be put under his feet.

The "world to come" is the renovated earth under the reign of the Messiah. In the spiritual arithmetic of Scripture the number of the earth is *four*, a number plainly stamped upon it: note the four seasons to its year, the four points to its compass. How striking is it to note, then, that the Word speaks of exactly *four* earths, namely, the pre-Adamic, the present, the Millennial (delivered from the curse), the new earth. The "world to come" is the time when Israel shall dwell in their own land in peace and blessing, when wars shall be made to cease, when oppression and injustice shall end, when all the outward creation shall manifest the presence of the Prince of peace.

Not unto the angels hath God "put in subjection" this world to come. "Put in subjection" is the translation of a single compound Greek word, meaning "to put under." In its simple form it signifies to appoint or ordain; in its compound, to appoint over. In the Millennial kingdom angels will not hold the position of rule:

instead, they will serve. Note the relative "He": God places in subjection whom He will and to whom He will. Because God hath not put the world to come in subjection to angels, therefore angels have no authority over it. "It is the good pleasure of God to use an angel where it is a question of providence, or law, or power; but where it comes to the manifestation of His glory in Christ, He must have other instruments more suited for His nature, and according to His affections" (W. Kelly). To whom, then, hath God subjected the world to come? Instead of supplying a categorical answer, the apostle leaves his readers to draw their answer from what an O.T. oracle had said.

Ere taking up the point last raised, let us now consider the bearing which the contents of this 5th verse has upon the apostle's argument. It opens with the word "for," which intimates that there is a glance backwards to and now a continuation of something said previously. This casual particle connects not with the first four verses of our chapter, for, as we have shown, they are of the nature of a parenthesis. The backward glance is to what was said in 1:14, where we are told, "Are they not all ministering spirits sent forth to minister for them who shall be heirs of salvation?" The Inheritance will not be governed by angels; they are but *ministers* to its "heirs." "*For* He (God) hath not put in subjection to angels the world to come" (the earthly inheritance) whereof we speak. Thus the connection is clear. The "whereof we speak" takes us back to 1:14, and is amplified in 2:6-9.

Before turning to that which follows, let us summarise that which has been before us in v. 5. In 1:14 the apostle had affirmed that the angels are in a position of *subjection to* the redeemed of Christ; now he declares that, in the Millennial era also, not angels, but the "heirs of salvation," shall occupy the place of governmental dominion. The "world to come" is mentioned here because it is in the next Age that the Inheritance of salvation will be entered into and enjoyed. In view of what follows from Psa. 8, Heb. 2:5 may possibly set forth a designed contrast from the pre-Adamic earth, which, most probably, was placed under the dominion of unfallen Satan and his angels. The *practical* bearings of this verse on the Hebrews was: Continue to hold fast your allegiance to Christ, *for* the time is coming when those who do so shall enter into a glory surpassing that of the angels.

"But one in a certain place testified, saying, What is man, that Thou art mindful of him? or the son of man, that Thou visitest him?" (v. 6). In seeking to discover the relevancy of this quotation and its bearing upon the apostle's argument, the scope and details of this remarkable and little-understood Psalm from which it is taken, need to be carefully studied. But observe, first, *how* the quotation is introduced, "But one in a certain place testified, saying." It suggests that the Hebrews were so familiar with the Holy Scriptures that it was not necessary to give the reference! The "But" intimates that the apostle is about to point a contrast from the angels: not "and," but "but!"

The *purpose* for which this quotation from Psa. 8 was made is to show *to whom* the "world to come" will be in subjection. The closing words of v. 5, "whereof we speak," supply the prophetic key to it; without this, we might not have realised that it looked forward to millennial times. And yet, literally understood, its opening verse could scarcely be applied to any other period. "O Lord, our Lord, how excellent is Thy name in all the earth! who hast set Thy glory above the heavens." In O.T. days the name of "Jehovah" was known to scarcely none save Israel. Even now there are many parts of the earth where the excellency of the Lord's name is yet unknown. But in the Millennium, when "the earth shall be full of the knowledge of the Lord, as the waters cover the sea" (Isa. 11:9), then shall His saints have full cause for saying, "O Lord, our Lord, how excellent is Thy name in *all* the earth!" The last verse of Psalm 8 repeats the same gladsome exclamation: the contents of vv. 2-7 show how this will be reached.

Before proceeding further, let us ponder the doctrinal teaching of Psa. 8. Upon this we cannot do better than reproduce the summary of it given by Dr. Gouge: "The main scope of the Psalm is, to magnify the glory of God: this is evident by the first and last verses thereof. That main point is proved by the works of God, which in general He declares to be so conspicuous, as very babes can magnify God in them to the astonishment of His enemies, v. 2. In particular He first produceth those visible glorious works that are above; which manifest God's eternal power and Godhead, v. 3. Then He amplifieth God's goodness to man (who had made himself a mortal miserable creature, v. 4), by setting forth the high advancement of man above all other creatures, not the angels excepted, vv. 5-7. This evidence of God's goodness to man so ravished the prophet's spirit, as with an high admiration he thus expresseth it, 'What is man?' etc. Hereupon he concludeth that

Psalm as he began it with extolling the glorious excellency of the Lord."

The force of the 4th verse of Psalm 8, the first here quoted in Heb. 2, may be gathered from the words which immediately precede: "When I consider Thy heavens, the work of Thy fingers, the moon and the stars which Thou hast ordained—What is man, that Thou are mindful of him? and the son of man, that Thou visitest him?" In view of the magnitude of God's creation, in contrast from the heavenly bodies, What is *man!* This is confirmed by the particular word which the Holy Spirit has here employed. In the O.T. He has used four different words, all rendered "man" in our English version. The one used here is "enosh," which signifies "frail and fallen man." It is the word used in Psalm 9:20! What is man, fallen man, that the great God should be mindful of him? Still less that He should crown him with "glory and honour?" Ah, it is *this* which should move our hearts to deepest wonderment, as it *will* fill us with ever-increasing amazement and praise in the ages yet to come.

"What is man that Thou art mindful of him? or the son of man that Thou visitest him?" (v. 6). The latter clause seems to be added in order to emphasise the preceding thought. "Son of man" is added as a *diminution* for "man": compare Job 25:6 for a parallel. Another reason why this second clause may be added to v. 6 is to show that it is *not* Adam who is here spoken of. From the contents of vv. 5, 6, 7 many have thought that Psalm 8 was referring to the father of the human family (see Gen. 1:26); but this second part of its fourth verse seems to have been brought in designedly to correct us. Certainly Adam was not a *"son* of man!"

"Thou madest him a little lower than the angels" (v. 7). This supplies additional proof that it is not Adam who is here in view. Both the Hebrew word used in Psa. 8:5 and the Greek word in Heb. 2:7 signify the failing or falling of a thing from that which it was before. "The word 'made lower' does not signify to be created originally in a lower condition, but it signifies to be brought down from a higher station to a lower" (Dr. J. Brown). The Hebrew word is used to denote the failing of the waters when Noah's flood decreased (Gen. 8:4); and, negatively, of the widow's oil that did not fail (1 Kings 17:14, 16). The Greek word is used of the Baptist when he said, "I must decrease" (John 3:30).

But to what is the Holy Spirit here referring in our 7th verse? First, it should be pointed out that both the Hebrew and Greek word here for "little" has a double force, being applied both to time and degree. In 1 Peter 5:10 it is rendered "a while," that is, a short space of time; so also in Luke 22:58 and Acts 5:34. Such, we believe, is in force here, as it certainly is in the 9th verse. Now in what particular sense has God made frail and fallen man a "little while" lower than the angels? With Dr. J. Brown we must answer, "We cannot doubt that man, even in his best estate, was in some respects inferior to the angels; but in some points he was on a level with them. One of these was immortality; and it deserves consideration, that this is the very point referred to when it is said of the raised saints, the children of the resurrection, 'Neither can they die any more: for they are equal unto the angels'" (Luke 20:36). Thus, for a season, man, through being subject to *death,* has been made "lower than the angels."

"Thou madest him a little lower than the angels; Thou crownedst him with glory and honour, and didst set him over the works of Thy hands" (v. 7). Just as in the first part of this verse reference is made to the humiliation of man, so the second part of it speaks of God's exaltation of man. "The verbs being expressed, not in the Future, but in the Past tense, will not be felt as an objection to its being considered as a prediction, this being quite common in the prophetic style. Most of the predictions, for example, in the 53rd chapter of Isa. are expressed in the Past tense" (Dr. J. Brown). To this we may add, all prophecy speaks from the standpoint of God's eternal purpose, and so certain is this of accomplishment, the Past tense is used to show it is as sure as if it were already wrought out in time: compare "glorified" in Rom. 8:30, and see Rom. 4:17. Thus we understand the second part of this 7th verse as referring to the coming glorification of Christ's redeemed.

"Thou crownedst him with glory and honour, and didst set him over the works of Thy hands." This is applied by the Spirit to the redeemed, the "heirs" of 1:14, "whereof we speak" (2:5). That the redeemed *are* to be "crowned" is clearly taught in the N.T. For example, in 2 Tim. 4:7, 8 the apostle says, "I have fought a good fight, I have finished my course, I have kept the faith: Henceforth there is laid up for me a *crown* of righteousness, which the Lord, the righteous Judge, shall give me at that day: and not to me only, but unto all them also that love His appearing." So also James declares, "Blessed is the man that endureth temptation: for when he is tried, he shall receive the *crown* of life, which the Lord hath promised to them that love Him" (1:12).

They are to be crowned with "glory and honour." In Scripture "glory" is put for the excellency of a thing: hence, what is here predicted is, that the dignity which God will place upon His saints will be the most excellent they could be advanced unto. The Hebrew word means that which is real and substantial, in contrast from that which is light and vain. The word for "honour" implies that which is bright: and in Psa. 110:3 is rendered "beauty." Its distinctive thought is that of being esteemed by others. Thus we have here a striking word upon the glorification of the redeemed. First, they are to be "crowned," that is, they are to be elevated to a position of the highest rank. Second, they are to be crowned with "glory," that is, they will be made supremely excellent in their persons. Third, they are to be crowned with "honour," that is, they will be looked up to by those below them.

"And didst set him over the works of Thy hands." This has reference to the rule and reign of God's saints in the Day to come. In Dan. 7:18, 27 we read, "But the saints of the Most High shall take the kingdom, and *possess* the kingdom forever, even forever and ever. . . . And the kingdom and dominion, and the greatness of the kingdom under the whole heaven, shall be given to the people of the saints of the Most High, whose kingdom is an everlasting kingdom, and all dominions shall serve and obey Him." So also in Rev. 2:26 we are told, "And he that overcometh and keepeth My works unto the end, to him will I give power over the nations."

"Thou hast put all things under his feet" (v. 8). The language here employed shows plainly the connection between this quotation from the 8th Psalm and what the apostle had declared in v. 5. There he had said, "For unto the angels hath He not put in subjection the world to come whereof we speak." Here we learn that unto "man" will the world to come be placed in subjection. Here we learn that "man," frail and fallen, but redeemed and exalted by the Lord, will have, in the world to come, "all things" put under his feet. It is the blessed sequel to Gen. 1:28 —the earthly Paradise regained. The *absoluteness* of this "subjection" of the world to come unto redeemed man, is intimated by the figure which is here used, "under his feet"; lower a thing cannot be put. It is not simply "*at* his feet," but "*under*." The *scope* of the subjection is seen by the "*all* things." This goes beyond the terms of Psa. 8:7, 8, for the last Adam has secured for His people more than the first Adam lost. All creation, even angels, will then be "in subjection" to man.

"For in that He put all in subjection under him, He left nothing that is not put under him" (v. 8). This is the apostle's comment on his quotation from Psa. 8. "Thou hast bestowed on man such honours as Thou hast bestowed on none of Thy creatures. Thou hast set him at the head of the created universe. From this passage it appears that, with the single exception of Him who is to put all things under him, i.e., God, all things are to be put under man. In the world to come even angels are subordinate to them. Man is next to God in that world" (Dr. J. Brown). In Rev. 21:7 we read, "He that overcometh shall inherit *all things;* and I will be his God, and he shall be My son." Our joint-heirship with Christ (Rom. 8:17) will be *manifested* in the world to come. What a prospect! O for faith to lay hold of it and *enjoy* it, even now. Were it more real to us, the trifling baubles of this world would fail to attract us. Were it more real to us, the trials and troubles of this life would be unable to sadden or move us. May the Lord enable each of His own to look away from the things seen to the things unseen.

"But now we see not yet all things put under him" (v. 8). This is the language of an hypothetical objector, which confirms and establishes what was said in the opening paragraphs of this article. The "him" here is the "man" of v. 6. Anticipating the objection that Jesus of Nazareth could not be superior to the angels, seeing that He was Man, the apostle met it by showing that one of God's ancient oracles declared that he who, for a short season, was made lower than the angels, has been crowned with glory and honour and set over the works of His hands; yea, that *all* things, and therefore angels, have been "put in subjection under him." But how can this be? says the objector: "Now we *see not* yet all things put under him." What you have said is belied by the testimony of our senses; that which is spread before our eyes refutes it. Why, so far from "all things" being in subjection to man, even the wild beasts will not perform his bidding! Unanswerable as this difficulty might appear, solution, satisfactory and complete, is promptly furnished. This is given in our next verse.

"But we see Jesus, who was made a little lower than the angels . . . . crowned with glory and honour" (v. 9). It is most blessed to observe how the apostle meets the objector: he does so by pointing at once and directly to Him who is the Centre of all our hopes and in whose Person all our interests and blessings are bound up. "The following appears to me to be the track of the apostle's thoughts: 'In the world to come, men, not angels, are to occupy the first place. An ancient oracle, which refers to the world to come, clearly proves this. The place to be occupied by man in that world is not only a high place, but is the first place among creatures. The words of the oracle are unlimited. With the exception of Him who puts all things under man, everything is to be subjected to him. This oracle must be fulfilled. In the exaltation of Christ, after and in consequence of His humiliation, we have the begun fulfilment of the prediction, and what, according to the wise and righteous counsels of heaven, were necessary, and will be the effectual means of the complete accomplishment of it in reference to the whole body of the redeemed from among men" (Dr. J. Brown).

"But we see Jesus." What is meant by this? To what was the apostle referring? *How* do we "*see* Jesus?" Not by means of mysterious dreams or ecstatic visions, not by the exercise of our imagination, nor by a process of visualisation; but by *faith*. Just as Christ declared, in John 8:56, "Abraham rejoiced to see My day, and he *saw* it, and was glad." Faith is the eye of the spirit, which views and enjoys what the Word of God presents to its vision. In the Gospels, Acts, Epistles, Revelation, God has told us about the exaltation of His Son; those who receive by faith what He has there declared, "*see* Jesus crowned with glory and honour," as truly and vividly as His enemies once saw Him here on earth "crowned with thorns."

It is this which distinguishes the true people of God from mere professors. Every real Christian has reason to say with Job, "I have heard of Thee by the hearing of the ear: but *now* mine eye *seeth* Thee" (42:5). He has "seen" Him leaving Heaven and coming to earth, in order to "seek and to save that which was lost." He has "seen" Him as a sacrificial Substitute on the cross, there bearing "our sins in His own body on the tree." He has "seen" Him rising again in triumph from the grave, so that because He lives, we live also. He has "seen" Him highly exalted, "crowned with glory and honour." He has "seen" Him *thus* as presented to the eye of faith in the sure Word of God. To him the testimony of Holy Scripture is infinitely more reliable and valuable than the testimony of his senses.

The name by which God's Son is here called is that of His humiliation. "Jesus" is *not* a title; "Saviour" is an entirely different word in the Greek. "Jesus" was His human name, as Man, here on earth. It was as "Jesus of Nazareth" that His enemies ever referred to Him. But not so His own people: to the apostles He said, "Ye call Me Master and Lord: and ye say well; for so I am" (John 13:13). Only once in the four Gospels do we ever find any of His own speaking of Him as "Jesus of Nazareth" (Luke 24:19), and that was when their faith had completely given way. It was the language of unbelief! That He is referred to in the narratival form in the Gospels as "Jesus" is to emphasise His humiliation.

When we come to the Acts, which treats of His exaltation, we read there, "God hath made this same Jesus . . . . both Lord and Christ" (2:36). So in the Epistles: God has "given Him a name which is above every name," and that name is "Lord" (Phil. 2:9, 10). Thus, it is either as "Christ," which *is* a title, or as the Lord Jesus Christ, that He is commonly referred to in the Epistles: read carefully 1 Cor. 1:3-10 for an example. It is thus that His people should delight to own Him. To address the Lord of glory in prayer simply as "Jesus," or to speak of Him to others thus, breathes an unholy familiarity, a vulgar cheapness, an irreverence which is highly reprehensible.

After the four Gospels the Lord Christ is never referred to in the N.T. simply as "Jesus" save for the purpose of historical identification (Acts 1:11, e.g.), or to stress the humiliation through which He passed, or when His enemies are speaking of Him. Here in Heb. 2:9 "Jesus" rather than "the Lord Jesus" is used to emphasise His humiliation: it was the One who had passed through such unparalleled shame and ignominy that had been "crowned with glory and honour." May Divine grace enable both writer and reader to entertain such exalted views of this same Jesus that we may ever heed the exhortation of 1 Peter 3:15: "But sanctify in your hearts Christ as Lord" (R.V.).

Now that which it is of first importance for us to observe is the *use* which the apostle here makes of the Saviour's glorification. The exaltation of Jesus is both the proof and pledge of the coming exaltation of all His redeemed. The prophecy of Psa. 8 has already begun to receive its fulfilment. The crowning of Jesus with glory and honour is the ground and guarantee of the ultimate glorification of all His people. Christ has entered Heaven as the "First-fruits," the earnest of the coming harvest. He has passed within the veil as the "Forerunner" (Heb. 6:20), so that there *must be* others to follow.

Here, then, is, we believe, the true interpretation and application of Psa. 8. The verses quoted from it in Heb. 2 refer not to Adam, not to mankind as a whole, nor to Christ Himself considered alone, but to His redeemed. The Holy Spirit, through the Psalmist, was looking forward to a *new order of man*, of which the Lord Jesus is the Head. In the Man Christ Jesus, God has brought to light a new order of Man, One in whom is found not merely innocence, but *perfection*. It is of *this* "man" that Eph. 2:15 speaks: "To make in Himself of twain (redeemed from among the Jews and from among the Gentiles) one *new man*"; and also Eph. 4:13: "Till we all come in the unity of the faith, and of the knowledge of the Son of God unto *a perfect man*, unto the measure of the stature of the fulness of Christ." As God looks at His incarnate Son He sees, for the first time, a perfect Man, and us in Him. And as we, by faith, "see Jesus crowned with glory and honour," we discover both the proof and pledge of ourselves yet being "crowned with glory and honour."

"But we see Jesus, who was made a little lower than the angels . . . . crowned with glory and honour," as the ground and guarantee of our approaching exaltation. Here then is the Divine answer to the question asked by the Psalmist long ago: "When I consider Thy heavens, the work of Thy fingers, the moon and the stars which Thou hast made—What is man, that Thou art mindful of him?" Ah, brethren in Christ, when you go out at night and view the wondrous heavens, and then think of your own utter insignificance; when you meditate upon the glory of God's majesty and holiness, and then think of your own exceeding sinfulness, and are bowed into the dust; remember that up there is a Man in the glory, and that that Man is the measure of God's thoughts concerning *you*. Remember, that by wondrous and sovereign grace, you have been not only predestinated to be conformed to His image, but that you should, as a joint-heir with Him, share *His inheritance*. May the Lord grant each Christian reader that faith which will enable him to grasp that wonderful and blissful prospect which the Word of God sets before him.

—*Arthur W. Pink*.

GLEANINGS IN EXODUS.

56. *The Anointing Oil.* *Ex.* 30:22-33.

Having completed His description of the Tabernacle and its furniture, the Holy Spirit now makes mention of the holy anointing oil and the fragrant incense, without which the sanctuary Moses was to erect for Jehovah would have been unacceptable. As the "incense" has already been considered in our study of the golden-altar, we shall dwell here only on the "oil." This was composed of olive oil, into which were compounded four principal spices. It was designed for the anointing of the Tabernacle and its sacred vessels, and was also used at the consecration of Aaron and his sons to their priestly office. Strict instructions were given prohibiting any of the people from making any like unto it, which emphasises its uniqueness.

Like everything else connected with the service of Jehovah's house, the holy anointing oil, with its fragrant ingredients, pointed forward to the person of the Lord Jesus and the excellencies which are to be found in Him, particularly, to those graces which the Holy Spirit manifested through Him. Though there may be some difficulty in determining the precise spiritual import of some of the details, yet the main truth here foreshadowed is too plain to miss. May our eyes now be "anointed" with spiritual "salve" (Rev. 3:18) that we may be enabled to behold and enjoy wondrous things out of God's Law. Let us consider:

1. *Its Ingredients.*

"Moreover the Lord spake unto Moses, saying, Take thou also unto thee principal spices, of pure myrrh five hundred shekels, and of sweet cinnamon half so much, even two hundred and fifty shekels, and of sweet calamus, two hundred and fifty shekels, and of cassia five hundred shekels, after the shekel of the sanctuary, and of oil olive an hin: And thou shalt make it an oil of holy ointment, an ointment compounded after the art of the apothecary, it shall be an holy anointing oil" (vv. 22-25).

Thus, the ingredients were four in number, blended together; their fragrance being borne along in the power of the oil. Scholars tell us that the Hebrew word for "spices" is from a root meaning to "smell sweetly." Therefore, the basal thought in the ointment is its sweet scent. "*Principal spices*" signifies those which exceeded others in their rich odor, pre-eminent in their aroma. Surely it is evident that they speak to us of Christ. Our minds at once turn to Psa. 45 where God says to Him, "Thou lovest righteousness, and hatest wickedness; therefore God, Thy God, hath *anointed* Thee with the oil of gladness above Thy fellows. All Thy garments smell of myrrh, and aloes, and cassia, out of the ivory palaces, whereby they have made Thee glad" (vv. 7, 8).

"*Myrrh*" is the first ingredient mentioned. "This was the gum from a dwarf tree of the terebinth family, growing in Arabia. The gum exudes from the trunk either spontaneously or through incisions made for the purpose. That prescribed for the ointment was 'pure,' literally, 'free'—the best, what had flowed spontaneously. . . . It is fragrant to the smell, but very bitter to the taste" (Mr. Ridout). To the Scriptures we must turn to learn its typical significance.

It is striking to note that the word itself is found just fourteen times therein, 2 x 7, or a witness unto perfection. Eight of the references are in the Song of Solomon, which at once suggests that the prominent thought emblemised by it is *love*. The keynote is struck in its first occurrence: "A bundle of myrrh is my Well-beloved" (1:13). Further proof that "myrrh" is an emblem of love is found in 5:13, "His cheeks are a bed of spices, as sweet flowers; His *lips* lillies, dropping sweet-smelling myrrh." Significant is the final reference, found in connection with the *death* of Christ (John 19:39)—expressing the *love* of His disciples for Him. Thus, love poured out in a bitter but fragrant death is what was prefigured by the "myrrh." Beautifully is this brought out in the following quotation:

"Flowing spontaneously from the tree, as well as through incisions, would suggest on the one hand how willingly He offered all that He was, even unto death, to God, and on the other the 'piercing' to which He was subjected by man, but which only brought out the same fragrance. The bitterness of the myrrh suggests the reality of the *sufferings* through which He went. It was not physical discomfort and pain, nor even death, which gave intensity to His suffering, but the 'contradiction of sinners against Himself' (Heb. 12:3). His very presence in a world where all was against God was bitter to Him. How His perfect soul, enjoying fullest communion with His Father, recognised what an evil and bitter thing it was for men to forsake the Lord! Who could measure sin like the sinless One? He it was who tasted, and drank to the dregs, the bitter cup of God's wrath against sin.

"But all this bitter experience only furnished the occasion for the manifestation not only of a devotedness to God which was perfectly fragrant to Him, but of a love to His own which was as strong as death. And what has been the measure of this love? The myrrh again, from its association with death, may well tell us that it 'passeth knowledge' (Eph. 3:19). 'The Son of God who loved me and gave Himself for Me' (Gal. 2:20)—a measure which cannot be measured, freely flowing from Him whose heart was pierced by and for our sins. Feeble indeed is the estimate we put upon that love at best; but One estimates it at its full value" (Mr. Ridout).

"*Cinnamon.*" Remarkable indeed are the contrasts presented by the four passages in which this word is found. Here in Ex. 30 it pointed to the person of Christ. In Song of Solomon 4:14 it is used in the Bridegroom's description of His bride—referring to that which grace has imputed to her. In the third and fourth references this sweet spice is seen connected with the harlot: Prov. 7:17; Rev. 18:13. There, it is a hypocritical love for souls, used by the usurper of Christ to attract the ungodly. Upon the "cinnamon" Mr. Ridout has said:

"There seems to be no doubt that this spice is the same that is familiar to us under the same name; it is the bark of a small evergreen tree of the laural family. Another tree of the same family is the fragrant camphor. The odor of the cinnamon is sweet and its taste agreeable; it is largely used for flavouring. A valuable essential oil is extracted from the bark, having these properties in an intensified form. It is obtained chiefly from Ceylon, and probably brought from India in the times of the Exodus. The bark is obtained from the young shoots. As a medicine, it is a stimulant and cordial.

"Seeking for light as to its spiritual significance from the etymology of the word, we are met with uncertainty" (Mr. Ridout). But in a footnote he tells us that, one writer has suggested "a possible derivation from two well-known Hebrew words: *Kinna*, 'jealousy' from the root to glow or burn, or be zealous; and *min*, 'form' or 'appearance.' The 'appearance of jealousy.'" To which Mr. Ridout adds, "We need not say, what burning zeal marked our Lord's entire life—'the zeal of Thy house hath eaten Me up' (John 2:17). And this was shown in the holy form of jealousy which would purge that house of all the carnal traffic which had been introduced there. 'Love is strong as death; jealousy is cruel as the grave; the coals thereof are the coals of fire, which hath a most vehement flame' (Song of Sol. 8:6). This gives, at least, a beautiful and significant meaning, and accords with the character of our Lord—a love which was zeal for God's glory and for 'the place where Thine honour dwelleth' (Psa. 26:8). In love for that He would let His own temple, His holy body, be laid low in death. Here was indeed a jealousy of a new form—jealousy for God alone, without one element of selfishness in it. Cruel it was, only in the sense of bearing cruelty rather than suffer one blot to rest upon God's glory—it burned with 'a most vehement flame.'" We believe that this brings out the distinctive thought suggested by the "cinnamon."

"It is well, too, to recall the fact that this tree was an evergreen, passing through no periods of inertness. So our Lord was ever the unchanging devoted One, whose leaf did not wither in time of drought or cold. In the midst of the arid waste of unbelief—as at Chorazin and Bethsaida and Capernaum—there were no marks of feebleness upon Him: 'I thank Thee, O Father,' was His language there as everywhere. Here, too, is medicine, a spiritual tonic and cordial for the faint-hearted. This love and devotedness of our Lord, which knew no change, is not only a most powerful example, but in His grace that which cheers and encourages the fainting of His beloved people" (Mr. Ridout).

"*Sweet calamus.*" The Hebrew word means a "reed" or "cane," being derived from a root-term meaning "to stand upright." Once more we shall take extracts from Mr. Ridout's helpful remarks: "The 'sweet' as in the case of the cinnamon, tells of its fragrance, and this would seem to give us the clue to the article intended. A 'sweet cane' is said to be found in Lebonan, in India and Arabia. It usually grows in miry soil, from which it sends up the shoots from which its name is derived. The fragrant cane of India is supposed to have been the 'spikenard' of Scripture. The fragrance was obtained by crushing the plant.

"Its growth in the mire may remind us of One who in the mire of this world grew up erect and fragrant for God. Man grows in the mire and gravitates toward it—like the man with the much-rack, who was bowed to earth and saw not the crown of glory offered to him. But our Lord had His eyes and heart only on the heaven above. The mire of earth was but the place where He has come for a special work. Men might grovel in that mire, as, alas, we have! A Job finds that his self-righteousness was covered with the mire of the ditch (Job 9:31). But His surroundings were only the contrast to that erect and perfect life which ever pointed heavenward. His treasure, His all, was with the Father. And wherever He found a 'bruised reed,' to lift it from the mire and establish it erect was the purpose of His heart—'Neither do I condemn thee' (John 8:11).

"This reed was crushed. Wicked men took Him, bound and bruised Him. But what fragrance has filled heaven and earth through that bruising. Again, the aromatic odor of the calamus reminds us that in our Lord there was nothing negative or insipid. That weak word 'amiable' is unsuitable in connection with Him. Thus when the high priest commanded that He be smitten, our Lord neither resents it nor cowers under it; but with what holy dignity did He rebuke that unrighteousness, and bear witness of His kingship before Pilate. A heavenly fragrance pervaded the judgment-hall—the vital fragrance and energy of Holiness, bearing witness to the truth (John 18:33-37)."

"*Cassia.*" Gesenius tells us that the Hebrew name of this spice is derived from a root signifying "to stoop," to "bow down," as in worship. Thus, what was foreshadowed here was the perfect Man's submission to and worship of God. In Luke 4:16 we read that, "As His custom was, He went into the synagogue on the Sabbath day." In the Psalms we find many out-breathings of His worship. In the great Temptation, He refused to fall down before the Devil, reminding him that it was written, "Thou shalt worship the Lord thy God, and Him *only* shalt thou serve."

The only other passage in which "cassia" is mentioned is Ezek. 27:19. There we learn that this was one of the articles in which Tyre—the great merchant nation of the ancients—traded. Like Egypt, Tyre stands for the world. Typically, this tells us that even the world will traffic in the excellencies of Christ in order to further its sordid ends. It is very striking to note that in the very next chapter, Ezek. 28:12-19, Satan is presented as the "king of Tyre." Thus we are there shown that the arch-enemy of God ever seeks to rob Christ, so far as he is permitted, of that worship which is His alone due.

Summarising the emblematic significations of these four principal spices, we learn that, the "myrrh" pointed to the outpouring of Christ's love in a bitter but fragrant death; the "cinnamon" to His holy jealousy for the honour and glory of God; the "calamus" to His uprightness and righteousness in a world of sin and wickedness; the "cassia" to His submission to and worship of God.

2. Its Proportions.

These are given in vv. 23, 24: of the "myrrh" there was five hundred shekels, of the "sweet cinnamon" and the "sweet calamus" two hundred and fifty shekels, and of the "cassia" five hundred shekels. First of all, we must note that there were *four* sweet spices mingled with the oil, and that each of them was taken from *plant* life, which ever speaks of man here on earth. Our minds turn instinctively to the four Gospels, where the Divine record of Christ's earthly life is given. Each of them reveals some special perfection of Christ, yet all are perfectly blended together by the all-pervading "oil," the Holy Spirit.

The *quantities* used of the spices were not of equal weight: of two there were 500 shekels, of two but 250. Thus, we have here a suggestion that there is some truth or aspect of Christ's perfections *common* to the "myrrh" and "cassia," and some truth *common to* the "cinnamon" and "calamus." The *order* in which they are given is 500, 250, 250, and 500 shekels. Comparing them thus with the Gospels, we are hereby bidden to look for some definite link uniting Matthew and John (the First and Fourth) and something shared in common by Mark and Luke, the two middle Gospels. Let us now look, very briefly, first at Matthew's and John's, and then at Mark's and Luke's.

The first and the fourth Gospels present the *highest* glories of Christ, namely, His kingship and His Godhood, agreeing with the *double* quantity of the first and fourth mentioned "spices." Moreover, the *distinctive* character of each Gospel exactly corresponds with the *nature* of the two spices. As already said, the "myrrh" symbolised a bitter death, the death of Christ. It was *this* of which the Israelites were reminded on the Passover-night: the "lamb" must be eaten with "bitter herbs" (Ex. 12:8)! How remarkable then to find that *Matthew*, and he alone, records the wise men presenting to the infant Saviour their gifts of "gold and frankincense and *myrrh*" (Matt. 2:11)! So, it is in this first Gospel that the bitterness of Messiah's experience in being despised and rejected by His brethren according to the flesh, is most fully set out. The etymology of "cassia," the fourth spice, signifies "worship," which at once introduces the *Divine* element. *This* is exactly what we have in the *fourth* Gospel: there Christ is portrayed as the Son of God!

The second and third Gospels both present the *lowliness* of Christ, the one as Servant, the other as Man—the One who had not where to lay His head; and this is in striking accord with the fact that the second and third "spices" were only *half* the quantity of the others! Yet mark how the Holy Spirit here, as ever, guarded the *glory* of Christ, even in His humiliation: the second and third spices alone were termed "sweet"!—telling us that *God* found peculiar delight in His Son's voluntary and obedient condescension. That which is highly esteemed among men is abomination in the sight of God (Luke 16:15); and that which is despised by men is of great price in His sight (1 Peter 3:4). It was when Christ was first "numbered with transgressors," taking His place among those who were "confessing their sins" (Mark 1:5), that the voice of the Father was heard saying, "This is My beloved Son, in whom I am well-pleased" (Matt. 3:17).

The figures 500, 250, 250 and 500 show, at a glance, that the perfections of Christ were all perfectly balanced. In this we behold His uniqueness. Even in His people, in their present state, one grace or other is found predominating. Not so with Christ. Everything was in lovely proportion in Him. The total weight of the spices was fifteen hundred shekels or 5x3x100—the last being 10x10. Five is the number of grace, three is manifestation and also the number of God, ten the measure of responsibility. Thus we have, the grace of God manifested in perfect human responsibility. This is to be found in Christ alone.

Each of the spices was apportioned by weight, "after the shekel of the sanctuary" (v. 24). This was before us in our article on the Atonement-money (30:13). "God is a God of knowledge, and by Him actions are weighed (1 Sam. 2:3). The proud king of Babylon was weighed and found wanting (Dan. 5:27). And 'all have sinned and come short of the glory of God.' The Old Testament word for 'glory' is 'weight,' derived from a word 'to be heavy.' So by God's standard, all have come short of the full weight which alone can glorify Him. There is therefore but One in whom, when tested, full and true weight was found, who could say I have glorified Thee upon the earth; I have finished the work which Thou gavest Me to do' (John 17:4)." (Mr. Ridout.)

3. Its Vehicle.

This was the "oil olive," a figure of the Holy Spirit: "God *anointed* Jesus of Nazareth with the Holy Spirit and with power" (Acts 10:38). The spices gave fragrance to the oil, and the oil was the element by which their aroma was borne along. So the lovely graces manifested by Christ when He was upon earth were all according to the Spirit (Isa. 11:1, 2), and were all in the power of the Spirit (Luke 4:1, 14, etc.). It was by means of the oil that the sweet spices were blended together; the oil pervaded all and united all. The fragrance of the spices was to be evenly diffused through the whole hin of oil olive, so that no one took precedence over the other; but the oil sent forth the sweetness of each alike. So Christ, ever filled with the Spirit, blended the various fragrances of His character into one holy perfume: His name (that which represents and reveals the person) was, and ever is "as *ointment* poured forth" (Son of Sol. 1:3)!

4. *Its Use.*

It was employed in the anointing of the Tabernacle and all its furniture (Ex. 30: 26-29), and at the consecration of the priests (30:30). That which speaks of the sweet savor of Christ was put on all that foreshadowed Him. The vessels of the sanctuary represented various offices and services of our great High Priest, some performed by Him when here on earth, others in which He is now engaged on High. The same eternal Spirit by which He offered Himself as the sacrifice without spot unto God (Heb. 9:14) is still the power of His service in resurrection—cf Acts 1:2:

Very blessed is it to behold the anointing of Aaron's sons with this holy oil, for this, in figure, shows us the people of Christ having communicated to them the selfsame "sweet savour" which gives their Head acceptance before God. It is the Spirit of God graciously equipping us for priestly ministry. Remarkable is it to note that the instructions concerning the "holy oil" in Ex. 30 follow right after mention of the laver (30:18-21). The "laver" is negative in character, a type of that which *removes* all that would hinder our approach unto God; the "oil" gives us the positive side, *bringing in* that which gives us acceptance before Him. The antitype comes out most preciously in 2 Cor. 2:14, 15, "Thanks be unto God, which always causeth us to triumph *in Christ,* and maketh manifest the savour of His knowledge *by us* in every place. For *we* are unto God a sweet savour of Christ."

5. *Its Prohibitions.*

"Upon man's flesh it shall not be poured" (v. 32). Only those belonging to the priestly family were anointed. Typically, this means that only the people of God, those in Christ (the "Anointed") are "anointed"—have the Spirit of God. "Because ye *are* sons, God hath sent forth the Spirit of His Son into your hearts" (Gal. 4:6). "Now He which stablisheth us with you *in Christ* and hath anointed us, is God" (2 Cor. 1:22). This is something which man in the flesh has not, and cannot have. "The graces of the Spirit can never be connected with man's flesh, the Holy Spirit cannot own nature. Not one of the fruits of the Spirit has ever yet produced 'in nature's barren soil.' We must be 'born again.' It is only as connected with the new man, as being part of that 'new creation,' that he can know anything of the fruits of the Spirit" (C.H.M.).

"Neither shall ye make any other like it, after the composition of it: it is holy, and it shall be holy unto you" (v. 32). The type must not be imitated or it would not figure that which was *inimitable,* even the perfections of Christ! As no strange altar must be built (Ex. 20:25), as no "strange fire" must be used (Lev. 10:1, 2), so there must be no strange oil. How this word condemns the imitations of Divine worship, the Spirit's operations, the fragrance of Christ, in present-day religious Christendom! Mere head knowledge, ritualism, exquisite music, soulical excitements, are so many human substitutes for the true ministry of Christ in the power of the Spirit.

Unspeakably solemn is the final word: "Whosoever compoundeth any like it, or whosoever putteth any of it upon a stranger, shall even be cut off from his people" (v. 33). "It is thus a heinous sin to imitate the action of the Spirit. Ananias and Sapphira did this when they professed to devote the whole proceeds of the property they had sold to the Lord's service (Acts 5). The same penalty, observe, was attached to putting it upon a stranger, upon those who had no title to it. God is holy, and He jealously guards His sovereign rights, and cannot but visit any infringement of them with punishment. If He seem now to pass by such sins unnoticed, it is owing to the character of the present dispensation being one of grace; but the sins themselves are no less in His sight" (Mr. Ed. Demnett).

—*Arthur W. Pink.*

GREAT PEACE.

"And all Thy children shall be taught of the Lord; and great shall be the peace of Thy children" (Isa. 54:13).

Thus far, in our examination of this text, we have considered two points, namely: Who are the members of this favoured family? What is it that all of them are taught? Now we are to ponder the closing clause of the verse, and meditate upon the "great peace" which is the portion of this family.

Peace; what a blessed word is this! We are living in a world of turmoil and strife. We are told that at the beginning of the present world-system "In six days the Lord made heaven and earth, the sea, and all that in them is, and *rested* the seventh day" (Ex. 20:11). But alas, sin came in, and this world has seen no "rest" since then. A part of the curse which sin entailed was that man should obtain his bread by the sweat of his face (Gen. 3:19). All Nature has shared in and suffers from the disastrous consequences of Adam's fall: "For we know that the whole creation groaneth and travaileth in pain until now" (Rom. 8:22). But the heaviest penalty has fallen upon man. "A *fugitive* and a vagabond shalt thou be in the earth" (Gen. 4:12), said God to Cain; and a "fugitive"—a wanderer, a disconcerted rover—has man been ever since; seeking satisfaction and finding it not.

How blessed, then, is the contrast pointed in our text: "and great shall be the peace of Thy children." We have been much impressed while preparing this sermon to find how much there is in the Scriptures about "peace." The name Jerusalem signifies "the foundation of peace." Christ is called "the Prince of peace." When He was born into this world the angels said, "Glory to God in the highest, and on earth peace, good will toward men" (Luke 2:14). While on earth, more than once, He said to a believing sinner "thy faith hath saved thee; go in peace" (Luke 7:50). In His paschal discourse Christ said to the apostles, "Peace I leave with you, My peace I give unto you: not as the world giveth, give I unto you" (John 14:27).

After His resurrection the Lord Jesus appeared to His apostles in the upperroom and said, "Peace be unto you" (John 20:19). And we are told, "then said Jesus unto them *again*, Peace be unto you" (John 20:21). One of the names for the Evangel of Christ is "the Gospel of peace" (Eph. 6:15). The grand salutation found at the beginning of all the Pauline Epistles is "grace be to you, and peace, from God our Father, and from the Lord Jesus Christ." One of the very titles of Deity is "the God of peace" (Heb. 13:20).

"And great shall be the peace of Thy children." This presents to us, then, a sharp and blessed contrast. We might also say a *solemn* contrast: it all depends upon the angle from which we speak. The contrast is this: "There is *no* peace, saith my God to the wicked" (Isa. 57:21). The soul of man has lost its anchorage: "the wicked are like the troubled sea, when it cannot rest, whose waters cast up mire and dirt" (Isa. 57:20). Their very minds are unstable—"tossed too and fro, and carried about with every wind of doctrine by the sleight of men, and cunning craftiness, whereby they lie in wait to deceive" (Eph. 4:14). As saith Rom. 3:17, "The way of peace have they not known." Their lives make it manifest; their very countenances show it. Now with these dark shadows as a background let us consider the restful, blessed, tranquilising words of our text.

"And great shall be the peace of Thy children." Following my usual custom, I have asked the text a number of questions: thus—What is the nature of this peace? Wherein lies the "greatness" of it? If the peace of Christians is so "great," then why are so many of them often perturbed, discontented and unhappy? What hinders them from the enjoyment of it? As the Lord shall enable we will now endeavour to suggest answers to these questions.

1. *The Nature of this Peace.*

That "great peace" which is the portion of all the members of this favoured family is two-fold in its character: judicial and experimental. There is a peace outside of them; there is also a peace within them. Our text includes both.

1. *A judicial peace.* When sin entered into this world the peace which had existed between God and His unfallen creatures was broken; a state of war was declared. All sin is a species of rebellion against and defiance of God. He says, "thou shalt"; sin says, "I will not." God says, "Thou shalt not"; the sinner says, "I will." As Isa. 53:6 declares, "We have turned every one to *his own* way. Sin is spiritual anarchy: it is raising the red flag against the throne of God; it is revolt against His righteous government. In their unregenerate days the members of this favored family were engaged in active warfare against God. Therefore, He

and they were alienated—"you that were sometime alienated and enemies in your mind by wicked works" (Col. 1:21).

In order for reconciliation to be effected between these alienated parties, in order for peace to be established on a righteous basis, the government of God must be vindicated and the requirements of His law fully met. A righteous God could not gloss over things: peace at any price is contrary to His holy nature: a patched up peace would not satisfy His claims. Anarchy is a serious thing, and this must be plainly shown by the costliness of the satisfaction required. Law and order must be upheld; the claims of justice must be met; sin must be punished.

Now only the Prince of peace could make peace between an offended God and His rebellious and alienated people. Therefore we read in Rom. 3 that Jesus Christ has been, by God, "set forth to be a propitiation through faith in His blood, to declare His righteousness" (v. 25). The word "propitiation" means "an appeasement, a satisfaction rendered to placate an offended party." Christ was appointed to be "a propitiation," that is, a satisfaction rendered unto the outraged law of God; and this in order that He might righteously acquit and receive the sinner who believes in His Son. Hence we are reminded that Christ is "first King of righteousness, and after that also King of peace" (Heb. 7:2). "When we were enemies we were reconciled to God by the death of His Son" (Rom. 5:10).

Sinners are sometimes asked, "Have you made your peace with God?" Unless the terms of this question be clearly defined it is a misleading one. For His own people Christ has "made peace—through the blood of His cross" (Col. 1:20). Therefore He "is our peace" (Eph. 2:14). This is something outside of us altogether. It is entirely objective. It is what Christ has done for us. He has appeased the anger of God's holiness against us as rebels. And this peace is "great" because it is perfect.

2. *An Experimental Peace*. In Isa. 27:5 God said to each of His people, "Let him take hold of My strength, that he may make peace with Me; and he shall make peace with Me." Parallel with this is that word in Psa. 2:12, "Kiss the Son, lest He be angry, and ye perish from the way, when His wrath is kindled but a little. Blessed are all they that put their trust in Him." To make our peace with God, to "Kiss the Son," means to throw down the weapons of our warfare, to cease fighting against Him, to sue for peace with Him. It is written, "He that covereth his sins shall not prosper: but whoso confesseth and *forsaketh* them shall have mercy" (Prov. 28:13). It is only when this is done that the peace of God fills the soul. Peace is a state of rest; a cessation of striving against God.

That which we have referred to above is wrought in each of God's elect by the Holy Spirit. He brings them to the realisation that they have been fighting against God. He subdues their enmity against Him, and puts into their hearts a desire to serve and please Him, and thus are they, experimentally, reconciled to God. Thus it is written, "Therefore being justified by faith, we have peace with God through our Lord Jesus Christ" (Rom. 5:1). The words "peace *with* God" signify that there is peace *between* God and the believing sinner—enmity has been destroyed.

The *effects* of this experimental peace reach to every part of the Christian's being. He now has peace of *conscience*. When the Holy Spirit convicted him of his lost condition, showed him that his sins were more than the hairs of his head, revealed to him the awfulness of his state in fighting against the Almighty, his conscience was burdened beyond endurance. The load upon him was intolerable, and he groaned beneath it day and night. But when the Spirit led him to the cross, and showed him that Christ fully atoned for all his sins, the load fell off. The precious blood having been once and for all applied to such, the word now is, "Let us draw near with a true heart in full assurance of faith, having our hearts sprinkled *from* an evil (guilty) conscience" (Heb. 10:22).

The Christian enjoys an *intellectual* peace. His mind is no longer "tossed to and fro, and carried about with every wind of doctrine" (Eph. 4:14). As it is written, "Thou wilt keep him in perfect peace whose mind is stayed on Thee: because he trusteth in Thee" (Isa. 26:3). There are thousands of people to-day who claim to be "Seekers *after* Truth." Not so with the Christian. He *has* it. He is thoroughly satisfied with the explanation which the Holy Scriptures give of the origin of the universe, of man, of sin, of how to be saved, and of the future. He has no doubts on these things. His mind is at rest.

He also has peace of *heart*. Once the very mention of God and of Christ made him uneasy. Instead of seeking His presence, he desired to flee from it. He had rather read anything than His blessed

Word. But now "fellowship" with the Father and His Son is his greatest delight. All dread has gone; his heart is at rest in His presence. He can now say with the Psalmist, "Whom have I in heaven but Thee, and there is none upon earth that I desire beside Thee." For the coming of Christ he looks and longs. To be "forever with the Lord" is his blissful expectation.

2. *The Grounds of this Peace.*

As already stated, the ground of our peace, judicially, is the blood of Christ. The ground of our peace, experimentally, is the work of the Holy Spirit within, subduing the native enmity of our hearts. The Christian's peace is based upon the knowledge that *all* his sins are remitted. The words of Christ to him are, "Thy sins are forgiven . . . . thy faith hath saved thee; go in peace" (Luke 7:48, 50). "Peace, perfect peace, in this dark world of sin; the blood of Jesus whispers peace within."

But there are collateral grounds or contributory causes to the Christian's experimental peace. His peace of heart is based upon the knowledge that "all things work together for good to them that love God, to them who are the called according to His purpose" (Rom. 8:28). How it tranquilises the heart to know that even losses are our gains, that disappointments are His appointments, that our chastenings are regulated by Divine love! Nothing provides such a refuge for our restless hearts than the realisation that God is upon the throne, directing all things, working out all things according to His eternal purpose.

Again; the knowledge of the unending bliss awaiting us fills with a peace which passeth all understanding. The more we are occupied with that inheritance unto which we have been begotten, "an inheritance incorruptible, and undefiled, and that fadeth not away" (1 Peter 1:4). the more are our hearts sustained while passing through this "howling wilderness." The ungoldly wish to remain here forever; the Christian has a desire "to depart, and to be with Christ, which is far better" (Phil. 1:23). When in our right minds we know that "the sufferings of this present time are not worthy to be compared with the glory which shall be revealed in us" (Rom. 8:18).

3. *The Greatness of our Peace.*

"And great *shall be* the peace of Thy children." It is to be noted that the words, "shall be," are in italics. The original is wider in its scope than is the rendering in our English Bibles. The added words of the translators serve to restrict this great peace to the future. The Holy Spirit has left it abstract, because, "great peace" is the portion of God's children both now and forever.

Our God gives with no niggardly hand. He is a great God and the redemption He has provided is a great one. In Heb. 2:3 His salvation is called a "great salvation." In Heb. 4:14 Christ is called our "great High Priest"; and a "great peace" is the portion of His people. I like the word "great" coming in here. The Holy Spirit is very sparing in His use of adjectives. One of the features of Holy Scripture which distinguishes it from all other books is its *sober* tone. It is very rare that flights of oratory are indulged in. It is very seldom that the superlative degree is used. Hence, when the Holy Spirit *does* use the word "great," it has a force which would be lost if He were always using it.

The peace of God's children is "great" in many respects. It is "great" in its *power.* This is seen in the way in which a Christian can review the whole of his awful past: though this causes him sorrow. yet has it no terror for him. Though the remembrance of his former wickedness brings grief and bows him in contrition before God. yet, knowing that his sins are all blotted out, his peace with God is not disturbed. It is "great" in its *depths.* This aspect of the saint's peace may be likened unto the ocean. Though the surface of the sea is often disturbed by the wind. yet the depths below remain unmoved. Thus with the Christian: though his outward composure is frequently ruffled, though circumstances may often disquieten, yet, deep down in his heart there is a peace which is undisturbed. It is "great" in its *duration*: it will never end. It is the peace of God: therefore will it last forever.

4. *The enjoyment of this Peace.*

Here we touch upon the practical side of our theme. Though God's children have a great peace as their portion, they do not always enjoy it. Just as heavy clouds sometimes hide the sun, so our peace is often obscured. The sun still remains there, unchanged, in the heavens, but the clouds prevent us from basking in its comforting and warming rays. In like manner, the peace which Christ has purchased for His people, and the peace which the Holy Spirit has communicated to them, never changes; but unless we are in daily communion with God we fail to walk in its blissful power.

Among the things which *hinder* our enjoyment of God's peace we may mention, carelessness of walk, the allowance of worldliness in our lives, disobedience to God's precepts, failure to use the means of grace which God has provided for us, and the inevitable backslidings to which these lead. God says, "Whoso *hearkeneth* unto Me shall dwell safely, and shall be quiet from fear of evil" (Prov. 1:33). But if we fail to "hearken" unto what God hath said, then the opposite will be our state. God has told us, "Be ye not unequally yoked together with unbelievers" (2 Cor. 6:14): many Christians have not heeded this, and therefore they have lost their enjoyment of God's peace. God has said, "Be content with such things as ye have" (Heb. 13:5), but instead, many Christians have coveted earthly riches, and consequently they have "pierced themselves through with many sorrows" (1 Tim. 6:10).

What a word is that in Isa. 48:18, "O that thou hadst *hearkened* to My commandments, then had thy peace been as a river, and thy righteousness as the waves of the sea." God has said, "He that is surety for a stranger shall smart for it: and he that hateth suretyship is sure" (Prov. 11:15). And again, "Be *not* thou one of them that strike hands, or of them that are sureties for debts" (Prov. 22:26): how many a child of God would have been spared much "smarting" had he heeded this Divine commandment! Once more, God says, "Owe no man anything" (Rom. 13:8), yet many Christians deliberately run into debt and suffer severely for it.

"I will hear what God the Lord will speak: for He will speak peace unto His people, and to His saints: but let them not turn again to folly" (Psa. 85:8). How watchful we need to be! We shall "hear" more clearly, if we seek to walk more closely with God in our daily lives—in separation from the world's attractions and distractions. O that Divine grace may keep both reader and writer from "turning again to folly," then shall we be kept in the enjoyment of the "great peace" which is the portion of God's family.

—*Arthur W. Pink.*

UNCLOTHED OR CLOTHED.

2 Corinthians 5:1.

The object of the Christian's hope and desire is not a vague and shadowy idea of happiness. This, we know, however pleasing, cannot, from the constitution of the human mind, be influential. Nothing proves this more conclusively than the substitution of an imaginary heaven for the hope set before us in the Gospel by a secularized church. Such a heaven arrests no thoughts of worldliness, but rather sheds a charming light upon its hours of ease. Let it be added that it affords no support in the hour of temptation and trial; and that it cannot be said, "Every one that hath this hope purifieth himself."

The hope of the Christian is definite in its object and assured in its certainty, because it is *in Christ;* or, to state it in the converse aspect, "Christ in you is this hope of glory." A natural man may say, "I do not care what or where heaven is. It is enough for me if I am to be happy for ever." This satisfies the man whose desires centre in self. So a Christian with low and perverted views of the grace of God may say with affected humility, "I know nothing of the nature of heaven's glory or blessedness. It is enough for me if I may sit for ever as a doorkeeper at the gate. Only assure me that I shall be there." And well it might be when the alternative is hell. This, too, is but nature's selfishness, which knows nothing of the mind of Christ, cares nothing for the glory of God, and makes no response to the love that promised, "I will come again to receive you to myself; that where I am there ye may be also." To the heart in which the love of God is shed abroad by the Holy Spirit given unto us, there can be no heaven without Christ. If Christ be in you the hope of glory, the object of it must be His glory, and the desire enkindled must be to be like Him as well as to see Him as He is. The mere desire to be happy, without caring how, is selfish and degrading. It is transforming, purifying, and ennobling when faith and love find heaven anticipated in the assurance, "So shall we be for ever with the Lord," and in the thought that then "He shall be glorified in His saints and admired in all them that believe."

In harmony with this is the view which the inspired records afford of the hope that animated and sustained the early Christians in their holy, unworldly, and self-sacrificing course. They waited for the Son of God from heaven, leaving out none of the revealed consequences of His appearing. But in nothing is the hope which was so influential in their lives more distinguished from the vague dream which, to a large extent, has supplanted it, and which is so uninfluential on the lives of professing Christians in our day, than in the prominence which the resurrection from the dead stood out in its consummation before their minds.

According to modern views, we should have expected an apostle standing in jeopardy every hour and always delivered unto death for Jesu's sake, to exult in the thought of the day of death as his better natal day, and of an escape from the body as, in itself, the most desirable enlargement to the imprisoned soul, and as the immediate entrance upon a glory and blessedness which are incompatible with an embodied state. But their views and the very phraseology in which they are expressed are borrowed, not from the apostles, but from the philosophers who despised them. Nature's longings, its fond desires, its unsatisfied aspirations, sought refuge in these dreams of immortality for which death was the only preparation. But we find those who had received the first-fruits of the Spirit "waiting for the adoption, to wit, the redemption of the body." Though for the time of waiting they regarded it as far better to depart and to be with Christ, yet this was not their hope; and there were blessed results of suffering and service which more than reconciled them to remain in the body, even when troubled on every side, perplexed, persecuted, and cast down.

That which sustained and cheered Paul in all that he was called to endure, he thus expresses, "For we know that if our earthly house of this tabernacle were dissolved, we have a building of God, an house not made with hands, eternal in the heavens."

In considering such a prospect as influential in the apostle's life, it is necessary to observe the confidence with which he speaks of it, "We know." The word is used in Scriptures, especially by Paul and John, to express the highest certainty to which the mind can attain. Here we perceive how the word "hope" changes its meaning when it is transferred from earthly to heavenly things—from human probabilities to divine verities. From the uncertainty which invests all the future to man's frailty and short-sightedness, hope acquires a secondary meaning in which we use it to convey a doubt or suspicion. But the Christian's hope is as certain as the word and throne of Jehovah, and his knowledge will not be more real and assured when he stands amidst the glory revealed, than it is now when the things hoped for are substantiated by faith resting on the Word of God. But in order to such knowledge no human reasonings must be allowed a place beside the Word of God as its evidence, and no human fancies must be permitted to mingle with what God has revealed as its matter.

It must be observed than when the apostle says, "We know," he has in view not only the certainty of the things hoped for as glorious realities in the future of the redeemed; but also his own personal interest in these realities. "We know that *we have* a building of God, an house not made with hands, eternal in the heavens." He knows that they are *his*. It avails little, for any practical result, to know that there is an inheritance for the children of God, unless we can say, "Now are we the sons of God." And here is another point in which we observe a marked difference between apostolic and modern Christians. With the latter, not only are the things hoped for vague shadows, but their interest in them, such as they are, is a matter of doubt; and for the simple reason that human reasonings come into the place of God's word, human emotions into the place of the testimony of the Spirit, human attainments and experiences into the place of Christ's work, and the contemplation of our love to God into the place of the contemplation of the manner of love the Father hath bestowed upon us that we should be called sons of God. All must rest upon a divine foundation—the inheritance and our sonship, the glory and our title to it; in other words, it must be "Christ in you the hope of glory," before it can be removed from the region of human probability into the region of divine certainty, where we can say with the apostle, *"We know."*

"Our earthly house of this tabernacle" is the apostle's description of this mortal body. The apostle Peter also speaks of the body as a tabernacle, and with reference to his approaching decease says, "Knowing that shortly I must put off my tabernacle." The figure expresses the idea of fraility, in contrast with a substantial building; a temporary rest for a pilgrim, in contrast with a permanent home. But we would now rather direct attention to the manner in which Peter and Paul regard it, as apart from their own proper personality—from that which a man calls *himself*. He is but a dweller there. Peter speaks of putting it off, and Paul speaks of its being dissolved; but Peter and Paul remain. This appears more distinctly in the chapter before us, where Paul speaks of being unclothed and being absent from the body.

"Tabernacle," as a temporary resting-place, seems opposed to "house," as a permanent abode; and so it appears a solecism to speak of "our earthly *house* of this *tabernacle*." But the propriety of speaking of the tabernacle as a house is justified when it is described as an *"earthly* house," in contrast with a building of God;" for that word earthly retains the characteristics of frailty and temporary residence. It is of the earth, earthy; according to the sentence of God, "Dust thou art and to dust thou shalt return." The earthly house is but a tabernacle soon to be dissolved. And especially in view of all that afflicted and threatened it in the apostle's case, it was an abundant consolation to know that "we have a building of God, an house not made with hands, eternal in the heavens."

When the apostle elsewhere would express the dignity, perfection, and glory of the church, he says, "Ye are God's building." This is another illustration of an important truth, that, in all vital and essential points, whatever is affirmed of the whole may be affirmed of every part; what is true of the church is true of every believer. Thus, keeping near to the present figure, the church is the temple of God, builded together as a habitation of God through the Spirit. But the individual believer also is a temple of the Holy Spirit. In the case before us, where the glorified body that awaits the saints in resurrection is spoken of as "a building of God," we are assured of its perfection and permanence. "Not made with hands" expresses the fact that it does not come to us at second hand, or through any creature instrumentality by which it might be marred, but directly from God Himself, its beauty undefaced even by the touch of a messenger bearing the gift. "Eternal" expresses its duration, not only in itself, but as the saint's abode. "In the heavens" contrasts both its nature and the scene of its enjoyment with the former house, which was earthly. And, besides this, we may understand faith's upward glance to Him who had passed into the heavens—the man Christ Jesus, who shall change our vile body and fashion it like unto His own glorious body—when Paul spoke of the thing hoped for as already ours; though out of sight, reserved in heaven for us.

The contrast between these two bodies —the earthly tabernacle and the building of God—will recall the apostle's contrast of the natural with the spiritual body in his argument on the resurrection in 1 Cor. 15, "Howbeit that was not first which is spiritual, but that which is natural, and afterward that which is spiritual. The first man is of the earth, earthy; the second man is the Lord from heaven. As is the earthy, such are they that are earthy; and as is the heavenly, such are they that are heavenly. And as we have borne the image of the earthy, we shall also bear the image of the heavenly." Whatever else we may learn from this statement, it is evident that the resurrection from the dead, which is our hope, is by no means a resuscitation of the body which returns to dust. The earthly house is dissolved, not to be repaired or restored, but that it may be replaced by a heavenly; it is put off, not to be put on again; but, instead of it, we shall be clothed upon with our house which is from heaven. The preservation of personal identity, as we pass from our humiliation and into glory, does not depend on the identity of the bodily structure, any more than it now does upon the clothes which we wear. The personal identity resides in that which is not dissolved, but which is invested *now* with a vile body, and will be *then* with a glorious body. The body which we now inhabit, derived from the first man, is adapted to the life which we shared in common with him, but is ill-adapted to the new life which we have in the Second Man, the Lord from heaven. That body, therefore, is to be dissolved, and in its place we shall receive a body suited to the new life, God will give to that spiritual life its own body; and, since Christ is our life, evidently it must be a body fashioned like unto His glorious body. "We shall bear the image of the heavenly."

With a heavenly life so inadequately housed, it is no wonder that it should be written, "For in this we groan, earnestly desiring to be clothed upon with our house which is from heaven." The life seeks investment with that which becomes it, which will be a fit organ for its powers, a fit medium for the manifestation of what God has wrought, and a vessel capable of receiving all that grace has destined and prepared for the sons of God. In other words, we desire to be "like Christ; for we shall see Him as He is." And now observe the consequence: "If so be that, being clothed, we shall not be found naked." This means more than that, being clothed, we shall not be found unclothed. We can scarcely suppose that an apostle was inspired to write such a mere truism. It will be remembered that Adam's guilty consciousness in the presence of God found this first expression, "I was afraid because I was *naked;* and I hid myself." And the apostle here means that the last trace of sin's shame will be effaced, and redemption will be complete when, in the perfect likeness of Christ, the believer shall stand forth unabashed in the unveiled radiance of the presence of God.

There is a reference to the sin which made the earthly house a shame to us, as well as to the condition of the house itself in consequence of sin, in the statement, "For we that are in this tabernacle do groan, being burdened." The body, curiously and wonderfully made, is marred by sin, and the word "mortal" expresses more than the fact of liability to death. Not to speak of the sufferings which it includes, and the ills which flesh is heir to; the cares and sorrows that beset man's path from the cradle to the grave; the unfitness of such a body to be the organ and medium of the life of which we have spoken, there are the appetites and tendencies which, in nature's disorder, hinder the heavenly affections, and encumber the energies of the new man. And, in addition to all this, although the fallen and marred body be not itself sin, yet, in indissoluble connection with it, there is the law in our members warring against the law of the mind; all that is born of the flesh being still flesh lusting against the Spirit, though sin ought not to reign in our mortal bodies that we should obey it in the lusts thereof. From all this, the universal and necessary experience of believers in this life, "We that are in this tabernacle do groan, being burdened." Nor can it be otherwise till the burdened and imprisoned life shall be set free. How welcome to the groaning believer the prospect that is as sure as the exaltation of Jesus to the right hand of God—the accomplishment of the purpose of Him who hath predestined us to be conformed to the likeness of His Son—when we shall not only be freed from the bondage of corruption, but brought into the glorious liberty of the sons of God!

Paul was not a mere weary-of-the-world, discouraged because of the way, seeking to be discharged from the warfare, and to escape toil and service. "Not for that we would be unclothed, but clothed upon, that mortality may be swallowed up of life." It is not death that he seeks, but immortality. Not the repose even of those who sleep in Jesus and are comforted, but resurrection glory, the manifestation of sons of God, the body fashioned like unto Christ's glorious body, in which the life which is now obstructed and repressed shall find an organ of its mighty energies, and a channel of the joy of Christ's presence and the companionship of all saints. But the manner in which Paul here speaks of being clothed upon without being unclothed, and of mortality being swallowed up of life, must find explanation in a mystery which he had showed to the church of God at Corinth, in 1 Cor. 15, from which we have already quoted, "Behold, I show you a mystery; we shall not all sleep, but we shall all be changed, in a moment, in the twinkling of an eye, at the last trump: for the trumpet shall sound, and the dead shall be raised incorruptible, and we shall be changed."

Believers are no longer under the original doom by which "it is appointed unto men once to die, and after this the judgment." It is indeed most true, joyously true, that the mortal must be put off; that which belongs to earth cannot rise to heaven. All that is of the flesh must be left behind. Now, indeed, until the number of God's elect shall be completed, believers put off this tabernacle and await the accomplishment of God's purposes in their brethren that are in the world. But, to believers as such, death is not a necessity; they are not subject to it as a penalty which justice must exact. By the laws of a new nature, and the rights of an accomplished redemption, they are heirs of immortality; and, while the day of the manifestation of the sons of God is concealed, it was Paul's privilege and proper attitude, in common with all believers, to speak as one whose portion is life, not death, not knowing but that any day, in any instant, the transition may be made from mortality to immortality.

It is not a just construction of Paul's language, "We shall not all sleep, but we shall all be changed," or "we which are alive and remain at the coming of the Lord, to say that it expresses a confidence that the Lord's coming would be in his day, or that he should not sleep. His epistles abound with expressions which show that he contemplated the possibility, and even more than the probability, of dying. Paul spoke, and every believer is entitled to speak as a member of a body which is not under the iron necessity of dying, but whose proper hope is a glorious immortality. As a member of that body he says, "We shall not all sleep." And if his ignorance of the day when Christ will come the second time without sin unto salvation forbade him to count positively that this great event should occur in his day, it equally forbade to conclude positively that it could not occur in his day. In this uncertainty of the day of "our gathering together unto Him," it was most natural, and it showed where his heart was fixed, that he should associate himself with the body of whom he testifies, "We shall not all sleep."

In either case, the result is the same: "This corruptible must put on incorruption, and this mortal must put on immortality"; whether it be sown a natural body and raised a spiritual body, or whether by an instantaneous change we are "clothed upon with our house which is from heaven.' There is something peculiarly inspiriting in the contemplation of this final display of the Lord's victory over death—this proof of the divine energy of the God-given life—when in a moment, in the twinkling of an eye, mortality shall be swallowed up of life; and not a single trace of earthliness, or decay, or frailty shall be left to burden the energies or stain the glory of children of the resurrection. While, if the Lord has so willed that any of us shall be called to die, we accept His will in the confidence that death as well as life is ours, let us still associate ourselves with the scenes of that victory in the manifestation of sons of God.

The ground of the apostle's confidence in this hope is, "He that hath wrought us for the self-same thing is God, who also hath given unto us the earnest of the Spirit."

We are God's workmanship, and since He has had this end in view, the perfection of the Workman assures us of the perfect adaptation to the end. So the apostle elsewhere speaks of "giving thanks unto the Father, which hath made us meet to be partakers of the inheritance of the saints in light." It is no longer a question of the completeness of our preparation for glory, but of the perfection of God's workmanship. And if we think what the glory is—even Christ's glory—it will at once be seen that as no creature righteousness could give a title to it, so no creature attainments could constitute meetness for it. We do not speak unadvisedly when we say that holy angels could never make themselves meet for it. Only God's workmanship could meet its requirements, and that, too, only when God hath wrought us for the self-same thing.

But this also brings assurance of the certainty of the result. If God has wrought us for the self-same thing, then the attainment of it is infallibly sure. There can be no failure in the wisdom and power of God to accomplish His purpose. To bring this home to our hearts, He has "given us the earnest of the Spirit." The disposition of men is to seek an earnest of the coming glory in some work of the Spirit, just as they seek such a work as the seal which the Spirit, as the active agent of the divine purpose, impresses on the heart. The search for such an earnest and seal ends either in disappointment or delusion; for it proceeds in a misapprehension of the truth of God. The Spirit Himself is both the earnest and the seal. By the gift of the Holy Spirit, God stamps the believer as His own, and gives both an assurance and a fore-taste of that which will be completed in glory. The Spirit given is the Spirit of adoption, and is therefore the seal of sonship and the pledge of the inheritance. For we are taught to argue, "If sons, then heirs; heirs of God, and joint-heirs with Christ." More particularly with reference to the resurrection, the apostle argues, "But if the Spirit of Him that raised up Christ from the dead dwell in you, He that raised Christ from the dead shall also quicken your mortal bodies by His Spirit that dwelleth in you." This is a true earnest, not merely security for the fulfilment of a promise, but such a security as consists in a part-payment; since the Spirit which now dwells in you will be the agent of that mighty work, and will so quicken your mortal body that the mortal will be swallowed up of life.

While with grateful delight we dwell upon the security of our hope and the completeness of our preparation for its enjoyment, since it is God that hath wrought us for the self-same thing, let us not forget that all the praise of salvation belongs to God. To the truth that it is God who hath wrought us for the self-same thing, let us join the truth that the thing for which He hath wrought us is "a building of God," and see that, from first to last, all is God's work. It originated in the eternal counsels of His love, and He hath charged Himself with the accomplishment of His purpose. We speak not alone of that display of love by which He opened up a righteous way for the fulfilment of it and laid a foundation for our faith, but also of all the steps in the salvation of every believer. As the Lord expresses it, He came not only to save, but "to *seek* and to save that which was lost." Or, as He illustrates it in the parable of the lost sheep, the good

Shepherd does not wait merely to open the door to the returning wanderer. He goes forth to seek that which was lost; and when He finds it, He does not drive it home by the compulsion of His rod, but lays it on His shoulders and carries it home, rejoicing every step of the way. What blessed security! Though the way may seem long, and dark, and dreary, and surrounded by dangers, none can pluck the found one from the shoulders of the Shepherd, and He can neither fail nor err in the homeward way. Hark! how He rebukes thy fears: "Hast thou not known, hast thou not heard that the everlasting God, the Lord, the Creator of the ends of the earth, fainteth not, neither is weary? There is no searching of His understanding."

Some of the wise men after the flesh have thought to vindicate both God and man by representing that the sacrifice of Christ was for the sins of none in particular, but accomplished as much for all as for any. It set before all an open door, it provided a feast for all, and then it is left to themselves to enter in and enjoy the feast. But what will an open door avail for the dead? What will a provided feast avail while the carnal mind is in enmity against God? It availed nothing that the stone was rolled away from the door of the sepulchre, till the Life-Giver called with a loud voice, "Lazarus, come forth." So it is He who raised up the Lord Jesus who must call and quicken the dead in trespasses and sins—a work not less truly divine than to raise the dead and clothe the mortal with immortality. He who thus begins the good work carries it on, and will perfect it in the day of the Lord Jesus. It is all His. The perfect masterpiece of the heavenly Workman, showing forth the resources of His wisdom and power more resplendently than all the shining worlds around us, than the glory and beauty of the principalities and powers of the heavenlies, will be that "building of God," the glorified body of the saints, or rather, we should say, the glorious body of Christ, according to which theirs will be fashioned.

We challenge the undivided praise of the whole work, from first to last, to the God of our salvation. We are lost in wonder before the glory which He hath prepared for us, and for which He hath prepared us. We do not attempt to picture that glory, or the scenes of eternal joy amid which it shall be displayed. A dying saint said to a visitor, "I have longed to see you, that I might tell you of all the love He has revealed to me; and now, when I see you, I can tell you nothing; for it would not be the love of God if my poor tongue could tell it." And just so with the glory. It would not be the glory which Christ has gotten and given, if our words could express it. Heaven would not be heaven if our imagination could picture it. But what must be the glory of the saints, if it will not be out of place on the throne of Christ! What the glory of the church, when she is made ready as the queen to be brought to the King, and be the partner of His reign and His joy for ever!

This, believer, is what is set before your hope, amidst the humiliation, trials, conflicts of the present; and in view of it, you might well say, "None of these things move me." And what an antidote is here to the attractions by which the world would draw you aside from your heavenly calling. "May the God of our Lord Jesus Christ, the Father of glory, give unto you the spirit of wisdom and revelation in the knowledge of Him; the eyes of your understanding being enlightened, that ye may know what is the hope of His calling, and what the riches of the glory of His inheritance in the saints, and what is the exceeding greatness of His power to usward, who believe according to the working of His mighty power which He wrought in Christ when He raised Him from the dead and set Him at His own right hand in the heavenly places, far above all principality, and power, and might, and dominion, and every named that is named, not only in this world, but also in that which is to come; and hath put all things under His feet, and gave Him to be Head over all things to the church, which is His body, the fulness of Him that filleth all in all."

—Waymarks in the Wilderness, 1871.

Do you know of a lonely, or bed-ridden, or starved Christian who would probably value this little magazine? If so, write us, and, D.V., we will gladly send each such a sample copy.

GODLINESS AND A SUFFICIENCY.

"But godliness with contentment is great gain."—*1 Tim. 4:6.*

Is not contentment an essential in godliness? Is not one godly only so far as he is pleased with God? When discontent fills our hearts, has not Satan so far prevailed against us? Elijah was a godly man; but there was not godliness in his pleading against God's seven thousand; it was only his impatient, ignorant, indignation; and when his God revealed to him the number of His "reserved ones," he knew the God of Israel better than before; his godliness grew and was strengthened, for his discontent was gone.

Jonah was angry even unto death, because of his gourd, and thought he did well in being so. His honour as a prophet seemed gone, when Nineveh was spared; and when the worm which God prepared killed his only remaining comfort, and the east wind blowing on his head made him faint, he said, "It is better for me to die than to live," and maintained his foolish fancy before God Himself. He spoke like the fool who saith in his heart, "There is no God;" and nothing but the love of the Saviour of the babes and cattle of Nineveh saved the faith of His prophet from eternal shipwreck.

No; godliness and grumbling cannot live together: so far as godliness lives it kills grumbling, and so far as grumbling prevails, it eats out the heart of godliness. How then does Paul say, "'Godliness with contentment is great gain?" as if there were two things, and the one needed the other to make a man truly rich.

There is a great mistake here; nor is the mistake less dangerous that, in the English versions, it seems universal and inveterate. Many years ago, it fell to the writer's lot to revise the Pastoral Epistles for the American Bible Union: and he felt compelled to change the translation thus: "But godliness is a great means of gain, with a sufficiency, *or enough,* for one's self." But the old version has been restored by Dr. Conant. Now, while he cordially acknowledges the great learning and ability of Dr. Conant, he cannot perceive, after a careful consideration of the whole matter, either the consistency or the correctness of the revised version. And that for the following reasons:—

1. Contentment is only the secondary meaning of the last word autarkeia; its proper meaning being *sufficiency,* or, more strictly, *sufficiency for one's self.* In 2 Cor. 9:11, the only other place where it occurs, it is rendered *sufficiency.* Now, no rule is more binding, in translating, than that which requires us to keep to the strict and primary meaning, unless the sense demands a secondary one.

2. The following context plainly demands the proper meaning of *a sufficiency for one's self.* For the Apostle immediately gives the reason for his assertion, vv. 7, 8, "For nothing have we carried into the world, and clear it is that neither can we carry any thing out: but having food and raiment—*victuals and coverings* —we shall with these have enough." For such is the proper reading and rendering of the last verb. It is plain therefore that the Apostle by the word autarkeia is referring to food, raiment, etc., which are all that we need: they form a sufficiency for man. But how is the child of God sure that his godliness must infallibly bring him such a sufficiency? This brings us to our third reason.

3. Because our Lord at great length in His Sermon on the Mount assures us of this connection. After insisting that His followers shall not be anxious about what they shall eat, and what they shall drink, and wherewithal they shall be clothed, He winds up His divine expostulation by adding: "Seek ye first the kingdom of God and His righteousness," that is godliness "and these things" (food and raiment), that is "a sufficiency for us," "shall be added unto you." The kingdom of God and the righteousness of God, are the great gain; but He who calls us to these will never deny us food and raiment. These are God's *incast.*

4. The doctrine of Christ and His Apostle, as thus explained, is the uniform declaration of the Old Testament as well as the New. Psa. 34:9, 10, "O fear the Lord, ye His saints; for there is no want to them that fear Him. The young lions do lack, and suffer hunger: but they that seek the Lord shall not want any good." Psa. 37:3, 4, "Trust in the Lord and do good; so shalt thou dwell in the land (earth), and verily thou shalt be fed. Delight thyself in God, and He will give thee the desires of thine heart."

5. While the great truth pervades both Testaments, it is believed they will be searched in vain for a parallel to the common version in 1 Tim. 6:6.

It may be objected to our doctrine, that it failed in Paul's own experience; for, godly as he was, he tells the Corinthians, "Even unto this present time, we both hunger and thirst, and are naked" (1 Cor. 4:11). And in that unparalelled eleventh chapter of his second Epistle to the Corinthians, amid all his other trials, he again mentions, "hunger and thirst, and cold and nakedness." Where then was his *sufficiency?* Yet this very Paul tells the Philippians (4:11), "I have learned, in whatsoever state I am, to be—'content'? nay, but to be an autarkes, one who has enough for himself; what we call an independent man. Still the question may seem to press, How could he have enough, if he had neither bread nor water, nor clothes? I answer, If these were denied him, he knew well it was the Great Physician who denied them; He whose eye was ever on him, and whose hand held the riches of the universe for *him,* and in due time would bestow them on *him.* But *then* was not the time. The hunger, the thirst, the cold, were necessary for his soul's health, and his world-wide work of bringing them to the Lord. He could say, in his own measure, after his Master, even more than all the apostles, "My meat and My drink is to do the will of Him who sent Me, and to finish His work."

—Waymarks in the Wilderness.

N.B.

The promise of Phil. 4:19 is the word of Him who "cannot lie," and therefore must be made good. But here, too, Scripture has to be interpreted by Scripture. An important principle of God's dealings with His people is illustrated in 2 Chron. 16:7-9, "And at that time Hanani the seer came to Asa, king of Judah, and said unto him, Because thou hast relied on the king of Syria, and not relied on the Lord thy God, therefore is the host of the king of Syria escaped out of thine hand. Were not the Ethiopians and the Lubims a huge host, with very many chariots and horsemen? yet, because thou didst rely on the Lord, He delivered them into thy hands. For the eyes of the Lord run to and fro throughout the whole earth, to show Himself strong in the behalf of them whose heart is perfect toward him. Herein thou hast done foolishly: therefore, from henceforth thou shalt have wars."

"My God shall supply all your need according to His riches in glory by Christ Jesus" (Phil. 4:19). It is not our "greed," but our "need" God promises to supply. And it must be left to *His* unerring wisdom to determine *what* it is that we really "need." Oftentimes we "need" to be brought low, brought to our wits' end (Psa. 107:27); oftentimes we "need" chastisement. Whatever the need may be, God shall "supply" it.

—A.W.P.

"My God *shall* supply all your need according to His riches in glory by Christ Jesus" (Phil. 4:19)—that covers the future! Then "Trust in the Lord with all thine heart." A very large part of this consists in calmly and confidently counting upon God *to continue* supplying our every need.

A blessed illustration of whole-hearted trust, fully authenticated, came before us in a book which we recently read. Some years ago, in Germany, there was a daughter of God who was very poor in this world's goods; so poor that she literally lived from hand to mouth; yet unmurmuringly, and with confidence in the Lord. One afternoon several Christian friends called to see her; they, too, were very poor, and much fatigued from the journey, and looked in sore need of some refreshment. But in this sister's cupboard was neither bread nor coffee; it was empty. She lifted up her heart unto Him from whom every good and every perfect gift cometh, and felt sure her fervent desire to entertain, not angels, but some of His children, was granted. She filled the kettle with water and put it on the fire, and presently it began to boil. The sister silently thanked the Lord for granting her request, and laid the table, though nothing was in sight. But still the hand of God was withheld, for "patience must have her perfect work." Again, she lifted up her heart to God, and said, "Lord, the kettle is boiling!" Just then came a knock at the door, and other friends, who knew nothing of the urgency of her case, appeared with baskets on their arms. Soon the table was filled with good things. God never disappoints real faith in Him! Then "Trust in the Lord with all thine heart."

—*Arthur W. Pink.*

child trust there is no reasoning, he simply takes his parent's words at their face value, he **has** implicit confidence that his father will make good what he has said; he dwells not **on the** difficulties in the way, but expects a fulfilment of what is promised. So it should be with us and our heavenly Father's words. Third, it means with our *affections* going out to Him. As we read in 1 Cor. 13:7, "Love believeth all things, hopeth all things. Thus, to trust in the Lord with all our heart is *love's* reliance: it is the affections going out to Him in believing dependency and expectation.

It is blessed to ponder a number of examples, recorded in Scripture for our encouragement, of men who did trust in the Lord with all their heart. Abraham upon Mount Moriah is a case in point. He had received commandment to take his well-beloved son and present him to Jehovah as a burnt offering. His response not only evidenced his obedience, but his whole-hearted trust or confidence in God. The Lord had said, "In Isaac shall thy seed be called." But how could that be, if he were slain? Instead of leaning unto his own understanding, he fully trusted in the Lord, and left Him to harmonise His promise with His precept.

Another illustration equally striking, though perhaps less known, is found in the response made by Hezekiah to the threatening letter which he had received from the King of Assyria. A most critical situation confronted him. That heathen monarch aspired to world conquest. One kingdom after another had fallen before him; now he blatantly threatened Israel. What was Hezekiah's response? Did he wring his hands in despair? No; what then? Did he confer with his generals, or set about strengthening his army. No; instead, "Hezekiah went up into the house of the Lord, and spread it before the Lord" (2 Kings 19:14, and read his prayer in vv. 15-19).

An urgent crisis, similar to the last, confronted Asa. "There came out against them Zerah the Ethiopian with an host of a thousand thousand, and three hundred chariots; and came unto Mareshah" (2 Chron. 14.9). It is easy to read this, but endeavour to visualise that vast hostile force. What was the king's response? This, "And Asa cried unto the Lord his God, and said, Lord, it is nothing with Thee to help, whether with many, or with them that have no power: help us, O Lord our God; for we *rest on Thee*, and in Thy name we go against this multitude. O Lord. Thou art our God; let not man prevail against Thee" (v. 11). *That* illustrates and exemplifies the meaning of our text.

Let us seek now to apply this Divine admonition to the details of our daily lives, particularly to the mysteries of providence therein. "Many are the afflictions of the righteous," and some of them are very trying and painful to the flesh. Oftentimes they bring us to wit's-end corner. Perhaps our experience is like that of the disciples on the storm-tossed sea: it is dark, and the wind is contrary to us. Even so, the call comes, "Trust in the Lord with all thine heart." Remember that the winds and the waves obey *His will*.

Or, possibly our circumstances resemble those of Israel at the Red Sea: the enemy threatens at our rear, and before us stands a cold and unfriendly ocean; there seems no way of escape. Even so, "Trust in the Lord with all thine heart." Or, the lot of some Christian reader may be that of the widow to whom God's prophet was sent—the barrel of meal is almost empty; your circumstances are critical to the last degree, and your heart faints within.

What is such an one to do? Why, turn to the sure promises of God, or, better still, look up to the Promiser Himself. *"Hitherto* hath the Lord helped us" (1 Sam. 17:12): then will He fail them now? *"Remember* all the way which the Lord thy God led thee" (Deut. 8:2): let the memory of past mercies and deliverances reassure thee now. God is still the same. Is it not written, "He shall deliver thee in six troubles: yea, in seven there shall no evil touch thee" (Job 5:19)? True, the afflictions of the righteous are many, yet the very verse which affirms this, adds, "But the Lord delivereth him out of them all" (Psa. 34:19).

Possibly some reader is saying, "But I am growing old and feeble; soon I shall no longer be able to work; then what will become of me?" To you also the word is, "Trust in the Lord with all thine heart." God hath placed on record a special promise for your comfort: "And even to your old age I am He; and even to hoar hairs will I carry you: I have made, and I will bear; even I will carry, and will deliver you" (Isa. 46:4). Then can you not fully trust Him!

Perhaps another is thinking, "It is the prospects of *to-morrow* which renders me so uneasy and fearful. I know that God says 'sufficient unto the day is the evil thereof,' but I cannot help looking forward and anticipating the pressing emergency ahead of me." Very well, if you must look forward, look upward, too. *God* is on the throne, and He will not vacate it when the morrow arrives! Is it not written,

STUDIES IN THE SCRIPTURES

"Search the Scriptures" John 5: 39

Copyright in all English-speaking Countries.

Editor: Arthur W. Pink, 7 The Crescent, Surbiton, Surrey, England.
Hon. Agent in U.S.A.: Mr. C. S. Pressel, 559 Dupont Avenue, York, Penna.
Hon. Agent in Australia: Mr. G. Ardill, The Christian Workers' Depot. Commonwealth and Reservoir Streets, Sydney.

FREE TO ALL WHO WILL READ IT

REASONING REPUDIATED.

"And lean not unto thine own understanding."—Prov. 3:5.

To "lean unto our own understanding" is to trust in our own wisdom, it is to be guided by what the world calls "common sense," it is to rely upon the dictates of human reason. The objector may reply, "God has endowed me with the reasoning faculty, shall I not use it?" To which we reply, The highest act of reason is to bow before the wisdom of God and be controlled by His unerring Word. But, alas, fallen men, in the pride of their hearts, had rather walk by sight than by faith: "having the understanding darkened, being alienated from the life of God through the ignorance that is in them, because of the blindness of their heart" (Eph. 4:18).

The connection between the words of our text and the first clause in the verse, is not difficult to trace; it forms a supplementary word of warning. It is this very leaning unto our own understanding, or reasoning things out, which so often hinders us from trusting in the Lord with all our hearts. A similar supplementary warning is found in Matt. 21:21: added to "if ye have faith" is "and doubt not," which shows the danger of unbelief coming in afterwards and preventing the fruits of faith. So the great obstacle against *continued* whole-hearted trust in the Lord is leaning unto our own understanding.

To lean unto our own understanding is to rest upon a broken reed, for it has been deranged by sin. That is why we need to constantly seek counsel and instruction from the Scriptures, which are given not only to reveal the way to heaven, but also to guide us through this dark world (2 Peter 1:19). God's Word is given to be "a lamp unto our feet, and a light unto our path," and it is because we have failed to use this Divine provision that we have had so many slips and falls. Experience shows that more grace is needed to repudiate our own wisdom than to abandon our own righteousness.

It is both solemn and humbling to see how many of the most eminent saints have failed at this point. Abraham, at the very time he responded to God's call to leave the land of his birth, instead of fully trusting the Lord to care for his wife as well as himself, leaned unto his own understanding, and instructed her to pose as his sister (Gen. 20:13). Jacob, instead of trusting the Lord to make good His promise, relied upon human expediency and trickery. Moses, after God had graciously supplied the Cloud to guide them by day and by night (Num. 9:18-20), said to Hobab, "We are journeying unto the place of which the Lord said, I will give it you: come thou with us, and we will do thee good: for the Lord hath spoken good concerning Israel. And he said unto him, I will not go; but I will depart to mine own land, and to my kindred. And he said, Leave us not, I pray thee; forasmuch as thou knowest how we are to encamp in the wilderness and *thou* mayest be to us instead of eyes" (Num. 10:29-31).

The policy of Moses was dictated by natural prudence. Knowing that his father-in-law was thoroughly familiar with the wilderness, he concluded that he would be a suitable and competent guide. It is hard to imagine Moses being so foolish, yet

(Continued on Page 216.)

IMPORTANT NOTICES

Back numbers of each year of the magazine are yet obtainable at 5/- (1.25) per year. Bound at 7/6 (1.75) post paid. They will soon be out of print. Those in U.S.A. wanting them, please purchase from Mr. Pressel (see front cover page).

Advise promptly of change of address. This Magazine is published as a work of faith and labour of love. The Editor gladly gives his services. It is freely sent to all who will read it. No charge is made for it.

Christians who feel definitely led to do so, may have fellowship with us in this Ministry. Send only *Inter-National M.O.*

CONTENTS.

	Page.
Hebrews	194
Gleanings in Exodus	200
Scope of Matt. 24	205
Our Greatest Need	209

THE EPISTLE TO THE HEBREWS.

9. Christ Superior to Angels (Heb. 2:9-11.)

In our last article we were obliged, through lack of space, to break off our exposition of Heb. 2 in the middle of a verse; to have continued further would have required us to go to the end of v. 11, and this would have made it much too long. However, the point at which we left off really completed the first thought which the apostle establishes in our present section. As we sought to show, at v. 5 the apostle begins meeting an objection which might be, and most probably was, made against what he had set forth in chapter one, namely, the immeasurable superiority of the Mediator, Israel's Messiah, above the angels. Over against this, two difficulties stood in the way, which needed clearing up.

First, How could Christ be superior to angels, seeing that He was *Man?* Second, How could He possess a greater excellency than they, seeing that He had died? The first difficulty was satisfactorily removed by an appeal to Psalm 8, where God had affirmed, in predictive language, that He had crowned "man" with glory and honour and had put "all things in subjection under his feet." To this the objector would rejoin, "But now we see not yet all things put under him" (v. 8), how, then, does Psalm 8 prove your point? In this way, answers the apostle, In that even now, "we see (by faith) *Jesus* crowned with glory and honour," and in *His* exaltation we find the ground and guarantee, the proof and pledge, of the coming exaltation of all His people.

In the remainder of this most interesting portion of Heb. 2, we shall see how the Holy Spirit enabled the beloved apostle to meet and dispose of the second difficulty of the Jews in a manner equally convincing and satisfactory as He had dealt with their first objection. Though it be true that angels do not and cannot die (Luke 20:36), and though it be a fact that Jesus had died, yet this by no means went to show that He was inferior to them. *This* is the particular point which the apostle is here treating of and which it will now be our object to consider.

First, he shows *why* it was necessary for Christ to die, namely, in order that He should taste death for every son, or, as it reads in the A.V., "for every man" (v. 9). Second, he declares that God had a benevolent design in suffering His Son to stoop so low: it was by His grace that He so "tasted death" (v. 9). Third, he affirms that such a course of procedure was *suited* to the nature and honouring to the glory of Him who orders all things: it "became Him" (v. 10). Fourth, he argues that this was inevitable because of Christ's oneness with His people (v. 11). Fifth, he quotes three O.T. passages in proof of the union which exists between the Redeemer and the redeemed. Let us now turn to our passage and attentively weigh its details.

"But we see Jesus, who was made a little lower that the angels, for the suffering of death, crowned with glory and honour; that He, by the grace of God, should taste death for every man" (v. 9). The central thought of this verse was before us in the preceding article, namely, the exaltation of the once-humbled One. Now we must examine its several clauses and note their relation to each other. Really, there are five things in this verse, each of which we shall consider. First, the humiliation of the Mediator: "But we see Jesus, who was made a little lower than the angels." Second, the character of His humiliation: "For," or much better "by the suffering of death." Third, the object of His humiliation: to "taste death for every man," better "every son." Fourth, the moving cause of His humiliation: "by the grace of God." Fifth, the reward of

His humiliation: "crowned with glory and honour."

"But we see Jesus, who was made a little lower than the angels." How these words should melt our hearts and move our souls to profoundest wonderment! That He, the Creator of angels, the Lord of them, the One who before His incarnation had been worshipped by them, should be "made lower" than they; and this for *our* sakes! Our hearts must indeed be dead if they are not thrilled and filled with praise as we ponder that fathomless stoop. As was pointed out under our exposition of v. 7, the Greek word here for "little" is used in the N.T. in two senses: sometimes where it is a matter of degree, at others where it is a case of time. Here it is the latter, for "a little season." In what particular sense the apostle is here contemplating Christ's being "made lower" than the angels, the next clause tells us.

"For the suffering of death." Many have experienced difficulty with this clause. That which has exercised them is whether the words "for the suffering of death" state the *purpose for which* Christ was "made a little lower than the angels," or, whether "for the suffering of death" gives the *reason why* He has been "crowned with glory and honour." Personally, we are fully satisfied that neither of these give the real thought.

The difficulty mentioned above is self-created. It is occasioned by failure to rightly define the reference to Christ's being made "a little lower than the angels." As already stated, we believe this signified "for a little while." If the reader will turn back again to our comments on 2:7 he will see we have adopted the suggestion of Dr. J. Brown to the effect that the specific reference is to *mortality*, the angels being incapable of dying. This, we are assured, is the meaning of the verse now before us. All ambiguity concerning this clause of v. 9 disappears if the first word be rendered "by" instead of "for." The English translators actually give "by" in the margin. The Greek preposition is "dia," and is translated "by" again and again, both when it governs a noun in the accusative or the genitive case.

Thus by altering "for" to "by" it will be seen that in this third clause the Holy Spirit has graciously defined His meaning in the second: (1) "But we see Jesus;" (2) "who was made a little season lower than the angels;" (3) "by the suffering of death." It was in *this* particular that Jesus was made for a season lower than the angels, namely, by His passing through a death of sufferings—an experience which, by virtue of the constitution God had given them, they were incapable of enduring. Therefore, the point here seized by the Holy Spirit in affirming that Jesus had been made lower than the angels, was *His mortality*. But here we must be very careful to explain our terms. When we say that Christ, by virtue of His incarnation, became "mortal," it must not be understood that He was subject to death in His body as the fallen descendants of Adam are. His humanity was holy and incorruptible: no seed or germ of death was in it, or could attack it. He laid down His life of Himself (John 10:18). No; what we mean is, and what Scripture teaches is, that in becoming man Christ took upon Him a nature that was *capable of* dying. This the angels were not; and in *this* respect He was, for a season, made lower than they.

"By the suffering of death." This expression denotes that Christ's exit from the land of the living was no easy or gentle one, but a death of "suffering"; one accompanied with much inward agony and outward torture. It was the "death of the cross" (Phil. 2:8). It was a death in which He suffered not only at the hands of men and of Satan, but from God Himself. It was a death in which He fully satisfied the demands of infinite holiness and justice. This was a task which no mere creature was capable of performing. Behold here, then, the wonder of wonders: Christ undertook a work which was far above the power of all the angels, and yet to effect it He was made lower than them! If ever power was made perfect in weakness, it was in this!

"Crowned with glory and honour." This is the dominant clause of the verse. Concerning it we cannot do better than quote from Mr. C. H. Welch: "The crowning with glory and honour is the consecration of Christ as the Priest after the order of Melchizekek. 'And no man taketh this *honour* unto himself. . . . So also Christ *glorified* not Himself' (Heb. 5:4, 5). We shall find an allusion to this in 3:3, for this man was counted worthy of more *glory* than Moses, inasmuch as He who builded the house hath more *honour* than the house.' Thus we find Christ superior in honour and glory to both Moses and Aaron; and when we see Him crowned with honour and glory we are indeed considering Him who is the Apostle (Moses) and High Priest (Aaron) of our profession."

Here, then, is the first part of the apostle's answer to that which was, for the Jews, the great "stumbling-block" (1 Cor. 1:23). He who by the suffering of death had been made, for a little season, lower than the angels, has, because of His humiliation and perfect atoning sacrifice, been "highly exalted" by God Himself. He has been "raised far above all principality and power, and might and dominion, and every name that is named, not only in this world, but also in that which is to come" (Eph. 1:21). It is not simply that this exaltation followed the Mediator's suffering and death, but, as the "therefore" in Isa. 53:12 and the "wherefore" of Phil. 2:9 plainly denote, were the meritorious reward thereof. Thus, so far from the Cross needing an apology, it has magnified the Saviour. So far from Christ's degradation and death being something of which the Christian need be ashamed, they are the very reason why God has so signally rewarded Him. The "crown of thorns" which man gave Him, has been answered by the "crown of glory and honour" that God has bestowed upon Him. The humbled Christ is humiliated no longer; the Throne of the Universe is where He is now seated.

Ere passing on to the next verse, let us ask the reader, Have *you* "crowned with glory and honour" Him whom the world has cast out? Do you, in a practical way, own Him as your Lord and Master? Is *His* glory and honour ever the paramount consideration before you? Is He receiving from you the devotion and adoration of a worshipping heart? *"Worthy* is the Lamb." O may He, indeed, occupy the throne of our hearts and reign as King over our lives. In what esteem does the Father hold His once humiliated Son: He has crowned Him with glory and honour; then what *must* He yet do with those who "despise and reject" Him?

"That He by the grace of God should taste death for every man." Here is the second part of the apostle's answer to the Jews' objection. God had a benevolent design in permitting His Son for a season, to become lower than the angels. The end in view fully justified the means. Only by the Son tasting death could the sons of God be delivered from the ruins of the fall; only thus could the righteousness and mercy of God be reconciled. This, we take it, indicates the relation of this final clause to the remainder of the verse: God's *design* in making His Son lower than the angels was that He might become the Redeemer of His people. The opening conjunction "that" (hopos, meaning "to the end that"), expressing purpose, is conclusive.

There has been considerable discussion as to the precise import of the expression "tasted death." Here, as ever in Scripture, there is a fulness in the language used which no brief definitions of man can ever embrace. The first and most obvious thought suggested by the language is, that the Saviour consciously, sensibly, experienced the bitterness of death. "The death of our Lord Jesus Christ was a slow and painful death; He was 'roasted with fire' as was prefigured by the Paschal lamb. But it was not merely that it lasted a considerable time, that it was attended with agony of mind as well as pain of body; but that He came, as no finite creature can come, into contact with death. He tasted death; all that was in death was concentrated in that cup which the Lord Jesus Christ emptied on the cross" (Saphir).

He tasted that awful death *by anticipation*. From the beginning of His ministry (yea, before that, as His words in Luke 2:49 plainly show), there was ever present to his consciousness the Cross, with all its horror, see Matt. 16:21, John 2:4, 3:16, etc. At Calvary He actually drained the bitter cup. The death He tasted was, "The curse which sin brings, the penalty of the broken law, the manifestation of the power of the devil, the expression of the wrath of God; and in all these aspects the Lord Jesus Christ came into contact with death, and tasted it to the very last" (Saphir).

"That He by the grace of God should taste death for every man." The opening words of this clause set forth the efficient cause which moved the Godhead in sending forth the Son to submit to such unparalleled humiliation: it was the free favour of God. It was not because that the ends of Divine government required mercy should be shown to its rebels, still less because that they had any claim upon Him. There is nothing whatever outside God Himself which moves Him to do anything: He "worketh all things after the counsel of His *own* will" (Eph. 1:11). It was solely by the grace and good pleasure of God, and not by the violence of man or Satan, that the Lord Jesus was brought to the Cross to die. The appointment of that costly sacrifice must be traced back to nothing but the sovereign benignity of God.

"For every man." This rendering is quite misleading. "Anthropos," the Greek word for "man" is *not* in the verse at all. Thus, one of the principal texts relied upon by Arminians in their unscriptural contentions for a general atonement vanishes into thin air. The R.V. places the word "man" in italics to show that it is not found in the original. The Greek is "panta" and signifies "every one," that is, every one of those who form the subjects of the whole passage—every one of "the heirs of salvation" (1:14), every one of the "sons" (2:10), every one of the "brethren" (2:11). We may say that this is the view of the passage taken by Drs. Gouge and J. Brown, by Saphir, and a host of others who might be mentioned. Theologically it is demanded by the "tasted death *for* every one," i.e., substitutionally, in the room of, that *they* might not. Hence, every one for whom He tasted death shall themselves never do so (see John 8:52), and this is true *only* of the people of God.

What we have just said above is confirmed by many Scriptures. "For the transgression of *My people* was He stricken" said God (Isa. 53:8), and all mankind are not His "people." "I lay down My life *for the sheep* said the Son" (John 10:10), but every man is not of Christ's sheep (John 10:26). Christ makes intercession on behalf of those for whom He died (Rom. 8:34), but He prays not for the world (see John 17:9). Those for whom he died are redeemed (Rev. 5:9), and from redemption necessarily follows the forgiveness of sins (Col. 1:14), but all have not their sins forgiven.

"For it became Him, for whom are all things, and by. whom are all things, in bringing many sons unto glory, to make the captain of their salvation perfect through sufferings" (v. 10). This gives the third part of the apostle's reply to the objection which he is here rebutting, and a most arresting statement it is: he now takes still higher ground, advancing that which should indeed bow our hearts in worship. The word "became" means suited to, in accord with, the character of God. It was consonant with the Divine attributes that the Son should, for a season, be "made lower than the angels" in order to "taste death" for His people. It was not only according to God's eternal purpose, but it was also suited to all His wondrous perfections. Never was God more Godlike than when, in the person of Jesus, He was crucified for our sins.

"For it became Him, for whom are all things, and by whom are all things, in bringing many sons unto glory, to make the captain of their salvation perfect through sufferings." There are five things in this verse claiming our reverent and diligent attention. First, the particular character in which God is here viewed; as the One "for whom are all things and by whom are all things." Second, the manner in which it "became" the Most High to bring many sons unto glory by giving up His beloved Son to the awful death of the cross. Third, the particular character in which the Son Himself is here viewed: as "The Captain of our salvation." Fourth in what sense He was, or could be, "made perfect through sufferings." Fifth, the result of this Divine appointment: the actual conducting of many sons "unto glory."

First, then, the special character in which God is here viewed. "For it became Him, for whom are all things, and by whom are all things." This expression sets forth the high sovereignty of God in the most unqualified and absolute manner: "all things" without exception, that is, all creatures, all events. "For whom are all things" affirms that the Most High God is the Final Cause of everything: "The Lord hath made all things *for* Himself" (Prov. 16:4), i.e., to fulfill His own designs, to accomplish His own purpose, to redound to His own glory. So again we read in Rev. 4:11, "Thou art worthy, O Lord, to receive glory and honour and power: for Thou hast created all things, and *for* Thy pleasure they are and were created." This blessed, basic, yet stupendous truth is to be received with unquestioning and unmurmuring faith. He who maketh the wrath of man to praise Him (Psa. 76:10) will not only vindicate His broken law in the punishment of the wicked, but His justice and holiness shall be magnified by their destruction. Hell itself will redound to His glory.

"And by whom are all things." Every creature that exists, every event which happens, is by God's own appointment and agency. Nothing comes to pass or can do so without the will of God. Satan could not tempt Peter without Christ's permission; the demons could not enter the swine till He gave them leave; not a sparrow falls to the ground apart from His decree. This is only another way of saying that God actually *governs* the world which He has made. True, there is much, very much in His government which *we* cannot understand, for how can the finite comprehend the Infinite? He Himself tells us that His ways are "past finding out," yet His own infallible word declares, "For of Him, and through Him, and to Him are all things: to whom be glory forever" (Rom. 11:36).

"For whom are all things, and by whom are all things." Nothing so stirs up the enmity of the carnal mind and evidences the ignorance, the sin, and the high-handed rebellion of fallen man as the response which he makes when this great fact and solemn truth is pressed upon him. People at once complain, if this be so, then we are mere puppets, irresponsible creatures. Or worse, they will blasphemously argue, If this be true, then God, and not ourselves, is to be charged with our wickedness. To such sottish revilings, only one reply is forthcoming, "Nay but, O man, who art thou that repliest against God? Shall the thing formed say to Him that formed it, Why hast Thou made me thus?" (Rom. 9:20).

Consider now the *appropriateness* of this title or appellation of Diety. The varied manner in which God refers to Himself in the Scriptures, the different titles He there assumes are not regulated by caprice, but are ordered by infinite wisdom; and we lose much if we fail to attentively weigh each one. As illustrations of this principle consider the following. In Rom. 15:5 He is spoken of as "The God of patience and hope": this, in keeping with the subject of the four preceding verses. In 2 Cor. 4:6 He is presented thus: "God who commanded the light to shine out of darkness hath shined in our hearts," which is in beautiful keeping with the theme of the five preceding verses. In Heb. 13:20 it is "The God of Peace" that brought again from the dead our Lord Jesus. Why? Because His holy wrath had been placated at the cross. So in Heb. 2:10 the apostle would silence the proud and wicked reasoning of the Jews by reminding them that they were replying against the Sovereign Supreme. For Him are all things and by Him are all things: His glory is the end of everything, His will the law of the universe; therefore, to quarrel with *His method* of bringing many sons unto glory was insubordination and blasphemy of the worst kind.

And what are the *practical bearings* upon us of this title of God? First, an *acknowledgement* of God in this character is due from us and required by Him. To believe and affirm that "for Him are all things, and by Him are all things" is simply owning that He *is* God—high above all, supreme over all, directing all. Anything short of this is, really, atheism. Second, *contentment* is the sure result to a heart which really lays hold of and rests upon this truth. If I really believe that "all things" are for God's glory and by His invincible and perfect will, then I shall receive submissively, yea, thankfully, whatsoever He ordains and sends me. The language of such an one must be, "It is the Lord: let Him do what seemeth Him good" (1 Sam. 3:18). Third, *confidence and praise* will be the outcome. God only does that which "becomes" Him; therefore, whatsoever He does must be right and best. Those who truly recognise this "*know* that all things work together for good to them that love God" (Rom. 8:28). True it is that our short-sighted and sin-darkened vision is often unable to see *why* God does certain things, yet we may be fully assured that He always has a wise and holy reason.

"For it became Him." More immediately, the opening "for" gives a reason for what has been advanced at the close of v. 9. Should it be reverently inquired why God's "grace" chose *such* a way for the redeeming of His elect, here is the ready answer: it "became Him" so to do. The Greek term signifies the answerableness or agreement of one thing to another. Thus, "speak thou the things that *become* sound doctrine" (Titus 2:1), i.e., that are agreeable thereto. So, too, the Greek term implies the *comeliness* of a thing. Thus, "which *become* women professing godliness (1 Tim. 2:10). The adorning of Christian women with good works is a comely thing, yea, it is the beauty and glory of their profession. In like manner the grace of God which gave Christ to taste death for His people, answered to the love of His heart and agreed with the holiness of His nature. Such an appointment was suited to God's character, consonant with His attributes, agreeable to his perfections. Never did anything more exhibit, and never will anything more redound to the glory of God than His making the Son lower than the angels in order to taste death for His people. A wide field of thought is here set before us. Let us, briefly, enter into a few details.

It "became" God's *wisdom*. His wisdom is evidenced in all His works, but nowhere so perspicuously or conspicuously as at Calvary. The cross was the masterpiece of Omniscience. It was there that God exhibited the solution to a problem which no finite intelligence could ever have solved, namely, how justice and mercy might be perfectly harmonised. How was it possible for righteousness to uphold the claims of the law and yet for grace to be extended to its transgressors? It seemed impossible. These were the things which the angels desired to look into, but so profound were their depths they had no line with which to fathom them. But the cross supplies the solution.

It "became" the *holiness* of God. What is His holiness? It is impossible for human language to supply an adequate definition. Perhaps about as near as we can come to one is to say, It is the antithesis of evil, the very nature of God hating sin. Again and again during O.T. times God manifested His displeasure against sin, but never did the white light of God's holiness shine forth so vividly as at Calvary, where we see Him smiting His own Beloved because the sins of His people had been transferred to Him.

It "became" His *power*. Never was the power of God so marvellously displayed as it was at Golgotha. Wherein does this appear? In that the Mediator was enabled to endure within the space of three hours what it will take an eternity to expend upon the wicked. All the waves and billows of Divine wrath went over Him (Psa. 42:7). Yet was He not destroyed. There was concentrated into those three hours of darkness that which the lost will suffer forever and ever, and nothing but the power of God could have upheld the suffering Saviour. Yea, only a Divine Saviour could have stood up under that storm of outpoured wrath; that is why God said, "I have laid help upon One that is *mighty*" (Psa. 89:19).

It "became" His *righteousness*. He can by no means clear the guilty. Sin must be punished where ever it is found. God's justice would not abate any of its demands when sin, through imputation, was found upon Christ: as Rom. 8:32 says, He "spared not His own Son." Never was the righteousness of God more illustriously exhibited than when it cried, "Awake, O sword, against My Shepherd, and against the Man that is My Fellow saith the Lord of hosts: smite the Shepherd" (Zech. 13:7).

It "became" the *love* and *grace* of God. Innumerable tokens of these have and do His children receive, but the supreme proof of them is furnished at the cross. "Herein is love, not that we loved God, but that He loved us, and sent His Son to be the propitiation for our sins" (1 John 4:10). The mercy of God is over all His works, but never so fully and so gloriously was it manifested as when Christ became Man and was made a curse for His people, that theirs might be the blessing.

We must next consider the special character in which the Saviour Himself is here contemplated: "The Captain of their salvation." This is one out of more than three hundred titles given to the Lord Jesus in the Scriptures, each of which has its own distinctive meaning and preciousness. The Greek word is "Archegos," and is found four times in the N.T. It signifies the "Chief Leader." It is the word rendered "Author" in Heb. 12:1, though that is an unhappy rendition. It is translated "Prince" in Acts 3:15 and 5:31. Thus, it is a title which calls attention to and emphasises the dignity and glory of our Saviour, yet, in His mediatorial character.

It needs to be borne in mind that in N.T. days the "captain" of a regiment did not remain in the rear issuing instructions to his officers, but took the lead, and by his own personal example encouraged and inspired his soldiers to deeds of valour.

Thus the underlying thoughts of this title are, Christ's going before His people, leading His soldiers, and being in command of them. He has "gone before" them in three respects. First, in the way of obedience, see John 13:15. Second, in the way of suffering, see 1 Peter 2:21. Third, in the way of glory: He has entered heaven as our forerunner, so that faith says, "Thanks be unto God which giveth us the victory through our Lord Jesus Christ." Thus it will be seen that v. 10 continues the same thought as v. 9.

"The Captain of their salvation." The plain and necessary implication of this title is that we are passing through a country full of difficulties, dangers, oppositions, like Israel in the Wilderness on their way to the promised inheritance; so that we need a Captain, Guide, Leader, to carry us safely through. This title of Christ's, then, is for the *encouragement* of our hearts: the grace, the faithfulness, and the power of our Leader guarantees the successful issue of our warfare. It teaches us once more that the *whole* work of our salvation, from first to last, has been committed by God into the hands of Christ.

"To make the Captain of their salvation perfect through sufferings." This sentence has occasioned real trouble to many: how can a perfect person be "made perfect?" But the difficulty is more imaginary than real. The reference is not to the person of Christ, but to a particular office which He fills. His character needed no "perfecting." Unlike us, no course of discipline was required by Him to subdue faults and to develop virtues. We believe that Heb. 5:9 supplies the key to the words we are now considering: "being made perfect, He became the author of eternal salvation unto all them that obey Him." The previous verse speaks of Christ "learning obedience" by the things which He suffered," which does not mean that He learned to obey, but rather that He learned by experience what obedience is. In like manner it was by the experiences through which He passed that Christ was "perfected," not experimentally, but officially, to be "the Captain" of our salvation. A striking type of this is furnished by the case of Joshua, who, as the result of his experiences in the wilderness, became experimentally qualified to be Israel's "captain," leading them into Canaan.

"To make the Captain of their salvation perfect through sufferings." Two other things need to be borne in mind: the particular design of this passage, and the special purpose and aim of the Epistle as a whole. The special design of the apostle was to remove the scandal of Christ's humiliating death, which was such a stumbling-block to the Jews. Therefore, he here affirms that the sufferings of Christ eventuated not in ignominy but glory: they "perfected" His equipment to be the "Captain" of His people, v. 18 amplifies. In regard to the scope of the Epistle as a whole, this word of the apostle's was well calculated to *comfort* the afflicted and sorely-tried Hebrews: their own Captain had reached glory via sufferings—sufficient for His soldiers to follow the same path. Thus, this word here is closely parallel with 1 Peter 4:1.

It should be added that the Greek word for "perfected" is rendered "consecrated" in 7:28. By His sufferings Christ became qualified and was solemnly appointed to be our Leader. It was *by* His sufferings that He vanquished all His and our foes, triumphing gloriously over them, and thus He became fitted to be our "Captain." What reason have we then to *glory* in the Cross of Christ! The eye of faith sees there not only consummate wisdom, matchless mercy, fathomless love, but victory, triumph, glory. By dying He slew death.

"In bringing many sons unto glory." This is both the Captain's work and reward. The term "glory" is one of the most comprehensive words used in all the Bible. It is almost impossible to define; perhaps "the sum of all excellency" is as near as we can come to it. It means that the "many sons" will be raised to the highest possible state and position of dignity and honour. It is *Christ's own* "glory" into which they are brought: "And the glory which Thou gavest Me I have given them; that they may be one, even as we are one" (John 17:22, and see Col. 3:4).

Into this "glory" *many* sons are to come. Some have difficulty in harmonsing this word with "many be called, but *few* chosen" (Matt. 20:16). In contrast from the vast multitudes which perish, God's elect are indeed "few" (Matt. 7:14); His flock is only a "little" one (Luke 12:32). Yet, considered by themselves, the redeemed of all generations will constitute "many."

Into this "glory" the many sons do not merely "come," but are *"brought."* It is the same word as in Luke 10:34 where the Good Samaritan "brought" the poor man that was wounded and half dead, and who could not "come" of himself, to the "inn." Let the reader consult these additional passages: Song of Sol. 2:4; Isa. 42:16; 1 Peter 3:18. This "bringing" of the many sons "unto glory" is in distinct stages. At regeneration they are brought from death unto life. At the Lord's return they will be brought to the Father's House (1 Thess. 4:16, 17). The whole is summarised in the parable of the lost sheep; see Luke 15:4-6.

In closing, let us ask the reader, Are *you* one of these many "sons" whom Christ is bringing "unto glory"? Are you quite sure that you are? It is written, "As many as are led by the Spirit of God, they are the sons of God" (Rom. 8:14). Is *this* true of you? Can others see the *evidences* of it? Is your daily life controlled by self-will, the ways of the world, the pleasing of your friends and relatives, or by the *written Word*, for that is what the Spirit uses in leading His sons.

Above we have contemplated that which "became" God; let our final consideration be that which "becomes" His favoured children. "Let your conversation (manner of life) be as it *becometh* the Gospel of Christ" (Phil 1:27). If we are now light in the Lord, let us "walk *as* children of light" (Eph. 5:8). Let us seek grace to "walk worthy of the vocation wherewith we are called" (Eph. 4:1).

—*Arthur W. Pink.*

GLEANINGS IN EXODUS.

57. *The Appointed Artificers: Ex.* 31:1-11.

The 31st of Exodus is an important chapter, both in its typical teachings and its practical lessons. There are three things in it: first, we are shown the Divine provision which was made for the carrying out of Jehovah's instructions concerning the building of the tabernacle and the making of its furniture; second, the Divinely-appointed Sabbath in its special relation to Israel is here defined; third, the actual giving to Moses of the two tables of the testimony, on which were written, by the finger of God, the ten commandments, is here recorded.

Full instructions concerning all the details of the tabernacle had now been given; the provision for the execution of them is next made known. Nothing is left to chance, no place allowed for human scheming. All is of God. Though skilled in all the wisdom of the Egyptians, Moses was not left to draw the plans for Jehovah's dwelling-place; instead, he was bidden to make all things after the pattern shown him in the mount. Now that the "pattern" had been completely set before him, the Lord makes known *who* are to be the principal workmen. The choice of them was His, not Moses'; and their equipment for the work was Divine and not human.

The appointed artificers were Bezaleel and Aholiab, one from the tribe of Judah, the other from the tribe of Dan. We do not have here the actual making of the tabernacle, that is seen in chapters 36 to 39; rather is it the Divine calling and making competent of those who were to engage in that work. That Christ is the One here foreshadowed is evident, for "in the volume of the book it is written of *Me*" is His own express declaration. None but He was capable of building a House for God, and every detail of our present type clearly establishes that fact. May the Spirit of God grant us eyes to see.

"And the Lord spake unto Moses, saying, See, I have called by name Bezaleel, the son of Uri, the son of Hur, of the tribe of Judah: And I have filled him with the Spirit of God, in wisdom, and understanding, and in knowledge, and in all manner of workmanship, to devise cunning (skilful) works, to work in gold, and in silver, and in brass, and in cutting of stones, to set them, and in carving of timber; to work in all manner of workmanship" (vv. 1-5).

In the above verses we have three things: the workman appointed, the workman equipped, the workman's task. Here, as ever in Holy Writ, the proper nouns are pregnant with spiritual significance. The first of the two principal artificers here mentioned is Bezaleel, which means "In the shadow of God" or "the protection of God." He was the son of Uri, which means "light"; the grandson of Hur, which means "free"; from the tribe of Judah, which means "praise." The suitability of these names for one who foreshadowed the person of our Saviour is at once evident.

The similarity of thought between "shadow" and "protection" may be seen by a reference to a number of scriptures in which the former is found. "Hide me under the shadow of Thy wings" (Psa. 17:8); "In the shadow of Thy wings will I make my refuge" (Psa. 57:1); "In the shadow of Thy wings will I rejoice" (Psa. 63:7). The "shadow of Thy wings" speaks of the place of intimacy, of protection, of fellowship. This is the place which the Lord Jesus has ever occupied in His relationship to the Father: "The only begotten Son which is in the *bosom* of the Father" (John 1:18).

Bezaleel was the son of Uri, "light," viz., "the light of Jehovah." The "urim" of the high priests's breastplate is the same word, in the plural number. Now, as the name "Bezaleel" suggests the *place* occupied by the perfect Workman, the Builder of the "true tabernacle," so the "son of Uri" defines His *person*, telling us who He is. The "Son of Light" at once announces that He is the Son of God, for "God is light, and in Him is no darkness at all" (1 John 1:5). Yes, He is "the Brightness of His glory, and the very impress of His substance" (Heb. 1:3). While here on earth, He was "The Light of the world" (John 9:5). When He returns to it, it will be as "the Sun of Righteousness."

Bezaleel was the son of Uri, the son of "Hur," which means "free," or "at liberty." This is very blessed. As the first name speaks of Christ's relation to the Father, and the second tells who He is, so this third one makes known the *manner* in which He entered upon His Divinely-appointed work. That which was here foreshadowed is told out in plain terms in Heb. 10:9, "Then said He, I come to do Thy will, O God." The Lord Jesus *voluntarily* entered upon the great work which He undertook. True it is that the Father "sent" Him (John 9:4, etc.); yet, equally true is it that He "came." Perfectly does this come out in our type: Bezaleel was "called" by God to his work (v. 2), yet was he a son of "liberty."

"Of the tribe of Judah." Beautiful line in the picture is this. Judah was, of course, the royal tribe, as also the one who took the lead when Israel journeyed. But it is the meaning of his name which it is so blessed to note: Judah signifies "praise." Does not this tell us the *spirit* in which the Redeemer entered into His work, that work which involved such humiliation, such suffering, such a death! Listen to His own words in Psalm 40:8, "I *delight* to do Thy will, O God." Behold Him at the very time He was being despised and rejected of men: "In that hour Jesus *rejoiced* in spirit, and said, I thank Thee O Father, Lord of heaven and earth, that Thou hast hid these things from the wise and prudent" (Luke 10:21). Let it be added that while there are not a few of the Psalms which breathe out the sorrows and sufferings of Christ, there are also many of them which express thanksgiving and praise.

Next we have the equipment or qualification of the typical artificer for his work: "And I have filled him with the Spirit of God, in wisdom, and in understanding, and in knowledge, and in all manner of workmanship." This at once makes us think of Isa. 11:1-4, "And there shall come forth a rod out of the stem of Jesse, and a branch shall grow out of his roots: And the Spirit of the Lord shall rest upon Him, the Spirit of wisdom and understanding, the Spirit of counsel and might, the Spirit of knowledge and the fear of the Lord; and shall make Him of quick understanding in the fear of the Lord: and He shall not judge after the sight of His eyes, neither reprove after the hearing of His ears. But with righteousness shall He judge the poor, and reprove with equity for the meek of the earth."

"To work in gold." As it has been pointed out so frequently in previous articles, "gold" speaks of Divine glory, the Divine glory manifested. Ah, only one filled with "the Spirit of God, in wisdom and understanding and in knowledge" was competent to "work in gold." Now, it is in the Gospel of John that the antitype of this is most plainly seen. There, at the close of His public ministry, we find the Son saying to the Father, "I have *glorified* Thee on the earth: I have finished *the work* which Thou gavest Me to do." Details of that "work" are given in the verses that follow: "I have manifested Thy name" (v. 6), "I have given unto them the words which Thou gavest Me" (v. 8), "I have kept them in Thy name" (v. 12), etc.

"And in silver." This symbol has also been before us again and again. It speaks of *redemption*. And who was qualified to "work in silver?" None but He who came from the Father's bosom as the Son of Light. The work of redemption was a more stupendous and wondrous one than the work of creation. It was a work far beyond the power of those who were to be redeemed: "None of them can by any means redeem his brother nor give to God a ransom for him: for the redemption of their soul is precious" (Psa. 49:7, 8). Yes, the redemption of their soul *is* "precious," so precious that naught but the "the precious blood of Christ, as of a lamb without blemish and without spot" (1 Peter 1:19) could avail. The blessed outcome of His "work in silver" is seen in Rev. 5:9, "And they sung a new song, saying, Thou art worthy to take the book, and to open the seals thereof: for Thou was slain, and hast *redeemed* us to God by Thy blood out of *every* kindred, and tongue, and people, and nation."

"And in brass." This is ever the symbol of Divine *judgment*. Here, too, a Divinely-qualified workman was called for, for no mere creature as such was capable of enduring the entire weight of God's judgment upon the sins of His guilty people. Therefore, did God lay help upon One that is "Mighty". (Psa. 89:19). Unspeakably solemn is this aspect of our type. It tells of our blessed Redeemer being "made sin for us" (2 Cor. 5:21), which signifies that He became sacrificially what we were personally. It tells of Him being "made a curse for us" (Gal. 3:13), suffering the inflexible penalty of God's righteous law on our behalf, receiving the wages of sin in our stead. It tells of Him being "lifted up" as Moses lifted up the serpent of brass (John 3:14). The "work in brass" was completed when He cried "It is finished," bowed His head, and breathed forth His spirit (John 19:30).

"And in cutting of stones." The local reference is to the jewels which were to adorn the shoulders and breastplate of Israel's high priest, as he appeared before God on their behalf, jewels on which were engraved the names of all their twelve tribes. Thus, those gems spoke of the people of God, presented before Him in all the merits and excellency of that blessed One whom Aaron foreshadowed. The antitype of this is found in 1 Peter 2:5, "Ye also as living *stones,* are built up a spiritual house." The next words of Ex. 31. "and in carving of timber" look forward, we believe, to the Lord's future dealings with Israel. "To work in all manner of workmanship," which is repeated from v. 3, at once reminds us of that word in Eph. 2:10, "For we are His *workmanship,* created in Christ Jesus unto good works." How blessedly significant to observe that the work of this artificer is given (vv. 4, 5)—in *five* details—all is of Divine grace!

"And I, behold, I have given with him Aholiab, the son of Ahisamach, of the tribe of Dan: and in the hearts of all that are wise-hearted I have put wisdom, that they may make all that I have commanded thee" (v. 6). Many human characters were needed to foreshadow the varied and manifold perfections of the God-man. Creation demonstrates the Creator. Some things in creation manifest His mighty power, some His consummate wisdom, others His abiding faithfulness, still others His abundant mercy. Each and all are required to exhibit the different attributes of their Maker. In like manner, Abel, Noah, Moses, Aaron, David, are all types of Christ, each one pointing to some distinctive aspect of His person, offices, or work. Thus it is in our present type: Aholiab supplements Bezaleel.

"And I, behold, I have given with him Aholiab, the son of Ahisamach, of the tribe of Dan." The meanings of these names are also significant. Aholiab signifies "The Tent of the Father." In the light of John 1:14, "And the Word became flesh and dwelt (Greek, *tented*) among us, and we beheld His glory," the force of this name is clear. Just as of old Jehovah took up His abode in the tabernacle in the wilderness, so did He again find a Dwelling-place on this earth when the Son became incarnate: "God was in Christ reconciling the world unto Himself" (2 Cor. 5:19). The Lord Jesus walking among men was "God manifest in flesh" (1 Tim. 3:16). So perfect and complete was that manifestation He could say, "he that hath seen Me, hath seen the Father" (John 14:9).

Aholiab was the son of Ahisamach, and the latter name signifies "Brother of Support." As another has said, "Probably this name primarily refers to the fact that Aholiab was a fellow-helper to Bezaleel in the work of the tabernacle. But is it not worthy of remark that while we have in Aholiab the name *Father*, we have in the name Ahisamach, the word *Brother;* and may there not be in this a little prophetic hint of that truth contained in Heb. 2:9-11, in which we find the Lord Jesus raised from the suffering of death to a place of exaltation, where everything is put under His feet, and in which also it is declared that 'he (the Lord Jesus) who sanctifieth and they who are sanctified, are all of one, for which cause He is not ashamed to call them brethren.' He is the Dwelling-place of God, and He is the Brother of support to His brethren" (H. W. Soltau).

Aholiab was of the tribe of Dan. As Judah took the lead when Israel was on the march, so Dan brought up the rear. Thus, the spiritual principle here exemplified was that, in the two men appointed to be the chief artificers, all Israel were *represented*. So the Lord Jesus, in the glorious work which He accomplished, represented *all* God's people, the feeblest as well as the strongest. The name Dan signifies "Judge." "The tabernacle of God is a place for worship and *praise*, because therein is revealed God's great act of *judgment* upon sin in the sacrifice of the Lamb of God" (H.W.S.).

"That they may make all that I have commanded thee" (v. 6), words repeated in v. 11. Significant line in the typical picture is this. Every detail of their work was Divinely appointed beforehand. No room was there for the exercise of self-will; all was to be the working out of that which God had willed. Most blessed is it to behold the fulfilment of this in the Antitype. Very explicit are His words: "For I came down from heaven, not to do Mine own will, but the will of Him that sent Me" (John 6:38); "Therefore, doth My Father love Me, because I lay down My life, that I might take it again. No man taketh it from Me, but I lay it down of Myself. I have power to lay it down, and I have power to take it again. This *commandment* have I received from My Father" (John 10:17, 18).

There is no need for us to comment separately on each of the details mentioned in vv. 7-11 as they have all been before us in previous articles. It should be noted, though, that *fourteen* things are specified: (1) "The tabernacle of the congregation (the tent of meeting); (2) And the ark of the testimony; (3) and the mercy-seat that is thereupon; (4) and all the furniture of the tabernacle (the pillars, sockets, pins, etc.); (5) and the table, and his furniture," etc. In vv. 4, 5 a fivefold work was mentioned; in vv. 7 to 11 the making of fourteen articles is referred to. This tells us that the work of Christ was founded upon Divine grace, and that in the execution of it He displayed a perfect witness to the perfections of God.

Turning now to the *practical* teaching of our passage, it is at once evident that here we have most important instruction upon the subject of Divine *service*: note how the "See!" (v. 2) and "Behold!" (v. 6) direct attention to the weightiness of what follows. The first thing is God's *selection* of His servants. Bezaleel and Aholiab did not presume to intrude into this holy office of themselves, nor were they appointed by Moses, or by a committee made up of the leading Levites; instead, they were "called" by God (v. 2). "This principle runs through all dispensations. The apostle adduces it when speaking of the priesthood of Christ. He says, 'So also Christ glorified not Himself to be made an high priest; but He that said unto Him, Thou art My Son, to-day have I begotten Thee. As He saith also in another place, Thou art a priest forever after the order of Malchizedek' (Heb. 5:5, 6). In like manner he speaks of himself as an 'apostle by the will of God' (1 Cor. 1:1; 2 Cor. 1:1, etc.)" (Mr. Dennett).

This lies at the foundation of all true service. Those who run without being sent, those who undertake work (though in the name of the Lord) without being called to it by God, are *rebels*, not "servants." Yet how many there are in these days—days which are characterised by self-will and lawlessness—occupying prominent positions in Christendom, yet who have never been called of God. Many, attracted by the prestige and honour of the position, others because it is an easy way of making a living, have thrust themselves into an holy office. Many, influenced by men with more zeal than knowledge, or advised by admiring friends or doting mothers, have been pressed into service for which they had no call from Heaven. Fearful presumption and sin is it for any man to profess to speak in the name of Christ if he has received no call from Him.

The second principle of service which receives both illustration and exemplification in our present passage is God's *equipment* of His servants. It is by this that God's people may identify *His* sent servants, and in this way that an exercised heart may ascertain whether or no a call to service has been received from the Lord. God never calls a man to any work without fitting him for it. If God calls one to be an evangelist, He will fill his heart with compassion for the lost, and so burden him with a sense of the doom awaiting the wicked, that he will cry "Woe is me, if I preach not the Gospel." If God calls a man to be a pastor, He will bestow upon him the necessary gifts; if to be a missionary, He will endow him with a special aptitude for learning a foreign language; and so on.

What is still more to the point, and so essential for us to note is that, when God calls a man to be His servant, He fills him with "the Spirit of God, in wisdom, and in understanding, and in knowledge" (v. 3). For other examples of this, see 1 Kings 7:13, 14; Luke 1:5; Acts 10:38; 2:4; 6:3. Vastly different is this from the expedients and substitutes of men. Colleges, universities, theological seminaries, Bible-training schools do not and cannot impart these spiritual gifts. God alone can bestow them. And where He *has* done so, then all the schools of men are needless. The servant who has been endowed with power and wisdom from on High is entirely independent of men. Human wisdom is of no avail in the service of God. This is all very humbling to the flesh, but it is God's way, for He is a jealous God, and will not share His glory with another.

The third important principle in connection with service to be noted in our passage is God's *appointment* of the servant's work: "that they may make all that I have commanded them" (vv. 6, 11). The very essence of all real service lies in obedience, obedience to the will of our master. So it is in connection with Divine service. Listen again to the words of the perfect Servant, "I came down from Heaven, not to do Mine own will, but the will of Him that sent Me" (John 6:38). Bezaleel and Ahoilab were not left free to pick and choose what they should do or not do; all was ordered for them. Thus it is with the Lord's servants to-day: the Word sets forth his marching-orders—what he should preach, what he should do, how he should do it.

A very simple but searching principle is this. As another has said, "The Word is both the guide of the servant and the test of his service—the proof of its being done with divine wisdom and according to the divine mind." God's work must be done in God's way, or we cannot count upon *His* blessing thereon. He has promised, "them that honour Me, I will honour," and the only way to honour God is to keep His precepts diligently, to preach nothing but His Word, to employ no methods save those expressly sanctioned by Holy Writ. Anything other than this is self-will, and that is *sin*. O what need is there for pondering the basic principles of service as made known in Exodus 31!

Finally, we may observe here the Divine *sovereignty* exercised in the selection of the servants called. One was from the tribe of Judah, the other from the tribe of Dan. This is the more striking in the light of the history of those tribes. The former was the one from which Christ, according to the flesh, came; the other is the tribe from which, most probably, the Antichrist shall arise (Gen. 49:17). At any rate, Dan was the tribe that took the lead in apostasy. "Such a selection speaks of divine sovereignty. God has taken pains to show by many examples that He acts for Himself, and that He does not find His motive in the character, conduct, or genealogy of those whom He blesses. It is a comfort to see that a man from Dan comes in as well as from Judah. It shows the principle on which *all* really comes in; that is, as 'vessels of mercy'" (C. A. Coates).

Dan was the very last tribe from which the natural understanding would expect to find a man selected to be one of the principal artificers of the tabernacle. Yes, and fishermen and publicans are the last classes among whom one would look for the apostles of the Lamb! Ah, God's thoughts and ways are ever different from man's. The one chosen to deliver Egypt from an unparalleled famine-crisis, was called from the dungeon. He who was to lead Israel's hosts across the desert was called from the back-side of the wilderness. The man after God's own heart who was to sit on Israel's throne, was taken from the sheepcote.

It is not without reason that Christians are enjoined to "condescend of men of low estate," for *that* is God's way. It is still His way. "That which is highly esteemed among men is abomination in the sight of God" (Luke 16:15). And, conversely, those who are rated lowest by the world are often the ones through whom God performs His greatest wonders. "For God hath chosen the foolish things of the world to confound the wise; and God hath chosen the weak things of the world to confound the things which are mighty; And base things of the world, and things which are despised, hath God chosen, and things which are not, to bring to naught things that are" (1 Cor. 1:27, 28). Why? "That no flesh should glory in His presence." May the Lord bless His own truth to His poor and needy people.

—*Arthur W. Pink.*

THE PROPHETIC SCOPE OF MATTHEW 24.

The prophetic discourse of Christ found in Matthew 24 and 25 was delivered by Him in private to a few of His disciples less than a week before the Crucifixion. He had left the Temple for the last time. His public ministry was completed. He had announced to the leaders of the nation that, "your house is left unto you desolate," and had declared, "Ye shall not see Me henceforth, till ye shall say, Blessed is He that cometh in the name of the Lord."

As Christ left the Temple, accompanied by His disciples, they, no doubt, awed and puzzled by what He had just said, directed His attention to the magnificent buildings of the Temple, particularly to the massive stones of which they were constructed, saying, "Master, see what manner of stones and what buildings are here!" (Mark 13:1 and compare John 2:20). To which He responded, "See ye not all these things? verily I say unto you, There shall not be left here one stone upon another, that shall not be thrown down" (Matt. 24:2). Then, as He sat upon the Mount of Olives, in full sight of the City and Temple, the disciples asked, "Tell us, when shall these things be? and what shall be the sign of Thy coming, and of the end of the world?" (Matt. 24:3).

Each of the first three Gospels supply us with an inspired acccount of our Lord's prophetic discourse, but it is only by diligently comparing them and noting their *differences* that we can discover the scope and design of each, for there is no mere repetition in Scripture. Luke's account differs from Matthew's and Mark's in two important respects—what is related and what is omitted. Matthew's account is based upon a *threefold* question, see 24:3; whereas Luke's is based upon a *twofold* question, see 21:7. It is most important that the student should carefully note the *omission* of any reference to Christ's "coming" in Luke's account. The second main difference is connected with the *time* for "fleeing." In Matt. 24:15, 16 we read, "When ye therefore shall see the abomination of desolation, spoken of by Daniel the prophet, stand in the holy place, (whoso readeth, let him understand), *then* let them which be in Judea *flee* into the mountains." Whereas in Luke 21:20, 21 we read, "And when ye shall see Jerusalem compassed with armies, then know that the desolation thereof is nigh. *Then* let them which are in Judea *flee* to the mountains." That part of our Lord's prophetic discourse recorded in Luke 21 (to the middle of v. 24) was all fulfilled by the year A.D. 70. First, Jerusalem was invested by Cestius Gallus, who was repulsed. Later, it was attacked by Titus, the emperor's son, who was successful. But between the two besiegements, there is good reason to believe that, all *Christians* "fled," and that none of them perished in Jerusalem. Luke's "sign" is past, Matthew's is yet future. It is most important to observe that in Matt. 24 no reference is made to the destruction of Jerusalem after v. 2; while, on the other hand, in Luke 21 no reference at all is made to "the abomination of desolation."

Now the first thing to do in taking up the study of Matt. 24 is to pay careful attention to its *context*, namely chapter 23. There, a sevenfold "woe" is uttered, and solemn sentence of doom is pronounced by the Lord Jesus upon the apostate nation of Israel. This is found in vv. 34-38, closing with those fearful words, "Behold, *your* house is left unto you *desolate.*" Then the Lord added, "For I say unto you, ye shall not see Me henceforth, till ye shall say, Blessed is He that cometh in the name of the Lord" (v. 39). This last verse is most important. The "coming" of Christ which is there referred to is not His descent into the air to catch up the Church, but His return to the earth unto the people of Israel. It is *this* which supplies the key to Matt. 24:3, and shows that everything in Matt. 24 is yet future and is wholly Jewish.

"And Jesus went out, and departed from the Temple" (v. 1). Mark the first word of this verse: the "and" denotes that what follows gives a continuation, without any break, of that which is recorded in the closing verses of chapter 23. It supplies a solemn confirmation of what was there announced: "Your house is left unto you desolate" is verified by the words "And Jesus *went out*, and *departed from* the temple."

"And His disciples came to Him for to show Him the buildings of the temple. And Jesus said unto them, see ye not all these things? verily I say unto you, There shall not be left here one stone upon another, that shall not be thrown down" (vv. 1, 2). This foretold the destruction of Jerusalem, or more specifically, the razing of the Temple. It is most important to observe that this was said *before* the prophetic discourse of Christ's which is recorded in Matt. 24:4 and onwards.

"And as He sat upon the Mount of Olives, the disciples came unto Him' privately, saying, Tell us, when shall these things be?" (v. 3). That this question was asked separately from "And what shall be the sign of Thy coming, and of the end of the world?" or "age," shows plainly that the "when shall *these things* be?" referred specifically to the overthrow of the Temple, which implied the destruction of the City. It is to be noted that *only Luke* records Christ's answer to *that* question, see Luke 21:20-24. *This* part of our Lord's prediction *Matthew* was guided to omit.

"And what shall be the sign of Thy coming?" (v. 3). *What* did the disciples have in mind when they asked this question? Surely there cannot be the slightest difficulty for us now to discover the true answer. So far as the inspired records go, up to this point the Lord had said nothing whatever to His disciples about His going to the Father's house to prepare a place for His people, and of His coming again to receive them "unto Himself." No hint whatever had been given of His future descent into the air for the purpose of removing His saints from this earth. Therefore *this* aspect of the Lord's "coming" could not have been in the mind of the disciples at that time. It should be obvious to every honest heart and impartial mind that when they asked, "What shall be the sign of Thy coming?" they had before them what He had just said to the nation of Israel, namely, "Ye shall not see Me henceforth, till ye shall say, Blessed is He that *cometh* in the name of the Lord" (23:39); which was His coming back *to the earth*. One other thing enables us to fix the meaning of this question of the disciples, "What shall be the *sign* of Thy coming?" *No* "signs" are now given to or for those whose calling is a heavenly one. How could there be, when of them it is written, "we walk by faith, not by sight"? (2 Cor. 5:7). God's people to-day are *not* to be looking for "signs," but listening for a sound, namely, the "shout" of the Lord (1 Thess. 4:16)!

"And of the end of the age?" To *what* "age" did the disciples refer? Surely there can be only one answer: that associated with Christ's "coming" to the earth itself. It should be carefully borne in mind that this question was asked by the disciples, as Jews, *before* the Cross, before the *Christian* dispensation began. It is of the greatest importance that this fact should be kept before us, for a mistake on that point necessarily involves an erroneous interpretation of what follows. If we remember that at this time the apostles had no thought of (or, at any rate, no real belief in) Christ's death and resurrection, it should help us to see that the Christian "age" could not have been in their minds. They were *Jews*, in spirit, hopes, expectations—the very first verse of Matt. 24 (following right after 23:38) more than hints at that. It is failure at this very point which has led so many to imagine that Matt. 24 teaches that "the Church" will pass through the great Tribulation.

It is to be carefully observed that in His answer the Lord referred the disciples to Daniel: "When ye therefore shall see the abomination of desolation, spoken of by Daniel the prophet, stand in the holy place" (v. 15). It is interesting to note that the expressions "the end" or "time of the end" occur in Daniel just thirteen times, and that they are found nowhere else in the Old Testament. These expressions refer to the unfulfilled 70th "week" of Daniel 9:24-27, which brings to a close Israel's national servitude under Gentile domination. The new "Age" will be introduced by the second advent of the Messiah to this earth and the consequent placing of Israel at the head of the nations. References to *that* "Age" are found in Heb. 2:5, 6:5. Thus the disciples rightly connected the "end of the age" with the "Coming" of Christ; for His return to this earth and the ending of the "Age," i.e. the "Times of the Gentiles" synchronise. What is so important to note is that in 23:39 Christ did not connect His "coming" with the destruction of Jerusalem and the overthrow of the Temple, but with the glorious epoch of Israel's national conversion.

"And Jesus answered and said unto them, take heed that no man deceive you. For many shall come in My name, saying,

I am Christ; and shall deceive many" (vv. 4, 5). The Lord was here addressing His disciples as the representatives of the godly Jewish remnant of the future. Matthew does not record Christ's answer to their first question, that being given in Luke. There is nothing at all in Matt. 24 parallel with Luke 21:20. Nor is there anything in it which falls, directly, within the scope of the Christian dispensation. The whole of *this* parenthetical dispensation is ignored, coming in as it does between the 69th and 70th "weeks" of Daniel 9. Verses 4-14 of Matt. 24 treat of the first half of the 70th "week"; vv. 15-30 of its second half. Though vv. 4-7 describe conditions which have obtained, more or less, all through the centuries of this Christian era, yet will they appear in a much more intensified form during the Tribulation period.

Fuller and further details concerning the time covered by Christ's prophetic discourse in Matt. 24 are furnished in the Revelation, the major portion of that book treating of the same period. At the close of this present dispensation Christendom is spued out (Rev. 3), the saints are raptured (4:1), and then the united company of the redeemed are seen in Heaven worshipping God (Rev. 4:4-11). Following this, the Lamb as the "Lion" of the "*tribe of Judah*" takes "the book" (Rev. 5), and Israel at once appears on the scene. As soon as the "seals" of that book are broken we find that which corresponds exactly with what we have in Matt. 24. Marvellous, minute, and many are the parallels between the two chapters. At a few of them only shall we now glance.

"And Jesus answered and said unto them, take heed that no man deceive you. For many shall come in My name, saying, I am Christ; and shall deceive many" (Matt. 24:4, 5). This was the *first* part of the Lord's reply to the questions asked by His disciples. "And I saw when the Lamb opened one of the seals, and I heard, as it were the noise of thunder, one of the four living creatures saying, Come and see. And I saw, and behold a white horse: and he that sat on him had a bow; and a crown was given unto him: and he went forth conquering, and to conquer" (Rev. 6:1, 2). These words picture the Anti-christ deceiving men, posing as the true Christ—cf. Rev. 19:11.

"And ye shall hear of wars and rumours of wars: see that ye be not troubled: for all must come to pass, but the end (i.e. of the 70th "week") is not yet. For nation shall rise against nation, and kingdom against kingdom" (Matt. 24:6, 7).

"And when He had opened the second seal I heard the second beast say, Come and see. And there went out another horse that was red: and power was given to him that sat thereon to take peace from the earth, and that they should kill one another: and there was given unto him a great sword" (Rev. 6:3, 4). Thus the contents of the second seal correspond exactly with the second part of Christ's prophecy.

"And there shall be famines" (Matt. 24:7). "And when he had opened the third seal, I heard the third beast say, Come and see. And I beheld, and lo a black horse (the colour of *famine*, see Lam. 4:8; 5:10); and he that sat on him had a pair of balances in his hand. And I heard a voice in the midst of the four living creatures say, A measure of wheat for a penny (a day's wage, see Matt. 20:2) and three measures of barley for a penny" (Rev. 6:5, 6).

"And pestilences, and earthquakes, in divers places" (Matt. 24:7). "And when he had opened the fourth seal, I heard the voice of the fourth living creature say, Come and see. And I looked, and behold a pale horse: and his name that sat on him was Death, and Hell followed with him. And power was given unto them over the fourth part of the earth, to kill with sword, and with hunger, and with death, and with the beasts of the earth" (Rev. 6:7, 8).

"All these are the beginnings of sorrows" or "birthpangs" (Matt. 24:8). These "birth-pangs" are the travail which shall yet precede the birth of a regenerated Israel. If the reader desires to trace out the remaining correspondences between the two chapters let him compare Matt. 24:8-28 with Rev. 6:9-11; and then Matt. 24:29, 30 with Rev. 6:12-17.

Passing on now to v. 15: "When ye therefore shall see the abomination of desolation, spoken of by Daniel the prophet, stand in the holy place, whoso readeth let him understand." This is the point which marks the *division* between the two halves of the 70th "week," compare Daniel 9:27. These words were addressed by Christ to His apostles, but the "ye" need occasion no difficulty. The Lord was speaking to them as Jews, as the *representatives* of those who shall be on earth at the time these things are fulfilled. That this is *not* a "begging of the question" should be clear by a reference to Matt. 23:39: the word "Ye" there was spoken to the scribes and pharisees as the *representatives* of the Nation both present and future, that is, of the nation as a unit. A similar instance is found in 1 Thess. 4:17, "Then *we* which are alive." The apostle did not say "they," but addressed those Thessalonian saints, including himself, as the *representatives* of all believers who shall be alive on the earth at the Lord's coming in the air.

The "abomination of desolation" is the image of Anti-christ (Rev. 13) which will yet be set up in the re-built Temple at Jerusalem. The reference here in Matt. 24:15 is *not* to the defiling of the Temple by Titus, as Daniel 9:27, 11:31, 12:11 clearly show. It is in "the midst of the week" that "sacrifice and oblation" are made to cease. It is then that the pseudo-Christ will throw off his mask and appear as an opposing Christ, demanding that Divine honours shall be paid to him alone: an Old Testament type of this is found in Daniel 3:1-7.

"For then shall be great tribulation, such as was not since the beginning of the world to this time, no, nor ever shall be. And except those days should be shortened, there should no flesh be saved: but for the elect's sake (i.e. the sake of the godly Jewish remnant) those days shall be shortened" (Matt. 24:21, 22). The double reference to "those days," and there is a third one in v. 19, finds its interpretation in the *"when* ye therefore shall see the abomination of desolation" of v. 15. It was not the destruction of Jerusalem by Titus of which Christ here spoke. His words in v. 22 are clearly parallel with Daniel 12:1, "And at that time shall Michael stand up, the great prince which standeth for the children of thy people: and there shall be a time of trouble, such as never was since there was a nation, even to that same time: and at *that* time thy people shall be *delivered*, everyone that shall be found written in the book" i.e. God's "elect" among the Jews. Thus the "great tribulation" of Matt. 24:21 instead of referring to the time when Jerusalem was destroyed and Israel dispersed, speaks of that which shall immediately precede the day when they shall be "delivered."

"*Then* if any man shall say unto you, Lo, here is Christ, or there, believe not" (Matt. 24:23). This has in view the time when the Man of Sin shall sit in the Temple of God "showing himself that *he* is God" (2 Thess. 2:3, 4).

"For as the lightning cometh out of the east, and shineth even unto the west; so shall the coming of the Son of man be" (Matt. 24:27). Never once is this title of Christ's used in any of the Pauline Epistles which are addressed to the members of the Body of Christ. We are waiting the call of "the Son of God" (1 Thess. 1:9, 10).

"For wheresoever the carcase is, there will the eagles be gathered together" (Matt. 24:28). The "carcase" refers to the apostate mass of Israel; the "eagles" are the symbols of Divine judgment: see Deut. 28:26, Ezek. 39:17, Rev. 19:17.

"Verily I say unto you, This generation shall not pass, till all these things be fulfilled" (Matt. 24:34). With this should be carefully compared Matt. 12:43-45. Not only would not the Jewish nation ("generation") pass away, but it would not cease as a "wicked generation." But when Matt. 24 has been completely fulfilled then that "wicked generation" *shall* "pass away," and be followed by a *new* Nation: see Psa. 22:30, 31; 102-18; Deut. 32:5, 20.

The reference to "the days of Noah" in vv. 37-39 are in striking accord with the rest of this prophetic discourse, and at once fix the scope thereof. First, Noah lived at the very *close* of the antedeluvian age: so Matt. 24 describes conditions at the very end of the Jewish age. Second, Noah and his house were saved through a great and sore judgment of God: so an elect Jewish remnant will be preserved through the great Tribulation (Rev. 12:6, 14). Third, Noah and his house came forth from the ark on to an earth which had been swept clean by the besom of destruction, and entered into a *new* Age: so the godly Jewish remnant pass through the great tribulation, and from them will spring millennial Israel. Fourth, judgment consumed the ungodly: "So shall also the coming of the Son of man be." But how blessed for the Christian to remember that *before* the Flood began, Enoch—type of the Church—was translated! May this blessed hope be the stay of our hearts, and the purifying power for our walk. May we, instead of looking for "signs," be listening for that Sound of all sounds; instead of dreading the swiftly approaching Tribulation, be found praising God that *we* shall be high above it all; instead of studying the character of Mussolini or others to find in them marks of the Man of Sin, may we be "looking for that blessed hope and the glorious appearing of the great God and our Saviour Jesus Christ" (Titus 2:13).

—*Arthur W. Pink.*

THE CHRISTIAN'S GREATEST NEED.

"But one thing is needful" (Luke 10:42).

What is the Christian's greatest need? Is it to be more liberal in his giving? to be more zealous in service? to be more orthodox in doctrine? to be more fervent in prayer? to cultivate a greater humility? to seek a filling of the Holy Spirit? to render more implicit obedience to Christ? to give more time to the study of the Word of God? No; the Christian, *every Christian*, has a deeper need, a need more desperate than any of these. What is it? Before answering, let us turn and consider Luke 10:38-42.

"Now it came to pass, as they went, that He entered into a certain village: and a certain woman named Martha received Him into her house. And she had a sister called Mary, which also sat at Jesus's feet, and heard His word. But Martha was cumbered about much serving, and came to Him, and said, Lord, dost Thou not care that my sister hath left me to serve alone? Bid her therefore that she help me. And Jesus answered and said unto her, Martha, Martha, thou art careful and troubled about many things; But one thing is needful; and Mary hath chosen that good part, which shall not be taken away from her."

Both of these women were genuine believers. Martha not only received the Lord into her house, but she had already received Him into her heart. Moreover, she was busy serving Him, and let us not forget that there were very few in Palestine, at that time, who cared to serve *Him*. He was the One who "had not where to lay His head." He was the One that was "despised and rejected of men," He was the One "from whom men hid their faces; He was despised, and they esteemed Him not."

Now Martha was busy "serving" this One, and it is this which makes so solemn what follows. Martha had faith, was serving the Saviour, and yet Christ Himself puts her in disparaging contrast with Mary, her sister—Mary who simply "sat at His feet." Martha's service Christ reproves, Mary's sitting He approves. Now let us notice carefully each statement here.

"But Martha was cumbered about much serving." The word "cumbered" means distracted; she was encumbered, that is to say, she was weighted down. Not only was she "cumbered," but she was dissatisfied, for she went to the Lord with a complaint—"And came to Him, and said, Lord, dost Thou not care that my sister hath left me to serve alone? bid her therefore that *she help* ME." Poor Martha! She began by seeking to serve the Lord, and she ends with wanting to get Mary to serve her. But it is the Lord's answer to Martha that we would now carefully consider—"And Jesus answered and said unto her, Martha, Martha, thou art careful and troubled about many things: *But one thing is needful*: and Mary hath chosen that good part, which shall not be taken away from her."

What did the Lord mean? Are there not many things needful? No! The Lord said, "But one thing is needful" and this "one thing" is that which the Saviour here terms "that good part" which, said He, "Shall not be taken away from her." "But one thing is needful"—how that would banish care if we only apprehended it! How many distractions would our hearts be free from, did we but recognise and bow to the truth of Christ's words! Do we really believe them? Do you, dear friend? Do you believe that *only* "one thing is needful"? But again we ask, What is this "one thing"? And the answer to our question is found in verse 39 —"Mary, which also sat at Jesus's feet, and heard His word." There are a great many needs in this busy world; there are a great many duties which the Christian has to perform; but the Lord would bring our hearts from everything simply to this one, and that one, to sit at His feet and there to *receive from Him*. If we are really receiving from Christ, service, and everything else, will take care of itself. Here is the key to true spirituality. Here is the secret of practical holiness. This "one thing" embraces everything else, because it lies at the base of everything else, it is the ground of everything else.

What God wants from us is *receptiveness*, that is, the capacity to receive—to receive from Him. In John 7:37 we read, "In the last day, that great day of the feast, Jesus stood and cried, saying, If any man thirst, let him come unto Me and drink." The occasion when the Lord Jesus uttered these words is exceedingly striking. Men were busily engaged in observing a religious "feast"; they were busy with their empty forms and ceremonies, which, after all, left the heart just where it was at the beginning—empty. The Lord stood up on "that great day of the feast," when its hollowness was most manifested. And in this "great day," when men showed how little they could do to procure the happiness they were seeking, the Son of God stood forth and said, "If any man thirst, let him come unto Me and drink." What is "drinking"? It is receiving, receiving from Him: it is having our emptiness ministered unto from His fulness. Now mark, carefully, the consequence of coming to Him and "drinking"—"He that believeth on Me, as the Scripture hath said, out of his belly shall flow rivers of living water. But this spake He of the Spirit, which they that believe on Him should receive" (John 7:38, 39).

The majority of our readers profess to be "believers," yet how many of them would say, confidently, that out of their innermost parts *are* flowing "rivers of living water"? How many would venture to say that this is being fulfilled through them? Now what is the "belly"? It is that part of man which constantly craves. It is that part which, in his fallen condition, is the natural man's "god." "Whose god is their belly" (Phil. 3:19) says the apostle. It is that part of man which is never satisfied, because it is constantly crying for something to appease its cravings. Now the remarkable thing is, we would say, the blessed thing is, that not only is the believer himself satisfied, but he overflows with that which satisfies, for, from out of his innermost parts "flow rivers of living water." The thought is a striking one. It was not from him, that is, the believer, shall "flow rivers of living water," but, said the Saviour, "out of his belly" shall flow rivers of living water, namely, from that very part of our constitution which, in the natural man, is never satisfied.

Now *how* is the believer satisfied? The answer is, by coming to Christ, and "drinking." But does this refer only to a single act? Is this something that is done once and for all? never to be repeated? This seems to be the common idea. Many imagine that grace is a sort of thing that God puts into a soul like a seed, and that it will grow and develop into more. Now do not misunderstand me: I am not denying that the believer grows. The believer grows "in grace": it is not the grace in him which grows. Dear friends, we are to continue, as we began. Where was it that we found rest and peace? It was in Christ. And how did we obtain these? It was by being conscious of our need of them, it was by coming to Christ for them, it was by faith appropriating them, from Him. But why should we stop there? Are we to find experimental holiness in another way? Surely not. Experimental holiness is advanced by sitting at the Saviour's feet, by looking into His blessed face, by rejoicing in Him—*that* is experimental holiness! To be occupied with Christ is to be satisfied, and *this* is the "good part" which shall never be "taken away." The "fulness" is in the Lord Jesus, and from Him we need to draw daily. This was just what Mary was doing. She was sitting at His feet, and drinking in His words. But alas, alas, so many of us are Martha's, "cumbered with much serving" and the last thing we think of doing is to come to Christ, and find heart-rest and satisfaction in Him alone.

Just as the last thing which the sinner does is to come to Christ for salvation of soul, so the last thing that the believer usually does is to come to Him for satisfaction of heart. We allow the Devil to continue getting the better of us. When we were yet in our sins, Satan occupied us with ourselves and our works; and the sad thing is that he is now doing this with many a believer. How many there are who have seen their need of Christ to deliver them from the wrath to come, and who will go to Him when they are in deep trouble, but who, ordinarily, give Him little or no place in their daily lives.

We are not only to "grow in grace," but also "in the knowledge of our Lord and Saviour Jesus Christ." Nothing can make up for, or take the place of, *personal intercourse* with the Saviour.

"O fix our earnest gaze,
So wholly, Lord, on Thee,
That with Thy beauty occupied,
We elsewhere none may see."

What is the root of all the dishonour done to Christ by His people? It is because they are not where Mary was—in the place of occupation with Himself. *That* is what the Lord Jesus wants. He has come all the way from heaven to earth to attract our hearts unto Himself. He wants us to "receive" out of His fulness, that He may enrich us; not to say after a while, "I must be doing something new." He wants us to "receive" from Him. We cannot minister to others until we have received from Him. Our own souls must first be fully satisfied. The vessel must be filled, before it can overflow. It is not the vessel that is partly filled that overflows. We must sit at the Lord's feet for ourselves; that is the first thing. When I have been filled myself, no effort will be required, for then, out of my belly *will* flow, "rivers of living water"—lifegiving streams which will refresh others. But, alas, pride comes in. We want to make God our debtor, and give to Him instead of receiving from Him.

Here, then, is the one thing needful—fellowship with Him. It is to be occupied with Christ. It is to cultivate companionship with Him. It is the contemplating of His excellencies. It is to be able to say, out of a heart experience, "My beloved is mine, and I am His." It is the being able to say with Paul, "For me to live is Christ." It is to be able to say in truth, "Thou O Christ art all I want, more than all *in Thee* I find." It is to know and enjoy Christ. It is to have our eyes fixed upon His face, and our ears opened to His voice. It is to be able to say,

"I have heard Thy voice, Lord Jesus,
 Tell me not of ought beside;
I have seen Thy face, Lord Jesus,
 All my soul is satisfied."

This is what we have been saved for, and this is what we have been saved unto —unto "fellowship with the Father, and with His Son Jesus Christ" (1 John 1:3.) If this "one thing" be attended to daily everything else will be cared for. To particularise:—

1. *This will prevent backsliding.* Take Peter as an illustration, He sees the Saviour coming towards him, walking on the waters. At once he steps out of the boat, and essays to walk to Him. But suddenly he begins to sink. And when was this? What was the cause of it? Peter began to sink when he took his eye off Christ. Take Peter again; his boast is, that though all men should forsake the Lord, yet he would remain faithful. But did he? You know he did not. He denied Him, denied Him with an oath. And how is that to be explained? It was because he had followed the Lord Jesus "afar off"—that was the explanation. Reader, settle this in your mind once and for all, that you cannot sin in the presence of Christ. To abide in Him, to walk with Him, to remain in communion with Him is *the only thing* that will keep any of us from backsliding, and doing that which is dishonouring to His holy name. Again,

2. *This will equip us for true service.* We must be much with Him before we can do anything for Him. Did you ever notice that striking word in Mark 3:14? "He ordained twelve that they should be with Him, and that He might send them forth to preach." Notice the order: First, they must be *with Him,* second, "*and* that He might send them forth to preach." Ah! how different would our service be if this were heeded. Apart from this, so-called Christian service is nothing but the restless energy of the flesh, and in the day to come will prove but "wood, hay and stubble."

One of the great curses of the day is too much activity, and too little "sitting at the feet of the Lord Jesus Christ and hearing His word." Men are so busy doing things for Christ, that they have no time to cultivate fellowship with Christ. But O, dear reader, what God wants is quality, not quantity. The service which He desires is that which does not separate from Him, that service which flows freely, almost unconsciously, from the joy of His presence, and which is the direct outcome of His service to us. But the trouble is, that we are constantly exalting ourselves, and He has to abase us. Because He would have us in the place of blessing, He has to put us down. How slow we are to recognise that grace, when received, not only fills us, but overflows to others. How slow we are to learn that grace never requires, but always gives!

Brethren, what is service? Is it not testimony for Christ? And what is testimony for Christ? Is it not the overflowing of a full heart? And the heart is only full in His presence. And again we say, How little we realize our need of being served by Him, and being served by Him all the way through. What we need for effective service is wisdom, grace, power, unction, and these are the fruit of spending much time in His presence. If I am in fellowship with Him, then shall I have that wisdom which cometh from above. If I am in fellowship with Him, then I shall have His compassion for the lost. If I am in fellowship with Him, then shall I have that power which will enable me to do even "greater works." But again we say, That if we are out of fellowship with Him, then all our service, no matter how successful we may deem it, nor how highly valued it may be by fellow-believers, nor how wonderful the "results" we get, yet, nevertheless, our service will have been performed in the energy of the flesh, and in the day to come will simply go up as smoke. And O what a bonfire there will be in that day!

3. *This is the one great condition of fruit-bearing.* In John 15:5 we read, "I am the Vine, ye are the branches: he that abideth in Me, and I in him, the same bringeth forth much fruit: for without Me ye can do nothing." "Without Me" signifies "apart from Me" or, "severed from Me." This severance from Christ has no reference whatever to the vital union which exists between the Saviour and the one who has believed in Him, for

nothing can sever *that* union. The severance in John 15 refers not to the severance of relationship but of fellowship: and the one great condition of fruit-bearing is the maintaining of this fellowship. How many believers there are who bemoan their spiritual barrenness! Here then is the explanation: here is the cause. There is a worm at the root of their spiritual life—fellowship with Christ has been neglected. This must be the case, for the language of Christ here is positive and unequivocal: He distinctly states that if we abide in Him, that is, maintain fellowship with Him, and He abides in us, then, "the same bringeth forth much fruit." "But one thing is needful!"

4. *Here is the fundamental requirement of power in prayer.* Quoting again from John 15 we find that the Lord declares, "If ye abide in Me, and My words abide in you, ye shall ask what ye will, and it shall be done unto you" (v. 7). How many Christians there are who have become utterly discouraged because they have received so few answers to their prayers; and how many others there are who get so little joy out of prayer, finding it an irksome duty, and a profitless occupation! Here then is the key to it. If we were really in communion with Christ, if we had received from Him, our heart would be full, and it would no longer be a duty but a delight to tell out to Him the joy of our heart. But more; if we were in communion with Him we should have the mind of God, and in such case, would ask only those things which were in accord with His mind, and these would be granted us. How necessary it is to attend to these qualifying terms which precede the promise, "Ye shall ask what ye will, and it shall be done unto you." There are some who have wondered how to harmonise these words with what we find in 1 John 5:14, "And this is the confidence that we have in Him, that, if we ask any thing according to His will, He heareth us." But John 15:7 is in perfect accord. If we are abiding in Christ, that is, if we are in real fellowship with Him, then the only requests that we shall make of God will be those that are "according to His will."

5. *This is the secret of abounding joy.* "That which we have seen and heard declare we unto you, that ye also may have fellowship with us; and truly our fellowship is with the Father, and with His Son Jesus Christ. And these things write we unto you, that your joy may be full" (1 John 1:3, 4). A beautiful illustration of this is found in John 20:19, 20, "Then the same day at evening, being the first day of the week, when the doors were shut where the disciples were assembled for fear of the Jews, came Jesus and stood in the midst, and saith unto them, Peace be unto you. And when He had so said, He showed them His hands and His side. Then were the disciples glad when they saw the Lord." Notice two things here: it is the work of Christ which is the ground of the believer's "peace," denoted by the Lord Jesus calling the attention of His disciples unto "His hands and His side." And it is the person of Christ which is the source of our "joy," for it was when the disciples "saw the Lord" that they were glad. This is the precious secret for our hearts. There are many of the Lord's people who suppose that they cannot be glad so long as they are in circumstances of sorrow. O what a mistake it is! It is not true. Mark it carefully in connection with the above incident that the Lord did not change the circumstances of those disciples. They were still "shut in for fear of the Jews," but He showed them Himself, and thus raised them above their circumstances.

In 1 Peter 1 we see the same thing. There we are given to behold the saints of God enduring a great trial; they are persecuted, scattered abroad, homeless. But what do we read of them? What was their spiritual conditions? The apostle says of them, "Wherein ye greatly rejoiced, though now for a season, if need be, ye are in heaviness, through manifold trials; That the trial of your faith, being much more precious than of gold that perisheth, though it be tried with fire, might be found unto praise and honour, and glory at the appearing of Jesus Christ." Then, after having mentioned the person of Jesus Christ, he at once adds, "whom having not seen, ye love; in whom, though now ye see Him not, yet believing, ye rejoice with joy unspeakable, and full of glory." Their circumstances were not changed, but their hearts were lifted above them. In like manner, this is the key to the experience of Paul and Silas. They were in prison, they were there wrongfully and unjustly; they were there simply because they had been preaching the Gospel. They had been scourged, their backs were bleeding, their feet were fast in the stocks. And what were they doing? How were they occupying themselves? Were they moralising about the injustice of human law? Were they complaining against God? Not at all. They were singing praises. And the only way in which this can be explained is by the fact that their hearts were so occupied with Christ, that they were so absorbed with His loveliness, that their souls were so satisfied with His perfections, they overflowed with "songs in the night."

6. *This is the key to experimental holiness.* The deepest longing of the heart of every believer who is walking in the Spirit, that is, who is in fellowship with Christ, is that he may be conformed to His image. And innumerable are the prescriptions furnished by the religious doctors of the day for attaining this end. And sad it is to witness the heart-rending effects of those who attempt to follow out such prescriptions. Pitiable it is to witness many of God's dear children groping after that which eludes them—the secret to a holier life. Some pray for many hours a day; others try fasting; others deny themselves the legitimate comforts of life; others read every book and booklet they can find on the subject of sanctification; others go from one convention to another—holiness conventions, victorious-life conventions, deepening-of-spiritual-life conventions, etc., etc.—others have gone forward to the front of a church and in response to some preacher's invitation have knelt down, and have sought to "lay their all on the altar" and "consecrate" their life to God; still others have sought a filling, an anointing, or a baptism of the Spirit; and so we might go on indefinitely. But after all these rules for holy living and requirements of religious teachers have been met, the heart still remains unsatisfied, and the secret still defies the most diligent efforts of the earnest believer. What then is the remedy? Is there any? Thank God there is. What is it? And again we reply, in the language of the text, "But one thing is needful." And what that is, you need go to no convention to find out, consult no preacher to ascertain, and read no treatise of man to discover. Here is the secret told out—"But we all, with open face beholding as in a glass the glory of the Lord, are changed into the same image from glory to glory, even as by the Spirit of the Lord."

The order of this verse in the Greek is as follows: "But we all beholding as in a mirror the glory of the Lord with unveiled face, are changed into the same image from glory to glory, even as by the Spirit of the Lord" (2 Cor. 3:18). The context contrasts the "glory" of this present dispensation with that of the previous, namely, the dispensation of the law. The glory of the Lord shone in the face of Moses, the mediator, but Israel could not steadfastly behold his face, and therefore Moses "put a veil over his face." That veil we are told in 3:14 is "done away in Christ." The mirror in which the glory of the Lord is beheld is the mirror of the Word. The figure is taken from the mirrors of the ancients, which unlike ours were not made of glass, but of some metal highly polished. In order to use this mirror a brilliant light was required, and as the light fell upon the mirror, not only did the person beholding it see in it his own countenance, but upon his face was reflected the glow from the mirror itself. If the mirror was made of gold, then the reflection would be a yellow one; if the mirror were of silver, then the reflection would be white.

The historical reference of the above passage is to Moses. This servant of the Lord had been up in the mount for forty days, speaking face to face with Jehovah. And when he descended from the mount, the glory of the Lord was reflected upon his face; and so bright was this, he had to veil himself. Now, says the apostle, in like manner as we behold in the mirror of the Word, the glory of the Lord, that is, the perfections and excellencies of Jesus Christ as therein revealed, we, too, "are changed into the same image from glory to glory." In other words, as we are occupied with Christ as He is revealed to us in the written Word, we become conformed to His image, we reproduce faintly, His excellencies. How blessedly, divinely, simple this is. There is no striving, there is no agonising, there is no having to work ourselves up into a frenzy, there is in fact nothing at all except— "*Beholding*"! Just as we "beheld" the Lamb of God when we first sought the Saviour; that is, just as we turned away from ourselves and from everything else, and came in all our wretchedness and need, empty-handed, to Christ Himself; so now we are to continue "beholding." And as we do this, God says we "*are* changed." We may not feel it, we may not be conscious of it—as Moses "knew not that the skin of his face shone"—but others will know it, and that, without us boastfully telling them about it.

7. *This is the secret of a contented and satisfied heart.* What a beautiful example we have of this in connection with John the Baptist! Here is what he said, "The friend of the Bridegroom, which standeth and heareth him, rejoiceth greatly because of the Bridegroom's voice; this my joy

therefore is fulfilled" (John 3:29). John was occupied with Christ, and therefore was he satisfied. He found his joy fulfilled, that is filled full, by standing and hearing the voice of Christ. And this is the only way in which any heart can be satisfied. Did you ever ponder the reason why the Holy Spirit has placed the books of Ecclesiastes and the Song of Solomon side by side? They seem to have nothing whatever in common; in fact, a greater contrast between two books could scarcely be imagined. In the former, the plaintive cry is repeated, again and again, "All is vanity and vexation of spirit." Solomon is seeking everywhere for a *satisfying object*, but he seeks in vain. He roams through many a field, he explores every realm, he experiments with many an object; but what he seeks he finds not. Over Ecclesiastes should be written as its theme-title, "Whosoever drinketh of this water, shall thirst again." But how striking and how blessed is the contrast presented in the Song of Songs! Here we have the very opposite from what is before us in Ecclesiastes. Instead of "vanity and vexation of spirit" we have joy and satisfaction of heart. Here a satisfying portion *is found*. Over the Song of Solomon should be written as its theme-title, "Whosoever drinketh of this water that I shall give him shall never thirst."

And now, brethren, *"What think ye of Christ?"* This is still the test question, not only for sinners, but for believers, too. Do you think of Him only as the One who supplies your need? What would you think of a man whose only thought of his wife was as the one who cooked his meals and mended his clothes? You would say he had very little love for her. The man who really loves his wife desires her companionship and enjoys her company. After the evening meal he wants to sit with her and enjoy heart-communion. And surely this should be so with the believer in Christ. What think ye of Christ? Do you think enough of Him to seek a better acquaintance and a more intimate fellowship with Him?

Coming back again to Mary, let us turn to John 12:3. "Then took Mary a pound of ointment of spikenard, very costly, and anointed the feet of Jesus, and wiped His feet with her hair; and the house was filled with the odour of the ointment." Here again Mary is seen at the Saviour's feet; not now as a learner, but as a worshipper. The dark shadow of the cross fell athwart that happy gathering in Bethany; an enemy was there, with vile plan in mind. Mary, with the true instinct of love, recognises that "shadow," and uses the opportunity to express her devotion. And how lavishly she gave! It is the Holy Spirit who tells us that her gift was "very costly." The Lord Jesus interprets her act as follows, "Against the day of My burying hath she kept this" (John 12:7). Mary was the one who anointed the Lord's body before His death, because she "believed" that He would die. The other women were preparing to "anoint" the Lord's body after His death, because they did not "believe" that He would rise again. But notice, dear friends, that it was Mary and not Martha who acted thus. At every point the sisters are contrasted. Martha was troubled over "many things," but Christ said, *"one thing* is needful," and this was what Mary had chosen. Martha was busy *for* Him; Mary was occupied *with* Him!

"That I may know Him." That was Paul's deepest longing. Is it yours? To the apostle, Christianity was all summed up in Christ, and this both for time and eternity. When he said, "I have a desire to depart" he did not add "and go to Heaven," but, I have a desire to depart "and to be with Christ" (Phil. 1:23). And again he said, "Willing rather to be absent from the body," and—and what? translated to glory? No, but—"to be present with the Lord" (2 Cor. 5:8). This is the desire of Christ, too. Notice His response to the dying thief: "To-day shalt thou be" —not merely in Paradise, but—*"with Me* in Paradise." So again He says to His disciples, "I go to prepare a place for you; and if I go and prepare a place for you, I will come again and receive you" —not into the place prepared, but—*"unto Myself;* that where I am there ye may be also" (John 14:2, 3).

May Divine grace cause writer and reader to "choose that good part," that "one thing needful"—the Christian's greatest need—which "shall not be taken away" from us.

—*Arthur W. Pink.*

"It is the Lord enthroned in light,
 Whose claims are all Divine,
Who has an undivided right,
 To govern me and mine."

"GET THEE OUT."—Acts 7:3.

The Lord has made it clear to us that the work for which He brought us to Australia has been accomplished. All praise to Him, for His counsel "shall stand" (Isa. 46:10). The next place in which we believe He would have us pitch our tent is London, England. We have received no human call or invitation; there is no "open door" apparent to sight. We are acquainted with very few of the Lord's people in London, and most of them who have heard of us are likely to be prejudiced because we are on the outside of every thing ecclesiastical. For all of this we are truly thankful, as it affords another opportunity to prove the faithfulness of Him who *never* disappoints those whose "expectations" are (by grace) in Him alone.

At the time of writing this (June 25) we know no more than the reader what may be before us. But we rejoice to know that our "times are in *His* hands" (Psa. 31:15). Like Abraham of old we are literally going forth "not knowing within" (Heb. 11:8). Yet are we fully assured that He who makes "all things *work together* for good to them that love God, to them who are the called according to His purpose" is, even now, ordering every thing for us. We shall much value the daily prayers of God's people that the Lord will graciously make good for us Phil. 2:13, Eph. 2:10, Heb. 13:21.

God willing, this little magazine will be published and mailed out as hitherto. We sail, D.V., July 21. On the front cover page appears our temporary London address. With joyous anticipations, till He come.—*A.W.P.*

---

to hold in view, is the glory of God; and the only "means" becoming His servants are those which are prescribed in the Scriptures. Implicit confidence in God's promise that *His* Word shall not return unto Him void, and unquestioning obedience to all *His* arrangements, are what constitute all acceptable service. When Moses built a house for the Lord, though skilled in all the wisdom of the Egyptians, he was not permitted to use his own ingenuity, but had to make *all* things according to the pattern showed him in the mount. And this is written for our learning.

The teaching of Scripture on the subject of Service and the thoughts of many professing Christian thereon, differ widely. The Word teaches that the measure in which we glorify God is the measure in which we obey Him. But how many gauge it by *apparent results!* Those preachers who do most visible good in the conversion of souls and the edification of Christians, are regarded as having brought most glory to their Master. But *that* is a false standard of measurement; it is walking by sight; it is leaning unto our own understanding. Again, those methods which seem to secure the best returns are almost everywhere looked upon as being most blessed of God, and therefore as most pleasing to Him. But the value of any action can only be ascertained through testing it by Scripture.

So many reason backward from effect to cause: the effect is good, therefore it is supposed the cause must be. God is giving blessing, therefore He must be pleased. Ah, it is so easy to lean unto our own understanding. Have we forgotten what happened when Moses was bidden to speak to the rock? Instead of so doing, in his anger, he smote it. In this he sinned, and God judged him for it. Nevertheless, the water flowed forth! Did *that* "result" prove Moses was in the right? Certainly not. And it is recorded as a solemn warning against our arguing from effect to cause, against reasoning from results. It is so easy to persuade ourselves that we have God's *approval* because we appear to have His *blessing*. If we leave the path marked out for us in His Word, we may have visible "results," but we shall not have God's approval. If we desire the latter, then we must give constant heed to the Divine injunction, "'Trust in the Lord with all thine heart, and lean not unto thine own understanding."

—*Arthur W. Pink.*

how often have we acted in a similar fashion! Other examples of this sad failing are to be found in what is recorded concerning the twelve apostles. For example, when the Lord first announced to them His approaching death, Peter rebuked Him, saying, "Be it far from Thee, Lord" (Matt. 16:22). When He bade them give the multitude "to eat," they said, "Shall we go and buy two hundred pennyworth of bread?" (Mark 6:37). Yes, the exhortation of our text is much needed by us.

"Lean not unto thine own understanding" *when interpreting the Scriptures.* God's Word is not addressed to the intellect, but to the conscience and heart; and as soon as we begin reasoning over its contents, we land into a bog of error. The majority, if not all, of the false systems in Christendom, are the outcome of the natural mind of men taking up the things of God. People single out certain fragments of Scripture, ignoring or repudiating all else, and by a process of reasoning have based thereon their schemes. Some dwell on the fact that God is gracious and that His mercy endureth forever, and from this premise they reason that there can be no eternal punishment for anybody. Others single out the statements that "God so loved the world that He gave His only begotten Son" (John 3:16), and "whosoever will, let him take the water of life freely" (Rev. 22:17), and from these, reason that there cannot be such a thing as God having, from all eternity, chosen or elected certain ones to salvation. On the other hand, some appear to be very jealous of God's glory and imagine it is sullied when we press the responsibility of man. Because "Salvation is of the Lord" (Jonah 2:9), they can see neither need nor warrant for the preacher to urge the ungodly to seek the Saviour. Because repentance and faith are the gifts of God it seems senseless to hyper-calvinists to call upon the unregenerate *to* repent and believe. All of these people are doing the very thing which our text forbids.

"Lean not unto thine own understanding" *by seeking to solve the mysteries of Providence.* God has told us that His thoughts and ways are very different from ours (Isa. 55:8, 9), yea, that they are "past finding out" (Rom. 11:33). When a finite creature attempts to comprehend the Infinite, he is not only guilty of presumptuous sin, but is working against his own well-being. To philosophise about our lot, to reason about our circumstances, is fatal to our rest of soul and peace of heart. We cannot by searching find out God.

In His Word God has placed on record example after example to warn us against the folly and futility of reasoning about His providences. Take the case of Jacob: when Joseph seemed lost to him, Simeon had been left behind in Egypt, and request was made for Benjamin to leave too, he said, "All these things are against me" (Gen. 42:36). He was walking by sight, judging things from their outward appearance, reasoning from what he saw. *God* was left out of his calculation and consideration. As the sequel showed, all those things were, really, working together for his good. What a warning for us! Take the children of Israel after their exodus from Egypt: "When Pharaoh drew nigh, the children of Israel lifted up their eyes, and, behold, the Egyptians marched after them; and they were sore afraid. . . . And they said unto Moses, Because there were no graves in Egypt, hast thou taken us away to die in the wilderness?" (Ex. 14:10, 11). Instead of trusting in the Lord with all their hearts, they leaned unto their own understanding. Once more: consider the apostles after the Crucifixion: the death of their Master, was the death of their hopes. Why? Because instead of trusting in the Lord with all their heart, they leaned unto their own understanding. Once again we say, What a warning for us!

Ah, Christian readers, when shall we learn that God's dealings with us are designed to wean us *from* leaning unto our own understanding. If it takes us a long time to discover that we have no might of our own, and must draw strength from above; it takes us longer still to realise that we have no wit of our own, and must seek wisdom from on high.

> "Judge not the Lord by feeble sense,
>   But trust Him for His grace;
> Behind a frowning providence
>   He hides a smiling face.
>
> "Blind unbelief is sure to err,
>   And scan His work in vain;
> God is His own interpreter,
>   And He will make it plain."

"Lean not unto thine own understanding" *when engaged in the work of the Lord.* Alas, how much failure is there here! How much of the flesh enters into "Christian service"! how frequently worldly methods are employed! how often it is assumed that the end justifies the means! The only "end'" which is worthy for any Christian

(Concluded Page 215.)

STUDIES IN THE SCRIPTURES

"Search the Scriptures" John 5: 39

Copyright in all English-speaking Countries.

Editor: Arthur W. Pink, 7 The Crescent, Surbiton, Surrey, England.
Hon. Agent in U.S.A.: Mr. C. S. Pressel, 559 Dupont Avenue, York, Penna.
Hon. Agent in Australia: Mr. G. Ardill, The Christian Workers' Depot. Commonwealth and Reservoir Streets, Sydney.

FREE TO ALL WHO WILL READ IT

OWNERSHIP OWNED.

"In all thy ways acknowledge Him" (Prov. 3:6).

We are frequently the losers through failure to observe the *order* in which Divine truth is set before us. For example, how obvious is the progression to be observed in and how necessary it is that we should lay to heart the fourfold injunction of Psa. 37:3-7. First, "Trust in the Lord, and do good" (v. 3); second, "Delight thyself also in the Lord" (v. 4); third, "Commit thy way unto the Lord" (v. 5); fourth, "Rest in the Lord" (v. 7). So it is in the book from which our text is taken. These "proverbs" are not so many maxims strung together at random, but instead they are presented according to a Divine plan; and the more they are prayerfully pondered, the more will the wisdom and love which lie behind their arrangement be perceived by the anointed eye. Prov. 3:5, 6 is a case in point.

"Trust in the Lord with all thine heart." This comes first because it is the primary duty; without *this*, everything else is vain. "Trust" in His loving kindness. Can He who is Love withhold anything which is really for thy good? "Trust" in His wondrous power. Is anything too hard for the Almighty? No matter how critical your situation, "Trust in the Lord." "Trust" in His unchanging faithfulness. Hath He not promised? then will He not perform! Hath He said? then will He not also do it!

"And lean not unto thine own understanding." This comes next to put us on our guard concerning the principal enemy of faith. Just as we cannot serve *two* masters, so we cannot trust in the Lord and lean unto our own understanding. It is a word of warning against the inveterate tendency of our evil hearts. To rely upon our own wisdom, to follow the dictates of common sense, is the chief obstacle in our way against whole-hearted trust in the Lord. Thus, we are bidden to repudiate our own reasoning-powers.

Then comes the word, "In all thy ways acknowledge Him." This goes much further than trusting in the Lord with all the heart, though, of necessity, it must be preceded by that. Unless our hearts are completely occupied with God, the acknowledgment of Him in our outward ways will be nothing more than a perfunctory performance, which is of no value in His sight. That which the Lord requires and desires is the obedience of love. Confidence in the Lord is now to be translated into conformity to His will. Faith without works is dead. Our "ways," that is, all the details of our walk, are to make manifest our unreserved trust in the Lord. His Ownership of us is to be owned, in a practical way, by that faith which "worketh by love." To "acknowledge" the Lord in all our ways, signifies:—

1. *Seek His permission for everything you do.* Dare we be so presumptuous as to act *without* His leave? We are but creatures, He is God. We are but servants, He is our Lord and Master. We are but purchased property, He is our Redeemer. "Ye are not your own" (1 Cor. 6:19). Therefore, we are not free to please ourselves, but under deepest obligations to be in subjection to the Divine will. God's leave should be *asked* even when a thing is lawful and right. A striking illustration of this is furnished in the prayer which Christ taught His disciples, and that so many have

(Continued on Page 240.)

IMPORTANT NOTICES

Back numbers of each year of the magazine are yet obtainable at 5/- (1.25) per year. Bound at 7/6 (1.75) post paid. They will soon be out of print. Those in U.S.A. wanting them, please purchase from Mr. Pressel (see front cover page).

Advise promptly of change of address.

This Magazine is published as a work of faith and labour of love. The Editor gladly gives his services. It is freely sent to all who will read it. No charge is made for it.

Christians who feel definitely led to do so, may have fellowship with us in this Ministry. Send only *Inter-National M.O.*

CONTENTS.

	Page.
Hebrews	218
Gleanings in Exodus	224
Path of the Just	229
Way of the Wicked	231
The Saving Look	235

THE EPISTLE TO THE HEBREWS.

10. *Christ Superior to Angels: Heb. 2:11-13.*

Inasmuch as we feel led to break up the second half of Heb. 2 into shorter sections than is our usual habit (so that we may enter more into detail), it will be necessary to begin each article with a brief summary of what has already been before us. Though we dislike using valuable space for mere repetitions, yet this seems unavoidable if the continuity of thought is to be preserved and the scope of the apostle's argument intelligently followed. Moreover, as we endeavour to study the holy Word of God, it is ever the part of wisdom to heed the Divine injunction, "he that believeth shall not make haste" (Isa. 28:16). To pause and review the ground already covered, serves to fix in the memory what otherwise might be crowded out. As said the apostle to the Philippians, "to write the *same* things to you, to me indeed is not grievous, but for you it is safe" (3:1).

In the opening chapter of our Epistle, from vv. 4 to 14, seven O.T. passages were quoted for the purpose of showing the superiority of Israel's Messiah over the angels. The first four verses of chapter 2 are parenthetical, inasmuch as the argument of that section is broken off in order to make a searching application to the conscience of what has already been said. At 2:5 the discussion concerning the relative positions of the Mediator and the celestial creatures is resumed. Two objections are now anticipated and dealt with—this is made clear by the last clause of v. 8, which is the interjecting of a difficulty. The objections are: How could Christ be superior to angels, seeing that He was *Man?* and, How could He possess a grater excellency than they, seeing that He had *died?*

In meeting these objections appeal was first made to the 8th Psalm, which affirmed, in predictive language, that God has crowned "man" (redeemed man) with "honour and glory," and that He has put "all things under *his* feet"; and in the exaltation of Jesus faith beholds the ground and guarantee, the proof and pledge, of the coming exaltation of all His people (v. 9). Second, the necessity for the Mediator's humiliation lay in the fact that He must "taste death," as the appointed Substitute, if "every son" was to receive eternal life (v. 9). Third, the apostle affirmed that God had a benevolent design in suffering His Son to stoop so low: it was by His "grace" that He tasted death (v. 9). Fourth, it is announced that such a course of procedure was suited to the nature and honouring to the glory of Him who ordains all things: it "became Him" (v. 10). Fifth, the Divine love and wisdom in causing the Captain of our salvation to be perfected "through sufferings" was fully vindicated, for the outcome from it is that many sons are brought "unto glory."

In Heb. 2:11, which begins our present portion, the needs-be for the Son's humiliation is made still more evident: "For both He that sanctifieth and they who are sanctified, are all of one: for which cause He is not ashamed to call them brethren." The opening "for" at once intimates that the Holy Spirit is still advancing confirmation of what He had said previously, and is continuing to show *why* the Lord of angels had been made Man. It may help the reader to grasp the force of this verse if we state it thus: It was imperative that Christ should be made, for a season, "lower than the angels" if ever He was to have ground and cause to call *us* "brethren." *That* is a title which presupposes a *common* state and standing; for this He must become "one" with them.

In other words, the Redeemer must identify Himself with those He was to redeem.

We may add that the opening "for" of v. 11 supplies an immediate link with v. 10: a further reason is now advanced why it "became" God to make the Captain of His people perfect through sufferings, even because He and they are "all of one." Herein lies the *equity* of Christ's suffering. It was not that an innocent person was smitten in order that guilty ones might go free, for that would be the height of injustice, but that an innocent Person, voluntarily, out of love, *identified Himself with* transgressors, and so became answerable for their crimes. Therefore, "in all things it behooved Him to be made like unto His brethren" (Heb. 2:17). How this should endear Him to us!

"All of one," is very abstract, and for this reason not easy to define concretely. "Observe that it is only of sanctified persons that this is said. Christ and the sanctified ones are all of one company, men together in the same position before God; but the idea goes a little farther. It is not of one and the same Father; had it been so, it could not have been said, 'He is not ashamed to call them brethren.' He could not then do otherwise than call them brethren. If we say 'of the same mass' the expression may be pushed too far, as though He and others were of the same nature as children of Adam, sinners together. In this case Jesus would have to call every man His brother; whereas it is only the children whom God hath given Him, 'sanctified' ones, that He so calls. But He and the sanctified ones are all as men in the same nature and position together before God. When I say 'the same' it is not in the same state of sin, but the contrary, for they are the Sanctifier and the sanctified, but in the same proof of human position as it is before God as sanctified to Him; the same as far forth as man when He, as the sanctified One is before God" (Mr. J. N. Darby).

Though the above quotation is worded somewhat vaguely, nevertheless we believe it approximates closely to the thought of the Spirit. They, Christ and His people, are "all of one." Perhaps we might say, All of one class or company. If Christ were to be the Saviour of men, He must Himself be Man. This is what the quotations from the O.T., which immediately follow, go to show. We do believe, however, that the "all of one" is a little fuller in scope than that brought out by Mr. Darby's comments. The remainder of Heb. 2 seems to show it also has reference to the oneness in *condition* between the Sanctifier and the sanctified, i.e., in this world. The Shepherd went before the sheep (John 10:4): the path they follow is the same He trod. Thus, "all of one" in position, in sufferings, in trials, in dependency upon God.

"For both He that sanctifieth and they who are sanctified are all of one." Many of the commentators have quite missed the meaning of this "all of one." Had sufficient attention been given to the context they should have seen that the apostle is *not* here treating of the oneness of Christians with Christ in acceptance before God and in glory—that, we get in such passages as Eph. 1: and 2; instead, he is bringing out the oneness of Christ with His people in their humiliation. In other words, the apostle is not here speaking of our being lifted up to Christ's level, but of His coming down to ours. That which follows clearly establishes this.

But what is meant by "He that sanctifieth and they who are sanctified"? The Sanctifier is Christ Himself, the sanctified are the many sons who are being brought to glory. "The source and power of sanctification are in the Son of God our Saviour. We who were to be brought unto glory were far off from God, in a state of condemnation and death. What could be more different than our natural condition and the glory of God which we are awaiting? Condemned on account of our transgressions of the law, we lived in sin, alienated from God, and without His presence of light and love. We were dead; and by 'dead' I do not mean that modern fancy which explains death to mean cessation of existence, but that continuous, active, self-developing state of misery and corruption into which the sinner has fallen by his disobedience. Dead in trespasses and sins, wherein we *walked;* dead while living in pleasing self (Eph. 2:1, 2, 1 Tim. 5:6). What can be more opposed to glory than the state in which we are by nature? and if we are to be brought into glory, it is evident we must be brought into holiness; we must be delivered and separated from guilt, pollution, and death, and brought into the presence of God, in which is favour, light, and life—that His life may descend into our souls, and that we may become partakers of the Divine nature.

"Christ is our sanctification. 'By one offering He hath perfected forever them that are sanctified' (Heb. 10:14). By the offering of His body as the sacrifice for sin, He has sanctified all that put their trust in Him. To sanctify is to separate unto God; to separate for a holy use. We who were far off are brought nigh by the blood of Christ. And although our election is of God the Father (who is thus the Author of our sanctification, Jude 4), and the cleansing and purification of the heart is generally attributed to the Holy Spirit (Titus 3:4, 5), yet is it in Christ that we were chosen, and from Christ that we receive the Spirit, and as it is by the constant application of Christ's work and the constant communication of His life that we live and grow, Christ is our sanctification.

"We are sanctified through faith that is in Him (Acts 26:18). By His offering of Himself He has brought us into the presence of God. By the Word, by God's truth, by the indwelling Spirit, He continually sanctifies His believers. He gave Himself for the church, 'that He might sanctify and cleanse it by the washing of water by the Word' (Eph. 5:26). 'Sanctify them through Thy truth' (John 17:17; 15:3).

"Christ Himself is the foundation, source, method, and channel of our sanctification. We are exhorted to put off the old man and to put on the new man day by day, to mortify our members which are upon the earth. But in what way or method can we obey the apostolic exhortations, but by our continually beholding Christ's perfect sacrifice for sin as our all-sufficient atonement? In what other way are we sanctified day by day, but by taking hold of the salvation which is by Him, 'The Lamb that is slain'? Jesus is He that sanctifieth. The Holy Spirit, the Comforter, is sent by Christ to glorify Him, and to reveal and appropriate to us His salvation. We are conformed to the image of Christ by the Spirit as coming from Christ in His glorified humanity" (Saphir).

"For which cause He is not ashamed to call them brethren" (v. 11). Because Christ became Man, He is not ashamed to own as "brethren" those whom the Father had given to Him. The community of nature shared by the Sanctifier and the sanctified furnishes ground for Him to call them "brethren." That He did so in the days of His humiliation may be seen by a reference to Matt. 12:49; John 20:17. That He will do so in the Day to come, appears from Matt. 25:40. That He is "not ashamed" to so own them, plainly intimates an act of condescension on His part, the condescension arising out of the fact that *He* was more than Man, none other than "the Lord of glory." There is, no doubt, a latent contrast in these words: the world hated them, their brethren according to the flesh despised them, and called them "apostates"; but the Son of God incarnate was not ashamed to call them "brethren." So, too, He owns us. Therefore, if *He* is "not ashamed" to own us, shall *we* be "ashamed" to confess Him! Moreover, let us "not be ashamed" to own as "brethren" the poorest of the flock!

"For which cause He is not ashamed to call them brethren." Ere passing from these blessed words, it needs to be said, emphatically, that this grace on the part of Christ *does not* warrant His people from being so presumptuous as to speak of Him as their "Brother." Such a thing is most reprehensible. "Question, May we by virtue of this relation, call the Son of God our Brother? Answer, We have no example of any of the saints that ever did so. They usually gave titles of dignity to Him, as Lord, Master, Saviour. Howsoever the Son of God vouchsafes this honour unto us, yet we must retain in our hearts an high and reverent esteem of Him, and on that ground give such titles to Him as may manifest as much. Inferiors do not use to give like titles of equality to their superiors, as superiors do to their inferiors. It is a token of love in superiors to speak to their inferiors as equals; but for inferiors to do the like, would be a note of arrogancy" (Dr. Gouge). The same principle applies to John 15:15. Christ in His condescending grace may call us His "friends," but this does *not* justify us in speaking of Him as our "Friend"!

"Saying, I will declare Thy name unto My brethren" (v. 12). Once more the apostle appeals to the written Word for support of what he had just affirmed. A quotation is made from Psa. 22, one which not only substantiated what had been said in v. 11, but which also made a further contribution towards removing the objection before him. As is well known, the 22nd is the great Cross Psalm. In vv. 20, 21, the suffering Saviour is heard crying, "Deliver My soul from the sword (of Divine justice, cf. Zech. 13:7), My darling from the power of the dog (the Gentiles, cf. Matt. 15:24-26). Save Me from the lion's (the Devil's, cf. 1 Peter 5:8) mouth." Then follows faith's assurance, "For Thou *hast* heard Me from the horns of the unicorn." This is the turning point of the Psalm: the cries of the Sufferer are heard on High. What a conclusive and crushing reply was this to the objecting Jew! God's own Word had foretold the humiliation and sufferings of their Messiah. There it was, unmistakably before them. What could they say? The Scriptures *must* be fulfilled. No reply was possible.

But more: not only did the 22nd Psalm announce beforehand the sufferings of the Messiah; it also foretold His victory. Read again the last clause of v. 21: "Save Me from the lion's mouth: for Thou *hast* heard Me." Christ *was* "saved," not from death, but out of death, cf. Heb. 5:7. Now what is the very next thing in Psalm 22? This: "I will declare Thy name unto My brethren" (v. 22). Here the Saviour is seen on resurrection ground, victorious over every foe. It is *this* which the apostle quotes in Heb. 2:12.

Now that which it is particularly important to note is that in this verse from Psa. 22 Christ is heard saying He would declare the Father's name unto His "brethren." *That* could only be possible on resurrection ground. Why? Because by nature they were "dead in trespasses and sins." But as "quickened together with Christ" (Eph. 2:5) they were made sons of God, and therefore the "brethren" of the risen Son of God. Hence the great importance of noting carefully the very point at which v. 22 occurs in the 22nd Psalm. The Lord Jesus never called His people "brethren" on the other side of the Cross! He spoke of them as "disciples," "sheep," "friends," but never as "brethren." But as soon as He was risen from the dead, He said to Mary, "Go to My brethren, and say unto them, I ascend unto My Father and to your Father" (John 20:17). Here, then, was the unanswerable reply to the Jews' objection: Christ could reach *resurrection* ground only by passing through death, cf. John 12:24.

"I will declare Thy name unto My brethren." Here the Son is heard addressing the Father, promising that He would execute the charge which had been given Him. The Greek word for "declare" is very emphatic and comprehensive. It means, To proclaim and publish, to exhibit and make known. To declare God's "Name" signifies to reveal what God is, to make known His excellencies and counsels. This is what Christ came here to do: see John 17:6, 26. None else was competent for such a task, for none knoweth the Father but the Son (Matt. 11:27). But only to His "brethren" did Christ do so. They are the "babes" unto whom heavenly things are revealed (Matt. 11:25); they are the ones unto whom are made known the "mysteries of the kingdom of heaven" (Matt. 13:11). From all others these blessed revelations are "hid," to those "without" they are but "parables."

"In the midst of the church will I sing praise unto Thee" (v. 12). This completes the quotation from Psalm 22:22. No doubt the first fulfilment of this took place during the "forty days" of Acts 1:3: mark how Acts 1:4 brings in the assembly; though its ultimate fulfilment is yet future. The *position* in which Christ is here viewed is very blessed, "in the midst": it is the Redeemer leading the praises of His redeemed. Strangers to God may go through all the outward forms of mere "religion," but they never *praise* God. It is only upon resurrection ground that worship is possible. A beautiful type of this is found in Ex. 15:1: it was only after Israel had crossed the Red Sea, and the Egyptians were dead upon the shore, that "Then sang Moses and the children of Israel this song." Note how Moses, the typical mediator, *led* their praises!

"And again, I will put My trust in Him" (v. 13). The apostle is still replying to the Jews' objection, How could Jesus of Nazareth be the superior of angels, seeing that He was Man and had died? Here, in vv. 12, 13, he quotes Messianic passages from the O.T. in proof of the statements made in vv. 10, 11. First, Psalm 22:22 is cited, in which Christ is heard addressing His redeemed as "brethren." The implication is unmistakable: that is a title which presupposes a common position and a common condition, and in order to that the Lord of glory had to be abased, come down to their level, become Man. Then, in the same passage, the Saviour is heard "singing praise" unto God. This also views Him as incarnate, for only as Man could He sing praise unto God! Moreover, it is not as Lord over the church, but as One "in the midst" of it He is there viewed. Thus "all of one" is illustrated and substantiated.

A second quotation is now made, from Isa. 8:17, according to the Septuagent version. The passage from which this is taken is a very remarkable one. Beginning at v. 13 the exhortation is given, "Sanctify the Lord of Hosts Himself; and let Him be your fear, and let Him be your dread." This means, give Him His true place in your hearts, recognise His exalted dignity, bow before His ineffable majesty, submit to His high sovereignty, tremble at the very thought of quarrelling with Him.

Then, in v. 14, the Lord of Hosts is brought before us in a twofold character: "And He shall be for a sanctuary; but for a stone of a stumbling and for a rock of offence to both the houses of Israel, for a gin and for a snare to the inhabitants of Jerusalem." These expressions, Sanctuary and Stone of stumbling, define the relation of the Lord to the elect and to the non-elect. To the one He a Refuge, a Resting-place, a Centre of worship; to the other, He is an offence. "The Stone" is one of the titles of Christ, and it is most interesting and instructive to trace out the various references, the first being found in Gen. 49:24. Here in Isa. 8 it is Christ in His *lowliness* which is in view. Israel was looking for One who would be high among the great ones of the earth, therefore when One who was born in a manger, who had toiled at the carpenter's bench, who had not where to lay His head, appeared before them, they "despised and rejected" Him. The figure used here is very affecting. How *low* a place must the Lord of glory have taken for Israel to "stumble" over Him, like a stone lying at one's feet! Thus, once more, the Holy Spirit refers to an O.T. passage in which the Messiah was presented in humiliation, as it were "a stone" lying on the ground.

It is scarcely necessary to add that the very lowliness into which the Saviour entered, coming here not to be ministered unto but to minister, and give His life a ransom for many, is that which makes Him a "precious Stone" (1 Peter 2:6) to all whose faith sees the Divine glory shining beneath the humiliation. What is more moving to our hearts, what is more calculated to bow them in worship before God as we behold His Son in John 13?—verily, "a Stone" at the feet of His disciples, washing them! Blessed is it to know that the very Stone which the builders rejected "is become the head of the corner" (Psa. 118:22), that is, has been exalted.

Returning now to Isa. 8, v. 15 amplifies what was said in the previous one: "And many among them shall stumble, and fall, and be broken, and be snared, and be taken." How solemnly and how literally this was fulfilled in the history of the Jews we all know. Then, in v. 16, we have stated the *consequences* of Israel's rejection of their Messiah: "Bind up the testimony, seal the law among My disciples." Ever since there has been a veil over Israel's heart, even when reading the Holy Scriptures (2 Cor. 3:15).

Now comes the word in Heb. 2:13, "I will put My trust in Him" (Isa. 8:17, Sept. version). A most blessed word is this. It reveals the implicit confidence of the Saviour in God. Notwithstanding the treatment which He met with from both the houses of Israel, His trust in Jehovah remained unshaken; He looked away from the things seen to the things unseen. The *relevancy* of this citation in Heb. 2 is obvious: such a thing could not have been unless Christ had become Man—considered simply as God the Son, to speak of Him "trusting" was unthinkable, impossible. Wonderful proof was this of what had been affirmed in 2:11 concerning the oneness which exists between Christ and His people: He, like they, was called on to tread the path of faith.

"I will put My trust in Him." This is indeed a word which should bow our hearts in wonderment. What a lowly place had the Maker of heaven and earth taken! How these words bring out the reality of His humanity! The Son of God had become the Son of Man, and while here on earth He ever acted in perfect accord with the place which He had taken. He lived here a life of faith, that is, a life of trust in and dependence upon God. In John 6:57 we hear Him saying, "I live by the Father." *This* is what He pressed on Satan when tempted to manufacture bread for Himself.

Isa. 8:17 is not the only O.T. passage which speaks of Christ "trusting" in God. In Psalm 16:1 He cries, "Preserve Me, O God: for in Thee do I put My trust." As Man it was not fitting that He should stand independent and alone; nor did He. The whole of this Psalm views Him in the place of entire dependency—in life, in death, in resurrection. Strikingly will this appear if vv. 10 and 11 be compared with John 2:19 and 10:18. In the passages in John's Gospel, where His *Divine* glory shines forth through the veil of His humanity, He speaks of raising Himself from the dead. But here in Psa. 16, where the perfections of His manhood are revealed, He is seen trusting in God to raise Him again. How important it is to get the Spirit's viewpoint in each passage!

"I will put My trust in Him." This perfection of our Lord is not sufficiently pondered by us. The life which Jesus Christ lived here for thirty-three years was a life of faith. That is the meaning of that little-understood word in Heb. 12:2: "Looking off unto Jesus (His name, as Man), the Author (Greek, same as "Captain" in 2:10) and Perfecter of faith." If these words be carefully weighed in the light of their context, their meaning is plain. In Heb. 11 we have illustrated, from the O.T. saints, various aspects of the life of faith; but in Jesus we see *every* aspect of it *perfectly* exemplified. As our Captain or Leader, He has gone before His soldiers, setting before them an inspiring example. The path we are called on to tread, is the same He trod. The race we are bidden to run, is the same He ran. And we are to walk and run as He did, by faith.

"I will put my trust in Him." This was ever the expression of His heart. Christ could say, and none but He ever could, "I was cast upon Thee from the womb: Thou art My God from My mother's belly" (Psa. 22:10). Never did another live in such complete dependence on God as He: "I have set the Lord always before Me; because He is at My right hand, I shall not be moved" (Psa. 16:8) was His language. So evident was His faith, even to others, that His very enemies, whilst standing around the Cross, turned it into a bitter taunt: "He trusted on the Lord that He would deliver Him, let Him deliver Him, seeing He delighted in Him" (Psa. 22:8). How blessed to know that when *we* are called on to walk by faith, to submit ourselves unto and live in dependency on God, to look away from the mists of time to the coming inheritance, that Another has trod the same path, that in putting forth His sheep, the Good Shepherd went before them (John 10:4), that He bids us to do nothing but what He has Himself first done.

"I will put My trust in Him." This is *still* true of the Man Christ Jesus. In Rev. 1:9 we read of "the kingdom and *patience* of Jesus Christ": that is the patience of faith, cf. Heb. 11:13. Heb. 10:12, 13 interprets: "But this Man, after He had offered one sacrifice for sins forever, sat down on the right hand of God; from henceforth *expecting* till His enemies be made His footstool." That is the expectation of *faith*, awaiting the fulfilment of God's promise. Ah, dear reader, fellowship with Christ is no mystical thing, it is intensely practical; fellowship with Christ means, first of all, walking by faith.

"And again, behold I and the children which God hath given Me" (v. 13). This completes the quotation made from Isa. 8:17, 18. The pertinency of these words in support of the apostle's argument is evident: it is Christ's taking His place before God as Mediator, owning the "children" as His gift to Him; it is Christ as Man confessing His oneness with them, ranking Himself with the saints—"I and the children," compare "My Father and your Father" (John 20:17). It is the Lord Jesus presenting Himself to God as His Minister, having faithfully and successfully fulfilled the task committed to Him. He is here heard addressing the Father, rejoicing over the fruits of His own work. It is as though He said, "Here am I, O Father, whom Thou didst send out of Thine own bosom from Heaven to earth, to gather Thine elect out of the world. I *have* performed that for which Thou didst send Me: behold I and the children which Thou hast given Me." Though He had proved a stone of stumbling and a rock of offence to both the houses of Israel, yet was He not left without a people; "children" had been given to Him, and these He owns and solemnly presents before God.

Who are these "children?" First, they are those whom the Mediator brings to God. As we read in 1 Peter 3:18, "For Christ hath also once suffered for sins, the Just for the unjust, that He might *bring us to God*." This is what Christ is seen doing here: formally presenting the children to God. Second, they are here regarded as the "children" *of Christ*. In Isa. 53:10, 11 it was said, "He shall see His seed, He shall prolong His days, and the pleasure of the Lord shall prosper in His hands. He shall see *of the travail* of His soul, and shall be satisfied." In John 13:33 and 21:5 He is actually heard *owning* His disciples as "children." Nor was there anything incongruous in that. Let the reader ponder 1 Cor. 4:14, 15: if they who are converted under the preaching of God's servants may be termed *their* "children," how much more so may they be called "children" of Jesus Christ whom *He* has begotten by His Spirit and by His Word!

"Behold I and the children which God hath given Me." Those whom God hath given to Christ were referred to by Him, again and again, during the days of His public ministry. "All that the Father giveth Me shall come to Me" (John 6:37). "I have manifested Thy name unto the men which Thou gavest Me out of the world: Thine they were, and Thou gavest them Me. . . . I pray for them: I pray not for the world, but for them which Thou hast given Me" (John 17:6, 9). They were given to Christ before the foundation of the world (Eph. 1:4). These "children" are God's elect, sovereignly singled out by Him, and from the beginning chosen unto salvation (1 Thess. 2:13). God's elect having been given to Christ "before the foundation of the world," and therefore from all eternity, throws light upon a title of the Saviour's found in Isa. 9:6: "The everlasting Father." This has puzzled many. It need not. Christ is the "everlasting Father" because from everlasting He has had "children!"

Why were these "children" given to Christ? The first answer must be, For

His own glory. Christ is the Centre of all God's counsels, and His glory the one object ever held in view. Christ will be eternally glorified by having around Him a family, each member of which is predestined to be "conformed to His image" (Rom. 8:29). The second answer is, That He might save them: "All that the Father giveth Me shall come to Me, and him that cometh to Me I will in no wise cast out" (John 6:37).

"Behold I and the children which God hath given Me." We doubt not that the ultimate reference of these words looks forward to the time anticipated by that wonderful doxology found at the close of Jude's Epistle: "Now unto Him that is able to keep you from falling, and to *present* you faultless before the presence of His glory with exceeding joy, to the only wise God our Saviour, be glory and majesty, dominion and power, both now and ever." When the Lord Jesus shall, in a soon-coming Day, gather the company of the redeemed unto Himself and *"present* it to Himself a glorious church, not having spot, or wrinkle, or any such thing" (Eph. 5:27), then shall He triumphantly exclaim, "Behold I and the children which God hath given Me." In the meantime let us seek to take unto our hearts something of the blessedness of these words that, even now, the "joy of the Lord" may be our strength (Neh. 8:10).

"Behold I and the children which God hath given Me." Let us endeavour to point out one or two plain implications. First, *how dear,* how precious, must God's elect be unto Christ! They are the Father's own "gift" unto Him. The value of a gift lies not in its intrinsic worth, but in the esteem and affection in which the giver is held. It is in this light, first of all, that Christ ever views His people—as the expression of the Father's own love for Himself. Second, how certain it is that Christ will continue to care for and minister unto His people! He cannot be indifferent to the welfare of one of those whom the Father has given to Him. As John 13:1 declares, "having loved His own which were in the world, He loved them unto the end." Third, *how secure* they must be! None of His can possibly perish. Beautifully is this brought out in John 18:8, 9, where, to those who had come to arrest Him, Christ said, "If therefore ye seek Me, let these go their way: that the saying might be fulfilled, which He spake, Of them which Thou gavest Me have I lost none."

Inexpressibly blessed is that which has been before us in Heb. 2:12, 13. The Lord's people are there looked at in a threefold way. First, Christ owns them as His "brethren." O the wonder of it! The ambitious worldling aspires to fleshly honours and titles, but what has he which can, for a moment, be compared with the honoured title which Christ confers upon His redeemed? Next time you are slandered by men, called some name which hurts you, remember, fellow-Christian, that *Christ* calls you one of His "brethren." Second, the entire company of the redeemed are here denominated "the church," and Christ is seen in the midst singing praise. There, they are viewed corporately, as a company of worshippers, and He who is "a Priest forever" leads their songs of joy and adoration. Third, the Lord Jesus owns us as His "children," children which have been given to Him by God. This speaks both of their nearness and dearness to Himself. Surely the contemplation of these wondrous riches of grace must impel us to cry, "To Him be glory and dominion for ever and ever. Amen" (Rev. 1:6).

—*Arthur W. Pink.*

GLEANINGS IN EXODUS.

58. *The Sabbath and Israel. Ex.* 31:13-18.

As was pointed out at the commencement of our last article, the contents of Ex. 31 fall under three clearly-defined divisions. First, the provision made by Jehovah for the carrying out of the instructions which He had given to Moses concerning the making of the tabernacle. This, as we have seen, was His calling and equipping of the principal artificers and the appointing of their work. Second, the mention, once more, of God's holy Sabbath, and the defining of its special relation to Israel. Third, a brief word in v. 18 of the actual giving to Moses of the tables of testimony, on which were inscribed the ten commandments. It is the last two divisions we are about to consider; may the Spirit of God graciously preserve us from all error and guide us into all truth.

"And the Lord spake unto Moses, saying, Speak thou also unto the children of Israel, saying, Verily My sabbaths ye shall keep: for it is a sign between Me and you throughout your generations; that ye may know that I am the Lord that doth sanctify you. Ye shall keep the sabbath therefore for it is holy unto you: every one that defileth it shall surely be put to death: for whosoever doeth any work therein, that soul shall be cut off from among his people. Six days may work be done; but in the seventh is the sabbath of rest, holy to the Lord: whosoever doeth any work in the sabbath day, he shall surely be put to death. Wherefore the children of Israel shall keep the sabbath, to observe the sabbath throughout their generations, for a perpetual covenant. It is a sign between Me and the children of Israel forever: for in six days the Lord made heaven and earth, and on the seventh day He rested, and was refreshed" (vv. 12-17). In pondering what is here said concerning the Sabbath we propose to look first at its typical significance, then at its dispensational bearings, and lastly at the judicial aspects of our passage.

It may strike the thoughtful reader as strange that any reference should be made here to the Sabbath: coming right after the description of the tabernacle, its furniture, its priesthood and its artificers; the more so, as full mention of it had already been made in Ex. 20:8-11. There are no mere repetitions in Holy Writ, and though a thing may be mentioned more than once, or the same command or ordinance be given again and again, yet it is always with another end in view, or for the purpose of enforcing a different design, or with the object of bringing in fuller details. Generally the Spirit's purpose may be discerned by taking note of the *connection* in which each statement occurs.

The first time the Sabbath is mentioned in Exodus is in 16:23-29, from which it should be quite apparent that this holy day unto the Lord was no new appointment at that time: the words of v. 28 (occasioned by Israel's desecration of the Sabbath, see v. 27) are too plain to be misunderstood: "And the Lord said unto Moses, How long refuse ye to keep My commandments and My laws?" Thus, the initial reference to the Sabbath in Exodus contains the Lord's expostulation with His people for having disregarded His commandments—referring no doubt to the evil way in which they had, for centuries, conducted themselves in Egypt: see Ezek. 20:5-9.

The second time the Sabbath is found in Exodus is in chapter 20, where we have the ten commandments given to Israel orally. They were given to Israel as a redeemed people, which the Lord had brought "out of the house of bondage." They expressed the rights of God, His claims upon His people, that which He righteously required from them. Those commandments were not a yoke grievous to be borne, but the making known of a path in which love was to walk. In them God promised to show mercy unto thousands (*not* "millions") of them that love Me and keep My commandments" (v. 6). God's commandments are just as truly the expressions of His love as are His promises, and a heart that loves Him in return should rejoice in the one as much as in the other. God's commandments express both His authority over and His solicitude for His people. It is in that light this second mention of the Sabbath in Exodus is to be viewed.

The third reference in Exodus to the Sabbath is found in chapter 31, a section of the book where everything speaks loudly of Christ. Unless this be carefully noted the meaning of our present passage will be missed. It should be evident at once that the *typical* significance of the Sabbath is the first thing to be looked at here. True, that by no means exhausts the scope and value of these verses, yet it does supply the key which unlocks for us their primary meaning. Here, again, we have another example of a principle which holds good of every part of the Word, namely, if we ignore the *context* we are sure to err in our interpretation.

Now in seeking to discover the typical meaning of the Sabbath we cannot do better than turn back to the first mention of it in Scripture: "And on the seventh day God ended His work which He had made; and He rested on the seventh day from all His work which He had made. And God blessed the seventh day, and sanctified it: because that in it He had rested from all His work which God created and made" (Gen. 2:2, 3). It will be observed that three actions of God in connection with the Sabbath are here mentioned: He ended His work which He had made and "rested on the seventh day," He "blessed the seventh day," He "sanctified" it. We believe the order in which these three things are mentioned is the order of spiritual importance—confirmed by the first thing mentioned being repeated.

In order to apprehend aright the spiritual import of the Sabbath, it is most necessary to observe that the first thing of all connected with it is *the rest of God*. The fact that God rested on the seventh day is undoubtedly recorded for the purpose of teaching that the Creator graciously condescended to set an example before His creatures of how to spend and enjoy the Sabbath; yet that there is also a deeper meaning to this statement will scarcely be denied. Nor do we think that the reference is solely to the Creator's delight and satisfaction in the works which He had made during the six days preceding; rather would it appear (from subsequent scriptures) that this "rest" was *anticipatory*—spiritually, of that rest which the Christian enjoys now; dispensationally, of the millennial Sabbath; typically, of the eternal Sabbath.

Now in the light of what is before us in the first eleven verses of Ex. 31, is there any difficulty in discovering the perfect propriety of a reference to *the Sabbath* in what immediately follows? What else *could* have been more appropriate? In the first part of the chapter we have a most lovely foreshadowing of Him who had ever dwelt in the bosom of the Father, the Son of Light, voluntarily undertaking to "work in gold, silver, brass, and of precious stones." The stupendous work therein typified having been gloriously completed, we have at once mentioned that which speaks of the rest of God. How suitable, how blessed the connection! As cause stands to effect, so is the relation between the labours of the tabernacle-artificers and the mention here of the Sabbath. The rest of God is the consequence of the finished Work of Christ: first, that in which God Himself finds complacency; second, that into which His redeemed are brought.

The wicked are like the troubled sea which cannot rest (Isa. 57:20). And why? Because they are away from God. Away from God, they are seeking satisfaction in that which cannot provide it. Theirs is a ceaseless quest after that which will give peace and joy. But over all the varied cisterns to which they have recourse, is written these words, "Whosoever drinketh of this water shall thirst again" (John 4:13). "There is *no* peace, saith my God, unto the wicked" (Isa. 57:21), for they are strangers to the Prince of peace. It is not until the Spirit of God has shown us that all under the sun is but "vanity and vexation of spirit," has convicted us of our sinful and lost condition, has shown us our desperate need of the Saviour, and drawn us to Him, that we hear the Lord Jesus saying, "Come unto Me, all ye that labour and are heavy laden, and I will give you rest." Then it becomes true that, "we which have believed *do* enter into rest" (Heb. 4:3).

"Verily My sabbaths ye shall keep: for it is a sign between Me and you throughout your generations; that ye may know that I am the Lord that doth *sanctify* you. Ye shall keep My Sabbaths *therefore*, for it is holy unto you" (vv. 13, 14). Surely the meaning of this is too plain for us to miss. The Sabbath was now, for the first time, appointed as a "sign" between Jehovah and Israel that they were His "sanctified" people—a people set apart unto Himself. So, also, that of which the Sabbath spoke—the rest of God—was also the portion of a sanctified people, a people "chosen in Christ before the foundation of the world" (Eph. 1:4). This people was sanctified by God the Father before they were called (Jude 1), even from all eternity. They were sanctified by God the Son "with His own blood" (Heb. 13:12). They are sanctified by God the Spirit (2 Thess. 2:13) when they are quickened into newness of life, and thus separated from those who are dead in sins. And the "sign" between God and His sanctified people is still the "Sabbath," i.e., the fact that they have entered into *rest*.

Turning back from the antitype to the type, we can see at once why the Sabbath should be the appointed "sign" between Jehovah and Israel. At the time He entered into covenant relation with them, all other nations had been given up by God (Rom. 1:19-26). Not liking to retain Him in their knowledge, they gave themselves unto idolatry. For this cause God gave them up to a reprobate mind. The heathen nations, therefore, kept no Sabbath, and, in all probability, by that time knew not that the Creator required them to. But to Israel God made known His laws, and the appointed sign or token that they were His peculiar people was their observance of the Sabbath. So that of which, spiritually, the Sabbath speaks, is still the portion of none but God's chosen people.

Dispensationally, the *rest* to which the Sabbath pointed, was the Millennial era, the seventh of earth's great "days." In view of the inspired declaration, "But, beloved, be not ignorant of this one thing, that one day is with the Lord as a thousand years, and a thousand years as one day" (2 Peter 3:8) we believe, with many others, that the "six days" of Gen. 1 give us a prophetic forecast of the world's history, and that the "seventh day" of Gen. 2:2, 3 points to the final dispensation. This is confirmed by Rev. 20 where, again and again, the reign of Christ and His saints over this earth is said to be of a "thousand years" duration. The Millennium will be the earth's great Sabbath. Then shall this scene which has witnessed six thousand years of strife, turmoil, bloodshed, enjoy an unprecedented era of rest. The Prince of peace shall be here; Satan shall be in the bottomless pit; war shall be made to cease to "the end of the earth" (Psa. 4:6:9);

the curse which now rests upon the lower orders of creation shall be lifted (Isa. 11: 6-9).

But not only did the original Sabbath of Gen. 2:2, 3 anticipate the spiritual rest which is, even now, the portion of God's people; not only did it forecast the millennial peace which this earth will yet enjoy; but it also typified an eternal Sabbath, into which nothing shall ever enter to disturb and mar its perfect tranquility and bliss. *This* is what the Work of Christ (adumbrated in Ex. 31:1-11) has secured, and toward which all things are moving. When the present heaven and earth shall have passed away, and a new heaven and earth shall have come into existence, then shall be fulfilled that precious word of Rev. 21: 3-5, "And I heard a great voice out of heaven saying, Behold, the tabernacle of God is with men, and He will dwell with them, and they shall be His people, and God Himself shall be with them, and be their God. And God shall wipe away all tears from their eyes; and there shall be no more death, neither sorrow nor crying, neither shall there be any more pain, for the former things are passed away. And He that sat upon the throne said, Behold, I make all things new."

A beautiful foreshadowing of this is to be found in Zeph. 3:17, "The Lord thy God in the midst of thee is mighty; He will save, He will rejoice over thee with joy; He will rest in His love, He will joy over thee with singing." The immediate reference is to the restoration of Israel to God's favour, to their land, and to the fulfilment of His purpose and promises concerning them. But the ultimate reference, we believe, is to that which shall characterise the Eternal State. Then, in the midst of His redeemed, and as the fruit of His Son's perfect work, God Himself shall rejoice over His people with joy and *"rest* in His love."

Once more we pause to admire the striking and lovely *order* in which God's truth is presented before us. In the first part of Ex. 31 we behold the Divine provision made for giving effect to all that was in the will of God; therefore, in the very next section, that which speaks of Divine rest, is brought before us. In keeping with this it is most blessed to take note of one word which is found here, and nowhere else: "In six days the Lord made heaven and earth, and on the seventh day He rested, *and was refreshed"* (Ex. 31:17). The fact that these words are found not in Gen. 2: 2, 3, or Ex. 20:8-11, but here, right after what is typically in view in 31:1-11, tells, unmistakably, of that refreshment, that joy, that resting in His love, which shall be the eternal portion of God—Father, Son, and Holy Spirit. What is here in view is that rest of God which is the consequence of the bringing into effect, the actual realisation, of the whole will of God as set forth in the tabernacle. When "the tabernacle *of God* is with men" (Rev. 21:3), then shall there be an holy, unbreakable, eternal rest. God will rest in His love, and His sanctified people will rest with Him.

"I think it is in the light of the tabernacle system, and of its taking form for the pleasure of God, that He adds the words, 'And was refreshed.' God was refreshed because even in the material creation He was forming a sphere where all His own blessed thoughts of grace and glory in Christ could be worked out. Those thoughts first came to light in a definite, though figurative, form in the tabernacle, and in the light of them all being brought into effect God could, as it were, carry back into Gen. 2 a secret not revealed. When God made the heavens and the earth He had 'the holy universal order' of the tabernacle in His mind. He was making a material universe, and this in itself could not afford Him refreshment. But He was making it so that it might be the scene for the introduction of 'the holy order of the tabernacle,' which represented the vast scene in which God's glory is displayed in Christ, and in view of the introduction of this He was 'refreshed'! The Sabbath speaks of things being brought to completion, so that there is no more work to be done; all is finished, and there is holy rest for God and His people" (C. A. Coates).

Having pondered the typical significance of the Sabbath's being mentioned in Ex. 31, having sought to point out its dispensational application, it now remains for us to consider the judicial aspect of our passage. This is brought before us in vv. 14, 15, "Ye shall keep the Sabbath therefore; for it holy unto you: every one that defileth it shall surely be put to death: for whosoever doeth any work therein, that soul shall be cut off from among his people. Six days may work be done; but in the seventh is the Sabbath of rest, holy to the Lord: whosoever doeth any work in the Sabbath day, he shall surely be put to death." A solemn example of this threat is recorded in Num. 15:32-36, "And while the children of Israel were in the wilderness they found a man that gathered sticks upon the Sabbath day. And they that found him gathering sticks brought him unto Moses and Aaron, and unto all the congregation. And they put him in ward, because it was not declared what should be done to him. And the Lord said unto Moses, "The man shall surely be put to death: all the congregation shall stone him with stones without the camp. And all the congregation brought him without the camp, and stoned him with stones, and he died."

It seems strange that so many have experienced a difficulty with the above passages. The key to them is surely found in noting the character and design of the Mosaic economy. *That* Dispensation was a legal and a probationary one. It was preparatory to the fuller and final revelation which God made of Himself in and through Christ. It is a mistake to look upon it as a stern regime of unmixed law. True, it was marked at the beginning by the proclamation of the Ten Commandments, but it should not be forgotten that this was immediately followed by the revelation concerning the Tabernacle and the institution of the priesthood, and (see the book of Leviticus) by the Divine appointment of a series of offerings and sacrifices, wherein provision was made for God's people to approach unto Him through their representatives. Though all of this was a typical foreshadowing of that which was to be made good and secured by and through the person and work of Christ, yet it should not be forgotten that it was also a most gracious provision of God for His people at that time.

On the other hand, there was not, and, in the nature of the case, could not be, a full and perfect revelation of the *grace* of God during the Mosaic economy. Law is law, and righteousness requires the strict enforcing of its terms and penalties. Mercy might, and did, make provision for "sins of ignorance" (Lev. 4:2-4; Num. 15:27, 28), and for the unavoidable contact with that which defiled (Num. 19:11-19); but for pre-meditated or deliberate transgressions no sacrifice was available—"he that *despised* Moses' law died without mercy" (Heb. 10:28). A notable case in point which illustrates this distinction is to be found in connection with the requirement of the Mosaic law when a man had been slain. We refer to the "cities of refuge": let the reader carefully consult Num. 35:9-24. If any person had been killed "unawares" (vv. 11, 15)—that is, without "malice aforethought"—then he might find an asylum in one of those cities; but if that person had been deliberately slain, then the word was, "the murderer shall surely be put to death" (vv. 16:17).

What has just been said explains a reference in Psalm 51, which, though very familiar, is understood by but few. That Psalm records the deep penitence of David. He was guilty of murder, the murder of Uriah. In v. 16 he says, "For Thou desireth not sacrifice; else would I give it: Thou delightest not in burnt offering." No "sacrifice" was *available* for murder! What, then, could poor David do? This: cast himself on the "mercy" of God (v. 1), acknowledge his transgression (v. 3), and cry for deliverance from "blood-guiltiness" (v. 14). That his cry was heard, we all know, and the very hearing of it testified to the blessed truth that "mercy rejoiceth against judgment" (James 2:13).

What has just been pointed out should greatly modify the prevailing conception of the harshness of the Mosaic dispensation. True, the Law, as such, showed no mercy; but side by side with the Law was the Levitical sacrifices, and over and above these was the mercy of God, available for those who sought it out of a broken heart. Thus, unless we keep both of these facts in mind, and learn to distinguish between things that differ, confusion of thought and conception must necessarily ensue.

"Whosoever doeth any work on the Sabbath day, he shall surely be put to death." This was the exaction of Law as such, the righteous enforcement of its penalty. Nor was this peculiar to the fourth commandment; it obtained equally with the other nine. The following passages may serve as illustrations and proofs, "And he that smiteth his father, or his mother, shall surely be put to death" (Ex. 21:15); "And the man that committeth adultery with another man's wife, even he that commiteth adultery with his neighbour's wife, the adulterer and the adulteress shall surely be put to death" (Lev. 20:10); "And he that blasphemeth the name of the Lord, he shall surely be put to death" (Lev. 24:16); see also Deut. 13:6-10, etc.

Our chapter closes with the mention of God's giving the tables of testimony unto Moses: "And He gave unto Moses, when He had made an end of communing with him upon Mount Sinai, two tables of testimony, tables of stone, written with the finger of God" (v. 18). This completes the section of the book of Exodus begun at 24:18. For forty days Moses had been in the mount receiving instructions from Jehovah. That those instructions closed with the giving of these two tables of stone is most significant. Coming here after the appointing of the tabernacle-artificers and the mention of the Sabbath it announces, typically, that the rights and claims of God have been made good and eternally secured by and through the person and work of the Lord Jesus. Grace now "reigns," but "through righteousness" (Rom. 5:21). That there is also a close connection between Ex. 31:18 and what follows will, D.V., be shown in our next article.

—*Arthur W. Pink.*

THE PATH OF THE JUST.

"But the path of the just is as the shining light, that shineth more and more unto the perfect day" (Prov. 4:18). Like many another verse which has a pleasant or comforting sound to it, this is one which is often seized without any exercise of soul and appropriated by those who have no title to it. It is the sort of verse which is found in a "Promise-box." Possibly most of our readers have seen them. Many of the Divine promises are printed separately on slips of stiff paper which automatically curl up. These are placed together in a box. Such a box is often to be found in homes professedly Christian. When visitors or friends drop in, the hostess hands this box to them, much as she might a box of chocolates, and says, "Have a promise." What a terrible cheapening of the Divine words of Holy Writ is this! If the reader possesses such a box, he ought to burn it at once. Most of God's promises are *conditional,* but people don't like those conditions. They want the promises, but without exercise of heart. They are not honest. To seize the promises of Scripture without regard to their qualifying context is to be guilty of spiritual theft. We have never seen a box of God's Curses, nor even one of His Commandments! O, what a state of heart this reveals!

Now in connection with the promise contained in Prov. 4:18 we must note carefully *to whom* it is addressed. It is not "The path of the redeemed," nor "the path of the saints," but "the path of the *just.*" The Hebrew word for "just" is translated "righteous" one hundred and sixty-four times, and might have been so here. Now a "righteous" man is one who is right with God, and because of this, he *does* right, his life is right; and in consequence, the path of such an one is "as the shining light." You know there may be light *without* it "shining." The electric light is not always shining; when the current is switched off it does not shine at all. The sun is not always shining, on us, at any rate; clouds obscure it, night falls, and it is dark. But when the child of God *is* treading the "path of the righteousness," it is, to him, "as the *shining* light." Not only so, it "shineth more and more." The further he progresses along that path—that is, the more he really walks with God—the more light has he upon his path.

This should be the portion and the experience of every Christian. As the Lord Jesus declared, "I am the light of the world: he that followeth Me shall not walk in darkness, but shall have the light of life" (John 8:12). Every true Christian has "life," but comparatively few, it is greatly to be feared, enjoy the "light of life." *That* is dependent on "following" Christ; following Him in a practical way. Multitudes of professing Christians are following their own inclinations; that is to say, they are pursuing a course of self-will. Some are following the ways and fashions of the world. Still others are followers of men, perhaps Christian men, but almost always *worldly* Christians. Being almost total strangers to real exercise of heart before God for themselves, they reason that if a certain Christian or a number of other Christians do certain things, then it is quite right for *them* to do the same. Others take some preacher for their pattern. But none of these are "following" *Christ,* and of none of them can it be said that *their* path "is as the shining light, which shineth more and more unto the perfect day."

Oftentimes this becomes apparent to others. For example: a servant of God presses upon them something of the *claims* of his Master, something which requires the denial of self. What he says is quite clear to those who *are* treading the path of the righteous, who are walking in the "shining light," but to others, even though Christians, what he is bringing before them is far from being plain. Their own language reveals where they are. There is no need for others to sit in judgment on them. Their own words place them, condemn them. They say, "I cannot see that"! Ah, my brethren, if you cannot, that is very sad, and ought to lead to deep searchings of heart before God. If it does, He will show you that you *have not* been walking with Him. "God is light" (1 John 1:5), and as we walk with Him our path is "as the shining light," and everything is plain and clear. Such Christians prove the truth of that word in Psa. 36:9, "In Thy light shall we see light." Depend upon it, that if you are saying there are some things, that some of your brethren see from the Word, which you cannot see, then you are *away from* God; you are not "following" Christ, and therefore not enjoying the "light of life."

"The way of the wicked is as darkness:

they know not at what they stumble" (Prov. 4:19). This is in sad and fearful contrast from what has been before us in the preceding verse. These words do not describe the wicked themselves, nor their conduct—what they do; but instead, the path they are treading. God is light, but the wicked are far from Him—in the "far country" (Luke 15:13); therefore, have they no light. "They meet with darkness in the daytime, and grope in the noonday as in the night" (Job 5:14). When the Sun of Righteousness came to this world, "the people which *sat in darkness* saw a great light and to them which sat in the darkness and shadow of death, light is sprung up" (Matt. 4:16). The way of the wicked is as darkness, because they are away from God. They have no sense of His majesty, no conception of His holiness, no concern for His glory, no respect for His will. The path they tread is entirely one of self-will, self-seeking, self-pleasing, self-gratification; they have "turned every one to *his own way*" (Isa. 53:6). God is not in all their thoughts" (Psa. 10:4), yea, "the fool hath said in his heart, no God" (Psa. 14:1). Such is their determination, such is their desire. They wish to have no dealings with Him, no interference from Him. Not being in subjection to God, they have no light from Him: "the way of the wicked is as darkness."

Now the searching and solemn thing for the Christian is that *he is in* grave danger of turning into this same path. What an unspeakably dreadful thing for a child of God to be found treading the *same* way as the wicked! What a terrible calamity for a child of light to be found walking in a path of darkness! Do you think I am a pessimist, an alarmist, talking of a danger that has no real existence? Then turn to verses 1 to 15 of Prov. 4. Those are not my words, but God's. As a glance at vv. 1, 10 will show, the Lord is addressing His own children, and it is not without reason that the plural number in v. 1 is changed to the singular number in v. 10; it is an intensely individual matter which is in view. In v. 14 God says to His son, "Enter not into the path of the wicked, and go not in the way of evil." Thus, God Himself exhorts us against this very thing. Then in v. 15 He says, "Avoid it, pass not by it, turn from it, and pass away." Note how definite, how emphatic, is this repeated command. Is God multiplying words for no reason? Certainly not.

Alas! alas! many of God's own children *have not* heeded this word. Let us be specific. If I go and spend a social evening with some ungodly friends or relatives, I *have* "entered into the path of the wicked." I need not go to the theatre with them; if I visit them, or ask them to my home for a musical evening, or for light talk, then I have *disobeyed* this command. Think of a child of God laughing and joking with one whom he knows is on the way to an eternal Hell! If the world condemns Nero for fiddling while Rome was burning, what must the thrice holy God think of His fleshly, worldly, careless children! So again, if I go away with the ungodly for a holiday, I have entered into "the path of the wicked." Do you say, "I certainly cannot see *that*"? Then that is sure proof that you are, even now, *in* that path, for "the way of the wicked *is* as darkness"! Ah, my brethren, the Way which we are called on to tread *is* a Narrow one, much narrower than the flesh likes, much narrower than many a Christian desires to realise or is willing to admit. I know full well the haughty reply which the natural and desperately-wicked heart will make: "Are we to live like hermits in this world"? No; but we *are* commanded by God to live here as "strangers and pilgrims." Again, the objection will be raised: "Are we to have no innocent pleasures, no recreation?" *That* must be determined between the individual's soul and God. But with this qualification: no recreation or innocent pleasure is right for a Christian if it will contribute to the false happiness and peace of the lost.

What is the consequence of a Christian entering the path of the wicked? We speak not now of the awful dishonour done to Him whose name we bear, but of the sad consequence to himself. The answer is, He walks in Darkness. He has no light on his path, no spiritual discernment, no intelligence in the things of God or the ways of God. *That* is why things which are clear and plain to those who *are* treading the path of the righteous, are *not* clear to you. You say, "I cannot see it for myself." You speak the truth, you *cannot;* and there is a reason why. This is what we are here seeking to point out: "The path of the just is as the shining light, which shineth more and more unto the perfect day. The way of the wicked is as darkness; they know not at what they stumble." *You* have entered the path of the wicked, have done wickedly, and "darkness" is your present portion. Let it be repeated once more, the Way of the Wicked is the path of self-will, self-seeking, self-gratification.

Is there a Christian who *has* been convicted by this piercing word? Is he asking, "What can I do?" The answer is: "Unsparingly judge yourself; get right with God; confess your sins in detail before Him. Ask Him to give you the spirit of repentance, and own before Him that you *have* departed from the path of the righteous, that you have been living to please self, that you have compromised with the world, that your whole life is a reproach and a dishonour to Him. Ask Him to reveal this to you yet more fully; ask Him to expose to you the desperate wickedness of your deceitful heart; ask Him to show you how little your daily walk is really regulated by His Word. Mourn it before Him, beg Him to save you from *yourself,* and to work in you both to will and to do of *His* good pleasure. "If we would judge ourselves, we should not be judged. But when we are judged, we are chastened of the Lord, that we should not be condemned with the world" (1 Cor. 11: 31, 32). May the Lord add His own blessing to His own Word.

—*Arthur W. Pink.*

THE WAY OF THE WICKED.

"The way of the wicked is as darkness: they know not at what they stumble" (Prov. 4:19).

The subject which I believe God would have us consider to-night is exceedingly solemn, and one which should fill us with horror and sadness: horror, at that hideous monster, *sin,* which has brought about such a fearful condition of things; sadness, to think that the vast majority of our fellow-men and women are in the terrible plight described in our text—"The way of the wicked is as darkness: they know not at what they stumble."

The present theme is not calculated to be an inspiring one, rather will it be repellant to the flesh, a weariness to the carnal mind; and should the preacher dwell upon it for fifty or sixty minutes, instead of the time seeming to fly by, it is far more likely to appear as moving on leaden wings. Particularly is this apt to be the case with you who are unregenerated, for there are few things which the ungodly are more unwilling to look squarely in the face than the fearful condition and terrible plight of the natural man.

Man has not always walked in the way of darkness. At the beginning it was not so. Man was made in the image and likeness of God, and "God is light, and in Him is no darkness at all" (1 John 1:5). But, alas, man turned his back upon God. He became a rebel against his Maker, and fearful was his fall, and dreadful were the consequences of it. Sin has closed every window of man's soul, so that darkness completely enshrouds him. He is born into a land of darkness, over which hangs the shadow of death; and his life is lived in a world over which reigns the Prince of Darkness. Therefore, "the way of the wicked is as darkness: they know not at what they stumble.

This was clearly evident as soon as that awful monster Sin entered this world. What was the "Way" in which our fallen first parents went? What is the first thing recorded of them after their wilful disobedience? This: as soon as they heard the voice of Him who is omnipresent, they attempted to flee from Him. Think of it: they supposed they could hide themselves from the eyes of the All-seeing One! They imagined that a few trees would conceal them from Him who is Light. Verily "the way of the wicked *is* as darkness: they know not at what they stumble." Thus it has been ever since.

After the Fall, God gave a gracious revelation of the coming of the woman's Seed to bruise the Serpent's head (Gen. 3:15): so, too, He made known the way back unto Himself (Gen. 4:4). And what use did the human race make of these Divine revelations in the early days of human history? Even then it was shown that "the way of the wicked is as darkness: they know not at what they stumble." The darkness over the heart and mind of man prevailed to such a fearful extent that by Noah's time his family was the only one that had not corrupted its way upon the earth, or that had any experimental knowledge of the true God. Therefore the Flood was sent and carried them all away.

Surely that terrible judgment of the Deluge would prove an effective and lasting warning unto men of the madness of departing from God! Divine providence saw to it that Noah himself lived for another three hundred years and his son Shem for five hundred years after the Flood. What solemn warnings must they have given to each succeeding generation of their descendants! But, even in those days the solemn truth of our text was demonstrated—"The way of the wicked is as darkness." "Professing themselves wise, they became fools, and changed the glory of the uncorruptible God into an image made like to corruptible man" (Rom. 1:22, 23). That period of human history was closed by God's judgment at the Tower of Babel, when He confounded their speech and scattered men abroad over the face of the earth.

Following this, God called out Abraham and made to him and his son Isaac and his grandson Jacob special manifestations of Himself. He "appeared" to them, made Himself known, gave them promises, revealed to them His will. What followed? This: their descendants settled in Egypt. And what became of *their* knowledge of the true and living God? Joshua 24:14 tells us: "Put away the gods which your fathers served on the other side of the flood (see Josh. 24:2), *and in Egypt,* and serve ye the Lord." Plainer still is Ezek. 20:5-8, "Thus saith the Lord God, In the day when I chose Israel, and lifted up Mine hand unto the seed of the house of Jacob, and made Myself known unto them in the land of Egypt, when I lifted up Mine hand unto them, saying, I am the Lord your God: In the day that I lifted up Mine hand to them, to bring them forth of the land of Egypt unto a land that I had espied for them, flowing with milk and honey, which is the glory of all lands: then said I unto them, Cast ye away every man the abominations of his eyes, and defile not yourselves with the idols of Egypt: I am the Lord your God. But they rebelled against Me: they did not every man cast away the abomination of their eyes, neither did they forsake the idols of Egypt: then I said, I will pour out My fury upon them to accomplish My anger against them in the midst of the land of Egypt." Truly, "the way of the wicked *is* as darkness." In consequence of their idolatry, they were made to labour and groan beneath the merciless lash of their taskmasters in the brick-kilns of Egypt.

At the end of that period God acted again in sovereign grace and brought them forth from the House of Bondage and displayed His power on their behalf at the Red Sea. Surely they would now walk in His light. Alas, how short a time was it before they were found worshipping the golden calf! So it was later: notwithstanding the fact that Jehovah made a wondrous revelation of Himself at Sinai, giving to Israel His laws, which expressly and severely prohibited all idolatry, yet soon after they entered the promised land they adopted the gods of Canaan and bowed down to idols. Yes, "the way of the wicked is as darkness."

Concerning the wisest of Israel's kings it is recorded, "Solomon went after Ashtoreth the goddess of the Zidonians, and after Milcom the abomination of the Ammonites. . . . Then Solomon built an high place for Chemosh the abomination of Moab, in the hill that is before Jerusalem, and for Molech the abomination of the children of Ammon. And likewise did he for all his strange wives, which burnt incense and sacrificed unto their gods. And the Lord was angry with Solomon, because his heart was turned from the Lord God of Israel, which had appeared unto him twice" (1 Kings 11:5-9). Some of Solomon's successors did still worse.

How was it with the Gentiles during that period? Rom. 1 tells us: "That which may be known of God is manifest to them; for God hath showed it unto them. For the invisible things of Him from the creation of the world are clearly seen, being understood by the things that are made, His eternal power, and Godhead; so that they are without excuse" (vv. 19, 20). Man has been endowed with faculties whereby he is fully capable of inferring the being of the Creator through His creation, and the perfections of His Divine nature are very manifest in the works of His hands. Yet what *were* the conceptions of Deity which obtained in Egypt, Babylon, Persia, etc.? Instead of worshipping the living God, they manufactured and worshipped idols. Instead of worshipping the one true Deity they invented a multitude of gods.

"Because that, when they knew God, they glorified Him not as God, neither were thankful; but became vain in their imaginations, and their foolish heart was darkened. Professing themselves to be wise, they became fools, and changed the glory of the incorruptible God into an image made like to corruptible man, and to birds, and fourfooted beasts, and creeping things" (Rom. 1:21-23). Many, in fact most, of the idols and images which the Gentiles worshipped, were of the most frightful and revolting shapes which their darkened and filthy heart could devise: in fact, the more hideous and horrible they appeared, the better were they supposed to serve them *as* "gods." Men held such sottish delusions that they cut themselves with knives, and tortured their children as an act of devotion, yea, even burned them to death as a sacrifice to their self-chosen deities. Yes, "the way of the wicked is as *darkness*."

Take the Greeks, who are looked upon to this day as the most cultured of the ancients. They had a veritable pantheon of gods, principal among which were Orpheus, Bacchus, and Venus; these were simply the vices defied. They ascribed drunkenness, theft, unchastity, to their gods. Prostitution was practised in their temples as a part of divine worship, and unmentionable things were done by their priests as religious rites. Verily, "the way of the wicked *is* as darkness."

Of course, all of this was in Old Testament times. How was it, then, when God's Son came here? A new and fuller revelation of God was then made. For thirty-three years Emmanuel walked this earth. The Sun of Righteousness arose upon this dark world. But the more the light shone, the more the horrible things of darkness were exposed. So great was that darkness, when Christ said to a master in Israel, "Except a man be born again he cannot see the kingdom of God," the answer he received was, "How can a man be born when he is old? can he enter the second time into his mother's womb, and be born?" (John 3:3, 4)! So great was that darkness that when He had healed paralytics, expelled demons, cleansed lepers, the religious leaders came to Him and said, "Show us a sign!" So great was that darkness, they deemed the Son of God an enemy to Caesar, and a blasphemer against Heaven, and so condemned Him to a malefactor's death. Yes, "the way of the wicked is as darkness."

Even then God did not cease His activities in exposing and exhibiting the terrible and inveterate darkness in which men are determined to walk. He raised up and sent forth the apostles, who preached the Gospel far and wide. In their days the Word of God grew mightily and multiplied on every side, until its light penetrated all countries. The commission Christ gave His disciples to "make disciples of all men" was carried out in the first century: "The word of the truth of the gospel which is come unto you, as in *all* the world. . . . Be not moved away from the hope of the Gospel, which ye have heard, which *was* preached to every creature which is under heaven" (Col. 1: 5, 6, 23).

But O how soon that light was quenched! Even before Paul ended his career he had to say, "All they which are in Asia be turned away from me" (2 Tim. 1:15). Tares were soon sown among the wheat; the corrupt leaven was placed in the meal; the little mustard-seed developed into a monstrosity, so that the fowls of the air found lodgment in its branches; and very soon the grossest of idolatry was practised in the very name of Christ. Then followed a thousand years which have rightly and most significantly been named "The Dark Ages!"

Coming now to our own days, Have things changed for the better, or is it still true that "the way of the wicked is as darkness?" The unspeakably awful fact is that at this very moment more than half of the human race know no more about the true God, who is Light, than do the chairs on which you are sitting. There are at this very day over two hundred millions of Mahommedans who believe when they die they shall go to that paradise which their false prophet promised them, a paradise in which they shall live in all manner of sensual pleasures, and spend their time in the unbridled gratification of the lusts of the flesh. So, too, there are in India, in this so-called day of enlightenment, men of the higher casts, lying upon beds of spikes, doing so because they imagine God requires it, and that such self-tortures will bring them into His favour. Verily, "the way of the wicked is as darkness."

Let me come nearer home. Half of Christendom is walking in Popish darkness, and hold such gross delusions that they worship images of a woman and of a multitude of dead men whom they have canonised as saints, some of them real saints, others monsters of iniquity. Many of their monks and nuns whip themselves, starve themselves, and do all sorts of ridiculous penances and sufferings in order to appease the anger of God against their sins. For those to whom such austerities do not appeal, another method is provided —they *pay* the priests for their forgiveness. Yes, "the way of the wicked is as darkness."

Worse than that, there are almost countless millions of professing Christians who are walking in such gross darkness that they bow down before a piece of bread and worship it. Yea, unless the law of the land intervenes at almost the eleventh hour, or God Himself prevents it, here in Sydney, a wafer of bread will, ere long, be carried through the streets in solemn procession, asserting that piece of bread to be Christ Himself, both in His Deity and humanity. Truly, "the way of the wicked is as darkness."

Before coming to the individual application of our text, we add two more solemn considerations to what has been already before us. First, the terrible fact that the wicked *are* "walking in darkness" is further seen in that men fall into the most sottish delusions and awful superstitions *soon after* they have been favoured with light from God. History abounds in examples of those who *have* received the knowledge of the truth, yet forsaking it for the most barbarous and brutal notions. Illustrations of this have already been before us in connection with the nation of Israel: though blest with a revelation from the living God such as the Gentiles possessed not, yet that people forsook Jehovah again and again, and turned unto the false gods of the heathen. So, as previously pointed out, the same sad thing has been repeated in the history of Christendom: the Gospel preaching of the apostles and their disciples was followed by the Dark Ages. Now in the fifteenth and sixteenth centuries of the Christian era, the light of God shone forth again with power and blessing. In the days of Luther, Calvin, Knox, etc., there was a most blessed Reformation: God restored the light of the Gospel to large portions of Christendom. But what was the almost immediate sequel? Again it was demonstrated that "men *loved* darkness rather than light" (John 3:10). Soon almost all of Europe lapsed back again into popery, or atheism and arminianism. These examples show how addicted men are to darkness. This is the inveterate tendency of the unregenerated heart: to extinguish light when it is given, to sink lower and lower in darkness.

Second, there is not a single case on record of any nation or people ever delivering themselves from their gross darkness. No single case can be pointed to of a people who had fallen into heathen darkness, who have, by their own powers, discovered a remedy. As the centuries have proceeded men have not grown wiser. Those parts of the earth which are not now evangelised are as sottish and bruitish as they were five hundred years ago—there are still countless millions praying to idols which cannot hear, and turning to gods which cannot help; while in Christendom, to-day, popery is more popular than it was before the Reformation.

Coming now to the *individual* application of our text: "The way of the wicked is as darkness: they know not at what they stumble." Such is *thy* state, my unconverted hearer. So blind are you, that you cannot guide yourself; yea, so blind that you are unable to see your need *for* a Guide. Walking in darkness, yea, loving the darkness rather than the light, because your deeds are evil; therefore the things of God seem "foolishness" unto you, "neither can you discern them" (1 Cor. 2:14).

That is why you cannot see your awful state. If God were to bring you into His own marvellous light, you would abhor yourself, for you would see that there was "no soundness" in you (Isa. 1:6), you would see that you were a mass of corruption, that everything about you is polluted; that you are lost and undone. But "the way of the wicked is as darkness": you are enveloped in a pall of midnight gloom, and therefore *cannot* see yourself.

That is why you cannot see that everything under the sun is "vanity and vexation of spirit." You cannot see that you are spending your strength for naught, feeding on the husks which the swine eat, running after cisterns which hold no water. You are ever snatching at shadows but missing the substance, ever pursuing that which is not and slighting that which is, and ever shall be. But you cannot see that the course you are following is unable to satisfy your heart. You hear the preacher say these things, but they make no impression. Why? You cannot see the truth of them for yourself. Why? Because "the way of the wicked is as darkness."

That is why you cannot see that you have to do with the thrice holy God, who will judge thee, who will review the whole of thy life with all its wicked works, and sentence you accordingly. Yea, you *hate* the very One who gave you being, who preserves your unprofitable life, Who supplies your every need; for it is written, "the carnal mind is enmity *against* God" (Rom. 8:7).

That is why you are blind to your terrible peril: you *cannot* see what lies ahead. You do not realise that you are building your house on the sand, with no sure foundation beneath, so that when the Day of Testing comes your whole life's structure will collapse, and you will stand before a holy and an angry God with *no* refuge to flee into. You cannot see what lies ahead. You do not perceive that the Broad Road which you are treading is leading to certain destruction, *eternal* destruction. The Pit stands yawning before you, but you cannot see it. Hell is ready, even now to receive you; its fires are kindled, but you realise it not. Why? because "the way of the wicked is as darkness."

That is why you "see no beauty" in the altogether lovely One that you should desire Him (Isa. 53:2). If you did, you would hate yourself for having so long slighted Him, and would wonder if such an enormous sinner as you are *could* be pardoned. O how loathsome must you appear in the eyes of the Almighty! He is "Light"; then what a vile and repulsive object must *you* appear to His holy eyes!

The marvel is that He has not cast you out of His sight into Hell long ago. Unless God Himself delivers you from the path you are treading the "blackness of darkness" forever will be your awful lot. That is the sure and dreadful portion of every one who continues treading the path of self-will, be he a professing Christian or no, a church-member or not.

O what need is there for you to cry unto the Sun of Righteousness that He will not cast you into the Outer Darkness (Matt. 22:13). O what need is there for you to implore God, for Christ's sake, to "bring you out of darkness into His marvellous light." May His gracious Spirit cause some present to cast themselves before Him as self-confessed and Hell-deserving sinners, begging Him to have *mercy* on them.

N.B.—The above is a sermon preached by the Editor in Summer Hill.

THE SAVING LOOK.

"Look unto Me, and be ye saved, all the ends of the earth: for I am God, and there is none else" (Isa. 45:22).

In the context reference is made to the false gods of the heathen, and the sad condition and fate of those who worship them. "They shall be ashamed, and also confounded, all of them: they shall go to confusion together that are makers of idols. . . . they have no knowledge that set up the wood of their graven image, and pray unto a god that cannot save" (vv. 16, 20).

In the present-day application of these Scriptures we must not limit our thoughts to those in China and Japan, India and Africa. They speak with solemn force to multitudes in this Land. Idolatry is just as rampant here as in any heathen country. There are many thousands in Sydney now bowing and scraping to crucifixes and images of Mary. Nor is Protestantism guiltless, though the form of idolatry is different. Instead of praying to Mary and invoking the help of patron saints, many make "gods" out of the ordinances. Baptism and the Lord's supper are objects in which many put their trust. Others have created a "god" out of their own sentiments and imaginations. He is a "god" who loves everybody, but his power is limited; his intentions are benevolent, but he is unable to carry them out; he wants to save everybody, but the Devil is one too many. People "pray" to this imaginary "god," but *he* "cannot save them." Now in our text we are bidden to look away from all false gods. The great Jehovah says, "Look unto *Me*, and be ye saved, all the ends of the earth: for I am God, and there is none else."

I want to address myself to-night mainly to the unconverted, but ere doing so would first apply our text to a certain class of Christians. Many times during the past few months I have asked myself the question, Why is it that many of the Lord's own people never seem to get rid of their doubts, fears, and questionings of their acceptance? Sometimes they seem to have assurance, and are bright and happy; but they soon become depressed, doubt their interest in Christ, and become most unhappy. Some are almost on the borders of despair, and even if they should enjoy a measure of peace, they are in fear that this will not last long.

No doubt this lack of assurance proceeds from different causes in different persons. But I believe in the case of not a few it is due to their faint and feeble desires after a deeper knowledge of Christ. It is because they breathe so faintly after fellowship with the Lord Jesus that the Holy Spirit is grieved, for remember that He is here to glorify Christ. The sad thing is that so many are occupied, in one way or another, with *themselves,* rather than with Christ: their faith, their feelings, their evidences, their clouds or gleams of sunshine, constantly engage their minds. The person of Christ and His wondrous love are so little dwelt upon either in meditation or in conversation that He is little known, loved, or prized. Consequently, the Holy Spirit is *grieved* and so Christ is not revealed to the soul, and therefore darkness and feebleness necessarily follow. If self were only set aside, and *Christ* became all in all to the heart, the soul would grow and become more like Him: "But we all, with open face, *beholding* (as in a glass) the glory of the Lord, *are changed* into the same image from glory to glory, as by the Spirit of the Lord" (2 Cor. 3:18). O to value more what He is in Himself and in all His wondrous love to us, and to pant after a deeper communion with Him our living Head in glory. Then would our souls enjoy the happy liberty of His love.

"Look unto Me" is ever the Lord's word to His saints. "Looking off unto Jesus the Author and Finisher of faith" (Heb. 12:2). We need to continue as we began: to be constantly occupied with Him who is

fairer than the children of men, to delight ourselves in the Lord, to have our minds stayed upon Him. To meditate upon His love, His power, His faithfulness, His grace, is the secret of peace and joy. Let us commence each day by earnestly asking the Holy Spirit to stay our mind upon the Lord, to draw out our affections to Christ, to take of the things of the Saviour and reveal them unto us, to bring us into heart-fellowship with our blessed Redeemer.

No doubt much of the Christian's depression and gloom are to be attributed to Satan. But this *ought not* to be. It is a cause for shame and humiliation for any child of God to be defeated by the Devil. We are not ignorant of his devices, God having fully exposed them in His Word; complete armour is provided for us; and the Divine promise is, "Resist the Devil and he will flee from you." But the great Enemy constantly seeks to persuade the Christian, especially the young one, that his conversion is all a delusion, and in reality he has no part or lot in the matter. Now such fiery darts can only be quenched by the shield of faith: not by reasoning, nor by referring back to the date of our conversion; but by trusting in Christ. *"Look unto Me"* is the word for the young Christian. It is only as the eye remains steadfastly fixed on Christ that Satan's darts all fall to the ground. Let us now consider:

1. The Call to Salvation.

How humbling and solemn is this—"Look unto Me and be ye saved." None ought to *need* such a call. It should be our chief delight and occupation *to be* looking unto —contemplating, worshipping, loving, serving—the One who daily loadeth us with His benefits. But instead, our eyes and hearts are elsewhere: objects which are worthless engage our attention. By nature we love darkness rather than light. Because of this we need to be called upon *to* "look." How very humbling and solemn!

How condescending and amazing is this —"Look unto Me and be ye saved." God knows that men are occupied with other things rather than Himself. God is fully aware that *He* has little place in His creatures' thoughts, and still less in their hearts; yet does He not turn away in disgust. He is not too insulted to bid sinners turn to Him, nor does He leave them alone, as they so fully deserve. Instead, the great God calls to them and says, "Look unto Me and be ye saved." What condescension! what amazing mercy!

How definite and explicit is this—"Look unto Me and be ye saved." The language of our text is so plain that it scarcely needs any explanation, and I am fearful lest I should darken counsel by a multitude of words. Our text contains a call for the sinner to take his heart off from every other exercise and to fix its undivided attention upon the Saviour-God. It bids us turn away from all creature confidences and look only unto Him who thus invites us. This brings us to:

2. The Simplicity of the Gospel.

Our text is a very simple one, and I am trying to preach a very simple sermon from it. We ought to be deeply and increasingly thankful for the plainness of God's Way of Salvation. The Gospel presents no intricate system of philosophy which only the wise of this world can comprehend, and here, it is in striking and blessed contrast from many of the schemes and religions of men. That which God calls upon the sinner to do, requires no university course as a necessary equipment. "Believe on the Lord Jesus Christ" (Acts 16:31); "Come unto Me all ye that labour and are heavy laden" (Matt. 11:28); "If any man thirst let him come unto Me and drink" (John 7:37); "Whosoever shall call upon the name of the Lord shall be saved" (Rom. 10:13).

But perhaps our text puts the Gospel even more simply than elsewhere. *"Look unto Me and be ye saved."* A baby can "look" long before it is able to speak. A sick person may "look" when he is too ill or too weak to do anything else. That which so impresses me in our text is the blessed simplicity of its terms. It is this plainness of the Gospel which suits it to all classes and conditions of men. O that the Spirit of God may awaken some poor sinner here to-night, and show him its suitability to his case. And now let us ponder:

3. The Way of Salvation.

Notice that it is not "Live unto Me," but, "Look unto Me." Salvation does not come by altering our manner of life. No one has ever been saved because of his right living. Salvation by works is a universal delusion. If sinners could be saved by living as they ought, then the Cross of Christ was unnecessary. "Not by works of righteousness which we have done, but according to His mercy He saved us" (Titus 3:5) is the united confession of all God's people.

The first word of our text is *"Look,"* but observe that it is not "look *at your sins."* There is no relief by that method.

As well might I attempt to produce heat by looking at ice, light by looking at darkness, wealth by looking at poverty, as produce salvation by looking to self. When I look at myself I see something that God has condemned, for God has written the sentence of death upon the flesh. No, our text bids the sinner to look away from self, and look only unto the Lord.

Nor is it "look at *your convictions.*" If you are trying to make a righteousness out of your feelings you are just as far from the true Way to God as if you sought to make a righteousness out of your works. The sinner is no more saved by his conscious miseries than he is by his conscious merits. If you try to make a Saviour out of your convictions you will no more obtain forgiveness than if you sought pardon from God by means of ceremonies. To imagine that a deep sense of sin constitutes a *claim* on Divine mercy would be placing a premium on sin.

"Could your tears forever flow,
Could your grief no respite know,
These for sin could not atone,
Thou must save, and Thou alone."

To tell sinners that they must have a certain sense of sin, a certain degree of contrition, a certain brokenness of heart, *before* they may rightly apply to Christ, is turning the sinner away from the Saviour *to self.* The remedy does not lie at the seat of the disease, but in the great Physician Himself. Look to Christ then just as you are, and wait no longer for a preparation manufactured out of your miseries. The publican did not say, "God be merciful to me a *penitent* sinner!"

"But ought I not to have a godly sorrow which worketh repentance *before* trusting in Christ?" Certainly not. You cannot have "godly sorrow" until you are a godly man, and you cannot be a godly man until you have *submitted to God* and obeyed His call; and His call is "Look unto Me and be ye saved." Faith is the *beginning* of all godliness, for it is written "without faith it is impossible to please Him" (Heb. 11:6). If your heart is hard, come to the Lord and confess it as the greatest of your sins. If you cannot come to Christ *with* a broken heart, then come to Him *for* one.

Nor does our text bid the sinner to *look at his faith,* nor look within to see if he has faith. That is the mistake that many are making to-day, and consequently they have no assurance. Looking within produces nought but sadness. It is the look *without* which brings peace *within.* I greatly fear that some of you are resting upon your faith, instead of upon Christ. Remember the serpent-bitten Israelites. They were ordered to look away from self, and to fix their gaze upon the Divinely-appointed object set before them.

Nor does our text say *"pray unto God."* How many in these modern Evangelistic Campaigns have "gone forward," prayed to God for the forgiveness of sins, and asked Him to make them better men and women. No doubt some of them, because they have done this, supposed God had accepted them because of their earnest cries. Having "made a start for heaven," they no doubt "felt happy," and resolved by the help of God to hold out to the end. But if praying be substituted for "looking" to Christ, then God's way of salvation is missed and the seeking soul, though sincere in the belief that he has "got religion," is sincerely deluded. Believing that I am a millionaire will not make me one, and believing that I am saved when I am not will not save me.

What is signified by "looking?" It implies concentrated attention: not a mere passing "glance," but a definite "look." It signifies the abandonment of all creature confidence and the heart turning to a Saviour-God. It denotes the exercise of faith, for God is invisible, and therefore cannot be seen with the outward eye. It is the acknowledgment that from Him alone can salvation come. There was only one refuge from the flood, only one way of escape from the angel of death in Egypt, only one remedy for the bitten Israelites in the wilderness; so is there only one way of salvation. To look unto the Lord means turning away from all other confidences to Christ Himself. "I am the Way, the Truth, and the Life, no man cometh unto the Father but *by Me*" (John 14:6) is His own declaration. To look unto the Lord means to *put your trust* in the Saviour, relying solely on Him because of what God says in His Word. When a man says to his friend "I am looking to you to help me," he means, I am *counting* on you. Thus, to look to the Lord Jesus means to *depend upon* what He did for poor sinners. That is why the text says, "look *unto*" not simply "at." There are many who look "at" Him, perhaps with admiration, but this does not save them. To "look unto" signifies, to cast yourself upon Him.

Now mark the *universality* of the call of our text: "Look unto Me, and be ye saved, *all the ends of the earth.*" In view of such plain language as this none can truthfully say that God has excluded *them* from His Gospel call. What could possibly be more inclusive? It is not only "the ends of the earth," but "*all* the ends of the earth." If there is an *unlimited* expression in the Bible it is here. As God says in Prov. 8:4, "Unto you, O men, I call; and My voice is to the sons of men." And the call is a bona-fide one, too. In other words, the text means what it says. To everyone in this congregation to-night, without any exception whatsoever, God says, "Look unto Me and be ye saved." I will allow no man-made system of theology to tie my hands in preaching the glorious Gospel of God's grace. I refuse to make my commission any narower than the one my Master has given me, and He has said "preach the Gospel to *every* creature." And while God preserves my health and strength I shall (by His grace) declare "*all* the counsel of God," and an intrinsic part of that "counsel" is to hold up before all Him who "died for the ungodly" (Rom. 5:6), and to announce that He is willing and ready to receive and pardon *every* sinner who comes to Him.

Finally, mark the *encouragements* contained in our text for sinners *to* "look." First, this is *God's command*. Never say, May *I* look? Am *I* included in the call? Most certainly you are. "God now commandeth all men everywhere to repent." and He bids you look unto Him, and warns you that if you do not and will not you shall eternally perish. Second, our text contains more than a bare call. It is accompanied by *a sure promise:* "Look unto Me *and* be ye saved." This is the affirmation of One who cannot lie, whose Word is forever settled in heaven. Just as surely as you "look" to Christ you *shall* "be saved." Then put this promise to the proof. Many others have done so, and have experienced the blessedness of it in their own souls. Then why should you not do so? Third, it is followed by a *convincing reason:* "For I am God, and there is none else." This should meet every objection and solve every difficulty. You may feel like saying, "But I am so unworthy"; God replies, "I am the God of all grace!" Then, "look" unto Him. You may answer, "But I am so helpless"; God replies, "I am the Almighty, with Me all things are possible." Then, "look" unto Him. You may object, "But I am so sinful and wicked"; God replies, "With Me is plentious redemption." Then, "look" unto Him and be ye *saved*. May the Spirit of God remove the scales from your eyes and give you to see that Christ is willing and ready and "mighty to save."

—*Arthur W. Pink.*

NO CONTRADICTION.

"No man hath seen God at any time" (John 1:18). In Gen. 18:1 we are told that the Lord "appeared" unto Abraham, and even condescended to eat in his presence. In Exodus 24:9, 10 we read, "Then went up Moses and Aaron, Nadab and Abihu, and seventy of the elders of Israel: and they saw the God of Israel." These passages form one of the stock arguments of infidels and atheists. They appeal to them as furnishing a 'flat contradiction' in the Bible. But the child of God, assured that the Scriptures are Divinely inspired, knows that there cannot be any contradictions in them.

But what is the earnest seeker after truth to do with the above objection? How is he to set about the solving of this problem? First, by confessing to God his ignorance and crying unto Him for light. Second, by diligently "comparing" other passages, for Scripture never interprets Scripture.

If the reader will turn back again to John 1:18 and read the remainder of the verse, he will find help there toward the solution of the difficulty. The whole verse reads, "No man hath seen God at any time; the only begotten Son, which is in the bosom of the Father, He hath declared," or made Him manifest. Thus, the first part of the verse is speaking of God the Father. In John 5:37 we are told, "And the Father Himself which hath sent Me, hath borne witness of Me. Ye (Jews) have neither heard His voice at any time, nor seen *His* shape." Thus it is clear that the One who appeared unto Abraham and others of the patriarchs, and the "God of Israel" who was seen upon the mount, was not God the Father.

Other passages confirm what we have said above. For example, in Dan. 3:25 the "form of the fourth," which Nebuchadnezzar saw walking in the midst of the fire with the three Hebrews, was said to be "like the *Son* of God." So in 1 Cor. 10:9 Israel in the wilderness are said to have tempted "Christ." So again in Heb. 11:26 we are told that Moses esteemed "the reproach of *Christ* greater riches than the treasures in Egypt." Thus the solution to the above difficulty is very simple: no one in O.T. times ever saw God the Father; the One who was manifested to Israel was God the Son!

—*A. W. Pink.*

GRACIOUS SPEECH.

"Let your speech be *always* with grace."—Col. 4:6.

Surely Christians should have a higher standard for conversation. Few, very few, ever broach the subject which *should* lie next to the heart, and when it is done, there is little or no response. Have they nothing to say of all the wonderful works of God? Is there no pleasure in speaking of "the might of His marvellous acts," or telling of the hourly, daily mercies received? no delight in uttering merely the name of our Beloved, or making mention of His banqueting-house, and banner of love? "What are words," says one; "we may feel as much without them." Ah, yes,—perhaps—but "out of the abundance of the heart the mouth speaketh"; and let him who makes the remark consider if the topics *most interesting* are not chosen for converse with friends. What are the occurrences of the day—political or domestic affairs—or even personal feelings, so silently cherished! Away with such excuses! If there were love for Christ, love worthy of the name, if there were communion with Him in real experience, depend on it, the subject would be often on the tongue—like the prophet's message, it would be fire shut up in the bones, and we would weary of forbearance.

—Grace and Truth.

---

thy pitcher, I pray thee, that I may drink; and she shall say, Drink, and I will give thy camels drink also, let the same be she that Thou hast appointed for Thy servant Isaac; and thereby shall I know that Thou hast showed kindness unto my master" (Gen. 24:10-14).

Third, the outstanding case of one who sought God's *glory* was His incarnate Son: "Glorify Thy Son, that Thy Son also may glorify Thee" (John 17:1)—this ever actuated Him. Fourth, in Rom. 1:10 we find the apostle Paul seeking God's *blessing* on his journey.

On the other hand, Scripture mentions not a few instances where the Lord's people *failed* to "acknowledge" Him in all their ways, and records the disastrous consequences which attended their self-will. After Abraham had entered Canaan "there was a famine in the land," sent, no doubt, to chasten and to test him. But, alas! as is so often the case with us, he failed. Instead of seeking guidance from the Lord, he "went down into Egypt, to sojourn there" (Gen. 12:10). Ultimately he was delivered, but for many years after he reaped an unpleasant harvest through Hagar, whom he acquired in Egypt. Concerning the Gideonites who deceived Israel it is written, "And the men took of their victuals and *inquired not* at the mouth of the Lord. And Joshua made peace with them, and made a league with them" (Josh. 9:13, 14). The sequel shows they became a thorn in Israel's side. These are written for our learning.

How solemn are the words of Isa. 30:1, 2, "Woe to the rebellious children, saith the Lord, that take counsel, but not of Me; and that cover with a covering, but not of My spirit, that they may add sin to sin; that walk to go down into Egypt, and have not asked at My mouth; to strengthen themselves in the strength of Pharaoh, and to trust in the shadow of Egypt!" Egypt is a type of the world, and how frequently Christians are found accepting its counsels, trusting its expedients, and following its ways! But what sorrows they bring upon themselves by so doing! To lean unto our own understanding, to turn to our fellows for counsel and help, to fail in acknowledging the Lord in all our ways, is a certain forerunner of trouble, chastisement, anguish.

"In all thy ways acknowledge Him." This precept applies to the arrangements of the home, our business affairs, our social life, our church relations, our service for Christ; and our obedience thereto determines the measure in which our lives are pleasing to God, glorifying to Him, and really blest by Him. Then let us, more earnestly, daily seek grace to conform to it in everything.

—*Arthur W. Pink.*

been puzzled by it only reveals the wicked independency of our hearts. We refer to the clause, "Give us this day our daily bread."

Numbers of times has the inquiry been put to us, How can I sincerely ask this, when bread for the day is already in hand? Let us draw a homely analogy. Here are cakes and tarts in the pantry: shall a boy or girl enter and help themselves? Not if they have been properly brought up. Though the food is there, they should first ask mother's permission before they take any. In like manner, God requires that we first ask of Him: "*Give* us this day our daily bread," lest like thieves we take without His leave. O how far have we all departed from the standard which God has set before us in His holy Word! To "acknowledge" the Lord in "all our ways" means, seek His permission in everything we do, as dutiful and respectful children.

2. *Seek His guidance in every undertaking.* Not to do so is to act in a spirit of independency, which is as the worldling does. "The wicked, through the pride of his countenance, will not seek after God: God is not in all his thoughts" (**Psa. 10:4**). The clear implication of this is that God *ought to be* in all his thoughts, and that it is through pride He is not. No matter how great or how small the undertaking may be, Divine guidance should be definitely sought: "in *everything* by prayer and supplication" (Phil. 4:6). It is only as we so act that God's lordship is owned by us in a practical way, and that He is really honoured.

We are not only to "trust in the Lord," count upon Him, but also to "acknowledge Him," seek His direction and help. Has not Christ, here as everywhere, left us an example? "I have set the Lord always before me" (Psa. 16:8) was His confession. Ah, fellow-Christians, is there any wonder that so many of our "ways" have turned out so disastrously? God has said, "Them that honour Me I will honour" (1 Sam. 2:30). But if we do not "honour" Him, then He will not prosper us. Then let us daily seek grace to heed this word, "In all thy ways acknowledge Him."

3. *Seek His glory in everything.* That this also must be regarded as being included within the scope of the word "acknowledge" is clear from 1 Cor. 10:31, "Whatsoever ye do, do all to the glory of God." Ah, if only we did so, how very different many of our "ways" would be! If we more frequently paused and enquired, Will *this* be to God's glory? we should be withheld from much sinning and saved from much foolishness, with all its painful consequences. Yet, right here, we need to give diligent heed to the clause preceding our text: "Lean not unto thine own understanding" has a close connection with what follows, as well as with that which goes before. God has not left *us* to decide and determine *what* will be to His "glory." No, in His loving kindness He has supplied us with an unerring standard, by which everything may be tested, namely, His Word. Only that is to the glory of God which the Scriptures enjoin and approve. If we are anxious to learn God's mind for us, then His promise holds good, "Seek, and ye shall find."

4. *Seek His blessing upon everything.* Surely *this* is what the Christian desires above everything else. Without it, temporal prosperity, the approval and applause of our fellows, or the fleeting pleasure anything may bring you, is worse than worthless. But what right have we to expect God's blessing, if we have not prayerfully sought it? On the other hand, if we have truly sought God's permission, guidance, glory, and blessing, then may we assuredly count upon His blessing. Note how in Deut. 14:29; 15:10, 18 the Lord's blessing is promised to those who *have* acknowledged Him in their ways by carrying out His revealed will. O what business worries, domestic heartaches, social disappointments, and spiritual failures had been spared us had we but sought God's permission, God's guidance, God's glory, God's blessing on everything! The past is beyond recall; for the present "consider your ways" (Hag. 1:5).

Let us now observe that the Scripture records examples of how men of God "acknowledged" Him in the manner indicated above. First, behold how David, on two occasions, sought the Lord's *permission* concerning his actions: "And David inquired at the Lord, saying, Shall I pursue after this troop?" (1 Sam. 30:8); "And it came to pass after this, that David inquired of the Lord, saying, Shall I go up into any of the cities of Judah? And the Lord said unto him, Go up" (2 Sam. 2:1).

Second, in the case of Abraham's servant we have a blessed illustration of one who sought Divine *guidance* on his undertaking: "And the servant . . . . Arose, and went to Mesopotamia, unto the city of Nahor. And he made his camels to kneel down without the city by a well of water at the time of the evening, the time that women go out to draw. And he said, O Lord God of my master Abraham I pray Thee, send me good speed this day, and shew kindness unto my master Abraham. Behold, I stand by the well of water; and the daughters of the men of the city come out to draw water: And let it come to pass, that the damsel to whom I shall say, Let down

(Concluded on Page 239.)

STUDIES IN THE SCRIPTURES

"Search the Scriptures" John 5 : 39

Copyright in all English-speaking Countries.

Editor: Arthur W. Pink, Sidmouth Road, Seaton, Devon, England.
Hon. Agent in U.S.A.: Mr. C. S. Pressel, 559, Dupont Avenue, York, Penna.
Hon. Agent in Australia: Mr. G. Ardill, The Christian Workers' Depot.
Commonwealth and Reservoir Streets, Sydney.

FREE TO ALL WHO WILL READ IT.

GUIDANCE GUARANTEED.

"*And He shall direct thy paths.*"—Prov. 3 : 6.

We come now to what is, in one sense, both the simplest and yet the most difficult clause of Prov. 3 : 5, 6. Paradoxical as it may sound, it is often the case that the simplest things are the most profound, and the profoundest things which are the most simple. What is more simple than the Gospel : "Through this Man is preached unto you the forgiveness of sins, and by Him, all that believe are justified from all things" (Acts 13 : 38, 39) ! And yet what is more profound ? Does not the Gospel make known things which even "the angels desire to look into" (1 Peter 1 : 12) ! What is more profound than the truth of God's sovereignty ? As we seek to contemplate it, we are made to cry with the Psalmist, "Such knowledge is too wonderful for me ; it is high, I cannot attain unto it" (139 : 6). And yet, what is, really, more simple and obvious ? If God be *God* then He must be sovereign, high above all, supreme over all.

"And He shall direct thy paths." This *is* the simplest part of our text as a whole, inasmuch as it is a plain and definite assurance given to all who meet and conform to the conditions named in the preceding clauses. This Divine promise needs no analyzing or philosophising about. It is presented for our faith to lay hold of and our hearts to rest upon. "Believe on the Lord Jesus Christ and thou shalt be saved" is plain enough. It needs to be received and obeyed, not discussed or reasoned about. But that is no plainer than if we (1) "Trust in the Lord with all our hearts" ; if we (2) "lean not unto our own understandings" ; if we (3) "acknowledge the Lord in all our ways"—then most assuredly, "He *shall* direct our paths." Under such circumstances we have a sure word from God that we may count upon and draw peace from.

The sense in which the last clause of Prov. 3 : 6 presents a difficulty is that it treats of a subject which is one of the profoundest and most complicated which can engage our thoughts, namely, that of Divine guidance, God regulating the details of our daily lives. *How* does God "direct" my paths ? How may I know that He *is* directing them ? The problem of attaining assurance that we are in the current of God's will is often an acute one to a sensitive conscience and a devoted heart, which longs, above all else, to please the Lord. To know that I am in the will of God is essential to real peace of soul, but how to obtain the certainty that I have His guidance taxes and exercises many.

The *need* for being "directed" by the Lord is real and pressing. The children of Adam are fallen and ruined creatures, "alienated from the life of God through the ignorance that is in them, because of the blindness of their hearts" (Eph. 4 : 18). The natural man is like a rudderless ship, or a motor-car without a steering-wheel. Scripture emphatically affirms "the way of man is not in himself : it is not in man that walketh to direct his steps" (Jer. 10 : 23). True, it is otherwise with the Christian, for the Spirit of God indwells him ; yet the "flesh" is still in him, too, and this world is a "dark place" (2 Peter 1 : 19), a trackless desert. It is not without reason that the Lord's people are termed "sheep," for no other creature is so apt to stray or has such a propensity to wander. Of old God said concerning Israel, "Thus have they loved to wander, they have not refrained their feet" (Jer. 14 : 10). And this is recorded for our learning and warning.

"And He shall direct thy paths." The Hebrew word for "direct" means "to

(Continued on Page 264.)

IMPORTANT NOTICES

Back numbers of each year of the magazine are yet obtainable at 5/- (1.25) per year. Bound at 7/6 (1.75) post paid. They will soon be out of print. Those in U.S.A. wanting them, please purchase from Mr. Pressel (see front cover page).

Advise promptly of change of address.

This Magazine is published as a work of faith and labour of love. The Editor gladly gives his services. It is freely sent to all who will read it. No charge is made for it.

Christians who feel definitely led to do so, may have fellowship with us in this Ministry. Send only *Inter-National M.O.*

CONTENTS.

	Page
Hebrews	242
Gleanings in Exodus	248
Worship	252
Christ in us	255
Privilege and Responsibility	258
Touch not Mine Anointed	260

THE EPISTLE TO THE HEBREWS.

11. *Christ Superior to Angels* (Heb. 2 : 14-16.)

The closing verses of Heb. 2 are so rich and full in their contents and the subjects with which they deal are of such importance that we feel the more disposed to devote extra space for the exposition of them. More and more we are learning for ourselves that a short portion of Scripture prayerfully examined and repeatedly meditated upon, yields more blessing to the heart, more food to the soul, and more help for the walk, than a whole chapter read more or less cursorily. It is not without reason that the Lord Jesus said in the parable of the Sower, "that on the good ground are they, which in an honest and good heart, having heard the Word, keep, and bring forth fruit with *patience*" (Luke 8 : 15). The only way in which the Word is "kept" or held fast is through prolonged meditation and patient or persevering study.

The verses which are to be before us on this occasion form part of the apostle's inspired explanation of "the Son's" becoming Man and suffering the awful death of the cross. If the reader will turn back to the third paragraph of the preceding article he will there find five reasons (substantiated in vv. 9, 10), as to why Christ endured such humiliation. In vv. 11 to 13 four more are advanced. It was necessary for the second Person of the holy Trinity to be made lower than the angels if He were to have ground and cause for calling us "brethren" (vv. 11, 12), for that is a title which pre-supposes a common ground and standing. Then, it was necessary for the Lord of glory to become "all of one" with His people if, in the midst of the church, He should "sing praise" unto God (v. 12); and this, the O.T. scriptures affirmed, He would do. Again, it was necessary for Him who was in the form of God to take upon Him "the form of a servant" if He was to set before His people a perfect example of the life of faith; and in Isa. 8 : 17 He is heard saying, by the Spirit of prophecy, "I will put My trust in Him" (v. 13). Finally, His exclamation "Behold I and the children which God hath given Me" (v. 13), required that He should become Man and thus rank Himself alongside of His saints.

In vv. 14 to 16 we have one of the profoundest statements in all Holy Writ which treats of the Divine incarnation. For this reason, if for no other, we must proceed slowly in our examination of it. Here too the Holy Spirit continues to advance further reasons as to why it was imperative that the Lord of angels should, for a season, stoop beneath them. Three additional ones are here given, and they may be stated thus: first, that He might render null and void him who had the power of death, that is, the Devil (v. 14); second, that He might deliver His people from the bondage of that fear which death had occasioned (v. 15); third, Abraham's children could only be delivered by Him laying hold of Abraham's seed (v. 16).

"Forasmuch then as the children are partakers of flesh and blood He also Himself likewise took part of the same; that through death He might destroy him that had the power of death, that is, the devil" (v. 14). The connection between this verse and the preceding context may be stated thus: Since it became Him for whom are all things and by whom are all things, in bringing many sons unto glory, to make the captain of their salvation perfect through suffering; and since, according to Old Testament prophecies, the Sanctifier and the sanctified, the Saviour and the saved, must be of the same race; and since the saved are human beings,—the Son of God, the appointed Saviour, assumed a nature capable of suffering and death—even the nature of man, when He came to save, that in that nature He might die, and by dying accomplish the great purpose of His appointment, the destruction of the power of Satan, and the deliverance of His chosen people" (Dr. J. Brown).

The opening words of our verse denote that the Holy Spirit is drawing a conclusion from the proof-texts just cited from the O.T. The Greek words for "forasmuch then" are rendered "seeing therefore" in 4 : 6, and their force is, "it is evident hereby" that the Son of God became the Son of Man for the sake of those whom God had given Him.

"Forasmuch then as the children are partakers of flesh and blood He also Himself likewise took part of the same ; that through death He might destroy him that had the power of death, that is, the devil" (v.14). Here we have the eternal Word becoming flesh, the Son of God becoming the Son of man. Let us consider, first, the Wonder of it ; second, the Needs-be of it ; third, the Nature of it ; fourth, the Perfection of it ; fifth, the Purpose of it.

The tragic thing is that, for the present, our minds are so beclouded and our understandings so affected by sin, it is impossible for us to fully perceive the *wonder* of the Divine incarnation. As the apostle wrote, "But now we see through a glass darkly" (1 Cor. 13 : 12). But thank God this condition is not to last for ever soon, very soon, we shall see "face to face." And when by God's marvellous grace His people behold the King in His beauty, they will not, we think, be bewildered or dazed, but instead, filled with such wonderment that their hearts and whole beings will spontaneously bow in worship.

Another thing which makes it so difficult for us to grasp the wonder of the Divine incarnation is that there is nothing else which we can for a moment compare with it ; there is no analogy which in any wise resembles it. It stands unique, alone, in all its solitary grandeur. We are thrilled when we think of the angels sent forth to minister for those who shall be heirs of salvation : that those wondrous creatures, which so far excel us in wisdom and strength, should have been appointed to be our attendants ; that those holy creatures should be commissioned to encamp round about poor sinners ; that the courtiers of Heaven should wait upon worms of the earth ! Truly, that *is* a great wonder. But O my brethren, that wonder pales into utter insignificance and, in comparison, fades away into nothingness, before this far greater wonder—that the Creator of angels should leave His throne on High and descend to this sin-cursed earth ; that the very One before whom all the angels bow should, for a season, be made lower than they ; that the Lord of glory, who had dwelt in "light unapproachable," should Himself become partaker of "flesh and blood"! *This* is the wonder of wonders.

So wonderful was that unparalleled event of the Divine incarnation that the heavenly hosts descended to proclaim the Saviour newly-born. So wonderful was it that the "glory of the Lord," the ineffable Shekinah, which once filled the temple, but had long since retired from the earth, appeared again for "the glory of the Lord shone round about" the awe-struck shepherds on Bethlehem's plains. So wonderful was it that chronology was revolutionised, and anno mundi became anno domini : the calendar was changed, and instead of its dating from the beginning of the world, it was re-dated from the birth of Christ ; thus the Lord of time has written His very signature across the centuries. Passing on now, let us consider ; the *needs-be* for the Divine incarnation.

This is plainly intimated both in what has gone before and in what follows. If the "children" which God had given to His Son were to be "sanctified" then He must become "all of one" with them. If those children who are by nature partakers of flesh and blood were to be "delivered from him that had the power of death, that is the devil," then the Sanctifier must also "likewise take part of the same." If He was to be a merciful and faithful High Priest in things pertaining to God, He must in all things "be made like unto His brethren." If He is to be able to "succor them that are tempted," then He must Himself, "suffer, being tempted " ; and, as God Himself "cannot be tempted," He had to become Man in order to that experience.

The needs-be was real, urgent, absolute. There was no other way in which the counsels of God's grace towards His people could be wrought out. If ever we were to be made "like Him," He first had to be made like us. If He was to give us of His Spirit, He must first assume our flesh. If we were to be so joined unto the Lord as to become "one spirit" (1 Cor. 6 : 17) with Him, then He must first be joined with our flesh, so as to be "all of one" with us. In a word, if we were to become partakers of the Divine nature, He must be made partaker of human nature. Thus we perceive again the force of the apostle's reply to the objection which he is here removing—How could it be that a Man was superior to angels ? He has not only shown from the Jews' own scriptures that the Man Christ Jesus had been given a name more excellent than any pertaining to the celestial hierarchies, but here he shows us the needs-be for the Lord of glory to become Man. If we were to be "conformed to His image" then He must be "made in the likeness of sin's flesh." If the children of Abraham were to be redeemed, then He must take on Him the "seed of Abraham."

The *nature* of the Divine incarnation is

here referred to in the words "flesh and blood." That expression speaks of the frailty, dependency, and mortality of man. This is evident from the other passages where it occurs. The words "flesh and blood" are joined together five times in the N.T.: Matt. 16:17, 1 Cor. 15:50, Gal. 1:16, Eph. 6:12, Heb. 2:14. It is a humbling expression, emphasising the weakness of the flesh and limitations of man : note how in Eph. 6:12 "flesh and blood" is contrasted from the mightier foes against which Christians wrestle.

"Flesh and blood" is the present state in which is found those children whom God has designed to bring unto glory. By their natural constitution and condition there is nothing to distinguish the elect from the non-elect. The Greek noun for "partakers" is derived from a root signifying "common": in Rom. 15:27 Gentile believers are said to be "partakers" of Israel's spiritual blessings, that is, they enjoy them in common, one with another. So God's children are "partakers," equally with the children of the Devil, of "flesh and blood." Nor does our regeneration effect any change concerning this : the limitations and infirmities which "flesh and blood" involve still remain. Many reasons for this might be suggested : that we may not be too much puffed up by our spiritual standing and privileges ; that we might be rendered conscious of our infirmities, and made to feel our weakness before God ; that we might abase ourselves before Him who is Spirit ; that the grace of compassion may be developed in us—our brethren and sisters are also partakers of "flesh and blood," and often we need reminding of this.

In the words "He also Himself likewise took part of the same" we have an affirmation concerning the *reality* of the Saviour's humanity. It is not merely that the Lord of glory *appeared* on earth in human form, but that He actually became "flesh and blood," subject to every human frailty so far as these are freed from sin. He knew what hunger was, what bodily fatigue was, what pain and suffering were. The very fact that He was "the Man of sorrows" indicates that "He also Himself likewise took part of the same." Thereby we see the amazing condescension of Christ in thus conforming Himself to the condition in which the children were. How marvellous the love which caused the Lord of glory to descend so low for us sons of men ! There was an infinite disparity between them: He was infinite, they finite ; He omnipotent ; they frail and feeble ; He was eternal, they under sentence of death. Nevertheless, He refused not to be conformed to them; and thus He was "crucified through weakness" (2 Cor. 13:4), which refers to the state into which He had entered.

The *perfection* of the Divine incarnation is likewise intimated in the words "He also Himself likewise took part of the same." These words emphasise the fact that Christ's becoming Man was a *voluntary* act on His part. The "children" were by nature subject to the common condition of "flesh and blood." They belonged to that order. They had no say in the matter. That was their state by the law of their very being. But not so with the Lord Jesus. He entered this condition as coming from another sphere and state of being. He was the Son who "thought it not robbery to be equal with God." He was all-sufficient in Himself. Therefore it was an act of condescension, a voluntary act, an act prompted by love, which caused Him to "take part of the same."

These words also point to the *uniqueness* of our Lord's humanity. It is most blessed to observe how the Spirit here, as always, has carefully guarded the Redeemer's glory. It is not said that Christ was a "*partaker* of flesh and blood," but that "He likewise took part of the same." The distinction may seem slight, and at first glance not easily detected ; yet is there a real, important, vital difference. Though Christ became Man, real Man, yet was He different, radically different, from every other man. In becoming Man He did not "partake" of the foul poison which sin has introduced into the human constitution. *His* humanity was not contaminated by the virus of the Fall. Before His incarnation it was said to His mother, "That *Holy* Thing which shall be born of thee" (Luke 1:35). It is the sinlessness, the uniqueness of our Lord's humanity which is so carefully guarded by the distinction which the Holy Spirit has drawn in Heb. 2 ; 14.

The *purpose* of the Divine incarnation is here intimated in the words that "through death He might destroy him that had the power of death, that is, the devil." It was with *this* end in view that the Son of God took part in "flesh and blood." In the several passages where the Divine incarnation is referred to in the New Testament different reasons are given and various designs are recorded. For example John 3:16 tells us that one chief object in it was to reveal and exhibit the matchless love of God. 1 Tim. 1:15 declares that "Christ Jesus came into the world to save sinners." But here in Heb. 2:14 it is the destroying of him that had the power of death that is mentioned.

The object of the Holy Spirit in our present passage is to display the glorious and efficacious side of that which was most humbling —the infinite stoop of the Lord of glory. He is pointing out to those who found the Cross such a stumbling-block, how that there was a golden lining to the dark cloud which hung over it. That which to the outward eye, or rather the untaught heart and mind, seemed such a degrading tragedy was, in reality, a glorious triumph; for by it the Saviour stript the Devil of his power and wrested from his hands his most awful weapon. Just as the scars which a soldier carries are no discredit or dishonour to him if received in an honourable cause, so the cross-sufferings of Christ instead of marking His defeat were, actually, a wondrous victory, for by them He overthrew the arch-enemy of God and man.

"That through death He might destroy him that had the power of death, that is, the devil." It is most blessed to note the bearing of this statement upon the special point the apostle was discussing. The Jews were stumbled by the fact that their Messiah had died. Here the Holy Spirit showed that so far from that death tarnishing the glory of Christ, it exemplified it, for by death He overthrew the great Enemy and delivered His captive people. "Not only is He glorious in heaven, but He hath conquered Satan in the very place where he exercised his sad dominion over men, and where the judgment of God lay heavily upon men" (Mr. J. N. Darby).

"That through death He might destroy him that had the power of death, that is, the devil." Three things here claim attention: First, what is meant by the Devil having "the power of death"? Second, what "death" is here in view? Third, in what sense has Christ "destroyed" the Devil? From the words of the next verse it is clear that the reference is to what particularly obtained before Christ became incarnate. That it does not mean the Devil had absolute power in the infliction of physical death in O.T. times is clear from several scriptures. Of old Jehovah affirmed, "See now that I, even I, am He, and there is no god with Me: I kill, and I make alive" (Deut. 32:39). Again, "the Lord killeth, and maketh alive; He bringeth down to the grave, and bringeth up" (1 Sam. 2:6). And again, "unto God the Lord belong the issues from death" (Psalm 68:20). These passages are decisive, and show that even during the Mosaic economy the giving of life and the inflicting of death were in the hands of God only, no matter what instruments He might employ in connection therewith.

The particular kind of "death" which is here in view is explained for us in the words 'that through death He" etc. The death which Christ died was "the wages of sin"— the penal infliction of the law, suffering there wrath of a holy God. The point raised here is a deeply mysterious one, yet on it Scripture throws some light. In John 8:44 Christ declared that the Devil was "a murderer" (literally "man-slayer") from the beginning In Zech. 3:1 we are shown Satan standing at Jehovah's right-hand to resist Israel's high priest. Upon the subject Saphir has said, "But which death did Christ die?" That death of which the Devil had the power. Satan wielded that death. He it was who had a just claim against us that we should die. There is justice in the claim of Satan.

"It is quite true that Satan is only a usurper; but in saving men God deals in perfect righteousness, justice, truth. According to the Jewish tradition the fallen angels often accuse men, and complain before God that sinful men obtain mercy. Our redemption is in harmony with the principles of righteousness and equity, on which God has founded all things. The prince of this world is *judged* (John 16:11); he is conquered not merely by power, but by the power of justice and truth. ... He stood upon the justice of God, upon the inflexibility of His law, upon the true nature of our sins. But when Christ died our very death, when He was made sin and a curse for us, then all the power of Satan was gone. ... And now what can Satan say? The justice, majesty, and perfection of the law are vindicated more than if all the human race were lost for ever. The penalty due to the broken law Jesus endured, and now, as the law is vindicated, sin put away, death swallowed up, Christ has destroyed the Devil."

Inasmuch as the Devil is the one who brought about the downfall of our first parents, by which sentence of death has been passed upon all their posterity (Rom. 5:12); inasmuch as he goeth about as a roaring lion "seeking whom he may devour" (1 Peter 5:8); inasmuch as he challenged God to inflict upon the guilty the sentence of the law (Zech. 3:1); and, inasmuch as even the elect of God are, before their regeneration, under "the power of darkness" (Col. 1:13 and cf. Acts 26:18), dead in trespasses and sins, yet "walking according to the Prince of the power of the air"; the Devil may be said to have "the *power* of death."

The word "*destroy* him that had the power of death" does not signify to annihilate, but means to make null and render powerless. In 1 Cor. 1:28 this same Greek word is rendered "bring to nought"; in Rom. 3:3 "without effect"; in Rom. 3:31 "make void." Satan has been so completely vanquished by Christ the Head that he shall prevail against none of His members. This is written for the glory of Christ, and to encourage His people to withstand him. Satan is an enemy bespoiled. Therefore is it said, "Resist the Devil, and he will flee from you" (James 4:5). To such as believe there is assurance of victory. If the Devil gets the upper hand of us, it is either because of our timidity, or lack of faith. "To 'destroy him that had the power of death' is to strip him of his power. It is said by the apostle John, 'for this purpose was the Son of God manifested, to destroy the works of the Devil,' i.e. ignorance, error, depravity, and misery. In the passage before us, the destruction is restricted to the peculiar aspect in which the Devil is viewed. To destroy him, is so to destroy him as having 'the power of death'—to render him, in this point of light, powerless in reference to the children; i.e., to make death cease to be a penal evil. Death, even in the case of the saints, is an expression of the displeasure of God against sin; but it is not—as but for the death of Christ it must have been—the hopeless dissolution of his body; it is not the inlet to eternal misery to his soul. Death to them for whom Christ died consigns, indeed, the body to the grave; but it is 'in the sure and certain hope of a glorious resurrection,' and it introduces the freed spirit into all the glories of the celestial paradise" (Dr. J. Brown).

This stripping Satan of his power of death was accomplished by the laying down of the Saviour's life, "that through death He might destroy." "The means whereby Christ overcame Satan, is expressly said to be death. To achieve this great and glorious victory against so mighty an enemy, Christ did not assemble troops of angels, as He could have done (Matt. 26:53), nor did He array Himself with majesty and terror, as in Exodus 19:16; but He did it by taking part of weak flesh and blood, and therein humbling Himself to death. In this respect the apostle saith, that Christ 'having spoiled principalities and powers, made a show of them openly, triumphing over them in the cross' (Col. 2:15), meaning thereby, His death. The apostle there resembleth the cross of Christ to a trophy whereon the spoils of enemies were hanged. Of old conquerors were wont to hang the armour and weapons of enemies vanquished on the walls of forts and towers." (Dr. Gouge.)

"That through death He might destroy him that had the power of death, that is, the devil." A striking type of this is furnished in Judges 14:12-19—will the reader please turn to this, before considering our brief comments. The riddle propounded by Samson prefigured what is plainly declared here in Heb. 2:14. The greatest "eater" (Judges 14:14), or "consumer," is Death. Yet out of the eater came forth meat: that is, out of death has come life; see John 12:24. Note in Judges 14 how, typically, the natural man is, of himself, utterly unable to solve this mystery. The secret of the death of Christ, the Lion of the tribe of Judah, must be *revealed*. Finally, note how that a change of raiment was provided for those to whom the riddle was explained—a foreshadowment of the believer's robe of righteousness!

"And deliver them who through fear of death were all their life-time subject to bondage" (v. 15). It needs to be carefully borne in mind that throughout this passage the apostle has in view a particular class of persons, namely, the "heirs of salvation," the "sons" of God, the "brethren" of Christ. Here they are described according to their unregenerate condition: subject to bondage; so subject, all their unregenerate days; so subject through "the fear of death." It was to deliver them from this fear of death that Christ died. Such we take it is the general meaning of this verse. 2 Tim. 1:7 gives the sequel: "For God hath not given us the spirit of fear; but of power, and of love, and of a sound mind."

The opening "And" and the verb "deliver" (which is in the same mood and tense as "destroy" in the previous verse) intimate that Christ's death had in view these two ends which cannot be separated, namely, destroying the Devil, delivering us. Just as Abraham destroyed those enemies who had taken Lot captive together with the other inhabitants of Sodom, that he might "deliver" them (Gen. 14:14), and as David destroyed the Amelekites, that he might "deliver" his wives and children and others out of their hands (1 Sam. 25:9), so Christ vanquished the Devil, that he might "deliver" those who had (by yielding to his temptations) fallen captive to him. What thanks is due unto Christ for thus overthrowing our great adversary!

To the "fear of death," *i.e*, that judgment of God upon sin, all men are in much greater bondage than they well own or than they imagine. It was this "fear" which made Adam and Eve hide themselves from the presence of God (Gen. 3:8), which made Cain explain, "my punishment is greater than I can bear" (Gen. 4:13), which made Nabal's heart to die within him (1 Sam. 25:37), which made Saul fall to the ground as a man in a swoon (1 Sam. 28:20), which made Felix to tremble (Acts 24:25), and which will yet cause kings and the great men of the earth to call on the mountains to fall on them (Rev. 6:15, 16). True, the natural man, at times, succeeds in drowning the accusations of his conscience in the pleasures of sin, but "as the crackling of thorns under a pot, so is the laughter of the fool" (Ecc. 7:6). It is from this fearful bondage that Christ delivered His people: through His grace, by His Spirit filling them "with all joy and peace in believing" (Rom. 15:13).

A beautiful and most complete type of the truth in our present verse is to be found in 1 Sam. 17. Will the reader turn to that chapter and note carefully the following details: First, in vv. 4-8 there we have, in figure, Satan harassing the O.T. saints. Second, where was David (type of Christ) during the time Goliath was terrifying the people of God? Verses 14, 15 answer: In his father's house, caring for his sheep. So through the Mosaic economy Christ remained on High, in the Father's House, yet caring for His sheep. Third, Goliath defied Israel for "forty days," v. 16—figure of the forty centuries from Adam to Christ, when the O.T. saints lived in fear of death, for "life and immortality" were only brought "to light through the Gospel" (2 Tim. 1:10). Fourth, next we see David leaving his father's house, laden with blessings for his brethren, vv. 17, 18. Note the "early in the morning," v. 20, showing his *readiness* to go on this mission. Fifth, mark the sad reception he met with from his brethren, v. 28: his efforts were unappreciated, his purpose misunderstood, and a false accusation was brought against him. Sixth, in vv. 32, 38-49, we have a marvellous type of Christ defeating Satan in the wilderness: note how David went forth in his *shepherd* character (v. 40 and compare John 10). He took "five" stones out of the brook (the place of running water—figure of the Holy Spirit) but used only one of them; so Christ in the Wilderness selected the Pentateuch (the first five books of Scripture) as His weapon, but used only one of them, Deuteronomy. Note David *slew* him not with the stone! He stunned him with that, but slew him with his *own* sword: so Christ vanquished him that had the power of death "*through death*." Read again v. 51 and see how accurate is the figure of Christ "bruising" the Serpent's *head* Finally, read v. 52 and see the typical climax: those "in fear" *delivered*. What a marvellous Book is the Bible!

"For verily He took not on angels; but He took on the seed of Abraham" (v. 16). This verse, which has occasioned not a little controversy, presents no difficulty if it be weighed in the light of its whole context. It treats not of the Divine incarnation, that we have in v. 14; rather does it deal with the purpose of it, or better, the consequences of Christ's death. Its opening "for" first looks back, remotely to vv. 9, 10; immediately, to vv. 14, 15. The Spirit is here advancing a *reason* why Christ tasted death for every son, and why He destroyed the Devil in order to liberate His captives; because not angels, but the seed of Abraham, were the objects of His benevolent favour. The "for" and the balance of the verse also, looks forward, laying a foundation for what follows in v. 17: the ground of Christ's being made like to His brethren and becoming the faithful and merciful High Priest was because He would befriend the seed of Abraham.

The Greek verb here translated "He took on" or "laid hold" is found elsewhere in some very striking connections. It is used of Christ's stretching out His hand and rescuing sinking Peter, Matt. 14:31, there rendered "caught." It is used of Christ when He "took" the blind man by the hand (Mark 8:23). So of the man sick of the dropsy. He "took" and healed him (Luke 14:4). Here in Heb. 2:16 the reference is to the almighty power and invincible grace of the Captain of our salvation. It receives illustration in those words of the apostle's where, referring to his own conversion, he said, "for which also I am (was) *apprehended* (laid hold) of Christ Jesus" (Phil. 3:12). Thus it was and still is with each of God's elect. In themselves, lost, rushing headlong to destruction; when Christ stretches forth His hand and delivers, so that of each it may be said, "Is not this a brand *plucked* from the burning" (Zech. 3:2). "Laid hold of" so securely that none can pluck out of His hand!

But not only does our verse emphasise the invincibility of Divine grace, it also plainly teaches the absolute sovereignty of it. Christ lays hold not of "the seed of Adam," all mankind, but only "the seed of Abraham" —the father of God's elect people. This expression, "the seed of Abraham," is employed in the N.T. in connection with both his natural and his spiritual seed. It is the latter which is here in view: "Now to Abraham and his seed were the promises made. He saith not, And to seeds, as of many, but as of one, And to thy seed which is Christ" (Gal. 3:16)—not only Christ personal, but Christ mystical. The last verse of Gal. 3 shows that: "And if ye be Christ's, then are ye Abraham's seed, and heirs according to promise."

This verse presents an insoluble difficulty to those who belive in the *universality* of God's love and grace. Those who do so deny the plain teaching of Scripture that Christ laid down His life for "the sheep," and for them alone. They insist that justice as well as mercy demanded that He should die for all of Adam's race. But why is it harder to believe that God has provided no salvation for part of the human race, than that He has provided none for the fallen angels? They were higher in the scale of being; they, too, were sinners needing a Saviour. Yet none has been provided for *them*! He "laid not on" angels.

But more: Our verse not only brings out the truth of election, it also presents the solemn fact of reprobation. Christ is not the Saviour of angels. "And the angels which kept not their first estate, but left their own habitation, He hath reserved in everlasting chains under darkness unto the judgment of the great day" (Jude 6). On this Dr. J. Brown has well said:

"What an overwhelming subject of contemplation is this! He is not the Saviour of angels, but of the elect family of men. We are lost in astonishment when we allow our minds to rest on the number and dignity of those whom He does not lay hold of, and the comparative as well as real vileness of those of whom He does take hold. A sentiment of this kind has engaged some good, but in this case not wise men, in an inquiry why the Son of God saves men rather than angels. On this subject Scripture is silent, and so should we be. There is no doubt that there are good reasons for this, as for every other part of the Divine determinations and dispensations; and it is not improbable that in some future stage of our being these reasons will be made known to us. But, in the meantime, I can go no further than, 'even so, Father, for so it hath seemed good in Thy sight.' I dare not 'intrude into things which I have not seen,' lest I should prove that I am 'vainly puffed up by a fleshly mind.' But I will say with an apostle, 'Behold the goodness and severity of God: on them that fell, severity'—most righteous severity; 'but to them who are saved, goodness '— most unmerited goodness." (Dr. J. Brown.)

May the Lord add His blessing to what has been before us.—*Arthur W. Pink.*

GLEANINGS IN EXODUS.

59. *The Golden Calf* (*Ex.* 32 : 1-10.)

Our present portion, which runs on to the end of chapter 34, commences a new and distinct section of Exodus, a section which, in one sense, is parenthetical in its character and contents. This will at once appear if Ex. 32 to 34 be omitted and chapter 35 be read right after chapter 31. In Ex. 24 to 31 inclusive we have recorded the communications which Moses received from Jehovah while he was with Him in the mount, instructions which concerned the making of the tabernacle and the institution of the priesthood. In chapter 35 Moses makes known to the people the revelations which he had received from the Lord, and forthwith the making of the holy vessels and the house for them is proceeded with. But in chapters 32 to 34 the flow of the tabernacle theme is interrupted, and a very different subject is brought before us. Here we are given to see what transpired among the Congregation while Moses was in the mount. Here we behold the awful sin of Aaron and the people during the interval of their leader's absence, with the fearful consequences which it entailed.

A more frightful contrast than that which is presented in these two sections in the book of Exodus is scarcely possible to imagine. In the former we are permitted to witness the condescending grace of Jehovah as He spoke with Moses; in the latter we are called upon to gaze at that which exhibited the awful depravity of fallen man. In the one we are occupied with that which unveils to us the manifold glories of Christ; in the other we have exposed the awful abominations which Satan produces. First we are shown the povisions which God made for His people to worship Him, according to His own holy appointments; then we witness the idolatrous manufacture of a golden calf, and the children of Israel bowing down before it in worship. Verily, truth *is* stranger than fiction. "God hath made man upright," *but* they have sought out many inventions (Eccl. 7 : 29), inventions which only serve to make manifest the exceeding sinfulness of sin and the fearful depths of depravity into which fallen man has descended.

Above, we have stated that Ex. 32 to 34 forms a parenthetical section of the book, inasmuch as the contents of these chapters break in upon the narrative concerning the tabernacle. But looked at from another standpoint they contain the historical sequel to what is recorded in Ex. 19. There we see the children of Israel, in the third month after their going forth out of Egypt, encamped before Sinai. They were bidden to sanctify themselves, wash their clothes, and come not at their wives, and then on the third day, the Lord came down " in the sight of the people upon Mount Sinai." Most awe-inspiring was the Divine manifestation: "There were thunders and lightnings, and a thick cloud upon the mount, and the voice of the trumpet exceeding loud; so that all the people in the camp trembled. . . And Mount Sinai was altogether on a smoke, because the Lord descended upon it in fire: and the smoke thereof ascended as the smoke of a furnace, and the whole mount quaked greatly" (19: 16, 18).

Moses was then called up into the mount, where he received the laws enumerated in Ex. 20-23. Then, in 24 : 3 we read, "And Moses came and told the people all the words of the Lord, and all the judgments: and all the people answered with one voice, and said, All the words which the Lord hath said will we do." This vow of the people was most solemnly ratified: Moses wrote all the words of the Lord in a book, " And he took the book of the covenant and read it in the audience of the people: and they said, All that the Lord hath said will we do, and be obedient. And Moses took the blood and sprinkled it on the people, and said, Behold the blood of the covenant, which the Lord hath made with you concerning all these words (24: 7, 8).

Following this, we are told, "And the Lord said unto Moses, Come up to Me into the mount, and be there. . . . And Moses rose up, and his minister Joshua: and Moses went up into the mount of God. And he said unto the elders, Tarry ye here for us, until we come again unto you: and, behold Aaron and Hur are with you: if any man have any matters to do, let him come unto them. . . . And Moses went into the midst of the cloud, and gat him up into the mount: and Moses was in the mount forty days and forty nights" (24: 12-14, 18). It was while Moses was on the mount on this occasion that he received the Divine communications recorded in chapters 25 to 31. And what of the people during the interval? How were they conducting themselves during this most solemn period? Our present portion contains the answer; to it we are now ready to turn.

"And when the people saw that Moses delayed to come down out of the mount, the people gathered themselves together unto Aaron, and said unto him, Up, make us gods, which shall go before us; for this Moses, the man that brought us up out of the land of Egypt, we wot not what is become of him" (v. 1). The key to this incident is found in part of Stephen's address, recorded in Acts 7: "This is He that was in the church in the wilderness . . . to whom our fathers would not obey, but *thrust from them*, and in their hearts turned back again into Egypt, saying unto Aaron, Make us gods to go before us" (vv. 38-40). It was not that they were peeved at the lengthy absence of Moses, but that they had cast off their allegiance to Jehovah, their hearts had departed from Him.

What we have said above is confirmed by Israel's reference to Moses on this occasion as "the man that brought us up out of the land of Egypt." Instead of owning their Divine Deliverer, their vision was narrowed to the human instrument which had been employed. It is ever thus with a people whose hearts are divorced from God. Compare the words of apostate Israel at a later date: "Then the men of Israel said unto Gideon, Rule thou over us, both thou, and thy son, and thy son's son also: for *thou* hast delivered us from the hand of Midian" (Judges 8: 22). Here in Ex. 32 the human instrument was contemptuously referred to as "this Moses," so little did they appreciate his unwearied service and prayers on their behalf.

It is not without reason that our present portion is immediately preceded by these words: "And He gave unto Moses, when He had made an end of communing with him upon Mount Sinai, two tables of testimony, tables of stone, written with the finger of God" (31: 18). On those tables of stone were written the ten commandments, the first of which was, "Thou shalt have no other gods before Me." And the second, "Thou shalt not make unto thee any graven image" (20: 3, 4,). It is the deliberate, public and united disobedience of these commandments which our lesson records. Man must have an object, and when he turns from the true God, he at once craves a false one.

What we have here has been perpetuated in every generation; nor has Christendom proved any exception to the rule. As another has said, "Alas! alas! it has ever been thus in man's history. The human heart lusts after something that can be seen; it loves that which meets and gratifies the senses. It is only faith that can 'endure as seeing Him who is invisible.' Hence, in every age, men have been forward to set up and lean upon human imitations of Divine realities. Thus it is we see the counterfeits of corrupt religion multiplied before our eyes. Those things which we know, upon the authority of God's Word, to be Divine and heavenly realities, the professing Church has transformed into human and earthly inventions. Having become weary of hanging upon an invisible arm, of trusting in an invisible sacrifice, of having recourse to an invisible Priest, of committing herself to an invisible Head, she has set about 'making' these things; and thus from age to age, she has been busily at work, with 'graving tool' in hand, graving and fashioning one thing after another, until we can at length recognize as little similarity between much that we *see* around us, and what we *read* in the Word, as between a 'molten calf' and the God of Israel" (C.H.M.)

Israel had served false gods in Egypt (Joshua 24: 14), and the flesh in them was still unchanged. It is true that Israel as a nation were only typically redeemed—the vast majority of them being children in whom was *no* faith (Deut. 32: 20)—yet we must never forget when reading their history that, "These things were our examples, to the intent we should not lust after evil things, as they also lusted" (1 Cor. 10: 6). Yea, does not the apostle at once follow this with, "Neither be ye idolators as were some of them" (v. 7). And again he says, "Wherefore, my dearly beloved, flee from idolatry" (v. 14). So, too, John, whose Epistle is addressed to those to whom he could say, "truly our fellowship is with the Father, and with His Son Jesus Christ," closes with the exhortation, "Little children, keep yourselves from idols." May God grant us hearts to heed these solemn and needed warnings. There is but one safeguard and preventative, and that is, being constantly occupied with Christ.

What has just been before us is of such immense practical importance that ere passing on we feel we must add a further word. The typical picture is unmistakably plain in its present-day application to God's people. Moses was away from Israel, up in the mount; so Christ is away from the earth, on High before God. But before He went away, He said to His disciples, "Ye believe in God, believe also in Me" (John 14:1). He is the Object of faith, and it is only as our affections are set upon Him, as we are in daily communion with Him, that our hearts are kept from idols. But just as surely as Israel's turning away from Jehovah was at once followed by the making of the golden calf, just as surely as (in the history of the corporate Christian profession) the leaving of first love (Rev. 2:4) was followed by the setting up of the "synagogue of Satan" (Rev. 2:9), so now, the estranging of the heart from Christ opens the door for all sorts of abominable idolatries.

"And Aaron said unto them, Break off the golden earrings, which are in the ears of your wives, of your sons, and of your daughters, and bring unto me" (v. 2). As Ex. 24:18 informs us, Moses was absent from Israel for forty days, a number which, in Scripture, is almost always connected with *probation*. It hardly needs to be said that such a length of time was not needed by God: had He so pleased He could within the space of a few hours (or even in a moment) have told Moses all that is recorded in Ex. 25 to 31 and made him understand it. Why, then, those forty days? For the testing of Israel—to make manifest whether or no they would patiently wait for the ordinances they had promised to observe. But so far from keeping their solemn vows, they would not even wait to hear what God said.

Aaron, with Hur, was left to adjudicate upon any question that might arise while Moses and his minister, Joshua, was away (24:14). Aaron is now put to the test. It was the first time he had been left in charge of the Congregation, and wretchedly did he acquit himself. Instead of putting his trust in the Lord, the fear of man brought him a snare. Instead of boldly withstanding the people, he, apparently without any struggle, yielded to their evil designs. Alas, it but supplies another tragic illustration of the fact that when responsibility is committed to man, he betrays his trust. Thus it has been in the history of Christendom: instead of the leaders refusing to follow the worldly wishes of their people, they have heeded, and oftentimes encouraged them.

"And all the people brake off the golden earrings which were in their ears, and brought them unto Aaron. And he received them at their hand, and fashioned it with a graving tool, after he had made it a molten calf: and they said, These be thy gods, O Israel which brought thee up out of the land of Egypt" (vv. 3, 4). Another has pointed out an analogy between what we have here and that which is recorded in Matt. 17:1-18. "There is a striking resemblance, in one aspect, between this scene and that witnessed at the foot of the mount of transfiguration. In both alike Satan holds full sway. In the one before us, it is the nation who have fallen under his power, in the other it is the child whom he has possessed; but the child again is a type of the Jewish nation of a later day. The absence of Christ on high (shown in figure also by Moses on Sinai) is the opportunity seized by Satan—under God's commission—for the display of his wicked power, and man (Israel) in the evil of his heart becomes his wretched slave." (Ed. Dennett.)

The calf, or ox, was the principal Egyptian god—"Apis"—with which they had been familiar in the land of bondage. "These be thy gods" is expounded in Neh. 9:18 as meaning, "This is thy god." The inspired comment of the Psalmist is very solemn, "They made a calf in Horeb, and worshipped the molten image. They changed their Glory into the similitude of an ox that eateth grass. They forgat God their Saviour, which had done great things in Egypt" (106:19-21). The making of that idol and the rendering worship to it was an act of open apostasy, the bitter harvest from which continued to be reaped until they were carried into Babylon (Acts 7:43). Such is the flesh: ever ready to forget God's deliverances, despise the light He has given us, disobey His commands, act in self-will, and bring in that which effectually shuts Him out.

"And when Aaron saw it, he built an altar before it" (v. 5). Still darker become the clouds which hang over this awful scene. Not content with substituting a false god for the true One, they must, perforce, cover up their wickedness under the cloak of religion. An "altar" is now erected. Thus it has always been, and still is: man ever seeks to hide the shame of his idolatry by putting over it the name of Deity. Therefore the next thing that we read here is that, "Aaron made proclamation, and said, To-morrow is a feast to the Lord" (v. 5). As a fact, this was a pretence, for there were no "feasts" in either the third or fourth months. (See Lev. 23.)

What is before us in this 5th verse but

gives the prototype of what is now going on almost everywhere in Christendom. Men have set up their idols and then sought to dignify and sanctify their inventions by worshipping them in the name of Christ. Romanism and Ritualism give us one form of it. Worldliness and fleshly indulgencies another. Just as Aaron proclaimed the honours paid to the calf and the carnal merriment that followed as "a feast unto the Lord," so many a "church supper," bazaar, religious carnival, whist drive, &c., is officially carried out under the name of Christianity. What a mockery it all is! Aaron had no Scripture to justify his proclamation, nor have the present-day leaders any word from God to warrant their doings.

"And they rose up early on the morrow, and offered burnt offerings and brought peace offerings" (v. 6). Terrible travesty was this. Those offerings which spoke of the devotedness of Christ unto the Father, and the fellowship which He has made possible between a holy God and His people, were now presented to this fetish of their own corrupt imaginations. It is significant to mark the absence of any *sin* offering! But that had no place in their thoughts. How could it? When there is departure from God, the conscience becomes calloused: "The way of the wicked is as darkness, they know not at what they stumble" (Prov. 4:19). That is why the unscriptural and Christ-dishonouring performances in the churches occasion no uneasiness to those engaged in them.

"And the people sat down to eat and to drink, and rose up to play" (v. 6). Having formally presented their offerings, they now felt free to indulge the lusts of the flesh. And, be it remembered, what we have here is something more than the inspired record of an incident which happened long ago. God's Word is a *living* Word, describing things as they actually are. It was in the "early" hours that the burnt and peace offerings were presented. So the early morning mass or "communion" remains popular, and is still followed by the offerers spending the remainder of the day eating, drinking, and playing: "As in water face answereth to face, so the heart of man to man" (Prov. 27:19)!

"And the Lord said unto Moses, Go, get thee down; for thy people which thou broughtest out of the land of Egypt have corrupted themselves" (v. 7). These words of the Lord must be read in the light of what is recorded in Ex. 24:6-8. There we read of a "covenant" which the Lord made with Israel on the ground of His law and their avowal to keep it. It was a purely legal compact between the two contracting parties. Israel had now broken their agreement: they had disowned their Deliverer (32:1), they had broken His law (32:6) Therefore the Lord now, in view of the broken covenant, disowns them: He speaks of them to Moses as "*thy* people."

"They have turned aside quickly out of the way which I commanded them: they have made them a molten calf, and have worshipped it, and have sacrificed thereunto, and said, These be thy gods, O Israel, which have brought thee up out of the land of Egypt" (v. 8). Alas how "quickly" had they departed from the path of obedience and loyalty! Less than five months before they had declared, "The Lord is my strength and song, and He is become my salvation: He is my God, and I will prepare Him an habitation: my father's God, and I will exalt Him" (15:2). Instead of so doing, they had raised up that which effectively shut Him out, and instead of exalting Him they had debased themselves. It is solemn to note the Lord here quotes to Moses the identical language the people had used with Aaron: though engaged in "communing" with His servant, He had heard the very words of His wayward people down below. And He still hears and records all our words!

"They have turned aside quickly out of the way which I commanded them." It has been thus all through the piece. How "quickly" Adam "turned aside" from the way of his Creator's command! How "quickly" Noah failed after he came out from the Ark! How "quickly" Nadab and Abihu did that which the Lord "commanded them not" (Lev. 10:1) after the priesthood was instituted! How "quickly" sin entered Israel's camp after Canaan was entered (Josh. 7). And so we might go on. Alas, how "quickly" the young Christian leaves his "first love" and loses his early joy! Failure is written large across every page of human history. And what is the chief cause of all such failure? Do not the next words of Jehovah to Moses make known the answer?

"And the Lord said unto Moses, I have seen this people, and, behold, it is a stiff-necked people" (v. 9). What is signified by this oft-used figure? It signifies a state of insubordination: note the order in Deut. 31:27. "I know thy rebellion, and thy stiff neck." It is the opposite of submission to the will of God: "Be ye not stiff-necked, as your fathers were, but *yield yourselves unto* the Lord" (2 Chron. 30:8). It is a state into which we may bring ourselves: "They obeyed not, neither inclined their ear, but *made* their necks stiff, that they might not hear, nor receive instruction" (Jer. 17:23). It is brought about by not yielding ourselves to God: "Ye stiff-necked and uncircumcised in hearts and ears, ye do always resist the Holy Spirit" (Acts 7:51). A stiff-necked person is one who bows not to

God: he is one in whom self-will is at work. This was the state of Israel, therefore did God go on to say:

"Now therefore let Me alone, that My wrath may wax hot against them, and that I may consume them: and I will make of thee a great nation" (v. 10). Having by their sins forfeited all the blessings engaged to them on the terms of their own covenant, the Lord at once stands against them, disclaims them, and threatens to execute consuming judgment upon them. "Thus Israel, if dealt with according to the righteous requirements of the law which they had accepted, and to which they had promised obedience as the condition of blessing, were lost beyond recovery, and would perish through their own wilful sin and apostasy" (Ed. Dennett). The reason why God did not totally destroy His stiff-necked people on this occasion we must leave for consideration, D.V., to our next article. In the meantime let us seek grace to heed this solemn warning. By nature none of us are a whit better than Aaron and the Israelites. Were God to withdraw His grace from us, we, too, would surely and speedily fall into as great and gross sin as they did. Then let us cry with the Psalmist, "Hold Thou me up, and I shall be safe, and I will have respect unto Thy statutes continually" (119:117).

—*Arthur W. Pink.*

WORSHIP.

One of the most solemn and soul-destroying fallacies of the day is that unregenerate souls are capable of worshipping God. Probably one chief reason why this error has gained so much ground is because of the widespread ignorance which obtains concerning the real nature of true worship. People imagine that if they attend a religious service, are reverent in their demeanor, join in the singing of the hymns, listen respectfully to the preacher, and contribute to the collection, they have really worshipped God. Poor deluded souls, a delusion which is helped forward by the priest-craft and preacher-graft of the day. Over against this delusion are the words of Christ in John 4:24, which are startling in their plainness and pungency: "God is Spirit: and they that worship Him must worship in spirit and in truth."

In seeking to develop this most important theme, we shall take it up under the following heads: 1, The vanity of false worship. 2, The exclusiveness of true worship. 3, The nature of worship. 4, The pre-requisites of worship. 5, The power of worship. 6, The place of worship. 7, Hindrances to worship.

1. THE VANITY OF FALSE WORSHIP.

"Well hath Isaiah prophesied of you hypocrites, as it is written. This people honoureth Me with their lips, but their heart is far from Me. Howbeit in vain do they worship Me, teaching for doctrines the commandments of men" (Mark 7:6-7). These solemn words were spoken by the Lord Jesus to the scribes and Pharisees. They had come to Him with the complaint that His disciples did not conform to their traditions and practices in connection with ceremonial washings and cleansings. In His reply, Christ exposed the worthlessness of their religion.

The service of Christ was many-sided. In the second part of Mark 7 He is seen ministering to the need of a poor woman who cast herself on His mercy; but in the first section of the chapter we behold Him unmasking the hypocrisy of man. Before man can be blest spiritually his heart must be reached and revealed to himself. Before his heart can be bared, the specious coverings behind which he vainly seeks to hide from the light of God have to be stripped off. But man prefers anything to exposure in the presence of God. Why? Because he can never feel at home in that Presence till he takes his true place before God as a needy and acknowledged sinner. The wondrous and the blessed thing is that the more I am conscious of my wretchedness and own my deep need before the Lord, the more I feel at home in His presence. But these are experiences to which the mere religionist is a total stranger.

It makes a world of difference whether men bring their religiousness or their need to Christ. The former is met with exposure and rebuke; the latter with unqualified grace and unlimited supply. At the beginning of Mark 7, the scribes and Pharisees are seen bringing their religiousness to Christ, quoting the decrees of the elders for their authority. In reality they were seeking to cloke their fallen condition and hide their awful depravity behind the garb of ritualism. The worst thing a poor sinner can do is to parade his religious performances before God. The best thing he can do is to bring his sins to Christ, confess them before Him, and thus get rid of his awful burden.

These scribes and Pharisees were raising the question of the ceremonial "washing of hands," while their *hearts* remained filthy before God. Ah, dear reader, the traditions of the elders may be diligently attended to, their religious ordinances strictly observed, their doctrines devoutly upheld, and yet the conscience have never been searched in the presence of God as to the question of sin.

The fact is that *religion* is one of the greatest hindrances against the truth of God blessing men's souls.

God's truth addresses us on the ground that God and man are as far apart as sin is from holiness; therefore his first great need is cleansing and reconciliation. But "religion" proceeds on the assumption that depraved and guilty man *may have* dealings with God, approach unto Him, yea, worship and serve Him. The world over, human religion is based on the fallacy that fallen and sinful man can have dealings with God. Religion is the principal means used by Satan to blind men to their true and terrible condition. It is the Devil's anaesthetic for making lost sinners feel comfortable and easy in their guilty distance from God. It hides *God* from them in His real character—as a holy God who is "of purer eyes than to behold evil, and canst not look on iniquity" (Hab. 1:13).

A flood of light is thrown upon this side of our subject if we weigh attentively the awful incident recorded in Matt. 4:8, 9, "Again, the Devil taketh Him up into an exceeding high mountain, and shewed Him all the kingdoms of the world, and the glory of them; And said unto Him, All these things will I give Thee if Thou wilt fall down and worship me." The Devil seeks worship. How few in Christendom are aware of this, or realize that the principal activities of the Enemy are carried on in the religious sphere!

Listen to the testimony of Deut. 32:17, "They sacrificed unto *demons*, not to God; to gods whom they knew not." That refers to Israel in the early days of their apostasy, Listen again to 1 Cor. 10:20, "But I say that the things which the Gentiles sacrificed, they sacrificed to demons and not to God." What light does that cast on the idolatries and abominations of heathendom! Listen, again, to 2 Cor. 4:4, "In whom the *god* of this world hath blinded the minds of them which believe not, lest the light of the glorious Gospel of Christ, who is the image of God, should shine unto them." This means that Satan is the inspirer and director of the world's religion. Yes, *he* seeks worship, and is the chief promoter of all false worship.

2. THE EXCLUSIVENESS OF TRUE WORSHIP.

"God is spirit, and they that worship Him must worship Him in spirit and truth." This "must" is final: there is no alternative, no choice in the matter. It is not the first time that we have this very emphatic word in John's Gospel. There are two notable verses where it occurs previously. "Marvel not that I said unto thee, Ye *must* be born again" (John 3:7); "As Moses lifted up the serpent in the wilderness, even so *must* the Son of Man be lifted up" (John 3:14). Each of these three "musts" is equally important and unequivocal. The first has reference to God the Spirit, for He it is who regenerates. The second refers to the work of God the Son, for He it was who made atonement for sin. The third has reference to God the Father, for He it is that seeketh worshippers (John 4:23). This order cannot be changed: it is only those who have been born of the Spirit, and who are resting upon the atoning work of Christ, that can worship the Father.

To quote again the words of Christ to the religionists in His day, "This people honoureth Me with their lips, but their heart is far from Me: howbeit *in vain* do they worship Me" (Mark 7:6, 7). Ah, my reader, the worldling may be a generous philanthropist, a sincere religionist, a zealous denominationalist, a devout churchman, a regular communicant, yet is he no more capable of *worshipping* God than a dumb man is of singing. Cain tried it, and failed. He was not irreligious. He "brought of the fruit of the ground an offering unto the Lord" (Gen. 4:4). But "unto Cain and his offering He had not respect." Why? Because he refused to own his undone condition and his need of an atoning sacrifice.

In order to worship God, God must be *known*; and He cannot be known apart from Christ. Much may be predicated and believed about a theoretical or a theological "God," but He cannot be known, apart from the Lord Jesus. Said He, "I am the way, the truth and the life, no man cometh unto the Father but by Me" (John 14:6). Therefore it is a sinful make-believe, a fatal delusion, a wicked farce, to cause unregenerate people to imagine that *they* can worship God. While the sinner remains away from Christ, he is the "enemy" of God, a child of wrath; how then can he worship God? While he remains in his unregenerate state, he is "dead in trespasses and sins"; how then can he worship God?

What has just been said above is almost universally repudiated to-day, and repudiated in the name of Religion. And, we repeat, Religion is the principal instrument used by the Devil in deceiving souls, for it insists—whether it be the "Buddhist religion" or the "Christian religion"—that man, yet in his sins, *can* have dealings with and approach unto the thrice holy God. To deny this is to stir up the enmity and call down upon the one so doing the opposition of all mere religionists. Yea, it was that very thing which brought down upon Christ the merciless hatred of the religionists of His day. He refuted their claims, exposed their hypocrisy, and so incurred their wrath.

To the "chief priests and the elders of the temple" (Matt. 21:21), Christ said, "The publicans and harlots go into the kingdom of God before you" (Matt. 21:31); and at the close of His discourse, it is added, "They sought to lay hands on Him" (v. 46). They attended to outward things, but their inward state was neglected. And why was it that the "publicans and harlots" entered the kingdom of God before them? Because no religious pretentions stood in their way; they had no self-righteous profession to maintain at all costs, no pious reputation to keep up. Under the preaching of the Word they were convicted of their lost condition, so took their true place before God and were saved. Only such can be worshippers.

3. THE NATURE OF TRUE WORSHIP.

"God is Spirit: and they that worship Him must worship Him in spirit and truth" (John 4 : 24). First of all there is, no doubt, a dispensational reference here. To worship "in spirit" stands contrasted from the fleshly rites and imposing ceremonies of Judaism. To worship "in truth" stands opposed to the superstitions and idolatrous delusions of the heathen. To worship God "in spirit and in truth" means in a manner suited to the full and final revelation which God has now made of Himself in Christ. It means to worship spiritually and truly. It means giving to Him the homage of an enlightened understanding and the love of a regenerated heart.

To worship "in spirit and in truth" stands opposed to a carnal worship which is external and spectacular. It bars out all worshipping of God with the senses. We cannot worship Him who is "Spirit" by gazing on ornate architecture and stained-glass windows, by listening to the beautiful peals of a costly organ, by smelling sweet incense or "telling" of beads. We cannot worship with our eyes and ears, or nose and hands, for *they* are "flesh," not "spirit." "*Must* worship in spirit and in truth" excludes everything that is of the natural man.

To worship "in spirit and in truth" bars out all *soulical* worship. The soul is the seat of the emotions, and very much of the so-called worship of present-day Christendom is only soulical. Touching anecdotes, stirring appeals, thrilling oratory of a religious character, are all calculated to produce this very thing. Beautiful anthems by a well-trained choir, rendered in such a way as to move to tears or to ecstacies of joy, may stir the soul, but will not and cannot affect the new man.

True worship is the adoration of a redeemed people, occupied with God Himself. The unregenerate look upon "worship" as an obeisance which God exacts from them, and wh ch gives them no joy as they seek to proffer it. Far different is it with those who have been born from above and redeemed with precious blood. The first time the word 'redeemed" occurs in Scripture is in Ex. 15, and it is there also, for the first time, we behold a people "singing," worshipping, adoring God Himself. There, on the far shores of the Red Sea, that Nation which had been brought out from the house of bondage and delivered from all their enemies united in praising Jehovah.

"Worship" is the new nature in the believer, stirred into activity, turning to its divine and heavenly Source. It is that which is "spirit" (John 3 : 6) turning to Him who is "Spirit." It is that which is the "workmanship" of Christ (Eph. 2 : 10) turning to Him who re-created us. It is the children, spontaneously and gratefully turning in love to their Father. It is the new heart crying out, "Thanks be unto God for His unspeakable Gift" (2 Cor. 9 : 15). It is sinners, cleansed by blood, exclaiming, "Blessed be the God and Father of our Lord Jesus Christ, who hath blessed us with all spiritual blessings in the heavenlies in Christ" (Eph. 1 : 3). *That* is worship: assured of our acceptance in the Beloved, adoring God for what He has made Christ to be unto us, and what He has made us to be in Christ.

It is worthy of our closest attention to observe that the only time the Lord Jesus ever spoke on the subject of Worship was in John 4. Matt. 4 : 9, and Mark 7 : 6, 7, were but *quotations* from the Old Testament. It should indeed stir our hearts to discover that the sole occasion when Christ made any direct and personal observations on worship was when He was speaking, not to a religious man like Nicodemus, nor even to His apostles, but to a woman, an adulteress, a Samaritan— a semi-heathen! Truly God's ways *are* different from ours!

To that poor woman our blessed Lord declared, "The hour cometh, and now is, when the true worshippers shall worship the Father in spirit and in truth; for the Father seeketh such to worship Him" (John 4 : 23). And *how* did the Father "seek" worshippers? Does not the whole of the context supply the answer? At the beginning of the chapter, the Son of God is seen taking a journey (vv. 3, 4). His object was to seek out one of His lost sheep, to reveal Himself to a soul that knew Him not, to wean her from the lusts of the flesh, and fill her heart with His satisfying grace; and this, in order that *she* might meet the longings of Divine love and give in return that praise and adoration which only a saved sinner can give.

Who can fail to see in the journey which He took to Sychar's well in order to meet that desolate soul and win her to Himself, that we have a most blessed adumbration of that still greater journey which God's Son took—leaving Heaven's peace and bliss and light, coming down to this world of strife and darkness and wretchedness. He came here seeking sinners, not only to save them from sin and death but to give them to drink in and enjoy the love of God as no angel can enjoy it; that from hearts overflowing with the consciousness of their indebtedness to the Saviour and thankfulness to the Father for having given His dear Son for them, they, realising and accepting His superlative excellency, might pour forth unto Him the sweet incense of praise. *That* is worship, and the remembrance of God's seeking love and Christ's redeeming blood are the *springs* of it.

One of the most blessed and beautiful examples recorded in the New Testament of what worship is is found in John 12 : 2, 3, "There they made Him a supper; and Martha served: but Lazarus was one of them that sat at the table with Him. Then took Mary a pound of ointment of spikenard, very costly, and anointed the feet of Jesus, and wiped His feet with her hair: and the house was filled with the odour of the ointment." As another has said, "She came not to hear a sermon, though the Prince of preachers was there. To sit at His feet and to hear His Word was not now her object, blessed as that was in its proper place. She came not to meet the saints, though precious saints were there; but fellowship with them, though blessed, was not now her object. She came not, after a week's toil, for refreshment; though none knew better the blessed springs of refreshment which are in Him. No, she came to pour out upon Him that which she had long treasured up, which was the most valuable of all her earthly possessions. She thought not of Simon the leper, sitting there a cleansed man; she passed by the apostles; so, too, Martha and Lazarus, her sister and brother in the flesh and in Christ. *The Lord Jesus* filled her thoughts: He had won her heart and now absorbed all her affections. She had eyes for no-one but Him. Adoration and homage was now her one thought: to pour out her heart's devotion before Him." *That* is worship.

We must leave for another sermon the remaining sections of our subject. May the Holy Spirit bless to each renewed heart what has been before us.

—*Arthur W. Pink.*

CHRIST IN US.

Col. 3 : 9-25 ; 4 : 1.

This portion of the Word of God brings out in a very simple and practical way the life we have in Christ, and the manifestations of it in us down here in this world—Christ in us.

In Colossians 1 : 26 - 27 (which I do not dwell on now), the apostle speaks of "the mystery," and presents to us there this aspect of it, "*Christ in you.*" This characterizes every Christian. This agrees with the words of the Lord in John 14 : 20, "At that day ye shall know that I am in My Father, and ye in Me, and *I in you.*" Also in Col. 3 : 11, we read, "Christ is *in* all"; that is, Christ is in every individual who belongs to the new creation. In verse 9-12 we have, first, what we are cleared from, and afterwards what we are brought into as having "put on the new man." Then follows the practical exhortations, and these are really the expression of what Christ was upon earth, so that what we are exhorted to be is exactly what Christ was down here. Some might think this high truth, and could not be carried out in the every-day relationships of life; but it is interesting to notice, that, in the latter part of this chapter, these very relationships are spoken of—wives, husbands, children, fathers, servants, masters.

Now let us look at verse 9. There it is very clearly shown, that though a person may be truly saved, there is still the old sinful nature in him which never improves, and which he will never lose till he is with the Lord. Many Christians have been surprised that such an exhortation as this, "Lie not one to another," should have been written to those who were addressed as "saints" and "faithful brethren in Christ" (1 : 2). What! a saint of God having to be told that he must not lie! Yes, but we must remember that these Colossian saints had all been heathen, and had not the knowledge that we have. Still the exhortation "Lie not one to another" is in force. "Why," it may be asked, "is a Christian not to tell a lie"? Not for fear of being lost, or of coming into judgment; but, "Lie not one to another, *seeing ye have put off the old man with his deeds;* and have put on the new man." It is an important thing to see that in Scripture we are never exhorted to walk like Christians in order to become Christians; but on the contrary, we are brought into full and perfect blessing through God's sovereign grace, and then comes the exhortation to walk worthy of the place of blessing we are brought into.

Suppose you were to be asked, Have you put off the old man? What would you answer? Some might say, I don't quite understand what the old man is. Well, I suppose "old man" means ourselves as children of Adam, born in sin, with a sinful nature—a nature which hates God and loves sin, and which is utterly dark and ignorant of God. Have you put that off? A person may answer, without thinking, No, indeed I have not, for I often find workings of that "old man" in me; in fact, I am not at all what I should wish myself to be. To such a one we would say, If you look at these verses in Colossians 3 you will see that we are not exhorted to " put off the old man," but are told " that *ye have* put off the old man with his deeds."

It is true of the weakest believer that he has " put off the old man with his deeds." There are two things—" The old man " and ' 'the deeds " of " the old man." There is a parallel verse in Eph. 4 : 21, 22, " As the truth is in Jesus : that ye put off concerning the former conversation the old man." This passage as we have it in our Bibles, might lead us to suppose that we have not put off the old man. It should, however, read thus : " Your having put off the old man " ; and in verse 24 : " Your having put on the new man."

In passing I would call your attention to that expression, " As the truth is in Jesus." Mark, it does not say " Lord Jesus." Jesus is His personal name, the name of His humiliation down here on earth ; and here on earth was perfectly expressed in Him that life which we possess as Christians. Have you ever, in reading the Gospels, seen all the path of the Lord Jesus—seen all His goodness and perfection, and said to yourself, that is my life, that is the life I have now, and which was thus perfectly expressed in a Man on earth ? Therefore it is important to see that in Eph. 4 it says, " As the truth is in *Jesus* "—the name of His humiliation here ; and now that He has died and risen again, we share His life and have part in the risen Man (Christ).

Now let us return to Colossians. In verse 9 we read, " Ye have put off the old man with his deeds." Oh, what a mercy to know this ! It is not every Christian that knows it. In other words, God says to you and to me, I do not see you now as a child of Adam at all ; but all that you have done (your sins), and all that you were as a sinful child of Adam, is gone forever from before Me. That is the only annihilation Scripture speaks of. " Our old man has been crucified with Him, that the body of sin might be destroyed " (Rom. 6 : 6).

I wonder if you have got hold of that blessed truth. Are you troubled about sin that is within you ? I don't mean troubled at its presence there ; but does it hinder your peace at all ? Did you think, after you believed, that you would have nothing but peace and joy ? Well, you found very soon it was not so ; something of the world that you had been fond of presented itself, and you felt the old desire that you used to have for it before you were converted.

Then perhaps the Devil came and suggested that after all you had only heard the Word with joy, and perhaps you were but a stony-ground hearer, and there had never been a real work of God in your soul. Many have no doubt thought, if not said it. Perhaps you have.

Well, just a word as to this. I think the first thing to see is that the Lord Jesus was on the cross not only on account of what we have done, but also because of what we are. Perhaps you and I are learning by degrees how bad we are by nature. Many are thinking that for the first time God is finding out how bad they are, just in the same proportion as they are discovering it for themselves. Oh, if God had only known how badly I should have turned out, He would never have taken me up at all ! This is quite a mistake. God knew all about you long ago. Is it not blessed to know this ? The Lord Jesus knew exactly what we were, and what we should do ; and when He knew it all, knew the worst about us, He gave Himself for us in the love of His own heart, to bear our sins and to be made sin for us. What a wonderful thing to see that the blessed Lord was not only on the cross for our sins, but that He was made sin for us ; and there is nothing left but the sweet savour of His sacrifice to God in which we are accepted ! God condemned sin in the flesh. What is that ? Why, the sinful nature that we have got. Is it not a blessed thing to see that all the depth of the evil of our nature came out before God at the cross more than 1800 years ago, and the blessed Lord bore the judgment due to us, there the fire of God's judgment consumed all the sin ? When the Lord Jesus laid down His life, it was the life of One who had already borne upon the cross the judgment of God against sin. He cried out, " My God, My God, why hast Thou forsaken Me ? "

We know this much, that there He bare in His own soul the whole weight of God's judgment against sin without mercy, and then He died ; and Scripture says that we died with Him. *With Him.* We need not go further than this chapter of Colossians to see that. We read in v. 3 " Ye have died." This is the correct way of reading it. There would be no sense in saying to a dead man, You are dead. He would not be alive to hear it. If you had been at the supper-table where Lazarus was, who had been raised from the dead, you would not have said to him, You are dead ; but, You have died, and now you are alive. Therefore when the Spirit of God says to us, " You have died," He supposes that we are alive to God in Christ, or, as we read in the remainder of the verse, " Your life is hid with Christ in God." Now it is wonderful how this verse is misapplied. Most people think it means our life is so safe that no-one can take it away, which, thank God, is blessedly true. The context shows what the meaning is. "Your life is hid" means that it is not yet outwardly manifested what it will be in glory. At the present time Christ is hidden, and so consequently is our life. When Christ shall appear in glory, then it will be no longer hidden; but the life will be manifested because He is manifested (compare 1 John 3 : 2).

And now we have seen that when Jesus died, we died, and that there on the cross the whole question of sin was gone into, and we can each say, by God's grace, There was an end of me, as a sinful child of Adam, before God. "Knowing this, that our old man was crucified with Him." Now God says, "My thoughts are not your thoughts," and the thought of a great many Christians is, that because we have this old sinful nature in us we cannot be children of God, and that God is always angry with us. It is not so; for He sees us as having only one life, and that the life of Christ, the life of a risen Christ; a life that is beyond death, beyond judgment, beyond Satan's power; a life that sin has nothing to do with. That is the life of Christ risen from the dead; that is the life we have as believers. It is the life out of reach of judgment, a life hid with Christ in God.

Then there is the positive side what we have "put on." We have "put on the new man"; that is, Christ now glorified. Think of Him there as a Man before God ! What delight must God now find in Him ! What a place of favour and acceptance is he in Him who so glorified the Father on earth ! Twice was the Father's voice heard from heaven, saying of Him while here, "This is My beloved Son, in whom I am well pleased," or "in whom I have found all My delight." How much more now must God the Father find delight in Him, who has not only glorified Him in life, but also in death, where he went for us ! He brought infinite glory to God, and His obedience unto death was a fresh motive (so to speak) for the love of the Father to be drawn out towards Him. "Therefore doth My Father love Me, because I lay down My life that I might take it again." And to think that He is our life and that "as He is, so are we in this world" (1 John 4 : 17). And because He is our life the very expressions the Holy Spirit can use of us are those applied to Christ Himself, "Put on therefore as the elect of God, holy and beloved." Think of these words, "The elect of God, holy and beloved." What expressions for the Holy Spirit to use of such poor things as we are ! and they are the same as those used of Christ Himself, because we are in Christ before God. First,

the elect of God, "Behold My servant, whom I uphold: Mine elect, in whom My soul delighteth" (Isa. 42 : 1). Second, "Thou wilt not suffer Thy Holy one to see corruption" (Psalm 16 : 10). Third, Beloved, "This is My beloved Son, in whom I am well pleased" (Matt. 3 : 17).

We shall see in the following verses of our chapter, verses 12, &c., that what we are exhorted to be is just what Christ was in all His perfection when He was on earth; for here it is that "the life was manifested." "Put on therefore (now comes the practical part, we have put off the old man and have put on the new; that is our place before God as Christians, and because that this is true of us we are practically to put on) bowels of mercies, kindness." How this was seen in the Lord Jesus here ! How His heart went out in compassion to the poor leper ! For we read that, "Jesus' moved with compassion, put forth His hand, and touched him." How kind He was ! always at the call of every sinner that needed Him, always ready to serve others. Are we like Him in this ?

"Humbleness of mind." We know how He humbled Himself. As another has said, "Humble: He would teach us to take the lowest place, but that He has taken it Himself, the privilege of His perfect grace. Blessed Master, may we at least be near to and hidden in Thee."

"Meekness." He was meek and lowly in heart. A person may be outwardly meek yet very proud at heart; but he was meek and lowly in heart. Are we like Him in this ?

"Long suffering; forbearing one another. . . if any man have a quarrel against any: even as Christ forgave you, so also do ye." We are to act towards others as Christ has to us. "Above all these things put on charity (love), which is the bond of perfectness." Oh, may the life of Jesus be more manifested in our mortal flesh ! "Let the peace of Christ (it should read) rule in your hearts,"; that is, the peace which the Lord Jesus had here, as a Man, in communion with the Father, is to preside in our hearts. And in v. 16 "the Word of Christ" is to dwell in us richly; for in the new creation, in which we are, "Chirst is all and in all."

In verse 17 : "Whatsoever ye do in word or deed, do all in the name of the Lord Jesus, giving thanks to God and the Father by Him." And then, in the verses that follow, the life of Jesus is to be manifested in all the relationships of life—wives submit themselves to their own husbands, husbands to love their wives, children to obey their parents, fathers not to provoke their children to anger, servants to obey in all things their masters, and masters to give them that which is just and equal. May the Lord grant we may know more what it is practically in every-day life to be " always bearing about in the body the dying of Jesus, that the life also of Jesus might be made manifest our in body," for His name's sake.

—*Simple Testimony*, 1887.

PRIVILEGE AND RESPONSIBILITY.

(*Read Deuteronomy* 20 : 1-9.)

Privilege and responsibility ! Yes, this is the Divine order ; and how important it is, in dealing with the things of God, to place them in the order in which He places them, and leave them there ! The human mind is ever prone to displace things ; and hence it is that we so frequently find the responsibilities, which attach to the people of God, pressed upon those who are yet in their sins. This is a great mistake. I must be in a position before I can fulfil the responsibilities attaching thereto. I must be in a relationship before I can know the affections which belong to it. If I am not a father, how can I know or exhibit the affections of a father's heart ? Impossible. I may descant upon them, and attempt to describe them ; but in order to feel them, I must be a father.

Thus it is in the things of God. I must be in a position before I can enter into the responsibilities which belong to it. I must be in a relationship before I can understand the affections which flow out of it. Man has been tested in every possible way. He has been tried in creation. He has been tried under divine government. He has been tried under law. He has been tried with ordinances. He has been tried by the ministry of the prophets. He has been tried by the ministry of righteousness, in the person of John the Baptist. He has been tried by the ministry of grace, in the Person of Christ. He has been tried by the ministry of the Holy Spirit. What has been the result ? Total failure ! An unbroken chain of testimoney from Paradise to Pentecost has only tended to make manifest man's utter failure in every possible way. In every position of responsibility, in which man has been set, he has broken down. Not so much as a single exception can be adduced.

So much for man's responsibility. He has proved himself unfaithful in every thing. He has not a single inch of ground to stand upon. He has destroyed himself, but in God is his help. Grace has come in, in the Person of Christ, and perfectly met man's desperate case. The cross is the Divine remedy for all the ruin, and by that cross the believer is introduced into a place of Divine and everlasting privilege. Christ has met all the need, answered all the demands, discharged all the responsibilities, and, having done so by His death upon the cross, He has become, in resurrection, the basis of all the believer's privileges. We have all in Christ, and we get Him, not because we have fulfilled our responsibilities, but because God loved us even when we had failed in every thing. We find ourselves, unconditionally, in a place of unspeakable privilege. We did not work ourselves into it ; we did not pray ourselves into it ; we did not weep ourselves into it ; we did not fast ourselves into it. We were taken up from the depth of our ruin, from that deep, deep pit into which we had fallen, in consequence of having failed in all our responsibilities ; we have been set down, by God's free grace, in a position of unspeakable blessedness and privilege, of which nothing can ever deprive us. Not all the powers of hell and earth combined ; not all the malice of Satan and his emissaries ; not all the power of sin, death, and the grave, arrayed in their most terrific form, can ever rob the believer in Christ of that place of privilege in which, through grace, he stands.

My reader cannot be too simple in his apprehension of this. We do not reach our place of privilege as the result of faithfulness in the place of responsibility. Quite the reverse. We have failed in everything. " All have sinned and come short of the glory of God." We deserved death ; but we have received life. We deserved hell ; but we have received heaven. We deserved eternal wrath ; but we have received eternal favour. Grace has entered the scene, and it " reigns through righteousness, unto eternal life, by Jesus Christ our Lord."

Hence then, in the economy of grace, privilege becomes the basis of responsibility, and this is beautifully illustrated in the passage of Scripture which stands at the head of this paper. I shall quote it for my reader, lest he should not have " The Word " at hand. " When thou goest out to battle against thine enemies, and seest horses, and chariots, and a people more than thou, be not afraid of them ; for the Lord thy God is with thee, which brought thee up out of the land of Egypt. And it shall be, when ye are come nigh unto the battle that the priest shall approach, and speak unto the people, and shall say unto them, Hear, O Israel ; ye approach this day unto battle against your enemies ; let not your hearts faint ; fear not, and do not tremble, neither be ye terrified because of them ; for the Lord your God is He that goeth with you, to fight for you against your enemies, to save you."

Here we have Israel's privileges distinctly set forth. "The Lord thy God is with thee," and that, moreover, is the very character in which He had brought them up out of the land of Egypt. He was with them in the power of that sovereign grace which had delivered them from the iron grasp of Pharaoh, and the iron bondage of Egypt, which had conducted them through the sea, and led them across "the great and terrible wilderness." This made victory sure. No enemy could possibly stand before Jehovah acting in unqualified grace on behalf of His people.

And let my reader note carefully, that there is not a single condition proposed by the priest in the above quotation. He states, in the most absolute way, the relationship and consequent privilege of the Israel of God. He does not say, " The Lord thy God will be with you, if you do so and so." This would not be the proper language of one who stood before the people of God as the exponent of those privileges which grace had conferred upon them. Grace proposes no conditions, raises no barriers, makes no stipulations. Its language is, "The Lord thy God is with thee . . . . He goeth with you. . . . to fight for you. . . . to save you." When Jehovah fights for His people they are sure of victory. "If God be for us, who can be against us"? Grant me but this, that God is with me, and I argue full victory over every spiritual foe.

Thus much as to the question of privilege ; let us now turn, for a moment, to the question of responsibility.

"And the officers shall speak unto the people, saying, What man is there that hath built a new house, and hath not dedicated it? Let him go and return to his house lest he die in the battle, and another man dedicate it. And what man is he that hath planted a vineyard, and hath not yet eaten of it? Let him also go and return to his house, lest he die in the battle, and another man eat of it. And what man is there that have betrothed a wife, and hath not taken her? Let him go and return to his house, lest he die in the battle, and another man take her. And the officers shall speak further unto the people, and they shall say, What man is there that is fearful and faint-hearted ? Let him go and return unto his house, lest his brethren's heart faint as well as his heart ?"

There is uncommon moral beauty in the order in which the priest and the officer are introduced in this passage. The former is the exponent of Israel's privileges ; the latter, of Israel's responsibilities. But how interesting it is to see that, before the officers were permitted to address the assembly on the grand question of responsibility, the priest had established them in the knowledge of their precious privilege. Imagine the case reversed. Suppose the officer's voice had first been heard, what would have been the result ? Fear, depression, and discouragement. To press responsibility before I know my position—to call for affections ere I am in the relationship, is to place an intolerable yoke upon the neck—an insufferable burden upon the shoulder. This is not God's way. If you search from Genesis to Revelation you will find, without so much as a single exception, that the Divine order is privilege and responsibility. Set me upon the rock of privilege, and I am in a position to understand and fulfil my responsibility ; but talk to me of responsibility while yet in the pit of ruin, the mire of legality, or the slough of despond, and you rob me of all hope of ever rising into that hallowed sphere upon which the sunlight of Divine favour pours itself in living lustre, and where alone responsibilities can be discharged to the glory of the name of Christ.

Some there are who talk to us of "gospel conditions." Who ever heard of a gospel fenced with conditions ? We can understand law conditions, but a gospel with conditions is "a different gospel, which is not another" (Galatians 1 : 6, 7). Conditions to be fulfilled by the creature pertain not to the Gospel but to the law. Man has been tried under all possible conditions. And what has been the issue ? Failure ! Yes, failure only—failure continually. Man is a ruin—a wreck—a bankrupt. Of what use can it ever be to place such an one under conditions, even though you should call them by the anomalous title of "gospel conditions"? None whatever. Man, under any kind of conditions, can only prove unfaithful. He has been weighed in the balance and found wanting. He has been condemned, root and branch. "They that are in the flesh cannot please God." It does not say "they that are in the body." No ; but "they that are in the flesh." But the believer is not in the flesh, though in the body. He is not looked at in his old-creation standing—in his old Adamic condition, in which he has been tried and condemned. Christ has come down and died under the full weight of his guilt. He has taken the sinner's place, with all its liabilities, and by His death settled every thing. He lay in the grave after having answered every claim and silenced every enemy. Justice, law, sin, death, wrath, judgment, Satan, every thing, and every one. There lay the Divine Surety in the silent tomb ; and God entered the scene, raised Him from the dead, set Him at His own right hand in the heavens, sent down the Holy Spirit to testify to a risen and exalted Saviour, and to unite to Him, as thus risen and exalted, all who believe in His name.

Here, then, we get on to new ground altogether. We can now listen to the officer as he tells out in our hearing the claims of Christ upon all those who are united to Him. The priest has spoken to us, and told us of the imperishable ground which we occupy, the indestructible relationship in which we stand, and now we are in a position to listen to the one who stands before us as the exponent of our high and holy responsibilities. Had "the officer" come first, we should have fled from his presence, discouraged and dismayed by the weight and solemnity of his words, and given utterance to the despairing inquiry, "Who then can be saved?" But, inasmuch as "the priest"—the minister of grace—the exponent of privilege, has set us upon our feet in the new creation, and strengthened our hearts by unfolding the unconditional grace in which we stand, we can listen to the "commandments" of the officer, and find them "not grievous," because they come to us from off the mercy-seat.

And what does the officer say to us? Just this: "No man that warreth entangleth himself with the affairs of this life." This is the sum and substance of the officer's message. He demands, on the part of God's warriors, a disentangled heart. It is not a question of salvation, of being a child of God, of being a true Israelite; it is simply a question of ability to wage an effectual warfare; and, clearly, a man cannot fight well if his heart is entangled with "a house," "a vineyard," or "a wife."

Nor was it a question of having these things. By no means. Thousands of those who went forth to tread the battlefield, and gather the spoils of victory, had houses, and lands, and domestic ties. The officers had no quarrel with the possessors of these things; the only point was, not to be entangled with them. The apostle does not say, "No man that warreth engages in the affairs of this life." Had he said this, we should all have to live in idleness and isolation, whereas he distinctly teaches us, elsewhere, that, "If any man will not work, neither shall he eat." The grand point is to keep the heart disentangled. God's warriors must have free hearts, and the only way to be free is to cast all our care upon Him who careth for us. I can stand in the battlefield with a free heart when I have placed my house, my vineyard, and my wife, in the Divine keeping.

But, further, God's warriors must have courageous hearts as well as free hearts. The fearful and the faint-hearted can never stand in the battle, or wear the laurel of victory. Our hearts must be disentangled from the world, and bold by reason of our artless confidence in God; and, be it well remembered, that these things are not "gospel conditions," but gospel results—a deeply important distinction. What a mistake to speak of gospel conditions! It is simply the old leaven of legality presented in a new and strange form, and dubbed with a name which, in itself, involves a contradiction. If those precious clusters which are the result of union with the Living Vine be set forth as the necessary conditions of that union, what must become of the sinner? Where shall we get them if not in Christ? And how do we become united to Christ? Is it by conditions? Nay; but by faith.

May the Holy Spirit instruct my readers as to the Divine order of "Privilege and Responsibility."

(" *Things New and Old,*" 1861.)

TOUCH NOT MINE ANOINTED.

Deacon Lee, who was a kindly, silent, faithful, gracious man, was one day waited upon by a restless, ambitious, worldly Church member, who was labouring to create uneasiness in the Church, and especially to drive away the preacher. The deacon came in to meet his visitor, who, after the usual greetings, began to lament the low state of religion, and inquire as to the reason why there had been no conversions for two or three years past.

"Now, what do you think is the cause of things being dull here; Do you know?" he persisted in asking. The deacon was not ready to give his opinion, and, after a little thought, frankly answered, "No I don't."—Do you think the Churches are alive to the work before them?—"No I don't." "Do you think the minister fully realises the solemnity of his work?"—"No I don't." A twinkle was seen in the eye of this troubler in Zion; and taking courage he asked, "Do you think Mr. B—— a very extraordinary man?"—"No I don't."—"Do you think his sermon on 'Their eyes were holden,' anything wonderfully great?" "No I don't."

Making bold, after all this encouragement in monosyllables, he asked, "Then don't you think we had better dismiss this man and 'hire' another?" The old deacon started as if shot with an arrow, and, in a tone louder than his wont, shouted, "No I don't." "Why," cried the amazed visitor, "you agree with me in all I have said, don't you?"—"No I don't."—"You talk so little, sir," replied the guest, not a little abashed, " that no one can find out what you do mean." " I talked enough once," replied the old man, rising to his feet, " Thirty years ago I got my heart humbled and my tongue bridled, and ever since that I've walked softly before God. I then made vows solemn as eternity, and don't you tempt me to break them ! "

The troubler was startled at the earnestness of the hitherto silent, unmovable man, and asked " What happened to you thirty years ago ?

" Well, sir, I'll tell you. I was drawn into a scheme just like this of yours, to uproot one of God's servants from the field in which He had planted him. In my blindness I fancied it a little thing to remove one of the " stars " which the Lord holds in His right hand, if thereby my ear could be tickled, and the pews filled with those who turned away from the simplicity of the Gospel. I and the men that led me—for I admit that I was a dupe and a fool— flattered ourselves that we were conscientious. We thought we were doing God service when we drove that holy man from his pulpit and his work, and said we considered this work ended in B——, where I then lived. We groaned because there was no revival, while we were gossiping about, and criticising, and crushing, instead of upholding, by our efforts and our prayers, the instrument at whose hand we harshly demanded the blessings. Well, sir, he could not drag on the chariot of the Gospel with half-a-dozen of us taunting him for his weakness, while we hung as a dead weight to the wheels ; he had not the power of the Spirit, and could not convert men ; so we hunted him like a deer till, worn and bleeding, he fled into a covert to die. Scarcely had he gone, when God came among us by His Spirit to show that He had blessed the labours of His dear rejected servant. Our own hearts were broken, and our wayward children converted, and I resolved at a convenient season to visit my former pastor and confess, my sin, and thank him for his faithfulness to my wayward sons, which, like long-buried seed, had now sprung up. But God denied me that relief, that He might teach me a lesson that " he who toucheth one of His servants toucheth the apple of His eye." I heard my former pastor was ill, and taking my oldest son with me, set out on a twenty-five miles ride to see him. It was evening when we arrived, and his wife, with a spirit which any woman ought to exhibit towards one who had so wronged her husband, denied me admittance to his chamber. She said— and her words were arrows to my soul— " He may be dying, and the sight of your face might add to his anguish ! " " Had it come to this, I said to myself, that the man whose labours had, through Christ, brought me into His fold : who had consoled my spirit in a terrible bereavement ; and who had, till designing men had alienated us, been to me as a brother—that this man could not die in peace with my face before him ? God pity me ! " I cried, " What have I done ? I confessed my sins to that meek woman, and implored her for Christ's sake to let me kneel before His dying servant, and receive his forgiveness. What did I care then whether the pews by the door were rented or not ? I would have gladly taken his whole family to my home for ever, as my flesh and blood ; but no such happiness was in store for me.

" As I entered the room of the blessed warrior, whose armour was falling from his limbs, he opened his languid eyes, and said ' Brother Lee, Brother Lee ! ' I bent over him and sobbed out, ' My pastor, my pastor," Then raising his white hand, he said, in a deep, impressive voice, ' Touch not Mine anointed, and do My prophets no harm.' I spoke tenderly to him, and told him I had come to confess my sin, and bring some of his fruit to him, calling my son to tell him how he had found Christ. But he was unconscious of all around ; the sight of my face had brought the last pang of earth to his troubled spirit.

" I kissed his brow, and told him how dear he had been to me. I craved his pardon for my unfaithfulness, and promised to care for his widow and fatherless little ones ; but his only reply, murmured as if in a troubled dream, was ' Touch not Mine anointed, and do My prophets no harm.'

" I stayed by him all night, and at daybreak I closed his eyes. I offered his widow a house to live in the remainder of her days ; but, like a heroine, she said ' I freely forgive you ; but my children, who entered deeply into their father's anguish, shall never see me so regardless of his memory as to take anything from those who caused it. He has left us all with his Covenant God, and He will care for us.'

" Well, sir, those dying words sounded in my ears from that coffin and from that grave. When I slept Christ stood before my dream, saying ' Touch not Mine anointed, and do My prophets no harm.' These words followed me until I fully realised the esteem in which Christ holds those men who have given up all for His sake, and I vowed to love them evermore for His sake, even if they are not perfect ; and since that day, sir, I have talked less than before, and have supported my pastor, even if he is not a ' very extraordinary man.' My tongue shall cleave to the roof of my mouth, and my right hand forget her cunning, before I dare put to asunder what God has joined together. When a minister's work is done in a place, I believe God will show it him. I will not join you, sir, in the scheme that brought you here; and, moreoever, if I hear another word of this from your lips, I shall ask my brethren to deal with you as with those who cause divisions. I would give all I own to recall what I did thirty years ago. Stop where you are, and pray God if perhaps the thought of your heart may be forgiven you."

This decided reply put an end to the newcomer's efforts. There is often great power in the little word "No," but sometimes, and in some circumstances, it requires not a little courage to speak it so resolutely as did the silent deacon.

Author, unknown.

CHRIST FOR ALL.

I dare say you feel, find, and experience yourself to be a sinner. You have proof in yourself, and can testify of yourself, that you are inwardly guilty and helpless. It may be you are at times strangely puzzled and perplexed what to think, or say, of yourself. Is it really so? Have I read your heart, and expressed your case as it is? What, do you see sin in yourself? Do you feel it to be your very self? What, cannot you think one good thought, if you could gain heaven for it? Are you in your own person, nature, temper, walk, in all, sinful, perfectly, entirely sinful? Blessed are ye of the Lord, and blessed be the Lord for ever and ever if you really and inwardly, spiritually and practically, experience the truth of all this. Because it fits you for receiving Christ into your heart and mind, as a perfect Saviour. This, my good friend, is the office and work of the Holy Spirit in the souls of all the elect and called people of God. He quickens their souls with spiritual life. He gives them spiritual light, He shews them clearly and gives them truly to feel what they are, as the apostate descendants of guilty, fallen Adam. The Holy Spirit sets before them, as thus convinced, the salvation of Jesus; showing them how exactly suited it is for them, and how all-sufficient Christ is, to heal every wound sin has given us, to supply every want it hath brought upon us; and happy would it be for us, if we made use of every sin we have, and feel in us, of every corruption and misery experienced by us, of every trial, pain and grief we are the subjects of, *to show us* our exceeding *need* of Jesus. And were constrained by it to look off ourselves wholly, and look immediately and steadfastly to the holy immaculate Lamb of God, whose blood cleanseth us from all sin, and whose righteousness is to and on all them that believe. Surely this is, and must be, the highest attainment in Christian experience, to *make use of Christ* for the healing of *all* our wounds and the supply of *all* our wants: to set Christ against all our sins and miseries, against all our temptations and corruptions. To *live on Him* for the whole of our salvation, and to trust Him with our all. Casting all our care on Him, because He careth for us. If we were not what we are, we should not need Christ. If we had not that sinfulness in us which we actually have, nor those wounds which we feel, Christ could not be exalted in us, as giving us spiritual life, health and cure. It is a most blessed part of the Divine Spirit's teachings, to lead us to view the everlasting sufficiency of Christ's blood and righteousness, as the whole of our salvation, and as being completely sufficient to save us from all sin, and to present us in the sight of God every moment, righteous, and spotless in Jesus; Who is our "wisdom, righteousness, sanctification, and redemption." It is our blessedness to receive into our understandings, and believe in our hearts, this immutable truth contained in the Word of revelation, that "God hath made Christ sin for us, who knew no sin, that we might be made the righteousness of God in Him." In this the whole, and all our salvation consists, in the imputation of our sins on Christ, and in the imputation of His righteousness unto us. It is in our believing in Christ that the efficacy of His righteousness and blood is made known, and believing the everlasting worth, virtue, and efficacy of Christ's blood cleanseth the conscience, purifies the heart, produces peace with God, and boldness before Him.

May the Lord the Spirit lead you wholly off yourself, both good and bad self, and fix your mind wholly on Christ, and teach you the love of His heart, the mercy which He shows to such as feel and find themselves to be just what you are, and help you to survey the perfect and everlasting efficacious salvation of the worthy Lamb, and keep you looking so to Jesus, that you may say of Him, and His work, He, this adorable Immanuel, His righteousness and blood, "is all my salvation and all my desire." And remember, Christ would neither be fit for you, nor you for Him, if you were one jot better than you are in yourself. Oh! that the Holy Spirit may establish this point in your mind, and give you the real experience of it in your soul, and that you must not expect to feel less of sin, see less of it, that you may be better for Christ, and be better suited to come to Him. You are as fit as ever you will be. You should go to Him with all that you are, with your sins; He hath promised to take away all iniquities,

It is only a "*good* man's steps" which are said to be "ordered by the Lord" (Psa. 37 : 23).

That there *are* "conditions" which we must meet if we are to enjoy God's immediate ordering of our path, is clear not only from Prov. 3 : 5, 6, and John 8 : 12, but from many other Scriptures. Take the order of truth brought before us in that familiar 23rd Psalm: "He *leadeth* me beside the still waters" (v. 2), is preceded by "He maketh me to lie down in green pastures." There must be an implicit and complete resting in God's authoritative Word (of which the "green pastures" are the figure), before I can count upon His "leading me." So again in the next verse: "He *leadeth* me in the paths of righteousness" is preceded by "He *restoreth* my soul." Not until His grace brings me into right relationship, experimentally, with Himself, is the "leading" given. How solemnly searching is this!

Again, in Psa. 25, which reveals so much on the subject of Divine guidance, in v. 9 (where we have God's response to the prayer of vv. 4, 5) we are told, "The meek"—they who are subject to God's will—"will He guide in judgment, the meek will He teach His way." So v. 12: "What man is he that *feareth* the Lord? *him* shall He teach in the way that He shall choose." How searching is the verse which immediately precedes that oft-quoted (frequently, *lightly* quoted, we fear) 105th verse in Psalm 119. It is only when through God's "precepts" we get understanding, and by them are made to hate "every false way" that God's Word becomes to us, experimentally, "a lamp unto our feet, and a light unto our path."

"I will instruct thee and teach thee in the way which thou shalt go: I will guide thee with Mine eye" (Psa. 32 : 8). Here again we have what is both blessed and searching. A person cannot guide another with his "eye" unless that other is near to him, and unless the eyes of that other are steadfastly fixed upon him. The immediate context (vv. 6, 7) speaks of subjection and confidence in God. If these be lacking, then we become "as the horse or as the mule, which have no understanding; whose mouth must be held in with bit and bridle" (v. 9). Even then, the Lord, in His mercy, does not give us up; He keeps His hand on the reins, and uses *circumstances* to check, restrain, and guide us. But this is a painful experience when compared with the blessedness of being "guided by His eye."

Yes, there *are* "conditions" if we are to have God's immediate guidance, and these "conditions" are summed up in Prov. 3 : 5, 6. If we exercise whole-hearted trust in the Lord, lean not unto our own understandings (cease to be controlled or influenced by the dictates of "common sense"), acknowledge Him in *all* our ways (seek His permission, and have before us His glory in everything), then "He *shall* direct our paths." May the Lord, in His abounding grace, work in writer and reader "both to will and to do of His good pleasure."—*Arthur W. Pink.*

---

to receive graciously, to love freely; go to Him with all spots and filthiness; He hath promised to sprinkle clean water upon us. And He says, and ye shall be clean, from all your filthiness and from all idols will I cleanse you. Go to Christ with your heart as hard as adamant, with your mind as cold as ice, with your fresh wounds and innumerable wants, carry all to Jesus, His love will warm your cold heart, His blood will cleanse your conscience, and soften your hard heart. Jesus, by putting forth continually the efficacy of His death in you, will heal your fresh wounds, His fullness will supply and more than supply all your wants. After all I have wrote on this subject, I conceive I see you drawing back, and saying, "But I am afraid to deal thus with Christ, I wish I was in myself better, less sinful, less polluted, less helpless, and more worthy." Is it thus? Are these your sentiments? Then, my good friend, you and I widely differ, for instead of wishing myself to be otherwise than I am, "a fallen, sinful, guilty, polluted creature," all which I really am in my natural self, I would rejoice that though in myself, *i.e.*, in my fallen nature, I am this very moment, as perfectly sinful as sin can be, and cannot be exceeded therein, no, not by the damned in hell! yet Christ is "Jehovah, self-existent, an Almighty Saviour." He can get Himself an everlasting name, and eternal glory, in "saving me just as I am, the vilest of the vile, from every spot and stain of sin, in His own blood and righteousness." Nay, blessings on Him, He hath saved me in Himself with an everlasting salvation, and this is my evidence of it. I am brought from His Word, and by His Spirit, to believe the everlasting purity and perfection of His sacrifice and righteousness, to heal, purify, justify and sanctify my whole person, and to present me before God, as perfectly righteous and spotless, as though I had never sinned. If it please the Lord the Spirit to open the eyes of your mind, and give you to see the freeness, fullness, nature, and perfection of Christ's salvation, your heart will leap for joy, then you will see there is nothing worse than legality and unbelief. You will, in beholding Christ, see there is no purity in His blood, but 'tis *for you*; yea, it is your purity before the Lord. There is no perfection in His righteousness, but it is *your* perfection in the sight of God. And as long as Immanuel continues to be the object of the Father's everlasting love and complacency, so long His love and complacency will be continued to you. May you see yourself in yourself to be nothing, and see yourself out of yourself in Christ, as holy, righteous, and pure, as His holiness, righteousness, and blood can make you.

—*Extract from Letters of S. E. Pierce*, 1796.

make straight." We are living in a world where everything is crooked. Sin has thrown everything out of joint, and, in consequence, confusion worse confounded reigns all around us. Even the natural man, who is thoughtful and serious, is often bewildered by the conflicting opinions and theories concerning present-day life. Old standards are forsaken; the ways of our forefathers are looked upon as the product of an ignorant age. This is true of every realm. Take the medical world; remedies which proved effective a generation ago, are now condemned as harmful. Take the domestic circle; we are told the methods used by our grandparents were all wrong; they kept children in the nursery too long, they repressed development. Parents are told now (but not by Scripture) that if they are strict with their little ones, in a few years they will be hated by them. The result is that, everywhere, thoughtful people are bewildered.

How blessed, how comforting, how re-assuring is the language of our text to the child of God! If I really desire to please the Lord, He will not allow me to remain in ignorance of His will: "He *shall* direct my paths." He will make clear to me the course of duty. But remember that this promise is *conditional*; it is only given to those who comply fully with the preceding admonitions. Scripture interprets Scripture. In the N.T. we have a word parallel to Prov. 3 : 5, 6, "I am the light of the world; he that followeth Me shall not walk in darkness, but shall have the light of life" (John 8 : 12). What does it signify to "follow" Christ? First, it means full confidence in Him, for I would not take as guide one I did not trust—trusting Him with all my heart. Second, it means completely resigning myself to His directions—leaning not unto my own understanding. Third, it means unqualified submission to Him—acknowledging Him in all my ways. Then, but only then, have I the Divine assurance that I "shall not walk in darkness, but have the light of life."

As another has said, "A believer's course indicates where he is in his soul, and sooner or later exposes the motives that control him. It is pretty easy to see when a man has the Lord before him. You find him regulated by Divine motives, and ordering his ways with reference to the will of God and the interests of Christ. He will not be occupied with Guidance, but his whole course will evidence that his steps are ordered by the Lord. On the other hand, if a man be carnal and worldly, it will come out in his ways. He will have no Divine judgment about things—no spiritual sensibilities or tastes—and, though he may maintain a certain degree of outward correctness it will be manifest that he is not guided by the Lord. It is in having to do with the Lord that we are enlightened and our spiritual intelligence developed, so that we are enabled to discern the path that is pleasing to Him. God would guide us, as a rule, by forming our souls in the intelligence of His will, and thus enabling us to exercise a spiritual judgment about things.

"Many would like to have guidance without any reference to their spiritual condition; but this is never the Lord's way. I have often been amazed at the devices to which even converted people will resort in a moment of perplexity. A favourite plan is to open the Bible haphazard or put a pin between the leaves, and read the text which happens to turn up. This savours more of witchcraft and superstition than of godliness. As we go on with the Lord, and become acquainted with His mind, our vision is cleared in a wonderful way" (C.A.C.).

Let us seek to add a few more words upon the *conditions* of Divine guidance. The word "conditions" in this connection would be objected to by some, namely, hyper-Calvinists, who deny human responsibility. Restricting themselves to the Divine side of things, they have so lost the "balance" of Truth that they are really "Fatalists." Confining all their thoughts to the fact that God has, from the beginning, mapped out the whole of our course, they see no need for being *exercised* in heart as to guidance, still less are they aware of "conditions" governing it. On the other hand, some are so much occupied with the *human* side of things, and dwell so exclusively upon Christians themselves being responsible for their walk, that Divine foreordination has little or no place in their thoughts. These people need reminding of such passages as Prov. 21 : 1 ; Rom. 11 : 36 ; Eph. 1 : 11.

Still others are confused when they hear of *both* sides and are puzzled to know where the sovereignty of God ends and human responsibility begins in relation to our daily walk. Without attempting now to explore this great deep, let us humbly offer two remarks for prayerful consideration. First, whatever of good there is in our lives, unreservedly give God the glory for it; whatever there is of sin, we must unqualifiedly take the blame unto ourselves. I must never charge God with my folly and sin, but unsparingly condemn myself for it. Second, learn to distinguish sharply between God's *ordaining* our course, and God *directing* our paths. God *has* foreordained everything that comes to pass; but He does not, by direct agency bring everything to pass. God has predestinated that we should taste the bitter consequences of self-confidence and reap the awful sowings of self-will, in order to wean us from self and sin. But He does not, personally and immediately, lead us into such things; our own evil lusts are responsible for that.

(Continued on Page 263.)

STUDIES IN THE SCRIPTURES

"Search the Scriptures" John 5 : 39

Copyright in all English-speaking Countries.

Editor: Arthur W. Pink, Sidmouth Road, Seaton, Devon, England.
Hon. Agent in U.S.A.: Mr. C. S. Pressel, 559, Dupont Avenue, York, Penna.
Hon. Agent in Australia: Mr. G. Ardill, The Christian Workers' Depot. Commonwealth and Reservoir Streets, Sydney.

FREE TO ALL WHO WILL READ IT.

A GRACIOUS GREETING.

"*Mercy unto you, and peace, and love be multiplied.*"—*Jude 2.*

This is the final salutation of the apostolic epistles, and as this issue is the last one in the seventh year of this publication—thus completing a cycle—it strikes us as a suitable greeting to our brethren and sisters in Christ. It is addressed to those who are "sanctified by God the Father, and preserved in Jesus Christ, called." The reference to our being "sanctified (set apart) by God the Father" takes us back before the foundation of the world, when He chose us in Christ (Eph. 1—4.) As it is written "God hath from the beginning chosen you to salvation" (2 Thess. 2 : 13). Next we have, "preserved in (or *by* Jesus Christ." This precedes our being "called," and refers, we believe, to His *temporal* preservation of us during the days of our unregeneracy. The subject is deeply interesting, but one, we fear, that is little pondered by the saints. There was never a moment in our wildest and most wicked days but the eye of our covenant God was upon us and His powerful hand protected us. The cases of Moses preserved in infancy, the Hebrew maid in childhood (2 Kings 5), David in his youth (1 Sam. 17 : 34-37), come to mind. Let our Christian readers thank God for having "preserved" them by Jesus Christ ere they were brought to a saving knowledge of the truth. "Called" points to that effectual call which each of God's elect receives when he is brought out of darkness into God's marvellous light.

It will be noted that there is a distinct reference to the work of each of the three Persons of the Godhead in the opening verse of Jude. Sanctified by the Father, protected by the Son, called by the Holy Spirit. Thus we have, in turn, predestination, preservation, and regeneration, for our "calling" occurs when we are born again, which is effected by the Spirit (John 3 : 5, 6). So in the second verse we may also perceive a latent reference to the Holy Trinity. This salutation is a three-fold one, calling down blessing from Father, Son and Holy Spirit. "Mercy," from Him who is "the Father of mercies" (2 Cor. 1 : 3); "peace," from Him who is "our peace" (Eph. 2 : 14); "love," from Him by whom the love of God is "shed abroad" in our hearts, even the Holy Spirit (Rom. 5 : 5). May these rich blessings of our triune God rest abundantly upon each Christian reader, and upon all who are, by sovereign grace, members of the Household of Faith.

The *order* of these three Divine qualities and gifts will well repay prolonged meditation. That "mercy" comes first shows that *this* is the fount from which all our blessings proceed. This was the first thing we were made to feel our need of: "God be merciful to me, the sinner," is ever the initial cry of an unawakened soul—awakened from the sleep of death. As transgressors of God's righteous law, "mercy" is our only hope; and even now, as Christians, we are in daily need of coming to the throne of grace that we may "obtain *mercy*" (Heb. 4 : 16). How blessed to know that "mercy" will be regnant at our Saviour's return: as we read in this same epistle of Jude, "*Looking for* the mercy of our Lord Jesus Christ unto eternal life" (v. 21)—ah, it is only then we shall enter into the full and unhindered enjoyment of Eternal Life. And who among the redeemed will be beyond the need of "mercy" when we first behold, face to face, the King in His beauty? Certainly not the writer. Our prayer for each reader is that of Paul's for Onesiphorus, "The Lord grant unto him that he may find mercy of the Lord in that day" (2 Tim. 1 : 18).

Continued on Page 288.

IMPORTANT NOTICES

Back numbers of each year of the magazine are yet obtainable at 5/- (1.25) per year. Bound at 7/6 (1.75) post paid. They will soon be out of print. Those in U.S.A. wanting them, please purchase from Mr. Pressel (see front cover page).

Advise promptly of change of address. This Magazine is published as a work of faith and labour of love. The Editor gladly gives his services. It is freely sent to all who will read it. No charge is made for it.

Christians who feel definitely led to do so, may have fellowship with us in this Ministry. Send only *Inter-National M.O.*

CONTENTS.

	Page
Hebrews	266
Gleanings in Exodus	271
Worship (2)	276
Worship	279
Sobriety	283
Christ as Master	284
Qualifications of a Preacher ...	285
Anxious Care	287

THE EPISTLE TO THE HEBREWS

12. *Christ Superior to Angels*: 2:17-18.

The verses which are now to be before us complete the second main division of the Epistle, in which the apostle has set forth the superiority of Christ over angels, and has met and removed a double objection which might be made against this. In showing that it was necessary for the Son of God to become Man in order to save His people from their sins, the Holy Spirit took occasion to bring out some striking details concerning the real and perfect humanity of Christ. In 2:11 He affirms that Christ and His people are "all of one." This receives a sevenfold amplification, which is as follows: First, they are one in sanctification, v. 11. Second, they are one in family relationship, vv. 11, 12a. Third, they are one in worship, v. 12b. Fourth, they are one in trust, v. 13. Fifth, they are one in nature, v. 14. Sixth, they are one in the line of promise, v. 16. Seventh, they are one in experiencing temptation, v. 18.

It is remarkable to notice, however, that in this very passage which sets forth. Christ's identification with His people on earth, the Holy Spirit has carefully guarded the Saviour's glory and shows, also in a sevenfold way, His uniqueness: First, He is "the Captain of our salvation" (v. 10), we are those whom He saves. Second, He is the "Sanctifier," we but the sanctified (v. 11). Third, the fact that He is "not ashamed to call us brethren" (v. 11), clearly implies His superiority. Fourth, He is the Leader of our praise and presents it to God (v. 12). Fifth, mark the "I, and the children" in v. 13. Sixth, note the contrast between "partakers" and "took part of" in v. 14. Seventh, He is the Destroyer of the enemy, we but the delivered ones vv. 14, 15. Thus, here as everywhere, *He* has the "pre-eminence in all things."

Another thing which comes out strikingly and plainly in the second half of Heb. 2 is the distinguishing grace and predestinating love of God. Christ is His "Elect" (Isa. 42:1), so called because His people are "chosen in Him" (Eph. 1:4). Mark how this also is developed in a sevenfold manner. First, in "bringing many *sons* unto glory" (v. 10). Second, "the Captain of *their* salvation" (v. 10). Third, "they who are sanctified," set apart (v. 11). Fourth, in the midst of the church" (v. 12). Fifth, "the children which God hath given me" (v. 13). Sixth, "He took on Him the seed of Abraham" (v. 16), not Adam, but "Abraham," the father of God's chosen people. Seventh, "to make reconciliation for the sins of *the* people" (v. 17).

If the reader will turn back to the third paragraph in article 10, and the second and third in article 11, he will find that we have called attention to twelve distinct reasons set forth by the apostle in Heb. 2:9—16, which show the meetness and necessity of Christ's becoming man and dying. In the verses which we are now to ponder, **two** more are advanced: First, the incarnation and death of the Saviour were imperative if He was to be "a merciful and faithful High Priest" (v. 17). Second, such experiences were essential that He might be able to "succor them that are tempted" (v. 18). Thus, in the fourteen answers given to the two objections which a Jew would raise, a *complete* demonstration is once more given of the two leading points under discussion.

Though our present portion consists of but two verses yet are they so full of important teaching that many more pages than what we shall now write might well be devoted to their explication and application. They treat of such weighty subjects as the incarnation of Christ, the priesthood of Christ, the atoning-sacrifice of Christ, the temptation of Christ, and the succour of Christ. Precious themes indeed are these, may the Spirit of truth be our Guide as we prayerfully turn to their consideration.

"Wherefore in all things it behoved Him to made like unto His brethren, that He might be a merciful and faithful High Priest in things pertaining to God, to make reconciliation for the sins of the people" (v. 17). The Holy Spirit here adduces a further reason why it was necessary for the Son of God to become incarnate and lay down His life for His people: it behoved Him so to do that He might be an effectual High Priest. As the priesthood of Christ will come before us again and again in the later chapters, D.V., we shall not here discuss it at length. Let us now ponder the several words and clauses of our present verse.

"Wherefore" is the drawing of a conclusion from what has been said in the previous verses. "It behoved Him": the Greek word is not the same as for "it became" Him in 2:10. There the reference is to the Father, here to the Son; that signified a comeliness or meetness, this has reference to a necessity, though not an absolute one, but in conjunction with the order of God's appointment in the way sinners were to be redeemed, and His justice satisfied, cf. Luke 24:46. "To be made like unto His brethren" is parallel with "all of one" in v. 11 and "He also Himself likewise took part" in v. 14. The expression goes to manifest the reality of Christ's human nature; that He was Man, such a man as we are.

The words "it behoved Him in *all* things to (His) brethren to be made like" are not to be taken absolutely. When the writer points out that, in view of other scriptures, the word "all" must be limited in such passages as John 12:32, 1 Tim. 2:4, 6, &c., some people think we are interpreting the Bible so as to suit ourselves. But what will *they* do with such a verse as Heb. 2:17? Can the words "in *all* things it behoved Him to be made like unto His brethren" be understood *without* qualification? Was He made like unto us in the depravity of our natures? Did He suffer from physical sicknesses as we do? Emphatically no. How do we know this? From other passages. Scripture needs to be compared with Scripture in order to understand any verse or any expression. The same Greek words here rendered "all things" (kapa panta) occur again in Heb. 4:15, where we are told that Christ "was in all points (things) tempted like as we are sin *excepted*" for thus the Greek word should be rendered. Thus the Holy Spirit expressly declares that the "all things" is *not* universal!

What then does the "all things" signify and include? We answer, everything which Scripture does not except or exclude. "When people saw Him, they did not notice in His outward appearance anything superhuman, glorious, free from earthly weakness and dependency. He did not come in splendour and power. He did not come in the brightness and strength which Adam possessed before he fell. 'In all things He became like unto us' In His body, for He was hungry and thristy; overcome with fatigue, He slept; in His mind, for it developed. He had to be taught. He grew in wisdom concerning the things around Him; He increased, not merely in stature, but in mental and moral strength. In His affections, for He loved. He was astonished; He marvelled at men's unbelief. Sometimes He was glad, and 'rejoiced in spirit'; sometimes He was angry and indignant, as when He saw the hypocrisy of the Jews. Zeal like fire burned within Him: 'The zeal for the house of God consumed Me'; and he showed a vehement fervor in protecting the sanctity of God's temple. He was grieved; He trembled with emotion; His soul was straitened in Him. Sometimes He was overcome by the waves of feeling when He beheld the future that was before Him.

"Do not think of Him as merely *appearing* a man, or as living a man only in His body, but as Man in body, soul, and spirit. He exercised faith; He read the Scriptures for His own guidance and encouragement; He prayed the whole night, expecially when He had some great and important work to do, as before setting apart the apostles. He sighed when He saw the man who was dumb; tears fell from His eyes when at the tomb of Lazarus He saw the power of death and of Satan. His supplications were with strong crying and tears; His soul was exceeding sorrowful" (Saphir). Thus, the Son of God was made like unto His brethren in that He became Man, with a human spirit, and soul and body; in that He developed along the ordinary lines of human nature, from infancy to maturity; and, in that He passed through all the experiences of men, sin, and sickness excepted.

"That He might be a merciful and faithful High Priest in things pertaining to God, to make reconciliation for the sins of the people." The Son of God became the Son of Man in order that He might be an High Priest. There was an absolute necessity for this. First, because of the infinite disparity there is between God and men: He is of infinite glory and majesty, and dwells in that light which no man can approach unto (1 Tim. 6:16); they are but dust and ashes (Gen. 18:27). Second, because of the contrariety of nature between God and men; He is most pure and holy, they most polluted and unholy. Third, because of the resultant enmity between God and men

(Rom. 5 : 10; Col. 1: 21). Hence we may observe: there is no immediate access for any man to God without a priest; there is no priest qualified to act for men in things pertaining to God, but Jesus Christ, the God-man. Thus has He been appointed " Mediator between God and men " (1 Tim. 2 : 6).

Because of the perfect union between His two natures, the Lord Jesus is " a merciful and faithful High Priest ": " merciful " manwards, " faithful " Godwards. To be " merciful " is to be compassionate, ever ready, under the influence of a tender sympathy, to support, comfort, and deliver. Having trod the same path as His suffering and tried people, Christ is able to enter into their afflictions. He is not like an angel, who has never experienced pain. He is Man; nor are His sympathies impaired by His exaltation to heaven. The same human heart beats within the bosom of Him who sits at God's right hand as caused Him to weep over Jerusalem! To be " faithful " means that His compassions are regulated by holiness, His sympathies are exercised. according to the requirements of God's truth. There is a perfect balance between His maintenance of God's claims and His ministering to our infirmities.

" To make reconciliation for the sins of the people." It is a pity that the translators of the A.V. rendered this clause as they did. The Revisers have correctly given: " to make *propitiation* for the sins of the people." The Greek word here is " Hilaskeothai," which is the verbal form of the one found in 1 John 2 : 2 and 4 : 10. The word for " reconciliation " is " katallage," which occurs in 2 Cor. 5 : 18, 19, and Rom. 5 : 10, though the word is there wrongly rendered " the atonement." The difference between the two terms is vital though one which is now little understood. Reconciliation is one of the effects or fruits of propitiation. Reconciliation is between God and us; propitiation is solely Godward. Propitiation was the appeasing of God's holy anger and righteous wrath; reconciliation is entering into the peace which the atoning sacrifice of Christ has procured.

" To make propitiation for the sins of the people." Here is the climax of the apostle's argument. Here is his all-conclusive reply to the Jews' objection. Atonement for the sins of God's elect could not be made except the Son became Man; except He became " all of one " with those who had, from all eternity, been set apart in the counsels of the Most High to be " brought unto glory "; except He took part in " flesh and blood," and in all things be " made like unto His brethren." Only thus could He be the *Redeemer* of the " children " which God had given Him.

In Scripture the first qualification of a redeemer was that he must belong to the same family of him or her who was to be redeemed : " If thy brother be waxen poor, and hath sold away of his possession, and if any of his kin come to redeem it, then shall he redeem that which his brother sold " (Lev. 25 : 25). The redeemer must be a " kinsman ": this fact is fully and beautifully illustrated in the book of Ruth (see 2 : 20; 3 : 12, 13; 4 : 1, 4, 6). Neither pity, love, nor power were of any avail till *kinship* was established. The important bearing of this on what immediately follows we shall now endeavour to show.

" To make propitiation for the sins of the people." This word, in the light of its setting, is one of the most vital to be found in all Holy Writ on the subject of the Atonement, bringing out, as it does, the absolute righteousness of God in connection therewith. At the back of many minds, we fear, there lurks the suspicion that though it was marvellous grace and matchless love which moved God to give His Son to die for sinners, yet that, strictly speaking, it was an act of *un*-righteousness. Was it really just for an *innocent* person to suffer in the stead of the guilty ? Was it right for One who had so perfectly honoured God and kept His law at every point, to endure its awful penalty ? To say, It *had* to be, there was no other way of saving us, supplies no direct answer to our question; nay, it is but arguing on the jesuitical basis that " the end justifies the means."

Sin must be punished; a holy God could not ignore our manifold transgressions; therefore, if we are to escape the due reward of our iniquities a sinless substitute must be paid the wages of sin in our stead. But will not the Christian reader agree that it had been infinitely better for all of us to be cast into the Lake of Fire, than that God should act *un*-righteously to His Own Beloved ? Has, then, our salvation been secured at the awful price of a lasting stigma being cast upon the holy name of God ? This is how the theological schemes of many have left it. But not so the Holy Scriptures. Yet, let us honestly face the question : Was God *just* in taking satisfaction from His spotless Son in order to secure the salvation of His people ?

It is at this point that so many preachers have shown a zeal which is *not* " according to knowledge " (Rom. 10 : 2). In their well-meant but carnal efforts to simplify the things of God, they have dragged down His holy and peerless truth to the level of human affairs. They have sought to " illustrate " Divine mysteries by references to things which come within the range of our senses. God has said, " The natural man receiveth not the things of the Spirit of God :

for they are foolishness unto him: neither can he know, because they are spiritually discerned" (1 Cor. 2 : 14). Why not believe what He has said? You cannot teach a corpse, and the natural man is dead in sin. If the Word of God does not bring him life and light, no words of ours can or will. And to go outside of Holy Writ for our "illustrations" is a piece of impertinency, or worse. When a preacher attempts to simplify the mystery of the three Persons in the Godhead by an illustration from "nature" he only exhibits his foolishness, and helps nobody.

Thus it has been with the sacred truth and holy mystery of the Atonement. Good men have not hesitated to ransack the annals of history, both ancient and modern, to discover examples of those who, themselves innocent of the crime committed, volunteered to receive the penalty due to those who were guilty. Sad, indeed, is it to behold this unholy cheapening of the things of God; but what is far worse, most reprehensible is it to observe their *mis*-representations of the greatest transaction of all in the entire history of the universe. An innocent man bearing the punishment of a guilty one may meet the requirements of a human government, but such an arrangement could never satisfy the demands of the righteous government of God. Such is its perfection, that under it no innocent person ever suffered, and no guilty person ever escaped; and so far from the atonement of the Son of God forming an exception to this rule, it affords the most convincing evidence of its truth.

Once we perceive that the Atonement is founded upon the *unity* of Christ and His people, a unity formed by His taking part in flesh and blood, the righteousness of God is at once cleared of the aspersion which the illustrations of many a preacher has, by necessary implication, cast upon it. The propitiation rendered unto God was made neither by a stranger, nor an intimate friend, undergoing what another merited; but by the Head who was responsible for the acts of the members of His spiritual body, just as those members had been constituted guilty because of the act of their natural head, Adam—when "by the offence of one, judgment came upon all men to condemnation" (Rom. 5:18). It is perhaps worthy of notice in this connection that, in the overruling providence of God, it is the *head* of a murderer's body which is dealt with when capital punishment is inflicted—either decapitation as in France, hanging by the neck as in England, or being gassed as in some parts of U.S.A. Thus the head is held responsible for the feet, which were swift to shed blood, and the hand which committed the lethal crime.

However great the dignity of the substitute, or however deep his voluntary humiliation atonement for us would not have been possible unless that substitute became actually, as well as legally, one with us. In order to ransom His church, in order to purge our sins, Christ must so unite Himself with His people, that their sins should become His sins, and that His sufferings and death should become their sufferings and death. In short, the union between the Son of God and His people, and theirs with Him, must be as real and as intimate as that of Adam and his posterity, who all sinned and died in him. Thus did He, in the fullness of time, assume their flesh and blood, bear their sins in His own body on the tree, so that they, having died to sin, may live unto righteousness, being healed by His stripes. Therefore, no human transaction can possibly illustrate the suretyship and sacrificial death of Christ, and any attempt to do so is not only to darken counsel by words without knowledge, but is, really, to be guilty of presumptuous impiety. Probably more than one preacher will be led to cry with the writer, "Father, forgive me, for I knew not what I did."

Here, then, is the answer to our question: so far from the salvation of God's elect having been procured at the unspeakable price of sullying the holy name of Deity, the manner in which it was secured furnishes the supremest demonstration of the inexorable justice of God; for when sin was found upon Him, God "spared not His own Son" (Rom. 8 : 32). But it was against *no* "innocent Victim" that God bade His sword awake. It was against One who had graciously condescended to be "numbered *with* transgressors," who not only took their place, but had become one with them. Had He not first had a real and vital relation to our sins, He could not have undergone their punishment. The *justice* of God's imputation of our sins to the Saviour's account rested upon His *oneness* with His people.

It is this fact which is iterated and reiterated all through the immediate context. "Both He that sanctifieth and they who are sanctified are all of one" (v. 11), "Behold I and the children which God hath given Me" (v. 13), "Forasmuch then as the children are partakers of flesh and blood, He also Himself likewise took part of the same" (v. 14), "Wherefore in all things it behoved Him to be made like unto His brethren" (v. 17). Why? Why? Here is the inspired answer: "*To* make propitiation for the sins of the people." That was only possible, we say again, because of His union with them. When Christ became one with His people their guilt became His, as the debts of a wife become by marriage the debts of the husband. This itself is acknowledged by Christ, "For innumerable evils hath compassed Me about

Mine iniquities have taken hold upon Me, so that I am not able to look up; they are more than the hairs of Mine head: therefore My heart faileth Me" (Psa. 40:12).

"To make propitiation for the sins of the people." In the light of all that has gone before in the Epistle, this statement is luminous indeed. The whole context shows us His *qualifications* for this stupendous work, a work which none but He could have performed. First, He was Himself "the Son," the brightness of God's glory and the very impress of His substance. Thus it was the dignity or Deity of His person which gave such infinite value to His work. Second, His moral perfections as Man, loving righteousness and hating iniquity (1:9), thus fulfilled every requirement of the law. Third, His union with His people which caused Him to be "made sin for us, that we might be made the righteousness of God in Him."

The "propitiation" (which is the N.T. filling out of the O.T. "to make an atonement") which Christ made, was the perfect satisfaction that He offered to the holiness and justice of God on behalf of His people's sins, so that they could be righteously blotted out, removed for ever from before the face of God, "as far as the east is from the west." This sacrificial work of the Saviour's was a priestly act, as the words of our present verse clearly enough affirm.

For "the sins of *the* people" is parallel with Matt. 1:21; John 10:11. They plainly teach that atonement has been made for the sins of God's elect only. "The people" are manifestly parallel with the "heirs of salvation" (1:14), the "many sons" (2:10), the "brethren" (2:12), the "seed of Abraham" (2:16). It is with them alone Christ identified Himself. The "all of one" of 2:11 is expressly defined as being only between "He that sanctifieth and they who are sanctified." He laid hold of "the seed of Abraham," and not "the seed of Adam." He is the "Head" not of mankind, but of "the church which is His body" (Eph. 1:21—23). A *universal* atonement, which largely fails of its purpose, is an invention of Satan, with the design of casting dishonour upon Christ, who would thus be a defeated Saviour. A *general* atonement, abstractly offered to Divine justice, which is theoretically sufficient for everybody, yet in itself efficient for nobody, is a fictitious imagination, which finds lodgment only in those who are vainly puffed up by a fleshly mind. A *particular* atonement, made for a definite people, all of whom shall enjoy the eternal benefits of it, is what is uniformly taught in the Word of God.

"For in that He Himself hath suffered being tempted He is able to succour them that are tempted" (v. 18). Here is the final reason given why it was necessary for the Son to become Man and die: He is the better able to succour His tried people. It was not simply His having been "tempted" that qualified Him, for God Himself may be tempted (Num. 14:22), though not with evil (James 1:13). So men may be tempted, yet as to be moved little or nothing thereby. But such temptations as make one *suffer*, do so work on him, as to draw out his pity to other tempted ones, and to help them as far as He can. It is *this* point which the Spirit has here seized.

"For in that He Himself hath suffered, being tempted." The subject of Christ's being tempted is an important one, for erroneous conceptions thereof necessarily produce a most dishonouring conception of His peerless Person. If the Lord wills, we hope to discuss it more fully when we come to 4:15, yet feel we must offer a few remarks upon it now. That the temptations to which our blessed Lord was subjected were *real* ones is evidenced from the inspired declaration that He "suffered" from them, but that they involved a conflict *within* Him, or that there was any possibility of His yielding thereto, must be emphatically denied. That He became Man, with a human spirit and soul and body, and therefore possessed a human will, we fully believe; but that there was the slightest inclination for His heart or will to yield to evil solicitations, is wicked to so much as imagine. Not only was *His* humanity sinless, but it was "holy" (Luke 1:35), and His inherent holiness repelled all sin as water does fire.

The temptations or trials which Christ suffered here on earth must not be limited to those which came upon Him from Satan, though these are included. First, Christ suffered bodily hunger (Matt. 4:1, 2), &c. Second, His holy nature suffered acutely from the very presence of the foul Fiend, so that He said, "Get thee hence" (Matt. 4:10). Third, the temptations from the Pharisees and others "grieved" Him (Mark 3:5). Fourth, from the words of His own disciples, which were an "offence" unto Him (Matt. 16:23). Fifth, His greatest sufferings were from His Father's temptings or tryings of Him. (See John 12:27; Matt. 26:38, 39; 27:46.) Note how in Luke 22:28, "My temptation," the Saviour spoke of His whole life as one unbroken experience of trial! How real and deep His "sufferings" were, many of the Messianic Psalms reveal.

The very fact that He *suffered* when "tempted" manifests His uniqueness. "He suffered, never yielded. *We* do not 'suffer' when we yield to temptation: the flesh takes pleasure in the things by which it is tempted. Jesus suffered, being tempted. It is important to observe that the flesh, when acted upon by its desires, does not suffer. Being tempted it, alas, enjoys. But when, according to the light of the Holy Spirit and fidelity of obedience, the spirit resists the attacks of the enemy, whether subtle or persecuting, then one suffers. This the Lord did, and this we have to do " (Mr. J. N. Darby).

" He is able to succour them that are tempted." Having passed through this scene as the Man of sorrows, He can, experimentally, gauge and feel the sorrows of His people, but let it be clearly understood that it is not the " flesh " in us which needs " succouring," but the new nature, the faithful heart that desires to please Him. We need " succour " *against* the flesh, to enable us to mortify our members which are upon the earth. Not yet has the promised inheritance been reached. We are still in the wilderness, which provides nothing which ministers to us spiritually. We are living in a world where everything is opposed to true godliness. We are called upon to " run the race which is set before us," to " fight the good fight of faith," and for this we daily need His " succour."

The Greek word for " He is able " implies both a fitness and willingness to do a thing. Christ is both competent and ready to undertake for His people. If we have not, it is because we ask not. The Greek word for " succour " here is very emphatic, and signifies a running to the cry of one, as a parent responding to the cry of distress from a child. A blessed illustration of Christ's " succouring " one of His own needy people is found in Matt. 14 : 30, 31, where we read that when Peter saw the wind was boisterous he was afraid, and began to sink, and cried " Lord, save me." And then we are told, " And *immediately* Jesus stretched forth His hand and caught him."

On one occasion the Lord Jesus asked His disciples, " Believe ye that I *am* able to do this ? " (Matt. 9 : 28). And thus He ever challenges the faith of His own. To Abraham He said, " Is anything too hard for the Lord ? " (Gen. 18 : 14). To Moses, who doubted whether the Lord would give flesh to Israel in the wilderness, He asked, " Is the Lord's hand waxed short ? " (Num. 11 : 23). To Jeremiah the searching question was put, " Is there anything too hard for Me ? " (Jer. 32 : 27). So He still asks, " Believe ye, that I am able to do this ? " Do *what*? we may ask. Whatever you are really in need of—give peace, impart assurance, grant deliverance, supply succour.

" He is able to succour them that are tempted." Remember who He is, the God-man. Remember the experiences through which He passed ! He, too, has been in the place of trial : He, too, was tempted—to distrust, to despondency, to destroy Himself. Yes, He was tempted " in all points like as we are, sin excepted." Remember His present position, sitting at the right hand of the Majesty on high ! How blessed then to know that He *is* " able " both to enter, sympathetically, into our sufferings and sorrows, and that He has power to " succour."

" As Man, a man of sorrows,
Thou hast suffered every woe,
And though enthroned in glory now,
Canst pity all Thy saints below."

Oh, what a Saviour is ours ! The allmighty God ; yet the all-tender Man. One who is as far above us in His original nature and present glory as the heavens are above the earth : yet One who can be " touched with the feeling of our infirmities." One who is the Creator of the universe ; yet One who became Man, lived His life on the same plane ours is lived, passed through the same trials we experience, and suffered not only as we do, but far more acutely. How wellfitted is such a One to be our great High Priest ! How self-sufficient He is to supply our every need ! And how completely is the wisdom and grace of God vindicated for having appointed His blessed Son, to be made, for a season, lower than the angels ! May our love for Him be strengthened and our worship deepened by the contemplation of what has been before us in these first two chapters of Hebrews.

—*Arthur W. Pink.*

GLEANINGS IN EXODUS.

60. *The Typical Mediator* (*Ex.* 32 : 11-14)

In our last article we were occupied with the inspired account of Israel's idolatrous worship of the golden calf. It was the first time that they were guilty of this awful sin since their leaving of Egypt as a nation. The subject of idolatry is both solemn and important, and as the nature and cause of it are so little understood we propose to offer here a few general remarks on the subject.

Man is the only creature who lives on the earth that was originally created with faculties capable of apprehending God, and with a sentiment of veneration for Him. True, all creation is to the praise of the Creator, but man's praise is the homage of an intelligent heart and of a conscious choice or preference. But this capacity to offer intelligent praise is necessarily accompanied by responsibility. This was made evident in connection with Adam. The tree of the knowledge of good and evil was the visible means of the first man's paying homage to God: abstention from its fruit was the witness of his subjection to the authority of his Maker. Obedience to God's command concerning that tree would not only secure to him all the blessings of Eden, but was also the link which bound him to the Creator. Thus, that which united man to God at the beginning was the obedience of the will, subjection of heart. Whilst this was maintained God was honoured and man was blest.

But that link was broken. Through disobedience man became "alienated *from* the life of God" (Eph. 4:18), and thus he lost his happiness and was turned out of the Garden. The original link being broken, it could never be reformed. If man was ever again to be in relationship with God, it must be on entirely new ground, namely, redemption-ground, resurrection-ground, the ground of new creation. Into Eden fallen man could never re-enter. It was a garden of delights for innocence alone; and guilt once incurred made a return to it impossible. But for His own people God has provided a new garden, the " paradise of God " (Rev. 2:7), where the guilty are restored to more than the pleasures of Eden. That new garden is anticipated by faith, and there is found forgiveness of sins and eternal life.

Now when man fell, though he became alienated from God (which is what spiritual " death " is) he lost none of his original faculties, nor was his responsibility destroyed. In his essential nature man remained after the Fall all that he was before it. True, his nature became vitiated by sin, and, in consequence, his whole being was corrupted; nevertheless, the " breath of life " which God had breathed into him at the beginning, remained his portion after his expulsion from Eden. True, all the faculties of his being now became the " instrument of unrighteousness unto sin " (Rom. 6:13), yet none of them had ceased to exist or to function.

It is the very character of man's nature (that which distinguishes him from and elevates him above the beasts) which has made his fall his ruin. It has been rather vulgarly said that " Man is a religious animal," by which is meant that man, by nature, is essentially a religious creature, *i.e.*, made, originally, to pay homage to his Creator. It is this religious nature of man's which, strange as it may sound, lies at the root of all idolatry. Being alienated from God, and therefore ignorant of Him, he falls the ready dupe of Satan. It was to this fact of fallen man's essential nature that Christ had reference when He said, " If therefore the light that is in thee be darkness, how great is that darkness " (Matt. 6:23). The " light " in man is that which distinguishes him from the beasts, and that which is (potentially) capable of communing with God. But, as we have said, that faculty in man which is capable of communion with God, is, as the result of sin, put to a wrong use, and thus the " light " in him has become " darkness." Instead of worshipping God, he now serves his own lusts, and honours idols which are patterned after his lusts.

Man must have his god, otherwise he would not be man, and because the " natural man "—what he now is as a fallen creature—has lost his knowledge of the true God, he turns to the resources of his own mind to fill the void. And, as another has said (from whom part of the above has been condensed), " From the mental image formed in a corrupt mind, it is but a short step to the golden or wooden idol in the temple. Every shape and form had its prototype in the imagination, which to the philosopher was supplemented by the material things of nature; but to the vulgar, surrounding objects were the basis upon which the superstructure of idolatry rested. Through the senses their imagination was fed by the things seen and felt; and though these be not the sole source of idolatry, they greatly modified its form and multiplied its gods. For the mountain and the valley, the river, the grove, the heavens above and the waters beneath had their divinities, and everywhere that which in nature most impressed man soon took rank as a god.

" Nor let us forget the greatest factor which produced this confused mass of superstition and credulity. Not only did man not like to retain the knowledge of God and thus became the dupe of his senses, but over all was the delusive power of Satan, who held man in captivity through his fears and lusts. The loss of the knowledge of the true God, to a creature endowed with religious faculties, must result in subjective idolizing. Satan, the god of this world, presented himself in a tangible form and made it objective.

" The religious element in man's nature was not eradicated by sin, but while every faculty of his mind and every instinct of his nature is debased and perverted, man's complete ruin and his greatest guilt are seen in the degradation of those same faculties, originally given as the means of worshipping God. The endowments which placed him above all other creatures, now sink him beneath them " (" The Bible Tresury, 1882).

What has been said above not only serves to explain the universality of idolatry, but supplies the key to what is recorded in Exodus 32. There we behold the favoured Israelites making and worshipping a golden calf. It was inexcusable, open, blatant, united idolatry. For a very good reason, the first command which God had written, with His own finger, upon the tables of stone, was " Thou shalt have no other gods before Me "; and here was the deliberate and concerted violation of it. What, then, must be the sequel? Jehovah turns to Moses, acquainted him with the awful sin of the people down below, and says, " Now therefore let me alone, that My wrath may wax hot against them, and that I may consume them: and I will make of thee a great nation."

Solemn and fearsome as those words sound, yet a closer examination reveals a door of hope opened by them. When the Lord said to Moses, " Let Me alone . . . I will make of thee a great nation," it was as though He placed Himself in the hands of the typical mediator. " Let Me alone " plainly suggests that Moses stood between Jehovah and His sinful people. This was indeed the case. But for Moses they were surely lost: he only stood between the holy wrath of God and their thoroughly merited doom. What would he do? When menaced by the Egyptians at the Red Sea, Moses had cried unto the Lord on their behalf (14: 15). So, too, at the bitter waters of Marah he had supplicated Jehovah for them (15: 25). When at Rephidim they had no water, yet again Moses had cried unto the Lord and obtained answer on their behalf (17: 4). When Amelek came against Israel, it was the holding up of Moses' hands which gained them the victory (17: 11). But now a far graver crisis was at hand. Would Moses fail them now? or would he again intervene on their behalf?

" And Moses besought the Lord his God, and said, Lord, why doth Thy wrath wax hot against Thy people, which Thou hast brought forth out of the land of Egypt with great power, and with a mighty hand?" (v. 11). Moses did not fail his people in this hour of their urgent need. Most blessed is it to behold how he conducted himself on this occasion: God had said to him, " Let me alone, that My wrath may wax hot against them . . . and I will make *of thee* a great nation," but Moses uses his place of nearness to God not on his own behalf, but for the good of the people.

At an earlier date he had " refused to be called the son of Pharaoh's daughter, choosing rather to suffer affliction with the people of God than to enjoy the pleasures of sin for a season; esteeming the reproach of Christ greater riches than the treasures in Egypt: for he had respect unto the recompense of the reward " (Heb. 11: 24-26). So now he declines to be made the head of another nation, choosing rather to be identified with this stiff-necked and disobedient people. Is there not here a blessed foreshadowing of Him who " made Himself of no reputation " (Phil. 2: 7), and who became one with His sinful people? Yes, indeed; and, as we shall see, in more respects than one.

" And Moses besought the Lord his God, and said, Lord, why doth Thy wrath wax hot against Thy people, which Thou hast brought forth out of the land of Egypt with great power, and with a mighty hand?" This was the typical mediator's response to what Jehovah had said to him in v. 7, " Go, get thee down; for *thy* people, which *thou* broughtest out of the land of Egypt have corrupted themselves." We believe there is a double force to these words. In their local significance they furnish God's answer to the wicked declaration of Israel recorded in v. 1. There the people had disowned their Divine Deliverer; here He righteously disclaims them. But there is a *typical* meaning, too, and most precious is it to contemplate this.

In v. 7 the Lord practically turns the Nation over to Moses, calling them " thy people "; here in v. 11 the typical mediator, as it were, gives them back again unto God, saying " Thy people." Was not this a plain adumbration of what we find in John 17? First, in v. 2, the antitypical Mediator speaks of a people whom God had given to Him: " As Thou hast given Him power over all flesh, that He should give eternal life to as many as Thou hast *given Him*." Then, in v. 9, we behold Him giving back that people to God, " I pray for them: I pray not for the world, but for them which Thou hast given Me; for they *are Thine*."

Let us notice now the various *grounds* upon which Moses pleaded before " the Lord *his* God." They are three in number: he appealed to the grace of God, the glory of God, and the faithfulness of God. His appeal to God's grace is found in v. 11, " Lord, why doth Thy wrath wax hot against Thy people, which Thou hast brought forth out of the land of Egypt?" It was grace, pure and simple, which had actuated Jehovah when He delivered the Hebrews from the House of Bondage. There was absolutely nothing in them to merit His esteem; rather was there everything in them to call forth His wrath. It was sovereign benignity, unadulterated grace, the Divine favour shown to them, unasked and unmerited.

But let it not be overlooked that the Divine grace which was shown to unworthy Israel was not exercised at the expense of the claims of justice, for it is ever true that grace reigns " through righteousness " (Rom. 5: 21). So it was in Egypt: the passover-lamb had been slain, its blood shed and applied. Thus, it is on the ground of *redemption* that grace flowed forth. And it is still the same, " Being justified freely by His grace *through* the redemption that is in Christ Jesus " (Rom. 3: 24).

Now it was to *this* that Moses made his first appeal. Israel had sinned, sinned grievously, and Moses made no effort to deny or excuse it. Later, we find him acknowledging the Lord's charge against

His people, owning "it *is* a stiff necked people" (34 : 9). Nevertheless, they were *God's* people—His by redemption. They were His purchased property. Unworthy, unthankful, unholy; but yet, the Lord's redeemed. Blessed, glorious, heart-melting fact: O may the realisation of it create within us a greater hatred of sin and a deeper appreciation of the precious blood of the Lamb. Is it not written, "If any man (Greek "any one"—of those spoken of in 1 John 1 : 3) sin, we have an Advocate with the Father, Jesus Christ the righteous" (1 John 2 : 1)? And what is the ground of His advocacy? What but His blood shed once for all!

"Wherefore should the Egyptians speak, and say, For mischief did He bring them out, to slay them in the mountain, and to consume them from the face of the earth? Turn from Thy fierce wrath, and repent of this evil against Thy people" (v. 12). Here is the second ground on which Moses pleaded with God: he appealed to His glory. Where would be His honour in the sight of the heathen were He to consume the children of Israel here at Sinai? Would not reproach be cast upon His name by the Egyptians? The thought of this was more than Moses could endure; therefore did he beseech Jehovah to relent against His erring people.

"Spite of their shameful apostasy, the plea of Moses was that they were still Gods' people, and that His glory was concerned in sparing them—lest the enemy should boast over their destruction, and thereby over the Lord Himself. In itself it was a plea of irresistible force. Joshua uses one of like character when the Israelites were smitten before Ai. He says "the Canaanites and all the inhabitants of the land shall hear of it, and shall environ us round, and cut off our name from the earth: *and what wilt Thou do unto Thy great name?* ' (Joshua 7 : 9. In both cases it was faith taking hold of God, identifying itself with His own glory, and claiming on that ground the response to its desires—a plea that God can never refuse ". (Ed. Dennett).

This ground of appeal to God is not made by any of us to-day nearly as much as it should be. The prayer of Moses here in Ex. 32 is also recorded for our learning. It brings before us the essential elements of those " effectual fervent prayers of a righteous man" which "availeth much." This was not the only occasion on which Moses appealed to the glory of the Lord's name: let the reader consult carefully Numbers 14 : 13-16, and Deut. 9 : 28, 29; for others who used this plea, see Psa. 25 : 11; Joel 2 : 17, &c. It is the glory of His own name, which God ever has before Him in all that He does.

It was for the honour of His name that He had, originally, brought Israel out of Egypt: " I wrought for My name's sake, that it should not be polluted before the heathen, among whom they were, in whose sight I made Myself known unto them, in bringing them forth out of the land of Egypt " (Ezek. 20 : 9). So, at a later date in Israel's sinful history He declared, " For My name's sake will I defer Mine anger, and for My praise will I refrain from thee, that I cut thee not off. . . . For Mine own sake, even for Mine own sake, will I do it : for how should My name be polluted ?" (Isa. 48 : 9, 11). It is " for *His* name's sake " "that He leads His people in the paths of righteousness" (Psa. 23 : 3).

Blessed is it to behold the Lord Jesus in His high priestly prayer, recorded in John 17, using this same plea before God. In that prayer He is heard presenting many petitions, and varied are the grounds upon which He presents them. But underlying all, first and foremost He asked, " glorify Thy Son, *that* Thy Son also may glorify Thee" (v. 1) ! Here is one of the prime secrets in prevailing prayer. Just as bowing of the heart to God's sovereign will is the first requirement in a praying soul, so the having before us the glory of God and the honour of His name is that which, chiefly, ensures an answer to our petitions. " Whatsoever ye do, do all to the glory of God" (1 Cor. 10 : 31) applies as strictly to our praying as to any other exercise. Let us take to heart, then, this important lesson taught us in this successful prayer of Moses.

"Remember Abraham, Isaac, and Israel, Thy servants, to whom Thou swearest by Thine own self, and saidst unto them, I will multiply your seed as the stars of heaven, and all this land that I have spoken of will I give unto your seed, and they shall inherit it forever " (v. 13). Here is the third ground which Moses took in his intercession before Jehovah. He appealed to His faithfulness; he pleaded His promises; he reminded Him of His oath. There was no ground to go on and no plea which he could make from anything that was to be found in Israel, so he fell back upon that which God is in Himself.

"In the energy of his intercession—fruit surely of the action of the Spirit of God—he goes back to the absolute and unconditional promises made to Abraham, Isaac and Jacob, reminding the Lord of the two immutable things in which it was impossible for Him to lie (Heb. 6 : 18). A more beautiful example of prevailing intercession is not to be found in the Scriptures. Indeed, in the emergency which had arisen, everything depended on the mediator, and in His grace God had provided one who could stand in the breach, and plead His people's cause—not on the ground of what they were, for by their sin they were exposed to the righteous indignation of a holy God—but on the ground of what God was, and on that of His counsels revealed and confirmed to the patriarchs, both by oath and promise " (Ed. Dennett).

But let us look a little more closely at this third feature of Moses' prayer. In the above quotation there are two slight inaccuracies: it was not God's promises to " Abraham, Isaac and *Jacob*," but " and Israel "—the difference intimating the height to which Moses' faith had risen; nor were God's revealed counsels confirmed to the patriarchs " both by oath and by promise," but, instead, by promise and oath—note the order in Heb. 6 : 13-18, which is the same as in Gen. 12 : 3, and then Gen. 22 : 15, 16. But that which we would here dwell upon is that Moses made these the final grounds of his pleading before God.

The *Word* of God is " quick and powerful " (Heb. 4 : 12), not only in its effects upon us, but also in its moving power with God Himself. If this were more realized by Christians, the very language of Holy Writ would have a larger place in their supplications, and more answers from above would be obtained. God has magnified His Word above all His name (Psa. 138 : 2), and so should we. He has expressly declared, " Them that honour Me, I will honour," and how can we more honour Him in our prayers than by employing the very words of Scripture, *His* words, rather than our own ? Ah, here too, our speech betrays us. If the Word of Christ dwelt in us more richly, it would find fuller expression in our intercessions, for " out of the abundance of the heart the mouth speaketh." Christ has left us a perfect example : His prayers were the outbreathing of the Psalms, and a close examination of the one which He taught His disciples reveals the fact that every clause of it was a quotation from the O.T. ! And He explicitly enjoined His disciples, " after *this* manner therefore pray *ye* " (Matt. 6 : 9). But we do not; hence so many unanswered prayers.

Now that which Moses pleaded before God from His Word were the *promises* which He had made to the patriarchs. This, too, is recorded for our learning. It is the humble, simple, trustful spreading of the Divine promises before the throne of grace which secures the ear of God. *That* is what real prayer is : a presenting of our need before the Lord, and then reverently reminding Him of His own declaration that He will supply it. It is a confident asking with David, " Do as Thou hast said " (2 Sam. 7 : 25).

This is what the " exercise of faith " signifies : a laying hold of God's promises, an " embracing " (Heb. 11 : 13) of them, a counting upon them. " Hath He said, and shall He not do it ? or hath He spoken, and shall He not make it good ? " (Num. 23 : 19).

Men like a written agreement in " black and white," and the great God has condescended to give us such. How strange, then, that we do not treat His promises as *realities*. Jehovah never trifles with His words : His engagements are always kept: Joshua reminded Israel, " This day I am going the way of all the earth : and ye know in all your hearts and in all your souls, that not one thing hath failed of all the good things which the Lord your God spake concerning you ; *all* are come to pass unto you, not one thing hath failed thereof " (Joshua 23 : 14). Then let us seek grace to emulate Abraham, the father of all them that believe, of whom it is recorded, " He staggered not at the promise of God through unbelief ; but was strong in faith, giving glory to God ; and being fully persuaded that, what He had promised, He was able also to perform " (Rom. 4 : 20, 21).

" And the Lord repented of the evil which He thought to do unto His people " (v. 14). These words do not mean that God changed His mind or altered His purpose, for He is " *without* variableness or shadow of turning " (James 1 : 17). There never has been and never will be the smallest occasion for the Almighty to affect the slightest deviation from His eternal purpose, for everything was foreknown to Him from the beginning, and all His counsels were ordered by infinite wisdom. When Scripture speaks of God's repenting it employs a figure of speech, in which the Most High condescends to speak in our language. What is intended by the above expression is that Jehovah answered the prayer of the typical mediator.

" And the Lord repented of the evil which He thought to do unto His people " (v. 14). Blessed is it to note how Israel is still spoken of as " *His* people." " What encouragement to faith ! If ever there was an occasion when it seemed impossible that prayer should be heard, it was this ; but the faith of Moses rose above all difficulties, and grasping the hand of Jehovah claimed His help ; and, inasmuch as He could not deny Himself, the prayer of Moses was granted " (Ed. Dennett). May this little meditation be blest of God to many to the enriching of thier spiritual lives.

We shall much value the continued prayers of God's people that His way may be made plain before our face, and grace given to walk therein.

WORSHIP (2).

Having pointed out the vanity of false worship and the exclusiveness of true worship, having also dwelt briefly on the nature of worship, we are now ready to consider,

4. The prerequisites of worship.

It may help us to examine with some little care the first example of worship recorded in the New Testament. This is found in Matt. 2, where we have the inspired account of the wise men journeying in search of, finding, and worshipping the infant Saviour. That incident is recorded for our instruction, and there is much in it which should search our hearts. By noting carefully what the Holy Spirit has there said, we may discover not a little which bears directly upon that aspect of worship which we are now considering.

First, we are told that these earliest worshippers of the incarnate Son of God were "wise men" (Matt. 2:1). Now in Scripture a "wise" man is not one whose head is filled with the learning which human schools supply. A "wise" man is one who is moved by godly awe and reverence, for "the fear of the Lord is the beginning of wisdom." A wise man is the opposite of a fool, who says in his heart "no God." Only to the extent that we are really walking with God, are we "wise"; and none but "wise" men can truly worship.

Second, they were "from the east" (v. 1). This is the quarter in which the sun rises; it is there it starts its daily journey on its circuit through the heavens. Thus, the wise men "from the east" suggests the thought that they were following the light, for they were moving in the direction in which the sun was going. Spiritually speaking, that means, they were men who *responded* to the illumination which they had received from God. This is another essential prerequisite for worship. Before I am capable of worshipping God I must be brought out of darkness into His marvellous light, and continue yielding to His revealed will.

Third, they came "to Jerusalem" (v. 1). This tells us that they conformed to God's arrangements, for it was there the Temple stood. They did not lean unto their own understanding and say, We can worship God in our own country, just as well as in Palestine. They were not like those who argue, We can go away on a holiday and worship God on the mountains, or by the seaside, just as truly as among His people. *That* would be the very reverse of conforming to God's arrangements, for He has expressly commanded us *not* to forsake "the assembling of ourselves together, as the manner of some is" (Heb. 10:25).

Fourth, they were men who owned the Kingship of Christ (v. 2). Unless we do this in a practical way, worship is impossible. To own Christ's kingship means to be in subjection to His rule, to bow to His authority, to keep His commandments. As the Lord said of old, "To obey is better than sacrifice, and to hearken than the fat of rams" (1 Sam. 15:22). Then do you think that He will accept the formal worship of a disobedient heart? To His refractory people He still asks, "Why call ye Me Lord, Lord, and do not the things which I say?" (Luke 6:46).

Fifth, they were men who considered not their own ease and comfort. They deemed no trouble, no expense, no sacrifice too great, to go to where the Lord Jesus was. They journeyed all the way from Chaldea to Bethlehem, and in those days travel was a very different matter from what it now is. They were willing to set aside their physical ease. Why? Because the person of Christ attracted them. And where is Christ to be found to-day? Do not His own words tell us: "For where two or three are gathered together in My name, there am I in the midst" (Matt. 18:20)?

Sixth, they were men who continued following the heavenly light, the "star" (v. 9). It is striking to note that this is the only line in this spiritual picture which is repeated—because, no doubt, it is the most important for us to be exercised about. Those wise men were *tested*. The star led them as far as Jerusalem. When they arrived there, it was to find the Saviour was elsewhere. After inquiry, they learned, from the testimony of Holy Writ, that He was to be found in Bethlehem. Then it was that the star moved on again; and following it, they arrived at where the young Child was. Such is the situation which confronts many of God's people to-day. Christ is not to be found in the "temples" of Christendom. Where, then, is the place in which He graciously manifests Himself? Often it is only by diligent inquiry, and following the testimony of Scripture, that this place can be found; but it is always "*outside* the camp" (Heb. 13:13).

Seventh, they were men who "rejoiced with exceeding great joy" (v. 10). Notice where the Holy Spirit has placed *this* line in the picture: not at the beginning, but following the six already pointed out. This is very searching. Unless I am acting as a "wise" man, following God's light, conforming to His arrangements, owning His Kingship, setting aside my own ease and comfort, "exceeding joy" will not be my portion. But if, by grace, I am in this blessed state, then worship will be the spontaneous outflow. And *what* was it that occasioned their "exceeding joy"? Heavenly light on their path again. But if our hearts are not right and our ways are not pleasing to God, we shall not have this.

Finally, they were men laden with "treasures" to present to Christ (v. 11). They brought to Him rich "gifts." This is what real worship is. It is not a coming to receive *from* Him, but to render *unto* Him. It is the pouring out of the heart's adoration. Blessed climax to that typical scene was this: it was to present to Christ their "treasures" that these wise men had come all the way from Chaldea to Bethlehem. O that more of our readers may bring to the Saviour "gold, frankincense and myrrh," *i.e.*, adoring Him because of His Divine glory, His moral perfections, His fragrant death.

Let us call attention to another spiritual picture, the central subject of which is Worship. This is to be found in Luke 1. There we are shown four things: the prerequisites of worship, the exercise of worship, the ceasing of worship, the restoration of worship.

"There was in the days of Herod, the king of Judea, a certain priest named Zacharias" (Luke 1:5). This is very solemn, and yet very blessed. The time-mark here is most important. The Holy Spirit has prefaced what follows by telling us that it occurred in the days when Herod was king of Judea. A fearful state of affairs obtained: one which must have sorely troubled and deeply exercised the hearts of God's people— Jehovah was no longer King in Zion; a usurper was ruling over Israel. There is a close parallel with this to-day. The Lord Jesus is not King in Christendom: corporately it has apostatised. This should sadden us. That is the solemn side of the introduction to what follows.

The bright and blessed side is, that, even in those evil days, God had reserved to Himself a faithful remnant. There were those whose affections He had drawn unto Himself. Though a heathen ruled over Judea, there was still left a little company of true worshippers, prominent among them being the parents of John the Baptist. Their names are significant. Zacharias means "God remembers"; Elizabeth signifies, "the oath of God." Ah, everything turns upon that. (Compare Ex. 2:23-25.) This comes first here because it is the foundation of everything. The N.T. parallel is found in Heb. 6:13-20. God will not belie Himself. Though a usurper (Satan) is now on the throne of this world, yet God will not forget His oath.

Zacharias was "of the course of Abia." This detail is not without meaning. If the reader will consult 1 Chron. 24 he will find that Solomon divided Israel's priesthood into twenty-four "courses" who took turns in ministering before God. The course of "Abia" was the eighth, which is the number of the *new creation*. Thus, in this typical picture the Divine side is presented first; worship is the outcome of God's remembering His oath, and as the result, creating anew in Christ His own elect. Only such can worship God.

"And they were both righteous before God, walking in all the commandments and ordinances of the Lord blameless" (v. 6). This brings in the human side of things, and very searching it is. This comes before v. 9, where a typical picture of *worship* is before us. The contents of v. 6 tell us what must precede worship, what is the necessary prerequisite of it. If I am walking in a course of self-will, of disobedience, then, obviously, I cannot worship God. I may go through the forms of it, I may be in the midst of a worshipping people, yet *I* cannot worship God, for "they that worship Him *must* worship Him in spirit *and in truth*" (John 4:24).

"And they had no child" (v. 7). This seems to present a difficulty, a real one. Typically, "no child" means there was *no fruit*. But is it possible to be a worshipper and yet remain fruitless? Remember that this is a typical picture—that is, Divine truth presented under a figure—and all of God's pictures are flawless. In the light of what follows the difficulty vanishes. Pass on for a moment to v. 13: "Fear not, Zacharias: for thy prayer is heard, and thy wife Elizabeth shall bear thee a son." Look beyond the figure to what is spiritually depicted: they were *exercised* before God about the matter of their fruitlessness. Are we? Are we deeply concerned in our souls about this important matter? Are those words of Christ constantly before us: "Herein is My Father glorified, that ye bear much fruit; so shall ye be My disciples" (John 15:8)?

Let us return now to v. 7: "And they had no child, because that Elizabeth was barren, and they both now were well stricken in years." What is the lesson which God would here teach us? This, mere nature cannot produce fruit. The power of God must come in for *that*: as said Jehovah of old, "From Me is thy fruit found" (Hos. 14:8). But ere the power of God comes in to produce "fruit," there must be real and deep exercise of heart before Him (note the word "exercised" in Heb. 12:11), and *preceding* such exercise on the part of Zacharias and Elizabeth we are told, "They were both righteous before God, walking in all the commandments and ordinances of the Lord blameless"! Yes, all of this *is* very searching.

What do we read of next? This: "And it came to pass, that while he executed the priest's office before God in the order of his course, according to the custom of the priest's office, his lot was to burn incense when he went into the temple of the Lord, and the whole multitude of the people were praying without at the time of incense" (vv. 8—10). Observe the time-mark, "While": while he was conforming to God's arrangements (note "in the *order* of his course"), while he was keeping the Divine ordinances, while the whole multitude was praying—what? "There appeared unto him an angel of the Lord" (v. 11). Of course! This is ever God's way: He has promised "them that honour Me, I will honour." Thus, Zacharias was now granted a Divine communication.

"And when Zacharias saw him he was troubled, and fear fell upon him" (v. 12). This is very solemn. Many may be tempted, at first, to regard this line as a marring of the typical picture. Alas, does not the experience of many of us testify to its accuracy? Zacharias was *not prepared* for the Divine communication which he was about to receive. Ah, it is sadly possible to rise to the high level of true worship before God, to be in the very place and act of presenting, spiritually, "sweet incense" to God, and yet to be made uncomfortable, to be "troubled" when God appears to us with a new and further revelation of His will and purpose concerning us.

The communication which was made by the angel to Zacharias is recorded in Luke 1:13 to 17. It was a blessed message which should have filled God's servant with thanksgiving. Assurance was now granted that the desired fruit would be given, and that this fruit should signally redound to God's glory and the blessing of His people. But instead of Zacharias rejoicing at such tidings, we are told that he said "Whereby shall I know this? for I am an old man, and my wife well stricken in years?" (v. 18). This is very solemn, exceedingly grave, as the immediate sequel plainly shows. This priest of Aaron, this worshipper of God, is now heard advancing objections against the Divine messenger and his message. Zacharias was occupied with himself and the state of his wife. The things of the flesh, the ties of nature, filled his vision, and so an evil heart of unbelief possessed him.

"And the angel answering said unto him, I am Gabrial, that stand in the presence of God, and am sent to speak unto thee, and to show thee these glad tidings. And, behold, thou shalt be dumb, and not able to speak, until the day that these things shall be performed, because thou believest not my words, which shall be fulfilled in their season" (vv. 19, 20). Zacharias was chastised, chastised in his own flesh. But let us, again, seek to look behind the figure to what is here depicted. Zacharias was stricken with dumbness, his lips could no more sing the praises of God; there could be no more active worship. Forever? No; until the fruit appeared.

There is one very striking and searching detail for us to note concerning that fruit for which worship must wait. Go back to v. 15: "he shall be great in the sight of the Lord, and shall drink neither wine nor strong drink." Does that need interpreting? The fruit was to be a *Nazarite* (see Num. 6:1—6), one separated wholly to God, one apart from nature's joys, one devoted to the Lord in a practical way. Till *this* fruit was born Zacharias must remain dumb. That fruit was John the Baptist, who dwelt in the wilderness, with no thought for self; instead of living on the fat of the land, his garment was of camel's hair; his food, locusts and wild honey.

Ah, Christian reader, does the history of Zacharias describe yours? In earlier days your walk was pleasing to God, your heart was full of praise, and in consequence you were a joyous worshipper. But, "first love" was left (Rev. 2:4), fuller light from the Word was not responded to, and now the songs of praise are no longer heard from you. Is it not so? Then what is needed? A pouring out of your heart unto God in penitent prayer; a bringing forth (by His power) of that fruit which is marked by separation from the world in devotedness unto Him.

The sequel in Luke 1 is very blessed. It is found in vv. 57-67. Here we behold the fruit produced (v. 57), and inseparably connected therewith entire submission to the revealed will of God (vv. 60, 63). Then we are told "and his mouth was opened immediately, and his tongue loosed, and he spake, and praised God" (v. 64). Worship was restored. O may the Spirit of God produce in and through His people to-day this same precious fruit of separation from the world and consecration unto the Lord, so that the spirit of worship may again be found in many a Christian whose lips have for so long a time been "dumb."

—*Arthur W. Pink.*

At the time of going to press (Nov. 7), we are still very much exercised before God about His open door for oral ministry in England.

WORSHIP

The subject of worship is most important, yet it is one upon which many have but the haziest ideas. It is because of this we feel constrained to devote yet another article to it. Worship may be contemplated from various angles, and there is so much bearing upon it in the Scriptures, both directly and indirectly, that it is impossible to exhaust our present theme. Thus far we have sought to contrast true worship with false, to point out the character of worship, and to call attention to some of the prerequisites of worship. We shall now consider,

5. *The Power of Worship.*

The object of worship is God; and the inspirer of worship is God. Only that can satisfy God which He has Himself produced. "Without faith it is impossible to please Him" (Heb. 11:6), yet faith is His own gift (Eph. 2:9). He it is who worketh in us "both to will and to do of His good pleasure" (Phil. 2:13). The fruit which the Christian bears is "the fruit of the Spirit" (Gal. 5:22). So also we "have access by one Spirit unto the Father" (Eph. 2:18). Therefore do the saints affirm, "Lord, Thou wilt ordain peace for us: for Thou also hast wrought all our works in us" (Isa. 26:12).

Now there is a beautiful type of the *power* of worship in Ex. 30:7, 8, "Aaron shall burn thereon sweet incense every morning; when he dresseth the lamps, he shall burn incense upon it. And when Aaron lighteth the lamps at even he shall burn incense upon it." The "burning of incense" was one of of worship unto God. Now what is to be particularly noted in this passage is that God has linked together two things: the lighting of the lamps and the burning of the incense.

The *connection* between those two things is not hard to trace. Every fresh measure of light which the Spirit of God grants concerning the person and work of Christ causes fresh outbursts of praise unto the Father. And this supplies us with the surest test for ascertaining whether the preaching we sit under is of the Holy Spirit or not. That which magnifies Christ, that which affords such a view of His manifold excellencies and causes our hearts to be drawn out in praise and thanksgiving to God, is of the Spirit. Contrariwise, that which exalts the poor human instrument, or which flatters the hearers, is not of God. It is only as the Lamb is exalted in the power of the Spirit that saints are made to cry, "My soul doth magnify the Lord, and my spirit hath rejoiced in God my Saviour" (Luke 1:46, 47).

What has been brought out above supplies the explanation to so very much of what is now going on all around us in the religious world. The general and conspicuous absence of that worship which is "in spirit and in truth" is due to an order of things over which the Spirit of God does not preside, where the world, the flesh and the Devil have free play. But even in circles where worldliness, in its grosser forms at least, are not tolerated, and where outward orthodoxy is still preserved, there is, almost always, a noticeable absence of that unction, that freedom, that joyousness, which are inseparable from the spirit of true worship. Why is this? Why is it that in numbers of "churches," meeting-houses, Brethren "assemblies," where the letter of God's Word is ministered, that we now so rarely find those overflowings of heart, those spontaneous outbursts of adoration, that "sacrifice of praise," which should ever be found among God's people? Ah, is the answer hard to find? It is because there is a *grieved Spirit* in the midst.

The Holy Spirit has been given to God's people to take of the things of Christ and show them unto them (John 16:15). But, alas, how rarely is He free to do so! Just as it is in His work in the unregenerate, so it often is with the regenerate. Before a sinner is ready to appreciate the great Physician, he must be shown that he is sick; before he is ready to hear of One that is mighty to save, he must be made to feel his need of Him. Thus, the initial work of the Spirit is to convict of sin, to reveal to us our lost condition, to wound before He heals. Then it is that He leads the awakened and contrite soul to the foot of the Cross. And is it not the same, in principle, in His dealings with those who are converted? While I am really "following" Christ, the Spirit will reveal Him to me more and more. But if I have turned aside into a path of self-will and self-pleasing, for Him to then set before me the glories of Christ would only be placing a premium on loose walking, on sin. To the one who has *left* his "first love" the Spirit's word is, "Repent and do the first works." Ah, my brethren, there is a reason why there is so little living, refreshing, worship-producing ministry of Christ to-day. There is a *grieved* Spirit in our midst.

Many are aware that something is wrong, that something is lacking; but having no discernment to discover the real cause, they have betaken themselves to the wrong remedy. Realizing the absence of those manifestations of the Spirit of God which, at the beginning, took the form of "tongues of fire," they have had recourse to *other* "fire." The sin of Nadab and Abihu has been repeated, and is being perpetuated all around us. Of them it is written, "And Nadab and Abihu, the sons of Aaron, took either of them his censer, and put fire therein, and put incense thereon, and offered *strange fire* before the Lord, which He commanded them not" (Lev. 10 : 1).

What is the typical meaning of that "strange fire"? To answer this, let us point out again the significance of the legitimate "fire." The "incense" was an emblem of worship, of the praises and prayers which ascend to God from the hearts of His redeemed. But before the incense could go up as a sweet savour to Heaven, it had to be kindled, set aglow, and for this, live coals of fire were needed. Those "live coals" were the power behind the incense. They were taken from off the brazen altar, where the sin-offering had been consumed by fire from heaven (Lev. 16 : 12 ; Num. 16 : 46). What were those "live coals," then, but a figure of the Holy Spirit, who warms our hearts, kindles our praises, and is the power of all true worship; that blessed Spirit which has been given to us on the ground of the atoning work of Christ! Ah, we can no more worship without the direct empowering of the Spirit than the incense could ascend in fragrant fumes to God until the live coals were first placed beneath it.

What is recorded at the beginning of Lev. 10 is in solemn and glaring contrast from what is found in the two preceding chapters, which belong together: their theme being, The consecration of the priesthood. Note the repeated words, "As the Lord commanded," in 8 : 9, 13, 17, 21, 36; 9 : 5, 7, 10, 21. Hence in 9 : 23, 24, we read, "And Moses and Aaron went into the tabernacle of the congregation, and came out, and blessed the people: and the glory of the Lord appeared unto all the people. And there came a fire out from before the Lord, and consumed upon the altar the burnt offering and the fat: which, when all the people saw, they shouted, and fell on their faces." But at the beginning of chapter 10 we are told, "And Nadab and Abihu, the sons of Aaron, took either of them his censer, and put fire therein, and put incense thereon, and offered strange fire before the Lord, which He commanded them not. And there went out fire from the Lord, and devoured them, and they died before the Lord" (vv. 1, 2).

Man spoils everything. No matter what God entrusts to him, he betrays that trust. Place him in the position of highest dignity and he will disgrace himself; endow him with the greatest of privileges, and he will abuse them. Thus it was here. Hardly had the shouts of praise of 9 : 24 died away than the elements of a spurious worship were introduced. No sooner had those sons of Aaron been inducted into their holy office, than they failed miserably in their sacred functions. They departed from the explicit instructions of Jehovah; they did that which "He commanded them not."

The consequences of their disobedience were unspeakably solemn: fire came out from the Lord and consumed them. What a contrast was that from what is recorded in 9 : 24! There we behold Jehovah's acceptance of the true sacrifice; here we witness His judgment upon the false worship of self-willed priests. There the fire fed on that which spoke of Christ; here it is seen destroying that which was of the flesh. The sons of Aaron departed from God's arrangements, and substituted their own devices. No fire was to be used for the burning of the incense save that which was the gift of God, kindled from off His own altar. Because Nadab and Abihu introduced "strange (foreign) fire" they were slain. And this is placed on lasting record for our learning and warning!

As we have pointed out the fire or live coals beneath the incense foreshadowed the power of the Holy Spirit behind all true and Divinely-acceptable worship; for even the believer can no more work himself up into a frame of worship than he can create a world. Yet this basic fact is almost universally denied to-day—in action, in reality, if not in words. And that is why we now witness, on every side, those "having a form of godliness but denying the *power* thereof" (2 Tim. 3, 5). Instead of praying down Divine blessing, men attempt to work up religious fervour. Instead of humbly seeking the presence, power and blessing of the Holy Spirit, modern preachers seek to "create an atmosphere of worship." Instead of maintaining the simplicity that is in Christ (2 Cor. 11 : 3), all the adjuncts of a man-made religion are called in—costly organs, trained choirs, a godless orator in the pulpit; or so-called "speaking in tongues" or "faith-healings" (?) are brought in to stir the emotions. All these things are but modern forms of this "strange fire." The result is that the Spirit of God is resisted, grieved, quenched.

Contrast things at the beginning of the dispensation: what made the ministry of the apostles so effective? Why was it that the Word of God through Peter and Paul, Barnabas and Apollos, grew so rapidly and prevailed so mightily? Not because of their eloquence or gifts of human learning; nor because of an elaborate and expensive organization, with its complex machinery, behind them. It was because they were "filled with the Spirit"! And why are things now at such a low ebb through the whole of Christendom? It is because of the "strange fire" which now burns in almost every pulpit. Nor is the whole of the blame to be laid at the preachers' doors. The majority of the members in the average church (?) demand it. They stipulate for a man who can draw and hold a crowd, and are willing to pay him at the market rates. They insist that "bright music" should be provided, and goddess soloists be employed to entertain the people. What are these things but bringing "strange fire" into what is professedly the house of God."

For their daring impiety Nadab and Abihu were slain, and to the offering of "strange fire" to-day there is attached spiritual death. Few expressions are now more commonly used when describing existing conditions than to say that such a "church" is *dead*, or the services were *lifeless*. Ah, where there is a cessation of the Divine workings of the Holy Spirit, things quickly droop, wither, die. And the remedy for these evils is not *more* "strange fire," though at the present hour this is what is commonly resorted to. One minister is asked to resign that another of more popular talents may be secured. Or, new God-dishonouring means are used to make the services more attractive to worldlings. Or, sensational novelties are introduced to work up interest and excitement as a substitute for spiritual life.

Oh, what a solemn warning was pointed by the contents of the opening verses of Lev. 10! God will own no substitute for the One whom He has given to prompt and direct the worship of His people. Then let us honour the person, presence, and power of the Holy Spirit by owning that He alone can supply the energy for true worship—supply it by occupying our hearts with Christ. Let us confess our sins and get right with God, that the Spirit may be free to perform this His highest office. Let us not insult Him by bringing into the public services any fleshly devices. Let us feed the heavenly flame with the fuel God has provided, even His own Word. Let us adhere strictly to His arrangements, changing nothing, omitting nothing, adding nothing. Let us *seek* more the help and blessing of the Spirit, and then shall we enter into the good of that promise, "Them that honour Me, I will honour."

6. *The place of worship.*

A separate article might well be devoted to this particular aspect of our theme, for upon it the greatest ignorance and confusion prevails generally. But a few words only must now suffice. Let it be said emphatically and without qualification that, there is *no* "place" of worship, as such, anywhere on earth. During O.T. times there was. When the Lord Jesus was here there was, though He plainly intimated that the order of things which existed was, even then, on the very eve of passing away. To the Samaritan woman who had raised this very point with Him, He declared, "Woman, believe Me, the hour cometh, when ye shall neither in this mountain, nor yet at Jerusalem, worship the Father" (John 4 : 21). In a few years Jerusalem would be over-run by the Romans and the Temple destroyed, and since that time there has been no Divinely-appointed place of worship anywhere on earth.

Obviously, the place of worship is where God is, and that is, in Heaven. Where a man's treasure is, there will his heart be also ; and, as the Redeemer is now seated at the right hand of God, the Divine admonition to the redeemed is, " If ye then be risen with Christ, seek those things which are above. . . . Set your affection on things above, not on things on the earth " (Col. 3 : 1, 2).

The *place* of worship was plainly foreshadowed in connection with the Tabernacle. As we have seen, the emblem of worship was the incense, which was burned and ascended in fragrant clouds. And *where* was it burned ? In the outer court ? No, indeed ; inside the holy place. But into it, none save the priests were allowed to enter. The antitype of this is plainly revealed in the N.T. Believers in the Lord Jesus have been made " kings and priests unto God " (Rev. 1 : 6), and a " new and living way " has been opened for them, " through the veil," that is, through the rent body of Christ, Therefore is it written, " Having therefore brethren, boldness to enter into the holiest by the blood of Jesus, and having a High Priest over the house of God ; Let us draw near with a true heart in full assurance of faith " (Heb. 10 : 19-22). Thus, the true place of worship is in Heaven, within the veil, whither, in spirit, in faith, all the blood-bought family are bidden to draw near.

7. *Hindrances to worship.*

What is worship ? Praise ? yea, more ; it is the adoration flowing forth from a heart which is fully assured of the excellency of Him before whom it bows, expressing its profoundest gratitude for His unspeakable Gift. Therefore it is at once apparent that the first hindrance to worship in a child of God is *lack of assurance.* Whilst I entertain doubts as to my acceptance in Christ, as long as I remain in a state of uncertainty as to whether *my* sins were atoned for at Calvary, I cannot, really, praise and adore Him for His death for me ; I cannot actually say " my Beloved is mine, and I am His." It is one of the favourite devices of the enemy to keep Christians in the " Slough of Despond," his object being that Christ should not receive from them the homage of their hearts.

Lack of assurance in the Christian is generally due to two things : failure to rest in simple confidence on the bare Word of God, and failure to go on with Christ, the heart being daily occupied with Him. The Saviour has expressly declared, " him that cometh to Me, I will in no wise cast out " (*John* 6—37). If then I have " come to Him," come as a poor, lost, hell-deserving sinner; come to Him empty-handed as the sinner's only hope, then it is my privilege, yea my duty, to rely upon His promise. Again: God has said, " Whosoever shall call upon the name of the Lord shall be saved " (Rom 10—13). If then I have called, called upon Him for mercy, then I have His own infallible word for it that I " shall be saved." What more do I want? It is not a question of feelings, nor of looking within, for confirmatory " evidences "; it is a matter of resting on something *outside* myself, namely, the infallible Word of Him that cannot lie. *That* is how assurance is obtained.

And how is it *maintained*? By continuing as I began. By going on with Christ. By making *Him* my all in all. By feeding on the Word, and thereby " growing in grace and in the knowledge of our Lord and Saviour Jesus Christ " (1 Peter 2:2; 2 Peter 3:18). But many are hindered at this point through sitting under a defective ministry, a ministry which is mainly of a subjective or " experimental " character. The preaching they listen to is largely upon the depravity and helplessness of men. The result is that the Christian's eyes are taken off Christ, and he becomes occupied with self, either his sinful self or his religious self. And then peace, experimentally, is at an end. So, too, is worship! And the tragic thing is that thousands are taught that this state of despondency and doubting is a good sign, that it is an evidence of humility, that it is the very thing to be desired. Such expressions as " Rejoice in the Lord alway " (Phil. 4:4), and " By Him therefore let us offer the sacrifice of praise " (Heb. 13:15) are passed over as if they were not in the Word at all.

The fact of the matter is that many of God's children, to use the language of the Tabernacle types, get no further than the brazen-altar. But *that* stood not in the holy place, but in the outer court. No incense was burned upon it. The brazen altar was where the question of *sin* was dealt with, and where the atoning offering for it was presented unto Jehovah. And it is there that so many of God's dear children stop short. They are still wondering whether or not Christ died for *their* sins. They are still in the outer court. There is no real approach unto God Himself within the veil.

How many of God's people are still crying " God be merciful to me a sinner," and imagine that such a petition is very acceptable to God and most becoming to themselves. They forget that that was the prayer of one who stood " afar off " (Luke 18:13). Such words are perfectly proper from one who has just been convicted of sin; but they are most dishonouring to God from one who has already cried to Him for mercy, cast himself upon Christ, and therefore has been " accepted in the Beloved." The prodigal son, when he discovered what a sinner he was, did not remain in the " far country," but " arose and came to his Father " (Luke 15:20). And the Father did not allow him to remain on the outside, still in his rags; no, He clothed him, brought him inside, and seated him at His table—which is the place of communion and worship. O that His people to-day would *enjoy* that wondrous place into which grace has *already* brought them. So the priests of Israel did not remain at the brazen altar, but passed into the holy place, and there burned incense on the golden altar. O may we who have already been " made kings and priests unto God " (Rev. 1:6) *exercise* our priestly privileges and pass, in spirit, within the veil, and there worship Him who is seated upon the Throne of Grace.

Another great hindrance to worship is *failure to judge ourselves* by the Holy Word of God. Above, we have stated that the priests did not remain at the brazen altar in the outer court. But it needs to be pointed out that *before* they passed into the holy place, there to burn incense, they were required to *wash* at the laver. As we have already written thereon (see Gleanings in Exodus for July, 1928), a very brief reference here must suffice. Approach unto the laver of brass speaks of the believer's unsparing judgment of and upon himself (cf. 1 Cor. 11:31). The using of its water points to the application of the Word to all our works and ways. Of old the question was asked, " Wherewithal shall a young man cleanse his way? " And the unchanging answer is " By taking heed thereto according to Thy Word " (Psa. 119:9).

Now just as the sons of Aaron were required under pain of death (Ex. 30:20) to wash at the laver before they entered the holy place to burn incense, so must the Christian to-day have the defilements of the way removed before he can suitably approach unto God as a worshipper. Failure at this point brings in death, that is, I remain under the contaminating power of dead things. The defilements of the way are the results of my passing through a world which is " alienated from the life of God " (Eph. 4:18). If these are not removed, then I continue under the power of death in a spiritual way, and worship becomes impossible. This is brought out fully in John 13, where the Lord said to Peter, " If I wash thee not, thou hast no part *with* Me." How many Christians there are who, through failure to place their feet in the hands of Christ for cleansing, are hindered from exercising their priestly functions and privileges!

One other fatal hindrance to worship needs to be mentioned, and that is *worldliness*, which means the things of the world obtaining a place in the Christian's affections, and, as the result, his ways becoming " conformed to this world " (Rom. 12 : 2). A solemn example of this is found in the history of Abraham. When God called him to leave Chaldea and go into Canaan, he compromised : he went only as far as Haran (Gen. 11 : 31 ; Acts 7 : 4) and settled down there. Haran was Half-way House, the wilderness lying between it and the borders of Canaan. Later, Abraham fully responded to God's call and entered Canaan, and " there he builded an altar (which speaks of worship) unto the Lord " (Gen. 12 : 7). But there is no mention of his building any " altar " during the years he dwelt in Haran ! O how many children of God to-day are compromising, dwelling at Half-way House, and in consequence they are not worshippers.

O that the Spirit of God may be graciously pleased to deliver many a Christian reader of these pages from these God-dishonouring hindrances. O that He may so work upon and within all of us that the language of our lives, as well as of our hearts and lips, may be " worthy is the Lamb "—worthy of whole-hearted consecration, worthy of unstinted devotion, worthy of that love which is manifested by keeping His commandments, worthy of real worship. May it be so for His name's sake.

—*Arthur W. Pink.*

SOBRIETY.

This little paper does not profess to do more than bring under the notice of our readers a few texts out of God's Word bearing upon the above subject.

The time has come to a very large extent indeed, which is spoken of in 2 Tim. 4 : 3, 4, which says, " For the time will come when they will not endure sound doctrine ; but after their own lusts shall they heap to themselves teachers, having itching ears ; and they shall turn away their ears from the truth, and shall be turned unto fables." If we look at much of the so-called ministry of our day, how strikingly true this all is. The tendency nowadays is to gloss over the truth of God with man's philosophy, and to bring in a large spice of humour, to be what is called a *popular* preacher. A man who preaches God's truth in a plain, unvarnished way and who tells man the whole truth about himself, as seen in the Word of God, has often to be content with a very small audience.

But we can thank God that we have very plain instructions in His own Word, which the Psalmist declares " is a lamp unto my feet, and a light unto my path " (Psa. 119 : 105). Whatever the consequences of following the Word are to sight, we know by faith that we have God's own approval, which is much to be preferred to man's. 1 Sam. 15 : 22, says, " Behold, to obey is better than sacrifice, and to hearken than the fat of rams." I am afraid that a large number of Christians practically by their lives quote the above text the other way about. You may say that I am taking up this subject in regard to public ministry principally. I believe in these perilous times we may be tempted to follow the ways of those whom we spoke of, on the principle that the end justifies the means—a principle entirely contrary to the teaching of Scripture. Thus the hearers are leavened by the conduct of those who profess to be leaders. A little of ourselves introduced into the things of God is graphically described in Eccl. 10 : 1, " Dead flies cause the ointment of the apothecary to send forth a stinking savour : so doth a little folly him that is in reputation for wisdom and honour."

Titus 2 presents to us, in a very remarkable way, the mind of the Spirit on the point of sobriety. You will find, on reading it, that *all* classes of Christians are here plainly exhorted to soberness. Verse 2 exhorts that " the aged men be sober, grave, &c." ; verse 3, that the " aged women likewise." Then in verse 4, the aged women are exhorted to teach the young women to be sober. In verse 6, Titus is told to exhort the young men to be sober-minded ; and in verse 7 the Apostle Paul exhorts Titus himself to gravity. Finally, in verse 12, it speaks about the grace of God " teaching us that, denying ungodliness and worldly lusts, we should live soberly, righteously, and godly in this present world."

If we look at the Epistles to Timothy and Titus, we shall find that bishops and deacons, with their wives, are exhorted to gravity. This subject is not confined to speaking publicly, but applies also to speaking privately, to the way we adorn our homes, and our persons, and to all our actions down here ; for 1 Tim. 2 : 9, in proof of this, speaks about dressing with sobriety. 1 Peter 4 : 7 gives us one reason why we should be sober : " But the end of all things is at hand : be ye therefore *sober*, and watch unto prayer." As the end of all things draws near, and all, both in the world and the Church, is undergoing a disintegrating process, it behoves us to be sober and watchful, that we have the mind of the Lord as we go on.

1 Peter 5:8 gives us a second reason: "Be *sober*, be vigilant; because your adversary the devil, as a roaring lion, walketh about, seeking whom he may devour." We find the same principle at work in worldly matters. The soldiers who guard a camp, hourly expecting an attack, do not sit down, laughing, joking, and amusing themselves. We find every sense on the alert, and complete sobriety, in order to detect the least movement of the enemy. So we, as Christians, should be in a similar condition in a spiritual sense. Our enemy is more subtle than a natural one, and we are more ignorant of his devices than of those of an enemy of flesh and blood. Christians may say that they don't want to become misanthropes. I would say to such, the Word of God should be our standard in these matters, and should judge and correct our ways. The sobriety of Scripture does not allow us to conduct ourselves in a light, frivolous way, but it admits of a true joy and rejoicing, as Phil. 4:4, says, "Rejoice in the Lord alway; and again I say, rejoice."

I have heard Christians ridiculing the idea of a sober joy as a paradox, but I think the Scriptures bears us out on this point. Again, many dear Christians excuse themselves and others on the plea of nature. They say it is natural amd they cannot help it. Sin is natural to the old man, and yet that never excuses or palliates it. Let us allow the Word of God a true place in our hearts, and let it govern our ways, whether it is against nature or not. In fact, the teaching of the Word of God is entirely opposed to the natural man, as 1 Cor. 2:14 says, "The natural man receiveth not the things of the Spirit of God."

This has been written in no spirit of fault-finding or spiritual pride, for the writer knows that it applies more to himself than to most of his readers. May God bless it for His own name's sake, is our earnest prayer.

Simple Testimony, 1887

CHRIST AS MASTER

There are seven different titles given to our Lord, all of which are rendered in our English Bible by the word Master. Each of these has its own proper meaning, and is applied to Him appropriately, thus furnishing one of ten thousand proofs of verbal inspiration. The sacred writers make no mistake, but in every instance use the term that is suitable to Him in the character, and for the purpose, which led various persons on various occasions to address Him, or led Him to speak of Himself under one or another of the many names that have the common translation of Master.

First, we find an excellent young man running to Him with the cry, "Good Master, what shall I do that I may inherit eternal life?" Our Lord met him on the ground of his own choosing, and told him, if it was a question of doing, to keep the commandments. "Master," was the reply, "all these have I kept from my youth up" (Mark 10:17, 20). Here the word is didaskolos, teacher, and it is so rendered in the remark of Nicodemus, "We know that Thou art a teacher come from God" (John 3:2). It occurs forty-six times in the Gospels, and always implies one who is competent to show the way of salvation, or to teach the Truth. It is blessed to know that we have such a Master, and that under His instructions we can make no mistake, and fall into no error.

Second, He is called epistatees, from a verb which signifies "to stand by or near, to come near, to be at hand." Thus we find Peter saying to Him, "Master, we have toiled all the night, and have taken nothing" (Luke 5:5). The disciples awoke Him in the storm with the shriek of alarm and despair, "Master, Master, we perish" (Luke 8:24); and the poor lepers who stood afar off, lifted up their voices and said, "Jesus, Master, have mercy on us" (Luke 17:13). It is easy to see in these incidents how appropriate is the title, which represents Him as standing by, as at hand, to comfort and encourage and deliver those in need.

Third, He is also called katheegeetees, from a verb meaning "to lead, conduct." In the light of this fact, new significance is imparted to His command, "Neither be ye called masters; for one is your Master (your leader), even Christ" (Matthew 23:10). He thus strikes directly at the root of the ambition, which causes so many to aspire to leadership among their brethren, and at the servility which follows. There are thousands in the church and the ministry who can give no better reason for their faith than the fact that Dr. So-and-So holds the view they advocate, or that it is the written or unwritten creed of the ecclesiastical organisation to which they belong. Christ as Master is the only leader, and to His Word alone we are to be in subjection at the peril of our souls.

Fourth, kurios, Lord, is the title He assumes when He says "Watch ye therefore; for ye know not when the master of the house cometh, at even, or at midnight, or at the cock-crowing, or in the morning" (Mark 13:35). He seems here to anticipate the discoveries of modern astronomy, for when

He descends into the air, and pauses in His journey to the earth long enough to summon His sleeping saints from the grave, and to transform living believers into His glorious likeness, that stupendous event will take place to some at even, to others farther east at midnight, to others still farther east at morning, and to others still farther east at mid-day. It is not strange that the Master that comes in the pomp of that tremendous day speaks of Himself as Lord.

Fifth, rabbi, is another title by which He was addressed, as when Peter said to Him on the mount of transfiguration, " Master, it is good for us to be here" (Mark 9 : 5) ; and again, " Master, behold, the fig tree which Thou cursedst is withered away " (Mark 11 : 21). The name is from the Hebrew, signifying " great, chief, mighty," and it is peculiarly appropriate when given to Him in connection with a scene which was designed to afford us a glimpse of His millennial kingdom, in which Israel shall once more become the head of the nations, and when the fig-tree was cursed, the symbol of Israel's shame and rejection, until that kingdom shall be established in its regal splendour and power.

Sixth, He is the despotees, not of course a cruel and tyrannical despot, but absolutely sovereign in His sway, and exercising supreme authority in the service He demands at the hands of His followers. In the last epistle the devoted Paul was inspired to write, he views the professing Church as a great house, containing not only " vessels of gold and silver, but also of wood and of earth ; and some to honour, and some to dishonour. If a man therefore purge himself from these, he shall be a vessel unto honour, sanctified, and meet for the Master's (despotees) use, and prepared unto every good work " (2 Timothy 2 : 20, 21). He claims service at the hands of every one He has purchased with His precious blood, and He claims it with the imperious demand of an infinitely good and wise and independent monarch. Let us at once respond to the calls of a Master who will brook no disobedience.

Seventh, the last of these suggestive titles is oikodespotees, denoting His undisputed authority over His own house. With this in view we are comforted by the thought, that " if they have called the master of the house Beelzebub, how much more shall they call them of his household " (Matthew 10 : 25) ; and we are searched by the solemn announcement, " When once the Master of the house is risen up, and hath shut to the door, and ye begin to stand without, and to knock at the door, saying, Lord, Lord, open unto us ; and He shall answer and say unto you, I know you not whence ye are : then shall ye begin to say, We have eaten and drunk in Thy presence, and Thou hast taught in our streets. But He shall say, I tell you, I know you not whence ye are ; depart from me all ye workers of iniquity " (Luke 13 : 25-27). Well would it be to recognise Him as our Master in these various relations suggested by these various titles, and as we remember the present, certain, and eternal salvation He so freely bestows upon the believer, to enter into the measure of the apostle's happy and sustained consecration, when he wrote, " the love of Christ constraineth us " (2 Corinthians 5 : 14).

—"*The Truth,*" Vol. 13.

QUALIFICATIONS OF A PREACHER.

You requested me to give you my thoughts concerning what I conceive to be a qualification and call to the ministry. I will, with pleasure, communicate my views on the subject, which are these. I take it for granted a person is not fit to minister in holy things, except he be regenerated and born of God. He should be a partaker of Christ, who attempts to speak in the name of Christ.

He is not fit to feed the flock of God, who is not one of the flock ; if he be one of the flock and in the kingdom of God's dear Son, and the Lord designs him for the ministry, He will fit and qualify him accordingly. I do not look on myself, or any other, sent out immediately by the Lord as the apostles and evangelists were. It is now more under the direction and influence of the Holy Spirit in a *providential* way. The Lord fits such as He means to make use of with gifts, whereby they are suited to instruct and direct others. This is *taken notice of* by some company or other of God's people, or by a regular church of Jesus Christ. Hereby the person is called forth to exercise the gifts the Lord hath bestowed upon him. He is not a proper judge of himself ; it is for those who engage him to judge of his qualification ; and if they find real spiritual edification in what he delivers from the Scriptures of truth, I think it follows of course, he has a right to go forth in the strength of the Lord, to preach the everlasting Gospel of the ever-blessed God. Whomsoever the Lord calls to be a preacher, He bestows on him gifts to fit him for the work designed. These gifts are spiritual ones ; they do not make the person on whom they are bestowed spiritual, but being bestowed on a spiritual person, he is enabled, by the teachings of the Holy Spirit, to exercise them to the praise and glory of God. All have not gifts alike, nor do they require them. The Lord confers on all His sent servants, just such a measure of them as is needful, and to answer the end He pleases. These increase by the use and exercise thereof. They are given for the benefit of others, not to make any man shine on whom they are bestowed, but that the grace of God may be displayed towards His church, for the sake of which He hath bestowed them. Ministers, and spiritual gifts, are the fruits of Christ's ascension, and are bestowed for the edifying of the body of Christ. With respect to a man's real call to the ministry, I think the voice of the people is, in this case, the voice of God; and let him be ever so unwilling to preach, yet if the Lord thrusts Him out by His holy providence, and by repeated calls of persons of truth, understanding, and godliness, it is his duty to preach and minister as of the ability which God giveth, that God in all things may be glorified through Jesus Christ, to whom be glory and dominion for ever and ever. Amen.

A man whom the Lord qualifies to preach, is one who loves our Lord Jesus Christ in sincerity. Next to his love for Christ he loves such as love Christ, and is desirous of serving the cause and interest of Christ, and His church. He should never look at the gift the Lord hath bestowed on him, so as to be discouraged. It would be well to know it, so as to improve it for the particular purpose given. If it be a doctrinal gift it should be followed. In opening the truths, doctrines, and mysteries of the everlasting Gospel, much light will be increasingly let into the mind of the preacher, and he will in the exercise of his gift, increase with the increase of God. If the gift be of an awakening sort, the Lord will set home the worth of souls on the mind, and such portions of the Word, too, as shall fill the preacher's mind with holy arguments, to plead with sinners, and from knowing the terrors of the Lord, to persuade men to enter into a serious consideration of their state and case as sinners in the sight of a most holy God; and also to attend closely and thoroughly to what the Lord God hath set before them in His written Word. If the gift be of an experimental kind, and consist in opening and explaining the operations of the Holy Spirit on the minds of the regenerate; in describing how the Holy Spirit reveals Christ; in what way He testifies of Jesus, and forms Him in the heart; this gift should be exercised with immediate design to answer this end, to show what is the real work of God on the soul and what is not: and this gift, more or less exercised, will be owned of God. If the gift be particularly designed and calculated to show the deceitfulness of the heart, the workings of sin and Satan, or his malice against the saints of the Most High, let it be pursued. Every man should exercise the particular gift God hath given him; and he should be content with it; he should not drop it, but improve it. No one man, let him be who or what he may be in the church of Christ, hath all man's gifts. Every one whom the Lord sends, is useful in the Lord's church, and among His people, just as He pleases. There is as much need of small gifts as great ones, and the Lord will, and at times does, bless a man of very slender abilities, more than a real saint of greater, to show His sovereignty, and to prove that power belongeth unto God. As it would be a sin to speak against a man sent of God because his gifts are not great, so it is equally sinful to speak against a man whose gifts are great: in both cases there is too much self-importance.

If it be required of men to give answer to such a question as this: How shall a person know that he is called to preach the Word of truth? I would reply, by the persons who call Him. Are they the Lord's? Do they spiritually discern the things of God? Have they a spiritual relish? Do they spiritually digest the Word, and are they nourished by it? Do their love and faith in Christ abound in consequence of what they hear? Then surely a person can have no reason to doubt of his call to preach unto such; and if unto these, he need not be backward in preaching to others also, when and where desired. I would also add, it is truly delightful to preach Jesus Christ; to recommend Him to others, to spread His fame, to be aiming to gain Him glorious praise. Surely these are as good evidences of being called to the work of the ministry as can be given. It is an honour to speak for Christ, if sent by the Lord to do so. It will always be proved by this. We shall never want to be exalted, but only aim to set forth Christ; our best sermons will always fill us with shame and confusion of face; we shall never take state to ourselves, or want great I to be exalted.

Now, my good friend, these are my views of the subject, and I believe you will find no difficulty in saying, I have in a brief way and manner said enough. As the Lord has given you a *desire*, a *gift*, and an *opportunity* to speak for Him, go on, and the Lord be with you. You can do no harm in preaching and teaching Christ. Do not look at your gift, whether great or small, so as to be encouraged or discouraged; look at it so as to know wherein it consists, and look up to the Lord, that you may be taught how to lay it out, and to improve it to real advantage. Have nothing to do with what people whom you have no concern with may say or think: you have one qualification which the Lord hath bestowed on you, and which I am sure is very rarely found and wondrously did our faithful God answer: as Mrs. Pink expressed it, "God wrought miracles for us every day." We were on the mighty deep for forty days, yet though passing through the Pacific, Indian, and part of the Atlantic Oceans, the Arabian and Mediterranean Seas, the Bay of Biscay, &c., we never encountered so much as a squall. This was the more remarkable, as it was the monsoonal trip, and storms were predicted and expected. The three days and nights we were in the Red Sea (the hottest part of the trip), our gracious God caused a fresh and cool head-wind to blow all the time.

We arrived in London August 30th. As stated in a previous issue, we had received no human invitations or calls, and no "open door" was apparent to sight. Following six weeks' oral silence on ship (we encountered not a single Christian among our five hundred fellow passengers), a further period of four weeks' inactivity followed our landing. But our hearts were kept in perfect peace. By Divine grace we were enabled to "rest in the Lord, and wait patiently for Him" (Psa. 37:7). We are His servants, therefore it is His to command, ours to obey. At the end of September, without any knocking on doors or seeking brethren to use their influence on our behalf, quite unsought on our part, a Devonshire reader of this Magazine kindly opened his home to us and opportunities to minister the Word in that neighbourhood are now being afforded. It is in this district we felt that the Lord would have us first pitch our tent. We shall value the earnest prayers of God's people that the Good Shepherd will graciously grant us access to many of His hungry sheep, and enable us to lead them into the green pastures of His Ward.

We are counting on God enabling us to continue this publication. As our present movements are so uncertain, we would ask our friends to wait patiently for the next few issues. We shall do our best to publish and mail out as promptly as possible. The 1928 Vol. has to be bound in Australia, so copies will not be ready for mailing for many weeks. Those who have ordered bound volumes should not look for them D.V., any earlier than March 1, 1929,—they will be 3s. (75 cents) each, which is cost price. We are still very desirous of increasing circulation, and shall value the names and addresses of those who would welcome this publication. With hearty greetings to all, we remain, by God's wondrous grace,

A. W. & V. E. PINK.

---

in our day and times, and that is a simplicity of mind, which I most highly esteem and love you for. I am persuaded the Lord bestowed it on you, and considered as a gift from Him, it is invaluable. Lay it out to His praise. I suppose you are never fully satisfied with any one sermon you preach: so much the better, it is of God, for He does not mean you should be. Neither am I. I am always satisfied with the subject, not with myself for delivering it. You will, again and again, have trials in preaching, and think you will never preach more. This is a temptation, which, if you are not exercised with you must differ vastly from others; but do not give place to the devil in acquiescing in it.

My good friend, as you look to Jesus, there is nothing to discourage you; but if you regard the people, yea, the very people of the Lord, you will have abundant discouragements. It is the case with all who preach, you must therefore leave them all out, and say, I will look to the Lord, I will wait for the God of my salvation, my God will hear me.

May the Lord Jesus Christ shine upon you. May He bless, direct, and keep you, and so shine on your mind as to give you a clear knowledge of His own counsel and will concerning you.

A letter of S. E. Pierce, 1810.

ANXIOUS CARE.

In a published letter of Luther's to his wife, he reproves her with gentle irony for her anxious care for him. Here is an extract from the letter: "We thank you very fondly for the great care for us which has prevented you sleeping. Since the time you have taken this care upon you, the fire all but consumed us in our inn, breaking out outside my chamber door. And yesterday, no doubt in consequence of these cares of yours, a stone all but fell on our head and crushed us; in our room two days since, the lime and plaster crumbled away; for this also, we should have to thank your holy care, if the angels had not hindered. I fear, lest, if thou dost not give up thy anxieties, at the length, the earth itself may swallow us up, and all the elements turn against us."

Do thou pray, and leave God to care; has He not said "*Casting all your care upon Him, for He careth for you.*"

Next comes "peace," which is the product or fruit of mercy. First, peace of *conscience*, which is the result of knowing that all my sins have been removed from before God " as far as the east is from the west " : " Therefore being justified by faith, we have peace with God through our Lord Jesus Christ " (Rom. 5 : 1). Peace, perfect peace, in this dark world of sin ; the blood of Jesus whispers peace within ! Second, peace of *mind*. It is written, " Thou wilt keep him in perfect peace, whose mind is stayed on Thee : because he trusteth in Thee " (Isa. 26 : 3). Stayed upon Jehovah, hearts are fully blessed ; finding, as He promised, perfect peace and rest. To be thus, " Stayed upon Jehovah " means to leave everything with Him to work out as He sees best (see Phil. 4 : 6, 7). Third, peace of *heart*, such as Christ Himself enjoyed, as Man, when on earth. That, we believe, is the meaning of His word in John 14 : 27. " Peace I leave with you, *My peace* I give unto you ; not as the world giveth, give I unto you. Let not your *heart* be troubled, neither let it be afraid." This is maintained by child-like and unshaken confidence in the fact that " all things work together for good to them that love God, to them who are called according to His purpose " (Rom. 8 : 28).

Last, but not least, comes " love." As 1 Cor. 13 : 13 says " And now abideth faith, hope, love, these three ; but the greatest of these is love," for " God is love." Then why should " love " be mentioned last here in Jude 2 ? Because it is only as we are the recipients of Divine mercy, and as peace is our experimental portion, that we are able to enter into the realisation and enjoyment of Divine love. And it is only as we ourselves are " merciful " (Matt. 5 : 7) and " follow peace with all " (Heb. 12 : 14), that we are capable of exercising that love which " suffereth long and is kind," which " seeketh not her own, is not easily provoked, thinketh no evil," which " beareth all things, believeth all things, hopeth all things, endureth all things " (1 Cor. 13). Yes, it is " love " which needs to be " *multiplied* unto " us !

And now, as this number is the closing one of Vol. 7, we must make mention of the Lord's goodness to us through another year. " Hath He said, and shall He not do ? or hath He spoken, and shall He not make it good ? " (Num. 23 : 19). He has promised that He would supply *all* our need (Phil. 4 : 19), and He has. Through another twelve months our gracious God has sustained both the editor and his wife in health and strength. Notwithstanding many preaching engagements, we have been enabled to keep as busy as ever with our pen. By the Lord's goodness and the clerical help of a few self-sacrificing friends, we have, in spite of having to cross from one end of the earth to the other, been permitted to issue and mail out the " Studies " as usual, without any break. Prayer has been answered for an enlarged circulation, and we are deeply thankful for that grace which has brought us into touch with several hundreds more of the Lord's needy people, affording us the unspeakable privilege of setting before them some of the treasures to be found in God's wondrous Word.

During 1928 our expenses increased quite a little, but so also have the gifts from God's stewards, so that by the abounding mercy of Him whom we serve, we close another year with a balance to the good. We have no regrets for having removed the subscription price, nor have we had a single moment's anxiety as to the incoming of funds to continue sending out this magazine free to all who will read it. We make no appeal for funds. Yet Christian readers should be reminded that it is both their privilege and responsibility to have fellowship in the maintenance of this work of faith and labour of love. Neither of us take out a penny for ourselves, and any surplus at the end of the year is used to send out free tracts and books to those unable to purchase them. We are receiving an increased number of requests from refugee Armenians, native workers in India and China who can read English, and lonely Missionaries, for some of our larger works, such as " The Sovereignty of God," " Redeemer's Return," " The Anti-Christ," " The Seven Sayings of the Saviour on the Cross," &c. During 1928 we sent out free well over £100's ($500) worth of such literature, and we are fully assured that those who had part with us in this much-needed ministry have laid up for themselves " treasure in heaven."

In these days of deepening apostasy, conscientious Christians are finding it an increasingly difficult matter as to where to place their gifts for God's glory. His Word plainly teaches us to " have *no* fellowship with the unfruitful works of darkness." As so many are departing from the faith (1 Tim. 4 : 1), it behoves us to be doubly on our guard, lest we be found supporting that which is dishonouring to Christ. There are hundreds of unregenerate missionaries now out on the field, and being unsaved themselves, they can only be " blind leaders of the blind." But God has His own sent-servants who are seeking out His lost sheep. These it is our happy privilege to support and encourage in every way possible. During 1928 we had the joy of forwarding to those sound in the faith over £100, sent in by the Lord's stewards—most of it for the translation and circulation of the pure Word of God. Will not each Christian reader definitely look to the Lord to see if He would have *you* have a part in this work.

We desire to heartily thank our many Christian friends who daily prayed for " journeying mercies " for us during our 12,500 miles' trip from Sydney to London. Abundantly

Continued on page 287.

STUDIES IN THE SCRIPTURES

"Search the Scriptures" John 5 : 39

Copyright in all English-speaking Countries.

Editor: Arthur W. Pink, Sidmouth Road, Seaton, Devon, England.
Hon. Agent in U.S.A.: Mr. C. S. Pressel, 559, Dupont Avenue, York, Penna.
Hon. Agent in Australia: Mr. G. Ardill, The Christian Workers' Depot.
Commonwealth and Reservoir Streets, Sydney.

FREE TO ALL WHO WILL READ IT.

DEDICATION.

"*And this they did, not as we hoped, but first gave their own selves to the Lord, and unto us by the will of God.*" (2 Cor. 8: 5).

Before attempting to open-up the theme of this verse, a few words require to be said upon its setting. In 2 Cor. 8 the apostle sought to stir up the local saints to more liberality in giving. He begins by setting before them the encouraging example furnished by their fellow-Christians in the Macedonian churches. He says, " Moreover, brethren, we do you to wit of the grace of God bestowed on the churches of Macedonia." The words " we do you to wit," is an archaic expression meaning " we make known to you." The noble generosity and abounding liberality of those Christians the apostle attributes to the " grace of God," thus giving Him the glory for it—a needful reminder for us. 2 Cor. 8: 1 presents a blessed contrast from Acts 16: 9: there it was the Macedonians calling on a converted Jew to come and help them; here the converted Macedonians were sending help to their Jewish brethren in Jerusalem.

" How that in a great trail of affliction the abundance of their joy and their deep poverty abounded unto the riches of their liberality " (v. 2). The reference here is to the social condition which then obtained. The state of Greece at that time was one of desolation and destitution. It had never recovered from the Roman conquest. Then too they had suffered long from the civil wars between Caesar and Pompey, Brutus and Cassius, Augustus and Antonius. The Macedonians had been heavily taxed to pay off the national debt, and were, financially, desperately poor.

" For to their power I bear, record, yea, and beyond their power, they were willing of themselves; Praying us with much intreaty that we would receive the gift, and take upon us the fellowship of the ministering to the saints " (vv. 3, 4). This tells us not a little about the spirit and nature of the giving of those early Christians. First, they gave " Beyond their power," denying themselves the bare necessities of life. Second, they did this " willingly," spontaneously, without being asked. Third, they earnestly pressed their gift upon Paul: " praying us with much intreaty "—which intimates that, under their distressing circumstances, the apostle was reluctant to accept their gifts.

" And this they did, not as we hoped, but first gave their own selves to the Lord." " Not as we hoped " means, far more than we expected or desired, " First *gave their own selves* to the Lord," explains it all. They had, unreservedly, dedicated themselves to God. They could truly say, " Naught that I have I call my own, I hold it for the Giver; For He is mine, and I am His, Forever and forever." Whole-hearted consecration to Christ is always evidenced by freely giving to His cause, His service, His people.

As this is the first number of our *eighth* volume, these words seem an appropriate introduction to it : " But *first* gave their own selves to the Lord." May this be the initial act of both writer and reader at the commencement of 1929. But perhaps our text sets forth an aspect of God's truth which many Calvinists know little or nothing about, for one fears that it will hardly fit in to one-sided creed of some. Not a few have been so repelled by Arminian preachers urging the unconverted to give their hearts to Christ, that probably some would receive quite a shock were they to discover that our text is in the Word of God. The fact is that Arminians have made a wrong use of a right thing : they have applied to unbelievers what belongs only to believers. Our text speaks of a dedication rendered, not by sinners in order to be saved, but by Christians because they were saved. It was the answering response of their hearts to the wondrous love of Him who " gave " Himself for them.

Continued on Page 24.

IMPORTANT NOTICES

Back numbers of the last four years of this magazine are yet obtainable, nicely and strongly bound at 7/6 each, post paid. They will soon be out of print. Those in U.S.A. wanting them, please purchase from Mr. Pressel (see front cover page).

Advise promptly of change of address otherwise copies will be lost in the mails.

This Magazine is published as a work of faith and labour of love. The Editor gladly gives his services. It is freely sent to all who will read it. No charge is made for it.

Christians who feel definitely led to do so, may have fellowship with us in this Ministry. Send only *Inter-National M.O.* made out to Seaton, Devon, England.

CONTENTS.

	Page
Hebrews	2
Gleanings in Exodus	7
Abraham's Call	11
Romans 7	15
The Sympathy and Grace of Christ	17
One of Christ's Little Ones	20
Jerusalem and Cyprus	22

THE EPISTLE TO THE HEBREWS.

13. *Christ Superior to Moses*: 3 : 1-6.

Our present portion introduces us to the third division of the Epistle, a division which runs on to 4:6. The first division, comprising but the three opening verses of the first chapter, evidences the superiority of Christ over the prophets. The second division, 1 : 4 to the end of chapter 2, sets forth the superiority of Christ over the angels. The one we are now commencing treats of the superiority of Christ over Moses. "The contents of this section may be stated briefly thus: That the Lord Jesus Christ, the mediator of the new covenant, is high above Moses, the mediator of the old dispensation, inasmuch as Jesus is the Son of God, and Lord *over* the house; whereas Moses is the servant of God, who is faithful *in* the house. And upon this doctrinal statement is based the exhortation, that we should not harden our hearts lest we fail to enter into that rest of which the possession of the promised land was only an imperfect type. This section consists of two parts—a doctrinal statement, which forms the basis, and an exhortation resting upon it" (Saphir).

Of all the godly characters brought before us in the O.T. scriptures, there is not one who has higher claims on our attentive consideration than the legislator of Israel. Whether we think of his remarkable infancy and childhood, his self-sacrificing renunciation (Heb. 11 : 24-26), the commission he received from God and his faithfulness in executing it, his devotion to Israel (Ex. 32 : 32), his honoured privileges (Ex. 31 : 18), or the important revolutions accomplished through his instrumentality; "it will be difficult to find," as another has said, "in the records either of profane or sacred history, an individual whose character is so well fitted at once to excite attachment and command veneration, and whose history is so replete at once with interest and instruction."

The history of Moses was remarkable from beginning to end. The hand of Providence preserved him as a babe, and the hand of God dug his grave at the finish. Between those termini he passed through the strangest and most contrastive vicissitudes which, surely, any mortal has ever experienced. The honours conferred upon him by God were much greater that any bestowed upon any other man, before or since. During the most memorable portion of their history, all of God's dealings with Israel were transacted through him. His position of nearness to Jehovah was remarkable, awesome, unique. He was in his own person, prophet, priest and king. Through him the whole of the Levitical economy was instituted. By him the Tabernacle was built. Thus we can well understand the high esteem in which the Jews held this favoured man of God—cf John 8 : 28, 29.

Yet great as was Moses, the Holy Spirit in this third section of Hebrews calls upon us to consider One who so far excelled him as the heavens are above the earth. First, Christ was the immeasurable superior of Moses in His own *person*: Moses was a man of God, Christ was God Himself. Moses was the fallen descendant of Adam, conceived in sin and shapen in iniquity; Christ was sinless, impeccable, holy. Again; Christ was the immeasurable superior of Moses in His *Offices*. Moses was a prophet, through whom God spake; Christ was Himself "the Truth," revealing perfectly the whole mind, will, and heart of God. Moses executed priestly functions (Ex. 24 : 6; 32 : 11); but Christ is the "great High Priest." Moses was "king in Jeshurun" (Deut. 33 : 5); Christ is "King of kings." To mention only one other comparison, Christ was the immeasurable superior of Moses in His *work*. Moses delivered Israel from Egypt, Christ delivers His people from the everlasting burnings. Moses built an earthly tabernacle, Christ is now preparing a place for us on High. Moses led Israel across the wilderness but not into the Canaan itself; Christ will actually bring many sons "unto glory." May the Holy Spirit impress our hearts more and more with the exalted dignity and unique excellency of our Saviour.

"Wherefore, holy brethren, partakers of the heavenly calling, consider the Apostle and High

Priest of our profession, Christ Jesus" (v.1). There are three things in this verse which claim our attention: the exhortation given, the people addressed, the characters in which Christ is here contemplated. The exhortation is a call to "consider" Christ. The people addressed are "holy brethren, partakers of the heavenly calling." The characters in which the Saviour is viewed are "the Apostle and High Priest."

"Wherefore." This word gives the connecting link between the two chapters which precede and the two that follow. It is a perfect transition, for it look both ways. In regard to that which goes before, our present verse makes known the *use* we are to make of it; we are to "consider" Christ, to have our hearts fixed upon Him who is "altogether lovely." In regard to that which follows, this basic exhortation lays a foundation for the succeeding admonitions: if we render obedience to *this* precept, then we shall be preserved from the evils which overtook Israel of old—hardening of the heart, grieving the Lord, missing our "rest."

The exhortation given here is, "Wherefore... consider the Apostle and High Priest of our profession." Three questions call for answers: what is meant by "considering" Him; why we should do so; the special characters in which He is to be considered. There are no less than eleven Greek words in the N.T. all rendered "consider," four of them being simple ones; seven, compounds. The one employed by the Holy Spirit in Heb. 3 : 1 signifies to thoroughly think of the matter, so as to arrive at a fuller knowledge of it. It was the word used by our Lord in His "consider the ravens, consider the lilies" (Luke 12 : 24, 27). It is the word which describes Peter's response to the vision of the sheet let down from heaven: "I considered and saw fourfooted beasts" (Acts 11 : 6). It is found again in Matt. 7 : 3, Rom. 4 : 19, Heb. 10 :24. In Acts 7 : 31 "katanoeo" is rendered "to behold." In Luke 20 : 23 it is translated "perceived." In all, the Greek word is found fourteen times in the N.T.

To "consider" Christ as here enjoined means, to thoroughly ponder who and what He is; to attentively weigh His dignity, His excellency, His authority; to think of what is *due* to Him. It is failure to thoroughly weigh important considerations which causes us to let them "slip" (Heb. 2:4). On the other hand, it is by diligently pondering things of moment and value that the understanding is enabled to better apprehend them, the memory to retain them, the heart to be impressed, and the individual to make a better use of them. To "consider" Christ means to *behold* Him, not simply by a passing glance or giving to Him an occasional thought, but by the heart being fully occupied with Him. "Set Me as a seal upon thine heart "(Song of Sol. 8 : 7), is His call to us. And it is our failure at this point which explains why we know so little about Him, why we love Him so feebly, why we trust Him so imperfectly.

The motive presented by the Spirit here as to *why* we should so "consider" Christ is intimated in the opening "Wherefore." It draws a conclusion from all that precedes. Because Christ is the One through whom Deity is now fully and finally manifested, because He is the Brightness of God's glory and the very Impress of His substance; because, therefore, He has by inheritance obtained a more excellent name than the angels; because He, in infinite grace, became "all of one" with those that He came to redeem, having made propitiation for the sins of His people; because He is now seated at the right hand of the Majesty on High, and while there is "a merciful and faithful High Priest;" because He has Himself suffered being tempted and is able to succor them who are tempted;—therefore, He is infinitely worthy of our constant contemplation and adoration. The opening "Wherfore" is also an anticipatory inference from what follows: because Christ is worthy of more honour than Moses, therefore, "consider" Him.

There are two special characters in which the Holy Spirit here bids us contemplate Christ. First, as "the Apostle." This has reference to the *prophetical* office of Christ, the title being employed because an "apostle" was the highest minister appointed in N.T. times. An apostleship had more honours conferred upon it than any other position in the church (Eph. 4 : 11): thus the excellency of Christ's prophetic office is magnified. The term apostle means one "sent forth" of God, endowed with authority as His ambassador. In John's Gospel Christ is frequently seen as the "Sent One," 3 : 34, 5 : 36, etc. The general function of Christ as a prophet, an apostle, a minister of the Word, was to make known the will of His Father unto His people. This He did, see John 8 : 26 etc. His special call to that function was immediate: "as My Father hath sent Me, so send I you" (John 20: 21).

Christ is more than an apostle, He is *"the* Apostle," that is why none others, not even Paul, are mentioned in this Epistle. He eclipses all others. He was the *first* apostle, the twelve being appointed by Him. His apostolic jurisdiction was more extensive than others; Peter was an apostle of the circumcision, Paul of the Gentiles; but Christ preached both to them that were nigh *and* to them that were far off (Eph. 2 : 17). He received the Spirit more abundantly than any other (John 3 : 34). With Him the Messenger was the message: He was Himself "the Truth." The miracles He wrought (the "signs of an apostle" Cor. 12 : 12) were mightier and more numerous than those of others. Verily, Christ is "the Apostle," for in *all* things He has the preeminence. The special duty for us arising therefrom is, "Hear ye Him" (Matt. 17 : 5)—cf Deut. 18 : 15, 18

The second character in which we are here bidden to "consider" Christ Jesus, is as the "High Priest of our profession." As the priesthood of Christ will come before us, D.V., in detail in the later chapters, only a few remarks thereon will now be offered. As we have already been told, the Lord Jesus is "a merciful and faithful High Priest in things pertaining to God" (2 : 17). This at once gives us the principal feature which differentiates His priestly from His prophetic office. As Prophet, Christ is God's representative to His people; as "Priest," He is their representative before God. As the Apostle He speaks *to* us from God, as our High Priest He speaks *for* us to God. The two offices are conjoined in John 13 : 3, "He was from God, and went to God." Thus He fills the whole space between God and us: as Apostle He is close to me; as Priest, He is close to God.

"Of our profession." The Greek word here is a compound and properly signifies "a consent." In the N.T. it is used for the confession of a thing (1 Tim. 6 : 12, 13), and to set forth the faith which Christians profess (Heb. 4 : 14). Here it may be taken either for an act on our part—the confessing Christ to be "the Apostle and High Priest," or, the subject matter *of* the faith we profess. Christians are not ashamed to own Him, for He is not ashamed to own them. The apostleship and priesthood of Christ are the distinguishing subjects of our faith, for Christianity centers entirely around the person of Christ. The confession is that which faith makes, see Heb. 10 : 23. The cognate of this word is found in Heb. 11 : 13 and 13 : 15, "giving thanks:" these two references emphasising the "stranger and pilgrim" character of this profession, of which Christ Jesus is the Apostle and High Priest.

It remains now for us to notice the people to whom this exhortation is addressed: they are denominated "holy brethren, partakers of the heavenly calling." These Hebrews were addressed as "brethren" because they belonged spiritually to the family of God. "He evidently refers to the blessed truth just announced, that Jesus, the Son of God, is not ashamed to call us brethren" (2 : 12). He means therefore those who by the Spirit of God have been born again, and who can call God their Father. He addresses those of God who are in Christ Jesus, who were quickened together with Him; for when He rose from the dead He was 'the first-born among many brethren'. He calls them 'holy brethren,' because upon this fact of brotherhood is based their sanctification: 'He that sanctifieth and they who are sanctified are all of one' (Saphir). No doubt the "holy brethren" was also designed to distinguish them from their brethren according to the flesh, the unbelieving Jews. By his use of this appellation the apostle to the Gentiles evidenced his interest in and love for the Hebrews: he acknowledged and esteemed them as "brethren."

"What an interesting and delightful view is thus presented to our minds of genuine Christians scattered all over the earth—belonging to every kindred, and people, and tongue, and nation—distinguished from one another in an almost infinite variety of ways, as to talent, temper, education, rank, circumstances, yet bound together by an invisible band, even the faith of the truth, to the one great object of their confidence, and love, and obedience, Christ Jesus—forming one great brotherhood, devoted to the honor and service of His Father and their Father, His God and their God! Do *you* belong to this holy brotherhood? The question is an important one. For answer, note Christ's words in Matt. 12 : 50" (Dr. J. Brown).

"Partakers of the heavenly calling." This at once serves to emphasise the superiority of Christianity over Judaism, which knew only an earthly calling, with an earthly inheritance. The word "partakers" signifies "sharers of." The calling wherewith the Christian is called (Eph. 4 : 1) is *heavenly*, because of its origin—it proceeds from Heaven; because of the means used—the Spirit and the Word, which have come from Heaven; because of the sphere of our citizenship (Phil. 3 : 20); because of the end to which we are called—an eternal Heaven. Thus would the Holy Spirit press upon the sorely-tried Hebrews the inestimable value of their privileges.

Finally, the whole of this appellation should be viewed in the light of the relation between those addressed and Christ. How is it possible for sinful worms of the earth to be thus denominated? Because of their union with the incarnate Son, whose excellency is imputed to them, and whose position they share. We are partakers of the heavenly calling because He, in wondrous condescension, partook of our earthly lot. What He has, we have; where He is, we are. He is the Holy One of God, therefore are we holy. He has been "made higher than the heavens," therefore are we "partakers of the heavenly calling!" Just so far as our hearts really lay hold of this, shall we walk as "strangers and pilgrims" here. Where our "Treasure" (Christ) is, there will our hearts be also. That is why we are here bidden to "consider" Him.

"Who was faithful to Him that appointed Him, as also Moses was in all His house" (v 2). "To speak of Moses to the Jews was always a very difficult and delicate matter. It is hardly possible for Gentiles to understand or realize the veneration and affection with which the Jews regard Moses, the man of God. All their religious life, all their thoughts about God, all their practices and observances, all their hopes of the future, everything connected with God, is with them also connected with Moses. Moses was the great apostle unto them, the man sent unto them of God, the mediator of the old covenant" (Saphir). Admire then the perfect wisdom of the Holy Spirit so plainly evidenced in our passage. Before taking up Christ's superiority over Moses, He points first to a resemblance between them, making mention of the "faithfulness" of God's servant. Ere taking this up let us dwell on the first part of the verse.

"Who was faithful to Him that appointed Him." The chief qualification of an apostle or ambassador is, that he be *faithful*. Faithfulness signifies two things: a trust committed, and a proper discharge of that trust. "Our Lord had a trust committed to Him…this trust He faithfully discharged. He sought not His own glory, but the glory of Him that sent Him; He ever declared His message to be not His own, but the Father's; and He declared the whole will or word of God that was committed unto Him" (Dr. J. Owen). Christ was ever faithful to the One who sent Him. This was His chief care from beginning to end. As a boy, "I must be about My Father's business" (Luke 2:49). In the midst of His ministry, "I must work the works of Him that sent Me" (John 9:4). At the finish, "Not as I will, but as Thou wilt" (Matt. 26:39).

"As also Moses was faithful in all His house." "The key to the whole paragraph is to be found in the meaning of the figurative term 'house,' which so often occurs in it (just seven times, A.W.P.). By supposing that the word 'house' here is equivalent to *edifice*, the whole passage is involved in inextricable perplexity. 'House' here signifies a family or household. This mode of using the word is an exemplification of a common figure of speech, by which the name of what contains is given to what is contained. A man's family usually resides in his house, and hence is called his house. This use of the word is common in the Bible: 'The House of Israel,' 'the House of Aaron,' 'the House of David,' are very common expressions for the children, the descendents, the families of Israel, Aaron and David. We have the same mode of speech in our own language, 'the House of Stuart,' 'the House of Hanover.' Keeping this remark in view, the verse we have now read will be found, short as it is, to contain in it the following statements:—Moses was appointed by God over the whole of His family: Moses was faithful in discharging the trust committed to him. Jesus is appointed by God over the whole of His family: Jesus is faithful in the discharge of the trust committed to Him" (Dr. J. Brown).

"The house, the building, means the children of God, who by faith, as lively stones, are built upon Christ Jesus the Foundation, and who are filled with the Holy Ghost; in whom God dwells, as in His temple, and in whom God is praised and manifested in glory. The illustration is very simple and instructive. We are compared unto stones, and as every simile is defective, we must add, not *dead* stones, but *lively* stones, as the apostle in his epistle to the Ephesians speaks of the building *growing*. The way in which we are brought unto the Lord Jesus Christ and united with Him is not by building, but by *believing*. The builders rejected the 'chief corner-stone' (Psa. 118:22); but 'coming unto Christ' (1 Peter 2:4:5), simply believing, 'ye also, as lively stones, are built up a spiritual house.' When we go about the works of the law we are trying to build, and as long as we build we are not built. When we give up working, then by faith the Holy Ghost adds us to Christ, and grafts up into the living Vine, who is also the Foundation. We are rooted and grounded. The house is one, and all the children of God are united in the Spirit" (Saphir).

That which the Spirit has here singled out for mention in connection with Moses, the typical "apostle," is that he was *faithful* in all God's house, faithful in the discharge of his responsibilities concerning the earthly family over which Jehovah placed him. Although he failed personally in his faith, he was faithful as an "apostle." He never withheld a word which the Lord had given him, either from Pharoah or from Israel. In erecting the tabernacle all things were made "according to" the pattern which he had received in the mount. When he came down from Sinai and beheld the people worshipping the golden calf, he did not spare, but called for the sword to smite them (Ex. 32). In all things he conformed to the instructions which he had received from Jehovah (Ex. 40:16).

"For this Man was counted worthy of more glory than Moses, inasmuch as He who hath builded the house hath more honour than the house" (v. 3). The apostle now proceeds to present Christ's superiority over Moses. But ere considering this, let us admire again the heavenly wisdom granted him in the method of presenting his argument. In the previous verse he has acknowledged the greatness of Moses, and here he also allows that he was worthy of glory, or praise. This would at once show that Paul was no enemy of Judaism, seeking to disparage and revile it. Equally striking is it to note how, in now turning the eyes of the Hebrews to One who is infinitely greater than Moses, he does not speak of his *failures*—his slaying of the Egyptians (Ex. 2), his slowness in responding to the Lord's call (Ex. 3, 4), his angered smiting of the rock (Num. 20); but by presenting the *glories* of Christ.

This third verse presents to us the first of the evidences here furnished of the superiority of Christ over Moses: He is the Builder of God's house; this, Moses never was. Its opening "For" looks back to the first verse, advancing a reason or argument *why* the Hebrews should "consider" the Apostle and High Priest of their confession, namely, because He is worthy of more glory than Moses the typical apostle. "The phrase, 'to build the house,' is equivalent to, be the founder of the family. This kind of phraseology is by no means uncommon. It is said, Ex. 1:21, that God 'made houses' to those humane women who refused to second the barbarous policy of Pharaoh in destroying the opening verses of our present passage, "How different is this from what we see in Christ! He came down from the bosom of the Father, not with the tables in His hands, but with the law in His heart. He came down, not to be made acquainted with the condition of the people but with a perfect knowledge of what that condition was. Moreover, instead of destroying the memorials of the covenant and executing judgment, He magnified the Law and made it honourable and bore the judgment of His people in His own blessed Person, on the cross" (page 316). Here is a case in point which shows the need for all of us to heed the Divine admonition, "*Prove* all things; hold fast that which is good" (1 Thess. 5 :,21)—which applies to our own writings equally as much as any others—for only thus shall we be able to "take forth the precious from the vile" (Jer. 15 : 19).

In the first place, what we have here is *not* a type, either by comparison or contrast, of the first advent of God's Son to this earth, coming here to seek and to save that which was lost. How could it be, when the section immediately preceding gives us a picture of His intercession on High? In the second place, when Christ was here, He *did* come with the ten commandments in His hands, came to enforce their righteous demands, though not to execute their inexorable penalty. He came here, full not only of "grace," but of "truth" as well (John 1 : 14), saying, "Think not that I am come to destroy the law or the prophets: I am not come to destroy, but to fulfill" (Matt. 5 : 17). In the four Gospels we see the tables of stone in the hands of Christ again and again: see Matt. 5 : 27-32; 15 : 3-6; 19 : 16-19; 23 : 2-3. In the third place, Moses did *not* come down from the mount " to *be* made acquainted with the condition of the people," instead, he already had full knowledge of their awful state and sin before he descended, as vv. 7-9 clearly enough show.

That what is before us in the second half of Ex. 32 possesses a deep and wondrous typical significance we are fully assured, though nought but Divine guidance will enable us to rightly divide this portion of the Word of Truth. We believe that this type has a twofold application, first to Israel, second to Christendom. Its application to Israel has already been pointed out at the close of our comments upon Ex. 24 (Article 32), but as many of our present readers have not seen them, we shall here repeat briefly what was then said.

First, in Ex. 24 : 18 we behold Moses entering the glory (the "cloud") consequent upon his having erected the altar and sprinkled the blood (vv. 4-8). If the reader will consult 24 : 16, 18 he will find that it was after "six days"—which speaks of work and toil, on the seventh day, which tells of *rest*, that the typical mediator was called by God to enter the glory. Beautiful foreshadowment was this of Christ, as it is said of Him in Heb. 4 : 10, "He that is entered into His rest, He also hath ceased from His works, as God from His." And what was the "rest" into which He entered? Does not His own request in John 17 : 4, 5 tell us! Thus, Moses going up into the mount and entering the cloud to commune with Jehovah is a type of the *ascension* of Christ, following the triumphant completion of the work which had been given Him to do. That which formed the subject of communion between the Lord and Moses in the mount was the revelation concerning the Tabernacle and its priesthood, which, coming in at *this* place in the book, tells of the provision of God's grace for His people, secured to them by and in Christ during His absence.

Now the next event, chronologically, was Moses' *descent*, recorded in Ex. 32. He did not end his days on the mount, but, in due time, returned unto the people. In like manner, the One whom Moses foreshadowed, is not to remain on High forever, but will come back again as truly and as literally as He went away. It is indeed striking to observe that Moses came down from Sinai *twice* after he had entered the glory. First, as recorded in 32 : : 15; second, in 34 : 29, having of course returned thither in the interval. So also will there be *two* stages in the second advent of Christ: the first when He descends into the air, to catch up His saints away from this scene (1 Thess. 4 : 16, 17); the second when He returns to the earth itself (Zech. 14 : 4). These two stages in the Redeemer's return will affect Israel very differently: the first will be followed by terrible judgment, the second will usher in an era of unparalleled blessing, even the Millennium.

That which we have in our present passage is what immediately followed the *first* descent of Moses. During his absence in the mount, the people had gathered themselves unto Aaron, saying "Up, make us gods which shall go before us out of the land of Egypt, we wot not what is become of him" (32 : 1). Is not that an accurate description of the spiritual state of the Jews all through this Day of Grace? They are all at sea over the long absence of their Messiah, not knowing what to think. While Moses was away, they made and worshipped a golden calf. And has not history again repeated itself? That which has characterised the Jews has not been the love of conquest or the lure of pleasure, as it has been with the Gentiles, but the lust for *gold*.

Now just as at his first descent Moses found Israel worshipping the golden calf, so at the first stage in the second advent of our Saviour, Israel will still be pursuing their mad quest after material riches; and just as Moses' response was to act in judgment, making them drink the dust of their idol and calling for the sword to smite them, so shall the

Christ "the Apostle" (v. 1). Moses was a member of an 'house,' Christ was the Buidler of one (v. 3). Moses was connected with a single house, Christ "built *all* things," being the Creator of the universe (v. 4). Moses was a man; Christ, God (v. 4). Moses was but a "servant" (v. 5); Christ, the "Son." Moses was a "testimony" of things to be spoken after (v. 5), Christ supplied the substance and fulfilment of what Moses witnessed unto. Moses was but a servant in the house of Jehovah, Christ was Son over His *own* house (v. 6). The Puritan Owen quaintly wrote, "Here the apostle taketh leave of Moses: he treats not about him any more; and therefore he gives him, as it were, an honourable burial. He puts this glorious epitaph on his grave: 'Moses, a faithful servant of the Lord in His whole house.'"

"But Christ as a Son over His own house, whose house are we" (v. 6). Here the "house" is plainly defined: it is a spiritual house, made up of believers in Christ. Not only are the "brethren" of v. 1 partakers of the heavenly calling, but they are members of the spiritual family of God, for in them He dwells. How well calculated to comfort and encourage the sorely-tried Hebrews were these words "whose house are we!" What compensation was this for the loss of their standing among the unbelieving Jews!

"If we hold fast the confidence and the rejoicing of the hope firm unto the end" (v. 6). Do these words weaken the force of what has last been said? In nowise; they contained a much-needed warning. "There were great difficulties, circumstances calculated especially to effect the Jew, who, after receiving the truth with joy might be exposed to great trail, and so in danger of giving up his hope. It was, besides, particularly hard for a Jew at first to put these two facts together: a Messiah come, and entered into glory; and the people who belonged to the Messiah left in sorrow, and shame, and suffering here below" (W. Kelly). The Hebrews were ever in danger of subordinating the future to the present, and of forsaking the invisible (Christ in heaven) for the visible (Judaism on earth), of giving up a profession which involved them in fierce persecution. Hence their need of being reminded that the proof of *their* belonging to the house of Christ was that they remained steadfast to Him to the end of their pilgrimage.

"If we hold fast the confidence and the rejoicing of the hope firm unto the end." As the same thought is, substantially, embodied again in v. 14, we shall now waive a full exposition and application of these words. Suffice it now to say that the Holy Spirit is here pressing, once more, on these Hebrews, what had been affirmed in 2 : 1, "Therefore we ought to give the more earnest heed to the things which we have heard, lest at any time we should let them slip." Let each Christian reader remember that our Lord has said, "If ye *continue* in My word, then are ye My disciples indeed" (John 8 : 31).

—*Arthur W. Pink.*

GLEANINGS IN EXODUS.

61. *The Righteous Judge* Ex. 32 : 15-29.

Our present section presents to us a vastly different scene than the one upon which we gazed in the preceding verses. There we beheld the typical mediator pleading so graciously and effectually before the Lord, turning away His wrath from His stiffnecked people. Here we see Moses coming down from the mount, where he had been in such wondrous and blessed communion with God, angered at the sin of idolatrous Israel, breaking the tables of stone, grinding the golden calf to powder, strewing it upon the water and making the people to drink. Here we see this man of prayer arraigning Aaron, the responsible and guilty leader, and then calling upon the Levites to put on their swords and "slay every man his brother." The contrast is so radical, so strange, that many have been perplexed, and grotesque have been some of the explanations attempted.

It is therefore pertinent to ask at once, Does our type now fail us? Is Moses in our present passage no longer a foreshadowing of Christ? Surely after all that has been before us in the previous chapters of Exodus we should be slow to answer these questions in the affirmative. If we are unable to perceive the spiritual meaning and application of this picture, certainly that is no reason why we should say or even imagine that there is a defect in the holy Word of God. Far better and becoming for us to confess the dimness of our vision and betake ourselves to the great Physician, that He may anoint our eyes with eyesalve that we may see (Rev. 3 : 18). It is only in His light that we ever "see light" (Psa. 36 : 9). If we who take up our pens to write upon the Oracles of God did this more faithfully and frequently, there would be far less of darkening "counsel by words without knowledge" (Job 38 : 2). Not that we dare to imply, though, that other writers have done this less than ourselves.

In his "Notes on Exodus," which are for the most part very spiritual and helpful, and from which, under God, the writer himself has received not a little help, C.H.M. says on the opening verses of our present passage, "How different is this from what we see in Christ! He came down from the bosom of the Father, not with the tables in His hands, but with the law in His heart. He came down, not to be made acquainted with the condition of the people but with a perfect knowledge of what that condition was. Moreover, instead of destroying the memorials of the covenant and executing judgment, He magnified the Law and made it honourable and bore the judgment of His people in His own blessed Person, on the cross" (page 316). Here is a case in point which shows the need for all of us to heed the Divine admonition, "Prove all things; hold fast that which is good" (1 Thess. 5 :,21)—which applies to our own writings equally as much as any others—for only thus shall we be able to "take forth the precious from the vile" (Jer. 15 : 19).

In the first place, what we have here is *not* a type, either by comparison or contrast, of the first advent of God's Son to this earth, coming here to seek and to save that which was lost. How could it be, when the section immediately preceding gives us a picture of His intercession on High? In the second place, when Christ was here, He *did* come with the ten commandments in His hands, came to enforce their righteous demands, though not to execute their inexorable penalty. He came here, full not only of "grace," but of "truth" as well (John 1 : 14), saying, "Think not that I am come to destroy the law or the prophets: I am not come to destroy, but to fulfill" (Matt. 5 : 17). In the four Gospels we see the tables of stone in the hands of Christ again and again: see Matt. 5 : 27-32; 15 : 3-6; 19 : 16-19; 23 : 2-3. In the third place, Moses did *not* come down from the mount " to *be* made acquainted with the condition of the people," instead, he already had full knowledge of their awful state and sin before he descended, as vv. 7-9 clearly enough show.

That what is before us in the second half of Ex. 32 possesses a deep and wondrous typical significance we are fully assured, though nought but Divine guidance will enable us to rightly divide this portion of the Word of Truth. We believe that this type has a twofold application, first to Israel, second to Christendom. Its application to Israel has already been pointed out at the close of our comments upon Ex. 24 (Article 32), but as many of our present readers have not seen them, we shall here repeat briefly what was then said.

First, in Ex. 24 : 18 we behold Moses entering the glory (the "cloud") consequent upon his having erected the altar and sprinkled the blood (vv. 4-8). If the reader will consult 24 : 16, 18 he will find that it was after "six days"—which speaks of work and toil, on the seventh day, which tells of *rest*, that the typical mediator was called by God to enter the glory. Beautiful foreshadowment was this of Christ, as it is said of Him in Heb. 4 : 10, "He that is entered into His rest, He also hath ceased from His works, as God from His." And what was the "rest" into which He entered? Does not His own request in John 17 : 4, 5 tell us! Thus, Moses going up into the mount and entering the cloud to commune with Jehovah is a type of the *ascension* of Christ, following the triumphant completion of the work which had been given Him to do. That which formed the subject of communion between the Lord and Moses in the mount was the revelation concerning the Tabernacle and its priesthood, which, coming in at *this* place in the book, tells of the provision of God's grace for His people, secured to them by and in Christ during His absence.

Now the next event, chronologically, was Moses' *descent*, recorded in Ex. 32. He did not end his days on the mount, but, in due time, returned unto the people. In like manner, the One whom Moses foreshadowed, is not to remain on High forever, but will come back again as truly and as literally as He went away. It is indeed striking to observe that Moses came down from Sinai *twice* after he had entered the glory. First, as recorded in 32 :: 15; second, in 34 : 29, having of course returned thither in the interval. So also will there be *two* stages in the second advent of Christ: the first when He descends into the air, to catch up His saints away from this scene (1 Thess. 4 : 16, 17); the second when He returns to the earth itself (Zech. 14 : 4). These two stages in the Redeemer's return will affect Israel very differently: the first will be followed by terrible judgment, the second will usher in an era of unparalleled blessing, even the Millennium.

That which we have in our present passage is what immediately followed the *first* descent of Moses. During his absence in the mount, the people had gathered themselves unto Aaron, saying "Up, make us gods which shall go before us out of the land of Egypt, we wot not what is become of him" (32 : 1). Is not that an accurate description of the spiritual state of the Jews all through this Day of Grace? They are all at sea over the long absence of their Messiah, not knowing what to think. While Moses was away, they made and worshipped a golden calf. And has not history again repeated itself? That which has characterised the Jews has not been the love of conquest or the lure of pleasure, as it has been with the Gentiles, but the lust for gold.

Now just as at his first descent Moses found Israel worshipping the golden calf, so at the first stage in the second advent of our Saviour, Israel will still be pursuing their mad quest after material riches; and just as Moses' response was to act in judgment, making them drink the dust of their idol and calling for the sword to smite them, so shall the

Jews be made to drink the outpoured vials of God's wrath and suffer beneath the sword. But just as the Nation was not completely exterminated under the anger of Moses, neither shall it be under the far sorer afflictions of the Tribulation period. In Ex. 33 and 34 that which followed the *second* descent of Moses anticipates millennial conditions.

Having dwelt on the application of our present type to Israel, let us view it now as it bears on Christendom. The action of Moses in the passage before us foreshadowed Christ in another character than that which was before us in our last article. There we viewed Him as the Mediator, making intercession for His people; here we behold Him as Judge, not consuming, but inspecting and executing *corrective* judgment. "Moses coming down from the mountain to expose and judge what was going on in the camp is very much like the Lord's attitude in Rev. 2, 3. He takes His place in the midst of the seven lamps to pass judgment upon what is evil and idolatrous, and also to take account of such faithfulness as might answer to what was found in the sons of Levi" (C. A. Coates). We believe it is the first three chapters of the Revelation which supply the key to the meaning of our present type.

"And Moses turned, and went down from the mount, and the two tables of the testimony were in his hand: the tables were written on both their sides; on the one side and on the other were they written. And the tables were the work of God, and the writing was the writing of God, graven upon the tables" (vv. 15, 16). This is not contradictory, but complementary, to that which precedes. First we have that which speaks of the *grace* of God, now that which brings out His *government*. The tables of stone in the hands of Moses announced that the righteous requirements of the law cannot be set aside. "Whatsoever a man soweth, that shall he also reap" was addressed not to worldlings, but to Christians. Let the reader note attentively the inspired description of Christ in Rev. 1 : 12-18. There we behold One "like unto the Son of *man*" (cf. John 5 : 27) in the midst of the seven lampstands, and "out of His mouth goeth a sharp two-edged sword, and His countenance was as the sun shineth in his strength" (v. 16)!

"And when Joshua heard the noise of the people as they shouted, he said unto Moses, There is a noise of war in the camp. And he said, It is not the voice of them that shout for mastery, neither is it the voice of them that cry for being overcome; but the noise of them that sing do I hear" (vv. 17, 18). An important spiritual principle here receives exemplification. If the reader will turn back to Ex. 24 : 13-18 it will be found that though both Moses and Joshua went up into the mount, leaving the congregation below at its base, yet Moses alone went into the midst of the cloud, to talk to Jehovah. For forty days Joshau had, apparently, been left alone, while Moses "communed" with the Lord (31 : 18). The *effect* of this we see in the verses before us: Moses, and not Joshua, is the one who discerns the true state of affairs in the camp. His ear was able to interpret aright the noise and din which came up to them. Ah, it is not only true that in God's light we alone see light, but only by much communion with Him do we acquire the *hearing* "ear."

"And it came to pass, as soon as he came nigh unto the camp, that he saw the calf, and the dancing: and Moses' anger waxed hot, and he cast the tables out of his hands, and brake them beneath the mount" (v. 19). A most appalling spectacle was spread before these servants of God. The very people who had only recently bowed before the manifested majesty of Jehovah, were now obscenely sporting around the golden image of a calf. In holy indignation Moses dashes the tables of stone to the ground, just as in the days of His flesh the Lord Jesus "made a scourge of small cords" and drove out of the Temple those who had desecrated His Father's house; and just as in Rev. 1 He is seen with "His eyes as a flame of fire" (v.14).

"And Moses' anger waxed hot, and he cast the tables out of his hands, and brake them beneath the mount." This affords a most striking illustration of what is said in James 2 : 10, "For whosoever shall keep the whole law, and yet offend in one point, he is guilty of all." Israel *had* offended "in one point." God had said to them, "Thou shalt not make unto thee any graven image, or any likeness of anything that is in heaven above or that is in the earth beneath, or that is in the water under the earth: thou shalt not bow down thyself to them, nor serve them (Ex. 20 :4, 5). This they had disobeyed, and the law being a unit, they are guilty of all"—hence the breaking of the two tables to show that the ten commandments, as a whole, had been violated.

"And he took the calf which they had made, and burnt it in the fire, and ground it to powder, and strawed it upon the water, and made the children of Israel drink of it" (v. 20). Some of the so-called "higher critics" with their customary scepticism have called into question the reference to Moses strawing the powder upon "the water;" but if these men would but take the trouble to "search the Scriptures," they would find that the Holy Spirit has granted light upon this point, though not in this chapter (for the Bible does not yield its meaning to lazy people), but in another book altogether. In Deut. 9 : 21 we read, "I took your sin, the calf which ye had made, and burnt it with fire, and stamped it, and ground it very small, even until it was as small as dust: and I cast the dust thereof into the *brook* that descended out of the mount." What that "brook" was that "descended out of the mount" Ex. 17 : 6 tells us.

Moses' actions here in grinding the idol to powder, strawing it upon the water, and making the children of Israel drink thereof, are very solemn. The Christian is bidden to keep himself from idols (1 John 5 : 21), which, we need scarcely add, covers very much more than bowing down to graven images. An "idol" is anything which displaces God in my heart. It may be something which is quite harmless in itself, yet if it absorbs me, if it be given the first place in my affections and thoughts, it becomes an "idol." It may be my business, a loved one, or my service for Christ. Any one or any thing which comes into competition with the Lord's ruling me in a practical way, is an "idol." And if I have set up an idol, then God, in His faithfulness and love, will break it down; not If I sow to the flesh, then of the flesh I must reap corruption (Gal. 6 : 8).

"And Moses said unto Aaron, What did this people unto thee, that thou hast brought so great a sin upon them?" Moses now arraigns the one who had been left in charge of the people, just as in Rev. 2, 3, Christ addresses, in each case, the responsible "angel" or "messenger" of the local church. Sad it is to hear the reply of the one who should have maintained the honor and glory of Jehovah.

"And Aaron said, Let not the anger of my Lord wax hot: thou knowest the people, that they are set on mischief. For they said unto me, Make us gods, which shall go before us: for this Moses, the man that brought us up out of the land of Egypt, we wot not what is be come of him" (vv. 22, 23). Very sad indeed is this. There was no sense of the terribleness of the sin committed, no sign of repentance; instead, there was a throwing of the blame upon others. Thus it was at the beginning: when the Lord arraigned Adam, he blamed his wife (Gen. 3 : 12); and when Eve was questioned, she blamed the Serpent. How often we hear the leaders in Christendom saying, "We have to make these concessions because the people demand it."

"What a contrast there is here between Aaron and Moses! Aaron afraid of the people, instead of protesting against their idolatrous wishes, actually making the calf; and then excusing himself in a way which is just a sample of the kind of excuses people make for doing evil (v 24). Moses comes down in an energy that could take a stand single-handed against six-hundred-thousand men, that could execute judgment on their sin, and maintain what was due to God. It is just the contrast between the servant who is *with men* and the servant who is *with God*. If a man acts with God he always acts in power. He may have plenty of exercise as to his own weakness in secret, but in public he acts in power and with no uncertainty or hesitation" (C.A.C.).

" And I said unto them, Whosoever hath any gold, let them break it off. So they gave it me: then I cast it into the fire, and there came out this calf" (v. 24). The breaking off of their "golden" ornaments was a figure of their being stript of their *glory*. This is ever what precedes all idolatry. What is man's "glory?" To be in subjection to his Maker and to be grateful for His mercies. Man is only in honor when God is given His true place. Just as we read of the Gentiles, in Rom. 1 : 21, "When they knew God, they glorified Him not as God, neither were thankful." What followed? This: they "changed the glory of the uncorruptible God into an image made like to corruptible man" etc. Nothing will preserve from idolatry but a will bowed to God's authority and a heart lifted up in thanksgiving for His bounties. If I do not bow to God, I shall quickly bow to something else that is of the creature, and thus be stript of my "gold," my glory.

"So they gave it me: then I cast it into the fire, and there came out this calf." In this purile manner did Aaron seek to deny all personal responsibility in the matter. Really, he told a downright lie, as a reference to v. 4 will show. Great indeed was his sin: marvellous the mercy which pardoned it. It is blessed to learn from Deut. 9 : 20 that the life of Aaron was spared in answer to the supplications of Moses. Thus we see in type, again, the efficacy of the Mediator's intercession for His people.

"And when Moses saw that the people were naked; (for Aaron had make them naked unto their shame among their enemies): Then Moses stood in the gate of the camp, and said, Who is on the Lord's side? let him come unto me" (vv. 25, 26). The situation called for drastic action. Having arraigned Aaron, Moses now considers the condition of the people, and beheld them naked and demoralised, having indulged in the idolatrous sensualism which they had so often witnessed in Egypt, and whose mad merriment they had, no doubt, remembered with many a sigh. They had been disturbed in their abominable orgies, and had yielded only to the terror of Moses' presence. A swift and summary vengeance must therefore be visited upon them, in order that the survivors might be brought to soberness and repentance, and that the Divine wrath, which had only been suspended by his intreaties, might be averted from utterly consuming the Nation.

" Who is on the Lord's side?" That was now the issue, clearly defined. " It was no time for concealment of the evil or for compromise. When there is open apostasy there can be no neutrality. Neutrality when the question is between God and Satan is itself apostasy. He that is not with the Lord, at such a time, is against Him. And mark, moreover, that this cry is raised in the midst of those who were the Lord's professing people. They were all

Israelites. But now there must be a separation, and the challenge of Moses, 'Who is on the Lord's side?' makes all manifest. He becomes the Lord's centre; and hence to gather to Him was to be *for*, to refuse his call was to be *against* the Lord" (Ed. Dennett).

"And all the sons of Levi gathered themselves together unto him" (v. 26). The Levites were the "overcomers" (cf. Rev. 2, 3) of that day. They had, apparently, been preserved from the awful sin of their nation, and now promptly responded to the call of God's servant. A most searching and severe test was presented to them: "And he said unto them, Thus saith the Lord God of Israel, put every man his sword by his side, and go in and out from gate to gate through the camp, and slay every man his brother, and every man his companion, and every man his neighbour" (v. 27).

Natural inclinations might well shrink from compliance with such a command. Sentiment would say, Not so, let us be gentle and gracious, we shall accomplish more by kindness than severity. Reason would argue, We can do no good by slaying people: there is far more power in love than in the sword; let us seek to woo and win them back to God. Such arguments sound very plausible, but the call was distinct and decisive, "Put every man his sword by his side." There was nothing else for it in view of that calf. So in preaching to idolators to-day it is the *wrath* of a holy God, and not His love (which is a truth for His own people only), which needs pressing upon them.

As another has said in his application of this verse to the saints to-day, "It was obedience at all costs to the divine call, and hence complete separation from the evil into which Israel had fallen. God often tests His people in the same way; and whenever confusion and declension have begun, the only path for the godly is that which is marked out by the course of Levi—that of full-hearted, unquestioning obedience. Such a path must be painful, involving for those who take it the surrender of some of the most intimate associations of their lives, and breaking many a tie of nature—of kindred and relationship; but it is only the path of blessing. Well may all challenge their hearts and inquire, if in this evil day they are apart from all that dishonours the Lord's name, in subjection to His Word."

The terrible sequel we must leave for our next article. May the Lord sanctify to our souls the solemn yet salutary lessons contained in the verses which have been before us.

—*Arthur W. Pink.*

ABRAHAM'S CALL.

Gen. 12.

The twelfth chapter commences the third section in the book of Genesis. As its name intimates this first portion of Holy Writ is the book of *beginnings*, and its literary structure is true to its title, for its contents centre around three "beginnings." First, there is the beginning of the human race in Adam. Second, a new beginning of the human race on the post-diluvian earth in Noah and his sons. Third, the beginning of the Chosen Nation in Abram.

At the beginning of the third section of Genesis we are introduced to *Abram,* who is the most illustrious person of ancient history. He was the progenitor of the Israelitish people He is the father of all them that believe. He is the one from whom, according to the flesh, the Saviour came (Matt. 1 : 1). He is called "the friend of God." There is no man, save the God-man, in whom Christians should be more interested.

Not a little is said about Abram in the N.T. The Lord Jesus declared that "Abraham rejoiced to see My day: and he saw it, and was glad" (John 8 : 56). In writing to the saints at Rome, the apostle speaks of Abraham as "our father" (4 : 1), and declares that they are those "who also walk in the steps of that faith of our father Abraham, which he had being yet uncircumcised" (4 : 12); and after recounting the patriach's faith in the promise of God, he goes on to say "it was not written for his sake alone......but for us also" (4 : 23, 24). So too in Gal. 3 : 29 we read, "And if ye be Christ's, then are ye Abraham's seed, and heirs according to promise."

From the above scriptures we gather that a study of what the Holy Spirit has recorded concerning the life of Abraham is a subject of deep interest. When we say "interest" we do not mean in a merely natural way—taking it up as human biography, or an item of ancient history—but spiritually. Inasmuch as Abram is "the father of us all," the account of his life, the inspired record of God's dealings with him, reveal to us the fundamental principles which underlie the life of faith. To the contemplation of it we propose devoting a series of articles. May the Holy Spirit be our Guide.

"Now the Lord had said unto Abram, Get thee out of thy country, and from thy kindred, and from thy father's house, unto a land that I will show thee" (Gen. 12 : 1). This verse records the Call which Abram received from God. To the examination of it we now turn our attention.

1. THE CALL ITSELF.

The very first thing which Holy Writ records concerning Abram is the Divine call of which he was the subject. Those who are really Christians need not to be told *why* this comes first: the "call" of God marks the beginning of our acquaintance with Him, for it is the starting-point of His dealings with us experimentally.

There are two "calls" from God to men mentioned in the Scriptures, and it is most important that we should distinguish between them. The one is general, the other is specific. The one is ineffectual, the other is invincible. The one is made to all who come under the sound of the Gospel, the other comes only to God's elect. The former is referred to in such passages as Prov. 8 : 4, Matt. 20 : 16. "Unto you, O men, I call; and My voice is to the sons of man;" "For many be called, but few chosen." The latter is mentioned in Rom. 8 : 28-30, "We know that all things work together for good to them that love God, to them who are *the called* according to His purpose...... Whom He did predestinate, them He also called: and whom He called, them He also justified: and whom He justified, them He also glorified—compare 1 Cor. 1 : 26-29.

The first, or general, of these two calls is addressed to human responsibility; the second is solely a matter of God's sovereign and efficacious grace. The first call is through the Word, addressed to the hearts of all who hear it. This call is universally refused, for an evil heart and a perverse will prefer the pleasures of sin to the ways of God. But in a coming day men will be called to account for their refusals of God's calls. He will say to men, "Because I have called, and ye refused; I have stretched out My hand, and no man regarded; But ye have set at nought all My counsel, and would none of My reproof; I also will laugh at your calamity, I will mock when your fear cometh; When your fear cometh as desolation, and your destruction cometh as a whirlwind, when distress and anguish cometh upon you" (Prov. 1 : 24-27).

The second call is something more than the voice of God addressing the heart through the Word. It is the Holy Spirit's *application* of that Word in mighty power, quickening the dead, giving sight to blind eyes, opening deaf ears. Such a call comes only to the elect. This distinguishing and effectual call corresponds with the new birth, and, as said above, marks the beginning of God's dealings, experimentally, with His own people. As said our blessed Saviour, "He calleth His own sheep by name and leadeth them out" (John 10 : 3). And again, "Other sheep I have which are not of this fold, them also I must bring, and they *shall* hear My voice" (John 10 : 6).

The call of God to a soul is a most wondrous thing. An all-powerful voice from the invisible world reaches our hearts, awakening from the sleep of death, and bringing us to the consciousness that we have to do with God. The object of that Voice is to call us apart from the things of self and earth—which hitherto entirely engrossed us—turning over thoughts, interests, hearts, to Him who created us, loved us, redeemed us: pressing upon us His claims, separating us from the world, introducing us to a realm where only Glory dwelleth. It was such a call that was received by the Samaritan adulteress at Sychars' well, by Matthew as he sat at the receipt of custom, by Zacchaeus in the tree, by Saul the persecutor on the Damascus road. Have *you*, my reader, in the infinite grace of a sovereign God, been the favoured recipient of it? It was such a call that Abram received.

The details of Scripture concerning Abraham's call are very brief, yet sufficient is said to furnish a summary of the essential features of every saving call from God. But these details are not all gathered together in a single passage, instead, they are scattered through the Scriptures, requiring diligence on our part to prayerfully collect them. The Bible was not written for lazy people, and the casual and careless reader of it will derive little profit. Truth has to be "bought" (Prov. 23 : 23), but few are willing to pay the price.

If we turn to Josh 24 : 2, 3, 14 we shall discover something of the conditions in which Abram lived both before and at the time God first called him: "Thus saith the Lord God of Israel. Your fathers dwelt on the other side of the flood in old time, Terah, the father of Abraham, and the father of Nachor: and they *served other gods*. And I took your father Abraham from the other side of the flood, and led him throughout all the land of Canaan, and multiplied his seed, and gave him Isaac......Now therefore fear the Lord, and serve Him in sincerity and in truth: and put away the gods which your fathers served on the other side of the flood." Thus Abram came of an idolatrous stock. Confirmation of this is found in the figurative but pointed language of Isa. 51 : 1, 2: "Hearken to Me, ye that follow after righteousness, ye that seek the Lord: look unto the rock whence ye are hewn, and *to the hole of the pit* whence ye are digged. Look unto Abraham your father, and unto Sarah that bare you."

Gen. 11 : 27, 28 informs us *where* Abram dwelt at the time God called him: "Terah begat Abram, Nahor and Haran......And Haran died before his father Terah in the land of his nativity, in Ur of the Chaldees." By linking these passages together we learn that Abram belonged to a heathen family and that he dwelt in a great city, until he was, approximately seventy years of age. No doubt he lived his life after the same manner as his fellow-citizens—satisfied with the husks which the swine feed upon, with little thought of and still less concern about God and the eternal hereafter. Thus it is with each of God's elect till the Divine call comes and arrests them in their self-willed, mad, and destructive course.

"The God of glory appeared unto our father Abraham, when he was in Mesopotamia, before he dwelt in Canaan" (Acts 7 : 2). All that is included in these words we shall not learn until the Day comes. As to *what form* this "appearing" of the Lord took we cannot be certain. But of two things we may be assured: for the first time in Abram's life God suddenly became a reality to him; second, he perceived that He was a glorious Being. Thus it is in the soul's experience of each and all of the true people of God. In the midst of our worldly self-seeking, one day Him of whom we had only the vaguest notions, Him whom we had tried to banish from our minds, suddenly appears before the heart, bowing us in wonderment, and becoming to us more than all the world. Such an one can say with Job, "I have heard of Thee by the hearing of the ear: *but now* mine eyes seeth Thee" (42 : 5).

From what has been before us in the above scriptures, one thing stands out with unmistakable clearness, namely, that the Call which Abram received from God was one of pure grace, sovereign grace, amazing grace. What was there in him to attract the notice of God? What was there in his circumstances to cause the great Jehovah to "appear" unto him? What had he done to entitle him to the inheritance which was given him? Nothing, absolutely nothing. It was *grace,* and grace alone, which moved God to act.

The fact that God "appeared" only to Abram, and not to any of his fellow-citizens, testifies to the *sovereignty* of His grace. There were countless thousands among his neighbours equally needy, but they were passed by. Let those who cavil against the truth of Divine foreordination, election unto salvation, ponder well the case of Abram. Why did not God give a similar call to his perishing fellows in Ur? Why was Abram thus singled out?—for mark well the Lord's own declaration concerning our patriarch in Isa. 51 : 2, "I called him *alone.*" Only one answer is forthcoming: "Even so, Father, for so it seemed good in Thy sight" (Matt. 11 : 26). God is not under obligations to save any. Were He so, salvation would not be by *grace.* Therefore has God affirmed, "I will have mercy on whom I will have mercy" (Rom. 9 : 15).

Let it not be forgotten that Abram's is a *pattern* case: he is "the father of us all." Let each Christian reader look back to the circumstances he was in when the Hand of Mercy plucked him as a brand from the burning. Go back to your school days: how many of your fellow-scholars have gone to a Christless grave? Recall the gay and giddy companions of your youth: how many of them are now rejoicing with you in God's great salvation? Perhaps the majority in your own family-circle are strangers to God. "Who hath made *thee* to differ?" (Cor. 4 : 7). There is only one answer: a sovereign God. Nor was it because your heart was more tender, your will less stubborn, or your sins less heinous than others. Grace, and grace alone—unsought and unmerited—is the spring from which flowed your salvation. Then ascribe *freely* all the glory unto Him to whom alone it belongs.

2. *THE TERMS OF HIS CALL.*

"Now the Lord had said unto Abram, Get thee out of thy country, and from thy kindred, and from thy father's house" (Gen. 12 : 1). It should be evident to every renewed mind, without any argument, that such a manifestation of God as Abram had received called for movement, response. After the "God of glory" had appeared to him, he could not continue his old manner of life. A new Object was before him, new desires filled his heart, new relationships now claimed him. It is thus with the Christian. The moment I realize that I have to do with God, I cannot go on in my former course: "Therefore if any man be in Christ, he is a new creature: old things are passed away; behold, all things are become new" (2 Cor. 5 : 17).

The Call which Abram received made a double demand upon him: he was to go out from the land of his natural birth, and he was to separate from his kindred, his father's house. Once again we would remind the reader that Abram's is a pattern case. Inasmuch as he is "the father of us all," each of his children must be conformed to the family likeness. Abram is a figure or prototype of those who have been, by infinite grace, made "partakers of the *heavenly* calling" (Heb. 3 : 1). Christians have been chosen out of the world (John 15 : 19); their citizenship is in heaven (Phil. 3 : 20); henceforth they are but "strangers and pilgrims" (1 Pet. 2 : 11) here on earth.

The Call which Abram received may be looked at from two view-points: as it typified the believer's position, and as it bears upon his condition. The call of God is a separating one, lifting me right out of the old order of things and bringing me into an entirely new realm and relationship. Col. 1 : 13 gives us the N.T. equivalent of Gen. 12 : 1: "Who hath delivered us from the power of darkness, and hath translated us into the kingdom of His dear Son." But let us examine the terms of Abram's call more in detail.

"Get thee out of thy country." This, as we have said, symbolized the believer's being called out of the world. The world is under God's curse (Rom. 3 : 19); the whole world lieth in the Wicked one (1 John 5 : 19); all its works are doomed to destruction (2 Pet. 3 : 10). Hence we read that Christ "gave Himself for our sins, that He might deliver us from this present evil world, according to the will of God and our Father" (Gal. 1 : 4). Another type of this is to be found in connection with God's dealings with Israel. At the beginning of their national history they were found in Egypt—figure of *the world*—and from that land God delivered them. The same principle is strikingly exemplified in connection with Christ Himself, who became "all of one" with those whom He came to redeem, entering into their circumstances, being numbered with transgressors. Hence, concerning Him it is said, "Out of Egypt have I called My Son" (Matt. 2 : 15).

"And from thy kindred, and from thy father's house." This speaks of the Christian's old standing in the flesh being annulled, or, as Rom. 6 : 6 expresses it, "knowing this that our old man was crucified with Him." God no longer sees the believer in Adam, but beholds him now in Christ. He is no longer numbered amongst the "children of wrath" (Eph. 2 : 3), for he has been made a member of the family of God (1 John 3 : 1). He now has a new "kindred," for all who have been born again are his brethren and sisters in Christ. A new position is now his; he is no longer viewed as a member of his earthly father's "house," but, like the prodigal son of Luke 15, has been brought into the Father's house, and given a place of welcome and of honor at His table.

Now all of this *is* an accomplished fact from the Divine side: such is the inalienable standing of every real Christian before God. But this is now to be entered into in a practical way. It is presented before us in the Word, for faith to lay hold of and make good in our daily walk. The terms of this Divine call which Abram received are addressed to *our* hearts today. Implicit obedience to them is required from us. A complete break with all that pertains to the old life, a practical separation from the world and from all the ties of the flesh (of which "Get thee out......from thy *kindred*" speaks)" is the first demand which God makes upon us.

Observe how the teaching of the Epistles confirms what has just been said. Take the one that heads the list. In the first eleven chapters of Romans we have, almost entirely, doctrinal exposition, whereas the last five chapters are hortatory. How striking then to observe that the opening admonition is, "I beseech you therefore, brethren, by the mercies of God, that ye present your bodies a living sacrifice, holy, acceptable unto God, which is your reasonable service. *And* be not conformed to this world" (12 : 1, 2). The Christian is not to be "conformed to this world's fashions and follies, its policies or politics, its ethics or religion. Why? Because "the friendship of the world is enmity with God" (James 4 : 4). Why? Because the world lies under the awful guilt of the murder of God's incarnate Son. Then, shall I be intimate with those who despise and reject Him? Shall I seek my satisfaction in that system which has cast Him out? No; rather must I "come out" and "be separate" as God bids me in 2 Cor. 6 : 17.

So too the *flesh* is to be given no rein. "They that are after the flesh do mind the things of the flesh; but they that are after the spirit the things of the Spirit. For to be fleshly minded is death; but so be spiritually minded is life and peace" (Rom. 8 : 5, 6). Hence the word to the Christian is "make not provision for the flesh, to fulfill the lusts thereof" (Rom. 13 : 14). The claims and calls of mere nature are to be rigidly eschewed; our members which are upon the earth are to be "mortified" (Col. 3 : 5). Sternly and drastically did our Lord and Master press this principle of the believer's walk when He said, "If any come to Me, and hate not his father, and mother, and wife, and children, and brethren, and sisters, yea, and his own life also, he cannot be My disciple" (Luke 14 : 26). His claims upon us are paramount. We are not our own, but "bought with a price;" then let us seek grace, daily, to glorify Him in the way of His own appointments.

"Get thee out......from thy kindred, and from they father's house." Terah, his father, was an idolator, whereas Abraham had now, by grace, been brought to a knowledge of the true God and of personal dealings with Him. His grace, His glory, His requirements had been revealed. Therefore not only must his idolatrous neighbours be left behind, but those near and dear in the flesh too, for, "Can two walk together except they be agreed?" (Amos 3 : 3). Thus we are told, " They that are Christ's have crucified the flesh with the *affections* and lusts" (Gal. 5 : 24).

Even the most intimate natural affections cannot unite souls who are sundered by entirely different interests, motives, and desires. For instance, a friendship may be formed between two real Christians, a purely fleshly or natural one; two people attracted to each other because of the same age, because they belong to the same class socially, or because possessing similar temperaments or tastes. But if one of them has, by grace, made considerable experimental progress in the things of God, and is walking with Him in a practical way, while the other knows little or nothing of obedience to Christ's word "If any one will come after Me, let him deny himself, take up his cross and follow Me," there can be *no fellowship* between them. How much less can there be fellowship between a Christian and a worldling! Natural ties, fleshly affections, have to be subordinated to the glory of God. *This* is what the Lord first pressed upon Abraham. And this is His path for us now, and if we walk not in it, we shall yet discover to our irreperable loss that "a man's foes *are* they of his own household."

The Call which Abram received was to separate himself from that which was, in figure, the world, and to sever all the ties of the natural man. God was now to be supreme in his affections. Henceforth he was to be a man who had no home here. Such a Call demanded absolute confidence in the Lord and implicit obedience to His Word. Thus in Abram we have exemplified the character and course of the life of faith. The life of faith *begins* only when the Christian completely separates himself from the world, and his place in it by nature—is separated in spirit, in heart, in interests, in motives, in all that actuates and regulates his conduct. There must be a clear and definite break, a right-about-face.

—Arthur W. Pink.

ROMANS 7.

(*This article is of the "heavy" type, and therefore needs to be read slowly. It will not appeal to all, but is inserted for those who value light from any portion of God's Word; it will repay re-reading. A.W.P.*).

Few parts of Scripture are read by the believer with more earnest interest than the central part of the seventh chapter of the Romans—its subject being the inherent, unchangeable evil of the nature of fallen man. There is nothing of which we are more acutely sensible, when taught by the Spirit of holiness and truth, than of the evil of our "flesh"—that word, when thus used, denoting all that *morally* characterises us, in body, soul and spirit, as the children, naturally of the first Adam who sinned. We constantly feel the power of that truth—"in me, that is, in my flesh, there dwelleth no good thing." Any passage therefore, that teaches us respecting our innate evil in its relation to the holiness of God, may well be read by us with feelings of the deepest and most solemn interest.

Yet, just in proportion to the importance of any truth, is the energy put forth by our great enemy to pervert or to destroy it. When the Philistines of old spread themselves over the land of Israel, they chiefly sought to seize the towers, and citadels, and strongholds of God's people. Just so in respect of the truths of God's holy Word. The foe longs to occupy, or to destroy, our chief citadels of strength : and of such citadels, this passage, taken in connection with the chapter that follows, is one.

Accordingly, it has been the subject of much controversy; and, not unfrequently, of great perversion. Many have said that the seventh of Romans from the 13th to the 24th verse, cannot, in any sense, be true of those in whom "the new man" is. They affirm that a description such as that given in these verses can pertain only to the unregenerate. Not a few have gone even further, and have said that a matured christian state is characterised by a cessation of inward conflict; that sin and its motions may be, and ought to be driven from the flesh by the power of God's Spirit; that in such a case, conflict ceases, and we sin no more.

We can scarcely wonder that some, in their eagerness to combat doctrines so dangerous, should have been betrayed into statements not altogether faultless. The soldiers of Truth may, in assailing the strongholds of error, be negligent in duly guarding their own position. Some in their desire to overthrow the deadly doctrine of the perfectability of the flesh, have, it must be admitted, in interpreting this chapter, advanced opinions antinomian in tendency, which have therefore been welcomed and adopted by others, who are, in deed and in truth, antinomians.

In considering this chapter, it should carefully be observed, that the first six verses have a distinct subject of their own; and should be read either as a separate chapter, or as a distinct section. The subject of these verses is analagous to that of the sixth chapter that precedes. In the sixth chapter, SIN, being personified is spoken of under the similitude of a master to whom and to whose household we, naturally, as slaves belong. Yet, says the apostle, although the bond that binds the slave to his master may be indissoluble *in life,* it must be dissolved *by death.* The title of the master ceases as soon as the slave dies. Therefore, seeing that in the courts of God, believers are regarded as having substitutionally died in Christ, their Representative; all the family of faith are judicially recognised as freed from the claims of their old master, SIN. We are considered as legally dead to our first master, and as living in Christ risen unto our new Master even God, and as enabled through Christ, to serve God.

The subject of the first six verses of the seventh chapter is analagous to this. As the sixth chapter has described our natural relation to *sin,* under the similitude of master and slave, so the first six verses of the seventh chapter describe our dispensational relation to *the Law* under the likeness of a marriage union—the Law being the husband, whilst those dispensationally under it are regarded as married thereunto. But this relation also is found by man to be one of ruin : "The motions of sin which were by the law did work in our members to bring forth fruit unto death" (v. 5). The result, therefore, of this union is destructive; nor can anything release from it but death. But as, in Christ, their Substitute, believers have judicially died to sin their first master, so likewise in Christ they have judicially died to the law, their first husband, and are now, "married to Another, even to Him that is raised from the dead, that we should bring forth fruit unto God" (v. 4). "Now therefore we are delivered from the law, having died to that wherein we were held; that we might serve in newness of spirit and not in the oldness of the letter." Such is the sixth verse of the seventh of Romans, and there the subject treated of in the preceding verses ends. At the seventh verse a new subject begins, that subject being first, the relation to the law of man as man (vv. 7-12); secondly, its relation to a regenerate person who had ceased to be dispensationally under it. After diverging, in order to trace out this new branch of truth, the apostle brings us back in the eighth chapter to the same point as had been reached in the sixth verse of the seventh chapter—for there we are spoken of as "serving in newness of spirit," and this is the subject of the eighth chapter. This habit of turning back in order to trace a new branch of the subject, and so bringing us by another path to the same point again, is constant in Scripture.

At the seventh verse a new subject begins: that subject indeed is not unconnected with the preceding; on the contrary, it is suggested by it. It might seem from what had been said, as if sin and the law had been placed in the same class together. Sin had been spoken of as a master, and the law as a husband; from both which it is a mercy to be delivered. Nay, more; the law had been declared to be the occasion of calling forth in us developments of sin—"the motions of sin which were by means of the law, did work in our members to bring forth fruit unto death" (v. 5). All this might seem to cast a kind of imputation of evil on the law, as if it were other than "holy, just and good." But this thought is instantly repelled by the apostle. "What shall we say then? Is the law sin? God forbid" (v. 7). It is "holy, just, and good;" and the reason why its effect on us is ruinous is not any defect in the law, but the cause is, our evil, which is unable to meet its perfectness. Light coming in the midst of darkness may manifest that darkness, but it creates it not. The law may make manifest the sin that is in us. It may arouse and exasperate the slumbering viper and cause it to show what its venom is; but it does not create either the viper or the venom.

The subject, therefore, of vv. 7—12 is the vindication of the law. The apostle in them supplies himself as an example of man (the reference of the apostle being *here* retrospective; looking back to that which he once was. The tenses accordingly are *here* past: "I WAS alive" etc; but in v. 14 the tense is *changed unto the present*, for there the view is not retrospective) for every man is like unto his fellow man: and the same elements of character are displayed in all who are placed in the same circumstances. The paraphrase of this passage may be given thus: "What shall we say then? Is the law sin? God forbid? on the contrary, so far from being sin, it makes manifest the presence of sin, and to do that must be good. Conscience would not have recognised sin as being in me, except by means of the law. To take as an example concupiscence (evil desire)—that first and chiefest and most essential of all the inward developments of sin—I should not have recognised concupiscene within me, unless the law had said 'thou shalt not have concupiscence.' From the moment I apprehended that the law forbad me to desire certain things, I began consciously to desire them; and thus, sin availing itself of the opportunity, used the commandment as the occasion of awakening in me desires after everything which the law commanded me *not* to desire. Up to that time, sin had lain hid within me, like a thing that was dead. Its energies were undeveloped; and I seemed and thought myself to be alive unto God. But as soon as the commandment came, sin revived; deceived me; brought me, *formally*, under the law's curse; and left me under its sentence of death. Thus the law made manifest the reality of my condition. It showed that sin lived in me, it showed that I was not alive unto God: it proved that I, as well as all other men, was under curse, and the sentence which righteousness awarded, it *formally* pronounced. Could that which thus detected sin and made it manifest, and pronounced on it the sentence which righteousness demanded, be other than "holy, just and good?"

Up to this point there has been, comparatively, little difference of judgment in the true Church of God. But here divergency begins. With respect to the immediately succeeding verses from the fourteenth onwards, (v. 13 being the transition verse), it has been earnestly debated, whether a believer can, or cannot, apply them to himself. Are they applicable to a regenerate person, or must they be considered as the description of an unregenerate state? If this question be patiently examined, little difficulty, I think, will be found in returning a decisive reply.

In vv. 18, 19, 22 I find such expressions as these: "*To desire* (viz., that which is good) is present with me" (v. 18). "The good that *I desire*" (v. 19). "*I delight in* (the expression in the original is still stronger: it means to have a sympathetic or common joy with another. The law rejoices in good, and "the new man" rejoices sympathetically with it) the law of God after the inner man " (v. 22). It is impossible, I think, for any instructed believer to ponder the force of these words, without acknowledging that no one, whilst he continues dead in trespasses and sins can be described as *desiring* that which is good, or as "delighting in" the law of God. Some have asked whether the natural conscience may not do this? I reply never. The natural conscience may, under the appeals of Truth, (as when Festus heard and trembled) be constrained to own that certain things are right and ought to be followed; and that certain other thing are wrong and ought to be eschewed. But the power of conscience goes no further. Even in its best condition, it is only as a hand that points out the way: it has no motive power of action. It may, sometimes, even in the unregenerate heart, speak loudly: but the very characteristic of such a heart is, that it does *not* "desire," much less "delight in," the things to which its conscience testifies as right. If there be in us, naturally, an innate 'desire" of good, and a "delight" in God and in His law, we certainly must be something more than flesh: for "in the flesh there dwelleth no good thing." Yet, naturally, we are nothing more than flesh: "that which is born of the flesh is flesh." When, therefore, the apostle says, "I delight in the law of God after the inner man," I must conclude that he is speaking of himself as a regenerate person, and that the condition described in this passage is a complex one—one in which "the new man created according to God," and "the old man corrupt according to the deceitful lusts," are alike present. An equally strong proof is found in the words, "in me, *that is, in my flesh*, dwelleth no good thing." If he had been speaking of himself as unregenerate, he would have said, "In me there dwelleth no good thing." The fact that he limits this statement respecting the absence of all good, to that which he is in the flesh, proves that there was *another* aspect of his condition of which this could *not* be affirmed.

A third aspect, therefore, of the condition of man is here presented to us. The two previously treated of are, to the believer, *past*. The apostle had first spoken of the condition of man before the law came: (i.e., in power to his heart. A.W.P.) "I was alive without the law once" (v. 9). Secondly, he had spoken of that proved condition of condemnation in which man was found after the law had been dispensationally (better "experimentally," by the Holy Spirit A.W.P.) applied to him: "I died—the commandment that was proposed for life was found to be to me unto death" (v. 10). This proved condition of condemnation he shared in common with other men. Man as man is left in death. But now we come to another question, and one that affects God's people only. Accordingly, here, as I have already noticed the tenses which up to this point have been *past*, change into the *present*—an additional proof that he is speaking of a condition that pertained to him as a believer.

It should be observed also that throughout this passage the apostle speaks of himself both as the contemplator and also as the subject contemplated. When he uses the oft-recurring expressions, "I know, I see, we know," and the like, he speaks of himself or of believers (for it is equally true of them) as endowed, through the Spirit, with a certain capacity to know respecting evil and respecting good, and to judge of their own relation thereunto. There are occasions (and that before us is one in which the believer may make himself the subject of his contemplating; just as a physiologist may treat of his own body or of his own mind, and supply himself as an example of what man's natural condition is. In such a case, we have, of course, to distinguish between him as contemplating, and him as contemplated.

The verses in which "I" or "we" is used to denote the place of the contemplator are, "I know" (v. 18), "I find" (v. 21), "I see" (v. 23), and 'we know" (8 : 22), 'we know" (8 : 28). On the other hand, "I" is used of that which is the *subject* of contemplation in such instances as the following "I am carnal," "I desire," "I do," "I allow," "I do not," and the like.

To be continued D.V.

THE SYMPATHY & GRACE OF CHRIST.

Matt. 14 : 1-21, Mark 6 : 30-44.

In these two parallel scriptures we are presented with two distinct conditions of heart which both find their answer in the grace and sympathy of Christ. Let us look closely at them; and may the Holy Spirit enable us to gather up and bear away their precious teaching.

It was, no doubt, a moment of deep sorrow to John's disciples when their master had fallen by the sword of Herod; when the one on whom they had been accustomed to lean, and from whose lips they had been wont to drink instruction, was taken from them after such a fashion. This, we may well believe, was indeed a moment of gloom and desolation to the followers of the Baptist.

But there was One to whom they could come, in their sorrow, and into Whose ear they could pour their tale of grief—One of whom their master had spoken, to whom he had pointed, and of whom he had said, "He must increase, but I must decrease." To Him the bereaved disciples betook themselves, as we read, "They came and took up the body, and buried it, and *went and told Jesus*" (Matt. 14 : 12). This was the very best thing they could have done. There was not another heart on earth in which they could have found such a response as in the heart—the tender, loving heart—of Christ. His sympathy was perfect. He knew all about their sorrow. He knew their loss, and how they would be feeling it. Wherefore, they acted wisely when "they went and told Jesus." His ear was ever open, and His heart ever at leisure to sooth and sympathise. He perfectly exemplified the precept afterwards embodied in the words of the Holy Spirit, "Rejoice with them that do rejoice, and weap with them that weep" (Rom. 12 : 15).

And oh! who can tell the worth of genuine sympathy? Who can declare the value of having one who can really make your joys and sorrows his own? Thank God! we have such an one in the blessed Lord Jesus Christ; and although we cannot see Him with the bodily eye, yet can faith use Him in all the preciousness and power of His perfect sympathy. We can, if only our faith is simple and child-like go from the tomb where we have just deposited the remains of some fondly-cherished object, to the feet of the Lord, and there pour out the anguish of a bereaved and desolate heart. We shall there meet no rude repulse, no heartless reproof for our folly and weakness, in feeling so deeply. No; nor yet any clumsy effort to say something suitable, an awkward effort to put on some expression of condolence. Ah! no; Christ knows how to sympathise with a heart that is crushed and bowed down beneath the heavy weight of sorrow. His is a perfect human heart. What a thought! What a privilege to have access, at all times, in all places, and under all circumstances, to a perfect human heart! We may look in vain for this down here. Yes; look in vain, not merely in the world, but even in the church. There may, in many cases, be a real desire to sympathise, but a total lack of capacity. I may find myself, in moments of sorrow, in company with one who knows nothing about my sorrow or the source thereof. How could he sympathise? And even though I should tell him, his heart might be so occupied with other things as to have no room and no leisure for me.

Not so with the perfect Man, Christ Jesus. He has both room and leisure for each and for all. No matter when, how, or with what you come, the heart of the Lord Jesus is always open. He will never repulse, never fail, never disappoint. If, therefore, we are in sorrow, what should we do? We should do as the disciples of the Baptist did, "go and tell Jesus." This, assuredly, is the right thing to do. Let us go straight from the tomb to His feet. He will dry up our tears, sooth our sorrows, heal our wounds, and fill up our blanks. In this way we shall be able to enter into the truth of Rutherford's words when he says, "I try to lay up all my good things in Christ, and then a little of the creature goes a great way with me." This is an experience which we may well covet. May the blessed Spirit lead us more into it!

We may now contemplate another condition of heart, as furnished by the twelve apostles, on their return from a successful mission. "And the apostles gathered themselves together unto Jesus, and told Him all things, both what they had done, and what they had taught" (Mark 6 : 30). Here, we have not a case of sorrow and bereavement, but one of rejoicing and encouragement. The twelve made their way to Christ to tell Him of their *success*, just as the disciples of the Baptist made their way to Him in the moment of their *loss*. The Lord Jesus was equal to both. He could meet the heart that was crushed with sorrow, and He could meet the heart that was flushed with success. He knew how to control, to moderate, and to direct both the one and the other. Blessings forever be upon His honoured name!

And He said unto them "Come ye yourselves apart into a desert place, and rest awhile : for there were many coming and going, and they had no leisure so much as to eat." Here, then, we are conducted to a point at which the moral glories of Christ shine out with uncommon lustre, and correct the selfishness of our poor narrow hearts. Here we are taught, with unmistakable clearness, that to make the Lord the depository of our thoughts and feelings will never produce in us a spirit of haughty self-sufficiency and independence, or a feeling of contempt for others. Quite the reverse. The more we have to do with Christ, the more will our hearts be open to meet the varied forms of human need which may present themselves to our view from day to day. It is when we come to Him and empty our whole hearts to Him, tell Him of our sorrows and our joys, and cast our whole burden at His feet, that we really learn how to feel for others.

There is great beauty and power in the words, "*Come* ye yourselves apart." He does not say, "Go ye." This would never do. There is no use in going apart into a desert place, if Christ be not there to go to. To go into solitude without Him is but to make our cold, narrow hearts colder and narrower still. I may retire from the scene around me in chagrin and disappointment, only to wrap myself up in impenetrable selfishness I may fancy that my fellows have not made enough of me, and I may retire in order to make much of myself. I may make myself the centre of my whole being, and thus become a cold-hearted, contracted, miserable creature; but when Christ says, "*Come*," the case is totally different. Our finest moral lessons are learned alone with Him. We cannot breathe the atmosphere of His presence without having our hearts expanded. If the apostles had gone into the desert without Christ, they would, no doubt, have eaten the loaves and fishes themselves; but having gone with Him, they learned differently. He knew how to meet the need of a hungry multitude, as well as that of a company of sorrowing or rejoicing disciples. The sympathy and grace of Christ are perfect. He can meet all. If one is sorrowful, he can go to Christ; if he is happy, he can go to Christ; if he is hungry, he can go to Christ. We can bring everything to Christ, for in Him all fulness dwells, and, blessed be His name, He never sends any one empty away.

Not so, alas! with His poor disciples. How forbidding is their selfishness when viewed in the light of His magnificent grace! "And Jesus, when He came out, saw much people, and was moved with compassion toward them, because they were as sheep not having a shepherd; and He began to teach them many things." He had gone to a desert place to give His disciples rest; but no sooner does human need present itself than the deep flowing tide of compassion rolls forth from His tender heart.

"And when the day was now far spent, His disciples came unto Him, and said, This is a desert place, and now the time is past: *send them away*." What words to drop from the lips of men who had just returned from preaching the Gospel! "Send them away." Ah! it is one thing to *preach* grace, and another thing to *act* it. No doubt it is well to preach; but it is also well to act. Indeed, the preaching will be little worth if not combined with acting. It is well to instruct the ignorant; but it is also well to feed the hungry. The latter may involve more self-denial than the former. It may cost us nothing to preach; but it may cost us something to feed; and we do not like to have our private store intruded upon. The heart is ready to put forth its ten thousand objections; "What shall I do for myself? What will become of my family? We must act judiciously. We cannot do impossibilities." These, and such-like arguments the selfish heart can urge when a needy object presents itself.

"Send them away." What made the disciples say this? What was the real source of this selfish request? Simply *unbelief*. Had they only remembered that they had in their midst the One who of old had fed "six hundred thousand footmen," for forty years in the wilderness, they would have known that He would not send a hungry multitude away. Surely the same hand that had nourished such a host for such a long time could easily furnish a meal for five thousand. Thus faith would reason; but alas! unbelief darkens the understanding and contracts the heart. There is nothing so absurd as unbelief, and nothing which so shuts up the bowels of compassion. Faith and charity always go together, and in proportion to the growth of the one is the growth of the other. Faith opens the flood-gates of the heart and lets the tide of charity flow forth. Thus the apostle could say to the Thessalonians, your faith groweth exceedingly, and the charity of every one of you all toward each other aboundeth." This is the divine rule. A heart that is full of faith can afford to be charitable; an unbelieving heart can afford nothing. Faith places the heart in immediate contact with God's exhaustless treasury, and fills it with the most benevolent affections. Unbelief throws the heart in upon itself, and fills it with all manner of selfish fears. Faith conducts us into the soul-expanding atmosphere of heaven Unbelief leaves us enwrapped in the withering atmosphere of this heartless world. Faith enables us to harken to Christ's gracious accents, "Give ye them to eat." Unbelief makes us utter our own heartless words, "Send the multitude away." In a word there is nothing enlarges the heart like simple faith; and nothing so contracting as unbelief. Oh! that our faith may grow exceedingly, so that our charity may abound more and more! May we reap much permanent profit from the contemplation of the sympathy and grace of Christ.

What a striking contrast between "Send the multitude away," and "Give ye them to eat." Thus it is ever. God's ways are not as our ways! and it is by looking at His ways that we learn to judge our ways—by looking at Him that we learn to judge ourselves. Christ, in this lovely scene corrects the selfishness of the disciples, first, by making them the channels through which His grace flowed to the multitude, and secondly, by making them gather up " twelve baskets full of the fragments" for themselves.

Nor is this all. Not merely is selfishness rebuked, but the heart is most blessedly instructed. Nature might say, "What need is there of the five loaves and two fishes at all? surely the One who can feed such a multitude with, can as easily feed them without, such an instrumentality." Nature might argue thus; but Christ teaches us that we are not to despise God's creatures. We are to use what we have with God's blessing. This is a fine moral lesson for the heart. "What hast thou in the house?" is the question. It is just that and nothing else that God will use. It is easy to be liberal with what he have not; but the thing is to bring out what we have, and with God's blessing, apply it to the present need.

So also in the gathering up of the fragments. The foolish heart might say, "What need of gathering up those scattered crumbs? Surely the one who has wrought such a miracle can have no need of fragments." Yes; but we are not to waste God's creatures. If in the using of the loaves and fishes we are taught not to *despise* any creature of God, in the gathering up of the fragments we are taught not to *waste* it. Let human need be liberally met, but let not a single crumb be wasted. How Divinely perfect! How unlike us! Sometimes we are penurious; at other times prodigal. Christ was neither the one nor the other. "Give ye them *to eat*." But, "Let nothing be *lost*." Perfect grace! Perfect wisdom! May we adore it, and learn from it. May we rejoice in the assurance that the blessed One who manifested all this wisdom and grace is our life. Christ is our life, and it is the manifestation of this life that constitutes practical christianity. It is not living by rules and regulations, but simply having Christ dwelling in the heart by faith—Christ the source of perfect sympathy and perfect grace.

C. H. M.

ONE OF CHRIST'S LITTLE ONES.

(Matt. 18 : 10).

A poor idiot, who was supported by his parish in the Highlands of Scotland, passed his time in wandering from house to house. He was silent and peaceful, and won pity of all kind hearts. He had little power to converse with his fellowmen, but seemed often in loving communion with Him who, while He in the high and Holy One, condescends to men of low estate.

Yeddie, as he was called, was in the habit of whispering and muttering to himself as he trudged along the highway, or performed the simple tasks which any neighbour felt at liberty to demand of him. The boys, while they were never cruel to him, often got a little fun out of his odd ways.

Once, when a merry boy heard him pleading earnestly with some unseen one asked, "What ghost or goblin are you begging favours of now Yeddie? "Neither the one nor the tither, laddie," he replied; "I was just having a few words wi' Him that neither yersel' nor I can see, and yet wi' Him that sees the baith o' us!" The poor fellow was talking to God, while the careless wise ones laughingly said, "He was talking to himself."

One day Yeddie presented himself in his coarse frock and his hob-nailed shoes before the minister, and making a bow, much like that of a wooden toy when pulled by a string, he said, "Please, minister, let poor Yeddie eat supper on the coming day wi' the Lord Jesus." The good man was preparing for the observance of the Lord's Supper, which came quarterly in that thin-settled region, and was celebrated by several churches together; so that the concourse of people made it necessary to hold the service in the open air. He was too busy to be disturbed by the simple youth, and so strove to put him off as gently as possible. But Yeddie pleaded, "Oh minister, *if ye but kenned how I love Him,* ye wud let me go where He's to sit at table." This so touched his heart that permission was given for Yeddie to take his seat with the rest. And although he had many miles to trudge over hill and moor, he was on the ground long before those who lived near and drove good horses.

As the service proceeded, tears flowed freely from the eyes of the poor "innocent," and at the name of Jesus he would shake his head mournfully and whisper, "But I dinna see Him." At length, however, after partaking of the hallowed elements, he raised his head, wiped away the traces of his tears, and, looking in the minister's face, nodded and smiled. Then he covered his face with his hands and buried it between his knees, and remained in that posture till the parting blessing was given, and the people began to scatter. He then rose, and with a face lighted with joy, and yet marked with solemnity, he followed the rest.

One and another from his own parish spoke to him, but he made no reply until he was pressed by some of the boys. Then he said, "Ah, lads, dinna bid Yeddie talk to-day! He's seen the face of the Lord Jesus among His ain ones. He got a smile fro' His eye and a word fro' His tongue; and he's afeared to speak lest he lose memory o't; for its but a bad memory he has at best. Ah! lads, lads, I ha' seen Him this day that I never seed before. I ha' seen wi' these dull eyes *yon lovely Man.* Dinna speak but just leave poor Yeddie to His company." The boys looked on in wonder, and one whispered to another, "Sure he's na longer daft! The senses ha' come into his head, and he looks and speaks like a wise one."

When Yeddie reached the poor cot he called "home," 'he dared not to speak to "granny" who sheltered him, lest he might, as he said, "lose the bonny face." He left his "porritch and treacle" untasted; and after smiling on and patting the faded cheek of the old woman, to show her that he was not out of humour, he climbed the ladder to the poor loft where his pallet of straw was, to get another look and another word "fro" yon lovely Man." And his voice was heard below in low tones: "Aye, Lord, its just poor me that has been sae long seeking ye; and now we'll bid togither and never part more! Oh, aye! but this is a bonny loft, all goold and precious stones. The hall o' the castle is a poor place to my loft this bonny night!" And then his voice grew softer and softer till it died away.

Granny sat over the smouldering peat below, with her elbows on her knees, relating in loud whispers to a neighbouring crony the stories of the boys who had preceded Yeddie from the service, and also his own strange words and appearance. "And beside all this," she said, in a hoarse whisper, "he refused to taste his supper—a thing he had never done before since the parish paid his keeping. More than that, he often ate his own portion and mine too, and then cried for more; such a fearful appetite he had; But to-night, when he cam' in faint wi' the long road he had come, he cried, "Na meat for me, granny; I had a feast, which I will feel within me while I live; I supped wi' the Lord Jesus, and noo I must e'en gang up the loft and sleep wi' Him."

"Noo, Molly," replied granny's guest, "doesna' that remind ye of the words o' our Lord Jesus Himsel' when He tell'd them that bid Him eat, 'I ha' meat to eat that ye know not of?' Who'll dare say that the blessed hand that fed the multitude when they were seated upon the grass, hasna' been this day feeding the hungry soul o' poor Yeddie as he sat at His table? Ah! Molly, we little know what humble work He will stoop to do for His ain puir ones who cry day and night to Him! We canna' tell noo but this daft laddie will be greater in the kingdom of heaven than the Earl himsel'—puir body—that looks very little noo as if he'd be able to crowd in at the pearly gate!"

"And oh, Janet, if you could ha' seen the face of yon puir lad as he cam' into the cot! It just shone like the light, and at first, even before he spoke a word, I thocht he was carrying a candle in his hand! I believe in my soul, good neebor, that Yeddie was in great company to-day, and that the same *shining* was on him as was on Moses and Elias when they talked with Jesus on the Mount. I e'en hope he broct the blessing home wi' him to 'bide on the widow that was too auld and feeble to walk to the table, but who has borne with him, and toiled patiently for him, because he was one of the Lord's little and feeble ones."

"Oo, aye, doubtless he did bring home the blessing, and that ye'll get the reward o' these many cups o' cold water ye've given him; for what are the few pence or shillings the parish grants ye, compared wi' the mother's care ye give him," said Janet. "Awell, awell," replied granny," if I get the reward it'll not be because I wrought for *that*. I seemed ne'er to ken, syne the day I took the daft and orphanted lad, that I was minding and feeding, and clothing one o' "these little ones," and I ken it better to-night than ever. I ha' strange new feelings mysel' too, neebor, and I'm minded of the hour when our blessed Master came and stood among His faithful ones, the door being shut, and said, "peace be unto you." Surely this strange heavenly calm can no' be of earth, and who shall say that Himsel' is not here beside us twa' come to this poor place more for the daft lad's sake than oor ain." And thus these lowly women talked of Him whom their souls loved, their hearts burning within them as they talked.

When the morrow's sun arose "granny," unwilling to disturb the weary Yeddie, left her poor pillow to perform her humble tasks. She brought peat from the stack, and water from the spring She spread her humble table and made her "porritch;" and then, remembering that he went supperless to bed, she called him from the foot of the ladder. There was no reply. She called again and again, but there was no sound above, but the wind whistling through the openings in the thatch. She had not ascended the rickety ladder for years; but anxiety gave strength to her limbs, and she soon stood in the poor garret which had long sheltered the half-idiot boy. Before the rude stool, half-sitting, half-kneeling, with his head resting on his folded arms, she found Yeddie. She laid her hand upon his head, but instantly recoiled in terror. The heavy iron crown had been lifted from his brow, and, while she was sleeping, had been replaced with the crown of the ransomed which fadeth not away. Yeddie had caught a glimpse of Jesus and could not live apart from Him. As he had supped so he had slept,—with Him.

A deep awe fell on the parish and the minister for this evident token that Christ had been among them; and the funeral of the idiot boy was attended from far and wide. A solemnity rarely seen was noticed there as if a great loss had fallen on the community, instead of the parish having been relieved of a burden. Poor "granny" was not left alone in her cot; for He who had come thither after that last supper with Yeddie, was with her, and Christ's promises to His disciples were fulfilled: "I will not leave you comfortless; I will come to you." "Lo I am with you alway, even unto the end of the world."

—J. D. C.

"I have heard the voice of Jesus,
Tell me not of ought beside;
I have seen the face of Jesus,
All my soul is satisfied."

JERUSALEM AND CYPRUS.
(*Acts* 13 : 13 *and* 15 : 38, 39).

The four Gospels furnish a narrative of the acts of the Lord Jesus Christ; and, in the Acts of the Apostles, we have a narrative of the acts of God the Holy Spirit who came down on the day of Pentecost, and has been labouring here ever since. The Lord Jesus acted in His own immediate Person; and, in this way, we have, frequently to bear in mind, as we pass along the inspired missionary record, the infirmity and failure of the various instruments who, though used of God, were, in themselves, feeble men. And not only have we to take into account the infirmity of man, but also the hostile influence of surrounding circumstances, as used of Satan, for the purpose of hindering the work, and cramping and ensnaring the workmen. Thus the study of the Acts is most interesting and practical. In it, we have men and things, localities and their influences looked at, and presented by the Holy Spirit, with direct reference to the great work which He was, at that time, and still is carrying on.

At the close of the 12th chapter of Acts, we read, "And Barnabas and Saul returned from Jerusalem, when they had fulfilled their ministry, and took with them John whose surname was Mark." In the next chapter we find this same John Mark accompanying Paul and Barnabas, on a mission and continuing with them, during their sojourn in the Island of Cyprus;

but on their leaving that and proceeding "to Perga in Pamphylia," we read that, "John departing from them returned to Jerusalem" (13 : 13). Home influences as well as religious privileges, would, no doubt, attract the heart of John Mark, and induce him to abandon the arduous path of missionary labour. In chapter 12 we read of the "house of Mary, *the mother of John,* whose surname was Mark; where *many were gathered together praying."*

Here, we have the two paths, namely, the power of natural affection, and the rare spiritual attraction of christian fellowship. Need we wonder that John vastly preferred a prayer-meeting in his mother's house at Jerusalem, to the hardships of a mission in Pamphylia or Pisidia? Ah! my dear reader, is but too well able to understand the preference. There was a vast difference between a comfortable home—regular habits—a mother's love and care—the peaceful charms of well-ordered domestic life, and all the roughness, severity, and hardship of a precarious missionary tour. Furthermore, there was a striking contrast, indeed, between an assembly of loving and united christian friends gathered for prayer, in the city of Jerusalem, and a synagogue of bigoted Jews, at Antioch, or a fickle mob at Lystra of Lycaonia.

However, the judgment which we form of the actings of John Mark will entirely depend upon the point of view from which we contemplate them. In the judgment of mere nature, in its amiability or even religiousness, there was nothing reprehensible, but in the judgment of a well-girt, single-eyed servant of Christ, he was all wrong. It is very evident that Barnabas and Paul looked to Mark's conduct from those opposite points. A passage in Acts 15 proves this very clearly. "And some days after, Paul said unto Barnabas, Let us go again and visit our brethren in every city where we have preached the Word of the Lord, and see how they do. And Barnabas determined to take with them John, whose surname was Mark. But Paul thought not good to take him with them, who departed from them from Pamphylia, and *went not with them to the work.* And the contention was so sharp between them, that they departed asunder one from the other: and so Barnabas took *Mark,* and sailed unto *Cyprus."* Thus we see that Mark, by yielding to the attractive influences of his home at Jerusalem, not only abandoned the work, but also snapped the link between two workmen.

But whether was Paul or Barnabas in the right? The sequel answers "Paul chose Silas and departed, being recommended by the brethren unto the grace of God. And he went through Syria and Cilicia, confirming the churches." We hear nothing of Barnabas being recommended to the grace of God, or of his confirming the churches. In fact, his name never again appears in the inspired missionary record. He took his nephew (Col. 4 : 10) with him and sailed to Cyprus, where, upon his first starting on the christian course, he had sold his land (Acts 4 : 36). All this is full of meaning, full of deep and solemn instruction—replete with salutary warning for every one, who desires to pursue a path of thorough devotedness to Christ and His service. The voice which it utters is distinctly this—"Beware how you allow home influences, nature's soft and enervating attraction, or even spiritual advantages, to draw you off from the stern realities of active labour in the vineyard of Christ." Jerusalem and Cyprus had charms for John Mark and his uncle Barnabas—charms sufficiently powerful to allure them from the side of that ever earnest, ever harnessed workman, Paul.

But some may say, "Could not Barnabas and Mark serve the Lord at Jerusalem or Cyprus as well as at Perga or Antioch?" Assuredly. Paul himself, as we know, served in both these places. But was it the service of Christ that led Mark back to Jerusalem, or Barnabas back to Cyprus? This is the question. Let the spiritual reader answer it in the light of the Acts of the Apostles. One thing is plain—they both travelled out of the current of the Spirit's action, and their names never again appear in the inspired annals of missionary labour. True, they were both children of God, and servants of Christ. Barnabas "was a good man, and full of the Holy Spirit and of faith;" and, as to Mark, we find some touching allusions to him in Paul's epistles, which would warrant the conclusion that he had somewhat regained his place in the apostle's heart. "Aristarchus, my fellow-prisoner, saluteth you, and Marcus, sister's son to Barnabas, (touching whom ye received commandment) if he come unto you receive him" Col. 4 : 10). And again, "Take Mark and bring him with thee, *for he is profitable unto me for the ministry"* (2 Tim. 4 : 11).

It is also well worthy of notice, that the Holy Spirit should have selected Mark as His instrument to write that Gospel, which so especially presents Christ as the true Workman—the faithful Minister—the self-denying Servant—the One whom no influence whatever could move a single hair's breadth from the straight line of devotedness to God and His work. Doubtless a more enlarged communion with that only perfect Servant, had rendered Mark "profitable for the ministry," so that Paul could say to his devoted son Timothy, "Take Mark, and bring him with thee." Lovely picture! Precious fruit of Divine grace on all sides. The Lord had raised up Timothy to be a faithful yoke-fellow for Paul when both Mark and Barnabas had forsaken him; and now Timothy is commanded to take this Mark and bring him to Paul, as additional profitable help in the ministry. Such are the marvellous ways of grace.

O for a deeper and more abiding communion with the blessed Master. May we live near to Him. May we drink into His spirit, and walk

Let us also remind the reader it is failure at this point which constitutes the principal stumbling-block to unbelievers. I cannot commend Christ to others if I am miserable and wretched myself. But if I am "alway rejoicing" (2 Cor. 6 : 10), if my life is an anthem of praise unto God, those around will want to know the secret of it. Has the reader ever pondered the implication of 1 Pet. 3 : 15, "Be ready always to give an answer to every man that *asketh* you a reason of the hope that is in you?" Are *you* ever "asked?" Ah, my brethren, just so far as we are living for self, we are misrepresenting our Saviour, who "pleased not Himself" (Rom. 15 : 3). Just to the extent that we find our pleasure in the world, are we denying the sufficiency of Christ to fill the heart. Just so far as these things are true of us, are we a stumbling-block, a hindrance, a curse, to those around us.

Finally, we ought to "give ourselves unto the Lord" because His second coming is imminent. Each year that passes brings His return that much nearer: "For yet a little while, and He that shall come, will come, and will not tarry" (Heb. 10 : 38). Ah, if you knew for certain that ere 1929 expired the Lord Jesus shall have come again to receive us unto Himself, how would you live? Would there not be many changes made in your daily life? Would you not be more devoted to Him, more zealous in His service, more faithful in witnessing for Him? Well, He *may* come even before this month has run its course! Then yet your loins be girded, and your lamps trimmed and burning. Do you wish to see a look of grief in His eyes at His appearing, or one of joy as He says, "Well done, thou good and faithful servant?" O may His love constrain us to *"first* give ourselves unto the Lord."

> Take my life and let it be,
> Consecrated, Lord, to Thee.
> Keep my life and let it be,
> Glorifying, Lord, to Thee.

—*Arthur W. Pink.*

---

in His footsteps! Then shall we be raised above very influence that would tend to withdraw us from His service, whether that influence rises from Jerusalem or Cyprus. May we be nabled, by the grace of the Holy Spirit, to ird on the harness, and go forth in whole-earted devotedness to Christ, and His cause. he Lord, in His great mercy, grant it. May "be profitable for the ministry," in me small degree. Let us aim at a higher aracter of devotedness than ever we have exbited. Jesus is worthy of the supreme place in our heart's affections. If, therefore, His service calls us to endure hardness and roughness, privation and trial, let us not sigh after the attractions of Jerusalem or Cyprus. Let neither nature nor earth entangle us; but may our language ever be—

> "Were the whole realm of nature mine,
> That were an offering far too small,
> Love so amazing, so Divine,
> Demands my heart, my life, my all."

—Things New and Old, Vol. 3.

A PERSONAL WORD.

Coming to England as we did, with no open door" visible before us, and being on the outside of every thing ecclesiastical—we knew that a season of severe testing lay before us. such it has proved. During our four months here we have had only two comparatively brief speaking engagements, and at present everything *seems* to be fast closed against us. But, *'My grace is sufficient for thee"* is being realised in a most blessed way. The Lord is keeping our hearts in perfect peace. We have rented a small cottage in a little sea-side town for the winter, where we are devoting ourselves to the work of this Magazine. We are looking to God to grant us access to companies of His hungry people, in His own good time and way, to whom we may have the privilege of ministering His Word orally. We shall much value the prayers of Christian readers to this same end. In the meantime, we are giving Bible readings in our home to the few here who care for such things. *Teachers* of the Word are not in much demand these days—what a sign of the times! Is it not the fulfillment of that word in 2 Tim. 4 : 3, "For the time will come when they will not endure sound doctrine." Entertaining preaching, bright and cheery evangelistic addresses, are still listened to; but solid teaching is, with very rare exceptions, no longer tolerated.

Will readers continue praying for an enlarged circulation of "Studies."

A.W.P.

But if extreme Calvinists are largely ignorant of the practical truth of personal dedication to God, it is to be feared that many other Christians are strangers to it experimentally. Does not the present state of the cause of Christ on earth bear witness to the fact? Does the reader suppose that there would be such a shortage of missionaries, that half of the human race would still know nothing of the glorious Gospel of Christ, had even one tenth of His people really "given themselves to the Lord?" Would so many departments of Christian enterprise be crippled through lack of funds? Why is there such a shortage of teachers and preachers, we mean really sound ones, not "blind leaders of the blind?" Is it because so few of our Christian young men have "given *themselves* unto the Lord?"

We are well aware that there is a Divine side in being called to minister God's precious Word, but there is a human side too. *What* constitutes a "call" to be an evangelist? God rarely speaks immediately and directly; He generally employs instruments and means. Suppose that late at night you saw a house on fire, and there was an axe and a hose to hand. Would you wait for a call before you attempted to help? Would not the very urgency of the case, your knowledge of the danger of those within that house, be sufficient? And would not the means to hand make it your bounden duty *to* help? In like manner, if God has granted to you a saving knowledge of His truth, and all around are men and women which you see are going down to Hell as swiftly as time can take them, is not *that* a "call" for you to bid them" flee from the wrath to come?"

Ah, the real trouble is that many Christians are afraid to "give themselves unto the Lord" lest He take them at their word. They are fearful that He might send them out to China or India. But, my reader, we have nothing to do with consequences. Our first duty is to "give ourselves unto the Lord:" *how* God responds, *what* use He makes of our gift, is *His* business, not ours. It is not for us to reason why, it is not for us to make reply: it is for us to do, and die, if needs be: "Hereby perceive we the love of God, because He laid down His life for us: and *we ought* to lay down our lives for the brethren" (1 John 3 : 16). We do not wish to imply that God *would* send out to China or India every young Christian who truly dedicated himself to His service, but we do say that this is his first privilege and duty.

What is meant by "giving ourselves unto the Lord?" Surely there is but little need for a lengthy explanation. It is the response of a regenerated soul to God's call, "My son, *give Me* thine heart" (Prov. 23 : 26). It is a compliance with the terms of Christian dicipleship: "And whosoever doth not bear his cross, and come after Me, cannot be My disciple" (Luke 14 : 26). It is something which *we* do, a voluntary act on our part. It is obeying that Divine exhortation, "I beseech you therefore, brethren, by the mercies of God, that ye present your bodies *a living sacrifice,* holy, acceptable to God, which is your reasonable service" (Rom. 12 : 1). It is the complete consecration of ourselves to Christ, an unreserved placing of ourselves at His disposal. It is *love's* response to God's unspeakable Gift. It is the glad return of a heart that has been *won* by Christ.

Truly, this *is* a "reasonable service" (Rom. 12 : 1). When we think of the Lord of glory leaving the perfect peace and bliss of heaven, and coming down to this world of sin and suffering; when we recall that while here, He "had not where" to lay His head; when we behold Him led as a lamb to the slaughter; when we go to Calvary, and see Him bearing our sin in His own body on the tree; unless gratitude within us is dead, can our hearts remain unmoved? Is there no response unto Him who cried, "Is it nothing to you, all ye that pass by? Behold, and see if there be any sorrow like unto My sorrow" (Lam. 1 : 12)? Surely the least we can do is to dedicate ourselves to Him, spirit and soul and body. Surely, Love so amazing, so Divine, *demands* my life, my love, my all.

Christ Himself has left us an example so to do: 'Who loved me, and *gave Himself* for me" (Gal. 2 : 20). Yes, that bearing shame and scoffing rude, that passing through such unparalleled suffering, that being forsaken both by God and man, was for *me*. And now that He has saved me at such tremendous cost, and with such a wondrous salvation, He has left me here in the world for a little while. What for? To make money? To enjoy selfish ease? No, to *represent Him,* to show unto others something of His spirit; and the starting-point of this is that, we "first *give ourselves* unto the Lord."

Again; it is only as we thus completely dedicate ourselves unto the Lord that a joyous life is possible. Why do so few Christians retain their first love? Why is it many so quickly lose the "joy of God's salvation?" Why is it that few have settled peace and full assurance? The answer is not far to seek: it is because they have failed to definitely and unreservedly "give themselves unto the Lord." We need hardly say that the man of the world has an altogether erroneous idea of both the nature and source of happiness. He supposes it lies in the possession of things, in the gratification of selfish desires. The Christian knows better: he has learned that all under the sun is "vanity and vexation of spirit." But he also needs to learn that satisfaction and joy are only to be found in Christ, and they, to the fullest extent, only through entire consecration to Him.

(Continued on Page 23.)

STUDIES IN THE SCRIPTURES

VOL. VIII.   FEBRUARY, 1929   NO. 2

"Search the Scriptures" John 5 : 39

Copyright in all English-speaking Countries.

Editor: Arthur W. Pink, Sidmouth Road, Seaton, Devon, England.
Hon. Agent in U.S.A.: Mr. C. S. Pressel, 559, Dupont Avenue, York, Penna.
Hon. Agent in Australia: Mr. G. Ardill, The Christian Workers' Depot.
Commonwealth and Reservoir Streets, Sydney.

FREE TO ALL WHO WILL READ IT.

THE DIVINE PRECEPTS.

The actual word "precepts" is found more frequently in Psalm 119 than in any other chapter in the Bible. Not only so, it occurs there oftener than all the other references in the Bible added together. It is very striking and profitable to trace through this lengthy Psalm the various references which are there made to God's "precepts." Here, as ever in Holy Writ, the *order* is perfect, and as we examine them it will be found their order is a *progressive* one.

The first reference is in verse 4: "Thou hast commanded us to keep Thy precepts diligently." The Holy Spirit begins by emphasising their authority. They are not to be treated lightly, but kept diligently. They are not the counsels of a fellow-mortal, but the decrees of the eternal and all—wise God. They are not merely commended to our notice, but we are commanded to keep them.

The next reference is in verse 15: "I will meditate in Thy precepts." This is what we *must* do if we are to "keep" them. They need to be frequently pondered, lest we "let them slip" (Heb. 2 : 1). A very searching word is this. We love to "meditate" on God's promises, are we equally fond of meditating upon His *precepts?* The answer to that question reveals the state of our hearts. We *are*, if really anxious to please Him.

Next in verse 27, we read, "Make me to understand the way of Thy precepts." The order is still progressive. As we meditate on God's precepts we begin to feel there is a breadth about them which we do not altogether grasp: as David says later on, "Thy commandment is exceeding *broad*" (v. 96). God's precepts are many-sided, of wide and varied applications. Thus, "meditation" thereon brings us to realise the need for Divine instruction—for guidance as to the application of them to all the varied details of our lives.

Then, in verse 40, "Behold I have looked after Thy precepts." That does not come first. If we are honest, we have to acknowledge with shame and sorrow, that we were far from "longing after" God's precepts at the beginning of our Christian lives. By Divine grace we were constrained to fear and respect them; but oftentimes we had a secret wish they were not there. But as we "meditate" upon them, as we *pray* over them, ask God to make us understand "the way" of them—i.e. the peace and blessing which ever attend the diligent keeping of them—we come to "long after" them.

"I will walk at liberty, for I seek Thy precepts" (v. 45). This is another decided advance; here the Psalmist contemplates the blessings consequent upon setting his heart on God's precepts. How different was the view he took from that which is ever entertained by the carnal mind. The natural man supposes that the keeping of God's commands means a foregoing of his freedom: that it means a fettering of him with a lot of restrictions which will rob him of his liberty. How this proves that Satan has blinded his mind (2 Cor. 4 : 4). It is not the man who obeys God, but he who disobeys Him who is in the "bonds of iniquity." The very freedom which the sinner *thinks he* is enjoying by indulging his fleshly propensities, is only additional proof that he *is* the "bond-slave of sin." Love of self, love of the world, love of money, love of pleasure, are the tyrants which rule over all who are away from God. The more we are serving God, the greater is our freedom.

(Continued on Page 48)

IMPORTANT NOTICES

Back numbers of the last four years of this magazine are yet obtainable, nicely and strongly bound at 7/6 each, post paid. They will soon be out of print. Those in U.S.A. wanting them, please purchase from Mr. Pressel (see front cover page).

Advise promptly of change of address otherwise copies will be lost in the mails.

This Magazine is published as a work of faith and labour of love. The Editor gladly gives his services. It is freely sent to all who will read it. No charge is made for it.

Christians who feel definitely led to do so, may have fellowship with us in this Ministry. Send only *Inter-National* M.O. made out to Seaton, Devon, England.

CONTENTS.

	Page
Hebrews	26
Gleanings in Exodus	32
Life of Abram	35
Romans 7	39
Grapes of Eschol	43
Laughter	46

THE EPISTLE TO THE HEBREWS.

14. *Christ Superior to Moses* Heb. 3 : 7-12.

In the first six verses of our present chapter four things were before us. First, the call to "consider" the Apostle and High Priest of our profession. Of old, Moses was God's apostle or ambassador to Israel, Aaron, the high priest. But Christ combines both these offices in His own person. Second, the superiority of Christ over Moses: this is set forth in **seven details** which it is unnecessary for us to specify again. Third, the one thing which the Spirit of God singles out from the many gifts and excellencies which Divine grace had bestowed upon Moses, was his "faithfulness" (vv. 2, 5); so too is it there said of Christ Jesus that He was "faithful to Him that appointed Him" (v. 2). Fourth, the assertion that membership in the household of Christ is evidenced, chiefly, by holding fast the confidence and rejoicing of the hope firm unto the end (v. 6). That there is an intimate connection between these four things and the contents of our present passage will appear in our exposition thereof.

"If we hold fast the confidence and the rejoicing of the hope firm unto the end." The "hope" mentioned here is that made known by the Gospel (Col. 1 : 23), the hope which is laid up for God's people in Heaven (Col. 1 :5), the hope of glory (Col. 1 : 27). Christians have been begotten unto a living hope (1 Peter 1 : 3), that "blessed hope" (Titus 2 : 13), namely, the return of our God and Saviour Jesus Christ, when He shall come to take us unto Himself, to make us like Himself, to have us forever with Himself; when all God's promises concerning us shall be made good. The reference to the holding fast the "confidence" of this hope is not subjective, but objective. It signifies a fearless profession of the Christian faith. It is to be "ready *always* to give an answer to every man that asketh you, a reason of the hope that is in you, with meekness and fear" (1 Peter 3 : 15). Stephen is an illustration. Then, this hope is also to be held fast with "rejoicing" firm unto the end: Paul is an example of this, Acts 20 : 24.

What follows in our present portion contains a solemn and practical application of that which we have briefly reviewed above. Here the apostle is moved to remind the Hebrews of the *un*-faithfulness of Israel in the past and of the dire consequences which followed their failure to hold fast unto the end of their wilderness pilgrimage the confidence and rejoicing of the hope which God had set before them. A passage is quoted from the 95th Psalm which gives most searching point to both that which precedes and to that which follows. The path in which God's people are called to walk is that of faith, and such a path is necessarily, full of testings, that is, of difficulties and trials, and many are the allurements for tempting us to wander off into "By-path meadow." Many, too, are the warnings and danger-signals which the faithfulness of God has erected; unto one of them we shall now turn.

"Wherefore" (v. 7). This opening word of our present passage possesses a threefold force. First, it is a conclusion drawn from all that precedes. Second, it prefaces the application of what is found in 3 : 1-6. Third, it lays a foundation for what follows. The reader will observe that the remaining words of v. 7 and all of vv. 8 to 11 are placed in brackets, and we believe rightly so, the sentence being completed in v. 12: "Wherefore take heed, brethren, lest there be in any of you an evil heart of unbelief, in departing from the living God."

The reasons for this exhortation have been pointed out above. First, because of the supreme excellency of our Redeemer, exalted high above all Israel's prophets, and given a name more excellent than any ever conferred on the angels; therefore, those who belong to Him should give good heed that they harden not their hearts against Him, nor depart from Him. Second, because the Apostle, Christ Jesus, is worthy of more honour than Moses, then how incumbent it is upon His people to be especially watchful that they be not, by any means, turned from that obedience which He requires and which is most certainly due Him. Third, in view of the lamentable history of Israel, who, despite God's wondrous favours to them, hardened their hearts, grieved Him, and so provoked Him to wrath, that He sware they should not enter into His rest, how much on our guard we need to be of "holding fast" the confidence and rejoicing of our hope "firm unto the end!"

"As the Holy Spirit saith." Striking indeed is it to mark the way in which the apostle introduces the quotation made from the O.T. It is from the 95th Psalm, but the human instrument that was employed in the penning of it is ignored, attention being directed to its Divine Author, the One who "moved" the Psalmist— cf 2 Peter 1 : 20, 21. The reason for this, here, seems to be because Paul would press upon these Hebrews the weightiness, the Divine authority of the words he was about to quote: consider well that what follows are the words of the Holy Spirit, so that you may promptly and unmurmuringly submit yourselves thereunto.

"As the Holy Spirit saith." This is the more forceful if it be linked up with Heb. 1 : 1 and 2 : 3. In the former it is God, the Father, who "spake." In 2 : 3, "How shall we escape if we neglect so great salvation, which at the first began to be *spoken* by the Lord?:" there it is the Son. Here in 3 : 7 the Speaker is the Spirit; thus, by linking together these three passages we hear all the Persons of the Godhead. Observe, next, the tense of the verb used here; it is not "the Holy Spirit said," but "saith:" it is an ever-present, living message to God's people in each succeeeding generation. "Whatever was given by inspiration from the Holy Ghost, and is recorded in the Scripture for the use of the Church, He continues therein to speak it unto us unto this day" (Dr. J. Owen). Let the reader also carefullly compare the seventimes-repeated, "he that hath an ear to hear, let him hear what the Spirit *saith* unto the churches" in Rev. 2 and 3.

"As the Holy Spirit saith." Dr. Gouge has pointed out how that this sentence teaches us four things about the Holy Spirit. First, that He is true God: for "*God* spake by the mouth of David" (Acts 4 : 25). "God" spake by the prophets (Heb. 1 : 1), and they "spake as they were moved by the Holy Spirit" (2 Peter 1 : 21). Second, the Holy Spirit is a distinct person: He "saith." An influence, a mere abstraction, cannot speak. Third, the Holy Spirit subsisted before Christ was manifested in the flesh, for He spake through David. True, He is called, "the Spirit of Christ," yet that He was before His incarnation is proven by Gen. 1 : 2 and other scriptures. Fourth, He is the Author of the O.T. scriptures, therefore are they of Divine inspiration and authority.

"To-day if ye will hear His voice, harden not your hearts" (vv. 7 : 8). Here begins the apostle's quotation from Psa. 95, the first portion of which records a most fervent call (vv. 1, 6) for the people of God to be joyful, and come before Him as worshippers. Most appropriate was the reference to this Psalm here, for the contents of its first seven verses contain, virtually an amplification of the "consider" of 3:1. There the Hebrews were enjoined to be occupied with Christ, and if their hearts were engaged with His surpassing excellency and exalted greatness, then would they "come before His presence with thanksgiving, and make a joyful noise unto Him with psalms" (Psa. 95 : 2).

Their Apostle and High Priest had "built all things" (Heb. 3 : 4), being none other than God. The same truth is avowed in Psalm 95 : 3-5, "For the Lord is a great God, and a great King above all gods. In His hand are the deep places of the earth: the strength of the hills is His also. The sea is His, and He made it: and His hands formed the dry land." The apprehension of this will prepare us for a response to what follows, "O come, let us worship, and bow down: let us kneel before the Lord our Maker. For He is our God; and we are the people of His pasture, and the sheep of His hand" (Psa. 95 : 6, 7).

The next thing in the Psalm is, "To-day, *if* ye will hear His voice harden not your heart." So the next thing in Heb. 3 is, "whose house are we *if* we hold fast the confidence and the rejoicing of the hope firm unto the end." Thus the Psalmist admonished those addressed in his day to hearken to the voice of the Lord, and not to harden their hearts against Him as had their ancestors before them. By quoting this here in Heb. 3, the apostle at once intimated what is the *opposite* course from holding fast their confidence.

"To-day" signifies the time present, yet so as to include a continuance of it. It is not to be limited to twenty-four hours, instead, this term sometimes covers a present interval which consists of many days, yea years. In Heb. 3 : 13 it is said, "But exhort one another daily, while it is called To-day." So in Heb. 13 : 8 we read, "Jesus Christ the same yesterday, and to-day, and forever." So in our text. As that present time wherein David lived was to him and those then alive "to-day", so that present time in which the apostle and the Hebrews lived was to them "to-day," and the time wherein we now live, is to us "to-day." It covers that interval while men are alive on earth, while God's grace and blessing are available to them. It spans the entire period of our wilderness pilgrimage. Thus the "end" of Heb. 3 : 6 is the close of the "today" in v. 7.

"If ye will hear His voice." "Unto you, O men I call; and My voice is to the sons of man" (Prov. 8 : 4). But no doubt the immediate reference in our text is unto those professing to be God's people. The "voice" of God is the signification of His will, which is the rule of our obedience. His will is made known in His Word, which is a *living* Word, by which the voice of God is now uttered. But, alas, we are capable of closing our ears to His voice. Of old God complained, "The ox knoweth his owner, and the ass his master's crib: but Israel doth not know, My people doth not consider" (Isa. 1 : 3). To "hear" God's voice signifies to attend reverently to what He says, to diligently ponder, to readily receive, and to heed or obey it. It is the hardening of our hearts which prevents us, really, hearing His voice, as the next clause intimates. To it we now turn.

"If ye will hear His voice, harden not your hearts." It is to the *heart* God's Word is addressed, that moral centre of our beings out of which are the issues of life (Prov. 4 : 23). There may be conviction of the conscience, the assent of the intellect, the admiration of the understanding, unless the heart is moved there is no response. A tender heart is a pliable and responsive one; a hard heart is obdurate and rebellious. Here hardening of the heart is attributed to the creature: it is due to impenitency (Rom. 2 : 5), unbelief (Heb. 3 : 12), disobedience (Psa. 95 : 8).

"It appears that unto this sinful hardening of the heart which the people in the wilderness were guilty of, and which the apostle here warns the Hebrews to avoid, there are three things that do concur: 1. A *sinful neglect*, in not taking due notice of the ways and means whereby God calls any unto faith and obedience. 2. A *sinful forgetfulness and casting out* of the heart and mind such convictions as God by His word and works, His mercies and judgments, His deliverances and afflictions, at any time is pleased to cast into them and fasten upon them. 3. An *obstinate cleaving of the affections* unto carnal and sensual objects, practically preferring them above the motives unto obedience that God proposeth unto us. Where these things are so, the hearts of men are so hardened, that in an ordinary way, they cannot hearken unto the voice of God. Such is the nature, efficacy and power of the voice or word of God, that men cannot withstand or resist it without a sinful hardening of themselves against it. Every one to whom the word is duly revealed, who is not converted to God, doth *voluntarily* oppose his own obstinancy unto its efficacy and operation. If men will add new obstinacy and hardness to their minds and hearts, if they will fortify themselves against the word with prejudices and dislikes, if they will resist its work through a love to their lusts and corrupt affections, God may justly leave them to perish, and to be filled with the fruit of their own ways" (Dr. J. Owen).

"Harden not your hearts, as in the provocation, in the day of temptation in the wilderness" (v. 8). The reference here is to what is recorded in the early verses of Ex. 17. There we are told that the congregation of Israel journeyed to Rephidim, where there was "no water for the people to drink." Instead of them counting on Jehovah to supply their need, as He had at Marah (Ex. 15 : 25) and in the wilderness of Sin (16 : 4), they "did chide with Moses" (v. 2), "and when they thirsted, the people murmured against Moses, (and said, Wherefore is this that thou hast brought us up out of Egypt, to kill us and our children and our cattle with thirst?" (v. 3). Though Moses cried unto the Lord, and the Lord graciously responded by bringing water out of the rock for them, yet God's servant was greatly displeased, for in v. 7 we are told, "And he called the name of the place Massah (Tentation) and Meribah (Strife), because of the chiding of the children of Israel and because they tempted the Lord, saying, Is the Lord among us, or not".

Once more we would point out the appositeness of this quotation to the case of the Hebrews. "The thought of Moses (in vv. 1 to 5 A. W. P.) naturally suggests Israel in the wilderness. Faithful was the mediator, through whom God dealt with them; but was Israel faithful? God spake: did they obey? God showed them wonder signs: did they trust and follow in faith? And if Israel was not faithful under Moses, and their unbelief brought ruin upon them, how much more guilty shall we be, and how much greater our danger, if we are not faithful unto the Lord Jesus" (Saphir).

It is not only true that the difficulties and trials of the way test us, but these testings reveal the state of our hearts—a crisis neither makes nor mars a man, but it does *manifest* him. While all is smooth sailing we appear to be getting along nicely, But are we? Are our minds stayed upon the Lord, or are we, instead, complacently resting in His temporal mercies? When the storm breaks, it is not so much that we fail under it, as that our habitual lack of leaning upon God, of daily walking in dependency upon Him, is made evident. Circumstances do not change us, but they do *expose* us. Paul rejoiced in the Lord when circumstances were congenial. Yes, and he also sang praises to Him when his back was bleeding in the Philippian dungeon. The fact is, that if we sing only when circumstances are pleasing to us, then our singing is worth nothing, and there is grave reason to doubt whether we are rejoicing "in *the Lord*" (Phil. 4 : 4) at all.

The reason Israel murmured at Meribah was because there was no water; they were occupied with their circumstances, they were walking by sight. The crisis they then faced only served to make manifest the state of their hearts, namely, an "evil heart of *unbelief*." Had their trust been in Jehovah, they would at once have turned to Him, spread their need before Him, and *counted* on Him to supply it. But their hearts were hardened. A most searching warning was this for the Hebrews. Their circumstances were most painful to the flesh. They were enduring a great fight of afflictions. How were they enduring it? If they were murmuring that would be the outward expression of unbelief within. Ah, it is easy to *profess* we are Believers, but the challenge still rings out, 'What doth it profit, my brethren, though a may say he hath faith, and have not works?'' (James 2 : 14).

"When your fathers tempted Me, proved Me, and saw My works forty years" (v. 9). The "when" looks back to what is mentioned in the previous verse. The "Day of Temptation in the wilderness" covered the whole period of Israel's journeyings from the Red Sea to Canaan. "The history of the Israelites is a history of continued provocation. In the wilderness of Sin they murmured for the want of bread, and God gave then manna. At Rephidim they murmured for the want of water, and questioned whether Jehovah was with them; and He gave them water from the rock. In the wilderness of Sinai, soon after receiving the law, they made and worshipped a golden image. At Taberah they murmured for want of flesh; and the quails were sent, followed by a dreadful plague. At Kadesh-barnea they refused to go up and take possession of the land of promise, which brought down on them the awful sentence referred to in the Psalm; and after that sentence was pronounced, they presumptuously attempted to do what they had formerly refused to do. All these things took place in little more than two years after they left Egypt. Thirty-seven years after this, we find them at Kadesh again, murmuring for want of water and other things. Soon after this, they complained of the want of bread, though they had manna in abundance, and were punished by the plague of fiery flying serpents. And at Shittim, their last station, they provoked the Lord by mingling in the impure idoltry of the Moabites. So strikingly true is Moses' declaration: "Remember, and forget not, how thou provokedst the Lord thy God to wrath in the wilderness: from the day that thou didst depart out of the land of Egypt, until ye came unto this place ye have been rebellious against the Lord' Duet. 9 : 7" (Dr. J. Brown).

"When your fathers tempted Me, proved Me, and saw My works forty years" (v. 9). Israel's terrible sins in the wilderness are here set forth under two terms: they "tempted" and "proved" Jehovah, the latter being added as an explanation of the former. To tempt one is to try or prove whether he be such as he is declared to be, or whether he can or will do such and such a thing. By tempting God Israel found out by experience that he was indeed the God He had made Himself known to be. In this passage the tempting of God is set down as a sin which provoked Him, and so is to be taken in its worst sense. Instead of believing His declaration, Israel acted as though they would discover, at the hazard of their own destruction, whether or not He would make good His promises and His threatenings.

"In particular men tempt God by two extremes: one is presumption, the other is distrustfulness. Both these arise from unbelief. That distrustfulness ariseth from unbelief is without all question. And however presumption may seem to arise from overmuch confidence, yet if it be narrowly searched into, we shall find that men presume upon unwarrantable courses, because they do not believe that God will do what is meet to be done, in His own way. Had the Israelites believed that God in His time and in His own way would have destroyed the Canaanites, they would not have presumed, against an express charge, to have gone against them without the ark of the Lord and without Moses, as they did, Num. 14 : 40 etc. Alas, what is man!

"Men do presumptuously tempt God, when, without warrant, they presume on God's extraordinary power and providence; that whereunto the devil persuaded Christ when he had carried Him up to a pinnacle of the temple, namely, to cast Himself down, was to tempt God; therefore, Christ gives him this answer, 'Thou shall not tempt the Lord thy God,' Matt. 4 : 5-7. Men distrustfully tempt God when in distress they imagine that God cannot or will not afford sufficient succor. Thus did the king of Israel tempt God when he said, 'The Lord hath called these three kings together, to deliver them into the hand of Moab,' 2 Kings 3 : 13. So that prince who said 'Behold, if the Lord would make windows in heaven, might this thing be' 2 Kings 7 : 2'' (Dr. W. Gouge).

"And saw My works forty years." This brings out the inexcusableness and heinousness of Israel's sin. It was not that Jehovah was a Stranger to them, for again and again He had shown Himself strong on their behalf. The "works" of God mentioned here are the many and great wonders which He did from the time that He first took them up in Egypt until the end of the wilderness journey. Some of them were works of *mercy*. In delivering them from enemies and dangers, and in providing for them things needful. Others were works of *judgment*, as the plagues upon the Egyptians, their destruction at the Red Sea, and His chastening of themselves. Still other were *manifestations* which He made of Himself, as by the Cloud which led them by day and by night, the awesome proofs of His presence on Sinai, and the Shekinah glory which filled the tabernacle. These were not "works" done in bygone ages, or in far-distant places, of which they had only heard; but were actually performed before them, upon them, which they "saw." What clearer evidence could they have of God's providence and power? Yet they tempted Him! The clearest evidences God grants to us have no effect upon unbelieving and obdurate hearts.

An unspeakably solemn warning is this for all who profess to be God's people to-day. A still more wonderful and glorious manifestation has God now made of Himself than any which Israel ever enjoyed. God has been manifested in flesh. The only-begotten Son has declared the Father. He has fully displayed His matchless grace and fathomless love by coming here and dying for poor sinners. When He left the earth, He sent the Holy Spirit, so that *we* now have not a Moses, but the third Person of the Trinity to guide us. God made known His laws unto Israel, but His complete Word is now in our hands. What more can He say, than to us He has said! How great is our responsibility; how immeasureably greater than Israel's our sin and guilt, if we despise Him who speaks to us!

A further aggravation of Israel's sin is that they saw God's wondrous works for "forty years." God continued His wonders all that time: despite their unbelief and murmuring the manna was sent daily till the Jordan was crossed! Man's incredulity cannot hinder the workings of God's power: "What if some did not believe? shall their unbelief make the faith of God without effect? God forbid" (Rom. 3 : 3). An incredulous prince would not believe that God could give such plenty as He had promised when Samaria by a long siege was famished; yet, "it came to pass as the man of God had spoken" (2 Kings 7 : 18). Nor would the Jews, nor even the disciples of Christ, believe that the Lord Jesus would rise again from the dead; yet He did so on the third day. O the marvellous patience of God! May the realization of it melt and move our hearts to repentance and obedience.

"Wherefore I was grieved with that generation" (v. 10). In these words, and those which follow, we learn the fearful consequences of Israel's sin. "When God says He 'was grieved' He means that He was burdened, vexed, displeased beyond that forbearance could extend unto. This includes the judgment of God concerning the greatness of their sin with all its aggravations and His determinate purpose to punish them. Men live, speak and act as if they thought God very little concerned in what they do, especially in their sins; that either He takes no notice of them, or if He do, that He is not much concerned in them; or that He should be grieved at His heart—that is, have such a deep sense of man's sinful provocations—they have no mind to think or believe. They think that, as to thoughts about sins, God is altogether as themselves. But it is far otherwise, for God hath a *concernment of honour* in what we do; He makes us for His glory and honour, and whatsoever is contrary thereunto tends directly to His dishonour. And this God cannot but be deeply sensible of; He cannot deny Himself. He is also concerned as a God of *Justice*. His holiness and justice is His nature, and He needs no other reason to punish sin but Himself" (Dr. J. Owen).

"And said, They do alway err in their heart" (v. 10). To err in the heart signifies to draw the wicked and false conclusion that sin and rebellion pay better than subjection and obedience to God. Through the power of their depraved lusts, the darkness of their understandings, and the force of temptations, countless multitudes of Adam's fallen decendents imagine that a course of self-will is preferable to subjection unto the Lord. Sin deceives: it makes men call darkness light, bitter sweet, bondage liberty. The language of men's hearts is, "What is the Almighty, that we should serve Him? and what profit should we have, if we pray unto Him?" (Job 21 : 15). Note Israel *alway* erred in their hearts," which evidenced the hopelessness of their state. They were radically and habitually evil. As Moses told them at the end, "Ye have been rebellious against the Lord from the day that I knew you" (Deut. 9 : 24).

And they have not known My ways (v. 10). The word "ways" is used in Scripture both of God's dispensations or providences and of His precepts. A way is that wherein one walks. It is not God's secret "ways" (Isa. 55 : 9, Rom. 9 : 33), but His manifest ways which are here in view. His manifest ways are particularly His *works*, in which He declares Himself and exhibits His perfections, see Psa. 145 : 17. The works of God are styled His "ways" because we may see Him, as it were, walking therein: "they have seen Thy goings, O God " (Psa. 68 : 24). Now it is our duty to meditate on God's works or "ways" (Psa. 143 : 5), to admire and magnify the Lord in them (Psa. 138 : 4, 5), to acknowledge the righteousness of them (Psa. 145 : 17. God's precepts are also termed His way and "ways" (Psa. 119 : 27, 32, 33, 35), because they make known the paths in which He would have us walk. Israel's ignorance of God's ways, both His works and precepts, was a wilful one, for they neglected and rejected the means of knowledge which God afforded them; they obstinately refused to acquire a practical knowledge of them, which is the only knowledge of real value.

"So I sware in My wrath, They shall not enter into My rest" (v. 11). This was the fearful issue of Israel's sin. The patience of God was exhausted. Their inveterate unbelief and continued rebellion incensed Him. The sentence He pronounced against them was irrevocable, confirmed by His oath. The sentence was that they should not enter into Canaan, spoken of as a "rest" because entrance therein would have terminated their wilderness trials and travels: "God's rest," because it would complete His work of bringing Israel into the land promised their fathers, and because His sojournings (see Lev. 25 : 23), with His pilgrims would cease.

"We may observe, 1. When God expresseth great indignation in Himself against sin, it is to teach men the greatness of sin in themselves. 2. God gives the same stability unto His threatenings as unto His promises. Men are apt to think the *promises* are firm and stable, but as for the threatenings, they suppose some way or other they may be evaded. 3. When men have provoked God by their impenitency to decree their punishment irrevocably, they will find severity in the execution. 4. It is the presence of God alone that renders any place or condition good or desirable 'they shall not enter into My rest'" (Dr. J. Owen).

"Take heed, brethren, lest there be in any of you an evil heart of unbelief, in departing from the living God" (v. 12). Here the apostle begins to make a practical application to the believing Hebrews of the solemn passage which has just been quoted from the 95th Psalm. He warns them against the danger of apostatising. This is clear from the expression "in departing from the living God." The same Greek verb is rendered "fall away" in Luke 8 : 13, and in its noun form signifies "apostasy" in 2 Thess. 2 : 3. Such apostasy is the inevitable outcome of giving way to an "evil heart of unbelief," against which the apostle bids those to whom he was writing to "take heed."

Thus the contents of this verse at once bring before us a subject which has been debated in Christendom all through the centuries—the possibility or the impossibility of a true child of God apostatising and finally perishing. Into this vexed question we shall not here enter, as the contents of the verses which immediately follow will oblige us taking it up, D.V. in our next article. Suffice it now to say that what is here in view is the *testing of profession;* whether the profession be genuine or spurious, the ultimate outcome of that testing makes evident in each individual's case.

"Take heed brethren." The introducing here of this blessed and tender title of God's saints is very searching. Those unto whom the apostle was writing, might object, The scripture you have cited has no legitimate application to *us;* that passage describes the conduct of unbelievers, whereas *we* are believers." Therefore does the apostle again address them as "brethren;" nevertheless, he bids them "take heed." They were not yet out of danger, they were still in the wilderness. Those mentioned in Psa. 95 began well, witness their singing the praises of Jehovah on the farther shores of the Red Sea (Ex. 15). They too had avowed their fealty to the Lord: "all the people answered together, and said All that the Lord hath spoken we will do" (Ex. 19 : 8); yet the fact remains that many *of them* apostatised and perished in the wilderness. Therefore the searching relevancy of this word, "take heed brethren lest there be in any *of you* an evil heart of unbelief."

"In departing from the living God." The reference here is plainly to the Lord Jesus Himself. In Matt. 16 : 16 the Father is denominated "the living God," here and in 1 Tim. 4 : 10 the Son is, in 2 Cor. 6 : 16 (cf 1 Cor. 3 : 16) the Holy Spirit is. The reason for the application of this Divine title to the Saviour in this verse is apparent: the temptation confronting the Hebrews was not to become atheists, but to abandon their profession of Christianity. The unbelieving Jews denounced Jesus Christ as an imposter, and were urging those who believed in Him to renounce Him and return to Judiasm, and thus return to the true God, Jehovah. That Christ is God the apostle had affirmed here, in v. 4, and he now warns them that so far from the abandonment of the Christian profession and a return to Judaism being a going back to Jehovah, it would be the "*departing from* the living God." That Christ was the true and living God had been fully demonstrated by the apostle in the preceding chapters of this epistle.

The extent to which and the manner in which the warning from Psa 95 and the admonition of Heb. 3 : 12 applies to Christians to-day, we must leave for consideration till next month, D.V. In the meantime let us heed the exhortation of 2 Peter 1 : 10, "Wherefore the rather, brethren, give diligence to make your calling and election sure," and while attending to this duty, let us pray the more frequently and the more earnestly for God to deliver *us* from "an evil heart of unbelief."

—*Arthur W. Pink.*

The following books by the Editor may be obtained from him:—

Gleanings in Genesis, (46 articles), the 2 Volumes, 12/6.
The Redeemer's Return, 400 pages ... ... 7/6.
The Sovereignty of God ... ... 7/6.
The 7 Sayings of Christ on the Cross ... ... 4/6.

GLEANINGS IN EXODUS.

62. *Israel Plagued Ex. 32 : 28 to 33 : 2.*

Our last article closed with the descent of Moses from the mount and, upon his beholding the idolatries of Israel, his giving a stern commission to the Levites: "Put every man his sword by his side, go in and out from gate to gate throughout the camp, and slay every man his brother, and every man his companion, and every man his neighbour." In their response we behold the spirit triumphing over the flesh, the claims of Jehovah's holiness over-riding all natural and sentimental considerations: "And the children of Levi did according to the word of Moses: and there fell of the people that day about three thousand men. For Moses had said, Consecrate yourselves to-day to the Lord, even every man upon his son, and upon his brother; that He may bestow upon you a blessing this day" (vv. 28, 29).

The above verses present several most striking contrasts. First, from what is recorded in Gen. 34 : 25, 26, where, too, the "sword" is seen in the hand of Levi, not for Jehovah's glory, but in fleshly anger—cf. Gen. 49 : 5-7. Second, from what is said in Ex. 28 : 41, where we read of the sons of Aaron being consecrated that they might minister unto the Lord in the priest's office. The word "consecrate" means to "fill the hand," the reference being to the sweet-savour offerings and fragrant incense with which they were to appear before Jehovah. But here in our present portion their hands were filled with swords, to slay those who had apostatised. Third, from what is recorded in Acts 2 : 41: on the day of Israel's idolatry there fell of the people "about three thousand men," on the day of Penticost "about three thousand souls" were saved!

Fearful was the ensuing carnage. Stupefied with terror and awed by the irresistable power with which Moses was known to be invested, and by the sight of the threatening Cloud upon the mount above them, the people offered no resistance, and three thousand of them were put to death. "And so they were left for the night: the day of sin had ended in lamentation and woe. The camp, which in the morning had resounded with unholy merriment and licentious song, was full of groans and sighs: the dead awaited burial, and the wounded cried for pain. And every soul was weighed down, if not with remorse for the sin, at least with dread, lest wrath should go forth from the Lord, and the destroying angel appear with sword outstretched to smite the wicked people, who, after hearing the law uttered by the awful voice of God Himself, and promising to do all that He had spoken, and then, even before the signs of His presence were removed, lightly passed over to idolatry and fornication" (G. H. Pember).

"Now all these things happened unto them for types" (1 Cor. 10 : 11), that is, types *for us;* "types" mark, not precedents, not examples for us to imitate. The weapons of our warfare "are not carnal," (2 Cor. 10 : 4), but "spiritual." No place for the literal sword is provided in the Christian's equipment. It is a perversion of the Scriptures, a failure to rightly divide the Word of Truth, to appeal to Israel's history as warrant for us to use physical force. No, No; the material things connected with them, were but figures of the spiritual things which belong to us. What, then, is the lesson for us in this solemn work committed to the Levites? Is not the answer obvious? Uncompromising and unsparing dealing with all that is dishonouring to God, with everything that savours of idolatry.

The Christian possesses a sword, but it is "the sword of the Spirit, which is the Word of God" (Eph. 6 : 17). With that sword we are called on to smite every enemy which lifts up its head against Christ. "The sword must be drawn against every influence that corrupts the people of God, even though it may have a place in those nearest us. It might seem very severe to treat brethren, friends, neighbours, in this way, but it was the only way to be consecrated to Jehovah, and to secure His blesing. When what *is* due to the Lord is in question, it is with those nearest to you that you have to be most decided. There is no particular conscration in drawing the sword against people you care little about. But to take a definite stand for the Lord against influences which are not of Him, even in those that you regard and truly love, secures great blessing. . . If I am going on with something that does not recognise the rights of Christ, or maintain what is due to God, the kindest thing we can do is to take a definite stand against it. I may, *now* call you narrow, uncharitable, bigoted! But when I meet you in the light of the judgment-seat of Christ I shall thank you for it?" (C. A. Coates).

As we said in the preceding article, these Levites were the "overcomers" of that day, and if the reader will consult Rev. 2 and 3 he will find that all the promises contained in those chapters were made to the overcomers. How blessed then to find that these Levites were richly rewarded for their faithfulness. In Deut. 33 : 8-11 we read, "And of Levi he said, Let thy Thummin and Urim be with thy holy one, whom Thou didst prove at Massah and with whom Thou didst strive at the water of Meribah; Who said unto his father and to his mother, I have not seen him; neither did he acknowledge his brethren, nor knew his own children : for they have observed Thy word and kept Thy covenant. *They* shall teach Jacob Thy judgments, and Israel Thy law: they shall put incense before Thee, and whole burnt sacrifice upon Thine altar." It was because they crucified the flesh "with its *affections* and lusts," (Gal. 5 : 24) ignoring natural ties, knowing no man according to nature, not even acknowledging their own brethren when it came to maintaining the claims of God's holiness; it was because they observed His word and kept His covenant, that unto this Tribe were committed the "Thummin and Urim," the gift of teaching, and the privilege of burning incense on the altar. Truly God *does* honour those who honour Him, but they who despise Him are lightly esteemed.

"And it came to pass on the morrow, that Moses said unto the people ye have sinned a great sin" (v. 30). It is solemn to note the absence of any recorded word of Israel's repentance. Nothing is said of their contrition and horror at having so grievously offended against the Lord. Ominous sign was that. The rod of chastisement had fallen heavily upon them, yet, so far as we can gather, they had not bowed in heart beneath it. But God will not be mocked: if His chastening be "despised" (Heb. 12 : 5) it will return in a more acute form. It did so here, as we shall see in the immediate sequel. May the Lord grant each of us the hearing ear.

Moses did not wink at their wickedness, nor did he attempt to minimise the enormity of it. Just as when he first came down from the mount he charged Aaron with having brought "so great a sin" upon Israel (v. 21), so now, on the morrow, he says unto the people, "Ye have sinned a great sin." That he truly and clearly loved his people, the verses that follow plainly testify; yet, this did not deter him from dealing faithfully with them. As the Holy Spirit declares in Heb. 3 : 5, "Moses verily was faithful in all his house, as a servant, for a testimony of those things which were to be spoken after." In this too was he a type of Christ, the Holy One of God, who ever stressed the heinousness of sin.

"And now I will go up unto the Lord; peradventure I shall make an atonement for your sin" (v. 30). Care needs to be exercised lest we read into these words what they do not really contain. It was not the penal sentence upon their sin, but, we believe, the remitting of the *governmental consequences* to which Moses referred. It must not be forgotten that we have already been told in v. 14 that "The Lord repented of the evil which He thought to do unto His people." In answer to the earnest supplications of the typical mediator, the wrath of God in utterly "consuming" the people (v. 10) had been averted, and this, we say, should be carefully borne in mind as we endeavour to understand that which follows—admittedly a most difficult passage.

"Peradventure I shall make an atonement for your sin." The "peradventure" here ought not to occasion any difficulty, though more than one commentator has tripped over it. The uncertainty was due to the character and circumstances of his mission. Moses was about to appear before God on behalf of a people who had evidenced no sorrow for their great sin; therefore it was doubtful whether or not the governmental consequences of it might be remitted. There are quite a number of similar cases recorded in Scripture. In 2 Sam. 16 : 12, following Shimei's cursing of him, we find David saying, "It *may be* that the Lord will look on mine affliction and that the Lord will requite me good for his cursing this day." When wayward Israel was threatened by the Assyrians, Hezekiah sent to Isaiah saying, "It *may be* the Lord thy God will hear all the words of Rabshakeh, whom the king of Assyia his master hath sent to reproach the living God."

Nor are such cases restricted to the O.T. In N.T. times we read of Peter saying to Simon the sorcerer, "Repent therefore of this thy wickedness, and pray God, *if perhaps* the thought of thine heart may be forgiven thee" (Act 8 : 22). While in 2 Tim. 2 : 25 we read, "In meekness instructing those that oppose themselves; *if God peradventure* will give them repentance to the acknowledging of the truth." The careful reader will observe two things common to all these instances: first, each had in view the governmental consequences of sin; hence, second, each emphasises the note of uncertainty —because forgiveness was dependent upon their repentance.

"And Moses returned unto the Lord" (v. 31). Very blessed is this. Moses was, pre-eminently a man of prayer. In every crisis we find him turning unto the Lord: see Ex. 5 : 22; 8 : 30; 9 : 33; 14 : 15; 17 : 4. Beautiful foreshadowing was this of the Apostle and High Priest of our profession, who, in the days of His flesh, ever maintained and manifested a perfect spirit of dependency upon the One who had sent Him.

"And Moses returned unto the Lord, and said, Oh, this people have sinned a great sin, and have made them gods of gold. Yet now, if Thou wilt forgive their sin;—and if not, blot me, I pray thee, out of Thy book which Thou hast written" (vv. 31 : 32). Let us consider first the practical lesson which this incident contains for our hearts. Most helpfully has this been brought out by another.

"But if we speak of drawing the sword in this way, let us remember that the same man who said in the camp, 'Slay every man his brother' went up to Jehovah and said, 'And now, if Thou wilt forgive their sin . . .but if not, blot me, I pray Thee, out of Thy book that Thou hast written.' It was the same spirit of Christ which led him to take a decided stand in public against those who had allowed what was contrary to God, that led him to go up and pray for them in secret with such intense yearning for their good. He went as far as it was possible for man to go in the way of self-sacrifice. He could not be made a curse for them; only the Blessed One could go to that depth; but he was truly in the Spirit of Christ. It might be thought that slaying the people and interceding for them were not consistent. But the same spirit of Christ that would stand for Jehovah even against the nearest and dearest, was the spirit that would plead with God to be blotted out rather than that they should not be forgiven. The man who takes the strongest ground against me when I am wrong, and when I have set aside what is due to the Lord, is probably the one who prays most for me" (C. A. Coates).

"And Moses returned unto the Lord, and said, Oh, this people have sinned a great sin, and have made them gods of gold. Yet now, if Thou wilt forgive their sin;—and if not, blot me I pray Thee, out of Thy book which Thou hast written." Unspeakably precious is the typical picture presented here. How it brings out the intense devotion of Moses both to Jehovah and to His people. No sin on their part could alienate his affections from them. "Many waters cannot quench love, neither can the floods drown it" (Song of Sol. 8 : 7). Superlatively was this manifested by the One whom Moses here foreshadowed: Having loved His own which were in the world, He loved them unto the end" (John 13 : 1). Yes, notwithstanding the fact that all would be offended because of Him that night, yea, that all would forsake Him and flee, yet, He "loved them unto the end."

Moses gave proof that his affections were bound up with Israel, though they were a sinful people. So much were their interests his, he was willing to be blotted out of God's book, if He would not forgive them. Here again we must be careful not to read into his words what is not there. Moses said, "Thy book," *not* "the book of life." In Psalm 69 : 28 we read, "Let them be blotted out of the book of *the living*, and not be written with the righteous." In Isa. 4 : 3 it is said, "And it shall come to pass, that he that is left in Zion, and he that remaineth in Jerusalem, shall be called holy, even every one that is written among *the living* in Jerusalem." Thus it seems clear from these references that the "book" mentioned by Moses was *not* "the Lamb's book of life" (Rev. 21 : 27), which was written "from the foundation of the world" (Rev. 17 : 8), but the Divine register in which are recorded the names of those living on the earth, whose names are "blotted out" at the death of each one. God has various "books:" see Mal. 3 : 16, Rev. 20 : 12.

"And the Lord said unto Moses, Whosoever hath sinned against Me, him will I blot out of My book" (v. 33). God was speaking here from the viewpoint of the unchanging principles of His righteous government. Is not Gal. 6 : 7, 8 a parallel passage? "Be not deceived; God is not mocked: for whatsoever a man soweth, that shall he also reap. For he that soweth to the flesh shall of the flesh reap corruption." Does not Rom. 8 : 13 sound-forth the same warning note? "For if we live after the flesh, we shall die?"

"Therefore now go, lead the people unto the place of which I have spoken unto thee: behold, Mine angel shall go before thee: nevertheless in the day when I visit I will visit their sin upon them" (v. 34). Here is further proof that their penal deserts were cancelled. Equally clear is it that the governmental consequences of their sin were not remitted. They were not consumed, yet in due time God would deal with them. Does then our type fail us at this point? Certainly not; it only serves to exhibit the perfect accuracy of it. In connection with the mediation of Christ, we find the same two things: His intercession averts the penal wrath of God, but does not remove the governmental consequences of His people's sins. The latter is conditioned upon our true repentance and confession, and the laying hold of God's restoring grace.

"And the Lord plagued the people, because they made the calf which Aaron made" (v. 35). In view of what we said in our last article, namely, that what is found here in Ex. 32 has a prohetic application not only to Israel in the Tribulation period, but also to Christendom in this present era, probably the reader is ready to ask, But how could this terrible sequel to Israel's sin ever have its counterpart in God's dealings with His own in this Dispensation of Grace? Surely Christ has never called for the "sword" to smite His own; surely He does not "plague" His redeemed! Ah, dear friend, the picture that is now before us was not drawn by man, and the heavenly Artist makes no flaws. If it be recalled that Rev. 1 to 3 supplies the key to the present application of our type, it will not be difficult to discover the antitype.

In the second of the seven epistles found there, we read, "Fear none of those things which thou shalt suffer: behold, the Devil shall cast some of you into prison, that ye may be tried." This epistle to Smyrna contemplates the second stage in the history of the Christian profession. It was a period marked by opposition and persecution, suffering and death. It was the martyr age, covering the last half of the first century A.D. and most of the second and third centuries. It was the time when the early Christians suffered so sorely under Nero and the other Roman emperors that succeeded him. It is unnecessary to enter into detail, most of our readers being doubtless aware of the fearful conditions that then prevailed, and of the fiery trials through which the people of God were called to pass. But what is not so well known, what in fact has been quite lost sight of by most Christian historians, is the *cause* of that era of suffering, as to *why* God permitted the Enemy to rage against His people—for, of course, neither the Roman emperors, or Satan who stirred them up, could move at all without *His* direct permission.

God does not afflict willingly (Lam. 3 : 33), nor are the sufferings of His people arbitary. The Scriptures expressly declare, "When a man's ways please the Lord, He maketh even his enemies to be at peace with him" Prov. 16 : 7). The reason *why* God sent such tribulation upon His people in the second era of Christendom's history was because of their evil conduct in the first period. The epistle which precedes the Smyrean in Rev. 2, namely, the Ephesian, makes known what that evil conduct was: "Thou hast left thy first love" (Rev. 2 : 4). Affection for Christ had waned: *He* was no longer, "all and in all" to them. And, inward decline was swiftly followed by outward corruption, as is evidenced by the fearful fact that by the time the Smyean era had dawned the "synagogue of Satan" (Rev. 2 : 9) had already become established in their midst. Thus, as cause stands to effect, the leaving of "first love" at the beginning, occasioned the sufferings of the second and third centuries. It was God *chastening* His backslidden people!

Had the people of God remained true to Christ, had not the love of the world crept into their hearts, how vastly different history would have been! Nor is this a mere conjecture of ours. After Israel had suffered so severely from their enemies (see the book of Judges) God said through the Psalmist, "Oh that My people had hearkened unto Me, and Israel had walked in My ways! I *should soon* have subdued their enemies, and turned My hand against their adversaries" (81 : 13, 14)! But they did *not* "hearken" unto Him, nor did they walk in His ways. Sadly did history repeat itself. Just as God chastened Israel with the sword and "plague" then, so did He chasten and plague the early Church, using the Roman emperors as His scourge. Thus, what is seen in our type in Ex. 32 finds its counterpart in the history of Christendom. When there was departure from the Lord, when the spirit of idolatry came in, He called for the sword to smite them.

"And the Lord said unto Moses, Depart, and go hence, thou and the people which thou hast brought up out of the land of Egypt, unto the land which I sware unto Abraham, to Isaac, and to Jacob, saying, Unto thy seed will I give it: And I will send an angel before thee: and I will drive out the Canaanite, the Amorite, and the Hittite, and the Perizzite, the Hivite, and the Jebusite: Unto a land flowing with milk and honey: for I will not go up in the midst of thee; for thou art a stiffnecked people: lest I consume thee in the way" (33 : 1-3). Thus Moses by his supplication secured the immediate safety of the people, and the promise of an angelic guide and protector to go before them; but the further chastisement of their sin must yet be visited upon them. Nor were they restored to their covenant relations with Jehovah.

Moses was next directed to return to the camp with a message from the Lord. The details of that message, its effect upon the people, with the sequel, we must leave for consideration till our next article. May what has been before us bring to each of our hearts a greater horror and hatred of sin, and a more earnest crying unto God to be delivered from it.

—*Arthur W. Pink.*

LIFE OF ABRAM.

2. HIS ENCOURAGEMENTS:
Gen. 12 : 1-3.

In our last article we contemplated the peremptory summons which Abram received from the Lord to leave both the land and the house of his father. There was to be a definite break from the old life, a complete separation from that which spoke, in figure, of the world and our place in it by nature. God's claims upon His people are paramount, and it is not until they are owned in a practical way that we really enter the path of faith, which is at once a path glorifying to God and of blessing to him who treads it. No man can serve two masters, and just so long as a Christian vainly strives to make the best of both worlds does he dishonour the One who has redeemed him and make against his own spiritual progress.

"Now the Lord had said unto Abram, Get thee out of thy country, and from thy kindred, and from thy father's house" (v. 1). If a worldling were to read this verse and ponder its exacting terms, probably he would say, "Poor Abram, that was hard lines for him; such a demand was asking a great deal from him." But God's commands are "not grievous" (1 Jo 1n 5 : 3), neither in themselves nor unto one whose heart is right with Him. To Wisdom's "children" (Luke: 7 : 35), Wisdom's ways are "ways of pleasantness, and all her paths are peace" (Prov. 3 : 17). But to the natural man and to a carnal Christian too, God's commands *"are* grievous, very grievous, for they cross his will, run counter to his desires.

are contrary to his plans. Thus the way in which we receive God's commands becomes a *test* of the state of our hearts, and the response which we make to them reveals our true spiritual state. That is why Christ said, "If ye love Me, keep My commandments."

It is very blessed to mark the manner in which the Lord dealt with Abram. We lose much when we fail to ponder His perfect "ways." God does not drag His people along the path of faith, the path of discipline, the path of separation; no, He *draws*. And how? By setting before them other objects, other inducements, other attractions. The Lord never asks any of us to give up anything without proffering something far better in return.

> Who leave the choice to Him."
> Nothing this truth can dim:
> He gives the very best to those
> Who leave the choice with Him."

And *what* were the encouragements given to Abram for him to step out in obedience to the Divine commands which he had received? First, an Object of surpassing attraction was set before him: as we read in Acts 7 : 2, "The God of glory appeared unto our father Abram, when he was in Mesopotamia, before he dwelt in Canaan." It was not only that the one true God now became a living reality to him, but that He made known His glory. From that moment, whatever attraction the idols of Chaldea had over him in the past, their power was now broken. This is what true conversion is, a "turning to God from idols, to serve the living and true God, and to wait for His Son from heaven" (1 Thess. 1 : 9, 10).

It was thus with the apostles of the Lord Jesus. As one of them wrote, "We beheld His glory, the glory as of the Only-begotten of the Father, full of grace and truth" (John 1 : 14). Ah, they had beheld the King in His beauty, and beholding Him, they promptly left their fishing-boats and nets to follow Him. It was thus with Saul of Tarsus: the Lord revealed Himself above that Damascus road in a glory so bright that it blinded him—so closed his eyes to every attraction of earth that henceforth he counted everything the world offered his as "dung." A heavenly glory now so engrossed his soul that it became his one purpose and desire to know better, to serve more faithfully, to glorify that One who is fairer than the children of men.

The unregenerate are utterly at a loss to understand devoted Christians: "the world knoweth us not, because it knew Him not" (1 John 3 : 1). The successful financier, the man of fame, or the society butterfly, perceives not why it is that the things which enthral them repel the genuine disciples of Christ, who "rejoice in hope of the glory of God" (Rom. 5 : 2). Their language is,

> "I have heard the voice of Christ,
> Tell me not of aught beside;
> I have seen the face of Christ,
> All my soul is satisfied."

Alas that such an experience is not constantly maintained. When our eyes are taken from off Him, and our communion is thus broken, our joy ceases. Thus the Christian needs to cry daily, "Lord, occupy my heart with Thyself; lift up the light of Thy countenance upon me; show me Thyself."

In addition to the manifestation of Divine glory, Abram received precious *promises*. God's commands are rarely accompanied by reasons, but they are nearly always so with His promises—direct or indirect. And, it is just in proportion as faith lays hold of these promises that His commands cease to be grievous, and obedience becomes easy and joyous, always providing that our hearts are right with God. A. N.T. parallel to Gen. 12 : 1-3 in found in 2 Cor. 6 : 14-18. If the sevenfold promise of the last three verses be laid hold of, then obedience to the preceding commands—"Be ye not unequally yoked together with unbelievers," and "Come out from among them, and be separate"—will not be difficult. To the promises made to Abram we now turn.

"Unto a land that I will show thee: and I will make of thee a great nation, and I will bless thee, and make thy name great, and thou shalt be a blessing; and I will bless them that bless thee, and curse him that curseth thee; and in thee shall all families of the earth be blessed" (vv. 2, 3). Were a worldling to read these words, coming right after verse 1, he would most probably argue: "Had I been Abram, I would have remained where I was; a bird in the hand is worth two in the bush. Why should I leave my own country, where I do have a home, for some unknown land, where all is obscure and uncertain?"

We have commenced our comments on Gen. 12 : 2, 3 in this way for the purpose of showing how incapable are the unregenerate of entering into the things of God. It is just as 1 Cor. 2 : 14 declares, "But the natural man receiveth not the things of the Spirit of God: for they are foolishness unto him : neither can he know them, because they are spiritually discerned." Ah, it is "spiritual discernment" which is so vitally necessary if we are to "receive" the things of God. Even a Christian who is *out of* communion with God, who is in a backslidden state, who has sunk to the level of the world, cannot enjoy the "things of God." If his eyes have become filmed by the things of time and sense, then is he quite incapable of perceiving the beauty and preciousness of many of God's promises. And such a person is doubly wretched: as a Christian he has been spoiled for the things of the world—they can no longer enthral him; as a backslider he has lost the joy of God's salvation, and so has no satisfaction at all.

Now just as the Divine commands which Abram received tested the state of his heart, so the Divine promises given him tested the strength of his faith. Those promises set forth the spiritual compensations which Abram received for what he was losing in a natural way. It was just like God to deal thus with the father of the faithful. He never asks us to relinquish any thing without proffering something far better in return. But alas, only too often our faith is so little in exercise that we largely fail to live in the enjoyment of what God has set before us. It is only *faith* which can enjoy the spiritual portion, the spiritual blessings, the spiritual inheritance, which are ours in Christ Jesus.

The Christian may be well versed in the letter of God's promises, he may have gone to much pains and trouble in memorising scores of them, he may have a thorough intellectual acquaintance with them; but unless the heart really lays hold of them, unless they are "embraced" by faith (Heb. 11 : 13), he does not enter into the good of them, nor receive the inspiration and strength they should bring him. But that is not God's fault; it is ours. *He* has been faithful, yea gracious, in giving us exceeding great and precious promises (2 Pet. 1 : 4). God has displayed His love by setting before us so many spiritual encouragements to compensate us for the loss of those things which the natural man hankers after, to nerve and energise us to "run with perseverance the race that is set before us." Had Abram's heart laid hold of the promises which were given when the God of glory first appeared to him, he had not clung so tenaciously to his natural kin, nor wasted the years in Haran which he did. But we must not anticipate.

"Unto a land that I will show thee." The wording of this promise was couched in such a way as to test Abram's faith. This appears in the *general* terms employed. Notice, first, "unto *a* land," not unto "a good land, which floweth with milk and honey." The land was not described, nor so much as named; hence it is said in Heb. 11 : 7 that Abram went forth "not knowing whither he went." Second, "unto a land that I will *show* thee:" as yet God gave no assurance that it would be given him, with which agrees, again, Heb. 11 : 7: "Unto a land which he was *after* to receive for an inheritance." Faith has to be developed. The path of the just is as the shining light, which shineth "more and more." God honours those who honour Him. He did Abram. When he obeyed God's command and actually entered Canaan, then God made known to him the fact that that land was his forever; but it was not till he had obeyed that this assurance was given him.

In a similar way God deals with His people now. Many a Divine promise is couched in general and abstract terms, for the testing of our faith. Take the well known words of Isa. 40 : 31: "They that wait upon the Lord shall renew their strength." At first glance that seems definite and specific. But is it? "Renew" which strength—physical or spiritual? Whichever our faith appropriates! The "strength" of what—our faith, our hope, our courage, our patience, our love, our zeal? Ah, does not the reader get the thought: it is for *faith* to fill in the blank! So it is with many another Divine promise; let the one quoted serve as an example.

"Unto a land that I will shew thee." Let us not lose sight of the grand fact that God's dealings with Abram temporally, foreshadowed that which is heavenly in connection with us. The vagueness of His words to our patriarch concerning the land of Canaan which he was *"afterward* to receive," illustrated a typical truth. Comparatively little has been made known to us concerning the nature and character of *our* inheritance. And that for a very good reason : if Heaven could now be described to us in language that we could understand, it would not be Heaven.

A closer examination of the promises which God gave to Abram reveals the fact that they correspond very closely with the commands he had received. A careful comparison of the two will show that the commands set forth a threefold requirement, while the promises make known a threefold blessing. First, God had said, "Get thee out of thy country:" now He added, "unto a land that I will shew thee." The latter was in return for the former. Second, God had said, "And from thy kindred:" now He adds, "and I will make of thee a great nation, and I will bless thee" etc. What compensation was this! The nation from which Abram sprang had fallen into idolatry, and was ultimately destroyed by the judgments of God; whereas the nation which should issue from Abram would be made the custodians of the oracles of God, and be the one from which the Saviour, according to the flesh, came. The "blessing" of Jehovah would more than make up for any carnal comforts and joys lost by forsaking his "kindred." Third, God had said, "and from thy father's house:" now He adds, "and in thee shall all families of the earth be blessed." God made him the head of a new house, even the House of Israel. Again we say, God never asks anyone to abandon anything without giving something far better in return.

"And thou shalt be a blessing" (v. 2). This became true of Abram, and ought to be so of each of his children. But is it true of you, my reader? Art *thou* "a blessing?" We are only, truly, made a blessing to others when we are ourselves walking with God. If I am not in the path of obedience, but, instead, following a course of self-will, then I am a hindrance, a curse to others. And the louder my profession and the loftier my pretentions, the more dangerous I am. O how few Christians *are* "a blessing to others; how many are stumbling-blocks!

"And thou shalt be a blessing:" may each Christian reader ponder these words with an exercised conscience. First, face the question honestly: *Am I* a "blessing?" Is my daily walk a help, an encouragement, a holy example to my brethren and sisters; or, is it a hindrance? Is my conversation spiritually refreshing, a benediction to them? Second, weigh this question in the presence of God: have I really sought *to be* a "blessing" to other Christians? or is my one and only thought the receiving of a blessing for myself? Third, How may I become a "blessing?" By getting right with God, which means, confessing to Him my wretched selfishness. By definitely asking God to make me a blessing to others: "Ye have not, because ye ask not" (James 4 : 2). By giving out His own unadulterated Word, for *that* is what God uses in "blessing" souls: "A word fitly spoken is like apples of gold in pictures of silver" (Prov. 25 : 11).

"And I will bless them that bless thee, and curse him that curseth thee" (v. 3). This inspired sentence sets forth an important spiritual principle, which is far-reaching in its consequences and effects. That principle may be stated thus: men are tested by their attitude and conduct toward that which is of God. Abram was the called of God, yea, the "friend of God" (James 2 : 23), and men would be tested by their dealings with him and his seed.

The dispensational application of this principle to the lineal descendents of Abram is well known. The conduct of the Gentiles toward the Jews and the governmental consequences thereof supplies one of the keys to the meaning of much of human history. Pharaoh and the Egyptians oppressed the Hebrews, and severely were they made to pay for it; and to this day the very nation which first enslaved the children of Abram are themselves little better than serfs. Haman, "the Jews' enemy," erected a gallows for Mordecai, yet he and his own sons were hanged thereon. So it has been through the centuries. The Anglo-Saxon race has shown more tolerance and kindness to the Jews than any other, and in return have been more "blessed." During the middle ages Spain was the most cruel of all in their treatment of Israel, and to-day that once mighty nation has sunk lower than any of the leading Powers of Europe. Latterly, Russia has persecuted the Jews the severest, and for the last fourteen years they have been reaping what they have sown.

Turkey's day of retribution is near at hand.

Yes, men are tested by their attitude and conduct toward that which is of God. This principle was most vividly exemplified in connection with the Lord Jesus. He was, in His own person, the great test. His very presence on earth tested all with whom He came into contact. No sooner was it announced that the king of the Jews was born, than we are told, "All Jerusalem was troubled" (Matt. 2 : 3). Take the scene presented in Luke 4. It was the sabbath day, and the synagogue at Capernaum was filled with devout worshippers. Ah, but all is not gold that glitters. In a short while "*all* they in the synagogue......were filled with wrath," and united in the attempt to commit murder (vv. 28, 29)! Christ had exposed them.

Everything that is of God becomes a test unto all who come into contact with it. It is most important we should take note of this. If God brings near to men what is of Himself, people receive either a blessing or a curse and *which* it is is determined by their reception or rejection of it. The preaching of the Gospel illustrates this same principle. God sends His servant to tell of a great Saviour for great sinners. One hearer rejoices at such good news, saying, "Such tidings is just suited to my poor heart." In consequence, he receives Christ as his Saviour and is saved. *That* illustrates "I will bless them that bless thee." The sinner blesses God for His Word of grace and so is blest. On the other hand, another hearer who is self-righteous says, "Such a sermon may be suited to the heathen or prisoners in jail, but not for me." If the preacher presses upon him *his* lost condition and imminent danger of Hell, he gets angry, "curses," and so *is* "*curst.*"

This same principle holds good in ministry to a company of saints. When God grants them light from His Word it acts in the same way: it becomes a *test* of the state of the hearts of those who hear. If God grants a ministry which is of Himself, then those who "bless" it—who speak well of it, thank God for it—get the blessing. On the other hand, those who speak evil of it, who criticise either the message or messenger, disclose *their* state of heart by so doing, and are in danger of a "curse." If, in the naughtiness of their heart, they are saying, "No man has the right to set such a standard before us;" or, "It is not so much what he says, but *how* he says it, that grates;" that shows, that instead of their ears and eyes being fixed upon God, they are occupied only with His servant.

The same principle holds good out in the world. If a worldling shows kindness to one of God's children, He will not let him be the loser. Contrariwise, if he "curses" God's people, he will surely suffer for his pains. It is on this basis the Lord will yet judge the nations: "Inasmuch as ye did it unto one of the least of these My brethren;" or, "Inasmuch as ye did it not unto" etc.

"And in thee shall all families of the earth be blessed" (v. 3). This was one of the great Messianic promises, for the primary reference of these words was to the coming of the Lord Jesus. From Abram was yet to issue, according to the flesh, Him who should be a "blessing" not only to his immediate and literal seed, but to "all families of the earth." That did not mean, all without exception, for, as a matter of fact, half of the human race was in Hell when Christ became incarnate, and far more than half of those born since then have never so much as heard of Him. No, "all families of the earth" refers to the *Gentiles* as such.

Is there also a present-day application of *this* word to Abram's spiritual seed? Most certainly there is. You say, I cannot see that: in what possible sense can I ever be a *blessing* to "all families of the earth?" First, through prayer: by spending much time before the Throne of Grace, interceding for the children of God "scattered abroad." My brother, *you* may be made a "blessing" to families in Africa, China, India if you will pray definitely, earnestly, daily for them! Second, by helping to send forth God's holy Word far and wide. According unto your faith be it unto you.

And now we must draw to a close. We have dwelt upon the encouragements Abram received to step out in implicit obedience to the call He had from God. We must not anticipate our next article further than by saying that, notwithstanding these precious promises, Abram *failed,* and failed miserably. Shall we? God forbid. Let us seek grace to heed that word in 2 Cor. 7 : 1, "*Having* therefore these promises, *let us* cleanse ourselves from all filthiness of the flesh and spirit, perfecting holiness in the fear of God."

—*Arthur W. Pink.*

ROMANS 7.

Continued from page 15.

Was it the design of God in giving the Law, that it should be everlasting destruction to His people? Was its holiness to be made abiding death unto *them*? No: they were to be delivered. But before he details the mode and character of the deliverance, he speaks of a further use of the Law in teaching God's people the exceeding sinfulness of sin by an experience peculiar to themselves. Such is the subject of vv. 14 to 23.

The Law is still spoken of in this passage as "holy, just, and good," but it is not spoken of (this should be most carefully observed) as that which was shunned or dreaded, but as that which is "consented to" (v. 16), "desired" (v. 19) and "delighted in" (v. 22). "The new man," seeing it is "created according to God in righteousness and true holiness," must, by the very necessity of its nature, rejoice in that which is "holy, just, and good." "I delight in the law of God after the inner man," are words that may be truthfully used (and where there is much practical grace they will be *realised*) by every one in whom "the new man" is. Yet the very fact of these new "desires" and "delights" being in the believer, is made the means of teaching him one of his deepest experimental lessons, respecting the sin that dwells within him. However intense may be our desire, in "the new man," to love God perfectly and to serve Him perfectly—however we may long to banish from our bosom every desire and every tendency that is contrary to His will, yet there is found in every regenerate heart an antagonistic principle of evil that meets every claim of God with unvarying, habitual resistance. The energy of this evil may in different hearts be developed in different degrees: but as to its essential character, it is alike in all. It acts *for* evil and *against* good. It obstructs and impairs every desire and every action that is directed towards God. None of our counsels, none of our deeds, are found to have the perfectness which the law of God requires, and which we, in "the new man," desire. Our desire in the new man is toward *absolute, unmixed* good: for *unmixed* good is the only thing that the law, in the strictness of its righteousness, can recognise, as good. But, however truly we may, in 'the new man," long after it we cannot DO it. Unmixed good is beyond us.

I beg it may be especially noticed that I use the expresion, "*unmixed* good;" by which I mean, that absolutely perfect good which was once found on earth, when the Holy One was here, but now is known only in heaven. This passage therefore, does not speak of that kind of good which believers, through grace, may, and do perform—good which, though not perfect, is accepted through Jesus Christ. It does not say that I can perform no good: what it asserts is, that I cannot perform *that perfect good* which the law commands and in which, I in the new man, "delight." "Good" in this passage is to be understood only of that which is perfect according to this perfectness: and "evil" is that which falls short in the least conceivable degree of such perfectness. It is the not observing the *kind* of good spoken of in this passage that has mainly caused the difficulty in understanding it. (Re-read this paragraph—A.W.P.)

It must be remembered too, that sin, throughout this passage is personified. It is regarded as a living agent with whom we, naturally, are indentified. The first result or *act* of sin in us is evil desire, or concupiscence, which can be no more separated from sin, than heat from fire; and which concupiscence, being in itself an inward *act*, precedes the deliberate choice of the soul and all developed action. Indeed concupiscence may be resisted and never go on to a deliberate intention or choice. Yet evil has been *done* by us the moment a wrong desire has been excited.

We are obliged, therefore, to say, "the good I desire, I do not," for unmixed good is beyond us. And when we further consider, how, (notwithstanding all our watchfulness) elements of infirmity and evil mingle with every thing we feel, or think, or do, we are obliged to add, "the evil I desire not that I do." To this many, perhaps, will be disposed to refuse their assent. "A Christian," they will say, "does not habitually Do what 'the new man' hates. To say that he will, would make him practically the servant of iniquity; and this we are expressly told in the sixth of Romans he is not."

It is indeed true that a Christian is not the servant of iniquity, he who is a doer of sin, says the apostle John—one, that is, who habitually walks in the path of evil, does thereby prove that he hath not seen Christ, neither known Him. Such an one does not resist, but indulges and follows, and that habitually, the impulses of sin that dwells within him. To say that a Christian thus—yields himself up to sin, and that he cannot help so obeying it; and to affirm that the words, "the evil I would not, that I do," mean that he does, in this sense, serve sin, is no doubt, antinomianism; and that antinomianism has been taught from this passage I do not deny. But are the words "to do evil" capable of no other meaning than that in which we apply them to the habitual service of sin? Does the eye of God, judging according to the strict holiness of His law, detect sin only in such developments of it as are outward and palpable, and have in them that character of *unmixed* evil which is found in the actions of the unregenerate world? Is there no inner man, no inward world of thought and feeling which His eye scrutinizes? Is not a thought of foolishness sin? Is not the slightest bias to evil, the slightest tendency towards anything false or wrong, or the slightest want of readiness or of capacity in *perfectly* following the path of holiness, sin? So the Scripture teaches. If, therefore, when a Christian seeks to serve God, it be found that sin within him puts forth the slightest power to obstruct the action, or to mar the mode of its performance—if it puts forth one desire or causes one momentary feeling that is contrary to or falls short of, the perfectness of God, that desire, or that feeling is in the sight of God, *an act*. Sin has wrought something in us, and by us; and we are identified (and but for grace should be identified forever) with that which is thus wrought in us; for sin is, naturally, a part of ourselves. We have therefore *done* something, which, in "the new man," we hate; and although the world will refuse to call it *"a deed,"* and will persist in extenuating human frailty (as they term it); and although they will not allow that evil desire is, if resisted, sin; yet the Law of God determines otherwise. Nor can there be a truer form of antinomianism than to say that the impulses and strugglings of sin, are, if resisted, *not* sin. Grace indeed does not impute them to a believer as sin. That is a different question. We are not now speaking of the pardoning power of grace; but we are speaking of what that is which grace pardons. If then there be an active power in us, that hinders, mars, and taints our efforts after all good, and renders the performance of perfect good hopeless; and if we cannot, though we would, free ourselves, either from the presence of this evil power, or from its working, then are we, in a very intelligible sense, subject to the doings and actings of an evil principle within us, which, in "the new man," we hate.

But again,—as we must beware of understanding the word "DO" in this passage—"the evil I would not that I do," as denoting that habitual willing service of evil that is seen in the world; so we must also remember that it is not to be understood of such sins as believers *may* indeed fall into, but which by greater faithfulness and watchfulness they might have avoided. When Peter temporized at Antioch, and virtually surrendered the truth of the Gospel, his sin was one which watchfulness and faithfulness would have prevented; and consequently, he had no title to say of his transgression, "It was not I that did it, but sin that dwelleth in me." To attempt to shelter deliberate transgressions (whether they be habitual as in the world, or occasional as in the case of believers) by bringing them within the scope of this passage is antinomianism. The workings of sin contemplated in this passage, are such as no watchfulness can hinder, no faithfulness avoid. The existence of sin within us entails on us certain consequences which we have no more power to evade, than the idiot has to change his look of idiocy; or the palsied hand has power to free itself from its torpor. The transgression of our first parents brought on us, not only the imputed guilt of that trangression, but has also entailed on us the hereditary possession of a depraved nature. There are certain effects of that depravation which are beyond the power of our control; and it is of *such* effects that *this* passage treats, and not of transgressions which the believer by watchfulness, could avoid. Any manifestation of evil to which we can truthfully apply the word, "so then it is no more I that do it, but Sin that dwelleth in me," is not to be included among the deeds referred to in this passage.

Is there not reason then to think that if our spiritual intelligence, or rather spiritual sensitiveness, were more acute, we should find less difficulty in understanding this passage? The energies of the "new man" must be lively in any soul that can practically say, "I delight in the Law of God; I desire and long after that *unmixed* good which holiness demands." The spiritual perceptions of the soul must be quick and sensitive when it habitually watches the risings and workings of indwelling Sin, and counts evil as a DEED, even though it may through grace be withstood and never become a deliberate purpose of the soul. We are so accustomed to judge after the manner of men, and to attach culpability only to deliberate counsels, or deliberate acts; that if an evil desire be resisted, we are far more ready to take credit to ourselves for the resistance, than we are to acknowledge, that evil desire is in itself sin, and a fruit of essential sin. The very holiness therefore, of the passage occasions our difficulty in understanding it. It recognises as *deeds*, things which men are not accustomed to regard as deeds. It teaches us that whenever Sin within us moves, some effect, either inward or outward, is produced, which not only frustrates our desire after the *unmixed* good which the Law requires, but would, except for grace, leave us forever in hopelessness and condemnation.

Grace has not as yet been mentioned in this passage. Our utter inability to attain to the performance of the good which in "the new man" we desire, and the guilt entailed on us by the workings of that Sin which causes this inability, is the only aspect, up to this point, presented. What if it had been appointed that we should be left in that condition? That thought is for a moment presented, and causes the sowerful bitter cry"—O wretched man that I am, who shall deliver me," etc. But the cry is but momentary—indeed it is only uttered in order to introduce the answer, and that answer speaks of peace and assured deliverance—"I thank God, through Jesus Christ our Lord," etc. Therefore, although the condition portrayed in the preceding verses, is not imaginary, but real; although it be true that every believer on earth does *actually* stand in that relation to "good," and in that relation to "Sin," which the passage we have been considering, describes, yet we are not hereby furnished with a *complete* view of a believer's condition. The aspect we have been considering is a real and true aspect: but it is a *partial* one. We have yet to ask the all-important question, How has God met this our condition? Does He teach us this lesson respecting our personal condition in the presence of the terrors of Sinai, or of the grace and peace of Zion? (It should be carefully remembered that when the Apostle says, "I delight in the Law of God," etc., he does not mean that he would delight in being dispensationally placed under the Law. That *had* been once his dispensational relation; but he had found no ground of joy in it: he had found in it death. To delight according to the new man in *the good* that the Law points out, is a very different thing from delighting in the Law as the ground of our hope towards God. The latter a believer never does, for grace would then be despised: the former he must do, and that forever, for it is the eternal immutable law of his new nature). That question has already been answered. He has met us in grace—not in judgment. We must, consequently, add to the picture presented in the seventh chapter, all that is subsequently detailed in the eighth respecting the deliverance. Thus, and thus only, we gain the complete aspect in which we are taught to view the condition of those who are in Christ Jesus.

The deliverance brought to us in Him respects first, the *pardon* of our sins. He hath borne, and by bearing hath removed, that wrath, which, if righteousness were to appoint our due, would be our everlasting portion. The sin of our first parent, the guilt of which, by imputation, rests on us naturally, deserves wrath: the Sin that dwells within us, and all its workings (even when resisted) deserve wrath: the many occasions on which we have voluntarily acquiesced in those workings and obeyed them, deserve wrath. But from all this wrath so justly due, the grace that comes through the one sacrifice once offered on Calvary, delivers, and that forever, all who come unto God thereby. This deliverance is a present, as well as a complete deliverance. "There is NOW" (that is at this present time) no condemnation to them who are in Christ Jesus." We have found in Him our "Deliverer from the wrath to come" (1 Thess. 1 : 10).

But secondly, there is another deliverance not less certain indeed, but as yet *future*; one for which we wait in patience of hope. A time coming, according to the sure promise of God, when we are to be delivered *actually* from our evil selves—when Sin, with its obstructive and defiling power, shall be in us no longer—when the aspirations of the "new man" after the performance of *perfect absolute* good, will be no longer disappointed—when we shall serve God worthily, because we shall have been changed into the glorious likeness of Christ. This will be what the apostle calls, "the *glorious* liberty of the children of God." At present we have *a* liberty, but not this perfect glorious liberty. Then the picture drawn in the seventh of Romans will cease to be true of believers. Then, the *full* deliverance included in those words, "who shall deliver," etc., will have come. We shall no longer have to submit to the presence and to the actings of a power within us which in "the new man" we hate.

But although our captivity to the power and presense of indwelling sin is not *in this sense* terminated as yet; yet there is another sense in which it is terminated: and here we find a third form of deliverance. We are so far freed from its practical power that "the law of sin in our members" ("the law of sin and death" as it is in this eighth chapter called) is no longer able to prevent us from rendering *acceptable*, though not perfect service unto God. To take a practical example. A believer desires in "the new man," to perform an action that is right—one to which the Holy Spirit that dwells within him leads. But the moment he desires it, he is sensible of an opposing bias: he feels a counteracting agency within him. His desire after that which is right is, more or less, resisted: his action impeded: wrong or imperfect motives are suggested: unbelieving doubts presented. If duty require him to meet and to deal with evil —evil perhaps in another, he feels that his appreciation of it, and the manner of his dealing with it, are alike imperfect. Sometimes he may be tempted to treat it with a severity and sternness inconsistent with either humility or grace: at another time he may be disposed to sympathize with and extenuate it in a manner inconsistent with holiness. Inadequacy of appreciation will no less mark his estimate of good; and as he pursues it, his steps will never be found *perfect* either in constancy or vigour; that is, if the only true standard be taken—the absolute perfectness of God. In many a way, he will find that the principle of Sin within him is mighty to put forth its power against the Spirit. But being under *grace*, and knowing how the guilt of this indwelling Sin (which if he were dispensationally under the Law would be imputed to him) has been borne for him by Christ, his Substitute, he struggles on. And as the Spirit of life puts forth His antagonistic power, Sin in the flesh is resisted, and the action is performed. Yet it will not be found to be a perfect action. A hand trembling from palsy, will never succeed in making a straight stroke. The action, therefore, will be found to have its flaws; and flaws of two kinds—those which, because of the living presence of indwelling Sin, no watchfulness can avoid; and likewise flaws which more perfect grace might have avoided or lessened. It will be in some degree or other marred, so as not to have the absolute unmarred perfectness that was found only in that Holy One in whom there was no sin. Yet although not absolutely perfect, such actions (seeing that they are the action of those who walk not after the flesh, but after the Spirit) *are accepted through Jesus Christ.* The incense of His name is added to all that is thus presented, and it becomes a sanctified and accepted offering. See 1 Peter 2 : 5.

Thus then "what the Law could not do, in that it was weak through the flesh," God has, through Christ, effected. The Law can exhibit to us good—good which in "the new man" we delight; but ability to perform that good it cannot give. The Law can neither accept anything that is short of *absolute* perfectness, nor can it remove the guilt of the Sin that hindereth that perfectness. But "what the Law could not do, in that it was weak through the flesh, God having sent His own Son in the likeness of sinful flesh, and concerning sin judged (i.e. visited with damnatory wrath) sin in the flesh (that is, ours, believers.") It was visited with the due award of wrath when Christ, as the Substitute of His believing people, died. There the believer sees the *judicial* end of the Sin that dwelleth in him, as well as all its results. Its guilt is no longer imputed to him, and as God accepteth his so He accepteth his services also for Christ's sake. Thus his capacity to sin is nullified. He is set free to serve God; not indeed with perfect, but with acceptable service: and thus in this new evangelical way, the claim or ordinance of the Law is in our case fulfilled in whatsoever we do as led by the Spirit.

If then it be asked, whether the seventh of Romans, from the fourteenth verse to the twenty-second verse inclusive, describes the experience of a believer, we answer that it describes *part*, but that it does not describe *all* of the experience proper to the believer. If in narrating the history of the apostle Paul, we described merely his sufferings and sorrows—if we spoke only of his "journeyings often, in perils of waters, in perils of robbers, in perils by mine own countrymen, in perils by the heathen, in perils in the city, in in perils in the wilderness, in perils in the sea, in perils among false brethren"—if we told of his "infirmities, and reproaches, and necessities, and persecutions, and distresses," we should no doubt present a very true and a very important part of his history; but if this were all our narrative, our hearers, if they knew nothing more, would probably be ready to say, "Surely then he was of all men most miserable." But if in addition to the tale of his sorrows, we told also of his consolation and rejoicing in Christ; of the triumph, and prosperity, and honour of his service; of his present joy, of his coming glory, we should *add* features to the picture which would materially change its aspect. Certain elements of darkness and sorrow would still remain; but light and joy would predominate. We should understand what he meant when he said, "though sorrowful, yet always rejoicing." So likewise in the case before us. The verses we have been considering in the *seventh* of Romans, present a faithful picture of a condition that *actually* pertains to us, and will continue to pertain to us, while we are in the flesh. But to this picture, which is dark and sorrowful, we have to add the light, and joy, and strength, and hope of the *eighth* chapter. The combination does not present to us the perfectness of Heaven, but it is an earnest of the perfectness of heaven. We know that the conflict, and sorrow, and bondage such as it is, pertain to the flesh, from which we already are judicially liberated—all such things will pass away. On the other hand we know that the light, and joy, and strength are of the Spirit, and that with the Spirit they will abide forever.

It will be seen, then, that it is essentially requisite, in interpreting the seventh chapter of Romans, to remember most carefully the sense in which "good" is used:—"the good I desire, I do not." "Good" here denotes *absolute* perfectness: such perfectness as the unmitigated holiness of the Law requires; and to the performance of such good no believer, whilst in the flesh, ever attains. The good that he does perform (for every believer is a doer of good) is mingled with imperfection: but such good, though the law must reject it, grace can, and does receive, through the redemption that is in Christ Jesus. It is of the *former* character of good that this passage speaks, when it says, "the good I desire, I do not."

Secondly, we have to remember that the evil spoken of in this chapter, is not *habitual* service of evil in which the unregenerate live: nor is it such evils as believers may, and do, fall into, but which greater grace and watchfulness would have enabled them to avoid. This passage speaks not of evil which might be, and ought to be avoided; but of evil which no watchfulness on our part could avoid—evil which flows from the adulterating, impairing power of Sin, insinuating itself into all our plans and deeds, and causing them to fall short of the absolute perfectness of God. Of such developments of Sin, and of such alone, can it be truthfully said, "So then, it is no more I that do it, but Sin that dwelleth in me." To apply these words to sins that *can* be avoided is antinomianism indeed.

A right view of this chapter will not encourage antinomianism. On the contrary, it will teach us to dread and avoid every thing which stimulates and gives effect to the power of evil that is within us. Experience teaches us that certain circumstances tend to increase, others, to weaken the power of its development. Nor will the humbling sense that we are at present withheld from doing that *perfect* good in which the new man, by the very law of its nature, delights, make us indifferent to, or unthankful for, the opportunity of doing a less perfect "good" which grace is pleased to acknowledge and to accept.

If on the other hand our dread of antinomianism or any other reason leads us to say that evil tendency or bias is not, (if resisted) sin—or if we say with Papists and others, that evil desire and tendency can be thoroughly extinguished from the flesh, we undermine the whole fabric of redemption. Whenever the soul refuses to bow to that which God testifies respecting Sin that dwells in us; His testimony to grace, to salvation, and to Christ will be refused also. The depth of nature and grace must be viewed in connection with the depth and nature of the Sin that it is designated to meet. He who denies that "concupiscence" (evil desire) is in the regenerate, or who affirms that such concupiscence is not in itself sin, as well as the operative cause of sin, lays the axe at the very root of Truth as it is revealed in Jesus. The thanksgiving of the believer is grounded on the fact that the guilt of this "concupiscence" (great as its evil is) is not imputed to him for Christ's sake: but he does not on that account (seeing that he has the Holy Spirit, and is led by the Spirit) acquiesce on that evil, or cease to struggle against and resist it: although well knowing that the perfect absolute good which is in "the new man" he desires, will never be "performed," "accomplished," or "done," by him until the "glorious" liberty of the children of God shall come; when, disrobed of his natural self and of all corruption, he shall stand clothed upon with the heavenly likeness of his risen Lord.

—B. W. Newton.

GRAPES OF ESCHOL.

(Numbers 13).

The grand principle of the divine life is faith—simple, earnest, whole-hearted faith—faith that just takes and enjoys all that God has given—faith that puts the soul in possession of eternal realities, and maintains it therein habitually. This is true in reference to the people of God in all ages. "According to your faith, so be it unto you," is ever the divine motto. There is no limit. All that God reveals, faith may have; and all that faith can grasp, the soul may abidingly enjoy.

It is well to remember this. We all live, far, very far, below our privileges. We are satisfied, many of us, to move at a great distance from the blessed Centre of all our joys. We are content with merely knowing salvation, while, at the same time, we taste but little holy communion with the Person of the Saviour. We are satisfied with merely knowning that a relationship exists, without earnestly and jealously cultivating the affections belonging thereto. This is the cause of much of our coldness and barrenness. As in the solar system, the further a planet is from the sun the colder its climate and the slower its movement; so in the spiritual system, the further one moves from Christ, the colder will be the state of his heart toward Christ, and the slower his movements for Christ. On the contrary, fervour and rapidity will ever be the result of felt nearness to that central Sun—the great Fountain of heat and light.

The more we enter into the power of the love of Christ, and the more we realize His abiding presence with us, the more intolerable we shall feel it to be one moment away from Him. Everything will be dreaded and avoided which would tend to withdraw our hearts from Him, or hide from our souls the light of His blessed countenance. The heart, that has really learnt aught of the love of Christ, cannot live without it; yea it can part with all for it. When away from Him, nought is felt save the gloom of midnight and the chilling breath of winter; but in His presence, the soul can mount upward like the lark, as he rises into the bright blue heavens to salute, with his cheerful song, the sun's morning beams.

Nothing exhibits more the deep-seated unbelief of our hearts than the fact that, while our God would have us enjoying communion with the highest truths, few of us ever think of aspiring beyond the mere alphabet. Our hearts do not sigh, as they should, after the walks of spiritual fellowship. We are satisfied with having the foundation laid, and are not as anxious as we should be, to add layer after layer to the spiritual structure. Not that we can ever do without the alphabet or the foundation. This would be, obviously impossible. The most advanced scholar must carry the alphabet along with him; and the higher the building is raised, the more the need of a solid foundation is felt.

But, let us look at Israel's case. Their history is full of rich instruction for us. It is "written, for our admonition" (1 Cor. 10 : 11). We must contemplate them in three distinct positions, namely, as sheltered by the blood; as victorious over Amalek; and as introduced into the land of Canaan.

Now, clearly, an Israelite in the land of Canaan had lost nothing of the value of the first two points. He was not the less shielded from judgment or delivered from the sword of Amalek, because he was in the land of Canaan. Nay, the milk and honey, the grapes, figs, and pomegranates of that goodly land would but enhance the value of that precious blood which had preserved them from the sword of the destroyer, and afford the most unquestionable evidence of their having passed beyond the cruel grasp of Amalek.

Still, surely, no one would say that an Isrealite ought to have sought nothing beyond the blood-stained lintel. It is plain he ought to have fixed his steady gaze on the vine-clad hills of the promised land and said, "There lies my destined inheritance, and by the grace of Abraham's God, I shall never rest satisfied until I plant my foot triumphantly thereon." The blood-stained lintel was the starting-post; the land of promise, the goal. It was Israel's high privilege not only to have the assurance of full deliverance from the hand of Pharaoh, and the sword of Amalek, but also to cross the Jordan and pluck the mellow grapes of Eschol. It was their sin and their shame that with the mellow clusters of Eschol before them, they could ever long after "the leaks, the onions, and the garlick" of Egypt.

But how was this? What kept them back? Just that hateful thing which, from day to day, and hour to hour, robs us of the precious privilege of treading the very highest stages of the divine life. And what is that? UNBELIEF. "So we see that they could not enter in because of unbelief" (Heb. 3 : 19). This it was which caused Israel to wander in the desert forty years. Instead of looking at Jehovah's power to bring them into the land, they looked at the enemy's power to keep them out of it. Thus they failed. In vain did the spies, whom they themselves proposed to send (Duet. 1 : 22) bring back a most attractive report of the character of the land. In vain did they display in their view a cluster of the grapes of Eschol, so luxuriant that two men had to bear it upon a staff. All was useless. The spirit of unbelief had taken possession of their hearts. It was one thing to admire the grapes of Eschol when brought to their tent doors by the energy of others; and quite another to move onward, in the energy of personal faith, to pluck those grapes for themselves.

And if "twelve men" could get to Eschol, why not six hundred thousand? Could not the same hand that shielded the one, shield the other likewise? Faith says, "Yes." But unbelief shrinks from responsibility, and quails before difficulty. The people were no more willing to advance after the spies returned, than before they set out. They were in a state of unbelief, first and last. And what was the issue? Why, that out of six hundred thousand, which came up out of Egypt, only *two* had sufficient energy to plant their foot in the land of Canaan. This tells a tale. It utters a voice. It teaches a lesson. May we have ears to hear, and hearts to understand!

It may, perhaps, be said by some, that the time had not yet arrived for Israel's entrance into the land of Canaan, inasmuch as "the iniquity of the Amorites was not yet full." This is but a one-sided view of the subject, and we must look at both sides. The apostle expressly declares that Israel "could not enter in because of unbelief." He does not assign as a reason "the iniquity of the Amorites," or any secret counsel of God, with respect to the Amorites. He simply gives as a reason, the unbelief of the people. They might have got in if they would. Nothing can be more unwarrantable than to make use of the unsearchable counsels and decrees of God, in order to throw overboard man's solemn responsibility. It will never do. Are we to fold our arms and lie back in the culpable indolence of unbelief, because of God's eternal decrees about which we know nothing? To say so can only be viewed as a piece of monstrous extravagance, the sure result of pushing one truth to such an extreme as to interfere with the range and action of some other truth equally important. We must give each and every truth its due place. We should not run one truth to seed while some other truth is not even allowed to take root. We know that unless God bless the labours of the husbandman there will be no crop at the time of harvest; does this prevent the diligent use of the plough and the harrow? Surely not, for the same God who has appointed the crop as the *end*, has appointed patient labour as the *means*.

Thus it is also in the spiritual world. God's appointed end must never be separated from God's appointed means. Had Israel trusted God and gone up, the whole assembly might have regaled themselves on Eschol's luxuriant clusters. This they did not do. The grapes were lovely no doubt. This was obvious to all. The spies were constrained to admit that the land flowed with milk and honey. But there was sure to be a "nevertheless." Why? Because they were not trusting in God. He had already declared to Moses the character of the land, and his testimony ought to have been amply sufficient. He had said, in the most unqualified manner, "I am come down to deliver them out of the hand of the Egyptians, and to bring them up out of that land unto a good land a large, unto a land flowing with milk and honey" (Ex. 3 : 8). Should not this have sufficed? Was not Jehovah's description much more trustworthy than man's? Yes, to faith; but not to unbelief. This latter can never be satisfied with divine testimony, it must have the testimony of the senses. God had said it was "a land flowing with milk and honey." This the spies admitted. But, then, hearken to the additions: "Nevertheless the people be strong that dwell in the land, and the cities are walled and very great; and, morever, *we saw the children of Anak there......and there we saw the giants, the sons of Anak, which come of the giants; and we were in our own sight as grasshoppers, and so were we in their sight*" (Num. 14 : 28).

Thus it was with them. They only "saw" the frowning walls and towering giants. They did not see Jehovah, because they looked with the eye of sense and not with the eye of faith.

God was shut out. He never gets a place in the calculations of unbelief. It can see walls and giants; but it cannot see God. It is only faith that can "endure as seeing Him who is invisible." The spies could declare what they were in their own sight, and in the sight of the giants, but not a word about what they were in God's sight. They never thought of this. The land was all that could be desired; but the difficulties were too great for *them*, and they had not faith to trust God. The mission of the spies proved a failure. Israel "despised the pleasant land," and, "in their hearts, turned back again into Egypt."

This is the sum of the matter. Unbelief kept Israel from plucking the grapes of Eschol, and sent them back to wander for forty years in the wilderness; and these things, be it remembered, "were written for our admonition." May we deeply and prayerfully ponder the lesson! Out of six hundred thousand that came up out of Egypt, only two planted their foot on the fruitful hills of Palestine! They passed the Red Sea, triumphed over Amalek, but quailed and retreated before "the sons of Anak," though these latter were no more to Jehovah than the former.

Now let the christian reader ponder all this. The special object of this paper is to encourage him to arise, and, in the energy of a full, unqualified trust in Christ, tread the very highest stages of the life of faith. Having our solid foundation laid in the blood of the cross, it is our privilege not only to be victorious over Amalek, or indwelling sin, but also to taste of the old corn of the land of Canaan, to pluck the grapes of Eschol, and delight ourselves in its flowing tide of milk and honey; or, in other words, to enter into the living and elevated experiences which flow from habitual fellowship with a risen Christ, with whom we are linked in the power of an endless life. It is one thing to know that our sins are cancelled by the blood of Christ. It is another thing to know that Christ has destroyed the power of indwelling sin. And it is still a higher thing to live in unbroken fellowship with Himself. It is not that we lose the sense of the two former when living in the power of the latter. Quite the opposite. The more closely I walk with Christ—the more I have Him dwelling in my heart by faith, the more I shall value all He has done for me, both in the putting away of my sins, and in the entire subjugation of my evil nature. The higher the superstructure rises the more I shall value the solid foundation beneath. It is a great mistake to suppose that those who move in the higher spheres of spiritual life could ever undervalue the title by which they do so. Oh! no; the language of those who have passed into the innermost circle of the upper sanctuary is, "Unto Him that loved us, and washed us from our sins in His own blood." They talk of the love of Christ's heart and the blood of His cross. The nearer they approach to the throne, the more they enter into the value of that which placed them on such sublime elevation. And so with us; the more we breathe the air of the divine presence —the more we tread, in the spirit, the courts of the heavenly sanctuary, the more highly shall we estimate the riches of redeeming love. It is as we pluck the grapes of Eschol in the heavenly Cannaan, that we have the deepest sense of the value of that precious blood which shielded us from the sword of the destroyer.

Let us not, therefore, be deterred from aiming after a higher consecration of heart to Christ by a false fear of undervaluing those precious truths which filled our hearts with heavenly peace when first we started on our christian career. The enemy will use anything and everything to keep the spiritual Israel from planting the foot of faith in the spiritual Canaan. He will seek to keep them occupied with themselves and with the difficulties which attend upon their upward and onward course. He knows that when one has really eaten of the grapes of Eschol, it is no longer a question of escaping from Pharaoh or Amalek, and hence he sets before them the walls and the giants, and their own nothingness, weakness, and unworthiness. But the answer is simple and conclusive. It is this, *trust! trust! trust!* Yes from the blood-stained lintel in Egypt, to the rare and exquisite clusters of Eschol, it is all simple, unqualified, unquestioning, trust in Christ. "By faith they kept the passover, and the sprinkling of blood;" and, "by faith the walls of Jericho fell down;" (Heb. 11). From the starting-post to the goal, and at every intermediate stage, "The just shall live by faith."

But, let us never forget that this faith involves full surrender of the heart to Christ, as well as the full acceptance of Christ for the heart. Reader, let us ponder this deeply. It must be wholly Christ for the heart and the heart wholly for Christ. To separate these things is, as some one has remarked, to be "like a boat with one side oar, which goes round and round, but makes no progress, only drifts with the stream, whirling as it drifts. Or like a bird with a broken wing, whirling over and over, and falling as it whirls. This is too-much lost sight of, and hence, the uncertain course and fluctuating experience. There is no progress. People cannot expect to get on with Christ in one hand and the world in the other. We can never feast on the "grapes of Eschol" while our hearts are longing after "the flesh-pots of Egypt."

May the Lord grant us a whole heart—single eye—an upright mind. May the one commanding object of our souls be to mount upward and onward. Having all divinely and eternally settled, by the blood of the cross, may we press forward, with holy energy and decision, "toward the mark, for the prize of our high calling of God in Christ Jesus."

"O wonderous grace! O love divine!
To give as such a home;
Let us the present things resign,
And seek the rest to come;
And gazing on our Saviour's cross,
Esteem all else but dung and dross:
Press forward till the race be run;
Fight till the crown of life be won."

—Things New and Old, Vol. 3.

LAUGHTER.

"God made me to laugh, so that all that hear will laugh with me" (Gen. 21 : 6). "Blessed are ye that weep now, for ye shall laugh" (Luke 6 : 21).

I used always to associate laughter with the boisterous mirth of carnality, but to use the dictionary term, it is, "a peculiar involuntary noise which joy and cheerfulness excites." But there are other forms of laughter according to the dispositions and passions of the individual. Seeing our Lord making use of the term we may safely conclude there is some rich teaching in it for our edification and comfort, especially as it is associated with the word "Blessed." Let us see what the Scriptures say concerning "laughter" and the form it takes.

In Matt. 9 : 24 we get the *scornful* laugh, our Lord being made the butt of it on His raising the ruler's daughter to life; and Psa. 22 :7 shows us also how He had to endure such on the cross. In Neh. 2 : 19 we get the *contemptible* or *hateful* laugh by the enemies of the builders of the walls of Jerusalem. We get the antithesis of this in Psa. 2 : 4; 37 : 13; 59 : 8; Prov. 1 : 26 and Luke 6 : 25, "Woe unto you that laugh now, for ye shall weep." There is also the laugh that comes through supreme heart-satisfaction, as Luke 6 : 21.

When our Lord put a little child in the midst of His disciples, to set forth certain lessons, it showed His marvellous wisdom, for in this living illustration we get help and light on many dark passages, and I know nothing that illustrates the above Scriptures better than "a little child." In every pain, disappointment, or desertion, the manifestation of it is seen by "weeping." But when happy, rewards at first glance this may not be perceived, prayerful meditation thereon will reveal a steady advancing through the whole series of the Psalmist's mentionings of the Divine precepts.

What we have sought to bring before our readers in this article is but an illustration of a principle which is exemplified all through Scripture, and we may add, all through Nature; for the God of revelation and the God of creation is one and the same. And He is a God of order. Not only is each word of Holy Writ given by inspiration of God, but the exact position occupied by every single statement therein evidences the perfect wisdom of its Author. Just as in the natural realm there is "first the blade, then the ear, then the full corn in the ear! so it is in the spiritual life; and so it is in the Word. Each phase of Divine truth is unfolded in an orderly manner, according to the law of progress, ever moving towards a climax or consummation. This illustration upon the Divine "precepts" of Psalm 119 is only one from hundreds of examples which might be cited. Others will be found in the same Psalm. May the Lord stir up both writer and reader to a more diligent and prayerful *searching* of the Scriptures.

Arthur W. Pink.

---

realized, it is all expressed by "laughter." How the child's tears give way to laughter when his outlook has been brightened by some precious promise of his fond mother, before he gets it the rippling laugh of faith is heard.

The laugh of *faith* brings us back to Gen. 17 : 17. After the Lord had renewed His covenant with Abraham, his faith was already embracing the joyous fact, and is expressed by his falling on his face, laughing. Faith was about to give way to sight, after waiting about 23 years. Sarah hearing such good news expressed her joy by laughing, though she doubted, but when her hopes were realized, and despair driven away, she said, "God made me to laugh, and all that hear will laugh with me." Is not this the answer to Luke 6 : 21. She had experienced her trials, now she was reaping a time of joy. Her case is typical of all those who will "hear." God has called many in paths they knew not, a voice behind them saying, "This is the way, walk ye in it." Those that know His voice and obey may have some time of weeping, but God will cause them to laugh. "He that hath ears to hear let him hear" was ever uttered when important truths and issues were at stake, but ever associated with the "hearing" were blessed and glorious results for those who heard: Rev. 2 : 3. In Psa. 126, when the captives were liberated, the great desire of their life consummated, we read, "then was our mouth filled with *laughter* and our tongue with singing." And as our Lord to-day binds up the broken-hearted, gives liberty to the captive, and comforts the mourners, "they get beauty for ashes, the oil of joy for mourning, and the garment of praise for the spirit of heaviness." What blessedness and joy is this! It is far better to have the trial and experience and His Presence and gracious help in it, than not to have the trial at all. It is better to have the howling wilderness and His sustaining hand seen and gracious help and power realized, than to be in Egypt without it. They that sow in tears shall reap in joy.

Ye heralds of the Cross may painfully realize the hardness of the heathen soil, the disappointing journeys and various perils. Listen! The voice that spake on Judah's plains floats down the centuries to you. "Blessed are ye that weep now, for ye shall laugh." Ye brokenhearted parents, who have been bereaved of that fair young flower of your family, how earthly hopes have been dashed to the ground, how that poignant grief is seen through bitter tears. Listen! "Weeping may endure for a night, but joy cometh in the morning." Faith will soon give way to sight, soon to be from this scene of death to endless life, and God shall wipe away all tears. "Blessed are ye that weep now, for ye *shall* laugh." "As for God His way is perfect" (Psa. 18 : 30). His Word is perfect Deut. 32 : 34, and His will is perfect Rom. 12 : 2. How the writer experienced the power of Luke 6 : 21 as his little girl received her Home-call, is more than tongue can tell or pen describe.

Ye godly toilers who are hard beset by the enemies of the Lord, who scoff and reject your faithful testimony; if troubled, be not in distress, if perplexed be not in despair, if cast down, you are not destroyed. The cloud is yet bright with the bow of promise. "This is the victory that overcometh the world, even our faith." He always causes us to triumph in Christ. Soon we shall be ushered into that scene without a cloud. "He that goeth forth weeping bearing precious seed, *shall* doubtless come again rejoicing, bringing his sheaves with him." So the tired feet and blistering hands, breaking heart and aching head and weeping eye will all be a thing of the past when we enter the joy of our great harvest-home.

J.E.

"This I had because I kept Thy precepts" (v. 56). As one of the best of the Puritan expositors (Manton) said, "Many of the sentences of this Psalm have no other connection than pearls strung on a string, though some are as links on the same chain, fastened one to another by an apt method of order." The sentence quoted at the beginning of this paragraph seems to be quite independent of the previous verse, as the sudden outburst of a gracious heart engaged in meditating on the fruit of obedience—"This I had because I kept Thy precepts." David does not tell us *what* he "had"—quickening, confidence, deliverance. "This I had"—each obedient believer may fill it in for himself—God's approval and blessing, peace of conscience, mind and heart.

But that which is germane to the present inquiry is what is said upon the subject of our present study: "I have *kept* Thy precepts." Once more we may observe the striking and progressive order: First, commanded to keep the precepts because they are from God; now a "keeping" of them. How blessed, but how searching the order! Second, meditating therein; third, praying for light thereon; fourth, longing after them.

"I am a companion of all them that fear Thee, and of them that keep Thy precepts" (v. 63). Surely this is so plain, and the point taken in advance of the previous references is so obvious, that no interpretation is needed. Commanded to keep God's precepts, meditating in them, praying over them, loving them, keeping them—now having fellowship with kindred souls! The one who, by grace, "keeps" God's precepts desires and seeks felllowship with others in whom he observes the fear and love of God.

"The proud have forged a lie against me; but I will keep Thy precepts with my whole heart" (v. 69). There is *opposition* now! and it is very striking to note the point at which this is introduced. There is no hint of opposition until after this keeper of the Divine precepts becomes the "companion" of God's people! But mark how this only deepens his resolution—"I will keep Thy precepts with my *whole* heart."

"Let the proud be ashamed, for they have dealt perversely with me without a cause; but I will meditate in Thy precepts" (v. 78). Here we see how the opposition the Psalmist encountered only served to make him renew his "meditation:" as his enemies assailed him, he felt the more need of further meditation. Thus God makes the wrath of man to praise Him and turns the attacks of the Enemy into blessing for His people.

"They had almost consumed me upon earth; but I *forsook* not Thy precepts" (v. 87). The opposition has grown fiercer; Reader, do you know anything about this from personal experience? If you do not, there is something wrong in your life. The reason why many Christians escape antagonism is because their daily walk is so little regulated by God's precepts. It still stands written, "*All* that will (are determined to) live godly in Christ Jesus *shall* suffer persecution" (2 Tim. 3 : 12)! The world loves its own; but it hates those whose ways contradicts theirs.

"They had almost consumed me upon earth; but I *forsook not* Thy precepts." That is the acid test of a genuine work of grace in the heart—how we conduct ourselves in the face of opposition and persecution. It does not take much to turn a mere professor aside: a few sneers and frowns, or a shrug of the shoulder is enough, and the white—washed worldling goes back to his own people, "When tribulation or persecution ariseth because of the Word, by and by he is offended" (Matt. 13 : 21). But where God has placed His fear in the heart, a man will stand and withstand, even though there was not another kindred soul in all the world to stand with him.

"I will not forget Thy precepts, for with them Thou hast quickened me" (v. 93). Here the Psalmist is heard expressing his appreciation of and his thankfulness for the Divine precepts; and that because of the value of them, what they had done for and meant to him. The term "quickened" here probably includes the initial act of his regeneration, and the subsequent renewals, revivings, refreshings he had received from God's precepts. As he recalled the blessings they had brought to him, he resolves never to forget God's precepts. This is more than "meditating" upon them. As the result of that, they have become so a part and parcel of his innermost being he would never forget them.

"I am Thine, save me; *for* I have sought Thy precepts" (v. 94). This is very striking and marks a further decided advance. Here the Psalmist not only makes his conscience of God's commands an encouragement to seek help from Him when he is in straits, but to ground an appeal thereon. Has not God said, "Them that honor Me, I will honor" (1 Sam. 2 : 30)? Here is David pleading the principle of that promise before the Throne of Grace. If we take care of our duty, God will take care of everything else.

There are yet nine other verses in this Psalm containing references to the Divine precepts, but these we will leave the student to follow out for himself. As they are carefully weighed it will be found, like those which we have already considered, the later ones also follow a progressive order, an expermental order, which evidences a steady advancement in the spiritual life. Though

(Continued on Page 47)

STUDIES IN THE SCRIPTURES

"Search the Scriptures" John 5 : 39

Copyright in all English-speaking Countries.

Editor: Arthur W. Pink, Sidmouth Road, Seaton, Devon, England.
Hon. Agent in U.S.A.: Mr. C. S. Pressel, 559, Dupont Avenue, York, Penna.
Hon. Agent in Australia: Mr. G. Ardill, The Christian Workers' Depot.
Commonwealth and Reservoir Streets, Sydney.

FREE TO ALL WHO WILL READ IT.

THE GAINS OF GODLINESS.

"No good thing will He withhold from them that walk uprightly" (Psa. 84 : 11).

It is indeed a sad evidence of the wickedness of our hearts that men should take such a blessed word as this and make it the occasion of cavilling and wrangling. Yet if this inspired statement were pressed and enlarged upon in quite a number of circles of professing Christians to-day, the one so doing would at once provoke an argument, and be regarded as a legalist. He would be told that this verse of scripture is found in the Old Testament, that it pertained to the Dispensation of Law, and that to insist it holds good as much now as then is to repudiate that *grace* which, in this age, characterises all the dealings of God. It is in no argumentative spirit that we would reply to these assertions, but with the object of presenting what we believe is the truth before some who may have been led into error or disturbed by ultra-dispensationalists.

Our text enunciates one of those principles which regulates God's governmental dealings with men, particularly with His own people. The thrice holy God is not indifferent to our conduct as every page of His Word clearly enough bears witness. God deals very differently with him who walks uprightly, than He does with one whose ways are evil. Those who honour Him, He honours; but those who despise Him, He lightly esteems (1 Sam. 2 : 30). So plainly is this fact taught in Scripture that probably the majority of our readers would deem it quite unnecessary for us to labour the point. Verily it is enforced by the Holy Spirit so clearly, so emphatically, so insistently, that only one blinded by the prejudice of a favorite theory could overlook it. Yet the sad thing is that in these degenerate times there are not a few, claiming to have considerable insight into the "deep things of God," who deny that He is now, in any wise, influenced by the conduct of His people.

The leaders of those circles referred to above have written extensively on the believer's perfect and unchanging standing before God, his completeness in Christ, his being blessed with all spiritual blessings in the heavenlies in Him. They have emphasised the fact that God treats with us according to the perfections of His beloved Son; that it is not our unworthiness, but Christ's worthiness that the Father is ever occupied with. Not for a moment would we seek to minimize the preciousness of the Christian's oneness with the Saviour, nor do we wish to weaken in any wise, his hold on the heart-sustaining and worship-provoking truth of our acceptance in the Beloved. Yet do we desire to point out that there are subjective as well as objective aspects of the truth to be weighed and appropriated; that there is much, very much, in God's Word, treating of our state as well as our standing, and that there are consequences issuing from the one as truly as from the other.

Before taking up, briefly, some of the consequences which our state and conduct on earth involve, we would point out that the principles which regulate God in His governmental dealings are the same in every dispensation. Necessarily so, for He is One "with whom is *no variableness*, neither shadow of turning" (James 1 : 17). God is not engaged in a series of experimentations during the course of the ages, nor is He,

Continued on page 72.

IMPORTANT NOTICES

Back numbers of the last four years of this magazine are yet obtainable, nicely and strongly bound at 7/6 each, post paid. They will soon be out of print. Those in U.S.A. wanting them, please purchase from Mr. Pressel (see front cover page).

Advise promptly of change of address otherwise copies will be lost in the mails.

This Magazine is published as a work of faith and labour of love. The Editor gladly gives his services. It is freely sent to all who will read it. No charge is made for it.

Christians who feel definitely led to do so, may have fellowship with us in this Ministry. Send only *Inter-National M.O.* made out to Seaton, Devon, England.

CONTENTS.

Hebrews	50
Gleanings in Exodus	56
Abram's Compromises	60
A Threefold Salvation	64
A Personal Word	71

THE EPISTLE TO THE HEBREWS.

15. *Christ Superior to Moses:* Heb. 3 : 13—19.

There are two great basic truths which run through Scripture, and are enforced on every page: that God is sovereign, and that man is a responsible creature; and it is only as the balance of truth is preserved between these two that we are delivered from error. The Divine sovereignty should not be pressed to the exclusion of human responsibility, nor must human responsibility be so stressed that God's sovereignty is either ignored or denied. The danger here is no fancied one, as the history of Christendom painfully exhibits. A careful study of the Word, and an honest appropriation of all it contains, is our only safeguard.

We are creatures prone to go to extremes: like the pendulum of a clock in motion, we swing from one side to the other. Nowhere has this tendency been more sadly exemplified than in the teachings of theologians concerning the security of the Christian. On the one hand, there have been those who affirmed, Once saved, always saved; on the other hand, many have insisted that a man may be saved to-day, but lost to-morrow. And both sides have appealed *to the Bible* in support of their conflicting contentions! Very unwise and unguarded statements have been made by both parties. Some Calvinists have boldly declared that if a sinner has received Christ as his Saviour, no matter what he does afterward, no matter what his subsequent life may be, he cannot perish. Some Arminians have openly denied the efficacy of the finished Work of Christ, and affirmed that when a sinner repents and believes in Christ he is merely put in a salvable state, on probation, and that his own good works and faithfulness will prove the deciding factor as to whether he should spend eternity in Heaven or Hell.

Endless volumes have been written on the subject, but neither side has satisfied the other; and the writer for one, is not at all surprised at this. Party-spirit has run too high, sectarian prejudice has been too strong. Only too often the aim of the contestants has been to silence their opponents, rather than to arrive at the truth. The method followed has frequently been altogether unworthy of the "children of light." One class of passages of Scripture has been pressed into service, while another class of passages has been either ignored or *explained away*. Is it not a fact that if some Calvinists were honest they would have to acknowledge there are some passages in the Bible which they wish were not there at all? And if some Arminians were equally honest, would they not have to confess that there are passages in Holy Writ which they are quite unable to fit into the creed to which they are committed? Sad, sad indeed, is this. There is nothing in the Word of God of which any Christian needs be afraid, and if there is a single verse in it which conflicts with his creed, so much the worse for his creed.

Now the subject of the Christian's security, like every other truth of Scripture, has *two* sides to it: into it there enters both God's sovereignty and human responsibility. It is failure to recognise and reckon upon this which has wrought such havoc and created so much confusion. More than once has the writer heard a renowned Bible-teacher of orthodox reputation say, "I do not believe in the perseverance of saints, but I do believe in the preservation of the Saviour." But that is to ignore an important side of the truth. The N.T. has much to say on the *perseverance* of the saints, and to deny or ignore it is not only to dishonour God, but to damage souls.

There have been those who boldly insisted

that, if God has eternally elected a certain man to be saved, that man *will be* saved, no matter what he does or does not do. Not so does the Word of God teach. Scripture says, "God hath from the beginning chosen you to salvation, through sanctification of the Spirit *and belief of the truth*" (2 Thess. 2 : 13), and if a man *does not* "believe the truth" he will never be saved. The Lord Jesus declared, "Except ye repent, ye shall all likewise perish" (Luke 13 : 3); therefore, if a sinner, *does not* "repent," he will not be saved. In like manner, there are those who have said, If a man is *now* a real Christian, no matter how he may live in the future, no matter how far or how long he may backslide, no matter what sins he may commit, he is sure of Heaven. Put in *such* a way, this teaching has wrought untold harm, and, at the risk of our own orthodoxy being suspected, we here enter a solemn and vigorous protest against it.

The writer has met many people who profess to be Christians, but whose daily lives differ in nothing from thousands of non-professers all around them. They are rarely, if ever, found at the prayer-meeting, they have no family worship, they seldom read the Scriptures, they will not talk with you about the things of God, their walk is thoroughly worldly; and yet they are quite sure *they* are bound for heaven! Inquire into the ground of their confidence, and they will tell you that so many years ago they accepted Christ as their Saviour, and "once saved always saved" is now their comfort. There are thousands of such people on earth to-day, who are nevertheless, on the Broad Road, that leadeth to destruction, treading it with a false peace in their hearts and a vain profession on their lips.

It is not difficult to anticipate the thoughts of many who have read the above paragraphs: "We fully agree that there are many in Christendom resting on a false ground of security, many professing the name of Christ, who have never been born again; but this in nowise conflicts with the declaration of Christ that no sheep of His shall ever perish." Quite true. But what we would here point out and seek to press on our readers is this: I have no right to appropriate to myself the blessed and comforting words of the Saviour found in John 10 : 28, 29, *unless I answer to* the description of His "sheep" found in John 10 : 27; and I have no warrant for applying His promise to those who give no evidence of being conformed to the characters of those He there has in view. Let no man dare separate what God Himself has there joined together.

The passage begins with, "My sheep *hear* My voice, and I know them, and they *follow Me.*" That is the Lord's own description of those whom *He* owns as His "sheep." Now if, to the contrary, I am "hearkening" to the seductive voice of this world, if I am "following" a course of self-will, self-seeking, self-gratification, what right have I to regard myself as one of the "sheep" of Christ? None at all. And if, notwithstanding, I do profess to be one of His, then my walk gives the lie to my profession. And any one who comes to me with words of comfort, pressing upon me the *promises* of God to His people, is only encouraging me in a course of wrong-doing and bolstering me up in a false hope.

It may be replied, "Yet a real Christian may leave his first love." True, and before a church that had done so, the Lord Jesus appeared and said—not, "It will be alright in the end," but—"Repent, and do the first works, or else I will come unto thee quickly, and will remove thy candlestick" (Rev. 2 : 4). "But a real Christian may backslide, and in a large measure become worldly again." Then if he does, *his* need is *not* to hear about the eternal security of God's saints, but the eternal and fearful consequences of giving way to an evil heart of unbelief if such a course be continued in. "Yes, but if he *is* one of God's people, he will be chastened, and grace will restore him; and therefore I cannot see the need or propriety of giving him to believe there is a danger of his being lost."

Ah, it is not without reason that the Lord Jesus declared, more than once, "he that *endureth to the end* shall be saved." And let it not be forgotten that in Matt. 13 : 20, 21, He spoke of some who "but dureth *for a while*"! Again it may be objected, "Such a pressing of the need of perseverance of God's elect is uncalled for: if a man *be* a Christian, he *will* persevere, and if he persevere then there is no need of urging him *to* persevere." Not so did the apostles think or act. In Acts 11 : 22, 23 we read, "they sent forth Barnabas, that he should go as far as Antioch. Who when he came, and had seen the grace of God, was glad, and *exhorted* them all, that with purpose of heart they would *cleave unto* the Lord." Again, in Acts 13 : 43 we read, "Paul and Barnabas: who, speaking to them, persuaded them to *continue* in the grace of God." Once more, in Acts 14 : 21, 22 we are told "And when they had preached the Gospel to that city, and had taught many, they returned again to Listra, and Iconium, and Antioch, Confirming the souls of the disciples, *exhorting them to continue* in the faith, and that we must through much tribulation enter into the kingdom of God."

According to the views of some, such earnestness on the part of the apostles was quite unnecessary. But the impartial Christian reader will gather from the above passages that the apostles believed in no *mechanical* salvation, wherein God dealt with men as though they were stocks and stones. No, they preached a salvation that needed to be *worked out* with "fear and trembling" (Phil. 2 : 12); in a salvation which calls human responsibility into exercise; in a Divine salvation effectuated by the *use* of the means of grace which God has mercifully provided for us. True we *are* "kept by the power of God," but the very next words afford us light on *how* God keeps—"*through* faith" (1 Peter 1 : 5). And not only does faith feed on the promises of God, but it is stirred into healthful exercise and directed by the solemn *warnings* of Scripture.

A real need then is there for such words as these, "But Christ as a Son over His own house; whose house are we, *if* we hold fast the confidence and rejoicing of the hope firm unto the end" (Heb. 3 : 6). "Oh, blessed word and promise of God, that *He* will keep us unto the end. But *how* is it that we are kept? Through faith, through watchfulness, through self-denial, through prayer and fasting, through our constant taking heed unto ourselves according to His Word. 'Hold fast' if you desire it to be manifested in that day that you are not merely outward professors, not merely fishes existing in the net, but the true and living disciples of One Master." (Saphir).

"But exhort one another daily, while it is called To-day; lest any of you be hardened through the deceitfulness of sin" (v. 13). "There is need of constant watchfulness on the part of the professors of Christianity, lest under the influence of unbelief they 'depart from the living God.' 'Take heed,' says the apostle. There is nothing, I am persuaded, in regard to which professors of Christianity fall into more dangerous practical mistakes than this. They suspect everything sooner than the soundness and firmness of their belief. There are many who are supposing themselves believers who have no true faith at all,—and so it would be proved were the hour of trial, which is perhaps nearer than they are aware, to arrive; and almost all who have faith suppose they have it in greater measure than they really have it. There is no prayer that a Christian needs more frequently to present than, 'Lord, increase my faith'; 'deliver me from an evil heart of unbelief.'

"All apostasy from God, whether partial or total, originates in unbelief. To have his faith increased—to have more extended, and accurate and impressive views of 'the truth as it is in Jesus'—ought to be the object of the Christian's most earnest desire and unremitting exertion. Just in the degree in which we obtain deliverance from the 'evil heart of unbelief' are we enabled to cleave to the Lord with full purpose of heart, to follow Him fully, and, in opposition to all the temptations to abandon His cause, to 'walk in all His commandments and ordinances blameless.' To prevent so fearful and disastrous a result of apostasy from the living God, the apostle calls on them to strengthen each other's faith by mutual exhortation, and thus oppose those malignant and deceitful influences which had a tendency to harden them in impenitence and unbelief" (Dr. J. Brown).

To "exhort one another daily" is to call attention to and stir up one another for discharging our mutual duties. But in performing this obligation we are sadly lax: like the disciples upon the mount of transfiguration (Luke 9 : 30) and in Gethsemane (Luke 22: 45), we too are very dull and drowsy and in constant need of both exhortation and incitation. As fellow pilgrims in a hostile country, as members of the same family, we ought to have "care for one another" (1 Cor. 12 : 25), to "love one another" (John 13 : 34), to "pray one for another" (James 5 : 16), to "comfort one another" (1 Thess. 4 : 18), to "admonish one another" (Rom. 15 : 14), to "edify one another" (1 Thess. 5 : 11), to have "peace one with another" (Mark 9 : 50). Only thus are we really helpful one to another. And, note, the exhorting is to be done "daily," for we must not be weary in well doing. "*While* it is called To-day" warns us that our sojourn in this scene is but brief; the night hastens on when no man can work.

"Lest any of you be hardened" adds force to the duty enjoined. In v. 8 the terrible damage which hardness of heart produces had been pointed out; here it is warned against. The implication is unmistakeable: hardness of heart is the consequence of neglecting the means for softening it—"lest." Clay and wax which are naturally hard, melt when brought under a softening power, but when the heat is withdrawn they revert again to their native hardness. The same evil tendency remains in the Christian. The flesh is "weak," our heart "deceitful"; only by the daily use of means and through fellowship with the godly are we preserved. Oftentimes the failure of a Christian is to be charged against his brethren as much as to his own unfaithfulness. How often when we perceive a saint giving way to hardness of heart we go about mentioning it to others, instead of faithfully and tenderly exhorting the offending one!

"Through the deceitfulness of sin." Here is the cause of the evil warned against and upon which we need to be constantly upon our guard. It is the manifold deceits of sin which prevail over men so much. The reference here is to the corruption of our nature, with which we are born, and which we ever carry about with us. It is that which, in Scripture, is designated the "flesh," the lustings of which are ever contrary to the Spirit. God's Word speaks of "deceitful lusts" (Eph. 4 : 22), the "deceitfulness of riches" (Matt. 13 : 22), for their innate depravity causes men to prefer material wealth to vital godliness and heavenly happiness. So we read of the "deceivableness of unrighteousness" (2 Thess. 2 : 10); philosophy (the proud reasoning of that carnal mind which is enmity against God) is termed "vain deceit" (Col. 2 : 8); and the lascivious practices of formal professors are called "their own deceivings" (2 Peter 2 : 13). This is one of the principal characteristics of sin: it deceives. "All the devices of sin are as fair baits whereby dangerous hooks are covered over to entice silly fish to snap at them, so as they are taken and made a prey to the fisher" (Dr. Gouge).

This deceitfulness of sin should serve as a strong inducement to make us doubly watchful against it, and that because of our foolish disposition and proneness of nature to yield to every temptation. Sin presents itself in another dress than its own. It lyingly offers fair advantages. It insensibly bewitches our mind. It accommodates itself to each individual's particular temperament and circumstances. It clothes its hideousness by assuming an attractive garb. It deludes us into a false estimate of ourselves. One great reason why God has mercifully given us His Word is to expose the real character of sin. By the deceitfulness of sin the heart is *hardened*. "To be hardened is to become insensible to the claims of Jesus Christ, so that they do not make their appropriate impression on the mind, in producing attention, faith, and obedience. He is hardened who is careless, unbelieving, impenitent, disobedient" (Dr. J. Brown).

In the light of the whole context the specific reference in the exhortation of v. 13 constitutes a solemn caution against apostasy. What we particularly need to daily exhort one another about is to cleave fast to Christ, lest something else supplant Him in our affections. The whole trend of our sinful natures is to depart from the living God, to grasp at the shadows and miss the substance. This was the peculiar danger of the Hebrews. Sin was trying to deceive them. It was seeking to draw them back to Judaism as the one true and Divinely-appointed religion. To guard against the insidious appeals being made, the apostle urges them to "exhort one another daily," that is, promptly and frequently. The importance of taking heed to this injunction is placed in its strongest light by what immediately follows.

"For we are made partakers of Christ, if we hold the beginning of our confidence steadfast unto the end" (v. 14). These words complete the exhortation commenced at v. 12. They are added as a motive to enforce the dissuasion from apostasy (v. 12), and also the warning against that which occasions it (v. 13). The contents of this verse are similar in their force to that which was before us in v. 6: in both instances it is profession which is being put to the proof. There are two classes on which such exhortations have no effect: the irreligious who are dead in trespasses and sins, and have no interest in such matters; and the self-righteous religionist, who, though equally dead spiritually, yet has an intellectual interest. Many a professing Christian, who is infected by the Laodicean spirit of the day, will shrug his shoulders, saying, Such warnings do not concern me, there is no danger of a real child of God apostatising. Such people fail to get the good of these Divine warnings, their conscience never being reached. But where there is a heart which is right with God, there is always self-distrust, and such an one is kept in the place of dependency through taking heed to the solemn admonitions of the Spirit. It is these very warnings against departure from God which *curb* the regenerate.

"Persistency in our confidence in Christ unto the end is a matter of great endeavour and diligence, and that unto all believers. It is true that our persistency in Christ doth not, as to the issue and event, depend absolutely on our own diligence. The *unalterableness of union with Christ*, on the account of the faithfulness of the covenant of grace, is that which doth and shall eventually secure it. But yet our own diligent endeavour is such an indispensable means for that end as that without it it will never be brought about. Hence are many warnings given us in this and other epistles, that we should take heed of apostasy and falling away; and these cautions and warnings are given unto all true believers, that they may know how indispensably necessary, from the appointment of God, and the nature of the thing itself, is their watchful diligence and endeavour unto their abiding in Christ" (Dr. J. Owen).

But it should be pointed out that these solemn warnings of Scripture ought not to be pressed upon weak Christians, who though anxious to walk acceptably before God, are lacking in assurance. "Observe here—for Satan, and our own conscience when it has not been set free, often make use of this epistle—that doubting Christians are not here contemplated, or persons who have not yet gained entire confidence in God: to those who are in this condition its exhortations and warnings have no application. These exhortations are to preserve the Christian in a confidence *which he has,* and to persevere, not to tranquillise fears and doubts. This use of the epistle to sanction such doubts is but a device of the enemy. Only I would add here that, although the full knowledge of grace (which in such a case the soul has assuredly not yet attained) is the only thing that can deliver and set it free from its fears, yet it is very important in this case practically to maintain a good conscience, in order not to furnish the enemy with a special means of attack" (J. N. D.).

For the right understanding of this verse it is of first importance that we should note carefully the tense of the verb in the first clause: it is *not* "we shall be made partakers of Christ if"—that would completely overthrow the gospel of God's grace, deny the efficacy of the finished Work of Christ, and make assurance of our acceptance before God impossible before death. No, what the Spirit here says is, "We *are* made partakers of Christ," and in the Greek it is expressed even more decisively: "For partakers we have become of the Christ." The word "partakers" here is the same as in 3 : 1, "partakers of the heavenly calling," and at the end of 1 : 9 is rendered, "fellows." Perhaps, "companions" would be a better rendering. It means that we are so "joined unto the Lord," as to be "one spirit" with Him (1 Cor. 6 : 17). It is to be so united to Christ that we are "members of His body, of His flesh, and of His bones" (Eph. 5 : 30). It is to be made by grace, "joint-heirs" with Him (Rom. 8 : 17). The word *"made* partakers of Christ" shows there was a time when Christians were not so. They were not so born naturally; it was a privilege conferred upon them when they "received" Him as their Saviour (John 1 : 12).

"If we hold the beginning of our confidence steadfast unto the end." This does not express a condition of our remaining partakers of Christ in the sense of its being a contingency. "What is the one thing which the Christian desires? What is the one great thing which he does? What is the one great secret which he is always endeavouring to find out with greater clearness and grasp with firmer intensity? Is it not this: 'my Beloved is mine, and I am His'? The inmost desire of our heart and the exhortations of the Word coincide. To the end we must persevere; and it is therefore with great joy and alacrity that we receive the solemn exhortations: 'He that endureth unto the end shall be saved'; 'No man, having put his hand to the plow, and looking back, is fit for the kingdom of God.' We desire to hear constantly the voice which saith from His Heavenly throne, 'To him that overcometh will I grant to sit with Me in My kingdom, even as I also overcame, and am set down with My Father in His throne' " (Saphir).

To hold fast the beginning of our confidence firm unto the end is to furnish evidence of the genuineness of our profession, it is to make it manifest both to ourselves and others that we have been made "partakers of Christ." Difficulties in the path are presupposed, severe trials are to be expected: how else could faith show itself? Buffetings and testings do but provide occasions for the manifestation of faith, they are also the means of its exercise and growth. The Greek word for "confidence" here is not the same as in v. 6: there the "confidence" spoken of is to make a bold and free confession of our faith; here, it is a deep and settled assurance of Christ's excellency and sufficiency, which supports our hearts. The one is external, the other is internal. To "hold fast the beginning of our confidence" signifies to "continue in the faith, grounded and settled" (Col. 1 : 23). It is to say with Job, "Though He slay me, yet will I trust in Him."

"Firm unto the end." This is the test. At the beginning of our Christian course, our confidence in Christ was full and firm. We knew that He was a mighty Saviour, and we were fully persuaded that He was able to keep that which we have committed unto Him against that day. But the roughness of the way, the darkness of the night, the fierceness of the storm into which, sooner or later, we are plunged, tends to shake our confidence, and perhaps (much to our sorrow now) we cried, "Lord, carest Thou not"? Yet, if we were really "partakers of Christ" though we fell, yet were we not utterly cast down. We turned to the Word, and there we found help, light, comfort. In it we discovered that the very afflictions we have experienced were what God had told us *would be* our portion for "we are appointed thereunto" (1 Thess. 3 : 3). In it we learned that God's chastenings of us proceeded from His love (Heb. 12). And now, though we have proved by painful experience to have less and less confidence in ourselves, in our friends, and even in our brethren, yet, by grace, our confidence in the Lord has grown and become more intelligent. Thus do we obtain experimental verification of that word, "Better is the end of a thing than the beginning thereof" (Eccl. 7 : 8).

"While it is said, To-day if ye will hear His voice, harden not your hearts, as in the provocation" (v. 15). The apostle continues to make practical application of the solemn passage he had been quoting from Psalm 95, pressing upon them certain details from it. That which is central in this verse is its directions for cleaving fast to Christ. Two things are to be observed: the duty to be performed, positively to "hear His voice," negatively not to "harden their hearts." This duty is to be performed promptly, "To-day," and is to persevered in—"*whilst* it is said to day" i.e. to the end of our earthly pilgrimage. The opportunity which grace grants us is to be eagerly redeemed, the improvement of it is to be made as long as the season of opportunity is ours. The admonition is again pointed by the warning of Israel's failure of old. Thus the sins of others before us are to be laid to heart, that we may avoid them.

"When we hear God's voice—and, oh, how clearly and sweetly does He speak to us in the person of His Son Jesus, the Word incarnate, who died for us on Golgotha! —the *heart* must respond . . . By this expression is meant the centre of our spiritual existence, that centre out of which thoughts and affections proceed, out of which are the issues of life, that mysterious fount which God only can know and fathom. Oh that Christ may dwell *there*! God's voice is to *soften* the heart. This is the purpose of the divine word—to make our hearts tender. Alas, by nature we are *hard*-hearted; and what *we* call good and soft-hearted is not so in reality and in *God's* sight . . . . When we receive God's word in the heart, when we acknowledge our sin, when we adore God's mercy, when we desire God's fellowship, when we see Jesus, who came to save us, to wash our feet and shed His blood, for our salvation, the heart becomes soft and tender. For repentance, faith, prayer, patience, hope of heaven, all these things make the heart tender: tender towards God, tender towards our fellow-men" (Saphir).

"For some, when they had heard, did provoke: howbeit not all that came out of Egypt by Moses" (v. 16). The apostle here begins to describe the kind of persons who sinned in the provocation, amplification being given in what follows. His purpose in making mention of these persons was to more fully evidence the need for Christian watchfulness against hardness of heart, even because those who of old yielded thereto provoked God to their ruin. The opening "for" gives point to what has preceded. The unspeakably solemn fact to which He here refers is that out of six hunderd thousand men who left Egypt, but two of them were cut off in the wilderness, Caleb and Joshua.

The Greek word "provoke" occurs nowhere else in the N.T., but the Sept. employs it in Psalm 78 : 17, 40; 106 : 7, 33; Jer. 44 : 8, etc. They "vexed" Him (Isa. 63 : 10), and this because of their contempt of His word. Hereby they showed they were not of God, see John 8 : 47, 1 John 4 : 6. Should any unsaved man or woman read these lines, we would say, Beware of provoking God by *thine* obstinacy. To them that believe not, the gospel becomes "a savor of death unto death."

"But with whom was He grieved forty years"? (v. 17). This being put in the form of a question was designed to stir up the conscience of the reader, cf. Matt. 21 : 28, James 4 : 5, etc. "Was it not with them that had sinned, whose carcases fell in the wilderness"? (v. 17). "He doth not say, 'they died,' but their 'carcases fell,' which intimates contempt and indignation. God sometimes will make men who have been wickedly exemplary in sin, righteously exemplary in their punishment. To what end is this reported? It is that we may take heed that we 'fall not after the same example of unbelief' (4 : 11). There is then an example in the fall and punishment of unbelievers" (Dr. J. Owen .

"And to whom sware He that they should not enter into His rest, but to them that believed not"? (v. 18). Having reminded the Hebrews in the previous verse that sin was the cause of Israel's destruction of old, he now specifies the character of that sin, unbelief. The order is terribly significant: they hearkened not to God's voice; in consequence, their hearts were hardened; unbelief was the result; destruction, the issue. How unspeakably solemn! The Greek word here rendered "believed not" may, with equal propriety, be rendered "obeyed not"; it is so translated in Rom. 2 : 8; 10 : 21. It amounts to the same thing, differing only according to the angle of view-point: looked at from the mind or heart, it is "unbelief"; looked at from the will, it is "disobedience." In either case it is the sure consequence of *refusal* to heed God's voice.

"So we see that they could not enter in because of unbelief" (v. 19). "The apostle does not single out the sin of making and worshipping the golden calf; he does not bring before us the flagrant transgressions into which they fell at Beth-peor. Many much more striking and to our mind more fearful sins could have been pointed out, but God thinks the one sin greater than all is *unbelief*. We are saved by faith; we are lost through unbelief. The heart is purified by faith; the heart is hardened by unbelief. Faith brings us nigh to God; unbelief is departure from God" (Saphir). There is no sin so great but it may be pardoned, if the sinner believe; but "he that believeth not shall be damned."

The application of the whole of this passage to the case of the sorely-tried and wavering Hebrews was most pertinent and solemn. Twice over the apostle reminded them (vv. 9, 17) that the unbelief of their fathers had been continued for "forty years."

Almost that very interval had now elapsed since the Son had died, risen again, and ascended to heaven. In Scripture, forty is the number of probation. The season of Israel's testing was almost over; in A.D. 70 their final dispersion would occur. And God changeth not. He who had been provoked of old by Israel's hardness of heart, would destroy again those who persisted in their unbelief. Then let *them* beware, and heed the solemn warning, "Take heed, brethren, lest there be in any of you an evil heart of unbelief, in departing from the living God." May God grant us hearts to heed the same admonitary warning.

—*Arthur W. Pink.*

GLEANINGS IN EXODUS.

63. *Outside the Camp*: Ex. 33 : 4—10.

In order to enter into the significance of of what is to be before us on this present occasion, and especially to discern its typical application to Christendom to-day, careful attention must be paid to the context. Moses' pitching of the tent "outside the camp," and the seeking unto it of "every one which sought the Lord" can only be interpreted aright by noting carefully the imperative necessity for such a drastic action, and that, in the light of all which occasioned it. The section of Exodus in which our present portion is found begins with 32 : 1. In that chapter, as we have already seen, Israel is shown committing the awful sin of making and worshipping the golden calf. That, in turn, was the consequence of their throwing off allegiance to Jehovah. Having, in their hearts, cast off the God they loved not, they now set up an idol patterned after their own evil lusts—a beast, graven in gold.

That the Lord did not there and then let loose the thunderbolts of His wrath and completely exterminate Israel is something which should bow our hearts before Him in wonder and worship, the more so when we observe what it was and who it was that averted His righteous anger against them, namely, the earnest and effectual supplications of the typical mediator. Blessed foreshadowment was this of Him who has entered into heaven itself, "now to appear in the presence of God for us" (Heb. 9 : 24), and who is "able also to save them unto the uttermost (to the last extremity) that come unto God by Him, seeing that He ever liveth to make intercession for them" (Heb. 7 : 25). Had there been no Moses to plead their cause, Israel had perished. And had we no High Priest to plead before God the merits of His atoning sacrifice on our behalf, we too would perish in this wilderness scene. It is the ministry of Christ on High which succors and sustains us while we journey to the promised inheritance.

How Moses must have *loved* his people! Do we not have more than a hint of this in the words of the Spirit in Heb. 11 : 24, 25, "By faith Moses, when he was come to years, refused to be called the son of Pharaoh's daughter: Choosing rather to suffer affliction *with* the people of God, than to enjoy the pleasures of sin for a season." His love for them is brought out again in Acts 7 : 23, "And when he was full forty years old, it came into his *heart* to visit his brethren the children of Israel." Blessed adumbrations were these of a greater than Moses, who refused not to lay aside His heavenly glory and come down to this sin-curst earth, where His "brethren" (Heb. 2 : 11) were in cruel bondage to sin and Satan. More blessed still is it to follow out the love of Moses for his people under the severest trials and testings. Though they appreciated him not, though they repeatedly murmured and rebelled against him, though they manifested their utter unworthiness of his unselfish devotion to them, yet nothing quenched his love for them. So too we read of Him to whom Moses pointed, "having loved His own which were in the world, He loved them *unto the end*" John 13 : 1). Nor could the awful sin of His people kill the affections of Moses: when unsparing judgment at the hands of a holy God was their only due, he stepped into the breech, and stood between them and His wrath.

But, as we saw in our last article, though the intercession of Moses averted the consuming wrath of God, yet it did not preclude the manifestations of His displeasure in a governmental way. The nation was not "consumed" (32 : 10), but it *was* "plagued" (32 : 35). This was due to no failure in the prayer of Moses, but to the lack of repentance on the part of the people. Most solemnly does this speak to us, and timely is its warning. How sadly neglected is this truth to day! If there be little or no preaching of "repentance" to the unsaved, there is still less to those who are saved. Yet, concerning the one we read "But, except ye *repent*, ye shall all likewise perish" (Luke 13 : 3); and of the other, it is to be noted, that the very first admonitory word of Christ to the seven churches in Rev. 2, 3 is, "Remember therefore from whence thou art fallen, and *repent*" (2 : 5)! It is because there is so little repentance among God's people to-day that His chastening hand is laid so heavily on many of them.

"And the Lord said unto Moses, Depart, go up hence, thou and the people which thou hast brought up out of the land of Egypt, unto the land which I sware unto Abraham, to Isaac, and to Jacob, saying, Unto thy seed will I give it" (33 : 1). In these words Jehovah presses upon Moses the solemn position which Israel occupied. Having broken the covenant which they had made only a few weeks before (Ex. 19 : 5, 8; 24 : 7), they had thus forfeited their relationship to God as *His* people. Having rejected Him, He speaks to them according to their transgression, saying to Moses, "The people which *thou* hast brought up out of the land of Egypt." Nevertheless, He promised them the land, according to His absolute and unconditional promises to the patriarchs—to which Moses had appealed in his intercession (32 : 13). "And I will send an angel before thee; and I will drive out the Canaanite, the Amorite, and the Hittite, and the Perizzite, the Hivite, and the Jebusite: unto a land flowing with milk and honey" (vv. 2, 3).

Next, the Lord added, "For I will not go up in the midst of thee; for thou art a stiffnecked people: lest I consume thee in the way (v. 3). Solemn word was this; a real test of Israel's heart. "At the beginning of this book, when the people were in the furnace of Egypt, the Lord could say, 'I have surely seen the affliction of My people which are in Egypt, and have heard their cry by reason of their taskmasters; for I know their sorrows.' But now he has to say, 'I have seen this people, and, behold, it is a stiffnecked people', An afflicted people is an object of grace; but a stiffnecked people must be humbled. The cry of the oppressed Israel had been answered by the exhibition of grace; but the song of idolatrous Israel must be answered by the voice of stern rebuke" (C.H.M.).

Then we read, "And when the people heard these evil tidings, they mourned" (v. 4). Here was the first hopeful sign that the people gave. The Hebrew word for "mourn" in this passage means to sorrow or lament. The threat that Jehovah Himself would not accompany them moved Israel to deep contrition. How sad is the contrast presented in Rev. 3! There too the Lord is viewed as *not* being "in the midst" of His people, but outside (v. 20). Yet Laodicea is indifferent, content without Him (v. 17). When the Lord is no longer "in the midst" of His people, it is high time for them to "mourn."

"And no man did put on his ornaments. For the Lord had said unto Moses, Say unto the children of Israel, ye are a stiffnecked people: I will come up in the midst of thee in a moment, and consume thee: therefore now put off thy ornaments from thee, that I may know what to do unto thee" (vv. 4, 5). The removal of their ornaments was for the purpose of evidencing the genuineness of their contrition. Outward adornment was out of keeping with the taking of a low place before God. Contrariwise, external attractions and displays show up the absence of that lowliness of spirit and brokenness of heart which are of great price in the sight of God. The more true spirituality declines, the more an elaborate ritual comes to the fore. All around us Christendom is *putting on* as many "ornaments" as possible.

"And the children of Israel stripped themselves of their ornaments by the mount Horeb" (v. 6). This was a still more hopeful sign. Here we see Israel obeying God's command to humble themselves. This is ever the ground of further blessing. The promise is, "he that humbleth himself shall be exalted." A New Testament parallel to what we have before us here, is found in the case of the Corinthians. To them the apostle wrote, "Now ye are full, now ye are rich, ye have reigned as kings" (1 Cor. 4 : 8). There we see them with all their "ornaments" on. Later he was able to write, "For though I made you sorry with a letter, I do not repent, though I did repent: for I perceive that the same epistle hath made you sorry, though but for a season. Now I rejoice, not that ye were made sorry, but that ye sorrowed *to repentance;* for ye were made sorry after a godly manner" (2 Cor. 7 : 8, 9). They had "stripped themselves" of their "ornaments"!

"And Moses took the tabernacle, and

pitched it without the camp, afar off from the camp, and called it the tabernacle of the congregation" (v. 7). This movement of Moses denoted three things: it was an act of *submission*, it was an act of *faith*, it was an act of *grace*. Let us enlarge a little upon these things. The going forth of Moses outside the camp was an act of submission, it was a bowing to God's righteous verdict. While Israel was a stiffnecked people, Jehovah could not remain in their "midst" (v. 3). While they continued in a state of impenitency He could not own them as His people (v. 1). Accordingly, Moses is here seen acquiescing in the Lord's holy judgment, and therefore leaves the place where He no longer was. Well would it be—both for God's glory and for their own good—if His people would act on this same principle to-day.

But more: the going forth of Moses outside the camp was an act of *faith*. This comes out plainly and most blessedly in what Israel's leader did on this occasion: he "*took*" the tabernacle and "pitched it without the camp." It should be pointed out that this was not the Tabernacle proper, with its three apartments, for this had not yet been erected. If the reader will refer back to Ex. 24 : 18 and 32 : 1 it will be found that Israel committed their great sin of worshipping the golden calf while Moses was up in the mount, during which time Jehovah had said to him, "Let them make Me a sanctuary: that I may dwell among them" (25 : 8)—details concerning which are found in the chapters that follow to the end of 31.

In the opening paragraphs of article 41 of this series (May 1927) on "The Coverings," we called attention to the distinction which is to be drawn between "the Tabernacle" (Heb. "mishkan") and "the Tent" (Heb. "Ohel"): the former signifies "dwelling-place"; the latter, simply "tent." The one refers to the abode of Jehovah, the other to the meeting-place for His people. The two are clearly distinguished in several scriptures, for example in Num. 3 : 25 we read of "the tabernacle *and* the tent." In the majority of passages where the A.V. has "tabernacle of the congregation," the Heb. reads "tent of the congregation." This holy building was Jehovah's place of abode, but Israel's place of assembly; they visited it, He remained there.

Now it was the "tent" and not the "tabernacle" which Moses here "took" and "pitched it outside the camp," for, as we have said, the tabernacle proper had not yet been built. In this action of Israel's leader we may discern the exercise of real faith. "Faith cometh by hearing, and hearing by the word of God" (Rom. 10 : 17). Moses had been hearing the word of God yonder in the mount, and now that he is down in the camp again his heart lays hold of, and anticipates, the actual erection of Jehovah's dwelling-place. It was a temporary provision to meet a pressing emergency. "It does not appear that Moses, in pitching the tabernacle outside the camp, was acting under any direct commandment from the Lord. It was rather spiritual discernment, entering into both the character of God and the state of the people. Taught of God, he feels that Jehovah could no longer dwell in the midst of a camp which had been defiled by the presence of the golden calf. He therefore made a place outside, afar off from the camp, and called it the 'tabernacle of the congregation' " (Ed. Dennett).

Again; the pitching of the tent outside the camp was an act of *grace*. This will be seen the more clearly if we revert once more to the context; "The Lord had said unto Moses, Say unto the children of Israel, Ye are a stiffnecked people: I will come up in the midst of thee in a moment, and consume thee: therefore now put off thy ornaments from thee, that I may know what to do unto thee." God was here speaking after the manner of men—just as He does when He is said to "repent." It was as though He were weighing the condition of His wicked people, waiting to see whether or not their "mourning" was genuine. Before He smote, He would furnish opportunity for repentance. The people availed themselves of His forbearance: humbled by their sin, awed by the solemn tidings of iminent destruction, they stripped themselves of their ornaments. Then, as another has said, "He who pronounced judgment upon the people for their sins, provided a way for their escape." Those who "sought the Lord" were not only spared, but permitted to go forth unto the tent. Thus, "where sin abounded, grace did much more abound."

"And it came to pass, that every one which sought the Lord went unto the tent of the congregation, which was without the camp" (v. 7). Once more we have a striking illustration of the word "even so might grace reign through righteousness" (Rom. 5 : 21). God is "the God of all grace," yet it ever needs to be remembered that He never exercises grace at the expense of righteousness. God forgives sins, but it is because they were atoned for by Christ. Israel was delivered from the avenging angel in Egypt, but only because they were sheltered beneath the blood. So here: God maintained His righteousness. Holiness forbade Him entering the defiled camp, but grace made it possible for the people to meet Him outside.

"And it came to pass, that every one which sought the Lord went out unto the tent of the congregation, which was without the camp" (v. 7). Let us now consider the typical significance of this. We think at once of Heb. 13 : 13, "Let us go forth therefore unto Him, without the camp, bearing His reproach." Obviously, the Holy Spirit here had Ex. 33 : 7 before Him, and it is in the light of what is there recorded that we must interpret this New Testament exhortation. What we have there is a call to separation, but unless we pay close attention to the type we shall err in our application of the antitype. The all-important thing is to bear steadily in mind the *circumstances* under which Moses pitched the Tent "outside the camp." It was not when Israel murmured (Ex. 16 : 2), when they desecrated the sabbath (16 27, 28), when the Amalekites fought against them (17 : 8); it was after Israel had disowned Jehovah and set up the golden calf. General and *open idolatry* in the camp constitutes the call to "go forth" outside it!

The same principle holds good in the interpretation of Heb. 13 : 13. This exhortation was not given to the Corinthians, where a sectarian spirit prevailed, where immorality had been condoned, and where the Lord's supper had been turned into a carnal feast. Nor was the call given to the Galatians, among whom false doctrine, of a serious character, had come in. Instead, it was addressed to "Hebrews." The believing Jews were enjoined to forsake the unbelieving Nation who had despised and rejected Christ. The "camp" was guilty of the murder of God's Son, hence the call to forsake it. What we would here press upon the Christian reader is that neither Ex. 33 : 7 nor Heb. 13 : 13 supplies any warrant for Christians forsaking "churches" or companies of God's professing people where Christ *is* owned, honoured, worshipped. There are those claiming to "gather unto the Lord," who insist they are the *only* people that are on true scriptural ground. They have separated themselves not only from false systems, but from the great majority of God's own people. Little wonder that to-day *they* are more sectarian than any of the denominations, and that God has blown upon their proud and pharisaical claims. To "go forth unto Him without *the camp*" is a vastly different thing than separating from *God's own people*. All who are dear to Christ should be dear to the Christian.

It was corporate idolatry which made Jehovah refuse to continue in Israel's midst. It was when the Lord Himself had been rejected, and not till then, that Moses pitched the Tent outside the camp. Nothing short of this ever warrants a Christian from breaking away from those who profess the name of Christ. Perfection will be found no where on this earth, and the loftier the pretentions of those claiming to come nearest to perfection, the least grounds for such a profession they will evidence. A drum makes a big noise, but it is very hollow inside! No, ideal conditions, a faithful carrying out of all the revealed will of God, are not to be met with among *any* company of Christians. Failure is stamped upon everything which God has committed to man. But that does not justify me in holding aloof from my erring brethren and sisters, and assuming an attitude of "I am holier than thou"; for in the sight of God I am probably a greater failure than they are. We are all of us quick to discover the mote in another's eye, while complacently impervious to the *beam* in our own eye.

"Strengthen the things which remain (not "pull down"), that are ready to die," is God's word to us (Rev. 3 : 2). "Lift up the hands which hang down, and the feeble knees" (Heb. 12 : 12): obedience to this will accomplish far more than criticising and condemning every body and every thing. "Forbearing one another in love" (Eph. 4 : 2), implies there is that in each of us which is a trial to the other. There will be much to test patience and love in any "church" or gathering, but if the Lord is there, that is the place for me too. *He* is "long-suffering," so must I be. But when He is disowned, when a *false* god is set up in His place, when "another Jesus" (2 Cor. 11 : 4) is preached (a "Jesus" who is not the God-man, born of a virgin, died for the sins of His people, rose again in bodily triumph over death), it is high time for me to get out. To remain in a place where He is denied would be for me to dishonour my Lord. It was on *this* principle that Moses here acted; and not Moses only, but "every one who sought the Lord."

Thus, the principle which is to guide us to-day in our application of Heb. 13 : 13 to any local situation, is simple and plain. If I am worshipping with a company of Christians where the Lord Jesus is owned as the Christ of God, as the alone Saviour for sinners, as the Exemplar of His people, though the preaching there may not be as edifying as I could desire, though my fellow-disciples may come far short of what I wish, that is no reason why I should desert them; rather it is an occasion for me to be much in prayer on their behalf, and by my own walk seek to show them the way of the Lord more perfectly. But, on the other hand, if I am in a place where the Christ of God is denied, the inspiration of the Scriptures repudiated, the Holy Spirit quenched through a false god having been set up, then no matter what my friends may do, no matter what may be the decision of my brethren, I am responsible before God to separate myself from what is so grossly dishonouring to Him.

"And it came to pass, when Moses went out unto the tabernacle, that all the people rose up, and stood every man at his tent door, and looked after Moses, until he was gone into the tabernacle" (v. 8). From this it appears that not many responded to the call of separation. "The majority stood at their tent doors, interested in Moses, and looking after him, and seeing the pillar of cloud stand at the entrance of the tent, but not going out! They seem to represent those who have reverence for divine things, and are interested in the truth, but who remain in the camp. God-fearing persons, but not knowing the presence of the Lord in its attractive and satisfying power" (C. A. Coates).

"And it came to pass, as Moses entered into the tabernacle, the cloudy pillar descended, and stood at the door of the tabernacle, and the Lord talked with Moses" (v. 9). The "cloudy pillar" was the visible symbol of Jehovah's presence. This is the third time in Exodus we find mention of it. First, in 13 : 21 we read, "And the Lord went before them by day in a pillar of a cloud, to lead them the way; and by night in a pillar of fire, to give them light." Second, in 14 : 19, 20 we are told, "And the pillar of the cloud went from before their face, and stood behind them: and it came between the camp of the Egyptians and the camp of Israel; and it was a cloud and darkness to them, but it gave light by night to these: so that the one came not near the other all the night." Third, "the cloudy pillar descended, and stood at the door of the tabernacle, and the Lord talked with Moses." Thus it was connected first with *guidance*, then with *protection*, now with *communion*.

"The cloudy pillar descended, and stood at the door of the tabernacle, and the Lord talked with Moses." Blessed answer of God was this to the confidence of His servant. How true are His words "them that honour Me I will honour." Moses was not put in confusion: his submission and faith were amply rewarded. God never disappoints those who seek His glory and count upon His grace. It is the compromisers, the fearers of men, and the unbelieving who are the losers. O for more single-eyed devotion to the Lord, then we shall have Him "talk with" (not "to") us.

"And all the people saw the cloudy pillar stand at the tabernacle door; and all the people rose up and worshipped, every man in his tent door" (v. 10). Nothing but a gracious manifestation of the Lord will produce real worship, and the more we are conscious of His *unmerited* favour, the more fervent will our worship be. Nor must we ignore the Spirit's notice of the *position* occupied by these prostrate Israelites: they "worshipped every man in his *tent* door." This has a voice for us if we have hearts to receive it. The "tent" is the symbol of the pilgrim, and it is only as *this* character is maintained that worship will be sustained. The blessed sequel we must leave for consideration till our next article. May the Lord exercise each of us by what has been before us.

—*Arthur W. Pink*.

---

3. ABRAM'S COMPROMISES.

Gen. 11 : 31, 32.

Two things have been before us concerning Abram: the Call which he received from God, and the encouragements which accompanied it. The call of God made a threefold demand upon him: he was to leave the land of his birth, his kindred, and his father's house. It was a call to complete separation from the old life. It was a call requiring him to sever his connections with that which spake, in figure, of the world and our place in it by nature. It was a call which insisted that the Lord should have the first place in his affections, all other claims being thoroughly subordinated. The encouragements which Abram received were an appearing of the God of glory, and the making to him of promises which corresponded to the sacrifices which the call demanded from him. Those promises set forth the spiritual blessings which were to be his as compensations for the temporal losses he was to suffer. Most gracious were those promises: Abram was assured that, following his obedience to God, he would not only be blessed personally but become a blessing even to all families of the earth. Thus would God establish the heart of that one to whom He had condescended to reveal Himself.

Now what is recorded here in Gen. 12 is far more than an interesting fragment of ancient history, even sacred history; it is recorded for our learning. Gen. 12 is an integral part of that Word of God which "liveth and abideth forever." Therefore nothing in it is obsolete or out of date. All is needed by us if we would be "thoroughly furnished unto all good works." Moreover, when we bear in mind that Abram is "the father of us all," a special and personal interest attaches to whatever is recorded concerning him.

Inasmuch as Abram is called "the father of all them that believe" (Rom. 4 : 12), we have more than a hint that God's dealings with him make known to us the fundamental principles which constitute and are to regulate the Life of Faith. This is a phrase which is well known to many, though it is much to be feared that those to whom it has been applied, has misled not a few. Men like Brainherd, Carey, Geo. Muller, Hudson Taylor, are looked upon as being among the few entitled to being called men who lived a life of faith; while the rank and file of God's people suppose that such is not for them. This is a grave mistake. The Christian in business, the wife in the home, is just as much called upon to live a life of faith as is the one who forsakes all and goes out as a missionary.

A life of faith is one of confidence in and dependence upon God. It is a turning away from all creature confidences, and casting one's self upon the living and faithful God, who never disappoints those whose "expectations" are (by grace) in Himself alone. But it is much more than that: it is a life of varied energies and graces. According to the teaching of Holy Writ, faith is that principle of action which not only believes in and trusts God, but also apprehends His way and acts in accord with His revealed will. It not only receives His promises and enjoys His favour, but performs His bidding. Thus a life of faith is a life that is lived in communion with God, walking in His light, and by His strength gaining victories over the flesh, the world and the Devil. It is a life formed by habitual walking with God. Such a life has only been perfectly exemplified by the perfect Man.

The life of faith then is one that is possessed of blessed and beautiful variety, and though Abram was far from perfectly exemplifying it, yet there is much in his life which all his spiritual children should earnestly and prayerfully seek to emulate. On some occasions in Abram's life of faith we find unshaken confidence in God was the grace manifested, as when he believed the promise concerning a son, considering not his body then incapable of begetting nor Sarah's incapacity to conceive, but "being fully persuaded that, what He had promised, He was also able to perform" (Rom. 4 : 17-21). On other occasions we find that implicit obedience to God's command was the fruit he exhibited, as when he laid his dearly-loved son on the altar to slay him. On yet other occasions rights were surrendered and wrongs submitted to were the virtues displayed, as in allowing Lot to make choice of pastorage. On still other occasions strength was put forth and glorious victories won, as when Lot was delivered from the enemy. All of these experiences formed part of the life of faith.

Above, we have said that Abram's walk was far from being an ideal setting forth of what the life of faith should be. The Holy Spirit has given us a faithful and true account of his experiences, recording his compromises, chronicling his failures, describing his sad falls. But let it here be said very emphatically that if *we* should seek to shelter behind Abram's faults, if we endeavour to make them the ground of excusing our own failings and falls, we are making a wrong and evil use of them. If in the naughtiness of our hearts we are saying, "Oh well, Abram was not perfect, *he* did not always do as God commanded him, therefore it cannot be expected that I should do any better than he did," such an attitude and such language betrays a sad state of soul, a heart that is very far from being right with God.

It is indeed solemnizing and saddening to take note of the response made by Abram to the call which he had received from Jehovah. The terms of that call were too positive and plain to be misunderstood, yet was his obedience far from being what it should have been. The Lord had said to Abram, "Get thee out of thy country, and from thy kindred, and from thy father's house, unto a land that I will show thee," and in three out of the four things required of him he failed. He did leave Chaldea, but instead of separating from his kindred, he suffered his nephew Lot to accompany him; instead of forsaking his father's house, Terah was permitted to take the lead; and, instead of entering Canaan, Abram stopped short at and settled down in Haran.

Above, we have pointed out that these sins of Abram are recorded not for us to shelter behind, but as *warnings* to prayerfully heed. If I hear that, of late, numbers of people have broken their limbs through slipping upon banana-skins on the streets, *that* should make me more careful where I put my feet; their falls ought to make me more diligent about my own walk. Or, if I read of an increasing number of people being knocked down by motor-cars, that should not make me more careless, but more careful to avoid them. So, when I read of Abram's sad falls, I should seek grace to avoid the things which ensnared him.

The falls of Abram are recorded for our *learning*. They show us what even a true believer is capable of: "As in water face answereth to face, so the heart of man to man." They are for us to take to heart, to be exercised before God concerning them, to examine ourselves and consider our ways and see if we have not already repeated some of his sad falls, and if we are not well on the way to become a victim to others of them. If we *have* already fallen, we must humble ourselves before God, confess our sins, seek His forgiveness. Only thus shall we really profit from what is thus written for our learning.

To attempt to explain away Abram's sins, or to apologise for them, is to miss God's salutary purpose in recording them. Probably every Christian reader has profitted by the Holy Spirit's recountal of Peter's denial of the Saviour. Our hearts instinctively realize that His recital of the apostle's terrible sin stands out on the pages of the N.T. as a beacon of warning, a danger-signal to diligently heed. Thus too we should regard the failures and falls of the O.T. saints. The sins of Noah, Abram, Isaac, Jacob, Moses, Joshua, David, are all recorded for our learning, and a conscience which is duly exercised will surely profit from them.

Finally, it should be pointed out that so far from the faults of Abram affording ground for us to extenuate our own sins, there is far less excuse for us now than there was for him then. Abram did not have the completed Word of God in his hands as we do. There was not then placed on record the falls of others who had gone before him, to serve as warnings, such as we have. Nor had he the inspired account of the earthly walk of the perfect Man as an example before him to be followed. Truly, *we have* every cause to bow our heads in deepest shame if we have been guilty of Abram's sins. If the grace of God has mercifully kept me from thus falling, then let me not be slow to freely ascribe all the glory unto Him to whom alone it rightly belongs.

It will be noted that Gen. 12 begins by saying, "Now the Lord *had* said unto Abram, Get thee out of thy country, and from thy kindred, and from thy father's house, unto a land that I will show thee." This call was received by Abram while he was yet in Mesopotamia, as Acts 7 : 2, 3 plainly shows. The response which Abram made is narrated in Gen. 11 : 31, "And Terah took Abram his son, and Lot the son of Haran his son's son, and Sarai his daughter-in-law, his son Abram's wife; and they went forth with them from Ur of the Chaldees, to go into the land of Canaan; and they came unto Haran, and dwelt there." Sad reading does this indeed make, yet can we admire the impartiality and faithfulness of the heavenly Artist who has painted the characters of Scripture in the colours of truth and reality.

Abram temporised. "Get thee out of thy country" he obeyed; but "and from thy kindred" he disregarded. Probably such a compromise appeared unto Abram as promising more than God had; in fact, it furnished less. No doubt Abram reasoned that it would be a big gain to carry his "kindred" along with him, and thus avoid a painful, and what to him doubtless seemed a needless separation. The same temptation or searching test often confronts a Christian to-day. The fellow-members of his household are unsaved. They may be moral, upright people, kind and amiable; but, though they may love him dearly, they have no love for that One who is the fairest of ten thousands to his soul. He knows full well that they are quite at a loss to appreciate the motives which now actuate him; he realises they do not understand his new interests, joys and desires. What then shall he do?

Or, to take a case which is even more testing : the other members of your household may be real Christians, but Christians who are not out and out for the Lord. They may not have responded to the light God has given so fully and freely as you have. They think you are too strict, too narrow, too extreme. What are you to do? It is at this point comes the temptation that Abram met with. Why should there be a break between you and your dear ones in any thing? Why not be patient, tolerant with their weakness; yea, tarry along with them, if they are lingering and lagging along the path of faith? Ah, my reader, sooner or later, most Christians have to learn experimentally that "a man's *foes* are they of his own household." It is not that they intend you harm, yet if there is more of unjudged self-will in them than there is in you, if they are not walking as closely with God as you are, then, for you to conform to their standard turns them into your spiritual enemies!

The subject is a searching and painful

one, yet plain speaking thereon is called for in these days of laxity, compromise, and abounding unfaithfulness on every hand. The Lord Jesus declared plainly, "Suppose ye that I am come to give peace on earth? I tell you, Nay; but rather division; For from henceforth there shall be five in one house divided, three against two, and two against three. The father shall be divided against the son, and the son against the father; the mother against the daughter, and the daughter against the mother; the mother-in-law against the daughter-in-law, and the daughter-in-law against her mother-in-law" (Luke 12 : 51-53).

The great responsibility of the Christian is, and his one desire and aim should ever be, to *please Christ,* to follow *Him,* obey Him, serve Him, glorify Him. And we cannot please Christ and men too, see Gal. 1 : 10. The path of faith is an *individual* one from start to finish: individual dealings with God, individual walking with Him, individual obeying Him. The path before us is so narrow that we can only walk it single file. And if you are walking ahead of other Christians who have not fully dedicated their lives to God, then you must expect to be misunderstood, criticised, and condemned for your "puritanism."

The God of glory had appeared to Abram and His peremptory call was, "Get thee out of thy country and from thy kindred." The sentiments and affections (though · *not* the responsibilities) of the flesh are to be set aside. The claims of God must over-ride all other considerations. The ties of nature are to be ignored whenever they clash with the revealed will of the Most High. The Christian is not his own, but bought with a price. The demand made upon Abram was neither peculiar nor exceptional. Our Lord has emphatically declared, "If any come to Me, and hate not his father, and mother, and wife, and children, and brethren, and sisters, yea, and his own life also, he cannot be My disciple" (Luke 14 : 26). Christ must have the preeminence in all things.

"And Terah took Abram his son, and Lot the son of Haran his son's son . . . and they went forth with him from Ur of the Chaldees." It is very solemn and searching to see that it was neither an attack from the Devil, nor the attractions of the world, but the ties of nature, which hindered Abram from fully responding to God's call. This should deeply exercise every renewed heart. Remember that *this* is written for *our* learning and warning. Instead of leaving his "kindred" behind, Abram took them with him, or rather, as Gen. 11 : 31 says, "Terah took Abram." This is very solemn: it shows that Abram was entirely controlled, dominated, by Terah. And how many a Christian to day is governed (especially in the home) not by the Word, but by natural love and respect for his relatives! Does not the reader see that this brings down the child of God to the level of many a worldling? Surely something higher than sentiment, however noble, is to govern an heir of heaven. Fleshly ties have to be subordinated to spiritual relationships. The sad *consequences* of Abram's failure soon became evident, for he must learn by sad experience, as most of God's people do, that "a man's foes *are* they of his own household."

"And they went forth with them from Ur of the Chaldees, to go into the land of Canaan; and they came unto Haran, and dwelt there" (Gen. 11 : 31). This is very sad. It records Abram's second compromise. God had commanded him to go "*Into* the land which I will shew thee" (Acts 7 : 3); instead of doing so, they "came unto Haran and *dwelt* there." There is much important instruction for us here if we note attentively the place at which Abram's party halted. Haran was Half-way House! It was an important town on the banks of the Euphrates, and lay on the edge of the Desert. Thus far their journey from Ur had been comparatively pleasant, within the bounds of "civilization." Haran lay at the dividing-line, where the cities were left behind and the desert began. A wilderness lay between Haran and Canaan, and this Terah was unwilling to cross.

What is typified here is this: the natural affections of our unsaved and uncalled kindred are ready to make certain concessions to a godly member of the family, but they are not prepared to, in fact cannot, go all the way with him. The "flesh" can be religious, but it never becomes spiritual. It may read the Bible, but it will not be governed by its precepts. Unregenerate people will attend meetings, even admire a logical and forceful exposition of the Word, and delight in the discoveries which another has made in it, but their life, their walk, is uninfluenced? Why? Because self has never been judged before God. "Except a man be born again he cannot see the kingdom of God."

Yes, the Word of God *is* a living Book; it describes living characters, it depicts things as they actually are, it exposes all the activities of an evil heart of unbelief. Terah was willing to leave Ur and accompany Abram as far as Haran. But further he would not go. Wilderness life appalled him, hence he stopped short at Halfway House.

He had no desire to cross the desert; and why? Because the life of a "stranger and pilgrim" repelled him. He craved the comforts and conveniences of this world. He was not willing to deny self and take up the cross. Terah is not difficult to understand; many of his tribe still survive. The solemn thing to note is that he never entered Canaan!

The sad thing is—and this is the chief lesson for every Christian to take to heart—that Terah influenced Abram. He too settled in Haran! It is worthy of notice that "Terah" means *delay;* and so it proved. Abram lost five years of his life in Haran. How many years have you, my reader, wasted there? "Ye did run well; *who* did hinder you that ye should not obey the truth"? (Gal. 5 : 7). Has it been a loved one, whose approbation you have esteemed more highly than that of your Lord's? Heed the warning ere it is too late.

Yes, Abram settled down in Haran. Not having obeyed God at the beginning and separated from that which spoke of the flesh, he was at once affected by his godless father. It is ever thus. If a Christian and a worldling become friendly and familiar, it is always the Christian who suffers, and never the worldling who is helped. The Holy Scriptures abound in examples of this fact, and human observation confirms it. And in what way does the Christian suffer? By failing to make progress along the path of faith, by becoming a compromising laggard; and thus his *witness* for Christ, as one of His "peculiar people," is spoiled.

Scholars are not agreed, but the majority of them say that "Haran" means *parched,* and we believe they are right. This is ever the place which an unfaithful, fleshly, worldly Christian, occupies. The "dew of the Lord" is not on him. Converse with him, and you quickly find that he has nothing with which to refresh you. He is wrapped up in self, occupied with the things of the world, and out of the abundance of his heart his mouth now speaks. He may tolerate *your* converse about Christ, he may have an idle curiosity to hear explained obscure passages of Scripture; but he has nothing himself with which to refresh his fellow-pilgrims. He is dwelling at Haran, and therefore is himself parched!

Now though Abram settled down in Haran, God would not allow him to continue there indefinitely. The Lord had purposed that he should enter Canaan, and no purpose of His shall fail. God therefore tumbled Abram out of the nest which he had made for himself (Deut. 32 : 11), and very, very solemn it is to observe the *means* which God used. "And Terah died in Haran" (Gen. 11 : 32). With this should be compared Acts 7 : 4; "Then came he out of the land of the Chaldeans, and dwelt in Haran: and from thence, *when his father was dead,* he removed him into this land." Death had come in before Abram left Halfway House! He never started across the *wilderness* until death severed that tie of the flesh which held him back. And this also is written for our learning and warning! O how often has history repeated itself. God's people are frequently so stiffnecked they will not heed His *commands* until His hand removes the idol which supplants Him in their affections. O Christian reader be warned. Will *death* have to enter your family circle before you become out and out for Christ?

—Arthur W Pink

A THREEFOLD SALVATION.

(This article was written by the editor some twelve years ago for young Christians, and was printed in booklet form, 5d. (10 cents.) a copy—still obtainable.

Salvation!—the most important word in human speech. Salvation!—the biggest word in the Bible. Salvation!—the sweetest word that ever falls on the ear of a penitent sinner. Salvation!—the most elementary word about Christianity, and yet, to-day, used more loosely than almost any other. Do we go too far when we say that the vast majority of believers have an altogether inadequate conception of the signification and scope of this word? We are not now thinking of its fullest and ultimate meaning, for who on earth can apprehend the breadth and length and depth and height of this precious Gospel term? No, we refer to its simplest and primary force and application.

The average person to-day, and the ordinary church-member, too, when they use the word salvation, think of little more than the forgiveness of sins. The believer knows that he has been saved from something and unto something. He knows that he has been delivered from the wrath to come and that he has been begotten to an inheritance which is "incorruptible, and undefiled, and that fadeth not away." But, speaking generally, if you were to ask him to explain the three tenses of salvation he would be unable to do so. Ask him to harmonise the following three passages: 2 Timothy 1 : 9; Philippians 2 : 12; Romans 13 : 11, (we quote them below) and he would be utterly at sea. Now, this ought not to be. If there is anything the Christian ought to be clear upon, it is the doctrine of salvation, i.e. the meaning and scope of the word salvation; and if there is anything the sinner needs to know, it is the way of salvation.

Let us now quote the three passages referred to above: "Who hath saved us, and called us with a holy calling, not according to our works, but according to His own purpose and grace which was given us in Christ Jesus before the world began" (2 Tim. 1 : 9). "Work out your own salvation with fear and trembling" (Phil. 2 : 12). "Now is our salvation nearer than when we believed" (Rom. 13 : 11). It will be seen that these three Scriptures bring before us the three tenses of salvation : the first refers to a past experience, the second to a present process, the third to a future prospect. Now these three verses do not refer to three different salvations, but to the three stages of our complete salvation, or, to put it in other words, the three phases of our one salvation. The word salvation always supposes deliverance from something, and the salvation or deliverance which the Bible treats of is salvation from sin.

To show how widespread is the ignorance upon this subject, and, at the same time, the need for some such tract as this, were we to say to many good people that salvation is a process, they would immediately look upon us with suspicion; were we to say, further, that our salvation is a future prospect, they would regard us as an heretic. And yet "work out your own salvation" unmistakably refers to a present process, and "Now is our salvation nearer than when we believed" unequivocally places our salvation in the future. What then are we to do with these verses? We answer, we must carefully define our terms and re-adjust our thinking. The whole trouble arises out of failure to define terms and from the wrong application of them.

Deliverance from the wrath to come, and the forgiveness of sins is not a process, neither is our acceptance with God or the being made His child a future prospect. But the being delivered from the body of this death, and the being made like Christ is. We repeat, the trouble is that many who ought to know better, bundle together these different truths and denominate them all by the one word 'salvation,' thus making it a kind of generic term. When speaking of forgiveness of sins or the new birth, they alternately use the term salvation, as though it were exactly synonymous, when it is not. It is true that in one sense, a born-again person is a saved person, but what we are now seeking to prove is that the word salvation is much wider in its Scriptural scope than the mere forgiveness of sins or of being made a new creature in Christ Jesus. We repeat, the word salvation is the biggest word in all the Bible, and in its widest sense includes our predestination, regeneration, justification, sanctification, and glorification.

As we have already said, salvation signifies, primarily, salvation from sin; and as we have shown, Scripture reveals a threefold deliverance from sin: a past, a present, and a future. In 2 Cor. 1 : 10, we have a statement which we can conveniently appropriate to our present discussion: "Who delivered us from so great a death, and doth deliver; and in whom we trust that He will yet deliver us." Here the apostle is referring to his experiences as an ambassador of Christ. His work had led him into manifold dangers, out of which God had graciously delivered him, out of which God was even then delivering him, and out of the future dangers he trusted that God would yet deliver him. Applying this passage to our present subject, we find the three tenses of our salvation brought together within the limits of a single verse. By substituting the word saved for delivered and applying it to ourselves, we learn that the believer has been saved, is now being saved, and will yet be saved. Using this threefold division, let us now consider each separately.

Our salvation is a thing of the past. We have been saved from the *penalty* of sin. By penalty, we mean the guilt, the punishment, the wages of sin. Every soul that has put his trust in the Lord Jesus Christ has been saved from the penalty of sin. All those Scriptures which present our salvation as an accomplished fact treat of this branch of our subject. For example, when we hear our Lord saying to the woman, "Thy faith hath saved thee; go in peace" (Luke 7 : 50), we understand Him to mean that her sins had been forgiven (verse 48), and forgiveness always has to do with the criminality and punishment of sin. To the same effect when we read, "By grace have ye been saved" (Eph. 2 : 5, R.V.) and "Who hath saved us" (2 Tim. 1 : 9) we understand them to mean that the Lord Jesus has already "delivered us from the wrath to come" (1 Thess. 1 : 10). This aspect of our salvation may be looked at from two viewpoints: the Divine and the human. The Divine side of it was accomplished by our blessed Redeemer on the cross, where He suffered the just for the unjust. There it was that He was "wounded for our transgressions and bruised for our iniquities." There it was that He, "His own self, bare our sins in His own body on the tree." There it was, while acting as our substitute, He was "smitten of God and afflicted." And, because He suffered in my stead, I go free.

The human side of salvation from the penalty of sin is effected by our repentance and faith. By repentance we mean, that we take the place of a lost and guilty rebel before God, and cry "God be merciful to me a sinner." By faith we mean, that we believe the record which God has given of His Son in the Holy Scriptures; that we appropriate His gracious promises unto our own hearts; that we receive His Son as our Saviour; that we commit our souls into His keeping, realising that we are unable to save ourselves or contribute anything at all toward our salvation. It is written, "Believe on the Lord Jesus Christ and thou shalt be saved (Acts 16 : 31), and the moment that any penitent sinner believes that God means what He says, and acts on it, acts by taking Christ as his personal Saviour, that moment his sins are all removed from God's sight, "as far as the east is from the west" (Psa. 103 : 12). Salvation from the penalty of sin—the wrath to come—is ours unconditionally and eternally the moment we believe.

We cannot do better here than quote those sublime lines of Toplady:

"From whence this fear and unbelief?
  Hast Thou, O Father, put to grief
     Thy spotless Son for me?
And will the righteous Judge of men
Condemn me for that debt of sin
     Which, Lord, was laid on Thee?
If Thou hast my discharge procured,
And freely in my place endured
     The whole of wrath Divine;
Payment God cannot twice demand,
First at my bleeding Surety's hand,
     And then again at mine.
Complete atonement Thou hast made,
And to the utmost farthing paid,
     Whate'er Thy people owed;
How then can wrath on me take place,
If sheltered in Thy righteousness,
     And sprinkled with Thy blood?
Turn, then, my soul, unto thy rest,
The merits of thy great High Priest
     Speak peace and liberty;
Trust in His efficacious blood,
Nor fear thy banishment from God,
     Since Jesus died for thee."

This aspect of our salvation is termed our *justification*. Justification is a legal term and has to do with the law-courts. Justification is the sentence or decision of the Judge. Justification is the opposite of condemnation. Condemnation means that a man is charged with a crime, his guilt is established, and the law sentences him to a term of punishment. Justification means that the accused is guiltless, that the law has nothing against him. He is, therefore, treated as an innocent man and acquitted—in other words, he leaves the court without a stain on his character. When we read, then, that believers are "justified from all things" (Acts 13 : 39), it signifies that their case has been tried in the high court of heaven, and that God, the Judge of all the earth, has pronounced them righteous. As we read in Rom. 8 : 1, "There is therefore now no condemnation to them which are in Christ Jesus," which is further explained in verses 33, 34 of the same chapter, "Who shall lay anything to the charge of God's elect? It is God that justifieth! Who is he that condemneth? It is Christ that died, yea, rather, that is risen again, who is even at the right hand of God, who also maketh intercession for us." But it may be objected that the sinner is guilty, therefore, God cannot treat him as an innocent person. The answer to this objection is as follows: It is true that every sinner is guilty in the sight of God, that His law convicts him of many transgressions; but, the moment a sinner believes, he is a new creature in Christ Jesus, he occupies a new standing or position before God. The sins of the believer have already been dealt with in the person of his Substitute. His sins have already been punished. The wages of sin is death, which means that the penalty of the broken law is death. This penalty was inflicted upon our adorable Saviour. He died for us. He bore the penalty due our iniquities. Hence our sins are put away for ever from the sight of God. Therefore, we say, the believer has been saved from the penalty of sin. The law cannot punish twice for the same crime. To do so would be unjust. Hence, because our sins have already been punished (on Christ), the law has nothing against us; and therefore, on this ground the Divine Judge pronounces us just. There is much more in justification than this, but what we have now written is sufficient for our present purpose.

In the Old Testament we have a beautiful type and illustration of this aspect of our salvation. We refer to Exodus 12, which records the institution of the Passover feast. Among others, two great truths stand out here with peculiar prominence, namely, substitution and security. On the Passover-night the angel of death was to pass through the land of Egypt and slay all the firstborn of the Egyptians. But why spare the firstborn of the Israelites? Was it because they were guiltless before God? Surely not, for "all have sinned and come short of the glory of God." In this respect there is "no difference." The Israelites, equally with the Egyptians, were sinners in the sight of the thrice holy God, and therefore, as such, liable to and deserving of judgment and death. But it was right at this point that the grace of God came in and met their need. Another was slain in their room, another died in their stead. A lamb was killed and its blood was shed, pointing, of course, to the coming One, which it foreshadowed—namely, the "Lamb of God, which taketh away the sin of the world." The head of each Israelitish household was commanded to take a lamb, slay it, and sprinkle its blood on the lintel and posts of his door. Here, then we have substitution— the lamb dying in the stead of the Israelitish firstborn. Having sprinkled its blood, all who were in that house were spared from the avenging angel. Here then is security under the blood. The angel passed over each house where the lamb had been slain, for God's own promise was, "When I see the blood I will pass over you" (Exodus 12 : 13). Israel in Egypt on the night of the Passover were saved from the penalty of sin on the ground of a lamb having died in their stead. We now take up the next phase of our subject and consider:

Our salvation a thing of the present. Upon this side of our subject the greatest confusion of thought prevails, especially among young Christians. Many there are who, having learned that Jesus Christ is the Saviour of sinners, have jumped to the erroneous conclusion that if they will exercise faith in Him and commit their souls into His keeping, He will change their hearts, remove their carnal nature, and destroy their sinful propensities. But after they *have* received Him as their Saviour, they find that evil is still present within them, their hearts are still deceitful and desperately wicked, and the things they would not, those they do, and how to perform the things they wish to do they know not, until, with hearts almost breaking, they cry, "O wretched man that I am, who shall deliver me from the body of this death"?

In our first main division we have dwelt upon salvation as a *past* experience, and this we defined as deliverance from the *penalty* of sin; now, we turn to consider salvation as a present process, and this we denominate deliverance from the *power* of sin. In the above paragraph, paradoxical as it may sound, we have pointed out the fact that sin still remains within a saved person. Even though a person has received Christ as his personal Saviour, yet the old evil nature continues to harass him. There are many Scriptures which prove this. Writing to the saints at Rome, the apostle Paul said, "Let not sin therefore reign in your mortal body" (6 : 12)—sin could not "reign" in their bodies if it had been completely expelled from them. Writing to the Corinthians, whom he addresses as "dearly beloved," the apostle says, "Let us cleanse ourselves from all filthiness of the flesh and spirit, perfecting holiness in the fear of God" (2 Cor. 7 : 1) —such an exhortation would be needless if Christ had already removed sin from their beings. In like manner the apostle Peter writes, "Humble yourselves therefore under the mighty hand of God, that He may exalt you in due time" (1 Peter 5 : 6)— what need of this word but for the fact that pride still lurks and works within our hearts? Finally, the apostle John writes, "If we say we have no sin we deceive ourselves and the truth is not in us" (1 John 1 : 8).

The old carnal nature remains in the believer, he is still a sinner, though a saved sinner. What, then, is the young Christian to do? Is he powerless? Must he resort to stoicism, and make up his mind that there is naught but a life of defeat before him? Certainly not! The first thing for him to do is to learn thoroughly the humiliating truth that in himself he is "without strength." It was here that Israel failed: when Moses made known to them the law of Jehovah, they boastfully declared, "All that the Lord hath said we will do and be obedient" (Exodus 24 : 7). Ah! how little did they realise "that in the flesh there dwelleth no good thing" (Rom. 7 : 18). It was here, too, that Peter failed. Peter was self-confident. His proud boast was that "Though all men be offended because of Thee, yet will I never be offended . . . though I should die with Thee, yet will I not deny Thee" (Matt. 26 : 33, 35). How little he knew his own heart! This boastful spirit lurks within every one of us. While we cherish the belief we can "do better next time," or think we can "turn over a new leaf," it is evident that we still have confidence in our own powers. It is not until we heed the word of the apostle and "have no confidence in the flesh" (Phil. 3 : 3); it is not until we heed the word of our Saviour, "Without Me ye can do nothing" (John 15 : 5), that we take the first step toward victory. It is only when we are weak (in ourselves) that we are strong (2 Cor. 12 : 10). It is not until we have discovered our own impotency that we shall look outside ourselves to another. Then shall we discover that deliverance is to be found in the Lord—"In the Lord have I righteousness and strength" (Isaiah 45 : 24). "The Lord will give strength unto His people (Psalm 29 : 11).

The believer still has the carnal nature within him, and he has no strength in himself to check its evil propensities, nor to overcome its sinful solicitations. But the believer in Christ also has another nature within him, a new nature. This is received at the new birth. "That which is born of the Spirit is spirit" (John 3 : 6), which means that by the quickening agency of the Holy Spirit a spiritual nature has been imparted to him. The believer, then, has two natures within him—the flesh and the spirit; one which is sinful, the other which is spiritual. These two natures being totally different in character are antagonistic to each other; to this antagonism or conflict the Apostle refers in Gal. 5 : 17 "The flesh lusteth against the spirit, and the spirit against the flesh." Now which of these two natures is to regulate the believer's life? It is manifest that both cannot, for they are contrary to each other. It is equally evident that the stronger of the two will exert the greater controlling power. It is also clear that in the young Christian the carnal nature is the stronger, because he was born with that, and hence it has had many years' start of the new spiritual nature, which he did not receive until he was born again. Further, it is unnecessary to argue at length that the only way by which we can strengthen and develop the new nature is by feeding it. In every realm growth is dependent upon food, suitable food, daily food. The food which God has provided for our spiritual nature is His own Word, for "Man shall not live by bread alone, but by every word that proceedeth out of the mouth of God" (Matt. 4 : 4). This is what Peter means when he says, "As newborn babes desire the sincere (pure) milk of the Word, that ye may grow thereby" (1 Peter 2 : 2). In proportion as we feed upon the Word of God, such will be our spiritual growth. Of course there are other things besides food necessary to growth. We must breathe, and breathe in a pure atmosphere; in a word, we need fresh air. This, translated into spiritual terms, means prayer. It is in the closet, when we approach the throne of God's grace and meet our Father face to face, that our spiritual lungs are filled with the ozone of heaven. Exercise is another essential to growth, and this finds its accomplishment in service unto the Lord. If, then, we observe and heed these primary laws of spiritual health, the new nature will develop. It is in this way that we shall "grow in grace and in the knowledge of our Lord and Saviour Jesus Christ" (2 Peter 3 : 18).

But not only must the new nature be fed, it is equally necessary for our spiritual well-being that the old nature should be starved. This is what the apostle had before him when he said, "Make not provision for the flesh, to fulfil the lusts thereof" (Rom. 13 : 14). To starve the old nature, to make not provision for the flesh, means that we abstain from everything that would stimulate or feed the natural man. It means we must avoid, as we would a plague, everything that is calculated to prove injurious to our spiritual welfare. Not only must we deny ourselves the "pleasures of sin" (Heb. 11 : 25), not only must we shun such things as the saloon, the theatre, the dance, the card-table, etc., but we must separate ourselves from worldly companions, we must cease reading the writings of unbelievers, we must cease everything upon which we cannot ask God's blessing. In a word, we must set our "affection upon things above, not upon things on the earth" (Col. 3 : 2). Does this sound impracticable? Does this seem a high standard? True, it is, and it is failure to conform to it, which is the cause and explanation of the lives of spiritual leanness and defeat experienced by so many Christians. It is true that we are still in this world, but we are not "of" it (John 17 : 14). It is true that we are forced to associate with godless people, but this is ordained of God in order that we may "let our light so shine before men, that they may see our good works, and glorify our Father which is in heaven" (Matt. 5 : 16). But there is a wide difference between associating with sinners as we go about our daily tasks and making them our companions and friends. Let the young believer settle it in his mind once for all that everything which does not help his spiritual life hinders it.

Here then, in brief, is the answer to our question. What is the young Christian to do in order to obtain the victory over indwelling sin? Negatively, he must starve the old nature by making no provision for the flesh; positively, he must develop the new nature by daily feeding on the Word, by prayer, and by service. Under these two heads can be readily grouped all the exhortations of the New Testament. It is only as we observe these laws pertaining to the spiritual life that we are enabled to heed that exhortation which summarizes the Christian's duty—"Put off concerning the former conversation (conduct) the old man, which is corrupt according to the deceitful lusts; and be renewed in the spirit of your mind, and that ye put on the new man, which, after God, is created in righteousness and true holiness" (Eph. 4 : 22-24).

Above, we have dealt only with the human side of the problem. How to obtain the victory over the power of sin. Necessarily there is a Divine side. It is only by God's grace we are enabled to use the means that He has provided for us, as it is only by the power of His Spirit which dwells within us that we can "lay aside every weight, and the sin which does so easily beset us, and (let us) run with patience the race that is set before us" (Heb. 12 : 1). These two sides are brought together in a number of Scriptures. We are bidden to "work out our own salvation with fear and trembling," but the apostle immediately adds, "For it is God which worketh in you both to will and to do of His good pleasure" (Phil. 2 : 12, 13). We are to work out that which God has placed within us; namely, the new nature or life which we received at the new birth.

It will be seen then, that this second branch of our subject, namely, salvation from the power of sin, is a process which goes on right through the believer's life. It is a growth in grace. It is to this Solomon referred, when he said, "The path of the just is as the shining light, which shineth more and more unto the perfect day" (Prov. 4 : 18). Hence we say, while it is true that the believer in Christ has been saved—saved from the penalty of sin; it is also true that the believer is now being saved (day by day)—saved from the power of sin.

Salvation from the penalty of sin is equivalent to our justification; salvation from the power of sin is the practical side of our *sanctification.* The word "sanctification" signifies "separation"—separation from sin. We need hardly say the word "holiness" is strictly synonymous with "sanctification"—being an alternative rendering of the same Greek word. As then the practical side of sanctification has to do with separation from sin, we read, "Let us cleanse ourselves from all filthiness of the flesh and spirit, perfecting holiness in the fear of God" (2 Cor. 7 : 1). That sanctification or holiness is a process, is progressive, is clear from the language of Heb. 12 : 14 "Follow . . . holiness, without which no man shall see the Lord." The fact that we are exhorted to "follow" holiness clearly intimates that we have not yet reached the Divine standard of practical sanctification. This is further seen in the passage quoted above, where we are bidden to "perfect" (make complete) holiness.

Ere we turn to the last question of our subject, we would, in a few sentences, point out how the history of Israel illustrates salvation as a present process. Israel under the blood of the lamb in Egypt foreshadowed our deliverance from the penalty of sin. Israel in their wilderness-journeyings toward the promised Land, typifies our deliverance from the power of sin. Israel did not enter Canaan immediately on their Exodus from Egypt; they had to face the trials and temptations of the wilderness, where they spent no less than forty years. But what a full provision God made there for His people! Manna was given them daily from heaven, typifying the food which God's Word now supplies for our spiritual nourishment. Water was given from the smitten rock; typifying the Holy Spirit (sent by the smitten Christ), who now dwells within us (John 7 : 38, 39). A cloud and a pillar of fire guided them by day and guarded them by night, reminding us of how God directs our steps and shields us from our foes. And, best of all, Moses, their great leader, was with them counselling, admonishing and interceding for them—foreshadowing the Captain of our salvation, who has said, "Lo, I am with you alway, even unto the end."

Our salvation a thing of the future. In our first main division, we treated salvation as a past experience, and this we defined as deliverance from the penalty of sin. In our second division, we have dwelt at length upon salvation as a present process, and this we defined as deliverance from the power of sin. There, we sought to prove two things: first, that the sinful nature abides still within the believer; second, that the way to obtain deliverance from the corruptions of this old nature is by developing the spiritual nature (received at the new birth), so that it becomes the stronger of the two, and thus the one that controls and regulates the believer's life. Now we turn to the consideration of that aspect of our salvation which is yet future, and this we define as deliverance from the *presence* of sin. By this we mean that sin shall yet be completely eradicated from the believer's being, so that he shall stand before God without spot or blemish.

Those Scriptures which present our salvation as a future prospect are concerned with our complete deliverance from the presence of sin. To this, the apostle Paul refers when he says, "Now is our salvation nearer than when we believed" (Rom. 13 : 11). It is of this that the apostle Peter writes when he states we are, "kept by the power of God through faith unto salvation ready to be revealed in the last time" (1 Peter 1 : 5).

Our salvation from the penalty of sin was accomplished by Christ on the cross, where He bore the punishment due our iniquities. Our salvation from the power of sin is effected by Christ dwelling within us (Gal.

2 : 20, Col. 1 : 27). Christ dwells within us by His Spirit, and He it is who empowers and illumines the new nature in the believer. Our salvation from the presence of sin will be secured by Christ at His second advent, for we read in Phil. 3 : 20, 21: "We look for the Saviour the Lord Jesus Christ, who shall change our vile body that it may be fashioned like unto His glorious body according to the working whereby He is able even to subdue all things unto Himself." And again, we are told, "We know that when He shall appear, we shall be like Him, for we shall see Him as He is" (1 John 3 : 2). It is all Christ. *He* is our Saviour—our Saviour from the penalty, the power, and the presence of sin.

Man was originally created in the image and likeness of God, but sin came in and man fell, and by that fall God's image in him was broken and His likeness defaced. But that image of God in man is to be restored: we are predestined "to be conformed to the image of His Son" (Rom. 8 : 29), and God's purpose in our predestination will not be completely realised until the second coming of our Lord. Then it will be that His people shall be emancipated from the thraldom and corruptions of sin. It is to this, the apostle refers when he says, "Unto them that look for Him shall He appear the second time without sin unto salvation" (Heb. 9 : 28).

Salvation from the penalty of sin is our justification; salvation from the power of sin is the practical side of our sanctification; salvation from the presence of sin is our *glorification*—"And whom he justified, them He also glorified" (Rom. 8 : 30). Not until the time of our Lord's return for His own shall we be glorified. As we read in 1 Cor. 15 : 51, 52, "We shall not all sleep, but we shall all be changed, in a moment, in the twinkling of an eye, at the last trump; for the trumpet shall sound, and the dead shall be raised incorruptible, and we shall be changed." That these verses have reference to the time of our Lord's second coming is clear from the reference to the "trumpet" in verse 52, as may be seen by comparing 1 Thess. 4 : 16, "For the Lord Himself shall descend from heaven with a shout, with the voice of the archangel, and with the trump of God; and the dead in Christ shall rise first; then we which are alive and remain (on earth at that time) shall be caught up together with them in the clouds, to meet the Lord in the air; and so shall we ever be with the Lord." At the time of our Lord's return, the believer will be completely delivered from the presence of sin; in other words, he will be "glorified." It was this the apostle had before him when he prayed, "I pray God your whole spirit and soul and body be preserved blameless unto the coming of our Lord Jesus Christ" (1 Thess. 5 : 23).

Referring once more to the typical significance of the history of Israel, it will be seen that, from one standpoint, their entrance into Canaan foreshadowed the consummation of our salvation. We say "from one standpoint," for the experiences of Israel in Canaan had a double significance. Israel had to overcome the present dwellers in Canaan before they could enjoy their inheritance, and in this respect they rather typify the continued conflicts of the believer while here in the flesh; but as entering the promised Land, they foreshadow our entrance into Heaven.

In John 8 we have an illustration of deliverance from the penalty of sin. A woman was taken in the act of adultery, the punishment for which was death. The Lord Jesus intervened and she escaped, because afterwards He endured the penalty on her behalf. In John 11 we have an illustration of deliverance from the power of sin: Lazarus was raised from the dead—typifying the new birth, which is a passing from death unto life. But, observe, that when Lazarus came forth from his tomb, he was still bound by the grave-clothes. The Lord said, "Loose him,"—typifying our emancipation from the dominion of sin. Elijah was taken to heaven without dying, and as such, typified the rapture of the saints at the time of our Lord's return. But, as he was ascending, his mantle fell off him and was left behind on the earth—foreshadowing the blessed fact that when our Lord comes for us, we shall leave behind us even "the garment spotted by the flesh" (Jude 23).

Thus it will be seen that our salvation is a threefold one. We have been saved from the *penalty* of sin; we are now being saved from the *power* of sin; we shall yet be saved from the *presence* of sin.

—*Arthur W. Pink.*

The printing and mailing out of this Magazine costs over £5 (25 dollars) every week. What is *your* responsibility? Seek the mind of God. "Studies" was sent throughout 1928 to over 1000 people who sent in no gift!

"No good thing will He withhold from them that walk uprightly." To walk "uprightly" is for our daily conduct to be regulated by the principles of holiness and righteousness. It is to act in all our dealings with our fellow-men in the fear of God. It is the reverse of that craftiness and crookedness which mark the conscienceless man of the world. An upright man is one of scrupulous honesty and integrity: his word, is his bond; he scorns lying and thieving. "A man of twisty, shifty, ways, of a crooked nature, is not saved, and in all probability will never be; for the ground which brings forth a harvest when grace is sown in it, may be weedy and waste, but our Lord tells us it is *honest* and good ground. Our observation has been that men of double tongues and tricky ways are the least likely of all to be saved: certainly when grace comes it restores man's mind to its perpendicular, and delivers him from being doubled up with vice, twisted with craft, or bent with dishonour" (C. H. Spurgeon).

"No good thing will He withhold from them that walk uprightly." Possibly some may say, This has not been my experience. By God's grace I have sought to do that which is right; I have conducted my business according to scriptural principles; yet have I not prospered to any thing like the same extent as some of my worldly competitors. Ah, dear friend, you must leave it with *God* to decide what is "good" for you. Earthly success and wealth is more often a curse than a blessing. The "good" things which God bestows on those whose walk is pleasing to Him are, peace of mind, a clear conscience, the spirit of contentment, the comfort of the Holy Spirit, a heart that rejoices in the Lord; and *these* are mercies which cannot be valued in silver and gold. Spiritual blessings are the true riches; but only a spiritual heart prizes them.

"No good thing will He withhold from them that walk uprightly." Those who walk uprightly shall live in the enjoyment of God's salvation, shall have their hearts garrisoned by His perfect peace, shall find their path shining "more and more, unto the perfect day." Those who walk uprightly abide in communion with God (Psa. 15 : 1, 2), have power in prayer (Psa. 34 : 15); yea, it is written, "he that walketh righteously, and speaketh uprightly . . . he shall dwell on high; his place of defence shall be the munitions of rocks: bread shall be given him; his waters shall be sure (Isa. 33 : 15, 16). Thus our text is written for the *encouragement* of God's saints, as an *incentive* to practical holiness. O that we may, the more earnestly, seek grace to heed that injunction "Ponder the path of thy feet, and let all thy ways be established. Turn not to the right hand nor to the left: remove thy foot from evil" (Prov. 4 : 26, 27); then shall we prove by experience that, "No good thing will He withhold from them that walk uprightly."

Arthur W. Pink.

A PERSONAL WORD.

As many friends are desirous of being kept posted with the Lord's present dealings with us, and so that interested ones may be enabled to pray the more intelligently for us, we are again writing a few lines concerning ourselves. Since Oct. 7 we have had no preaching engagements. A number of doors could have been entered, were we prepared to compromise a little; but we dare not. "Buy the truth, and *sell it not*" (Prov. 23 : 23), "*Hold fast* that which is good" (1 Thess. 5 : 21), are too plain to be disregarded. It costs something these days to be faithful to God! Yet, His spiritual gifts are rich compensations; *His* approval is of infinitely more worth than all the commendations of men.

We are devoting ourself to study and preparing articles for this magazine. The Lord is being pleased to grant us much light from His Word. Our daily prayer is that, in His own good time and way, He will give us access to some company of His people who really want "*all* the counsel of God" (Acts 20 : 27). "If we hope for that we see not, then do we with patience wait for it" (Rom. 8 : 25). In the meantime, God is faithful, and He is, in His own wondrous and gracious way, supplying our temporal need; and that peace which passeth all understanding is keeping our hearts and minds through Christ Jesus.

Spiritual conditions in England are in a very sad way, far worse than the majority imagine. Even among the professedly orthodox there is very little real subjection to the Word. A little handful gather for the Bible-readings in our home; others would like to attend them, but they are afraid to. How true it is that, "The fear of man bringeth a snare" (Prov. 29 : 25)! Subjection to priests is by no means restricted to the poor Papists. Profession is being tested in many ways to-day. "The righteous are bold as a lion" (Prov. 28 : 1), but their number is few indeed. May the Lord fulfill in us, through us, and by us, the good pleasure of *His* will: "Ye also helping together by prayer for us" (2 Cor. 1 : 11). May the Lord bless you all. —*V. E. & A. W. Pink.*

P.S.—*Will friends in Aust. and U.S.A. please communicate with us, so far as possible, directly. We wish to relieve our Hon. Agents as much as we can.*

like us, influenced by different factors at different times. "Justice and judgment are the habitations of Thy throne (Psa. 89 : 14)—ever have been, and ever will be; yet the Psalmist added, "mercy and truth shall go before Thy face," and these also are attributes of the Divine character which never have ceased and never will cease to operate. Let it not be forgotten that the same hand that penned our opening text also wrote, "He hath not dealt with us after our sins, nor rewarded us according to our iniquities" (Psa. 103 : 10), and this, be it noted, during the Dispensation of Law!

It appears to have been quite overlooked by many of those who pride themselves on their ability to "rightly divide" the Word of Truth, and who attempt to catalogue the Scriptures under their own arbitrary dispensational classifications, that even in Old Testament times, during the Mosaic economy, God was actuated by something in addition to the stern enforcement and infliction of the penalty of His law. What meant the Psalmist when he said, "If Thou, Lord, shouldest mark iniquities, O Lord, who shall stand?" (Psa. 130 : 2)? What meant all the many references to the *mercy* of God to be found on the pages of the Old Testament if the demands of righteousness over-rode everything else?

Should it be asked, How then do you harmonize the two classes of verses in the Old Testament? the one of which treats of God dealing with men according to their conduct, the other of which bases His actions upon His own goodness and grace? Our answer is, We make no attempt to reconcile them. We are fully assured that there is no conflict between them, yet we are also thoroughly convinced that what lies behind the actions of the Lord God is too far above human ken to be reduced to and explained by either a system of philosophy or theology. God's "ways" are "past finding out", and He Himself has told us so (Rom. 11 : 33). But man, in the pride of his heart, hates to acknowledge this, and by his intellectual searching seeks to "find out" the Almighty. But his attempts so to do exhibit not only his presumption but his madness, and foolishness is writ large across all his vain reasonings. Much more becoming is it for us to say with Job, "Lo, these are parts of His ways: but *how little* a portion is heard of Him" (26 : 14)!

"No good thing will He withhold from them that walk uprightly." What could be plainer than that? the character of our walk determines whether or not God will bestow upon us His good things. Of old he said to Israel, "Your sins have *withholden* good things from you" (Jer. 5 : 25). And is it not the same to-day? Why is there such a scarcity of Bible-teachers? Why are there so few pastors who lead the sheep of Christ into the green pastures of the Word? Why is it that many a "church" desires a godly, orthodox, old-fashioned preacher for its pulpit, and finds it most difficult if not impossible to secure such an one? We believe the reason lies in the worldliness and fleshliness of the great majority of professing Christians. While they are so indifferent to God's claims and so regardless of His glory, He is not likely to bestow His choicest gifts upon them. If God *were* to send one of His own servants to the average church of to-day, one who would, like the prophets of old, denounce the sins of its members and call upon them to repent before God, he would not be appreciated. No, the religious world wants those who will "prophesy *smooth* things"; and God will not cast His pearls before swine.

Was not the teaching of our Lord in perfect harmony with that of the Psalmist? Did He not say, "Seek ye first the kingdom of God, and His righteousness, *and* all these things shall be added unto you" (Matt. 6 : 33)? Do not these words plainly show that there is an inseparable connection between our conduct and God's bestowal of His gifts? Again; did He not affirm, "The light of the body is the eye: if therefore thine eye be single, thy whole body shall be full of light; but if thine eye be evil, thy whole body shall be full of darkness" (Matt. 6 : 22, 23)? God must be given His true place in our hearts and lives if we are to be the recipients of His bounties. A "single eye" means an undivided heart, which has only in view the honour and glory of God; and the one in whom this is found shall be blest with spiritual discernment, a knowledge of God's will, light upon his path.

The teaching of the Epistles gives expression to the same principle. In Rom. 8 : 13 it is said, "For if ye live after the flesh, ye shall die; but if ye through the Spirit do mortify the deeds of the body, ye shall live." In 1 Cor. 11 : 31 we are told, "For if we would judge ourselves, we should not be judged." In Eph. 6 : 8 we read, "Knowing that whatsoever good thing any man doeth, the same shall he receive of the Lord." Plainer still is the well-known word of Gal. 6 : 7, 8, "Whatsoever a man soweth, that shall he also reap" etc. Much more might be quoted to the same effect, such as conduct *hindering* our prayers (1 Pet. 3 : 7), etc.

Continued on page 71.

STUDIES IN THE SCRIPTURES

"Search the Scriptures" John 5 : 39

Copyright in all English-speaking Countries.

Editor: Arthur W. Pink, Sidmouth Road, Seaton, Devon, England.
Hon. Agent in U.S.A.: Mr. C. S. Pressel, 559, Dupont Avenue, York, Penna.
Hon. Agent in Australia: Mr. G. Ardill, The Christian Workers' Depot.
Commonwealth and Reservoir Streets, Sydney.

FREE TO ALL WHO WILL READ IT.

THE BOUNTIES OF GOD.

"Eye hath not seen, nor ear heard, neither have entered into the heart of man, the things which God hath prepared for them that love Him" (1 Cor. 2 : 9). How often this passage is quoted only so far as we have now quoted it; how rarely are the following words added, "But God *hath* revealed them unto us by His Spirit" (v. 10)! Why is this? Is it because so few of God's people search out and live in the enjoyment of what the Spirit has revealed in the Word concerning those things which God has prepared for them that love Him? If we were more occupied with God's riches instead of our poverty, Christ's fulness than our emptiness, the Divine bounties than our leanness, on what a different plane of experience should we live!

Of late we have been much impressed by noting some of "the *riches* of His grace" (Eph. 1 : 7). It is indeed striking to note that our Christian life starts at a marriage-feast (Luke 14 : 16-23 ; Matt. 22 : 2-10), just as Christ's first miracle was wrought at one (John 2). The word to us is, "Come, for all things are *now* ready" (Luke 14 : 17), "Behold I have prepared My dinner: My oxen and fatlings are killed, and all things are ready: come unto the marriage" (Matt. 22 : 4). Observe the "I have *prepared*," agreeing with "the things which God hath prepared for them that love Him" in 1 Cor. 2 : 9. Notice the "*are* ready," confirming the "God *hath* revealed them unto us" of 1 Cor. 2 : 10. Mark the "*My* dinner, *My* oxen and fatlings," for "all things are of God" (2 Cor. 5 : 18); the creature contributes nothing, all is provided for him. Finally, weigh the "come unto *the marriage.*" The figure is very blessed; it speaks of joy, festivity, feasting.

"He spread the banquet, made me eat,
Bid all my fears remove,
Yea, o'er my guilty, rebel head
He placed His banner—Love."

Practically the same figure was employed by Christ again in Luke 15. There He pictures the penitent prodigal welcomed home by the Father. No sooner is he clothed and fitted for the "house" than the words go forth, "Bring hither the fatted calf, and kill; and let us eat, and *be merry*" (v. 23); and, we are told, "they began to be merry." Since, in the parable, that merriment met with no reverse, since it is portrayed without a break and without a bound, then assuredly we may conclude that this new-born joy ought to go on characterising all who know that they are within this festive scene—as truly so now, as soon it will be in the glory.

A beautiful type of the lavish manner in which God bestows His bounties upon His people is found in Gen. 9 : 3: "Every moving thing that liveth shall be meat for you; even as the green herb, have I given you *all* things." This was Jehovah's response to the "sweet savor" which He had just smelled. It is most important that we should note the connection, and perceive the ground on which God so freely bestowed "all things" upon the patriarch. At the close of Gen. 8 we see Noah building an altar unto the Lord and presenting burnt-offerings thereon. Here at the beginning of Gen. 9 we learn God's answer thereto.

What has just been before us blessedly foreshadowed the unmeasured portion bestowed upon the new creation, the members of which have been "blessed with all spiritual blessings

(Continued on Page 96).

IMPORTANT NOTICES

Back numbers of the last four years of this magazine are yet obtainable, nicely and strongly bound at 7/6 each, post paid. They will soon be out of print. Those in U.S.A. wanting them, please purchase from Mr. Pressel (see front cover page).

Advise promptly of change of address otherwise copies will be lost in the mails.

This Magazine is published as a work of faith and labour of love. The Editor gladly gives his services. It is freely sent to all who will read it. No charge is made for it.

Christians who feel definitely led to do so, may have fellowship with us in this Ministry. Send only *Inter-National M.O.* made out to Seaton, Devon, England.

CONTENTS.

Hebrews	74
Gleanings in Exodus	80
Abram's Obedience	84
Provision for Perilous Times	88
A Model Christian	92

THE EPISTLE TO THE HEBREWS.

16.—CHRIST SUPERIOR TO JOSHUA —(Heb. 4 : 1—3).

The exhortation begun by the apostle in Heb. 3 : 12 is not completed till 4 : 12 is reached, all that intervenes consisting of an exposition and application of the passage quoted from Psa. 95 in Heb. 3 : 7-11. The connecting link between what has been before us and that which we are about to consider is found in 3 : 19, "So we see that they could not enter in because of unbelief." These words form the transition between the two chapters, concluding the exhortation found in vv. 12, 13, and laying a foundation for the admonition which follows. Ere proceeding, it may be well to take up a question which the closing verses of Heb. 3 have probably raised in many minds, namely, seeing that practically all the adults who came out of Egypt by Moses perished in the wilderness, did not the promises of God to bring them into Canaan fail of their accomplishment?

In Ex. 6 : 6-8 Jehovah said unto Moses, "Wherefore say unto the children of Israel, I am the Lord, and I will bring you out from under the burdens of the Egyptians, and I will rid you out of their bondage, and I will redeem you with a stretched out arm, and with great judgments: and I will take you to Me for a people, and I will be to you a God. . . And I will bring you in unto the land, concerning the which I did sware to give it to Abraham, to Isaac, and to Jacob, and I will give it you for an heritage: I am the Lord." We quote now from the helpful comments of Dr. J. Brown upon these verses:

"This is a promise which refers to Israel *as a people*, and which does not by any means necessarily infer that all, or even that any, of *that* generation were to enter in. No express condition was mentioned in this promise—not even the believing of it. Yet, so far as that generation was concerned, this, as the event proved, was plainly implied; for, if it had been an absolute, unconditional promise to *that* generation, it must have been performed, otherwise He who cannot lie would have failed in accomplishing His own word. There can be no doubt that the fulfilment of the promise *to them* was suspended on their believing it, and acting accordingly. Had they believed that Jehovah was indeed both able and determined to bring His people Israel into the land of Canaan, and, under the influence of this faith, had gone up at His command to take possession, the promise would have been performed to them.

"*This* was the tenor of the covenant made with *them*: 'Now therefore, *if* ye will obey My voice indeed, and keep My covenant, *then* ye shall be a peculiar treasure unto Me above all people: for all the earth is Mine: and ye shall be unto Me a kingdom of priests, and an holy nation' (Ex. 19 : 5, 6). ' Behold, I send an Angel before thee, to keep thee in the way, and to bring thee into the place which I have prepared. Beware of Him, and obey His voice, provoke Him not; for He will not pardon your transgressions: for My name is in Him. But *if* thou shalt indeed obey His voice, and do all that I speak; *then* I will be an Enemy unto thine enemies, and an Adversary unto thine adversaries' (Ex. 23 : 20-22).

"Their unbelief and disobedience are constantly stated as the reason why they did not enter in. 'Because all those men have seen My glory, and My miracles, which I did in Egypt and in the wilderness, and have tempted Me now these ten times, and have not hearkened to My voice; surely they shall not see the land which I sware unto their fathers, neither shall any of them that provoked Me see it' (Num. 14 : 22, 23), cf. Josh. 5 : 6. God promised to bring Israel into the land of Canaan; but He did not promise to bring them in whether they believed and obeyed or not. No promise was broken to *those* men, for no absolute promise was made to them.

"But their unbelief did not make the promise of God of none effect. It was accomplished to the next generation: 'And the Lord gave unto Israel all the land which He sware to give unto their fathers; and they possessed it, and dwelt therein' (Josh. 21 : 43). Joshua appealed to the Israelites themselves for the completeness of the fulfilment of the promise, see Josh. 23 : 14. *That* generation believed the promises that God would give Canaan, and under the influence of this fact, went forward under the conduct of Joshua, and obtained possession of the land for themselves."

This same principle explains what has been another great difficulty to many, namely, Israel's actual tenure of Canaan. In Gen. 13 : 14, 15 we are told, "And the Lord said unto Abram, after that Lot was separated from him, Lift up now thine eyes, and look from the place from where thou art northward, and southward, and eastward, and westward: For all the land which thou seest, to thee will I give it, and to thy seed *for ever*." This promise was repeated again and again, see Gen. 17 : 18, etc. How then came it that the children of Israel occupied the land only for a season? Their descendants, for the most part are not in it to-day. Has, then, the promise of God failed? In nowise. In His promise to Abraham God did not specify that any particular generation of his descendants should occupy the land "for ever" and herein lies the solution to the difficulty.

God's promise to Abraham was made on the ground of pure grace; no condition whatever was attached to it. But grace only superabounds where sin has abounded. Sovereign grace intervenes only after the responsibility of man has been tested and his failure and unworthiness manifested. Now it is abundantly clear from many passages in Deut., e.g., 31 : 26-29, that Israel entered Canaan not on the ground of the unconditional covenant of grace which Jehovah made with Abraham, but on the ground of the conditional covenant of works which was entered into at Sinai (Ex. 24 : 6-8). Hence, many years after Israel had entered Canaan under Joshua, we read, "And an Angel of the Lord came up from Gilgal to Bochim, and said, I made you to go up out of the land of Egypt, and have brought you unto the land which I sware unto your fathers; and I said, I will never break My covenant *with you*. And ye shall make no league with the inhabitants of this land; ye shall throw down their altars; *but ye have not obeyed* My voice: Why have ye done this? *Wherefore* I also said, I will not drive them out from before you; but they shall be a thorn in your sides, and their gods shall be a snare unto you" (Judges 2 : 1-3). The unconditional covenant of Jehovah with Abraham will be made good, completely and literally, during the Millennium: see Isa. 11 : 11-16, Jer. 31 : 31-40.

The same principles are in exercise concerning God's fulfilment of His *gospel* promises. "The gospel promise of eternal life, like the promise of Canaan, is a promise which will assuredly be accomplished. It is sure to all 'the seed.' They were 'chosen in Christ before the foundation of the world.' Eternal life was promised in reference to them before the times of the ages, and confirmed by the oath of God. They have been redeemed to God by 'the blood of the Lamb,' and are all called in due time according to His purpose. Their inheritance is 'laid up in heaven' for them, and 'they are kept for it by the mighty power of God, through faith unto salvation.' And they shall all at last 'inherit the kingdom prepared for them from the foundation of the world.'

"But the Gospel revelation does not testify directly to anyone that Christ so died for him in particular, that it is certain that *he* shall be saved through His death: neither does it absolutely promise salvation to all men; for in this case all must be saved,—or God must be a liar. But it proclaims, 'he that believeth shall be saved—he that believeth not shall be damned.' It is as believers of the truth that we are secured of eternal life; and it is by holding fast this faith of the truth, and showing that we do so, that we can alone enjoy the comfort of this security. 'The purpose of God according to election must stand,' and all His chosen will assuredly be saved; but they cannot know their election —they cannot enjoy any absolute assurance of their salvation—independent of their continuance in the faith, love, and obedience of the Gospel, see 2 Peter 1 : 5-12. And to the Christian, in every stage of his progress, it is of importance to remember, that he who turns back, turns 'back to perdition'; and that it is he only who believes straight onward—that continues in the faith of the truth—that shall obtain 'the salvation of the soul'" (Dr. J. Brown).

Our introduction for this article has already exceeded its legitimate limits, but we trust that what has been said above will be used of God in clearing up several difficulties which have exercised the minds of many of His beloved people, and that it may serve to prepare us for a more intelligent perusal of our present passage. The verses before us are by no means easy, as any one who will really study them will quickly discover. The apostle's argument seems to be unusually involved, the teaching of it appears to conflict with other portions of Scripture, and the "rest" which is its central subject, is difficult to define with any degree of certainty. It is with some measure of hesitation and with not a little trepidation that the writer himself now attempts to expound it, and he would press upon every reader the importance and need of heeding the Divine injunction of 1 Thess. 5 : 21, "Prove all things; hold fast that which is good."

It should be evident that the first thing which will enable us to understand our passage is to attend to the *scope* of it. The contents of this chapter are found not in Romans or Corinthians or Ephesians, but in Hebrews, the central theme of which is the superiority of Christianity over Judaism, and there is that in each chapter which exemplifies this. The theme is developed by the presentation of the superlative excellencies of Christ, who is the Centre and Life of Christianity. Thus far we have had Christ's superiority over the prophets, the angels, Moses. Now it is the glory of Christ which excels that attaching to Joshua.

Our next key must be found in noting the *connection* between the contents of chapter four and that which immediately precedes. Plainly, the context begins at 3 : 1, where we are bidden to "consider the Apostle and High Priest of our profession." All of chapter 3 is but an amplification of its opening verse. Its contents may be summarised thus: Christ is to be "considered," attended to, heard, trusted, obeyed: first, because of His exalted personal excellency: He is the Son, "faithful" over His house; second, because of the direful consequences which must ensue from not "considering" Him, from despising Him. This second point is illustrated by the sad example of those Israelites who hearkened not unto the Lord in the days of Moses, and in their case the consequence was that they failed to enter into the rest of Canaan.

In the first sections of Heb. 4, the principal subject of chapter 3 is *continued*. It brings out again the superiority of our "Apostle," this time over Joshua, for he too was an "apostle" of God. This is strikingly brought out in Deut. 34 : 9, "And Joshua the son of Nun was full of the spirit of wisdom; *for* Moses had laid his hands upon him; and the children of Israel hearkened unto him, and did as the Lord commanded Moses"—the prime thought of the "laying on of hands" in Scripture being that of *identification*. Let the reader compare Josh. 1 : 5, 16-18. The continuation of the theme of Heb. 3 in chapter 4 is also seen by the repeated mention of "rest," see 3 : 11, 18 and cf. 4 : 1, 3, etc. It is on this term that the apostle bases his present argument. The "rest" of 3 : 11 and 18 **refers to Canaan, and though Joshua actually** conducted Israel into this (see marginal rendering of 4 : 8), yet the apostle proves by a reference to Psalm 95 that Israel never really (as a nation) entered into the rest *of God*. Herein lies the superiority of the Apostle of Christianity: Christ *does* lead His people into the true rest. Such, we believe, is the line of truth developed in our passage.

"Let us therefore fear, lest a promise being left us of entering into His rest, any of you should seem to come short of it " (v. 1). The opening words of this chapter bid us seriously take to heart the solemn warning given at the close of 3. God's judgment upon the wicked should make us more watchful that we do not follow their steps. The "us" shows that Paul was preaching to himself as well as to the Hebrews. "Let us therefore *fear*" has stumbled some, because of the "Fear thou not" of Isa. 41 : 10, 43 : 1, 5. etc. In John 14 : 27 Christ says to us, "Let not your heart be troubled, neither let it be afraid." And in 2 Tim. 1 : 7 we read, "For God hath not given us the spirit of fear; but of power, and of love, and of a sound mind." On the other hand, believers are told to "Fear God" (1 Peter 2 : 17), and to work out their own salvation "with fear and trembling" (Phil. 2 : 12). How are these two different sets of passages to be harmonized?

The Bible is full of paradoxes, which, to the natural man, appear to be contradictions. The Word needs "rightly dividing" on the subject of "fear" as upon everything else of which it treats. There is a fear which the Christian is to cultivate, and there is a fear from which he should shrink. The fear of the Lord is the beginning of wisdom, and in Prov. 14 : 26, 27 we read, "In the fear of the Lord is strong confidence. . . . The fear of the Lord is a fountain of life"; so again, "Happy is the man that feareth always" (Prov. 23 : 14). The testimony of the New Testament inculcates the same duty: Christ bade His disciples, "Fear Him who is able to destroy both soul and body in hell" (Matt. 10 : 28). To the saints at Rome Paul said, "Be not high-minded, but fear" (Rom. 11 : 20). To God's people Peter wrote, "Pass the time of your sojourning here in fear" (1 Pet. 1 : 17). While in Heaven itself the word will yet be given: "Praise our God all ye His servants, and ye that fear Him both small and great" (Rev. 19 : 5).

Fear may be called one of the disliking affections. It is good or evil according to the object on which it is placed, and according to the ordering of it thereon. In Heb. 4 : 1 it is placed on the right object—an evil to be shunned. That evil is unbelief, which, if persisted in, ends in apostasy and destruction. About this the Christian needs to be constantly on his guard, having his heart set steadily against it. Our natural proneness to fall, the many temptations to which we are subject, together with the deceitfulness of sin, the subtlety of Satan, and God's justice in leaving men to themselves, are strong enforcements of this duty. Concerning God Himself, we are to fear Him with such a reverent awe of His holy majesty as will make us careful to please Him in all things, and fearful of offending Him. This is ever accompanied by a fearsome distrust of ourselves. The fear of God which is evil in a Christian is that servile bondage which produces a distrustful attitude, kills affection for Him, regards Him as a hateful Tyrant. This is the fear of the demons (James 2 : 19).

" Let us therefore fear." " It is salutary to remember our tendency to partiality and one-sidedness in our spiritual life, in order that we may be on our guard, that we may carefully and anxiously consider the ' Again, it is written'; that we may be willing to learn from Christians who have received different gifts of grace, and whose experience varies from ours ; above all, that we may seek to follow and serve the Lord Himself, to walk with God, to hear the voice of the Good Shepherd. Forms of godliness, types of doctrine, are apt to become substitutes instead of channels, weights instead of wings.

" The exhortations of this epistle may appear to some difficult to reconcile with the teachings of Scripture, that the grace of God, once received, through the power of the Holy Spirit by faith, can never be lost, and that they who are born again, who are once in Christ, are in Christ for ever. Let us not blunt the edge of earnest and piercing exhortations. Let us not pass them over, or treat them with inward apathy. ' Again it is written.' We know this does not mean that there is any real contradiction in Scripture, but that various aspects of truth are presented, each with the same fidelity, fulness and emphasis. Hence we must learn to move freely, and not to be cramped and fixed in one position : we must keep our eyes clear and open, and not look at all things through the light of a favourite doctrine. And while we receive fully and joyously the assurance of our perfect acceptance and peace, and of the unchanging love of God in Christ Jesus, let us with the apostle consider also our sins and dangers, from the lower yet most real earthly and time-point of view.

"When Christ is beheld and accepted, there is peace ; but is there not also fear? ' With Thee is forgiveness of sin, that Thou mayest be feared ' (Psa. 130 : 4). Where do we see God's holiness and the awful majesty of the law as in the cross of Christ? Where our own sin and unworthiness, where the depths of our guilt and misery, as in the atonement of the Lord Jesus? We rejoice with fear and trembling. . . It is because we know the Father, it is because we are redeemed by the precious blood of the Saviour, it is as the children of God and as the saints of Christ, that we are to pass our earthly pilgrimage in fear. This is not the fear of bondage, but the fear of adoption ; not the fear which dreads condemnation, but the fear of those who are saved, and whom Christ has made free. It is not an imperfect and temporary condition ; it refers not merely to those who have begun to walk in the ways of God. Let us not imagine that this fear is to vanish at some subsequent period of our course, that it is to disappear in a so-called ' higher Christian life.' No ; we are to pass the time of our sojourn here in fear. To the last moment of our fight of faith, to the very end of our journey, the child of God, while trusting and rejoicing, walks in godly fear " (Saphir).

" Lest a promise being left us." It is very striking to observe how this is expressed. It does not say, " lest a promise being made " or " given." It is put thus for the searching of our hearts. God's promises are presented *to* faith, and they only become ours individually, and we only enter into the good of them, as we appropriate or lay hold of them. Of the patriarchs it is said concerning God's promises (1) " having seen them afar off, (2) and were persuaded of them, (3) and *embraced* them " (Heb. 11 : 13). Certain promises of Jehovah were " left " to those who came out of Egypt. They were not " given " to any particular individuals, or " made " concerning that specific generation. And, as the apostle has shown in Heb. 3, the majority of those who came out of Egypt *failed* to " embrace " those promises, through hearkening not to Him Who spake, and through hardening their hearts. But Caleb and Joshua " laid hold " of those promises and so entered Canaan.

When the apostle here says, " Let us fear therefore lest a promise being left "—there is no " us " in the Greek—he addresses the *responsibility* of the Hebrews. He is pressing upon them the need of walking by faith and not by sight ; he is urging them to so take unto themselves the promise which the Lord has " left," that they might not seem to come short of it. But to what is the apostle referring when he says, " lest *a promise* being left "? Surely in the light of the context the primary reference is clear : that which the Gospel makes known. The Gospel proclaims salvation to all who believe. The Gospel makes no promise to any particular individuals. Its terms are " whosoever believeth shall not perish." That promise is " left," left on infallible record, left for the consolation of convicted sinners, " left " for faith to lay hold of. This promise of salvation looks forward, ultimately, to the enjoyment of the eternal, perfect, and unbroken rest of God in heaven, of which the " rest " of Canaan, as the terminal of Israel's hard bondage in Egypt and their wearisome journeyings in the wilderness, was the appropriate figure.

"Any of you should seem to come short of it". Passing over the word "seem" for a moment, let us inquire into the meaning of "to come short of it." Here again the language of Heb. 11 : 13 should help us. As pointed out above, that verse indicates three distinct stages in the faith of the patriarchs. First, they saw God's promises "afar off." They seemed too good to be true, far beyond their apprehension. Second, they were "persuaded of them" or, as the Revised Version renders it, "*greeted* them," which signifies a much closer acquaintance of them. Third, and "embraced them": they *did not* "come short," but took them to their hearts. It is thus the awakened and anxious sinner has to do with the Gospel promise. Wondrous, unique, passing knowledge as it does, that promise is "left" him, and the Person that promise points to is to be "greeted" and "embraced." "That which was from the beginning (1), which we have heard (2), which we have seen with our eyes (3), which we have looked upon (4), and our hands *have handled* of the Word of Life" (1 John 1 : 1).

At this stage perhaps the reader is ready to object against what has been advanced above, "But how can the 'promise' here refer to that presented in the Gospel before poor sinners, seeing that the apostle was addressing believers? Is not the 'promise' plainly enough defined in the 'of entering into His rest'"? Without attempting now to enter into a fuller discussion of God's "rest," it should be clear from the context that the primary reference is to the eternal sharing of His rest in heaven. *This* is the believer's hope, "the hope which is laid up for you in heaven, whereof ye heard before in the Word of the truth *of the Gospel*" (Col. 1 : 5). At first this "hope" appears "afar off," but as faith grows it is "greeted" and "embraced." But only so as faith is in exercise. If we cease hearing and heeding the Voice which speaks to us from heaven, and our hearts become hardened through the deceitfulness of sin, the brightness of our hope is dimmed, we "come short" of it; and if such a course be continued in, hope will give way to despair.

The whole point of the apostle's exhortation here is a pressing upon Christians the imperative need of persevering in the faith. Israel left Egypt full of hope, as their song at the Red Sea plainly witnessed, *see* Ex. 15 : 13-18. But, alas, their hopes quickly faded. The trials and testings of the wilderness were too much for them. They walked by sight, instead of by faith; and murmuring took the place of praising, and hardness of heart instead of listening to the Lord's voice. So too the Hebrews were still in the wilderness: their profession of faith in Christ, their trust in the Lord, was being tested. Some of their fellows had already departed from the living God, as the language of 10 : 25 clearly implies. Would, then, these whom the apostle had addressed as "holy brethren" fail, finally, to enter into God's rest? So it is with Christians now. Heaven is set before them as their goal: toward it they are to daily press forward, running with perseverance the race that is set before them. But the incentive of our hope only has power over the heart so long as faith is in exercise.

What is meant by "*seeming* to come short" of the Gospel promise of heaven? First, is not this word inserted here for the purpose of modifying the sharpness of the admonition? It was to show that the apostle did not positively conclude that any of these "holy brethren" were apostates, but only that they might appear to be in danger of it, as the "lest" warned. Second, was it not to stir up their godly fear the more against such coldness and dulness as might hazard the prize set before them? Third, and primarily, was it not for the purpose of showing Christians the *extent* to which they should be watchful? It is not sufficient to be assured that we shall never utterly fall away; we must not "seem" to do so, we must give no occasion to other Christians to think we have departed from the living God. The reference is to our *walk*. We are bidden to "abstain from all *appearance* of evil" (1 Thess. 5 : 22). Note how this same word "seem" signifies "appeared" in Gal. 2 : 9. The very appearance of backsliding is to be sedulously avoided.

"For unto us was the Gospel preached, as well as unto them: but the word preached did not profit them, not being mixed with faith in them that heard" (v. 2). The contents of this verse unequivocally establish our definition of the "promise" in v. 1, namely, that it has reference to the Gospel promise, which, in its ultimate application, looks forward to the eternal rest in heaven. Here plain mention is made of the "gospel." The obvious design of the apostle in this verse is to enforce the admonition of us fearing a like judgment which befell the apostate Israelites, by avoiding a like course of conduct in ourselves—unbelief.

The gospel preached unto Israel of old is recorded in Ex. 6 : 6-8, and that it was *not* "mixed with faith in them that heard it" is seen from the very next verse, "And Moses so spake unto the children of Israel, but they *hearkened not* unto Moses for anguish of spirit, and for cruel bondage." We need hardly say that was not the only time a gospel mesage was proclaimed to them, see Num. 13 : 26, 27, 30; and for their unbelief, 14 : 1-4. "But the word preached did not profit them." "They were none the better for it. They did not obtain the blessing in reference to which a promise was given them:

they did not enter into Canaan: they died in the wilderness" (Dr. J. Brown). The reason for this was, because they did not receive the good news in faith. The mere hearing of the Gospel is not enough: to profit, it must be believed. Thus Heb. 4 : 2 is parallel with 2 : 3.

"For we which have believed do enter into rest" (v. 3). Failure to rightly understand these words has led many of the commentators right off the track of the apostle's argument in this passage. It pains us to have to take issue here with some eminent expositors of Scripture, but we dare not call any man, however spiritual or well-instructed, our "father." We must follow the light which we believe God has granted us, though we would again press upon the reader *his* responsibility for "proving all things" for himself.

"For we which have believed do enter into rest." Many have taken these words as referring to a spiritual rest into which believers enter here and now. But we believe this is a mistake. The apostle did not say, "We which believe *have entered* into rest." To which it may be replied, "Nor did he say, 'We which have believed *shall* enter into rest.'" True, for to have put it thus would have weakened his argument. Moreover, it would be to evacuate the exhortation of v. 11 of its significance, "Let us labour therefore *to* enter into that rest, lest any man fall after the same example of unbelief." If then v. 3 does not refer to a spiritual rest into which believers now enter, what is its meaning?

Bagster's Interlinear (and we know of no English translation which is its equal) gives, "For we enter into the rest, who believe." This is a literal word for word rendering of the Greek into English. Put thus, the historical tense is avoided, and we have simply an abstract statement of a doctrinal fact. This verse gives us the positive side of v. 2, defining the characters of those who *will* enter God's rest, namely, Believers. Unbelieving Israelites did not, believing Christians shall. It is important to remember that the "rest" of this whole passage is as yet only "promised," v. 1.

"For we which have believed do enter into rest." "The apostle speaks of believers of all ages as a body, to which he and those to whom he was writing belonged, and says, 'It is we who believe, and we alone, who under any dispensation can enter into the rest of God'" (Dr. J. Brown). The opening "for" signifies that what follows is added as a reason to confirm what has been previously stated. The reason is drawn from the law of contraries, the inevitable opposites. Of contraries there must be opposite consequences. Now faith and unbelief are contraries, therefore their consequences are contraries. As then unbelievers cannot enter into God's rest (3 : 18), believers must (4 : 3), *that* is *their* privilege. Such we believe is the force of this abstract declaration.

"The qualification of such as reap the benefit of God's promise is thus set down, 'Which have believed.' To believe is to yield such credence to the truth of God's promise, as to rest on Him for participation of the thing promised. We can have no assurance of the thing promised till we do believe the promise: 'After that ye believed, ye were sealed with the Holy Spirit of promise' (Eph. 1 : 13). 'I know whom I have believed,' saith the apostle, and thereupon maketh this inference, 'and I am persuaded that He is able to keep that which I have committed unto Him against that day' (2 Tim. 1 : 12). This, Christ manifested by the condition which He required of those whom He cured, thus, 'If thou canst believe, all things are possible, Mark 9 : 23." (Dr. Gouge).

The second half of v. 3 we must leave for the next article, D.V. In the meantime, "Let *us* therefore fear." "The absolute safety, the fixed and unchanging portion of the chosen people of God can never be doubted. From the eternal, heavenly, divine point of view, saints can never fall; they are seated in heavenly places with Christ; they are renewed by the Spirit, and sealed by Him unto everlasting glory. But who sees the saints of God from this point of view? Not the world, not our fellow-Christians. They only see our character and walk . . From our point of view, as we live in time, from day to day, our earnest desire must be to continue steadfast, to abide in Christ, to walk with God, to bring forth fruit that will manifest the presence of true and Godgiven life. Hence the apostle, who says to the Philippians, 'Being confident of this very thing, that He which hath begun a good work in you will perform it until the day of Jesus Christ' (1 : 6), adds to a similar thought in another epistle, '*If* ye continue in the faith grounded and settled, and be not moved away from the hope of the gospel.' In the one passage Paul's point of view is the heavenly, eternal one ; in the other he looks from earth heavenwards, from time to eternity. And in what other way could he think, speak, exhort, and encourage both himself and his fellow - Christians but in this manner? For it is by these very exhortations and warnings that the grace of God keeps us. It is in order that the elect may not fall, it is to bring out in fact and time the (ideal and eternal) impossibility of their apostasy, that God in His wisdom and mercy has sent to us such solemn messages and such fervent entreaties, to watch, to fight, to take heed unto ourselves, to resist the adversary" (Saphir).

—ARTHUR W. PINK.

GLEANINGS IN EXODUS.

64.—GRACE ABOUNDING.

—Ex. 33 : 11-17.

Our present passage brings before us one of the most wondrous and blessed scenes described anywhere on the pages of the Old Testament Scriptures. Apart from the circumstances and occasion which gave rise to it, the character of this incident itself should move our hearts to profoundest wonderment and praise. Here we behold the typical mediator prevailing in his intercession for a sinful people, not only in averting the wrath of God, but in securing His continued presence in their midst. Here we are given to see not only the external symbol of His presence drawing near unto men, but the Lord Himself speaking to Moses "as a man speaketh unto his friend." Here we listen to the Lord not only promising to conduct Israel across the howling wilderness, but saying, "I will give thee rest." Verily, "Where sin abounded, grace did much more abound."

Let it be pointed out though, that this precious revelation of the abounding grace of God is recorded not only for our admiration, but also for our learning. Most valuable instruction is to be found here if we take to heart the *order* of events in this portion of the Divinely inspired account of the history of Israel. First, we have in Ex. 32 : 1-6 the narrative of their awful sin. Second, we have the intercession of Moses averting the "consuming" wrath of God (32 : 11-14). Third, we have the sore chastening of the people for it (32 : 25-28, 35). Fourth, we have the repentance of Israel (33 : 4-6). Fifth, we have Moses pitching the Tent "outside the camp," and every one "which sought the Lord," going forth unto it (33 : 7-10). Now we have Jehovah's response to this action of His servant: He speaks "face to face" with Moses. Such amazing condescension, such wondrous grace, was only manifested after sin had been owned and separation from it had been evidenced. The important practical lessons to be drawn from this will be pointed out in our exposition below.

At the beginning of Ex. 33 we hear Jehovah saying, "I will not go up in the midst of thee; for thou art a stiffnecked people; lest I consume thee in the way" (v. 3). Israel's terrible sin had necessitated the retirement of a holy God from them. To have remained among them would have required their total destruction. The mediation of Moses had averted the threatened storm of God's wrath, but until Israel repented the Lord could not come in among them again.

The same principle holds good to-day in connection with any company who profess to be the people of God. While gross sin is allowed, the Lord will not manifest Himself among them, and to such a people His word is "Draw nigh to God, and He will draw nigh to you. Cleanse your hands, ye sinners; and purify your hearts, ye double minded" (James 4 :

The next thing we read in our chapter is, "When the people heard these evil tidings, they mourned" (v. 4). The greatness of their sin began to be realized, and so their "drinking and playing" (32 : 6) was turned into sorrow. Then we are told "and the children of Israel stripped themselves of their ornaments" (v. 6). This evidenced the genuineness of their contrition; this was a bringing forth of "fruits meet for repentance" (Matt. 3 : 8); it was the outward expression of their having taken a lowly place before God. Finally, "It came to pass that every one which sought the Lord went out into the Tent of the congregation, which was without the camp" (v. 7). This corresponds with, "He that covereth his sins shall not prosper: but whoso confesseth and *forsaketh* them, shall have mercy" (Prov. 28 : 13).

Following Moses' going forth from the camp and his entrance into the Tent, which, by faith he had pitched, "the cloudy pillar descended, and stood at the door of the Tent, and the Lord talked with Moses." The effect of this upon the penitent and ornament-stripped people is blessed to behold: "And all the people rose up and worshipped, every man in his tent door" (v. 10). Jehovah was once more given His true place. The false god (the golden calf) was repudiated; the true God was now worshipped. Thus were they, in infinite grace, brought back from their wanderings and made to bow in wondering adoration before the manifested symbol of Jehovah's presence. The blessed sequel we are now to contemplate.

"And the Lord spake unto Moses face to face, as a man speaketh unto his friend" (v. 11). This was the most glorious moment in all the life of Moses, and the most blessed revelation he ever received from God. This even surpassed his experience in the Mount, when he received such wondrous communications from Jehovah. There was an intimacy of approach and a closeness of communion such as he had not been permitted to enjoy before. In the 12th of Numbers, where we read of Miriam and Aaron challenging the authority of Moses, Jehovah vindicated him by saying, "My servant Moses is not so, who is faithful in all Mine house" (v. 7); and then He added, "With him will I speak mouth to mouth, even apparently, and not in dark speeches."

"And the Lord spake unto Moses face to face, as a man speaketh unto his friend." These words must not be interpreted in such a way as to clash with the last verse of our chapter: "And thou shalt see My back parts, but My face shall not be seen." That which is before us here is free and intimate fellowship between the Lord and His servant. And this, be it noted, was the immediate sequel to his separation from what was dishonouring to Jehovah. Ah, dear reader, going forth unto Him without the camp may, yea, must, involve "bearing His reproach" (Heb. 13 : 13); but O the *compensation* — He rewards such faithfulness by manifestations of Himself, by the intimacies of His love, as are never enjoyed while we remain in associations which are derogatory to His honour.

"And the Lord spake unto Moses face to face, as a man speaketh unto his friend." That Moses, the mediator, is here also a blessed type of Christ, hardly needs saying. What we have here is a precious adumbration of the relations existing between the Father and the Son. Before the incarnation He could say, "That I was by Him, as one brought up with Him: and I was daily His delight, rejoicing always before Him" (Prov. 8 : 30). After the incarnation, we read of "the Only-begotten Son which is in *the bosom* of the Father" (John 1 : 18). And again, "For the Father loveth the Son, and showeth Him all things that Himself doeth" (John 5 : 20). And again, "I am not alone, because the Father is with Me" (John 16 : 32). So now, He is seated upon *the Father's* throne (Rev. 3 : 21)—the place of affection and intimacy.

"And he turned again into the camp: but his servant Joshua, the son of Nun, a young man, departed not out of the tent" (v. 11). Let us seek to ponder first the practical lesson exemplified for us in this statement, before we point out its typical signification. That which here receives illustration is most important to lay hold of, particularly for those who are called by God to occupy positions of leadership. Before a servant of God is qualified to minister unto His people he must himself seek unto the Lord; before he has any message for them, the Lord must speak "face to face" unto him. In other words, power for service is obtained only by maintaining intimate fellowship with God. But more: though he returns and ministers unto the people, yet in spirit he remains still inside the Tent. Here, as always in the book of Exodus, Moses and Joshua have to be considered *together*, as mutually complementing each other.

"This section closes with a double type— Moses returning to the camp, and Joshua departing not from within the Tent. Moses represents the energy of love that would serve the people of God. It is a man with whom Jehovah has spoken 'face to face, as a man speaketh with his friend' who can return to serve the people of God in all the holy separation of the spot where he has been, and of the communications which have been made to him. Such a man would not compromise the truth, nor would he allow himself to be entangled with what compromised the truth, but he would be in readiness to serve all in grace and faithfulness in relation to the will of God. But such service ever has as its attendant the spirit of Joshua. Whatever activities of service there may be, *in spirit* the servant does not leave his sweet retreat; he is always in spirit 'outside the camp.' His affections have their abiding place there; his satisfaction and rest is in the Lord" (C. A. Coates).

"And he turned again into the camp: but his servant Joshua, the son of Nun, a young man, departed not out of the camp." It is by no means an easy matter to work out the details of this type—due, no doubt, to the dimness of our spiritual vision. There are several passages in which Moses and Joshua are linked together in Exodus — the book which speaks of redemption. This is the more noticeable as Joshua is not mentioned at all in Leviticus. First, in Ex. 17, we find Moses and Joshua supplementing each other in connection with resisting the onslaught of Amalek. As we sought to show in article 25 of this series (Jan., 1926), Joshua there is a type of the Holy Spirit subjugating, but not exterminating, the "flesh" in the Christian. Then, in Ex. 24 : 13, we read, "And Moses rose up, and his *minister* Joshua: and *Moses* went up into the Mount of God." Here we have in figure the Holy Spirit as the Minister of an ascended Christ: during the present dispensation the Holy Spirit is maintaining the interests and glorifying Christ. Then, in 32 : 17, 18, we have, in type, the Holy Spirit taking note of the sins of God's people. Here in 33 : 11 it seems to be the Spirit's indwelling the true Church, compare 1 Cor. 3 : 16, Eph. 2 : 22.

"And Moses said unto the Lord, See, thou sayest unto me, Bring up this people; and thou hast not let me know whom Thou wilt send with me. Yet Thou hast said, I know thee by name, and thou hast also found grace in My sight" (v. 12). Here, and in the verses which immediately follow, we have another blessed foreshadowment of Christ as our Mediator, interceding before God, maintaining us in His *favour*. What is of first importance to take note of is, that it is as a man who has "found grace" in the sight of God, Moses here pleads. Mark how strikingly this particular feature is emphasised by its repeated mention: in vv. 12, 13, 16, 17 the words "found grace in Thy sight" or "found grace in My sight" are found.

How plainly this points to the Lord Jesus as the One who, on behalf of His poor people, has obtained favour before God. It is on the ground of His own acceptableness that Christ now pleads for us. It is the apprehension of this which gives peace to the heart. God's favour to His people is based upon nothing that He finds in them; it is solely the consequence of what He has obtained through Christ.

"And Moses said unto the Lord, See, Thou sayest unto me, Bring up this people: and Thou hast not let me know whom Thou wilt send with me." At first sight this may seem to clash with what the Lord had said to Moses in 32 : 34, "Therefore now go, lead the people unto the place of which I have spoken unto thee: behold, Mine Angel shall go before thee." But a closer reading will observe a notable distinction. In 32 : 34 Jehovah had spoken of His Angel going "*before* thee" for, while Israel remained impenitent the Lord Himself could not remain " in the midst of thee" (33 : 3). But now that the people had repudiated their sin, and had evidenced their separation from it, Moses says, "Thou hast not let me know whom Thou wilt send *with* me." Blessed distinction: may our hearts lay hold of it. Moses knew full well who *would go* with them, but, in view of Israel's sin, he here takes the place of a supplicant.

"Yet Thou hast said, I know thee by name, and thou hast also found grace in My sight." This carries us back to Ex 3. At the burning bush, where God first called Moses, He had addressed him by name: "God called unto him out of the midst of the bush, and said, Moses, Moses" (3 : 4). And *why is it* that Moses now refers to that memorable experience at the backside of the desert? Because it was there that Jehovah had made Himself known as "the God of Abraham, the God of Isaac, and the God of Jacob"; as the One who declared, "And I am come down to deliver them out of the hand of the Egyptians, and to bring them out of that land *unto a good land* and a large, unto a land flowing with milk and honey" (3 : 8). God having pledged Himself to this, His word must be fulfilled, His purpose accomplished, no matter what the contrariety of the people might be. Thus we behold the boldness of Moses' faith. Here, too, we should look from the type to the anti-type. It is on the ground of God's everlasting *covenant* with Christ that He now exercises mercy to His unworthy people.

"Now therefore, I pray Thee, if I have found grace in Thy sight, show me now Thy way, that I way know Thee, that I may find grace in Thy sight" (v. 13). Very blessed is this. The sad failure of Israel presented itself now to Moses only as an occasion for the unfolding of God's way, and of the knowledge of Him. God had made promises, He had sworn by Himself, and His promises ensured the actual entrance of Israel into Canaan, not their extermination in the wilderness. Moses therefore seeks unto Him now to learn His way. God's "way" is the course He takes in faithfulness in order to make good that which He has pledged.

A number of valuable practical thoughts are suggested by this verse. First, we are unable to discover God's "ways" for ourselves. This was recognized by the Psalmist when he prayed, "Show me Thy ways, O Lord; teach me Thy paths" (25 : 4). And again, "Teach me Thy way, O Lord, and lead me in a plain path" (27 : 11). Second, only God Himself can "show" us His way. Even the incarnate Son (having taken the place of perfect subjection) said, "Thou wilt *show* Me the path of life" (Psa. 16 : 11). Ah, it ever needs to be remembered that "the meek will He guide in judgment, and the meek will He teach His way" (Psa. 25 : 9). Third, it is as God condescends to show us His way that we get to know Him better: "Show me Thy way *that* I may *know* Thee."

"And consider that this nation is Thy people" (v. 14). This was Moses' answer to the word of Jehovah before the Tent had been pitched outside the camp. Then the Lord had said, "Depart, and go up hence, thou and the people which *thou* hast brought up out of the land of Egypt." Here was the response of faith: "Consider that this nation is Thy people." It was Moses casting himself back upon the word, the oath, the covenant of Jehovah to Abraham, Isaac and Jacob, renewed to himself at the burning bush. It is to be noted that Moses made the same plea at a later stage in Israel's history, when, in consequence of their unbelief at Kadesh-barnea, they again provoked the Lord to anger: see Deut. 9 : 26 and context. In a coming day, the godly Jewish remnant will repeat this argument: Joel 2 : 17. Finally, it is to be noted that our great High Priest makes this the ground of His plea too: "I pray not for the world, but for them which Thou has given Me; for they are *Thine*" (John 17 : 9).

"And He said, My presence shall go with thee, and I will give thee rest" (v. 14). We believe that the translators of our English Version have quite missed the point here. As it reads, the response of Moses in v. 15 wou'd be the language of doubt and unbelief. If Jehovah had positively affirmed that His presence *would* go with Moses, to answer, "*If* Thy presence go *not* with us" would be excuseless. So too his question in v. 16 is meaningless if God had already given him assurance. Finally, in such a case, the Lord's words in v. 17 would be a needless repetition. All difficulty is at once removed if, with the "Companion Bible" we punctuate v. 14 as a question: "Shall My presence go with thee? and shall I give thee rest?" It was as much as to say, How can My presence go with thee after this rejection of Me? The Lord was emphasising the enormity of Israel's sin, and pressing the claims of His holiness.

"And he said unto Him, If Thy presence go not with me, carry us not up hence" (v. 15). The issue was still in the balance. The Lord had bidden Moses say to Israel, "put off thy ornaments from thee, that I may know what to do unto thee" (v. 5). Israel had obeyed this command, and Moses had gone forth without the camp to seek unto the Lord (v. 7). His faith is now put to the test; not so much his faith in God personally, but in the superabounding of His grace. "Shall My presence go with thee? and shall I give thee rest?" was a challenge to his heart. The Lord frequently tests His people thus that He may the better discover to themselves the real ground of their confidence. When many of His disciples were forsaking Him, Christ asked the twelve, "Will ye also go away?" (John 6 : 66, 67). He knew, and they knew, that they would not; but He was drawing out their hearts unto Himself.

"And he said unto Him, If Thy presence go not with me, carry us not hence." Nobly did Moses rise to the occasion; or, shall we say, Blessedly did his heart respond to Jehovah's challenge. He felt that without the Lord's own presence with them, all was in vain. No confidence did he have in himself; nor was he satisfied with the prospect of the Angel going "before" them. It was the Lord's own presence, *communion* with Him, his soul craved. And is not this still the longing of every renewed heart? Very touching is it to behold Moses now identifying Himself with Israel: "Carry *us* not up hence." How blessedly did he again foreshadow Him who has said, "Behold I *and* the children which God hath given Me" (Heb. 2 : 13).

"For wherein shall it be known here that I and Thy people have found grace in Thy sight? Is it not in that *Thou* goest with us? So shall we be separated, I and Thy people, from all the people that are upon the face of the earth" (v. 16). It is to God's sovereign and illimitable grace (limited only by the bounds which our lack of faith puts upon it) that Moses now appeals. It was all he could appeal to, but, as the next verse shows, it was enough; his appeal was not in vain. Again we see him identifying himself with the sinful and penitent nation: twice over in this verse he says, "I and Thy people." "This is no mean adumbration of the heart of Christ—this intense love of Moses for Israel, linking them with himself in *his* place of favour before God. And not only so, but rising higher, he now links them with God. We have remarked that God took Israel on their own ground, and since they had rejected Him, He had said to Moses, 'thy' people. But now—now that Moses acts as mediator, has gained the ear of God, he says again, 'Thy people'" (Ed. Dennett).

"So shall we be separated, I and Thy people, from all the people that are upon the face of the earth." This is very important. The Lord's presence in the midst of His people is for the purpose of *separating* them from all others who are not His people. How little this is apprehended to-day. But let us return again to the blessed typical picture here: "he thus claims, as it were, as proof of Divine favour—restoration of favour—God's own presence with His people. It could not be otherwise known, and the fact of His presence would separate them off from all other people. It is the same in principle during this dispensation. The presence of the Holy Ghost on earth, building His people into an habitation for God, separates from all else, and so completely, that there are but two spheres — sphere of the presence and action of the Holy Ghost, and sphere of the action and power of Satan" (Ed. Dennett).

"And the Lord said unto Moses, I *will do* this thing also that thou hast spoken: for thou *hast* found grace in My sight, and I know thee by name" (v. 17). The mediation of Moses completely prevailed. This word of Jehovah's was His own answer to the questions He had asked in v. 14: "My presence shall go with thee, and I will give thee rest." This was the Lord's own response to the pleas of His servant, and it was all that was needed for the assurance of his heart and as the guaranty of Israel's safe conduct across the wilderness. It was grace pure and simple, sovereign and long-suffering grace. Grace vouchsafed to a people who had forfeited every claim upon God. Grace granted in response to the prevailing intercession of the mediator. Reference to this was made long after by Jehovah through one of the prophets, "Thus saith the Lord, The people which were left of the sword found grace in the wilderness; even Israel, when I went to cause him to rest" (Jer. 31 : 2).

How blessed to know that Israel's God is the Christian's God. "My presence shall go with thee": this same precious assurance is given to us while we journey through this world. No matter what the roughness of the path may be, no matter what the trials and disappointments of the way, the Lord Himself is with us. Has He not said, "Lo I am *with* you alway, even unto the end of the age" (Matt. 28 : 20)! With us to guard and protect, to lead and guide, to counsel and cheer. Ever with us, "a very *present* help in trouble" (Psa. 46 : 1). O for faith to realize this. O for a faith to *act* upon it—an ever-present, all sufficient Christ, by our side.

How differently should we conduct ourselves did we but live in the enjoyment and power of this! "Fear thou not, for I am *with* thee: be not dismayed, for I am thy God" (Isa. 41 : 10). "When thou passest through the waters, I will be *with* thee; and through the rivers, they shall not overflow thee: when thou walkest through the fire, thou shalt not be burned; neither shall the flame kindle upon thee" (Isa. 43 : 2). Was He not with the three Hebrews in Babylon's furnace! Then let us exclaim, "Yea, though I walk through the valley of the shadow of death, I will fear no evil: for Thou art *with* me" (Psa. 23 : 4). Yes, His own promise is, "I will *never* leave thee nor forsake thee" (Heb. 13 : 5). Praise and glory be to His name.

"My presence shall go with thee, and I will give thee rest." There are two things here: the Lord's "presence" for the present, "rest" assured for the future. What more can we ask? Blessed promise! Glorious prospect! "Rest," the rest of God (Heb. 4 : 1). Rest from sin, rest from toil, rest from sorrow. O for faith to anticipate it. O for hope to enjoy it even now, for "faith is the substance of things hoped for, the evidence of things not seen" (Heb. 11 : 1). Gird up thy loins, fellow-pilgrims. This wilderness journey is not to last for ever. A few more years at most, perhaps only moments, and thou shalt be where the wicked cease from troubling and where the weary are at rest. In the meantime, He will deal with us as He dealt with Israel of old: "He redeemed them, and He bare them, and *carried* them all the days of old" (Isa. 63 : 9). This was grace, grace abounding over all their sin. And this God is our God, "the God of all *grace*" (1 Peter 5 : 10). May our hearts adore Him and our lives show forth His praise.

—ARTHUR W. PINK.

4.—ABRAM'S OBEDIENCE.

—*Gen.* 12 : 4-7.

Three things have been before us in the preceding articles. First, the appearing of the God of glory unto Abram in Mesopotamia, and the call which he then received; a call which foreshadowed God's demand upon the Christian to live in separation from the world, and to walk not after the flesh, but after the spirit. Second, the encouragements which were given Abram to whole-heartedly respond to that call. God made promise to him that He would make of him a great nation, bless him and make him a blessing, to such an extent that in him all families of the earth should be blessed. Third, the sad failure of Abram, in compromising with God's requirements. Though he left Chaldea, he did not forsake his "kindred" as ordered; and instead of crossing the wilderness and entering Canaan, he tarried at Halfway House, settling down in Haran; and not till the hand of God removed Terah did he fully respond to His call.

The inspired record of the removing of Terah from this earth contains something more than a solemn warning that the disobedient Christian is in danger of having his idol rudely taken from him: it typifies a most important spiritual truth which is writ large across the pages of the New Testament epistles. The influences of nature, even natural affections, are ever *hostile* to our practically entering into the calling of God. And there is only one thing which can deliver a Christian from their baneful effects, and that is *the cross*—the cross appropriated as the principle of discipleship. Death must come in before there is real deliverance from the old order of things. This is little apprehended to-day by the rank and file of God's professing people, most of whom are living on the low plane of self-indulgence and self-gratification.

Judicially, the Christian *is* dead to the old order of things: "Knowing this, that our old man is (Greek, "was") crucified with Him" (Rom. 6 : 6). Every believer in the Lord Jesus has full title to say, "I am (I have been) crucified with Christ" (Gal. 2 : 20). So too may he exclaim, "But God forbid that I should glory, save in the cross of our Lord Jesus Christ, by whom the world is (was) crucified unto me, and I unto the world" (Gal. 6 : 14). Legally, we have died to sin, to the world, to all that pertains to the old creation. But this has to be laid hold of by faith and made practically good in our daily lives. Therefore are we told to "reckon ye also yourselves to be dead (*to have died*) indeed unto sin, but alive unto God through Jesus Christ our Lord" (Rom. 6 : 11). And again, "Because we thus judge, that if One died for all, then the all died: And He died for all, that they which live should not henceforth live unto themselves, but unto Him which died for them, and rose again" (2 Cor. 5 : 14, 15).

"They that are Christ's have crucified the flesh with the affections and lusts" (Gal. 5 : 24). This too is to be appropriated and incorporated into our daily walk: "Henceforth know we no man after the flesh" (2 Cor. 5 : 16). Only that which is spiritual is to have any weight with the Christian; only that which pertains to the new creation is to govern him. Affections are now to be set upon things above, and not upon things on the earth. But observe carefully what precedes that: "If ye then be *risen* with Christ, seek those things which are above" (Col. 3 : 1). Ah, *death* has come in. O that this may be, increasingly, the longing, the aim, and realization of all God's people— to "know Him, and the power of His resurrection, and the fellowship of His sufferings, being *made conformable unto* His death" (Phil. 3 : 10).

We are now to look at that which attended and immediately followed Abram's vacating of Haran. "So Abram departed, as the Lord had spoken unto him; and Lot went with him: and Abram was seventy and five years old when he departed out of Haran. And Abram took Sarai his wife, and Lot his brother's son, and all their substance that they had gathered, and the souls they had gotten in Haran; and they went forth to go into the land of Canaan, and into the land of Canaan they came" (Gen. 12 : 4, 5). We fear to express ourselves dogmatically upon these verses, as to whether or not they record a third compromise on the part of our patriarch.

Whether or not Abram now did wrong in taking his nephew Lot along with him, we are not prepared to say. Undoubtedly he sinned in first allowing Lot to accompany him from Chaldea, for God's command was very plain: he was not only bidden to leave his "father's house" but also his "kindred." Moreover, Isa. 51 : 2 expressly declares that God called Abram "alone"! On the other hand, it is difficult, if not impossible, to ascertain from the Scripture records what happened during the interval while Abram and his company dwelt in Haran. 2 Pet. 2 : 7 speaks of "*just* Lot," who was "vexed with the filthy conversation of the wicked." But as to when Lot was really saved we do not know. God may have met with him in Haran, or, it may have been after he entered Canaan. But one thing we do know, namely, that Lot became a thorn in Abram's side, and ultimately had to separate from him. In truth, they had little in common.

"And Abram passed through the land unto the place of Sichem, unto the plain of Moreh" (v. 6). Every word here is profoundly suggestive, and calls for prolonged and prayerful meditation. At last Abram had complied with the terms of God's call, and the verse now before us makes mention of his first stopping-place after his entrance into Canaan. A most significant place it was, and important are the instructions it contains for us, if we have hearts to receive them.

"Sichem" is the "Shechem" of later Scriptures, and means *shoulder*, which at once suggests to us the yoke and burden-bearing. The Hebrew for "plain" of Moreh is rendered by a number of reliable translators as the "oak" of Moreh, and this at once speaks of *strength*. The name "Moreh" signifies "instruction." Much-needed and valuable lessons are here recorded for our learning. First of all, we are here taught that it is only as the called of God separates himself from the world and subordinates the affections of the flesh to the claims of the Lord, that he is in the way to the things spoken of, typified, here. It is only as I am walking in the path of God's revealed will that I arrive at that of which Sichem and Moreh foreshadowed. There are three things connected with the point at which Abram had now arrived which are to be carefully noted: it was the place of the shoulder, of strength, and of instruction.

In the next place, it is of first moment that we should attend to the *order* of these three things. Of what does the believer's "strength" consist? In receiving "instruction" from the Lord. And *how* is that instruction to be obtained? By bowing the "shoulder" before Him. The New Testament parallel to Gen. 12 : 6 is the well-known, but, perhaps little understood, words of our Redeemer in Matt. 11 : 29, 30, "Take My yoke upon you, and learn of Me; for I am meek and lowly in heart: and ye shall find rest unto your souls. For My yoke is easy, and My burden is light."

That the believer's *strength* lies in being "instructed" by the Lord is evident from a number of Scriptures. Both in the natural and in the spiritual realms strength comes from food, suitable food, properly masticated and assimilated. The spiritual food for the Christian is to be found in the Word of God. That which nourished and sustained the children of Israel during all their wilderness journeyings, was the daily supply of manna which Jehovah rained down from heaven for them; and that manna was an outstanding figure and type of the spiritual food upon which God's people are now feeding. In 1 Pet. 2 : 2, we read, "As new-born babes, desire the sincere milk of the Word, that ye may grow thereby."

And *how* are we "taught" or "instructed" by the Lord? Observe carefully the order in Christ's words: (1) "Take My yoke upon you, (2) and learn of Me, (3) and ye shall find rest (in which strength is renewed) unto your souls." Observe particularly that our Lord did not speak of a yoke which His disciples are to *bear*; it is not a yoke which He lays upon us, but a yoke which He bids us "take"! To take Christ's yoke upon us means, to bow to God's will, to submit to His ways, to be in subjection to His commands. It is only as this is done that we shall, or can, "learn of" Christ: as said the Psalmist, "The *meek* will He guide in judgment: and the *meek* will He teach His way" (25 : 9). And, we repeat, strength comes through instruction: "strengthen Thou me according unto Thy Word" (Psa. 119 : 28). As another has aptly put it, "The oak of Moreh grows at Shechem still."

It should need no lengthy argument from us to convince the reader that "instruction" was an imperative need on the part of Abram. Having entered a strange land in which he had no friends; having started along a path in which he had had no previous experience; knowing not what might lie ahead; Divine instruction, Divine wisdom for the regulation of his walk, was now an imperative requirement. And this is, typically, what he *sought*, by making at once for Sichem, where grew the oak of Moreh. Equally urgent is the need of each of Abram's children to-day. His temporal circumstances were but a figure of our spiritual ones. Our first and ever-recurring need is to take upon us the "yoke" of Christ and learn of Him, for it is only as we do so that we obtain light for our path and strength to walk therein.

"And the Canaanite was then in the land" (v. 6). It is important that we should take note of the precise point in the sacred narrative at which this statement is introduced. One would naturally have thought that it had been found at the end of v. 5, thus: "And they went forth to go into the land of Canaan, and into the land of Canaan they came. And the Canaanite was then in the land." But not thus has the Holy Spirit expressed it. Instead, He has said, "And Abram passed through the land unto the place of Sichem, unto the plain of Moreh. And the Canaanite was *then* in the land." What then are we to learn from this? That we have here something more than a mere historical reference scarcely needs to be said. But what is the spiritual truth that is illustrated?

The *connection* between the two statements found in Gen. 12 : 6—Abram's journeying to Sichem, the presence of the Canaanite "then" in the land—strikingly linked together by the word "and," is highly significant and suggestive. That which is foreshadowed at the end of the verse emphasises the need for the child of God doing that which is portrayed at the beginning of the verse. The land through which Abram was called to pass as a "stranger and pilgrim" was already inhabited — not by brethren or friends, but by aliens, by heathen-idolators, with whom he had nothing in common. So too though the Christian has, by amazing grace, been made a partaker of the heavenly calling, he is still here in a land filled with those who despise and reject his Lord. Though he has been called out of the world, and is required to live in heart-separation from it, yet he is still in it, and friendship with it is "enmity with God" (James 4 : 4).

The "Canaanite" was the concrete expression of the presence of Satan. To enable the reader to grasp the better that which is here typified, let us put it this way: at the cross Christ settled every question which sin has raised or can raise between God and His people. *That* is a past and accomplished thing. But what of the future? *That* is resplendent with the glory of God, into which His people shall be brought according to the infinite value of Christ's work for them. But there is another thing, and that is the *interval* between the Cross and our entrance into the Glory. Now Satan cannot invalidate the worth and success of the redeeming sacrifice of Christ; nor can he, to the slightest degree, mar the perfection of the eternal glory. But the whole of his power is put forth to hinder a *present* result for Christ.

The great aim of the enemy is to prevent God's people bringing forth that which shall, even now, give delight to the heart of Christ. There is nothing which the Devil hates worse than to see the Lord Jesus being magnified and glorified through His followers, and his present efforts are concentrated—so far as God permits—to the thwarting of this. Nor are we ignorant of his devices (2 Cor. 2 : 11). Yet, though we know this, how readily and how frequently do we lend ourselves to the accomplishment of his vile purpose! Satan is a defeated foe; already he has been judged (John 16 : 11), and soon shall that judgment be executed. But even now it is the Christian's privilege to be completely victorious over him and all his machinations. "Resist the Devil, and he *shall* flee from you" (James 4 : 7) is the sure promise of God. But observe well what immediately precedes that promise: "Submit yourselves therefore to God"! Ah, here is the *same* order as in Gen. 12 : 6: first, Sichem, and the mention of the Canaanite; first submission to God (taking His "yoke" upon us), and thereby obtaining power with which to "Resist the Devil"!

Yes, the "Canaanite" is still "in the land," ready to contest every forward move, to oppose each step in the path of faith, ever seeking to hinder God's people from entering into their spiritual inheritance. But it may be objected that nothing is said in Gen. 12, or elsewhere either, of the Canaanites *attacking* Abram. Perfectly true, and in the omission we may discern the blessed accuracy of our type. The Word of Truth declares, "When a man's way please the Lord, He maketh even his enemies to be at peace with him" (Prov. 16 : 7). Satan is powerless to do a thing against us while we keep away from his ground; nor will God suffer him to molest one of His while he is living in dependence upon and submission to Him. Read through the books of Joshua and Judges and observe how and while Israel's ways pleased the Lord, the Canaanites were powerless before them; but as soon as Israel's ways displeased Him, the Canaanites prevailed against them.

Thus the reader will perceive by now, we trust, the connection between the last sentence of Gen. 12 : 6 and the clauses that precede, and what was meant when we said that this final sentence *emphasises the need* of the believer doing that which is typified by Abram making for Sichem. The Canaanite in the land speaks of the presence of the Enemy in this scene through which we are called to pass. And there is only one way of being fortified against him, and that is by complete submission to God, bowing the shoulder and taking His yoke upon us. In other words, it is only as we flee to Christ for refuge, and cast ourselves upon His sufficiency, that we are safe. While we are living in simple dependency upon God, having "no confidence in the flesh" (Phil. 3 : 3), we are safe, and the Devil cannot harm us. It is only when we leave this place of acknowledged weakness, and rely upon our own strength to overcome temptation, that we fall victims to Satan. While we are in communion with the Lord, the Devil cannot touch so much as a hair of our heads; but when we get away from Him, and cross over into the Enemy's territory, we are already as good as defeated.

It only remains for us to point out that the word "Canaanite" means "trafficer," and in the light of later Scriptures it is not difficult to discover *what* it is in which the Devil traffics. In the last verse of the prophet Zechariah we read, "And in that day there shall be no more the Canaanite in the house of the Lord of Hosts." It needs to be borne in mind that the sphere in which the Enemy's principal activities are conducted is the *religious* one, therefore it is in that which professes to be the "house of the Lord" that the believer needs most to be on his guard. "Beloved, believe not every spirit, but try the spirits whether they are of God: because many false prophets are gone out into the world" (1 John 4 : 1).

There are many of Satan's agents to-day trafficking in holy things, "transforming themselves into the apostles of Christ," and as "the ministers of righteousness" (2 Cor. 11 : 13, 15). They are men who run "greedily after the error of Balaam *for reward*" (Jude 11), who "corrupt the Word of God" (2 Cor. 2 : 17), and of whom it is said, "And many shall follow their pernicious ways, by reason of whom the way of truth shall be evil spoken of; and through covetousness shall they with feigned words make *merchandise* of you" (2 Pet. 2 : 2, 3). Yes, the Canaanite is still in the land.

"And the Lord appeared unto Abram" (Gen. 12 : 7). This is very blessed and precious, coming in at this point. It tells of the Divine provision which Divine grace has made for us, a provision which is more than sufficient to offset the presence of the Enemy. It was as though God said to His servant, "Be not occupied with the Canaanite, look unto Me." *That* is the secret of victory, of peace, and of blessing. Instead of dwelling upon Satan's efforts to keep us from the enjoyment of that which God hath given us, let us seek grace to appropriate power from Him to bring us into the good of it. "If God be for us, who can be against us?" (Rom. 8 : 31)! But if we *are* to have "God *for* us" in connection with all the affairs of our daily lives, then we must be in our proper place—not in the way of self-will, but in the path of humble submission to Him. God will not fight our battles for us if we are rebellious and disobedient. His "salvation" or "deliverance" is "nigh them that *fear* Him," and He hath promised to "show Himself strong in the behalf of them whose *heart* is perfect towards Him" (2 Chron. 16 : 9).

"And the Lord appeared unto Abram." God had "appeared" unto Abram, or manifested Himself before Him, when He first called him, while he was yet an idolator in Ur of the Chaldees (Acts 7 : 2). And now that he had, at last, fully responded to the terms of His call, He appeared to him again. It is very solemn to note that there is no mention of Abram's being favoured with any manifestation of God during the years he had dwelt in Haran! No, that could not be. For the Lord to have lifted up the light of His countenance upon our patriarch while he lingered at Halfway House, would have been setting a premium upon his compromises. Not thus does the thrice holy God act. But now that Abram had actually entered Canaan, now that he had sought out Sichem, the Lord was free to once more reveal Himself to him.

What has been before us in the last paragraph illustrates an important practical principle in the "ways" of God with His people. God's dealings are never capricious nor arbitrary. It is true that He is sovereign Most High, doing as He pleases; yet it needs to be ever kept in mind that *all* His actions are regulated by perfect wisdom and holiness, and in connection with His own people, by *love* as well. But because God is holy, He can never wink at sin—no, not even in His saints. Until we act upon and walk in the light which He has already given us, He will not grant us more. To His disciples Christ said, "For whosoever hath (i.e., in reality, manifesting it in his walk) to him shall be given, and he shall have more abundance: but whosoever hath not (who hides his light under a bushel) from him shall be taken away even that he hath (by mere profession)": Matt. 13 : 12. It is on this principle that God ever deals with us.

God does not treat with us as stocks and stones, but as responsible creatures, as those who are accountable to put into practice that which He has revealed to us. As one of His prophets declared long ago, "Then shall we know, if we follow on to know the Lord" (Hosea 6 : 3); and if we do not "follow on," if we do not respond to His voice, we shall not know the Lord in the intimacies of His love, in His heart-satisfying sufficiency. The "secret of the Lord is with them that fear (respect and honour) Him" (Psa. 25 : 14), but if we fear *men* instead, fear what they will think and say about us, fear their sneers and frowns, we shall lose irreparably. "I understand more than the ancients, because I *keep* Thy precepts" (Psa. 119 : 100)! Therefore, if I am *not* receiving further revelations from and gracious manifestations of God, then the cause, the fault, must be sought *in myself*.
—ARTHUR W. PINK.

PROVISION FOR PERILOUS TIMES.

It is of the very last importance, for the servant of Christ, in all ages, to have a clear, deep, abiding, influential sense of his position, his path, his portion, and his prospects—a divinely wrought apprehension of the ground which he is called to occupy; the sphere of action which is thrown open to him; the divine provision made for his comfort and encouragement, his strength and guidance; and the brilliant hopes held out to him. There is uncommon danger of our being allured into a mere region of theory and speculation, of opinion and sentiment, and dogmas and principles. The freshness of first love is frequently lost by contact with men and things, of what may be called "the religious world." The lovely verdure of early personal Christianity is often destroyed by a wrong use of the machinery of religion, if we may be allowed to use such a term.

In the kingdom of nature, it frequently happens that some stray seed has dropped into the ground, taken root, and sprung up into a tender plant. The hand of man had nothing to do with it. God planted it, watered it, and made it grow. He assigned it its position, gave it its strength, and covered it with beauteous verdure. By and by, man intruded upon its solitude and transplanted it to his own artificial enclosure, there to wither and droop. Thus it is, too often, alas! with the plants of God's spiritual kingdom. They are often injured by man's rude hand. They would be far better, if left to the sole management of the Hand that planted them. Young Christians frequently suffer immensely from not being left to the exclusive training of the Holy Spirit, and the exclusive teaching of Holy Scripture. Human management is sure to stunt the growth of God's spiritual plants. It is not, by any means, that God may not use men as His instruments in watering, culturing, and caring for, His precious plants. He assuredly may and does; but, then, it is God's culture and care, not man's. This makes all the difference. The Christian is God's plant. The seed which produced him was Divine. It was directed and planted by God's own hand, and that same hand must be allowed to train it.

Now, what is true of the individual believer, is equally true of the Church, as a whole. In the First Epistle to Timothy, the Church is looked at in its original order and glory. It is there viewed as "The house of God"—"The church of the living God"—"The pillar and ground of the truth." Its office-bearers, its functions, and its responsibilities, are there minutely and formally described. The servant of Christ is instructed as to the mode in which he is to conduct himself in the midst of such a hallowed and dignified sphere. Such is the character, such the scope and object of Paul's first Epistle to Timothy.

But, in the second Epistle, we have something quite different. The scene is entirely changed. The house which, in the first epistle, was looked at in its *rule*, is here contemplated in its *ruin*. The church, as an economy, set up on earth, had, like every other economy, utterly failed. Man fails in everything. He failed amid the beauty and order of Paradise. He failed in that favoured land "that floweth with milk and honey, the glory of all lands." He failed amid the rare privileges of the gospel dispensation; and he will fail amid the bright beams of millennial glory. (Compare Gen. 3; Judges 2; Acts 20 : 29; 3 John 9; Rev. 1 : 3; Rev. 20 : 7-9).

The remembrance of this will help us in the understanding of 2 Timothy. It may, very properly, be termed, "a divine provision for perilous times." The apostle seems, as it were, to be weeping over the ruins of that once beautiful structure. Like the weeping prophet, he beholds, "the stones of the sanctuary poured out in the top of every street." He calls to remembrance the tears of his beloved Timothy. He is glad to have even one sympathizing bosom into which to pour his sorrows. All that were in Asia had turned away from him. He was left to stand alone before Cæsar's judgment-seat. Demas forsook him. Alexander, the coppersmith, did him much evil. All around him, so far as man was concerned, looked gloomy and dark. He begs of his beloved Timothy to bring him his cloke, his books, and his parchments. All is strongly marked. "Perilous times" are anticipated. "A form of godliness without the power"—the mantle of profession thrown over the grossest abominations of the human heart—men not able to endure sound doctrine—heaping to themselves teachers after their own lusts, having itching ears which must needs be tickled by the fabulous and baseless absurdities of the human mind. Such are the features of the Second Epistle to Timothy. Who can fail to notice them? Who can fail to see that our lot is cast in the very midst of the evils and dangers here contemplated? And is it not well to have a clear perception of these things? Why should we desire to blind our eyes as to the truth? Why deceive ourselves with vain dreams of increasing light and spiritual prosperity? Is it not better far to look the true condition of things straight in the face? Assuredly; and the rather when the self-same epistle which so faithfully points out "the perilous times," fully unfold the divine provision. Why should we imagine that man, under the Christian dispensation, would prove a single whit better than man under all dispensations which have gone before, or under the millennial dispensation which is yet to follow? Would not analogy even in the absence of direct and positive proof, lead us to expect failure under one economy as well as under all others? If we, without exception, find judgment at the close of all dispensations, why should we look for aught else at the close of this? Let my reader ponder these things, and then accompany me, for a few moments, while I seek, by the grace of God, to unfold some of the divine provisions for "perilous times."

I do not attempt to expound this most touching and interesting epistle in detail. This would be impossible in an article like the present. I shall merely single out one point from each of the four chapters into which the epistle has been divided. These are, first, "unfeigned faith" (1 : 5). Secondly, "the sure foundation" (2 : 19). Thirdly, "the holy scriptures" (3 : 15). Fourthly, "the crown of righteousness" (4 : 8). The man who knows aught of the power of these things, is divinely provided for "perilous times."

1. And, first, as to "unfeigned faith" that priceless possession, the apostle says, "I thank God, whom I serve from my forefathers with pure conscience, that without ceasing I have remembrance of thee in my prayers night and day; greatly desiring to see thee, being mindful of thy tears, that I may be filled with joy; when I call to remembrance the unfeigned faith that is in thee, which dwelt first in thy grandmother Lois and thy mother Eunice; and I am persuaded that in thee also." Here, then, we have something above and beyond every thing ecclesiastical—something which one must have, ere he is introduced to the Church, and which will stand good though the Church were in ruins around him. This unfeigned faith connects the soul immediately with Christ, in the power of a link which must, of necessity, be anterior to all ecclesiastical associations how important soever they may be, in their due place—a link which shall endure when all earthly associations shall have been dissolved for ever. We do not get to Christ through the Church. We get to Christ first, and then to the Church. Christ is our life, not the Church. No doubt Church fellowship is most valuable; but there is something above and beyond it, and it is of that something that "unfeigned faith" takes possession. Timothy had this faith dwelling in him before ever he entered the house of God. He was connected with the God of the house previous to his manifested association with the house of God.

It is well to be clear as to this. We must never surrender the intense individuality which characterises "unfeigned faith." We must carry it with us through all the scenes and circumstances, the links and associations of our Christian life and service. We must not traffic in mere Church position, or build upon religious machinery, or be upborne by a routine of duty, or cling to the worthless props of sectarian sympathy or denominational predilection. Let us cultivate those fresh, vivid and powerful affections which were created in our hearts when first we knew the Lord. Let the beauteous blossom of our spring-time be succeeded, not by barrenness and sterility, but by those mellow clusters which spring from realized connection with the root. Too often, alas!

it is otherwise. Too often the earnest, zealous, simple-hearted young Christian is lost in the bigoted, narrow-minded member of a sect, or the intolerant defender of some peculiar opinion. The freshness, softness, simplicity, tenderness, and earnest affection of our young days, are rarely carried forward into the advanced stages of vigorous manhood, and mature old age. Very frequently one finds a depth of tone, a richness of experience, a moral elevation, in the early stages of the Christian life which too soon gives place to a chilling formalism in one's personal ways; or a mere energy in the defence of some barren system of theology. How rarely are those words of the Psalmist realized, "They shall bring forth fruit *in old age;* they shall be fat and flourishing" (Psa. 92 : 14).

The truth is, we all want to cultivate, more diligently, an "unfeigned faith." We want to enter, with more spiritual vigour, into the power of the links which bind us, individually to Christ. This would render us "fat and flourishing," even in old age. "The righteous shall flourish like the palm tree ; he shall grow like a cedar in Lebanon. Those that be planted in the house of the Lord, shall flourish in the courts of our God." We suffer materially by allowing what is called Christian intercourse to interfere with our personal connection and communion with Christ. We are far too prone to substitute intercourse with man for intercourse with God—to walk in the footsteps of our fellow, rather than in the footsteps of Christ—to look around, rather than upward, for sympathy, support and encouragement. These are not the fruits of "unfeigned faith." Quite the opposite. That faith is as blooming and vigorous amid solitudes of a desert as in the bosom of an assembly. Its immediate, its all engrossing business is with God Himself. "It endures as seeing Him who is invisible." It fixes its earnest gaze upon things unseen and eternal. "It enters into that within the veil." It lives amid the unseen realities of an eternal world. Having conducted the soul to the feet of Jesus, there to get a full and final forgiveness of all its sins, through His most precious blood, it bears it majestically onward through all the windings and labyrinths of desert life, and enables it to bask in the bright beams of millennial glory.

Thus much as to this first precious item in the divine provision for "perilous times" —this "unfeigned faith." No one can ever get on without it, let the times be peaceful or perilous, easy or difficult, rough or smooth, dark or bright. If a man be destitute of this faith, deeply implanted and diligently cultivated in his soul, he must, sooner or later, break down. He may be urged on, for a time, by the impulses of surrounding circumstances and their influence. He may be propped up and borne along by his co-religionists. He may float down along the stream of religious profession. But, most assuredly, if he be not possessed of "unfeigned faith," the time is rapidly approaching when it will be all over with him for ever. The "perilous times" will soon rise to a head, and then will come the awful crisis of judgment, from which none can escape save the happy possessors of "unfeigned faith." God grant my reader may be one of these! If so, all is eternally safe.

2.—We shall, now, consider, in the second place, "The sure foundation." "Nevertheless the foundation of God standeth sure, having this seal the Lord knoweth them that are His. And let every one that nameth the name of Christ depart from iniquity" (2 : 19). In the midst of all the "trouble," the "hardness," the "striving about words," the "profane and vain babblings," the errors of "Hymenaeus and Philetus"—in the midst of these varied features of the "perilous times," how ineffably precious to fall back upon God's sure foundation. The soul that is built upon this, in the divine energy of "unfeigned faith," is able to resist the rapidly rising tide of evil—is divinely furnished for the most appalling times. There is a fine moral link between the unfeigned faith in the heart of man, and the sure foundation by the hand of God. All may go to ruin. The Church may go to pieces, and all who love that Church may have to sit down and weep over its ruins ; but there stands that imperishable foundation, laid by God's own hand, against which the surging tide of error and evil may roll with all its fury, and have no effect, save to prove the eternal stability of that rock and of all who are built thereon.

"The Lord knoweth them that are His." There is abundance of false profession, but the eye of Jehovah rests on all those who belong to Him. Not one of them is, or ever can be forgotten by Him. Their names are engraven on His heart. They are as precious to Him as the price He paid for them, and that is nothing less than the "precious blood" of His own dear Son. No evil can befall them. No weapon formed against them can prosper. "The eternal God is their refuge, and underneath are the everlasting arms." What rich, what ample provision for "perilous times"! Why should we fear? Why should we be anxious? Having "unfeigned faith" within, and God's foundation beneath, it is our happy privilege to pursue, with tranquillized hearts, our upward and onward way, in the assurance that all is, and shall be well.

"I know My sheep," he cries,
My soul approves them well :
Vain is the treacherous world's disguise,
And vain the rage of hell."

It has been well remarked that the seal on God's foundation has two sides: one, bearing the inscription, "The Lord knoweth them that are His"; and the other, "Let every one that nameth the name of Christ depart from iniquity." The former is as peace-giving as the latter is practical. Let the strife and confusion be ever so great—let the storm rage and the billows arise—let the darkness thicken—let all the powers of earth and hell combine, "the Lord knoweth them that are His." He has sealed them for Himself. The assurance of this is eminently calculated to maintain the heart in profound repose, let the "times" be ever so "perilous."

But, let us never forget that each one who "names the name of Christ," is solemnly responsible to "depart from iniquity" wherever he finds it. This is applicable to all true Christians. The moment that I see anything that deserves the epithet of "iniquity," be it what or where it may, I am called upon to "depart from" that thing. I am not to wait till others see with me, for what may seem "iniquity" to one, may not seem to be so, at all, to another. Hence, it is entirely a personal question. "Let every one." The language used in this epistle is very personal, very strong, very intense. "If a man purge himself." "Flee also youthful lusts." "From such turn away." "Continue thou." "I charge thee." "Watch thou in all things, endure afflictions." "Of whom be thou ware also." These are solemn, earnest, weighty words—words which prove, very distinctly, that our lot is cast in times when we must not lean upon the arm or gaze upon the countenance of our fellow. We must be sustained by the energy of an "unfeigned faith," and by our personal connection with the "sure foundation." Thus shall we be able, let others do or think as they will, to "depart from iniquity"—to "flee youthful lusts"—to "turn away" from the adherents of a powerless "form of godliness," wherever we find them, and to "beware" of every "Alexander the coppersmith." If we suffer our feet to be moved from the rock—if we surrender ourselves to the impulse of surrounding circumstances and influences, we shall never be able to head against the special forms of evil in these "perilous times."

3.—This introduces us, naturally, to our third point, namely, "The holy scriptures"—that precious portion of every "man of God." "But continue thou in the things which thou hast learned and hast been assured of, knowing of whom thou hast learned them; and that from a child thou hast known the holy scriptures, which are able to make thee wise unto salvation through faith which is in Christ Jesus. All scripture is given by inspiration of God, and is profitable for doctrine, for reproof, for correction, for instruction in righteousness; that the man of God may be perfect, THOROUGHLY furnished unto ALL good works" (3:14-17). Here, then, we have a rich provision for "perilous times." A thorough knowledge of the One from "whom we have learned"—an accurate, personal, experimental acquaintance with the "holy scriptures"—that pure fountain of divine authority—that changeless source of heavenly wisdom, which even *a child* may possess, and without which *a sage* must err. If a man is not able to refer all his thoughts, all his convictions, all his principles, to God as their living source—to Christ as their living centre, and to the "holy scriptures" as their divine authority, he will never be able to get on through "perilous times." A second-hand faith will never do. We must hold truth directly from God, through the medium, and on the authority of "the holy scriptures." God may use a man to show me certain things in the Word; but I do not hold them from man, but from God. It is, "knowing of *whom* thou hast learned"; and when in this case I am able, through grace, to get on through the thickest darkness, and through all the devious paths of this wilderness world. Inspiration's heavenly lamp emits a light so clear, so full, so steady, that its brightness is only made the more distinctly manifest by the surrounding gloom. "The man of God" is not left to drink of the muddy streams that flow along the channel of human tradition; but with the vessel of "unfeigned faith," he sits beside the limpid and ever-gushing fountain of "holy scripture," there to drink of its refreshing waters, to the full satisfaction of his thirsty soul.

It is worthy of remark that, although the inspired apostle was aware, when writing his first epistle to Timothy's "unfeigned faith" and of his knowledge, from childhood's earliest dawn, of the "holy scriptures," yet he does not allude to these things until, in his second epistle, he contemplates the appalling features of the "perilous times." This reason is obvious. It is in the very midst of the perils of the "last days," that one has the most urgent need of "unfeigned faith" and "the holy scriptures." We cannot get on without them. When all around is fresh and vigorous—when all are borne onward as by one common impulse of genuine devotedness—when every heart is full to overflowing of deep and earnest attachment to the Person and cause of Christ—when every countenance beams with heavenly joy—then, indeed, it is comparatively easy to get on. But the condition of things contemplated in the Second Epistle to Timothy is the very reverse of all this. It is such, that unless one is walking closely with God, in the habitual exercise of "unfeigned faith"—in the abiding realization of the link which connects him, indissolubly with "the foundation of God"—and in clear, unquestionable, accurate knowledge of "the holy scriptures," he must, assuredly, make shipwreck. This is a deeply solemn consideration, well worthy of my reader's undivided, prayerful, attention. The time has, verily, arrived in which each one must follow the Lord, according to his measure. "What is it to thee? Follow thou Me." These words fall on the ear with peculiar power as one seeks to make his way amid the ruins of every thing ecclesiastical.

But, let me not be misunderstood. It is not that I would detract, in the smallest degree, from the value of true Church fellowship, or from the divine institution of the assembly and all the privileges and responsibilities attaching thereto. Far be the thought. I believe, most fully, that Christians are called to seek the maintenance of the very highest principles of communion; and, moreover, we are warranted, from the epistle which now lies open before us, to expect that, in the darkest times, the "purged vessel" will be able to "follow righteousness, faith, charity, peace, *with all* that call on the name of the Lord out of a pure heart" (2:22).

All this is plain, and has its due place and value; but it, in no wise, interferes with the fact that each one is responsible to pursue a path of holy independence, without waiting for the countenance, the sympathy, the support, or the company of his fellow. True, we are to be deeply thankful for brotherly fellowship, when we can get it on true ground. Of such fellowship no words can tell the worth. Would that we knew more of it! The Lord increase it to us a hundredfold. But let us never stoop to purchase fellowship at the very heavy price of all that is "lovely and of good report." May the name of Jesus be more precious to our hearts than all beside; and with all those who truly love His name may our happy lot be cast on earth, as it shall be, throughout eternity, in the regions of unfading light and purity, above.

4.—And, now, one closing word as to "the crown of righteousness." "For I am now ready to be offered, and the time of my departure is at hand. I have fought a good fight, I have finished my course, I have kept the faith. Henceforth there is laid up for me a crown of righteousness, which the Lord, the righteous judge, shall give me at that day; and not to me only, but unto all them that love His appearing" (4: 6-8). Here the venerable pilgrim takes his stand on the summit of spiritual Pisgah, and with undimmed eye surveys the bright plains of glory. He sees the crown of righteousness glittering in the Master's hand. He looks back over the course which he had run, and over the battle-field whereon he had fought—he stands on the confines of earth, and in the very midst of the ruins of that church whose rise and progress he had watched with such intense solicitude, and over whose decline and fall he had poured forth the tears of tender though disappointed affection—he fixes his eye on the goal of immortality which no power of the enemy can prevent him from reaching, in triumph; and whether it were by Cæsar's axe that he was to reach that goal, or by any other means, it mattered not to one who was able to say, "I AM READY." What true sublimity! What moral grandeur! What noble elevation is here! And yet there was nothing of the ascetic in this incomparable servant, for though his vision was filled with the crown of righteousness—though he is ready to step like a conqueror into his triumphal chariot—he, nevertheless, feels it perfectly right to give minute directions about his cloke and books. This is divinely perfect. It teaches us that the more vividly we enter into the glories of heaven, the more faithfully we discharge the functions of earth—the more we realize the nearness of eternity the more effectively shall we order the things of time.

Such, then, beloved reader, is the ample provision made, by the grace of God, for the "perilous times" through which you and I are now passing. "Unfeigned faith"—"The sure foundation"—"The holy scriptures," and "The crown of righteousness." May the Holy Spirit lead us into a deep sense of the importance and value of these things! May we love the appearing of Jesus, and earnestly look out for that cloudless morning when "the righteous judge" shall place a diadem of glory upon the brow of each one who really loves His advent!

—Things New and Old (Vol. 3).

A MODEL CHRISTIAN.

This third chapter of Philippians gives us the model of a true Christian—a model on which every Christian should be formed. The man who is here introduced to our notice could say, by the Holy Spirit, "Brethren, be ye followers together of me." Nor is it as an apostle that he here speaks to us—nor as one endowed with extraordinary gifts, and privileged to see unspeakable visions. It is not to Paul, the apostle, nor Paul, the gifted vessel, that we listen, in verse 17 of our chapter; but to Paul, the Christian. We could not follow him in his brilliant career, as an apostle. We could not follow him, in his rapture to Paradise; but we can follow him in his Christian course, in this world; and it seems to us that we have in our chapter, a very full view of that course, and not only of the course itself; but also the starting-post and the goal. In other words, we have to consider, first, the Christian's *standing*; secondly, the Christian's *object*; and thirdly, the Christian's *hope*. May God the Holy Spirit be our Teacher, while we dwell for a little on these mighty and most interesting points! And first, as to

THE CHRISTIAN'S STANDING.

This point is unfolded, in a double way, in our chapter. We are not only told what the Christian's standing is, but also what it is not. If ever there was a man who could boast of having a righteousness of his own in which to stand before God, Paul was the man. He was a Jew, of pure pedigree, in orderly fellowship, of blameless walk, of fervid zeal and unflinching devotedness. He was, in principle, a persecutor of the Church.

Hence Saul, as an earnest Jew, could not but be a zealous persecutor of the Church of God. It was part of his religion—of that in which he "excelled many of his equals in his own nation"—of that in which he was "exceedingly zealous." Whatever was to be had, in the shape of religiousness, Saul would have it; whatever height was to be attained, he would attain. He would leave no stone unturned in order to build up the superstructure of his own righteousness—righteousness in the flesh—righteousness in the old creation. He was permitted to possess himself of all the attractions of legal righteousness in order that he might fling them from him amid the brighter glories of a divine righteousness. "But what things were gain to me, those I counted loss for Christ. Yea, doubtless, and I count all things but loss, for the excellency of the knowledge of Christ Jesus my Lord; for whom I have suffered the loss of all things, and do count them but dung, that I may win Christ, and be found in Him, not having mine own righteousness, which is of the law, but that which is through the faith of Christ, the righteousness which is of God by faith."

And we should note here that the grand prominent thought, in the above passage, is not that of a guilty sinner betaking himself to the blood of Christ for pardon, but rather of a legalist casting aside, as dross, his own righteousness, because of having found a better. We need hardly say that Paul was a sinner—"the chief of sinners"—and that, as such, he betook himself to the precious blood of Christ, there found pardon, peace and acceptance with God. This is plainly taught us in many passages of the New Testament. But it is not the leading thought in the chapter now before us. Paul is not speaking of his *sins*, but of his *gains*. He is not occupied with his necessities, as a sinner, but with his advantages as a man—a man in the flesh—a man in the old creation—a Jew—a legalist.

True it is, most blessedly true, that Paul brought all his sins to the cross, and had them washed away in the atoning blood of the divine sin-offering. But, in this noble passage, we see another thing. We see a legalist flinging far away from him his own righteousness, and esteeming it as a worthless and unsightly thing in contrast with a risen and glorified Christ who is the righteousness of the Christian—the righteousness which belongs to the new creation. Paul had sins to mourn over, and he had a righteousness to boast in. He had guilt on his conscience, and he had laurels on his brow. He had plenty to be ashamed of, and plenty to glory in. But the special point to be presented in Phil. 3 : 4-8 is not a sinner getting his sins pardoned, his guilt cleared, his shame covered, but a legalist laying aside his righteousness, a scholar casting away his laurels, and a man abandoning his vain glory, simply because he had found true glory, unfading laurels, and an everlasting righteousness in the Person of a victorious and exalted Christ. It was not merely that Paul, the sinner, *needed* a righteousness, because, in reality, he had none of his own; but that Paul, the Pharisee, *preferred* the righteousness which was revealed to him in Christ, because it was infinitely better and more glorious than any other.

No doubt, Paul, as a sinner, needed, like every other sinner, a righteousness in which to stand before God; but that is not what he is bringing before us in our chapter. We are anxious that the reader should clearly apprehend this point. It is not merely that my sins *drive* me to Christ, but His excellencies *draw* me to Him. True, I have sins and therefore I need Christ; but even if I had a righteousness, I should cast it from me, and gladly hide myself "*in Him*." It would be a positive loss to me to have any righteousness of my own, seeing that God has graciously provided such a glorious righteousness for me in Christ. Like Adam, in the garden of Eden, he was naked, and therefore he made himself an apron, but it would have been a "loss" to him to retain the apron after the Lord God had made him a coat. It was surely better to have a God-made coat than any man-made apron. So thought Adam, so thought Paul, and so thought all the saints of God whose names are recorded upon the sacred page. It is better to stand in the righteousness of God, which is by faith, than to stand in the righteousness of man which is by works of law. It is not only mercy to get rid of our sins, through the remedy which God has provided, but to get rid of our righteousness, and accept instead, the righteousness which God has revealed.

Thus, then, we see that, the standing of the Christian is in *Christ*. "Found in Him." That is Christian standing. Nothing less, nothing lower, nothing different. It is not partly in Christ, and partly in the law—partly in Christ, and partly in ordinances. No; it is "Found in Him." This is the standing which Christianity furnishes. If this be touched, it is not Christianity at all. It may be some ancient *ism*, or some mediæval*ism*, or some modern*ism*; but most surely it is not the Christianity of the New Testament if it be aught else than this, "Found in Him."

We must press this upon the reader. We feel a solemn responsibility resting upon us, at the present moment. We believe we have far more to do than to furnish the necessary *amount* of matter for each month's Magazine. It is not the quantity but the quality that we have to attend to. Our business is not merely to furnish articles for the Magazine, but right articles, necessary articles, profitable articles for our readers. It were a comparatively easy matter to fill a monthly serial such as "Things New and Old." But this would never do. We must keep our eye upon the times in which we live—upon the consciences of our readers. We have to ponder the difficulties of the times, and the necessities of the conscience. We have to look to God to give us the right thing to say to our readers.

We do, therefore, earnestly exhort the reader to look well to this our first point, "In Christ it is we stand." He is our righteousness. He Himself, the crucified, risen, exalted, glorified Christ. Yes; He is our righteousness. To be found in Him is proper Christian standing. It is not Judaism, Catholicism, nor any other *ism*. It is not the being a member of this church, or that church, or the other church. It is to be in Christ. This is the great foundation of true practical Christianity. In a word, this is the standing of the Christian.

THE CHRISTIAN'S OBJECT.

Here again, Christianity shuts up to Christ. "That I may *know* Him," is the breathing of the true Christian. If to be "found in Him" constitutes the Christian's standing, then "to know Him" is the Christian's proper object. The ancient philosophy had a motto which it was continually sounding in the ears of its votaries, and that motto was "know thyself." Christianity, on the contrary, has a loftier motto, pointing to a nobler object. It tells us to know Christ—to make Him our object—to fix our earnest gaze upon Him.

This, and this alone, is the Christian's object. To have any other object is not Christianity at all. Alas! Christians have other objects. And that is precisely the reason why we said, at the beginning of this paper that we desire to hold up the view to our readers. It matters not, in the least, what the object is: if it is not Christ, it is not Christianity. The true Christian's desire will ever be embodied in these words, "That I may know Him, and the power of His resurrection, and the fellowship of his sufferings, being made comfortable unto His death." It is not that I may get on in the world—that I may make money—that I may attain a high position—that I may aggrandize my family—that I may make a name—that I may be regarded as a great man, a rich man, a popular man. No; not one of these is a Christian object. It may be all very well for a man, who has got nothing better, to make such things his object. But the Christian has got Christ. This makes all the difference. It may be all well enough for a man, who does not know Christ as his righteousness. To do the best he can in the way of working out a righteousness for himself; but to a man whose standing is in a risen Christ, the very fairest righteousness that could be produced by human efforts would be an actual loss. So is it exactly in the matter of an object. The question is not, What harm is there in this or that? but, Is it a Christian object?

It is well to see this. We may depend upon it, beloved reader, that one great reason of the low tone which prevails amongst Christians will be found in the fact that the eye is taken off Christ and fixed upon some lower object. It may be a very laudable object for a man of the world—for one who merely sees his place in nature, or in the old creation. But the Christian is not this. He does not belong to this world at all. He is in it, but not of it. "They," says our Lord, "are not of the world, even as I am not of the world" (John 17). "Our citizenship is in heaven"; and we should never be satisfied to propose to ourselves any lower object than Christ. It matters not, in the least, what a man's position may be. He may be only a scavenger, or he may be a prince, or he may stand at any one of the many gradations between these two extremes. It is all the same, provided Christ is his only real object. It is a man's object, not his position, that gives him his character.

Now, Paul's one object was Christ. Whether he was stationary, or whether he travelled; whether he preached the gospel, or gathered sticks; whether he planted churches, or made tents, Christ was his object. By night and by day, at home or abroad, by sea or by land, alone or in company, in of the Spirit" (Rom. 15 : 13), for it is only here that hope finds its sphere of exercise, as it is only in the saints it will receive its full fruition. If God speaks thus uniformly of the varied character of our blessing—whether it be His grace, His love, His life imparted to us, His confidences, His power, His mercy (1 Pet. 1 : 3), etc.—as being so "abundant," it must be because He would impress our hearts with the exuberance of the bounties He has bestowed upon us. And the practical effect of this on our souls should cause us to "joy in God through our Lord Jesus Christ" (Rom. 5 : 11), to draw out all that is within us in true worship, to fit us for closer and deeper fellowship with Himself. "And God is able to make all grace abound toward you; that ye always having all sufficiency in all things, may abound to every good work" (2 Cor. 9 : 8). May it be so, for His Name's sake.

—ARTHUR W. PINK.

---

public or in private, he could say, "One thing I do." And this, be it remembered, was not Paul the laborious apostle, or Paul the raptured saint, but Paul the living, acting, walking, Christian—the one who addresses us in these words, "Brethren, be ye followers together of me." Nor should we ever be satisfied with anything less than this. True, we fail sadly ; but let us always keep the true object before us. Like the schoolboy at his copy, he can only expect to succeed by keeping his eye fixed upon his headline. His tendency is to look at *his own* last written line, and thus each succeeding line is worse than the preceding one. Thus it is in our own case. We take our eye off the blessed and perfect head-line, and begin to look at ourselves, our own productions, our own character, our interests, our reputation. We begin to think of what would be consistent with our own principles, our profession, or our standing, instead of fixing the eye steadily upon that one object which Christianity presents, even Christ Himself.

But some will say, "Where will you find this?" Well, if it be meant, where are we to find it amongst the ranks of Christians, nowadays, it might be difficult indeed. But we have it in the third chapter of the epistle to the Philippians. This is enough for us. We have here a model of the true Christian, and let us ever and only aim thereat. If we find our hearts going after other things let us judge them. Let us compare our lines with the head-line, and earnestly seek to produce a faithful copy thereof. In this way, though we may have to weep over constant failure, we shall always be kept occupied with our proper object, and thus have our character formed ; for, let it never be forgotten, it is the object which forms the character. If money be my object, my character is covetous ; if power, I am ambitious ; if books, I am literary ; if Christ, I am a Christian. It is not, here, a question of life or salvation, but only of practical Christianity. If we were asked for a simple definition of a Christian, we should at once say, a Christian is a man who has Christ for his object. This is most simple. May we enter into its power and thus exhibit a more healthy and vigorous discipleship in this day, when so many, alas! are minding earthly things.

THE CHRISTIAN'S HOPE.

This, our third and last point, is presented in our chapter in a manner quite as characteristic as the other two. The *standing* of the Christian is to be found in Christ ; the *object* of the Christian is to know Christ ; and the *hope* of the Christian is to be like Christ. How beautifully perfect is the connection between these three things! No sooner do I find myself in Christ as my righteousness, than I long to know Him as my object, and the more I know Him, the more ardently shall I long to see Him as He is. Having a perfect righteousness, and a perfect object, I just want one thing more, and that is to be done with everything that hinders my enjoyment of that object. "For our conversation (or citizenship, Phil. 3 : 20) is in heaven ; from whence also we look for the Saviour, the Lord Jesus Christ, who shall change our vile body, that it may be fashioned like unto His glorious body, according to the working whereby He is able even to subdue all things unto Himself."

Now, putting all these things together, we get a very complete view of Christianity. We cannot attempt to elaborate any one of these three points above referred to ; for, it may be truly said, each point would demand a volume to treat it fully. But we would ask the reader to pursue the marvellous theme for himself. Let him rise above all the imperfections and inconsistencies of Christians, and gaze upon the moral grandeur of Christianity as exemplified in the life and character of the model man presented to our view in this chapter. And may the language of his heart be, "Let others do as they will, as for me, nothing short of this lovely model shall ever satisfy my heart." Let me turn away my eye from men altogether, and fix it intently upon Christ Himself, and find all my delight in Him as my righteousness, my object, my hope. Thus may it be with the writer and reader, for Jesus' sake.

"Oh! fix our earnest gaze
So wholly, Lord, on Thee ;
That with Thy beauty occupied,
We elsewhere none may see."

—THINGS NEW AND OLD (Vol. 5).

in the heavenlies in Christ" (Eph. 1 : 3). These "blessings" are based upon God's estimate of the value of Christ's sacrifice of Himself. The abiding worth of that sacrifice is immeasurable and illimitable: as immeasurable as the personal excellency of the Son, as illimitable as the Father's delight in Him. How the nature and extent of those blessings, which accrue to God's elect on the ground of Christ and His finished work, are intimated by the substantives and adjectives employed by the Holy Spirit when describing the profuseness of the Divine bounties which have already been bestowed upon us, and which we shall enjoy forever and forever!

Take first God's *grace*. Not only are we told of the "riches of His grace" (Eph. 1 : 7), and of the "exceeding riches of His grace" (Eph. 2 : 7), but we read that it has "*abounded* unto many," and that we receive "abundance of grace," yea that grace has (Greek) "super-abounded" (Rom. 5 : 15, 17, 21). It is the limitless wealth of divine grace flowing forth and mutliplying itself in its objects. The foundation or moving cause of this is made known in John 1. When the Only-begotten of the Father became flesh and tabernacled here for a season, it was as One who was "*full* of grace and truth," and because we have been made joint-heirs with Him it is written, "And of His *fulness* have all we received, and grace upon grace" (v. 16).

Take again God's *love*. There has been neither reserve nor restraint in the outflow of His love to its loveless and unlovely objects. He has loved His people with an everlasting love (Jer. 31 : 3), and wondrously has He manifested it; for when the fulness of time was come, He sent forth His Son, born of a woman ; yea, He did so love the world as to give His only-begotten Son, "that whosoever believeth in Him should not perish, but have everlasting life"; and therefore do we read of his "*great* love wherewith He loved us" (Eph. 2 : 4). The Greek word which is there translated "great" is rendered "plenteous" in Matt. 9 : 37, and "abundant" in 1 Pet. 1 : 3. O love unmeasured, that passeth knowledge, filling our lives with its unceasing ministrations, ever active in priesthood and advocacy on high, how truly is it "love abundant"!

Our present theme is inexhaustible. Our blessed Lord came here that His people "might have *life*, and that they might have it more *abundantly*" (John 10 : 10). This was first made good when Christ, as the Head of the new creation, the "Beginning of the creation of God" (Rev. 3: 14), breathed on His disciples and said "receive ye the Holy Spirit" (John 20 : 22). It was the risen Saviour communicating His resurrection-life to His own—compare Gen. 2 : 7 for the beginning of the old creation. So too when that same blessed One, Who down here received the Spirit without measure (John 3 : 34), ascended on high as the glorified Man, He baptized His people in the Holy Spirit (Acts 2), and which as the apostle Paul assures Gentile saints "He shed on us *abundantly*" (Titus 3 : 5, 6). Here, once more, is emphasized the profuseness of God's bounties

Consider now His *confidences*. Said the Lord Jesus to His disciples, "Henceforth I call you not servants ; for the servant knoweth not what his lord doeth: but I have called you friends, for *all* things that I have heard of My Father I have made known unto you" (John 15 : 15). There are things which the angels "desire to look into" (1 Pet. 1 : 12), yet have they been made known to us by God's Spirit. What a word is that in Eph. 1 : 8, 9, "Wherein He hath *abounded* towards us in all wisdom and prudence; having made known unto us the mystery of His will"! This may be termed the abundance of His counsels.

Once more, take the exercise and display of His *power*. The apostle prayed that we might know, "What is the *exceeding greatness* of His power to usward, who believe according to the working of His mighty power, which He wrought in Christ, when He raised Him from the dead, and set Him at His own right hand in the heavenlies" (Eph. 1 : 19, 20). Here was the might of God working transcendently in an objective way; its correlative is recorded in Eph. 3 : 20. "Now unto Him that is able to do exceeding abundantly above all that we ask or think, according to the power that worketh *in* us"—clearly this is the highest forth-putting of energy, working subjectively.

In such lavish measure then has God blest His people. As the apostle wrote to the Colossians concerning Him Who is our life, "For in Him dwelleth all the fulness of the Godhead bodily, and *ye are filled full* (complete), in Him" (2 : 9, 10). But it is one thing to know, intellectually, of these bounties of God; it is quite another, by faith, to make them our own. It is one thing to be familiar with the letter of them, it is another to live in the power of and be the personal expression of them.

What shall be our response to such Divine munificence? Surely it is that, "the abundant grace might through the *thanksgiving* of many redound to the glory of God" (2 Cor. 4 : 15). Surely it is that *we* should "*abound in hope* through the power

(Continued on Page 95).

STUDIES IN THE SCRIPTURES

"Search the Scriptures" John 5 : 39

Copyright in all English-speaking Countries.

Editor: Arthur W. Pink, Morton's Gap, Kentucky, U.S.A.
Hon. Agent in England: Mr. A. Winstone, 2, Lennox Villas, Hewlett Road, Cheltenham.
Hon. Agent in Australia: Mr. G. Ardill, The Christian Workers' Depot.
Commonwealth and Reservoir Streets, Sydney.

FREE TO ALL WHO WILL READ IT.

LOVE FOR THE BRETHREN.

On this subject, as on almost every other, the thoughts of God and the thoughts of the natural man are as far apart as the poles, and unless we bow to the teachings of Holy Scripture our ideas thereon will be all wrong. The fact is that we need to abandon our own ideas on this matter and let our thoughts be moulded by the Word of God.

In writing upon "Love for the Brethren" we have in mind *spiritual* love, Divine love. The sad thing is that, today, most of God's people are so unspiritual, they are unable to recognise the manifestations of true brotherly love even when they see it. They are so fleshly, so controlled by that which is merely of nature, that ofttimes they mistake carnal pleasantries and human sentimentality for spiritual love. The truth is, that there is much today which is regarded as the manifestation of Christian love which has no title whatever to that holy name.

It should be remembered that there are worldlings, those who make no profession of being Christians, people who are warm-hearted and sometimes with most unselfish dispositions; people who are ever thinking of others, who would give away almost their last shilling to one in dire need. There are daughters who have, for years, shown an untiring devotion to afflicted parents. There are mothers who have willingly sacrificed most of a life-time's comforts in order to wait on suffering children. Yet, if these same people should, without any genuine conversion, profess the name of Christ, they would not only be received by many a circle of Christians, but would be regarded as exemplars of Christian love and paragons of spirituality. Ah, it is so easy to be deceived if we fail to test everything by the Word of God.

On the other hand, if the average professing Christian attends a "church" or a religious meeting, and no one shakes hands with him or inquires after the state of his health, he at once concludes that such a "church" is cold, and that little or no love is in exercise there. But, my reader, the shaking of one another's hand and talking about 'our aches and pains, are neither evidences of spirituality nor marks of Divine love. And the proof of this is that such customs or courtesies are to be met with among those who make no profession of being Christians; such things occupy a prominent place in worldly gatherings.

John, the apostle of love, begins his third Epistle thus: "The elder unto the wellbeloved Gaius, whom I love in the Truth." What a needed word is this today! One of the present cries of the religious world is to this effect: Though many of us differ in our opinions, let us sink them, and come together in love. In the City of Sydney, on what they called "Good Friday," Presbyterians, Congregationalists, Baptists, Methodists, and others, held a united "Communion" (?) service. Their idea was, If we all come together and express love for each other, what else matters! But *alas* it is love at the *expense* of the Truth: it is not only a burlesque of "love," but a travesty and a mockery when those claiming to be orthodox commune with Modernists and Evolutionists. "The wisdom which is from above is *first* pure, *then* peaceable" (James 3: 17).

Now true Christian love is neither human in its origin, its nature, its characteristics, nor its manifestations. Christian love is neither the 'milk of human kindness' nor mere

(Continued on Page 120).

IMPORTANT NOTICES

Back numbers of the last four years of this magazine are yet obtainable, nicely and strongly bound at 7/6 each, post paid. They will soon be out of print.

Advise promptly of change of address otherwise copies will be lost in the mails.

This Magazine is published as a work of faith and labour of love. The Editor gladly gives his services. It is freely sent to all who will read it. No charge is made for it.

Christians who feel definitely led to do so, may have fellowship with us in this Ministry. Send only *Inter-National M.O.*

CONTENTS.

	Page
Hebrews	98
Gleanings in Exodus	104
Abram's Worship	109
The Willfull King	113

THE EPISTLE TO THE HEBREWS.

17. *Christ Superior to Joshua*: Heb. 4 : 3-10.

There has been so much confusion in the minds of commentators, so many conflicting interpretations of Heb. 4 in the past, that we deem it the more necessary to go slowly, and endeavour to supply full proof of the exposition which we are here advancing. That which appears to have occasioned the most difficulty for many is the statement made at the beginning of v. 3, "For we which have believed do enter into rest," or, more literally, "for we enter into the rest, who believed." Having regarded this verse as setting forth a spiritual rest into which believers now enter, they have altogether failed in their understanding of the second part of v. 1. That sinners do enter into rest upon believing is clear from the promise of Christ in Matt. 11 : 28. That the measure in which this is *enjoyed*, subsequently, will be determined by the degree and frequency with which faith is kept in exercise, we fully allow. But these things are not the subjects of which Paul is treating here in Heb. 4.

Considering that Heb. 4 : 3 speaks of the believer's present rest, many expositors have read this into the opening verse of the chapter, and have regarded its admonition as meaning, Let Christians be on their guard lest, through carelessness and backsliding, they "seem to come short" in their experimental enjoyment of Christ's rest. In other words, they look upon the "rest" of the opening verses of Heb. 4 as signifying *communion* with the Lord. They argue that this *must* be what was in the apostle's mind, for he was not addressing the unconverted, but "holy brethren, partakers of the heavenly calling." With considerable ingenuity they have appealed to the context, the contents of the closing verses of Heb. 3, as supporting their contention. Those who failed to enter into Canaan (which they consider was a figure of the saints' present portion) were not heathen, but Israelites, the covenant-people of God. We must therefore expose the error of this interpretation before proceeding farther.

First, we would remind the reader once more that the apostle was not here writing to Gentile Christians, but to Hebrews, whose circumstances and temptations were peculiar, unique. There was a very real and grave danger menacing them, not so much of interrupting their spiritual fellowship with Christ, but of shaking their faith in Him altogether. The temptation confronting them was the total abandonment of their Christian profession, of their faith in Jesus of Nazareth, now exalted at the right hand of God; and returning to Judaism. This fact must be kept in mind as we take up the study of each chapter of this Epistle. To lose sight of it, courts certain disaster in our interpretation.

Second, while it is true that the apostle's warning in Heb. 3 is taken from the history of Israel, the covenant people of God, it needs to be borne in mind that in connection with Israel there was an election within an election, a spiritual one within the national. Rom. 9 : 7, 8 distinctly affirms, "Neither because they are the seed of Abraham, are they all children: but, In Isaac shall thy seed be called. That is, They which are the children of the flesh, these are not the children of God: but the children of the promise are counted for the seed." Unless this fact be steadily remembered, much misunderstanding and error will ensue. The fact is that Israel *as a Nation*, in O.T. times, is *not* a type of God's elect in this N.T. dispensation (as so many have wrongly supposed), but a figure of *Christendom* as a whole. It was only the spiritual remnant, the elect of God within the nation, who foreshadowed His saints of today.

Third, close attention to what is said of the Israelites in Heb. 3 shows conclusively that they were an illustration not of true Christians out of communion with God, but instead, of nominal professors who were never born again. In proof of this note in 3: 19 it is said of them, "They do alway err in heart;" now though believers err frequently they do not so "alway;" then it is added, "they have not known My ways"—could this be said of the spiritual election of God? Surely not. Again, in v. 11 We are told, "So I sware in My wrath, They shall not enter into My rest:" but God is never wrathful with His own children. Further, in v. 17 it is not simply said that "they died" but that their "carcases fell" in the wilderness, sure proof is such language that they were not children of God, for "precious in the sight of the Lord is the death of His saints" (Psa. 116: 15). Finally, the words of the apostle in 3: 19 admit of no misunderstanding, "So we see that they could not enter in because of unbelief." Thus, they were "children in whom is *no* faith" (Deut. 32: 20).

Now at the beginning of chapter 4 the apostle applies this solemn warning to *test* the profession of those who were in danger of "departing from the living God." First he says, "Let us *therefore* fear." The "therefore" would have no real force if after referring to *un*-believers he should apply their example to warn believers of the tendency and danger of ceasing to have communion with the Lord; in such a case his illustration would be strained and irrevelant. No, when he says, "Let us therefore *fear*" he obviously has in mind the danger of an empty profession, and sets them to a testing of their faith, which test is answered by perseverance. "*Lest* a promise being left us *of* entering into His rest, any of you should seem to come short of it." It was *not* a "rest" of communion into which they *had* entered but were warned against leaving, or failing to enjoy; but instead, a rest that was *promised*. What follows clearly defines "His rest" and confirms what we have said above. It has to do with the Gospel, and not with precepts to saints! And the point insisted on is the presence or absence of *faith*.

The order of thought in Heb. 4, so far as we discern it, is as follows: First, there is a searching exhortation made (v. 1) to all who profess to be Christians, that they should work out their salvation with fear and trembling, and that their walk should be such as to give no one the impression that they "seem" to be departing from Christ. This is followed by a solemn warning (v. 2) that, the mere hearing of the Gospel is not enough; to profit us, it must be received by faith. Third, this is followed by the declaration that only believers enter into the rest of God. In the remainder of our passage the Spirit makes further comment on Psa. 95 and shows (by negative inference) what the "rest" of God is, and how that the believer's entrance into it is yet future.

"For we which believed do enter into rest, as He said, as I have sworn in My wrath, if they should enter into My rest" (v. 3). The relation of these two clauses the one to the other, is denoted by "as He said," what follows being a quotation from the 95th Psa.; their connection with the opening words of the verse being that they supply proof of what is there said. As pointed out in the previous article, "For we enter into the rest, who believed," simply informs us *who* are privileged to enter God's rest, namely, Believers. Corroboration of this is now furnished. Upon the second clause of this verse we cannot do better than quote from Dr. Gouge:

"These words 'as He said' may have a double reference. One immediate, to the words next before. Considered thus, they furnish a proof by the rule of contraries. The force of the argument resteth on that ruled case, which the apostle taketh for grant, v. 6, namely, that 'some *must* enter' into that rest which God hath promised. Hereupon this argument may be made: If some 'must enter,' then believers or unbelievers: But not unbelievers, for God by oath hath protested against them; Therefore believers shall enter."

"The other reference is more remote to the latter part of the former verse. If the first clause of v. 3 be included in a parenthesis, the reference of this unto the former verse will appear to be the more fit. For it showeth unbelievers reap no benefit by the word of promise, because God hath sworn that such shall not enter His rest. The relative 'He' is to God. That which He said was in and by David, in Psa. 95: 11." Upon the words here quoted from the Psa. Dr. J. Brown said, "according to the Hebrew idiomatical elliptical mode of expressing an oath, 'they shall not enter into My rest'."

"Although the works were finished from the foundation of the world" (v.3). It is at this point the real difficulty of our passage begins, due in part to its peculiar grammatical structure. "The passage that follows wears a peculiarly disjointed appearance, and has occasioned perplexity to interpreters. I apprehend that the last clause of the 3rd verse should be disconnected from the words immediately preceding, and should be connected with those which immediately follow. Along with the 4th and 5th verses, it appears to be a kind of explanatory note on the expression, 'the rest of God'. With this explanation the writer is in full accord, indeed, it seems to him impossible to see in the passage any connected sense unless it be taken thus. Continuing to quote from Dr. Brown:

"A promise is left us of entering into *His rest*. The 'rest' of God, in its primary use in the Old Testament scriptures, is descriptive of that state of cessation from the exercise of creating energy, and of satisfaction in what He hath created, into which God is represented as entering on the completion of His six days' work, when in the beginning 'He formed the heavens and the earth, and all their hosts.' In this sense the phrase was plainly not applicable to the subject which the apostle is discussing; but in these words he shows that the phrase, the *rest of God* is not in the scriptures so appropriated to the rest of God after the creation as not to be applicable, and indeed applied, to other subjects.

"Vv. 4, 5, Although the works were finished from the foundation of the world (for He spake in a certain place of the seventh day on this wise, 'And God did rest the seventh day from all His works'), yet in this place again, 'If they shall enter into My rest.' In this way the three apparently disjointed members are formed into one sentence; and that one sentence expresses a sentiment calculated to throw light on the language which the apostle has employed."

"Although the works were finished from the foundation of the world." This sentence is introductory to what immediately follows, in which the apostle, step by step, leads the Hebrews to the consideration of an higher and better rest than ever was enjoyed in this world. There were two "rests" frequently mentioned in the O.T. as special pledges of God's favour: the sabbath and the land of Canaan: the former being styled " the sabbath of rest to the Lord " (Ex. 35: 2), and " the sabbath of the Lord " (Ex. 20: 10); the latter, " the rest which the Lord gave them " (Deut. 12: 9; Josh. 1: 15). In view of these the Hebrews might well say, We have always enjoyed the Lord's sabbath, and our fathers have long occupied Canaan, why then do you speak so much about entering into God's rest? The verses which follow meet this objection, showing that neither of those " rests " was meant by David in Psa. 95, nor by himself here in Heb. 4.

The " rest " to which the apostle was pointing the Hebrews was so blessed, so important, so far surpassing anything that Judaism had known, that he was the more careful they should not be mistaken in connection with *its* nature and character. First, he clears the way for a definition of it by pointing out what it *does not* consist of. He begins with the sabbath which is the first " rest " mentioned in Scripture. Second, he passes on to the rest of Canaan. The rest of the sabbath *did* foreshadow the heavenly rest, and Canaan *was*, in an important sense, a figure of it too; but Paul would turn them from types and shadows to contemplate and have them press forward to the antitype and substance itself.

This reference to " the works " being " finished from the foundation of the world " takes us back to Gen. 2: 1, 2. It is the works of creation and restoration, detailed in Gen. 1. The word "foundation" here carries with it a double thought: stability and beginning. As pointed out in our remarks upon Heb. 1: 10, "foundation" denotes the *fixity* of that which is reared upon it: it is the lowest part of an edifice, upon which the whole of the structure rests. As the " foundation " is the first thing attended to in connection with a building, so this term is used here to denote the *beginning* of this present world-system.

" For He spake in a certain place of the seventh day on this wise, And God did rest the seventh day from all His works " (v. 4). God's rest on that primitive seventh day possesses at least a fourfold significance. First, it denoted His own complacency, His satisfaction in what He had made: " And God saw everything that He had made and, behold, it was *very good*." Second, it was the Creator setting before His creatures an example for them to follow. Why had God taken " six days " to make what is described in Gen. 1? Had He so pleased, all could have been done in one day, yea, in a moment! Obviously it was for the purpose of teaching *us*. Just as the great God employed in works of usefulness, in providing for the temporal necessities of His creatures, so should we be. And just as God was ceased from all the works of those six days and on the seventh day " rested," so must we. Third, that primitive sabbath was the prophetic pledge of the thousand-years' " rest " which this earth shall enjoy during the millennial reign of Christ. Fourth, it was a foreshadowing and earnest of the eternal sabbath, when God shall " rest in His love " (Zeph. 3: 17). For a fuller exposition of " the sabbath " we must refer the reader to Article 58 of the " Gleanings in Exodus."

Perhaps it needs to be added that the words " and God did rest " do not signify, absolutely, that He remained in a state of inactivity. The " rest " of Scripture is never a condition of inertia. The words of our Saviour in John 5 : 17 respecting the sabbath day, "My Father worketh hitherto" in nowise conflict with Gen. 2 : 3. God's " rest " there was from creating new kinds of creatures; what Christ speaks of is His work in doing good to His creatures; it concerns God's providences, which never cease day or night, preserving, succoring, governing His creatures. From this we learn that *our* keeping of the sabbath is not to consist of a state of idleness, but is forebearing from all the ordinary works of the preceding six days. The Saviour's own example in the Gospels teaches us that works of absolute necessity are permissable, and works of mercy proper. Isa. 58 : 13, 14 informs us *how* the sabbath is to be kept. John 5 : 17 linked to Gen. 2 : 3 also contains a hint of the eternal " rest " of heaven : it will be a ceasing from all the carnal works in which we were engaged here, yet it will not be a state of idleness as Rev. 22 : 3 proves.

" And in this again, If they shall enter into My rest " (v. 5). The line of argument which the apostle is here pursuing will the more readily be perceived if due attention be paid to the word " again ". He is proving that there was *another* "rest" of God beside that which followed upon His works of creation. This is evident from the language of Psa. 95, upon which he comments in the next verse. Thus the Holy Spirit warns us that each expression used in Holy Writ must be interpreted strictly in harmony with its context. A great deal of unnecessary confusion had been avoided if expositors heeded this simple but fundamental rule. Take the oft-quoted words of James 5 : 16, " The effectual fervent prayer of a righteous man availeth much." How often the " righteous man " here is regarded as synonymous with "Christian," one who is " righteous " *in Christ*. But such a view ignores the context. This statement is found not in Romans, but James. The epistle of James does not give us the believer's standing, so much as his state. The prayers of a Christian whose ways are *not* " right " before God, " avail" little or nothing. So all through the book of Proverbs the " righteous " man is not regarded there as one who is righteous imputatively, but practically.

Take again the believer's present experimental " rest." There are numbers of passages in the N.T. where the *same* word "rest" is found, but they by no means all refer to the same thing or experience. Each reference needs to be studied in the light of its immediate context, in the light of the particular book in which it is found, (remembering the special theme of that book), and in connection with what is predicated of that "rest." "Come unto Me, all ye that labour and are heavy-laden, and I will give you rest. Take My yoke upon you, and learn of Me; for I am meek and lowly in heart: and ye shall find rest unto your souls " (Matt. 11 : 28, 29). Here it is obvious, almost at first glance, that two distinct " rests " are before us. The first may be designated rest *of conscience*, which the convicted sinner, groaning beneath the intolerable load of his conscious sins, obtains when he casts himself on the mercy of Christ. The second is rest *of soul*, which alas, many professing Christians know very little, if anything, about. It is obtained by *taking* Christ's " yoke " upon us and " learning " of Him.

" Seeing therefore it remaineth that some must enter therein, and they to whom it was first preached entered not in because of unbelief" (v. 6). The first words give intimation of an inference being drawn from what has gone before. In v. 5 God's protestation against unbelievers is recorded, here the apostle infers therefrom that there is a rest for believers to enter into. Since God has made promise of some entering into His rest, then they *must* do so: if not unbelievers, then believers. The words, " it remaineth " here signify " it followeth," for no word of God can fall to the ground. No promise of His can be utterly made void. Though many reap no good thereby, yet others shall be made partakers of the benefit of it. Though the vast majority of the adult Israelites perished in the wilderness, yet Caleb and Joshua entered Canaan.

" And they to whom it was first preached entered not in because of unbelief." The word " preached " here means " evangelise." The same rootword is rendered " gospel " in v. 2. This shows us, first, that God has employed only one instrument in the saving of sinners from the beginning, namely, the preaching of the gospel, cf. Gal. 3: 8. Second, that the demand of the Gospel from those who hear it is *faith*, taking God at His word, receiving with childlike simplicity and gladness the good news He has sent us. Third, that " unbelief " shuts out from God's favour and blessing. In Heb. 11 : 31 we are told, " By faith the harlot Rahab perished not with them that believed not." It was not because the others were Canaanites, heathen, wicked people, but because they *believed not* that they "perished." Solemn warning was this for the Hebrews whose faith was waning.

"Again, He limiteth a certain day, saying in David, Today" (v. 7). It is evident that v. 6 is an incomplete sentence, finished, we apprehend, in v. 11. What follows in vv. 7 to 10 is a parenthesis, and to its consideration we must now turn. The purpose of this parenthesis is to *establish* the principle on which the exhortation is based, namely, that since there is a "rest of God" for believers to enter, and seeing that Israel of old failed to enter therein, it behoves us today to give the more earnest heed to the word of the Gospel which we have heard, and to "labour to enter into that rest, lest any man fall after the same example of unbelief."

"Again He limiteth a certain day, saying in David, Today, after so long a time; as it is said, Today if ye will hear His voice, harden not your hearts" (v. 7). This may be called the text which the apostle goes on to expound and apply. The R.V. rendering of it is much to be preferred: 'He again defineth a certain day, To-day, saying in David, so long a time afterward (even as hath been said before), To day if ye will hear" etc. Having drawn an argument from Psa. 95: 11 to show that the promise of rest which is "left" (v. 1) Christians, is not the same as that mentioned in Gen. 2: 3, the apostle now proceeds to point out that there is another "rest" to be sought after than the land of Canaan—let us not deem the demonstration of this *needless*, lest we be found impugning the wisdom of the Holy Spirit.

The apostle's argument here turns on the word "Today" found in Psa. 95: 7. *This* was what was "limited" or "defined." The "after so long a time" refers to the interval which elapsed after the Israelites perished in the wilderness and the writing of that Psalm, which contained a Divine exhortation for God's people living then. Betwixt Moses and David was a period of five centuries (Acts 13: 20). "The apostle's argument may thus be framed: That rest wherewith men are invited to enter four hundred and fifty years after a rest possessed, is another rest than that which Israel possessed. But the rest intended by David is a rest wherein he inviteth men to enter four hundred and fifty years after Canaan was possessed. Therefore Canaan is not that rest" (Dr. Gouge).

"For if Joshua had given them rest, then would He not afterward have spoken of another day" (v. 8). It is plain that the apostle is here anticipating a Jewish objection, which may be stated thus: Though many of the Israelites which were in the wilderness entered not into Canaan, yet others did; for Joshua conducted their children thither. To obviate this, the apostle proves that the O.T. Scriptures spoke of another "rest" besides that. He does not deny Canaan to be a rest, but he denies that it was the only rest, the rest to be so rested in as no other was to be sought after. The "then would he have not afterward have spoken of another day" is the proof that *Joshua* did not settle God's people in the "rest" which David mentioned.

It is right here that we may discern the point to which the apostle would direct the Hebrews' attention, though to spare their feelings he does not state it explicitly. It was a glorious thing when Joshua led Israel's hosts out of the wilderness, across the Jordan, into the promised land. Truly that *was* one of the outstanding epochs in their national history. Nor would the apostle, directly, deprecate it. Yet if the Hebrews would but meditate for a moment on the *nature* of that rest into which the illustrious successor of Moses led their fathers, they must see that it was very far from being the perfect state. It was only an earthly inheritance. It was filled with enemies, who had to be dispossessed. Its continued tenure was dependent on their own faithfulness to God. It was enjoyed comparatively only a short time. Different far is the rest of God into which the Apostle of Christianity will yet lead His people. Listen to His own words, "In My Father's house are many mansions: if it were not so I would have told you. I go to prepare a place for you. And if I go and prepare a place for you, I will come again, and receive you unto Myself; that, where I am, there ye may be also" (John 14: 2, 3). Here, then, we may see the superiority of Christ over Joshua, as the rest into which He brings His people excells that into which Joshua conducted Israel.

"There remaineth therefore a rest to the people of God" (v. 9). This verse gives the conclusion drawn from the preceding argument. The apostle had shown that the "rest" mentioned by David was neither the rest of the primitive sabbath in Gen. 2 nor the rest of Canaan into which Joshua had conducted the second generation of Israel. *Therefore* there "remaineth a rest to the people of God:" that is, there is some other rest for God's people to look forward to. Thus, the "therefore" here is, first of all, a general inference drawn from all that precedes. A "promise is left" of entering into God's rest (v. 1). That promise must be appropriated, "mixed with faith" in those who hear it (v. 2). Only believers will enter that rest, for God hath sworn that unbelievers shall not enter therein (v. 3). Although there is a rest of God mentioned in Gen. 2 (vv. 3, 4), and although Joshua led Israel into the rest of Canaan (v. 8), yet neither of these "rests" was what is promised Christians (v. 8). Hence, we can only conclude there is *another* "rest" for God's people (v. 9).

That the Christian's perfect "rest" is yet future is clear from the language of v. 11, where the Hebrews were admonished to "labour therefore to enter into that rest." Thus, regarding v. 9, first, as a general conclusion drawn from the whole of the context, we understand it to mean: "Thus it is evident there is a rest for the people of God." These words were designed to *re-assure* the hearts of the Hebrews. In turning their backs on Judaism the "rest" of Canaan was relinquished, but this did not mean that they had, because of their faith in Christ, *ceased to be* "the people of God," nor did it involve the forfeiture of all privileges and blessings. Nay, the apostle had warned them in 3: 6,12,14 that it was impossible to retain the privilege of belonging to the people of God except through faith in Christ. Now he assures them that only for such people was there a rest of God remaining.

Above, we have pointed out that the "therefore" of v. 9 denotes, first of all, that the apostle is here drawing a general conclusion from all he had said in the context. We would now call attention to a more specific inference pointed by that word. It needs to be most carefully observed that in this verse the Holy Spirit employs an entirely different word for "rest" than what he had used in vv. 1,3,4,5, and 8. There the Greek word is rightly rendered "rest," but here it is "sabbatismos" and its meaning has been properly given by the translators in the margin—"keeping of a Sabbath." The R.V. gives in the text itself, "There remaineth therefore a sabbath rest for the people of God."

The purpose of the Holy Spirit in employing this term here is not difficult to discover. He was writing to Hebrews, Jews who had professed to become Christians, to have trusted in the Lord Jesus. Their profession of faith involved them in sore trials at the hands of their unbelieving brethren. They denounced them as apostates from the faith of their fathers. They *disowned* them as the "people of God." But as we have said the apostle here re-assures them that now only believers in Christ had any title to be numbered among "the people" of God." Having renounced Judaism for Christ the question of the "sabbath" must also have exercised them deeply. Here the apostle sets their minds at rest. A suitable point in his epistle had now been reached when this could be brought in: he was speaking of "rest," so he informs them that under Christianity also, "there *remaineth* therefore a sabbath-keeping for the people of God." The *specific* reference in the "therefore" is to what he had said in v. 4: *God did rest* on the seventh day from all His works, *therefore* as believers in Christ are the "people of God" they must rest too.

"There *remaineth* therefore a sabbath-keeping for the people of God." The reference is not to something future, but to what is present. The Greek verb (in its passive form) is never rendered by any other English equivalent than "remaineth." It occurs again in Heb. 10 : 26. The word "remain" signifies "to be left after others have withdrawn, to continue unchanged." Here then is a plain, positive, unequivocal declaration by the Spirit of God: "There remaineth therefore a sabbath-keeping." Nothing could be simpler, nothing less ambiguous. The striking thing is that this statement occurs in the very epistle whose theme is the superiority of *Christianity* over Judaism; written to those addressed as "holy brethren, partakers of the *heavenly* calling." Therefore, it cannot be gainsaid that Heb. 4 : 9 refers directly to *the Christian Sabbath*. Hence we solemnly and emphatically declare that any man who says there is no Christian Sabbath takes direct issue with the *N.T.* scriptures.

"For he that is entered into his rest he also hath ceased from his own works, as God from His" (v. 10). In this verse the apostle expressly defines the *nature* of that excellent rest of which he had been speaking: it is a cessation from our works, as God from His. The object in thus describing our rest is to show that it is not to be found in this world, but is reserved for the world to come. The argument of this verse—its opening "for" denotes that further proof is being supplied to confirm what had been said—is taken from the self-evident principle that rest is not enjoyed till work is ceased from. This world is full of toil, travail and trouble, but in the world to come there is full freedom from all these.

"Thy commandment is exceeding broad" (Psalm 119 : 96). There is a breadth and fullness to the words of God which no single interpretation can exhaust. Just as v. 9 has at least a double application, containing both a general conclusion from the whole preceding argument, and also a specific inference from what is said in v. 4, so is it here. Not only does v. 9, state a general principle which serves to corroborate the apostle's inference in v. 9, but it also has a specific reference and application. The change in number of the pronoun here is not without meaning. In v. 1 he had used a plural, "us," so in v. 3 "we," and again in v. 11 he uses "us;" but here in v. 10 it is "he and his." "It appears to me that it is the rest of Christ from His works, which is compared with the rest of God from His works in creation." (Dr. J. Owen).

The reference to Christ in v. 10 (remember the section begins at 3 : 1 and concludes with 4 : 14-16) completes the positive side of the apostle's proof of His superiority over Joshua. In v. 8 he had pointed out that Jousha *did not* lead Israel into the perfect rest of God; now he affirms that Christ, our Apostle, *has* entered it, and *His* entrance is the pledge and proof that His people shall—"whither the Forerunner is *for us entered*" (Heb. 6 : 20). But more: what is said of Christ in v. 10 clinches our interpretation of v. 9 and gives beautiful completeness to what is there said: "There remaineth therefore a sabbath-keeping to the people of God. *For* He that is entered into His rest, He also hath ceased from His own works, *as* God from His."

Thus, the Holy Spirit here teaches us to view Christ's rest from His work of Redemption as parallel with God's work in creation. They are spoken of as parallel in this respect: the relation which each " work " has to *the keeping of a sabbath!* The opening " for " of v. 10 shows that what follows furnishes a reason *why* God's people, now, must keep the sabbath. That reason invests the sabbath with a fuller meaning than it had in O.T. times. It is now not only a memorial of God's work of creation, and a recognition of the Creator as our Proprietor, but it is also an emblem of the rest which Christ entered as an eternal memorial of His finished work; and inasmuch as Christ ended His work and entered upon His " rest " by rising again on the *first* day of the week, we are thereby notified that the Christian's six workdays must run from Monday to Saturday, and that his sabbath must be observed on Sunday. This is confirmed by the additional fact that the N.T. shows that after the crucifixion of Christ the first day of the week was the one set apart for Divine worship. May the Lord bless what has been before us.

—*Arthur W. Pink*

GLEANINGS IN EXODUS.

65. Sovereign Mercy: Ex. 33 : 18-23.

In studying the varied contents of Ex. 33 we need to remind ourselves of the particular book in which these events are recorded. They are found not in Leviticus, but in Exodus. Everything has been placed by the Holy Spirit in each book of Scripture according to a principle of selection: only that which was in perfect accord with the special design of that book, only that which contributed directly to its theme, is given a place; every thing irrelevant, every thing which did not illustrate or amplify the purpose and character of it, being excluded. This is true not only of the Gospels (see our book " Why Four Gospels?"), where each evangelist was guided by the Inspirer of Scripture to include only that which was in full accord with the particular character in which he was setting forth the Lord Jesus, but it holds good just as truly and strikingly of the four books dealing with the early history of the nation of Israel. It is only by recognising this that we can appreciate the perfections of the Spirit's handiwork, and as we do so, often the key is found which opens the deeper meaning of many a passage.

Genesis is the book wherein we have illustrated the foundation-truth of Divine *election*. This is seen in God's singling out of Abram, and making him the progenitor of His chosen people. Exodus sets forth the blessed truth of Divine *redemption*, God ransoming and emancipating an enslaved people from the house of bondage, and bringing them into a place of nearness to Himself. Leviticus is the book of Divine *worship*, of priestly privileges and exercises, revealing to us the provisions which God has made for His people to approach unto Him. Thus, in these first three books of Holy Writ we have wrought before us that which relates, peculiarly, to each of the Persons in the Godhead. The Father's predestination, the Son's propitiation," the Spirit's inspiration to worship.

As we have just said, the great subject which is unfolded in the book of Exodus is that of *redemption*. This was pointed out by us several times in the earlier articles of this series, but we mention it again because it throws light on the chapter now before us. What we would here call attention to is, that redemption not only procures deliverance from surfdom and slavery, not only brings its favoured objects into a place of nearness to God, but, through the mediation of the Redeemer, it secures a *continuance* of God's grace and mercy while His redeemed are still journeying to the purchased inheritance; and it ensures the *continued* presence of the Lord in the midst of His feeble and failing people. In 33 : 13-16 Moses is found pleading for God's continued presence with them. In v. 17 the Lord answers, "I will do this thing also that thou hast spoken." At the close of our book, we behold the fulfilment of this. After Moses had erected the tabernacle, the visible symbol of Jehovah's presence descended and filled it, and we read, "The cloud of the Lord was upon the tabernacle by day, and fire was on it by night, in the sight of all the house of Israel, throughout *all* their journeys" (40 : 38).

In our last few articles we have been occupied with the love of Moses for his people, and his prevailing intercession on their behalf before God. In this present one we find him a beautiful type of the Lord Jesus. But what we would here emphasise is the fact that the record of this is found in the book of *Exodus,* teaching us that the intercession of Christ on our behalf, with all the blessings which it secures, is the fruit of that *redemption* which He has wrought out for His people. Now as we have seen, the first great blessing which the prayer of Moses obtained for his people was the averting of God's consuming wrath (32 : 10, 14). The second grand privilege his supplications won for them—on the ground of having *himself* found favour in the eyes of God—was the securing of Jehovah's continued presence with them (32 : 12-17). Keeping these things in mind, let us now turn to the seventh and last recorded thing in Ex. 32 and 33—compare the second paragraph in the preceding article.

"And he said, I beseech Thee, show me Thy glory" (v. 18). Our pen falters as we take up such a verse as this, for what sinful creature is competent to write upon such an exalted theme as the glory of God? Nevertheless, some blessed thoughts are suggested by this request of Moses. First of all, contemplating it in the light of the book in which it is found, are we not taught thereby that this is both the longing of the redeemed and the goal of their redemption—to behold the glory of God! That this longing is yet to be fully realised, that this wondrous goal will be reached. we know from the last chapter but one of Holy Writ, for of the Eternal City we read, "And I saw no temple therein, for the Lord God Almighty and the Lamb are the temple of it. And the city had no need of the sun, neither of the moon, to shine in it: for the *glory* of God did lighten it, and the Lamb is the light thereof" (Rev. 21 : 22, 23).

"And he said, I beseech Thee, show me Thy glory." Pondering this verse next in the light of its immediate context, we are shown what is the sure product of intimate fellowship with God. The great Jehovah had condescended to draw very near to the one who had separated himself from evil, for we are told, "the Lord spake unto Moses face to face, as a man speaketh unto his friend" (v. 11). And what was the consequence of this upon Moses? Not only did he have freedom in supplicating His grace, but there was a holy longing to know more of Himself. Such is ever the outflow of real and close communion with God: the more we know of Him, the more we desire to know. The closer God deigns to draw near to His people, the more constrained are they to cry, "Lord, lift Thou up the light of Thy countenance upon us" (Psa. 4 : 6).

"And he said, I beseech Thee, show me Thy glory." If the connection between this and the previous verse be noted, we are taught here another valuable lesson on prayer, one which we do well to take to heart. In the previous verse we read, "And the Lord said unto Moses, I will do this also that thou hast spoken: for thou hast found grace in My sight, and I know thee by name." Twice Moses had petitioned Jehovah: first not to consume His people; then, to beg His continuance in their midst. Each of these supplications had been graciously granted. Emboldened by his success, instead of being content therewith, Moses presents (we may well say) a still greater petition. And, as the Lord's response denotes, He was not displeased at his servant's importunity. Oh to remember in prayer that "We are coming to a *King,*" then let us *"large* petitions with us bring." It is thus that we *honour* Him.

"And He said, I will make all My goodness pass before thee" (v. 19). How striking to learn here that God's "glory" is His "goodness," His "goodness" His "glory." And what is the goodness of the Lord? Ah, who is capable of returning answer: human definitions are worthless. Shall we say that His "Goodness" is what He *is* in Himself, the sum of His personal excellencies? But has not the Lord Himself answered our question, and fulfilled His promise to Moses when He declared, "The

Lord, The Lord God, merciful and gracious, long-suffering, and abundant in goodness and truth, Keeping mercy for thousands, forgiving iniquity and transgression and sin, and that will by no means clear the guilty; visiting the iniquity of the fathers upon the children" (34: 6, 7).

"And I will proclaim the name of the Lord before thee" (v. 19). Was not this the renewal and confirmation of what He had announced at the beginning, when, at the burning bush, He first called Moses? Moses had asked, "When I come unto the children of Israel, and shall say unto them, The God of your fathers hath sent me unto you; and they shall say unto me, *what is His name?* What shall I say unto them?" He made answer, "I am that I am: and He said, Thus shalt thou say unto the children of Israel, I AM hath sent me unto you;" and then He added, "Thus shalt thou say unto the children of Israel, The Lord God of your fathers, the God of Abraham, the God of Isaac, and the God of Jacob, hath sent me unto you; *this is My name forever,* and this is My memorial unto all generations" (Ex. 3 : 13-15).

"And will be gracious to whom I will be gracious, and will show mercy on whom I will show mercy" (v. 19). These words bring before us one of the most precious truths found in Scripture for the comfort of God's people, yet is it one that is little understood to-day. In 2 Tim. 2 : 15 the servant of God is bidden, "Study to show thyself approved unto God, a workman that needeth not to be ashamed, *rightly dividing the word of truth."* But how few "rightly divide" between the *grace* of God and the *mercy* of God! How many regard them as being virtually synonymous. How much we lose by failing to distinguish between things that differ, by confusing in our thoughts things which are perfectly distinct. Scripture never confuses the grace and mercy of God, and it is to our deep loss if we do so.

The *order* in which these two attributes of God are here mentioned supplies the key to the distinction between them: "mercy" comes in after the "grace" of God. Why is this? Because mercy is the wondrous provision of God to meet the desperate needs of a people who have failed to respond to His grace. And *this* is what is so blessedly brought out here in Ex. 33. From Egypt to Sinai God had dealt with Israel on the ground of pure *grace.* In themselves they were no better than the Egyptians, yet had God, in His sovereign benignity, brought them out of the house of bondage, conducted them through the Red Sea, separated them unto Himself, supplied their every need in the wilderness.

But how had the people requited such favours and blessings? They had revolted against Him, they had repudiated Him, they had set up an idol in His place. Was, then, their case hopeless? True they had "mourned," stripped themselves of their ornaments, and bowed in worship before the symbol of His manifested presence by the Tent. But could a God whose favours had been so lightly esteemed go on with them any further?

As we have seen, the typical mediator had interceded on behalf of the people who had sinned so heinously. And now it was that the Lord made one of the most blessed revelations of His character to be found anywhere in Holy Writ. Something was here made known of God's nature which had never before been revealed in its real depths, namely, His *mercy.* It is true we have mention of that precious word in the book of Genesis, but the full interpretation of its meaning is not there discovered. It was here in Ex. 33 that this deep and blessed spring in God's Being was made manifest— so rich, so full, so blessed. Man's extremity was God's opportunity. The Divine outflow of *grace* had been abused, His righteous law had been broken, the relation entered into by the Sinaitic covenant (Ex. 24) had been disrupted by the rebellion of Israel. Now, "mercy" sovereign and absolute, was the resource of Him who retires into Himself and acts from Himself; only by the exercise of *mercy* could sinning Israel be extricated from their merited doom.

As we have said above, from the time when Jehovah first took up His enslaved people in the land of Pharoah, till the waters gushed out of the smitten rock at Rephidim, all was a stream of pure grace, that is, free gifts, Divine favours to a people who had no worthiness or merits of their own. But here in Ex. 33 Israel were given cause to praise God on an altogether different ground, and from this time onwards we find that ground the great theme of Israel's songs—" O give thanks unto the Lord, for He is good: for His *mercy* endureth forever " (Psa 106 : 1). In proof of this contrast, note the contents of Psa. 105 and 106. Let the reader turn to them and mark carefully how that in Psa. 105, which also opens with " O give thanks unto the Lord," that the *grace*-history of Israel is taken up, beginning with Jehovah's dealings with the patriarchs (v. 9), and recounting what God had done for their descendants, till Rephidim was reached. In v. 41 we read, " He opened the rock, and the waters gushed out," and there the Psalmist stops. It will be observed that the word " mercy " does not occur in it a single time.

Now let the reader turn to Psalm 106, where we have the *mercy*-history of Israel's journeyings. Observe how frequently this Psalm makes mention of Israel's sins:—their unbelief (v. 7), their impatience (v. 13), their lusting (v. 14), their envy of Moses (v. 16), their idolatry (v. 19), their murmuring (v. 25), their unfaithfulness (v. 28), their provoking the Lord (v. 33), their disobedience (v. 34), their wickedness (vv. 35, 37). As v. 43 summarises it, "Many times did He deliver them; *but* they provoked Him with their counsel." Thus did Israel evilly requite the wondrous grace of God. What then? Did He annihilate them? Well He might have done so. But instead, we are told, "And He remembered for them His covenant, and repented according to the multitude of His *mercies*" (v. 45)!

From Sinai and onwards Israel's songs never recounted God's *grace*. No, it was too late for that after the golden calf had been set up. His grace had been abused, flung back, as it were, into His face. His law had been violated, His covenant broken. But His *mercy* "endureth forever." Hallelujah! Mercy, then, is that blessed quality of God's nature which meets the deep and dire needs of those who have sinned against His grace. The background of God's grace is our emptiness, poverty, worthlessness. The foil for His mercy is our sinfulness, wickedness, vileness. That is why we are bidden to come to the Throne of *Grace* that we may "obtain *mercy* and find grace to help in time of need" (Heb. 4: 16).

The distinction just drawn above serves to explain what is found in the opening salutation of the N.T. epistles. We would urge the reader to consult for himself each passage now to be referred to. In Rom. 1: 7, 1 Cor. 1: 1, 2, 2 Cor. 1: 1, 2, Gal. 1:3, Eph. 1: 2, Phil. 1:2, Col. 1: 2, 1 Thess. 1: 1, 2, 2 Thess. 1: 2, each Christian company is saluted with "*grace* be unto you." But when we turn to 1 Tim. 1: 2, 2 Tim. 1: 4, Titus 1: 4 we find "mercy" is added: "grace, *mercy* and peace." Why is this? We know of no writer that has ever advanced what we believe is the true answer. But does not the history of Israel supply the key? Alas, has not history repeated itself? has not the course of Christendom corresponded to that of Israel? Has not Christendom, too, *abused* the wondrous "grace" of God? And has He not, most blessedly, fallen back upon His *mercy* in His dealings with us?

It should be carefully observed that when we come to the epistles of Timothy (see 1 Tim. 4: 1, 2 Tim. 3: 1) we are brought down to the *closing* days of this dispensation. Ah, were it not for that mercy which "endureth forever" where would God's unfaithful, backslidden, and lukewarm people be! Still more significant is it to note that the salutation of Jude's epistle, the *last* one (treating of conditions in the end-time) *opens* with "*mercy* unto you." Verily, "mercy" *is* our last hope. Nor does it fail us. Yea, we are "looking for the *mercy* of our Lord Jesus Christ unto eternal life" (Jude 21)—the reference being to His second advent: compare 2 Tim. 1: 18.

Oh Christian readers, have our *own* souls understood and apprehended this glorious attribute of mercy in which our God is so "rich" (Eph. 2: 4)? Have we not often confused it with His grace, and thereby failed to perceive its distinctive glory and blessedness? Have we not only broken His holy law again and again, but despised His very grace? What then is left but to fall back upon His *mercy*, which very attribute supposes this is our last resource! Well aware are we that this very truth may be misappropriated and misused, but for those whose hearts *desire* to please and glorify God, it is unspeakably precious. The mercy of God can only be truly apprehended by those who have been made to feel how grievously they have sinned against His grace. It is such who will welcome the invitation to come boldly ("freely") to the Throne of Grace, that there they may "obtain mercy" for the unrequited grace of yesterday, and there also find fresh supplies of grace for the needs of today.

In perfect accord with all that has been said above, is the *first* mention of God's "mercy" in Holy Writ: "And while he lingered, the men laid hold upon his hand, and upon the hand of his wife, and upon the hand of his two daughters; the Lord being *merciful* unto him: and they brought him forth and set him without the city" (Gen. 19: 16). This regarded Lot, and it is blessed to note his own acknowledgment of it, "Behold now. Thy servant hath found grace in Thy sight, and Thou hast magnified Thy mercy, which Thou hast showed unto me in saving my life" (v. 19). Yes, he had "found grace" in God's sight, for he was one of the Lord's people (2 Peter 2: 7). But O how basely had he treated that grace! He had not only forsaken Abraham, but had settled down in wicked Sodom. The *only* hope for such an one was mercy, and this God had "magnified."

It only remains for us now to point out how that in Ex. 33: 19 the Lord emphasises His *sovereignty* in the exercise of this attribute, saying, "I will show mercy on whom *I will* show mercy." Necessarily it must be so. Mercy is that which none can claim as a right: might they justly do so, it would cease to be *mercy*. Hence God reserves to Himself the right to extend it to whom He pleases, and to withold it from whom He pleases. To this principle the apostle, when treating at length of the sovereignty of God, called attention in Rom. 9: 18. Nor is God unrighteous in this. None is wronged if "mercy" be witheld. God is therefore free to act as He pleases. "Is it not lawful for Me to do what I will with Mine own?" (Matt. 20: 15).

"And He said, thou canst not see My face: for there shall no man see Me, and live" (v. 20). We must ever distinguish between God's absolute character and His relative making known of Himself. In His absolute character and essence no man hath seen nor can see God, for He is "Spirit" (John 4: 24), and therefore unseeable. But relatively He has made Himself known to us by His many names and titles, by the manifestation of His many and varied attributes, and more fully and blessedly still, by and in the person of Christ. Yet it remains true that, absolutely, God is the invisible God, "dwelling in the light which no man can approach unto; whom no man hath seen, nor can see" (1 Tim. 6: 16). In O.T. times, when God made Himself known to Abraham, Moses, Joshua, Gideon it was the second Person of the Trinity, yet not in His essential Deity, but in human or angelic form. No human creature is capable of perceiving the infinite and eternal Spirit in all His majesty and ineffable glory.

"And the Lord said, Behold there is a place by Me, and thou shalt stand upon a rock: And it shall come to pass while My glory passeth by, that I will put thee in a clift of the rock, and will cover thee with My hand while I pass by: And I will take away Mine hand, and thou shalt see My back parts: but My face shall not be seen" (vv. 21-23). This is most blessed. In order for sinful man to be able clearly to contemplate the Divine perfections of an infinitely righteous, holy God, it is necessary that he should be put into a place of security and peace. This God *has*, in His infinite condescension and grace, provided for us. To faith that "rock" is Christ. Augustus Toplady beautifully represented this in his well-known hymn,

"Rock of Ages cleft for me,
Let me hide myself in Thee."

Or, as we prefer to sing it,

"Rock of Ages cleft for me,
Grace hath hid me safe in Thee."

God graciously permitted Moses to have an impression and perception of His presence such as he was capable of. A beautiful illustration of what we have in view here, we borrow from Dr. Cuyler's work on the Holy Spirit:—

"I was talking about Christ to an impenitent neighbour the other day. He said 'Why can't I feel about Him as you do? I have read the Bible a good deal—I have heard a good deal of preaching, yet I can't get up any enthusiasm in regard to this Saviour that you talk so much about.' I said to him, 'You make me think of my visit to the White Mountains some years ago. We were told that there was a wonderful piece of natural statuary there—a man's face chiselled out of a granite cliff. When we went to see it, we found what we supposed was the cliff, but there was no appearance of human features—no form or comeliness such as we had been told of. We were about to turn away disappointed when a guide came along and said. 'You are not looking from the right point.' He led us up the road a few rods, and then said, 'Turn and look!' We did so, and there was the face as distinct as any of ours, though of gigantic size. Until we reached the right spot we could see only a jagged rock, and not a symmetrical face. The vision of the form and comeliness *depended upon the angle of observation*. And it is so with you, my friend. Come with me under the shadow of the Cross. Come there as a penitent sinner. Look there upon that visage so marred more than any man. Realize that the mangled, thorn-crowned Sufferer is dying for you, and you will see in Him a beauty that will ravish your soul."

By linking together a clause out of v. 21 with what is stated in v. 22 we get a beautifully-complete type of the believer's absolute security. First, "thou shalt stand upon a rock." This at once reminds us of, "By faith we have peace with God through our Lord Jesus Christ; by whom also we have access by faith into this grace wherein we *stand*" (Rom. 5: 1, 2). Second, mark well the words, "*I will put thee* in a clift of a rock," for no sinner of himself can do this. Blessed figure was it of an elect soul being "*created in* Christ Jesus" (Eph. 2: 10). Third, "and will cover thee with My hand." "He that dwelleth in the secret place of the most High shall abide *under the shadow of the Almighty*" (Psa. 91: 1). Not only is the believer in Christ, but he is also protected by the Father's hand (John 10: 29). Finally, observe it is only as we are in the "clift of the rock" that God's "goodness" passes before us (v. 22). His "glory" can only come into view as the flesh is altogether *hidden*; that is, as we are made "new creatures in Christ."

"And I will take away Mine hand, and thou shalt see My back parts: but My face shall not be seen" (v. 23). This was in keeping with the Legal economy: the law had only "a shadow of good things to come, and not the very image of the things" (Heb. 10 : 1). But how blessed the contrast now: "For God who commanded the light to shine out of darkness, hath shined in our hearts, to give the light of the knowledge of the glory of God in *the face* of Jesus Christ" (2 Cor. 4 : 6)! O may Divine grace enable both writer and reader to walk worthy of such a God, and such a revelation of Himself (1 Tim. 3 : 16) as He has now made to us in and through Christ (John 14 : 9).

—Arthur W. Pink.

5.—ABRAM'S WORSHIP.
—Gen. 12 : 7, 8.

In our last article we pondered the obedience of Abram, his ultimate response to the terms of that call which he had received from the Lord in Ur of Chaldea. Three things were then before us: first, his making for Sichem, where grew the oak of Moreh. This tells us, in figure, that it is only as the believer bows his shoulder and submits to the yoke of Christ, that he is able to learn of Him who is meek and lowly in heart, and through such instruction, to be strengthened with might by His Spirit in the inner man. Second, we sought to point out the spiritual significance of the inspired statement, "And the Canaanite was then in the land." This speaks of the presence of the Enemy, ready to oppose our progress along the path of faith; yet, powerless to do a thing against the Christian while his heart and ways are right before God. Third, we took up briefly the announcement, "And the Lord appeared unto Abram." This intimates that the Christian is not to be occupied with the power of Satan, but to keep his eyes steadfastly fixed upon the Lord.

"And the Lord appeared unto Abram" (Gen. 12 : 7). Let us bear in mind that Abram is here to be looked at as a typical and representative character, "the father of all them that believe." What then is the N.T. parallel to this? Or, to put it another way, What is there in the present experiences of the Christian which corresponds to this gracious and wondrous blessing vouchsafed unto Abram? Do, *you,* my reader, know what it means for the Lord, today, to "appear" unto one of His own? Or does such language strike you as savouring of mysticism? Alas for your state of soul, if such be the case. You may reply, "But we are living in an entirely different dispensation from Abram's, everything now is altered." But God has not altered! Has He not said, "for I am the Lord, I change not" (Mal. 3 : 6)? Do you suppose that He is less willing to manifest Himself to His own now that His beloved Son has told out the wonders of His love, than He was in those early days of the unfolding of His counsels of grace? Surely not.

"He that hath My commandments, and keepeth them, he it is that loveth Me: and he that loveth Me shall be loved of My Father, and I will love him, and will *manifest Myself* to him" (John 14 : 21). These are the words of Christ to His beloved people, and they are plain enough, are they not? They speak of our blessed Lord drawing near to one of His own and revealing Himself to that soul in the precious intimacies of His love. Ah, but note well the first part of this verse: observe the *character* of the one to whom He thus, "manifests" Himself. It is not to the self-willed and self-pleasing one, who evidences little or no concern as to whether or not his life is pleasing to Him whose name he professes. Nor is it to one who is walking arm in arm with those who despise and reject the Saviour. No indeed, no such blessed promise is placed on record concerning them.

The words of our Lord are too plain to be mistaken: "he that *hath* My commandments (committed to memory, stored up in the heart as the welcome intimations of His will, frequently meditates thereon), and *keepeth* them"—who is not merely a hearer, but also a "doer of the Word." This is the one who really loves Christ, who is loved by Him in return (not only with a love of compassion, but also a love of complacency—finding His *delight* in such an one) and to whom He "manifests" Himself. It was thus with Abram. It was when he had obeyed the "commandments" of Jehovah, that He "appeared unto him" again! Let those murmur who will against the so-called *legality* of this teaching—they do but make manifest a will which is not yet subdued and a heart that is not broken before God.

Do we not have a parallel passage in that oft-quoted but little understood word of Christ's in Rev. 3: 20, "Behold, I stand at the door, and knock: if any man hear My voice, and open the door, I will come in to him, and will sup with him, and he with Me?" Does not the "I will *come in to him,*" correspond to the " and will manifest Myself to Him" of John 14: 21? And do not the introductory and qualifying words "*if* any man *hear* My voice and will open the door" remind us very pointedly of the "he that hath My commandments and keepeth them?" Ah, dear brethren and sisters, does not what has just been before us supply the key to our *lack* of such an experience as Abram was favoured with! The "manifestation" of Christ to the soul should be a daily experience, and if it is not, our hearts ought to be deeply exercised before Him. If we are not the regular recipients of such "appearings" of the Lord, it must be because we have wandered from the path of obedience!

"And the Lord appeared unto Abram, and said, Unto thy seed will I give this land" (v. 7). This was a decided advance on what is recorded in the opening verse of our chapter. There we read, " The Lord had said unto Abram, Get thee out of thy country and from thy kindred, and from thy father's house, unto a land that I will *shew* thee." Here Jehovah declared, "unto thy seed will I *give* this land." This also illustrates a principle in God's dealings with His own. This was the Divine *reward* for Abram's faith and obedience in leaving Chaldea and journeying into Canaan. In the revelations which God makes of Himself, and in the exercises of His grace toward His people, He acts upon the principle of "first the blade, then the ear, then the full corn in the ear." Or, as Prov. 4: 18 expresses it, "The path of the just is as the shining light, that shineth *more and more* unto the perfect day." God's commands are not grievous, and in keeping of them "there is great reward" (Psa. 19: 11).

"And there builded he an altar unto the Lord, who appeared unto him. And he removed from thence unto a mountain on the east of Bethel, and pitched his tent, having Bethel on the west, and Hai on the east: and there he builded an altar unto the Lord, and called upon the name of the Lord" (vv. 7, 8). This recounts the *response* made by Abram to the Lord's "appearing" unto him. Five things are to be noted. First, he built an altar. Notice carefully the word in italics—" and *there* builded he an altar." The Holy Spirit has thus called our attention to and emphasised the place at which Abram had now arrived. No mention was made of his having an "altar" in Haran. Of course not! for the " altar " speaks of worship, and no dweller at Halfway House can really be a worshipper. God is Spirit and they that worship Him "must worship Him in Spirit and in truth." By noting carefully our context we are shown what, ever, *precedes* true worship.

Worship can only proceed from one who has been Divinely called, regenerated, as Abram had been. The natural man can no more worship God than he can create a world. Go through the forms of it he may, yea, many do; but of them it stands written, " This people draweth nigh unto Me with their mouth, and honoureth Me with their lips; but their heart is far from Me. But in vain they do worship Me, teaching for doctrines the commandments of men" (Matt. 15: 8, 9). Again; worship can only proceed from one who has separated himself from the world and subordinated to God the claims of the flesh. That is why Moses was requested to go unto Pharoah and say "Now let us go three days' journey into the wilderness, that we may *sacrifice* to the Lord our God" (Ex. 3: 18). Not until God has the first place in our affections do we ever really worship Him. Again; worship can proceed only from one who has recognised and responded to the claims of Him who has called us, i.e., entered the path of obedience: "Behold, to obey is better than sacrifice and to harken than the fat of rams" (1 Sam. 15: 22)—the former *must* precede the latter.

Yet again, worship can only proceed from one to whom the Lord has "appeared." It is most important that we should observe the connection between the two things mentioned here in v. 7. Real-occupation with Him, the beholding (with the eyes of faith) the King in His beauty, is what alone draws out the adoration of the heart. It is only as we are enjoying the intimacies of His love that we are bowed before Him in true worship. When there is an experimental estrangement between the heart and God, we cannot "delight" ourselves in Him (Psa. 37: 4), and then praise ceases. This order is unchanging: the "appearing" of the Lord before us, and then the " building of an altar " unto Him.

"And he removed from thence unto a mountain." This was the second response made by Abram to the Lord's "appearing" unto him. We believe there is a double force to what is here suggested by the " mountain." First, it is a striking figure of those "heavenly places" to which the Christian belongs. Israel's portion is an earthly one; not so ours: we are "holy brethren, partakers of the *heavenly* calling" (Heb. 3: 1). It was *this* company that Abram represented: not the earthly, but the heavenly people of God, of whom it is written "for *our* citizenship is in heaven; from whence also we look for the Saviour, the Lord Jesus Christ" (Phil. 3: 20). Well may we exclaim, "Blessed be the God and Father of our Lord Jesus Christ, who hath blessed us with all spiritual blessings *in the heavenlies* in Christ" (Eph. 1: 3).

Thus we may admire the beautiful accuracy of our typical picture. As soon as Abram had taken his place in the path of obedience, and the Lord had "appeared" to him, the *mountain* is the very next thing which is seen. The first "appearing" of the Lord to Abram in Ur was for the purpose of calling him out from the place he was in, and to bring him into the path of obedience. Now that Abram was in that path, the Lord revealed Himself again, this time for communion—speaking to him, unfolding His wondrous counsels of grace. Ah, we are called to enjoy fellowship with a risen and exalted Saviour: "God is faithful, by whom ye were called, unto the fellowship of His Son Jesus Christ our Lord" (1 Cor. 1: 9); but such fellowship is only enjoyed by *seeking* "those things which are above, where Christ sitteth on the right hand of God" (Col. 3: 1).

Experimentally the "mountain" speaks of elevation of spirit, soaring above the low level in which a perishing world lies. It tells of our affection being set upon things above. It denotes a heart detached from this scene, attracted and attached to Him who has passed within the veil. It is very striking and most blessed to note in this connection how often, in the four Gospels, the Lord Jesus is seen "in the mount." It was in the mount that He gave to His disciples His first connected discourse (Matt. 5—7). It was from the mount He fed the hungry multitudes (John 6: 3-13). It was to the mount He retired for prayer (Mark 6: 46). It was in the mount He spent His nights with God (John 7: 53, 8: 1). It was on the mount He was transfigured (Matt. 17: 1, 2). It was on the mount that He gave his wondrous prophetic discourse (Matt. 24-25). It was from the mount He ascended (Acts 1: 9, 12). It is to the mount He will return: "And His feet shall stand in that day upon the Mount of Olives" (Zech. 13: 4).

Yes, Christ was distinctively the Man of the Mount. And if *we* are really "following" *Him*, if like Abram we have left the world behind and are in communion with the Lord, we shall be dwellers on the mountain too. Is it not written, "But they that wait upon the Lord shall renew their strength; they shall *mount up* with wings as eagles" (Isa. 40: 31)! Here is the secret of deliverance from the Slough of Despond. And how may this "mountain" experience be *maintained*? Is such a thing possible? We believe it is, and at it we should constantly aim, not being content with anything that falls short of it. The answer to our question is revealed in what immediately follows.

"And pitched his tent, having Bethel on the west, and Hai on the east." This is the third thing recorded in Abram's response to the Lord's "appearing" unto him. What is here in view is in perfect accord with the spiritual significance of the "mountain," whether we view that as a figure of the heavenlies of which the Christian's calling has made him a partaker, or whether we regard it as pointing to that elevation of spirit which ever characterises one who is in fellowship with the Most High. The "tent" is, of course, the symbol of the "pilgrim," of him who is a "stranger" here, of him who has no home, no abiding-place in this scene which has cast out from it the Lord of Glory. Abram never built him an "house" in Canaan: he was but a sojourner, and his "tent" was the evidence, the proof, the demonstration of it.

In Heb. 11 it is said of Abram, "By faith he sojourned in the land of promise, as in a strange country, dwelling in tabernacles (tents) with Isaac and Jacob, the heirs with him of the same promise: For he looked for a city which hath foundations, whose builder and maker is God" (vv. 9-10). Mark how the second of these verses supplies the key to the conduct of our patriarch in the previous one. *His* heart was set upon things above; therefore, having food and raiment, he was content to tarry in a tent down here. In this respect there was a marked contrast between Abram and his worldly-minded nephew. Of him we read, "And Lot lifted up his eyes and *beheld all the plain* of Jordan, and it was well watered everywhere . . . . Then Lot chose him all the plain of Jordan" (Gen. 13: 10, 11). Lot started in a "tent" (13: 12), but he soon forsook it for an "house" as Gen. 19: 1, 2, clearly shows. Again we would remind ourselves that Abram is the father of all them that believe, therefore are his children exhorted as follows, "Dearly beloved, I beseech you *as strangers and pilgrims*, abstain from fleshly lusts, which war against the soul" (1 Pet. 2: 11).

From this point onwards two things characterised Abram, his "tent" and his "altar." In addition to the present reference in Gen. 12: 8, observe the mention of them again in 13: 3, 4, "And he went on his journeys from the south even to Bethel, unto the place where his tent had been at the beginning, between Bethel and Hai; unto the place of the altar;" and again in 13: 18 "Then Abram removed his tent, and came and dwelt in the plain of Mamre, which is in Hebron, and built there an altar unto the Lord." Observe too that in each of these three passages the "tent" is mentioned before the "altar." This should speak loudly to our hearts: we cannot truly and acceptably worship God on high, unless we are walking as "strangers and pilgrims" here below. Ah, is it not at this very point that we may detect so much sad failure in ourselves and in our fellow-Christians? It is easy to *sing* "I'm a pilgrim and I'm a stranger," but do our *lives* witness to the fact? Does our daily conduct make it evident that we *are* "partakers of the heavenly calling?" Do our manners, our ways, our speech, make it plain to all around us that *"our citizenship is* in heaven?" Oh, how much empty profession there is in these degenerate times!

Ah, right here, my reader, we have the simple explanation of why it is that a "mountain" experience is so little maintained by us. We descend to the plains, we come down to the level of the unregenerate, we set our affection upon things below, and in consequence, we become "conformed to this world." We have been "chosen out of the world" (John 15: 19), "translated into the kingdom of God's dear Son" (Col. 1: 13), begotten unto a heavenly inheritance (1 Pet. 1: 3, 4). Shall we then, in a practical way, *deny* all this and be like him of whom Paul wrote, "Demas hath forsaken me, having *loved* this present world" (2 Tim. 4: 10)? Shall we now find our enjoyments in a world that crucified our Redeemer, and which still hates Him?

We *are* "strangers" here, and we are called upon to conduct ourselves as such. We no longer belong to the world, but to Him who has redeemed us with His precious blood. The world has no claims upon us, rather is it under a deep debt of obligation to those who are "the salt of the earth"—serving as a preservative, a check to its going to utter corruption. Because we are strangers, we are also "pilgrims," passing through this scene unto "a better Country." This fact should mould every detail of our lives. An Englishman who was journeying through China or some other land, would at once be marked as a foreigner. His dress, his habits, his speech, everything about him, would at once differentiate him. So it should be with the Christian. That Englishman would take no part in the politics of China, nor would he interfere with its national institutions or religion. If he did his duty, he would be loyal to his majesty, King George, attend to his own affairs, be satisfied with a stranger's portion, and long for the time of his home-going. Such are the qualities which should mark God's people as "strangers and pilgrims" here.

Of Abram and his fellow-sojourners it is recorded that they "*confessed*" that they were strangers and pilgrims on the earth" (Heb. 11: 13), and concerning them it is said, "But now they desire a better country, that is an heavenly: wherefore God is not ashamed to be called their God" (v. 16). Of how many of His people on earth today must God be "ashamed!" Only too often *they* are "ashamed," ashamed to confess that they *are* "strangers and pilgrims" on earth. They shrink from being known as "a peculiar people" (Titus 2: 14). They are afraid that their godless associates will deem them queer, straitlaced, fanatical, etc. So they compromise, hide their light under a bushel, come down to the level of the world, and, in many things, conform to their ways. *That* is why the "mountain" experience is not maintained.

Let us observe next *where* Abram pitched his tent: "having Bethel on the west, and Hai on the east." Nothing in Holy Writ is meaningless. Its minutest details have a meaning and message for us, if our hearts are open to receive then. "For *whatsoever* things were written aforetime were written for our learning" (Rom. 15 : 4). What then is the lesson to be learned from the *location* of Abram's tent? Bethel means "the house of God," and Hai signifies "a heap of ruins." It was *between* these that Abram pitched his tent. The "tent" speaks of the sphere where the believer lives his pilgrim life. Ah, no interpreter is needed, is he? My present lot is cast with "a heap of ruins"—all that pertains to the old creation —on the one hand, but with "the house of God"—on High—on the other.

"And there he builded an altar unto the Lord." This is the fourth thing recorded in Abram's response to God's "appearing" unto him. It is surely significant that this is the only item which is repeated, teaching us, emphasising the great truth that, worship is the spontaneous outcome of a saint's being in the path of obedience, and the Lord's manifesting of Himself to that soul. As another has aptly expressed it, "The tent and the altar give us the two sides of Abram's character—a stranger in the world, a worshipper of God. Having nothing on earth, he found his all in God." But let it not be overlooked that his "altar" was by *Bethel*. This is the place where faith enters and worships, where priestly privileges are enjoyed and priestly actions performed. "Having an High Priest over the house of God, let us draw near with a true heart in full assurance of faith, having our hearts sprinkled from an evil conscience" (Heb. 10 : 21, 22).

"And called upon the name of the Lord." This is the final response made by Abram to the Lord's "appearing." To "call upon the name of the Lord" means that he prayed. Prayer is the expression of dependency it betokens a soul that is cast upon God, who is looking to Him for the supply of every need. Prayer is, to carnal reason, one of the paradoxes of the Christian life, for it is at once the expression of weakness and the outbreathing of strength: it is an acknowledgment of creature-insufficiency, and it is the evidence of firm confidence in God. Just as in Gen. 12 the priestly action of Abram is at once followed by his calling upon the name of the Lord, so in Psa. 99 : 6 the Spirit has linked the two things together, "Moses and Aaron among his priests, and Samuel among them that call upon His name." May each Christian reader know in his experience, more and more these five things here found in Abram.

—*Arthur W. Pink.*

THE WILFUL KING.

Saul: 1 Sam. 8—31.

There is scarcely a character in Scripture which furnishes us with more solemn warning than that of King Saul. As we follow his history from stage to stage we should be awed at such exhibitions of the treachery and corruption of the heart of man. The history of Saul is one out of the many things which have been recorded "for *our* learning" (Rom. 15 : 4), and we may be thankful to God for the solemn warning it gives us, and seek grace from Him to read it to spiritual profit.

The first book of Samuel has a very distinct character: it strikingly sets forth the casting out of what is of man, and the bringing in of that which is of God. Accordingly, it opens with a barren woman, receiving a child from the Lord—an O.T. figure of Divine grace and power acting on the impotency of the creature. Next we have the priesthood corrupting itself, and removed by judgment, which is answered by God's promise to bring in the faithful Priest after His own heart (1 Sam. 2 : 35). Then we have the kingdom set up, first according to man's heart, corrupting itself, removed by judgment, followed by the bringing in of God's king, for whom He would build a sure house. Thus the first book of Samuel shows us two things: everything while it is in man's hand, whether in the sanctuary or on the throne, is brought to ruin; but everything is ultimately committed into the hand of God's anointed. Blessed foreshadowment is this of all the counsels of God made good in and by Christ, to whom has been given an untransferable priesthood and a kingdom that shall never be moved.

The history of Saul properly begins at the 8th chapter. There we behold the revolted heart of Israel, which had departed further and further from Jehovah, desiring a human king in His stead. The failure of Samuel's sons was given as their excuse. They had acted corruptly, and probably Samuel had been at fault in making *them* "judges"—consulting, perhaps, too much with flesh and blood, and too little with the Lord's honour and Israel's welfare. How often has Samuel's principle been acted on! Man's ways are ever different from God's. Mr. Spurgeon's son filled the pulpit of the Metropolitan Tabernacle after his father's decease, but the mantle which had been on the one did not fall on the other. Mr. Moody's son succeeded his sire as the head of Northfield, but how different the two administrations! The Booth's have sought to keep the leadership of the Salvation Army in their own family, but disaster has been the consequence.

The Lord made known to Samuel Israel's *real* reason for wanting a king: "Hearken unto the voice of the people in all that they say unto thee: for they have not rejected thee, but they have rejected Me, that I should not reign over them." Like Moses before him (Ex. 6 : 7), Samuel was nothing that the people should murmur against him for his sons; their murmurings were against Jehovah. "But My people would not hearken to My voice; and Israel would none of Me. So I gave them up unto their own hearts' lusts: and they walked in their own counsels" (Psa. 81: 11, 12). They should have what their soul was now wishing after, but they would find it to be their plague (1 Sam. 8: 11-18). Their king should be their sorrow and ruin, as all *our* own things are, if we follow and obtain them. As God said to Israel at a later date, "He feedeth on ashes: a deceived heart hath turned him aside" (Isa. 44: 20). And what but "ashes"—sorrow and death—does the labour of our hands gather for us? So is it always, try it in what way you may; and so Israel was now to find it to their bitter cost.

Very solemn is it to note how that God most graciously gave His people space to repent of this their evil choice, before they reaped the painful fruit of it. Samuel is sent to faithfully warn them of what would be the consequences, but they heeded him not: "Nevertheless the people refused to obey the voice of Samuel; and they said, Nay; but we will have a king over us; that we also may be like all the nations; and that our king may judge us, and go out before us, and fight our battles" (8: 19, 20). Ah, this too is recorded for *our* admonition. Was not Israel's way here, only too often our way? How often God (by His Spirit and by His providences) warns us against following a certain line of conduct. Often He graciously puts an obstacle in our path, but so determined are we to have our own way, we force a passage through or over it. And what is, ever, the end of a course of self-will, but confusion, loss and sorrow!

Such was Israel's case: determined now to have a king of their own at all costs. This at once prepares us for the type of person their king was—the willful people must have a willful king. Yet in the divine economy such a time as the reign of Saul had its appointed uses. It shows us what the kingdom is in man's hand, it serves to set off the kingdom in God's hand—mischief, corruption, and disaster marking the one; honour, blessing, and rest the other. The kingdom brought in by their own desire would but let them see how unequal they were to provide for their own happiness, just as "this present evil world" which our own lusts have formed and fashioned, is found unequal to satisfy us. But with all this, God's workmanship will stand in blessed contrast. The kingdom under Saul, in all its wretchedness and shame, only served to set off the glory and peaceful days of David and Solomon, as this world of ours will set off "the world to come" in the days of the Son of Man.

But however the Lord may thus serve His own glory, and His people's comfort by this, it is Israel that now brings this season of shame and sorrow on themselves: they sow the wind to reap the whirlwind. Saul comes forth, the chosen one of a willful and revolted nation, to do his evil work. And thus he stands ranked with another more wicked than himself; the type of that king who, in the latter day, is to "do according to his will" and "exalt himself" (Dan. 11: 36); the one who is to come "in his own name" (John 5: 43), and say in his heart, "no God." Saul was now coming forth the first of that line of shepherds or rulers who were to "feed themselves and not the flock," to eat the fat, and clothe them with wool (Ezek. 34). Into the hand of such shepherds Israel is now cast, seeing they have rejected the Lord their good Shepherd, and desired one after their own heart. The first of them, as we here find, was of that tribe of which it had been said of old, "Benjamin shall ravin as a wolf: in the morning he shall devour the prey, and at night he shall divide the spoil" (Gen. 49: 27). And Saul was of that city, and in that tribe, which had already wrought such mischief in Israel (see Judges 19-21).

But we further learn of him that though belonging to the least of all the families of his tribe, and that too, the smallest tribe in Israel, his father Kish was "a mighty man of substance" (9: 1). And from this description we gather that Saul and his father had prospered in this world, people of that class who "will be rich," though nature, and family, and circumstances are all against them. Saul is first presented to us seeking for his father's asses (not "sheep")! Something of the family property was missing, and must be searched for. But though thus careful of his own things, he seems, as yet at least, to have no care for the things of God, for he did not at that time so much as know the person of Samuel, who was then God's principal witness in the land. Later, his neighbours who had "known him aforetime" (10: 11) wondered with great wonder that *he* should be found among the prophets, so that he became a proverb. These notices are sufficient to tell us of what generation Saul was, and that, though as yet in an humble sphere, he and his father's house had been formed rather by the low principles of the world, than by worthy thoughts of the Lord of Israel. Such an one was well fitted to be Israel's king at that time—his mind on the asses, the world set in his heart.

In full accord with these incidental references, let us note the absence of any mention of moral or spiritual qualities in him: "And there was not among the children of Israel a goodlier person than he: from his shoulders and upward he was higher than any of the people" (9: 2). Only thus is he described. He is judged of simply after the flesh, looked at only in the outward man; and therefore was well suited for those who desired him. Hence, when the people were introduced to him, and saw his *stature*, and nothing more, they cried, "God save the king" (10: 24).

This was the king after their own heart. He was of the world, and the world loves his own. But if Saul be thus the one after man's heart, and David the one after God's heart, we learn in the former what *we* are, and in the latter what *Christ* is: Saul would have everything his own way, and be everything himself; David was willing to be nothing and have nothing, and be ever the unselfish servant of others. And thus man, to our *shame*, is presented in the narrow-heartedness of Saul, but God to our *comfort* in the generous self-abasement of David.

To have given Israel a king, appears to have been God's purpose from the beginning: Gen. 49: 10, Num. 24: 17. But things were not ready for the king all at once; various previous courses must be accomplished ere that topstone in the divine building could be brought forth. Israel at first had to be redeemed from bondage, then to be carried through the wilderness to learn the ways and secrets of God's love; then to get their promised inheritance delivered out of the hand of the usurper. Till these things were done, all was not in readiness for the king. Had these things been simply accomplished, the king without delay would have appeared to crown the whole work with the full beauty of the Lord. But every stage in this way of the Lord, Israel had sadly interrupted and delayed. After their redemption from Egypt, they had given themselves, through disobedience, forty years' travel in the wilderness; after taking the inheritance, they had, again through disobedience, brought pricks into their sides and thorns in their eyes; and now they forestal God's king, and, through disobedience again, bring their own king, as another plague upon them.

But this is the way of man, the way of us all by nature. Through unbelief and willfulness we refuse to wait God's time, and we procure a Saul for ourselves. It was thus that Sarah brought Ishmael into her house, and Jacob his twenty and one years of exile and servitude upon himself. Our own crooked policy and unbelief are the cause of many sorrows. God, if waited on, would bring the blessing that maketh rich and which *addeth no sorrow with it*, but our own way only teaches us that he which soweth to the flesh must of the flesh reap corruption. To this day Israel is learning this, and reaping the fruit of the tree they planted, learning the service of the nations which, like Saul, they have set over themselves; and their only real joy lies in this, that God's counsel of grace, in spite of all, is to stand (Isa. 46: 10), and His own King shall sit on His holy hill of Zion (Psa. 2).

In spite of Israel's self-will, God proved that there was nothing wanting on His part. He had not only signified Saul to Samuel, and Samuel in turn had anointed him, but the Spirit of the Lord came upon him as faculty for his office, and an "occasion" for proving that God was with him would be afforded (10: 6, 7). This "occasion" was soon given, in the insult of Nahash the Ammonite towards Jabesh-gilead, and the Lord gave Israel complete victory over him by the hand of their king (1 Sam. 11). Thus here, as in ancient days, the Lord displayed His grace and power, notwithstanding the stiffneckedness of the people.

In the 13th chapter of Samuel we find Saul tried and found wanting. There is a close analogy with the testing of Israel at Sinai. There, the people grew impatient at the delay of Moses (Ex. 32: 1), and, in violation of the very first article of the covenant into which they had just entered, made a golden calf. So here: Samuel had left Saul for a few days, telling him to go to Gilgal and wait for him there till he should come and offer the sacrifices. But, petulent and presumptuous, Saul offers them himself (vv. 7, 8). Thus he forsook the word of the Lord, and violated the first command he had received. But beside this great sin, note how at this same time the character of Saul began to exhibit itself: "Saul chose *him* three thousand men of Israel. . . and the rest of the people *he* sent every man to his tent" (v. 2). Thus he treated them as his property—compare "And when Saul saw any strong man, or any valiant man, he took him *unto him*" (14: 52). All his ways now were in the same tone of self-will: exalting himself above his brethren, he speaks with the voice more of a god than of a man, blowing the trumpet, and saying, "Let the Hebrews hear" (v. 3). Moreover, as we have seen, he would be priest as well as king—type of him who shall not only sit on the throne, but also in the Temple of God (2 Thess. 2).

Such was Saul, yet in spite of his wickedness God did not allow the enemy to triumph over Israel. He wrought deliverance for them from the Philistines, as He had promised (9: 16), and that too in a manner that displayed *His* hand more conspicuously than in the day of Gideon or Samson: see chapter 14. But a sorry figure did Saul cut. He had no courage in the Lord's cause: "And Saul tarried in the uttermost part of Gibeah under a pomegranate tree" (14: 2). Jonathan, not Saul, is the instrument God used to vanquish his enemies. Saul raged after the fight, but struck no blow in it; instead, he sacrifices the honour of Israel to his own will, adjuring the people not to touch any food till the evening—a thing which hindered the full overthrow of the Philistines (14: 30).

But with all his self-will and pride Saul could be very religious, when religion did not affect his own interests, when, like Jehu, he could serve himself by it. When the famished people offended by eating the blood with the flesh, he is the one to throw up hands of holy horror, and then builds an altar unto the Lord (14 : 34, 35). Thus he took to himself, again, the honour of the priesthood. Yet, almost the very next thing recorded is his willingness to sacrifice Jonathan his son (v. 44).

In chapter 15 the king is tested again by a command from the Lord: "Thus saith the Lord of hosts, I remember that which Amalek did to Israel, how he laid wait for him in the way, when he came up from Egypt. Now go and smite Amalek, and utterly destroy *all* that they have, and spare them not; but slay both man and woman, infant and suckling, ox and sheep, camel and ass" (vv. 2, 3). Again Saul fails: "But Saul and the people spared Agag, and the best of the sheep, . . . and would not utterly destroy them" (v. 9). The solemn sequel is recorded in vv. 23, 35: "Because thou hast rejected the word of the Lord, He hath also rejected thee from being king . . . And Samuel came no more to see Saul until the day of his death: nevertheless Samuel mourned for Saul: and the Lord repented that He had made Saul king over Israel."

All is now ruin under the hand of the proud king: the ground is cursed again, and thorns and thistles shall it bring forth. Saul now sought to turn the conquest of Amalek to his own profit and glory, utterly regardless of the word and glory of Jehovah. First he had coveted the cattle (v. 9) instead of destroying them. Next he erected a sort of monument to his own name: "Saul came to Carmel, and, behold, he set him up a place" (15 : 12). It is true that, when taken to task by Samuel, he said "I have sinned"—but so said Balaam before him, and Judas after him. Even in his confession, the desire of his heart was not towards God's forgiveness, but for his own glory before men: "Then he said, I have sinned: yet *honour me* now, I pray thee before the leaders of my people" etc. (15 : 30). This was his lust: he craved the praise of men. He would, at all costs, have the honour that cometh from man, and Samuel now delivers him over to a reprobate mind.

The judgment of God now lay upon him: "The Spirit of the Lord departed from Saul, and an evil spirit from the Lord troubled him" (16 : 14). And now the time had arrived for revealing again "the secret of God," for in all seasons of man's destruction of himself, there has been another thing going on in the outworking of the purpose of God. At the beginning (Gen. 3 : 15), the promise of God's Son was first given when Adam had rebelled against his Maker. While his brethren were filling up their sins and sorrows in Canaan, Joseph, unknown to them, was growing up in Egypt for their help. While Israel was in the heat of Pharaoh's furnace, God was preparing their deliverer in the distant solitudes of Midian. While disasters followed sin in quick succession, the Judges were raised up as God's deliverers for the people. While, at last, when the priesthood was defiled, and the glory gone into the enemy's land, Samuel the child is brought forth to minister before Jehovah.

Thus had it been before, and so is it now again. Saul and the kingdom are bringing ruin on themselves, but David, the "secret of God," is under preparation to establish the throne in honour, and the kingdom in order and strength. And what are all these things but notices to us of Him who is the true secret of God? For as such, the blessed Son of God is now, though flesh and blood decay, the hidden seed in the believer, that is to burst forth in the resurrection a plant of glory. And as such He will bye and bye bear up the pillars of the earth, when all things else are dissolving. He will then come forth out of His secret chambers, as Joseph or Moses, as Samuel or David, and shall be as the light of the morning, after a dark and dreary night, when the sun riseth, even a morning without clouds. And this is always the way of grace—it comes into exercise after man has been convicted of entire insufficiency. And grace ever takes for its instruments the weak and foolish things of the world. Such was Jesus of Nazareth, such was Paul with the thorn in his flesh, and such was David now.

"Man looketh on the outward appearance, but the Lord looketh on the heart." Man had already looked on the outward appearance and found his object in Saul, who in stature was the greatest in Israel. But God's choice is not ordered by such a measure (Psa. 147: 10). A rod out of the stem of Jesse was His object, a root out of a dry ground, in which there was no comeliness before the eye of man: the one of whom his father scornfully said, "There remaineth yet the youngest, and, behold, he keepeth the sheep" (16: 11)—the one, who like a greater than he, man was thus despising and the nation abhorring (Isa. 49: 7). This one, this youngest son of Jesse, the keeper of a few sheep in the wilderness, is now God's object. "Arise, anoint *him*: for this is he" says the Lord to Samuel.

Here we would notice the difference of condition in Saul's house and David's house as they are severally brought before us. Saul's house, as we have seen, was of no repute in Israel, but had made a fortune, as people speak. David's, on the other hand, had once been in honour, was of the tribe of Judah, and in its genealogy bore the distinguished name of Boaz, who had been, perhaps, the first man in his generation. But now it seems to be otherwise with them, for David and his father's house have no distinction now, but simply take their place among the many thousands of Israel (Micah. 5: 2). Thus the world finds its object in Saul—" Men will praise thee, when thou doest well to thyself " (Psa. 49: 18)—but God, in David. And these things teach us that when God will exalt, He first abases; when He will glorify, He first humbles. He puts the sentence of *death* in the children of *resurrection*. Saul went through no sorrow up to the throne as David did. Esau, the man of the earth, had dukedoms in his family, while Jacob's children were homeless strangers on the earth (Gen. 36), yet is it written, " Jacob have I loved, but Esau have I hated. God's way in this is hard indeed for flesh and blood to learn.

God's hand thus found its object in David, and we now have, accordingly, a new feature in the scene before us. We have God's chosen, as well as Saul within and the Philistine without. David is set before us in the strength of the Spirit of God, and he soon gives proofs of his ministry, both upon the rejected king and upon the uncircumcised. Both are made to own the power of the Lord that was in him. Whether it were the harp or the sling, his hand is skilled to use either. The king had an evil spirit in him, and the uncircumcised is breathing out slaughter, but David stands above both in the strength of the Lord. The unclean spirit goes out from the king at the bidding of his harp, and the Philistine giant falls under his sling (16, 17). It might be thought that Saul's evil course was interrupted by this, but it soon appears that this was rather only another stage in his downward way. The sow was to return to her mire. The unclean spirit only goes out to bring back seven others more wicked.

And in all this we see Israel. The way of Saul under David's harp, has been the way of Israel under God's ministers. Elijah raised among them, for a moment, the cry, " The Lord He is God"; but all was quickly " Baal " again. In the light of John the Baptist they afterwards rejoice, but it was only for a season (John 5: 35); and when the Son of God Himself was among them to heal and bless, for a while they flocked to Him in thousands; and when He preached, they wondered at His gracious words (Luke 4: 22); and when He entered their city, they cried "Hosanna"; but all soon ended in the Cross! The evil spirit had been charmed, the unclean spirit had gone out, but the house was still ready for it, and for it only. And thus the harp of David and the gracious ministry of Christ were only the same stage in the downward paths of the king and the people. They were both of them disobedient and gainsaying still.

But Saul's sin is not to hinder God's mercy. David has a work to do with the Philistine, which must be done, be the king ever so unworthy. And in this too we see a foreshadowing of the Son of God. He came to destroy the power of the Enemy, as well as to heal the daughter of Zion; and though she, like Saul, may refuse to be healed, the Son of God must do His great work upon Goliath. He must lead captivity captive. He must make an end of sin, He must break down the middle wall of partition. He must abolish death. He must accomplish all this glorious triumph over the full power of the Enemy, though He find none in Israel who were His own to receive Him, nor any in the world, that He had made, to know Him.

This again is shame and comfort to us —shame, that we could thus treat His love; comfort, that His love survived such treatment. And upon this we should notice (for it carries another lesson for ourselves), that though Saul knew the power of David's harp for a time, he never knew *David himself*—David was still a stranger to him (17: 56). How this exhibits man, and Israel still! Man will enjoy the rain from heaven, and fruitful seasons; but remain ignorant of the One who orders all this for him. Many in Israel were healed by Jesus, but did not learn Him; many *pressed* upon Him in the throng, but did not *touch* Him. And all this is like Saul who could be refreshed by David's music, but still have to ask " whose son is this youth"? Truly sad and solemn is it to meditate on this wretched Saul. He portrays a child of this world, who goes on in self-will, with desperate purpose of heart to take this world for his portion at all costs.

Through the next chapters (18-27) David becomes the principal object, and all that we see in Saul is only the course of a vexed and disappointed man of the world, who, by the goading of his own lusts, rushes on to destruction, as a horse to the battle (cf. Prov. 29: 1). He feels that he is losing the world, and that is everything to him. He cared nothing for the kingdom, for its own sake; and valued its welfare only so far as it served the world in his heart and his own honour among men. The evil spirit now returns with others more wicked than himself. Before, it was a spirit that *troubled* him, now it *irritates his lusts*, and is too strong for the harp of David (18:

10, 11). He had now become one of that generation who will not hearken to the voice of charmers, charming never so wisely (Psa. 58: 5). The song of the women had the rather awakened all the evil passions of his soul, and envy and wounded pride and hatred of the righteous express themselves fearfully through all these scenes. That fatal song was to Saul what Joseph's dream had been to his brethren, and what the testimony of the wise men was afterwards to Herod—it stirred up all his enmity (19: 8-10).

His ruling passion was strong even unto death: while he confessed that David would soon have everything, and he himself be laid in the grave, still he says, "Sware now therefore unto me by the Lord, that thou wilt not cut off my seed after me, and that thou wilt not destroy my name out of my father's house" (24: 21). Truly this is all a solemn warning unto us. Saul's eye was set on fire of hell, and he fixed it on the righteous as its prey (18: 9). And it is not in the prospect or even the approach of death to heal the "evil eye." The spirit of envy and strife will work in us, even to the very last gasp; and the only divine cure for it is to learn, through the Holy Spirit, with enlarged hearts, to cease looking to our own personal honour or interests, and to take our place in God's interests; to know that we have our honour, our enduring honour, only in *God's* approval and reward. That will give victory over the world. But the world was Saul's aim: he knew nothing beyond "his own things." He knew not, as believers do, that if we be Christians "*all things*" are ours (1 Cor 3: 21).

Saul would have David fall, but by the hand of another, rather than by his own, for he had some stings of conscience; and besides, he saw that David was "accepted in the sight of all the people." He plots against his life, first by the Philistines, then by his daughter, and at last solicits even Johnathan to be the executioner. But these failing, and only forcing David out from the court, he then proclaims him a traitor; and would have his people treat him as an outlaw. But no weapon formed against him could prosper. So when the officers of the Jews came to take Jesus, they had to return saying, "Never man spake like this Man" (John 7: 46).

The more wisely David carried himself, and showed that God was with him, the more the infatuated heart of Saul feared and hated him, and sought his destruction. In all this he traversed the way of Satan, who, knowing the Son of God in His day, trembled before Him, and yet sought to destroy Him. And yet Saul could weep when he met David; so too did Esau when he met Jacob. But there is no trusting these tears When many were believing in the Lord Jesus, beholding the miracles which He did, He would not commit Himself unto them (John 2: 24). And Saul prophesied too; yet so have others of the same generation. Balaam did so while loving the wages of unrighteousness. Caiaphas did so (John 11: 51) while thirsting for innocent blood. Judas could work miracles while he carried the heart of a traitor. A new heart, or "another heart," as a gift for *office*, had been imparted to each of them, and through them the Holy Spirit prophesied and wrought miracles. But all this tells us that it is not gifts which make us what we should be; nothing will avail if the heart be not right with God.

But we must hasten now to the closing scenes of this solemn and affecting history. The night of Israel was setting in with many a dark and dreary cloud (chap. 28). Saul was doomed; the Philistines as strong and threatening as ever; David, the deliverer of the people, forced without the camp; and our poor king, the slave of his lusts, full of fear and confusion. He enquires of God, but there is no answer, for it is written, "Because I have called, and ye refused . . . I also will laugh at your calamity . . . Then shall they call upon Me, but I will not answer" (Prov. 1: 24 28).

There was now a forsaking of the living for the dead, and a seeking unto wizards that peep and mutter. At different seasons of the ripening of man's iniquity there has been a confederacy of kings and their counsellors against the Lord. Thus Pharaoh took counsel with the magicians to withstand Moses. Balak sent for Balaam to curse Israel. The Jews with Caiaphas as their counsellor raged against the Lord. And so in the latter day, we read of the Beast *and* the false Prophet. And, we may add, have we not witnessed a most striking and solemn example in our own times. When Russia had filled up the measure of her iniquity, when God's judgment was about to fall for her long-continued cruelty against the Jews, the last of her Czars had Rasputin, a spiritist, for his counsellor; but only to his own destruction.

So here we find another instance of the same desperate efforts of man to obtain help from the powers of evil when his own sin is consummated, and his doom nigh at hand. Saul and the witch of Endor exhibits another apostate king in consultation with an evil counsellor. His cup was almost full, and judgment, at the door, was ready to enter. It is to be noted that Saul had never set up an idol in the land, though *that* had been the principal sin of Israel, both before and after him. He had rather been moved with the desire of setting *himself* up, thus more clearly imaging forth the Man of Sin. Moreover he had cleared the land of wizards and witches (28: 9) but this "light" was really darkness in him, for it was himself and not the God of Israel that he would exalt. Now that he was losing himself and the world, as he fears, is departing from him, he will readily enough strike hands with any helper.

The way which the Lord now takes in hand to deal with this confederacy is very striking. By His prophet He has said, "Every man of the house of Israel that setteth up his idols in his heart, and putteth the stumbling-block of his iniquity before his face, and *cometh to* the prophet; I the Lord will answer him that cometh *according to* the multitude of his idols" (Ezek. 14 : 4). This was the way of the Lord here. Saul was a corrupt man, in whose heart and before whose face the world, as his idol and stumbling-block, was set; and because of this, the Lord now answers him Himself. He takes the business out of the hand of the witch altogether, gives Samuel for a moment according to Saul's desires; but it is only in *judgment*, only "according to the multitude of his idols;" only to tell him of the vengeance that was now at his door. And thus, this appearance of Samuel was only another hand-writing upon the wall, marking judgment against another profane king *with the finger of God Himself*.

The Lord thus in Saul illustrates His own principle of action as revealed by Ezekiel. It was now too late for anything but an answer of judgment. Like Esau, Saul might have had God for his portion. The birthright was his, but he sold it. For the honour that cometh from man, he sold it, as Esau did for a mess of pottage. And now there is no place of repentance for him. He beseeches Samuel, but the Master of the house had risen up, and the door was shut. The prophet from among the dead will not persuade, where the living prophet has been refused. For a while Saul was troubled, lay on the earth, refused to be comforted; but the trouble passes, he takes of the woman's hand, and is refreshed by her dainties. Like Israel afterwards, the raising of Lazarus did but strengthen the enmity against Christ, and carried them onward only the more rapidly to finish their sin at Calvary (John 1 : 47).

And now we have only to follow our infatuated king to his "day of visitation." He had rejected the word of the Lord, and the Lord had rejected him. His sin had gone before unto judgment—no inquiry after it need now be made. Every part of his evil reign had declared it, and now he has only to meet the judgment. In the strength of that food which he had received at the hand of his evil counsellor, he goes out against the uncircumcised, but only to fall before them (31). He dies as a fool dies, slain by his own sword; his sons fall with him, and his army is routed by the enemies of the Lord (vv. 6, 7), for it was *God* who had a controversy with him. Thus all ends on the fearful day of Mount Gilboa. Saul has presented us with a fearful warning of the apostate and his end. Chosen, anointed, gifted for office; but by transgression he fell, and his office another takes. Lost child of this world. Here was death, the wages of sin.

Surely we have reason to "remember" Saul, as well as Lot's wife. In him we see the man of the earth perishing in his own corruptions. Of him we may say, "Lo, this is the man that made not God his strength; but trusted in the abundance of his riches, and strengthened himself in his wickedness" (Psa. 52 : 7). Truly "the friendship of the world is enmity against God" (James 4 : 4). Saul sought its honour, and what it had to give him; and that he might make sure of it, gave up God. And are not we pressed and tempted by the same world that ruined him? O that God may, by His grace, set the hearts of reader and writer upon Himself, and our eyes upon *His* glory, and then, when this poor world and all its works have been burned up, shall we find that, in His presence there is "fulness of joy" and at His right hand "pleasures forever more."

The above is condensed from an article in "The Christian Witness" of 1839, with a few alterations, and additions of our own.

—Arthur W. Pink.

A PERSONAL WORD.

April 11. The Lord has now made it plain that He would have us return to the U.S.A. where, in the past, we laboured in the Gospel for upwards of twelve years. Quite unsought by us, several invitations have come to hand from America, asking the editor to conduct Bible conferences in different places. As all doors in England remain fast closed, we take it that the above requests are intimations of God's will concerning us. We believe, too, they have come in answer to the prayers of many Christian friends who have sought the Lord on our behalf; to whom we are deeply grateful. God willing, we sail from Southampton on May 2, by the "Majestic." Continue, dear readers, to supplicate the throne of grace on our behalf. Kindly turn to page 143 of the *June* issue for a further word.

—A. W. Pink.

creature good-will perfected by grace. True Christian love is the love *of God* shed abroad in our hearts by the Holy Spirit (Rom. 5: 5). It is no refinement of the flesh; it is no product of " religion." It is the " fruit of the Spirit " (Gal. 5: 22). It is altogether supernatural, Divine. It is the most beautiful thing to be seen on this earth, though, as we have said, few have eyes to recognise it even when it is manifested before them.

How do we know that we love the brethren? By feeling our hearts drawn out to them? No. Through being attracted by their sweet temperaments and amiable dispositions? No. Appearances are ever deceptive. A winsome smile, a warm handshake, a kiss, proves nothing—as Judas' kissing of Christ demonstrated, and *that* is also " written for our learning"! Nor do honied-mouthed expressions prove anything, in fact the Christian needs to be doubly on his guard against people who say smooth things and flatteries to him. Let the reader ponder prayerfully and diligently Prov. 20: 19; 26: 28; Psa. 12: 3.

In this connection we do well to also consider Prov. 27: 5, 6: " Open rebuke is better than secret love. Faithful are the wounds of a friend; but the kisses of an enemy are deceitful." Ah, my reader, the one who " wounds " you most frequently, is probably your best friend, and has the most true love for you. But the one who winks at your faults, ignores your failings, is silent about your sins, and does not reprove for what is dishonouring to Christ, is an " enemy " to you. O for grace to say with the Psalmist, " Let the righteous smite me; it shall be a kindness: and let him reprove me; it shall be an excellent oil, which shall not break my head " (141: 5).

How shall we know whether or not we really love the brethren? Let the Word of Truth answer, " By this we know that we love the children of God, when we love God, and keep His commandments " (1 John 5: 2). Go back for a moment to the preceding verse: " Whosoever believeth that Jesus is the Christ, is born of God; and every one that loveth Him that begat loveth him also that is begotten of Him." We love the brethren because they have been made " partakers of the Divine nature." It is *that, and not* anything pertaining to the flesh, which is the uniting bond. How that lifts us entirely out of the realm of nature, into the spiritual sphere! The awful thing is that today so much that bears the name of " love " shuts *God* out altogether.

" By this we know we love the children of God, when we love God and keep His commandments." And what is the touchstone of my own personal love to God? It is my keeping of His commandments: John 14: 15,21,24; 15: 10. The strength of my love to God is to be gauged not by pious words, nor by the lustiness with which I sing His praises; but by my obedience to His word. The same principle holds good in my relations with my brethren.

" By *this* we know that we love the children of God, *when* we love God and keep His commandments." If I am glossing over the faults of my brethren and sisters, if I am walking with them in a course of self-pleasing and self-will, then I am *not* " loving " them. Love is to be exercised in a Divine way. I must never love my brethren at the expense of failing to love God; in fact, it is only when God has His true place in my heart that spiritual love can be exercised by me toward them. True spiritual love does not consist in gratifying them, but in pleasing God and helping them, and I can only *help* them in the path of God's commandments.

" By this we know that we love the children of God, when we love God and keep His commandments." O how far have God's people departed from *His* standard! Surely when those who are partakers of " the heavenly calling " come together, some higher ambition than worldly courtesies and fleshy amenities should occupy their thoughts. True we are to " greet " one another, but it is with " a *holy* kiss," i.e. with a greeting of holy affection. Petting and pampering each other is not Christian love. Exhorting one another to pressforward in the race that is set before us, and speaking words that will encourage each to " look off unto Jesus," would be much more helpful.

Love to one another is to be a holy thing, not a fleshy sentiment, not a loose indifference as to the path we are treading. God's " commandments " are expressions of *His* love, as well as His authority, and to ignore them, even while seeking to be kindly affectioned one to another, is not to "love" at all. The *exercise* of love is to be in practical conformity to the revealed will of God. Much that is called " Brotherly love " is only fleshy amiability and affability, the sentimentality of nature. There is nothing truly *Divine* in it. May the Holy Spirit search the hearts of both writer and reader with this important word, " By this we know that we love the children of God, when we love God, and keep His commandments."

—*Arthur W. Pink.*

VOL. VIII.   JUNE, 1929   NO. 6
STUDIES IN THE SCRIPTURES
"Search the Scriptures" John 5 : 39

Copyright in all English-speaking Countries.

Editor: Arthur W. Pink, Morton's Gap, Kentucky, U.S.A.
Hon. Agent in England: Mr. A. Winstone, 2, Lennox Villas, Hewlett Road, Cheltenham.
Hon. Agent in Australia: Mr. G. Ardill, The Christian Workers' Depot.
Commonwealth and Reservoir Streets, Sydney.

FREE TO ALL WHO WILL READ IT.

ACCEPTING CHRIST.

What we are about to write is designed chiefly for preachers, particularly the younger ones, though it should not be lacking in interest to any who are concerned about the proclamation of God's truth. To preach the Word faithfully and profitably is the most solemn, the most honourous, and the most difficult task which can fall to the present lot of any one. After twenty years' experience the writer is conscious that he knows nothing yet as he ought to know, and that his best performances need the atoning blood of Christ to cleanse them. May writer and reader heed, more and more, the Divine injunction, " Prove all things; hold fast that which is good " (1 Thess. 5: 21).

Some evangelists are very fond of urging their unconverted hearers to "Accept Christ" as their personal Saviour. With almost monotonous frequency this phrase is constantly on their lips. It is rare that they employ any alternate one. Probably the majority of our readers have heard this expression so often that they have mechanically endorsed it without giving it a serious thought. Or, perhaps, they have heard it used by preachers who were so renowned for their orthodoxy that it never occurred to them to challenge it.

On the other hand, there exist companies of professing Christians to-day who take serious exception to this expression. To them it savours of " free will," implies creature ability, and shuts out the work of the Holy Spirit. Should they hear a preacher making use of this phrase they would at once question his orthodoxy and look upon him as an Arminian, which is a synonym for a heretic. They imagine that to speak to unconverted souls of " accepting Christ " is to employ language which is foreign to Holy Writ and grossly dishonouring to God.

Without a desire to provoke any controversy on the matter, but rather with the hope of making a helpful though brief contribution to the subject, we feel led to write a few lines thereon. First of all, we would press the fact that the Gospel is to be preached to " every creature ": not only to those who give evidence of being among God's elect, not simply to those who show signs that they have been quickened by the Spirit, but to all men everywhere. And " the Gospel " is both the proclamation and presentation of a Saviour who is mighty to save. The Gospel is that " Christ Jesus came into the world to save *sinners*."

Second, we would point out that there is no real rest for any soul until the Gospel is heartily believed. To the sinful woman of Luke 7, Christ said, " Thy *faith* hath saved thee: go *in peace* " (v. 50)—hers was a personal, present, perfect salvation. Just so long as an anxious sinner is occupied with himself, concerned about his frames and feelings, looking at his sins or his repentance of them, will he remain a stranger to that peace which " passeth all understanding." As it is written, " Therefore being justified *by faith*, we have peace with God through our Lord Jesus Christ " (Rom. 5: 1). And again, " Now the God of Hope fill you with all joy and *peace in believing* " (Rom. 15 : 13).

Third, if the preacher is aware of an anxious soul in his congregation who is earnestly longing for peace, he should spare no pains in seeking to be God's instrument for pointing that sinner to the Prince of peace. He should preach, pray, and labour to that end. He should diligently seek from his Master a special message for

(Continued on Page 144).

IMPORTANT NOTICES

Back numbers of the last four years of this magazine are yet obtainable, nicely and strongly bound at 7/6 each, post paid. They will soon be out of print.

Advise promptly of change of address otherwise copies will be lost in the mails.

This Magazine is published as a work of faith and labour of love. The Editor gladly gives his services. It is freely sent to all who will read it. No charge is made for it.

Christians who feel definitely led to do so, may have fellowship with us in this Ministry. Send only *Inter-National M.O.*

CONTENTS.

Hebrews	122
Gleanings in Exodus	128
Abram's Failure	133
The Servant-King	137

THE EPISTLE TO THE HEBREWS.

18. *Christ Superior to Joshua*: Heb. 4:11-16.

The verses which are to be before us complete the present section of our Epistle, a section which begins at 3:1 and which has two main divisions: the first, setting forth the superiority of Christ over Moses; the second, His superiority over Joshua. In the last six verses of chapter 4 a practical application is made of what had previously been said. That application begins with an exhortation for Christians to "labour therefore to enter into that rest." Both the nature and the place of this "rest" have been defined in the earlier verses. As the opening verse of the chapter shows, it is the "rest of God" which is, in promise, set before us. Beautifully has another said:

"But what did God mean by calling it *His* rest? Not they enter into *their* rest, but His own. Oh, blessed distinction! I hasten to the ultimate and deepest solution of the question. God gives us *Himself*, and in all His gifts He gives us Himself. Here is the distinction between all religions which men invent, which have their origin in the conscience and heart of man, which spring up from the earth; and the truth, the salvation, the life, revealed unto us from above, descending to us from heaven. All religions seek and promise the same things: light, righteousness, peace, strength, and joy. But human religions think only of creature-light, creature-righteousness, of a human, limited, and imperfect peace, strength, and blessings. They start from man upwards. But God gives us Himself, and in Himself all gifts, and hence all His gifts are perfect and divine.

"Does God give us righteousness? He Himself is our righteousness, Jehovah-Tsidkenu. Does God give us peace? Christ is our peace. Does God give us light? He is our light. Does God give us bread? He is the bread we eat. As the Son liveth by the Father, so he that eateth Me shall live by Me (John 6). God Himself is our strength. God is ours, and in all His gifts and blessings He gives Himself. By the Holy Spirit we are one with Christ, and Christ the Son of God is our righteousness, nay, our life. Do you want any other real presence? Are we not altogether 'engodded,' God dwelling and living in us, and we in Him? What more real presence and indwelling, awful and blessed, can we have than that which the apostle described when he said: 'I live; yet not I, But Christ liveth in me?' Or again, 'I can do all things through Christ which strengtheneth me.' Thus God gives us *His* rest as our rest" (Saphir).

Following the exhortation to labour to enter into God's rest, reference is made to the living, powerful, and piercing character of the Word of God, and the effects it produces in regeneration. In the light of the solemn warning which follows in v. 13, the contents of v. 12 seem to be brought in for the purpose of enabling the Hebrews to test the genuineness of their Christian profession: sufficient is there said for them to discover whether or not they had been born again. Then the chapter closes with one of the most precious passages to be found in our Epistle, or indeed in the whole of the N.T. It makes known the gracious provisions which God has made for His poor people while they are yet in the place of testing. It brings before us the sufficiency and sympathy of our great High Priest, in view of which Christians are bidden to "come boldly unto the throne of grace," that they "may obtain mercy, and find grace to help in time of need." May the Spirit of God condescend to open up to us this portion of His Word.

"Let us labour therefore to enter into that rest, lest any man fall after the same example of unbelief" (v. 11). As pointed out in the preceding article, this verse completes the sentence begun at v. 6. It is in view of the solemn fact that the great majority of those Israelites to whom the Gospel of Rest was first preached did not receive it in faith, and so perished in the wilderness, and hence because that only true believers will enter into God's rest, the Hebrews were now enjoined to spare no efforts in making sure that they would not fail and miss it. This 11th verse is also the complement to v. 1.

The verb for "let us labour" is derived from another verb meaning "to make haste." It is designed to point a contrast from "any of you should seem to come short of it" in v. 1. There the word is derived from a root meaning "afterwards," and some able linguists declare that the word for "come short of" means, literally, "be a day late." We believe the Spirit's designed reference is to what is recorded in Num. 14. Israel had already crossed the wilderness, and had reached Kadesh-barnea. From thence Moses had sent the twelve spies to view the land of Canaan. They had returned with a conflicting report. Ten of them magnified the difficulties which lay ahead, and discouraged the people; but Caleb said, "Let us go up *at once*, and possess it" (Num. 13: 30). The congregation listened only to the ten, and "wept that night" and "murmured against Moses and against Aaron: and the whole congregation said unto them, Would God we had died in the land of Egypt! or would God we had died in this wilderness! And wherefore hath the Lord brought us unto this land, to fall by the Sword, that our wives and children should be a prey? were it not better for us to return into Egypt? And they said one to another, Let us made us a captain and let us return into Egypt" (Num. 14 : 1-3).

Then it was that the wrath of Jehovah was kindled against His unbelieving people, saying, "How long shall I bear with this evil congregation which murmur against Me? I have heard the murmurings of the children of Israel, which they murmur against Me. Say unto them, As truly as I live, saith the Lord, *as* ye have spoken in Mine ears, *so* will I do to you: Your carcases shall fall in this wilderness" (Num. 14 : 27-29). But instead of bowing to the Lord's solemn sentence, we are told, "And they rose up early in the morning, and gat them up into the top of the mountain, saying, Lo, we be here, and *will* go up unto the place which the Lord hath promised" (v. 40). Moses faithfully expostulated with them, "Wherefore now do ye transgress the commandment of the Lord? but it shall not prosper. Go not up, for the Lord is not among you; that ye be not smitten." But they heeded him not: "They presumed to go up unto the hill top ... Then the Amelekites came down, and the Canaanites which dwelt in that hill, and smote them, and discomfited them, even unto Hormah" (vv. 44, 45). *They were a day late!* They had delayed, they had failed to trust the Lord and heed His voice through Caleb the previous day, and now they "came short" of entering the promised rest of Canaan.

It was in view of Israel's procrastination at Kadesh-barnea that the apostle admonished the Hebrews, "Let us therefore fear, lest a promise being left of entering into His rest, any of you should seem to come short of it." As we pointed out the word "seem" regarded their *walk*: let there be nothing in their ways which gave the appearance that they were halting, wavering, departing from Christ. For Christians to *seem* to come short, be a day late, in laying hold of the promise "left" them of entering into God's rest, means to sink to the level of the ways of the world, to settle down *here*, instead of going forward as "strangers and pilgrims." It means to look back to and long for the flesh-pots of Egypt. Ah, my reader, to which does your daily life witness? to the fact that you have *not yet* entered your "rest," or that you *have* found a substitute for it *here*? If so, heed that solemn word, "Arise ye, and depart; for *this* is not your rest: because it is polluted, it shall destroy, even with a sore destruction" (Micah 2 : 10).

Having then warned the Hebrews in v. 1 what to *avoid*, the apostle now tells them in v. 11 what to *essay*. They were to "labour" to enter into that rest. As stated above, the Greek word is derived from another verb meaning "to make haste;" the one used here signifies to "give diligence" and is so rendered in the R.V. In 2 Tim. 2 : 15 it is translated "study." "The word 'labour' is equivalent to 'eagerly and perseveringly seek.' The manner in which the Hebrew Christians were to 'labour to enter into that rest,' was by believing the truth, and continuing 'steadfast and unmoveable' in the faith of the truth, and in the natural results of the faith of the truth" (Dr. J. Brown). It is human responsibility which is here being addressed again, and Heb. 4 : 11 is closely parallel with the exhortations of 1 Cor. 10 : 10-12 and 2 Pet. 1 : 5-10.

Our real "rest" is yet to come, it is but "promised" (v. 1); in the meantime we are to press forward to it. "This world is not a fit place, nor this life a fit time, to enjoy such a rest as is reserved in heaven.

Rest here would glue our hearts too much to this world, and make us say, 'It is good to be here' (Matt. 17 : 4). It would slack our longing desire after Christ in heaven. Death would be more irksome, and heaven the less welcome. There would be no proof or trial of our spiritual armour, and of the several graces of God bestowed on us. God's providence, prudence, power, mercy, could not be more so well discerned. This rest being to come, and reserved for us, it will be our Wisdom, while here we live, to prepare for trouble, and to address ourselves to labour: as the soldiers in the field and as the labourers in the daytime. Yet withal to have our eye upon this rest to come; that thereby we may be the more encouraged and incited to hold out to the end" (Dr. Gouge).

"Lest any man fall after the same example of unbelief." To enforce the previous exhortation the apostle points out the danger and damage that would follow a neglect thereof. The "rest" is a word of caution and calls for cimcumspection as a preventative against apostasy. The lest "any man" intimates that this care and circumspection is not to be restricted to one's own self, but extended to our fellow-pilgrims. The word "fall" signifies to fall utterly: it is used in Rom. 11 : 22. Professors may fall away; many have done so (see 1 John 2:19 etc); then let *us* be on our guard. The "example" of others having fallen through unbelief should make us wary.

"We may well observe from this exhortation, 1. That great oppositions will and do arise against men in the work of entering into God's rest ... But notwithstanding all these difficulties, the promise of God being mixed with faith will carry us safely through them all. 2. That as the utmost of our endeavour and labours are required to our obtaining an entrance into the rest of Christ, so it doth very well deserve that they should be laid out therein. Men are content to lay themselves out to the utmost and to spend their strength for the 'bread that perisheth,' yea 'for that which is not bread.' But the rest of the Gospel deserves our utmost diligence and endeavour. To convince men thereof is one of the chief ends of the preaching of the Gospel" (Dr. J. Owen).

As was the case with the contents of vv. 9 and 10, so we are assured there is a *double* reference to the words of v. 11: a general and a specific. The general, refers to the future and perfect rest of the christian in heaven; the specific, being to that which is the emblem and type of it, namely, the weekly sabbath. This, we believe, is why the Holy Spirit here says, "Let us give diligence therefore to enter into *that* rest," rather than "into *His* rest," as in v. 1. "*That* rest" designedly includes both the eternal rest of God, and the sabbath rest, spoken of in v. 10. This we are to "give diligence" to enter, not only because the sabbath-desecration of worldlings is apt to discourage us, but also because there are professing Christians who loudly insist that there is no such thing *as* a "Christian sabbath." Beware lest we fail to heed this word of God, and "fall through the same example of unbelief" as Israel in the wilderness, who failed to listen to God.

"For the Word of God is quick, and powerful, and sharper than any two edged sword, piercing even to the dividing asunder of soul and spirit, and of the joints and marrow, and is a discerner of the thoughts and intents of the heart" (v. 12). The first word of this verse (which has the force of " because ") denotes that the apostle is here furnishing further reason *why* professing Christians should give diligence in pressing forward to the rest which is set before them. That reason is drawn from the nature of and the effects produced by the Word of God. This verse and the one which follows appear to be brought in for the purpose of *testing* profession and enabling exercised souls to discover whether or not they have been born again.

"Let us give diligence therefore to enter into that rest ... *For* the Word of God is quick and powerful, and sharper than any two-edged sword, piercing even to the dividing asunder of soul and spirit, and of the joints and marrow, and is a discerner of the thoughts and intents of the heart." It should be evident that the first thing emphasised here is that Christianity consists not so much of external conduct, as the place which the Word of God has *within* us. The Word of God "piercing even to the dividing asunder of soul and spirit" is the effect which it produces, under the application of the Lord, when a sinner is regenerated. Man is a tripartite being, consisting of spirit and soul and body. This, we believe, is the first and deepest meaning of Gen. 1: 26, "And God said, Let *us* make man in Our image, after Our likeness." God Himself is a Trinity in Unity, and such He made man to be.

The "spirit" is the highest part of man, being the seat of God-consciousness. The "soul" is the ego, the individual himself, and is the seat of self-consciousness; man *has* a "spirit," but he *is* "a living soul." The "body" is his house or tabernacle, being the seat of sense-consciousness. In the day that man first sinned, he died spiritually. But in Scripture "death" never means extinction of being; instead, it always signifies *separation* (see Luke 15: 24). The nature of man's spiritual " death " is intimated in Eph. 4: 18, *" alienated from the life of God."* When Adam disobeyed his Maker, he became a fallen creature, separated from God. The first effect of this was that his " spirit " no longer functioned separately, it was no more in communion with God. His spirit *fell* to the level of his soul.

The " soul " is the seat of the emotions (1 Sam. 18: 1, Judges 10: 16, Gen. 42: 21, etc). It is that part of our nature which stirs into exercise the " lust of the flesh, the lust of the eyes, and the pride of life." The unregenerate man is termed " the *soulical* man " (1 Cor. 2: 14), the Greek word there being the adjectival form of "psuche" or "soul." That is to say, the unregenerate man is entirely dominated by his soul, his lusts, his desires, his emotions. Spiritual considerations have no weight with him whatsoever, for he is " alienated from the life of God." True, he *has* a "spirit," and by means of it he is capable of perceiving all around him the evidences of the " eternal power and godhead " of the Creator (Rom. 1: 20). It is the " candle of the Lord " (Prov. 20: 27) within him; yet has it, because of the fall, *no* communion with God. Now at regeneration there is, literally, a " dividing asunder of soul and spirit." The spirit is restored to communion with God, made *en-rapport* with Him, " reconciled." The spirit is raised from its immersion in the soul, and once more functions separately : " For God is my witness, whom I serve with my *spirit*" (Rom. 1: 9); " my *spirit* prayeth " (1 Cor. 14: 14) etc.

The first consequence of this is intimated in the closing words of v. 12, " And is a discerner of the thoughts and intents of the heart." The Word of God now exposes his innermost being. Having eyes to see, he discovers, for the first time, what a vile, depraved and hell-deserving creature he is. Though, in the mercy of God, he may have been preserved from much outward wickedness in his unregenerate days, and so passed among his fellows as an exemplary character, he now perceives that there dwelleth *" no good thing "* in him, that every thought and intent of his desparately-wicked heart had, all his life, been contrary to the requirements and claims of a holy God. The Word has searched him out, and discovered him to himself. He sees himself a lost, ruined, undone sinner. This is ever the first conscious effect of the new birth, for one who is still " dead in trespasses and sins " has *no* realization of his awful condition before God.

Ere passing on let us earnestly press upon the reader what has just been before us, and ask, has the Word of God thus "pierced" you? Has it penetrated, as no word from man ever has, into your innermost being? Has it exposed the workings of your wicked heart? Has it detected to you the sink of iniquity which dwells within? Make no mistake about it, dear friend, the thrice holy God of Scripture " requireth truth in the *inward* parts " (Psa. 51: 6). If the Word of God *has* searched you out, then you cried with Isaiah " Woe is me! for I am undone " (6: 5); with Job, " I abhor myself " (42: 6); with the publican, "God be merciful to me the sinner " (Luke 18: 13). But if you are a stranger to these experiences, no matter what your profession or performances, no matter how highly you may think of yourself or Christians think of you, *God* says you are still *dead* in sin.

Let it not be supposed that we have attempted to give above a *complete* description of all that takes place at the new birth; not so, we have confined ourself to what is said in Heb. 4: 12. Nor let it be thought that the language of this verse is to be *restricted* to what occurs at regeneration, not so. that is only its initial reference. The activities of the Word of God therein described are repeated whenever a Christian gets out of communion with Him, for then he is dominated to a large extent by his soul rather than his spirit. It should not need pointing out, yet the terrible ignorance of Scripture prevailing today makes it necessary, that when a child of God is walking in communion with Him, His word does not come to *him* as a " sword " rather is it " a lamp" unto his feet. If the reader will compare Rev. 2: 12 and 19: 15 he will obtain confirmation of this.

The relation of this 12th verse to the whole context is very striking, and its contents divinely appropriate. It brings out the dignity and Deity of " The Apostle " of our profession. It shows the *sufficiency* of His Word. It is striking to note that just *seven* things are here said of it. First, it is the " Word of God." Second, it is living, or " quick." Third, it is mighty, "powerful." Fourth, it is effectual, "sharper than any two edged sword." Fifth, it is penetrating, " piercing." Sixth, it is regenerative, " even to the dividing asunder of soul and spirit." Seventh, it is revealing and exposing, bringing to light the "thoughts and intents of the heart, etc." The reference to the Word piercing to the dividing asunder of "the joints (external) and marrow" (internal) tells of its discriminating power over every part of our being. The more we submit ourselves unto its searching and convicting influence the more shall we be blest.

"Neither is there any creature that is not manifest in His sight: but all things are naked and opened unto the eyes of Him with whom we have to do" (v. 13). The rendering of the A.V. here is faulty, the opening "Neither" being quite misleading. The R.V. gives "And there is no creature that is not manifest in His sight" etc. Thus the first word denotes that a reason is being given for the power and efficacy of the Word, a reason which is drawn from the nature of Him whose Word it is, namely, God; who being Himself the Searcher of the heart and the Discerner of all things, is pleased to exercise that power in and by the ministry and application of His Word. The two verses taken together supply a further reason why Christ's voice should be heeded, even because, as God, He is the omniscient One.

"Seeing then that we have a great High Priest, that is passed into the heavens, Jesus the Son of God, let us hold fast our profession" (v. 14). The connection between this and what has gone before is most blessed. The closing verses of our chapter contain precious words of encouragement. They tell of the wondrous provisions of God's grace for His people while they are still in the place of testing. They assure us that none of those who are really the people of God shall, finally, miss the perfect and eternal rest.

The R.V. reads, "Having then a great High Priest"; Bagster's interlinear gives, "Having therefore a High Priest, great" The general reference is back to what was said in 1: 3, 2: 17, 3: 1: the Divine sonship the incarnation, the exaltation of Jesus, our High Priest, is the supreme motive for holding fast our profession. The particular reference is to the apostle's main point in this chapter: if the question be asked, What hope have we poor sinners got of entering into God's rest? The answer is, Because Christ, our High Priest, has already entered heaven, and we also must do so in and by Him. The immediate reference is to what had been said in vv. 12, 13: we shall be assuredly found out if we fall from our profession, therefore it becomes us to hold it fast.

As the priesthood of Christ will, D.V., come before us more fully in the chapters that follow, we shall offer here only a few brief remarks on the verse now before us. First, it is to be noted that the Holy Spirit here designates Christ the "great High Priest," no other, neither Aaron nor Melchizedec, is so denominated. Its use emphasises the supreme dignity, excellency, and sufficiency of our High Priest. Second, He has "passed in (Greek "through") the heavens." "This word signifies to pass through notwithstanding any difficulties that may seem to hand. Thus it is said that an angel and Peter 'passed the first and second wards' (Acts 12: 10). Our Lord Christ having assumed our nature, passed through the virgin's womb; and being born, in His infancy, childhood, and manhood, passed through many difficulties, temptations, afflictions, persecutions, yea, death itself and the grave; after His resurrection He passed through the air and the stellar heavens, entering the heaven of heavens. Thus we see that nothing could hinder Him from that place where He intended to appear as our Priest before His Father" (Dr. Gouge).

"For we have not an High Priest which cannot be touched with the feeling of our infirmities; but was in all points tempted like as we are, yet without sin" (v. 15). Most blessed is this. The third thing said in v. 14 of our exalted High Priest is that He is "the Son of God." Well may poor sinners, conscious of their unworthiness and vileness, ask, How may we, so weak and worthless, approach unto and seek the mediation of *such* an One? To re-assure our poor hearts, the Holy Spirit at once reminds us that albeit Christ *is* such a great and glorious Priest, yet, withal, He is full of sympathy and tender compassion for His afflicted people. He is "merciful" (2: 17), as well as omnipotent. He is Man, as well as God. He has Himself been tempted in all things, like ourselves, sin excepted.

"But was in all points tempted like as we are, yet without sin," or literally, "who has been tempted in all things according to our likeness, apart from sin" i.e. in spirit, and soul, and body. "He was tempted—tried, exercised—for no more doth the word impart. Whatever is the moral evil in temptation is due to the depraved intention of the tempter, or from the weakness and sin of the tempted. In itself, it is but a trial, which may have a good or bad effect. He was tempted like as we are, yet without sin. Sin may be considered as to its principle, and as to its effect. Men are tempted to sin by sin, to actual sin by habitual sin, to outward sin by indwelling sin. And this is the greatest source of sin in us who are sinners. The apostle reminds us of the holiness and purity of Christ, that we may not imagine that He was liable unto any such temptations unto sin from within as we find ourselves liable unto, who are never free from guilt and defilement. Whatever temptation He was exposed unto or exercised withal, as He was with all and of all sorts that can come from without, they had none of them in the least degree any effect upon Him. He was absolutely in all things ' without sin'; He neither was tempted by sin, such was the holiness of His nature; nor did His temptation produce sin, such was the perfection of His obedience" (Dr. J. Owen).

The Man Christ Jesus was the Holy One of God, and therefore He *could not* sin. But were not Satan and Adam created without sin, and did not they yield to temptation? Yes; but the one was only a created angel the other merely man. But our Lord and Saviour was not a created being; instead, He was " God manifest in flesh." In His humanity He was " holy " (Luke 1: 35) and, as such, as high above unfallen Satan or Adam as the heavens are above the earth. He was not only impeccable God, but impeccable Man. The prince of this world came, but found *nothing* in Him (John 14: 30). Thus, He is presented before us not only as an example to be followed, but as an Object upon which faith may rest with unshaken confidence.

"Let us therefore come boldly unto the throne of grace, that we may obtain mercy, and find grace to help in time of need " (v. 16). This verse sets before us the second use we are to make of the priesthood of Christ. The first is named in v. 14, to " hold fast our profession "; here, to " come boldly unto the throne of grace." In relation to the whole context this verse makes known the wondrous and blessed provision God has made for His wilderness people. Herein, too, we may behold again the immeasurable superiority of Christianity over Judaism. The Israelites were confined to the outer court; none at all save the high priest was permitted to draw near to God within the vail. But all Christians, the youngest, weakest, most ignorant, have been " made nigh " (Eph. 2: 13); and in consequence, freedom of access to the very throne of Deity is now their rightful and blessed portion.

" And having such a High Priest in heaven, can we lose courage? Can we draw back in cowardice, impatience, and faintheartedness? can we give up our profession, our allegiance, our obedience to Christ? Or shall we not be like Joshua and Caleb, who followed the Lord fully? Let us hold fast our profession; let us persevere and fight the good fight of faith. Our great High Priest in the highest glory is our righteousness and strength. He loves, He watches, He prays, He holds us fast, and we shall never perish. Jesus is our Moses, who in the height above prays for us. Jesus our true Joshua, who gained the victory over our enemies. Only be strong, and of a good courage; be not afraid, neither be thou dismayed. In that mirror of the Word in which we behold our sin and weakness, we behold also the image of that perfect One who has passed through the conflict and temptation, who as the High Priest bears us on His loving heart, and as the Shepherd of the flock holds us in safety forever more. Boldly we come to the throne of grace. In Jesus we draw near to the Father. The throne of majesty and righteousness is unto us a throne of grace. The Lord is our God. There is not merely grace on the throne, but the throne is altogether the throne of grace. It is *grace* which disciplines us by the sharp and piercing Word; it is grace which looks on us when we have denied Him, and makes us weep bitterly. Jesus always intercedes: the throne is always a throne of grace. The lamb is in the midst of the throne. Hence we come boldly.

" Boldly is not contrasted with reverently and tremblingly. It means literally ' saying all,' with that confidence which begets thorough honesty, frankness, full and open speech. 'Pour out your heart before Him.' Come as you are, say what you feel, ask what you need. Confess your sins, your fears, your wandering thoughts and affections. Jesus the Lord went through all sorrows and trials the heart of man can go through, and as He felt all affliction and temptation most keenly, 'so in all these difficulties and trials He had communion with the Father. He knows therefore, how to succor them that are tempted, how fully and unreservedly, then, may we speak to God in the presence and by the mediation of the man Christ Jesus!

" The Lord Jesus is filled with tender compassion and the most profound, lively, and comprehensive sympathy. This belongs to the perfection of His high-priesthood. For this very purpose He was tempted, He suffered. Our infirmities, it is true, are ultimately connected with our sinfulness; the weakness of our flesh is never free from a sinful concurrence of the will; and the Saviour knows from His experience on earth how ignorant, poor, weak, sinful, and corrupt His disciples are. He loved them, watched over them with unwearied patience; prayed for them that their faith fail not; and reminded them the spirit was willing, but the flesh is weak. He remembers also His own sinless weakness; He knows what constant thought, meditation, and prayer are needed to overcome Satan, and to be faithful to God. He knows what it is for the soul to be sorrowful and overwhelmed, and what it is to be refreshed by the sunshine of Divine favour, and to rejoice in the Spirit. We may come to Him expecting full, tender, deep sympathy and compassion. He is ever ready to strengthen and comfort, to heal and restore, He is prepared to receive the poor, wounded, sin-stained believer; to dry the tears of Peter weeping bitterly; to say to Paul, oppressed with the thorn in the flesh, ' My grace is sufficient for thee.'

" We need only understand that we are sinners, and that He is High Priest. The law was given that every mouth may be shut, for we are guilty. The High Priest is given that every mouth may be opened . . . . We come in faith as sinners. Then shall we obtain mercy; and we always need mercy, to wash our feet: to restore to us the joy of salvation, to heal our backslidings, and bind up our wounds. We shall obtain help in every time of need. For God may suffer Satan and the world, want and suffering, to go against us; but He always causes all things to work together for our good. He permits the time of need, that we may call upon Him, and, being delivered by Him, may glorify His name " (Saphir).

" We should come therefore with boldness to the throne of grace " (Bagster). Then let us do so, in the full confidence of our acceptance before God in the person of His Beloved (Eph. 1 : 6). The verb in 4 : 16 is not in the aorist tense, but the present—let us "come" constantly, continually; let us form the habit of doing so. This is the first of seven occurences of this blessed word in our epistle: the other references are 7 : 25; 10, 1, 22; 11 : 6; 12 : 18, 22, To " *obtain* mercy " is passive, and refers to past failures. "*Finding* grace " is active, and signifies that we humbly, earnestly, and believingly seek it. To "help in time of need:" this is daily, yea, hourly. But whatever the need may be, spiritual or temporal, grace all-sufficient is ever -available. May it be ours to constantly *seek* it, for the unchanging promise is, " Seek, and ye shall find."

—*Arthur W. Pink.*

GLEANINGS IN EXODUS.

66. *God's Governmental Principles*: *Ex.* 34 : 1-7.

Our present passage gives the sequel to what was before us in Ex. 19 and Ex. 24. Up to Ex. 19 God had dealt with Israel on the ground of His unconditional covenant with Abraham: see Gen. 15 : 18; Ex. 2 : 24; 6 : 3, 4. The last thing recorded before Israel reached Sinai was the miraculous giving of the water at Rephidim, and concerning that the Psalmist tells us, "He opened the rock, and the waters gushed out; they ran in the dry places like a river. *For* He remembered His holy promise, Abraham His servant" (105 : 41, 42). But at Sinai, God's relationship to Israel was placed upon a different basis.

In Ex. 19 : 5 we find God, from the mount, bidding Moses say unto the people, "Now therefore, if ye will obey My voice indeed, and keep My covenant, then ye shall be a peculiar treasure unto Me above all people: for the earth is Mine." In connection with the covenant that He had made with Abraham there was nothing which Israel *could* "keep;" there were no conditions attached to it, no stipulations, no proviso's. It was unconditional so far as Abraham and his descendants were concerned. It was a covenant of pure grace, and it was on the ground of *that* covenant God will again take up Israel after this dispensation is over. But at Sinai God proposed another covenant, to which there should be two parties—Himself and Israel: It was a *conditional* covenant, a covenant which Israel must "keep" if they were to enjoy the blessings attached thereto; note carefully the "if" in 19 : 5.

The *charter* of the Siniatic covenant was the two tables of stone, upon which were engraved the ten commandments, see Ex. 34 : 27, 28, Deut. 4 : 13. The terms of this covenant Israel freely accepted (19 : 8, 24 : 3), and accordingly, it was solemnly ratified by blood (24 : 4-8). In proposing this covenant, God had two things before Him: the maintaining of His own rights, and the good of His people. Grace ever reigns "through righteousness" (Rom. 5 : 21), and in His sovereign benignity to Abraham's seed, God must uphold the claims of His throne. But this was also for their good: God's commands " are not grievous " (1 John 5 : 3), and in keeping of them there is great reward. In article 28 of this series we sought to show that, so far from redemption setting aside the rights of God over His creatures, it supplies an additional motive for recognising and meeting them.

Now at the close of Ex. 24 we hear Jehovah saying to Moses, "Come up to Me into the mount, and be there: and I will give thee tables of stone, and a law, and commandments which I have written;

that thou mayest teach them" (v. 12). Accordingly Moses, accompanied by his minister Joshua, goes up into the mount, and as v. 18 tells us, he was "in the mount forty days and forty nights." The next seven chapters are occupied with a description of the Tabernacle, details of which God also gave to Moses on that occasion. Then, in Ex. 32, we learn how the people below had been conducting themselves during the absence of their leader: the great sin of the golden calf, with its idolatrous worship, had been committed. Nothing but the intercession of the typical mediator had saved them from utter extermination by the wrath of God. As we have seen, they were severely chastised for their wickedness, the Tent of meeting was removed outside the camp, and following Israel's repentance and Moses' repeated supplication, they were restored again to communion with God.

Therefore the next thing we read is, "And the Lord said unto Moses, Hew two tables of stone like unto the first: and I will write upon these tables the words that were on the first tables, which thou breakest. And be ready in the morning, and come up in the morning unto mount Sinai, and present thyself there to Me in the top of the mount. And no man shall come up with thee, neither let any man be seen throughout all the mount; neither let the flocks nor herds feed before that mount" (34 : 1-3). Thus, as we have said in the opening sentence of this article, our present passage gives the sequel to what was before us in Ex. 19 and 24. Though Israel had, during the interval, sinned so grievously, Moses *must* return to Jehovah and receive from Him the inscribed tables of stone. No purpose of the Most High can fail. To the outward eye it may appear that the wickedness of the creature *is* thwarting, or at least hindering, the execution of His counsels. But it is only *seeming*; in reality it is not so: "My counsel shall stand, and I will do all My pleasure" (Isa. 46 : 10), in His sure and unchanging declaration.

The ground we have sought to review above is especially rich in its typical teaching. The first tables of stone were broken (32 : 19) in view of Israel's sin—a figure of man's inability to keep God's Law. The first tables of stone were provided by Jehovah Himself "I will give thee" (24 : 12), but the second were to be supplied by Moses himself: "hew *thee*" (34 : 1)—type of Christ the Mediator who declared, "Think not that I am come to destroy the law, or the prophets: I am not come to destroy, but to fullfill" Matt. 5 : 17). Accordingly, the second set of tables were securely deposited in the ark (Deut. 10 : 5)—type, again, of Him who said, "I delight to do Thy will, O My God: Yea, Thy law is *within* My heart" (Psa. 40 : 8).

Again; the covenant which God made with Abraham at the beginning (Gen. 15), and on the ground of which He had delivered Israel from Egypt and brought them unto Himself, foreshadowed that eternal covenant which God made with Christ (2 Tim. 1 : 9; Titus 1 : 2; Heb. 13 : 20), on the basis of which God's people are saved and blest (Eph. 1 : 3, 4). The covenant God made with Israel at Sinai, which brought in the establishing of His rights and the good of His people on earth, foreshadowed the present *government* of God over His people, pressing upon us our responsibilities and obligations, making known to us the terms on which we receive blessings from Him in this life, and revealing the principles which regulate God Himself in His dealings with us. As these will receive amplification in what follows, we pass on now to notice one other typical feature of importance and preciousness.

In the interval between the two ascents of Moses into the mount to receive from Jehovah the engraved tables of stone, we have the solemn account of Israel's wickedness; but, where sin abounded "grace did much more abound." Very blessed is it to see illustrated there that word in Psa. 76 : 10, "Surely the wrath of man shall praise thee." Israel's sin, so far from defeating the purpose of God, only provided occasion for Him to reveal the wondrous provisions which He has made for His failing people: seen in the unfailing love and prevailing intercession of the typical mediator. It is this which has been before us in the last few articles, finding its glorious climax in the making known of the *mercy* of God—that wondrous spring in the Divine character which ministers to those who have failed to respond to His grace—and the making of His "goodness" to pass before Moses (33 : 19). That "goodness" was inseparably connected with the proclamation of "the name of the Lord," and what *that* signified we shall learn from our present passage.

"One other remark should be made. Satan had come in, and for the moment seemed as if he had succeeded in frustrating the purposes of God with respect to His people. But Satan is never so completely defeated as in his apparent victories. This is nowhere so fully illustrated as in the cross, but the same thing is perceived in connection with the golden calf. This was Satan's work; but the failure of Israel becomes the occasion through the mediation of Moses, which God in His grace had provided, of the fuller revelation of God, and of His mingling grace with law. The activity of Satan does but work out the purposes of God, and his wrath is made to praise Him against whom all his malice and enmity are directed" (Ed. Dennett).

"And he hewed two tables of stone like unto the first; and Moses rose up early in the morning, and went up unto mount Sinai, as the Lord had commanded him, and took in his hand the two tables of stone" (v. 4). The typical teaching of this verse brings out an important truth which is now very frequently denied, namely, that God's redeemed are still under law: not as a condition of salvation, but as the Divine rule for their walk. Let it be remembered that what we have here in Ex. 34 follows right after what is recorded in chapter 33, where we have a most manifest and lovely foreshadowing of the intercession of our great High Priest on high.

Many are the New Testament passages which give us the antitype of this. Said the Lord Jesus to His disciples, "If ye *love Me, keep My commandments*" (John 14: 15), which is, obviously, paralell with, "Showing mercy unto thousands of them that *love Me*, and keep My commandments" (Ex. 20: 6). In perfect accord with this, is that word in Rom. 13: 10, "Love is the fulfilling of the law." The law has not been abrogated, nor is love lawless. Equally plain is that word in 1 Cor. 9: 21, where the apostle affirms that New Testament saints are "under the law to Christ." Nor does Rom. 6: 14 set this aside, for God's Word does not contradict itself. When the apostle there says, "Ye are not under the law, but under grace," he is referring to our justification, not to our walk as believers.

"And the Lord descended in the cloud, and stood with him there, and proclaimed the name of the Lord" (v. 5). This at once introduces to us a subject of much importance, but, alas, like many another, sadly neglected today: the teaching of Holy Writ concerning *the Name of the Lord*. God is very jealous of His name as the third commandment in the decalogue shows: the Lord will not hold guiltless that one who taketh His name in vain. In the prayer which Christ taught His disciples, the *first* petition is "Hallowed be Thy name." In Prov. 18: 10 we read, "The name of the Lord is a strong tower: the righteous runneth into it and is safe." From Mal. 3: 16 we learn that God has written a book of remembrance "for them that feared the Lord and that *thought upon His name*." While the last chapter of Scripture tells us that God's name shall be in the foreheads of His people (22: 4).

"And the Lord descended in the cloud, and stood with him there, and proclaimed the name of the Lord." This was the fulfillment of the promise which He had made to Moses in 33: 19. There He had said, "I will make all My goodness pass before thee, and *I will* proclaim the name of the Lord before thee." To proclaim His "name" signified to *reveal* Himself, to make Himself known. Just as the angel said to Joseph concerning the Child Mary was to bear, "Thou shalt call His name Jesus, *for He shall save His people from their sins*" (Matt. 1: 21): the "name" Jesus revealed what He was—the Divine Saviour. Or, just as Christ commanded His disciples to baptize "in the name of the Father, and of the Son, and of the Holy Spirit" (Matt. 28: 19), because it is thus that the Triune God now stands revealed.

The *particular character* in which Jehovah was about to reveal Himself to Moses is best perceived by noting the place and circumstances of this gracious manifestation of Himself. It was upon Sinai, in connection with the giving of the Law. It was, as we have said above, at the time when the Lord was enforcing His own rights on the people, following upon the exercise of His grace toward them. It was when Jehovah took His place in Israel's midst as their king. It was there, upon *the Mount* that He made known that "righteousness and judgment are the habitation of His throne" (Psa. 97: 2). Many are the scriptures which connect the "mount" with Divine government. For example, it was upon the mount (Matt. 5: 1) that the Lord Jesus proclaimed the principles which are to regulate those who are the subjects of "the kingdom of heaven." It was on the "holy mount" that He was transfigured (Matt. 17), which set forth in vivid tableau the features which shall attend the establishment of His Messianic kingdom here on earth. While in Zech. 14: 4 we are told, that when He returns with the "government upon His shoulder" (Isa. 9: 6), "His feet shall stand in that day upon the mount of Olives."

At the burning bush Jehovah proclaimed His name, but there it was not a making known of the principles which regulate Him in the government of His people, rather was it a revelation of what He *is* in Himself—the great "I AM," the all-sufficient, self-subsisting One, "with whom is no variableness neither shadow of turning" (James 1: 17). How appropriate was such a revelation of Himself on that occasion!

Moses was about to appear, first, to his oppressed brethren, who would, at the onset, welcome him, but subsequently blame him because of their increased burdens; later before Pharaoh, who would first display an haughty and defiant spirit, and then a vacillating and temporising one. Well was it for Moses to lay firm hold of the glorious fact that he was an ambassador of the great "I AM."

"And the Lord descended in the cloud, and stood with him there, and proclaimed the name of the Lord." With this should be compared, or rather contrasted what we read of in John 17. There we find our Saviour rendering an account of His work to the One who had sent Him here; and, as He entered into detail, the first thing that He says is, "I have *manifested Thy name*." But how different was this from what we have in Ex. 34: There it was God making Himself known *in government*; here it was God made manifest by the Son *in grace*. This is at once evidenced by the words immediately following, "I have manifested Thy name unto the men which *Thou gavest Me* out of the world: Thine they were, and Thou gavest them Me"; it was grace, pure and simple, eternal and sovereign, which gave us to Christ. So again in the 26th verse we hear our great High Priest saying to the Father, "I have declared unto them Thy name, and will declare it: *that* the love wherewith Thou hast loved Me may be *in them*." Ah, that was grace, the "riches of His grace" (Eph. 1: 7), yea, "the *glory* of His grace" (Eph. 1: 6).

"And the Lord passed by before him, and proclaimed, The Lord, The Lord God, merciful and gracious, longsuffering, and abundant in goodness and truth, Keeping mercy for thousands, forgiving iniquity and transgression and sin, and that will by no means clear the guilty; visiting the iniquity of the fathers upon the children, and upon the children's children, unto the third and fourth generation" (vv. 6, 7). These are the most important as well as the most blessed verses in our passage. In them the Lord makes known the principles or attributes which are exercised in the government of His people. The *perfections* of that government appear in that *seven* principles are here enumerated. A careful study of them supplies the key to and explains all the subsequent dealings of God with Israel.

It is a most profitable exercise to go through the remainder of the Old Testament in view of these verses: by them much light is thrown upon the later history of Israel. Many are the passages in the prophets which have their roots in Ex. 34: 6, 7; many are the prayers whose appeals were based upon their contents. But that which is the most important for us to heed is that, here we have proclaimed what marked the "ways" of Jehovah with Israel. As we trace His dealings with them from Sinai onwards, it will be found that each one of these seven attributes were in constant exercise. Let us now consider, though briefly, each one separately.

"The Lord God merciful." How unspeakably precious is it to mark that *this* is mentioned first. It is, we might say, the fount from which all the others flow: because God is *merciful*, He is "gracious, longsuffering, abundant in goodness" etc. Mercy was the hope of David when he had sinned so grievously: "Let us fall now into the hand of the Lord, for His *mercies* are great" (2 Sam. 24: 14. Solomon owned God's "mercy" to Israel (1 Kings 3: 6: 8: 23). So Jehosaphat (2 Chron. 20: 21). So too Nehemiah at a later date: mark how he recalled the constant mercy of God to Israel: 9: 19, 27, 28, 31. So too did Daniel encourage himself in the mercy of God: 9: 9, 18. To Jeremiah God said, "Go and proclaim these words toward the north, and say, return, thou backsliding Israel, saith the Lord; and I will not cause Mine anger to fall upon you: *for I am merciful*, saith the Lord" (3: 12).

It is on the ground of "mercy" that God will take up Israel again in a coming day. He shall say, "For a small moment have I forsaken thee; but with *great mercies* will I gather thee" (Isa. 54: 7). "And I will show mercies unto you, that he may have mercy upon you, and cause you to return to your own land" (Jer. 42: 12). So the Lord Jesus shall yet say "And I will strengthen the house of Judah, and I will save the house of Joseph, and I will bring them again to place them; for I have *mercy* upon them: and they shall be as though I had not cast them off" (Zech. 10: 6).

"And gracious." This tells us the ground on which God bestows His mercies: it is not for anything in man or from him, but solely because of His own benignity. All of God's mercies are gifts, free favours to a people entirely devoid of any worthiness. Many are the appeals to the grace of God recorded in the Old Testament. David cried, "O God, the proud are risen against me, and the assemblies of violent men have sought after my soul; and have not set Thee before them. But Thou O Lord, art a God full of compassion, and *gracious*" (Psa. 86: 14, 15).' Hezekiah appealed to the Divine clemency (2 Chron. 30: 9). So did Jonah (4:2). Isaiah assured the people in his day, "And therefore will the Lord wait, that He may be *gracious* unto you" (Isa. 30: 18). Through Joel God said to Israel, "Rend your heart, and not your garments, and turn unto the Lord your God: for He is *gracious*" (2: 13). While in the last book of the Old Testament the prophet exhorted, "And now, I pray you, beseech God that He will be *gracious* unto us" (1: 9).

"Longsuffering." How strikingly did the whole history of Israel bear witness to the wondrous patience of God! The word longsuffering signifies "slow to anger." It was to the "longsuffering" of Jehovah that Moses first appealed when Israel had sinned so grievously at Kadesh-barnea (Num. 14: 18). It was the realisation of God's great patience which stayed David's heart (Psa. 145: 8). To it Nehemiah referred when reviewing Israel's history and God's long forebearance with them (9 : 18). In Nahum's brief but powerful message we read, "The Lord is slow to anger and great in power" (1: 3). The Lord Jesus pointed to the same perfection when He said to the Jews. "O Jerusalem, Jerusalem, thou that killest the prophets, and stonest them which are sent unto thee, *how often* would I have gathered thy children together" (Matt. 23: 37).

"Abundant in goodness." The Hebrew word for goodness is more frequently translated "kindness." David acknowledged it when he said, "Blessed be the Lord; for He hath showed me His marvellous *kindness* in a strong city" (Psa. 41: 21). So too Nehemiah (9: 17). In a coming day the Lord will say to Israel, "In a little wrath I hid My face from thee for a moment; but with everlasting *kindness* will I have mercy on thee" (Isa. 54 : 8). The Hebrew word is also rendered "loving-kindness." Frequent mention of it is made in the Psalms: "For Thy lovingkindness is before mine eyes" (26: 3); "How excellent is Thy lovingkindness, O God!" (36: 7); "We have thought of Thy lovingkindness, O God, in the midst of Thy temple" (48: 9). Isaiah said, "I will mention the lovingkindnesses of the Lord" (63: 7). Through Jeremiah God said, "But let him that glorieth glory in this, that he understandeth and knoweth Me, that I am the Lord which exercise *lovingkindness*, judgment, and righteousness, in the earth: for in these things I delight" (9: 24).

"And truth." The Hebrew word signifies "stedfastness." It is rendered "verity" in Psalm 111: 7: "The works of His hands are verity and judgment." It is translated "faithful" in Nehemiah 7: 2. To the men of Jabesh-gilead David said, "The Lord show kindness and truth unto you" (2 Sam. 2: 6). Unto Jehovah the Psalmist sang, "For Thy mercy is great above the heavens: and Thy *truth* reacheth unto the clouds" (Psa. 108: 4). God is faithful to His covenant-engagements, true to both His promisings and His threatenings.

"Keeping mercy for thousands—*forgiving* iniquity and transgressions and sin." How often God pardoned Israel for her sins! "And they remembered that God was their rock, and the high God their redeemer. Nevertheless they did flatter Him with their mouth, and they lied unto Him with their tongues. For their heart was not right with Him, neither were they stedfast in His covenant. *But He*, being full of compassion, *forgave* their iniquity, and destroyed them not: yea, many a time turned He His anger away" (Psa. 78: 35-38). So in a coming day the Lord will say, "I will *forgive* their iniquity, and I will remember their sin no more" (Jer. 31: 34).

"And that will by no means clear the guilty; visiting the iniquity of the fathers upon the children, and upon the children's children, unto the third and fourth generation." Though God pardons, often He does not remit the consequences of sin: "Thou wast a God that forgavest them, *though* Thou tookest vengeance of their inventions" (Psa. 99: 8). To this day the Jews are suffering because of the sins of their forefathers.

It only remains for us to add that, inasmuch as God changes not, the seven principles contemplated above *now* regulate His government of Christendom corporately and the Christian individually. How merciful, how gracious, how longsuffering, has God been to those who profess His name! How good, how faithful, how forgiving, all through these nineteen centuries! Yet the sins of the fathers have also been visited upon their children. Today we are suffering from the compromisings, unfaithfulness, sectarianism, pride, and wickedness, of those who went before us. May the Lord bless to the reader what has been according to His own Word.

—*Arthur W. Pink.*

PRAY DAILY FOR THE MINISTRY OF THIS MAGAZINE.

6. ABRAM'S FAILURE.
—*Gen.* 12 : 9, 10.

In our last article we contemplated Abram's worship: that which preceded it, that which accompanied it, and that which maintained it. It is only as we observe diligently the *order* of things here in Gen. 12 that many valuable lessons will be laid hold of by our hearts. God is a God of order, and perfect wisdom, arrangement, precision, mark alike His works and His Word. His truth is ever presented to us in spiritual and logical sequence, though an anointed eye is required to perceive this. The chief trouble is that most of us are in too big a hurry, and fail to prayerfully meditate upon the details of Scripture.

That which *preceded* Abram's worship, denoted by his erecting an "altar," was his response to the terms of God's call. We re-iterate because until the Christian has entered the path of obedience he cannot be a worshipper in the true sense of the word. Upon entering Canaan, Abram seems to have made at once for Sichem, where grew the oak of Moreh; which speaks, in figure, of the Christian taking upon him the yoke of Christ and learning of Him who is meek and lowly in heart. This too has to be made good in our experience before true worship will ascend from us to God. Then we are told, "the Lord appeared unto Abram." The N.T. equivalent of this is found in John 14 : 21 : Christ manifesting Himself to the one who evidences his love by keeping the Lord's commandments. This is another prerequisite of worship.

That which *accompanied* Abram's worship was his removal "unto a mountain on the east of Bethel." Experimentally, the "mountain" speaks of elevation of spirit, the heart seeking those things which are above, delighting itself in the Lord. As the believer is occupied with Him who is "altogether lovely," he is lifted out of himself, and soars high above the poor things of this perishing world. A notable example of this is found in Acts 16, where we behold the apostles, with bleeding backs, their feet in the stocks, incarcerated in the dark and damp Philippian dungeon. Yet were they full of joy, singing praises unto God! Ah, beloved reader, just so long as you dwell upon the difficulties of the way, the unpleasantness of your circumstances, or the infirmities and sins of your wretched self, gloom and groans will be your experience. Only as the heart turns unto Him who is "fairer than the children of men" are we able to say, "My soul doth magnify the Lord, and my spirit hath rejoiced in God my Saviour." Only by frequent meditation on His amazing grace, His boundless love, His unchanging faithfulness, His infinite perfections, is the heart drawn out in adoring thanksgiving.

It is to be noted that the mountain to which Abram betook himself was "on the east of Bethel." Now Bethel signifies "the house of God." Our mind turns at once to Luke 15. It was into the Father's "house" that the repenting prodigal was brought. It was there that the best robe, the ring, shoes for his feet, were placed upon him. It was there that the fatted calf was feasted upon—figure of our enjoyment of Christ who was slain for us. It was there "they began to be merry." But what meaneth "on the *east* of Bethel"? Ah, the east is that quarter which heralds the dawn of another day. It is that point of the compass where new light bursts upon a darkened earth. Is not the spiritual application evident? It is the spirit of worship which keeps us in the *freshness* of all that God's "house" speaks of!

That which *maintained* Abram's worship is intimated in the words "and pitched his tent." The tent is the temporary abode of a sojourner: it is the emblem of a "pilgrim." It speaks of separation from the world. Abram dwelt in Canaan for upwards of seventy-five years, but so far as we can gather, both from the book of Genesis and Heb. 11 : 9, he was content to tarry, all that time, in a tent. Now it is only as the stranger-and-pilgrim-spirit is maintained by the Christian, that worship can be sustained. Just as soon as he settles down here, and his desires, interests, pleasures, are centered upon earthly things, is the spirit of worship quenched. Find a worldly-minded Christian and, every time, you will discover a worshipless Christian. The reason why so few are found today offering a "sacrifice of *praise*" (Heb. 13: 15) unto God, is because so few are walking in separation from that world whose very atmosphere stifles the regenerated soul. Back to thy tents, O Israel; then shall we hear again the singing of birds in our Zion.

In our last article we called attention to the fact that Abram's building of an altar is the one item which is repeated in vv. 7, 8. We sought to show the reasons for this are, because the Holy Spirit would thereby make the altar the central figure upon which our attention is to be fixed; because He would thus emphasise the importance of its spiritual import; and because of the double line of truth which is suggested by it. First, the altar stands for *worship.* The primary thought connected with the "altar" in scripture is not that of atonement made for sin, but of presenting to God an offering of thanksgiving. The first time the altar comes before us in the O.T. is in Gen. 8: 20, where we read "And Noah builded an altar unto the Lord; and took of every clean beast, and of every clean fowl, and offered burnt offerings on the altar." This was Noah's first act after emerging from the ark, and it plainly enough evidenced his gratitude unto God. Immediately following we are told, "And the Lord smelled a sweet savour."

The next reference to the "altar" is in Gen. 12: 7, 8, and there is nothing to show that Abram presented to God a sin-offering from it. Plainer still is the teaching of Gen. 22. There we read of Abram's laying his son Isaac on the altar: how significant then to observe that before doing so he said to his servant, "I and the lad will go yonder and *worship,* and come again to you" (v. 5)! The first altar mentioned in Exodus was not for the reception of a sacrifice for sin, but was for "burnt offerings and the peace offerings" (20: 24). So the last time that we have the "altar" mentioned in Scripture we read, "And another Angel came and stood at the altar, having a golden censer; and there was given unto Him much incense, that He should offer it with the prayers of all saints upon the golden altar which was before the throne" (Rev. 8: 3).

Closely connected with the thought of worship, the "altar" was also the place of *priestly exercise.* Abram's erection of an altar denoted his taking a priestly place before God. This is something which is almost entirely absent today, and necessarily so, due to the fact that the vast majority of Christians are now living on such a low spiritual plane. All true believers *have been* made "kings and priests unto God" (Rev. 1: 6), have access to Him through Christ (Heb. 10: 21, 22), and all are privileged to come before Him with "spiritual sacrifices" (1 Pet. 2: 5). But how few Christians are there who ever exercise these privileges! To take a priestly place before God means ministering to *His* pleasure. Yet how little is there of this today!

Even when the saints come together on the Lord's day, the spirit of worship is conspicuous by its absence. It seems that their thoughts rarely rise above themselves. Even where they are not nursing their doubts and fears, and groaning over their sins and infirmities, it is generally their *needs* which absorb them—food for their souls, the strengthening of their faith, the seeking of fresh blessings *from* God. Few of them appear to have ever realised the concept that it is their happy privilege (and their bounden duty too) to present something *to* God—the thanks of their hearts, the joy of their souls, the adoring of Himself for all that He is. Nor is it much better in the pulpit: more petitions than praises are presented, and rarely do we hear a servant of God exclaiming with loving fervour, "Bless the Lord, O my soul: and all that is within me, bless His holy name" (Psa. 103: 3).

Few however can remain inactive; the feverish energies of the flesh *must* find an outlet somewhere. Consequently, where there is little or no ministering to the delight of God, there is now an abundance of so-called "service" for man. One of the popular slogans of the hour is that, "we are saved to serve." It would be far more accurate to say, "We are saved to worship." The Father is not seeking servants, but "worshippers" (John 4: 23). Service is proper enough in its place, but if it is allowed to oust worship, it is pressed into a wrongful place. Nor is it difficult to understand why "service" is so prominent today: seeking to minister unto the needs of fellow-sinners calls for far less exercise of heart and demands much less spirituality of life than does ministering unto the thrice holy God. Moreover, it affords more scope for pride being given a place, it makes me self-important; whereas worship *bows* me before God in the adoring contemplation of Himself.

Exodus 30: 30 gives us God's thought of the "priest": "And thou shalt anoint Aaron and his sons, and consecrate them, that they may *minister unto Me* in the priest's office." But mark it well, that there must be "consecration" before there is entering into priestly exercises. This is one of the great practical truths which Gen. 12 sets before us. It cannot be emphasised too strongly or repeated too often that Abram's "altar," his taking a priestly place before God, is not mentioned until *after* his entrance upon the path of implicit obedience to God, and his coming to Sichem. This is still God's unchanging order: there must be complete separation from the world, the subjugation of the affections and lusts of the flesh to the claims of Him who has called us, the taking of Christ's yoke upon us and learning of Him, the walking in communion with Him, if we are to enter into our priestly privileges and perform our priestly functions by ministering to the pleasure of God.

From this bright picture of Abram's entrance into his priestly privileges, we are now to turn unto a very sad episode in the life of our patriarch, which is recorded for our learning, and which should occasion every true Christian reader deep exercise of heart. That which follows is so entirely out of harmony with what has just been before us, the remaining verses of Gen. 12 present such a sad contrast from the contents of vv. 6 to 8, that it seems difficult to reconcile the one with the other. From Abram's *worship* we now turn to Abram's *failure*, and from that to his *sin*!

Many would argue that one who was now in the path of obedience, who was going on with God so whole-heartedly, who was the man of the " tent " and the " altar," would be immune from such a terrible fall as the remainder of Gen. 12 describes. Should there be those who would modify such an optimistic expectation, and, going to the opposite extreme, would say, " Departures from the path of righteousness on the part of God's people are only to be expected; there has only been one perfect Man who has trode this earth." We would earnestly remind such objectors that it is written, " he that sayeth he abideth in Him, ought himself also so to walk, even as He walked" (1 John 2 : 6). Others, in seeking to minimise the gravity of Abram's conduct, may say, "The flesh still remained in him, and therefore we need not be surprised to find him giving way to it." To them we would reply, *God* has said, "But let not sin therefore reign in your mortal body, that ye should obey it in the lusts thereof. Neither yield ye your members as instruments of unrighteousness unto sin: but yield yourselves unto God, as those that are alive from the dead, and your members as instruments of righteousness unto God" (Rom. 6 : 12, 13). And again, "Mortify therefore your members which are upon the earth " (Col. 3 : 5).

Sin is always sin, no matter in whom it is found; and it is never to be excused, least of all in the Christian. The standard which God has set before us is, "Awake to righteousness, and sin not" (1 Cor. 15 : 34); and, "But as He which hath called you is holy, so be ye holy in all manner of conversation" (1 Pet 1 : 15). There is no honest method of evading the plain force of such words as these. Nor has God failed to make full provision for us to measure up to His standard. He has said, "walk in the Spirit and ye shall not fullfill the lusts of the flesh" Gal. 5 : 16). He has promised, "My grace is sufficient for thee, for My strength is made perfect in weakness" (2 Cor. 12 : 9). And a man subject to the same temptations we are, a man of like passions with ourselves, declared,"I can do all things through Christ which strengtheneth me" (Phil. 4 : 13). Therefore instead of excusing our sins, let us penitently and frankly confess them to God; instead of telling ourselves that a certain amount of fleshly indulgence is inevitable, let us seek grace to aim more diligently and ambitiously at conforming to the standard which God has set before us.

Let us point out, once more, that the failures and falls of the O.T. saints are not designed by God as so many excuses behind which we may shelter. Instead, they are recorded as so many pitfalls in the path of faith which we should sedulously avoid, so many danger-signals which we should diligently heed, so many solemn warnings which we should take to heart. And the way *to profit* from them is to prayerfully and carefully seek into the occasions and causes of them. There is an old adage that "Forewarned is forearmed," and if we take the trouble to find out what led up to each failure, then we should be the more on our guard. If the captain of a ship knows from his chart that there lies ahead of him submerged rocks and low-lying coral islands, he will, if he is a wise man, change his course. So if the Christian today, through a study of the O.T. Scriptures, learns that certain things preceded the culminating sins of various saints of old, he should shun those things as he would a plague.

This principle is allowed by all when it comes to the cases of N.T. saints. Take Peter's denial of Christ: we mention this because it is, perhaps, the best known example of all. Probably every reader of these lines is aware that in the hour of testing, this favoured apostle repudiated his Master with oaths. And most of us know that the Holy Spirit has placed upon record the various steps in his downward course which culminated so tragically. That which *preceded* Peter's great sin really accounts for what he did. The apostle had been filled with self-confidence: he had boasted that though all the others forsook the Lord Jesus yet would not he. Then, instead of heeding his Master's warning " watch and pray lest ye enter into temptation " he went to sleep. Next, he had followed Christ "afar off." Then he had entered the company of the wicked, warming himself at their fire. Finally, when challenged, he had denied his allegiance to the Lord.

Now it is by carefully noting, by taking to heart these preliminary steps in Peter's backslidings that we may personally profit from the record of his fearful fall. We observe that self-confidence was the root from which such evil fruit issued, and this should press upon us the solemn force of such words as, "Pride goeth before destruction, and a haughty spirit before a fall" (Prov. 16: 18), and "Wherefore let him that thinketh *he* standeth, take heed lest he fall" (1 Cor. 10: 12); and should cause us to cry earnestly to God that we may be delivered from pride, and daily ask Him for a spirit of entire dependency upon Himself. And so we should take up and translate into exercise of heart and earnest prayer the other points in Peter's departure from Christ. *In like manner* we should study the contexts of Noah's drunkenness, Isaac's gluttony, Moses' anger, David's adultery, for the purpose of discovering what *preceded* their sins, that we may be the more on our guard against falling into them. It is thus that we propose to take up what the Holy Spirit has recorded as immediately preceding Abram's going *"down into Egypt,"* where he lied unto Pharoah.

"And Abram journeyed, going on still toward the south, and there was a famine in the land; and Abram went down into Egypt to sojourn there; for the famine was grievous in the land" (vv. 9, 10). A careful reading of these verses reveals the fact that there were four things which preceded Abram's going down into Egypt, each of which needs to be attentively weighed, each of which followed in logical order downwards, each of which is recorded for our admonition. May the Spirit of God prepare our hearts to ponder them as in the prescence of the thrice holy One.

"And Abram journeyed." What does this tell us? Unless we here ponder each word slowly we are very liable to miss most important instruction for our conscience. The treasures of Scripture are not revealed to lazy people: it is the man who meditates in God's law "day and night" who becomes like a tree " planted (fixed and stable) by the rivers of water (the place of refreshment), that bringeth forth his fruit in his season " (Psa. 1: 2, 3). So here: unless we move slowly, we shall miss the most important point of all. To learn the first spiritual lesson which v. 9 points, we need to refer back to the preceding one. Let us set it forth thus: "And Abram removed from thence unto a mountain on the east of Bethel . . . and there he builded an altar unto the Lord. . . . and Abram journeyed." Now does the reader perceive the starting point in our patriarch's path of declension. *Abram left Bethel*!

This is the first thing for us to carefully note and lay well to heart. Abram turned away from "the house of God," which speaks of communion, and left his "altar," the place of worship! All that follows is recorded for the purpose of warning us what is surely to be expected if *we* leave "Bethel." Abram's leaving of Bethel was the root cause of failure; what follows makes known the effects of such a course. Here the Spirit has exposed the root, later we see the bitter fruit which sprang from it. "Bethel," we repeat, was the place of communion and priestly privileges; once that was left, the path moved downwards swiftly. *That* was the place that Peter left, for he followed Christ "afar off." *That* was the place which the Christian profession forsook in the early days of this dispensation: "Thou hast left thy first love" (Rev. 2: 4), explains all that follows in the remainder of Rev. 2 and throughout Rev. 3.

Ah, Christian reader, make no mistake upon this vitally-important point: moving away from Bethel, getting out of communion with the Lord, leaving our first love, is the root cause of all our failures. No man can sin in the presence of Christ. The heart cannot be engaged with two objects at the same time. If my heart is occupied with the Beloved, then the things of the world have no attraction for me, and Satan has no power over me. If I am walking in the Spirit I shall not, cannot, fulfill the lusts of the flesh. The whole secret of the Christian life is being able to say daily, "for me to live is *Christ* "—to be absorbed with Him, learning of Him, obeying Him, glorifying Him.

It may be replied, nothing is said in Gen. 12: 9 about Abram leaving Bethel. Directly, no; by clear and necessary implication, yes. But to show that we have not read into v. 9 what is not there, let the reader turn with us to what is recorded in Gen. 13: 1-4. Ah, that is plain enough, is it not! When Divine grace restored Abram to the paths of righteousness, he retraced his steps to the place where he had been at the beginning, and that place was *Bethel,* the house of God, over which is the Lord Jesus; as it is written, " But Christ as a Son over His own house." (Heb. 3: 6).

There is only space left for us to touch briefly upon the second cause of Abram's sad failure: "And Abram journeyed, going on" (v. 9)—a *restless spirit* now possessed him. The Hebrew here is more expressive and emphatic. "And Abram journeyed, in going and journeying still toward the south." This was a sure sign of loss of communion. Psa. 37: 7 says, " Rest in the Lord." Yes, but note *before* that, comes " Delight thyself also in the Lord" (v. 4). This is a day of restlessness, of feverish bustle and excitement, of rushing about hither and thither. It has ever been true that "the wicked are like the troubled sea, which *cannot* rest" (Isa. 57 : 20), but it is sad indeed to see so many of God's people in the same miserable plight. And the cause of it is the same now as it was in the days of Abram: leaving Bethel is the certain precursor of a spirit of restlessness taking possession of us. "He that hath an ear to hear let him hear." "Be still and know that I am God"!

"There is perhaps no moment in the life of a believer when he has more need to watch, than when he has been enabled to reach some point of desired and honoured attainment in the path of his pilgrimage. It was a great thing for Abram to have left the land of his fathers, and to have followed on obediently until at last he entered the Land into which it was the object of God to bring him. His obedience was so far complete. He felt, perhaps, that he had done great things. Self-complacency not unfrequently attends successful obedience. He may have expected too, now that he had reached Canaan, to enjoy present rest. Could it be needful now, that there should be the same anxious vigilance as during the days of his wearing journeyings? Was the end of those journeyings to come without bringing with it any result of present good? Nature soon becomes impatient, disappointed, fretful—a condition very adverse to the calm, quiet exercise of faith. Patient endurance, and the sorrow of hope long deferred, were among the lessons to be taught to Abram—and finally he learnt them. Now, however, he went journeying on, no longer waiting on the guidance of his heavenly Friend." (B. W. Newton).

—*Arthur W. Pink.*

THE SERVANT-KING.

In this article we propose taking up the histories of David and Solomon, with a view to noting their striking and blessed foreshadowings of the Lord Jesus Christ. Ere turning to a few details concerning them, let us point out (more especially for the benefit of those who wish to make a study of the types) that, again and again, *two* objects were selected by the Spirit to prefigure the person and work of Christ. Well-known illustrations of this are seen in the "two turtle-doves" (Lev. 14: 22) and the "two goats" (Lev. 16: 7). So too the same principle applies to persons. Noah and Abraham together portray the *headship* of Christ: the former as Lord and Heir of the earth in its fulness (Gen. 9: 1-3); the latter as Father of the family of God (Rom. 4: 16; Heb. 2: 13). Moses and Aaron are united to set forth the prophetic and priestly offices of Christ. In like manner, David and Solomon adumbrate the *kingship* of Christ. The order and character of their respective reigns supply the needed key to unlock the distinctive typical significance of each. David's must be considered before we are prepared to contemplate Solomon's.

Now in many respects was David a wonderful type of Christ: not in that which was sinful and exceptional about him, but in that which marked him generally and in the even tenor of his ways. Born in Bethlehem of Judea, given a name which signifies "the Beloved," designated "the man after God's own heart," we see at once an unmistakable foreshadowing of David's Son and Lord. A "shepherd" they despised; a man of sorrows as few have been; suffering chiefly from those who were related to him by ties of flesh; he aptly prefigured the One who is still "despised and rejected of men." As one who vanquished the great adversary of God's people (Golioth), who was exalted from the sheepcote to the throne, and as the one who reigned till he had subdued all Israel's enemies, David clearly pointed to Him who is the Captain of our salvation, our triumphant Redeemer, and exalted Lord.

But there is one feature in David's character which marked him in every scene through which he passed, one lovely grace which no change of circumstances could affect, and that was, at all times and at all seasons, he was the *servant*. No matter what the sphere of his life might be *that* was his character. The very first time he is introduced to us in Scripture, we behold him thus. There we see him slighted and well-nigh forgotten. He was the youngest of his father's sons, scarcely given a place among his children, treated rather *as* a servant: "And he said, There remaineth yet the youngest, and, behold, he *keepeth the sheep*" (1 Sam. 16: 11).

Though lightly esteemed by his brethren, David had found favour in the eyes of God. He was the one chosen by Him to occupy the throne, and Samuel was sent to anoint him (1 Sam. 16: 13). Striking indeed is it to mark the immediate sequel. There we see him in Saul's house, not so much as occupying a position of honour, still less exercising those prerogatives to which his "anointing" entitled him; but acting as a *servant*: "And it came to pass, when the evil spirit from God was upon Saul, that David took an harp, and played with his hand: so Saul was refreshed, and was well, and the evil spirit departed from him" (1 Sam. 16: 23). Thus we see him *waiting on* Saul; not ministered unto, but ministering to him.

The next mention of him is equally striking. In 1 Sam. 17: 15 we are told, "But David went and returned from Saul to feed his father's sheep at Bethlehem." Thus, his comforting ministry to Saul completed, he leaves the palace and returns to the farm, not to rule over it, but to care for the sheep. In what immediately follows we find a further exemplification of his lowly spirit.

The Philistines were menacing Israel, and the older sons of Jesse had joined themselves to the army of Saul. Anxious for their wellfare, their father sends one to enquire how it fared with them. The one selected was his servant-son. Accordingly we read, "And David rose up early in the morning, and left the sheep with a keeper, and took, and went, as Jesse had *commanded* him; and he came to the trench, as the host was going forth to the fight" (1 Sam. 17: 20). Sad indeed is it to see how little David's brethren appreciated his kindness on their behalf: "And Eliab his eldest brother heard when he spake unto the man; and Eliab's anger was kindled against David, and he said, Why camest thou down hither? and with whom hast thou left those few sheep in the wilderness? I know thy pride, and the naughtiness of thine heart; for thou art come down that thou mightest see the battle" (1 Sam. 17: 28). Different far was the errand of David. He had come carrying provisions for them (vv. 17. 18); he had come to *minister* to them; he was there as the *servant* of their needs.

Arriving at the camp, he learns of the haughty challenge of the Philistine giant, and the timidity of Israel's hosts to accept it. Then it was that he proffered himself as the *servant* of Israel's necessities and of Jehovah's glory. The Lord had been dishonoured by this blatant Gentile, and His people threatened. Mark the character in which our hero presented himself before the king: "Let no man's heart fail because of him, thy *servant* will go and fight with this Philistine" (v. 32)—not as a warrior, but as a "servant" would he advance to the conflict. Nor was his confidence in himself: said he, "*The Lord* that delivered me out of the paw of the lion and out of the paw of the bear, *He* will deliver me out of the hand of this Philistine" (v. 37).

In view of Eliab's taunt (1 Sam. 17: 28), the beautiful suggestion has been made by another that it may well have been on this very occasion, there on the plains of Elah, that those words of David in Psalm 131 first found place in his heart, "Lord, my heart is not haughty nor mine eyes lofty: neither do I exercise myself in great matters, or in things too high for me." And then, in the confidence that Jehovah was the strength of His people, he went forth to meet Golioth, encouraging his soul in the closing words of that same Psalm: "Let Israel hope *in the Lord* from henceforth and forever" (v. 3).

Saul had promised unto the one who should slay Golioth, "great riches" and his daughter in marriage" (1 Sam. 17: 25). But it was not the prospect of these things which moved David. It was the fact that "reproach" had been brought upon Israel, and that "the living God" had been defied (v. 26), that caused him to serve the one and glorify the Other. Nor do we read of him, after his memorable victory, claiming the promised reward, flattering and tempting though it might seem—yea, the very things to be most desired had he been one who sought his own glory. Instead, when, later, Saul said, "Behold my elder daughter Merab, her will I give thee to wife," David answered, "*Who am I?* and what is my life, or my father's family in Israel, that I should be son-in-law to the king?" (1 Sam. 18: 18).

Very striking, too, it is to observe David's conduct later, when he suffered so cruelly at the hands of Saul. There was ever the same beautiful spirit of *submission*. Instead of standing up for his own rights, or attempting to avenge his own wrongs, he *yielded* to the enmity of the king. When Saul determined to kill him, David retired from the court: "So David fled, and escaped, and came to Samuel to Ramah, and told him all that Saul had done" (1 Sam. 19: 18). Blessed is it to observe that instead of stating his case to the army, which we may safely assume would readily have responded to the justice of his cause, he betook himself to the prophet of God.

Later, when Saul relentlessly persued him, David entertained no thought of ridding himself of his persecutor: rather than that, he would be as "a partridge in the mountains" all his days. Though knowing full well that he had been appointed and anointed unto the throne of Israel, yet he freely enters into covenant with the rival house of his enemy, regardless of how they tended to exalt them and debase him (1 Sam. 20: 17; 24: 22). When ultimately his enemy fell, and the way to the throne was made simple for him, he rejoiced not on his own account, but was full of grief at the fall of Saul: "The beauty of Israel is slain upon thy high places: how are the mighty fallen! Tell it not in Gath, publish it not in the streets of Askelon; lest the daughters of the Philistines rejoice, lest the daughters of the uncircumcised triumph" (2 Sam. 1 : 19, 20).

The one who brought to him the tidings of Saul's death did not understand David. He supposed, no doubt, that he had brought joy to the king-elect, and that he would be rewarded for his pains; but David looked on the sadness of Israel's dishonour and on the sin of an Amalekite for lifting up his hand against the anointed of Jehovah (2 Sam. 1 : 14-16). How strikingly did this incident illustrate those words, "Therefore the world *knoweth us not*" (1 John 3 : 1)!—their griefs are not our griefs, nor their joys our joys.

But we may trace the *servant*-character of David still further, for no change of scene or circumstance had any power to affect him on whom the Spirit of God abode; changing scenes and circumstances only served to set forth his character more brightly. And should it not be so with us, Christian readers? There is only one thing which will be rewarded in the kingdom—that which is the product of lowliness: "Whosoever shall exalt himself shall be abased; and he that shall humble himself shall be exalted" (Matt. 23 : 12). Nothing but *service* shall be honoured hereafter. Is it not written, "Whosoever will be great among you, shall be your *minister*" (Mark 10 : 43)? And again; "If any man *serve* Me, him will My father *honour*" (John 12 : 26).

We are now to look at David on the throne; having received it, though, not by his own seeking, but called to it by the Lord Himself. And *how* does David conduct himself now? Alas, how many a servant of God might trace *his* fall to a rise, his poverty to prosperity, his loss from gain! For this reason we may well pray, "Give me neither poverty nor riches" etc., (Prov. 30 : 8, 9). But with David it was far otherwise. He still exercised the spirit of self-abnegation. That which had characterised him as a boy in Bethlehem, as a youth on Elah's plains, and as a member of Saul's household; just that which had marked him in the caves and holds of the wilderness, now signalized him as seated upon the throne of Israel. He was still the servant, doing Jehovah's pleasure alone, seeking only *His* glory. He gave himself no rest. He paused not in his course till the enemies of the Lord and His people were all subdued (2 Sam. 22 : 38).

So too, later, the time of peace, as well as the time of war, was marked by *service* on the part of the king: at home or abroad, he was ever the same. Blessed is it to behold how he was occupied in his declining years. Hear him as he says, "Surely I will not come into the tabernacle of my house, nor go up into my bed; I will not give sleep to mine eyes, or slumber to mine eyelids, *Until I find out a place for the Lord*, an habitation for the mighty God of Jacob" (Psa. 132 : 3-5). Therefore do we find him making provision and preparation for it, and bringing up the ark of Jehovah—which had been neglected in the days of Saul (1 Chron. 13 : 3)—to the place in the tabernacle which he had pitched for it. Yea, more; *he* waits on it himself, offering burnt and peace offerings. Beautiful too is it to see him blessing the people in the name of the Lord, and, as a girded servant, making them to sit down to meat, while *he* served them (2 Sam. 6 : 19).

At the end, unwearied in serving as at the beginning, he proposes to build a temple for the ark of the Lord (1 Chron. 22 : 14), Not only so, but he gave patterns of all things to Solomon. *He* numbered and distributed the Levites into courses, for the service of the house. He appointed the offices of the singers, instructed in the songs of the Lord; settled the divisions of the porters and judges. And then, when all his service was ended, and nothing remained but to reap the fruit of it all, and the glory of the kingdom for which all these things had been prepared, *he retires*. He ceased to be, when he must cease to serve. The throne of Jerusalem was no more to him then the sheepcote at Bethlehem; in both, all his desire was to fill *as an hireling* his day.

"The king also said unto them, Take with you the servants of your lord, and cause Solomon my son to ride upon mine own mule, and bring him down to Gihon: And let Zadok the priest and Nathan the prophet anoint him there king over Israel: and blow ye with the trumpet, and say, God save king Solomon. Then ye shall come up after him, that he may come and sit upon my throne; for he shall be king *in my stead*" (1 Kings 1 : 33-35). Thus he gave up the throne which his own hands had established, with all the honours of it, for these were nothing in his account —he had finished his work of service, and *that* was everything to him.

The moment that everything was ready for the full display of glory, he *disappeared*. He had sown, another would now reap. He had laboured, and he was willing that another should now enter into his labours. He appointed Solomon his son king over Israel. "Then Solomon sat on the throne of the Lord as king instead of David his father, and prospered; and all Israel obeyed him" (1 Chron. 29 : 23). Such was David. But in Solomon we see another thing altogether. Solomon enjoyed *by inheritance* the honours and the name which David in his trouble and toil had gotten. In the sight of Israel the Lord magnified Solomon exceedingly, and bestowed upon him such royal majesty as had not been on any king before him. He excelled all the kings of the earth in riches and wisdom, and God made the name of Solomon better than David's name, and his throne greater than David's throne (1 Kings 1 : 47). David did the Lord call his *servant*, but Solomon He called His *son*, saying, "I will be to him a Father, and he shall be to Me a son." As heir of the fruit of David's service, Solomon appears before us full of peace and prosperity; not as David had been,—the scorn of others; but the boast and joy of his people, and the very centre of the world's attention, for his fame went abroad into all the earth.

Solomon's was the time of rest. No enemy remained for him to conquer, no work of toil and trouble was laid upon him. His was the time of joy also. Therefore, then for the first time, did *songs* break forth from the midst of the congregation of Israel. Moses had appointed sacrifices, but no songs had been heard in the Tabernacle. David had ordered the singers, given them their charge, and settled them in their course, but all this was prepared for Solomon: it was in the House that *he* builded that the trumpeters and singers first awakened the praises of Jehovah in Israel. And glorious, above all, was the Cloud which filled the Temple. These things were characteristic of Solomon's days: nothing was there but peace and joy, glory and praise (2 Chron. 5 : 12-13).

Now this double type of David and Solomon finds its fulfilment in the Lord Jesus Christ. He too is the perfect Servant before He reigns as the glorious King. From the beginning, His *servant* character is seen. What was His work of creation but a glorifying of the Father and a ministry unto His creatures! When He entered this world it was "in the form of a *servant*" (Phil. 2). He came here "not to be ministered unto, but to minister." At all times He could say, "I seek not mine own glory."

When challenged by His brethren according to the flesh "show thyself to the world," He answered, "My time is not yet come" (John 7 : 6). When He had been engaged in wondrous works of grace, and the people were astonished, His disciples (desirous that He should be magnified in the eyes of the world) said, "All men seek for Thee," but His only answer was that of a *servant*—"Let us go into the next towns, that I may *preach* there also" (Mark 1 : 38). And such was He throughout.

As a Child He was subject to His parents, thus fulfilling all righteousness. When "anointed" by God (Acts 10 : 38) at the Jordan, like David, He still went forth only to serve. Whether in solitudes by night, or in abundant labours by day, the Father could ever say of Him, "Behold My *servant*" (Isa. 42 : 1). He ever performed the works of Him that sent Him. The vows of His God were on Him, and He did all, till He was entitled to say, "It is finished:" He was obedient unto death, even the death of the cross."

Not only did the fact of His death, but all the circumstances of it as well, attest the place which He had taken. The demands which were made upon Him at Calvary were just those which the fallen creature in his pride, would make: "And they that passed by reviled Him, wagging their heads and saying, Thou that destroyest the temple, and buildest it is three days *save Thyself*. If Thou be the Son of God, come down from the cross" (Matt. 27 : 39). But such was the perfection of this Servant, He utterly resisted those demands. He had met this same temptation from Satan, when he sought to get Him to glorify Himself (Matt. 4 : 6); and now man, moved by the pride which had been his transgression in Eden, sought the same. But in vain.

And wherein lay the *necessity* for this humiliation of the Son of God? It was that He might undo the mighty mischief that our pride wrought when, in the person of our first representative, we sought to be as God (Gen. 3 : 5, 6). But this was only possible by the Highest emptying Himself, and the Brightness of God's glory being manifested in flesh, veiling Himself in Servant form. The first Adam sought his own glory; the last Adam laid His by (John 17 : 5). To be "as God" was the daring design of the first man—a creature of yesterday; to take the form of a servant was the willing humiliation of the second Man—whose goings forth had been from eternity. Thus the attempted dishonour to God by the one was abundantly repaired by the Other.

He was "crucified through weakness" (2 Cor. 13 : 4). Everything that the pride of the fallen creature would scorn and reject, and count as weakness, was in Him. But in this was God's delight and honour: for the Son of man thus, in the loss of reputation and life, in the cross and its shame, met all the reproaches and enmity of man's pride and apostasy. "For *Thy* sake I have borne reproach; shame hath covered My face;" "The reproaches of them that reproached *Thee* are fallen upon Me" (Psa. 69 : 79) was the language of the Son to the Father.

Thus can He as Son of man hold glory and a kingdom in *righteousness*. In His person, through His perfect life and by His obedient death, He had made answer to all the pride and assumption of man, and He can therefore take the honour of dominion which man had forfeited. He loved righteousness, and hated iniquity; therefore shall His throne be forever and ever. He was once crucified through weakness, yet He liveth by the power of God now, and the kingdoms of this world shall be His hereafter (Rev. 11 : 15). And ought not we, fellow-Christians, be ready to be "weak" for Him—accounted of the world vile, that our present life may be more in the same power of God, and our coming glory, glory at the hand of our God in company with the once despised and rejected Christ?

But not only was He the perfect Servant, both of the Father and of sinners, while here on earth, even unto death and all its circumstances, but now in heaven the Son of God is waiting on the Father and ministering to us. He is "A *Minister* of the sanctuary" (Heb. 8 : 2), continually making intercession for us, till He shall present His people faultless before the presence of His glory with exceeding joy. And even then, when He comes forth in manifested glory, it will be as *Servant*: "He shall gird Himself, and make them to sit down to meat, and will come forth and serve them" (Luke 12 : 37); "For the Lamb which is in the midst of the throne shall feed them, and shall lead them unto living fountains of waters" (Rev. 7 : 17).

Thus is He the true David: no change of scene or circumstances ever produced any change in His character as the Servant of Jehovah's glory and His people's joy. But God has also highly exalted Him as Solomon, and given Him a name which is above every name, to which every knee shall bow, of things in heaven and things on earth, and things under the earth. God has crowned Him with glory and honour, and put all things under His feet. He will bring Him forth into this world a second time and all the angels of God shall worship Him. On His thigh and on His vesture shall His name be written " King of kings and Lord of lords." To Him whom men despised, to this Servant of servants, kings shall pay homage, princes also shall worship, and all nations shall call Him blessed. He has been anointed with the oil of gladness above His fellows, and "The God of the whole earth" shall He be called.

The King shall be seen in His beauty then: He shall bless the people like Solomon, and sustain them in all their needs (2 Chron. 6). On His breastplate and on His shoulders He will bear their names continually. And like as Solomon builded cities, and fenced them with walls and bars, so that "Judah and Israel dwelt safely, every man under his vine and under his fig tree, from Dan even to Beer-sheba, all the days of Solomon" (1 Kings 4 : 25), so says the King by His prophet, "And My people shall dwell in a peaceable habitation, and in sure dwellings, and in quiet resting places" (Isa. 32 : 18). The word of knowledge was with Solomon, and largeness of heart, even as the sand that is on the sea-shore was given to him, and the spirit of understanding to discern judgment: so on the greater than Solomon shall the Spirit of Jehovah rest, "And shall make Him of quick understanding in the fear of the Lord: and He shall not judge after the sight of His eyes, neither reprove after the hearing of ears: But with righteousness shall He judge the poor, and reprove with equity for the meek of the earth" (Isa. 11 : 2-4).

And Zion shall be in her beauty too. King Solomon made silver to be in Jerusalem as stones, and cedars as the sycamore trees that are in the vale for abundance; but when the glory of the Lord rises in Zion, she shall shine in fulness of beauty—every land shall deck her forth—gold from Sheba, and incense, the treasures of the Midianites and Kedar, and the glory of Lebanon shall be there; " I will make the place of My feet glorious " says the King, " for brass I will bring silver, and for wood brass, and for stones iron, I will also make thy officers peace, and thine exactors righteousness" (Isa 60). And upon her citizens shall blessings again be pronounced—" Happy is that people whose God is the Lord " (Psa. 144 : 15). Such and far beyond the range of our poor thoughts, will be the *kingly* glory of our Beloved. First, it will be the Kingdom of *the* Son. It is the " son " and not the " servant " who is to establish and inherit it. The temple was built by Solomon, not David. It therefore has the value of the Son upon it and above it, and this is everything; for this is the charter of its *stability*. This Kingdom cannot have an end.

Second, throughout the Kingdom, there will be a constant remembrance of "the Man of Sorrows," just as everything in the temple, the stones that fitly framed it together, the gold, silver, brass and iron, all spoke increasingly of David: for David *in his trouble* had prepared them all (1 Chron. 2: 18). It was on *this* ground Solomon pleaded with God: "Lord, remember David, and, all his afflictions... Arise, O Lord into Thy rest; Thou, and the ark of Thy strength" (Psa. 132: 1, 8). The afflictions of David were thus known amid the glories of Solomon, and so the Lamb that was slain shall be "in the midst of the throne." As our fallen earth bears upon it every where the trail of the Serpent, so will the Kingdom wear the traces of the blood of the Lamb.

Third, the Kingdom shall be the place of thanksgiving and praise, and God, even our God, shall accept this worship, and rest in it as His honour forever. As when the temple was finished the ark was in its place under the wings of the cherubim, and everything was in due order, then, "It came even to pass, as the trumpeters and singers were as one, to make one sound to be heard in praising and thanking the Lord; and when they lifted up their voice with the trumpets and symbols and instruments of music, and praised the Lord, saying, For He is good; for His mercy endureth forever: that then the house was filled with a cloud, even the house of the Lord; so that the priests could not stand to minister by reason of the Cloud; for the glory of the Lord had filled the house of God" (2 Chron. 5: 13, 14). So, in the Kingdom, shall all be displaced to make room for the glory of Christ, all be silenced save the ceaseless and unwearying songs of joy and praise. Blissful prospect! Oh for faith and hope to anticipate it.

—*Arthur W. Pink.*

N.B.—Quite a little in this article has been suggested by another, which we read recently, from the pen of J. G. Bellett, that appeared in "The Christian Witness" Jan. 1836.

HIDDEN IN THE HEART.

"Thy word have I hid in mine heart that I might not sin against Thee" (Psa. 119: 11).

This truly is a wise and safe thing to do. Let us ponder it. Let us imitate it. There are three special points suggested, namely, *What* have I hid? *Where* have I hid it? *Why* have I hid it? The reader will easily remember what? where? why?

1. *What have I hid?* "Thy Word." It is not man's word, but the Word of God, that liveth and abideth forever. This is the thing to hide. It is a treasure worth hiding. No thief can steal it, no moth corrupt it. It increases by being hidden in the way here spoken of, We cannot set too high a value upon the Word of God. So the Psalmist thought when he "*hid*" it. This expression sets forth how intensely he prized the Word. "I have hid it." He placed it out of the reach of every one and everything that could deprive him of it. May we ponder it—may we understand it—may we imitate it.

2. *Where have I hid it?* "In my heart." It was not in his head, or in his intellect; but in his heart—the seat of his affections—the centre of his moral being—the source of all the influences that swayed his entire career. This is the right place to hide the Word. It is not hiding it under a bed, or under a bushel, or in the earth. It is not basely cushioning it, through a slavish dread of men, lest they should sneer at us, or oppose us. No, my reader, this will not do. We must hide the Word where the Psalmist hid it, even in the heart. May we ponder this—may we understand it—may we imitate it.

3. *Why have I hid it?* For a very weighty reason—a most important reason. "That I might not sin against Thee." It was not that he might have a rich fund of new ideas to talk about and show off upon. Nor yet was it that he might be able to confound in argument all his opposers, and silence them. The Psalmist did not care about any of these things. He had a horror of sin—a holy horror; he knew that the most effectual safeguard against sin was the Word of God, and therefore he hid it in his heart. May we ponder this—may we understand it—may we imitate it.

—Things New and Old, Vol. 3.

not found upon the pages of Holy Writ, but in 1 Tim. 1: 15 we do have that which, virtually, amounts to the same thing: "This is a faithful saying, and worthy of all *acceptation*, that Christ Jesus came into the world to save sinners." So also in 2 Cor. 11: 4 we read, "For if he that cometh preacheth another Jesus, whom we have not preached, or ye receive another spirit, which ye have not received, or another gospel, which ye have not *accepted*, ye might well bear with him." Personally, we prefer to employ the language of John 1: 12, "As many as *received Him*, to them gave He power to become the sons of God, to them that *believe* on His name." To bid sinners, "receive" Christ is, we believe, the preacher's solemn obligation, pointing out that, "he that believeth on Him is not condemned; but he that believeth not is condemned already, *because he hath not believed* in the name of the only-begotten Son of God" (John 3: 18). Further than this we do not see that the scriptures warrant us in going.

The two chief aims of the preacher should be, under God, by means of the Scriptures: first, to show the sinner his ruined and lost condition, the awfulness of his state, the reality of eternal punishment, and thus set before him his *need* of the Saviour. Second, to expose the vanity of every creature-confidence, to declare the impossibility of salvation by self-efforts, to announce that all his righteousness are as filthy rags, to bring before him Christ as the sinner's only hope. His happy task is to set before him One who is "mighty to save," and to leave him face to face with Him. It is his duty to discourage and dispel the sinner's dream that the preacher can help him. Seek to be like John the Baptist. A "voice" —heard, but not seen!

The preacher, as much as any other Christian, is to "walk by faith, not by sight" (2 Cor. 5: 7). He has the Divine assurance that, "Let us not be weary in well doing: for in due season we *shall* reap, *if* we faint not" (Gal. 6: 9). On this he should confidently rest. After he has delivered his message he should retire as quietly and quickly as possible, leaving the Holy Spirit to *apply* the Word in His own sovereign way. He should get alone with God, and, in the name of the Lord Jesus, plead His promise: "So shall My Word be that goeth forth out of My mouth: it shall not return unto Me void, but it *shall* accomplish that which I please, and it *shall* prosper in the thing whereto I sent it" (Isa. 55: 11); saying, "Do as Thou hast said" (2 Sam. 7: 25).

May the Lord stir up all His sent servants to a more faithful, hearty, and Christ-honouring proclamation of the Gospel of His Grace.

ARTHUR W. PINK.

A PERSONAL WORD.

"Come ye yourselves apart into a desert place, and rest a while" (Mark 6: 31). These words sum up the Lord's dealings with us during the past six months. When we left Australia last July, *we* thought the Lord was bringing us to England for active service. But *He* had other designs. Since October 7 not a single door for public preaching has been opened to us. "Rest" was what He saw we personally needed, and "rest" is what, in His infinite grace and tender mercy, He provided for us. Since Dec. 1 we have been in complete seclusion, and, from a spiritual viewpoint, in a "desert place." But O how wondrously and blessedly has the Lord manifested Himself to us! He did not say "Go," but "Come"—We have been *with Him*.

The next place in which our tent is to be pitched, God willing, is Morton's Gap, Kentucky, U.S.A. (this is our *full* postal address), to which we would ask our friends to address their communications. There, we hope to devote most of our time to the work of this magazine, going out occasionally (as the Lord leads) for Bible Conference and Evangelistic work. Morton's Gap is but a small town, but there is a company of God's elect there to whom we are well known, and with whom we anticipate precious seasons of fellowship.

D.V. the July and August issues of "Studies" will be printed in U.S.A. and mailed by us as early as possible: friends kindly be patient. Readers in Great Britain kindly note that Mr. Winstone (address on front cover page) can supply any of our published works. He will be glad to send out sample copies of the Magazine on request, to any of your Christian friends. Please enclose stamped addressed envelope when writing him. Be much in prayer for us and the work the Lord has given to us.

Yours by grace alone,

—*A. W. and V. E. Pink.*

that soul, that he may be enabled to speak "a word in due season" (Prov. 15: 23). Spurgeon used to say, "Some preachers aim at nothing, and they are very good at hitting it." Let us aim directly at the conscience and then at the heart, counting on the Holy Spirit to direct our shafts.

Now the question which is before us for consideration and (attempted) elucidation, really concerns the preacher's efforts to "win souls" (Prov. 11:30), and as to how far the Word warrants him going toward the realisation of his longings to see sinners converted under his ministry. And here, it seems to the writer, there are two extremes to be guarded against. On the one hand, we believe those preachers come short of discharging their duties who rest content with simply setting forth in an abstract and impersonal way what are termed "the Doctrines of Grace." To say, "I have faithfully declared all the counsel of God, and now I must leave results with Him," sounds very pious, but it leaves the way open for several serious questions. It is perfectly true that "results" rest entirely with God, for He alone, "giveth the increase" (1 Cor. 3: 7). But, *have we* declared *all* the counsel of God when we have fully expounded the "five points" of Calvinism? We trow not. The preacher is something more than a human gramophone, mechanically repeating a scriptural formula.

Of the forerunner of Christ it is said that he was "A *burning* and a shining light" (John 5: 3). He was "the voice of one *crying* in the wilderness." No correct but cold formalist was he. Of our Saviour it is recorded that, He wept over Jerusalem because her children would not come to Him. No heartless fatalist was He. The great apostle to the Gentiles wrote, "Knowing therefore the terror of the Lord, we *persuade* men" (2 Cor. 5: 11). Do *you* do this, brother preacher? Query: were Paul on earth to-day saying, "*We* persuade men" would his orthodoxy be suspected? Again; he announced, "Now then we are ambassadors for Christ, as though God did *beseech* by us; we *pray* (plead) in Christ's stead, be ye reconciled to God" (2 Cor. 5: 20). Do *these* methods characterise *our* evangelical ministrations? Surely we all have need to pray earnestly for more devotion to Christ, more love for souls, more fervour and power in preaching the Gospel.

On the other hand, we must not allow our fervour to run away with us. There is a zeal which is not according to knowledge. There is a concern for souls which is not regulated by the Word. And this is to be deplored just as much as a cold and stilted preaching which repells rather than attracts. After a preacher has delivered his message —warned his hearers to flee from the wrath to come, called upon them to forsake their evil ways, presented an all-sufficient Saviour who is ready and able to save all that come to Him; what more can he do? He should press upon his hearers such words as, "Repent and believe the Gospel" (Mark 1: 15). He should remind them that God has said, "*To-day* if ye will hear His voice, harden not your hearts" (Heb. 3: 7, 8). He should warn them, "See that ye *refuse not* Him that speaketh. For if they escaped not who refused Him that spake on earth, much more shall not we escape, if we turn away from Him that speaketh from heaven" (Heb. 12: 25).

Perhaps some will say, "All this is very good, but is not the preacher to press for a decision, there and then?" Much depends upon what is meant by this expression. If what is intended be, the calling upon the sinner to perform some outward act in order to make it evident that he is desirous of being saved—inviting him to come forward and take the preacher's hand, kneel at a penitent-form, sign some card, raise his hand to be prayed for, etc., etc.; we at once ask, Where is the scripture which authorises the preacher to make such a demand or request? Where do we find that our Lord or any of His apostles so acted? And the answer is, Nowhere. "But many godly preachers have employed these methods, and with much success." Answer: the Day to come will show whether or not this is true; in the meantime, we insist most emphatically that the methods of no preacher are any guide or criterion for us. The Word of God is our *only* court of appeal.

But waiving now the matter of any outward demonstration on the part of a seeking sinner, Is it, or is it not, the responsibility of the preacher to aim at his immediate conversion? Though fully assured that a sovereign God has appointed, from all eternity, the very moment when each of His elect shall be brought out of darkness into His marvellous light, yet we also believe that each time a servant of Christ stands up in His name, he should "Preach as a dying man to dying men, as one who never may preach again." It is his bounden duty to cry out, "Boast not thyself of tomorrow; for thou knowest not what a day may bring forth" (Prov. 27: 1) It is part of his God-given commission to say to his hearers, The Feast is spread, "Come, for all things are *now* ready" (Luke 14: 17). It is his privilege to say, at any time, to any awakened and anxious soul, "Believe on the Lord Jesus Christ and thou shalt be saved" (Acts 16: 31).

"But ought he not bid the sinner to accept Christ?" This particular expression is

(Continued on Page 143).

STUDIES IN THE SCRIPTURES

"Search the Scriptures" John 5 : 39

Copyright in all English-speaking Countries.

Editor: Arthur W. Pink, Morton's Gap, Ky., U. S. A.
Hon. Agent in England: Mr. A. Winstone, 2, Lennox Villas, Hewlett Road, Cheltenham.
Hon. Agent in Australia: Mr. G. Ardill, The Christian Workers' Depot.
Commonwealth and Reservoir Streets, Sydney.

FREE TO ALL WHO WILL READ IT.

WHY THIS MAGAZINE IS PUBLISHED

For the encouragement and joy of those who are interested in "the works of the Lord"—which are "sought out of all them that have pleasure therein" (Ps. 111:2)—we usually devote one editorial each year to the giving of some information which illustrates how God is being pleased to bless our labours: Scriptural warrant for such a practice may be found in Acts 14:27, "They rehearsed all that God had done with them." Out of gratitude and love unto those who help us bear the burdens which the publishing of this magazine entails, we feel that we cannot do less than that. It is due unto them that they should know, in part at least, how God is answering their prayers and transmuting their financial gifts into spiritual blessings to fellow-members of the household of faith. It is for this reason we depart from our general rule and insert that which is different from our other articles.

It is true that our motive in publishing these details is liable to be misunderstood that some may think we are actuated by self-importance, moved by a spirit of boasting, or are indirectly but really appealing for funds. Yet, "Unto the pure all things are pure; but unto them that are defiled and unbelieving is nothing pure; but even their mind and conscience is defiled" (Titus 1:15). Whether we be judged rightly or wrongly we must leave in the hands of Him who understandeth our thoughts afar off (Ps. 139:2), and who "weigheth the spirits" (Prov. 16:2). Oftentimes we are ignorant of the real motives which do prompt us, for our hearts are deceitful above all things, and much of self enters into our most spiritual performances. Nevertheless, while we dare not claim that no self-interest lies at the springs of our actions, yet, He who is our God and Lord knows it is our earnest desire and prayer to seek only His glory and the good of His people.

It was from these considerations that we first entered upon this work. We were in touch with numbers of God's children who longed to have His Word opened up to them, but who knew not where to turn for such a ministry. With very rare exceptions, the preaching of the day completely fails to meet this need. Even where the faith once delivered to the saints is not denied, there is little real **exposition** of the Holy Scriptures. One may hear a couple of topical sermons every Sunday the year round, and know nothing more of the Bible at the end of twelve months than was known at the beginning. Mere generalizations, the re-iterating of platitudes, striking anecdotes, the recounting of personal experiences, will not feed the soul, nor impart that instruction which is essential to vital godliness. "Preach the Word" (2 Tim. 4:2) is God's command to His servants, yet apart from the text how much of "the Word" does the average sermon contain?

It is the same with nearly all of the literature published today. Even the soundest of it is sadly lacking in a spiritual and helpful **exposition** of the Scriptures. There is much to interest the curious, much that appeals to the intellect, but little that searches the conscience or that feeds the soul. The best of the Magazines, though giving much of the religious news of the day, are, for the most part, sadly lacking in that which promotes a closer walk with God. "Signs of the Times" may make exciting reading, but they do not lead to more intimate communion with Christ. If the Editors would insert some of the sermons of C. H. Spurgeon, or give extracts from the best of the Puritans, their pages would be more edifying. If they would take up a book of Scripture and give a verse by verse interpretation, with its present-day application to the needs of God's people, more would be truly helped.

It was because of the lack of expository ministry, both oral and written, that seven and a half years ago we were asked and consented to publish a magazine

(Continued on Page 168)

IMPORTANT NOTICES

Please advise promptly of change of address, otherwise copies will be lost in the mails.

We are glad to send a sample copy to any of our friends whom you believe would be interested in such a publication.

Send to Mr. I. C. Herendeen, 433-435, The Arcade, Cleveland, Ohio, for a list of our publications. He has published many of our books and booklets.

This Magazine is published as a work of faith and labour of love. The Editor and his wife gladly give their services. It is freely sent to all who will read it. No charge is made for it.

Christians who feel definitely lead to do so, may have fellowship with us in this ministry. Those outside the U. S. A., please send only INTERNATIONAL Money Orders made out to Morton's Gap, Kentucky, U. S. A. See that it is made out in American money.

Mailing Permit applied for.

CONTENTS

Hebrews	146
Gleanings in Exodus	152
Abram's Sin	157
Book of Nehemiah	161
A Personal Word	163
Self-Control	164

THE EPISTLE TO THE HEBREWS

19. Christ Superior to Aaron: Heb. 5:1-4.

We are now to enter upon the longest section of our Epistle (5:1-10:39), and a section which is, from the doctrinal and practical viewpoints, perhaps the most important of all. In it the Holy Spirit treats of our Saviour's **priesthood.** Concerning this most blessed and vital subject the utmost confusion prevails in Christendom today. Yet this is scarcely to be wondered at. For not only has the time now arrived when the majority of those who profess the name of Christ "will not endure sound doctrine," who after their own fleshly and worldly lusts have heaped to themselves teachers that tickle their itching ears with God-dishonoring novelties, but they have turned away their ears from the truth, and are "turned unto fables" (2 Tim. 4:3, 4). Never were there a time when true God-fearing Christians more needed to heed that Divine admonition, "**Prove** all things, hold fast that which is good" (1 Thess. 5:21). Our only safeguard is to emulate the Bereans and search the Scriptures daily to ascertain whether or not the things we hear and read from men—be their reputation for scholarship, piety, and orthodoxy never so great—are according to the unerring Word of God.

Romanists, and with them an increasing number of Anglicans (Episcopalians), virtually set aside the solitary grandeur of the Priesthood of Christ and the sufficiency of His Atonement, by bringing in human priests to act as mediators between God and sinful men. Arminians are in fundamental error by representing the priestly office and ministry of Christ as having a relation to and a bearing upon the whole human race. Most of the leaders among the Plymouth Brethren have wrested the Scriptures by denying the **priestly** character of Christ's death, by insisting that He only entered upon His priestly office after His ascension, and by affirming that it bears no direct relation to sin or sins, but is only a ministry of sympathy and succor for weakness and infirmities. But as it will serve no profitable purpose to deal with the errors of others, let us turn to the positive side of our subject.

Three references to the High Priesthood of Christ have already been before us in the preceding chapters of our Epistle. First, in 2:17 we read, "Wherefore, in all things it behoved Him to be made like unto His brethren, that He might be a merciful and faithful High Priest in things pertaining to God, to make propitiation for the sins of the people." This, of itself, is quite sufficient to expose the sophistries of those who teach that the priestly work of Christ has nothing to do with "sins." Second, in 3:1 we have been exhorted to, "consider the Apostle and High Priest of our profession, Christ Jesus." Third, in 4:14 we are told, "We have a great High Priest, that is passed into the heavens, Jesus the Son of God." Here again is a single statement which is alone sufficient to prove that our Saviour entered upon His priestly office **before** His ascension, for it was **as** the "great High Priest" He "passed into the heavens."

Supplementing our previous comments on Heb. 4:14 and introducing what is to be before us, let us note that the Lord Jesus is designated a "**great** High Priest." This word at once emphasises His excellency and pre-eminency. Never was there, never can there be another, possessed of such dignity and glory. The "greatness" of our High Priest arises, first, from the dignity of His person: He is not only Son of man, but Son of God (4:14). Second, from the purity of His nature: He is "without sin" (4:15), "holy, (7:26). Third, from the eminency of His order: that of Melchizedek (5:6). Fourth, from the solemnity of His ordination: "with an oath" (7:20, 21)—none other was. Fifth, from the excellency of His sacrifice: "Himself, without spot" (9:14). Sixth, from the perfection of His administration (7:11, 25)—He has satisfied divine justice, procured Divine favour, given access to the Throne of Grace, secured eternal redemption. Seventh, from the perpetuity of His office: it is untransferable and eternal (7:24). From these we may the better perceive the blasphemous arrogancy of the Italian pope, who styles himself "pontifex maximus"—the **greatest** high priest.

"No part of the Mosaic economy had taken a stronger hold of the imaginations and affections of the Jews than the **Aaronical High-priesthood,** and that system of ritual worship over which its occupants presided. The gorgeous apparel, the solemn investiture, the mysterious sacredness of the high priest, the grandeur of the temple in which he ministered, and the imposing splendour of the religious rites which he performed,—all these operated like a charm in riveting the attachment of the Jews to the now overdated economy, and in exciting powerful prejudices against that simple, spiritual, unostentatious system by which it had been superseded. In opposition to those prejudices, the apostle shows that the Christian economy is deficient in nothing excellent to be found in the Mosaic; on the contrary, that it has a more dignified High Priest, a more magnificent temple, a more sacred altar, a more efficacious sacrifice; and that, to the spiritually enlightened mind, all the temporary splendours of the Mosaic typical ceremonial, wax dim and disappear amid the overwhelming glories of the permanent realities of the Christian institution" (Dr. John Brown).

But once more we would feign pause and admire the consummate wisdom of the Spirit of God as exhibited in the method pursued in presenting the truth in this Epistle. Had it opened with the declaration of Christ's superiority over Moses and Aaron, the prejudices of the Jews had been at once aroused. Instead, the personal dignity of the mediatorial Redeemer has been shown (from their own Scriptures) to be so great, that the glory of the angels was so far below His,

it follows as a necessary consequence that, the honour attaching to the most illustrious of earth's mortals most be so too. Moreover, at the close of chapter 4 the High Priesthood of Christ is presented in such a way that every renewed heart must be won by and to it. There the apostle had announced not only that our High Priest is Divine (v. 14), holy, (v. 15), and has passed into the heavens, but also that He is One filled with tender sympathy toward our infirmities, having Himself been tempted in all points like as we are (sin excepted); and, moreover, that through Him we have obtained free access to God's throne of grace, so that there we may obtain mercy (the remitting of what is due us) and find grace (the receiving that to which we are **not** entitled) to help in time of need. How we should **welcome** such a Priest! How thankful we should be for Him!

Having thus comforted the hearts of God's children by assuring them of the tender compassion of Christ as the pledge of His effectual intercession for them on high, the apostle now proceeds to set forth more precisely the nature and glory of the priesthood of the Incarnate Son. He pursues the same method as was followed in the previous sections. As in chapters 1 and 2 He has been compared and contrasted with angels, and in chapters 3 and 4 with Moses and Joshua, so now in the present and succeeding chapters the order and functions of the Aaronic priesthood are examined, that the way may be paved for a setting forth of the more excellent order to which **our** High Priest belongs. "In the course of the section he makes it evident, that whatever was essential to the office of a high priest was to be found in Christ Jesus, that whatever imperfections belonged to the Aaronical high priesthood were not to be found in Him, and that a variety of excellencies were to be found in Him of which none of the Aaronical priests were possessed." (Dr. J. Brown).

"For every high priest taken from among men is ordained for men in things pertaining to God, that he may offer both gifts and sacrifices for sins: Who can have compassion on the ignorant, and on them that are out of the way, for that he himself also is compassed with infirmity. And by reason hereof he ought, as for the people, so also for himself, to offer for sins. And no man taketh this honour unto himself, but he that is called of God, as was Aaron" (vv. 1-4). Here we have defined the intrinsic nature of the priestly office.

The verses just quoted above contain

a general description of the Levitical high priests. Five things are here said concerning them. First, he must be "taken from among men," that is, he must partake of the nature of those on whose behalf he acts. Second, he acted not as a private individual, but as a public official: "is ordained for men." Third, he came not empty-handed before God, but furnished with "gifts and sacrifices for sins." Fourth, he himself was not exempt from infirmity, so that he might the more readily succour the distressed (vv. 2, 3). Fifth, he did not presumptuously rush into this office of himself, but was chosen and approved of God (v. 4). Let us look at each of these more closely.

"For every high priest taken from among men." First, then, his humanity is insisted upon. An angel would be no fitting priest to act on behalf of men, for he possesses not their nature, is not subject to their temptations, and has no experimental acquaintance with their sufferings; therefore is he unsuited to act on their behalf: therefore is he incapable of having "compassion" upon them, for the motive-spring of all real intercession is heart-felt sympathy. Thus, the primary qualification of a priest is that he must be personally related to, possess the same nature as, those for whose welfare he interposes.

"For every high priest taken from among men." Bearing in mind to whom this Epistle was first addressed, it is not difficult for us to discern why our present section opens in this somewhat abrupt manner. As was pointed out so frequently in our articles upon Heb. 2, that which so sorely perplexed the Jews was, that the One who had appeared and tabernacled in their midst in human form should have claimed for Himself divine honours (John 5:23, etc.). But if the Son of God had never become **man,** He could never have officiated as priest, He could never have offered that sacrifice for the sins of His people which Divine justice required. The Divine Incarnation was an imperative necessity if salvation was to be secured for God's elect. "It was necessary for Christ to become a real man, for as we are very far from God, we stand in a manner before Him in the person of our Priest, which could not be were He not one of us. Hence, that the Son of God has a nature in common with us does not diminish His dignity, but commends it the more to us; for He is fitted to reconcile us to God, because He is man" (John Calvin).

"Is ordained for men." This tells us the reason why and the purpose for which the high priest was taken "from among men:" it was that he might transact on behalf of others, or more accurately, in the stead of others. To this position and work he was "ordained" or appointed by God. Thereby, under the Mosaic economy, the Hebrews were taught that men could not directly and personally approach unto God. They were sinful, He was holy; therefore was there a breath between, which they were unable to bridge. It is both solemn and striking to observe how at the very beginning, when sin first entered the world, God impressed this awful truth upon our fallen parents. The "tree of life," whose property was to bestow immortality (Gen. 3:22), was the then emblem and symbol of God Himself. Therefore when Adam transgressed, we are told, "So He drove out the man; and He placed at the east of the garden of Eden cherubim, and a flaming sword which turned every way, to keep the way of the tree of life" (Gen. 3:24). Thereby man was taught the awful fact that he is **alienated from** the life of God." (Eph. 4:18).

The same terrible truth was pressed upon the Israelites. When Jehovah Himself came down upon Sinai, the people were fenced off from Him: "And thou shalt set bounds unto the people round about, saying, Take heed to yourselves, that ye go not up into the mount, or touch the border of it: whosoever toucheth the mount shall be surely put to death" (Ex. 19:12). There was the Lord upon the summit, there were the people at the base: separated the One from the other. So too when the Tabernacle was set up. Beyond the outward court they were not suffered to go; into the holy place, the priests alone were permitted to enter. And into the holy of holies, where God dwelt between the cherubim, none but the high priest, and he only on the day of atonement, penetrated. Thus were the Hebrews, from the beginning, shown the awful truth of Isa. 59:2—"Your iniquities have **separated** between you and your God."

But in the person of their high priest, through his representing of them before God, Israel might approach within the sacred enclosure. Beautifully is that brought out in the 28th chapter of Exodus, that book whose theme is **redemption**. There we read, "And thou shalt take two onyx stones, and grave on them the names of the children of Israel . . . and thou shalt put the two stones upon the shoulders of the ephod for stones of memorial unto the children of Israel: and Aaron shall bear their names before the Lord

". . . And thou shalt make the breastplate of judgment . . . and thou shalt set in it setting of stones . . . and the stones shall be with the names of the children of Israel . . . And Aaron shall bear the names of the children of Israel in the breast-plate of judgment upon his heart when he goeth in unto the holy, for a memorial before the Lord continually" (vv. 9, 12, 15, 17, 21, 29). Concerning the high priest being "ordained for men" we are told, "Aaron shall lay both his hands upon the head of the live goat, and confess over him all the iniquities of the children of Israel, and all their transgressions in all their sins, putting them upon the head of the goat, and shall send him away by the hand of a fit man into the wilderness" (Lev. 16:21).

"Is ordained for men." The application of these words to the person and work of Christ is patent. He not only became Man, but had received appointment from God to act on behalf of, in the stead of, men: "Lo I come, to do Thy will, O God" (Heb. 10:9), announce both the commission He had received from God and His own readiness to discharge it. What that commission was we learn in the next verse: "By the which will we are sanctified through the offering of the body of Jesus Christ once for all." He came to do what men could not do—satisfy the claims of Divine justice, procure the Divine favour. Note, in passing, "ordained for **men**," not mankind in general, but that people which God had given Him—just as Aaron, the typical high priest, confessed not the sins of the Canaanites or Amalekites over the head of the goat, but those of Israel only.

"In things pertaining to God," that is, in meeting the requirements of His holiness. The activities of the priests have God for their object: it is His character, His claims, His glory which are in view. In their application to Christ these words, "in things pertaining to God" distinguishes our Lord's priesthood from His other offices. As a prophet, He reveals to **us** the mind and will of God. As the King, He subdues **us** to Himself, rules over and defends **us**. But the object of His priesthood is not us, but **God**.

"That He may offer both gifts and sacrifices for sins." To "offer" is the chief function of the high priest. He offers to God for men. He offers both gifts and sacrifices; that is, eucharistic or thanksgiving offerings, and sacrificial or propitiatory sacrifices. "The first word includes, as I think, various kinds of sacrifices, and is therefore a general term; but the second denotes especially the sacrifices of expiation. Still the meaning is, that the priest without a sacrifice is no peace-maker between God and man, for without a sacrifice sins are not atoned for, nor is the wrath of God pacified. Hence, whenever reconciliation between God and man takes place this pledge must ever necessarily precede Thus we see that angels are by no means capable of obtaining for us God's favour, because they have no sacrifice" (John Calvin).

"That He may offer both gifts and sacrifices for sins." The application of these words to the Lord Jesus, our great High Priest, calls attention to a prominent and vital aspect of His death which is largely lost sight of today. The sacrificial death of Christ was a **priestly** act. On the Cross Christ not only suffered at the hands of men, and endured the punitive wrath of God, but He actually "accomplished" (Luke 9:31) something: He **offered** Himself as a sacrifice to God. At Calvary the Lord Jesus was not only the Lamb of God bearing judgment, but He was also His Priest officiating at the altar. "For every high priest is ordained to offer gifts and sacrifices: wherefore it is of necessity that this Man have somewhat also **to offer**" (Heb. 8:3). As Heb. 9:14 also tells us, He "**offered** himself without spot to God."

Christ on the Cross was far more than a willing victim passively enduring the stroke of Divine judgment. He was there **performing** a work, nor did He cease until He cried in triumph, "It is finished." He "loved the Church and **gave** Himself for it" (Eph. 5:25). He "**laid down** His life" for the sheep (John 10:11, 18)—which is the predicate of an active agent. He "**poured out** His soul unto death" (Isa. 53:12). He "dismissed His spirit" (John 19:30). "Hell's utmost force and fury gathered against Him: heaven's sword devouring Him, and heaven's God forsaking Him: earth, and hell, and heaven, thus in conspiring action against Him, unto the uttermost of heaven's extremest justice, and earth's and hell's extremest injustice:—what is the glory of the Cross if it be not **this**: that with such action conspiring to subdue **His** action, His action outlasted and outlived them all, and He did not die subdued and overborne in the dying, He did not die till He **gave** Himself in death" (H. Martin on "The Atonement").

"Who can have compassion on the ignorant, and on them that are out of the way; for that he himself also is compassed with infirmity" (v. 2). Passing now from the design of the Levitical priesthood, we have a word upon their qualifications, the first of which is **compassion** unto those for whom he is to act. "The word here translated 'have compassion' is rendered in the margin 'reasonably bear with.' A person could not be expected to do the duties of a high priest aright if he could not enter into the feelings of those whom he represented. If their faults excited no sentiments in his mind but disapprobation—if they moved him to no feeling but anger, he would not be fit to interpose in their behalf with God—he would not be inclined to do for them what was necessary for the expiation of their sins, and the accomplishment of their services. But the Jewish high priest was one who was capable of pitying and bearing with the ignorant and erring; for 'he himself also was compassed with infirmity.' 'Infirmity,' here, plainly is significant of sinful weakness, and probably also of the disagreeable effects resulting from it. The Jewish high priest was himself a sinner. He had personal experience of temptation, and the tendency of man to yield to it—of sin, and of the consequences of sin; so that he had the natural capacity, and ought to have had the moral capacity, of pitying his fellow-sinners" (Dr. J. Brown).

And what, we may enquire, was the Spirit's design in here making mention of this personal qualification in the Levitical high priest? We believe His purpose was at least fourfold. First, implicitly, to call attention to the failure of Israel's high priests. It is very solemn to mark how that the last of them failed, most signally, at this very point. When poor Hannah was "in bitterness of soul," and while she was in prayer, weeping before the Lord, Eli, because her lips moved not, thought that she was drunken, and spoke roughly to her (1 Sam. 1:91-14). Thus, instead of sympathizing with her sorrows, instead of making intercession for her, he cruelly misjudged her. True, it is 'human to err;' equally evident is it that the ideal priest would never be found among the sons of men. Second, was not the Spirit of God here paving the way for a contrast of the superiority of our great High Priest over the Aaronical? Third, does not this statement of v. 2 show, once more, that the value and efficacy of his work was inseparably connected with the **personal** qualifications of the priest himself, namely, his moral perfections, his human sympathy? Fourth, thus there was emphasized again the necessity for the Son of God becoming man, only thus cou'd He acquire the requisite human compassion.

"This compassionate, loving, gentle, all-considerate and tender regard for the sinner can exist in perfection only in a sinless one. This appears at first sight paradoxical; for we expect the perfect man to be the severest judge. And with regard to **sin**, this is doubtless true. God charges even His angels with folly. He beholds sin where we do not discover it. And Jesus, the Holy One of Israel, like the Father, has eyes like a flame of fire, and discerns everything that is contrary to God's mind and will. But with regard to the **sinner**, Jesus, by virtue of His perfect holiness, is the most merciful, compassionate, and considerate Judge. For we, not taking a deep and keen view of sin, that central essential evil which exists in all men, and manifests itself in various ways and degrees, are not able to form a just estimate of men's comparative guilt and blameworthiness. Nay, our very sins make us more impatient and severe with regard to the sins of others. Our vanity finds the vanity of others intolerable, our pride finds the pride of others excessive. Blind to the guilt of our own peculiar sins, we are shocked with another's sins, different indeed from ours, but not less offensive to God, or pernicious in its tendencies. Again, the greater the knowledge of Divine love and pardon, the stronger faith in the Divine mercy and renewing grace, the more hopeful and the more lenient will be our view of sinners. And finally the more we possess of the spirit and heart of the Shepherd, the Physician, the Father, the deeper will be our compassion on the ignorant and wayward.

"The Lord Jesus was therefore most compassionate, considerate, lenient, hopeful in His feelings toward sinners and in His dealings with them. He was infinitely holy and perfectly clear in His hatred and judgment of sin; but He was tender and gracious to the sinner. Beholding the sinful heart in all, esteeming sin according to the Divine standard, according to its real inward character, and not the human, conventional, and outward measure; Jesus, infinitely holy and sensitive as He was, saw often less to shock and pain Him in the drunkard and profligate than in the respectable, selfish, and ungodly religionists. He looked upon sin as the greatest and most fearful evil, but on the sinner as poor, lost, and helpless, Thus, while Jesus, in perfect holiness, judges most truly, lovingly, and tenderly of us. He knows by experience the weakness of the flesh, and the difficulty and soreness of the struggle. What a marvelous fulfilment of the Priest's requisite, that he should be taken from men! one to whom we can look with full and calm trust, our Representative, the Man Christ

Jesus, possessed of perfect, Divine love and compassion" (Abbreviated from A. Saphir).

Those for whom the high priest was deputed to act are here described as 'the ignorant and them that are out of the way." These are not two different classes of people, instead, those words give a twofold description of sinners. It has been rightly said that "in the Bible all sin is represented as the result of ignorance, but of blameable ignorance." "The way of the wicked is as darkness: they know not at what they stumble" (Prov. 4:19). "There is none that understandeth, there is none that seeketh after God" (Rom. 3:11). Every sinner is a fool. "Out of the way" means that men have turned aside from that path which the Word of God has marked out for them to walk in: "All we like sheep have gone astray, we have turned every one to his own way" (Isa. 53:6).

"And by reason hereof he ought, as for the people, so also for himself, to offer for sins" (v. 3). "There was none who could offer sacrifice for the sins of the high priest; therefore, he must do it for himself. He was to offer for himself in the same way and for the same reasons as he offered for the people, and this was necessary, for he was encompassed with the same infirmities and was obnoxious as to sin, and so stood in no less need of expiation or atonement than did the people" (Dr. John Owen). For scriptures where the high priest was bidden to present an offering for his own sin, let the reader consult Lev. 4:3, 9:7, 16:6, 24.

"And by reason hereof he ought, as for the people, so also for himself, to offer for sins" (v. 3). Here again we may observe the Spirit of God calling attention to the imperfections of the Levitical priests that the way may be prepared for presenting the infinitely superior perfections of Christ. But that is not all we have in this verse. It is the personal **qualifications** of the one who exercises this office which is now before us. Before Aaron could present an offering on behalf of Israel, he must first bring a sacrifice for his own sins, that he might be purified and stand accepted before Jehovah. In other words, the one who was to come between a holy God and a sinful people must himself have no guilt resting upon him, and must be an object of Divine favour. Thus, personal fitness was an essential qualification of the priest: in the case of the Levitical, a ceremonial fitness: with Christ, a personal and inherent.

"And no man taketh this honour unto himself, but he that is called of God, as was Aaron" (v. 4). "The foregoing verses declare the personal functions of a high priest, but these alone are not sufficient to invest any one with that office; for it is required that he be lawfully called thereunto. Aaron was called of God immediately, and in an extraordinary way. He was called by the command of God given to Moses, and entrusted to him for execution; he was actually separated and consecrated unto the office of high priest, and this was accomplished by special sacrifices made by another for him; and all these things were necessary unto Aaron, because God, in his person, erected a new order of priesthood" (Dr. J. Owen).

"And no man taketh this honour to himself." The expression "this honour" refers to the high priestly office, for one to approach unto the Most High, to have personal dealings with Him, to transact on behalf of others before Him, obtaining His favour toward them, is a signal privilege and great favour indeed. To mark this distinguishing honour, Aaron was clothed in the most gorgeous and imposing vestments (Ex. 28). Looking beyond the type to the Antitype, we may discern how that the Spirit is, once more, bringing before the Hebrews that which was designed to remove the offence of the Cross. To carnal reason the death of Christ was a humiliating spectacle; but the spiritually enlightened see at Calvary One performing the functions of an office with high "honour" attached to it.

"But he that is called of God, as was Aaron." This was the ultimate and most important qualification: no man could legitimately act as high priest unless he was Divinely called to that office. "The principle on which the necessity of a Divine calling to the legitimate exercise of the priesthood rests is an obvious one. It depends entirely on the will of God whether He will accept the services and pardon the sins of men; and suppose again that it is His will to do so, it belongs to Him to appoint everything in reference to the manner in which this is to be accomplished. God is under no obligation to accept of every one, or of any one who, of his own accord, or by the choice of his fellow-men, takes it upon him to offer sacrifices or gifts for himself or for others; and no man in these circumstances can have reason to expect that God will accept of his offerings, unless He has given him a commission to offer them, and a promise He will be appeased by them. This, then, from the very nature of the case, was necessary to the legitimate discharge of the functions of a high priest" (Dr. J. Brown). What the apostle is here leading up to was the proof that **God** was the Author of Christ's Priesthood. As that will come before us in the verses which follow, we pass it by now.

"But he that is called of God, as was Aaron." That which makes an office lawful is the personal call of God. A most important principle is this to recognize, but one which, in these days of abounding lawlessness, is now flagrantly ignored. The will of man is to be entirely subordinated to the will of God. Everything connected with His work is to be regulated by the Divine appointments. Expediency, convenience, popular customs, are ruled out of court. Nor is any one justified in rushing into a holy office uncalled of God. To elect myself, or to have no higher authority than the election of fellow-sinners, is to usurp the authority of God.

All ministry is in the hand of Christ (Rev. 2:1). He appointed the twelve apostles, and later the seventy disciples, to go forth. He bids us "Pray ye therefore the Lord of the harvest, that **He** send forth labourers into His harvest" (Matt. 9:38). When He ascended on high **He** "gave some, apostles; and some, prophets; and some, evangelists, and some pastors and teachers" (Eph. 4:11). In the days of Paul it was said, "How shall they preach, except they be sent?" (Rom. 10:15). But in these days, how many there are who run **without** being "sent!" Men have taken it upon themselves to be evangelists, pastors, teachers, who have received no call from God to such a work. The **absence** of His call, is evidenced by the absence of the qualifying gift. When God calls, He always equips.

Returning to the call of Aaron, we may observe that a time came when his official authority was challenged (Num. 16:2). The manner in which God vindicated His servant is worthy of our most thoughtful attention. The record of it is found in Num 17: Aaron's rod budded and brought forth almonds. **Supernatural fruit** was the sign and pledge that he had been called of God. Let this be laid well to heart. Judged by **this** standard, how many today stand accredited as God's sent-servants? When God calls a man, He does not send him forth on any fruitless errand.

It is a solemn thing for one to obtrude himself into a sacred office. The tragic case of Uzzah (2 Chron. 26:16-21) is a lasting warning. Alas, how rarely is it heeded; and how grievously is God dishonored! There are those who decry a "one-man ministry," and cut themselves off from many an edifying message from God's true servants; but after twenty years' experience on three continents, the writer much prefers that which some so unchristianly condemn, to the lawlessness and fleshly exhibitions of an "every-man ministry" which is their alternative. Again: how many are urged to become Sunday School teachers and open-air speakers who have received neither call nor qualification from God to such work! Again: how many go forth as missionaries, only a few years later, at most, to abandon the work: what a proof that they were not "sent" or "called" by God! Let every reader weigh well Heb. 5:4. Unless **God** has called you, enter not into any work for Him. Let restless souls seek grace to heed that Divine command, "Be swift to hear, **slow to speak**" (James 1:19).

—Arthur W. Pink.

GLEANINGS IN EXODUS

67 A Jealous God—Ex. 34:8-17

We turn now to contemplate a portion of the further communication which Jehovah made to Moses in the Mount. It is not easy to break up this chapter into sections of suitable length for these comparatively brief articles, and therefore we are obliged to spend a little time in reviewing the ground covered in the previous one, that the continuity of thought may be preserved. In our last, we beheld God asserting His rights over those whom He had redeemed unto Himself: Moses being called to receive the Law at His hands. There we heard Him enunciating the principles of His government. These are seven in number, and close attention to them is called for if we would appreciate His "ways" with Israel of old, and enter intelligently into that which regulates Him in His dealings with us now.

God is "light" (1 John 1:5), as well as "love" (1 John 4:8), and therefore we are exhorted, "Behold therefore the goodness **and** the severity of God" (Rom. 11:22). The two sides to the Divine character shine forth in all His dealings with man. In Eden we behold His "goodness" in making promise of the coming of the woman's Seed to bruise the Serpent's head (Gen. 3:15), but we also see His "severity" in that "He drove out the man" (3:24). God as Love provided a shelter for Noah and his house; God as Light sent the flood and destroyed those who had corrupted their way on earth. The "goodness" of God commissioned two angels to deliver Lot, but His "severity" rained-down fire and brimstone and consumed wicked Sodom. God as Love preserved His people under blood in Egypt, God as Light slew all the firstborn of the Egyptians. The "goodness" of God, in response to the intercession of Moses, spared the idolatrous Nation from utter extermination, but His "severity" called for the sword to do its work (Ex. 32:27).

We may observe the clear display of these two sides of the Divine character in the ministry of the incarnate Son. The Lord Jesus came here "full" not only of grace, but "of grace **and truth**" (John 1:14). He was the Friend of publicans and sinners, but He was the Enemy of self-righteous hypocrites. The same One who was "moved with compassion" as He beheld the multitude (Matt. 14:14), "looked round upon them with anger" (Mark 3:5) as He beheld the hard-hearted critics of the synagogue. He who wept over Jerusalem, "made a scourge of small cords" and drove out of the temple the defilers of the Father's house (John 2:15). He who "blessed His disciples" (Luke 24:51), cursed the fig tree (Matt. 21:19). His "beatitudes" in Matt. 5 are balanced by His denunciatory "woe's" in Matt. 23. If we read of the "love of Christ" (Eph. 3:19), we read also of "the wrath of the Lamb" (Rev. 6:16).

The same conjunction of these Divine perfections is to be discerned in the proclamation of the name of the Lord, which He gave to Moses on the Mount in connection with the enunciation of His governmental principles. He is both "abundant in goodness **and truth**" (v. 6). If He "keeps mercy for thousands," yet He declares that He will "by no means clear the guilty." Though He **forgives** "iniquity, transgression, and sin," yet He also **visits** "the iniquity of the fathers upon the children." The sin of Ham was visited upon his descendants (Gen. 9:25): the sin of Korah and his company resulted in the earth opening its mouth and swallowing them up **and** their houses (Num. 16:32). When Achan was punished for his sin, there were stoned with him "his sons and his daughters" (Josh. 7:24, 25). When the Jews crucified Christ, they cried, "His blood be upon us, and upon our children" (Matt. 27:25), and God took them at their word.

And what is the practical application to us of these things? This: God is a God to be loved, but He is also a God to be feared, for "**our** God is a consuming fire" (Heb. 12:29). Did we perceive that God is Light as well as Love, we should stand more in holy awe of Him. Did we behold His "severity" as readily as we do His "goodness," we should be more fearful of displeasing Him. Did we bear in mind that He not only pardons, but also visits the iniquities of the fathers upon the children, we should be more careful about our walk than we are. "God is greatly to be feared in the assembly of the saints, and to be had in reverence of all them that are about Him" (Psa. 89:7): In Heaven itself the saints not only sing the praises of God, but they "fall down before Him" (Rev. 4:10). Then let us seek grace to heed that word, "work out your own salvation with fear and trembling" (Phil. 2:12).

"And Moses made haste, and bowed his head toward the earth, and worshipped" (v. 8). It is blessed to note the effect upon Moses of the wondrous and glorious communication which he had just received from the mouth of Jehovah: filled with adoration and awe he takes his place in the dust before Him. No formal or perfunctory homage was it that Moses now rendered. The words "made haste" seem to point to the spontaneity of his worship; the bowing of his head toward the earth shows how deeply his spirit was stirred. And if our hearts really lay hold of the perfections of God's administration, we too will be bowed before Him as worshippers.

"And Moses made haste, and bowed his head toward the earth, and worshipped." This is ever the result when the Lord condescends to reveal Himself to one of His own. When He appeared before Abram and said, "I am the Almighty God; walk before Me, and be thou upright," we are told that "Abram fell on his face" (Gen. 17:3). When He appeared before Joshua as "Captain of the host of the Lord," we are told that "Joshua fell on his face to the earth, and did worship" (Josh. 5:14). When His glory filled the temple which Solomon had built, all the children of Israel "bowed themselves with their faces to the ground upon the pavement, and worshipped and praised the Lord" (2 Chron. 7:3).

"And Moses made haste, and bowed his head toward the earth, and worshipped." Let us not lose sight of the immediate link between this and the close of the preceding verse. The last things mentioned there are that God will by no means clear the guilty, and that He visits the sins of the fathers upon the children. Instead of showing resentment, Moses acquiesced; instead of challenging the righteousness of these things, he worshipped. Well for us if we follow his example.

"And he said, If now I have found grace in Thy sight, O Lord, let my Lord, I pray Thee, go among us; for it is a stiffnecked people; and pardon our iniquity and our sin, and take us for Thine inheritance" (v. 9). Very beautiful is this. Moses continues to use the favour which he had personally found before God for the good of others. His affections were bound up with His people. Blessedly does he identify himself with them: "Let my Lord, I pray Thee, go among **us.**" How this brings to mind that wondrous word of our Redeemer's when, presenting Himself for baptism, He said to His amazed forerunner, "Thus it becometh **us** to fulfill all righteousness" (Matt. 3:16). Verily, "He that sanctifieth and they who are sanctified are all of **one**" (Heb. 2:11).

Let us note carefully the **reason** now presented by Moses for the Lord's accompanying His people: "Let my Lord, I pray Thee, go among us, **for** it is a **stiffnecked** people." This is very striking, though to some of the commentators it has presented a difficulty. It was their **need** which Moses spread before Jehovah; it was His **grace** to which he appealed. Seeing that God was "merciful, gracious, longsuffering," He was just the One suited to a "stiffnecked" people. None but He could bear with them. At the very time that Israel were worshipping the golden calf the Lord Himself had said to Moses, "I have seen this people, and, behold, it is a **stiffnecked** people: Now, therefore, let Me alone, that My wrath may wax hot against them" (32:9, 10). Now, Moses not only acknowledged the truth of God's charge, but, in wondrous faith, turns it into a plea **for** Him to continue in Israel's midst! Beautifully has another commented on this:

"The relationship between Moses personally and God, was fully established, so that he could present the people such as they were, because of his (Moses' own) position, and, consequently, make of the difficulty and sin of the people a reason for the presence of God, according to the character He had revealed. It is the proper effect of mediation; but it is exceedingly beautiful to see, grace having thus come in, the reason God had given for the destruction of the people, or at the very least of His absence, becoming the motive for His presence. We know this ourselves; my sinfulness in itself would be the reason for God's giving me up. But now I am in grace, I can plead it with God as a reason, blessed be His name, for His going with me, never should I overcome and get safe across the wilderness, if He was not with me. Surely the flesh is there, but it is wondrous grace" (Mr. J N. Darby).

Verily, it is all of grace from first to last. Christ came here not to call the righteous, but sinners to repentance (Matt. 9:13). The proud Pharisees resented it, murmured, and said, "This man receiveth sinners and eateth with them" (Luke 15:2). Thank God He still does so, and the more the Holy Spirit reveals to us the "plague" of our heart (1 Kings 8:38), the more we are enabled to apprehend the wondrous grace of God, the more shall we crave His presence with us, and that because we are, by nature, a "stiffnecked" people. The more we discover the true character of the "flesh"—its unimprovableness, and our own powerlessness to contend against it, the more shall we long for an Almighty arm to lean on. So, too, the more we realize that this world is a "wilderness," affording nothing for our souls, the more shall we perceive the need of the presence of Him who—all praise to His name—is the Friend that "sticketh closer than a brother" (Prov. 18:24).

"And pardon our iniquity and our sin, and take us for Thine inheritance." Here again we perceive the boldness of Moses' faith. This was the climax of his petitions on Israel's behalf. First, he had besought the Lord that His wrath should not wax hot against them (32:11). Then, he had pleaded for the Lord's continued presence in their midst (33:15, 16). Now he asks that the Lord will pardon their iniquity (note how graciously he identifies himself with his sinning people: "**our** iniquity and **our** sin") and "take us from Thine inheritance." When Sinia had first been reached, God had said, "Now therefore, if ve will obey My voice indeed, and keep My covenant, then ye shall be a peculiar treasure unto Me above all people" (19:5). But the sin of the golden calf had severed every relationship. But here Moses as their mediator and intercessor pleads that **everything** should be restored.

That his prayer was answered we know from other scriptures. In Deut. 32:9 we find him saying, "For the Lord's portion is His people; Jacob **is** the lot of His inheritance." So also we find David declared, "Blessed is the nation whose God is the Lord; and the people whom He hath chosen for His own **inheritance**" (Psa 33:12). Blessed is it to know that Israel, though temporarily cast aside for our sakes, is God's "inheritance" forever: "For the Lord will not cast off His people, neither will He forsake His **inheritance**" (Psa. 94:14). In a coming day the word shall go forth, "Sing and rejoice, O daughter of Zion: for, lo, I come, and I will dwell in the midst of thee saith the Lord, and many nations shall be joined to the Lord in that day and shall be My people: and I will dwell in the midst of thee, and thou shalt know that the Lord of hosts hath sent Me unto thee. And the Lord shall **inherit** Judah His portion in the holy land, and shall choose Jerusalem again" (Zech. 2:10-12).

"And take us for Thine inheritance." Again we would remind the reader that we are dealing with the contents of that book whose theme is **redemption.** How blessed then to learn that, through redemption, God has obtained for Himself an "inheritance!" Eph. 1:18 speaks of the "riches of the glory of **His** inheritance in the saints." A truly marvelous concept is that, one to which our poor minds are quite incapable of rising—that the great and selfsufficient God should deem Himself **enriched** by worms of the earth whom He hath saved by His grace. This "inheritance," like all others, has come in **through death,** the death of God's own Son. That death not only vindicated Divine justice by putting away the sins of His people, but it has brought in that which shall **glorify** God through the endless ages of eternity. God will **occupy** His "inheritance" forever. "Behold, the tabernacle of God is with men, and He will **dwell with them,** and they shall be His people, and God Himself shall be with them, and be their God." (Rev. 21:3).

"And He said, Behold, I make a covenant, before all thy people, I will do marvels, such as have not been done in all the earth, nor in any nation: and all the people among which thou art shall see the work of the Lord: for it is a terrible thing that I will do with thee." (v. 10). This verse presents a difficulty, which is by no means easy of solution. God here promised that He would do unprecedented miracles on Israel's behalf, "marvels such as have not been done in all the earth" Had these words been spoken at the burning bush, before Moses first interviewed Pharaoh, their application had been obvious; but here, at Sinai, their meaning is not easy to fix. God had already wrought great **"marvels"** on Israel's behalf: the plagues upon Egypt, when water was turned into blood, dust into lice, frogs entering the homes of the Egyptians, but avoiding those of the Israelites, a supernatural darkness lasting for three days, though "all the children of Israel had light in their dwellings." (Ex. 10:22, 23); the dividing asunder the Red Sea; the raining of manna from heaven, and in such quantities as to supply the needs of two million souls; the bringing of water out of the rock—these were, one and all, prodigies of power. But here God announces still greater wonders!

We believe that the last book of the Bible describes the fulfillment of this word of Jehovah's to Moses. There we read of plagues more dreadful and wondrous than those which came upon Pharaoh and his people. Upon Egypt God sent natural "locusts," but in a soon-coming day the bottomless pit shall be opened, and from it shall issue **infernal** "locusts," who instead of consuming vegetation, shall torment men, so that "in those days shall men seek death, and shall not find it." (Rev. 9:6.) In Rev. 15:1 we read, "And I saw another sign in heaven, great and marvelous, seven angels having the seven last plagues; for in them is filled up the wrath of God." How little the world dreams of what is shortly coming upon it!

In the past God put forth His power and delivered Israel from Egypt, but in a coming day He will, with still greater displays of His might and by means of judgments of far sorer intensity, deliver the scattered Jews from all countries among which they are now dispersed: "And it shall come to pass in that day, that the Lord shall set His hand again the second time to recover the remnant of His people, which shall be left, from Assyria, and from Egypt, and from Pathros, and from Cush, and from Elam, and from Shinar, and from Hamath, and from the Islands of the sea. And He shall set up an ensign for the nations, and shall assemble the outcasts of Israel, and gather together the dispersed of Judah from the four quarters of the earth." (Isa. 11:11-12). "And I will gather the remnant of My flock out of all countries whither I have driven them, and will bring them again to their folds; and they shall be fruitful and increase . . . Therefore they shall no more say, The Lord liveth, which brought up and which led the seed of the house of Israel out of the north country, and from all countries whither I had driven them; and they shall dwell in their own land." (Jer. 23:3, 7, 8)

Of old, God divided the Red Sea for His people to pass through; but in a coming day He shall completely **dry it up** for them. "And the Lord shall utterly destroy the tongue of the Egyptian sea; and with His mighty wind shall He shake His hand over the river, and shall smite it in the seven streams, and make men go over dry shod. And there shall be an highway for the remnant of His people, which shall be left from Assyria, like as it was to Israel in the day that he came up out of the land of Egypt." (Isa. 11:15, 16, compare also Zech. 10:11). So too we read. "And the sixth angel poured out his vial upon the great river Euphrates; and the water thereof was **dried up,** that the way of the kings of the east might be prepared." (Rev. 16:12).

But not only will God perform mighty miracles on Israel's behalf, but as Ex. 34. 10 adds, "It is a terrible thing that I will do **with** thee." Clearly this refers to the Great Tribulation, when God will deal with Israel for their sins. As Jeremiah predicted, "Alas! for that day is great so that none is like it: it is even the time of Jacob's trouble." (30:7). Of that dreadful period Christ declared, "For in those days shall be affliction, such as was not from the beginning of the creation which God created unto this time, neither shall be. And except that the Lord had shortened those days, no flesh should be saved." (Mark. 13:19, 20.)

At Sinai God appeared before Israel with the most awe-inspiring manifestations: "And mount Sinai was altogether on a smoke, because the Lord descended upon it in fire: and the smoke thereof ascended as the smoke of a furnace, and the whole mount quaked greatly." (Ex. 19:18) But when the incarnate Son returns to this world, we are told that He "Shall be revealed from heaven with His mighty angels, in flaming fire taking vengeance on them that know not God, and that obey not the Gospel of our Lord Jesus Christ." (2 Thess. 1:7, 8). To this grand event the Apostle Paul referred when quoting from Haggai: "Whose voice then shook the earth: but now He hath promised, saying, Yet once more I shake not the earth only, but also heaven." (Heb. 12:26.)

Should it be asked, What is **the connection** between the awful contents of this 10th verse of Ex. 34 and its context? The answer is not far to seek. At the close of v. 9 we find Moses beseeching Jehovah, "Take us for thine inheritance." The next thing we read is, **"And** He said, Behold I make a covenant," etc. With His omniscient eye, God looked down the centuries, and then made known to His servant what must, ultimately, take place before Israel became His "inheritance" in fact. When this Covenant of Marvels has been fulfilled, the prayer of Moses will receive its final answer. It is in the Millennium, following the awful judgment of the Great Tribulation, that the Lord will enter upon His heritage. Then shall it be said, "Sing, O daughter of Zion; shout, O Israel, be glad and rejoice with all the heart, O daughter of Jerusalem. The Lord hath taken away thy judgments, He hath cast out thine enemy; the King of Israel, even the Lord is in the midst of thee: thou shalt not see evil any more. In that day it shall be said to Jerusalem, Fear thou not: and to Zion, Let not thine hands be slack. The Lord thy God in the midst of thee is mighty; He will save, **He will rejoice** over thee with joy; **He will rest** in His love, He will joy over thee with singing." Zeph. 3:14-17.)

"Observe thou that which I command thee this day: behold, I drive out before thee the Amorite, and the Canaanite, and the Hittite, and the Perizzite, and the Hivite, and the Jebusite." (v. 11). Here the Lord returns to the more immediate present. Note the **"this** day," and the change from the "I will do marvels" and "it is a terrible thing that I **will** do with thee" of the previous verse, to "I drive out." It should also be observed that the extermination of the Canaanites is attributed not to the military prowess of Israel, but to the alone power of Jehovah.

"Take heed to thyself, lest thou make a covenant with the inhabitants of the land whither thou goest, lest it be for a snare in the midst of thee." (v. 12.) This was a call to separation. There must be no unequal yoke uniting the people of God with the children of the Devil. The Lord was taking Moses at his word: in 33:16 he had said, "Is it not in that Thou goest with us? so shall we be **separated,** I and Thy people, from all the people that are upon the face of the earth." It is solemn to discover how Joshua, at a later date, disobeyed this very exhortation, see Joshua 9:14, 15. Centuries after, serious trouble issued from Joshua's sin, see 2 Sam. 21:1-9.

"But ye shall destroy their altars, break their images, and cut down their groves." (v. 13.) This also has its **spiritual** application to us. Not that Christians are called upon to reform society and improve the world, by engaging in crusades against vice and drunkenness. The counterpart in our experience to what we have here in v. 13 is that we should wage an unsparing war upon that which prevents us from enjoying our inheritance in Christ. Everything that would displace God in our lives and in our affections must be demolished. Every idol—that which comes between the Lord and my heart—must be ruthlessly hewn down.

"For thou shalt worship no other God: for the Lord, whose name is Jealous, is a jealous God." (v. 14). Very searching, but very blessed is this. First, God is "jealous" of **His own glory.** Through Isaiah He has declared, "I am the Lord: that is My name; and My glory will I not give to another" (42:8). That is why God has chosen the foolish things of this world, weak things, things which are despised, yea, non-entities **"that** no flesh should glory in His presence.' (1 Cor. 1:27-29).

Second, God is "jealous' of the **affections of His people.** He is grieved when our love is given to another. "My son, **give Me** thine heart." (Prov. 23:26) is His appeal. "Set **Me** as a seal upon thine heart." (Song of Sol. 8:6) is His call to each of us.

Third, God is "jealous" of **His people:** "He that toucheth you toucheth the apple of His eye." (Zech. 2:8) is His own avowal.

As we have practically reached the limits of our space, we refrain from commenting in any detail upon v. 15, 16. The more so because what is there said has been before us in Ex. 13 and 23. That which is therein enjoined is separation from the Canaanites themselves, from their ways, and from their worship. In view of what had so recently taken place, the closing words of our passage are very solemn: "Thou shalt make thee no molten gods." (v. 17.) May the Lord grant both writer and reader that purpose of heart to cleave fully unto Himself, and that singleness of eye that has in view nought but His own glory, ever remembering that our God is a jealous God.

ARTHUR W. PINK.

ABRAM'S SIN
Gen. 12:10-13

The respective titles of our last article and of the present one—Abram's failure and Abram's sin—suggest a little overlapping in the ground covered by them. In articles 4 and 5 we were occupied with Abram's obedience and worship, and from them we turned to contemplate a sad episode in our patriarch's history, an episode which is described in some detail in the second half of Gen. 12. That episode may be divided into three parts: the causes which led up to it, the consequences that it entailed, and Abram's deliverance out of it. We shall now examine, again, that which preceded Abram's sad fall, and also some of the disastrous consequences which followed; completing these, D. V., together with God's gracious recovery of Abram, in our next and closing article.

That which occasioned Abram's going down into Egypt is detailed in Gen. 12:9,10. There are four things to be noted there. First, Abram left Bethel. This was the starting-point in his path of declension. His departure from Bethel was a figure of the Christian losing his communion with the Lord, leaving his "first love." (Rev. 2:4.) This is evident from the words of Gen. 13:3, 4, "And he went ... unto the place of the altar which he had made there **at the first."** Bethel signifies "the house of God," and the center and glory of that "house" is Christ. This is the first solemn warning of the passage which we need to take to heart. Once our eyes are removed from Christ (like Peter's when walking on the sea), we begin to sink. As soon as He ceases to fill our vision and satisfy the heart we have commenced on a course which, unless Divine mercy intervenes, will issue in what is dishonouring and grieving to Him. Hence the force of that injunction, "Keep thy heart with all diligence, for out of it are the issues of life." (Prov. 4:23); and the only way to do so is to heed His own loving appeal, "My son, give Me thine heart." (Prov. 23:26.)

The second step in Abram's downward course is described in the words, "And Abram journeyed, in going and journeying." (v. 9): a spirit of restlessness now possessed him. This, and all that follows, is the inevitable consequence of leaving Bethel. Once we depart from the place of Divine fellowship, our soul has lost its anchorage. "The wicked are like the troubled sea, which cannot rest." And why? Because they are alienated from, are strangers to, the only One who can give them rest (Matt. 11:28). To the saint the word is, "Rest in the Lord." (Psa. 37:7), as it also is, "Rejoice in the Lord alway." (Phil. 4:4.) But if something has come in between the heart and the Lord, then, till we return to Him, both rest and joy are at an end. The only antidote to the discontented and restless spirit, which now obtains on every side of us, is the daily cultivation of fellowship with the God of peace.

The third step in Abram's backslidings of heart is plainly to be seen in the **direction** which he took: "going on still toward the south." (v. 9.) Southward was **Egyptward!** Most suggestive and solemnly accurate is this line in our typical picture. Turning Egyptwards is ever the logical and inevitable outcome of leaving Bethel and being possessed with a spirit of restlessness. As most of our readers are aware, Egypt is the outstanding symbol in the O. T. for the **world**. The language of its king is, "Who is the Lord, that I should obey His voice to let Israel go? I know not the Lord, neither will I let Israel go." (Ex. 5:2). Consequently, it is the place of hard bondage, though it has much that is imposing and attractive to the outward eye. In Scripture it is ever presented as a menace to the people of God. Yet it was thither that Abram had now turned his feet.

It is "out of the world" that God has called His people (John 15:19) and against it that He forbids them to be conformed. (Rom. 12:2). And what has this poor perishing world to offer to a child of God, a joint heir with Christ? The answer to this question depends upon the practical state of his heart. If he is so absorbed with his Redeemer that the language of his soul is, "Thou O Christ art all I want, more than all in Thee I find," then the world has no appeal for him. But if he becomes dissatisfied with Bethel, then some other object will be sought. Disastrous indeed, as most of us have proved from painful experience, are the consequences of getting away from "the House of God."

No Christian gets right back again into that world, out of which Divine grace has called him, at a single step. Nor did Abram. Before he went down into Egypt to sojourn there" (v. 10), he "journeyed **toward** the south," (v. 9), which, as we have said, was in the direction of Egypt. No young Christian returns at once to novel-reading, card playing, theatre-going, etc. No, while he is in the bloom of "first love," his heart overflowing by the discovery which has been made to him of the grace of God in Christ Jesus, he is wholly taken up with his newly-found Saviour. He wishes that there were a spiritual gathering of God's people which he could attend every night in the week; and when there is not, he spends his time in communing with the Lord over His Word. While this state is maintained, all is well. While he continues seeking the company of spiritually-minded Christians, his soul will prosper. But if, after a while, he forms associations with worldly-minded professors, if he neglects to feed daily on the heavenly manna, if he frequents less and less the "secret place of the Most High," if he remains in bed Sunday mornings instead of attending the assembly of the saints, or tells himself that he is too tired to go to the weekly prayer meeting, this is sure proof that his heart has already left Bethel, and a spirit of restlessness will possess him.

Cannot the reader now perceive the **connection** between these three things in Abram, which preceded his going down into Egypt? Just as the leaving of Bethel was the inevitable precursor of his "going and journeying," so that was sure to be followed by his turning "southwards." Ah, it is the spirit of restlessness which occasions the going Egyptwards. Once the soul loses its anchorage, once it ceases to "rest in" and "delight itself" **in the Lord**, discontent takes possession of it; and the sure consequence of this is that the world is turned to for relief. Just as there is no vacuum in nature, so the heart cannot remain devoid of an object, and if Christ does not fill it, the world will. Ah, my reader, does time begin to hang heavily on thine hands, art thou almost at thy wits' end to devise some diversion? Beware, the spirit of restlessness already holds thee and unless you, penitently, seek a return to Bethel, then Egyptwards **your** feet will swiftly turn. Remember that Eve "desired" the fruit before she took it, and ere that, she "looked" upon it.

There is a fourth thing for us now to consider: "And there was a famine in the land: and Abram went down into Egypt to sojourn there; for the famine was grievous in the land." (v. 10). The significance of this line in our typical picture has been missed by most expositors of Gen. 12. Even such a helpful writer as C. H. M. goes astray here, and in our own work "Gleanings in Genisis," (written ten years ago), we were guilty of echoing his views without having first thoroughly "proved" (1 Thess. 5:21) them for ourself.

Almost all the commentators regard this "famine" as a testing of Abram's faith; but the immediate context is altogether against such a theory. The first key which unlocks for us the spiritual meaning of this "famine" is found by noting the exact place in Gen. 12 that it is mentioned. At the end of v. 5 we are told, "And into the land of Canaan they came." Now had the next statement been "And there was a famine in the land," this would undoubtedly have lent credence to the popular view. But nothing is said about any "famine" when Abram first entered the land. Of course not, the one who is in the path of obedience to God, encounters no such thing! Nor was there any "famine" at Sichem. Of course not; there is no shortage of food for the one who has taken Christ's yoke upon him. Nor was there any famine at Bethel. Of course not; there is always plenty of bread in the house of God. The analogy of scripture is also directly against the thought of "famines" being sent for the testing of faith. See Gen. 26:1; Ruth 1:1; 2 Sam. 22:1, etc. In each case the famine was a Divine judgment.

Once again it is by noting the **order** in which Divine truth is set before us that we are enabled to enter into the meaning of it. The different steps or stages in Abram's experience are here marked out for us plainly enough. First, he left Bethel, the place of communion and worship. Second, in consequence, he became possessed of a spirit of restlessness. Third, and again in consequence of what precedes, he turned his face southwards—figure of a believer who no longer finds his satisfaction in Christ, turning to the world for relief. Fourth, he encountered a "famine."

This is still the unchanging order of spiritual experience. Christ is the Bread of life, and to wander from Him in our affections necessarily involves a famine in the soul. So far from the "famine" recorded in Gen. 12:10 being sent for a testing of Abram's faith, it was a Divine **chastisement.**

There was no famine while Abram remained at Bethel! No, there is never any shortage of food there. There is always "bread" to be found in the place of Divine fellowship. Even the prodigal son, after he "came to himself," knew that. Did he not say, "How many hired servants of my Father's have bread enough and to spare" (Luke 15:17)? Ah, my brethren, if you are conscious of a shortage of food where you now are, that is sure proof that you are not in your right place. How many Christians today are complaining that they are not being fed; that the church, chapel or assembly they attend, provides no food for the soul. Such a state of affairs, goes to show, most probab'y, that they are in their wrong place, and while they continue there, God will not feed them.

The same principle holds good individually as well as coporately. I may be connected with a company of God's people where there is a ministry of blessing by the Holy Spirit, yet I may not personally be getting the good of it. To me that ministry may be quite dry and barren. But the fault lies in myself. If I am out of communion with God, if I am personally dwelling at Bethel, then, though a rich feast of Divine grace be spread before me. I have no appetite for it, and derive no benefit from it. If through the week I have been journeying "southward"

then I cannot take my place as a real worshipper before God on His holy Sabbath. I may be in my accustomed seat, and go through the outward forms of worship, but I have nothing to **present** unto the Lord for His delight, nor have I any capacity to receive food at His hands.

"Hear, O My people, and I will testify unto thee: O Israel, if thou wilt hearken unto Me. There shall no strange god be in thee, neither shalt thou worship any strange god. I am the Lord thy God, which brought thee out of the land of Egypt: open thy mouth wide, and I will fill it. But My people would not hearken to My voice; and Israel would none of Me. So I gave them up unto their own heart's lust: they walked in their own counsels. O that My people had hearkened unto Me, and Israel had walked in My ways! I should soon have subdued their enemies, and turned My hand against their adversaries. . . He should have fed them also with the finest of the wheat, and with honey out of the rock should I have satisfied thee" (Psa. 81:8-16). Thus it was of old: God **withheld** from Israel these rich dainties because they "walked in their own counsels." Selah!

So it was with Abram. The "famine" was a sure sign of God's displeasure. It evidenced that he was no longer in his proper place. It was sent as a Divine chastisement, but as Heb. 12:11 teaches us, these diciplinary dealings of our faithful God avail us nothing unless we truly lay them to heart: "Now no chastening for the present seemeth to be joyous, but grievous: nevertheless afterward it yieldeth the peaceable fruit of righteousness unto them which are **exercised** thereby." But if we treat God's chastenings as a matter of course, as part of the inevitable troubles which man is born unto, this is to "despise" them (Heb. 12:5), and we fail to get the good of them.

Alas, the first thought with the average Christian is not to be "exercised" over the chastisement, but, How may I most easily and quickly get from under the rod? If it be in the form of financial reverses, we rack our brains to devise some plan to make good our loss. If it be illness, we send for the doctor to give us quick relief. Instead, we ought first to seek unto the Lord and say with Job, "Show me wherefore Thou contendest with me?" (10:2). We should humbly ask God to show us **why** He is chastening us, what is the lesson He would have us learn, what there is in our walk which needs putting right. If we do not, we shall fail to benefit from the chastisement, and may bring down His rod still more heavily upon us.

When Abram encountered that famine he should have at once suspected that there was something wrong, wrong in himself! He should have argued, **God** called me into Canaan, why then this famine? In the face of such a trial he ought to have sought unto the Lord, not as to the speediest way out of his trouble, but as to the cause of it. God does not act arbitrarily, neither does He "afflict willingly" (Lam. 3:33). Nor would Abram's duty be to seek **direction** from God. He might have cried earnestly for relief, so too for instruction as to what he should do; and it would have been easy under the circumstances—probably inevitable—to have persuaded himself that it was right for him to turn to Egypt for succor. It would have been easy for Abram to have imagined that "providence" had led him "southward," so why not enter Egypt! In like manner, it is equally **natural** for a Christian who has lost his position to advertise for another, for a sick one to call in the doctor, for one who has suffered a monetary reverse to acquaint influential friends of his need. But what place has **God** in these things? Ah, our hearts **are** "deceitful above all things." Suppose I am pressed financially, and I spread my need before God. A little later a fellow-Christian, in affluent circumstances, pays me a visit. How easy to persuade myself that the Lord has sent that friend so that I might acquaint him with the urgency of my situation! Instead, God has sent that friend, most probably, to make it manifest whether or not my soul is waiting **only** on God (Psa. 62:5)!

The fact is that Abram failed to trust God in the time of famine, and the reason for this is not far to seek—he was away from Bethel. Abram could not trust God with his temporal affairs because he was out of communion with Him spiritually. The same principle which obtains in the physical life holds good in the spiritual: when the heart is out of order, the whole body is affected and suffers. So, if our **heart** is not delighting itself in the Lord, resting in Him, then all our **ways** are wrong. The outward is but the reflex of the inward. See a Christian who is following a course of self-will and self-gratification, and that is sure proof that his soul is out of touch with God. It is only as communion with Him is maintained, that our conduct will be pleasing unto Him.

"And Abram went down into Egypt to sojourn there, for the famine was grievous in the land" (v. 10). Here is the initial consequence of Abram's failures. This is the first time that "Egypt" is mentioned in Scripture, and like most of its subsequent references, so here, it stands for that which is a constant menace to God's people. "Woe to the rebellious children, saith the Lord, that take counsel, but not of Me; and that cover with a covering, but not of My Spirit, that they may add sin to sin; That walk to go down into Egypt, and have not asked at My mouth; to strengthen themselves in the strength of Pharaoh, and to trust in the shadow of Egypt!" (Isa. 30:1, 2). "Woe to them that go down to Egypt for help and stay on horses, and trust in chariots, because they are many; and in horsemen, because they are very strong, but they look not unto the Holy One of Israel, neither seek the Lord" (Isa. 31:1). Thus it will be seen that looking to Egypt for help becomes a substitute for relying alone on the Lord.

Notice carefully the word placed in bold: "And Abram went down into Egypt to sojourn there: **for** the famine was grievous in the land." Yes, it was the "famine" which caused Abram to go down into Egypt. Shortage of food, that is, lack of satisfaction of heart—the consequence of loss of communion—is a serious matter. It is hungry people who turn to the world for relief. This is a most important line in our picture, and we do well to ponder it prayerfully. What we have here supplies a sure key to much that is going on around us. On every side are hungry souls, people who have an aching void within; restless, discontented, turning from one thing to another in their quest for satisfaction. Yes, we are surrounded by those who are **seeking satisfaction**, but the vast majority are seeking it in things of the world, which are but "vanity and vexation of spirit."

So it is **hunger** which causes God's people to turn to the world. Make no mistake on that point. When was it that Jacob sent **his** sons to Egypt? It was when there was a "famine" in Canaan! And if you will read attentively the history of Jacob and his children, you should have no difficulty in discovering **why** there was a famine there. Ah, Christian reader, if you are nourished with spiritual food, if you are finding your satisfaction in Christ, if the "joy of the Lord" is your strength (Neh. 8:20), then you will not crave the world's food, which is but the "husks" that the **swine** feed upon. But if Christ is not the "Bread of life" to you in a practical way, then Egyptwards you will turn. The heart must have an object.

This explains what is going on in many of the so-called churches. There are, most probably, churches in your city, where, years ago, a spiritual man occupied the pulpit, and where God's people were fed with spiritual food. But that pastor resigned, or died, and a worlding succeeded him. What happened? Why, of course, there was no longer any spiritual food; and so, because the people must be given something, the world's food was brought in. That "church" has gone down to Egypt, and so concerts, socials, bazaars, etc., are the consequences. So it is with the Christian individually: if he is not feeding on Christ daily, then novels, the movies, etc., become necessary to satisfy his cravings.

"And it came to pass, when he was come near to enter into Egypt, that he said unto Sarai his wife, Behold I know that thou art a fair woman to look upon: Therefore it shall come to pass, when the Egyptians shall see thee, that they shall say, This is his wife: and they will kill me, but they will save thee alive. Say, I pray thee, thou art my sister; that it may be well with me for thy sake; and my soul shall live because of thee" (vv. 11-13). Unspeakably solemn is this. As soon as Abram got near to Egypt he began to be afraid: the dark shadows of that land fell across his soul before he actually entered it! Prov. 29:25 tells us, "The fear of man bringeth a snare," and here we see this most sadly exemplified.

There is much in the verses just quoted from Gen. 12 which we cannot now dwell upon. But observe the extent to which Abram was occupied with himself: "They will kill **me**. Say, I pray thee, thou art **my** sister, that it may be well with **me** . . . and **my** soul shall live because of thee." What an illustration is this of the inspired declaration of Prov. 14:14, "The backslider in heart shall be filled with his own ways!" Fearful of his own physical safety, Abram tempts his wife to repudiate her marriage to him. And what is the spiritual principle here exemplified? This: Abram was **afraid to avow his true relationship.** That is always what happens when a Christian goes down into Egypt. When the child of God forsakes the path of separation, he at once begins to compromise and equivocate. When he fellowships the world, he is afraid to fly his true colours. He knows full well that the wicked hate the name of Christ, so he sedulously avoids confessing it. Yes, the child of God in Egypt **is** afraid to avow his true relationship. How fearful are the consequences of getting away from Bethel!

—Arthur W. Pink.

THE BOOK OF NEHEMIAH
Blessing in Days of Apostasy

We may be quite sure that God has exercised His own perfect wisdom, in determining what parts of the world's history, and of His own people's history, should or should not be recorded in His Word; and though we may be often unable to discern the bearing of certain passages or books of the divine record, yet we may surely ascribe this to the dimness of our own sight, and rest satisfied that whatever is recorded of the things that happened of old, is written for our admonition, upon whom the ends of the world are come. Any one who can look back upon the time when he saw nothing respecting the Lord's earthly reign, and Israel's blessing in the latter day, and can compare his thoughts on Scripture then, with those which he has had since a knowledge of the Lords second coming opened on his mind, will be able to say how many parts of Scripture have become full of interest and light, which once appeared uninteresting and obscure.

Again—when we have learned a little to turn off our thoughts from resting only on ourselves, and to regard the Scripture as unfolding the thoughts of God respecting the Church, and Israel, and the world, in their present and future histories, we find that many parts from which we failed to draw any definite instruction, when we read the Scripture as isolated individuals selfishly, have assumed quite another character, when we have learned to see that our interests are indissoluably united to one body, even the Church, whose welfare and interests cannot be separated from our own. And thus we are by our own experience, furnished with many proofs, that when we have found Scripture in any part unintelligible, it has arisen from our own ignorance and want of wisdom in applying it aright.

It has already been remarked in a former paper, how every dispensation whose history is recorded in Scripture, bears marked upon it the same sad features of man's continual propensity to depart from God, and be false to those principles of blessing, by preserving which, his fidelity would have been manifested, and his happiness secured. But amidst these sorrowful relations of progressive evil, we have several times brought before us a more cheering and blessed subject of contemplation, and that is the power of the Spirit of God, even in the midst of apostasy and evil, to raise up and find a path for those who desire to return and to serve God in righteousness and truth.

Of this we find one instance in Hezekiah. He lived at a time when the tribes of Israel had long ceased to care about everything that marked them as distinct from the nations around, and which gave them oneness together as the blessed people of the Lord. Their paschal feast, the pledge and evidence of these blessings, had altogether been neglected; but Hezekiah re-establishes and summons all Israel to its celebration. The great part mock—but a few obey. He sanctifies the priests for worship, and the Levites for service; supplies them with sacrifices that they may have wherewith to offer, and intercedes that they and their offerings, though deficiently sanctified and imperfect, may yet be accepted: and they are. Here is one blessed type of the Spirit of Christ leading a little remnant, (whilst all others are careless) into power of manifested obedience and worship, supplying means of service, which through intercession finds, with all its weakness and imperfection, acceptance and conscious blessing.

But it is not to this period that I wish to draw our attention now, but to the later period of Nehemiah, a period which furnishes I believe, some important principles which will be useful in directing our judgment in many questions about which the Church is anxious. Nehemiah lived at a time when "the wall of Jerusalem was broken down, and the gates thereof burned with fire;" i.e., the chosen city—the city with His name there—the only place where He could be worshipped—the city which once laughed all her enemies to scorn, was now defenceless and deserted, and the people which should have been most blessed, were scattered and in reproach. It was the sense of this—the sense of God's being dishonoured, and of His people's being despoiled of their blessing; it was this that moved the faithful heart of Nehemiah and caused it to sorrow, when he might have enjoyed all the luxury and splendor of the Persian palace. He had one desire—to see Jerusalem restored, and worshipped in by her own separated people, that Jerusalem might become again palpably distinguished from the nations around.

And are **we** not living at a time when that which ought to be seen as the separated portion of the Lord, the Church of the living God, is scattered—its unity broken—itself undefended and unseparated by its proper bulwarks of truth? Nehemiah's anxiety was to restore the walls of Jerusalem—a wall is that which separates and defends; and this, the truth is to the Church—"Girt about with truth." "Sanctify them through Thy truth." Doctrinal truth—the very first knowledge of the blood of the paschal Lamb separates from the world unto God. Practical truth—any one precept of Jesus received and acted upon-separates from the world and brings into the paths of God. And while it separates, it defends, for it gives a strength in God which Satan is not able to overthrow,—"And who is he that will harm you, if ye be followers of that which is good?" (1 Peter 3:13). Only let the Church enfeebled as it is, and scattered, realize the truth of her heavenly calling—let them live the precepts of Christ, and the world will soon see that a separating wall is builded.

There were many things to discourage Nehemiah in his work. In the first place, there were his many enemies saving, "What do these feeble Jews?" etc. "If a fox should go over, he would break down their stone wall." And in answer to these taunts, there was not divine interference as of old—no manifestation of the presence and glory of God—nothing which to the outward eye could give the least sanction to their work, or prove that God regarded it with favour. With one hand they builded, and with another held a weapon to resist the foe.

Again; it might have been said to Nehemiah, By what authority doest thou these things? Those of old who had delivered Israel—such as Gideon, for example, had received the plain and manifested appointment of the Lord. David and Solomon were the Lord's anointed, the **ordained** rulers of His people. But Nehemiah had no such appointment, though the very circumstances of destitution and uncertainty in which they were, seemed to render such an appointment the more desirable. But we do not read of the people's stumbling at this difficulty, and questioning his authority, and refusing to obey. Instead, we read, "the people had a mind to work." Here was the great secret of their energy; they desired the restitution of Jerusalem, because they believed it was pleasing to God, and blessed for themselves, and therefore the superior fitness and zeal of Nehemiah for the work was sufficient to secure the obedient submission of all, who really desired that the work should prosper. His authority was over the obedient mind, I mean the mind obedient to God; and doubtless he who had refused to obey Nehemiah, thus labouring for the Lord, would have no less displeased Him, than if he had refused submission to David or Solomon, who were manifestedly and declaredly the Lord's anointed.

There are few things more important in regarding the circumstances of the Church, at any given period, than to consider in what part of the dispensation we are; for many things may befit one period of it, which would ill befit another. If Nehemiah had said, it will be useless for me to labour, unless the glory is first restored, and unless the ancient order of Israel in her kings and priests is restored, he never would have laboured at all. But would such a claim have been seemly in the mouth of one, who knew that rebellion and apostasy had forfeited these blessings? And that if the divine sanction had been palpably given as of old, it would have been given to a little, and in many respects still disobedient remnant, very small in comparison of the multitudes of their brethren who were scattered in distant lands, and little able to maintain the proper position of God's Israel in the earth. Surely it rather became him without any unseemly pretensions of right to power and blessing, which had justly been taken away, to do what he did, namely, seek to restore the fallen people of God to separateness, and purity, and obedience.

And his labour was not in vain, for although the glory never came back to the city, and though suffering and conflict were the portion of those who dwelt in it, yet it was the place in which some with fasting and prayer were enabled to serve God, until they could say, "Lord, now lettest Thou Thy servant depart in peace, for mine eyes have seen Thy salvation."

—The Christian Witness, 1838.

N. B.

Those who desire to follow up the present-day application of the book of Nehemiah will do well to procure "Notes on Nehemiah" by H. A. Ironside (Twenty-five cents in paper; seventy-five cents in cloth) from Cleveland Bible Truth Depot, Mr. I. C. Herendeen, 433-433 The Arcade, Cleveland, Ohio, U. S. A.

A PERSONAL WORD

Ere leaving Seaton, England, on May 1, we sought the prayers of many of our brethren and sisters in Christ (Phil. 4:6), that God would graciously grant us full journeying mercies, give us favour in the eyes of the Amercian officials, and make plain His way before our face. We therefore feel the least we can do now is to let them know how blessedly their prayers have been answered. Our object in writing is not to gratify the curiosity of any, but to provoke praise and thanksgiving unto Him who doeth all things well. May our remembrancers at the Throne of Grace be as earnest in acknowledging Jehovah's gifts, as they were in seeking them in our behalf.

We sailed from Southhampton on May 2, and once more the Lord made the sea calm for us (Psa. 107:29). All the way across the Atlantic we were favoured with a smoth passage, not even encountering so much as a squall (Rom. 1:10). This was the more striking, because in the two weeks immediately following, storms and heavy seas were reported daily (Psa. 115:3). On our arrival at New York, we experienced no difficulty in landing. The immigration officer was glad to admit us. He enquired if we intended to pursue our calling as a minister of the Gospel? To which we replied, Yes, by the grace of God. Then he added, You are coming here to mend broken souls? To which we responded, No, sir; instead, as an instrument in the Lord's hands, to bring life to those who are dead in sin. His face lit up, and he exclaimed, Atta boy; that's the talk! Nor did we meet with any trouble in the Custom's house (Gen. 39:21).

After a few days with our Brother and Sister Pressel at York, Pa., who have so kindly attended to the interests of "Studies" in this Country, during the four and a half years we have been absent from it; and a short visit with another Brother and Sister at Altoona, we completed the last stage of our long journey, arriving at Mortons Gap May 30. Here we received a hearty and loving welcome from a little company of God's people, to whom it has been our privilege to minister the Word of Life several times in the past. We solicit the earnest prayers of the saints on behalf of Brother Cole and his wife. Brother Cole is the pastor of the local Baptist Church here, and has been much hated and persecuted for his faithful preaching of God's truth. This is a favored section of the Lord's vineyard, and we long to see it copiously watered from on High, that there may be much fruit borne to the honour and glory of the Triune Jehovah (1 Cor. 12:13).

God willing, we expect to devote most of our time to the work of this magazine. O that the Lord may condescend to teach us so that we may be fitted to teach His people. Much wisdom is needed, wisdom which God only can give, to discern the messages most suited to these "perilous times." The sustaining grace of the Spirit is also required that we may preserve the **balance** of Truth, so that we shall be enabled to rightly divide the Word, and expound parts of it in their scriptural proportions. More and more are we convinced that stress should now be laid on the application of the Word to our **daily walk.**

"If ye know these things, happy are ye **if** ye **do** them." There are opportunities to be a "fellow-helper" in the Truth with the local pastor. In addition, we hope to go out in occasional meetings, as the Lord may lead. Quite a number of invitations are to hand for Bible conference work.

We are thankful to say the Lord has preserved us both in full health and has ministered freely to our every need. "Blessed be the Lord, who daily loadeth us with benefits, even the God of our salvation" (Psa. 68:19). With all good wishes and loving greetings to every brother and sister in Christ Jesus,

Yours by the Grace and Mercy of God,
A. W. and V. E. Pink.

SELF-CONTROL

The word "temperance" in 2 Peter 1:6, means a great deal more than what is usually understood by that term. It is customary to apply the expression "temperance" to a habit of moderation in reference to eating and drinking. No doubt it fully involves this, but it involves very much more. Indeed, the Greek word used by this inspired apostle, may, with strict propriety, be rendered "self-control." It gives the idea of one who has **self** habitually **well reined in.**

This is a rare and admirable grace, diffusing its hallowed influence over the entire course, character, and conduct. It not only bears directly upon one, or two, or twenty selfish **habits,** but upon **self,** in all the length and breadth of that comprehensive and most odious term. Many a one who would look, with proud disdain, upon a glutton or drunkard, may himself fail, every hour, in exhibiting the grace of self-control. True it is that gluttony and drunkenness should be ranged with the very vilest and most demoralizing forms of selfishness. They must be regarded as amongst the most bitter clusters that grow on that wide-spreading tree. But, then, **self** is a tree, and not a mere branch of a tree, or a cluster on a branch; and we should not only **judge** self when it works, but **control** it that it may not work.

Some, may, however ask, "How can we control self?" The answer is blessedly simple: "I can do **all** things through Christ which strengtheneth me" (Phil. 4). Have we not gotten salvation in Christ? Yes, blessed be God, we have. And what does this wondrous word include? Is it mere deliverance from the wrath to come? Is it merely the pardon of our sins, and the assurance of exemption from the lake that burneth with fire and brimstone? It is far more than these, precious and priceless though they be. In a word, this "salvation" implies a full and hearty acceptance of Christ as my "wisdom," to guide me out of folly's dark and devious paths, into paths of heavenly light and peace: as my "righteousness," to justify me in the sight of a holy God; as my "sanctification," to give me final deliverance from all the power of death, and entrance upon the eternal fields of glory.

Hence, therefore, it is evident that "self-control" is included in that salvation which we have in Christ. It is a result of that practical sanctification with which divine grace has endowed us. We should carefully guard against the habit of taking a narrow view of salvation. We should seek to enter into all its fulness. It is a word which stretches from everlasting to everlasting, and takes in, in its mighty sweep, all the practical details of daily life. I have no right to talk of salvation, as regards my **soul,** in the **future,** while I refuse to know and exhibit its practical bearing upon my **conduct,** in the **present.** We are saved, not only from the guilt and condemnation of sin, but also, and as fully, from the power, the practice, and the love of it. These things should never be separated, nor will they by any one who has been divinely taught the meaning, the extent, and the power of that precious word "salvation."

Now in presenting to my reader a few practical sentences on the subject of "self-control," I shall contemplate it under the three following divisions, namely— the thoughts, the tongue, the temper. I take it for granted that I am addressing a saved person. If my reader be not that I can only direct him to the one true and living way, "Believe on the Lord Jesus Christ, and thou shalt be saved, and thy house" (Acts 16). Put your whole trust in Him, and you shall be as safe as He is Himself. This grand theme is largely dwelt upon, and variously illustrated, throughout the pages of this magazine, and to them I would refer the unconverted sinner, or the anxious inquirer, while I proceed to deal with the practical and much-needed subject of "self-control."

1. And, first, as to our thoughts, and the habitual government thereof. I suppose there are few Christians who have not suffered from evil thoughts—those troublesome intruders upon our most profound retirement—those constant disturbers of our mental repose, that so frequently darken the atmosphere around us, and prevent us getting a clear, full view upward into the bright heaven above. The Psalmist could say, "I hate vain thoughts." No wonder. They are truly hateful, and should be judged, condemned, and expelled. Some one, in speaking of the evil thoughts, has said, "I cannot prevent birds flying over me, but, I can prevent their alighting upon me. In like manner, I cannot prevent evil thoughts being suggested to my mind, but I can refuse them a lodgment therein."

But how can we control our thoughts? No more than we can blot out our sins, or create a world. What are we to do? To look to Christ. This is the secret of self-control. He can keep us, not only from lodgment, but also from the suggestions of the evil thoughts. We could no more prevent the one than the other. He can prevent both. He can keep the vile intruders, not only from getting in, but even from knocking at the door. When the divine life is in energy—when the current of spiritual thought and feeling is deep and rapid—when the heart's affections are intensely occupied with the Person of Christ, vain thoughts do not trouble us. It is only when spiritual indolence creeps over us that evil thoughts—vile and horrible progeny!—come in upon us, like a flood; and then our **only** resource is to look straight at Jesus. We might as well try to cope with the marshalled hosts of hell, as with a horde of evil thoughts. Our refuge is in Christ. He is made unto us sanctification. We can do all things through Him. We have just to bring the name of Jesus to bear upon the flood of evil thoughts and He will, most assuredly, give full and immediate deliverance.

However, the more excellent way is, to be preserved from the suggestions of evil, by the power of pre-occupation with good. When the channel of thought is decidedly upward, when it is deep and well-formed, free from all curves and indentations, then the current of imagination and feeling, as it gushed up from the deep fountains of the soul, will naturally flow onward in the bed of that channel. This, I repeat, is, unquestionably, the more excellent way. May we prove it in our own experience. "Finally, brethren, whatsoever things are true, whatsoever things are honorable, whatsoever things are just, whatsoever things are lovely, whatsoever things are of good report, if there be any virtue, and if there be any praise, **think** on these things. Those things which ye have both learned and received, and heard and seen in me, do; and the God of peace shall be with you" (Phil. 4:8, 9). When the heart is fully engrossed with Christ, the living embodiment of all those things enumerated in verse 8, we enjoy profound peace, unruffled by evil thoughts. This is true self-control.

2. And, now, as to the tongue, that influential member, so fruitful in good, so fruitful in evil—the instrument whereby we can either give forth accents of soft and soothing sympathy, or words of bitter sarcasm and burning indignation. How deeply important is the grace of self-control in its application to such a member! Mischief, which years cannot repair, may be done by the tongue in a moment. Words, which we would give the world, if we had it, to recall, may be uttered by the tongue in an unguarded hour. Hear what the inspired apostle saith on this subject: "If any man offend not in word, the same is a perfect man, and able also to bridle the whole body. Behold, we put bits in the horses' mouths, that they may obey us; and we turn about their whole body. Behold also the ships, which though they be so great, and are driven of fierce winds, yet are they turned about with a very small helm, whithersoever the governor listeth. Even so the tongue is a little member and boasteth great things. Behold, how great a matter a little fire kindleth! And the tongue is a fire, a world of iniquity: so is the tongue among our members, that it defileth the whole body, and setteth on fire the course of nature; and it is set on fire of hell. For every kind of beasts, and of birds, and of serpents, and of things in the sea is tamed, and hath been tamed of mankind. But the tongue can **no man** tame; it is an unruly evil, full of deadly poison" (James 3:2-8). Who, then, can control the tongue? "No man" can do it, but Christ can; and we have only to look to Him, in simple faith which implies, at

once, the sense of our own utter helplessness and His all-sufficiency. It is utterly impossible that we could control the tongue. As well might we attempt to stem the ocean's tide, the mountain torrent, or the Alpine avalanche. How often, when suffering under the effects of some egregious blunder of the tongue, have we resolved to command that unruly member somewhat better next time: but, alas! our resolution proved to be like the morning cloud that passeth away, and we have only to retire and weep over our lamentable failure in the matter of self-control. Now, why was this? Simply because we undertook the matter in our own strength, or, at least, without a sufficiently deep consciousness of our own weakness. This is the cause of constant failure. We must cling to Christ as the babe clings to its mother. Not that our clinging is of any value; still we must cling. Thus, and thus alone, can we successfully bridle the tongue. And oh, let us remember, at all times, the solemn searching words of the same apostle James, "If **any one** (man, woman, or child) among you seem to be religious, and bridleth not his tongue, but deceiveth his own heart, this man's religion is vain" (1:26). These are wholesome words for a day like the present, when there are so many unruly tongues abroad. May we have grace to attend these words! May their holy influence appear in our ways!

3. The last point to be considered is the temper, which is intimately connected with both the tongue, and the thoughts. Indeed, all three are very closely linked. When the spring of **thought** is spiritual, and the current heavenly, the **tongue** is only the active agent for good, and the **temper** is calm and unruffled. Christ dwelling in the heart by faith regulates everything. Without Him, all is worse than worthless. I may possess and exhibit the self-command of a Franklin or a Socrates, and, all the while, be wholly ignorant of the "self-control" of 2 Peter 1:6. The latter is founded on "faith;" the former on philosophy, two totally different things. We must remember that the word is **"Add to your faith."** This puts faith first, as the **only** link to connect the heart with Christ, the living source of all power. Having Christ, and abiding in Him, we are enabled to add "courage, knowledge, self-control, patience, godliness. brotherly-kindness, charity." Such are the precious fruits that follow from abiding in Christ. But I can no more control my temper than my tongue or my thoughts; and if I set about it, I shall be sure to break down every hour. A mere philosopher without Christ, may exhibit more self-control as to tongue and temper, than a Christian, if he abides not in Christ. This ought not to be, and would not be, if the Christian simply looked to Jesus. It is when he fails in this that the enemy gains the advantage. The philosopher, without Christ, seems to succeed in the business of self-control, only that he may be the more effectually blinded as to the truth of his condition, and carried headlong to eternal ruin. But Satan delights to make a Christian stumble and fall, only that he may thereby blaspheme the precious name of Christ.

Christian reader, let us remember these things. Let us look to Christ to control our thoughts, our tongue, and our temper. Let us "give **all** diligence." Let us think how much is involved. "If these things be in you and abound, they make you that ye shall neither be barren nor unfruitful in the knowledge of our Lord Jesus Christ. But he that lacketh these things is blind, and cannot see afar off, and hath forgotten that he was purged from his old sins." This is deeply solemn. How easy it is to drop into a state of spiritual blindness and forgetfulness! No amount of knowledge, either of doctrine or the letter of Scripture, will preserve the soul from this awful condition. Nothing but "the knowledge of our Lord Jesus Christ" will avail; and this knowledge is to be increased in the soul by "giving all diligence to add to our faith" the various graces to which the apostle refers in the above eminently practical and soul-stirring passage. "Wherefore the rather, brethren, give diligence to make your calling and election sure: for if ye do these things ye shall never fail: for so an entrance shall be ministered unto you abundantly into the everlasting kingdom of our Lord and Saviour Jesus Christ."

—Things New and Old, Vol. 3.

IMPORTANT NOTICE

Many of our older readers will rejoice to hear that Vol. 3 of our Exposition of John's Gospel is now on the press, and, we expect, will be ready for sale within the next few days. Those who wish to secure a copy please send $2.00 (8-6) to the publisher, Mr. I. C. Herendeen, 433-435 The Arcade, Cleveland, Ohio, U. S. A.

For the benefit of many new readers

regularity in coming to me, and I am very grateful for the great spiritual blessing and help they have been to me in my study and reading of the Word."—A Missionary in Morocco.

"I have enjoyed pretty close reading of your Studies in the Scriptures since their beginning. The Lord is mightily using you in that ministry. Many times have your discussions of various sections of the Word anchored me in times of floundering.' They came as the steadying hand of God to hold me from the very snares of the Devil. May God give you many years for this work."—A pastor in Kentucky. A reader in Canada, who finds little or no real fellowship with professing Christians, and who gets little food for her soul in the church she attends, writes, "All this makes the 'Studies' doubly precious, and I pray the Lord earnestly that He will enable you to continue and open many doors for them." A brother in the wilds of Brazil writes, "I have been blessed in the reading of the Studies. I know you give all the glory to God, but still I thank you for what your paper has been to me." "Your teachings have been an inestimable blessing in my own ministry of the Word."—A pastor in West Virginia.

Additional quotations, similar in character to those given above, might be made from letters received from Belgium, France, Spain, Sweden, Siberia, India, Japan, British W. Indies, Bolivia, Costa Rica, and various parts of Australia. But sufficient has been said, we trust, to bow the hearts of many readers in fervent praise to God, for having condescended to bless our writings to quite a number of His scattered people. It is indeed a privilege and a joy to set before them some of the riches of His grace. Such acknowledgements of help and blessing received are ample compensation for the many hours of hard study which the preparation of the articles entail. Only the Day to come will reveal the full fruitage— all the product of Divine grace alone.

And now what shall be the response of the reader? Ah, dear brother, dear sister, we desire you to be **more than** a "reader;" we want you to be a fellow-helper in this blessed work of ministering to God's starved sheep: "Ye also helping together by prayer for us, that for the gift bestowed upon us by the means of many persons, **thanks** may be given by many on our behalf" (2 Cor. 2:11). Will you daily supplicate the throne of grace, first, for the Lord's blessing on the editor and his wife, that they may be sustained in this "work of faith and labour of love;" that we may be taught of Him, and thus qualified to teach others? Second, that we may be permitted to reach an increasing number of those who **are** hungry for spiritual food, and for those in isolated places? Third, that God will continue to move His stewards to have financial fellowship with this work, that they may lay up for themselves "treasures in heaven" (Matt. 6:26)? Yours by God's wondrous grace,

—ARTHUR W. PINK.

---

of this little magazine, we may say that for six years we printed a section of our Exposition of John's Gospel in each issue of "Studies." They were similar in style and tone to the series we are now inserting on the Epistle to the Hebrews. For some time they have been out of print in their original form. But we are thankful to say Mr. Herendeen has undertaken, at very heavy expense, to publish the whole of these seventy-two articles in separate form. They have been carefully revised by us. The Lord was pleased to bless this effort to interpret and apply the Fourth Gospel to many of His dear people, and numerous have been the letters testifying to help received.

This Exposition of John's Gospel is being printed in a better sized type. When completed it will make over fourteen hundred pages. It is divided into four volumes. These sell at two dollars each, post paid— a lower price is not practicable, as the demand for such works is so pitiably small. Vols. 1 and 2 are now on the market, and Vol. 3 is almost ready. This work is invaluable for preachers, S. S. teachers and Christian workers. It is the product of ten years' prayer and hard work. Purchasers may take these Volumes one at a time to suit their convenience. We trust that many will avail themselves of this opportunity.

devoted solely to studies in the Scriptures. This trust we have sought to fulfill. We have spared no pains to the discharge of this duty, having given the largest part of our time to this important work. But we have learned that there are not so many who welcome a ministry of this type as we had thought. There are fewer prepared to "**Buy** the Truth" (Prov. 23:23)—sacrifice time and personal recreation, subordinate temporal interests to the acquiring of that which is spiritual—than is commonly assumed. The vast majority of those who read today, do so to while away an hour or for recreation, rather than for edification and spiritual profit. Hence, a magazine which treats only with the Word of God, does not appeal to them; it is "dry" or "too heavy." People have not the requisite "time" to take up a publication which has to be read slowly, carefully, and prayerfully, to be of real benefit.

During the last seven years "Studies in the Scriptures" has been sent to many hundreds of missionaries, preachers, S. S. teachers, and Christian workers, besides large numbers of others that our friends **thought** would be interested. We have retained them on our mailing-list for one, two and three years, though we never received a line of acknowledgment from them. Then we dropped their names, but we have had requests from only a fractionaal minority asking us to again send them the magazine. For this reason, when we now receive from a friend the name and address of some one to whom they desire us to send "Studies," we mail to them only one or two issues, marked "Sample Copy," with an arrow pointing to "Free to all who will read it," and another to our name and address. If the recipient enjoys these sample copies and would like further issues, surely it is not asking too much of him that he should make personal application.

But though many who received this magazine in the past have, apparently, failed to value it, the Lord has, in answer to many prayers, brought us into touch with several hundreds of those who are deeply thankful to Him for what He has enabled us to write and circulate. For the most part these reside in widely different places, for as John 11:52 tells us, the children of God are "scattered abroad." The letters received from them have not only cheered our hearts, shown that our labour "is not in vain" (1 Cor. 15:58), and thus encouraged us to "be not weary in well doing" (Gal. 6:9); but it has caused us to praise the Lord "with a loud voice" (2 Chron. 20:19), bowing our hearts before Him in fervent gratitude and daily thanksgiving. God does not always permit His servants to see the fruits of their labours, for they are to "walk by faith, not by sight" (2 Cor. 5:7): but when He does, it is to be regarded as a signal mark of His grace. We now append extracts from some of the letters recently received:—

"I have received much help from your Studies in the Scriptures, and have been able to pass on to the Chinese believers in our little assembly here some of the precious truths with which you have dealt. The Gleanings in Exodus have been of special value."—A Missionary in Chefoo. "Have only recently been receiving Studies in the Scriptures, but wish to take this opportunity to give my testimony as to what a help and a blessing this leaflet is to me in my ministry."—A pastor in Tennessee. "May I take this opportunity to thank you personally for the very real spiritual strength and encouragement which I have received, as I have followed you through your works 'The Redeemer's Return,' 'The Sovereignty of God,' and 'The Divine Inspiration of the Scriptures.' They have helped me much, and I trust others also through my ministry."—A pastor in Worces, England.

"I received Vols. 3, 4, 5, of Studies of the Scriptures, they are a precious treasure for me. Two or three days ago I studied your article on the Manna, a type of the written and personal Word. What new light I received! I love very much these type studies: to read the O. T. in the light of the New is a great joy, especially to see the Lord Jesus' sufferings and glories in them. I appreciate all your Studies very much; the more I read them, the more I understand the deeper meaning of the Bible.'—A Syrian Christian. "The Nov. and Dec. issues of Studies came to me in this morning's mail, and I have been rejoicing all day in the wonderful expositions you have given of portions of God's Word. The 'Studies' have meant much to me. I have every copy from the first you published, and have found them exceedingly profitable and instructive."—An Evangelist in North Carolina.

"Your Studies have been an enormous help and blessing to my soul, and I have rejoiced exceedingly in the clearness of God's messages through you; and I can assure you that I co-operate with your blessed ministry by my prayers. The messages rejoice my heart because they are written with the sole aim of exalting the Lord Jesus, without the trammelling of sectarian differences."—A young brother in Liverpool. "It has been in my mind for some time now to write you a note in appreciation of Studies in the Scriptures. I thank you very much for their

(Continued on Page 167)

Vol. VIII. AUGUST, 1929 No. 8

STUDIES IN THE SCRIPTURES

"Search the Scriptures" John 5:39

Copyright in all English-speaking Countries.

Editor: Arthur W. Pink, Morton's Gap, Ky., U. S. A.
Hon. Agent in England: Mr. A. Winstone, 2, Lennox Villas, Hewlett Road, Cheltenham.
Hon. Agent in Australia: Mr. G. Ardill, The Christian Workers' Depot.
Commonwealth and Reservoir Streets, Sydney.

FREE TO ALL WHO WILL READ IT.

FEEDING ON THE WORD

"**Thy words were found, and I did eat them; and Thy Word was unto me the joy and rejoicing of mine heart**" (Jer. 15:16).

Four things are here told us about the Word. First, the Holy Scriptures are not of human origination, but of Divine inspiration (inbreathing): "**Thy** words." Therefore do they merit our reverent, loving, daily attention. Second, the Holy Scriptures call for diligent and prayerful **study**. "Search the Scriptures" was the command of Christ (John 5:39; Acts 17:11). This is what the word "found" in our text implies. The Word is to be searched daily for the needed and suited message from God to our souls. For the most part, God's truth is not classified and tabulated. Its full teaching on a given subject is never found in a single chapter. The promises of God are not all grouped together, but distributed through the sixty-six books. One reason for this is, that the reader is made to search, and search diligently. This is what Jeremiah had done. Third, God's words are to be **fed upon**: "I did eat them." How very few there are who know what this means; fewer still act thus. Fourth, it is this which turns a duty into a delight: "and Thy Word was unto me the joy and rejoicing of mine heart." The Bible was no longer difficult and dry. It is the third of these points we propose to develop.

"Thy words were found and I did eat them." One of the surest tests as to the condition of a person's health is his appetite; true spirituality, as well as physically. Where the appetite fails, weakness and sickness inevitably follow. Strength goes down the throat. As the body is nourished by that which is extraneous to itself, so it is with the soul. Food must come from without. The **only** food for the soul is the Word of God. "As newborn babes, desire the sincere milk of the Word, that ye may grow thereby" (1 Peter 2:2). In the Word there is food of all kinds: milk for babes, meat for the fully-grown, medicine for the sick, reviving cordials for the faint.

It is only by feeding on the Word of God that the new nature can be nourished. There is no nutriment in man's thoughts or words. Therefore, we need not wonder that so many Christians are weak and sickly, fruitless and useless. It could not be otherwise. Instead of feeding on God's Word for themselves, too many are attempting to thrive on the results of **another's** study of it. It cannot be done. I may attend lectures on dietics and learn all about the chemistry of food, but if this becomes a substitute for three or four good meals a day, I should have no vitality for life's duties. Others feed on devotional books, and the biographies of eminent saints; but if these crowd out the devotional reading and feeding on the Word itself, it is like attempting to exist on cakes and candies in the natural world. Still others attempt to feed on their own inward experiences; no wonder they are so lean and aenemic.

Now the Bread which God has provided for His people contains in it all that is needed by us. But, as another has remarked, "The Word of God is too often treated like wheat now is. In the grinding of wheat, man has so constructed his mills, that he eliminates from it, automatically, nearly all God has put in it. And what is left is mostly starch, and this is so out of proportion to other substance, that the diastase—that part of the saliva which alone can digest it—is overtaxed, and the bread ferments in the stomach, instead of being digested: hence, rather than doing us good, it does us harm. Meanwhile, our system is so poorly nourished, our general health is affected, we feel 'out of sorts', and then we resort to widely-

(Continued on Page 192)

IMPORTANT NOTICES

Please advise promptly of change of address, otherwise copies will be lost in the mails.

We are glad to send a sample copy to any of our friends whom you believe would be interested in such a publication.

Send to Mr. I. C. Herendeen, 433-435, The Arcade, Cleveland, Ohio, for a list of our publications. He has published many of our books and booklets.

This Magazine is published as a work of faith and labour of love. The Editor and his wife gladly give their services. It is freely sent to all who will read it. No charge is made for it.

Christians who feel definitely lead to do so, may have fellowship with us in this ministry. Those outside the U. S. A., please send only INTERNATIONAL Money Orders made out to Morton's Gap, Kentucky, U. S. A. See that it is made out in American money.

Mailing Permit applied for.

CONTENTS

Hebrews	170
Gleanings in Exodus	176
Abram's Restoration	181
Sanctification by the Blood	185

THE EPISTLE TO THE HEBREWS

20 Christ Superior to Aaron
Heb. 5:5-7

The central design of the Holy Spirit in this Epistle needs to be kept steadily before the mind of the reader: that design was to prove the superiority of Christianity over Judaism. The centre and glory of Judaism was the divinely appointed priesthood: what, then, had Christianity to offer at this point? "The unbelieving Jews would be apt to say to their Christian brethren, 'your new religion is deficient in the very first requisite of a religion—you have no high priest. How are your sins to be pardoned, when you have none to offer expiatory oblations for you? How are your wants to be supplied, when you have none to make intercession for you to God?' The answer to this cavil is to be found in the apostle's word, 'We **have** a High Priest' 4:14" (Dr. J. Brown).

That God has provided His people with a High Priest is the fulfilment of His own promise. On the demonstrated failure of the Aaronical priesthood in the days of Eli and his sons (1 Sam. 1:14, 2:12-17, 22), the Lord declared, "And I will raise Me up a faithful Priest, that shall do according to that which is in Mine heart and in My mind: and I will build Him a sure house" (1 Sam. 2:35). The fulfilment of this is found in the person and work of the Lord Jesus Christ. But in taking up the study of the priesthood of Christ it is of the greatest possible importance to perceive that **both** the typical persons of Aaron and Melchizedek were required to prefigure the varied actions and excellencies of the great High Priest who is the centre and heart of Christianity. It was failure to recognize this which has resulted in so many inadequate and faulty treaties on the subject.

Both Aaron and Melchizedek were needed to set forth the various phases of Christ's priestly ministry., But before the apostle could take up the latter, he had first to show that Christ fulfilled all which was adumbrated by the former: before he could dwell upon the points in which Christ's excelled the Levitical priesthood, he must first establish its parallels and similarities This the apostle does in Heb. 5. In its first four verses we have a description of the Levitical high priest: first with respect to his nature (v. 1), second his employment (v. 1), third his qualification (v. 2), fourth his duty (v. 3), fifth, his call (v. 4). In the verses which immediately follow, an application of this is made, more directly, to Christ. In so doing the Holy Spirit had before Him a double design:

He first shows the **fulfilment of the type.** God's purpose in appointing Israel's high priests was to foreshadow the person and work of the Lord Jesus. Thus, there must be some resemblance between the one and the other. Second, that the Hebrews might know that the ministry and service of the Levitical order had **terminated.** Their purpose having been served, they were no longer needed; now that the Substance had come, the shadows were superfluous. Nay, more, their very retention would repudiate the design of their institution: they were **prefigurative,** therefore to perpetuate them would deny that the Reality had come. For the Levitical priesthood to go on functioning would argue that it had a value and a use apart from Christ. Hence the necessity of showing the relation of Aaron's priesthood to Christ's, that it might the more plainly appear that a continuance of the former was not only useless but pernicious.

That there **was** a close conection between the priesthood of Aaron and that of Christ is evident from the opening verse of our present passage. Having stated, "No man taketh this honour unto himself, but he that is called of God, as Aaron," the apostle now adds, "**So also** Christ" (v. 5), or, "In like manner Christ." Thus, unmistakably, a parallel is here drawn. **As** it was with the Levitical high priests in all things necessary to that office, **so**, in like manner, was it with the Christ. In vv. 5-10 the same five things (personal sin excepted) predicated of Aaron and his successors were found in our great High Priest. That there were, also, dissimilarities was inevitable from the personal imperfections that appertained to Aaron and his descendants: had there been anything in Christ which corresponded to their blemishes and failures, He had been disqualified.

"So also Christ glorified not Himself to be made an high priest" (v. 5). In 2:17, 3:1, 4:14 it had been affirmed that Christ **is** High Priest. A difficulty is now anticipated and met. Considering the strictness of God's law, and the specified requirements for one entering the priestly office, and more especially seeing that Jesus did not belong to the tribe of Levi, **how** could He be said to be "Priest?" In meeting this difficulty, the apostle emphasises the fact that the **chief** requirement and qualification was a Divine **call**: "No man taketh this honour unto himself, but he that is called of God" (v. 4): applying that rule the apostle now shows, from Scripture itself, our Lord's right and title to this office. Ere weighing the proof for this, let us note that He is here designated "the Christ": the apostle's design was to demonstrate that the promised Messiah, the Hope of the fathers, was to be High Priest forever over the house of God. The "Anointed One" signified His unction unto this office.

"So also Christ glorified not Himself to be made an high priest." He did not take this dignity unto Himself; He did not obtrude Himself into office. As He declared, "If I honour Myself, My honour is nothing: it is My Father that honoureth Me." (John 8:54). No, He had made Himself of no reputation; He had taken upon Him the form of a servant (Phil. 2:6), and He ever acted in perfect subjection to the Father. Nor was there any need for Him to exalt Himself: He had entered into a covenant or compact with the Father, and He might be safely trusted to fulfill His part of the agreement. "He that shall humble Himself shall be exalted (Matt. 23:12) was no less true of the Head than of His members.

"So also Christ glorified not Himself to be made an high priest." He to whom the authority belonged, invested Christ with the honours of priesthood, as He had Aaron. An ellipsis needs supplying to complete the implied antithesis: "But **He** glorified Him," or "**He** (God) made Him to be High Priest." That Christ was **glorified** by being invested with the high priesthood is here plainly inferred. It was a high honour bestowed upon His mediatorial person, that is, upon His **humanity** (united unto His deity). Scripture plainly teaches that His mediatorial person was capable of being glorified, with degrees of glory, by augmentation of glory: see John 17:1; 1 Peter 1:21. This honour appears more plainly when we come to consider the **nature** of the work assigned Him as Priest: this was no less than healing the breach which sin had made between God and men, and this by "magnifying the law and making it honourable." It appears too when we contemplate the **effects** of His work: these were the vindicating and glorifying of the thrice holy God, the bringing of many sons unto glory, and the being Himself crowned with glory and honour. By that priestly work Christ has won for Himself the love, gratitude, and worship of a people who shall yet be perfectly conformed to His image, and shall praise Him world without end.

How wonderful and blessed it is to know that the honour of Christ and the procuring of our salvation are so intimately connected that it was His **glory** to be made our Mediator! There are three chief offices which Christ holds as Mediator: He is prophet, priest and potentate. But there is an importance, a dignity and a blessedness (little as carnal reason may be able to perceive it) attaching to His **priestly** office which does not belong to the other two. Scripture furnishes three proofs of this. First, we never read of "our **great** prophet," or "our **great** King," but we **do** of "our great High Priest" (Heb. 4:14)! Second, the Holy Spirit nowhere affirms that Christ's appointment to either His prophetic or His kingly office "glorified" Him; but this **is** insisted upon in connection with His call to the sacerdotal office (5:5)! Third, we read not of the dread solemnity of any divine "oath" in connection with His inauguration to the prophetic or the kingly office, but we **do** His priestly—"The Lord hath sworn, and will not repent, thou art a priest forever." (Psa. 110:4)! Thus the priesthood of of Christ is invested with supreme importance.

"So also Christ glorified not Himself to be made an high priest; but He that said unto Him, Thou art My Son, today have I begotten Thee." (v. 5). The apostle here cites the testimony of the 2nd Psalm: but **how does** this quotation confirm the priesthood of Christ or prove His "call" to that office? That the quotation here **is** adduced as proof-text is clear from the next verse—"As He saith **also** in **another** Psalm," which is given as a further confirmation of His call. In weighing carefully the purpose for which Psalm 2:7 is here quoted, observe, first, it is not the priesthood but His **call** thereunto which the apostle has before him. Second, his object was simply to show that it was from **God** Christ had all His mediatorial authority. Third in Psalm 2:7 God declares the incarnate Christ to be His Son. The proclamation, "Thou art My Son," testified to the Father's **acceptance** of Him in the discharge of all the work which had been committed to Him. This solemn approbation by the Father intimated that our Redeemer undertook nothing but what God had appointed. The Father's owning of Christ in human nature as "My Son," acclaimed Him Mediator—Priest for His people. In other words, Christ's "call" by God consisted of the formal and public owning of Him as the incarnate Son. Ps. 2:7 describes the "call."

It is to be observed that Psa. 2:7 opens with the words, "I will **declare** the decree," which signifies a public announcement of what had been eternally predestinated and appointed in the everlasting covenant. It was God making known that the Mediator had received a Divine commission, and therefore was possessed of all requisite authority for His office. The deeper meaning, in this connection, of the proclamation, "Thou art My Son," tells us that Christ's sufficiency as Priest lies in His **Divine** nature. It was the dignity of His person which gave value to what He did. Because He was the Son, God appointed Him High Priest: He would not give this glory to another. Just as, because He is the Son, He has made Him "Heir of all things." (Heb. 1:3).

"Thou art My Son." The application of these words to the call which Christ received to His priestly office, refers, historically, we doubt not, to what is recorded in Matt. 3:16:17. There we behold a shadowing forth on the lower and visible plane of that which was to take place, a little later, in the higher and invisible sphere. There we find the antitype of what occurred on the occasion of Aaron's induction to the priestly office. In Lev. 9 we find three things recorded of the type: First, his call (v. 1, 2). Second, his anointing (v. 12). Third, his consecration, (v. 22.) These same three things, only in inverse order again (for in **all** things He has the preeminence) are found on the occasion of our Saviour's baptism, which was one of the great crises of His earthly career. For thirty years He had lived in retirement at Nazareth. Now the time had arrived for His public ministry. Accordingly, He consecrates, dedicates Himself to God—presenting Himself for baptism at the hands of God's servant. Second, it was at the Jordan He was anointed for His work: "God **anointed** Jesus of Nazareth with the Holy Spirit" (Acts 10:38). Third, it was there and then He was owned of God. "This is my beloved Son in whom I am well pleased." That was the Father's attestation to His acceptance of Christ for His priestly office and work.

Above, we have pointed out the first historical fulfillment of the prophetic word recorded in Psa. 2:7. As all prophecy has at least a double accomplishment, we find, accordingly, this same word of the Father's approbation of the Son recorded a second time in the Gospel narratives. In Matt. 17:5 we again hear the Father saying, "Thou art My Son," or "This is My Beloved Son." Here it was upon the mount, when Christ stood glorified before His disciples. It was then that God provided a miniature tableau of Christ's millenial kingdom. As Peter says, "We are eye-witnesses of His **majesty**" (2 Peter 1:16). And no doubt this is the profounder reference in Heb. 5:5, for the 2nd Psalm, there quoted, foretells the setting up of Christ **as** "King." Yet, let it not be forgotten that the priesthood of Christ is the basis of His kingship: "He shall be a priest unto His throne." (Zech 6:13). It is as the "Lamb" He holds His title to the throne (Rev. 22:1)—cf. the "wherefore" of Phil 2:9. He is a Priest with royal authority, a King with Priestly tenderness.

"As He saith also in another, Thou art a priest forever after the order of Melchizedek" (v. 6). A further proof of God's call of Christ to the priestly office is now given, the quotation being from the 110th Psalm, which was owned by the Jews as a Messianic one. There the Father had by the Spirit of prophecy, said these words to His incarnate Son. Thus a double testimony was here adduced. The subject was of such importance that God deigned to give unto these Hebrews confirmation added to confirmation. How graciously He bears with our dullness: compare the "twice" of Psalm 62:11, the "again" of the Lord Jesus in John 8:12, 21 etc., the "many" proofs of Acts 1:3. "As He saith" is another evidence that God was the Author of the Old Testament. Here, the Father is heard speaking through David; in Psalm 22:1, the Son; in Heb. 3:7 the Spirit. "As He saith," namely unto the Son. The Father's here speaking to Him was His "call," just as in 7:21 it is His "oath." "**Thou art** a priest" was declarative of His eternal decree, of the everlasting covenant between the Father and the Son, wherein He was designated unto this office. Thus was Chrsit "called of God as was Aaron."

"Who in the days of His flesh, when He had offered up prayers and supplications with strong crying and tears unto Him that was able to save Him from death, and was heard in that He feared." (v. 7.) In seeking to expound this verse three things require attention. To ascertain its scope, or theme, to discover its relation to the context and its own contribution unto the apostle's argument, and to define its solemn terms. Its theme is the priestly ministry of Christ: this is evident from the expression "offered up." "As the theme of vv. 4-6 is, 'Jesus Christ has been divinely appointed to the priestly office, so the theme of vv. 7-9 is Jesus Christ has successfully executed the priestly office.'" (Dr. J. Brown). Its relation to the context is that the apostle was here showing the "compassed with infirmity" (v. 2) is found in the Antitype: the "strong crying and tears" being the proof. Its terms will be weighed in what follows. Ere submitting our own interpretation, we first subjoin the helpful analysis of Dr. Brown.

"The body of the sentence (vv. 7-10) divides itself into two parts: 1. 'He.' Christ in the character of a Priest 'learned obedience by the things which He suffered.' 2. 'He', in the same character, 'has become the Author of eternal salvation to all that obey Him.' The clauses, 'In the days of His flesh,' and 'though He were a Son,' qualify the general declaration, 'He' learned obedience by the things which He suffered', and the clauses, 'when He had offered up,' or 'having offered up', 'prayers and supplications with strong crying and tears, unto Him that was able to save Him from death,' and 'when He had heard —or having been heard—'in that He feared,' contain in them illustrations both of the nature and extent of those sufferings by which Christ learned obedience; whilst the clause, 'being made perfect,' qualifies the second part of the sentence, connecting it with the first, and showing how His 'learning obedience by the things which He suffered', led to His being 'the Author of eternal salvation to all who obey Him.'"

In this 7th verse two other of the qualifications of Israel's high priest are accommodated to Chrsit. First, his being "compassed with infirmity" (v. 2) so as to fit him for having compassion on those for whom he transacted. In like manner was the Son, when He entered upon the discharge of His office, compassed with sinless infirmity. This is here exemplified in a threefold way. First, the time when He fulfilled the Aaronic type, namely, "**in the days of** His flesh," which was before He was "crowned with glory and honour." Second, from His condition, "in the days of His **flesh**," which signifies a state of weakness and humiliation. Third, from the manner of His deportment: "with strong crying and tears," for these proceed from the "infirmity" of our nature—angels do not weep. Second, Israel's high priest was appointed to "offer." (vv. 1, 2). This is what Christ is here seen doing: **offering** up to God—"**to** Him that was able to save Him." This was a sacerdotal act, as is clear from the fact that the declaration of v. 7 is immediately preceded (v. 6), and succeeded (v. 10) by a reference to His **priesthood**. Let us now examine our verse clause by clause.

"Who in the days of His flesh." "Flesh as applied to Christ, signifies human nature not yet glorified, with all its infirmities, wherein He was exposed unto—hunger, thirst, weariness, labour, sorrow, grief, fear, pain, death itself. Hereby doth the apostle express what he had before laid down in the person of the high priest according to the law—he was 'compassed with infirmity.' (Dr. J. Owen.) The word "flesh" is often used in Scripture of a man as a poor, frail, mortal creature: Psalm 78:39, 62:27. The "days of His flesh" is antithetical to "made perfect." They cover the entire period of our Lord's humiliation, from the manger to the grave—cf. 2 Cor. 5:16. During that time Christ was "a man of sorrow," filled with them, never free from them; "and acquainted with grief," as a companion that never departed from Him. No doubt there is special reference to the close of those days when His sorrows, and trials came to a head.

"The 'days of His flesh' mean the whole time of His humiliation—that period when He came among men as one of them, but still the Son of God, whose majesty was hid. As applied to Christ 'flesh' intimates that He put on a true humanity, but a humanity under the weight of imputed guilt, with the curse that followed in its train— a sinless, yet a sin-bearing humanity. The

Lord felt the weakness of the flesh in His whole vicarious work, and though personally spotless, was in virtue of taking our place, subjected to all that we are heir to. We do not, indeed, find in Him the personal consequences of sin, such as sickness and disease, but the consequences which could competently fall to the sinless substitute; for He never was in Adam's covenant, but was Himself the last Adam. As He took flesh for an official purpose, He submitted to the consequences following in the train of sin-bearing—hunger and thirst, toil and fatigue in the sweat of His brow, persecution and injustice, arrest and sufferings, wounds and death." (Prof. Smeaton on the Atonement.)

"When He had offered up prayers and supplications." The Greek word for "offer up" signifies "to bear toward." It occurs in this Epistle sixteen times, and always as a **priestly** act See 8:3, 9:7, 14. 10:11, 14, 18, etc. Prayers and supplications are expressive of the frailty of human nature, for we never read of angels praying. "Prayers" are of two kinds: petitions for that which is good, requests for deliverance from that which is evil; both are included here. The Greek word for "supplications" occurs nowhere else in the New Testament; in its classical usage it denotes an olive bough, lifted up by those who were supplicating others for peace. What is here in view is Christ "offering" **Himself** unto God (9:14), His offering being accompanied with priestly prayers and supplications. These are mentioned to exemplify His "infirmity," and to impress upon us how great a work it was to make expiation for sin. These prayers and supplications are not to be restricted to the agony of Gethsemane, or the hours of torture on the Cross; they must be regarded as being offered by Him through the entire period of His humiliation. "The pressure of human guilt habitually weighed down His mind and He was by way of eminence a Man of prayer, as well as a Man of sorrows." (Dr. Brown.)

"With strong crying and tears." These words not only intimate the intensity of the sufferings endured by our Priest, but also the extent to which He felt them. The God-man was no stoic, unmoved by the fearful experiences through which He passed. No, He suffered acutely, not only in body, but in His soul too. The curse of the law, under which He had spontaneously placed Himself, smote His soul as well as His body, for **we** had sinned in both, and He redeemed both. These cryings and tears were evoked not by what He received at the hands of man, but what imputed guilt had brought down upon Him from the hand of God. He was overwhelmed by the pressure of horror and anguish, caused by the Divine anger against sin.

"With strong crying and tears" These were, in part, the fulfilment of that prophecy in Psa 22:1: "the words of My roaring." A part of those "strong cryings" are recorded in the Gospels. To His disciples He said, "My soul is exceeding sorrowful, even unto death" (Matt. 26:38). To the Father He prayed, "If Thou be willing, remove this cup from Me" (Luke 22:42). There we read of Him "being in an agony," that "He prayed more earnestly," that "His sweat was as it were great drops of blood falling down to the ground." Such was the "**travail** of His soul" that He cried for deliverance. He voluntarily entered the place into which sin had brought us: one of misery and wretchedness. No heart can convince the terribleness of that conflict through which our Blessed Substitute passed. "Jesus cried with a loud voice, My God, My God, Why hast Thou forsaken Me?" (Matt. 27:46): here again we witness the "strong crying" accompanying His sacrifice. And what is the application of this to us? If His sacrifice was offered to God with "strong crying and tears" let none of us imagine we are savingly interested therein if our hearts are unmoved by the awfulness of sin, and are in the coldness of impenitence and the sloth of unbelief. Let him who would approach unto Christ ponder well how He approached unto God on behalf of sinners.

"Unto Him that was able to save Him from death." The particular character in which our suffering Surety here viewed God, calls for close attention. These words reveal to us how Christ contemplated Deity at that time: "unto Him that is able." Ability or power is either natural or moral. Natural power is strength and active efficacy; in God, omnipotence. Moral power is right and authority; in God, absolute sovereignty. Christ looked toward both. In view of God's omnipotence He sought deliverance; in view of His sovereignty, He meekly submitted. The former was the object of His faith; the latter, of His fear. These two attributes of God should ever be before us when we approach unto His footstool. A sight of His omnipotence will encourage our hearts and strengthen our faith; a realization of His high sovereignty will humble us before Him and check our presumption.

"Unto Him that was able to save Him from death." This also makes known the **cause** of His "strong crying and tears:" it was His sight of death. What "death?" Not merely the separation of the soul from the body, but the "wages of sin," that curse of the law which God, as a just Judge, inflicts on the guilty. As the Surety of the covenant, as the One who had voluntarily taken upon Himself the debts of all His people, the wrath of a holy God must be visited upon Him. To this Christ referred when He said, "I am afflicted and ready to die from youth up: I suffer Thy terrors, I am distracted" (Psa. 88:15). Fiercer grew the conflict as the end was neared, and stronger were His cries for deliverance: "The sorrows of death compassed Me, and the pains of hell gat hold upon Me: I found trouble and sorrow. Then called I upon the name of the Lord; O Lord, I beseech Thee, deliver My soul" (Psa. 116:3, 4).

But what was the "deliverance" which He sought? Exemption from suffering this death? No, for He had received commandment to endure it (John 10:18, Phil. 2:8). What then? Note carefully that Christ prayed not to be delivered from **dying**, but from "death." We believe the answer is twofold. First, He sought to be **sustained** under it. When death as the penal visitation of God's anger upon Him for our sins was presented to His view, He had deep and dreadful apprehension of the utter inability of frail human nature bearing up under it, and prevailing against it. He was conscious of His need of Divine succour and support, to enable Him to endure the incalculable load which was upon Him. Therefore it was His duty, as perfect yet dependent Man, to pray that He might not be overwhelmed and overborne. His confidence was in "Him that is able." He declared, "For the Lord God will help Me, therefore shall I not be confounded" (Isa. 50:17)

"And was heard in that He feared." The best commentators differ in their understanding of these words. Two interpretations have been given, which, we believe, need to be combined to bring out the full meaning of this clause. Calvin gave as its meaning that the object of Christ's "fear" was the awful judgment of God upon our sins, the smiting of Him with the sword of justice, His desertion by God Himself. Arguing against the "fear" here having reference to Christ's own piety, because of which God answered Him, this profound exegete points out the **absence** of the possessive "His fear;" that the Greek preposition "apo" (rather than "huper") signifies "from," not "on account of;" and that the word for "fear" means, for the most part, anxiety—"consternation" is its force as used in the Sept. His words are, "I doubt not that Christ was 'heard' **from that** which He feared, so that He was not overwhelmed by His evils or swallowed up by death. For in this contest the Son of God had to engage, not because He was tried by unbelief (the source of all our fears), but because He sustained as a man in the flesh the judgment of God, the terror of which could not have been overcome without an arduous effort"—and, we may add, without a Divine strengthening.

The sufferings of Christ wrung His soul, producing sorrow, perplexity, horror, dread. This is shown by His exercises and agony in Gethsemane. While He suffered God's "terrors," He was "distracted" (Psa. 88:15). "I am poured out like water," He exclaimed, "and all My bones are out of joint: My heart is like wax. it is melted in the midst of My bowels. My strength is dried up like a potsherd; and My tongue cleaveth to My jaws" (Psa. 22:14, 15). And again, He cried, "Save Me, O God; for the waters are come in unto My soul. I sink in deep mire, where there is no standing . . . . Let not the waterflood overflow Me, neither let the deep swallow Me up" (Psa. 69:1, 2, 15). Fear, pain, torture of body and soul, were now His portion. He was then enduring that which shall yet cause the damned to weep and wail and gnash their teeth. He was deserted by God. The comforting influences of His relation to God were withdrawn. His relation to God as **His** God and Father were the fount of all His comfort and joy. The sense of this was now suspended. Therefore was He filled with heaviness and sorrow inexpressible, and, "and with strong crying and tears" He prayed for deliverance.

"And was heard." This means, first of all, God's approval or acceptance of the petitioner himself. Christ's prayer here was answered in the same way as was Paul's request for the removal of the thorn in his flesh—not by exemption, but by Divine succour which gave enablement to bear the trial. In Gethsemane "There appeared an angel unto Him from heaven, **strengthening** Him" (Luke 22:43). So too on the Cross. "His mind and heart were fortified and sustained against the dread and terror which His humanity felt, so as to come to a perfect composure in the will of God. He was heard insofar as He desired to be heard; for although He could not but desire deliverance from the whole, as He was man, yet He desired it not absolutely as the God-man, as He was wholly subject to the will of the Father" (Dr. J. Owen).

"And was heard in that He feared." Other commentators have rightly pointed out that the Greek word for "fear" here signifies godly reverence or piety: cf. Heb. 12:28, where it is found in its noun form. Having from godly fear offered up prayers and supplications, He was heard. His personal perfections made His petition acceptable-. This was His own assurance, at the triumphant completion of His sufferings: "Thou hast heard Me from the horns of the unicorns" (Psa. 22:21). This brings us to the second and ultimate meaning of the Saviour's petition to be delivered "from death," and the corresponding second response of the Father. "To 'save from death' means, to deliver from death after having died. God manifested Himself as 'Him who was able to save Him from death,' when, as 'The God of peace'—the pacified Divinity—'He brought again from the dead our Lord Jesus, that great Shepherd of the sheep, by the blood of the everlasting covenant. Heb. 13:20" (Dr. J. Brown).

Thus, to summarise the contents of this most solemn and wonderful verse, we here learn: First, that our blessed Substitute, in the discharge of His priestly work, encountered that awful wrath of God which is the wages of sin—'death." Second, that He encountered it in the frailty of human nature, compassed with infirmity—"in the days of His flesh." Third, that He felt, to an extent we are incapable of realizing, the visitation of God's judgment upon sin —evidenced by His "strong crying and tears." Fourth, that He cried for deliverance: for strength to endure and for an exodus from the grave. Fifth, that God answered by bestowing the needed succour and by raising Him from the dead.

Many are the lessons which might be drawn from all that has been before us. Into what infinite depths of humiliation did the Son of God descend! How unspeakably dreadful was His anguish! What a hideous thing sin must be if such a sacrifice was required for its atonement! How real and terrible a thing is the wrath of God! What love moved Him to suffer so on our behalf! What must be the portion of those who despise and reject such a Saviour! What an example has He left us of turning to God in the hour of need! What fervour is called for if our prayers are to be answered! Above all, what gratitude, love, devotion and praise are due Him from those for whom the Son of God died!

—ARTHUR W. PINK.

GLEANINGS IN EXODUS

68. God's Claims: Ex. 34:18-21

The verses which are now to be before us seem, at first sight, very disconnected, presenting, apparently, a series of miscellaneous duties which the Lord enjoined upon Israel. First, mention is made of "The feast of unleavened bread" (v. 18). Next, we have the redemption of the firstborn, both of beasts and Israel's sons (vv. 19, 20). Then reference is made to the sabbath (v. 21). This is followed by instruction concerning the observance of the feast of weeks and the feast of ingathering (vv. 22-24). Next we have prohibitions concerning the offering of leaven with God's sacrifices, and the leaving over of the passover feast till the next morning (v. 25). Finally, God's claims upon all the first-fruits of the land is made, and command is given that a kid is not to be seethed in its mother's milk (v. 26). Thus, no less than seven different things are brought before us in these few verses. What, then is the link which binds them together? Wherein lies the unity of our passage?

We believe the answer to our question is to be found in the promise which the Lord gave when He first appeared to Moses at the burning bush: "And He said, certainly I will be with thee; and this shall be a token unto thee, that I have sent thee: When thou hast brought forth the people out of Egypt, ye shall **serve God** upon this mountain" (Ex. 3:12). The sequel to this is found in 19:3,4: "And Moses went up unto God, and the Lord called unto him out of the mountain, saying, Thus shalt thou say to the house of Jacob, and tell the children of Israel; Ye have seen what I did unto the Egyptians, and how I bear you on eagles' wings, and brought you **unto Myself**." Here in Ex. 34 Jehovah makes known the **character** of that "service" which He required from Israel.

First of all, we have the two tables of stone, on which were inscribed the ten words of the Law. Submission to Himself, obedience to His revealed will is what God requires from His people. Second, Jehovah made known the principles which regulate the government of His people (vv. 6, 7). Third, the call to absolute separation from the heathen (v. 12), from their religion (v. 15), and from intermarriage with them (v. 16) is next given. No unequal loke must be formed between the children of God and the children of the Devil: compare 2 Cor. 6:14-18. God had brought them unto Himself (see 1 Peter 3:18), and this wondrous and glorious fact must now be witnessed to in all their ways. In the verses that follow, comprising our present portion, we have the **positive** side brought out.

"The feast of unleavened bread shalt thou keep. Seven days shalt thou eat unleavened bread, as I commanded thee, in the time of the month Abib: for in the month Abib thou camest out from Egypt" (v. 18). How blessedly this tells forth God's grand design in redemption: it is not only for the purpose of emancipating His people and bringing them unto Himself, but also that they may be happily gathered around Himself. That is what the "feast" speaks of, communion and joy. God gathered His redeemed around Himself in holy convocation, Himself the centre of peace and blessing.

The feast of unleavened bread was inseparably connected with the Passover. The passover provided that sacrifice upon which the feast itself was based. The antitype of it is found in 1 Cor. 5:7, 8: "For even Christ our passover is sacrificed for us: therefore let us keep the feast, not with old leaven, neither with the leaven of malice and wickedness; but with the unleavened bread of sincerity and truth." The two together tell us that **holiness is the consequence of redemption.** The two cannot be separated. It is because our sins have been put away, that God can now take us into communion with Himself. First, **God** counts us to have "died with Christ" (Rom. 6:4-8). Second, **we** are to "reckon" upon this fact (Rom. 6:11; 2 Cor. 5: 14): faith is to appropriate it. Third, there is to be the **practical expression** of this in our daily lives: "Always bearing about in the body the **dying** of the Lord Jesus, that the life also of Jesus might be made manifest in our body" (2 Cor. 4:10).

We must distinguish between what the "unleavened bread" itself emblemized, and what Israel's actual feasting thereon typified. The bread was the Divinely-appointed symbol of Him who declared, "I am the living bread which came down from heaven: if any man eat of this bread, he shall live forever: and the bread that I will give is My flesh, which I will give for the life of the world" (John 6:51). Hence, because His person is holy, **unleavened** bread was appointed: "Seven days shall ye eat unleavened bread; even the first day ye shall put away leaven out of your houses: for whosoever eateth leavened bread from the first day until the seventh day, that soul shall be cut off from Israel" (Ex. 12:15). If then God gave such explicit instructions to His people of old, to use only that kind of bread which suitably and accurately represented the immaculate body of His blessed Son, by what right may we today be less particular in the loaf selected for "the Lord's supper?"

The Lord Jesus Himself instituted that "Supper" as a memorial of Himself, given in death for His pepole. Concerning the emblems which **He** appointed, if we are subject to the Scriptures, there cannot be the slightest room for question. They were, first, bread, **unleavened**, as is clear from the fact that this "Supper" was instituted right after the paschal one (Matt. 26:29)—therefore, when all leaven was rigidly excluded from their houses. The second was the "cup," containing "the fruit of the vine" (Matt. 26:29). Therefore when reminding the Corinthians of these, the apostle Paul wrote, "As often as ye eat (not simply "bread," any bread, but) **this** bread, and drink **this** cup, ye do show the Lord's death till He come" (1 Cor. 11:26). Alas, in this day of laxity, compromise and departure from the written Word, man's substitutes for God's appointments are received in most places without a murmur.

In Central Africa, where flour is difficult to obtain, one company of professing native-Christians, with their white missionaries, use cocoanut in lieu of bread, and its milk for the cup. Another company known to us in Australia, use raspberry-juice. And why not? If we are justified in changing unleavened bread into leavened bread, prepared pieces of bread cut into cubes instead of a loaf **broken**—to remind us of the body of Christ broken for us; and an evening feast, a "supper," into a morning ordinance; then who has the right to say **where** the line of departure shall be drawn? Personally, the writer had far rather never partake of the Lord's supper again, than be a party to the sin of setting forth the blessed person of Christ by means of bread which has in it that which, in Scripture, is always the symbol of **evil**. If the loaf on the table has any symbolic significance at all, then a **leaven-**

ed one portrays a Christ with a corrupt humanity, and such is **not** the Christ of Holy Writ.

We are well aware of the objection which is likely to be made, namely, We must not be occupied too closely with the symbols themselves, lest the heart be taken off Christ. Such language may sound very pious, but it ill-becomes those who use it. Precisely the same objection is made by many pedo-baptists against immersion. They say, It is not the mere outward form, but the **spirit** behind the act that matters. But our Lord has said, "**This** do in remembrance of Me:" then how dare we "do" something else? If the outward symbols are of little or no moment, then why not be consistent and follow the "Quakers," and abandon the external ordinances altogether? We can and do "remember" Christ at other times than when we are gathered around His table. But we can only "**show the Lord's** death" (1 Cor. 11:26), when we adhere strictly to His own appointments. And is our obedience in this, a small matter to Him who commanded Moses to "make **all** things" (even the pins and cords) for the Tabernacle "after the pattern shown him in the mount?" It still stands written, "Behold, to obey is better than sacrifice, to hearken than the fat of rams" (1 Sam. 15:22).

Others object, If you are going to be such a stickler for the particular kind of bread used at the Lord's table, you might just as well insist that we select an "upper room," and partake of it sitting on the ground as the first disciples did. Our reply is, These details contributed nothing to the **showing forth** of "the Lord's death," which is the central design of the Supper. For that reason nothing whatever is said about **these** details in 1 Cor. 11, where the bread and the cup **are** particularized. Had the apostle mentioned them **there**, then we should have been under obligation to heed and emulate them. But he has not. Really, such an objection is nothing more than an idle quibble. Let those who are responsible for making the arrangements at the Lord's table, weigh in **His** presence what we have written. Let them ask, What kind of bread, leavened or unleavened, is the more scriptural? is the more appropriate as an emblem of the holy person of Christ? And which is least calculated to distress and stumble those of His people who, by grace, desire to be subject the Word in **all** things?

Returning now to our type. That which was prefigured by the "unleavened bread" was the person of Him who is "without blemish and without spot" (1 Peter 1:19). Israel's **participation** in the feast itself typified that holiness which is the believer's in Christ. Note how Paul could say, to the failing Corinthians, "ye **are unleavened**" (1 Cor. 5:7). But we must daily seek grace from on high to make this good in our lives, by walking in separation from all that defiles and corrupts: "Be ye holy, for I am holy" (1 Peter 1:16), is the unchanging demand of God upon us. And that upon which His demand is based is, "Ye are not your own, ye are bought with a price." If we are, by His wondrous grace, washed in the precious blood of Christ, He surely looks that we should keep our garments undefiled. If then we delight to contemplate the Passover, let us also keep, in a practical way, "the feast of unleavened bread," and that for "seven days"—a complete period, the whole of our life on earth.

"The feast of unleavened bread must be kept; God has provided us with it in Christ. He has brought in a new character of Manhood that we might feed upon it, and purge out all that is contrary to it. We see every where in the world an inflating principle, giving importance to that which has no true value before God. But in Christ we see One marked by purity, holiness, sincerity and truth; all that is delightful to God; and nothing inflated—nothing appearing to be greater than it really was. When they said to Him, Who art thou? He answered, 'Altogether that which I also say to you.' That is unleavened bread, and as we appreciate it and feed upon it, we shall become unleavened; we shall hate and purge out every kind of leaven" (C. A. Coates).

"All that openeth the matrix is Mine" (v. 19). God is the universal Proprietor. As the Creator of all, His rights are beyond question. But how little are they recognized and owned in a practical way! Our present verse is one which ought to be much before those who are parents. Listen fond mother, doting father, that little one in the cradle is not **yours** absolutely; in reality, it belongs to God. "Lo, children are an heritage of the Lord" (Psa. 127:3). Have you acknowledged this? Have you dedicated your litlte one to God? "Thou shalt **set apart unto the Lord** all that openeth the matrix" (Ex. 13:12) was God's word to His people of old, and it has never been repealed. O that you may be able to say with the mother of Samuel, "For this child I prayed; and the Lord hath given me my petition which I asked of Him: Therefore also I have returned him to the Lord" (1 Sam. 1:27, 28).

This is a subject of great practical importance, and there is much need to press it upon parents today. Scripture does not teach infant "christening," or infant baptism, but it does infant dedication. Even the parents of Christ, when He was a child, "brought Him to Jerusalem to present Him to the Lord" (Luke 2:22). And note that both here and in Samuel's case, it was the parents personally, and not a priest, who performed the solemn act. The act of dedication is the formal acknowledgment that the child belongs to God: it is saying, as David said, "For all things come of Thee; and of Thine own have we given Thee" (1 Chron. 29:14). The whole subsequent training of the child should be in the remembrance of this fact. Hold your children in trust from God, and "bring them up in the nurture and admonition (mark the 'balance of Truth') of the Lord" (Eph. 6:4).

"All that openeth the matrix is Mine; and every firstling among thy cattle, or sheep" (v. 19). Clearly it is God here pressing His claims upon His people. The cattle upon a thousand hills are His. So too He declares, "The silver is Mine, and the gold is Mine, saith the Lord of hosts" (Haggai 2:8). How often we forget this! Ah, it is one thing to sing, 'Naught that I have I call mine own, I hold it for the Giver; For I am His, and He is mine, Forever and forever," but it is quite another matter to recognize that we are but stewards, holding everything in trust from Him and for Him: "Moreover it is required in stewards, that a man be found faithful" (1 Cor. 4:2). If we shall be called to account for "every idle word" that we have uttered (Matt. 12:36), how much more shall we for every pound or dollar that we have wasted!

It is very striking and solemn to observe that in the three parables which our Lord gave on the subject of service and its reward, that, in each instance, He selected a coin to illustrate His theme. First, in the parable of the labourers in the vineyard, a "penny" (Matt. 20). Second, in the parable of the Nobleman, "He called His ten servants and delivered them ten pounds, and said unto them, Occupy till I come" (Luke 19:13). Third, in the parable of the Man travelling into a far country He called His own servants, and delivered unto them His goods: and unto one He gave five talents, to another two, and to another one; to every man according to his several ability" (Matt. 25:14, 15). The word talent signifies "a sum of money." With it His disciples were to trade during the time of His absence. If the teaching of these parables were more before our hearts, Christians would be more diligent and faithful in laying up for themselves "treasure in heaven" (Matt. 6:20).

"But the firstling of an ass thou shalt redeem with a lamb: and if thou redeem him not, then shalt thou break his neck. All the firstborn of thy sons thou shalt redeem" (v. 20). This is a repetition of what was before us in Ex. 13:13. As so many of our present readers have not seen what we wrote thereon, almost four years ago, we deem it advisable to go over the same ground again, or at least to review what we then said.

The words "the firstling of an ass thou shalt redeem with a lamb," at once carry our minds back to the Passover night, when the firstborn of the Hebrews was "redeemed with a lamb." Thus the Lord has linked together the redemption of His own people with the redeeming of asses. Again, it is to be noted that, "if thou redeem not (the "ass"), thou shalt break his neck," just as the Israelites would most certainly have been smitten by the avenging Angel unless they had slain the lamb and sprinkled its blood. Thus God here compares the natural man with the ass! Deeply humbling is this! As we read in Job 11:12 "For vain man would be wise, though man be born like a wild ass's colt."

Under the Mosaic law, the "ass" was an unclean animal, neither chewing the cud nor dividing the hoof. So too the natural man is unclean: "But we all as an unclean thing" (Isa. 64:4). Though a man may be most particular about his habits, yet within is he full "of uncleanness" (Matt. 23:27). The "divided hoof" symbolizes a separated walk, a life that is lived with God and for God. The "chewing of the cud" speaks of rumination, meditation,—meditating in God's Law day and night (Psa. 1:2). But to these two things the natural man is a total stranger. Thus, the "ass" accurately represents him. He is unclean. But thank God there is a fountain opened "for sin and for uncleanness" (Zech. 13:1).

Again, the "ass" is a stupid and senseless creature. It has less of what we call "instinct" than has almost any other beast. In this too it resembles the natural man. Proudly as he may boast of his powers of reason, conceited as he may be over his intellectual attainments, the truth is, that he is utterly devoid of any spiritual intelligence: "But the natural man receiveth not the things of the Spirit of God: for they are foolishness unto him; neither can he know them, because they are spiritually discerned" (1. Cor. 2:14). And again, "Walk not as other Gentiles walk, in the vanity of their mind, having the understanding **darkened**, being alienated from the life of God through the ignorance that is in them, because of the blindness of their heart" (Eph. 4:17, 18). How thankful Christians should be that, "We know that the son of God is come. and hath **given us an understanding**, that we may know Him that is true" (1 John 5:20).

Once more; the "ass" is a **stubborn and intractable** animal. Often he is as hard to move as a mule. Such also is fallen man. He is a rebel against God. The history of every descendant of Adam is summed up in those terrible words, "we have turned every one to his **own** way" (Isa. 53:6). "There is none that seeketh after God" (Rom. 3:11). When God became incarnate and tabernacled among men, He had to say, "Ye will not come to Me, that ye might have life" (John 5:40). When a sinner does come to Christ, it is because Divine power has "drawn" him (John 6:44). And after we become Christians, the Holy Spirit has to take us in hand and "lead" us in "the paths of righteousness" (Psa. 23:3. Rom. 8:14).

Most unpalatable to our proud hearts is such a line of truth as the above. Yet is it blessed if we bow to it and take our true place before God—in the dust. Only the illumination of the Holy Spirit can bring any of us to realize **how** ass-like we are. For this reason Solomon wrote, "I said in mine heart concerning the estate of the sons of men, that God might manifest them, and **that they might see** that they themselves are beasts" (Eccl. 3:18). Has God opened your eyes, my reader? Do you **own** that the "ass" accurately portrays all that you are in yourself—unclean, senseless, intractable, fit only to have your neck broken? If so, you can appropriate and appreciate those blessed words, "Christ died for the ungodly" (Rom. 5:6). How marvelous the grace that has provided salvation for such: "The firstling of an ass thou shalt redeem with a lamb!"

"And none shall appear before Me empty" (v. 20). How can they! Once a poor sinner has had his eyes opened to see the ruin which sin has wrought in him, once he learns that he was "redeemed by the Lamb," his heart is filled to overflowing, filled with gratitude and praise. The language which best expresses his thankfulness is, "Bless the Lord, O my soul: and all that is within me, bless His holy name" (Psa. 103:1). No, the redeemed cannot appear before the Redeemer "empty." Spontaneously must they heed that word, "By Him therefore, let us offer the sacrifice of praise to God continually, that is, the fruit of our lips giving thanks to His name' (Heb. 13:15).

"And none shall appear before Me empty." If this were expressed in its positive form, it would read, "They shall come before Me as worshippers," för worship is the presenting of something to God. As we have recently had three articles upon this subject in our magazine, there is the less need for us now to enlarge upon it. The **first** mention of "worship" in the O. T. gives us the basic and central thought in connection with the subject. In Gen. 22:5 we read that Abraham said, "I and the lad will go yonder and worship." Abraham was about to **offer** his son unto the Lord! So the first time we read of worship in the N. T. we find the wise men presenting **gifts** to the infant Saviour (Matt 2). Our hearts should be filled with love and our mouths with praise as we appear before our gracious God.

"Six days thou shalt work, but on the seventh day thou shalt rest: in earing time and in harvest thou shalt rest" (v. 21). The **order** of Truth presented in our passage is very beautiful. First, we have had that which speaks of absolute separation unto God (v. 18). Next, dedication unto God (vv. 19:20). Then, worship before, or the adoration of, God (v. 20). Now we get mention of the sabbath, the Lord's provision of mercy for our soul's occupation with Himself. It is to be observed that here a word is added to the previous references to the Sabbath which were before us in Ex. 16, 20, 31. Upon this Mr. Coates has said:

"The rest of the sabbath must be observed, and the distinctive feature of it in this case is that 'in ploughing-time and in harvest thou shalt rest.' It intimates the necessity for recurring periods in which we cease from activity to contemplate in rest what God has done. The sabbaths must be kept, no matter what the needs of the Lord's work may be; for I suppose that ploughing-time and harvest might typify the most exacting and strenuous times in His work. The soul must know what it is to lay aside its activities, and have its rest with God. I am afraid we do not always keep our sabbaths. We are either doing something, or occupied with what we are going to do. There is not enough restfulness with God."

ARTHUR W. PINK.

ABRAM'S RESTORATION
Gen. 12:14-13:4

Four things contributed toward Abram's going down into Egypt: his leaving Bethel, his becoming possessed of a restless spirit, his journeying southwards, his encountering a grievous famine. Here was a man who had come all the way from Chaldea to Canaan on the bare word of Jehovah, yet now afraid to trust Him when there was a shortage of food. But this was the sure consequence of his leaving Bethel: being out of communion with God, Abram was unable to trust Him in connection with his temporal affairs. It is ever thus. If I am not walking by faith, I must by sight. If I am not enduring as "seeing Him who is invisible" (Heb. 11:27), I shall faint under the difficulties of the way. Thus it was with our patriarch. Instead of trusting in the Lord with all his heart, he leaned unto his own understanding; instead of crying unto God for help, he turned for relief unto that which is a figure of the world.

As was pointed out in our last article, the famine which Abram encountered was a Divine warning. Something must be wrong: "for there is **no** want to them that fear God" (Psa. 34:9); and again, 'No good thing will He withhold from them that walk uprightly" (Psa. 84:11). Alas, how often is it true of us, as with Israel, "your sins have withholden good things from you" (Jer. 5:25)! The famine ought to have made Abram call a halt in the path he was following. It should have exercised his heart before God. But he failed to profit from this Divine chastisement. Instead of seeking unto the Lord for the **cause** of it, he sought to flee from the consequences of his own failures. Instead of casting his burden upon the Lord, he took matters into his own hands; therefore, he not only missed the good of the chastisement, but was made to smart still more for his sins. This is ever the way: "Be not deceived; God is not mocked: for whatsoever a man soweth, that shall he also reap. For he that soweth to his flesh shall of the flesh reap corruption; but he that soweth to the spirit shall of the spirit reap life everlasting" (Gal. 6:7, 8).

The downward path is very slippery, and one wrong step quickly leads to another. As soon as Abram drew nigh to Egypt, he began to quake and tremble. Its very shadows fell across his soul before he actually entered that land. He adopted its principles and ways while yet on its borders. He was prepared to sacrifice Sarah's honour, rather than endanger his own life (Gen. 12:11-13). The application of this to ourselves is obvious. When a Christian gets out of communion with God and becomes worldly-minded, he is, he must be, unfaithful to his true relationship. In "Egypt" he has to conceal the fact that he belongs to Christ. He is afraid of what will follow were he to avow it. He knows full well that worldlings would sneer at and taunt him for his inconsistencies. Thus it was with Peter. But a most blessed contrast is found in Daniel.

Once more it is deeply important that we should notice the **order** here. First Abram's turning to Egypt for help; then the repudiation of his wife! Failures seldom come singly. The first departure from God, the first step out of the path of faith and separation, seldom brings fully out into the light the secret evil which caused it. It is generally God's way with His people to allow the whole evil to be **manifested** before He begins to restore the soul; and this, in order that it may be judged in its deepest depth, for He will have "truth in the **inward** parts" (Psa. 51:6). Peter, again, illustrates this principle.

Another lesson to be learned from the **order** here—Abram's turning to Egypt for help, and then, denying his vital relationship—is not only that one sin quickly leads to another, but that failure in our love to God ever results in failure in our love to our neighbor. It is only as God has **His** right place in my affections, that I am enabled to discharge my responsibilities manwards. Down in Egypt Abram was going to practice deception, deny that Sarai was his wife, and thus endanger the one who should have been nearest and dearest to him on earth. Alas, what is man! What is the saint when he gets away from God! Abram's bounden duty was to protect Sarai, yet was he prepared to sacrifice her in order to protect himself—note the "me" and "my" in vv. 12, 13. Solemn warning is this for all of us, especially for the young Christian. Fearful are the consequences of getting away from Bethel. This is written for our learning; have we hearts to receive it?

Now the Holy Spirit has recorded one other thing which more specifically explains this particular sin of Abram's denial of Sarai. It is found in Gen. 20:13, "And it came to pass, **when** God caused me to wander, from my father's house, **that I said unto her**, This is thy kindness which thou shalt shew unto me; at every place whither we shall come, say of me, He is my brother." Ah, that was something which Abram had carried in his heart all the way from Chaldea; and it had never been judged. Only a suitable occasion was needed for it to come to the surface. When the roots of unbelief and sin are not really and thoroughly judged by us, then their evil fruits will appear and re-appear. This evil root was not judged by Abram even in Egypt, hence we find its awful fruit displayed again in Gerah (Gen. 20).

A most important principle is here set before us. People imagine that it is "force of circumstances" which influence them. This is a great mistake: it is circumstances which **expose** us. Crises neither make nor mar a man, but they do make **manifest** what is in his heart. While circumstances are comparatively pleasant and easy, we appear to be going along all right; but when they suddenly become trying and painful, we murmur, rebel, sin. and then blame our "circumstances!" But, dear reader, it is the circumstances which have stripped us of the false veil of **seeming** godliness, and shown what we really are in ourselves. None of us has any more patience than we exhibit when we are provoked. We have no more real faith than what we evidence in the hour of trial. It is the provocation which **reveals** and the trial which **displays** how much patience and faith we really have.

This at once meets the petulent objection which is so often made: If only my circumstances were easier, I could live the Christian life much more perfectly! If instead of being the employee of a godless man, surrounded by wicked fellow-workers, I could be in business for myself, how much more readily could I serve God! If instead of having to work such long hours in the home, attending to the needs of all my children, and could only change places with sister So and So who has none, I would be an exemplary Christian. If instead of having a weakly body, suffering constantly, I was blessed with a healthy and vigorous constitution, I could do so much more for the Lord. If only I could be lifted out of poverty, my mind would be freed from worry, and I could cultivate fellowship with Christ. And so we might go on indefinitely. But each of these cases ignores the **person** amid the circumstances and indwelling the body. It is what I **am** which regulates what I do.

Strikingly was this brought out by Christ in those words of His, "He that is an hireling, and not the shepherd, whose own the sheep are not, seeth the wolf coming, and leaveth the sheep, and fleeth: and the wolf catcheth them, and scattereth the sheep. The hireling fleeth, **because he is an hireling,** and careth not for the sheep" John 10:12, 13). It was his character that regulated his conduct. The crisis revealed the man. It was not the "wolf" which caused him to act like an "hireling," instead, the wolf was needed to reveal the fact that he **was** an "hireling" all the time Probably no one suspected it till the wolf came. Probably he appeared to be very devoted to the sheep. But when the wolf appeared his mask was removed.

Thus it was, in principle, with Abram. It took the "famine" to make him flee into Egypt, and when there, the unjudged evil which had been in his heart from the beginning, became manifested outwardly. And what is the moral of this for our own souls? To judge ourselves unsparingly before God; to cry with the Psalmist, "Search me, O God, and know my heart: try me, and know my thoughts: And see if there be any wicked way in me, and lead me in the way everlasting" (Psa. 139:23, 24). It is written, "If we would judge ourselves, we should not be judged" (1 Cor. 11:31).

"And it came to pass, that, when Abram was come into Egypt, the Egyptians beheld the woman that she was very fair. The princes also of Pharaoh saw her, and commended her before Pharaoh: and the woman was taken into Pharaoh's house" (vv. 14, 14). This is the first thing mentioned after Abram went down into Egypt. The mother of Israel was now taken into the harem of a heathen monarch. What a contrast: in Gen. 12:8 we behold Abram and Sarai at Bethel, the "house **of God,**" now we see her in the "house of Pharaoh!" This is written for our learning.

What is recorded in Gen. 12:14, 15 illustrates a most important spiritual principle, one which all Christians, especially Christian **parents,** need to take to heart. If I, personally, give way to worldliness, then I must not be surprised if the world captures my loved ones. It still remains true that the sins of the fathers are "visited upon the children." If as a parent I am anxious for my daughter to be "accomplished" in the refinements of the world; if for example I pay for private dancing-lessons, so that she may carry herself gracefully, then I must be prepared for her becoming a society butterfly. Or, if I am ambitious that my son should be educated so as to "shine" in some profession (rather than to shine in this dark world for Christ), then I may expect him to be captured by "the house of Pharaoh." And if in spite of such worldly plannings on my part, I nevertheless pray that God will protect them in the evil surroundings to which I have introduced them, I am but **mocking** Him. "Thou shalt not tempt the Lord thy God" applies here, directly, with solemn force.

Yes, our sins involve terrible consequences for our loved ones. Noah got drunk, and the sequel led to one of his sons and all of his posterity being cursed (Gen. 9:25). Lot made him a home in Sodom, and in consequence, his daughters were corrupted (Gen. 19:30-37). Jacob settled down at Shalem, buying there a portion of ground, which was a repudiation of his pilgrim character; and right after we are told, "And Dinah the daughter of Leah . . . . went out to the daughters of the land. And when Shechem, the son of Hamor the Hivite, prince of the country saw her, he took her, and lay with her, and defiled her" (Gen. 34:1, 2). Moses fled from Egypt and went to dwell in Midian. While there he married a Gentile, and not only did she become a continued source of trouble to him, but she was made a curse to his children (Ex. 4:24-26). Achan sinned against the Lord, and in consequence, all his family perished with him. Each of these examples, and others might be added, are written for **our** admonition. It is an unspeakably solemn thing for a Christian to forsake the paths of righteousness. If **you** go down into Egypt, you may count upon your **loved ones** being captured by Pharaoh!

"And he intreated Abram well for her sake: and he had sheep, and oxen, and he asses, and men servants, and maid servants, and she asses, and camels" (v. 16). Does this line seem to spoil our typical picture? Ah, my reader, temporal prosperity is not always a mark of Divine blessing. It was not so here. Is it not written, "Better is little with the fear of the Lord than great treasure and trouble therewith" (Prov. 15:16)? And again, "Better is a little with righteousness than great revenues without right" (Prov. 16:8). Both penury and wealth have their respective snares, therefore we do well to pray, "Give me neither poverty nor riches; feed me with food convenient for me: lest I be full, and deny Thee, and say, Who is the Lord? Or lest I be poor, and steal, and take the name of my God in vain" (Prov. 30:8, 9).

Again it behooves us to mark the order of truth here. Abram turned to the world for help, denied his vital relationship, and then his temporal riches increased. But at what a cost! Though Abram obtained plenty of cattle and servants, there was no communion with God, no appearings of the Lord unto him, no "altar!" No, a Christian who has gone down into Egypt cannot be a worshipper of Him whom the world hates. Better far to emulate Moses, who, "chose rather to suffer affliction with the people of God than to enjoy the pleasures of sin for a season; Esteeming the reproach of Christ greater riches than the treasures in Egypt: for he had respect unto the recompense of the reward" (Heb. 11:25, 26). If we do not, though temporal prosperity smile upon us, it is most likely to be at the cost of our spiritual welfare.

And what good did Abram's cattle and servants do him? In the very next chapter we read, "And Lot also, which went (out of Egypt) with Abram, had flocks, and herds, and tents. And the land was not able to bear them, that they might dwell together: for their substance was great, so that they could not dwell together. And there was a strife between the herdmen of Abram's cattle, and the herdmen of Lot's cattle" (Gen. 13:5-7). While in Gen. 16 we learn what a snare one of these Egyptian maid-servants became to him. What point does this give to the warning of 1 Tim. 6:9, 10? "But they that will be rich fall into temptation and a snare, and into many foolish and hurtful lusts, which drown men in destruction and perdition. For the love of money is the root of all evil; which while some coveted after they have erred from the faith and pierced themselves through with many sorrows!"

"And the Lord plagued Pharaoh and his house with great plagues because of Sarai Abram's wife" (v. 17). There are three things which we would point out from this verse. First of all, it furnishes a decisive answer to those who argue that compromising is sometimes justified, yea, really necessary. There are those who reason that because the worldling cannot be expected to rise to our level, therefore the Christian, who wishes to help him, should descend to his. How often we have heard professing saints say, If you desire to win a careless, godless soul, you must be careful not to repel him by puritanical ways; descend to his plane, and try and lift him up to yours. To those who are ignorant of God's Word such advice may sound plausible; yet when examined in the light of Scripture it is merely a plea for, "Let us do evil that good may come." But my reader, good will never come. Instead, you will only cause a "plague" to descend on the very ones you have "gone down" to.

If we only believed what God says about the wicked, we should perceive how impossible it is for us to reach down to where they really are. They are in "an horrible pit," in the "miry clay" (Psa. 40:2). They are in their spiritual graves, "**dead**" in trespasses and sins" (Eph. 2:1). There is only One who can quicken them into newness of life and bring them on to resurrection ground, and that is the mighty God. And the only instrument which He employs in working this miracle of grace is His own "quick and powerful Word" (Heb. 4:12). Therefore did the apostle Paul write to the Corinthians, "I have (as God's chosen channel of communication) begotten you **through the Gospel**" (1 Cor. 4:15). And therefore is it written, "Of His own will begat He us with the Word of truth" (James 1:18). Then let us "hold forth the Word of life" (Phil. 2:16), relying upon God's unchanging promise that it shall not return unto Him void (Isa. 55:11).

Second, Gen. 12:17 warns us that the inevitable consequence of a Christian's going down into Egypt means that he becomes a "plague" to others. This is very serious, and should cause us to thoroughly "consider our ways" (Hag. 1:7). "Be not deceived, evil communications **corrupt** good manners" (1 Cor. 15:33). It is sometimes said that, One of the greatest blessings a boy or girl can have, is to be brought up by Christian parents. But that needs qualifying. It is true, if those parents are living godly lives. But if they are not, if instead their ways are worldly, if their walk gives the lie to their profession, most likely they will become a curse to their children. How many an observant youth or maid has been disgusted by the inconsistencies of parents who profess to be Christians, and who because of the living lie which was daily before them, have come to regard Christianity as a sham! O what watchfulness, what prayerfulness is needed, lest **we** bring down a "plague" upon others!

Third, this verse and the immediate sequel shows what strange means God employs in restoring His backsliding people. In what follows, we read, "And Pharaoh called Abram, and said, What is this thou has done unto me? why didst thou not tell me that she was thy wife? Why saidst thou, She is my sister? so I might have taken her to me to wife: now therefore behold thy wife, take her, and go thy way. And Pharaoh commanded his men concerning him: and they sent him away, and his wife, and all that he had" (vv. 18-20).

To such a low level had Abram sunk that even a Pharaoh had to rebuke him. Unspeakably sad and solemn is this, yet that also is recorded for our learning: "All Scripture is given by inspiration of God, and is profitable for doctrine, for **reproof**, for **correction**, for instruction in righteousness, that the man of God may be perfect, thoroughly furnished unto all good works" (2 Tim. 3:16, 17). How much then must we lose if we fail to study prayerfully and appropriate personally both the encouragements and the warnings supplied by the inspired record of the lives of the Old Testament saints! Shame on a child of God when a worldling has to rebuke him! Yet how often has this happened!

"And Abram went up out of Egypt, he, and his wife, and all that he had, and Lot with him, into the south. And Abram was vrey rich in cattle, in silver, and in gold. And he went on his journeys from the south even to Bethel, unto the place where his tent had been at the beginning, between Bethel and Hai; unto the place of the altar, which he had made there at the first: and there Abram called on the name of the Lord" (Gen. 13:1-4).

Our mind at once recalls those precious words, "**He restoreth** my soul: He leadeth me in the paths of righteousness for His name's sake" (Psa. 23:3). Many instances are recorded in Scripture of God's restoring grace unto His wandering people. The cases of Jacob in Padan-aram, Moses in Midian, David, Jonah, Peter, Thomas, will richly repay careful examination. So too, the coming restoration of Israel as described in Hos. 2. The **sovereignty** of God is displayed unmistakeably in connection with them: many and varied are the means and agents employed by Him. Sometimes it is a personal manifestation of Himself, or a direct word from Him. Sometimes it is His ordering of our circumstances. More often it is by chastenings. Here in the case of Abram it was the humiliating rebuke of a worldling.

God's restoring grace unto a backslidden saint is very wonderful, but that which occasions it is indeed dreadful. It is to be noted that Abram returned "unto the place where his **tent** had been at **the beginning**." He had to retrace his steps. So the N. T. word to those who have left their first love is, "Remember therefore **from whence** thou art fallen (the place of communion), and repent, and do the **first** works" (Rev. 2:5). But what is so solemn is that, the time Abram spent in Egypt was lost. Every day away from Bethel is wasted! As it is said of the Nazarite. "He shall consecrate unto the Lord the days of his separation . . . but the days that were before shall **be lost,** because his separation was **defiled**" (Num. 6:12). How many blanks will there be in your life, my reader? How much of "wood, hay, stubble" (1 Cor. 3:12)?

O what need has each of us for crying, "Uphold me according unto Thy Word, that I may live: and let me not be ashamed of my hope. Hold Thou me up, and I shall be safe: and I will have respect unto Thy statutes continually" (Psa. 119:116, 117). May the Lord sanctify to each Christian reader the solemn lessons which have been before us.

—ARTHUR W. PINK.

SANCTIFICATION BY THE BLOOD

"**Sanctified by the offering of the body of Jesus once for all**" (Heb. 10:10). "**Jesus that He might sanctify the people by His own blood, suffered without the gate**" (Heb. 13:12).

We have considered that great act of God's grace in having provided for His people a Substitute, who kept for them perfectly His holy Law, and who also bore the curse that was due to their transgressions against it. Thus, although we are criminals who deserve to be placed at the bar of God's justice, and to be condemned; yet, in virtue of the accepted service of our Substitute, we are not condemned, but on the contrary, "justified," that is, **pronounced righteous,** or **right,** in relation to all the claims of God's heavenly courts. Mercy has rejoiced against judgment; yet not without the governmental holiness of God, as expressed in His holy Law, having been adequately glorified: for Immanuel, as the Representative of His people, obeyed it, and Immanuel also, as the Representative of His people suffered and died beneath its curse. Not one jot or one tittle has passed from the Law: all has been fulfilled. As respects justifying righteousness therefore, believers have nothing to do with the Law. They are justified "apart from it" (Rom. 3:21), that is, apart from any personal fulfilment thereof. We could neither fulfill its righteousness, nor bear its curse. The claim of the Law was met and ended, once and forever, by the satisfaction of our great Substitute, and as a result, we have attained to righteousness without works, i.e., without personal obedience of our own. "By the obedience of the **One** shall many be constituted righteous" (Rom 5:19). There may be indeed, and there are, other relations in which we stand to the Law. It is the principle of our **new** nature to rejoice in its holiness: "I delight in the Law of God after the inward man" (Rom. 7:22). We know the comprehensiveness and the blessedness of those first two commandments on which all the Law and the Prophets hang. We know that "love is the fulfilling of the Law." We do not despise the guiding light of the holy and immutable commandments of God, livingly embodied, as they have been, in the ways and character of Jesus; but we do not seek to obey them with any thought of obtaining justice thereby. That which **has been** attained, cannot remain to be attained. Nor do we place so great an indignity on "the righteousness of our God and Saviour," as to put the partial and imperfect obedience which we render **after** we are justified, on a level with that absolute and perfect righteousness by which we **have been** justified. ..After we have been justified, grace may and does for Christ's sake, accept as well pleasing, our imperfect obedience; but this being a consequence of our perfected justification cannot be made a ground thereof. Nor can any thing that is in the least degree imperfect, be presented to God with a view of attaining justification. In respect of this, the Courts of God admit of nothing that falls short of His own absolute perfectness. .

The Epistle to the Romans, is, as is well known, that part of Scripture in which the question of justification is most full treated. There, especially, we are taught to think of God as a Judge presiding in the Courts of His holy judgment. Accordingly, the expressions employed throughout that Epistle are **forensic** or **judicial.** They refer to our relation to God, or His relation to us, in His **judicial** Courts—the great question there being, how criminals can be brought into such a relation to Him, as to have, not criminality, but righteousness, imputed to them.

But if, in the Epistle to the Romans we see God in the **Courts of His judgment,** equally in the Epistle to the Hebrews, we see Him in the **Temple of His worship.** "Sanctified" is a word that has the same prominence in the Epistle to the Hebrews, that "justified" has in the Epistle to the Romans. It is a **Temple**-word, descriptive of our relation to God in the Courts of His worship, just as "justified" is a **forensic word** descriptive of our relation to God in the Courts of His judgment. Before there can be any question about serving or worshipping God acceptably, the necessity of His holiness requires that the claims both of the Court of His judgment, and also the Court of His worship, should be fully met. He who is regarded in the judicial courts of God as an unpardoned criminal, or who, in relation to the temple of God, is regarded as having the stain of his guilt upon him, cannot be allowed to take his stand amongst God's servants. No leper that was not thoroughly cleansed could serve in the Tabernacle. The existence of one sin not adequately covered by compensatory atonement, shuts out from the presence of God. We must stand "uncharged" (unreproveable) in relation to the judicial Courts of God. And imputatively "without blemish" in relation to the Courts of His worship—in other words, we must be perfectly "justified," and perfectly "sanctified" before we can attempt to worship or serve Him. "Sanctification," therefore, when used in this sense, is not to be contrasted with justification, as if the latter were complete, but the former incomplete and progressive. Both are complete to the believer. The same moment that brings the complete "justification" of the fifth of Romans, brings the equally complete "sanctification" of the tenth of Hebrews—both being equally needed in order that God, as respects the claims of His holiness, might be "appeased" or "placated" (propitiated) toward us; and therefore equally needed as pre-requisites to our entrance on the worship and service of God in His Heavenly Temple: for until wroth is effectually appeased there can be no entrance there.

The complete and finished sanctification of believers by the blood of Jesus, is the great subject of the ninth and tenth chapters of the Hebrews. The "blood of bulls and of goats" gave to them who were sprinkled therewith, a title to enter into the Courts of the typical Tabernacle, but that title was not an abiding title. It was no sooner gained than it was lost by the first recurring taint. Repetition therefore of offering, and repetition of sprinkling was needed again and again, and again. The same circle was endlessly trodden and retrodden; and yet never was perpetuity of acceptance obtained. Nor was the typical Tabernacle Heaven itself. The Tabernacle and its services were but shadows; but they teach us that as "the blood of bulls and goats" gave to them who were sprinkled therewith a temporary title to enter into, that typical Tabernacle, so, the blood of Christ, once offered, gives to all those who are once sprinkled therewith (and all believers **are** sprinkled) a title, **not temporary,** but **abiding,** to enter into God's presence as those who are sanctified for Heaven. "Sanctified,' says the apostle "by the offering of the body of Jesus once" (Heb. 10:10). In close connection therewith follows the fourteenth verse, "By one offering He hath perfected forever (or in perpetuity) them that are sanctified," that is, them that are **so** sanctified—sanctified in the manner that the **tenth** verse has defined. And again, "Jesus that He might sanctify the people by His own blood, suffered without the gate."

The types to which the apostle more especially refers in Heb. 9, when he speaks of "the blood of bulls and goats, and the ashes of a heifer sprinkling the unclean" are, first, the ceremonies of the Day of Atonement as described in Lev. 16; and secondly, the ordinance respecting the ashes of the red heifer as given in Num. 19. The first of these refers to transgressions committed by God's people in respect of holy things whilst serving and worshipping in His Tabernacle; the second, refers to defilements contracted by them, not in the Tabernacle, but in the external world, where the presence and tainting power of moral death in all its fulness dwells.

Israel were yet in Egypt, when, in the ordinance of the Passover, they received their first great typical lesson respecting redemption. The doom of Egypt and their own deliverance therefrom, because of the blood sprinkled on their doors, were the thoughts there presented to their souls. It was not sin, as detected in the servants of God serving in the midst of Holy things, that was there made prominent to their thoughts. But when separated in the wilderness, a new sphere of knowledge was opened to them. In the wilderness they were brought nigh to God and to His Tabernacle, that they might find in His service new interests and new joys. That service, was indeed, a counterbalance to the travail and sorrows of their weary way; but it soon taught them new lessons respecting themselves. They had not, aforetime, been brought so nigh to God. The order and services of His house were in Egypt unknown to them. They had, aforetime, thought of themselves as in the presence of Egypt's abominations, but they had little thought of themselves as standing in the presence of God's holiness. But now, a new test of their condition was presented. They entered indeed God's Tabernacle, but they carried uncleanness with them, holy vestments and holy offices ill became those whose touch generated defilement. The uncleanness of Israel might be hidden in the midst of Egypt's darkness; but in the light of the presence of God's holiness it was hidden no longer. Blackness and every shade of blackness is made manifest in the presence of light. Nevertheless, God was present among them in mercy, and they were not consumed. The Day of Atonement was appointed to meet these trespasses in holy things. Every returning year, it spread over Israel the temporary perfection of its typical expiation. Otherwise they would have perished—cut off like Nadab and Abihu.

But whilst, in Lev. 16, we see Israel, in their connection with the Tabernacle, learning respecting unholiness by proximity to holiness, in Num. 19 we find another aspect of their defilement. An Israelite might quit the Tabernacle, as one temporarily atoned for and temporarily clean, and go forth into the mingled scene of good and evil around. He finds himself begirt with defiling influences. He breathed a tainted air. If he touched a dead body, or a bone, or a grave, or if haply, he entered a tent where death was, he became instantly unclean; and unless duly sprinkled, he became exposed to wroth, and to cutting off from his people. And even if he had not himself touched any unclean thing—if he had not himself breathed the atmosphere of death, yet duty might call him to go and sprinkle another who had breathed it: and then, even by the mere fact of being so brought into proximity to uncleanness, he became himself unclean. Thus even the discharge of social duties (for it might be a social duty to touch a dead body, or a grave), and the discharge of religious duties (for it was a religious duty to sprinkle the unclean) alike brought uncleanness on those who, because of their affinity with corruption, and could not go into the presence of corruption without being acted on thereby. Affinities are developed by contact. Kindred elements combine.

Can these things be strange to any believer who has considered the relation in which he stands to God and to sin? Let us view ourselves as placed in the midst of holy things. When delivered from Egypt—the scene of our unregenerate activities, new interests and employments are opened to us in the service of God and of His Truth. But are we satisfied with ourselves in these new relations? Do we deem our worship, and service, and testimony, to be worthy of God? Or, does the near presence of Light make manifest the darkness that is within us, and detect the iniquity of our most holy things?

And if, from occupation with the more immediate service of God we go forth into the busy scene of human life around us, do we not find it teem with corruption and moral death? "Death" is the name that faith writes on everything that will not, in the Day of Christ, be found included within the circle of life. Many things useful for mere present purposes of human life—many things that seem fair and goodly if judged of merely by the light of "man's day," are found to be as dead bones or "graves" when viewed in the light of the Day of God. A cup of cold water given to a disciple **in the name of a disciple** has in it the power of eternal life, but all that belongs to the mere circle of man's **unregenerate** energy—all the efforts of his taste, and intellect, and skill, to beautify the place of his banishment (for a fallen earth is not Eden)—all his endeavors to vail the corruption and ruin of a lost world, and to hide creation's groan—all such efforts and their results, however seemly fair—however commended and extolled by those who think only of earth, are "dead things" in the estimate of God. There is nothing in them of the power of the new creation: nothing that is of the spirit and mind of Christ: nothing that adapts itself to the garb of Nazareth: nothing that connects itself with the practical place of faith and going without the camp. Yet it is on these things of death that our fallen nature feeds. Nature gravitates towards earth. It cannot rise out of its own sphere: it is earthy, and to earthiness it cleaves—its affinities being with evil—not with God. And although grace in the believer may and does restrain these tendencies in us to separate himself from flowers that we know to belong only to the gardens of earth—that blossom not in the power of the new creation—is there no tendency in us to have fellowship with things, or persons, or books, or systems, from which the world's leaven of falsehood is not purged away?

And even when we approach evil with the intent of dealing with it according to the will of God, do we betray no moral infirmity in ourselves? We may be anxious perhaps to remove some stumblingblock or some temptation out of another's way. We may try to rescue another from some atmosphere of moral death. We may rebuke or admonish, or seek to bring back to God some one who has gone astray. In doing such things, are our appreciations of the evil wherewith we are dealing perfect according to the perfectness of God? Is our eye quite single? Is there no ignorance, no hastiness, no want of wisdom or of love? Is there within us no affinity with the evil which we are judging? Are we neither unduly lenient, nor unduly severe? Is our inward purpose and our mode of carrying that purpose into effect quite free from vacillation? Even saint Paul when dealing with the evil at Corinth, confessed that he had vacillated. He resolved to write with severity, and he wrote. Afterward he regretted that he had written; and then again he recalled the expression of his regret: 2 Cor. 7:8. What he had done was right. He had written in and according to the Spirit; but his nature shrunk from contemplating the pain that might be caused to others from that which he had rightly done, and for a little while he regretted that he had done it. Holiness according to the holiness of God is needed in order to deal either with evil or with good **perfectly**. Where ever the presence of moral infirmity lurks, such infirmity will be more or less developed before the eye of God, even in the execution of our best designs—even whilst we are really acting against evil, and on behalf of good.

There is only One who, having taken in the earth a place of service to God, brought into it the perfectness of Heaven. He served in holy things, but He brought to the holy things that He touched, a holiness equal to the holiness of God. The defilements of earth surrounded Him. He went forth and stood in their midst, but they tainted Him not; for there was in Him not only no affinity with defilements, but everything that was repellent thereof. **Morally** His feet were always "like fine brass as though they burned in a furnace." What symbol can more strongly denote perfect **repellency** of corruption? All His tendencies were toward God. His appreciation of all things, whether of truth or of falsehood, of evil or of good, of joy or sorrow, were perfect. His sensibilities too were perfect. They became in no degree deadened by long familiarity with scenes of woe; nor did He seek to relieve Himself from the painfulness attendant on their exercise, by turning away from the contemplation of sorrow. His ear heard, and sought to hear, the groan of creation. His heart meditated on the misery and doom of a lost world. If His righteous indignation was awakened, and He rebuked, there was no undue excess of severity toward His enemies, nor undue leniency towards His friends. If He pitied, He pitied without weakness; if He showed sympathy He sympathized without compromising the claims of holiness. All His appreciations, estimates, and feelings, were those of perfect righteousness, holiness and truth. The typical priest could not sprinkle another without contradicting defilement thereby, but Christ could eat and drink with publicans and sinners, could forgive sins, could minister consolation to the repentant sinner, could take upon Himself all the mighty load of the sins of His people, could bear all that righteousness inflicted as due to those sins, and yet remain the untainted One still; as pure and as holy and as precious in the sight of God, whilst groaning under the infliction of damnatory wrath on the accursed tree, as when He was in the bosom of the Father before all worlds—the very same place in which He was "bruised" and "made a curse" for us, being also that in which He offered Himself for us "an offering and a sacrifice to God for a sweet-smelling saviour" (Eph. 5:2). He was at once the Burnt-offering, and the Meat-offering: the Peace-offering, the Sin-offering, and the Trespass-offering. All these various aspects of the sacrificial work of Jesus were found united in His one offering on Calvary. The Cross was the great manifestation of the perfect voluntary obedience, and willing devotedness of God's righteous Servant. Never was the character of Jesus exhibited in more transcendent excellency, never were His relations to God and to man maintained in greater perfectness, than during the time that He suffered for us on the Tree. Never did the Father more delight in and appreciate the excellency of the Son of His love: never did the Son more love and honour and delight in the Father, than when He uttered that bitter cry, "My God, My God, why hast Thou forsaken Me?" The very circumstances which placed Jesus, outwardly, in the extremes of distance from Heaven and from God, only proved that there was an essential nearness, an everlasting moral nearness, which not even the fact of His being the bearer of damnatory wrath could for one moment alter. Such is the offering by which we, that is all who are of faith, are forever sanctified— "sanctified by the offering of the body of Jesus once for all."

"Sprinkled," "washed," "cleansed," "purged," and "sanctified," are the words which the Scripture employs to indicate the abiding condition that pertains to those who, as believers in Jesus, are recognized by God as standing under the value of His blood. On this ground we have a title to say, that although the uncleanness that is in us, and which spreads more or less its defiling influence over our most holy things, does in itself merit wrath, yet, because of the blood once offered, **it is not imputed unto us**. As to this we are "perfected forever, whereof the Holy Spirit, speaking in Jeremiah is a witness to us, for after that He had said before . . . He also saith, Their sins and iniquities will I remember no more." All the atoning efficacy indicated by the typical sacrifices of the Day of Atonement, together with all the cleansing efficacy indicated by the ashes of the red heifer and every other type, is concentrated in the blood of Jesus once offered, and therefore every believer, seeing that he stands abidingly under the full value of that blood, is once and forever atoned for, and, once and forever sprinkled—"sprinkled," being a **typical** word, implying that God recognizes us as standing under the applied efficacy of the blood of Jesus. As there can be no repetition of atoning offering, so there can be no repetition of sprinkling to one once sprinkled. The being "unsprinkled" implies the being under an imputation of guilt, rendering amenable to **wrath**, and this no believer ever is. Accordingly, our great High Priest who intercedes for us in Heaven, and thereby recognizes and upholds the governmental holiness of God, never makes confession or pleads for us as if we were un-atoned for and un-sprinkled but always pleads for us on the ground of our having been once and forever both atoned for and sprinkled. Believers may indeed through defective instruction, or through unbelief and sin, be ignorant or oblivious of that which the blood of Jesus hath effected for them; and when recovered from a backsliding or careless condition may seem to themselves to be sprinkled afresh; but it is not really so: they are only recovered to **the recognition** of a condition that pertained to them fixedly, from the first moment they believed.

Whilst therefore, all that is implied by the words "washed," "cleansed," etc., is included in the condition of "the sanctified," it would nevertheless be a mistake to suppose that "sanctified" implies nothing more than the being "washed" or "purified." Both in the Old and New Testaments different words are used to express the several notions, and not unfrequently, the being "sanctified" or "hallowed" emphatically marked as a condition that goes beyond that of being simply "washed" or "purified." Thus in the consecration of the priests they were early washed (v. 4), but it was not until they were arrayed in their priestly garments and sprinkled with blood, that they were said to be "sanctified" or "hallowed" (v. 21). The healed leper too after he had passed through certain ceremonies was said to be "cleansed" or "purified," but he was not thereby like the priests, "sanctified." And when we read of "the Temple sanctifying the gold," and "the Altar sanctifying the gift," it is evident that sanctified **thus** used expresses no mere negative condition, but implies the positive ascription to the thing hallowed of a holiness corresponding to the holiness of that by which and unto which it was hallowed. More, therefore, is expressed by "sanctified" or "hallowed" than is implied either by separation, purification, or dedication. The notions expressed by these three words are not to be excluded; but we have to add to them another thought, namely, that the sanctified or hallowed are regarded as hallowed with a sanctification corresponding to the holiness of that **whereby** and that **whereunto** they are hallowed; just as the priests and their garments were considered to be holy according to the holiness of that wherewith they were sprinkled. The same blood that appeases the wrath and covers the stain of our guilt, leaves in the place of that which it cancels, its own excellency, so that we are at the same moment regarded as not only spotless and uncharged, but as "hallowed."

The passage just referred to (Col. 1:21) is parallel to that which we have been considering in Heb. 1. The being presented "holy, spotless, and uncharged" is made **the result of the one sacrifice alone.** "Holy," therefore, here expresses the result of being sanctified by the blood as taught in Heb. 10. And, observe, it is not regarded as synonymous with "spotless," that word (also a Temple word) conveying the **negative** thought of the stain of our guilt being purged away: whereas "holy" conveys the positive thought of being also hallowed unto God. Some have endeavored to lower the meaning of "sanctify" into the sense of mere **separation,** but both in Hebrew and Greek we have other words to express separation, and these words would have been used had nothing more than "separation" been intended. Dedication and the attainment of a condition in which we are regarded as holy according to the holiness of that whereby, and **whereunto,** we are hollowed, are the thoughts involved in "sanctified" when that expression is **applied to us.** In Lev. 20:25, 27 we find, the three connected, yet distinct thoughts, of "separated," "clean," and "sanctified to Jehovah" contrasted.

It is true indeed that in speaking of sanctification by the blood of Jesus we may sometimes take the retrospective view, and direct the mind back to that from which we have been sanctified; and in that case, "purification" is a word that may sufficiently represent the thought. At other times we may seek to direct attention rather to the condition unto which we are sanctified, and in that case we shall soon see the importance of not limiting sanctification simply to the purgation of our stains. No one who beheld the priest of old encompassed and covered over by a cloud of incense, would doubt that the qualities and characteristics of that incense were regarded as ascribed to him. If the incense was holy, and it was "most holy," the priest was regarded as being hallowed according to its holiness. How then can it be otherwise with those who are sanctified by the once-offered sacrifice of Immanuel? As being cleansed and as being holy (Col. 1:21) they have a title to draw nigh even into the Holiest of all. Christ hath become to them "both righteousness and sanctification, as well as redemption" (1 Cor. 1:31).

Thus the sanctification which is the result of the one finished sacrifice of Calvary, is as perfect and abiding as the justification which results from it. In virtue of the one, we are accounted righteous in the Courts of God's judgment; in virtue of the other, we are looked on as hallowed for the Courts of His worship.

—B. W. NEWTON.

CHRIST OUR ALL IN ALL

"Looking unto Jesus—living on Him, in Him, to Him, and for Him in all things. I think you say, This is my prayer and desire also, but how are we to carry it into practice? By renouncing ourselves, by looking out of self entirely, by looking away from and above it; thus alone are we fitted for living on Christ. Self is our worst enemy—it works chiefly in vile legality, sly, subtle insinuations:—"I wish I was what I am not, I wish I did not feel what I do, I wish I had not so many wants, I wish I had more strength, I cannot be happy because I can see nothing in myself to be pleased with." My friend, these are the workings of a self-righteous legal mind. Such things as these make up almost all which passes under the title of sound experience; and few see that these are the very things which keep the mind from exercising itself on Christ. I trust our Lord has given you to view all this rightly, to reject it wholly, to cast it off entirely. Oh, bless the Lord for it, because you are nothing in your self but sin, darkness, disease, emptiness, misery, and death; therefore you are fit for and well-suited to receive Christ, and for Him to glorify Himself in you and by you; to be content to be what you are, and to be well pleased for Christ to be what He is—a free, full, complete, present, and everlasting Saviour: and to make use of Him continually for all the purposes of spiritual life and salvation. This is to glorify God; this is to give proof that we are taught by the Spirit of God; this is to live a life of faith on the Son of God. When we live thus, we honour the Holy Trinity: the Father, for His everlasting love, in believing He has treasured up every grace and blessing of it for our use, in the fulness of His Son. We honour Christ also by trusting in His everlasting precious righteousness and sacrifice and in drawing upon Him for everything. And we honour the Holy Spirit by receiving His testimony concerning Christ into our hearts.—Extracts From the Letters of S. E. Pierce 1806.

The pillar was a cloud of darkness to the Egyptians, but it gave light by night to Israel. How like the Cross of our Lord Jesus Christ! It forms the foundation of the believer's peace, and, at the same time, seals the condemnation of a guilty world. The self-same blood which purges the believer's conscience stains the earth and consummates its guilt. The very mission of the Son of God, which strips the world of its cloak, and leaves it wholly without excuse, clothes the Church with a fair mantle of righteousness, and fills her mouth with ceaseless praises. The Lamb, whose wrath terrifies the nations, will lead, by His gentle hand, His blood-bought flock through the green pastures, and beside the still waters forever.

C. H. M.

the more nourishment do we derive from it. So it is spiritually. "Thy **words** were found and I did eat them:" God's Word is made up of words. To miss a word from, to add one to, to change one in a verse, mars or perverts its meaning. What a difference there is between "Hear what the Spirit said unto the churches," and "**saith** unto the churches" (Rev. 2:7); between, "he that follows Me," and "he that **followeth** Me shall not walk in darkness" (John 8:12); between, "they who win souls are wise," and "**He** that winneth souls is wise" (Prov. 11:30)! Scores of other examples might be given; let these suffice for showing the importance of noting carefully and weighing prayerfully every word and letter of Holy Writ. But this can only be done by mastication.

Meditation stands to reading as mastication does to eating. In Luke 2:19 we read, "Mary kept all these things, and **pondered** in her heart." It is not sufficient to hear or read the words of God, they need pondering. Let each word in the verse before you be weighed separately. Ask God to write them upon your heart. Come back to the same verse again and again during the day; pray over it till its meaning is opened up to you. No matter how familiar the verse may be, or how simple the language, do not make the mistake of supposing you already understand all there is in it; spiritual food must be turned over and over again in the mouth before its full flavour and sweetness is discovered. It must be "mixed with faith" (Heb. 4:2)—the spiritual saliva—before it is ready for digestion.

David meditated in God's law "day and night" (Ps. 1:2). "In the plainest text there is a world of holiness and spirituality; and if we in prayer and dependency on God did sit down and study it, we should behold much more than appears to us. It may be, at one reading or looking, we see little or nothing; as Elijah's servant went once, and saw nothing, therefore was he commanded to look seven times. What now? says the prophet. 'I see a cloud rising, like a man's hand;' and bye and bye, the whole surface of the heavens was covered with clouds. So you may look lightly upon the scripture, and see nothing; **meditate often** upon it, and then you shall see a light, like the light of the sun" (J. Caryl, 1647). The great value of meditation and rumination (chewing the cud) is shown in Psa. 119:99.

Finally, eating is preparatory to **assimilation**. The food which I have appropriated and masticated now becomes a part of me. It imparts richness to my blood, strength to my nerves, flesh to my bones. It is thus my body is sustained and maintained. So it is with the new man: "This book of the law shall not depart out of thy mouth; but thou shalt meditate therein day and night, that thou mayest observe **to do** according to all that is written therein: for **then** thou shalt make thy way prosperous, and **then** thou shalt have good success" (Josh. 1:8). God's words are given us to live by, to mould our whole deportment, to regulate all our ways. Then, may we be "**doers of the Word**, and not hearers only" (James 1:22).

—ARTHUR W. PINK.

The Lord help you to be reviewing your riches every day; the Lord help you to be living upon them, and may you be receiving a fresh income out of the fulness of Christ continually. It is good to be looking at Christ continually; it is good to be viewing your person in Christ; it is good to be exercising your mind in considering what you are in Christ, and what views your heavenly Father takes of you in His beloved Son, and how, holy, righteous, and pure, you are in the Lord Jesus. Such views revive the mind, relieve the heart, cheer the spirits, make a cheerful countenance. It is life from the dead to live in the belief of Christ's love to us; to believe He rejoices over us with His whole heart, and with His whole soul, to do us good; to treasure up this word, "I will never turn away from you from doing good; I will put My fear in your heart, and ye shall not depart from Me." To receive these words of Christ into our minds, and give full credit to them, to mix faith with them, and honour the Lord's faithfulness by relying on Him for the fulfilment of them to us, it is the means whereby we glorify the Lord; and in thus believing He strengthens us with strength in our souls: and thus we have our spiritual strength renewed, and go on towards the city of habitation, strong in the Lord, and in the power of His might.—Extract From Letter by S. E. Pierce, 1796.

advertised medicines or special foods. Man is beginning to discover his mistake. But how does he attempt to remedy it? Instead of going back to what God has provided in the corn of wheat, which contains everything needful, and in right proportions, he concocts various kinds of breads, giving them wonderful names—which cost more, but do not provide the desired results."

Today it is almost impossible to procure really wholesome bread. And all of this has its counterpart in the spiritual realm. The spiritual Bread which God has provided for the nourishment of our souls, namely, His Word, is passed through the denominational mills, and what is not believed by this sect or that ism is either eliminated or avoided. Each have their own "line of things." Hyper-Calvinists reject the important truth of human responsibility. Arminians refuse to bow to the absolute sovereignty of God. Some are all for objective truth, others will tolerate nothing but the subjective side. Some harp all the time on the experimental string; others crave only doctrine. And so we might continue indefinitely. The **whole** wheat is needed by us if we are to be healthy and robust.

Though the whole Word of God is needed by us, we cannot feed upon it as a whole. Jeremiah did not say, "Thy Word was found and I did eat it," but "Thy words were found and I did eat **them**." The loaf must be sliced, and each slice divided into separate mouthfuls, and each mouthful chewed, before it is swallowed. Thus it is spiritually. More benefit is derived by the soul in **eating** a single verse of Scripture than in reading through a whole chapter or book of the Word. This is a very commonplace remark to make, yet is it much needed today, for very few Christians have formed the habit of daily **feeding** on the Bread of life. There may be much studying of the Bible, labourious efforts to "rightly divide" it, frequent consultation of men's commentaries upon it, and yet, after all, the heart remain famished.

"Thy words were found and I did eat them." What is meant by this? Eating is an act of **appropriation**. It is a placing in the mouth of that which is set before me. It is the taking up of a portion of food and making it mine own. This is a personal act, which cannot be performed by deputy. No one else can do it **for** me. You cannot feed by watching other people eat. You cannot be a Bible-student by copying into the margins of your Bible the results of others' studies. And you cannot be nourished in the inner man unless you personally appropriate portions of the Word to your own needs.

First of all, when you open and read the Scriptures, recognize that in them **God** is speaking to your heart. It is His message direct to **you.** It is the word of the living God to your own needy soul. Until this is realized most of the Bible will appear little more than records of things that happened thousands of years ago. But God has written those histories for **your** benefit, they have a message and meaning for you today. The characters portrayed in Holy Writ were men and women of like passions with yourself, subject to the same temptations, called on to fight the same good fight of faith. Where they triumphed, they are your examples and encouragements; where they failed, they are your warnings and admonitions. Through them God will instruct you, if your heart is open, if you are ready to **appropriate** their lessons.

Having recognized that the chapter or verse you are reading is God's present message **to** you, ask now, What is there here **for** me? Bow your head and supplicate His grace that you may "receive with meekness" (James 1:21) His holy Word. The heart must be emptied of pride before there is room for His truth to become an "engrafted Word." The "good-ground" hearer is he that receives it into "an honest and good heart" (Luke 8:15). An "honest" heart is one that is willing to be judged by the Word, searched by it, admonished, corrected. The verse before you, may not be relished by the flesh, and Satan would bid you turn from it to some pleasanter portion, but the Lamb was only to be fed on in conjunction with "bitter herbs" (Ex. 12).

Settle it then once for all that everything in the Word is **for you**. There is not a verse in the Bible which does not apply to you, either directly or indirectly, typically or literally. Then **appropriate** it day by day, meal by meal, mouthful by mouthful: "For precept must be upon precept, precept upon precept; line upon line, line upon line; here a little, and there a little" (Isa. 28:10). The manna, a "small round thing" (Ex. 16), had to be gathered grain by grain. God did not provide Israel in the wilderness with ready-baked loaves, but with manna which required collecting, grinding, cooking.

Again, "eating" is an act of mastication. The teeth have to be used. Food taken into the mouth has to be broken up into small pieces before it is ready for swallowing. The more chewing we do, the more our food is mixed with the saliva,

(Continued on Page 191)

STUDIES IN THE SCRIPTURES

"Search the Scriptures" John 5 : 39

Copyright in all English-speaking Countries.

Editor: Arthur W. Pink, Morton's Gap, Ky., U. S. A.
Hon. Agent in England: Mr. A. Winstone, 2, Lennox Villas, Hewlett Road, Cheltenham.
Hon. Agent in Australia: Mr. G. Ardill, The Christian Workers' Depot.
Commonwealth and Reservoir Streets, Sydney.

FREE TO ALL WHO WILL READ IT.

Love For the Brethren

Upon reconsidering the editorial which appeared on the cover pages of the May 1929, issue of "Studies in the Scriptures" we feel that some of our readers may have misunderstood what we there wrote on "Love for the Brethren." Possibly some may draw the inference that we **disparage** kindness and gentleness. Not so. What we then sought to bring out was that true Christian love is something very different from and vastly superior to the pleasantries and courtesies of the flesh, that it is something entirely spiritual, and that its exercise and manifestation are to be regulated by the Word of God. The chief thing that we dwelt upon was to call attention to 1 John 5:2, "By this we know that we love the children of God, when we love God, and keep His commandments."

The touchstone of love for our brethren is our love for God, for "everyone that loveth Him that begot, loveth him also that is begotten of Him" (1 John 5:1). I cannot truly love my heavenly Father without loving His children; conversely, the love I have for my fellow-Christians is no greater, stronger, purer, than is the degree and purity of my love for my Father. Furthermore, the Christian's love for God is to be guaged by the keeping of His commandments. The measure in which we are in practical subjection to His Word is the extent by which our love for Him is made manifest. It is not our talk, but our walk, which best expresses the state of our hearts. Pointed were those words of our Saviour's, "If a man love Me, he **will** keep My words. . . . . he that loveth Me not, keepeth not My sayings" (John 14:23, 24).

The previous article upon our present subject dealt more with the negative side. Our principal object was to show that much which is regarded by professing Christians as "love" really has no scriptural title to that holy designation. Spiritual love is one of the choicest fruits of the Divine nature in the believer, and therefore is something far more excellent than the etiquette of the natural man, something more blessed and beautiful than the amiability and affability of the flesh. Yet, before proceeding farther, let it be said very definitely and positively that gruffness and rudeness, moroseness and selfishness are no part of the Christian character. We are exhorted to "**adorn** the doctrine of God our Saviour in **all** things" (Titus 2:10), and to "give none offence, neither to the Jews, nor to the Gentiles, nor to the Church of God" (1 Cor. 10:32).

In the remainder of this article we shall turn to the positive side of our subject. That the Christian should love his brethren is clear from the words of the Saviour to His disciples, "A new commandment I give unto you, That ye love one another; as I have loved you" that ye also love one another" (John 13:34). The "**as** I have loved you" is very searching. Notwithstanding our many sins and faults, in spite of our unloveliness, **He** loves us with an unceasing, unchanging, unquenchable love: "having loved His own which were in the world He loved them unto the end" (John 13:1). This is the standard which He has set before us. Christians are to love their

(Continued on Page 216)

IMPORTANT NOTICES

Please advise promptly of change of address, otherwise copies will be lost in the mails.

We are glad to send a sample copy to any of our friends whom you believe would be interested in such a publication.

Send to Mr. I. C. Herendeen, 433-435, The Arcade, Cleveland, Ohio, for a list of our publications. He has published many of our books and booklets.

This Magazine is published as a work of faith and labour of love. The Editor and his wife gladly give their services. It is freely sent to all who will read it. No charge is made for it.

Christians who feel definitely lead to do so, may have fellowship with us in this ministry. Those outside the U. S. A., please send only INTERNATIONAL Money Orders made out to Morton's Gap, Kentucky, U. S. A. See that it is made out in American money.

Mailing Permit applied for.

CONTENTS

Hebrews	194
Gleanings in Exodus	200
The Holy Spirit's Work	205
Matters of First Importance	211

THE EPISTLE TO THE HEBREWS

21. Christ Superior to Aaron
Heb. 5:8-10.

The first ten verses of Heb. 5 present to us a subject of such vast and vital importance that we dare not hurry over our exposition of them. They bring to our view the person of the Lord Jesus and His official work as the great High Priest of God's people. They set forth His intrinsic sufficiency for the discharge of the honourable but arduous functions of that office. They show us His right and title for the executing thereof. They reveal His full qualifications thereunto. They make known the nature and costliness of His sacrificial work. They declare the triumphant issue thereof. Yet plain as is their testimony, the subject of which they treat is so dimly apprehended by most Christians today, that we deem it necessary to devote a lengthy introduction to the setting forth of the principal features belonging to the Priesthood of Christ.

Let us begin by asking the question. Why did God ordain the office of priesthood? Wherein lay the **necessity** for it? The first and most obvious answer is, Because of sin. Sin created a breech between a holy God and His sinful creatures. Were God to advance toward them in His essential character it could only be in judgment, involving their sure destruction; for He "can by no means clear the guilty" (Ex. 34:7). Nor was the sinner capable of making the slightest advance toward God, for he was "alienated from the life of God" (Eph. 4:18), and thus, "dead in trespasses and sins" (Eph. 2:1): and as such, not only powerless to perform a spiritual act, but completely devoid of all spiritual aspirations. Looked at in himself, the case of fallen man was utterly hopeless.

But God has designs of **grace** unto men, not unto all men, but unto a remnant of them chosen out of a fallen race. Had God shown grace to all of Adam's descendants, the glory of His grace had been clouded, for it would have looked as though the provisions of grace were something which were due men from God, because of His having failed to preserve them from falling into sin. But grace is **unmerited** favour, something to which no creature is entitled, something which he cannot in any wise **claim** from God. Therefore it must be exercised in a **sovereign** manner by the Author of it (Ex. 32:19). that grace may appear to be grace (Rom. 11:6).

But in determining to show grace unto that people whom He had chosen in Christ before the foundation of the world (Eph. 1:4. 2 Tim. 1:9), God must act in harmony with His own perfections. The sin of His people could not be ignored. Justice clamoured for its punishment. If they were to be delivered from its penal consequences, it could only be by an adequate satisfaction being made for them. Without blood shedding there is no remission of sins. An Atonement was a fundamental necessity. Grace could not be shown at the expense of justice; no. grace must "reign through righteousness" (Rom. 5:21). Grace could only be exercised on the ground of accomplished redemption (Rom. 3:24).

And **who** was capable of rendering a perfect satisfaction unto the law of God? Who was qualified to meet all the demands of Divine holiness, if a sinful people were to be redeemed consistently with its claims? Who was competent both to assume the responsibilities of that people, and discharge them to the full satisfaction of the Most High? Who was able both to honour the rights of the Almighty, and yet enter sympathetically into the weakness and needs of those who were to be saved? Clearly, the only solution to this problem and the only answer to these questions lay in a **Mediator**, one who had both ability and title to act on God's behalf and on theirs. For this reason was the Son of God appointed to be made in the likeness of sin's flesh, that as the God-man He might be a "merciful and faithful High Priest" (Heb. 2:17); for **mediatorship** is the chief thing in priesthood.

Now this is what is brought before us in the opening verse of Heb. 5. There we are shown three parties: on the one side God, on the other side men, and the high priest as the connecting link between: "For every high priest taken from among men is ordained for men in things pertaining to God, that he may offer both gifts and sacrifices for sins" (v. 1). No correct conception of priesthood can exist where this double relation and this double service are not perceived. In Christ alone is this perfectly made good. He is the one connecting link between Heaven and earth, the only Mediator between God and "men" (1 Tim. 2:5). From Deity above, He is the Mediator downward to men beneath; and from men below, He is the Head upward to God. Priesthood is the **alone channel** of living relationship with a holy God. Solemn and awful proof of this is found in the fact that Satan, and then Adam, fell because there was **no Mediator** who stood between them and God, to maintain them in their standing before Him.

Above we have said, that Christ is the one connecting link between Heaven and earth, that He alone bridges the chasm between God and His people, considered as fallen and ruined sinners. Our last sentence really sums up the whole of Heb. 1 and 2. There we have a lengthy argument setting forth the relation between the two natures in Christ, the Divine and the human, and the needs-be of both to fit Him for the priestly office. He must be the Son of God in human nature. He must "in all things be made like unto His brethren" in order that He might be "a merciful and faithful High Priest;" in order that He might "make propitiation for the sins of the people;" and in order that He might be "able to succour them that are tempted." Heb. 2:17, 18 brings us to the climax of the apostle's argument in those two chapters.

The priestly work of Christ was to "make propitiation for the sins of the people." It was to render a complete satisfaction to God on behalf of all their liabilities. It was to "magnify the law and make it honourable." (Isa. 42:21). In order to this it was necessary for the law to be kept, to be perfectly obeyed in thought, word and deed. Accordingly, the Son of God was "made under the law" (Gal. 4:4), and "fulfilled" its requirements (Matt. 5:17). And this perfect obedience of Christ, performed substitutionally and officially, is now imputed to His people: as it is written, "By the obedience of One shall many be (legally) made righteous" (Rom. 5:19). But "magnifying the law" also involved His enduring its penalty on the behalf of His peoples' violation of its precepts, and this He suffered, and so "redeemed us from the curse of the law" by "being made a curse for us" (Gal. 3:13).

To sum up now the ground we have covered. 1. The **occasion** of Christ's priesthood was sin: it was this which alienated the creature from the Creator. 2. The **source** of Christ's priesthood was grace: rebels were not entitled to it; such a wondrous provision proceeded solely from the Divine favour. 3. The **function** of Christ's priesthood is mediation, to come between, to officiate for men Godwards. 4. The **qualification** for perfect priesthood is a God-man: none but God could meet the requirements of God; none but Man could meet the needs of men. 5. The **work** of priesthood is to make propitiation for sin. To these we may add: 6. The **design** of priesthood is that the claims of God may be honoured, the person of Christ glorified, and His people redeemed. 7. The **outcome** of His priesthood is the maintaining of His people in the favour of God. Other subsidiary points will come before us, D.V., in the later chapters.

Verses 8, 9 of Heb. 5 complete the passage which was before us in the preceding article. That we may the better perceive their scope and meaning, let us recapitulate the teaching of the earlier verses. In this first division of Heb. 5 the apostle's design was to show how that Christ fulfilled the Aaronic type. First, He had been Divinely called or appointed to the priestly office (vv. 4-6). Second, to fit Him for compassion on behalf of those for whom He officiated, He was "compassed with (sinless) infirmity" (vv. 3, 7). Third, He had "offered" to God, as Priest, "as for the people so also for himself" (v. 3), "strong crying and tears" (v. 7). That which is now to be before us, brings out still other perfections of Christ which qualified Him to fill the sacredotal office, and also makes known the happy issues therefrom.

"Though He were a Son, yet learned He obedience by the things which He suffered" (v. 8). In view of His unspeakable humiliation, portrayed in the previous verse, the Divine dignity of our High Priest is here mentioned both to guard and enhance His glory. "The things discoursed in the foregoing verse seem to have an inconsistency with the account given us concerning the person of Jesus Christ at the entrance of this Epistle. For He is therein declared to be the Son of God, and that in such a glorious manner as to be deservedly exalted above all the angels in heaven. Here He is represented as in a low, distressed condition, humbly, as it were, begging for His life, and pleading with 'strong crying and tears' before Him who was able to deliver Him. These things might seem unto the Hebrews to have some kind of repugnancy unto one another. And, indeed, they are a 'stone of stumbling, and a rock of offence,' unto many at this day; they are not able to reconcile them in their carnal minds and reasonings. . . . .

"The aim of the apostle in this place is, not to repel the objections of unbelievers, but to instruct the faith of those who do believe in the truth of these things. For He doth not only manifest that they were all possible, upon the account of His participation of flesh and blood, who was in Himself the eternal Son of God; but also that the whole of the humiliation and distress therein ascribed unto Him was necessary, with respect unto the office which He had undertaken to discharge, and the work which was committed unto Him. And this he doth in the next ensuing and following verses" (Dr. J. Owen).

"Though He were a Son, yet learned He obedience by the things which He suffered" (v. 8). First, what relation does this statement bear to the passage of which it is a part? Second, what is the particular "obedience" here referred to? Third, in what sense did the Son "learn" obedience? Fourth, how did the things "which He suffered" teach Him obedience? Fifth, what are the practical lessons here pointed for us? These are some of the questions raised by our verse which call for answer.

"Though He were a Son" looks back more immediately to v. 5, where a part of Psa. 2:7 is quoted. "That quotation has also reminded us of the Divine dignity and excellence of Christ as the ground of His everlasting priesthood. Jesus had a Divine commission; He was appointed by the Father because He was the Son; and thus He was possessed of all requisite qualifications for His office. Nevertheless the Son had to 'learn obedience.' He must not only possess authority and dignity, but be able to sympathize with the condition of sinners. By entering the circle of human experience He was made a merciful and faithful High Priest, and through suffering fitted for compassionately guiding our highest interests, as well as conducting our cause. The bond of brotherhood, the identity of suffering and sorrow, fitted Him to be touched with the feeling of our infirmities. He was made like unto His brethren (2:17); He suffered, that He might be in a position to succour them that are tempted (2:18); He was made in all respects like us, with the single exception of personal sinfulness (4:15); and He learned obedience by what He suffered. The design of all this was, that He might be a compassionate and sympathizing High Priest" (Prof. Smeaton).

Here then is the answer to our first question. In the 8th verse the Holy Spirit is still showing how that which was found in the type (v. 3), is also to be seen in the Antitype. What could more emphatically exemplify the fact that our High Priest was "compassed with infirmity" than to inform us that He not only felt accutely the experiences through which He passed, but also that He "learned obedience" by those very experiences? Nor need we hesitate to go as far as the Spirit of truth has gone; rather must we seek grace to believe all that He has said. None were more jealous of the Son's glory than He, and none knew so well how His glory had been displayed by His voluntary descent into such unfathomable depths of shame. While holding firmly to Christ's absolute deity, we must not (through a false conception of His dignity) shrink from following Him in thought and affection into that abyss of humiliation unto which, for our sakes, He came. When Scripture says, "He learned obedience" we must not whittle down these words to mean anything less than they affirm.

"Yet learned He obedience" brings out, very forceably, the **reality** of the humanity which the Son assumed. He became true Man. If we bow to the inspired statement that "Jesus increased in wisdom and stature, and in favour with God and men" (Luke 2:52), why balk—as many have—at He "learned obedience?" True, blessedly true, these words do not signify that there was in Him a will which resisted the law of God, and which needed severe discipline to bring it into subjection. As Calvin well says, "Not that He was driven to this by force, or that He had need of being thus exercised, as the case is with oxen or horses when their ferocity is to be tamed; for He was abundantly willing to render to His Father the obedience which He owed." No, He declared, "I **delight** to do Thy will, O God" (Psa. 40:8). And again, "My **meat** is to do the will of Him that sent Me" (John 4:24).

But what is "obedience?" It is subjection to the will of another: it is an owning of the authority of another; it is performing the pleasure of another. This was an entirely new experience for the Son. Before His incarnation, He had Himself occupied the place of authority, of supreme authority. His seat had been the throne of the universe. From it He had issued commands and had enforced obedience. But now He had taken the place of a servant. He had assumed a creature nature. He had become man. And in this new place and role He conducted Himself with befitting submission to Another. He had been "made under the law," and its precepts must be honoured by Him. But more: the place He had taken was an official one. He had come here as the Surety of His people. He had come to discharge their liabilities. He had come to work out a perfect righteousness for them; and therefore, as their Representative, He must obey God's law. As the One who was here to maintain the claims of God, in the very scene where fy the law and make it honourable," by His rebellious creatures, He must "magnify the law and make it honourable," by yielding to it a voluntary, perfect, joyous compliance.

Again; the "obedience" of Christ formed an essential part of His priestly oblation. This was typified of old—though very few have perceived it—in the animals prescribed for sacrifice: they were to be "without spot, with blemsh." That denoted ther excellency; only the "choice of the flock" (Ezek. 24:5) were presented to God. The antitype of this pointed to far more than the sinlessness of Christ—**that** were merely negative. It had in view His positive perfections, His active obedience, His personal excellency. When Christ "offered Himself without spot to God" (Heb. 9:14), He presented a Sacrifice which had already fulfilled every preceptive requirement of the law. And it was as Priest that He thus offered Himself to God, thereby fulfilling the Aaronic type. But in all things **He** has the pre-eminence, for at the cross He was both Offerer and Offering. Thus there is the most intimate connection between the contents of v. 8 and its context, especially with v. 7.

"Yet learned He obedience." The incarnate Son actually entered into the experience of what it was **to** obey. He denied Himself, He renounced His own will, He "pleased not Himself" (Rom. 15:3). There was no insubordination in Him, nothing dis-inclined to God's law; instead, His obedience was voluntary and hearty. But by being "made under the law" as Man, He "learned" what Divine righteousness required of Him; by receiving commandment to lay down His life (John 10:18), He "learned" the extent of that obedience which holiness demanded. Again; as the God-man, Christ "learned" obedience experimentally. As we learn the sweetness or bitterness of food by actually tasting it, so He learned what submission is by yielding to the Father's will. "But, moreover, there was still somewhat peculiar in that obedience, which the Son of God is said to learn from His own sufferings, namely, what it is for a **sinless person** to suffer for sinners, 'the Just for the unjust.' The obedience herein was peculiar unto Him, nor do we know, nor can we have an experience of the ways and paths of it" (Dr. J. Owen).

"By the things which He suffered" announces the **means** by which He learned obedience. Everything that Christ suffered, from first to last, during the days of His flesh, is here included. His entire course was one of suffering, and He had the experience of obedience in it all. Every scene through which He passed provided occasion for the exercise of those graces wherein obedience consists. Meekness and lowliness (Matt. 11:29), self-denial (Rom. 15:3), patience (Rev. 1:9), faith (Heb. 2:13), were habitually resident in His holy nature, but they were only capable of exercise by reason of His suffering. As His suffering increased, so His obedience grew in extent and intensity, by the very pressure brought to bear upon it; the hotter the conflict grew, the more His inward submission was manifested outwardly (compare Isa. 50:6, 7). There was not only sufferings passively endured, but obedience in suffering, and that the most amazing and unparalleled.

To sum up now the important teachings of this wonderful verse: He who personally was high above all obedience, stooped so low as to enter the place of obedience. In that place He learned, by His sufferings, the actual experience of obedience—He obeyed. Hereby we learn what was required to the right discharge of Suretyship: there must needs be both an active and a passive obedience vicariously rendered. The opening word "though" intimates that the high dignity of His person did not exempt Him from the humiliation which our salvation involved. The word "yet" is a note of exclamation, to deepen our sense of wonderment at His infinite condescension on our behalf, for in His place of servitude He never ceased to be the Lord of glory. "He was no less God when He died, than when He was 'declared to be the Son of God with power, by the resurrection from the dead,' Rom. 1:4" (Dr. J. Owen).

And what are the practical lessons here pointed for us? First, our Redeemer has left us an example that we should follow His steps. He has shown us how to wear our creature nature: complete and unquestioning subjection to God is that which is required of us. Second, Christ has hereby taught us the extent to which God ought to be submitted unto: He was "obedient unto death." Third, obedience to God costs something: "Yea, and all that will live godly in Christ Jesus shall suffer persecution" (2 Tim. 3:12). Fourth, sufferings undergone according to the will of God are highly instructive. Christ Himself learned by the things which He suffered; much more may we do so, who have so much more to learn (Heb. 12:10, 11). Fifth, God's love for us does not exempt from suffering. Though the Son of His love, Christ was not spared great sorrows and trials: sufficient for the disciple to be as his Master.

"And being made perfect, He became the Author of eternal salvation unto all them that obey Him" (v. 9). "The apostle having declared the sufferings of Christ as our High Priest, in His offering of Himself, with the necessity thereof, proceeds now to declare both what was effected thereby, and what was the especial design of God therein. And this in general was that, the Lord Christ, considering our lost condition, might be every way fitted to be a 'perfect cause of eternal salvation unto all that obey Him.' There are, therefore, two things in the words, both which God aimed at and accomplished in the sufferings of Christ. 1. On His own part, that He might be 'made perfect;' not absolutely, but with respect unto the administration of His office in the behalf of sinners. 2. With respect unto believers, that He might be unto them the 'Author of eternal salvation' (Dr. J. Owen). This is a good epitome of the teaching of the 9th verse, but a number of things in it call for fuller elucidation.

"And being made perfect." The word, "perfect" is one which is found frequently in this Epistle. It signifies "to consummate" or "complete." It also means "to dedicate" or "fully consecrate." Our present passage contains its second occurrence, the first being in 2:10, to which we must refer the reader. There the verb is used actively with respect to the Father: it became Him to "make perfect" the Captain of our salvation. Here it is used passively, telling of the **effect** of that act of God on the person of Christ; by His suffering He was "perfected." It has reference to the setting apart of Christ as Priest. "The legal high priests were consecrated by the sufferings and deaths of the beasts which were offered in sacrifice at their consecration (Ex. 29). But it belonged unto the perfection of the priesthood of Christ to be consecrated in and by His **own** sufferings" (Dr. J. Owen). It is most important to note that the reference here is to what took place in "the days of His flesh," not at His resurrection or ascension—vv. 7-9 form one complete statement. The Greek is even more emphatic than the A.V.: "And having been perfected became to those that obey Him all, the Author of salvation eternal." It was not in heaven that He was "perfected," but **before** He "became the Author of salvation"—cf. 10:14, which affirms our oneness with Him in His approved obedience and accomplished sacrifice.

"And being made perfect" does not contemplate any change wrought in His person, but speaks of His being fully qualified to officiate as Priest, to present Himself to God as a perfect sacrifice for the sins of His people. His official "perfecting" was accomplished in and by means of His sufferings. By His offering up of Himself He was consecrated to the priestly office, and by the active presentation of His sacrifice to God He discharged the essential function thereof. Thus, the inspired declaration we are now considering furnishes another flat contradiction (cf. 2:17) of those who affirm that Christ was not constituted and consecrated High Priest till His resurrection. True, there were other acts and duties pertaining to His sacredotal office yet to be performed, but these depend for their efficacy on His previous sufferings; those He was now made meet for. The "being made perfect" or "consecrated" to the priestly office at the Cross, finds a parallel in our Lord's own words, "For their sakes I sanctify (dedicate) Myself" (John 17:19). "Here is the ultimate end why it was necessary for Christ to suffer: that He might thus become initiated into His priesthood" (J. Calvin).

"He became the Author of eternal salvation." "Having thus been made perfect through such intense, obediential, pious suffering—having thus obtained all the merit, all the power and authority, all the sympathy, which are necessary to the discharge of the high priestly functions of Saviour, 'He is become the Author of eternal salvation.' This is the second statement which the apostle makes in illustration of the principle, that our Lord has proved Himself qualified for the office to which He has been divinely appointed by a successful discharge of its functions, the subsidiary clause, 'being made perfect,' connects this second statement with the first; showing how our Lord's 'learning obedience by the things which He suffered in the days of His flesh'—His humbled state—led to His being now, in His exalted state, 'the Author of salvation to all who obey Him' . . . . 'Being made perfect' is just equivalent to 'having thus obtained' every necessary qualification for actually saving them" (Dr. J. Brown).

The "Author of salvation" conveys a slightly different thought than the "Captain of salvation" in 2:10. There it is Christ actually conducting many sons, by the powerful administration of His Word and Spirit, unto glory. Here it is the work of Christ as the meritorious and efficient Cause of their salvation. It was the perfect satisfaction which He rendered to God, the propitatory sacrifice of Himself, which has secured the eternal deliverance of His people from the penal consequences of their sins. By His expiation He became the purchaser and procurer of our redemption. His intercession and His gift of the Spirit are the effects and fruits of His perfect oblation. "He has done everything that is necessary to make the salvation of His people consistent with, and illustrative of, the perfections of the Divine character and the principles of the Divine government; and He actually does save His people from guilt, depravity and misery—He actually makes them really holy and happy hereafter" (Dr. J. Brown).

The salvation which Christ has procured and now secures unto all His people, is here said to be an "**eternal**" one. First of all, none other was suited unto us. By virtue of the nature which we have received from God, we are made for eternal duration. But by sin we made ourselves obnoxious to eternal damnation, being by nature "the children of wrath, even as others" (Eph. 2:3). Therefore an eternal salvation was our deep and dire need. Second, the merits of our Saviour being infinite, required from the hand of Justice a corresponding salvation, one infinite in value and in duration: cf. 9:12. Third, the salvation procured by our great High Priest is here contrasted with that obtained by the Levitical high priest: the atonement which Aaron made, held good for one year only (Lev. 16); but that which Christ has accomplished, is of eternal validity.

"To all them that obey Him" describes those who are the beneficaries of our High Priest's atonement. "The expression is emphatical. To all and every one of them that obey Him; not any one of them shall be exempted from a share and interest in this salvation; nor shall any one of any other sort be admitted thereunto" (Dr. J. Owen). It is not all men universally, but those only who bow to His sceptre. The recipients of His great salvation are here spoken of according to the terms of human accountability. All who hear the Gospel are commanded to believe (1 John 3:23); such is their responsibility. The "obedience" of this verse is an evangelical, not a legal one: it is the "obedience **of faith**" (Rom. 16:26). So also in Acts 5:32 we read of the Holy Spirit "whom God hath given to them that obey Him." But this "obedience" is not to be restricted to the initial act, but takes in the whole life of faith. A Christian, in contradistinction from a non-Christian, is one who **obeys** Christ (John 14:23). The "all them that obey Him" of Heb. 5:9 is in apposition to "yet learned He obedience" in the previous verse: it identifies the members with their Head!

Before taking up the next verse, let us seek to point out how that the passage which has been before us, not only shows Christ provided the substance of what was foreshadowed by the Levitical priests, but also how that He excelled them at every point, thus demonstrating the immeasurable superiority of Christ over Aaron. First, Aaron was but a man (v. 1); Christ, the "Son." Second, Aaron offered "sacrifices" (v. 1); Christ offered one perfect sacrifice, once for all. Third, Aaron was "compassed with infirmity" (v. 2); Christ was the "mighty" One (Psa. 89:19). Fourth, Aaron needed to offer for his own sins (v. 3); Christ was sinless. Fifth, Aaron offered a sacrifice external to himself; Christ offered Himself. Sixth, Aaron effected only a temporary salvation. Christ secured an eternal one. Seventh, Aaron's atonement was for Israel only; Christ's for "**all** them that obey Him."

"Called of God an high priest after the order of Melchizedek" (v. 10). This verse forms the transition between the first division of Heb. 5, and its second which extends to the end of chapter 7—the second being interrupted by a lengthy parenthesis. In the first section treating of our Lord's priesthood, the apostle has amplified his statement in 2:17, 18, and has furnished proof that Christ fulfilled the Aaronic type. In the second section wherein he treats of our Lord's sacerdotal office, he amplifies his declaration in 4:15, and shows that in Christ we have not only an High Priest, but "a **great** High Priest." The different aspects of his theme treated of in these two divisions of Heb. 5 is intimated by the variation to be noted in vv. 6, 10. In the former he says, "Thou art a priest forever after the order of Melchizedek," but in v. 10 he adds, "Called of God an High Priest after the order of Melchizedek."

The Greek word for "called" in v. 10 is entirely different from the one used in v. 5, "called of God." The former signifies to ordain or appoint; the latter to salute or greet to the right understanding of the purport of v 10, it is essential to observe carefully the exact point at which this statement is introduced: it is not till **after** the declarations that Christ had "offered up" (v. 7), had "learned obedience" v. 7), had been "made perfect," and had become "the Author of salvation" (v.9), we are told that God saluted Christ as "High Priest after the order of Melchizedek." What is found in v. 6 does not in any wise weaken the force of this, still less does it clash with it. In vv. 5, 6 the Spirit is not treating of the **order** of Christ's priesthood, but is furnishing proof that He had been called to that office by God Himself.

We do not propose to offer an exposition of the contents of this 10th verse on the present occasion, but content ourself with directing attention to the important fact that it was consequent upon His being officially "made perfect" and becoming "the Author of eternal salvation," that Christ was saluted by God as "High Priest after the order of Melchizedek." This act of God's followed the Saviour's death and resurrection. It was God's greeting of the glorious Conqueror of sin and death. Hence the propriety of His new title. If the reader refers to Gen. 14 he will find that the historical Melchizedek first comes on the scene to greet Abraham after his noteable conquest of Chedorlaomer and his allies. It was upon his "return from the slaughter" of the kings, that Melchizedek appeared and blessed him. Thus he owned Abraham's triumph. In like manner, God has greeted the mighty Victor. May the Spirit of God fit our hearts and minds for a profounder insight of His living oracles.

—ARTHUR W. PINK.

GLEANINGS IN EXODUS

69. The Sinaiatic Covenant: Ex. 34:22-27.

The key verse to the whole of Ex. 34 is the 27th: "And the Lord said unto Moses, Write thou these words: for after the tenor of **these** words I have made a **covenant** with thee and with Israel." Hence the title to our present article. In the verse following the one just quoted, we read, "And he was there with the Lord forty days and forty nights; he did neither eat bread, nor drink water. And he wrote upon the tables the words of **the covenant,** the ten commandments." Thus, the Sinaiatic covenant was a **legal** one, but as vv. 6, 7 have shown us, it was Law administered in mercy and patience, as well as righteousness and holiness.

We have already considered the Law as expressing God's government over His redeemed people; let us now look at it in its **dispensational** bearings. In Rom. 5:20 we read, "the law entered, that the offence might abound;" that is, that sin might appear "exceeding sinful" (Rom. 7:13); that the wickedness of the human heart might be manifested; that it should be the more fully demonstrated that men **are** sinners; and this in order that, "Every mouth might be stopped, and all the world may become guilty before God" (Rom. 3:19).

In the light of what has just been before us, we should carefully bear in mind that God gave the Law to Moses **twice**: Ex. 31:18; 34:1, 28. The first giving of the Law demonstrated that man is **ungodly.** As we have seen, before the Law was written upon tables of stone, it was first given to Moses orally (Ex. 20), and Moses then repeated it to Israel (24:3), and they affirmed, "all the words which the Lord hath said will we do." The first word He had said was, "Thou shalt have no other gods before Me." But, at the very time He was engraving those words on the stones, Israel was saying to Aaron, "Up make us gods which shall go before us" (32:1). And the next thing was that the golden calf was made and worshipped. The immediate sequel was the visitation of God's anger upon them (32:27, 28). Thus, the first trial of man—not of Israel only, for "As in water face answereth to face, so the heart of man to man" (Prov. 27:19)—ended in judgment.

As the first giving of the Law demonstrated that man was "ungodly," so the second giving of it was to be followed by a manifestation that he is "without strength" to keep it. These are the two things which characterize fallen man (Rom. 5:6), and these were what the double giving of the law was designed to show. The first was demonstrated speedily; the second was made evident more slowly, yet none the less surely. God gave man fair and full opportunity to show whether he had power to keep the law. In the nation of Israel he was represented and tested under the most favourable circumstances. Israel was separated from the heathen; Jehovah Himself dwelt in their midst. They were given a land flowing with milk and honey; and, as the apostle says, unto them pertained "the adoption, and the glory, and the covenants, and the giving of the law, and the service of God, and the promises" (Rom. 9:4). Well might Jehovah say to them at a later date, "What could have been done more to My vineyard, that I have not done in it? wherefore when I looked that it should bring forth grapes, brought it forth wild grapes?" (Isa. 5:4).

Yes, the vineyard of the Lord's planting brought forth only "wild grapes." Graciously and longsufferingly did He bear with them, sending one prophet after another to exhort, admonish, rebuke, and warn. But all to no purpose (see Mark 12:1-5). One generation after another was tested, but always with the same result, in that the Law was "weak through the flesh" (Rom. 8:3). Man had no ability to meet the righteous requirements of God. He was "without strength." Therefore, as was inevitable, this second testing of man under the Law also ended with Divine judgment. And most impressive was the longsuffering mercy of God seen in that too. The full and final stroke of His wrath did not fall upon guilty Israel all at once, but was meted out slowly and in stages.

First, God delivered up His people into the hands of the Chaldeans. As He said through Isaiah, "O Assyrian, the rod of Mine anger, and the staff in their hand is Mine indignation. I will send him against an hypocritical nation, and against the people of My wrath will I give him a charge, to take the spoil, and to take the prey, and to tread them down like the mire of the streets" (10:5,6). Israel's second testing under the Law had come to an end. The "glory of the Lord" (the Shekinah) had departed from the holy city (Ezek. 11:23, 24), and Israel's sons were carried down captive into Babylon; and through the prophet Hosea the Nation was disowned of God: "Then said God, Call his name Lo-ammi: for ye are not My people" (1:9).

Later, a remnant was permitted to leave Babylon and return to the land of their fathers, unto the city which had been ruined through their folly and rebellion, to raise it up again and to build the temple. But they came back not as God's people, but as "Lo-ammi." And though a temple was erected, yet no Shekinah glory abode in it. **It was empty!** God no longer dwelt in their midst. The prophets which He sent unto them at that period emphasized the ruin which had come in, and pointed forward to the advent of the Saviour. The great test then was no longer obedience to the Law (though that was not repealed), but an humble acceptance of the Divine judgment which was upon them, and a waiting in contrition of spirit for the Deliverer. But instead of humbling themselves before God, instead of repenting for their sins, instead of owning that they **were** "without strength," they were more self-righteous than ever. Ably has this been set forth by another:

"But now, alas! you find again what the power of Satan is, and how subtly he can blind, through man's folly, the heart of man. It is very striking, and people generally notice it as favorable to Israel, that after their return, they were no more idolators. It had been their special sin. The prophet asks, you remember, 'Hath a nation changed their gods, which are yet no gods? but My people have changed their glory for that which doth not profit.' Even from the wilderness they had. There was first the golden calf, and all through the wilderness they had taken up 'the tabernacle of Moloch, and the star of their god Remphan, figures which they made to worship them.' God had declared that he was the one God, but they were idolators to the core of the heart.

"But as soon as there was no god in their midst—as soon as the temple was empty and the glory had departed—as soon as they were in the ruin which their sin had brought about, then immediately Satan came forward, not in the garb of idolatry any more, but now to resist the sentence which God had pronounced upon them—now to persuade them that after all they were **not** as Lo-ammi—that they **were** God's people, and to say, 'The temple of the Lord, the temple of the Lord are we.' In fact, pharisaism was the growth of that period, and pharisaism was the self-righteousness which resisted God's sentence upon them, pretending to have a righteousness when God had emphatically declared that man had none. So it was when that Deliverer prophesied of came, and when the glory, in a deeper and more wonderful way than ever was once more in their midst,—aye, the 'glory of the only begotten Son, in the bosom of the Father'—the Antitype of the glory of that tabernacle of old,—when He who was to come did come, and was amongst them in love and grace, ready to meet them with all mercy and tenderness,—not coming to be ministered to, but to minister,—not requiring, but to give with both hands—to give without limit—to give as God,—alas! these phasisees could turn comfortably to one another and say, 'which of the pharisees have believed on Him?' Pharisees they were who slew the Lord of glory" (Mr. F. W. Grant).

Then it was, as a matter of course, that Judaism ended. The high priest's rending of his garments (Matt. 26:65), though unknown to himself (cf. John 11:51), intimated that the priesthood had served its day. Man's second trial under Law was over. Nothing now remained but judgment, yet even that lingered for a further forty years, till, in A.D. 70, Jerusalem was captured, the temple destroyed, and the Jews dispersed abroad. Even before that judgment fell, God's call to His own people was, "Save yourselves **from** this untoward generation' (Acts 2:40). And again, "Let us go forth therefore unto Him, **without the camp**" (Heb. 13:13). But we must now retrace our steps, and return to the point from which we started. The central thing in Ex. 34 is the "covenant" which Jehovah made with Israel at Sinai.

As we pointed out in the opening paragraphs of our last article, that covenant was based upon the ten words engraved upon the tables of stone. It was a covenant of law, but law administered in mercy, grace, patience, as well as holiness and righteousness. In that covenant God pressed His **claims** upon man. First, He demanded absolute separation, unto Himself (v. 18). Second, entire consecration for Himself (vv. 19, 20). Third, complete submission to His appointed sabbath, no exception being permitted even in harvesttime (v. 21). Here follows our present passage.

"And thou shalt observe the feast of weeks, of the first fruits of wheat harvest" (v. 22). The central thought in connection with each of Israel's "feasts" was the gathering together of the people around Jehovah Himself, on the ground of redemption accomplished. Thus, it was corporate responsibility which is here in view, and, we may add, corporate privilege, for there is no greater privilege enjoyed on earth than for God's saints to be gathered together, in festive assembly, around Himself.

The "feast of weeks," better known as "Pentecost," is described at greatest length in Lev. 23:15-21. Here it is connected with "the first fruits of wheat harvest." This at once makes us think of James 1:18: "Of His own will begat He us with the Word of truth, that we should be a kind of **firstfruits** of His creatures." Dispensationally, the feast received a partial fulfillment at the descent of the Spirit in Acts 2. We say "partial fulfillment," for Peter's words in Acts 2:16, "But this **is that** which was spoken by the prophet Joel," rather than "this is the **fulfillment** of that which was spoken by Joel," tell us that the complete realization is yet future; as indeed it is. The "two loaves" of Lev. 23:17 pointed, first, to Jew and Gentile now gathered together and made fellow-members of the Body of Christ; but, ultimately they foreshadowed the re-uniting of the two houses of Israel (cf. Ezek. 37:16) when, after this dispensation has run its course, the Jews will be restored once more to Divine favour.

"And the feast of ingathering at the year's end" (v. 22). This is better known as "the feast of tabernacles." It was the final one on Israel's religious calendar. Its dispensational fulfillment is therefore yet future. "The feast of tabernacles is the joy of the millennium, when Israel hath come out of the wilderness, where their sins have placed them: but to which will be added this first day (the "eighth day" of Lev. 23:36" A. W. P.) of another week

—the resurrection joy of those who are raised with the Lord Jesus, to which the presence of the Holy Spirit answers meanwhile. Consequently, we find that the feast of tabernacles took place after the increase of the earth had been gathered in, and, as we learn elsewhere, not only after the harvest, but after the vintage also; that is, after separation by judgment, and the final execution of judgment on the earth, when heavenly and earthly saints shall all be gathered in" (Mr. J. N. Darby).

"Thrice in the year shall all your men children appear before the Lord God, the God of Israel" (v. 23). The particular occasions specified were, "in the feast of unleavened bread, and in the feast of weeks, and in the feast of tabernacles" (Deut. 16:16). Really, those feasts contemplated three distinct dispensations: the first, the O. T., when Israel was separated unto the Lord. The second, this present interval, when in addition to the "remnant according to the election of grace" (Rom. 11:5) from the stock of Abraham, God is also visiting "the Gentiles, to take out of them a people for His name" (Acts 15:14). The third, to the millennium, when the Lord "will return, and will build again the tabernacle of David, which is fallen down; and will build again the ruins thereof, and will set it up: That the residue of men might seek after the Lord, and all the Gentiles, upon whom My name is called" (Acts 15:16, 17). We may add that each of the three persons in the Godhead are, distinctively, contemplated in these feasts. The feast of unleavened bread, which is inseparably connected with the Passover, speaks to us of God the Son. The feast of weeks or Pentecost is marked by the descent of the Spirit (Acts 2:2; Joel 2:28). The feast of tabernacles will witness the answer to that oft-prayed petition, "Our Father which art in heaven . . . Thy kingdom come" (compare Matt. 13:43; 16:27). The **order** is the same as in the three-one parable of Luke 15: the work of the Shepherd, the work of the Spirit, bringing into the Father's house. Thus it is experimentally.

As we have said, the "feasts" had to do with corporate responsibility, and corporate privilege too, for, "Behold, how good and how pleasant it is for brethren to dwell together in unity" (Psa. 133:1). But alas, history has repeated itself. At the beginning of Israel's national history, they were a united "congregation." So it was at the beginning of this dispensation: "And all that believed were together" (Acts 2:44). For a time all went well; then failure and sin came followed by Divine chastisement and judgment; true alike of Israel and Christendom. Ultimately Israel was carried captive into Babylon, so too, all through the 'dark ages' the "mystery Babylon" of Rev. 17 dominated Europe. A remnant of Israel returned from Babylon and the true worship of God was restored in Israel, though not after its primitive glory. So there was a Reformation, a remnant was delivered from the papacy, and God again was magnified, though the streams of truth was not as pure as it was at the beginning.

But at the end of the Old Testament period the corporate testimony of Israel was a complete wreck and ruin: the priesthood had "corrupted the covenant of Levi" (Mal. 2:7, 8); polluted bread was offered upon God's altar (Mal. 1:7). Judah had "profaned the holiness of the Lord" (Mal. 2:11), and Jehovah had to say, "I have no pleasure in you . . . neither will I accept an offering at your hand" (Mal. 1:10). In like manner, the corporate testimony of Christendom has long since fallen into ruins. The last of the Epistles to the churches depicts Christ as being on the **outside** (Rev. 3:20), and His voice is addressed to the individual only, "If any man hear My voice."

"For I will cast out the nations before thee and enlarge thy borders: neither shall any man desire thy land, when thou shalt go up to appear before the Lord thy God thrice in the year" (v. 24). How remarkably does this verse illustrate Prov. 16:7: "When a man's ways please the Lord, He maketh even his enemies to be at peace with him." God will not allow any man to be His debtor: He has promised, "Them that honour Me, I will honour" (1 Sam. 2:30). So it was here. These Israelites were going up to the temple to worship the Lord; in their absence He would guard their homes.

"Neither shall any man desire thy land, when thou shalt go up to appear before the Lord thy God thrice in the year." How strikingly does this demonstrate the absoluteness of God's control of His creatures! And man, though fallen and rebellious, is no exception. As Dan. 4:35 tells us, "He doeth according to His will in the army of heaven, and among the inhabitants of the earth: and none can stay His hand." So it was here. The male Hebrews were to leave their farms and go up to the temple in Jerusalm (Deut. 16:16)—for many of them, a long journey. They were surrounded by hostile heathen, but so complete is God's control of man, every man, that none shall be allowed to molest their families or flocks while they were away. Thus, we see that God not only restrains the activities of the wicked, but even regulates the desires of their evil hearts: "The king's heart is in the hand of the Lord, as the rivers of water: He turneth it whithersoever He will" (Prov. 21:1).

"Thou shalt not offer the blood of My sacrifice with leaven" (v. 25). God was very jealous of the types. Why? Because they pointed forward to the person and work of Christ. Thus, His jealousy of the types was His guarding of the glory of His beloved Son. Therefore, inasmuch as the sacrifices pointed forward to the Lord Jesus, leaven (which is an emblem of evil) must be excluded, for He is "holy, harmless, undefiled, separate from sinners" (Heb. 7:26).

"Thou shalt not offer the blood of My sacrifice with leaven." Very wonderful and blessed is it to observe how the Lord here refers to the sacrifice: He does not say "the blood of **thy** sacrifice," but "**My** sacrifice." This is also the language of the antitype: The Sacrifice "offered once for all," was of God's appointing, was of God's providing, was for God's satisfaction. Man had no part or lot in it whatsoever. "Salvation is of the Lord." Frequently is this same truth brought out in the types. In Gen. 22:8 we hear Abraham saying to his son's query of "Where is the lamb for the burnt offering?—God will provide **Himself** a lamb." In Ex. 12: 27 we are told, "It is **the Lord's** passover." In connection with the two goats on the day of atonement, lots were cast, "one lot **for the Lord**" (Lev. 16:8); and so on.

"Neither shall the sacrifice of the feast of the passover be left unto the morning" (v. 25). The paschal lamb was to be eaten on the same night it had been slain and roasted in fire, not left over to be partaken of on the morrow (see 12:10). The application of this detail of the type is very solemn and searching. To have eaten the lamb on the morrow, would have been to dissociate it from the import of its death. The eating of the lamb speaks to us of the believer (already sheltered by His blood) feeding on Christ: eating the lamb the same night it was killed, tells us that we are ever to feed upon Christ with a deep sense in our souls of what His death and bearing judgment for us ("**roast** with fire") really involved for Him. Note how Christ Himself emphasized this in John 6: first vv. 50, 51, then vv. 53-56!

"The first of the firstfruits of thy land thou shalt bring unto the house of the Lord thy God" (v. 26). This Divine ordinance receives amplification in Deut. 26: 1-11. The interested reader would find it profitable to prayerfully study in detail the whole of that passage for himself; we can but summarise its teaching here. First, it had to do with Israel's possession of their inheritance (v. 1). Second, this "first of the firstfruits of thy land" was the Divine pledge or earnest of the coming harvest (v. 2). Third, Israel acknowledged this by their presentation unto the priest (v. 3). Fourth, the Israelite was then required to look back and acknowledge his previous state of shame and bondage (v. 5-7). Fifth, he then owned the Lord's goodness in deliverance (v. 8). Sixth, he expressed his gratitude for the goodly portion the Lord had given him (v. 9). Seventh, he presented the "firstfruits" in worship before Him (vv. 10: 11).

All of the above is rich in its typical teaching, much of which has already been before us in other connections. That which is here distinctive, is the contrast presented between what we find in Ex. 34:22 and here in v. 26. The "firstfruits of wheat harvest" refers to Christ (cf. John 12:24 with 1 Cor. 15:23). But the "first of the fruits of thy land" or "inheritance" speaks, we believe, of the Holy Spirit, who is "the earnest of our inheritance until the redemption of the purchased possession" (Eph. 1:13, 14). Do we not get the antitype of Ex. 34:26 in Rom. 8:22, "Ourselves also, which have the **firstfruits of the Spirit!**" And in the light of Deut. 26:10, 11 are we not taught that we should thank God as heartily for the gift of the Spirit as for the gift of His Son? Do we realize that we are as much indebted to, and therefore have as much cause of praise for, the work of the Spirit **in** us, as the work of Christ **for** us!

"Thou shalt not seethe a kid in his mother's milk" (v. 26). Upon this we have nothing better to offer than the brief comment of Mr. Dennett: "This remarkable prohibition is found three times in the Scriptures (Ex. 23:19; 34:26; Deut. 14:21). God will have His people tenderly careful, guarding them from the violation of any instinct of nature. The milk of the mother was the food, the sustenance of the kid, and hence this must not be used to seethe it as food for others."

"And the Lord said unto Moses, Write thou these words: for after the tenor of these words have I made a covenant with thee and with Israel" (v. 27). This verse summarises all that has been before us in the previous verses of the chapter. An imperishable record was to be made of all that Jehovah had said unto His servant. The words, "I have made a covenant with thee (the typical mediator) and with Israel," gives assurance that all will yet be made good through the person and millennial administration of Christ. Israel failed in the past, but there will be no failure with Him who shall yet effectuate God's counsels and glorify Him in this very scene where His people have so grievously dishonoured Him. May the Lord hasten that glad day.

—ARTHUR W. PINK.

THE HOLY SPIRIT'S WORK.
1. In The Saviour

"Wherever Christianity has been a living power, the Doctrine of the Holy Spirit has uniformly been regarded, equally with the Atonement and Justification by faith, as the article of a standing or falling Church. The distinctive feature of Christianity, as it addresses itself to man's experience, is the work of the Spirit, which not only elevates it far above all philosophic speculation, but also above every other form of religion." These words of Professor Smeaton in his most excellent work on "The Doctrine of the Holy Spirit," written fifty years ago, serves to expose the evil character of the days in which our lot is cast. "Christianity" is nothing like the "liveing power" it was two or three generations ago, and therefore it is not to be wondered at that "the doctrine of the Holy Spirit," His offices and operations, has such a meager place in the pulpit ministrations of the present hour.

But though there is little teaching today on the person and work of the Holy Spirit in those places which, formerly, were looked upon as the centers of orthodoxy, there are some unscriptural and wild extravagances published concerning Him in other quarters. Nor is this to be wondered at. Whenever Christendom sows the wind it is made to reap the whirlwind. Last century the Spirit was largely grieved and quenched by a professional officaldom, which substituted the "enticing words of man's wisdom," learned in human schools, for dependency upon "the demonstration of the Spirit and power." In consequence, many of the hungry sheep of Christ turned elsewhere for real spiritual food. Nor did God disappoint them, for His promise ever holds good. "Blessed are they which do hunger and thirst after righteousness, for they shall be filled."

Men of God, taught of Him, were raised up to "lift up the hands which hang down, and the feeble knees" (Heb. 12:12).

But, alas, pride soon spoiled the work, and that which, at its inception, was of the Spirit, quickly degenerated into a thing of the flesh. Those who had been favored with a little light from God, looked down in contempt upon other Christians that joined not with them. Those who had gone forth "without the camp," formed a camp of their own. What was worse, they made the audacious claim that they alone were "gathered on true ground," that they alone were under the presidency of the Spirit. Thus was the third Person of the Trinity insulted, by having imputed to Him whatever was given out in their meetings. They too have reaped the whirlwind. The Spirit of the Lord has long since departed from them, though, like Samson of old, they "wist not that" he has (Judges 16:20). The awful thing is that any one who likes to hear his own voice, any novice, is free to jump up and give forth the most un-edifying utterances under the pretense of being moved by the Spirit. How close akin this is to blasphemy we hesitate to say.

In the present day, fresh cults are arising and new companies are being formed where the "baptism of the Spirit" and "Speaking in tongues" have a promient place. This too is a judicial visitation from Heaven, a judgment from God, because of the unfaithfulness of His own servants to teach the true and scriptural doctrine of the Spirit. Ignorance is easily imposed upon. Where the heart is not filled with the truth, error finds a ready entrance. Moreover, many who are dissatisfied by a formal and lifeless orthodoxy turn to the "strange fire" of these Satanic movements, hoping they may find the warmth and cheer which they are denied elsewhere. Thus, the Devil is taking full advantage of the opportunity which a degenerate and dead Christendom now presents to him. When the Spirit of the Lord departed from Saul, an evil spirit took possession of him. So it is today.

It is not now our purpose to write the lengthy series of articles which would be required, were we to attempt a comprehensive outline of the Scripture's teaching on the Deity, personality, offices, and operations of the Holy Spirit; much as they are needed. Instead, we shall confine ourselves to a consideration of His work, first, in connection with the Saviour; second, in salvation; and third, in the saved. May the Spirit of Truth direct our hearts and minds, enabling us to write that which shall be to His honor and praise, and the good of God's people.

In contemplating the Spirit's work in connection with the Lord Jesus there are three dangers to be guarded against—may God grant us His preserving grace. First, going beyond the actual testimony of Holy Writ: this is impious presumption. Second, refusing to go as far as the teaching of Scripture goes: this is unwarrantable unbelief. Tihrd, reasoning upon and attempting to draw logical deductions from the declarations of the Word: this is sinful pride of intellect.

Now Scripture teaches that in all the works of the Godhead everything is **from** the Father, **through** the Son, **by** the Spirit. It has, we believe, been rightly said that, "In all the work of the Trinity, the Holy Spirit is the Personal Agent of the Godhead. In creation, providence, and redemption, He is the Executive Agent and Active Administrator" (S. Chadwick). This has not been sufficiently recognized by theologians. Were this fact better known to-day among God's people, there would be little in the remainder of this article calculated to awaken surprise. We fear that many of our readers will be well-nigh startled (so little is the Word studied to-day) when we affirm concerning Christ that His body was prepared by the Spirit, His opening faculties as a Child were under the control of the Spirit, His public teaching was directed by the Spirit, His miracles were wrought in the power of the Spirit. Yet so it was. Let us now prove and amplify these assertions.

1. The body of Christ was formed by the Spirit.

As to ordination and designation, His body was prepared in the eternal counsels and love by the Father (Heb. 10:5). As to voluntary assumption, it was taken upon Him by the Son (Heb. 2:14). But as to Divine efficacy, it was created by the Holy Spirit (Matt. 1:18, 20; Luke 1:35). He was the Divine Producer of this glorious body. The "power of the Highest" refers to the Holy Spirit in His supernatural working. His act was a creative one: not something out of nothing, but out of the substance of the virgin, for Isaiah 7:14 ascribes the "conceiving" to Mary herself. Eve was "created," but out of the substance of Adam; so too Adam was "created," but out of the dust of the ground.

It is all important that we should hold fast to the truth that the Saviour's body was formed, by the Spirit, out of the substance of Mary, for only thus could He be, truly, the seed of the woman (Gen. 3:15), the "Seed" of Abraham (Gal. 3:16), the "Seed" of David (Rom. 1:3). Only thus could He be a **kinsman**-Redeemer (Ruth 4). Nor would the genealogy be true if He were not Mary's Seed. So too the language of Heb. 2:14 affirms the same, otherwise there would have been no foundation for imputation. The miraculous "conception" was efficaciously of the Spirit, mediatorially of Mary. If Christ's humanity were not of Mary's substance He would not be true Man, but would belong to another order of beings. But the conception being under the immediate superintendence and by the creative operation of the Holy Spirit, prevented the transmission or derivation of any corruption or taint of sin. The body of Christ being formed pure by the Holy Spirit, there was no disposition or tendency in His constitution to the least deviation from perfect holiness.

"Although He took on Him those infirmities which belong unto our human nature as such, and are inseparable from it until it be glorified, yet He took none of our particular infirmities which cleave unto our persons, occasioned either by the vice of our constitutions or irregularity in the use of our bodies. Those natural passions of our minds which are capable of being the means of affliction and trouble, are grief, sorrow, and the like, He took upon Him; as also those infirmities of nature such as are troublesome to the body, as hunger, thirst, weariness and pain,—yea the purity of His bodily constitution made Him more highly sensitive of these things than any of the children of men:—but as to our bodily disorders and distempers, which personally adhere unto us, upon the disorder and vice of our constitution He was absolutely free from them" (Dr. J. Owen).

2. The Humanity of Christ was sanctified by the Spirit.

"The human nature of Christ being thus formed in the womb of Mary by a **creating act** of the Holy Spirit, was, in the instant of its conception, **sanctified** and filled with grace according to the measuure of its receptivity. Being not begotten by natural generation, it derived no taint of original sin or corruption from Adam, and, not being represented by the first man, his sin could not be imputed to Him. The sins of His people were charged to Him as the Mediator and Surety of the everlasting covenant; but on His own account, He was obnoxious to no charge of sin, original or actual. His human nature, miraculously created, was absolutely spotless" (Dr. J. Owen).

But more; the human nature of Christ was, by the Spirit, endowed with all grace. And this of necessity. No **creature** is able to live unto God apart from the Spirit. Thus we read in the word of prophecy, "And there shall come forth a rod out of the stem of Jesse, and a Branch shall grow out of his roots: And the Spirit of the Lord shall rest upon Him, the Spirit of wisdom and understanding, the Spirit of counsel and might, the Spirit of knowledge and of the fear of the Lord; And shall make Him of quick understanding" (Isa. 11:1-3). The fulfillment of this prediction must not be projected forward to the descent of the Spirit upon Christ at His baptism, as its opening words show. The first and immediate reference is to what the Holy Spirit communicated to the humanity of Christ in Mary's womb, and thus' His very humanity was designated "that **holy** thing" (Luke 1:35). The **exercise** of those spiritual graces was seen later; the **infusion** of them was at His incarnation.

3. The development of His faculties was under the superintendence of the Holy Spirit.

Two things are here to be diligently observed:—First, that the Lord Christ, as man, did and was to exercise all grace by the rational faculties and powers of His soul, His understanding, will, and affections; for He acted grace as a man, 'made of a woman, made under the law.' His Divine nature was not unto Him in the place of a soul, nor did immediatley operate the things which He performed, as some of old vainly imagined; but being a perfect man, His rational soul was in Him the immediate principle of all His moral operations, even as ours are in us. Now, in the improvement and exercise of those faculties of His soul, He had and made a progress after the manner of other men; for He was made like unto us 'in all things,' yet without sin. In their increase, enlargement, and exercise, there was required a progression in grace also; and this He had continually by the Holy Spirit: 'The Child grew and waxed strong in spirit.' The other respects the confirmation of the faculties of His mind—He waxed strong in spirit.' So, Luke 2:52, He is said to 'increase in wisdom,' Greek, continually 'filling and filled,' with new degrees of 'wisdom,' so to its exercise, according as the rational faculties of His mind were capable thereof; an increase of these things accompanied His years. And what is here recorded by the evangelist contains a description of the accomplishment of the prophecy before mentioned, Isa. 11:1-3. And this growth in grace and wisdom was the peculiar work of the Holy Spirit; for as the faculties of His mind were enlarged by degrees and strengthened, so the Holy Spirit filled them up with grace for actual obedience.

"Second, the human nature of Christ was capable of having **new objects** proposed to its mind and understanding, whereof it had a **simple nescience** (absence of knowledge). And this is an inseparable adjunct of human nature as such, as it is to be weary or hungry, and no vice or blameable defect. Some have made a great outcry about the ascribing of ignorance by some protestant divines unto the human soul of Christ. Take 'ignorance' for that which is a **moral defect** in any kind, or an unacquaintedness with that which any one **ought to know,** or is necessary unto him as to the perfection of his condition or his duty, and it is false that ever any of them ascribed it unto Him. Take it merely for a nescience of some things, and there is no more in it but a denial of infinite omniscience,—nothing inconsistent with the highest holiness and purity of human nature. So the Lord Christ says of Himself that He knew not the day and hour of His coming (Mark 13:32); and our apostle of Him, that He 'learned obedience by the things which He suffered,' Heb. 5:8. In the representation, then, of things anew to the human nature of Christ, the wisdom and knowledge of it was **objectively** increased, and in new trials and temptations He **experimentally** learned the new exercise of grace; and this was the constant work of the Holy Spirit in the human nature of Christ. He dwelt in Him in fulness; for He received Him not by measure" (Dr. J. Owen).

4. The discharge of His Messianic office was by the enduement of the Holy Spirit.

The very title "Christ" means "The **anointed** One," and was given Him in consequence of the peculiar unction of the Spirit conferred on Him, an unction which was **unique** in nature and degree. The Holy Spirit endued Christ with all the extraordinary powers and gifts which were necessary for His work on earth. "The Spirit of the Lord God is upon Me; because the Lord hath anointed Me to preach good tidings unto the meek; He hath sent Me to bind up the broken hearted, to proclaim liberty to the captives, and the opening of the prison to them that are bound" (Isa. 61:1). The Redeemer appropriated these words to Himself in Luke 4:18, 19. The historical reference is to what took place in His baptism (Matt. 3:17). It was then that He was "sealed" by the Father (John 6:27), in that visible pledge of His vocation, setting the great seal of Heaven to His commision. It was then that God 'anointed Jesus of Nazareth with the Holy Spirit" (Acts 10:38). His **need** for this lay in the Servant-place which He had taken, and the humanity which He had assumed. He was now "full of the Holy Spirit" (Luke 4:1).

5. The Temptation-triumph was by the power of the Spirit.

"And Jesus being full of the Holy Spirit returned from Jerusalem, and was led by the Spirit into the wilderness" (Luke 5:1). The reason why God has informed us that Jesus was "**led by the Spirit** . . . to be tempted," seems to be for the purpose of making known to us that His human nature was confirmed by the Spirit and strengthened by His power. The word "driveth" in Mark 1:12 denotes a high and strong impression made by the Spirit upon His mind. The same Greek word is rendered "thrust forth" in Matt. 9:38, where the reference is to the Lord of the harvest **constraining** His servants.

In his remarks upon the great temptation and the relation of the Holy Spirit to Christ, Dr. Owen has said: 1. The Holy Spirit guided Him to begin His contest with and conquest of the Devil. 2. By His assistance was He carried triumphantly through the course of His temptations unto a perfect conquest of His adversary as to the present conflict. 3. The temptation being finished, He returned again out of the wilderness, to preach the Gospel 'in the power of the Spirit' (Luke 4:14). 4. By Him was He directed, strengthened, comforted, in His whole course, in all His temptations, troubles and sufferings, from first to last; for we know that there was a confluence of all these upon Him in His whole way and work, a great part of that whereunto He humbled Himself for our sakes in these things. In and under them He stood in need of mighty supportment and strong consolation. This God promised Him, and this He expected: Isaiah 42:4, 6; 49:5-8; 50:7, 8 (the reader will do well to weigh carefully these passages A. W. P.). Now, all the voluntary communications of the Divine nature unto the human were by the Holy Spirit."

6. The works of Christ were by the energy of the Spirit.

If the passages in John's Gospel where Christ refers to His "works" be consulted, it will be found that they consisted of His **teaching and** His miracles—cf. Luke 24:19. For His teaching see Isa. 61:1, 2: he was "anointed **to** preach." So again in John 3:34: "For He whom God hath sent speaketh the words of God (which is a clear reference to Christ Himself—see preceding verses), **for** God giveth not the Spirit by measure unto Him." For His miracles we would refer to Acts 2:22, Matt. 12:28.

7. The atoning sacrifice of Christ was offered to God through the agency of the Holy Spirit.

This is plainly stated in Heb. 9:14: "How much more shall the blood of Christ, who through the eternal Spirit offered Himself without spot to God, purge your conscience from dead works?" Those who look only at the external death of Christ can see nothing but suffering in it: wicked hands took Him, scourged and slew Him. But the anointed eye discovers, from the teaching of Scripture, that the principal thing about His death was that Christ offered Himself as a sacrifice unto God, as the great High Priest, to make satisfaction for the sins of His people; and this He did by "the eternal Spirit:" He was moved and energized by the Spirit. This was plainly foreshadowed in the types of old, by the "fire" (emblem of the Spirit) which wafted the "sweet savour" of the sacrifice heavenwards: Lev. 9:23, 24 cf. Acts 2:3, Dan. 7:10. "The Holy Spirit was the impelling power which animated Christ from within to response to the awful commission without" (Prof. Smeaton), see John 10:17. This reference to the "eternal Spirit" shows the unison of the Godhead in the great work of redemption. The same Spirit which led Him into the wilderness (Matt. 4:1), also led Him, as a willing Victim, to the cross.

8. The dead body of Christ was under the guardianship of the Spirit.

"There was a peculiar work of the Holy Spirit towards the Lord Christ while He was in the **state of the dead;** for here our preceding rule must be remembered,—namely, that notwithstanding the union of the human nature of Christ with the divine person of the Son, yet the communications of God unto it, beyond subsistance, were **voluntary**. Thus, in His death the union of His natures in His person was not in the least impeached; but yet for His soul or spirit, He commits that in an especial manner into the hands of the Father (Luke 23:46), for the Father had engaged Himself in an eternal covenant to take care of Him, to preserve and protect Him even in death, and to show Him again the 'path of life' (Psa. 16:11). Notwithstanding then, the union of His person, His soul in a separate state was in an especial manner under the care, protection, and power of His Father preserved in His love until the hour came wherein He showed Him again the path of life.

"His holy body in the grave continued under the especial care of the Spirit of God; and hereby was accomplished that great promise, that 'His soul should not be left in Hell, nor the Holy One see corruption' (Psa. 16:10). It is the body of Christ which is here called 'the Holy One,' as it was made a 'holy thing' by the conception of it in the womb by the power of the Holy Spirit. (Luke 1:35). And it is here spoken of in contradistinction unto His soul. This pure and holy substance was preserved in its integrity by the overshadowing power of the Holy Spirit. I deny not but that there was use made of the ministry of angels about the dead body of Christ whilst it was in the grave (John 20:12); by these was it preserved from all outward force and violation;—but this also was under the peculiar care of the Spirit of God." (Dr. J. Owen).

9. The resurrection of Christ was by the Spirit of God.

"This being the completing act in laying the foundation of the church, whereby Christ entered into His rest,—the great testimony given unto the finishing of the work of redemption, with the salvation of God therein, and His acception of the person of the Redeemer. It is, on various grounds, assigned distinctly to each person in the Trinity; and this not only as all the external works of God are undivided, each person being equally concerned in their operation, but also upon the account of their especial respect unto and interest in the work of redemption. Unto the Father it is ascribed, on the account of His authority: Acts 2:24. The same work Christ also took upon Himself: John 10:17, 18. But the peculiar efficacy in the re-uniting of His most holy soul and body was an effect of the power of the Holy Spirit" (Dr. J. Owen).

This is expressly affirmed in 1 Peter 3:18, "Being put to death in the flesh, but quickened by the Spirit." To the same purpose we are told, "If the Spirit of Him that raised up Jesus from the dead dwell in you, He that raised up Christ from the dead shall also quicken your mortal bodies by His Spirit that dwelleth in you." So too in Rom. 1:4 we are told that Christ was declared to be "the Son of God with power, acording to the Spirit of holiness by the resurrection from the dead." If verses three and four be read together, it will be found that they present a contrast, not between the two natures of Christ, but between two states He was in: His humiliation, His exaltation.

10. The glorifying of Christ's humanity was by the Spirit.

"It was the Holy Spirit that glorified the human nature of Christ, and made it every way meet for its eternal residence at the right hand of God, and a pattern of the glorification of the bodies of them that believe in Him. He who first made His nature **holy**, now made it **glorious**" (Dr. J. Owen). It was to this the ancient oracle of Psa. 45:7 looked forward: "Therefore God, Thy God, hath anointed Thee with the oil of gladness above Thy fellows." This was fulfilled at the ascension. That this prophecy included much more than the glorification of Christ's humanity is freely granted, but that **this** is the **first** thing referred to in it is our firm conviction.

11. The Ministry of Christ after His resurrection was by the Spirit.

Clear proof of this is furnished in Acts 1:2, upon which we make no attempt to enlarge.

12. The Bestowment of the Spirit by Christ.

Of old it was said, "Thou hast ascended on high, Thou hast led captivity captive; Thou hast received gifts for men" (Psa. 68:18). Reference was made to this by Peter on the day of Pentecost: "Therefore being by the right hand of God exalted, and having received of the Father the promise of the Holy Spirit, He hath shed forth this, which ye now see and hear" (Acts 2:33). This was the fruit of the atonement, for the inestimable blessing and ineffable gift of the Spirit was purchased for His people by Christ. This is clear from Gal. 3:13, 14: note carefully the second "that" (in order that) in v. 14. "The promised Spirit followed the great work of cancelling the curse as the effect follows the cause" (Prof. Smeaton).

A few lines need to be added so as to guard against the reader drawing erroneous conclusions from what has been said above. Let it not be imagined that our blessed Saviour was, personally, little more than an automaton in the "days of His flesh," or that we have leanings toward the blasphemous theory that when the Son of God took upon Him the form of a servant He was emptied of His Diety. Nor will we allow for a moment that His own Divine attributes and prerogatives were held in abeyance during the time He tabernacled on earth. Even as a Babe in the manger He was "Christ **the Lord**" (Luke 2:10)! In His "I will" of Matt. 8:3 and John 17:24 there was the exercise of Divine prerogative. No, the Scriptures quoted in this article have to do with the relation of the Holy Spirit to Christ's **humanity**, and to the discharge of **His** mediatorial **office**. In His **person** Christ was none other than "Immanuel" (Matt. 1:23).

Nor have we any sympathy with those who have **reasoned** from the above Scriptures and drawn erroneous conclusions that the power and gifts of the Holy Spirit are equally available for Christians if they have "appropriating faith." It is not without reason that we are told "God giveth not the Spirit by measure **unto Him**" (John 3:34). Christ has been anointed with the oil of gladness (a clear reference to the Holy Spirit according to the language of the types) **above** His fellows (Psa. 45:7). In **all** things He "has the preeminence." We have received **only** the "first fruits of the Spirit" (Rom. 8:23), an "earnest" (2 Cor. 1:22) of that which awaits us above, when "we all come in the unity of the faith, and of the knowledge of the Son of God, unto a perfect man, unto the measure of the stature of the fulness of Christ" (Eph. 4:13).

We cannot do better than conclude with another quotation from Prof. Smeaton: "That we may not be engulfed in one-sidedness, it must be also added that the Spirit, according to the order of the Trinity, interposes His power only to execute the will of the Son. And so far is this from interfering with the glory of the Son, it rather reveals Him more conspicuously, that in the work of redemption the operations of the Spirit are next in order to those of the Son. The two natures of our Lord **actively concurred** in every mediatorial act. If He assumed human nature in the true and proper sense of the term into union with His divine person, that position must be maintained.

"The Socinian objection that there could be no further need for the Spirit's agency and, in fact, no room for it,—if the Divine nature was active in the whole range of Christ's mediation—is meant to perplex the question, because these men deny the existence of any Divine nature in Christ's person. That style of reasoning is futile; for the question simply is, What do the Scriptures teach? Do they affirm that Christ **was anointed by the Spirit**? (Acts 10:38), that He was led out into the wilderness by the Spirit? that He returned in the power of the Spirit? No warrant exists for anything akin to that **Kenotic** or depotentiation theory which denudes Him of esential attributes of the Godhead, and puts His humanity on a near level with that of other men. And as little warrant exists for denying the Spirit's work on Christ's humanity in every mediatorial act which He performed on earth or performs in Heaven.

"The unction of the Spirit must be traced in all His personal and official gifts. In Christ the Person and the office coincide. In His Divine Person He was the substance of all the offices to which He was appointed; and these He was fitted by the Holy Spirit to discharge. The offices would be nothing apart from **Himself**, and could have neither coherence nor validity without the underlying Person. The Holy Spirit, supplying Christ's humanity with light and strength for His mediatorial work, was, according to the Divine order, only carrying out the will of the Son and interposing His power to execute the intimations of the Son. The Spirit's operations **revealed** the will and purpose of the Son.

"From the statements already adduced in reference to Christ's unction for all His offices, it sometimes appears as if He were in the subordinate position of needing direction, aid, and miraculous power for the purposes of His mission; at other times He is said to **give** the Spirit and to **send** the Spirit, as if the Spirit's operations were subordinated to the Son. It is however, evident from the whole tenor of Scripture, that there was a conjoined mission in which the Son and the Spirit acted together for the salvation of God's elect, according to the well known order of operation in the Trinity."

—ARTHUR W. PINK.

MATTERS OF FIRST IMPORTANCE

When we see religious worldings blindly reversing God's order—putting works before faith, and walk before life, and vainly attempting to reach Christ through the Church instead of reaching the Church through Christ—we rightly pity them, and should seek by all means to show such the way of God. But there is the same natural tendency in us all to overlook the weightier parts of the will of God while pressing some minor points into prominence. And shall we indulge that in ourselves which we deplore in others, and not rather honestly examine all our ways to bring them into conformity to the will of God?

In our Lord's discourse upon the Mount, as given in Matt. 5-7, we find the word **first** three times used and in striking connections, which, but a slight reference to our own hearts and some little acquaintance with the ways of saints show us, are of great importance as bearing on our worship, life and service.

1. Our Worship.

"If thou bring thy gift to the altar and there rememberest that thy brother hath ought against thee, leave there thy gift before the altar; go thy way, **first** be reconciled to thy brother, and then come and offer thy gift" (Matt. 5:23, 24). Although these lessons on the Mount were not intended to set forth the distinctive truths of Christianity as afterwards unfolded by our precious Lord to the circle of His "own" in John 13-17, and further developed through His servant Paul, yet do they enforce truths and principles of priceless worth to us as the children of "Our Father which is in heaven." Our double relationship comes out very clearly in Matt. 5-7, as no doubt that of Israel in coming kingdom days. The word "Father" in connection with us occurs sixteen times, and the word "brother" seven times in this discourse. God is **our Father** and every one of His children is **our brother.** The latter springs out of the former. For our relationship with each other as brethren rests upon our common relation to God as our Father. It was a happy day when I could first take my place before God in the full consciousness of my eternal relationship with Him as His child, through faith in Christ Jesus; to know the unspeakable joy of "fellowship with the Father, and His Son Jesus Christ." And it is a blessed thing too, to learn that there is a "brotherhood" formed of all such as know the riches of His grace to them in Christ— a redeemed, regenerated company upon the earth now; a heavenly circle in which no "stranger or foreigner" participates; a family unlike all the families of earth, all begotten of the same Father, quickened into the same life in Christ, and born of the same Spirit; dear to the Father's heart, whose love has called them to have and enjoy fellowship with Himself and with one another.

But how slow we are to realize, though in measure we recognise, this spiritual relationship! This arises, no doubt, from the fact that it is **a purely spiritual relationship,** while every one who forms it, though made "spiritual" (as a new creation in Christ), is still indwelt by the flesh, which lusteth against the Spirit. All our difficulties with each other as children of God spring from this old root. There would be no jarring discords or divisions among saints but for the allowance of the flesh in us; never would brother trespass against his brother but for this; never should we see "a brother offended" amongst us if this "old man" were kept practically under. But just because we who live in the Spirit are so liable to walk in the flesh, in some of its many forms, the very nearness of our relationship brings us into special danger. What a display of the corruption of the flesh does it make that the life and love of God within us should so little control and characterise our dealings with one another!

It is comparatively easy to bring our gift to the altar, and maintain the proper form and semblance of worship, for the flesh is not disturbed, but rather satisfied with its own form of worship. Cain was forward to bring his gift to the altar, and then went forth to slay his brother, and we are warned against his spirit by John, for "If a man say, I love God, and hateth his brother, he is a liar; for he that loveth not his brother whom he hath seen, how can he love God whom he hath not seen? And this commandment have we from Him, that he who loveth God love his brother also" (1 John 4:20, 21). This is the law of love in which we are commanded to walk, but if this has been violated, and my brother "hath ought against me," the **first** thing is to be reconciled to my brother. Not merely to feel willing, not merely to seek reconciliation, but so to act as to secure it, and that before drawing near to God publicly. To say, "Let him come and show me my fault," will not do; I must **go my way,** even from the altar, and leave the great question of approaching God in abeyance, until I have approached my brother and become reconciled. Until this is done God will have no respect to my offering, He will bear no testimony to my gifts. It is only when brethren "dwell together in unity" that the Holy Spirit is ungrieved amongst saints, and where the "unity of the Spirit" is kept, God's blessing rests.

Oh, what power and blessing might be ours still if, as brethren, we were together "with one accord!" But, in looking back at our history, or on present circumstances in many assemblies, instead of spiritual concord how often has brother been separated in heart and spirit from brother, while the outward form of fellowship has been well kept! And so wide has been the breach in some instances that brethren have "preached at" and "prayed at" each other in the meeting, only to drive each other further apart. If this sorrowful state of things continues everything spiritual must be paralyzed, and the whole assembly thrown into disorder, "For where envying and strife is there is confusion and every evil work" (James 3:16). How can the saints be edified and comforted, or the Gospel go forth with power, until estranged hearts are "knit together in love?" For if the channels are not clear the spiritual supply must be hindered.

We are instructed, therefore, how to set such a matter right, and nothing can be plainer or more binding than the rule here laid down by our Lord, "Go thy way, **first** be reconciled to thy brother, and then come and offer thy gift." Go **thy** way; each one concerned in the estrangement must be ready to act in grace, not waiting for the other to "come round." It is just here the difficulty comes in; we are so sure to find the greatest obstacle in our own selves; we are so loath to come down from our position, so eager to prove our side of it right, and to secure our own honour, that we forget the Lord's honour, or mistake our own for the Lord's glory. Whereas, if our hearts were set for His glory, we should at any cost to ourselves seek it by keeping His commandments to love one another (John 13:34).

"**First** be reconciled to thy brother." It may be a work that needs delicate handling and much prayerful diligence, for "A brother offended is harder to be won than a strong city, and their **contentions** are like the bars of a castle" (Prov. 18:19). But the extreme difficulty cannot relieve us from the obligation. However repugnant to flesh and blood, or humbling to our natural pride, our own feelings must be laid aside, with "all malice and all guile, and hypocrisies, and envies, and all evil speakings." We must by the grace of God conquer the greater difficulty——the flesh in ourselves, then it will be easier to overcome the lesser in the brother who has somewhat against us. May the Lord give us grace to obey His own Word.

In Matt. 18 we have the other side of the matter, "If thy brother **trespass against thee**, go and tell him his fault between thee and him alone." Putting the two sides together, we see that the **first** thing is for each to go to the other. The offender in chapter 5, and the offended in chapter 18 are both instructed, not to "go **for** one another," but to go **to** each other, and if this were more often done in the spirit of forgiveness reconciliation would follow, divisions would be healed, contentions cease, and untold evils be averted. The closing words, "Then come and offer thy gift," intimate that our offering of praise and service rendered would be acceptable to God, and thus the most blessed results would inevitably follow. Since our happiness is not secured by knowing, but by doing these things, may the Lord greatly help us to put them into constant practice.

2. Our Walk.

In our life before men, is there not a solemn evidence of a very general reversal of the Master's injunction, "Seek ye **first** the kingdom of God and His righteousness, and all these things (that ye have need of) shall be added unto you" (Matt. 6:33)?

In the last ten verses of this chapter the Lord gives us seven great reasons for not being **anxious** or "of doubtful mind" about the necessities of this life. First, He who gives us the greater—life and the body—will not withhold the lesser—food and raiment (v. 25). Second, He who feedeth the fowls of the air will **much more** care for His own children (v. 26). Third, besides, our anxiety will not really improve matters; it is of no avail, we cannot turn the wheels of providence (v. 27). Fourth, even God's lavish expenditure on things inanimate inspire confidence as to the certainty of our Father's care for us (v. 28). Fifth, and again, to be so concerned about earthly things is to act like the world, and is most unworthy of the children of God (vv. 31, 32). Sixth, is not the Father's knowledge of our needs, and well-known readiness to supply them, ever enough for faith? (v. 32). Seventh, beyond a doubt all these things **shall certainly be added** to all who seek

first the kingdom of God (v. 33). Surely this ought to be enough to set our minds at rest, and furnish us with some leisure and heart for the things of God. What can we want more?

"What meaneth, then, this bleating of the sheep in mine ears, and this lowing of the oxen which I hear?" Are there any Sauls in our day accumulating luxurious hoards of Amalekites' spoil, at the unspeakable loss of the Kingdom, which far outshines that forfeited by Saul? That strange noise in the camp is not the voice of them that shout for mastery, neither is it the voice of them that cry from being overcome. Spiritual warfare and victory are out of the question when the golden calf is set up and worshipped; for "He that warreth entangleth not himself with the affairs of this life." A sorry soldier was Achan, who, by coveteousness, brought death to himself, disaster to his house, and defeat to the whole army of Israel.

Oh, that the "Achan's" and the "Saul's" with all who today allow things of earth to govern the heart, could be persuaded, or at least reminded, that we are not called to live delicately on the earth, in self-indulgence, nourishing the heart in a day of slaughter (James 5:5), but to live soberly, righteously, and godly in this present world, nourishing our hearts, by looking for that blessed hope, so that we love His appearing.

It may be our blessed Lord threshed out this matter in such detail, in view of our special danger of allowing cares for today and anxieties for tomorrow, discontent with the necessaries and lust for the luxuries of life, as to crowd out of our minds and hearts "the kingdom of God and His righteousness," well knowing that the seed of the Kingdom is ofttimes choked with "the cares and riches and pleasures of this life;" and brings forth no fruit to perfection.

It is startling to see the tide of worldliness rising fast among Christians almost everywhere, with a coresponding ebb in the desire for spiritual prosperity; on all hands there are abounding symptoms of spiritual decay, which it is to be feared will be followed by increasing ambition for fleshly advantage. Our Master's question may well ring in our ears and consciences today: "What **do** ye more than others?" Not what **know** ye more than others? We may pride ourselves on knowing the things of God, which the poor worldling cannot possibly perceive, but if we spend all our energies, crowd our minds, engage our affections, and tax our wits for present worldly advantage, do not the men of this world the same? If we content ourselves with just the Lord's day observances and meetings, do not religious worldlings the same? If we do not bring forth the fruit of the Spirit in a godly walk, in faithful testimony, and devoted service, what do we more than others? The most convincing book to the worldling is our manner of living, but if, withal, we are as hard in our dealing, as keen for selfish gains, as inconsiderate for others' rights in our bargains, as shrewd and tricky in running our business as the most wide-awake worldling, he will not believe the book, for its author is a living contradiction.

But the sad result is that Christ is wounded again in the house of His friends, and His holy Name is dishonoured. He is misjudged by His foes, because misrepresented by His friends. It is one thing to be saved by Christ, and quite another to be satisfied with Him; but very many claim His as Saviour who never seem to make any further acquaintance with Him. As the one Centre in the midst of all, the one Lord above all, and the one Object above all, how little is He known; and while the conscience has been relieved by His work, the heart is not attracted to His Person, and therefore is not detached from the world and worldly aims. When Christ is engraven on the heart, we become His epistle, we speak for Him in our life before all men; but when the spirit of worldliness has seized the citadel Christ is either veiled, or so distorted is the view of Him, through us, that the unsaved are driven from Him rather than drawn to Him.

It is utterly impossible to run the heavenly and earthly business on the same level; one or the other must be on the top; the mind cannot be set on things above and on things on the earth with equal devotion. Both cannot be "**first**:" one or the other must be. One must increase, the other must decrease. The question is, Which shall I make my object?—"The kingdom of God and His righteousness," or "all these things" after which the world is seeking? Never was a greater mistake than to think I can compete with the worldling in the pursuits, the possessions, the pleasures, and the politics of earth, and finally come off as a Spiritual overcomer. No: that which ministers to the flesh wars against the soul, and it is impossible to secure the present without loss, both present and future, for "he that loveth his life shall lose it." Let us honestly examine our ways, as to which of the two objects is occupying the supreme place in our hearts—Christ or self. Do we "mind earthly things," or is "our conversation in heaven" (Phil. 3)? Have we counted the cost of true discipleship, to suffer the loss of all fleshly gain, for the surpassing gain of Christ? Which is it to be? May the earnest cry of our souls be: "search me, O God, and know my heart; try me and know my thoughts; and see if there be any wicked way in me, and lead me in the way everlasting."

3. Our Service.

We have looked at the matter of **first importance** in relation to our worship and walk. We come now to that which must be **first** in our service one to another (Matt. 7:3-5). In each of the three great spheres of our life as Christians—toward God, before men, and among brethren—we are reminded of what must ever be the primary necessity. There are three things noticeable in this passage. First, the discovery of a mote in a brother's eye (v. 3); next, the offer of a voluntary service to remove it (v. 4); and then the only way in which this can be effectually done, and what it involves (v. 5).

1. Beholding the mote in our brother's eye is intended to illustrate a very common tendency amongst us of turning our eyes toward our brethren for the discovery of their fault, instead of using them to search out our own; it also intimates that this is done, not occasionally through the attraction of some glaring mishap, but habitually. "**Beholdest**" means that it is a continuous thing. It further points out a most lamentable **weakness** in us, that proneness to overlook all the general features of a brother's character, however praiseworthy, and fasten the gaze upon the smallest spot and the least speck that is wrong with him, though it can hardly be discerned. But it does more, it proves that this is hypocrisy, for those who are quick-sighted and fore-sighted to spie out the mote in their brother's eye, do not, for lack of ability or lack of inclination, or perhaps honesty, consider the **beam** that is in their own eye.

It is easy and natural to point out a small sin in my brother, while allowing a very great one in myself, whereas my own faults should appear greater and graver to me than the same faults in a brother. If I cultivated the habit of self-judgment instead of being severe with the sin of others and indulgent with my own, I should then "**consider the beam**" in my own eye, that is, I should first deal with my own faults with unsparing judgment, and then with my brother's, if necessary, in the spirit of meekness.

How unconscious are we naturally of our personal failings. As with a mote or a beam in the eye, we are powerless to discover that which is lodged in our own flesh, and the greater the evil the less able are we able to perceive it in ourselves. Those who are the most faulty are too often the least conscious of it, and usually the first to find out the faults of others, and the most unsparing to condemn them. It was not the brother with a mote in his eye that discovered the beam in his brother's, but he with the **beam,** although, undoubtedly, the former could see more clearly of the two. May we have grace to examine ourselves, and to mortify our own members, for if we would judge ourselves, we should not be jjudged.

2. Then, "How wilt thou say to thy brother, Let me pull out the mote out of thine eye; and behold a **beam** is in thine own eye?" There is nothing wrong in offering to remove the mote surely, for it is offensive to us, how much more is it painful to the brother himself! In itself it is a brotherly action. We are not to be blind or indifferent to each other's welfare, but it must be by love that we serve one another and wash one another's feet.

If a brother be overtaken in a fault, to neglect him, or leave him alone to drift, would be most blameworthy, much less should we lend our tongues to retail the wrong; by all means seek to restore such, but the spiritual only are able, for this must be done in the spirit of meekness, by those who have learned to consider themselves, lest they also be tempted. It is not every one who is skillful enough to perform this difficult operation, for it requires a delicate touch. At the same time let no one excuse himself from the responsibility. "Thou shalt not hate thy brother; thou shalt in any wise rebuke thy neighbour, and not suffer sin upon him" was God's express command to the Israelite; so may we never forget that it is not the will of our Father that one of these little ones should perish. But from the extreme difficulty of doing this in a manner not to be a further cause of stumbling to an erring brother or sister, no service calls for more prayer, delicacy of feeling and meekness of wisdom. It must be done just to "relieve my own mind" and to have "a clear conscience." The motive must be nothing less than love, the manner nothing else than showing "the kindness of God."

Even a well-meaning word may be entirely out of place, and produce contempt rather than conviction. It must be a word in season, and "a word fitly spoken" from lips that know what is acceptable, if it is to be a blessing, for "as an earring of gold and an ornament of fine gold, so is a wise reprover upon an obedient ear" (Prov. 25:12).

3. "Thou hypocrit, first cast out the beam out of thine own eye, and then shalt thou see clearly to cast out the mote out of thy brother's eye." He who would point to a brother's wrong and seek to set him right, must first consider his own weakness, so as to be free in himself of that which he seeks to remove from another, or endless sorrow may result from an ungracious attempt to deal with another's faults by one who has worse forms of evil in himself "neither considered" nor "cast out." Zeal for judging evil without honesty and impartiality enough to detect and judge personal errors, is indeed grievous hypocrisy, for to deal with another's fault supposes that I am free from (that) wrong myself, and an enemy to the evil in question.

Let us therefore have grace to diligently "consider" and "cast out" first our own beam, that we may "see clearly" to cast out the mote from our brother's eye, or our best attempts will be nothing better than an ungracious judgment of the sin in another, which has grown to more terrible proportions in ourselves.

E. VENN.
From "The Witness," 1901.

Jesus Christ being your life and light; your righteousness and purity; your peace and joy; your crown and glory; your salvation and blessedness; you have in Him everything which can make you happy on earth, and perfectly so in the heaven of heavens. It is given unto you to see from the Word, and by the Spirit, that your whole salvation is in the immaculate Lamb. That your everlasting all depends on His life of obedience, and death of expiation. Your faith consists in believing the Godhead of Jesus. The perfection of His life, the everlasting virtue and efficacy of His blood and death. The Father's delight and complacency, in the person and work of Immanuel, with His full acceptance of Him, as the Mediator, here your faith centres. In God, as reconciled unto you by the death of His Son, you triumph. Seeing yourself one with Christ, you know that you are complete with Him. What you are in Him is the foundation of all your hope and confidence in God. You are not so impure in yourself, as you are pure in Christ, You have not so much cause to distrust yourself, as you have cause to trust in Jesus. You have not that fulness of sin in you, that cannot be overmatched and exceeded by Christ's infinite, immutable, overflowing fulness. In Christ you are holy, righteous, and spotless in your heavenly Father's sight. Living in the belief of it, is a great part of our life of faith, I know, my dear sir, few will be found who so believe and live. With all the preaching and printing, 'tis few indeed who know Jesus, and the power of His resurrection. I have been, you are, tired in heart, to see how few know our Jesus in the Word, and have their minds enlightened by the glorious Gospel of the blessed God. Yet so it is, minds enlightened by the glorious Gospel of the blessed God. Yet so it is, 'tis but here and there a person is really taken with Jesus.

If we look into the churches, few preach Jesus. The people are taken with anything except Christ. Christ is too little known, and most awfully neglected. So that one would wish for long life, great strength of body, and much opportunity to set forth Christ, let the consequence be what it may.—Extract from Letters of S. E. Pierce, 1796.

He that hath Christ for his King and God, let him be assured he hath the Devil for his enemy, who will work him much sorrow, and will plague him all the days of his life. But let this be our comfort and great glory, that we poor people have the Lord of life and death, and of all creatures, clothed with our flesh and blood, sitting at the right hand of God the Father, who ever liveth to make intercession for us, defendeth and protecteth us.

—Martin Luther.

brethren fervently, faithfully, untiringly, after the same patient, unwearied, tender manner that Christ loves them. The Lord Jesus displayed a love which deemed no sacrifice too great.

"By this shall all know that ye are My disciples, if ye have love one to another" (John 13:35). Love is the **badge** of Christian discipleship. It is not knowledge, zeal, orthodoxy, or attention to ordinances, but **love**, which most clearly identifies a follower of the Lord Jesus. As the disciples of the Pharisees were known by their phylacteries, as the disciples of John were known by their baptism, and every school by its particular shibboleth, so the mark of a true Christian is **love**; and that, a spiritual, genuine, active love: not in words, but in deeds. Where such love is exhibited, then it is **known** that the exercisers of it are truly the disciples of the Lord of love; where such love is not seen, a doubt is raised.

"These things I command you, that ye love one another" (John 15:17). "There is something peculiarly searching and heart-rebuking in this. How humbling to find that Christ had to **command** us to love one another! How humbling to hear Him **repeating** this command, for He had already given this same command to His disciples (John 13:34)! And how humbling to find Him repeating it here, **again**, for He had just said, 'This is My commandment That ye love one another, as I have loved you' (1. 12)! Was it because He foresaw how little Christian love **would be** exercised among His people? Was it because He knew how much there is in each of us that is **unlovely**? Was it because He foresaw the Devil would stir up bitterness and strife among His followers, seeking to make them bite and devour one another?" (From the Editor's Exposition of John's Gospel).

"But as touching brotherly love ye need not that I write unto you; for ye yourselves are taught of God to love one another" (1 Thess. 4:9). This, too, though most blessed, is very humbling: Christians have to be "taught of God" **to** "love one another." This clearly shows us, once more, that the "love" of which the New Testament speaks is not the product of nature, but of grace. And **how** does God "teach" His children to love one another? By His written Word; in no other way. And that, in no mere mechanical or intellectual fashion, but by bringing home His Word in power to them, by writing it upon their hearts. In the case of the Thessalonian saints, there was no need for the apostle exhorting them to this duty: they were so filled with the Spirit, so putting into practice the oral teaching they had received, he could speak of their "labour of love" (1 Thess. 1:3). Alas that conditions are now so different, Because iniquity abounds, the love of many waxes cold (Matt. 24:12): selfishness is eating out the roots of spirituality; therefore God's people **have** "need" that one write them thereon.

Now true love ever seeks the good of its object, and grudges nothing that will promote its highest well-being. Spiritual love is operative, active, energetic. Love prays for, desires and labours to **serve** both the souls and bodies of our brethren and sisters in Christ. It goes about doing good; it is ever seeking opportunities to minister unto and edify another. Not that it pets and pampers, nor fawns and flatters. Love can be stern, as well as gentle. There are times when love has to wound (Heb. 12:6) as well as heal. Love is more than a sentiment, more than a beautiful ideal; it is intensely practical. It performs every good office in its power. Therefore "Love is the fulfilling of the law" (Rom. 13:10).

During our travels, we have heard many Christians complain that there is very little love exercised among the people of God today. That is all the more reason why **we** should show love to them. Mere talk is worthless; actions speak louder than words. "But whoso hath this world's good, and seeth his brother have need, and shutteth up his bowels from him, how dwelleth the love of God in him?" (1 John 3:17). How many professing Christians measure up to this standard? Numbers of God's children are poor, very poor in this world's goods. Alas, how few of their wealthier brethren think of ministering to their needs. It is not without reason that the apostle adds in the very next verse, "My little children, let us not love in word, neither in tongue; but in deed and in truth."

God is love; and the more we are in real communion with Him, the more shall we love His people. The one whose Epistles have the most to say about love, is the apostle who leaned upon the bosom of the Lord of Love! If we are brought into more intimate fellowship with Him then will it be our joy to minister rather than be ministered unto, to make ourselves of no reputation, to esteem no service too lowly. "Be kindly affectioned one to another with brother love; in honour preferring one another" (Rom. 12:10). May Divine grace make us more loving and loveable, conforming us daily to Him who is "Altogether Lovely."

—ARTHUR W. PINK.

Vol. VIII. OCTOBER, 1929 No. 10

STUDIES IN THE SCRIPTURES

"Search the Scriptures" John 5 : 39

Copyright in all English-speaking Countries.

Editor: Arthur W. Pink, Morton's Gap, Ky., U. S. A.
Hon. Agent in England: Mr. A. Winstone, 2, Lennox Villas, Hewlett Road, Cheltenham.
Hon. Agent in Australia: Mr. G. Ardill, The Christian Workers' Depot.
Commonwealth and Reservoir Streets, Sydney.

FREE TO ALL WHO WILL READ IT.

Profession Tested

"He that saith, I know Him, and keepeth not His commandments, is a liar, and the truth is not in him" (1 John 2:4).

There are, in all probability, a far greater number of nominal Christians on earth today than ever before. When we take into consideration the vast extensions which have been made in the boundaries of Christendom during the last century both at home and abroad, when we note the multiplication of "churches," seminaries, Bible institutes, etc., when we attempt to calculate the millions who are members of the numerous sects and denominations, and then compare them (as far as is possible) with those of previous generations, we believe we are quite safe in saying that there is a vastly larger number today who profess to be believers in and followers of the Lord Jesus Christ than ever before. On the other hand, we sincerely doubt whether there ever was a time during the last nineteen centuries when there were such multitudes of men and women whose lives belied their lips, whose walk repudiates their talk.

Not only are there hundreds of thousands of those whose names are yet preserved on "church-rolls" and "registers" who never attend a prayer-meeting and who are present at the Sabbath services only once or twice each year, not only are there millions of professing Christians who rarely if ever read the Scriptures for themselves, and who are in total ignorance of its most elementary teachings, not only is it evident to any God fearing man or woman with anointed eye that vain are the spiritual pretensions of the vast multitudes in Christendom who are "lovers of pleasure more than lovers of God" (2 Tim. 3); but, it is greatly to be feared that many, very many of those who **have** considerable head knowledge of God's truth, and who **be** regular attenders at preaching services, Bible conferences, etc., are, nevertheless, deceived souls. "There is a generation that is pure in their own eyes, and yet is not washed from their filthiness" (Prov. 30:12).

Yes, there are not only some isolated individuals who are "pure in their own eyes," who claim to have been cleansed from all sin by the precious blood of Christ, but there is a whole "generation" of such, who, nevertheless, "is not washed from their filthiness." As the Lord Jesus declared, "Many will say to Me in that day. Lord, Lord, have we not prophesied in Thy name? and in Thy name have cast out demons? and in Thy name done many wonderful works? And then will I profess unto them, I never knew you: depart from Me, ye that work iniquity" (Matt. 7:22, 23). The mere fact that a man believes the Bible to be the Word of God, proves nothing: "The demons also believe, and tremble" (James 2:19). That a person is sincere in regarding himself as on the road to Heaven, proves nothing: "There is a way which seemeth right unto a man, but the end thereof are the ways of death" (Prov. 14:12). A man may have "all knowledge," faith to "remove mountains," bestow all his goods "to feed the poor," yea, give his body "to be burned;" yet if he has not love—that love which is expressed and manifested by obedience to Christ's word (John 14:23)—then is he "nothing" (1 Cor. 13:2), and if "nothing," certainly not a regenerated child of God.

A tree is known by its fruits. This is an infallible criterion, both in the natural and spiritual realm. "Even so **every** good tree bringeth forth good fruit; but a

(Continued on Page 240)

IMPORTANT NOTICES

Please advise promptly of change of address, otherwise copies will be lost in the mails.

We are glad to send a sample copy to any of our friends whom you believe would be interested in such a publication.

Send to Mr. I. C. Herendeen, 433-435, The Arcade, Cleveland, Ohio, for a list of our publications. He has published many of our books and booklets.

This Magazine is published as a work of faith and labour of love. The Editor and his wife gladly give their services. It is freely sent to all who will read it. No charge is made for it.

Christians who feel definitely lead to do so, may have fellowship with us in this ministry. Those outside the U. S. A., please send only INTERNATIONAL Money Orders made out to Morton's Gap, Kentucky, U. S. A. See that it is made out in American money.

Mailing Permit applied for.

CONTENTS

Hebrews	218
Gleanings in Exodus	225
The Holy Spirit's Work	230
Separation	234
The History of a Stanza	237

THE EPISTLE TO THE HEBREWS

22. Christ Superior to Aaron.
Heb. 5:11-14.

At the close of our last article we pointed out that the 10th verse of Heb. 5 forms the juncture of the two divisions of that chapter. In the first section, vv. 1-9, the apostle has shown how Christ fulfilled that which was typified of Him by the Levitical high priests, and also how that He excells Aaron in His person, His office, and His work. The second section, which begins at 5:10 and extends, really, to the end of chapter 10, continues to display the superiority of Christ over Aaron, principally by showing that the Lord Jesus exercises a priesthood pertaining to a more excellent order than his. In substantiation of this the apostle, in 5:10, makes reference to Psa. 110:4. His purpose in so doing was twofold: first, to allow that Christ was not a high priest according to the constitution, law, and order of the Aaronic priesthood; second, to remind the Hebrews there was a priesthood antecedent unto and diverse from that of Aaron; which had also been appointed of God, and that for the very purpose of prefiguring the person of our great High Priest.

But at this point a difficulty has been presented to many students. We might state it thus: Seeing that this Epistle expressly declares, again and again, that Christ is priest "after the order of Melchizedek," how can it be true that Aaron, who belonged to a totally different order, could pre-figure His priestly office and work? This difficulty has largely resulted from failure to observe that the Holy Spirit has not said Christ is "an high priest **of** the order of Melchizedek," but, "**after** the order of," etc. The difference between the two expressions is real and radical. The word "of" would have necessarily **limited** His priesthood to a certain order. For when we say, as we must, that Phineas and Eli were "high priests **of** the order of Aaron," we mean that they had the very same priesthood that Aaron had. But it is not so with Christ. **His** priesthood is not restricted to any human order, for no mere man could possibly sustain or perform the work which pertains to Christ's priesthood.

As we have pointed out on previous occasions, it is of the very greatest importance, in order to a clear understanding of the priesthood of God's Son, to perceive that **both** Aaron and Melchizedek were needed to foreshadow His sacredotal office. The reason for this was, that the priestly work of Christ would be performed in two distinct stages: one in the days of His humiliation, the other during the time of His exaltation. Aaron prefigured the former, Melchizedek the latter. In perfect keeping with this fact Christ is not said to be a high priest "after the order of Melchizedek" in 2:17; 3:1, or 4:15. It was not until **after** the apostle has shown in 5:5-9 that Christ fulfilled that which Aaron typified (5:1-4), that He is "saluted of God" as an high priest after the order of **Melchizedek**. And, we would here point out again that, this was wondrously and blessedly adumbrated in Gen. 14, where Melchizedek is seen coming to meet and greet the **victorious** Abraham.

There were various things peculiar to the person of Melchizedek, above and beyond what appertained to Aaron, which rendered him an illustrious type of our great High Priest; and when Christ is designated Priest "after the order of

Melchizedek," the meaning of that expression is, according to the things revealed in Scripture concerning that O. T. character. "Because of the especial resemblance there was between what Melchizedek was and what Christ was to be, God called His priesthood Melchizedecian" (Dr. Owen). "After the order of Melchizedek" does not mean a limitation of His priesthood to that order—else it had said "of the order of Melchizedek"—but points to the particulars in which his priesthood also prefigured that of Christ's. The various details of which that resemblance consisted are developed in Heb. 7; all that we would now call attention to is, that nowhere in Scripture is Melchizedek ever seen offering a sacrifice, instead, we read, he "brought forth bread and wine" (Gen. 14:18)—typically, the **memorials** of the great Sacrifice already offered, once for all.

It was in death that Christ fulfilled the Aaronic type, making a full and perfect atonement for the sins of His people. It is in resurrection that He assumed the character in which Melchizedek foreshadowed Him—a **royal** Priest. It was after He had been officially "perfected" and had become "the Author of eternal salvation unto all them that obey Him" that the Lord Jesus announced, "All power is **given** unto Me in heaven and in earth" (Matt. 28:18). There was first the Cross and then the Crown: first He "offered up Himself" (7:27), then He entered "into heaven itself, now to appear in the presence of God for us" (9:24); and there He is seated "a Priest upon His throne" (Zech. 6:13)—the Millennial fulfillment of this on earth, will be but the outward demonstration in the lower sphere of what is true now in the higher yet invisible realm.

"Called of God an high priest after the order of Melchizedek" (v. 10). A most important point had now been reached in the apostle's argument, the central design of which was to exhibit the immeasurable superiority of Christianity over Judaism. The very center of the Jewish economy was its temple and priesthood; so too, the outstanding glory of Christianity, is its Priest who ministers in the heavenly sanctuary, officiating there in fulfillment of the Melchizedek type. But though the apostle had now arrived at the most important point in which treatise, it was also one which required the most delicate handling, due to the fleshly prejudices of his readers. To declare that, following His exodus from the grave, God Himself had greeted Christ as priest "after the order of **Melchizedek**," was tantamount to saying that the Aaronic order was thus Divinely set aside, and with it, all the ordinances and ceremonies of the Mosaic law. This was the hardest thing of all for a Hebrew, even a converted one, to bow to; for it meant repudiating everything that was seen, and cleaving to that which was altogether invisible. It meant forsaking that which their fathers had honoured for fifteen hundred years, and following that which the great majority of their brethren according to the flesh denounced as Satanic. In view of the difficulty created by this prejudice, the apostle interrupts the flow of his argument, and pauses to make a lengthy parenthesis.

"The apostle has scarcely entered on the central and most important part of his epistle, when he feels painfully the difficulty of explaining the doctrine of the heavenly and eternal priesthood of the Son, and this not merely on account of the grandeur and depth of the subject, but on account of the spiritual condition of the Hebrews, whom he is addressing. He had presented to their view the Lord Jesus, who after His sufferings was made perfect in His exaltation to be the High Priest in heaven. When he quotes again the 110th Psalm, 'Thou art a priest, forever after the order of Melchizedek,' the solemn and comprehensive words which are addressed by the Father to the Son, he has such a vivid and profound sense of the exceeding riches of this heavenly knowledge, of the treasures of wisdom and consolation which are hidden in the heavenly Priesthood of our ascended Lord, that he longs to unfold to the Hebrews his knowledge of the glorious mystery; especially as this was the truth which they most urgently needed. Here and here alone could they see their true position as worshippers in the true tabernacle, the heavenly sanctuary. Here and here alone was consolaiton for them in the trial which they felt on account of their excision from the temple and the earthly service in Jerusalem; while from the knowledge of Christ's heavenly priesthood they would also derive light to avoid the insidious errors, and strength to overcome the difficulties which were besetting their path" (A. Saphir).

In the course of his parenthesis which we are now about to begin, the apostle strikes two distinct notes: first he sounds a solemn warning, and then he gives forth a gracious encouragement. The warning is found in 5:11 to 6:8, the encouragement is contained in 6:9-20. Just so long as

Christians have the flesh in them and are subject to the assaults of the Devil, do they need constant warning; and just so long as they are harassed by indwelling sin and are left in an hostile world, do they stand in need of heavenly encouragement. All effective ministry to the saints proceeds along these two lines, alternating from the one to the other. Preachers will do well to make a careful note of this fact, fully exemplified in all the Epistles of the apostles; and every Christian reader will do well to take to heart the solemn and searching passage we are now to take up.

"Of whom we have many things to say" (v. 11). "Of whom:" concerning Christ as the fulfiller of the Melchizedek type, the apostle had much in mind, much that he desired to bring before his brethren. There were many things pertaining to this order of priesthood which were of deep importance, of great value, and most necessary to know; things which concerned the glory of Christ, things which concerned the joy and consolation of His people. But these things were "hard to be uttered," or as the R. V. has, "hard of interpretation." This does not mean that the apostle himself found it difficult to grasp them; nor does it mean they were of such a nature that he laboured to find language for expressing himself clearly. No, it was because the things themselves were **unpalatable** to the Hebrews, that the spirit of the apostle was straitened. This is seen from the next clause.

"And hard to be uttered, seeing ye are dull of hearing" (v. 11). "To be 'dull of hearing' is descriptive of that state of mind in which statements may be made without producing any corresponding impression, without being attended to, without being understood, without being felt. In a word, it is descriptive of mental listlessness. To a person in this state, it is very difficult to explain anything; for, nothing, however simple in itself, can be understood if it be not attended to" (Dr. J. Brown). The R. V. is again preferable here; "ye are **become** dull of hearing." They were not always so. Time was when these Hebrews had listened to the Word with eagerness, and had made diligent application thereof. "When the Gospel was first preached to them, it aroused their attention, it exercised their thoughts; but now with many of them it had become a common thing. They flattered themselves that they knew all about it. It had become to them like a sound to which the ear had been long accustomed—the person is not conscious of it, pays no attention to it" (Dr. J. Brown).

The Greek word for "dull" is translated "slothful" in 66:12. It signifies a state of heaviness or inertia. These Hebrews had become mentally and spiritually what loafers are in the natural world—too indolent to bestir themsleves, too lazy to make any effort at improvement. They were spiritual sluggards; slothful. Let the reader turn to Prov. 12:27, 19:24, 21:25, 24:30-34, 26:13-16, and remember these passages all have a **spiritual** application. To become, "dull of hearing" or "slothful," is the reverse of "giving diligence" in 2 Peter 1:5, 10. In such a condition of soul, the apostle found it difficult to lead the Hebrews on to the apprehension of higher truth. He had many things to say unto them, but their coldness, lethargy, prejudices, restrained him. And this is recorded for **our** learning; it has a voice for **us;** may the Spirit grant us an hearing ear.

"Ye are become dull of hearing." Of how many Christians is this true today! "Ye did run well: who did hinder you?" (Gal. 5:7). This is a cause of mourning unto all the true servants of God. Because iniquity abounds, the love of many waxes cold. Affections are set upon things below, rather than upon things above. Many who are deluded into thinking their eternal salvation is secure, evidence no concern over their present relationship to God. And Christians who mingle with these lifeless professors are injuriously affected, for "evil communications corrupt good manners" (1 Cor. 15:33). There is little "reaching forth unto those things which are before" (Phil. 3:13) and, consequently, little **growth** in grace and in the knowledge of the Lord. By the very law of our constitution, if we do not move forward, we slip backward.

There are few who seem to realize that truth has to be "bought" (Prov. 23:23), purchased at the cost of subordinating temporal interests to spiritual ones. If the Christian is to "increase in the knowledge of God (Col. 1:10), he has to give himself whole-heartedly to the things of God. It is impossible to serve God and mammon. If the heart of the professing Christian be set, as the heart of the nominal professor is, upon earthly comforts, worldly prosperity, temporal riches, then the "true riches" will be missed—sold for "a mess of pottage" (Heb. 12:16). But if, by Divine grace, through the possession of a new nature, there is a longing and a hungering for spiritual things, that longing can only be attained and that hunger satisfied by giving ourselves entirely to their ceaseless quest. "The loins of our minds" (1 Peter 1:13) have to be girded, the Word has to be "studied" (2 Tim. 2:15), the means of grace have to be used with "all diligence" (2 Peter 1:5). It is the diligent soul which "shall be made fat" (Prov. 13:4).

How many who sit under the ministry of a true servant of God are "dull of hearing!" There is little waiting upon God, little real exercise of heart, before the service, to prepare them for receiving His message. Instead, the average hearer comes up to the house of God with a mind full of worldly concerns. We have to "**lay aside** all filthiness and superfluity of naughtiness" if we are to "receive with meekness the engrafted Word" (James 1:21). We have to listen unto God's Word with a right motive; not out of idle curiosity, not merely to fulfill a duty, still less for the purpose of criticizing; but that we "may **grow** thereby" (1 Peter 2:2)—grow in practical godliness. And, if what we have heard is not to be forgotten, if it is really to profit the soul, it must be meditated upon (Psa. 1:2), and accompanied with earnest prayer for grace to enable us to "heed" what has been heard.

"For when for the time ye ought to be teachers, ye have need that one teach you again which be the first principles of the oracles of God; and are become such as have need of milk, and not of strong meat" (v. 12). The opening "for" intimates that the apostle is here substantiating the charge which he had preferred against the believing Hebrews at the close of the preceding verse. His reproof was with the object of emphasizing the sad state into which their inertia had brought them. Their condition was to be deplored from three considerations. First, they had been converted long enough to be of help to others. Second, instead of being useful, they were useless, needing to be grounded afresh in the A.B.C. of the Truth of God. Third, so far from having the capacity to masticate strong food, their condition called for that which was suited only to a stunted babyhood.

"For when for the time ye ought to be teachers." This, it seems to us, is only another way of saying, Consider how long you have been Christians, how long you have known the Truth, and what improvement of it ought to have been made! It was a rebuke for their having failed to "redeem the time" (Eph. 5:16). Most probably among these Hebrews were some who had been called during the days of Christ's public ministry, others no doubt were among the three thousand saved on the day of Pentecost, since which, about thirty years had passed. During that time they had the O. T. Scriptures which clearly testified to all they had been taught concerning Christ. The Gospel had been preached and "confirmed" unto them (2:1-3). Moreover, as the book of Acts shows, the apostles had laboured hard and long among them, and much of the N. T. was now in their hands. Hence, in 6:7 they are likened to the earth which drinketh in the rain that "cometh oft upon it." Thus, every privilege and opportunity had been theirs.

"Ye ought to be teachers." This tells us the improvement which should have been made of, and the use to which they ought to have put, the teaching they had received. The Gospel is given by God to the Christian, not only for his own individual edification and joy, but as a "pound" to be traded with for Christ's glory (Luke 19:13), as a "light" for the illumination of others (Matt. 5:15, 16). "You **ought** to be teachers" shows that this was a duty required of them. How little is this perceived by Christians today! How few listen to the ministry of the Scriptures with an ear not only for their own soul's profit, but also with the object of being equipped to help others. Instead, how many attend the preaching of the Word simply as a matter of custom, or to satisfy their conscience. Two aims should be prayerfully sought by every Christian auditor: his own edification, his usefulness to others.

"Ye ought to be **teachers**." Let not the searching point of this be blunted by saying, God does not want all His people to be public preachers. The N. T. does not limit "teaching" to the pulpit. One of the most important spheres is **the home**, and that should be a Christian seminary. Under the law God commanded the Israelite to give His words to the members of his household: "And thou shalt teach them diligently unto thy children, and shalt talk of them when thou sittest in thine house, and when thou walkest by the way, and when thou liest down, and when thou risest up" (Deut. 6:7). Does God require less from us now, in this dispensation of full light? No, indeed. Note, again, how in Titus 2:3-5 the older sisters are bidden to "**teach** the young women:" never was there a greater need for this than now. So in 2 Tim. 2:2 the brethren are to "teach others also." Yes, every Christian "ought to be" a teacher.

"Ye have need that one teach you again." The apostle continues his reproof of the listless Hebrews, and presses upon them the inevitable consequence of becoming "dull of hearing." Spiritual sloth not only prevents practical progress in the Christian's life, but it produces retrogression. It was not that they had lost, absolutely, their knowledge of Divine truth, but they had failed to lay it to heart, and live in the power of it. In 2 Peter 1 Christians are called on to **add** to their faith "virtue, and to virtue, knowledge; and to knowledge, temperance: and to temperance, patience; and to patience, godliness; and to godliness, brotherly kindness; and to brotherly kindness, love;" and then the apostle adds, "For if these things be in you, and abound, they make you that ye shall neither be barren nor unfruitful in the knowledge of our Lord Jesus Christ." On the other hand, we are solemnly warned, "But he that lacketh these things is blind, and cannot see afar off, and hath forgotten that he was purged from his old sins." This was the condition of the Hebrews.

"Which be the first principles of the oracles of God." Because of their unresponsiveness of heart, they had gone back so far that they were only fit to be placed in the lowest form of learners; they needed to be re-taught their A.B.C. Clear proof was this of their dullness and lack of proficiency. The "**first principles** of the oracles of God" signify the rudiments of our faith, the first lessons presented to our learning, the elementary truths of Scripture. Until these are grasped by faith, and the heart and life are influenced by them, the disciple is not ready for further instruction in the things of God. In the case of the Hebrews, those "first principles" or elementary doctrines were, that the O. T. economy was strictly a typical one, that its ordinances and ceremonies foreshadowed the person and work of God's Son, who was to come here and make an atonement for the sins of His people. He had thus come: the types had given place to the great Antitype, and therefore the shadows were replaced by the Substance itself. True, he had left this scene, gone into heaven, itself, there to appear in the presence of God for His people. Thither their faith and affections should have followed Him. But instead, they wanted to go back again to the temple-services in Jerusalem. They were setting their hearts upon the now effete types and figures, which the apostle hesitated not to call "the weak and beggarly elements" (Gal. 4:9).

Instead of walking by faith, the Hebrews were influenced by the things of sight. Instead of looking upward to an asceded and glorified Saviour, they were occupied with a system which had foreshadowed His work in the days of His humiliation. Thus they needed to be taught afresh the "first principles of the oracles of God." They needed to be reminded that that which is perfect had come, and therefore that which was in part had been done away. And what is the present-day application of this expression to Christians? This: the elementals of our faith are, that Christ Jesus came into this world to save sinners; that His salvation is perfect and complete, leaving nothing for us to add to it; that the only fitness He requires from sinners is the Spirit's discovery to them of their **need** of Him. The greater the sinner I know myself to be, the greater my need of Christ, and the more I am **suited** to Him, for He died for "the ungodly" (Rom. 5:6). It was the realization of my ruin and wretchedness which first drew me to Him. If I cast myself, in all my want and poverty, upon Him, then He **has** received me, for His declaration is, "him that cometh to Me, I will in no wise cast out." Believing this, I go on my way rejoicing, thanking Him, praising Him, living on Him and for Him.

But instead of living in the joyous assurance of their acceptance in the Beloved, many give way to doubting. They question their "interest in Christ;" they wonder, "Am I His, or am I not?" They are continually occupied with self, either their good self or their bad self. And thus their peace is at an end. Instead of affections set upon Christ, their attention is turned within, occupied with their faith or their lack of it. Instead of walking in the glorious sunshine of the conscious favour of God, they dwell in "Doubting Castle," or flounder in the "Slough of Despond." Thus, instead of themselves being teachers of others, they have need that one teach them again "which be the first principles of the oracles of God." They are fit only for the kindergarten. They require to be told once more that faith looks away from self, and is occupied entirely with Another. They need to be told that Christ, not faith, is the sinner's Saviour; that faith is simply the empty hand extended to receive from Him.

This clause is susceptible of various legitimate applications. Let us consider its bearing upon another class of Christians, among which may be numbers of our readers. Time was when, in the "far country," you sought to be filled with the husks which the swine fed on (Luke 15). But you found your quest was in vain. To change the figure, you sampled one after another of the world's cisterns, only to find that "whosoever drinketh of this water shall thirst again" (John 4:13). You discovered that the things of the world could not meet your deep need. Then, weary and heavy-laden, you were brought to Christ, and found in Him that "altogether lovely" One. O the joy that was now yours! "Thou O Christ art all I want," was your confession. But is this the language of your heart today? Alas, "thou hast left thy first love" (Rev. 2:4), and with it, peace and contentment are also largely a thing of the past. Like a sow that returns to her wallowing in the mire, many go back to the world for recreation, then for satisfaction. Ah, have not you, my reader, need to be taught again "which be the first principles of the oracles of God?" Do you not need reminding that nothing in this scene can minister to the new nature, a nature which has been created for heaven. Do you not need to relearn that Christ alone can satisfy your heart?

The "oracles of God" is one of many names given to the Holy Scriptures. Stephen called them the "living oracles" (Acts 7:28). "They are so in respect of their Author,—they are the oracles of 'the living God;' whereas the oracles with which Satan infatuated the world were most of them at the shrines and graves of dead men. They are so in respect of their use and efficacy: they are 'living' because life-giving oracles unto them that obey them (Deut. 32:47). Because they are 'the oracles of God,' they have supreme authority over the souls and consciences of us all. Therefore are they also infallible truth" (Dr. J. Owen).

"And are become such as have need of milk, and not of strong meat." Here the apostle continues to rebuke the Hebrews for their laxity, and sets before them their deteriorated condition under a figure designed to humble them: he likens them to infants. The same similitude is used in 1 Cor. 3:1, 2. "Milk" here signifies the same thing as the "first principles of the oracles of God." The "strong meat" had reference to the offices of Christ, especially His priesthood, as suited to our needs and affections. "Milk" is appropriate for babes, but Christians ought to grow and become strong in the Lord. They are exhorted to "be not children in understanding" (1 Cor. 14:20). They are bidden to "quit ye like men" (1 Cor. 15:13).

"For every one that useth milk is unskillful in the word of righteousness: for he is a babe" (v. 13). "Useth milk" means, lives on nothing else. By the "word of righteousness" is meant the Gospel of God's grace. In 1 Cor. 1:18 it is termed "the Word of the Cross," because that is its principal subject. In Rom. 10:8 it is designated "the Word of Faith," because that is its chief requirement from all who hear it. Here, the Word of Righteousness, because of its nature, use and end. In the Gospel is "the righteousness of God revealed" (Rev. 1:16, 17), for Christ is "the end of the law for righteousness unto every one that believeth" (Rom. 10:4). Now the Hebrews are not here said to be ignorant of or utterly without the Word of Righteousness, but "unskillful" or "inexperienced" in the use of it. They had failed to improve it to its proper end. Did they clearly apprehend the Gospel, they had perceived the needlessness for the perpetuation of the Levitical priesthood with its sacrifices.

The one unskilled in the Word of Righteousness is a "babe." This term is here used by way of reproach. A "babe" is weak, ignorant. A spiritual "babe" is one who has an inadequate knowledge of Christ, i. e. an experimental knowledge and heart-acquaintance with Him. Let the reader note that a state of infancy was what characterized God's people of old under Judaism (Gal. 4:1-6). They were looking forward to the Christ that was to come, and whose person and work was represented to their eyes by typical pictures and persons. Such was the ground to which these Hebrews had wellnigh slipped back. Earthly things were engrossing their attention. So it is still. A person may have been a Christian twenty or thirty years, but if he is not forgetting the things which are behind, and constantly pressing to the things before, he is, in actual experience and spiritual stature, but "a babe."

"But strong meat belongeth to them that are of full age, those who by reason of use have their senses exercised to discern both good and evil" (v. 14). Here the apostle completes the antithesis begun in the preceding verse, and describes the character of those to whom strong meat is suited. By necessary implication his statement explains to us **why** the Hebrews had become "dull of hearing." There is much here of deep practical importance. "Strong meat" is contrasted from "milk" or the "first principles" of God's Word, which we have defined above. This "strong meat" is the appropriate portion of those who have left infancy behind, who have so assimilated the "milk" of babyhood they have "grown thereby," grown in faith and love. This growth is produced and promoted by **using** our spiritual "senses" or faculties. Infants **have** "senses," but they know not how to exercise them to advantage. The proper use of our spiritual faculties enables us to distinguish between 'good and evil' It was here the Hebrews had failed so lamentably.

"A child is easily imposed upon as to its food. Its nurse may easily induce it to swallow even palatable poison. But a man, 'by reason of use,' has learned so to employ his senses as to distinguish between what is deleterious and what is nourishing" (Dr. J. Brown). The same holds good in the spiritual realm. There is in the new man that which corresponds to our "five senses" naturally, namely, understanding, conscience, affections. But these have to be trained and developed. It is only by the constant and assiduous exercise of our minds upon spiritual things, by the diligent study of the Word, by daily meditation thereon, by the exercise of faith therein, by earnestly supplicating the Spirit for light, that we acquire the all-important discernment to distinguish between good and evil, Truth and error. "Senses **exercised**" means ability or fitness acquired, as a disciplined soldier is equipped for his duty, or a trained athlete is for his work. Such capacity is only attained by the Christian through a constant and sedulous application of himself to the things of God. "By reason of use" refers not to spasmodic effort, but to a regular practice, a confirmed habit. The outcome is a spiritual ability to judge rightly of all that is presented to his notice.

It was here the Hebrews had failed, as, alas, so many Christians do now. "Their senses had not been exercised; that is, they had not walked closely with God, they had not followed the Master, listening earnestly to His voice, and proving what is that good, and acceptable, and perfect will of God. They had not conscientiously applied the knowledge which they had, but allowed it to remain dead and unused. If they had really and truly partaken of the milk, they would not have remained babes" (A. Saphir). Because of their slothfulness, they were unable to distinguish between "good and evil," i. e., between Truth and error, the promptings of the Spirit and the solicitations of Satan, the desires of the new nature and the lustings of the old. They were like babes are in the natural world, unable to discriminate between what is wholesome and what is hurtful; therefore were they unable to see the difference between what was right under the Judaic economy, and what was now suited to Christianity.

"Senses trained to discern both good and evil" has reference to what is set before a believer as food for his soul. The "good" is that which is nutritious and suited to his nourishment, "evil" is that which tends not to his edification, but to his destruction. Scripture itself is "evil" when wrongly divided and misapplied. This is seen in Satan's misuse of Scripture with Christ (Matt. 4:6). Truth becomes "evil" when it is not presented in its due and Divine **proportions**. The enemies of the Hebrews were appealing to the O. T. Scriptures, as Romanists now do to favour their elaborate form of worship and priesthood. In many other ways is Satan active today in setting before God's people both "good and evil," and unless their spiritual faculties have been diligently trained, through much waiting upon God, they fall easy victims to his half-lies.

"If people really **loved and cherished** what they so fondly called 'the simple gospel,' their knowledge and Christian character would deepen, and all the truths which are centered in Christ crucified would become the object of their investigation and delight, and enrich and elevate their experience. . . . There are no doctrines more profound than those which are proclaimed when Christ's salvation is declared. All our progress consists in learning more fully the doctrine which at first is preached unto us" (A. Saphir). It is **using** the light we already have, putting into **practice** the truth already received, which fits us for more. Unless this **is** done, we retrograde, and the light which is in us becomes darkness. Manna not used breeds worms (Ex. 16)! Milk undigested—not taken up into our system— ferments. A backslidden state deprives us of a sound judgment. The secret of "senses trained to discern good and evil" is revealed in Hos. 6:3. "Then shall we know, if we **follow on** to know the Lord." May His grace stir us up so to do.

—ARTHUR W. PINK.

GLEANINGS IN EXODUS

70. The Glorified Mediator.
Ex. 34:28-35.

The Law had "a shadow of good things to come" (Heb. 10:1). A beautiful illustration and exemplification of this is found in the closing verses of Ex. 34, in which we behold Moses descending from the mount with radiant face. The key to our present portion is found in noting the exact position that it occupies in this book of redemption. It comes after the legal covenant which Jehovah had made with Israel; it comes before the actual setting up of the tabernacle and the Shekinah-glory filling it. As we shall see, our passage is interpreted for us in 2 Cor. 3. What we have here in Ex. 34 supplies both a comparison and a contrast with the new dispensation, the dispensation of the Spirit, of grace, of life more abundant. But before that dispensation was inaugurated, God saw fit that man should be fully tested under Law, and that, for the purpose of demonstrating what he is as a fallen and sinful creature.

As was shown in our last article, man's trial under the Mosaic economy demonstrated two things: first, that he is "ungodly;" second, that he is, "without strength" (Rom. 5:6). But these are negative things: in Rom. 8:7 a third feature of man's terrible state is mentioned, namely, that he is "enmity against God." This was made manifest when God's Son became incarnate and tabernacled for thirty-three years on this earth. "He came unto His own, and His own received Him not" (John 1:11). Not only so, but He was "despised and rejected of men." Nay, more, they hated Him, hated Him "without a cause" (John 15:25). Nor would their hatred be appeased till they had condemned Him to a malefactor's death and nailed Him to the accursed cross. And, let it be remembered, that it was not merely the Jews that put to death the Lord of glory, but the Gentiles also; therefore did the Lord say, when looking forward to His death, "Now is the judgment of this world" (John 12:31)—not of Israel only. There the probation or testing of man ended.

Man is not now under probation. He is under condemnation: "As it is written, There is none righteous, no, not one: There is none that understandeth, there is none that seeketh after God. They are all gone out of the way, they are together become unprofitable; there is none that doeth good, no not one" (Rom. 3: 10-12). Man is not on trial: he is a culprit, under sentence. No pleading will avail; no excuses will be accepted. The present issue between God and the sinner is, will man bow to God's righteous verdict.

This is where the Gospel meets us. It comes to us as to those who are already "lost," as to those who are "ungodly, without strength, enmity against God." It announces to us the amazing **grace** of God—the only hope for poor sinners. But that grace will not be welcomed until the sinner bows to the sentence of God against him. That is why both repentance and faith are demanded from the sinner. These two must not be separated. Paul preached, "repentance toward God, and faith toward our Lord Jesus Christ" (Acts 20:21). Repentance is the sinner's acknowledgement of that sentence of condemnation under which he lies. Faith is the acceptance of the grace and mercy which are extended to him through Christ. Repentance is not the turning over of a new leaf and the vowing that I will mend my ways; rather is it a settine of my seal that God is true when He tells me that I am "**without** strength," that in myself my case is hopeless, that I am no more able to "do better next time" than I am of creating a world. Not until this is really believed (not as the result of my experience, but on the authority of God's holy Word), shall I really turn to Christ and welcome Him—not as a Helper, but as a **Saviour.**

As it was dispensationally so it is experimentally: there must be "a ministration of death" (2 Cor. 3:7), before there is a "ministration of spirit" or life (2 Cor. 3: 8); there must be "the ministration of condemnation," before "the ministration of righteousness" (2 Cor. 3:9). Ah, a "**ministration** of condemnation and death" falls strangely upon our ears, does it not? A "ministration of **grace**" we can understand, but a "ministration of condemnation" is not so easy to grasp. But this latter was man's first **need**: it must be shown what he is in himself: a hopeless wreck, utterly incapable of meeting the righteous requirements of a holy God—before he is ready to be a debtor to mercy alone. We repeat: as it was dispensationally, so it is experimentally: it was to this (his own experience) that the apostle Paul referred when he said, "For I was alive without the law once: but when the commandemnt came, sin revived, and I died" (Rom. 7:9). In his unregenerate days he was, in his own estimation "alive," yet it was "**without** the Law," i. e., apart from meeting its demands. "But when the commandment came," when the Holy Spirit wrought within him, when the Word of God came in power to his heart, then "sin revived," that is, he was made aware of his awful condition; and then he "died" to his self-righteous complacency—he saw that, in himself, his case was hopeless. Yes, the appearing of the glorified mediator comes not before, but after, the legal covenant.

"And he was there with the Lord forty days and forty nights; he did neither eat bread, nor drink water." And he wrote upon the tables the words of the covenant, the ten commandments" (v. 28). Our passage abounds in comparisons and contrasts. The "forty days" here at once recalls to mind the "forty days" mentioned in Matt. 4. Here it was Moses; there it is Christ. Here it was Moses on the mount; there it was Christ in the wilderness. Here it was Moses favoured with a glorious revelation from God; there it was Christ being tempted of the Devil. Here it was Moses receiving the Law, at the mouth of Jehovah; there it was Christ being assailed by the Devil to repudiate that Law. We scarcely know which is the greater wonder of the two: that a sinful worm of the earth was raised to such a height of honour as to be permitted to spend a season in the presence of the great Jehovah, or that of the Lord of glory should stoop so low as to be for six weeks with the foul Fiend.

"And it came to pass, when Moses came down from mount Sinai with the two tables of testimony in Moses' hand, when he came down from the mount, that Moses wist not that the skin of his face shone while he talked with Him." Very blessed is it to compare and contrast this second descent of Moses from the mount with that which was before us in the 32nd chapter. There we see the face of Moses diffused with anger (v. 19); here he comes down with countenance radiant. There he beheld a people engaged in idolatry, here he returns to a people abashed. There we behold him dashing the tables of stone to the ground (v. 19); here he deposits them in the ark (Deut. 10:5).

"And it came to pass, when Moses came down from mount Sinai with the two tables of testimony in Moses' hand, when he came down from the mount, that Moses wist not that the skin of his face shone while he talked with Him." This also reminds us of a N. T. episode, which is very similar, yet vastly dissimilar. It was on the mount that the face of Moses was made radiant, and it was on the mount that our Lord was transfigured. But the glory of Moses was only a reflected one, whereas that of Christ was inherent. The shining of Moses' face was the consequence of his being brought into the immediate presence of the glory of Jehovah; the transfiguration of Christ was the outshining of His own personal glory. The radiance of Moses was confined to his face, but of Christ we read, "His raiment was white as the light" (Matt. 17:3). Moses **knew not** that the skin of his face shone; Christ did, as is evident from His words, "Tell the vision to no man" (Matt. 17:9).

This 29th verse brings out, most blessedly, what is the certain consequence of intimate communion with the Lord, and that in a twofold way. First no soul can enjoy real fellowship with the all-glorious God without being affected thereby, and that to a marked degree. Moses had been absorbed in the communications received and in contemplating the glory of Him who spake with him; and his own person caught and retained some of the beams of that glory. So it is still: as we read in Psa. 34:5, "They looked unto Him, and their faces were radiant" (R. V.). It is communion with the Lord that conforms us to His image. We shall not be more Christlike till we walk more frequently and more closely with Him. "But we all, with open face, beholding as in a glass the glory of the Lord, are **changed** into the same image from glory to glory, by the Spirit of the Lord" (2 Cor. 3:18).

The second consequence of real communion with God is that we shall be less occupied with our wretched selves. Though the face of Moses shone with 'a light not seen on land or sea,' he wist it not. This illustrates a vital difference between self-righteous phariseeism and true godliness; the former produces complacency and pride, the latter leads to self-abnegation and humility. The pharisee (and there are many of his tribe still on earth) boasts of his attainments, advertises his imaginary spirituality, and thanks God that he is not as other men are. But the one who, by grace, enjoys much fellowship with the Lord, learns of Him who was "meek and lowly in heart," and says "Not unto us, O Lord, not unto us, but unto Thy name give glory" (Psa. 115:1). Being engaged with the beauty of the Lord, he is delivered from self-occupation, and therefore is unconscious of the very fruit of the Spirit which is being brought forth in him. But though **he** is not aware of his increasing conformity to Christ, **others** are.

"And when Aaron and all the children of Israel saw, Moses, behold the skin of his face shone; and they were afraid to come nigh him" (v. 30). This shows us the third effect of communion with God: though the individual himself is unconscious of the glory manifested through him, others are cognizant of it. Thus it was when two of Christ's apostles stood before the Jewish sanhedrin: "Now when they saw the boldness of Peter and John and perceived that they were unlearned and ignorant men, they marvelled; and they took knowledge of them, **that they had been with Jesus**" (Acts 4:13). Ah, we cannot keep company very long with the Holy One, without His impress being left upon us. The man who is thoroughly devoted to the Lord needeth not to wear some badge or button in his coat-lapel, nor proclaim with his lips that he is "living a life of victory." It is still true that actions speak louder than words.

"And when Aaron and all the children of Israel saw Moses, behold, the skin of His face shone; and they were **afraid** to come nigh him." The typical meaning of this is given in 2 Cor. 3:7, "But if the ministration of death, written and engraven in stones was glorious, so that the children of Israel **could not** steadfastly behold the face of Moses for the glory of his countenance." Concerning this another has said: "Why, then, were they afraid to come near him? Because the very glory that shone upon his face searched their hearts and consciences—being what they were, sinners, and unable of themselves to meet even the smallest requirements of the covenant which had now been inaugurated. It was of necessity a ministration of condemnation and death, for it required a righteousness from them which they could not render, and, inasmuch as they must fail in the rendering it, would pronounce their condemnation, and bring them under the penalty of transgression, which was death. The glory which they thus beheld upon the face of Moses was the expression to them of the holiness of God—that holiness which sought from them conformity to its own standards—and which would vindicate the breaches of that covenant which had now been estab'ished. They were therefore afraid, because they knew in their inmost souls that they could not stand before Him from whose presence Moses had come" (Mr. Ed. Dennett).

Typically (not dispensationally) the covenant which Jehovah made with Moses and Israel at Sinai, and the tables of stone on which were engraved the ten commandments, foreshadowed that new covenant which He will yet make with Israel in a coming day: "For I will take you from among the heathen, and gather you out of all countries, and will bring you into your own land. Then will I sprinkle clean water upon you, and ye shall be clean from all your filthiness, and from all your idols, will I cleanse you. A new heart also will I give you, and a new spirit will I put within you; and I will take away the stony heart out of your flesh, and I will give you an heart of flesh. And I will put My Spirit within you, and cause you to walk in My statutes, and ye shall keep My judgments and do them. And ye shall dwell in the land that I gave to your fathers; and ye shall be My people, and I will be your God" (Ezek. 36:24-28). "Behold, the days come, saith the Lord, that I will make a new covenant with the house of Israel, and with the house of Judah . . . After those days, saith the Lord, I will put My law in their inward parts, and write it **in their hearts;** . . . and they shall teach no more every man his neighbour, and every man his brother, saying, Know the Lord: for they shall all know Me, from the least of them unto the greatest of them, saith the Lord" (Jer. 31:31-34).

Spiritually, this is made good for Christians even now. Under the gracious operations of the Spirit of God **our hearts** have been made plastic and receptive. It is to this fact that Paul referred at the beginning of 2 Cor. 3. "The saints at Corinth had been 'manifested to be Christ's epistle ministered by us, written not with ink, but the Spirit of the living God; not on stone tables, but on fleshly tables of the heart.' Their hearts being made impressionable by Divine working, Christ could write upon them, using Paul as a pen, and making every mark in the power of the Spirit of God. But what is written is the knowledge of God as revealed through the Mediator in the grace of the new covenant, so that it might be true in the hearts of the saints—'They shall all know Me.' Then Paul goes on to speak of himself as made competent by God to be a new covenant ministry, 'not of letter, but of spirit'" (C. A. Coates).

"And Moses called unto them; and Aaron and all the rulers of the congregation returned unto him: and Moses talked with them. And afterward all the children of Israel came nigh: and he gave them in commandment all that the Lord had spoken with them in Mount Sinai. And till Moses had done speaking with them, he put a veil on his face" (vv. 31-33). Ah, does not this explain their fear as they beheld the shining of Moses' face? Note **what** was in his hands! He carried the two tables of stone on which were written the ten words of the law, the "ministration of condemnation." The nearer the light of the glory came, while it was connected with the righteous claims of God upon them, the more cause had they to fear. That holy Law condemned them, for man in the flesh could not meet its claims. "However blessed it was **typically**, it was **literally** a ministry of death, for Moses was not a quickening Spirit, nor could he give his spirit to the people, nor could the glory of his face bring them into conformity with himself as the mediator. Hence the veil had to be on his face" (C. A. Coates).

The dispensational interpretation of this is given in 2 Cor. 3:13: "And not as Moses, which put a veil over his face, that the children of Israel could not steadfastly look **to the end** of that which is abolished." Here the apostle is treating of Judiasm as an economy. Owing to their blindness spiritually, Israel was unable to discern the deep significance of the ministry of Moses, the purpose of God behind it, that which all the types and shadows pointed forward to. The **"end"** of 2 Cor. 3:13: is parallel with Rom. 10:4. "For Christ is **the end** of the law for righteousness to every one that believeth." "The veil on Israel's heart is self-sufficiency, which makes them still refuse to submit to God's righteousness. But when Israel's heart turns to the Lord the veil will be taken away. What a wonderful chapter Exodus 34 will be to them then! For they will see that **Christ** is the spirit of it all. What they will see, we are privileged to see now. All this had an 'end' on which we can, through infinite grace, fix our eyes. The 'end' was the glory of the Lord as the Mediator of the new covenant. He has come out of death and gone up on high, and the glory of all that God is in grace is shining in His face" (C. A. Coates).

"But when Moses went in before the Lord to speak with Him, he took the veil off, until he came out. And he came out, and spake unto the children of Israel that which he was commanded. And the children of Israel saw the face of Moses, that the skin of Moses' face shone; and Moses put the veil upon his face again, until he went in to speak with Him" (vv. 34, 35). Moses unveiled in the presence of the Lord is a beautiful type of the believer of this dispensation. The Christian beholds the glory of God shining in the face of Jesus Christ (2 Cor. 4:6), therefore, instead of being stricken with fear, he approaches with boldness. God's law **cannot** condemn him, for its every demand has been fully met and satisfied by his Substitute. Hence, instead of trembling before the glory of God, we "**rejoice** in hope of the glory of God" (Rom. 5:2).

"There is no veil now either on **His** face or **our** hearts. He makes those who believe on Him to **live** in the knowledge of God, and in response to God, for He is the quickening Spirit. And He gives His Spirit to those who believe. We have the Spirit of the glorified Man in whose face the glory of God shines. Is it not surpassingly wonderful? One has to **ask** sometimes, Do we really believe it? 'But we all, looking on the glory of the Lord with unveiled face, are transformed according to the same image from glory to glory even as by the Lord the Spirit' (2 Cor. 3:18). If we had not His Spirit we should have no liberty to look on the glory of the Lord, or to see Him as the spirit of these marvelous types. But we have liberty to look on it all, and there is transforming power in it. Saints under new-covenant-ministry are transfigured.

"This is the 'surpassing glory' which could not be seen or known until it shone in the face of Him of whom Moses in Exodus 34 is so distinctly a type. The whole typical system was temporary, but its 'spirit' abides, for **Christ** was the Spirit of it all. Now we have to do with the ministry of the Spirit and of righteousness, and all is abiding. The ministry of the new covenant subsists and abounds in glory" (C. A. Coates).

As a sort of appendix to this article we shall proffer, for the sake of those who may value it, an outline of the apostle's argument in 2 Cor. 3. The authority of Paul's apostleship had been called into question by certain Judaisers. In the first verses of this chapter he appeals to the Corinthians themselves as the proof of his God-commissioned and God-blessed ministry. In v. 6 he defines the **character** of his ministry, and this for the purpose of showing its superiority over that of his enemies. He and his fellow-gospellers were "ministers of the **new** testament" or covenant. A series of contrasts is then drawn between the two covenants, that is, between Judaism and Christianity. That which pertained to the former is called "the letter" that relating to the new, "the spirit," i. e., the one was mainly concerned with that which was external, the other was largely internal: the one slew, the other gave life—this was one of the leading differences between the Law, and the Gospel.

In what follows the apostle, while allowing that the Law was glorious, shows that the Gospel is still more glorious. The old covenant was a "ministration of death," for the Law could only condemn; therefore, though a glory was connected with it, yet was it such that man in the flesh could not behold (v. 7). Then how much more excellent would be, must be, the glory of the new covenant, seeing that it was "a ministration of the Spirit" (v. 8)—compare v. 3 for proof of this. If there was a glory connected with that which "concluded all men under sin" (Gal. 3:23), much more glorious must be that ministration which announces a righteousness which is "unto all and upon them that believe" (Rom. 3:22). It is more glorious to pardon than to condemn; to give life, than to destroy (v. 9). The glory of the former covenant therefore pales into nothingness before the latter (v. 10). This is further seen from the fact that Judaism is "done away," whereas Christianity "remaineth" (v. 11)—compare Heb. 8:7, 8.

At v. 12 the apostle draws still another contrast between the two economies, namely, the plainness or perspicuity over against the obscurity and ambiguity of their respective ministries (vv. 12-15). The apostles used "great plainness of speech," whereas the teaching of the ceremonial law was by means of shadows and symbols. Moreover, the minds of the Israelites were blinded, so that there was a veil over their hearers, and therefore when the writings of Moses were read, they were incapable of looking beyond the type to the Antitype. This veil remains upon them unto this day, and will continue until they turn unto the Lord (vv. 15, 16). **Literally** the covenant of Sinai was a ministration of condemnation and death, and the glory of it had to be veiled. But it had an "end" (v. 13), upon which Israel could not fix their eyes. They will see that "end" in a coming day; but in the meantime, **we** are permitted to read the old covenant without a veil, and to see that **Christ** is the "spirit" of it all, and that it had in view that which could only have its fulfillment under new covenant conditions, namely, God's glory secured in and by the Mediator.

The language of v. 17 is involved in some obscurity: "Now the Lord is that Spirit." This does not mean that Christ is the Holy Spirit. The "spirit" here is the same as in v. 6—"not of the letter, but of the spirit:" cf. Rom. 7:6. The Mosaic system is called "the letter" because it was purely objective. It possessed no inward principle or power. But the Gospel deals with the heart, and supplies the spiritual power (Rom. 1:16). Moreover, **Christ** is the spirit, the life, the heart and center of all the ritual and ceremonialism of Judaism. **He** is the key to the O. T. for, "In the volume of the Book" it is written of Him. So also Christ is the spirit and life of Christianity; He is "a quickening Spirit" (1 Cor. 15:45). And, "Where the Spirit of the Lord is, there is liberty." Apart from Christ, the sinner, be he Jew or Gentile, is in a state of bondage: he is the slave of sin and the captive of the Devil. But where the Son makes free, He frees indeed (John 8:32).

Finally the apostle contrasts the two **glories**, the glory connected with the old covenant—the shining on Moses' face at the giving of the Law (when the covenant was made)—with the glory of the new covenant, in the person of Christ. "But we all, with open (unveiled) face beholding as in a glass the glory of the Lord, are changed into the same image from glory to glory, even as by the Spirit of the Lord." Note here: first, "we **all**." Moses alone beheld the glory of the Lord in the mount: every Christian now beholds it. Second, we with "open face," with freedom and with confidence; whereas Israel were afraid to gaze on the radiant and majestical face of Moses. Third, we are "changed into the same image." The law had no power to convert or purify; but the ministry of the Gospel, under the operation of the Spirit, **has** a transforming power. Those who are saved by it, those who are occupied with Christ as set forth in the Word (the "mirror") are, little by little, conformed to His image. Ultimately, when we "see Him as He is" (1 John 3:2), we shall be "Like Him"—fully perfectly, eternally.

—ARTHUR W. PINK.

THE HOLY SPIRIT'S WORK

2. In Salvation

In the 19th of Acts we learn, that when the apostle Paul came to Ephesus he asked some disciples of John the Baptist, "Have ye received the Holy Spirit since ye believed?" (v. 2). And we are told, "They said unto him, We have not so much as heard whether there be any Holy Spirit." Sad to say, history has repeated itself. Without doubt, were the members of hundreds of so-called "churches"' (in which modernism and worldliness rule) asked this same question, they would be obliged to return an identical answer. The reason why those disciples at Ephesus knew not about the Holy Spirit was, most probably, because they had been baptized in Judea by the forerunner of Christ and then had returned to Ephesus, where they remained in ignorance of what had taken place on the day of Pentecost. But the reason why the members of the average "church" today know nothing about the third Person of the Godhead is because the preachers they sit under are silent concerning Him.

Nor is it very much better with many of the churches still counted as orthodox. Though the person of the Spirit may not be repudiated, and though His **name** may occasionally be mentioned, yet, with only rare exceptions, is there any definite scriptural teaching given out concerning the offices and operations of the Divine Comforter. As to His work **in salvation,** this is very little understood even by professing Christians. In the majority of places where the Lord Jesus is still formally acknowledged to be the only Saviour for sinners, the current teaching of the day is that Christ has made it possible for men to be saved, but they themselves must decide whether or not they **shall be** saved. The idea now so widely prevailing is that Christ is offered to man's acceptance, and that **he** must "surrender," "give his heart to Jesus," "take his stand for Christ," etc., if the blood of the cross is to avail for his sins. Thus, according to this conception, the Finished Work of Christ, the greatest work of all time, in all the universe, is left contingent on the fickle will of man as to whether it shall be a success or a failure.

Entering now a much narrower circle in Christendom, in places where it is yet owned that the Holy Spirit has a mission and ministry in connection with the preaching of the Gospel, the general idea that prevails even there, is that, when the Gospel of Christ is faithfully preached, the Holy Spirit convicts men of sin and reveals to them their need of a Saviour. But beyond this, very few indeed are prepared to go. The theory prevailing in these places is that the sinner has to **co-operate** with the Spirit, that he must himself **yield to** the Spirit's "striving" or he will not and cannot be saved. But this pernicious and God-insulting theory denies two things: to argue that the natural man is capable of co-operating with the Spirit is to deny that he is **"dead** in trespasses and sins," for a dead man is incapable of doing anything. And, to say that the operations of the Spirit in a man's heart and conscience may be resisted, withstood, is to deny His omnipotence.

Ere proceeding farther and in order to clear the way for what is to follow, a few words need to be said on "My Spirit shall not always strive with man" (Gen 6:3), and "ye do alway resist the Holy Spirit; as your fathers so ye" (Acts 7:51). Now these passages refer to the **external** work of the Spirit: that is, to His testimony through the preached Word. 1 Peter 3: 18-20 shows that it was the Spirit of Christ, **in Noah** who "strove" with the antediluvians, as that patriarch preached to them (2 Peter 2:5). So in Acts 7 the very next words explain v. 51—"Which of the **prophet**s have not your fathers persecuted?" As Nehemiah said, "Many years didst thou forebear them, and testifiedst against them by Thy Spirit **in Thy prophets**" (Neh. 9:30).

The external work of the Spirit, His testimony through the Scriptures as it falls on the outward ear of the natural man, is **always** "resisted" and rejected, which only affords solemn and full demonstration of the awful fact that "the carnal mind is enmity against God" (Rom. 8:7). But what we would now point out is that Scripture reveals another work of the Holy Spirit, a work that is internal, imperceptible, invisible. This work is always **efficacious.** ..It is the Spirit's work **in salvation,** begun in the heart at the new birth, continued or sustained throughout the entire course of the Christian's life on earth, and concluded and consummated in Heaven. This is what is referred to in Phil. 1:6: "He which hath begun a good work in you will finish it." This is what is in view in Psa. 138:8, "The Lord will perfect that which concerneth me." This work is wrought by the Spirit in each of God's elect, and in them alone.

It has been well said that "The part and office of the Holy Spirit in the salvation of God's elect consists in **renewing** them. He quickens the heirs of glory with a spiritual life, enlightens their minds to know Christ, reveals Him to them, forms Him in their hearts, and brings them to build all their hopes of eternal glory on Him alone. He sheds abroad the Father's love in their hearts, and gives them a real sense of it. In which experience of His gracious and effectual work in their souls, they are made to say with the Psalmist, 'Blessed is the man whom Thou choosest, and causeth to approach unto Thee, that he may dwell in Thy courts' (Psa. 65:4.)" —S. E. Pierce.

One of the delusions of the day is that an evangelical believing in Christ lies within the power of the **un**-renewed man, so that by performing what is naively called "a simple act of faith" he becomes a renewed man. In other words, it is supposed that man is the beginner of his own salvation. **He** takes the first step, and God does the rest; **he** "believes," and then God comes in and saves him. This is nothing but a bald and blank denial of the Spirit's work altogether. If there is one time more than another when the sinner lies in need of the Spirit's power it is **at the beginning.** "He who denies the need of the Spirit at the **beginning,** cannot believe in His work at the after stages —nay, cannot believe in the need of the Spirit's work at all. The mightiest and most insuperable difficulty lies at the beginning. If the sinner can get over **that** without the Spirit, he can easily get over the rest. If he does not need the Spirit to enable him to **believe,** he will not need Him to enable him to **love**" (H. Bonar).

They err greatly who think that **after** the Spirit has done His work in the conscience it still remains for man to say whether he shall be regenerated or not, whether he shall believe or no. The Spirit of God does not wait for the sinner to exercise his will **to** believe; instead, He works in the elect "**both to will** and to do" (Phil. 2:13). Therefore does Jehovah declare "I am found of them that sought Me **not**" (Isa. 65-1)—quoted by Paul in Rom. 10:20. To "believe" in Christ savingly is a supernatural act, the product of supernatural grace. There is no more power in fallen man to believe to the saving of his soul, than he has any merits of his own entitling him to the favour of God; thus, he is as dependent on the Spirit for power as on Christ for worthiness. The Spirit's work is to **apply** the redemption which the Lord Jesus purchased for His people, and the children of God owe their salvation to the One equally as much as to the Other.

In Titus 3:5 the **salvation** of the redeemed is expressly attributed to God the Spirit: "Not by works of righteousness which we have done, but according to His mercy He saved us, **by** the washing of regeneration, and renewing **of the Holy Spirit.**" "If it be asked in what sense can men be said to be 'saved' by the renewing of the Spirit, when the salvation is in Christ, the answer is obvious: There is a series of truths to which no link can be awanting. We are saved by the Divine purpose, for God hath chosen us to salvation; we are saved by the atonement, as the meritorious ground of all; we are saved by faith as the bond of union to Christ; we are saved by grace as contrasted with works done; we are saved by the truth, as conveying God's testimony; and, as here, we are saved by the renewing of the Holy Spirit, as producing faith in the heart" (Prof. Smeaton).

1. Regeneration is by the Spirit.

"And you hath He quickened, who were dead in trespasses and sins" (Eph. 2:1). The quickening of those who are dead in trespasses is the work of the third Person of the Trinity: "That which is born of the Spirit is spirit" (John 3:6). The natural man is spiritually dead. He is alive sinward and worldward, but dead Godward—"alienated from the life of God" (Eph. 4:18). If this solemn truth were really believed there would be an end to controversy on our present subject. A dead man **cannot** "co-operate" with the Spirit, nor can he "accept Christ." In 2 Cor. 3:5 we read, "Not that we are sufficient of ourselves to think anything." That is said of Christians. If the regenerate have no capaciy to "think" spiritually, still less are the unregenerate able to.

"The natural man receiveth not the things of the Spirit of God: for they are foolishness unto him; neither can he know them, because they are spiritually discerned" (1 Cor. 2:14). What could be plainer? The "natural man" is fallen man in his **un**regenerate state. Unless he is born from above he is completely devoid of spiritual discernment. Our Lord expressly declared, "Except a man be born again, he **cannot see** the kingdom of God" (John 3:3). The "natural man" cannot see himself, his ruin, his depravity, the filthiness of his own righteousness. No matter how plainly God's truth is presented to him, being blind, he cannot discern either its meaning, spirituality, or suitedness to his need.

A spiritual understand of the Gospel is as truly due to the operation of the Holy Spirit as that He is the Author of Divine revelation. Spiritual life must precede spiritual sight, and the Spirit Himself must enter the heart before there is "life:" "And shall put My Spirit in you, and ye shall live" (Ezek. 37:14).

The work of the spirit in regeneration is a Divine miracle which is the result of His forthputting of supernatural power. It is the quickening of a spiritual corpse; it is the bringing of a dead soul to life. The sinner himself can no more accomplish it by an act of his own will, than he can create a universe. This miracle of grace is spoken of in Scripture as "the exceeding greatness of His power to usward, who believe according to the working of His mighty power which He wrought in Christ when He raised Him from the dead" (Eph. 1:19, 20). "The same power which was put forth to raise Christ from the dead, is put forth in regeneration . . . Christ's resurrection is the exemplary pattern of our spiritual resurrection, according to which, as the Spirit wrought in Him, so He works in us a work conformed to His resurrection. As the resurrection of Christ was the great declaration of His being the Son of God, so is regeneration of our being the sons of God, being the evidence of our adoption, and also the first discovery of our election. As Christ's resurrection is the first step to His eternal kingdom and glory, so regeneration is the first open introduction into all the blessings of that state of grace into which the child of God is now introduced" (S. E. Pierce).

2. Meetness for Heaven is by the Spirit.

Our **title** to the glory lies solely in the righteousness of Christ; our personal **fitness** for it lies in the Holy Spirit's regenerating of us. All our meetness for the heavenly state was wrought in us in regeneration. Writing to the regenerated at Colosse the apostle said ,"Giving thanks unto the Father, which hath made us meet to be partakers of the inheritance of the saints in light." And then he shows **wherein** this "meetness" consists: "Who hath delivered us from the power of darkness, and hath translated us into the kingdom of His dear Son" (v. 13). Their title is without them; their "meetness" within. The Holy Spirit has created in them a nature which is capacitated to know and enjoy the Triune God.

In our unregenerate state we were completely under the power of darkness, that is, of sin and Satan, and we were less able to deliver ourselves from this bondage than Jonah was able to escape from the belly of the whale. We "sat in darkness" and "in the region and shadow of death" (Matt. 4:16). We were "captives," "bound" and "in prison" (Isa. 61:1). We were those "having no hope, and without God in the world" (Eph. 2:12). From this dreadful state every renewed soul hath been "delivered" by the gracious, sovereign, and invincible power of the Holy Spirit, and hath been "translated into the kingdom of God's dear Son." Then let each renewed reader give equal homage, adoration and worship to Him, as to the Father and to the Son.

3. Justification and Sanctification are by the Spirit.

"And such were some of you; but ye are washed, but ye are sanctified, but ye are justified in the name of the Lord Jesus, and **by the Spirit** of our God" (1 Cor. 6:11). This is a remarkable scripture, and little pondered. It would lead us too far away from our present theme were we to attempt a full exposition of it. Two things only would we here barely point out: the three saving blessings enumerated in this verse are referred, first, to the "name" or merits of Christ as the procuring cause; and then to the Holy Spirit who makes the elect partakers of them by His own effectual application. He it is who enlightens their minds and opens their hearts to take in and be assured that they **are** "washed, sanctified and justified."

4. Faith is from the Spirit.

A deeply taught servant of God once wrote to a young preacher, "Never represent faith as being an act so 'simple' that the work of the Spirit is not needed to produce it." Yet this is what has been commonly done. A great many of the evangelists of the past hundred years have displayed a zeal which was not according to knowledge (Rom. 10:2), and manifested a far greater concern to see souls saved than to preach the truth of God in its purity. In their efforts to show the **simplicity** of the "way of salvation," they have lost sight of the **difficulties** of salvation (Luke 18:24; 1 Peter 4:18); in their pressing of the responsibility of man to believe, they have ignored the fact that none can believe till the Spirit imparts faith. To present Christ to the sinner and then throw him back on his own will, is to mock him in his helplessness; the work of the Spirit in the heart is as real and urgent a need as was the work of Christ on the cross. For the heart to truly believe in and trust God is a **spiritual** act, a "good fruit," and if fallen man possesses inherent power to do good, then to present the Atonement to him is altogether needless.

There is no middle ground between death and life; no intermediate stage between conversion and non-conversion. The bestowal of eternal life is instantaneous; we are "**created** in Christ Jesus" (Eph. 2:10). It is a most serious error to suppose that after the Spirit of God has done His work in the sinner, it still remains for him to say whether he should be regenerated or not, whether he shall believe or no. All who are the recipients of His supernatural operations **are** regenerated, effectually converted, and actually believe. It is not that the Spirit imparts capacity to believe and then waits for the individual to exercise his will to believe; no, He works in the elect "both to will **and** to do" Phil. 2:13). I may tell a man that in the next room there is a lighted lamp, and he may not believe me; but let me bring it into the room where he is, so that he sees the light for himself, and he is irresistibly persuaded. So a servant of God may tell a man that Christ is sufficient for the chief of sinners, and he believes not; but when Christ is "revealed **in** him" (Gal. 1:16), he cannot but trust Him—see 2 Cor. 4:6.

How perversely men **reverses** the older of God's truth. They urge dead sinners to come to Christ, supposing they have power of will so to do. Whereas Christ has plainly and emphatically stated that "No man can come to Me, except the Father which has sent Me draw him" (John 6:44). "Coming to Christ" is the affections of the heart being drawn out towards Him, and how can one love a person he **knows** not? see John 4:10. Ah, it is the Spirit who must bring Christ to me, reveal Him in me, before I can truly know Him. "Coming to Christ" is an **inward** and **spiritual** act, not an outward and natural one. Truly "the natural man receiveth not the things of the Spirit of God: for they are foolishness unto him: neither can he know them, because they are spiritually discerned" (1 Cor. 2:14). We cannot so much as "see" Christ until we are born again (John 3:3).

Saving grace is something more than an objective fact presented to us; it is a subjective operation, wrought within us. As it is not by **natural** discernment that I discover my need of Christ, so it is not by my natural strength and will that I "come" to Him. There must be life and light (sight) before there can be motion. A babe has to be born, and have strength and sight too, before it is able to "come" to its parent. Believing in Christ is a supernatural act, the product of supernatural power. One may, by means of grammatical phrases and scriptural propositions teach spiritual truth to another, but he cannot illumine his mind with respect thereto. He may tell a man that God is holy, but he cannot impart to him a **consciousness** that God is holy. He may tell him that sin is infinitely heinous, but he cannot beget in him a **feeling** or heart-realization it is so. To those who were well acquainted with them outwardly, Christ said, "Ye neither know Me nor My Father" (John 8:19). A man may "know the way of righteousness" (2 Peter 2:21) theoretically, intellectually, but that is a vastly different matter (though very few are inwardly aware of it) from a spiritual and experimental acquaintance with it.

"We having the same Spirit of faith, according as it is written, I believe, and therefore have I spoken; we also believe, and therefore speak" (2 Cor. 4:13). Here the Spirit of God is spoken of accroding to the work whcih He performs. "The title **'Spirit of faith'** intimates that the Holy Spirt is the Author of faith; for all men have not faith; that is, it is not given to all and does not belong to all (2 Thess. 3:2). The designation means that the procuring cause of faith is the Holy Spirit, who produces this effect by an invincible call, an invitation which accompanies, according to the good pleasure of His will, the external proclamation of the gospel. The faith, therefore, of which **He** is the Author, is not effected by the hearer's own strength, or by the hearer's own effectual will . . . The special operation of the Spirit inclines the sinner, previously disinclined, to receive the invitations of the gospel; for it is He alone, acting as the Spirit of faith, that removes the enmity of the carnal mind to those doctrines of the cross which, but for this, would seem to him unnecessary, or foolish and offensive" (Prof. Smeaton).

Writing to the Philippian saints the apostle declared, "Unto you it is **given** . . . to believe on Him" (1:29). Faith is God's "gift" as Eph. 2:8, 9 positively affirms. It is not a gift **offered** for man's acceptance, but actually conferred upon God's children, breathed into them. It is imparted to each of God's elect, at His appointed time, by the Holy Spirit. It is not produced by the creature's will, but is "the faith of **the operation** of God" (Col. 2:12). We read of "the **work** of God's children, breathed into them. It is the "work" of the Spirit, by His supernatural action. The Holy Spirit is given by Christ to this end, that each of those for whom He died should be brought to a saving knowledge of the truth; therefore are we told "Who **by Him** (not by our wills) do believe in God" (1 Peter 1: 21). In 1 Cor. 3:5 it is said "by whom ye believed, even as the Lord **gave** to every man;" so in Eph. 6:23 it is declared, "Peace be to the brethren, and love with faith **from** God the Father and the Lord Jesus Christ." The very degree and strength of our faith is determined solely by God: "Think soberly, according as God hath dealt to every man the **measure** of faith" (Rom. 12:3). If by grace you are truly a "believer," let the reader give God the Spirit honor, glory and praise for it.

5. Salvation is wholly applied by the Spirit.

"We are bound to give thanks always to God for you, brethren beloved of the Lord, because God hath from the beginning chosen you to salvation **through sanctification of the Spirit** and belief of the truth" (2 Thess. 2:13). The mission of the Spirit in the earth is to apply to God's elect the redemption purposed by the Father and purchased by the Son for them. The Holy Spirit is here to make good in the souls of the heirs of glory the fruits of the travail of Christ's soul.

This He does by means of the gospel, by the written and oral ministry of the Scriptures, for the Word of God is the **only** instrument He employs or uses. The Word of God is "the Word of life" (Phil. 2:16), but it only becomes such in the experience of the individual soul by the immediate operation and application of the Spirit of God. As Paul wrote to the Thessalonian saints, "For our gospel came not unto you in word only, but also in power, and in the Holy Spirit" (1 Thess. 1:5). This is not to deny the efficacy of the Word itself, but is to insist that the direct agency of the Spirit on the heart is absolutley necessary in order to the **reception** of the Word. The Word is a lamp unto our path; but there must be an opening of the eyes of our understandings by the Spirit before we can **see** its light.

The salvation of God's elect was purposed, planned and provided by God the Father before the foundation of the world. It was procured and secured by the incarnation, obedience, death and resurrection of God the Son. It is made known, applied to, and wrought in them by God the Spirit. Thus "salvation is of the Lord" (Jonah 2:9), and man has no part or hand in it, at any point, whatsoever. The child of God is not the earner but the recipient of it. Faith is not a condition which the elect sinner must perform in order to obtain salvation, but is the means and channel through which he personally **enjoys** the salvation of the Triune Jehovah.

—ARTHUR W. PINK.

SEPARATION

How far is it compatible with faithful discipleship to the Lord Jesus, to seek or to retain stations of power and influence in the world? That the possession of power is not in itself evil, but that its righteous exercise is a thing excellent and blessed, is abundantly evident from scripture, as well as experience. Thus it is ascribed to God, as one of His distinguishing attributes: "Twice have I heard this —that power belongeth unto God." It is the endowment of the Lord Jesus, as the Son of Man glorified: "All power is given unto Me in heaven and in earth." And it will be communicated by Him to the saints in their glory;—"To him that overcometh and keepeth My works unto the end, to him will I give power, even as I received of My Father." Moreover the place assigned to Adam in innocency, when set over the creation which God had made, sufficiently indicates its adaption to the original constitution of our nature, and the anxiety evinced by mankind in every age to secure its healthful administration, shows how important they esteem its influence to be on the welfare and happiness of man. We cannot wonder therefore at the tenacity with which even believers are accustomed to cling to its possession. It is excellent in itself, and if any objection does really exist against its present exercise by the disciples of Christ, it can arise only from contingent circumstances connected with the present mode of administration.

There is only one test by which the character of these contingent circumstances can be rightly tried, and that is the New Testament. Some stations of authority are clearly sanctioned there, and rules distinctly given to guide us in its exercise. The father, the master, and the husband, are all directed how to use the authority which is entrusted to them; and thus it appears there are some circumstances in which power may fitly be exercised by the disciple of Jesus. And if it be asked how then are we to distinguish the circumstances in which power may rightly be used, is not the answer simply this? "It may be exercised whenever its exercise is guided only by the laws of Christ."

The master may control his household, or the parent his children without being himself constrained to forsake the laws of Christ, and to adopt others from men as the rule of his domestic government. He can reward or punish without being constrained to use the laws of man. He is simply the servant of Christ, and the apostles supply him with directions how to use the authority he holds. He can obey the scripture faithfully, and therefore govern others according to Christ.

In the Church, too, authority can be exercised according to the laws of Christ. The gathered company of saints which the apostles planted and watered, had each their rulers who watched over them; and these rulers owned no directory, except the laws of Christ, through His apostles, and now found in the Word; nor at that time was His Lordship denied by formally allowing the right of man to make laws for the Church of God. Here then are blessed spheres for the exercise of power. It is a comely and pleasing sight to see a parent training up his child in the nurture and admonition of the Lord —to see masters measuring to their servants that which they would desire to have measured back to themselves again by their Master who is in heaven, and to see the shepherds caring for the sheep. These are blessed but lowly spheres for the exercise of power. They may have been, and they have been, valued by some who silently and unregarded by the world, have sought that crown of glory which the chief Shepherd will give at His appearing. But the world values not and does not care to seek the exercise of a lowly authority restricted by the laws of Jesus of Nazareth. Power to be valued by the world, must be possessed and exercised according to the world's principles, and guided by its laws. Can such power be desirable for the servant of Christ?

Civil magistracy for example, is a thing eagerly sought for by the world. It is in itself a blessing,—a blessing from God, for "there is no power but of God." But yet the New Testament, whilst it directs the father, the husband, the master, gives no similar rules to guide the civil magistrate; because the civil magistrate was then, and still is according to the **present** arrangements of civil society the servant of the world, that is, he **must** administer the world's laws. A magistrate in the time of Trajan, was constrained to enforce the law of the empire for the proscription of Christians; and a magistrate may now be required to sign the warrant of impressment or any other similar edict, in which the supposed utilities of human society, bury every remembrance of what is owing to the laws of Christ.

If he could go to the seat of authority with his Bible in his hand, and drawing all the principles of his conduct from the New Testament act simply as the servant of Christ, a magistrate might retain his dignity and be a faithful servant still; but he is not there as the servant of Christ, he is there as the expositor and administrator of the world's laws, which are based on principles so entirely discordant with those of the Lord Jesus, that to admit the one is to nullify the other. Another code based upon principles of expediency and human selfishness, is brought in between him and the sermon of the mount; nor can he follow the plain precepts of the latter, without being false to his engagements to uphold the former; and therefore he has to choose which master he will obey.

For if we turn to facts—where is any nation to be found which dreams of receiving the laws of Christ as their directory? There may be in the midst of the nations many **individuals** who being children of faith, and instructed by the Holy Spirit, have esteemed the reproach of Christ greater riches than all the treasures of the world: but where can we find a nation, which in its collective capacity in its laws and social regulations, has esteemed the reproach of Christ? Let us take for any example, one branch only of Christian service, the meek forgiveness of those who despitefully use us according to the spirit of the command—"if any one smite thee on the right cheek, turn to him the other also." Where is the nation whose laws are not rather based upon principles of retaliation and revenge? whose fleets, and armies, and institutions, do not witness, that, as a nation, it is not subject to the laws of Him who by and bye shall be manifested as the Prince of Peace? when "nation shall not lift up sword against nation, neither shall they learn war any more;" and if this will be the result of His legislation then, who can doubt that it would be the consequence of its acceptance now? Can a believer then, when once he sees that the measures of nations are from the highest to the lowest departments of their control, regulated by other principles than those of Christ, assist in promoting their plans? Christ did not, neither His apostles. They rendered to the powers that were, custom, obedience, honour; but they neither held nor sought to hold authority in the world, and therefore free from having entailed upon them through the use of it, the necessity of acquiescing in the world's principles and habits.

The rejection of the Lord Jesus was the final manifestation that the systems of the world were hopelessly evil, or, to use the words of the apostle John, that the whole world was lying in the wicked one. The titles "god of this world," "prince of this world," are given by the scriptures to Satan only in connection with or after the rejection of the Son of God; for thereby the world's alienation from God and allegiance to Satan was fully shown. "To seek the things that the Gentiles seek, and to work the works of the Gentiles," are, in the language of our Lord and His apostles, equivalent to worldliness and sin; and if any one should acknowledge this but imagine that the preaching of the Gospel has produced a change, it may be again asked, how is this exhibited? When did the national systems of the Gentiles alter into conformity with the sermon on the mount? If an individual is rescued from his state of sin, and brought into the light of the gospel of Christ, and under the power of His before unrecognized precepts, the change is so great that it can only be described by saying—"Old things are passed away, and behold all things are become new." But when was it so with the systems of the nations?

If then the testimony of scripture be so very express as to the evil character of the Gentile systems at their close, if Babylon be the consummation, and Armageddon the end, of all the efforts of Gentile greatness, what can a believer hope respecting them? What can he do, except seek humbly to imitate the Lord Jesus, who, whilst He hated the world's evil systems, loved us sinners, who were in them, and directed towards us the gospel of His grace to save us, and to extricate us (for such is the true meaning of the word) from this present evil age (Gal. 1:4), an age whose darkness is elsewhere declared to be ruled by evil spirits (Eph. 2:2). Salvation therefore, is "extrication" from the principles and systems of this present evil age, and not permission to continue in them, as if sanatory measures were available. Salvation is extrication from these things and translation into another kingdom, even the kingdom of God's dear Son; the principles of which are not any of the old principles with which men have already been conversant, renovated or improved; but as strange and peculiar and new, as it was strange and peculiar for the Lord of glory to be born in a stable, and to die on the accursed tree.

This marvelous event produced a change in the manifested dispensations of God, which cannot be too carefully considered in its bearing upon the present position of the Christian. Pure, unmixed, untempered mercy, without an attempt to prosecute the just claims of righteousness upon the sinner; unmingled grace associated with the lowest abasement in the world, is the character of Christ, and of the new things which He came to declare. How could these things agree with the systems in which men were glorying? They did not agree, and therefore whilst the power of earth was still continued in the Gentile image, there was also constituted another system, viz., the Church of God, commanded to follow Jesus in the steps of suffering here, and to have their exaltation in a future world. The image which Nebuchadnezzar saw in vision, cannot symbolize the Church of God; for the Church will never be smitten with destruction, and therefore it follows that there is a system or systems of government in the world, which originally deriving their power from God, are using it in rebellion against Him. God may endure it, as He endures the actions of many a wicked man, who is indebted to Him as his Creator, for the very powers which he perverts to sin, but He neither Himself sanctions, nor would desire His saints to sanction by their aid in its evil course. And thus whilst we can truly say, "there is no power but of God, "the powers that be are ordained of God;" and as such are entitled to our submission and reverence; yet we can also say with equal truth, that power unguarded by the laws of Christ is power perverted, and therefore unsuited for His servant to exercise. This is exhibited in our Lord's conversation with Pilate.

Howevr possible then it may once have been for the servants of God, such as Daniel, to hold the stations of dignity in the world, when its systems had not finally proved the hopeless character of their evil, by the rejection of Christ, and when Christ had not yet taught His new and before unrecognized precepts; yet now Christ has taught, and **has been** rejected. And thus there are these two reasons why one who would faithfully follow Christ, is precluded from the present exercise of power in the world. The first is, that no one can exercise it without allowing human laws to intervene between Christ and themselves, whereby they subject themselves to a rule which never necessarily agrees with His will, and almost always is essentially discordant with it. This objection would hold even if Christ had not come in humiliation to be the servant of the Father in exhibiting grace to men: but how much more if it is not God in His exaltation, but Christ in meek and uncomplaining endurance and patient but active grace, that is presented to our imitation. The world would cease to be the world, and would be changed into the Church, if its laws and principles were changed into conformity with this pattern. The sword of the avenger cannot suit that hand which should bear only the ensign of peace; and accordingly it has been placed by God in the hand of other than those of the brethren of Christ. He has put it into the hands of the Gentiles, whether heathen, or nominally owning Christ, and they, whilst thinking only of themselves, will subserve His purposes for preserving order in the earth, and thus, even Nero, becomes to Paul the minister of God for good, though Paul was not the executor of Nero's laws. The giver and the gift are good, and though they who receive it may use it only to promote their selfish ends, yet even their use of it, may and will produce a result of blessing, far from being despised by those who desire not to strive nor to cry, but to lead a quiet and peaceable life in all godliness and honesty.

1. If the present principles of the nations are essentially opposed to those of Christ, we cannot serve two masters.

2. We cannot do unchristian things in a Christian way. If our professional employment, or the system whose credit we support, is in itself opposed to the principles of Christ, no personal holiness in ourselves can sanctify its evil, nor expel the poison of its influence.

3. In our own little sphere as individuals, we may be gathering with Christ; while in a more extensive one, by being linked with some evil system we may be scattering abroad.

4. It is not enough for us to be neutral (if that were possible) in the conflict which is now being carried on between Christ and Satan. He that gathered not with Me, scattereth abroad. Protestation against evil and separation from it, can alone satisfy the Spirit of Christ.

5. We cannot give ourselves two personalities. We cannot have an **official** existence, distinct from our existence as individuals and free ourselves from responsibility, whilst doing **officially** what individually we abhor. What kind of antinomianism can be more dangerous than that which flows from adopting the reverse principle of this? It allows us in our own persons to profess ourselves the disciples of Christ, but it sets our actions free from every moral restraint. Darius, the Persian, was sincerely anxious to save the life of Daniel, but **officially** he was bound to execute the laws of Persia. He might have resigned his throne rather than become an instrument in destroying Daniel; but this was too great a sacrifice, and therefore Daniel was cast into the den of lions.—Extracts from an article in "The Christian Witness," 1842.

THE HISTORY OF A STANZA

One Sunday evening, when I was Rector of St. Paul's Church, Halifax, "The Westminster Abbey of Canada," as the Govenor of Nova Scotia used to call it, I told towards the close of my sermon the following story:—Many years ago, Dr. Valpy, a well-known English scholar, wrote a little verse of four lines as the longing of his heart and the confession of his faith. This was the simple stanza:—

"In peace let me resign my breath,
And Thy salvation see;
My sins deserve eternal death,
But Jesus died for me."

Some time afterwards he gave this verse to his friend, Dr. Marsh, a well-known Church of England clergyman and the father of Miss Marsh, the author of the Life of Captain Hedley Vicars, and the verse became a great blessing to him. Dr. Marsh gave the lines to his friend, Lord Roden, who was so impressed wtih them that he got Dr. Marsh to write them out, and then fastened the paper over the mantlepiece in his study; and there, yellow with age, they hung for many years, a memorial of the beloved hand that traced them.

Some time after this an old friend—General Taylor, one of the heroes of Waterloo—came to visit him at Tollymore Park. Lord Roden noticed that the eyes of the old veteran were always fixed for a few moments on the motto over the mantlepiece. Lord Roden said, "Why General, you will soon know the verse by heart." The General replied with great emphasis of feeling, "I know it now by heart," and the simple words were the means of bringing him to know the way of salvation. Some two years afterwards, the physician, who had been with the old General while he lay a-dying, wrote to Lord Roden to say that his friend had departed in peace, and that the last words which fell from his lips were the words which he had learned to love in his lifetime:—

"In peace let me resign my breath,
And Thy salvation see;
My sins deserve eternal death,
But Jesus died for me."

Years afterwards, at the house of a neighbour, Lord Roden happened to tell the story of the old General and these lines, and among those who heard it was a young officer in the British Army who had recently returned from the Crimea. He listened carelessly enough, and no impression seemed to be made at the time. A few months later, however, Lord Roden received a message from the officer that he wanted to see him, as he was in a rapid decline. As the Earl entered the sickroom the dying officer extended both his hands to welcome him, repeating the lines:—

"In peace let me resign my breath,
And Thy salvation see;
My sins deserve eternal death,
But Jesus died for me."

And then he added, "These simple words have been God's message of peace and comfort to my heart in this illness, and they have been brought to my memory by the Holy Spirit, the Comforter, after days of darkness and distress."

As I said, I was telling this story in my sermon in old St. Paul's, but as I began to tell it I noticed that an old gentleman who was sitting in a pew not far from the pulpit just in front of me, a representative of one of the oldest families in Nova Scotia, was being overcome with an extraordinary emotion. His whole frame seemed to quiver with some unwonted excitement, and his eyes looked bright with a strange light. I thought for the moment that it was a transient attack of some physical affection. But as I went on telling the story there was no doubt that it had in some way seized upon the very soul of the listener and touched his feelings with some strange and indescribable suggestion. And when at last I came to the part about the Crimean Officer I thought that the old gentleman would have almost cried out in the church, so deeply was he affected. The story ended the sermon. After the singing of the hymn I went to the vestry. I had scarcely got there when a knock was heard at the door, and the old gentleman, with emotion still evident, came and said, "Where did you get that story? I told him I had read it in the work of a modern author whose works are widely read. He said, "I do not know whether you saw that I was very much touched by it, but it almost overcame me." And then, with tears streaming from his eyes, he told me this story:— "Years ago, when he was a young man, careless and indifferent in matters of religion, he sauntered one day in his walk into an old churchyard near Wolfville, Nova Scotia, in the land of Evangeline, and seeing a fallen gravestone, he overturned it in pure curiosity. And there he read at the foot, engraved in the stone, a verse of four lines that took such a hold upon him, and so clearly explained to him the way of salvation, that they were the means of his conversion. And from that day, nearly fifty years before, he had by God's grace as a result of those four lines, led a consecrated life for Christ."

"In peace let me resign my breath,
And Thy salvation see;
My sins deserve eternal death,
But Jesus died for me."

He said, "You can imagine my amazement, as well as my delight when I heard you tell the stroy about the lines. You brought back to me the wonderful way in which God was pleased to save my soul."

It was not long after that I was sent for to visit this old gentleman in a sickness, which gradually grew more serious. One of the last things he did before he died was to take my hand affectionately, and ask me, as his clergyman, to do him a favour; and that was, that at his funer-

"My little children, let us not love in word, neither in tongue; but in deed and in truth. Thus is profession tested, put to proof.

"He that saith I know Him, and keepeth not His commandments is a liar and the truth is not in him." There are many in these days who **do** say, "I know Him," who are loud in declaring that they have a saving knowledge of Him, but who keep not His commandments. Yet, so blatant is the Antinomian spirit of this age that there is a large section of professing Christians, headed by men claiming great proficiency in "rightly dividing the word of truth," who insist that grace and law are mortal enemies, that to press "commandments" (even the commandments of God) upon people, is seeking to bind on them a burden grievous to be borne. But apart from these extremists, the rank and file of professing Christians evidence little or no subjection to the commandments of God.

How few today respect the Sabbatic command! How grievously is the Lord's day desecrated! How few regard that word, "Owe no man anything" (Rom. 13:8)! Professing Christians run into debt, purchase things on the credit system, as freely as do non-professors. Christian parents are bidden to bring up their children "in the nurture and admonition of the Lord" (Eph. 6:4). Are they doing so? Servants are ordered to be obedient to their masters with fear and trembling "as unto Christ" (Eph. 6:5). Are they? Wives are bidden to submit themselves to their husbands, as unto the Lord, and this "in every thing" (Eph. 5:22-24). Do they? Husbands are commanded to love their wives as Christ also loved the Church (Eph. 5:25), and to give honour to the wife as the weaker vessel (1 Peter 3:7). Do they? Women are forbidden to have their hair bobbed (1 Cor. 11:5-15). And so we might go on almost indefinitely. The terrible thing is that violations of these and other commands of God are regarded as trifles, things of little moment. But, be not deceived: "He that saith, I know Him, and **keepeth not** His commandments, **is a liar,** and the truth is not in him." May the Holy Spirit apply this searching word to the hearts of the readers.

—ARTHUR W. PINK.

---

al and over his coffin I would tell the story of the lines in the hope that the prayer of a dying man might be answered, and that they might be a blessing to many souls more. Soon afterwards he died; and at his funeral, which was attended by some of the most distinguished citizens of Halifax, a large and representative body of prominent men, I told over his coffin, amidst the most profound and interested silence, the story of the stanza that had transformed so many lives. I ended by saying that it was the wish of the dear old man on his dying bed that the words, which would be distributed as his last memorial to all present, might become a blessing to their souls, and as each one passed from the house of mourning he received a beautiful card, elegantly printed in purple, with the name, and age, and burial date of that old saint of God, and on the other side the never-to-be-forgotten words:—

"In peace let me resign my breath,
And Thy salvation see;
My sins deserve eternal death,
But Jesus died for me."

The secret of the wonderful power that resides in these lines cannot be told. It may be that they were written in prayer and watered by tears of love. I only know that when I told this story in a vacation service in one of the charming hotels in the White Mountains, New Hampshire, an American gentleman, a prominent New Yorker, was so deeply impressed that he said, after hearing the words, "I have rarely heard anything that made such an impression upon me. Never in my life before have I so clearly grasped the way of salvation through faith in the Crucified." May they become the confession of faith of all who hear, and all who read.

—D. H.

corrupt tree bringeth forth evil fruit" (Mattt. 7:17). The test for love of Christ is obedience to His commandments. Profession is proved or disproved by the daily walk. If a man has no **love** for spiritual things, he is devoid of a spiritual nature. If a man is in an utterly prayerless state, he has not received the Spirit of adoption whereby the saved cries, "Abba, Father." If a man is thoroughly wrapped up in the things of this world, then his eyes must be closed to the glories of Heaven: "For where your treasure is, there will your heart be also" (Matt. 7:21). If a man prefers the company of worldlings to that of God's people, then is he a worlding himself. If a man lives to please self rather than God, he is yet dead in trespasses and sins.

"Faith if it hath not works is dead" (James 2:17). A faith which does not transform the life, which does not produce practical godliness, which does not issue in personal obedience to God in the daily walk, is not "the faith of God's elect" (Titus 1:1). The grace of God which brings salvation to a soul, also **teaches** that soul to deny ungodly and worldly lusts, and to live "soberly, righteously, and godly, in this present world" (Titus 2:11, 12). Christ gave Himself for a people who should be "zealous of good works" (Titus 2:14). Those born of the Spirit have been "created in Christ Jesus unto good works, which God hath before ordained that we **should** walk in them" (Eph. 2:10). If then I am **not** walking in "good works," I have no right to regard myself as a regenerated soul. If my professing brethren are not "zealous of good works," then, as yet, I have no scriptural reason to regard them as among that favoured number for whom Christ gave Himself. Good works are not required in order to salvation, but they **are** the certain fruit of salvation.

Near the close of the sermon on the mount, the Lord Jesus spoke of two foundations on which men build their houses, the one on the "rock," the other, on the "sand." Many professing Christians are familiar with this figure, but very few can define correctly (without looking up the passage) the **particular characters** whom the Lord describeth **as** building on these respective foundations. **Who** is the one who builds upon the "rock?" **Who** is the one who builds upon the "sand?" **What is it** that differentiates the one builder from the other? How many readers of this magazine can answer without consulting their Bibles? Christ did not there say that the builder on the "rock" was a **believer,** and the builder on the "sand" an **unbeliever.** Instead, He said, "Whosoever heareth these sayings of Mine and **doeth** them, I will liken him unto a wise man, which built his house upon a rock . . . And every one that heareth these sayings of Mine, and **doeth them not,** shall be likened unto a foolish man which built his house upon the sand" (Matt. 7:24, 26).

"He that saith, I know Him, and keepeth not His commandments, is a liar, and the truth is not in him." Does such language sound harsh to the reader? If so, his ears are too fastidious. Let none be found murmuring against them, for they are the words of the thrice holy God. Honesty is always outspoken; it is the jesuit who dissembles. Truth is always plain and to the point; it is error which needs the artifical elegancies of speech to embellish it. Faithfulness never flatters. Far better is it to be made miserable by Truth's exposure than to have a false peace maintained by the father of lies.

"He that saith I know Him, and keepeth not His commandments is a liar, and the truth is not in him." Let it not be overlooked that the one God first employed to pen these words was the apostle of love, the one who leaned upon the Master's bosom. But love is faithful, and faithfulness calls for a real endeavour to disillusion deluded souls. It is a spurious charity which, out of fear of hurting another's feelings, makes no effort to expose the lie on which he is resting, the more so because that lie will damn him for all eternity if not turned from. Better far to be made wretched now, while there is a hope of sorrow being turned into joy, than to weep and wail forever and ever.

Though such be not its central theme, nor its chief purpose, yet the 1st Epistle of John might well be designated, The Testing of Christian Profession. Much in it is exceedingly pertinent to the days in which our lot is cast, for these are the Perilous Times foretold in 2 Tim. 3, in which live multitudes "having a form of godliness, but denying the power thereof" (v. 5). Three times over in the first chapter we find the words "If we say," and three times in the second chapter, "he that saith." Each of these is followed by a statement which shows that the mere "saying" is not enough. Then in 3:7 we read, "Little children, let no man deceive you; he that **doeth** righteousness is righteous." Again, in 3:18 we are told,

(Continued on Page 239)

Vol. VIII.   NOVEMBER, 1929   No. 11

STUDIES IN THE SCRIPTURES

"Search the Scriptures" John 5:39

Copyright in all English-speaking Countries.

Editor: Arthur W. Pink, Morton's Gap, Ky., U. S. A.
Hon. Agent in England: Mr. A. Winstone, 2, Lennox Villas, Hewlett Road, Cheltenham.
Hon. Agent in Australia: Mr. G. Ardill, The Christian Workers' Depot. Commonwealth and Reservoir Streets, Sydney.

FREE TO ALL WHO WILL READ IT.

Increased Faith

"And the apostles said unto the Lord, Increase our faith" (Luke 17:5).

Faith is of the utmost importance to the Christian. There is nothing about which we ought to have a greater and more earnest concern than our faith. If a man lacks faith he lacks everything that is spiritual: "But without faith it is impossible to please God" (Heb. 11:6). Faith is the connecting link between the soul and God. Take that away, and all is gone. Remove faith and the Christian life is a non-entity: for "The just shall live by faith" (Heb. 10:38), and without faith how shall they live at all? The first thing for an awakened soul to make sure about is that he really **has** faith, that faith which is the gift of God.

"There are a thousand shams in the world, a thousand imitations of faith; but there is only one true, vital, saving faith. There are scores of notional faiths—a faith which consists of holding a sound creed; a faith which bids men believe a lie, by wrapping them up with assurances of their safety, when they are still in the gall of bitterness and the bonds of iniquity; a faith which consists in presumptuously trusting to ourselves. We ought to be more careful of our faith than anything else. True, we ought to examine our conduct, we ought to search our works; we ought to try our love; but, above all, our faith: for if faith be wrong, all is wrong" (C. H. Spurgeon).

Faith is the root grace upon which all other virtues depend. **Patience** cannot be exercised only as faith is in operation, for faith looks to "the recompence of the reward" (Heb. 11:26). ..**Courage** is weak when faith languishes, for unless my heart is confiding in the Captain of our salvation, I shall flee before my enemies. **Hope** is inactive when faith ceases to function, for this is a grace which is the fruit of eyeing God's promises. **Love** is feeble if faith be weak; I cannot love God at all if I do not believe in Him, and only as the heart is truly trusting Him are its affections drawn out towards Him. Thus, faith is the virtue which waters the roots of vital godliness. Faith is that vitality which imparts sap to all the branches of the Christian life. Faith is the golden thread upon which all the graces are to be strung.

"Faith is the only way whereby thou canst obtain blessings. If we want blessings from God, nothing can fetch them down except faith. Prayer cannot draw down answers from God's throne except it is the earnest prayer of the man who believes. Faith is the ladder on which my soul must walk to ascend to heaven. Faith is the telegraphic wire which links earth to heaven—on which God's blessings move so fast that before we call He answers, and while we are yet speaking He hears. But if that telegraphic wire be snapped, how can we receive the promise? O, then, Christian, watch well thy faith, for with it thou canst win all things, however poor thou art; but without it, thou canst obtain nothing" (C. H. Spurgeon).

"Lord, Increase our faith." The apostles realized that they could not increase their own faith. They knew it was useless to go to John the Baptist, eminent servant of God though he was. Faith's Author can alone increase it. A preacher may inflate the faith of his hearers, till it is turned into carnal presumption or

(Continued on page 264)

IMPORTANT NOTICES

Please advise promptly of change of address, otherwise copies will be lost in the mails.

We are glad to send a sample copy to any of our friends whom you believe would be interested in such a publication.

Send to Mr. I. C. Herendeen, 433-435, The Arcade, Cleveland, Ohio, for a list of our publications. He has published many of our books and booklets.

This Magazine is published as a work of faith and labour of love. The Editor and his wife gladly give their services. It is freely sent to all who will read it. No charge is made for it.

Christians who feel definitely lead to do so, may have fellowship with us in this ministry. Those outside the U. S. A., please send only INTERNATIONAL Money Orders made out to Morton's Gap, Kentucky, U. S. A. See that it is made out in American money.

CONTENTS

The Epistle to the Hebrews	242
Gleanings in Exodus	249
The Holy Spirit's Work	254
The Unity of Saints	259
Particular Redemption	263
Important Notice	263

THE EPISTLE TO THE HEBREWS

23. Infancy and Maturity: Heb. 6:1-3.

The interpretation which we shall give of the above verses is not at all in accord with that advanced by the older writers. It differs considerably from that found in the commentaries of Drs. Calvin, Owen and Gouge, and more recently, those of A. Saphir, and Dr. J. Brown. Much as we respect their works, and deeply as we are indebted to not a little that is helpful in them, yet we dare not follow them blindly. To "prove all things" (1 Thess. 5:21) **is ever our bounden duty.** Though it is against our natural inclination to depart from the exposition they suggested (several, with some diffidence), yet we are thankful to God that in later years He has granted some of His servants increased light from His wondrous and exhaustless Word. May it please Him to vouchsafe us still more.

The writers mentioned above understood the expression "the principles of the doctrine of Christ," or as the margin of the R. V. more accurately renders, "the word of the beginning of Christ," to refer to the elementary truths of Christianity, a summary of which is given in the six items that follow in the second half of v. 1 and the whole of v. 2; while the "Let us go on unto perfection," they regarded as a call unto the deeper and higher things of the Christian revelation. But for reasons which to us seem conclusive, such a view of our passage is altogether untenable. It fails to take into account the central theme of this Epistle, and the purpose for which it was written. It does not do justice at all to the immediate context. It completely breaks down when tested in its details.

As we have repeated so often in the course of this series of articles, the theme of our Epistle is the immeasurable superiority of Christianity over Judaism. Unless the interpreter keeps this steadily in mind as he proceeds from chapter to chapter, and from passage to passage, he is certain to err. This is the key which unlocks every section, and if attempt be made to open up any portion without it, the effect can only be strained and forced. The importance of this consideration cannot be overestimated, and several striking exemplifications of it have already been before us in our survey of the previous chapters. Here too it will again stand us in good stead, if we but use it. The apostle is not contrasting two different stages of Christianity, an infantile and a mature; rather is he opposing, once more, the substance over against the shadows. He continues to press upon the Hebrews their need of forsaking the visible for the invisible, the typical for the antitypical.

That in taking up our present passage it is also of first importance to study its **connection** with the immediate context, is evident from its very first word, "Therefore." The apostle is here drawing a conclusion from something said previously. This takes us back to what is recorded in 5:11-14, for a right understanding of which depends a sound exposition of what immediately follows. In these verses the apostle rebukes the Hebrews for their spiritual sloth, and likens them to little children capacitated to receive nothing but milk. He tells them that they have need of one teaching them again "**which** be the first principles of the oracles of God," which denoted they had not yet clearly grasped the fact that Judaism was but a temporary economy, because a typical one, its ordinances and ceremonies foreshadowing Him who was to come here and make an atonement for the sins of His people. Now that He had come and finished His work the types had served their purpose, and the shadows were replaced by the Substance.

The spiritual condition in which the Hebrew saints were at the time the Holy Spirit moved the apostle to address this Epistle to them, is another important key to the opening of its hortatory sections. As we showed in our last article, the language of 5:11-14 plainly intimates that they had gone backward. The **cause** of this is made known in the 10th chapter, part of which takes us back to a point in time prior to what is recorded in chapter 5. First in 10:32 we read, "But call to remembrance the former days, in which, after ye were illuminated, ye endured a great fight of afflictions." This "great fight of afflictions" they had, as v. 34 tells us, taken **"joyfully."** Very remarkable and rare was this. How was such an experience to be acounted for? The remainder of v. 34 tells us, **"Knowing** in yourselves that ye have in heaven a **better** and an enduring substance."

But this blessed and spiritual state which characterized the Hebrews in the glow of "first love" had not been maintained. While affections were set upon things above where Christ is seated at the right hand of God, whilst faith was in exercise, they realized that their real portion was on High. But faith has to be tested, patience has to be tried, and unless faith be maintained "hope deferred maketh the heart sick" (Prov. 13:12). Alas, their faith had wavered, and in consequence they had become dissatisfied to have **nothing** down here; they became impatient of waiting for an **unseen** and **future** inheritance. It was for this reason that the apostle said to them, "Cast not away therefore your confidence, which hath great recompence of reward. For ye have need of **patience,** that, after ye have done the will of God, ye might receive the promise" (10:35, 36).

Now it was this discontented and impatient condition of soul into which they had fallen, which accounts for the state in which we find them in 5:11, 12. So too it explains the various things referred to in chapter 6. That is why the apostle was moved to set before them the most solemn warning found in vv. 4-6. That is why we find "hope" so prominent in what follows: see vv. 11, 18, 19. That is why reference is made to "patience" in v. 12. That is why Abraham is referred to, and why **his** "patience" is singled out for mention in v. 15. And that is why in our present passage the Hebrews are urged to "go on unto perfection," and why the apostle interposes a doubt in the matter: "This will we do, **if** God permit" (v. 3), for there was good reason to believe that their past conduct had provoked Him. Thus we see again how wondrously and how perfectly Scripture interprets itself, and how much we need to "compare spiritual things with spiritual" (1 Cor. 2:13).

The sixth chapter of Hebrews does not commence a new section of the Epistle, but continues the digression into which the apostle had entered at 5:11. In view of the disability of those to whom he was writing receiving unto their edification the high and glorious mysteries which he desired to expound, the apostle goes on to set before them various reasons and arguments to excite a diligent attention thereunto. First, he declares his intention positively: to "go on unto perfection" (v. 1). Second, he names, what he intended to "leave," namely, "the word of the beginning of Christ" (vv. 1-3). Third, he warns of the certain doom of apostates (vv. 4-8). Fourth, he softens this warning in the case of the converted Hebrews (vv. 9-14). Fifth, he gives an inspiring encouragement to faith, taken from the life of Abraham (vv. 15-21).

"Therefore leaving the principles of the doctrine of Christ" (v. 1). As already pointed out, the first word of this verse denotes that there is a close link between what has immediately preceded and what now follows. This will appear yet more clearly if we attend closely to the exact terms here used. The word "principles" in this verse is the same as rendered "first" in 5:12. The word "doctrine" is found in its plural form and is translated "oracles" in 5:12. The word "perfection" is given as "of full age" in 5:14. Thus it is very evident that the apostle is here **continuing** the same subject which he began in the previous chapter.

"Therefore leaving the principles of the doctrine of Christ." The rendering of the A. V. of this clause is very faulty and misleading. The verb is in the past tense, not the present. Bagster's interlinear correctly gives "Wherefore **having left."** This difference of rendition is an important one, for it enables us to understand more readily the significance of what follows. The apostle was stating a positive fact, not pleading for a possibility. He was not asking the Hebrews to take a certain step, but reminding them of one they had already taken. They had left the "principles of the doctrine of Christ," and to them he did not wish them to return.

"Therefore leaving the principles of the doctrine of Christ." More accurately, "Wherefore having left the word of the beginning of Christ." Bagster's Interlinear, which gives a literal word for word translation of the Greek, renders it, "Wherefore, having left the of the beginning of the Christ discourse." This expression is parallel with the "first principles of the oracles of God" in 5:12. It has reference to what God has made known concerning His Son under Judaism. In the O. T. two things are outstandingly prominent in connection with Christ: first, prophecies of His coming into the world; second, types and figures of the work He should perform. These predictions had now received their fulfillment, those shadows had now found their substance, in the incarnation, life, death, resurrection and ascension of the Son of God. This, the "holy brethren" (3:1) among the Jews had acknowledged. Thus they had "left" the a.b.c for the Word Himself, the pictures for the Reality.

"Let us go on unto perfection." There is the definite article in the Greek, and "The Perfection" is obviously set in apposition to "The word of the beginning of Christ:" note, not of "the Lord Jesus," but of "Christ," i. e., the Messiah. It is the contrast, once more, between Judaism and Christianity. That which is here referred to as "The Perfection" is the full revelation which God now made of Himself in the person of His incarnate Son. No longer is He veiled by types and shadows, His glory is seen fully in the face of Jesus Christ (2 Cor. 4:6). The only begotten Son has "declared" Him here on earth (John 1:18); but having triumphantly finished the work which was given Him to do, He has been "received up into glory" (1 Tim. 3:16), and upon an exalted and enthroned Christ the affection of the believer is now to be set (Col. 3:1).

"**Wherefore** having left . . . let us go on unto perfection." The first word looks back to **all** that the apostle had said. It is a conclusion drawn from the contents of the whole preceding five chapters. Its force is: In view of the fact that God has now spoken to us in His Son; in view of who He is, namely, the appointed Heir of all things, the Maker of the worlds, the Brightness, of God's glory, and the very Impress of His substance, the One who upholds all things by the word of His power; in view of the fact that He has by Himself "purged our sins," and, in consequence, has sat down at the right hand of the Majesty on high, having been made so much better than the angels, as He hath by inheritance obtained a more excellent name than they; in view of the further fact that He was made in all things like unto His brethren, that He might be a merciful and faithful High Priest in things Godward, to make propitiation for the sins of the people, and having, in consequence of His successful prosecution of this stupendous work been "crowned with glory and honour;" and, seeing that He is immeasurably superior to Moses, Joshua and Aaron;—let us give Him His due place in our thoughts, hearts and lives.

"Let us go on unto perfection" has reference to the apprehension of the Divine revelation of the full glory of Christ in His person, perfections, and position. It is, from the practical side, a "perfection" of **knowledge,** spiritually imparted by the Holy Spirit to the understanding and heart. It refers to the mysteries and sublime doctrine of the Gospel. It is a perfection of knowledge in revealed truth. Yet, of course, it is only a relative "perfection," for an absolute apprehension of the things of God is not attainable in this life. Now "we know in part" (1 Cor. 13:10). "If any man think that he knoweth anything, he knoweth **nothing** yet as he ought to know" (1 Cor. 8:2). Even the apostle Paul had to say, "Brethren, I count not myself to have apprehended: but this one thing I do, forgetting those things which are behind, and reaching forth unto those things which are before, I press toward the mark for the prize of the high calling of God in Christ Jesus" (Phil. 3:13, 14).

"Let **us** go on unto perfection." Students are not agreed as to the precise force of the plural pronoun here. Some consider it to be the apostle linking on the Hebrews to himself in the task immediately before him; others regard the "us" as the apostle graciously joining himself with them in their duty. Personally, we think that both these ideas are to be combined. First, "let us go on;" it was his resolution so to do, as the remaining chapters of the Epistle demonstrate; then let **them** follow him. Thus considered it shows that the apostle did not look upon the condition of the Hebrews as quite hopeless, notwithstanding their "dullness" (5:11)—I shall therefore go on to set before you the highest and most glorious things concerning Christ. Second, the apostle condescends to unite himself with them in their responsibility to press forward. "Wherefore:" in view of the length of time we have been Christians, let us be diligent to grow in grace and in the knowledge of our Lord Jesus Christ. It was, thus, a call to stir them up.

"Let us go on" is passive, "be carried on." It is a word taken from the progress which a ship makes before the wind when under sail. Let us, under the full bent of our will and affections be stirred by the utmost endeavours of our whole souls, be borne onwards. We have abode long enough near the shore, let us hoist our sails, pray to the Spirit for His mighty power to work within us, and launch forth into the deep. This is the duty of God's servants, to excite their Christian hearers to make progress in the knowledge of Divine truth, to urge them to pass the porch and enter the sanctuary, there to behold the Divine glories of the House of God. Though the verb is passive, denoting the effect—"Let us be carried on" —yet it included the active use of means for the producing of this effect. "All diligence" is demanded of the Christian (2 Pet. 1:5). Truth has to be "bought" (Prov. 23:23). That which God has given us must be put into practice (Luke 8:18).

"Let us go on unto perfection." What, we may ask, is the application of this to Christians today? To the Hebrews it meant abandoning the preparatory and earthly system of Judaism, (which occupied their whole attention before believing in Christ as the sent Saviour) and, by faith, laying hold of the Divine revelation which has now been made in and through Him: set your affection on an ascended though invisible Christ, who now serves in the Heavenly Sanctuary on your behalf. For Christians it means, Turn away from those objects which absorbed you in the time of your unregeneracy, and meditate now on and find your joy and satisfaction in things above. Lay aside every weight and the sin which so easily besets, and run with perseverance the race that is set before us, "looking off unto Jesus"—the One who while here left us an example to follow, the One who is now enthroned on High because of the triumphant completion of His race.

To the Hebrews, this much-misunderstood exhortation of Heb. 6:1 was exactly parallel with the word which Christ addressed to the eleven immediately prior to His death: "Ye believe in God, believe also in Me" (John 14:1): Ye have long avowed your faith in "God," whom, though invisible, ye trust; now "believe also in Me," as One who will speedily pass beyond the range of your natural vision. I am on the point of returning to the Father, but I shall still have your interests at heart, yea, I am going to "prepare a place for you;" therefore, trust Me implicitly: let your hearts follow Me on high: walk by faith: be occupied with an ascended Saviour. For us today, the application of this important word signifies, Be engaged with your great High Priest in heaven, dwell daily upon your portion in Him (Eph. 1:3). By faith, behold Christ, now in the heavenly sanctuary, as your righteousness, life, and strength. See in God's acceptance of Him, His adoption of you, that you have been reconciled to Him, made nigh by the precious blood. In the realization of this, worship in spirit and in truth; exercise your priestly privileges.

Thus, the "perfection" of Heb. 6:1 is, strictly speaking, scarcely doctrinal or experimental, yet partakes of both. "The law made nothing perfect, but the bringing in of a better hope did" (Heb. 7:19). It is Christ who has ushered in that which is "perefect." It is in Him we now have a full revelation and manifestation of the eternal purpose and grace of God. He has fully made known His mind (Heb. 1:2). And, by His one all-sufficient offering of Himself, He has **"perfected** forever" (10:14), them whom God set apart in His everlasting counsels. Christ came here to fulfill the will of God (10:9). That will has been executed; the work given Him to do, He finished (John 17:4). In consequence, He has been gloriously rewarded, and in His reward all His people share. This is all made known to us for "the hearing of faith."

"Not laying again the foundation of repentance from dead works" (v. 1). It is most important to see that the contents of the second half of v. 1 and the whole of v. 2 are a parenthesis. The "Let us be carried on to perfection" is completed in **"this** will we do if God permit" in v. 3. That which comes in between is a definition or explanation of what the apostle intended by his "Having left the word of the beginning of Christ." The six items enumerated—"repentance from dead works," etc.—have nothing to do with the 'foundations of Christianity,' nor do they describe those things relating to the elementary experiences of a Christian. Instead, they treat of what appertained to

Judaism, considered as a rudimentary system, paving the way for the fuller and final revelation which God has now made in and by His beloved Son. Unless the **parenthetical** nature of these verses is clearly perceived, interpreters are certain to err in their exposition of the details.

"Not laying again the foundation," etc. It is to be remarked that there is no definite article in the Greek here, so it should be read, "a foundation," which is one of several intimations that it is **not** the 'fundamentals of Christianity' which are here in view. Had these verses been naming the basic features of the new and higher revelation of God, the Holy Spirit had surely said, "**the** foundation;" that He did not, shows that something less important was before Him. As said above, this "foundation" respects Judaism. Now there are two properties to a "foundation," namely, it is that which is first laid in a building; it is that which bears up the whole superstructure. To which we may add, it is generally lost to sight when the ground-floor has been put in. Such was the relation which Judaism sustained to Christianity. As the 'foundation' precedes the building, so had Judaism Christianity. As the 'foundation' bears the building, so the truth of Christianity rests upon the promises and prophecies of the O. T., of which the N. T. revelation records the fulfillment. As the 'foundation' is lost to sight when the building is erected on it, so the types and shadows of the earlier revelation are superceded by the substance and reality.

"Not laying again a foundation," etc. This is exactly what the Hebrews were being sorely tempted to do. To "lay again" this foundation was to forsake the substance for the shadows; it was to turn from Christianity and go back again to Judaism. As Paul wrote to the Galatians, who were being harassed by Judaisers, "Wherefore the law was our schoolmaster unto Christ, that we might be justified by faith" (3:24). To which he at once added, "But after that faith is come, we are no longer under a schoolmaster." Thus, under a different figure, he was here in Heb. 6:1 simply saying, Let us be carried on to maturity, and not go back again to the things which characterized the days of our childhood.

"Not laying again a founation," etc. It will be noted that the apostle here enumerates just **six** things, which is ever the number of man in the flesh. Such was what distinguished Judaism. It was a system which appertained solely to man in the flesh. Its rites and ceremonies only "sanctified to the purifying of the flesh" (Heb. 9:13). Had the fundamentals of Christianity been here in view, the apostle had surely given seven, as in Eph. 4:3-6. The first which he specifies is "repentance from dead works." Observe that it is not "repentance from **sins**." That is not what is in view at all. This expression "dead works" is found again in Heb. 9:14 (and nowhere else in the N. T.), where a contrast is drawn from what is said in v. 13: the blood of bulls and goats sanctified to the purifying of the flesh, then much more should the blood of Christ cleanse their conscience from dead works. Where **sins** are in question the N. T. speaks of them as "wicked works" (Titus 1:16), and "abominable works" (Col. 1:21). The reference here was to the unprofitable and in-efficacious works of the Levitical service: cf. 10:1, 4. Those works of the ceremonial law are denominated "dead works" because they were performed by men in the flesh, were not vitalized by the Holy Spirit, and did not satisfy the claims of the living God.

"And of faith toward God." Of the six distinctive features of Judaism here enumerated, this one is the most difficult to define with any degree of certainty. Nevertheless, we believe that if due attention be given to the particular people to whom the apostle was writing all difficulty at once vanishes. The case of the Jew was vastly different from that of the Gentiles. To the heathen, the one true God was altogether "unknown" (Acts 17:23). They worshipped a multitude of false gods. But not so was it with Israel: Jehovah had revealed Himself to their fathers, and given to them a written revelation of His will. Thus, "faith toward God" was a national thing with them, and though in their earlier history they fell into idolatry again and again, yet were they purified of this sin by the Babylonian captivity. Still, their faith was more of a form than a reality, a tradition received from their fathers, rather than a vital acquaintance with Him: see Matt. 15:8, 9, etc.

Israel's national faith "toward God" had, under the Christian revelation, given place to faith in the Lord Jesus Christ. A few references from the N. T. epistles will establish this conclusively. We read of "the faith of Jesus Christ," and "the faith of the Son of God" (Gal. 2:16, 20); "your faith in the Lord Jesus" (Eph. 1:15); "by faith of Jesus Christ" (Phil. 3:19); "your faith in Christ" (Col. 2:5); "the faith which is in Christ Jesus" (1 Tim. 3:13).

As another has said, "All the blessings of the gospel are connected with 'faith,' but it is faith which **rests in Christ**. Justification, resurrection-life, the promises, the placing of sons, salvation, etc., are all spoken of as resulting from faith which rests upon Christ . . . 'Hebrews' reveals Christ as the 'one Mediator between God and men.' It reveals Christ as 'a Priest forever after the order of Melchizedek,' and urges the divine claim of the Son of God. The apostle is directing his readers to look away from self to Christ, the Center, the Sum of all blessing. This is not merely 'faith toward God,' but it is faith which comes to God by the way of the mediation and merits of His Son."

"Of the doctrine of baptisms" (v. 2). Had the translators understood the scope and meaning of this passage it is more than doubtful if they had given the rendering they did to this particular clause. It will be observed that the word "baptism" is in the plural number, and if scripture be allowed to interpret scripture there will be no difficulty in ascertaining what is here referred to. It is neither Christian baptism (Matt. 28:19), the baptism of the Spirit (Acts 1:5), nor the baptism of suffering (Matt. 20:23), which is here in view, but the carnal ablutions which obtained under the Mosaic economy. The Greek word is "baptismos." It is found but four times on the pages of the N. T.: in Mark 7:4, 5 and Heb. 6:2; 9:10. In each of the other three instances, the word is rendered "washings." In Mark 7 it is the "washing of cups and pans." In Heb. 9:10 it is "meats and drinks and divers washings and carnal (fleshly) ordinances," concerning which it is said, they were "imposed until the time of reformation."

It is to be noted that our verse speaks of "the **doctrine** of baptisms." There was a definite teaching connected with the ceremonial ablutions of Judaism. They were designed to impress upon the Israelites that Jehovah was a holy God, and that none who were defiled could enter into His presence. These references in Heb. 6:2 and 9:10 look back to such passages as Ex. 30:18, 19; Lev. 16:4; Num. 19:19, etc. Typically, these "washings" denoted that all the defiling effects of sin must be removed, ere the worshipper could approach unto the Lord. They foreshadowed that perfect and eternal cleansing from sin which the atoning blood of Christ was to provide for His people. They had no intrinsic efficacy in themselves; they were but figures, hence, we are told they sanctified only "to the purifying of the flesh" (Heb. 9:13). Those "washings" effected nought but an external and ceremonial purification; they "could not make him that did the service perfect as pertaining to the conscience" (Heb. 9:9).

"And of laying on of hands." The older commentators quite missed the reference here. Supposing the previous clause was concerned with the Christian baptisms recorded in the Acts, they appealed to such passages as Acts 8:17; 19:6, etc. But those passages have no bearing at all on the verse before us. They were exceptional cases where the supernatural "gifts" of the Spirit were imparted by communication from the apostles. The absence of **this** "laying on of hands" in Acts 2:41; 8:38; 16:33, etc., shows plainly that, normally, the Holy Spirit was given by God altogether apart from the instrumentality of His servants. The "laying on of hands" is not, and never was, a distinctive Christian ordinance. In such passages as Acts 6:3; 9:17; 13:3, the act was simply a mark of **identification,** as is sufficiently clear from the last reference.

"And of laying on of hands." The key which unlocks the real meaning of this expression is to be found in the O. T., to which each and all of the six things here mentioned by the apostle look back. Necessarily so, for the apostle is here making mention of those things which characterized Judaism, which the Hebrews, upon their profession of their personal faith in Christ had "left." The "laying on of hands" to which the apostle refers is described in Lev. 16:21, "And Aaron shall lay both his hands upon the head of the live goat, and confess over him all the iniquities of the children of Israel, and all their transgressions in all their sins, putting them on the head of the goat, and shall send him away by the hand of a fit man into the wilderness." This was an essential part of the ritual on the annual Day of Atonement. Of this the Hebrews would naturally think when the apostle here makes mention of the "**doctrine** (teaching) . . . of laying on of hands."

"And of resurrection of the dead." At first glance, and perhaps at the second too, it may appear that what is here before us will necessitate an abandonment of the line of interpretation we are following. Surely, the reader may exclaim, you will not ask us to believe that these Hebrews had "left" the doctrine of the resurrection of the dead! Yet this is exactly what we do affirm. The difficulty which is seemingly involved is more imaginary than real, due to a lack of discrimination and failure to "rightly divide the Word of Truth." The resurrection of the dead was a clearly revealed doctrine under Judaism; but it is supplanted by something far more comforting and blessed under the fuller revelation God has given in Christianity. If the reader will carefully observe the preposition we have placed in bold type, he will find it a valuable key to quite a number of passages. "We make a great mistake when we assume that the resurrection as taught by the Pharisees, held by the Jews, believed by the disciples, and proclaimed by the apostles, was one and the same" (C. H. W.). The great difference between the former and the latter may be seen by a comparison of the scriptures that follow.

"After the way which they call heresy, so worship I the God of my fathers, believing all things which are written in the law and in the prophets: and have hope toward God, which they themselves also allow, that there shall be a resurrection of the dead, both of the just and unjust" (Acts 24:14, 15). That was the Jewish hope: "Martha saith unto Him, I know that he shall rise again in the resurrection at the last day" (John 11:24). Now in contrast, note, "He charged them that they should tell no man what things they had seen, till the Son of man were risen **from** the dead. And they kept **that** saying with themselves, questioning one with another what the rising **from** the dead should mean" (Mark 9:9, 10). It is this aspect of resurrection which the N. T. epistles emphasize, an elective resurrection, a resurrection of the redeemed a thousand years before that of the wicked: see Rev. 20:5, 6; 1 Cor. 15:22, 23; 1 Thess. 4:16.

"And of eternal judgment." In the light of all that has been before us, this should occasion no difficulty. The Jewish church, and, alas, most of Christendom now, believed in a General Judgment, a great assize at the end of time when God would examine every man's life, "For God shall bring every work into judgment with every secret thing, whether it be good or whether it be evil" (Ecc. 12:14). This is described in fullest detail in the closing verses of Rev. 20. It is the Great White Throne judgment. In to that judgment no child of God shall come. The Lord Jesus declared, "he that heareth My word and believeth on Him that sent Me, hath everlasting life, and **shall not come into condemnation**" (John 5:24). While the apostle Paul affirmed, "There is therefore now **no condemnation** to them that are in Christ Jesus" (Rom. 8:1). That which awaits the Christian is the Judgment-seat of Christ (2 Cor. 5:10), where his walk will be tried, and when his works will be rewarded or destroyed.

Let us now, very briefly, summarize what has just been engaging our attention. The Hebrews had confessed their faith in Christ, and by so doing had forsaken the shadows for the Substance. But hope had been deferred, faith hath waned, persecutions had cooled their zeal. They were being tempted to abandon their Christian profession and return to Judaism. The apostle shows that by so doing they would be laying **again** "a foundation" of things which had been left behind. Rather than this, he urges them to be carried forward to "perfection" or "full growth." That meant to substitute "repentance unto life" (Acts 11:18), for "repentance from dead works;" trust in the glorified Saviour, for a national "faith toward God;" the all-cleansing blood of the Lamb, for the inefficacious "washings" of the law; God's having laid on Christ the iniquities of us all, for the Jewish high-priest's "laying on of hands;" a resurrection "from the dead," for "a resurrection of the dead;" the Judgment-seat of Christ, for the "eternal judgment" of the Great White Throne. Thus, the six things here mentioned belonged to a state of things before Christ was manifested.

"And this will we do if God permit" (v. 3). Here we learn of the apostle's resolution as to the occasion before him, and the limitation of his resolution by an express subordination of it to the good pleasure of God. The "**this** will we do" has reference to "Let us go on unto perfection." The use of the plural pronoun is very blessed. Though a spiritual giant when compared with his fellow Chrsitians, the apostle Paul never imagined he **had** "attained" (Phil. 3:12). "This will **we do**" means, I in teaching, you in learning. In the chapters that follow, we see how the apostle's resolution was carried out. In 5:10 he had said, "an High Priest after the order of Melchizedek, of whom we **have** many things to say." By comparing 6:3 with 5:11, 12 we learn that no discouragement should deter a servant of God from proceeding in the declaration of the miystery of Christ, not even the dullness of his hearers.

"And this will we do, if God permit." This qualifying word may have respect unto the unknown sovereign pleasure of God, to which all our resolutions must submit: "I trust to tarry a while with you, if the Lord permit" (1 Cor. 16:7 and cf. James 4:13-15). Probably the apostle also had before him the sad state into which the Hebrews had fallen (5:11-14), in view of which this was a solemn and searching word for their conscience: because of their sloth and negligence there was reason to fear they had provoked God, so that He would grant them no further light (Luke 8:18). Finally, we believe the apostle looked to the Divine enablement of himself; were He to withdraw His assistance the teacher would be helpless: see 2 Cor. 3:5. To sum up: in all things we must seek God's glory, bow to His will, and recognize that all progress in the Truth is a special gift from Him (John 3:27).

ARTHUR W. PINK.

GLEANINGS IN EXODUS

71. The Lord's Dwelling-place.
Ex. 35-40.

In the last six chapters of Exodus four things are brought before us. First, mention is made once more of the Sabbath (35:1-3). Second, the people of Israel bring unto Moses all the materials required for the Tabernacle (35:4-29). Third, the setting to work of the appointed artificers with their assistants, and the actual making of the Tabernacle and its furniture (35:30—39:43). Fourth, the setting up of the Tabernacle and the glory of the Lord filling His house in Israel's midst (40). Nearly all that we have mentioned in 35-39 is a recapitulation of what has been before us in 25-31. As we pointed out in artcile 33 of this series, what we find in Ex. 25-31 is a description of the Tabernacle as it was given by Jehovah Himself directly to Moses in the mount; whereas 35-39 records what was actually made according to the pattern shown to Moses. Typically, this double account of that which, in every part, prefigured Christ, tells us that all which was originally planned in Heaven shall yet be accomplished on earth.

That which is central and distinctive about our present lengthy passage is the actual setting up of Jehovah's dwelling-place in the midst of His redeemed people. Before we attempt to bring out something of the deep and rich spiritual significance of this, a few remarks need to be made upon the opening sections of Ex. 35. In vv. 21-29 we behold the children of Israel bringing an offering unto the Lord, giving to Him of their substance. At the beginning of 36 we see the appointed artificers actively engaged in their work, the work of the Lord. But **before** these, at the very beginning of 35, mention is made of the sabbath as "a rest unto the Lord," in which no work was to be done. The **doctrinal** significance of this is: before we are fitted to work for Him, we must rest in Him; before we can bring to Him, we must receive from Him. Most important for our hearts is this seventh and last mention of the sabbath in Exodus. It was Solomon, "a man **of rest**" (1 Chron. 22), who alone could build a house to Jehovah's name.

It is to be noted that an additional feature is here added to the Sabbath restriction: "Ye shall kindle no fire throughout your habitations upon the Sabbath day." As another has said, "That speaks of the absence of consideration for one's own comfort in a natural way. In keeping a true sabbath one is neither occupied with one's own activity nor with one's natural consideration." That needs to be borne in mind in this day of fleshly ease and gratification. God's word to us on this point is: Thou shalt "call the sabbath a delight, the holy of the Lord, honourable; and shalt honour Him, not doing thine own ways, **nor finding thine own pleasure**, nor speaking thine own words: Then shalt thou delight thyself in the Lord; and I will cause thee to ride upon the high places of the earth, and feed thee with the heritage of Jacob thy father" (Isa. 58:13, 14).

In its deeper spiritual significance, this mention of the sabbath and the non-kindling of the fire in our dwelling, coming right after what is recorded at the end of Ex. 34, signifies that the privileges of the new covenant and our enjoyment of the glory of God as it shines in the face of Jesus Christ, calls for the **setting aside** of the desires of the flesh. Only as we rest in God, and only as we give heed to that word, "**Mortify** therefore your members which are upon the earth" (Col. 3:5), shall we be free to enter into the enjoyments and employments of the new-creation realm. On the other hand, the words "six days shall work be done" announce very distinctly that nought connected with our natural responsibility is to be neglected.

The second thing we have in Ex. 35 is the people's response to Jehovah's invitation in 25:1, 2. There we read, "Speak unto the children of Israel, that they bring Me an offering: of every man that giveth it willingly with his heart, ye shall take My offering." The materials out of which the Tabernacle was made were to be provided by the voluntary offerings of devoted hearts. Most blessed is it to read what is said in 35:21, 22, "And they came, every one **whose heart** stirred him up, and every one whom his spirit **made willing**, they brought the Lord's offering to the work of the Tabernacle of the congregation, and for all His service, and for the holy garments. And they came, both men and women, as many as were **willing hearted,** and brought bracelets, and earrings, and rings, and tablets, all jewels of gold: and every man offered an offering of gold unto the Lord." No unwilling donors were these, who had to be begged and urged to give. Spontaneously, freely, joyfully, did they avail themselves of their privilege.

Commenting on what has just been before us, Mr. Dennett has well said: "It is therefore of the first importance to remember that everything offered to God must proceed from hearts made willing by His Spirit, that it must be spontaneous, not the result of persuasion or of external pressure, but from the heart. The church of God would have been in a very different state today if this had been remembered. What has wrought more ruin than the many worldly schemes of raising money? and what more humbling than the fact that solicitations of all kinds are used to induce the Lord's people to offer their gifts? Moses was content with announcing that the Lord was willing to receive, and he left this gracious communication to produce its suited effect upon the hearts of the children of Israel. He needed not to do more; and if saints now were in the current of God's thoughts they would imitate the example of Moses, and would shun the very thought of obtaining even the smallest gift, except it were presented willingly, and from the heart, as the effect of the working of the Spirit of God. And let it be remarked, that there was no lack; for in the next chapter we find that the wise men who wrought came to Moses and said, 'The people bring much more than enough' (36:5-7).

"If the first Pentecostal days be excepted, there has probably never been seen anything answering to this even in the history of the church. The chronic complaint now is concerning the insufficiency of means to carry on the Lord's work. But it cannot be too often recalled—first, that the church of God is never held responsible to obtain means; secondly, that if the Lord gives work to do, He Himself will lay it upon the hearts of His people to contribute what is necessary; thirdly, that we are travelling off the ground of dependence, and acting according to our own thoughts, if we undertake anything for which the needful provision has not **already** been made; and lastly, that gifts procured by human means can seldom be used for blessing."

It is very beautiful to note the relation between the two things which have now been before us: first, the keeping of the sabbath; second, the bringing of an offering unto the Lord, an offering which was the outflow of a **heart** "stirred up." First the resting in, delighting itself in the Lord, then the affections drawn out towards Him. This too finds its accomplishment on new-covenant-ground. It is a redeemed people, a people who behold the glory of the Lord, that are devoted to His cause. The giving of their substance is not a legal thing, a mere matter of duty, but a privilege and a joy. Here too it is the love of Christ which "constraineth." We love Him because He first loved us, and we delight to give because **He** first gave to us. Nothing so moves the heart as the contemplation of the love and grace of God as now revealed to us in the glorified Mediator. In article 34 we have already pointed out the typical significance of each part of Israel's offerings; so we pass on now to notice, briefly, the work of the artificers.

Upon the two principal workmen, Bezaleel and Aholiab, we have already commented in article 57. There we dwelt upon the significance of the workmen's names, the equipping of them for their appointed tasks, and the particular service allotted them. Here we read, "**Then** wrought Bezaleel and Aholiab, and every wise hearted man, in whom the Lord put wisdom and understanding to know how to work all manner of work for the service of the sanctuary, according to all that the Lord had commanded" (36:1). Note carefully the opening word, and also the expression "every one whose heart **stirred him up** to come unto the work" in v. 2. Ah, wherever there is a spirit of devotion, manifested by a free and liberal offering unto the cause of God, He will not be backward in raising up qualified workers, whose hearts have been stirred by His Spirit, to make a wise and God-glorifying use of His peoples' gifts.

But let us now seek to take note of

the **connection** between this third item and what has gone before. First we have had the sabbath, the soul resting in God; second, we have had the free will offering of the people, the heart's affections drawn out to the Lord. Now we get active work. This puts **service** in its true position. Occupying as it does the **third** place, it shows us that acceptable service to God can only proceed from those who have passed from death unto life. Following, as it does, the other two, it intimates that the vital **prerequisites** for service are, delighting ourselves in the Lord and the affections flowing forth unto Him. Only then can we truly "abound in the work of the Lord." Anything else is either the outcome of the restless energy of the flesh, or is merely "bricks" produced under the whip of taskmasters.

There is one detail given us here that has not come before us in the previous chapters. "And all the women that were wise hearted did spin with their hands, and brought that which they had spun, of blue, and of purple, of scarlet, and of fine linen. And all the women whose hearts stirred them up in wisdom spun goats' hair" (35:25, 26). This brings in the thought of **co-operation** in the Lord's work: the sisters have their place and part too. Yet note it is a subordinate place: they "spun," not provided the material. The character of their work also shows us the legitimate **sphere** of their labours—in the home.

"And the rulers brought onyx stones, and stones to be set for the ephod, and for the breastplate" (35:27). The **leaders** set the people a godly example. This is as it should be. But, alas, how often is it otherwise. The preacher who sets before his people the teaching of Scripture on the subject of stewardship and the privilege of giving to the cause of God, but who is miserly himself, is not an honest man: he says one thing, but does another. God's word to pastors is, "Be thou an **example** of the believers, in word, in faith, in purity" (1 Tim. 4:12). "In all things showing thyself **a pattern** of good works" (Titus 2:7).

Before turning to the 39th chapter, there is one detail in the 38th which should be noted. In v. 21 we read, "This is the sum of the Tabernacle, even of the tabernacle of testimony, **as it was counted,** according to the commandment of Moses." Then we are told, "All the gold that was occupied for the work . . . was twenty and nine talents . . . and the silver of them **that were numbered** of the congregation was an hundred talents," etc. (vv. 24, 25). This conveys to us a most important practical lesson in connection with the work of the Lord. Everything was counted, weighed, numbered. What attention to detail was this! "People talk of essentials and non-essentials, but when they do, you may be sure they are only thinking of man's side. Every detail of the divine mind is essential to the glory of God in Christ. A missing peg would mean a slack cord, and a slack cord would mean a curtain out of place, and so the disorder would spread. Indeed the whole tabernacle would suffer if one detail were out of place" (C. A. Coates).

In the 39th chapter of Exodus the work of the Tabernacle is finished. Blessed is it to note that all was done "**as the Lord** commanded Moses." Mark how this expression occurs eight times in that chapter: vv. 1, 5, 7, 21, 26, 29, 31, 43; while in vv. 32, 42 it is added, "and the children of Israel did according to **all** that the Lord commanded Moses, so did they . . . According to all that the Lord commanded Moses, so the children of Israel made **all** the work." "The Lord had given the most minute instruction concerning the entire work of the tabernacle. Every pin, every socket, every loop, every tach, was accurately set forth. There was no room left for man's expediency, his reason, or his common sense. Jehovah did not give a great outline and leave man to fill it up. He left no margin whatever in which man might enter his regulations. By no means. 'See that thou make **all things** according to the pattern showed to thee in the mount' (Ex. 25:40). This left no room for human device. If man had been allowed to make a single pin, that pin would most assuredly have been out of place in the judgment of God. We can see what man's 'graving tool' produces in chapter 32. Thank God, it has no place in the tabernacle. They did, in this matter, just what they were told—nothing more, nothing less. Salutary lesson this for the professing church! There are many things in the history of Israel which we should earnestly seek to avoid,—their impatient murmurings, their legal vows, and their idolatry; but in two things we may imitate them: may our devotedness be more whole-hearted, and our obedience more implicit" (C. H. M.).

Yes, the obedience of Israel is recorded for our learning. We too have received commandment from the Lord concerning the work which He has given **us** to do. His complete Word is now in our hands. It is to be our guide and regulator in all things. It is given that "the man of God may be complete, thoroughly furnished unto all good works" (2 Tim. 3:17). If we desire God's blessing, then His work must be done according to **His** appointments. Human expediency, convenience, originality, are to have no place. The approval of God, not that of his fellows, is what every servant of the Lord must continually aim at. **Faithfulness,** not success, is what our Master requires. The quality of service is to be tested not by visible results, but by its conformity to God's Word.

There is one other detail in Ex. 39 which, in its spiritual application to ourselves, is very searching: "And they brought the tabernacle unto Moses, the tent, and all his furniture, etc. . . . And Moses did **look upon** all the work" (vv. 35, 43). Every thing was brought before the typical mediator for his inspection. All had to pass under the scrutiny of his eye. The typical significance of this is obvious. In 2 Cor. 5:10 we read, "For we must all appear before the judgment seat of Christ; that every one may receive the things done in his body, according to that he hath done whether it be good or bad." This does not refer to a **general** Judgment-day at the end of the world, but to that which follows the Lord's return for His people, and precedes His coming back to the earth to set up His millennial kingdom.

A further word on this same subject is found in 1 Cor. 3, "For other foundation can no man lay than that is laid, which is Jesus Christ. Now if any man **build upon** this foundation—gold, silver, precious stones; wood, hay, stubble. Every man's **work** shall be made manifest: for the day shall declare it, because it shall be revealed by fire; and the fire shall try every man's work of what sort it is. If any man's work abide which he hath built thereon, he shall receive a reward. If any man's work shall be burned, he shall suffer loss: but he himself shall be saved, yet so as by fire" (vv. 11-15). The reference here is to the Christian's **service:** 2 Cor. 5:10 treats more of his **walk.** Discrimination is made between two classes of service. On the one hand, "gold," the emblem of divine glory; "silver" which speaks of redemption; "precious stones" which are imperishable. Only that which has been done for God's glory, on the ground redemption, and which will stand the test of fire, shall abide and be rewarded. On the other hand, "wood, hay, stubble," which, though much greater in bulk. **will not** endure the coming fiery trial. The difference is between quality and quantity; that which is of the Spirit, and that which is of the flesh.

"And Moses did look upon all the work, and behold, they had done it as the Lord had commanded, even so had they done it: and Moses **blessed** them" (39:43). So will Christ in the coming Day. That which has been done in full accord with God's Word, though despised by man, shall be owned and rewarded of Him. His own words, in the final chapter of Holy Writ, are "And, behold, I come quickly; and My reward is with Me, to give every man according as his work shall be" (Rev. 22:12). In view of this, how earnestly and prayerfully should we heed that exhortation, "And now, little children, **abide in Him**; that, when He shall appear, we may have confidence, **and not be ashamed** before Him at His coming" (1 John 2:28).

In the last chapter of Exodus we have the actual setting up of the Tabernacle. Let us take note, first, of the **time** when it was erected: "And the Lord spake unto Moses saying, On the first day of the first month shalt thou set up the tabernacle" (vv. 1, 2). It was on the anniversary of Israel's departure from Egypt (12:2). This is very striking. As their deliverance from the house of bondage constituted the commencement of their spiritual history, so the dwelling of Jehovah in their midst marked an altogether new and most blessed stage in their experiences. That which was foreshadowed by this we shall point out later. Its spiritual application to Christians is given in Matt. 18:20, "For where two or three are gathered together in My name, there am I **in the midst** of them."

Next we would observe that Moses is the sole actor in this chapter: "And Moses reared up the tabernacle, and fastened his sockets, and set up the boards thereof, and put in the pillars thereof, and reared up his pillars" (v. 18). All subordinates disappear from view and only Moses is seen: read vv. 19-33, at the end of which we are told, "so Moses finished the work." The present application of this is given us in Heb. 3:3-6, "For this Man was counted worthy of more glory than Moses, inasmuch as He who hath builded the house hath more honour than the house. For every house is builded by some man; but He that built all things is God. And Moses verily was faithful in all His house, as a servant, for a testimony of those things which were to be spoken after; But Christ as a Son over His own house; whose house are we, if we hold fast the confidence and the rejoicing of the hope firm unto the end."

Finally, we read, "**Then** a cloud covered the tent of the congregation, and the glory of the Lord filled the tabernacle" (v. 34). The "then" points back to the "so Moses finished the work" of v. 33. The N. T. equivalent was what took place on the day of Pentecost: "And when the day of Pentecost was fully come, they were all with one accord in one place. And suddenly there came a sound from heaven as of a rushing mighty wind, and **it filled all the house** where they were sitting. And there appeared unto them cloven tongues like as **of fire**, and it sat upon each of them. And they were all filled with the Holy Spirit."

As an appendix to this glorious incident we are told in the closing verse of our book, "For the cloud of the Lord was upon the tabernacle by day, and fire was on it by night, in the sight of all the house of Israel throughout all their journeys." They needed only to keep their eyes on the Cloud. "The Lord thus undertook for His people. He had visited them in their affliction in Egypt; He had brought them out with a high hand and an outstretched arm; and had led them forth through the Red Sea into the wilderness. Now He Himself would lead them 'by the right way that they might go to a city of habitation.' 'Happy,' we might well exclaim, 'is that people that is in such a case; yea, happy is that people whose God is the Lord.' For surely there was nothing more wanted to the blessing of Israel. Jehovah was in their midst. The cloud of His presence rested upon, and His glory filled the tabernacle" (Mr. Dennett).

It only remains for us now to point out the most striking and lovely dispensational picture which is presented before the anointed eye in the last six chapters of Exodus. What is recorded there is that which followed the **second** descent of Moses from the Mount. In the opening paragraphs of article 61 we called attention to the fact that when Moses was called up unto Sinai to receive from Jehovah the tables of stone (the words of which formed the basis of His **new** covenant with Israel—the old one being the Abrahamic) Moses descended twice(having, of course, returned thither in the interval): see 32:15; 34:29. What immediately followed these two descents foreshadowed that which shall follow the two stages of the second coming of Christ, as these bear upon the Jews. Just as the first descent of Moses was succeeded by sore judgments on Israel, so the descent of Christ into the air to catch up His saints unto Himself (1 Thess. 4) will be succeeded by the great Tribulation, the Time of Jacob's trouble.

But let us now review that which attended the **second** descent of Moses. First, he appeared before them with radiant face: type of the glorified Mediator as He will come back to Israel (Col. 3:4). Second, the tables of stone were not broken this time, but deposited and preserved in the ark (Deut. 10:4): so when the Lord Jesus makes the new covenant with Israel, He declares, "I will put My law in their **inward** parts and write it in their hearts" (Jer. 31:33). Third, this last section of the book of Exodus opens with a reference to the sabbath (35:1-3), telling us that it is in **the Millennium** when all of this shall be made good. Fourth, the next line in the picture is the hearts of Israel flowing forth unto the Lord in free-will offerings (35:23, 24): the antitype of this is seen in Zeph. 3:9, 10, "Then will I turn to the people a pure language, that they may all call upon the name of the Lord, to serve Him with one consent. From beyond the rivers of Ethiopia My suppliants, even the daughter of My dispersed, shall bring Mine **offering**." Fifth, next we see Israel engaged in the work of Jehovah, doing all "as He had commanded:" so in Ezek. 36:27, we read, "And I will put My Spirit within you, and cause you to walk in My statutes, and ye shall keep My judgments and **do them**." Sixth, the tabernacle was now set up: compare with this, "Behold the Man whose name is the Branch; and He shall grow up out of His place, and He shall build the temple of the Lord ... and He shall bear the Glory" (Zech. 6:13). Seventh, the Lord then dwelt in Israel's midst: "Sing and rejoice, O daughter of Zion: for, lo, I come, and I will dwell in the midst of thee, saith the Lord" (Zech. 2:10). Eighth, the glory of the Lord was visibly displayed: "And the Lord will create upon every dwelling place of mount Zion, and upon her assemblies, a cloud and smoke by day, and the shining of a flaming fire by night: and above all **the glory** shall be a covering" (Isa. 4:5). May the Lord hasten that glad time.

Thus, in the closing chapter of this book of redemption we behold the full and perfect accomplishment of God's purpose of grace. Notwithstanding man's failure, notwithstanding Israel's sin of the golden calf, notwithstanding the broken tables of stone; in the end, grace superabounded over sin, and all the counsels of God were made good by the typical mediator. In its ultimate application what has been before us points forward to the new earth: "Behold, the tabernacle of God is with men, and He will dwell with them and they shall be His people and God Himself shall be with them, and be their God. And God shall wipe away all tears from their eyes; and there shall be no more death, neither sorrow nor crying, neither shall there be any more plague: for the former things are passed away" (Rev. 21:3, 4).

ARTHUR W. PINK.

THE HOLY SPIRIT'S WORK

3. In the Saved.

"The transcendent grace of God is the glorious subject of the everlasting gospel. It is revealed in it, proclaimed by the preaching of it, in its meridian splendor, in its utmost perfection, and with the utmost plainness and freeness **to sinners as sinners.** The gospel of salvation is accompanied by the Holy Spirit with life and light to elect sinners, and made the power of God unto their salvation. By it they hear Christ's voice, see His glory, behold how He loved them, receive Him into their hearts, live by faith on the Son of God, and find and enjoy every blessing of the Father's everlasting love and boundless mercies, flowing into their souls through the most precious bloodshedding, and inestimably valuable and everlastingly efficacious sacrifice of the worthy Lamb: all which give us a grand display and open discovery of the exceeding riches of grace. So saith the apostle: 'But God, who is rich in mercy, for His great love wherewith He loved us, Even when we were dead in sins, hath quickened us together with Christ, by grace ye are saved' (Eph. 2:4, 5).

"The Holy Spirit having, as the Spirit of life, quickened the elect with spiritual life in their souls, gives them to see, know, and understand, the fountain from whence all flows. He opens, explains, and applies with Divine power to the mind, what Paul, speaking of himself and Timothy hath declared, 'Who hath saved us, and called us with an holy calling, not according to our works, but according to His own purpose and grace, which was given us in Christ Jesus before the world began' (2 Tim. 1:9).

"The Holy Spirit agreeably to His office in the covenant of grace is pleased to take of the things of Christ and to 'shew' or make them manifest. He leads poor awakened sinners to behold the Lamb of God, and in a sight of Him as set forth in the Word, and testified of by the Spirit therein, they see salvation. On which they cannot forbear individually breaking out, saying, 'Behold, God is my salvation; I will trust, and not be afraid: for the Lord Jehovah is my strength and my song; He also is become my salvation' (Isa. 12:2). Perceiving how exactly suited Christ is to them, and how exactly suited they are for Him to glorify Himself in their eternal redemption, they cannot but prize and esteem Him as the Author and Finisher of their salvation.

"This knowledge concerning Christ they receive from the everlasting gospel, which is made effectual to them, as accompanied with the Divine energy of His Spirit. In it they find Christ, and know that His love passeth knowledge; that His mercy endureth forever; that His bloody sweat is their everlasting purification; His wounds and bruises, received in the day of the Lord's fierce anger, their everlasting healing; His soul travail, their peace; and His obedience unto death, even the death of the cross, their everlasting righteousness and perfection. This gladdens their hearts, and fills their minds with peace, so that in believing the everlasting worth, virtue, and efficacy of His blood and righteousness, they rejoice with joy unspeakable and full of glory" (S. E. Pierce).

Before the Lord Jesus left His disciples He declared, "And I will pray the Father, and He shall give you another Comforter, that He may abide with you forever" (John 14:16). That "Comforter" was henceforth, to be the Teacher of God's saints, giving to them the Holy Scriptures, opening them to their understanding, applying them to their hearts, supplying all their spiritual need. Yet how little do God's people realize the exceeding preciousness of this Gift! How faintly do they apprehend how much they owe, how deeply ther are indebted to the gracious operations of the third Person of the blessed Trinity! How rarely are their hearts engaged and their thoughts occupied with the Divine "Comforter!"

How scant is the honor, praise, and worship given to Him!

The mission of the Spirit in the earth is to bring and apply to the souls of God's elect that great and glorious redemption which was wrought out and purchased for them by the incarnate Son. "Salvation is of the Lord" (Jonah 2:9), entirely so from beginning to end. The Father purposed, planned and provided it. The Son procured and secured it. The Spirit imparts it. Faith perceives, understands and enjoys it. But faith is neither a faculty nor an act of the natural man. It is the result of "the operation of God" (Col. 2:12), namely, the inward, imperceptible, invincible workings of the Holy Spirit. Faith is one of the **senses** of the "new man." As the physical body has its five senses—sight, hearing, etc.—so has the "new man" his senses, that new man which is "created" (Eph. 2:10), by the Spirit, and is "spirit" (John 3:6). The "new man" has **eyes** to see that which the natural man cannot (1 Cor. 2:14); he has **ears** to hear that which the unregenerate are totally deaf to (Psa. 58:4, 5), and so on. But before there can be spiritual eyes and ears, there must be a "spiritual man" to see and hear.

A "new creature" (2 Cor. 5:17)—not the old one changed or renovated—has to be brought into existence. This is the product of the Spirit's creative work. He is here to give new and spiritual being to each of God's elect, who are, by natural birth, "dead in trespasses and sins" (Eph. 2:1). This is the Holy Spirit's work **in salvation**. The Holy Spirit is as truly the **Saviour** of God's people as Christ is. It is written, "Not by works of righteousness which we have done, but according to His mercy **He saved** us, **by** the washing of regeneration and renewing of **the Holy Spirit**" (Titus 3:5). And again, "God hath from the beginning chosen you to salvation through sanctification **of the Spirit** and belief of the truth" (2 Thess. 2:13). As Hell had been our eternal portion but for the work of Christ, so Heaven could never be our dwelling-place but for the work of the Holy Spirit. The Spirit not only shows the elect sinner his need **of** Christ, but "reveals" Him **in** him (Gal. 1:16). Christ is the "true light" (John 1:9), but the unregenerate love "darkness rather than light" (John 3:19); therefore, they will never, of themselves, come to the Light. No, the Light has to be brought to them; as it is written, "But God who commanded the light to shine out of darkness, hath shined in our hearts, to give the light of the knowledge of the glory of God in the face of Jesus Christ" (2 Cor. 4:6).

It is not till the sinner has been brought "out of darkness into His marvelous light" (1 Peter 2:9), that he "comes to Christ." Coming to Him, first, with his **mind** (Isa. 26:3): the spiritual "understanding" which has been "given" him (1 John 5:20), now apprehending Him. "Comes" to Him, secondly, with his **heart** (Rom. 10:10): his spiritual "affections" being drawn out to Him (1 Peter 1:8). "Comes" to Him, thirdly, with his **will** (Phil. 2:13): the new man surrendering completely to His lordship. "Coming to Christ" is **not** an outward, but is an inward act; it is **not** the act of the "natural man" (John 6:44), but of the new man (John 6:40—"see" spiritually, before "believe." And this new and spiritual man is the product of the sovereign and supernatural operations of the Spirit, to which **we** contribute nothing, and in which **we** have no part whatsoever.

The instrument which the Spirit employs, "the seed" which He uses, is the written Word of God. As long as that Word is only presented to us objectively, it makes no spiritual impression upon us; not until the Holy Spirit implants it **within** the soul, subjectively, does the Word **become to us** "quick and powerful" (Heb. 4:12). True, that Word is, in itself, the "Word of life" (Phil. 2:16), as the germ of life is in the living grain before it is sown in the ground; but it only **becomes** the "Word of life" **in** the individual, when the Holy Spirit imparts it to the soul itself. When He does so, that individual enters into a "saving knowledge of the truth:" God's great salvation is no longer a beautiful theory, but an experimental fact to the consciousness. Then it is that the Spirit takes of the things of Christ and **shows** them unto me—having previously given **eyes** to see. Then it is that, under the Spirit's **application** of the Scriptures to his understanding and heart, he gradually discovers more and more, what a vile and totally depraved sinner he is in himself. And then it is, and thus, he is brought to realize, by the Spirit, how well-suited is Christ, the Saviour of **sinners**, to him.

The "new man" having been formed in the Christian, his new "senses" and faculneed training and developing, as our natural ones did when we were little children. For this, too, the Christian is entirely dependent upon the power and operations of the third Person of the Godhead. He is in constant need of being "strengthened with might by His Spirit in the inner man" (Eph. 3:16). For this he should pray definitely, each day. In every thing and for everything, the Christian is absolutely dependent upon the Holy Spirit. In the remainder of this article we shall consider some of the works of the blessed Comforter in the soul.

1. He sheds abroad God's love in the heart.

"The love of God is shed abroad in our hearts by the Holy Spirit which is given unto us" (Rom. 5:5). The epistle to the Romans contains a full unfolding and exposition of the gospel of God (1:1). The verse we have quoted gives the first mention of the Spirit in it (except 1:4). Therefore this is the logical place to start in our consideration of the Spirit's work in the Christian. He it is who communicates to the heart of the elect sinner that wondrous love which has dwelt in the heart of God toward him from all eternity (Jer. 31:3). It is by the Spirit that a discovery is made to us of God's love; that which is revealed in Scripture, He seals to our personal consciousness.

No sinner has any real sense of the eternal and redeeming love of God for himself till it is actually communicated by the Spirit. To the unregenerate Christ said, "But I know you, that ye have not the love of God in you" (John 5:42). In his unconverted state the Christian dreaded God, feeling that He was against him. Yea, all men naturally hate God (Rom. 8:7). It is only when we see His love to us in Christ, by the Comforter, that we repent and love Him—"We love Him because He first loved us" (1 John 4:19). "The Lord thy God will circumcise thy heart and the heart of thy seed to love the Lord thy God" (Deut. 30:6). "Though sinners should hear ten thousand times of the love of God in the gift of His Son, they are never properly affected by it, till the Holy Spirit enters their hearts, and till love to Him is produced by the truth through the Spirit" (R. Haldane) —cf. 1 Cor. 2:10.

2. He assures us that the Word is God's.

"Now we have received, not the spirit of the world, but the Spirit which is of God; that we might know the things that are freely given to us of God" (1 Cor. 2:12). In v. 4 the apostle reminded the Corinthians that when he first preached to them it was not with "enticing words of man's wisdom"—vain philosophy—but "in demonstration of the Spirit and of power," i. e. with a God-given message.

And this was that, "Your faith should not stand in the wisdom of men but in the power of God" (v. 5). That which Paul had preached was "the wisdom of God in a mystery," i.e. a divine secret, but now disclosed, namely, "the hidden (counsels of grace) which God **ordained** before the world unto our glory" (v. 7). These counsels of grace, this electing love, which was to be accomplished through redemption, "None of the princes of this world knew" (v. 8). That the whole of this passage concerns the predestinating grace of God towards His elect, is clear from "the things God hath revealed unto us by His Spirit: for the Spirit searcheth all things, yea, the deep things of God" (v. 10), i.e. He is thoroughly cognizant of and conversant with the secret counsels of the Eternal Three in "the everlasting covenant."

In v. 11 the apostle points out that only the human spirit is capable of understanding human things; so Divine things are only known by the Divine Spirit. And we Christians have received "Not the spirit of the world," i.e. a mere reasoning faculty, but "the Spirit which is of God," the Comforter given to us, dwelling in us, and this, that "we might know the things that are freely given to us of God." Given to us now in the written Word for faith's instruction and encouragement. It is the Holy Spirit who works in the soul of the Christian, a firm persuasion, an unshakeable assurance that the Scriptures are the Word of God. It is not on the testimony and authority of "the church" he receives them as Divine. Godly men may present convincing arguments for their inspiration, and those arguments may win an intellectual assent, but they neither search the conscience nor beget in the soul a spiritual faith in them. The same Spirit who moved holy men to write them, must work in the heart a consciousness that they are **God's** Word. It is by the Spirit we are "stablished" in the faith: 2 Cor. 1:21.

3. He directs our walk.

This is the fulfillment of one of the many promises which God has given to His people: "And I will put My Spirit within you, and cause you to walk in My statutes, and ye shall keep My judgments and do them" (Ezek. 36:27). Even after God has imparted His Spirit to an elect soul, he has to be **caused** to "walk in God's statutes." As Jeremiah declared, "O Lord, I know that the way of man is not in himself: it is not in man that walketh to direct his steps" (10:23). Looked at according to the flesh, the old man, the Christian is not only ignorant of those paths pleasing to God, but he is averse to them. Looked at according to the spirit, the new man, the Christian, is but a "babe" in Christ, and needs a Guide and Supporter. Of old the Psalmist confessed, "He leadeth me in the paths of righteousness for His name's sake" (23:3). This is the acknowledgement of every true Christian.

"For as many as are led by the Spirit of God, they are the sons of God" (Rom. 8:14). This is the chief and distinguishing mark of a true Christian. He is **always** "led by the Spirit," for He never releases His hold of us. He leads, first, to Christ, then to the throne of grace, and then to practical godliness; ultimately to the glory. He "leads" by enlightening the understanding, by strengthening the desires of the new man, by inclining the will. It is the Spirit of God who keeps us in the Narrow Way, and delivers from the destructive snares of Satan.

4. He prompts all true obedience.

Christians have no more vital godliness than what the Holy Spirit has wrought in them. Some who would assent to this bare statement, would probably dissent did they pause to analyze it. We have no more faith than what the Holy Spirit has imparted to us, no more knowledge of God, no more hope or love, than what He has given. This is a very humbling confession to make, and proud flesh resents it. Yet the teaching of Holy Writ makes it unmistakably clear that the Author of all true godliness is the Divine Comforter. "By the grace of God I am what I am" (1 Cor. 15:10), namely, by what the Spirit of God hath imparted to me, wrought in me, produced through me. Without the Lord I can do **nothing** (John 15:5).

In the new nature, given at the new birth, there is a fitness and a readiness unto godly obedience, but **no power**. It has been well said that, "We are not in this world intrusted with any spiritual ability from God, as without farther actual assistance and aid to do anything that is good" (Dr. J. Owen). Thus, the Christian stands in daily and constant need of the Spirit's gracious operations. "Our sufficiency is of God" (2 Cor. 3:5), and He works in us not only to will, but also "to **do** of His good pleasure" (Phil. 2:13). Therefore we find the apostle praying that He would, "Make you perfect in every good work to do His will"—how? by—"working in you that which is well pleasing in His sight" (Heb. 13:21). And thus do the godly own, "For Thou also hast wrought all our works in us" (Isa. 26:12).

5. He produces all spiritual fruit.

Of old God said, "**From Me** is thy fruit found" (Hosea 14:8). Spiritual fruit is neither produced by nor does it issue from the natural man. It is produced by the Holy Spirit, and issues from the new man, "which after God is created in righteousness and true holiness" (Eph. 4:24). All that God works in and through His people is by the Spirit. For the Philippians Paul prayed that they might be, "filled with the fruits of righteousness which are by Jesus Christ, unto the glory and praise of God" (1:11)—in as much as the Holy Spirit is the Executive of the Godhead, **He** is to be understood as the Producer; they are "by Jesus Christ" as their meritorious cause.

The leading passage on fruit-bearing is found in John 15:1-8. There the Lord Jesus, under the figure of a vine and its branches, teaches us that "fruit" is the consequent and outcome of "abiding" in Him, which is one of the N. T. terms for intimate communion. But communion with Christ is produced and sustained by the Holy Spirit, who is here to glorify Christ. Yet faith has to be in exercise; there must be definite dependence on the Spirit for this. The result of such communion and faith is "fruit," i. e. "love, joy, peace, long-suffering, gentleness, faith, meekness, temperance;" and in Gal. 5:22 these are expressly called "the fruit **of the Spirit**."

6. He conforms us to Christ.

To this every believer has been predestinated (Rom. 8:29), and the decree of God is made good by the workings of His Spirit. Here again the only instrument which He uses is the written Word. He takes of the things of Christ, and shows them unto the Christian (John 16:13, 15). That is, He opens to our understandings and hearts the glories of Him who is Altogether Lovely. He shines upon the sacred page so that in His light we see light (Psa. 36:9). As our thoughts are occupied with Christ, as our hearts are engaged with Him, the features of His likeness are stamped upon us. This is the meaning of 2 Cor. 3:18, "But we all, with open face beholding as in a glass the glory of the Lord, are changed into the same image, from glory to glory, as by the Spirit of the Lord."

7. He inspires all true prayer.

A great deal of what passes for "prayer" to-day is nothing but the religiousness of the flesh. The Pharisees made long prayers; the Mahommedans and Papists do the same. Nor is Protestantism free from this plague. Again; much of our supposed praying is only the distress of the ntural man finding utterance. The most ungodly will cry unto the Lord in moments of real peril and acute pain. But this is nothing better than the cries which animals make when they are in distress. Thus did God complain about Israel of old: "They have not cried unto Me with their hearts when they **howled** upon their beds" (Hosea 7:14), which plainly intimates they **had** "cried unto Him", with the outward voice, yet was it a cry which was no more effectual than the "howling" of the wild beasts.

Of old the disciples of the Lord besought Him, "Teach us **to** pray" (Luke 11:1). This needs to be our daily request, for of ourselves we neither know **how** to pray nor **what** to pray for. But thank God, the Spirit is given to Christians "to help their infirmities" (Rom. 8:26). This He does by granting to them the "spirit of grace and of supplication" (Zech. 12:10), by showing them from the Scriptures what to ask for, and how to present their petitions so as to gain the ear of God. This is "praying in the Holy Spirit" (Jude 20). The Spirit is both the inspirer and inditer of all prayer. But His aid must be sought, His guidance importuned.

8. He preserves the Christian.

This He does by "renewing" him in the inner man "day by day" (2 Cor. 4:16), strengthening us with His might (Eph. 3:16 and cf. 3:20). It is by the Spirit we are kept from soul-destroying error, and preserved from making shipwreck of the faith. We are "kept by the power of God through faith" (1 Peter 1:5), that is, by the effectual operations of His Spirit maintaining and sustaining our faith. Thus it is by the Spirit that we are "**sealed** unto the day of redemption" (Eph. 4:30).

The competness of our dependency on the Spirit may be seen by those who will take the trouble to weigh carefully the following references. Apart from the Spirit we cannot even "remember" the things of God (John 14:26); we cannot "think" aright (2 Cor. 3:5); we cannot discern "things to come" (John 16:13): we cannot "cry Abba Father" (Rom. 8:15); we cannot know our Divine sonship (Rom. 8:16); we cannot "hope" (Gal. 5:5); we cannot "mortify" sin (Rom. 8:13).

Ere closing this article, which makes no pretensions to having presented anything like a **complete** outline of this important subject, perhaps some of our readers will welcome a few lines on what is termed the "Enduement of the Holy Spirit." Many of God's people have been sorely perplexed and harassed (Ezk. 13:22) by the deceptions of some who have asserted that Christians should seek from God a second work of grace, variously designated by them as the "Baptism of the Spirit," "Filling of the Spirit," etc. They have affirmed that the Holy Spirit is willing to come upon us in mighty power if we will but fulfill the conditions specified by these men, some of whom have been looked up to as eminent Bible teachers, and who claim that **they** have been thus endued by the Spirit. We have met, personally, numbers of God's people who have earnestly sought this blessing, who have done everything their teachers bade them do, only to find the desired "blessing" eludes them. Instead of blaming their teachers, they have blamed themselves. Instead of searching the Scriptures, they have sought to search their own hearts, with the result that some known to us have ended in the madhouse, others in a suicide's grave.

Of course appeal is made by these men to the Word of God; yet it does not support their errors. Let any exercised soul read carefully through the book of Acts, and he will not there find a single passage which tells of any of the apostles urging Christians to **seek** an enduement of the Spirit, still less are there any inspired directions as to how such an enduement may be obtained. This of itself is quite sufficient to expose the unscripturalness of these troublers of the saints. Neither their methods nor their message is apostolic. True, we do read in the Acts, of the **apostles** being filled with the Spirit, speaking in tongues, working signs and wonders; but that was **before** the New Testament was written and completed. Those divine gifts were the authentication of their mission. But those abnormal gifts were withdrawn before the last of the apostles passed from this scene.

Again; in the N. T. there are twenty-one Epistles, and with the one seeming exception of Eph. 5:18, none of them contain any exhortations for God' people to **seek** any further "anointing" or "enduement" other than what they already received when they were born again; still less are there any rules and regulations laid down for the obtaining of any "second blessing." Nor need Eph. 5:18 occasion the slightest difficulty. If vv. 18, 19 be read together it is obvious that the simple meaning of this passage is, "Let not Christians find their joy and delight in carnal intoxicants (such as worldlings do), but in spiritual enjoyments and employments. The definite article is not found here in the Greek; and "be filled with spirit" is interpreted for us in the parallel passage in Col. 3:16: "Let the word of Christ dwell in you richly," etc.

The responsibility of the Christian is to recognize that he is indwelt by the Spirit (Rom. 8:9), that his body is His "temple" (1 Cor. 6:19). It is to daily seek grace from God that he may be kept from "grieving the Spirit" (Eph. 4:30). It is to honor the Spirit by owning that **all** his springs are in Him, that He is the Author and Producer of all spiritual fruit in him. It is to render prayer, praise, and worship to the Spirit, equally as to the Father and to the Son. May the Lord the Spirit graciously add His blessing to what has been written, and cause each reader to "Prove all things; hold fast that which is good" (1 Thess. 5:21).

ARTHUR W. PINK.

THE UNITY OF SAINTS

In January 1924 we published an article entitled "The Saints of all ages Fellow-heirs." Our purpose in inserting it was to give proof that **all** of God's elect are common-sharers of the riches of His grace. The writer's object was to protest against the extravagancies of hyper-dispensationalists. There are those who, in their zeal to "rightly divide the Word of Truth," have wrongly divided the family of God. They have affirmed that the saints of this present dispensation are to have a higher position and enjoy grander blessings than will the saints of previous dispensations. We believe this is a mistake, and a grave one, for it really undermines the foundations of our faith. Hence this further article upon the subject. Pursuing our customary method we shall not examine the assertions and arguments of others for the purpose of refuting them, but instead, we shall (with one exception) endeavour to present the positive side of the subject from the Word of God itself.

First of all let it be pointed out that, from the beginning to the end of human history, God has **only one way of salvation,** namely, By grace, through faith, apart from any works of the sinner. During the course of the ages the Allwise has not been engaged in a series of experimentations, though He has tested man under a variety of vastly different circumstances, and this, with the object of making fully manifest the solemn fact that, under all conditions, man is a compete failure, a fallen and depraved creature. Yet, whether it were the generations before Moses, Israel under the Law, men during the days of Christ's earthly ministry, or since Pentecost under the preaching of the Gospel, there has been only one way of escape from the everlasting burnings, and that, through faith in the Lord Jesus Christ.

It is indeed sad that there should be any need to **press** this foundational truth yet the confusion around us, the babel of tongues in the religious world, calls for a clear statement thereon. The more so, when we find that men who, in the main, are contenders for the Faith once delivered to the saints, yet, nevertheless, teach that in bygone days God saved sinners on a different basis from what He does now. For example (and we could readily give others), we read in "The Scofield Bible," in a note under John 1:16—Grace (2) "As a dispensation, grace begins with the death and resurrection of Christ (Rom. 3:24-26; 4:24, 25). The point of of testing **is no longer** legal obedience **as the condition of salvation,** but acceptance or rejection of Christ:" compare also his note under Exodus 19:3. But this is a serious error. "Legal obedience" was **never** a "condition of salvation;" had it been so, not a single sinner from Moses to Christ had ever been saved. No, from Abel onwards (Heb. 11:4), salvation has always been through "faith in His blood" (Rom. 3:25). That the virtue and value of Christ's blood has been reckoned to all who believed prior to the Cross, equally with those since, is unmistakeably clear from Rom. 3:25: "To declare His righteousness for the remission of sins **that are past.**"

Let us now proceed one step further. The blessings which God's people are going to enjoy in the future were all purchased for them by the precious blood of God's Lamb, and what His sacrifice secured for one, it necessarily secured for all alike. The ground, and the only ground, upon which any redeemed sinner is favoured by God, is that of his **union with** that One in whom the Father is well pleased. As we read in 1 Cor. 3:21, "All things are yours . . . and ye are Christ's." Observe, not some distinctive and unique blessings, but, "**all** things are yours." Are **whose**? Those who belong to Christ; and Abel as much as John, Noah as much as Paul, the Old Testament saints as truly as the New Testament saints, belong to Him. Scripture knows of no salvation that does not involve **joint-heirship** with Christ, and joint-heirship involves the inheritance of "all things." The sacrifical work of Christ was wrought on behalf of the whole household of faith, that is, from Abel down to the last millennial saint who shall believe; and it is that Sacrifice which alone gives to any believer of any dispensation his title to all the grace, love, glory and blessing, which is the inheritance of the saints in light.

Well has another said, "What is it that gives title to enter into the Church, and all the Church's blessings? Is it not simply and only, the value of the blood of the Lamb? Is not the Church of God defined as being that Body "which He hath purchased with His own blood" (Acts 20:28)? The blood was shed, and the blood was offered—offered in all its preciousness to God. It was an offering that was meritorious—infinitely meritorious, for it was the result of the value and obedience of One 'Whose goings forth have been of old, from everlasting.' The imputation, therefore, of that meritoriousness was the greatest of gifts that could be granted by God to any creature, and this it is that has been appropriated by God to every member of the family of faith, so that they might have thereby community of blessing" (B. W. Newton).

The **unity** of all God's elect, and their **community** in His blessing, was brought out clearly in the High Priestly prayer of Christ's, recorded in John 17. There we find Him praying specifically for "them which Thou (the Father) hast given Me" (v. 9). Then He added, "Neither pray I for these alone, but for them also which shall believe on Me through their word" (v. 20). Thus He links together those who had been saved during His own ministry before Pentecost, with those who should be saved **after** Pentecost. And what is it that He requests the Father for these two companies? This: "That they all may **be one**" (v. 21)! That this is a **visible** unity in glory is clear from the remainder of the verse: "that the world may believe that Thou hast sent Me." The Father's answer to this petition will be evidenced at the return of Christ to this earth, "When He shall come to be glorified in His saints, and to be **admired** in all them that believe" (2 Thess. 1:10).

Speaking of this redeemed company, made "one," the Lord declared, "And the glory which Thou gavest Me, I have given them; that they may be one" (v. 22). What greater and grander blessing than **this** awaits any of God's redeemed? And is such wondrous "glory" reserved only for the New Testament saints, or, as some would restrict it still further, for only a special portion **of them**? Not so do the inspired Oracles teach. In Rom. 8:30 we are expressly told, "Moreover whom He did predestinate, them He also called, and whom He called, them He also justified: and whom He justified, them He also glorified." These Divine blessings are inseparable: the glorifying is co-extensive with the justifying. And then, that there should be no possible room for uncertainty as to what is included in the "gloryfying," the apostle at once adds, "What shall we say then to these things? If God be for us, who can be against us? He that spared not His own Son, but delivered Him up for us all, how shall He not with Him also freely give us all things?" (vv. 31, 32). On no principle of sound interpretation can the second "us" be made to exclude any from the first "us." The ones to whom God freely giveth all things are the same people for whom God delivered up His Son, namely, the entire company of His elect and redeemed, from Abel to the end of earth's history; and to each of them God has given "**all** things."

Into this blissful "glory," which Christ has won for and which He bestowed upon His people, He conducts them at the time of His return. In the writings of those who treat of prophetical and dispensational truth, we often find the expression, "The coming of Christ **for His Church**." If that term be limited to those who have been saved since Pentecost, it has no scriptural warrant whatever. The Word of God speaks of "they **that are Christ's** at His coming" (1 Cor. 15:23), and these words are not to be restricted to the New Testament saints: **all** who were chosen in Christ before the foundation of the world (Eph. 1:4) are included. The twentieth verse of this same 1 Cor. 15 announces, "But now is Christ risen from the dead, and become the firstfruits of them that slept." That those words include the entire company of all who were saved in Old Testament times cannot be gainsaid. If, then, Christ is **their** "firstfruits," is not that the guarantee **they** shall rise in the likeness of the same glory that He has?

What meaneth that oft-repeated word

that Christians are "Abraham's seed" (Gal. 3:29), unless we share together the same inheritance? The fourth of Romans makes it unmistakeably plain that Abraham was justified by faith, and if so, then all the merits of the Just One were imputed to him: he too had "**all** things!" But he not only belonged to the family of faith, he was himself the head of that family. And yet there are those would have us believe that in the chiefest of the blessings and glories of that family he will have no share. There are those who affirm that though Abraham is redeemed, yet will he be excluded from the grandest result of redemption which is revealed in Scripture. And why is he to be thus excluded? Because, forsooth, he is supposed not to belong to the Church of New Testament times.

It is no doubt true that the Old Testament saints were not favoured with the same fulness of light, nor the same dispensational privileges, as were possessed by the apostles of Christ. To quote again from Mr. Newton: "Neither the Old Testament saints, nor even John the Baptist, who came between the Old Testament and the New, were, **dispensationally,** in the kingdom of Heaven as an economy on earth. As regards dispensational position and the character of his service, the least in the kingdom of heaven was greater than John. It was the personal ministry of the Lord Jesus that introduced the kingdom of Heaven as an economy into the earth. He it was who first declared the great salvation (see Heb. 2:3). Every disciple, therefore of Jesus, as belonging to that kingdom, and able to bear testimony to its grace, was **dispensationally** greater and more privileged than John. But they whose service on earth terminated before the kingdom of heaven was dispensationally introduced on earth, were not therefore excluded from it as by and by manifested in glory. **Heaven is not become a transcript of the dispensational differences of earth**; and, therefore, we read that Abraham, and Isaac, and Jacob, who, like John the Baptist, were not in the kingdom of heaven as an economy on the earth, **will** be in it when manifested in glory: see Matt. 8:11."

Going back again to Abraham, as we have said, Romans 4 reveals him as a justified man. Now in Romans 5 the **privileges** of the justified are enumerated. Among them are mentioned, "peace with God" (v. 1), a standing in grace (v. 2), the love of God shed abroad in their hearts (v. 5), preserved by Christ's life (v. 10). But in addition to these, the justified are taught to "rejoice **in hope** of the **glory** of God" (v. 2), and the promise is that they "shall **reign** in life" (v. 17), and that as constituted righteous by the obedience of Christ. And all these things are predicated simply of those who are "justified by faith" (v. 1): hence, as Abraham was justified by faith, we maintain the conclusion is irresistible that Abraham also shall "reign in life" and participate in the "glory of God." Nor are we aware that the Holy Spirit promises any greater or grander blessings than these for any one.

There is much in the Epistle to the Galatians which furnishes clear proof of the truth for which we are contending. To quote from the "Prophetic Journal" of Dr. H Bonar: "They which be of faith are blessed with faithful Abraham' (Gal. 3:9). 'With' is not a word that implies **severence.** It implies **communion.** 'They which are of faith, the same are the children of Abraham' (Gal. 3:7). '**In thee** shall all nations be blessed' (3:8). 'To Abraham and his seed were the promises made' (3:16): 'That **the blessing** of Abraham might come on the Gentiles through Jesus Christ' (3:14); 'if ye be Christ's, then are ye Abraham's **seed** and heirs according to the promise' (4:29). From these quotations it is plain that the question discussed by the apostle was: Are believers in Christ really to **get up to** Abraham's privileges and standing? He takes for granted that the heirship was his; the kingdom his; the sonship his; the glory his—made over to him by the original promise; and his object is to show us that **we** are to enter on **Abraham's** privileges. 'The blessing of Abraham' he assumes to comprehend everything that God has promised to us in Christ, and he shows us that we are actually to get all that. He speaks of Abraham as so lofty and so glorious, that the highest place to be desired by us is simply to be **one of his seed.** This is the Church's privilege in consequence of her connection with Christ: 'If ye be Christ's, then are ye Abraham's **seed.**'"

To this may be added, "In the Galatians, too, the Old Testament saints, though placed for a season in the condition of pupilage under the Law, were, nevertheless, 'sons' of God. And what is the necessary consequence of being 'sons?' 'If sons then heirs: heirs of God and joint-heirs of God and joint-heirs with Christ.' In the same epistle we are taught that **all** the members of the household of faith, whether Jew or Gentile, are the chi'dren of Jerusalem that is above: 'But Jerusalem which is above is free, which is the mother of us all' (Gal. 4:26)" (B. W. Newton).

In Rom. 8:29 we are told, "For whom He did foreknow, He also did predestinate to be conformed to the image of His Son, that He might be the firstborn among many brethren." Who will dare confine the scope of this wondrous and blessed declaration to only a **portion** of the family of God? None, we trust. Then, who can conceive of any higher honour than conformity to the image of God's Son? That the Old Testament saints as well as the New Testament saints will experience this glorious transformation is clearly evident from the words of the Psalmist, "I shall be satisfied when I awake **with Thy likeness**" (17:15). Then, surely, no personal dissimilarities can exist among those who are equally alike to Christ.

True, there will be differences of **reward** among the members of the one redeemed family, as was evidenced by the words of Christ, "Have thou authority over ten cities . . . Be thou also over five cities" (Luke 19:17, 19). Just, as another has said, "But such differences interfere not with their common corporate blessings as the one family of God; and they are dependent, not on dispensational differences, not upon the fact that one has lived in a dispensation of great light, and another in a dispensation of lesser light. Differences of reward depend on differences of **faithfulness**: 'Every one shall receive his own reward according to his own works.' If Abraham, in his dispensation of lesser light, be more faithful than another who has lived in a dispensation of greater light, he will receive a higher reward.

"Can any one doubt that there have been few in Christendom whose works can compare with those recorded in the eleventh chapter of Hebrews, as wrought by Abel, and Enoch, and Noah, and the holy men of old, who, with less light, had greater faith and faithfulness than we? It is an humbling thought that Abraham, with his less extended scope of knowledge should, in faith and faithfulness, have so vastly exceeded us who live in a dispensation in which such fulness of light has been given. The apostles seem to have been **set forth last** to walk practically in the path of those 'appointed to death.' Since the apostles died, Christ's people have sought to reign rather than to suffer. It is humbling to think of this; yet it is still more humbling (might I not say terrifying) to think that we, so inferior to Abraham practically, in all our thoughts and ways, should yet venture to affirm, that because of his having, whilst on earth, lived in a dispensation less favoured as to light than ours, he will have no place **with** us in the final glory of the Church of God, but be placed forever in an inferior sphere" (B. W. Newton).

In the epistle to the Ephesians, where we have the fullest exposition of the calling and glory of the Church, the ultimate **community of blessing** of Old and New Testament saints is clearly enough stated. In 2:11, 12 we read, "Wherefore remember, that ye being in time past Gentiles in the flesh, who are called Uncircumcision by that which is called the Circumcision in the flesh made by hands; That at that time ye were without Christ, being **aliens from** the commonwealth of Israel, and strangers from the covenants of promise, having no hope, and without God in the world." This was the state by nature of these Gentile saints; but what has grace wrought? This: "Now therefore ye are no more strangers and foreigners, but **fellow-citizens** with the saints, and of the household of God" (v. 19). Thus we see here the fulfillment of Christ's words in John 10:16: "And other sheep I have, which are not of this (Jewish) fold: them also I must bring, and they shall hear My voice; and there shall be **one fold**, one shepherd."

Finally, observe how in Heb. 11:40 the union between the elder and younger members of God's one family is foretold: "God having provided some better thing for us (i. e. walking in conscious union with a risen Christ, whose promised coming **they** only saw "afar off") that they without us should not be made perfect." The spirits of the O. T. saints are already with Christ in Paradise (Heb. 12:23), but their bodies are yet in the graves. God has appointed that they shall not be perfected in resurrection apart from us. They await us. There is one Father, one Lord, one Spirit, one faith. And a oneness inconceiveable to us will attach to every member of the family of faith when together brought as the mystical body of Christ into their final glory.

—ARTHUR W. PINK.

PARTICULAR REDEMPTION

"He gave His life a ransom for many":
Matt. 20:28.

The doctrine of Redemption is one of the most important doctrines of the system of faith. A mistake on this point will inevitably lead to a mistake through the entire system of our belief. All Christians hold that Christ died to redeem, but all Christians do not teach the same redemption. We differ as to the nature of the Atonement, and as to the design of redemption. For instance, the Arminian holds that Christ, when He died, did not die with any intent to save any particular person; and they teach that Christ's death does not in itself secure, beyond doubt, the salvation of any one man living. They believe that Christ died to make the salvation of all men possible, or that by the doing of something else any man who pleases may attain unto eternal life; consequently, they are obliged to hold that if man's will would not give way and voluntarily surrender to grace, then Christ's atonement would be unavailing. They hold that there was no particularity and speciality in the death of Christ. Christ died, according to them, as much for Judas in hell, as for Peter who mounted to heaven. They believe that for those who are consigned to eternal fire, there was as true and real redemption made as for those who now stand before the throne of the Most High. Now, we believe no such thing. We hold that Christ, when He died, had an object in view, and that object will most assuredly, and beyond a doubt, be accomplished. We measure the design of Christ's death by the effect of it. If any one asks us, "What did Christ design to do by His death?" we answer that question by asking him another, "What has Christ done, or what will Christ do by His death?" For we declare that the measure of the effect of Christ's love is the measure of the design of it. We cannot so belie our reason as to think that the intention of Almighty God could be frustrated, or that the design of so great a thing as the atonement, can by any way whatever, be missed of. We hold —we are not afraid to say what we believe—that Christ came into this world with the intention of saving "a multitude which no man can number"; and we believe as the result of this, every person for whom He died must, beyond the shadow of a doubt, be cleansed from sin, and stand, washed in blood, before the Father's throne. We do not believe that Christ made any effectual atonement for those who are forever damned; we dare not think that the blood of Christ was ever shed with the intention of saving those whom God foreknew never could be saved, and some of whom were even in hell when Christ, according to some man's account, died to save them.

—C. H. SPURGEON.

IMPORTANT NOTICE

Numerous requests have been made for us to write something on the International Sunday School Lessons, many teachers being unable to find the kind of assistance they are desiring. After earnestly seeking the Lord's will on the matter, we feel that He would have us—counting on His enablement — undertake this important task. Our object is not to do the teacher's work for him, but to provide sufficient "seed-thoughts" for him to select from, and then prayerfully develop each. We shall endeavour to cover the principal points in each lesson, and give the most appropriate Scriptural references on them. We shall not attempt to furnish complete expositions, yet hope to give far more than bare outlines. God willing, each monthly issue will have eight pages in it, same size as these.

This magazine entitled "Helps on the Sunday-School Lessons", is being published by Mr. I. C. Herendeen, of the Cleveland, B. T. D.—433-435 The Arcade, Cleveland, Ohio,—at the nominal charge of fifty cents per year, which at once indicates that financial profit is not the object in view. To clear expenses a considerable number of subscribers will be needed: but if this is of the Lord He **will** send them in. Any readers of "Studies" who are Sunday School teachers will be well advised to procure at once these Helps on the Lesson. If you prefer you may send the subscription price to us, and we shall be glad to forward it. Above all pray God's blessing on it. Teachers in Australia can secure now from Mr. G. E. Ardill.

Will friends in Australia kindly note that letters to the U. S. A. require a three penny stamp.

fleshly fanaticism, but he cannot make it grow. It is **God's work** to feed faith, as well as to give it life at the first. O Christian reader, face the fact that **you** can no more increase your faith than you can create a universe. If, then, you are mourning the littleness and feebleness of your faith, go to Christ and beg Him to grant you more. If you have a little faith take it to Him and ask Him to multiply it as He did the loaves and fishes.

"Lord, Increase our faith." This is a petition which should be earnestly presented before the throne of grace daily. We cannot grow in grace and in the knowledge of the Lord, nor can we be strong in Him and in the power of His might unless our faith be increased. If the apostles felt it incumbent upon them to thus supplicate their Lord, how much more do we need to make this **our** prayer! As Spurgeon well said at the beginning of his sermon on this text, "If the twelve mightiest in the army of the Lord of hosts had need of such a supplication, what shall **we** say who are but the feeblest soldiers, the least of all saints?" Naught but indifference or pride will keep us from making this petition ours.

Our faith needs increasing in its **purity**. There is much of earth's dross mingled with this fine gold from heaven. Daily have we cause to say, "Lord, I believe; help Thou mine unbelief" (Mark 9:24). It is not without reason that Christ told His disciples, "If ye have faith, and **doubt not** . . . . . ye shall say to this mountain (of difficulty, of trial), be thou removed, and be cast into the sea; and **it shall be done**" (Matt. 21:21). So often, trusting in the Lord with all our hearts is hindered by leaning to our own understanding (Prov.3:5). That is why our faith has to be tried with fire (1 Peter 1:7)—that the dross may be removed. Lord, increase the purity of our faith.

Our faith needs increasing in its **extent**. A clear proof of this is furnished in those searching words of Christ's unto two of His disciples: "O fools, and slow of heart to believe **all** that the prophets have spoken" (Luke 24:25). Ah, we fail to believe **all** God has said to us. At the beginning of our Christian experience, our faith was restricted to the fact that Christ Jesus died for sinners. We trusted Him for salvation. Then, as we read God's Word we saw that the reason we believed was because God had ordained us unto eternal life (Acts 13:48). By grace, our faith was enlarged, and we laid hold of the blessed truth of election, that God chose us in Christ before the foundation of the world (Eph. 1:4), that He loved us with an everlasting love, and therefore with loving kindness drew us unto Himself. Thus our faith extends.

Thank God, dear reader, if the Holy Spirit has enabled you to lay hold of and enter into the blessedness of what men have termed "the doctrines of grace." But these are not all the Bible contains. Many who accept these, believe little more. Their faith is cramped by their creed. They fail to perceive that God has brought them into "a large place" (Psa. 18:19). They do not recognize human accountability. **We** are responsible to add to our faith, virtue, knowledge, temperance, patience, godliness, brotherly kindness, love (2 Peter 1:5-7). Those known as "Calvinists" have much need to pray, Lord, Increase the extent of our faith.

Our faith needs increasing in its **intensity**. We do not wish to act as some do with a river—break its banks, to let it spread over the pasture, and so make it shallower. No, while we long for its breadth to expend, we pray that it may also increase in its depth and strength. Many of us are so afraid to trust God **fully**. We are timid and half-hearted. We may not mistrust God, but we are frequently guilty of distrusting Him. We do not imagine for a moment that He would lie, yet we hesitate long to really rest on His Truth. Do we not need to say with Watts?—

"Oh! that I had a **stronger** faith,
To look within the vail;
To credit what my Saviour saith,
Whose word can never fail."

"Lord, Increase our faith." Let this be our daily prayer. Let us humbly, earnestly, believingly, beseech the Lord to increase the purity of our faith, the extent of our faith, the intensity of our faith, that we may honour and glorify Him, that we may be encouragements to our fellow-Christians, that we may be able to resist the Devil (1 Peter 5:9) and overcome the world (1 John 5:4).

—ARTHUR W. PINK

Vol. VIII.   DECEMBER, 1929   No. 12

STUDIES IN THE SCRIPTURES

"Search the Scriptures" John 5 : 39

Copyright in all English-speaking Countries.

Editor: Arthur W. Pink, Morton's Gap, Ky., U. S. A.
Hon. Agent in England: Mr. A. Winstone, 2, Lennox Villas, Hewlett Road, Cheltenham.
Hon. Agent in Australia: Mr. G. Ardill, The Christian Workers' Depot.
Commonwealth and Reservoir Streets, Sydney.

FREE TO ALL WHO WILL READ IT.

Praying For Death, Sinful.

"I pray not that Thou shouldest take them out of the world, but that Thou shouldest keep them from the evil" (John 17:15).

    As we take up our pencil to write the last editorial for the 1929 issues of this magazine, we are reminded again of the swift flight of time, and how that in a short while at most both writer and reader will receive an imperative summons to leave this earth. Yet, short as is our sojourn down here, it seems long, too long, for some of us. Not a few of our friends have been waiting for years past the return of their Saviour, but He has not yet come, and unless faith has been maintained "hope deferred maketh the heart sick." Numbers of them are feeling acutely the infirmities of old age, many of them are passing through deep waters of trial and affliction, many of them are almost quite cut off from fellowship with real saints. Ofttimes the language of their hearts is: "O that I had wings like a dove! for them would I fly away, and be at rest" (Psa. 55:6). Perhaps they have prayed, that the Lord would speedily send the angel of death and put an end to all their troubles. Such, we would tenderly remind of **Christ's** prayer in John 17:15.

    Christians are often made painfully conscious of their inability to pray aright, and of their ignorance as to what to pray for. Holy Writ itself affirms "We know not what we should pray for as we ought" (Rom. 8:26). The word "ought" here goes to intimate that our inability is excuseless and our ignorance blameworthy. The prayers found in Scripture are expressly recorded for our instruction, and did we pay more heed to them, we should pray more intelligently and more acceptably to God, and thus, more effectually. This, we believe, explains the first clause of Rom. 8:26: "Likewise the Spirit also helpeth our infirmities, **for** we know not what we should pray for as we ought." And **how** does the Spirit "help" us? Chiefly by directing our hearts and minds to the written Word, and particularly to the **prayers** recorded therein.

    In proof of what we have just said above about the ignorance and blameworthiness of much of our praying, we would point out one instance in particular, namely, the sinful request which most if not all saints present unto God, at some season of their lives, for Him to speedily remove them from this scene of sin, sorrow and suffering. The writer himself has to acknowledge with shame that more than once has he longed and prayed for death, and it is because he now sees the wickedness of this that he would endeavour to pass on to other tried and troubled souls what the Lord, in His infinite grace, has deigned to make a real blessing to his own soul; with the earnest prayer that God may condescend to sanctify it to others who are yet in this vale of tears.

    In John 17:15 we find our Saviour Himself saying to the Father, "I pray not that Thou shouldest take them out of the world." In view of these words of Christ's is it not evident that when a Christian asks to be delivered out of this present time-state and be taken at once to heaven, he is not praying according to the will of God? Is it not clear that our petulent impatience is a grievous failure to submit to the wisdom of Christ? Then is it not equally plain that we need to earnestly seek from God that grace which will reconcile us to living in this world

(Continued on page 288)

IMPORTANT NOTICES

Please advise promptly of change of address, otherwise copies will be lost in the mails.

We are glad to send a sample copy to any of our friends whom you believe would be interested in such a publication.

Send to Mr. I. C. Herendeen, 433-435, The Arcade, Cleveland, Ohio, for a list of our publications. He has published many of our books and booklets.

This Magazine is published as a work of faith and labour of love. The Editor and his wife gladly give their services. It is freely sent to all who will read it. No charge is made for it.

Christians who feel definitely lead to do so, may have fellowship with us in this ministry. Those outside the U. S. A., please send only INTERNATIONAL Money Orders made out to Morton's Gap, Kentucky, U. S. A. See that it is made out in American money.

CONTENTS

The Epistle to the Hebrews	266
Gleanings in Exodus	273
Justification	278
A Personal Word	284
Holy Horror	285

THE EPISTLE TO THE HEBREWS.

24. Apostasy. Heb. 6:4-6.

The passage which is now to occupy our attention is one of the most solemn in the Hebrews' epistle, yea, to be met with anywhere in the New Testament. Probably few regenerate souls have read it thoughtfully without being moved to fear and trembling. Careless professors have frequently been rendered uneasy in conscience as they have heard its awe-inspiring language. It speaks of a class of persons who had been highly privileged, who had been singularly favored, but who, so far from having improved their opportunities, had wretchedly perverted them; who had brought shame and reproach on the cause of Christ; and who were in such a hopeless condition that it was "impossible to renew them again unto repentance." Well does it become each one of us to earnestly lift up his heart to God, beseeching Him to prevent us making such a shipwreck of the faith.

As perhaps the majority of our readers are aware, the verses before us have proved one of the fiercest theological battlegrounds of the centuries. It is at this point that the hottest fights between Calvinists and Arminians have been waged. Those who believe that it is possible for a real Christian to so sin and backslide as to fall from grace and be lost eternally, have confidently appealed to these verses for proof of their theory. It is much to be feared their theory prejudiced them so much, that they were incapable of examining impartially and weighing carefully its varied terms. With their minds so biased by their views of apostasy, they have rather taken it for granted that this passage describes a true child of God, who, through turning his back upon Christ, ultimately perishes. But Scripture bids us "**Prove** all things" (1 Thess. 5:21), and this calls for something more than a superficial and hurried investigation of what is, admittedly, a difficult passage.

If on the one hand, Arminians have been too ready to read into this passage their unscriptural dogma of the apostasy of a Christian, it must be confessed that many Calvinists have failed to grapple successfully with and interpret satisfactorily the most knotty points in these verses. They are right in affirming that Scripture teaches, most emphatically and unequivocally the Divine preservation and the human perseverance of the saints, as they have also wisely pointed out that the Word of God does not and cannot contradict itself. If our Lord asserted that His sheep should "never perish" (John 10:28), then certainly Heb. 6 will not teach that some of them do. If through the apostle Paul the Holy Spirit assures us that nothing can separate the children from the love of their Father (Rom. 8:35-39), then, without doubt, the portion now before us does not declare that something will. It may not always be easy to discover the perfect consistency of one scripture with another, yet we must hold fast to the unerring harmony and integrity of God's Truth.

The chief difficulty connected with our passage is to make sure of the class of persons who are there in view. Is the Holy Spirit here describing regenerated or unregenerated souls? The next thing is to ascertain what is meant by, "If they shall **fall away**." The last, what is denoted by "It is **impossible** to renew them again unto repentance." Anticipating our exposition, we are fully assured that the "falling away" which is here spoken of signifies a deliberate, complete and final repudiation of Christ—a sin for which there is no forgiveness. So too we understand the "impossible" to renew them again to repentance, announces that their condition and case is beyond hope of recovery. Because of this, Calvinists have, generally, affirmed that this passage is treating of mere professors. But over against this there are two insuperable objections: first, mere professors have nothing from which to "fall away"; second, mere professors have **never** been "renewed" unto repentance.

In addition to the controversy which these verses have occasioned, not a few have turned them unto an unwarrantable use. "Misapprehension of this passage has also, I believe, in many cases occasioned extreme distress of mind to two classes of persons,—to nominal professors, who, after falling into gross sin, have been awakened to serious reflection; and to real Christians, on their falling under the power of mental disease, sinking into a state of spiritual languor, or being betrayed into such transgressions of the Divine law as David and Peter were guilty of: and this has thrown all but insurmountable obstacles in the way of both 'fleeing for refuge, to lay hold on the hope set before them' in the Gospel. All this makes it the more necessary that we should carefully inquire into the meaning of the passage. When rightly understood, it will be found to give no countenance to any of the false conclusions which have been drawn from it, but to be like every other part of inspired Scripture, 'profitable for doctrine, for reproof, for correction, for instruction in righteousness',—well-fitted to produce caution, no way calculated to induce despair" (Dr. J. Brown).

Before attempting an elucidation of the above-mentioned difficulties, and to prepare the way for our exposition of these verses, the contents of which have so sorely puzzled many, let us recall, once more, the condition of soul into which these Hebrew Christians had fallen. They had "become dull of hearing" (5:11), "unskilful in the Word of Righteousness" (5:13), unable to masticate "strong meat" (5:14). This state was fraught with the most dangerous consequences. "The Hebrews had become lukewarm, negligent, and inert; the gospel, once clearly seen and dearly loved by them, had become to them dull and vague; the persecutions and contempt of their countrymen a grievous burden, under which they groaned, and under which they did not enjoy fellowship with the Lord Jesus. Darkness, doubt, gloom, indecision, and consequently a walk in which the power of Christ's love was not manifest, characterized them. Now if they continued in this state, what else could be the result but apostasy? Forgetfulness, if continued, must end in rejection, apathy in antipathy, unfaithfulness in infidelity.

"Such was their danger. And if they succumbed to it their state was hopeless. No other gospel remains to be preached, no other power to rescue and raise them. They had heard and known the voice which saith, 'Come unto Me, and I will give you rest'. They had professed to believe in the Lord who died for sinners, and to have chosen Him as their Saviour and Master. And now they were forgetting and forsaking the Rock of their Salvation. If they deliberately and wilfully continued in this state, they were in danger of final impenitence and hardness of heart.

"The exhortation must be viewed in connection with the special circumstances of the Hebrews. After the rejection of the Messiah by Israel, the gospel had been preached unto the Jews by the apostles, and the gifts and power of the Holy Spirit had been manifested among them. The Hebrews had accepted the gospel of the once crucified and now glorified Redeemer, who sent down from heaven the Sipirt, a sign of His exaltation, and a pledge of the future inheritance. Having thus entered **into the sphere of new covenant manifestation,** any one who wilfully abandoned it could only relapse into that phase of Judaism which crucified the Lord Jesus. There was no other alternative for them, but either to go on to the full knowledge of the heavenly priesthood of Christ, and to the believer's acceptance and worship through the Mediator in the sanctuary above, or fall back into the attitude, not of the godly Israelites before Pentecost, such as John the Baptist and those who waited for the promised redemption, nor even into the condition of those for whom the Saviour prayed, 'for they know not what they do'; but into a state of wilful conscious enmity against Christ, and the sin of rejecting Him, and putting Him to an open shame" (A Saphir).

"The danger to which this spiritual inertness exposed the Hebrews was such as to justify the strongest language of expostulation and reproof. Apostasy from

Christ was a step more easy and natural to a Jewish than to a Gentile believer, because the way was always open and inviting them, as men, to return to those associations which once carried with them the outward sanctification of Jehovah's name, and which only the power of grace had enabled them to renounce. When heavenly realities became inoperative in their souls, the visible image was before them still, and here was the danger of their giving it the homage of their souls. If there were not an habitual exercise of their spiritual senses, the power of discernment could not remain: they would call evil good, and good evil. The ignorance which springs from spiritual neglect begins its own punishment of apathetic dulness on the once clear mind, and robs the spirit of its power to detect the wily methods of the Devil. It is in the presence of God alone that the Christian can exert his spiritual energies with effect. Abiding in Christ, maintains us in that presence. A more unhappy error cannot befal a believer than to separate, in the habit of his mind, acquired knowledge from the living Christ. Faith dies at once when separated from its object. Knowledge indeed is precious, but the knowledge of God is a progressive thing (Col. 1:10), whose end is not obtained this side of the glory (1 Cor. 8:2). The extreme experience of an advancing Christian is that of continual initiation. With a prospect ever-widening he has a daily deepening apprehension of the grace wherein he stands, and in which he is more and more established, by the word of righteousness. . . . .

"A clear and growing faith, in heavenly things was needed to preserve Jewish Christians from relapse. To return to Judaism was to give up Christ, who had left their house 'desolate' (Matt. 23:38). It was to fall from grace, and place themselves not only under the general curse of the law, but that particular imprecation which had brought the guilt of Jesus' blood on the reprobate and blinded nation of His murderers" (A. Pridham). It should be pointed out, however, that it is just as easy, and the attraction is just as real, for a Gentile Christian to return to that world out of which the Lord has called him, as it was for a Jewish Christian to go back again to Judasim. And just in proportion as the Christian fails to walk with God daily, so does the world obtain power over his heart, mind and life; and a continuance in worldliness is fraught with the most direful and fatal consequences.

"For it is impossible for those who were once enlightened" etc. (v. 4). Here the apostle continues the digression which he began at 5:11. The parenthesis has two divisions: the first, 5:11-14 is reprehensory; the second, 6:1-20 is hortatory. In chapter 6 he exhorts the Hebrews unto two duties: to **progress** in the Christian course (vv. 1-11); to **persevere** therein (vv. 12-20). The first exhortation is proposed in vv. 1, 2 and qualified in v. 3. The **motive** to obedience is drawn from the danger of apostasy (vv. 4-6). The opening "For" of v. 4 intimates the close connection of our present passage with that which immediately precedes. It draws a conclusion from what the apostle had been saying in 5:11-14. It amplifies the "if" in v. 3. It points a most solemn warning against their continuance in their present sloth. It draws a terrible contrast from the possibility of v. 3. "The apostle regards the retrogression of the Hebrews with dismay. He sees in it the danger of an entire, confirmed, wilful, and irrecoverable apostasy from the truth. He beholds them on the brink of a precipice, and he therefore lifts up his voice, and with vehement yet loving earnestness he warns them against so fearful an evil" (A Saphir).

Three things claim our careful attention in coming closer to our passage: the persons here spoken of, the sin they commit, the doom pronounced upon them. In considering the persons spoken of it is of first importance to note that the apostle does **not** say, "**us** who were once enlightened", nor even "you"; instead, he says "those". In sharp contrast from them, he says to the Hebrews, "Beloved, we are persuaded better things of you". "Afterwards, when the apostle comes to declare his hope and persuasion concerning these Hebrews that they were not such as those whom he had before described, nor such as would fall away unto perdition, **he doth** it upon three grounds whereon they were differenced from them as: 1. That they had such things as did 'accompany salvation'; that is, such as salvation is inseparable from. None of these things therefore had he ascribed unto those whom he describeth in this place (vv. 4-6); for if he had so done, they would not have been unto him an argument and evidence of a contrary end, that these should not fall away and perish as well as those. Wherefore he ascribes nothing to these here in the text that **doth** peculiarly 'accompany salvation'. 2. He describes them by their **duties of obedience** and fruits of faith. This was their 'work and labor of love' towards the name of

God, v. 10. And hereby, also, doth he differentiate them from those in the text, concerning whom he supposeth that they may perish eternally, which these fruits of saving faith and sincere love cannot do. 3. He adds, that, in the preservation of those there mentioned, the **faithfulness of God** was concerned: 'God is not unrighteous to forget'. For they were such he intended as were interested in the covenant of grace, with respect whereunto alone there is any engagement on the faithfulness or righteousness of God to preserve men from apostasy and ruin; and there is so with an equal respect unto all who are so taken into the covenant. But of those in the text he supposeth no such thing; and thereupon doth not intimate that either the righteousness or faithfulness of God was anyway engaged for their preservation, but rather the contrary" (Dr. J. Owen).

It is scarcely accurate to designate as 'mere professors' those described in vv. 4, 5. They were a class who had enjoyed great privileges, beyond any such as now accompany the preaching of the Gospel. Those here portrayed are said to have had **five** advantages, which is in contrast from the **six** things enumerated in vv. 1, 2, which things belong to man in the flesh, under Judaism. Five is the number of **grace**, and the blessings here mentioned pertain to the Christian dispensation. Yet were they not true Christians. This is evident from what is **not** said. Observe, they were not spoken of as God's elect, as those for whom Christ died, as those who were born of the Spirit. They are not said to be justified, forgiven, accepted in the Beloved. Nor is anything said of their faith, love, or obedience. Yet **these** are the very things which distinguish a real child of God. First, they had been "enlightened". The Sun of righteousness had shone with healing in His wings, and, as Matt. 4:16 says, "The people which sat in darkness saw great light, and to them which sat in the region and shadow of death light is sprung up". Unlike the heathen, whom Christ, in the days of His flesh, visited not, those who came under the sound of His voice were wondrously and gloriously illumined.

The Greek word for "enlightened" here signifies "to give light or knowledge by teaching". It is so rendered by the Sept. in Judges 13:8, 2 Kings 12:2, 17:27. The apostle Paul uses it for "to make manifest", or "bring to light" in 1 Cor. 4:5, 2 Tim. 1:10. Satan blinds the minds of those who believe not, lest "the light of the gospel should shine unto them" (2 Cor. 4:4), that is, give the knowledge of it. Thus, "enlightened" here means to be instructed in the doctrine of the gospel, so as to have a clear apprehension of it. In the parallel passage in 10:26 the same people are said to have "received the knowledge of the truth", cf. also 2 Peter 2:20, 21. It is, however, only a **natural** knowledge of spiritual things, such as is acquired by outward hearing or reading; just as one may be enlightened by taking up the special study of one of the sciences. It falls far short of that spiritual enlightenment which **transforms** (2 Cor. 3:18). An illustration of a **un**-regenerate person being "enlightened", as here, is found in the case of Balaam; Num. 24:4.

Second, they had "tasted of the heavenly gift. To "taste" is to have a personal experience of, in contrast from mere report. "Tasting does not include eating, much less digesting and turning into nourishment what is so tasted; for its nature being only thereby discerned it may be refused, yea, though we like its relish and savour, on some other consideration. The persons here described, then, are those who have to a certain degree understood and relished the revelation of mercy: like the stony-ground hearers they have received the Word with a transcient joy" (J. Owen). The "tasting" is in contrast from the "eating" of John 6:50-56.

Opinion is divided as to whether the "heavenly gift" refers to the Lord Jesus or the person of the Holy Spirit. Perhaps it is not possible for us to be dogmatic on the point. Really, the difference is without a distinction, for the Spirit is here to glorify Christ, as He came from the Father by Christ as His ascension "Gift" to His people. If the reference be to the Lord Jesus, John 3:16, 4:10, etc., would be pertinent references: if to the Holy Spirit, Acts 2:38, 8:20, 10:45, 11:17. Personally, we rather incline to the latter. This Divine Gift is here said to be "heavenly" because from Heaven, and leading to Heaven, in contrast from Judaism—cf. Acts 2:2, 1 Peter 1:12. Of this "Gift" these apostates had "tasted", or had an experience of: compare Matt. 27:34 where "tasting" is opposed to actual drinking. Those here in view had had an acquaintance with the Gospel, as to gain such a measure of its blessedness as to greatly aggravate their sin and doom. An illustration of this is found in Matt. 13:20, 21.

Third, they were "made partakers of the Holy Spirit". First, it should be pointed out that the Greek word for "partakers" here is a different one from that used in Col. 1:12 aand 2 Peter 1:4, where real Christians are in view. The word here simply means "companions", referring to what is external rather than internal. It is to be observed that this item is placed in the center of the five, and this because it describes the animating principle of the other four, which are all effects. These apostates had never been "born of the Spirit" (John 3:6), still less were their bodies His "temples" (1 Cor. 6:19). Nor do we believe this verse teaches that the Holy Spirit had, at any time, wrought **within** them, otherwise Phil. 1:6 would be contravened. It means that they had shared in the benefit of His supernatural operations and manifestations: "The place was shaken" (Acts 4:31) illustrates. We quote below from Dr. J. Brown:

"It is highly probable that the inspired writer refers primarily to the miraculous gifts and operations of the Holy Spirit by which the primitive dispensation of Christianity was administered. These gifts were by no means confined to those who were 'transformed by the renewing of their minds'. The words of our Lord in Matt. 7:22, 23 and of Paul in 1 Cor. 13:1, 2 seem to intimate, that the possession of these unrenewed men was not very uncommon in that age; at any rate, they plainly show that their possession and an unregenerate state were by no means incompatible".

Fourth, "And have tasted the good Word of God". "I understand by this expression the promise of God respecting the Messiah, the sum and substance of all. It deserves notice that this promise is by way of eminence termed by Jeremiah 'that good word' (33:14). To 'taste', then, this 'good Word of God', is to experience that God has been faithful to His promise—to enjoy, so far as an unconverted man can enjoy the blessings and advantages which flow from that promise being fulfilled. To 'taste the good Word of God', seems, just to enjoy the advantages of the new dispensation" (Dr. J. Brown). Further confirmation that the apostle is here referring to that which these apostates had witnessed of the fulfilment of God's **promise** is obtained by comparing Jer. 29:10, "After seventy years be accomplished at Babylon I will visit you, and perform My **good word** toward you, in causing you to return to this place".

Observe how studiously the apostle still keeps to the word "taste", the better to enable us to identify them. They could not say with Jeremiah, "Thy words were found and I did **eat** them" (15:16). "It is as though he said, I speak not of those who have received nourishment; but of such as have so far tasted it, as that they ought to have desired it as 'sincere milk' and grown thereby" (Dr. J. Owen). A solemn example of one who merely "tasted" the good Word of God is found in Mark 6:20: "for Herod feared John, knowing that he was just a man and an holy, and observed him; and when he heard him, he did many things, and heard him **gladly**".

Fifth. "And the powers of the world to come", or "age to come". The reference here is to the new dispensation which was to be ushered in by Israel's Messiah according to O. T. predictions. It corresponds with "these last days" of Heb. 1:2, and is in contrast from the "time past" or Mosaic economy. Their Messiah was none other than the "mighty God" (Isa. 9), and wondrous and glorious, stupendous and unique, were His miraculous works. These "powers" of the new Age are mentioned in Heb. 2:4, to our comments on which we would refer the reader. Of these mighty "powers" these apostates had "tasted", or had an experience of. They had been personal witnesses of the miracles of Christ, and also of the wonders that followed His ascension, when such glorious manifestations of the Spirit were given. Thus they were "without excuse". Convincing and conclusive evidence had been set before them, but there had been no answering faith in their hearts. A solemn example of this is found in John 11:47, 48.

"If they shall fall away". The Greek word here is very strong and emphatic, even stronger than the one used in Matt. 7:27, where it is said of the house built on the sand, "and great was the fall thereof". It is a complete falling away, a total abandonment of Christianity which is here in view. It is a wilful turning of the back on God's revealed truth, an utter repudiation of the Gospel. It is making "shipwreck of the faith" (1 Tim. 1:19). This terrible sin is not committed by a mere nominal professor, for he has nothing really to fall away from, save an empty name. The class here described are such as had had their minds enlightened, their consciences stirred, their affections moved to a considerable degree, and yet who were never brought from death unto life. Nor is it backsliding Christians who are in view. It is **not** simply "fall into **sin**", this or that sin. The greatest "sin" which a regenerated man can possibly commit is the personal denial of Christ: Peter was guilty of this, yet was he "renewed again unto repentance". It is the total renunciation of all the distinguishing truths and principles of Christianity, and this not secretly, but openly, which constitutes apostasy.

"If they shall fall away". "This is scarcely a fair translation. It has been said that the apostle did not here assert that such persons **did** or **do** 'fall away'; but that if they did—a supposition which, however, could never be realized—then the consequence would be they could not be 'renewed again unto repentance'. The words literally rendered are, 'And have fallen away', or, 'yet have fallen'. The apostle obviously intimates that such persons might, and that such persons did, 'fall away'. By 'falling away', we are plainly to understand what is commonly called apostasy. This does not consist in an occasional falling into actual sin, however gross and aggravated; nor in the renunciation of some of the principles of Christianity, even though those should be of considerable importance; but in an open, total, determined renunciation of all the constituent principles of Christianity, and a return to a false religion, such as that of unbelieving Jews or heathens, or to open infidelity and open godlessness" (Dr. J. Brown).

"It is impossible . . . . if they fall away, to renew them again unto repentance". Four questions here call for answer. What is meant by "renewed unto repentance"? What is signified by "renewed **again** unto repentance"? **Why** is such an experience "impossible"? To whom is this "impossible"? Repentance signifies a change of mind: Matt. 21:29, Rom. 11:29 establish this. It is more than a mental act, the conscience also being active, leading to contrition and self-condemnation (Job 42: 6). In the unregenerate, it is simply the workings of nature; in the children of God it is wrought by the Holy Spirit. The latter is evangelical, being one of the things which "accompany salvation". The former is not so, being the "sorrow of the world", which "worketh death" (2 Cor. 7:10). This kind of "repentance" or remorse receives most solemn exemplification in the case of Judas: Matt. 27:3, 5. Such was the repentance of these apostates. The Greek verb for "renew" here occurs no where else in the N. T. Probably "restore" had been better, for the same word is used in the Sept., for a Heb. verb meaning to renew in the sense of restore: Psa. 103:5; 104:30; Lam. 5:21. Josephus applies it to the renovation of the Temple!

But what is meant by "renewing unto repentance"? "To be 'renewed' is a figurative expression for denoting a change, a great change, and a change for the better. To be 'renewed' so as to change a person's mind is expressive of an important and advantageous alteration of opinion, and character and service. And such an alteration the persons referred to had undergone at a former period. They were once in a state of ignorance respecting the doctrines and evidences of Christianity, and they had been 'enlightened'. They had once known not of the excellency and beauty of Christian truth, and they had been made to 'taste of the heavenly gift'. They once misunderstood the prophecies respecting the Messiah, and were unaware of their fulfilment, and, of course, were strangers to that energetic influence which the N. T. revelation puts forth; and they had been made to see that that 'good word' was fulfilled, and had been made partakers of the external privileges and been subjected to the peculiar energies of the new order of things. Their view, and feelings, and circumstances, were materially changed. How great the difference between an ignorant, bigoted Jew, and the person described in the preceding passage! He had become as it were a different man. He had not, indeed, become, in the sense of the apostle, a 'new creature', His mind had not been so changed as unfeignedly to believe 'the truth as it is in Jesus'; but still, a great and so far as it went, a thorough change had taken place" (Dr. J. Brown).

Now it is impossible to "renew again unto repentance" those who have totally abandoned the Christian revelation. Some things are "impossible" with respect unto the **nature** of God, as that He cannot lie, or pardon sin without satisfaction to His justice. Other things which are possible to God's nature are rendered "impossible" by His **decrees** or purpose: see 1 Sam. 15: 28, 29. Still other things are "possible" or "impossible" with respect to the **rule or order** of all things God has appointed. For example, there cannot be faith apart from hearing the Word (Rom. 10:13-17). "When in things of duty God hath neither expressed command thereon, nor appointed means for the performance of them, they are to be looked upon then as impossible (as, for instance, there is no salvation apart from repentance, Luke 13:3. A. W. P.); and then, with respect unto **us**, they are so absolutely, and so to be esteemed. And this is the 'impossibility' here principally intended. It is a thing that God hath neither commanded us to endeavor, nor appointed means to attain it, nor promise to assist us in it. It is therefore that which we have no reason to look after, attempt, or expect, as being not possible by any law, rule, or constitution of God.

"The apostle instructs us no further in the nature of future events but as our own duty is concerned in them. It is not for us either to look or hope, or pray for, or endeavour the restoration of such persons unto repentance. God gives a law unto us in these things, not unto Himself. It may be possible with God, for aught we know, if there be not a contradiction in it unto any of the holy properties of His nature; only He will not have us to expect any such thing from Him, nor hath He appointed any means for us to endeavour it. What He shall do we ought trustfully to accept; but our own duty toward such persons is absolutely at an end. And indeed, they put themselves wholly out of our reach" (Dr. J. Owen).

It needs to be carefully observed that in the whole of this passage from 5:11 onwards the apostle is speaking of his own ministry. In God's hands, His servants are instruments by which He works and through whom He accomplishes His evangelical purpose. Thus Paul could properly say "I have begotten you through the gospel" (1 Cor. 4:15). And again, "My little children, of whom I travail in birth again until Christ be formed in you" (Gal. 4:19). So the servants of God had, through the preaching of the Gospel, "renewed unto repentance" those spoken of in Heb. 6:4. But they had apostatised; they had totally repudiated the Gospel. It was therefore "impossible" for the servants of God to "renew them again unto repentance", for the all-sufficient reason that they had no other message to proclaim to them. They had no other Gospel in reserve, no further motives to present. Christ crucified had been set before them. Him they now denounced as an Imposter. There was "none other name" whereby they could be saved. Their public renunciation of Christ rendered their case hopeless so far as God's servants were concerned. "Let them alone" (Matt. 15:19) was now their orders: compare Jude 22. Whether or not it was possible for God, consistently with His holiness, to same them, our passage does not decide.

"Seeing they crucify to themselves the Son of God afresh" (v. 6). This is brought in to show the aggravation of their awful crime and the impossibility of their being renewed again unto repentance. By renouncing their Christian profession they declared Christ to be an Imposter. Thus they were irreclaimable. To attempt any further reasoning with them, would only be casting pearls before swine. With this verse should be carefully compared the parallel passage in 10:26-29. These apostates had "received the knowledge of the truth", though not a saving knowledge of it. Afterward they sinned "wilfully": there was a deliberate and open disavowal of the truth. The nature of their particular sin is termed a "treading under foot the Son of God (something which no real Christian ever does) and counting (esteeming) the blood of the covenant an unholy thing", that is, looking upon the One who hung on the Cross as a common malefactor. For such there "remaineth no more sacrifice for sins". Their case is hopeless so far as man is concerned; and the writer believes, such are abandoned by God also.

"Seeing they crucify to themselves the Son of God afresh, and put Him to an open shame". "They thus identify themselves with His crucifiers—they entertained and avowed sentiments which, were He on earth and in their power, would induce them to crucify Him. They exposed Him to infamy, made a public example of Him. They did more to dishonour Jesus Christ than His murderers did. They never professed to acknowledge His divine mission; but these apostates had made such a profession—they had made a kind of trial of Christianity, and, after trial, had rejected it" (Dr. J. Brown).

Such a warning was needed and well calculated to stir up the slothful Hebrews. Under the O. T. economy, by means of types and prophecies, they had obtained glimmerings of truth as to Christ, called "the word of the beginning of Christ". Under those shadows and glimmerings they had been reared, not knowing their full import till they had been blessed with the full light of the Gospel, here called "perfection". The danger to which they were exposed was that of receding from the ground where Christianity placed them, and relaxing to Judaism. To do so meant to re-enter that House which Christ had left "desolate" (Matt. 23:38), and would be to join forces with His murderers, and thus "crucify to themselves the Son of God afresh", and by their apostasy "put Him to an open (public) shame". We may add that the Greek word here for "crucify" is a stronger one than is generally used: it means to "crucify up"

Attention is thus directed to the erection of the cross on which the Saviour was held up to public scorn.

Taking the passage as a whole, it needs to be remembered that all who had professed to receive the Gospel were not born of God: the parable of the Sower shows that. Intelligence might be informed, conscience searched, natural affections stirred, and yet there be "no root" in them. All is not gold that glitters. There has always been a "mixt multitude" (Ex. 12:38) who accompany the people of God. Moreover, there is in the real Christian the old heart, which is "deceitful above all things and desperately wicked", and therefore is he in constant need of faithful warning. Such, God has given in every dispensation: Gen 2:17; Lev. 26: 15, 16; Matt. 3:8; Rom. 11:21; 1 Cor. 10:12.

Finally, let it be said that while Scripture speaks plainly and positively of the perseverance of the saints, yet it is a perseverance of saints, not unregenerate professors. Divine preservation is not only in a safe state, but also in a holy course of disposition and conduct. We are "kept by the power of God through faith". We are kept by the Spirit working in us a spirit of entire dependency, renouncing our own wisdom and strength. The only place from which we cannot fall is one down in the dust. It is there the Lord brings His own people, weaning them from all confidence in the flesh, and giving them to experience that it is when they are weak they are strong. Such, and such only, are saved and safe forever.

—ARTHUR W. PINK.

GLEANINGS IN EXODUS.

72. Moses a type of Christ.

"The life of Moses presents a series of striking antitheses. He was the child of a slave, and the son of a king. He was born in a hut, and lived in a palace. He inherited poverty, and enjoyed unlimited wealth. He was the leader of armies, and the keeper of flocks. He was the mightiest of warriors, and the meekest of men. He was educated in the court, and dwelt in the desert. He had the wisdom of Egypt, and the faith of a child. He was fitted for the city, and wandered in the wilderness. He was tempted with the pleasures of sin, and endured the hardships of virtue. He was backward in speech, and talked with God. He had the rod of a shepherd, and the power of the Infinite. He was a fugitive from Pharaoh, and an ambassador from Heaven. He was the giver of the Law, and the forerunner of Grace. He died alone on mount Moab, and appeared with Christ in Judea. No man assisted at his funeral, yet God buried him. The fire has gone out of mount Sinai, but the lightning is still in his Law. His lips are silent, but his voice yet speaks" (Dr. I. M. Haldeman).

But the most striking thing of all in connection with this most remarkable man, is the wonderful way and the many respects in which he was a type of the Lord Jesus In the Introductory article of this series (Jan. 1924) we stated: "In many respects there is a remarkable correspondency between Moses and Christ, and if the Lord permits us to complete this series of articles, we shall, at the close, summarise those correspondencies, and show them to be as numerous and striking as those which engaged our attention when Joseph was before us"—see the last seven chapters in Vol. 2 of our work "Gleanings in Genesis". We shall now seek to fulfil that promise.

Ere we attempt to set forth some (for we do not profess to exhaust the subject) of these correspondencies, let us first appeal to the Word itself in proof that Moses was a type of Christ. In Deut. 18:15 we find Moses saying, "The Lord thy God will raise up unto thee a Prophet from the midst of thee, of thy brethren, like unto me; unto Him ye shall hearken". Thus it will be seen from these words that we are not trafficking in human imagination when we contemplate Moses as a type of Christ. Such is the plain teaching of Holy Writ.

As we desire to bring to a close these "Gleanings in Exodus" in the current issue, and therefore can devote but one article to our present theme, and as the points to be considered are so numerous, we cannot take up each one separately and comment upon it at length. Rather shall we, with a few exceptions, simply give the references, and ask the reader to look them up for himself.

1. His nationality.

Moses was an Israelite (Ex. 2:1, 2). So, according to the flesh, was Christ.

2. His Birth.

This occurred when his nation was under the dominion of a hostile power, when they were groaning under the rule of a Gentile king (Ex. 1). So the Jews were in bondage to the Romans when Christ was born (Matt. 2:1 cf. Luke 24:21).

3. His Person.

"In which time Moses was born, and was exceeding fair to God" (Acts 7:20). How blessedly did he, in this, foreshadow the Beloved of the Father! **His** estimate of the "fairness" of that Child which lay in Bethlehem's manger, was evidenced by the sending of the angels to say unto the shepherds, "Unto you is born this day in the city of David a Saviour, which is Christ the Lord" (Luke 2:11).

4. His Infancy.

In infancy his life was endangered, imperilled by the reigning king, for Pharaoh had given orders that, "Every son that is born ye shall cast into the river" (Ex. 1:22). How this reminds us of Matt. 2:16: "Then Herod . . . sent forth and slew all the children that were in Bethlehem, and in all the coasts thereof"!

5. His Adoption.

Though, previously, he was the child of another, he yet was made the son of Pharaoh's daughter: "And became her **son**" (Ex. 2:10). Thus he had a mother, but **no father**! What anointed eye can fail to see prefigured here the mystery of the Virgin-birth! Christ was the Son of Another, even the Son of God. But, born into this world, He had a mother, but no human father. Yet was He, as it were, adopted by Joseph: see Matt. 1:19-21.

6. His Childhood.

This was spent in Egypt. So also was Christ's: "Behold the angel of the Lord appeareth to Joseph in a dream, saying, "Arise, and take the young Child and His mother, and flee into Egypt, and be thou there until I bring thee word" (Matt. 2:13). Thus was fulfilled God's ancient oracle, "And called My Son out of Egypt" (Hos. 11:1).

7. His Sympathy for Israel.

He was filled with a deep compassion for his suffering kinsmen according to the flesh, and he yearned for their deliverance. Beautifully does this come out in Acts 7:23, 24, "And when he was full forty years old, it came into his heart to visit his brethren of the children of Israel. And seeing one of them suffer wrong, he defended him." So too Christ was filled with pity toward His enslaved people, and love brought Him here to deliver them.

8. His early knowledge of his Mission.

Long years before he actually entered upon his great work, Moses discerned, "how that God by his hand would deliver them" (Acts 7:25). So as a Boy of twelve, Christ said to His perplexed mother, "Wist ye not that I must be about My Father's business?" (Luke 2:49).

9. His condescending Grace.

Though legally the "son of Pharaoh's daughter", yet he regarded the Hebrew slaves as his **brethren**: "And it came to pass in those days, when Moses was grown, that he went out unto his brethren" (Ex. 2:11). So it is with Christ: "He is not ashamed to call them **brethren**" (Heb. 2:11).

10. His great Renunciation.

"By faith Moses, when he was come to years, refused to be called the son of Pharaoh's daughtetr; Choosing rather to suffer affliction with the people of God, than to enjoy the pleasures of sin for a season; Esteeming the reproach of Christ greater riches than the treasures in Egypt" (Heb. 11:24-26). What a foreshadowing was this of Him "Who, being in the form of God, thought it not robbery to be equal with God; But made Himself of no reputation, and took upon Him the form of a servant" (Phil. 2:6, 7)! Like Moses, Christ too voluntarily relinquished riches, glory, and a kingly palace.

11. His Rejection by his brethren.

"And the next day he showed himself unto them as they strove, and would have set them at one again, saying, Sirs, ye are brethren; why do ye wrong one to another? But he that did his neighbour wrong **thrust him away**, saying, Who made thee a ruler and a judge over us?" (Acts 7:26, 27). This is very sad; sadder still is it to read of Christ, "He came unto His own, and His own received Him not" (John 1:11). This same line in the typical picture was before us when we considered Joseph. But mark this difference: In the case of Joseph, it was his brethren's enmity against his **person** (Gen. 37:4); here with Moses, it was his brethren's enmity against his **mission**. Joseph was personally hated; Moses officially refused—"who made thee a ruler and a judge over us"? So it was with Christ. Israel said, "We will not have this Man to reign over us" (Luke 19:14).

12. His Sojourning among the Gentiles.

"But Moses fled from the face of Pharaoh, and dwelt in the land of Midian" (Ex. 2:15). Following Christ's rejection by the Jews, we read, "God at the first did visit the Gentiles, to take out of them a people for His name" (Acts 15:14).

13. His Seat on the well.

Away from his own land, we read of Moses, "And he sat down by a well" (Ex. 2:15). So the only time we read of the Lord Jesus seated by the well, was when He was outside Israel's borders, in Samaria (John 4:4, 6).

14. His Shepherdhood.

"Now Moses kept the flock of Jethro his father-in-law" (Ex. 3:1). This is the character which Christ sustains to His elect among the Gentiles: "And other sheep I have, which are not of this fold, them also I must bring, and they shall hear My voice; and there shall be one flock, one Shepherd" (John 10:16).

15. His Season of Seclusion.

Before he entered upon his real mission, Moses spent many years in obscurity. Who had supposed that this one, there "at the backside of the desert", was destined to such an honourable future? So it was with the incarnate Son of God. Before He began His public ministry, He was hidden away in despised Nazareth. Who that saw Him there in the carpenter's shop, dreamed that He was ordained of God to the work of redemption!

16. His Commission from God.

He was called of God to emancipate His people from the house of bondage: "Come now therefore, and I will send thee unto Pharaoh, that thou mayest bring forth My people the children of Israel out of Egypt" (Ex. 3:10). So Christ was sent forth into this world to "seek and to save that which was lost" (Luke 19:10).

17. His Apostleship.

Thus he was God's apostle unto Israel, for "apostle" signifies one "sent forth": "Now therefore go" (Ex. 4:12). So Christ was the Sent One of God (John 9:4 etc); yea, in Heb. 3:1 He is designated "the Apostle".

18. His Credentials.

His commission from God was confirmed by power to work miracles. So also Christ's mission was authenticated by wondrous signs (Matt. 11:4, 5). It should be noted that Moses is the first one mentioned in the O. T. that performed miracles; so is Christ in the N. T.—John the Baptist performed none (John 10:41).

19. His first Miracles.

Moses wrought many wonders, but it is most striking to observe that his first two miraculous-signs were power over the serpent, and power over leprosy (Ex. 4:6-9). So after Christ began His public ministry, we read first of His power over Satan (Matt. 4:10, 11), and then His power over leprosy (Matt. 8:3).

20. His Return to his own land.

In Ex. 4:19 we read, "And the Lord said unto Moses in Midian, Go, return into Egypt: for all the men are dead which sought thy life". The antitype of this is found in Matt. 2:19, "An angel of the Lord appeareth in a dream to Joseph in Egypt, saying, Arise, and take the young Child and His mother, and go into the land of Israel: for they are dead which sought the young Child's life"!

21. His Acceptance by his brethren.

This is recorded in Exodus 4:29-31. How different was this from his first appearing before and rejection by the Hebrews (Ex. 2)! How beautifully it prefigured Israel's acceptance of their Messiah at His second appearing!

22. His powerful Rod.

Moses now wielded a rod of mighty power: see Ex. 9:23; 10:13; 14:16. So also it is written of Christ, "Thou shalt break them with a rod of iron" (Psa. 2:9).

23. His Announcing solemn Judgments.

Again and again he warned Pharaoh and his people of the sore punishment of God if they continued to defy him. So also Christ declared, "Except ye repent, ye shall all likewise perish" (Luke 13:3).

24. His deliverance of Israel.

Moses perfectly fulfilled his God-given commission and led Israel out of the house of bondage: "The same did God send to be a ruler and a deliverer" (Acts 7:35). So Christ affirmed, "If the Son therefore shall make you free, ye shall be free indeed" (John 8:36).

25. His Headship.

Remarkably is this brought out in 1 Cor. 10:1, 2, "All our fathers were under the cloud, and all passed through the sea; and were all baptized unto Moses". So obedient Christians are "baptized unto Jesus Christ" (Rom. 6:3).

26. His Leadership of Israel's Praise.

"Then sang Moses and the children of Israel" (Ex. 15:1). Of Christ too it is written, "In the midst of the congregation will I praise Thee" (Psa. 22:22).

27. His Authority challenged.

This is recorded in Numbers 16:3; the antitype in Matt. 21:23.

28. His person Envied.

See Psa. 106:16, and compare Mark 15:10.

29. His person opposed.

Though Israel were so deeply indebted to Moses, yet again and again we find them "murmuring" against him: Ex. 15:24, 16:2, etc. For the N. T. parallel see Luke 15:2, John 6:41.

30. His life Threatened.

So fiercely did the ungrateful Hebrews oppose Moses that, on one occasion, they were ready to "stone" him (Ex. 17:4). How this brings to mind what we read of in John 8:59, 10:31!

31. His Sorrows.

Moses felt keenly the base ingratitude of the people. Mark his plaintive plea as recorded in Num. 11:11, 14. So too the Lord Jesus suffered from the reproaches of the people: He was "the Man of sorrows and acquainted with grief".

32. His unwearied Love.

Though misunderstood, envied, and opposed, nothing could alienate the affections of Moses from his people. "Many waters cannot quench love, neither can the floods drown it" (Song of Sol. 8:7). Beautifully is this seen in Ex. 32. After Israel repudiated Jehovah and had worshipped the golden calf, after the Lord has disowned them as His people (Ex. 32:7), Moses supplicates God on their behalf, saying "Oh, this people have sinned a great sin, and have made them gods of gold. Yet now, if Thou wilt forgive their sin—; and if not, blot me, I pray Thee, out of Thy book which Thou hast written" (vv. 31:32). How this reminds us of Him who "having loved His own which were in the world, He loved them unto the end" (John 13:1)!

33. His Forgiving spirit.

"And Miriam and Aaron spake against Moses . . . Hath the Lord indeed spoken only by Moses? Hath He not spoken also by us"? (Num. 12:1, 2). But he answered not a word. How this pointed to Him who, 'when He was reviled, reviled not again" (1 Peter 2:23). When Miriam was stricken with leprosy because of her revolt against her brother, we are told, "Moses cried unto the Lord, saying, Heal her now, O God, I beseech Thee" (Num. 12:13).

34. His Prayerfulness.

An example of this has just been before us, but many other instances are recorded. Moses was, pre-eminently, a man of prayer. At every crisis he sought unto the Lord: see Ex. 5:22, 8:12, 9:33, 14:15, 15:25, 17:4, etc. Note how often in Luke's Gospel Christ is also presented as a Man of prayer.

35. His Meekness.

"Moses was very meek, above all the men which were upon the face of the earth" (Num. 12:3) cf. Matt 11:29.

36. His Faithfulness.

"Moses verily was faithful in all his house" (Heb. 3:5). So Christ is "The faithful and true Witness" (Rev. 3:14).

37. His providing Israel with water.

See Num. 20:11 and compare John 4:14, 7:37.

38. His Prophetic office.

Deut. 18:18 and compare John 7:16, 8:28.

39. His Priestly activities.

"Moses and Aaron among His priests" (Psa. 99:6). Illustrations are found in Lev. 8: "And Moses took the blood, and put it upon the horns of the altar . . . and he took all the fat . . . and burned it upon the altar" (vv. 15, 16 and see 19:23). So Christ, as Priest, "offered Himself without spot to God" (Heb. 9:14).

40. His Kingly rule.

"Moses commanded us a law, even the inheritance of the congregation of Jacob. And he was king in Jeshurun" (Deut. 33:4, 5). So Christ is King in Zion, and will yet be over the Jews (Luke 1:32, 33).

41. His Judgeship.

"Moses sat to judge the people: and they stood by Moses from the morning until the evening" (Ex. 18:13). Compare 2 Cor. 5:10.

42. His Leadership.

Moses was the head and director of God's people, as He said to him, "Lead the people unto the place of which I have spoken" (Ex. 32:34). So Christ is called, "The Captain of their salvation" (Heb. 2:10).

43. His Mediation.

What a remarkable word was that of Moses to Israel, "I stood between the Lord and you" (Deut. 5:5): "There is one God, and one Mediator between God and men, the Man Christ Jesus" (1 Tim. 2:5).

44. His Election.

In Psa. 106:23 he is called, "Moses His chosen". So God says of Christ, "Behold My Servant, whom I uphold, Mine elect" (Isa. 42:1).

45. His Covenant-engagement.

"And the Lord said unto Moses, Write thou these words: for after the tenor of these words I have made a covenant with thee and with Israel" (Ex. 34:27): so Christ is denominated, "The Mediator of a better covenant" (Heb. 8:6).

46. His sending forth of the Twelve.

"These are the names of the men which Moses sent to spy out the land" (Num. 13:16 see previous verses). So Christ sent forth twelve apostles (Matt. 10:5).

47. His Appointing of the Seventy.

"And Moses went out and told the people the words of the Lord, and gathered the seventy men of the elders of the people" (Num. 11:24). So Christ selected seventy (Luke 10:1).

48. His Wisdom.

"Moses was learned in all the wisdom of the Egyptians" (Acts 7:22). Compare Col. 2:3.

49. His Might.

"And was mighty in words and in deeds" (Acts 7:22). Behold the antitype of this in Matt. 13:34: "They were astonished, and said, Whence hath this Man this wisdom, and these mighty works"?

50. His Intercession.

"And Moses brought their cause before the Lord" (Num. 27:5). Compare Heb. 7:25.

51. His Intimate Communion with God.

"And there arose not a prophet since in Israel like unto Moses, whom the Lord knew face to face" (Ex. 34:10). So, on earth, Christ was "The only-begotten Son, which is in the bosom of the Father" (John 1:18). It is striking to behold in Ex. 31 to 34 how Moses passed and repassed between Jehovah in the mount and the camp of the congregation: expressive of his equal access to heaven and earth—compare John 3:13.

52. His Knowledge of God.

See Psa. 103:7 and cf. John 5:29.

53. His holy Anger.

See Ex. 32:19 and cf. Mark 3:5, etc.

54. His Message.

He was the mouthpiece of God: "And Moses came and told the people all the words of the Lord" (Ex. 24:3). Compare Heb. 1:2.

55. His Commandments.

See Deut. 4:2 and cf. Matt. 28:20.

56. His Written Revelation.

See Ex. 31:13 and cf. Rev. 1:1.

57. His Fasting.

See Ex. 34:28 and cf. Matt. 4:2.

58. His Transfiguration on the mount.

See Ex. 34:29, 35 and cf. Matt. 17:2.

59. His Place Outside the Camp.

See Ex. 33:7 and cf. Heb. 13:13.

60. His Arraigning of the responsible head.

See Ex. 32:21 and cf. Rev. 2:12, 13.

61. His Praying for Israel's Forgiveness.

See Num. 14:19 and cf. Luke 23:34.

62. His Washing his Brethren with Water.

"And Moses brought Aaron and his sons, and washed them with water" (Lev. 8:6). Who can fail to see in that a foreshadowing of what is recorded in John 13:5: "After that He poureth water into a basin and began to wash the disciples' feet"!

63. His Prophecies.

See Deut. 28 and 33 and cf. Matt. 24 and Luke 21.

64. His Rewarding God's servants.

See Num. 7:6, 32:33, 40 and cf. Rev. 22:12.

65. His perfect Obedience.

"Thus did Moses according to all that the Lord commanded, so did he" (Ex. 40:16). What a lovely foreshadowing was this of Him who could say, "I have kept My Father's commandments" (John 16:10)!

66. His erecting the Tabernacle.

See Ex. 40:2, and cf. Zech. 6:12.

67. His Completing of his Work.

"So Moses finished the work" (Ex. 40:33). What a blessed prefiguration was this of Him who declared, "I have finished the work which Thou gavest Me to do" (John 17:4).

68. His Blessing of the People.

"And Moses blessed them" (Ex. 39:43). So too we read in Luke 24:50, "And He led them out as far as to Bethany, and He lifted up His hands, and blessed them".

69. His Anointing of God's House.

"And Moses took the anointing oil (the O. T. emblem of the Holy Spirit), and anointed the tabernacle and all that was therein" (Lev. 8:10). Carefully compare Acts 2:1-3, 33.

70. His Unabated Strength.

"His eye was not dim, nor his natural force abated" (Deut. 34:7): compare Matt. 27:50, and note the "loud voice".

71. His Death was for the benefit of God's people.

"It went ill with Moses **for their sakes**" (Psa. 106:32; "But the Lord was wroth with me **for your sakes**" (Deut. 3:26). What marvelous foreshadowings of the Cross were these!

72. His Appointing of another Comforter.

Moses did not leave his people comfortless, but gave them a successor: see Deut. 31:23 and cf. John 14:16, 18.

73. His giving an Inheritance.

"The land which Moses gave you on this side of Jordan" (Josh. 1:14): in Christ believers "have obtained an inheritance" (Eph. 1:11).

74. His Death necessary before Israel could enter Canaan.

"Moses My servant is dead; **now therefore** arise, go over this Jordan, thou, and all this people, unto the land which I do give to thee" (Josh. 1:2). "**Except** a corn of wheat fall into the ground **and die**, it abideth alone: but if it die, it bringeth forth much fruit" (John 12:24).

75. His Second Appearing.

Moses was one of the two Old Testament characters which **returned** to this earth in New Testament times (Matt. 17:3)—type of Christ's second coming to the earth.

Our space is already exhausted so we shall leave it with our readers to search the Scriptures for at least twenty-five other points in which Moses foreshadowed our Lord. The subject is well-nigh exhaustless. And a most blessed subject it is, demonstrating anew the Divine authorship of the Bible. May the Lord bless to many this very imperfect attempt to show that "in the volume of the Book" it **is** written of Christ.

—ARTHUR W. PINK.

JUSTIFICATION.

The first thought to which the mind should be directed in every question respecting Justification, respects the **Justifier.** To whom belongs the right to justify? The answer is very obvious to all who admit the sovereignty and almighty power of God. As there is only one supreme Ruler and Legislator, so there is only one Judge to whom alone it belongeth to justify or condemn.

Every question therefore, respecting Justification necessarily brings before us the judicial courts of God. The principles of those courts must be determined by God alone. Even to earthly governors we concede the right of establishing their own laws, and appointing the mode of their enforcement. Shall we then accord this title to man, and withhold it from the all-wise and almighty God? Surely no presumption can be greater than for the creature to sit in judgment on the Creator, and to pretend to determine what should, or should not be, the methods of His government. It must be our place reverently to listen to His own exposition of the principles of His own courts, and humbly to thank Him for His goodness in condescending to explain to us what those principles are. As sinners, we can have no claim on God. We have no claim to a revelation that should acquaint us with His ways.

The judicial principles of the government of God, are, as might be expected, based upon the absolute perfectness of His own holiness. This was fully shown both in the prohibitory and in the mandatory commandments of the Law as given at Sinai. That Law prohibited not only wrong deeds and wrong counsels of heart, but it went deeper still. It prohibited even wrong desires and wrong tendencies, saying, "Thou shalt not be concupiscent"—that is, thou shalt not have, **even momentarily,** one desire or tendency that is contrary to the perfectness of God. And then as to its positive requirements, it demanded the perfect, unreserved, perpetual surrender of soul and body, with all its powers, to God and to His service. Not only was it required, that love to Him—love perfect and unremitted should dwell as a living principle in the heart, but also that it should be developed in action, and that unvaryingly. The mode also of the development throughout, was required to be as perfect as the principle from which the development sprang.

If any among the children of men be able to substantiate a claim to perfectness such as this, the Courts of God are ready to recognize it. The God of Truth will recognize a truthful claim wherever it is found. But if we are unable to present any such claim—if corruption be found in us and in our ways—if in any thing we have fallen short of God's glory, then it is obvious that however willing the Courts of God may be to recognize perfectness wherever it exists, such willingness can afford no ground of hope to those, who, instead of having perfectness, have sins and short-comings unnumbered.

And if we see that such a mode of justification is, to us, hopeless, let us beware of murmuring against the strictness of the Divine requirements as if we were displeased with God for refusing to be satisfied with less than **perfectness**. Such murmuring is not only useless, but sinful. It has the sinfulness of rebellion, and of ingratitude too. It is in mercy that God has made known to us as the unalterable principle of His Courts, that they will not justify on the ground of personal righteousness any one who cannot prove the possession of a righteousness that is **perfect**—like His own, without intermission, and without flaw.

What then have we to do? We have to enquire whether the Courts of God permit that a claim to the possession of righteousness should be presented, based, not on the title of what we personally are, but on the title of what has been **substitutionally** effected by another. Do the Courts of God admit the principle of substitution? This question, like the previous one, can only be decided on the authority of God. He alone can determine, and He alone can reveal, the principles of His own Courts. But His declaration, respecting the holiness of His own unbending Law, is not more plain, than is His revelation respecting a means of justification provided through a Substitute. The same Courts which would be ready to recognize the claim of personal righteousness (if such a claim could be advanced) are also willing to admit of a claim being preferred on the ground of being beneficially interested in the substitutional righteousness of Another.

It is impossible, however, that the principle of substitutional righteousness could be recognized in the Courts of God on behalf of those who had broken God's Law, unless a provision were made for bearing its penalties, as well as for fulfilling its commandments. According to the appointment of the Law, if there be a falling short in any of its requirements, then there is not only failure in respect of the attainment of righteousness, but as a consequence of such failure, **guilt,** and upon all guilt the Law pronounces curse—"cursed is he that continueth not in all things that are written in the book of the Law to do them." Consequently, if, we are unable to prove the possession of personal perfect righteousness, that very inability leaves us under curse. We stand not merely as those who have failed in attaining the reward of righteousness, but as those who because of such failure are under the pronounced sentence of God's holy Law. He who has not **perfect** righteousness is a sinner, and every sinner is under curse.

If, therefore, grace is pleased to open a way of salvation through substitution, it is necessary that the Substitute should be One, able, both to meet all the demands of the Law in respect of righteousness, and also to bear the curse which the infraction of the Law entailed on those, whom as a Substitute, He represents. Such a Substitute, Christ is. He came to sustain the dignity and holiness of the Divine government, as well as to open a door of mercy. He magnified the Law by perfect obedience to all its requirements, so that not one jot or tittle passed therefrom till all was fulfilled: and He also bore in life and in death all that was appointed to be borne in order that mercy might be exercised with a due regard to the claims of justice. There may be, and there is, love in God towards sinners; but there is also wrath in God towards unpardoned sin, and that wrath demands an atoning or "appeasing" sacrifice. This "appeasement" Christ supplied, and thus the governmental holiness of God, before angels and men and Satan, was glorified, not only by the perfectness with which every commandment of His Law was kept, not only by the unswerving steadfastness with which its curse was borne, but also by the excellency and dignity of the Person of Him who undertook to obey it and to suffer under it: for that

Person was Immanuel—"the Man that is My fellow, saith the Lord of hosts". The dignity of the Person must not be overlooked while considering the perfectness of the work. All, therefore, who are recognized in the Courts of heaven as having such an One as their Substitute, must necessarily be regarded as effectually freed from the penalty of their guilt, seeing that their Substitute has borne the penalty for them; and as possessed of perfect righteousness in their stead.

Some modern writers, indeed, reject the doctrine of Christ's vicarious fulfillment of the Law on behalf of His people, as if it were not needed; and as if the righteousness referred to in such texts as, "He is the Lord our righteousness"—and "the righteousness of God which is by faith of Jesus Christ unto all and upon all them that believe", referred to something higher than any righteousness which could result from Christ's obedience to the Law. But let us beware of speaking or thinking lightly of the Law of God, or of the service of Him who undertook to obey it for His people. That Law was a transcript of the holiness of God; and none but One who was holy as God, and who was God, could meet its claims. Consequently, it is impossible that there can be any thing higher, any thing more perfect than the obedience rendered by Immanuel to the Law of God. Nothing can be more perfect than that which is perfect. Light that hath no darkness at all is light that hath no darkness at all; and such light can in no respect be surpassed or exceeded. Prolongation of development cannot make perfection more perfect. When a heavenly perfectness which had been from everlasting and shall be to everlasting, was manifested for thirty and three years here on earth, the perfectness so exhibited was in no respect less excellent than that which had been in the ages that preceded, or which shall be in the ages that succeed the period of its earthly development. The waters brought to David from the well at Bethlehem, and which he poured out before the Lord, were not less pure or less crystal because they were a part—a portion merely, of the well from which they were taken. As to purity and excellency there was no difference between the waters and the well. As was the well, such were the waters. Not indeed that such an illustration is adequate; for the fountain was, so to speak, present when He was in the earth who is "God over all, blessed forever". The development, however, of the fulness that is in Him was, no doubt limited during the days of His earthly service. It was limited as to time, and it was displayed but in part. Nevertheless, that limited period supplied the obedience by which believers are formally "constituted righteous"; and to that obedience attached the excellency of that heavenly and eternal Person whose obedience it was.

When, therefore, the righteousness which Christ provided by His vicarious fulfillment of the Law is reckoned to us, we become possessed of a righteousness no less excellent, no less perfect, no less precious, than the Person of Him whose righteousness it is. "By the obedience of One shall many be constituted righteous", is a statement sufficiently distinct. The obedience of which it speaks cannot be understood of anything save the obedience which was manifested on earth by that Holy One who was "born of a woman made under the Law": and that obedience is said to be the means, the necessary means, to our being constituted righteous. The fulfillment of the Law was no less necessary than was the bearing of its penalties to the maintenance of the governmental holiness of God: and consequently both were required of the heavenly Substitute—both were needed for our salvation. "Verily, I say unto you, till heaven and earth pass, one jot or one tittle shall in no wise pass from the Law till all be fulfilled". Did anyone so fulfill it but Himself? And did He fulfill it on His own behalf? That could not be, for He was essentially the Righteous One. He fulfilled it to provide a righteousness for His believing people. Well then may the righteousness so provided be said to be "the righteousness of God", for it is a righteousness in conformity with the requirements of His holy Law—a righteousness which He can acknowledge as failing in nothing short of His own perfectness. It was needful for our justification that such a righteousness should be formally provided, and formally acknowledged in the Courts of God. Accordingly there was a moment when the righteousness thus needed for the justification of God's people, **formally** began to be wrought out by their Surety, and there was a moment when the working out of that righteousness was **formally** accomplished. It began with the birth and terminated with the death of the Holy One: and it is in virtue of that which thus **formally** wrought out and accomplished in the days of His flesh, that Christ's people are said to be "constituted", by means of His obedience, "righteous".

Thus too is supplied the reason, why, in the Scripture, the non-imputation of sin is always spoken of as implying also the imputation of righteousness. In the arrangements of men, it is otherwise. Human tribunals may acquit or pardon; but their pardon is not accompanied by the imputation of righteousness, or by the reward of righteousness. Pardon, in human courts, is a negative act. It remits the penalty: but it bestows nothing. But in the Courts of God, pardon is always accompanied by the imputation of rigtheousness. And the reason is obvious. The sins of believers are remitted because the Holy One of God bore the appointed wrath: but in bearing it, He at the same moment presented His own spotless righteousness unto God. We cannot separate from Immanuel His own essential excellency. We may see Him bruised and given like beaten incense to the fire: but was incense ever burned without fragrance and only fragrance being the result? The name of Christ not only cancels sin; it supplies in the place of that which it has cancelled, its own everlasting excellency. We cannot have its nullifying power only: the other is the sure concomitant. So was it with every typical sacrifice of the Law. It was stricken: but as being spotless it was also burned on the altar for a sweet-smelling savour. The savour ascended as a memorial before God: it was accepted for, and its value was attributed or imputed to him, who had brought the vicarious victim. If therefore, we reject the imputation of righteousness, we reject sacrifice as revealed in Scripture; for Scripture knows of no sacrifice whose efficacy is so exhausted in the removal of guilt, as to leave nothing to be presented in acceptableness before God. It is on this account that the Apostle in the fourth chapter of Romans assumes the necessary concomitancy of the non-imputation of sin and the imputation of righteousness: for after saying that David describeth the blessedness of the man unto whom God imputeth righteousness without works, he quotes a passage which speaks not of the imputation of righteousness, but of the **non**-imputation of sin:—"Blessed are they whose iniquities are forgiven, and whose sins are covered: blessed is the man to whom the Lord will not impute sin". Thus, in the appointments of the Courts of God, wherever there is the non-imputation of sin, there, there is also the imputation of righteousness; nor have I ever heard any argument against the imputation of righteousness that is not equally capable of being used against the doctrine of vicarious atonement. The doctrines of vicarious atonement and vicarious righteousness stand or fall together.

"There is the very same need", says President Edwards, "of Christ's obeying the Law in our stead, in order to the reward, as of His suffering the penalty of the Law in our stead, in order to our escaping the penalty; and the same reason why one should be accepted on our account, as the other. There is the same need of one as the other, that the Law of God might be answered; for this the Scripture plainly teaches. This is given as the reason why Christ was made a curse for us, that the Law threatened a curse to us, Gal. 3:10, 13. But the same Law that fixes the curse of God as the consequence of not continuing in all things written in the Law to do them (verse 10), has as much fixed doing those things as an antecedent of living in them (verse 12). There is as much connection established in the one case as in the other. There is therefore exactly the same need, from the Law, of perfect obedience being fulfilled in order to our obtaining the reward, as there is of death being suffered in order to our escaping the punishment; or the same necessity by the Law, of perfect obedience preceding life, as there is of disobedience being succeeded by death. The Law is, without doubt, as much an established rule in one case as the other . . . It is absolutely necessary, that in order to a sinner's being justified, the righteousness of some other should be reckoned to his account; for it is declared, that the person justified is looked upon as (in himself) ungodly; but God neither will nor can justify a person without a righteousness, for justification is manifestly a **forensic** term, as the word is used in Scripture, and a judicial thing, or the act of a judge. So that if a person should be justified without righteousness, the judgment would not be according to truth. The sentence of justification would be a false sentence, unless there be a righteousness performed, that is, by the judge properly looked upon as his. To say, that God does not justify the sinner without sincere, though an imperfect obedience, does not help the case; for an imperfect righteousness before a judge is no righteousness. To accept of something that falls short of the rule, instead of something else that answers the rule, is no judicial act, or act of a judge, but a pure act of sovereignty. An imperfect righteousness is no righteousness before a judge: for 'righteousness (as one observes) is a relative thing, and has always relation to a law. The formal nature of righteousness, properly understood, lies in conformity of actions to that which is the rule and measure of them'. Therefore that only is righteousness in the sight of a judge that answers the law. The law is the judge's rule: if he pardons and hides what really is, and so does not pass sentence according to what things are in themselves, he either does not act the part of a judge, or else judges falsely. The very notion of judging is to determine what is, and what is not in any one's case. The judge's work is two-fold: it is to determine first what is fact, and then whether what is in fact be according to rule, or according to law. If a judge has no rule or law established beforehand by which he should proceed in judging, he has no foundation to go upon in judging; nor is it possible that he should do the part of a judge. To judge without a law, or rule by which to judge, is impossible; for, the very notion of judging, is to determine whether the object of judgment be according to rule; and therefore God has declared, that when He acts as a judge, He will not justify the wicked, and cannot clear the guilty; and by parity of reason, cannot justify without righteousness".

If then the Courts of God admit this mode of justification founded on the substitutional obedience and suffering of Another, the next question we have to consider is—What is the link that connects with the means of justification thus provided by God? The link is **faith**. In all questions respecting justification, men seem to delight in perplexing as much as possible themselves and others, and in nothing has their invention been more fertile than in multiplying difficulties respecting the nature and meaning of faith. But we may at once free ourselves from all these entanglements by remembering that faith in its connection with justification, means simply reliance and dependence on Another. And, in order to express this, the Scripture uses the words faith **in**, faith **on** or to believe **in**, or **on**—words which unequivocally express **"reliance"**, and utterly exclude the notion of justifying faith being the **mere** mental acknowledgement of a fact; or being any thing else than **reliance**, in the sense in which that word is universally understood. If I find myself confronted by a roaring torrent, and have no means of crossing the devouring flood except those provided and proffered by a friend—if I trust in **my** friend and in his competence, and prove my trust by committing myself (whether tremblingly or confidently) to his care, and spurn the thought of seeking any other means, no one questions that I rely on my friend, nor invent difficulties about the nature of such reliance, nor doubts that such reliance implies entire passivity on my part, and consequently excludes all thought of **my own** agency. The following text may be taken always, as a safe and sufficient guide to the meaning of faith in its connection with justification "who through Him (Jesus) de believe in God, that raised Him from the dead, and gave Him glory: that your faith and hope might be in God". It is very obvious that in these and similar passages the words "believe **in**" or "believe **on**", signify **reliance**. Wherever there is such reliance of soul, **there** there is justifying faith. And if in some passages that treat of justification we find simply the word "believe", without the addition of **"on"** or **"in"**, it equally denotes reliance; because in the connection in which it is used, it does not express the mere recognition of **a** fact, but it denotes that I believe in God in respect of something that He proposes and promises unto me: and he who so believes God relies on Him.

At the Reformation (and the habit is not yet extinct) "confidence" rather than "reliance" was the term often employed to denote that dependence of soul expressed by the words, "believe on". But of these two words "reliance", should be unhesitatingly adopted; because "confidence" is commonly understood to imply not reliance simply, but reliance to a certain degree of development and strength. Mere reliance, therefore, if it lacked sure strength would not be considered to be "confidence", and therefore would not be regarded as justifying faith. We cannot be too watchful against a doctrine like this. The Scripture emphatically states that we are justified by means **of faith**— not by faith of a particular degree or kind. The Scripture does not say that we are justified by appropriating faith, or confident faith, or assured faith, or realizing faith, but it simply says, that we are justified by faith. We must beware, therefore, of adding to the Word of God. She who with trembling finger touched the hem of the garment of Jesus, became as truly a recipient of the virtue that was in Him, as those who approached in fuller confidence of faith. They who, in expectation of the night of Egypt's judgment, marked their door-posts and doors with the blood of the Passover-Lamb, may have rested under it with different degrees of confidence. Some may have given way to unbelieving fears, whilst others were trustful and undismayed: but such differences however much they may have affected their peace, and the right tone and temper of their heart toward God, affected not their safety. Their reliance on God as their Deliverer was proved by the fact that they had credited His message and marked the appointed blood; and wherever the blood was found, there was found deliverance.

All then who despise not this salvation but who (it may be with feeble faith) cast themselves upon God according to the grace thus provided by Him in Christ, are believers, and are, in the Courts of Heaven, recognized as having obtained an interest in all the value, and in all the results, of the substitutional work of Christ. They are, to use the words of Scripture, "constitutetd righteous". "As by one man's disobedience many were constituted sinners, so by the obedience of One, shall many be constituted righteous" (Rom. 5:19). "Constituted" like "justification", is a forensic word, and equally brings before us the thought of God's judicial courts. The moment we are thus recognized as "constituted righteous", sentence to that effect is recorded on our behalf in the Courts above, and we are pronounced righteous—in other words, we are justified.

In considering therefore justification, three things should be presented to the mind—a Judge, one who presents a plea before that Judge, and an Adversary. If any were to plead that they were personally righteous, and were to claim to be so acknowledged, their claim, if proved, would be pronounced valid, and they would then be said to be justified by means of works. As soon as the Ethiopian can change his skin and the leopard his spots, then—but not before, lost man may talk about being justified thus. If, on the other hand, renouncing this folly, we enter our plea as sinners, (but sinners who have, through faith—which also is God's gift—obtained an interest in an atonement and in a righteousness substitutionally provided in Another) then, if our plea be recognized as valid (and it must be recognized unless the reality of our faith can be disproved), we are said to be justified by means of faith on account of Christ's vicarious obedience and suffering. In the first case, the plea would be, "I have worked"; in the second, "I have trusted" —trusted in that which God hath appointed to be trusted in for salvation.

But if the reality of the faith professed be contested; if the Adversary should urge that we have only a pretended faith— that we say indeed that we have faith, but that we have it not, then, it becomes necessary to show that certain results have sprung from our faith whereby it is evidenced to be true and living. Thus, whilst our claim to the non-imputation of guilt and the imputation of righteousness is grounded on faith alone (for we enter our plea on the ground of being through faith connected with the substitutional work of Another), yet our claim to have our faith pronounced genuine, is grounded on the fact of some practical result that can be shown to have flowed from it. With respect to our claim to the being beneficially interested in the work of the Substitute, we ground it on our having faith, and therefore when that claim is recognized in the Courts of God, we are said to be justified by means of faith: as respects our claim to having our faith recognized as **living**, that is grounded on our works, and therefore when that claim is recognized, we are said to be justified by works. One work, and that not perfect according to the perfectness of God, (for no work of any believer is perfect according to the perfectness of God) may be sufficient to prove that I have living faith: but if it become a question whether I am pronounced righteous on the ground of my works, then I must prove nothing less than that all my feelings, all my thoughts, all my words, and all my deeds, have been from the first moment of my existence, perfect according to the perfectness of God. One work, and that not in itself perfect, may suffice to justify me in respect of my claim to the possession of genuine faith; but one imperfect work, or one imperfect feeling would ruin my claim (if I dared to prefer it) to be pronounced righteous by works before God.

It must be evident also, that all who meet the claims of God on the ground of what their heavenly Substitute has done and suffered for them, must be **completely** justified. Nothing can be more perfect than the substitutional work of Christ. If He has borne the punishment due our sins He has perfectly borne it, and we are free: if He has presented His righteousness in our stead, then we have a righteousness in nothing short of the righteousness of God. Such is the provision of God's love and grace, and it pertaineth to all them that believe. Nor is this justification transitory. It is stable and everlasting—its sure end being glory. "Whom He justified, them He also glorified". Justification is the act of a covenant God. The consideration, however, of this I reserve for another occasion.

—B. W. NEWTON.

A PERSONAL WORD.

Another year has almost run its course. During its progress we have observed the steady advance of the Apostacy (2 Thess. 2:3) and the deepening darkness which now, like a pall, is spread over organized Christendom (Isa. 60:2). Increasing numbers are throwing off the mask of hypocrisy and openly departing from the Faith (1 Tim. 4:1). In the case of multitudes of others who still attempt to maintain a Christian profession (2 Tim. 3:5), the hollowness of their pretensions is becoming more and more evident to any one with a particle of spiritual discernment. Those who desire the sincere milk of the Word are a steadily diminishing minority (Matt. 13:23, Luke 18:8). Even at so-called Bible-conferences, solid exposition of Scripture has nearly disappeared (Amos. 8:11). Alleged servants of God who still command the attention of goodly crowds, are flesh-pleasing compromisers (Luke 6:26).

In view of the heart-saddening conditions, which prevail on every side, the world over, we cannot but be struck with wonderment and filled with praise to our faithful God, for His having made it possible for us, through the unsolicited gifts of His people, to continue this written ministry through another twelve months. It is only one here and there who has any appetite for the type of food which the Lord enables us to set before His people. It is therefore a miracle of grace that we have been brought into touch with a sufficient number of these to justify its continuance, and that sufficient offerings have been sent in to meet every obligation. Since the very first issue of "Studies" after we began to send them out free, not a bill has been left unpaid for forty-eight hours (Rom. 12:17).

During the past year we have been more severely tested, both in connection with the magazine finances and with our own path, than in any previous one. That is good for us, for any thing which exercises our hearts before God and drives us to our knees, is always a real blessing (Heb. 12:11). Thank God, our faith has never wavered (Luke 22:32), for (by grace) our confidence is in Him alone who never disappoints those who trust Him with all their hearts (Num. 23:19). With deep gratitude unto Him who is the Giver of every good and of every perfect gift, we are able to record that we close another year with a slight balance to the good, which will be used for publishing other literature: and throughout another year God has mercifully kept us both in splendid health. Let all who have sought to be our helpers in prayer fervently praise God for His goodness.

A very small supply of the material things of this life are sufficient to meet the requirements of those who seek and find all their satisfaction in the Lord Himself. It is astonishing to find how few are the real "needs" of our mortal existence: "having food and raiment let us be therewith content" (1 Tim. 6:8), is not difficult to heed if the "affection" be set upon things above. Though we are paying house-rent (Acts 28:30), the editor and his wife are getting along very comfortably on less than 50 dollars (ten pounds) a month. Our total receipts from all oral ministry during the past year have been less than 35 dollars (seven pounds), yet the Lord has moved different ones to send in little gifts for our "personal needs" to augment our small private income, so that we have been enabled to "owe no man anything" (Rom. 13:8). All praise to Him.

Were we walking by sight, the outlook would be dark indeed. The spiritual condition of the "churches"(?) in these parts is the same as everywhere else we have been: when weighed in the balances of Holy Writ, they are "found wanting". Those who are the loudest in their professions, exhibit the least grounds to justify them. Few indeed are willing to be shown "the way of God more perfectly" (Acts 18:26). About all that people will tolerate today is that which confirms their own ideas, or agrees with the "traditions" of their fathers. "Ichabod" (1 Sam. 4:21) is written over nearly all of them. When we receive an invitation to hold a meeting in a "church"(?) from which we are satisfied the Lord Himself has departed (Rev. 3:20), we decline it, for it is no place for the servant to be where his Master is not. If a "church'(?) is entirely or even mainly made up of worldlings, we dare not be a partaker of their evil deeds (2 John 11). We cannot fellowship the Christ-dishonouring mockery which now masquerades under the shelter of His holy name. We are therefore practically confined to the ministry of our pen. Almost all of our time is now being spent in prayerful study and in seeking to prepare written messages for the scattered and starved sheep of Christ. We are quite happy in this blessed work, and are receiving many encouragements to go in it; all praise to the God of all grace.

Each time we have been disappointed in a local company with whom we hoped to have spiritual fellowship, our hearts have turned the more to Him who never disappoints. "Cease ye from man" (Isa. 2:22) is a difficult precept to obey, and many hard knocks in the school of experience are needed before we are really weaned from the creature. We are slow to recognize that the Christian life, from start to finish, is an **individual** matter, a matter of personal dealings with the Lord Himself. The path we are called to walk is so "narrow" (Matt. 7:14) that it has to be trode single file. Believing on Christ is something none can do for another. Communion with the Lord is an individual experience (Rev. 3:20). The **only** real help that one Christian is to another, is when he points him to the Lord Himself.

The present issue contains the concluding article of the lengthy series of "Gleanings in Exodus". A number of friends are anxious for these to be re-issued in separate form. Complete, they would make two goodly-sized volumes. The cost would be considerable, and the demand today for such works is pitifully small, and will no doubt become much smaller. They would have to sell at $1.50 (6/3 or $2.00 (8/6) a volume. We shall be glad to hear from our readers how they feel about it.

Beginning in January 1930 (D. V.) will be a series of articles on the vitally-important and blessed subject of "The Atonement". There are many sides to this glorious truth which are very little understood today, even among God's people, for it is rarely preached from the pulpit. These articles will be of the "heavy" type, and will require prayerful and very careful reading and re-reading. But we are writing for those who desire to **study** the Scriptures, not to entertain those who read to "while away an hour". We covet the special prayers of God's people in the preparation of these articles.

During the past year we have received many new names for our Magazine mailing-list. To them were sent all twelve issues. From hundreds we have received no line of acknowledgement. We know not whether they have been helped or no. Therefore we are dropping them from our list. If you receive not the Jan. and February 1930 issues, and you desire them, we shall be glad to send (D. V.) providing you write us and express the intention of giving them a careful reading, unless we feel that on some they would be wasted. Will friends kindly note we are always glad to send sample copies to any they think would be interested.

We desire to express our gratitude to all the Lord's dear people who have had any fellowship with us in this work: "God is not unrighteous to forget your work and labour of love, which ye have showed toward His name" (Heb. 6:10). On the other hand, we have been obliged to refuse and even return gifts from those who gave no evidence of being His, for Scripture says "taking **nothing** of the Gentiles" (3 John 7), i.e., the unregenerate: contrast Gal. 3:28. And right here we earnestly beg those of our readers who know they are unsaved, or who are (which is the same thing) not daily seeking grace to **walk** in the Truth, **not** to send us in any gifts whatsoever. God will not own the offerings of such (Prov. 15:8), and we are forbidden to receive them. While the Lord has a use for this testimony, He **will** move His own people to support it.

Scripture does not supply the slightest grounds for expecting any improvement. Conditions are going to get worse, not better (2 Tim. 3:13). Yet, though this should sadden, it ought not to shake or discourage us: "God is our refuge and strength, a very present help in trouble. Therefore will we not fear, though the earth be removed, and though the mountains be carried into the midst of the sea" (Psa. 46:1, 2). May this be the God-given confidence of all His elect. "The Lord hath His way in the whirlwind and in the storm" (Nahum 1:3). How assuring, how stabalizing, how comforting to **know** this! All is well, for God Himself is **for** us (Rom. 8:31), **with** us (Psa. 23:4), **in** us (2 Cor. 6:16). Halleujah!

With loving greetings to all who belong to the Household of Faith.

Yours by God's abounding grace and mercy,

—A. W. and V. E. PINK.

HOLY HORROR

I wonder how many of us could honestly subscribe our names to the experience which the Psalmist declares he felt when he beheld the lawlessness of ungodly men. In Psa. 119 he employs three marvelous expressions which reveal the agony of his soul over the effrontery of the wicked.

Expression 1. "Horror hath taken hold upon me because of the wicked that forsake Thy law" (verse 53.) How many of us know any thing of this godly horror? How can we pretend to walk with God if we are not shocked and horrified at the highhanded doings of lawless men? Most of us are content to shake our heads and say: "What else are we to expect?" Does not Scripture say that: "Evil men and seducers shall wax worse and worse, deceiving and being deceived" (2 Tim. 3:13)? Yes, dear brethren, the Bible says all that and very much more, but that does not lessen our responsibility to be horror-stricken at the blasphemous utterances and actions of the wicked.

Expression 2. "Rivers of water run down mine eyes, because they keep not Thy law" (verse 136). How many of us have had this experience? When did we shed our last tear over the behaviour of those who openly defy God? Freed from the necessity of committing such sins ourselves, we have forgotten to be exercised concerning the dishonour done to God's Name through the violation of His laws. With what startling effect can Jeremiah 9:1 be introduced here: "Oh, that my head were waters, and mine eyes a fountain of tears"! Jeremiah is one of the few weeping willows to be found amongst the trees of the wood. Would to God there were more of them growing in the Lord's garden.

Expression 3. "I beheld the transgressors, and was grieved, because they kept not Thy Word" (verse 158). Again I reiterate, it is only folly of the most palpable order to pretend to have sympathy with God if the wickedness of the wicked is not a continual source of grief and vexation to us. It may be that we can do nothing to arrest the awful floods of ungodliness. On the contrary, we may see wickedness increasing and prospering, nevertheless it is our solemn duty to be horrified at its progress, to weep over its apparent success, and to be really grieved over its ascendency in the world. This, then, is one of the many tests which God applies to all professed spirituality. How does the sight of evil affect me? Do I look upon it as a necessity, and treat it with corresponding unconcern? Dear brethren, don't let us pretend to walk with God if the sight of evil does not pain our hearts.

"Oh may nothing ever **please us,**
He would **grieve** to look upon."

Even **worldly** Lot may be cited as an example for us. He was "vexed with the filthy conversation of the wicked." He "vexed his righteous soul from day to day with their unlawful deeds" (2 Peter 2:7, 8). **If we have fallen lower than Lot in these things, then we are low indeed.**—The Witness, 1903.

When we hear of communion with the Holy Three, we conceive it must altogether consist in high and exalted aspirations, in inconceiveable joy, in ecstasy and rapture. Indeed, we don't conceive it to be much as suits us when we feel sin, but when we are in very high, sublime, and spiritual frames. Whereas, communion with the Lord, whilst it is the greatest of all blessings, either in earth or heaven, yet we have this blessedness, when we ourselves overlook it. And as for myself, I conclude I have it most when I at least perceive it; for when I simply address the Lord Jesus, inwardly in my mind, saying, Lord, look upon me, take notice of all within me, take into Thine own hands all I am in myself, exercise Thy compassion on me, exactly as my necessities require, keep, Oh, keep, me; bless, Oh, bless, me; defend me for Thy mercy's sake, from sin, the world, and Satan; let me be contented to be nothing, do Thou be my all. I call this communion. If it be so, then I find this more or less to be my constant practice; because I cannot live but I must feel sin, so I cannot live, but I must look to Christ for salvation from it. Indeed I think the greatest communion with Christ, and the Father in Him, through the Spirit, in this present state, is and doth principally consist in a total renunciation of self, and in a real and actual dependence on the Lord, and the more simple this dependence, so much the better.—Extract from Letter by S. E. Pierce, 1796.

great love on the part of God to ease, heal, or speedily deliver them. Yet it would not be so, or otherwise He had done so, for most certainly He loves them too well to continue them one moment longer in the world than is for His praise and their benefit. Some saints lose all their worldly goods and friends, and are brought to a state of real poverty, and remain thus for many years; yet this is the will of the Lord for them. O suffering and tried Christian, fear none of these evils, leave yourself entirely in God's hands, His own unerring Word declares, "We know that all things work together for good to them that love God" (Rom. 8:28).

"A little stay on earth will make heaven all the sweeter to you. Nothing makes rest so sweet as toil; nothing can render security so pleasant as a long exposure to alarms and dangers. No heaven will be so blessed as a heaven which has been preceded by pains and torments. Methinks the deeper draughts of woe we drink here below, the sweeter will be those draughts of eternal glory which we shall receive from the golden bowls of bliss. Let us not, then, my brethren, fear to advance through our trials: they are for our good; to stop here is for our benefit. Why! we should not know how to converse in heaven if we had not a few trials and hardships to tell of, and no rescuing grace to report with joy" (C. H. Spurgeon).

These then are a few of the reasons why God leaves His people in this world of sorrows and afflictions: that His love may be displayed. His mercy extended, His power put forth, His promises fulfilled to them; that His name may be magnified through His grace succouring and sustaining them, that it may be exhibited His grace is "sufficient" for every case, every circumstance, every situation, every emergency which can possibly befall us; that we may be made a blessing to others; that we may learn more fully the nature of that sin from which we are saved; that we might be taught submission to God's holy will; that we may be fitted to enjoy heaven the more. May the Lord graciously bless this article to numbers of His suffering, tried, lonely and aged pilgrims.

—ARTHUR W. PINK.

Jesus Christ being your life and light; your righteousness and purity; your peace and joy; your crown and glory; your salvation and blessedness; you have in Him everything which can make you happy on earth, and perfectly so in the heaven of heavens. It is given unto you to see from the Word, and by the Spirit, that your whole salvation is in the immaculate Lamb. That your everlasting all depends on His life of obedience, and death of expiation. Your faith consists in believing the Godhead of Jesus. The perfection of His life, the everlasting virtue and efficacy of His blood and death. The Father's delight and complacency, in the person and work of Immanuel, with His full acceptance of Him, as the Mediator, here your faith centres. In God, as reconciled unto you by the death of His Son, you triumph. Seeing yourself one with Christ, you know that you are complete in Him. What you are in Him is the foundation of all your hope and confidence in God. You are not so unholy in your fallen nature, as you are holy in Christ. You are not so impure in yourself, as you are pure in Christ. You have not so much cause to distrust yourself, as you have cause to trust in Jesus. You have not that fulness of sin in you, that cannot be overmatched and exceeded by Christ's infinite, immutable, overflowing fulness. In Christ you are holy, righteous, and spotless in your heavenly Father's sight. Living in the belief of it, is a great part of our life of faith, I know, my dear Sir, few will be found who so believe and live. With all the preaching and printing, 'tis few indeed who know Jesus, and the power of His resurrection. I have been, you are, tried in heart, to see how few know our Jesus in the Word, and have their minds enlightened by the glorious Gospel of the blessed God. Yet so it is, 'tis but here and there a person is really taken with Jesus.

If we look into the churches, few preach Jesus. The people are taken with anything except Christ. Christ is too little known, and most awfully neglected. So that one would wish for long life, great strength of body, and much opportunity to set forth Christ, let the consequence be what it may.—Extract from Letters of S. E. Pierce, 1796.

just as long as He has ordained? Nothing is more becoming in the child of God than to submit to His Father's holy will. In this he is made conformable to Christ: He patiently and meekly awaited the appointed "hour" (John 17:1).

After the Lord has called His own people out of the world, and by His sovereign grace separated them from it, He has wise and good reasons for leaving them still in it—for His own glory, for the good of His cause, for the good of His people, for their own good. God is glorified in leaving His people here, that they may daily learn and know what they have been saved from. It is not until the Holy Spirit has regenerated us that we are in any wise capable of perceiving the awfulness and vileness of sin; and the longer a real Christian is left here, the deeper and fuller realization does he obtain of his inward depravity and the filthiness of his corruptions. This, in turn, makes him appreciate all the more his gracious Redeemer and value far more highly His precious blood that cleanses him from all sin. God leaves us here for a season that we may be the monuments of His perpetual mercy.

"Saints of all sorts are left here; amid all kinds of comforts and conveniences, and amid all kinds of temptations, sorrows, bodily diseases and trials. And Christ will have it so, that He may express His grace and royal mercy towards them in His own way, and hereby gain an everlasting name. It is not for us to prescribe to Him what He shall do. He gains glory where we see it not. He does good though we perceive it not. He gets honour and praise out of all His saints and called ones, where we have not the least idea of it. It is His glory to 'conceal a thing' (Prov. 25:2), yea, to conceal even from the eye of faith some of the glorious acts of His grace. We honour Him most by a **passive** reception of His truth, by a perfect **acquiescence** to His will, by being well pleased with all **His** good pleasure" (S. E. Pierce, 1810).

We are in hearty accord with the beloved Spurgeon when he said, "A tried saint brings more glory to God than an untried one. I do verily think in my own soul that a believer in a dungeon reflects more glory on his Maker than a believer in Paradise; that a child of God in the burning fiery furnace, whose hair is yet unscorched, and upon whom the smell of fire has not passed, displays more the glory of the Godhead than he who stands with a crown on his head and perpetually sings praises before the eternal throne. It honours Him when the saints preserve their integrity. Great glory is brought to Him when a saint cries, 'Though He slay me, yet will I trust Him' ".

Again; the Lord's people are left here that His **promises** may be fulfilled toward them, in them, and upon them. Peter says there is a "needs be" for our manifold trials (1 Peter 1:6), and a part of that "**needs be**" is that God may **manifest** His faithfulness, **demonstrate** His veracity, **make good** His own Word. For instance, "He giveth power to the faint; and to them that have no might He increaseth strength" (Isa. 40:29). What **experimental** acquaintance could a saint have with this word unless he be brought low, so low that his **own** strength completely gives out? So too, "When thou passest through the waters, I will be with thee; and through the rivers, they shall not overflow thee: when thou walkest through the waters, I wi'l be with thee; and through the rivers, they shall not overflow thee: when thou walkest through the fire, thou shalt not be burned; neither shall the flame kindle upon thee" (Isa. 43:2). Deep waters have to be passed through and the fiery trials suffered, if the soul is to have a **heart** knowledge of the fulfillment of this promise.

Descending lower: God's people are left here for the good of their fellow Christians. The Household of Faith sustains a real loss every time a member of it is taken away. Remember, dear Christian, that others are in the same case with you: they are fellow-pilgrims, fellow-soldiers, fellow-sufferers. They are to be profited by you: by your prayers for them, by speaking to them of Christ, by your godly and encouraging example. For all you know, God may be keeping you here because He will yet use you as His instrument to pluck some brand from the eternal burnings. These considerations should reconcile you to His will. It were well for each of us to ponder that word, "For none of us liveth to himself, and no man dieth to himself" (Rom. 14:7).

Finally, God leaves us here for our own good. Some saints experience great temptations and trials, and it is well for them to know that the Lord has a wise end in them. Some saints are continually exposed to the fiery darts of the Devil, and it is well for them to remember that these are not without Christ's own permission; He will promote their real good by them. Some are afflicted with sore diseases, grievous pains, long illnesses, and they are apt to think it would be

(Continued on page 287)

www.ingramcontent.com/pod-product-compliance
Lightning Source LLC
Chambersburg PA
CBHW072019240426
43667CB00044B/1476